海南统计年鉴
HAINAN STATISTICAL YEARBOOK

2007

（总第21期 No. 21）

海　南　省　统　计　局
国家统计局海南调查总队　编

Compiled by

Statistical Bureau of Hainan Province
Survey office of the National Bureau of Statistics in HaiNan

中国统计出版社
China Statistics Press

（京）新登字041号

图书在版编目（C I P）数据

海南统计年鉴. 2007 / 海南省统计局 国家统计局海南调查总队编.
—北京：中国统计出版社，2007.6
ISBN 978-7-5037-5133-2

Ⅰ.海… Ⅱ.海… Ⅲ.统计资料—海南省—2007—年鉴
Ⅳ.C832.66-54

中国版本图书馆CIP数据核字（2007）第049507号

海南统计年鉴—2007

作　　者/ 海南省统计局 国家统计局海南调查总队
责任编辑/郑淼淼
E-mail / yearbook@stats.gov.cn
责任校对/ 李 诚
封面设计/ 王志方
出版发行/ 中国统计出版社
通信地址/ 北京市西城区三里河月坛南街57号 中国统计出版社
邮　　编/ 100826
电　　话/ (010)63376907
印　　刷/ 海口景达鑫彩色印刷有限公司
经　　销/ 新华书店
开　　本/ 890×1240毫米 1/16
字　　数/ 1650千字
印　　张/ 46.875
印　　数/ 2000本
版　　别/ 2007年9月第1版
版　　次/ 2007年9月第1次印刷
书　　号/ ISBN 978-7-5037-5133-2/F·2433
定　　价/ 280元

《海南统计年鉴－2007》编辑委员会

Hainan Statistical Yearbook－2007 Editorial Board

编者说明

一、《海南统计年鉴》是一部以统计特有的语言全面、系统、量化地记录海南省经济和社会发展状况的大型资料性年刊。《海南统计年鉴 -2007》年刊辑录了海南省辖区内18个市、县、自治县和海南省农垦总局、洋浦经济开发区2006年经济社会发展各项统计数据及全省主要历史年份主要统计数据。

二、本年刊共分综合、经济核算、人口和就业、固定资产和房地产开发投资、能源和环境、财政、物价指数、居民生活、农业和农村经济、工业、建筑业、交通运输和邮电通讯业、批发零售贸易和住宿餐饮业、旅游业、对外经济贸易、金融和保险业、企业集团和景气、教育、文化和科技、卫生和体育、社会福利和保障等20个部分。每部分篇末附有主要统计指标解释条目,对主要统计指标的含义、统计范围、统计方法及历史数据的变动情况作了简要说明。

三、按照海南省现行行政管理体制和统计制度,各市、县、自治县辖区内的国有农垦系统经济社会活动由海南省农垦总局直接统计。本年刊所辑录之市、县、自治县统计数据,除人口、对外经济贸易、旅游业、交通运输和邮电通讯业、财政、金融和保险业、教育和文化、卫生和体育、科技等包含农垦数据或表中特别列示农垦数据外,其余部分均不包含农垦统计数据。农垦系统数据在"农垦""中单独列示。洋浦经济开发区作为一个经济活动单元,其统计数据单独列出。目前,海南省所辖西、南、中沙群岛经济活动较少,统计资料来源不易取得,本年刊除人口和就业包含西、南、中沙群岛数据外,其余部分均不计入。

四、本年刊使用的度量单位为国际统一标准计量单位。

五、本年刊指标口径和范围,基本上以国家现行统计报表制度为准,数据大部分来源于政府统计机构年度统计报表和抽样调查数据,少部分来源于政府或行业主管部门的年度统计报表。

六、由于第二次海南省农业普查结果尚未汇总完毕,故本年刊第九篇:农业和农村经济暂缺部分2006年度数据。该部分相关指标数据将在《海南统计年鉴 -2008》版予以补列。

七、本年刊部分指标合计数或相对数,由于四舍五入关系或核算单位不同,分项数字之和可能会与之有所出入。

八、本年刊使用的符号说明:"…"表示数据不足该表最小单位;"空格"表示该项指标数据不详或无数据;"#"表示其中部分项目。

Preface

Ⅰ. Hainan Statistical Yearbook 2006 is an annual statistics publication which comprehensively and systematically covers the social and economic development of whole Hainan Province. The yearbook has collected the social and economic development statistical data in year 2006 for 18 cities/counties, Hainan General Bureau of Land Reclamation (GBLR), Yangpu Economic Development Zone as well as major statistical data of whole province in importantly historical years.

Ⅱ. The book contains the following twenty parts, 1.General Survey; 2.Economic Accounts; 3. Population and Employment; 4.Investment in Fixed Assets and Real Estate Development; 5.Energy an Environment; 6.Finance; 7.Price Indices; 8.People's Livelihood; 9.Agriculture and Rural Economy; 10. Industry; 11.Construction; 12.Transpotion、Postal and Telecommunications; 13.Wholesale and Retail Trade、Hotel and Catering Services; 14.Tourism; 15.Foreign Trade and Economic Cooperation; 16.Finance and Insurance;17.Enterprise Groups and Business Climate Index;18.Education、Culture、Science and Technology; 19.Pubic Health and Sport; 20.Social Welfare and Security. Explanatory Notes on Main Statistical Indicators are provided at the end of each part to briefly describe the content of main statistical indicators, and the scope, and statistical methods and historical changes are concerned.

Ⅲ.According to the existing production management and administrative management system in Hainan province, the state owned land reclamation farms in the cities and counties are directly administrated by Hainan General Bureau of Land Reclamation. The data related with all cities and counties don't cover the data related with land reclamation sector except for the data in respect of population, foreign economy, tourism, transport, post and communication, finance and banking, culture, education, public health, science and technology as well as the data specially marked with data for land reclamation sector. The data related with land reclamation farms are separately listed in item "Land Reclamation". Statistical data related with Yangpu Economic Development Zone are separately listed since it is under direct administration of provincial government. Considering that economic activities are few in Xisha Islands, Nansha Islands and Zhongsha Islands and that it is difficult to obtain statistical data source, other data will are not covered except for population, labor force and wage for Xisha Islands, Nansha Islands and Zhongsha Islands

Ⅳ.The units of measurement used in this book are internationally standard measurement units.

Ⅴ. Path and scope of the data in this yearbook are basically based on the current national statistic system, the major data sources of this publication are obtained from annual statistical reports and sample surveys, and some from annual statistical reports of various departments responsible for the work.

VI. Because the results of the second census for Hainan agriculture have not been summarized, part data for year 2006 in Chapter 9 of the yearbook (Agriculture and Rural Economy) is absent for the time being. This part of data will be published in Hainan Statistical Yearbook for Year 2008 in supplementary form.

Ⅶ.Due to rounding or different accounting unit, the amount of separate number may not correspond with the aggregative or relative ones in this yearbook.

Ⅷ.Notations used in the yearbook: "…" indicates that the figure is not large enough to be measured with the smallest unit in the table, "blank space" indicates the data are unknown or are not available, "#" indicates a part of the total.

目 录

CONTENTS

第二篇　经济核算

Ⅱ National Accounts

第三篇　人口和就业

Ⅲ Population and employment

第四篇 固定资产和房地产开发投资

Ⅳ Investment in Fixed Assets and Real Estate Development

第五篇 能源和环境
V Energy and Environment Protection

第六篇 财 政
Ⅵ Government Finance

第七篇 物价指数
Ⅶ Price Indices

第八篇 居民生活
Ⅷ People' s Livelihood

第九篇 农业和农村经济
Ⅸ Agrlculture and Rural Economy

第十篇 工 业
X Industry

第十一篇 建筑业
XI Construction

第十二篇 交通运输邮电通讯业
XII Transportation, Postal and Telecommunications Services

第十三篇 批发零售贸易和住宿餐饮业
XIII Wholesale, Retail and Restaurant

第十四篇 旅游业
XIV Tourism

第十五篇 对外经济贸易
XV Foreign Economy and Trade

第十六篇 金融和保险
XVI Banking and Insurance

第十七篇 企业集团和景气

XVII Enterprises Group and Enterprises Business

第十八篇 教育、文化和科技

XVIII Education Culture Science and Technology

第十九篇 卫生和体育
XIX Health and Sports

第二十篇 社会福利和保障

XX Soclal Welfare and Social Security

2006年海南经济和社会发展综述

2006年，海南省委、省政府高举邓小平理论和“三个代表”重要思想伟大旗帜，以科学发展观为指导，带领全省各族人民认真贯彻国家宏观调控等一系列重大战略部署，积极稳妥推进“大企业进入、大项目带动”发展战略，进一步调整优化产业结构，努力转换经济增长方式，全省经济呈现出速度加快、结构优化、效益提高、活力增强、物价稳定的良好运行态势；深化改革、对外开放，加强交流合作取得新的进展；文化、教育、卫生、体育、社会保障等各项社会事业加快发展；计划生育、环境保护、生态省建设等取得了新的成效，城乡居民从经济社会发展中获得了实实在在的好处，实现了“十一五”良好开局，构建和谐海南迈出坚实的步伐。

经济社会发展中存在的主要问题是：农业基础薄弱的状况没有大的改变，现代农业水平仍较低；城乡发展不协调，“二元经济”特征仍较明显；经济发展中的结构性问题仍较突出，“三低一小”仍然是当前经济发展中的主要矛盾；城乡居民对公共产品不断增长的需求与政府财力供给的水平差距较大；粗放型经济增长方式仍未得到根本转变；对外开放水平有待进一步提高。

一、经济发展

（一）经济总量

整体经济加速增长，综合实力明显增强。2006年，全省生产总值（GDP）1052.85亿元，按可比价格计算，比上年增长12.5%，增速提高2.3个百分点，自2003年走出“房地产泡沫”阴影进入两位数增长平台后，创1994年以来生产总值增速新高，提前一年实现生产总值跨千亿目标；其中，第一产业增加值344.48亿元，增长9.1%；第二产业增加值287.86亿元，增长19.8%；第三产业增加值420.51亿元，增长11.0%。按常住人口计算，人均生产总值12654元，以当年平均汇率折算约合1617美元，增长11.3%。

产业结构进一步调整优化，新型工业和现代服务业得到大力发展。2006年，在全省生产总值中，第一产业所占比重由上年的32.97%降至32.72%，对经济增长贡献率为24.4%；第二产业所占比重由26.06%提高至27.34%，对经济增长贡献率为38.8%，居三次产业贡献率首位；第三产业所占比重由40.97%降至39.94%，对经济增长贡献率为36.8%。从各产业内部结构看，第一产业中优势农业加快发展，渔业、畜牧业、瓜菜、水果等四大优势农业对农业经济增长的贡献率达80.8%。第二产业中高新技术工业比重明显提高，石油加工、化肥、纸浆、汽车制造、制药、旋窑水泥等新型工业创造产值对规模以上工业经济增长贡献率达77.5%，经济增长的技术与知识含量显著提高。第三产业中现代服务业发展喜人。旅游客源结构发生新的变化，接待境外游客增幅较境内游客增幅快38.0个百分点；房地产市场在宏观调控中理性发展，销售面积大于竣工面积；金融环境进一步改善，资产质量明显提高，金融机构本外币存贷总量同步增长；会展产业方兴未艾，成功主办或协办博鳌亚洲论坛年会、两岸农业合作论坛、东亚海大会及部长会议、第一届世界海南青年大会等国际性大型会议。

宏观经济景气上扬，经济运行质量和效益提高。2006年，反映宏观经济运行质量的企业家信心指数为134.1，比上年提高9.6点，已连续四年处于较景气区间上行；反映微观主体运营状况的企业景气指数为131.7，提高5.2点，企业生产经营状况不断趋好，预期生产信心明显增强。全省全口径财政收入179.88亿元，比上年增长24.3%。其中，地方财政收入102.35亿元，增长20.6%，提前一年实现地方财政收入突破百亿元目标。在地方财政收入中，一般预算收入81.81亿元，比上年增长19.1%；基金收入20.54亿元，比上年增长26.7%。税收收入总额139.21亿元，比上年增长25.2%。按各项税收分，企业所得税比上年增长26.2%，增值税增长7.8%，营业税增长21.3%，个人所得税增长11.1%，房产税增长18.2%。上划中央“两税”收入54.69亿元，增长 37.7%；上划中央所得税收入 14.38 亿元，增长 18.9%。列入统计监测的 420 家规模以上工业企业经济效益综合指数205.65%，比上年提高 9.4 个百分点，创 1997 年建立工业企业综合效益指数统计制度以来新高；实现利润总额 41.50 亿元，增长 21.9%。

（二）农林牧渔业

农业内部结构继续调整优化，农业生产保持较快发展。加大支农力度，扎实推进社会主义新农村建设，农村和农业经济加快发展。2006 年，全省农业增加值 344.48 亿元，比上年增长 9.1%，增速提高 3.1 个百分点。在农业内部，渔业、畜牧业、瓜菜、水果等优势农业持续较快发展，所占比重明显提高，成为农业经济较快增长的主导力量。全年水产品产量 166 万吨，同比增长 10.7%；肉类总量 68.31 万吨，同比增长 6.6%；瓜菜产量 400.39 万吨，增长 10.2%；水果产量 187.85 万吨，增长 15.6%。渔业、畜牧业、瓜菜、水果四大优势产业对农业经济增长的贡献率达 80.8%。农业经济效益随着产业结构的调整和农产品价格上涨得到显著提高。

表 1　主要农产品产品产量

产品名称	单 位	2006 年实际	比上年增减%
粮食	万吨	186.61	22.0
糖蔗	万吨	361.46	42.5
油料	万吨	8.96	5.1
瓜菜	万吨	400.39	10.2
水果	万吨	187.85	15.6
其中:香蕉	万吨	108.63	19.0
菠萝	万吨	21.14	4.3
芒果	万吨	26.24	17.8
荔枝	万吨	8.85	25.9
龙眼	万吨	2.03	29.4
柑桔橙	万吨	2.66	34.9
石榴	万吨	5.94	-5.6
橡胶干胶	万吨	24.75	-0.1
椰子	亿个	2.14	-10.8
胡椒	万吨	3.14	0.9
槟榔	万吨	7.48	16.3
肉类总产量	万吨	68.31	6.6
其中:猪牛羊肉产量	万吨	45.48	7.9
禽肉产量	万吨	21.34	4.6
禽蛋产量	万吨	2.61	-1.4
水产品总产量	万吨	166.03	10.7
其中:海水产量	万吨	138.03	8.6
淡水产量	万吨	28.00	22.0

（三）工业和建筑业

工业"短腿"明显拉长，成为拉动经济增长"火车头"。"大公司进入、大项目带动"效应进一步显现，800 万吨炼油、60 万吨甲醇、110 万吨铁精粉、8 万吨苯乙烯、15 万台汽车发动机等一批大项目陆续投产并产生即期效益，石油加工、化肥、纸浆、汽车制造、制药、旋窑水泥等新型工业成为工业经济新的增长亮点，有效地推动了工业经济快速发展。2006 年，工业完成增加值 217.55 亿元，比上年增长 24.1%，增速提高了 7.1 个百分点，对经济增长贡献率为 33.6%，是全省经济增长的"火车头"，占生产总值比重由上年的 19.07%提高至 20.66%，提高 1.6 个百分点。其中，规模以上工业完成增加值 197.66 亿元，增长 26.5%。在规模以上工业增加值中，国有控股企业完成增加值 101.64 亿元，增长 14.6%。分轻重工业看，重工业完成增加值 137.85 亿元，增长 36.8%；轻工业完成增加值 59.81 亿元，增长 11.4%。分经济类型看，国有企业完成增加值 41.37 亿元，增长 8.5%；集体企业完成增加值 0.40 亿元，增长 23.7%；股份合作企业完成增加值 0.07 亿元，增长 24.9%；股份制企业完成增加值 79.16 亿元，增长 9.3%；外商及港澳台企业完成增加值 70.19 亿元，增长 66.7 %；其他经济类型工业完成增加值 6.47 亿元，增长 12.6%。工业产品国内外市场竞争力显著提高。工业产品出口交货值 46.05 亿元，增长 74.0%；工业产品产销率 96.8%，一批适应市场需求的工业产品较快增长。

表2 主要工业产品产量

产品名称	单 位	2006 年实际	比上年增减%
发电量	亿度	94.85	16.9
铁矿石原矿量	万吨	402.22	-4.5
原油加工量	万吨	179.86	1282.4
钢材(成品钢材)	万吨	14.15	-4.8
水泥	万吨	577.54	36.6
人造板	万 M3	17.81	-4.1
汽车	万辆	8.36	14.4
摩托车	万辆	13.37	98.2
塑料制品	万吨	2.12	9.7
化学纤维	万吨	5.59	21.1
服装	万件	22.79	-8.6
配混合饲料	万吨	79.01	7.5
糖	万吨	20.29	-22.6
原盐	万吨	18.25	9.4
卷烟	万箱	65.51	11.0
罐头	万吨	13.67	10.3
无酒精饮料	万吨	27.70	0.9
饮料酒	万吨	16.90	15.1
其中:啤酒	万吨	14.05	17.3
机制纸及纸板	万吨	1.36	7.0
油漆	万吨	0.46	21.2
氮肥	万吨	63.91	2.7
磷肥	万吨	0.36	-17.0
聚酯切片	万吨	23.79	457.1
天然原油	万吨	11.09	10.2
天然气	万 M^3	20501	23.7
纸浆	万吨	103.65	32.8
液化石油气	万吨	14.66	

建筑业稳定发展。2006 年,全省建筑业完成增加值 70.31 亿元,按可比价格计算,比上年增长 9.3%。房屋建筑施工面积 780.43 万平方米,比上年增长 12.7%;房屋建筑竣工面积 314.97 万平方米,比上年增长 53.2%;建筑企业全年实现利润总额 1.50 亿元,比上年减少 42.1%。

(四)固定资产与房地产开发投资

固定资产投资保持稳定增长。2006 年,全省全社会固定资产投资总额 426.01 亿元,比上年增长 12.3%。其中,城镇固定资产投资 397.00 亿元,增长 13.1%;农村固定资产投资 29.01 亿元,增长 3.9%。在城镇固定资产投资中,第一产业完成投资 14.60 亿元,增长 5.2%;第二产业完成投资 108.77 亿元,下降 15.6%;第三产业完成投资 273.63 亿元,增长 39.3%。全年施工项目 1493 个,比上年增长 5.2%。其中新开工项目 992 个,增长 8.6%。

大项目投资进展顺利。2006 年,完成投资 1500 万元以上投资项目共完成投资 261.40 亿元,占全社会固定资产投资总额的 61.4%。800 万吨炼油厂、15 万台汽车发动机、110 万吨铁精粉厂、60 万吨甲醇、8 万吨本乙烯、粤海西环铁路等一批大型项目相继建成投产或接近投产,福耀玻璃、华能“大代小”发电厂、海口绕城高速公路、凤凰机场二期扩建、神州半岛等项目稳步推进。

房地产市场健康运行。2006 年,房地产业完成增加值 34.29 亿元,比上年增长 0.3%。房地产开发投资 89.26 亿元,增长 26.0%。其中,商品房投资 67.94 亿元,增长 11.8%。房屋施工面积 995.2 万平方米,增长 8.0%;房屋竣工面积 125.9 万平方米,房屋销售面积 203.4 万平方米。

民间投资日趋活跃。2006 年,城镇固定资产投资到位资金 457.94 亿元,比上年增长 3.1%;资金到位率为 115.4%,投资活力显著增强。在固定资产投资到位资金中,国家预算内资金和债券投资 31.06 亿元,占 6.7%,利用外资和自筹资金分别为 67.59 亿元和148.66亿元，所占比重由上年的6.1%和30.1%提高到14.7%和32.5%，分别增长168.5%和18.6%，民间投资日趋活跃，经济增长活力显著增强。

（五）消费市场与物价

消费品市场持续旺销，消费结构加快升级。家乐福、大润发等一批著名零售企业进驻海南，连锁零售业竞相发展，带动了消费市场活跃走旺。2006年，批发零售和住宿餐饮业完成增加值122.18亿元，比上年增长12.3%，增速提高1.8个百分点；全省社会消费品零售总额达到308.30亿元，比上年增长14.8%。其中，城镇消费品零售额243.58亿元，比上年增长15.5%；农村消费品零售额64.72亿元，增长12.4%。分行业看，批发零售贸易业零售额241.14亿元，增长15.3%；住宿和餐饮业零售额55.33亿元，增长13.2%；其他行业零售额11.83亿元，增长11.8%。住房、汽车、旅游、通讯等消费热点继续升温，消费结构加快升级。

市场物价保持稳定，经济运行环境良好。2006年，居民消费价格总水平上涨1.5%，连续22个月维持较低水平，实现了高经济增长、低物价上涨的良好发展格局，为经济平稳、较快、健康发展创造了一个稳定的环境。其中，城市居民消费价格上涨1.2%，农村居民消费价格上涨2.3%。分类别看，居住类价格上涨7.7%，食品类价格上涨2.3%，交通和通讯类价格上涨1.2%，家庭设备用品及维修服务类价格上涨1.1%，烟酒及用品类价格上涨0.5%，衣着类价格下降4.2%，医疗保健和个人用品类价格下降1.2%，娱乐教育文化用品及服务类价格下降1.0%。全年商品零售价格上涨1.3%，工业品出厂价格上涨0.8%，原材料、燃料、动力购进价格上涨1.5%，固定资产投资价格上涨1.0%，农业生产资料价格上涨0.7%。

（六）交通运输、邮电通讯和旅游业

航权开放试点取得新进展，交通运输保持较快增长。2006年新增海南直达俄罗斯2条洲际航线，国际航线达30条，现代陆、海、空交通体系基本形成。主要交通运输周转量和港口吞吐量见表3。

表3 交通运输周转量和港口吞吐量

	单 位	2006年实际	比上年增减%
一、货物周转量	亿吨公里	612.82	32.9
铁路	亿吨公里	10.96	55.2
公路	亿吨公里	66.07	9.3
水运	亿吨公里	520.21	33.0
民航	亿吨公里	2.87	23.7
二、旅客周转量	亿人公里	283.52	31.7
铁路	亿人公里	1.84	50.8
公路	亿人公里	117.59	8.1
水运	亿人公里	2.25	55.2
民航	亿人公里	161.84	55.8
三、港口吞吐量			
货物吞吐量	万吨	5444	44.3
其中:出港货物	万吨	2922.29	59.2
旅客吞吐量	万人	1709.73	6.9

邮电业务较快增长，电信业得到长足发展。2006年，全省邮政业务量4.72亿元，比上年增长15.4%，电信业务量93.04亿元，比上年增长31.1%。年末全省固定电话用户249.01万户，比上年增长8.3%。其中城市电话用户179.72万户，增长5.7%；农村电话用户69.29万户，增长14.9%。年末移动电话用户239.89万户，增长17.7%。年末拥有互联网用户47.14万户，增长11.4%。

旅游市场整治和旅游结构调整取得明显成效，旅游效益明显提高。加大旅游市场"四黑"整治力度。出台了《海南省人大常委会关于进一步加强旅游市场监管的决定》，在整治旅游市场"四黑"取得成效的基础上，初步建立起旅游市场长效监管机制。2006年，全省旅游业创造增加值64.86亿元，比上年增长12.6%，增速提高0.3个百分点。全年接待旅游过夜人数1605.02万人次，比上年增长5.8%。其中，接待海外旅游者61.69万人次，增长42.8%；接待国内旅游者1543.33万人次，增长4.8%。旅游总收入141.43亿元，增长13.1%。其中，境外旅游收入17.86亿元，增长78.4%；国内旅游收入123.57亿元，增长7.9%。旅游饭店客房开房率52.5%。年末全省共有星级宾馆261家，比年初增加38家。其中，五星级宾馆13家，四星级宾馆50家，三星级宾馆115家。

（七）金融、证券和保险业

金融环境明显改善，信贷总量稳步增长。2006年末，全省金融机构本外币存款余额1560.30亿元，比上年末增长19.8%。其中，企事业单位存款余额538.21亿元，比上年末增长30.8%；城乡居民储蓄存款余额812.18亿元，比上年末增长12.5%。年末金融机构本外币贷款余额1123.34亿元，比上年末增长12.8%。其中，短期贷款247.13亿元，比上年末增长2.7%，中长期贷款824.87亿元，比上年末增长17.5%。

资本市场趋于活跃，证券业加快发展。2006年，全省20只上市A股市价总值为545.87亿元，比上年增长109.0%；证券营业部实现股票（含基金）交易量966.04亿元，增长187.4%；期货交易成交手数542.43万手，增长62.4%；期货交易成交额2705.45亿元，增长97.0%。

保险业务不断扩大，风险防范意识明显增强。2006年，保险机构承保金额8275.54亿元，比上年增长60.0%；实现保费收入17.72亿元，增长18.5%。其中，财产险收入6.99亿元，增长23.7%；寿险收入9.40亿元，增长15.1%；健康和意外伤害险收入1.33亿元，增长17.8%。全年各项赔款和给付金额4.26亿元，比上年增长9.6%。其中，财产险赔付2.72亿元，下降6.5%；寿险赔付1.28亿元，增长82.3%；健康和意外伤害险赔付0.25亿元，下降7.4%。

（八）人民生活

城乡居民收入较快增长，经济增长人民受惠。在经济发展的基础上，积极扩大城镇就业，加大农村劳动力转移力度，及时兑现粮食直补，完善城乡低保制度，关心弱势群体生活，使人民群众从经济社会发展中得到实惠。2006年，全省在岗职工年平均工资15890元，比上年增长10.2%；城镇居民年人均可支配收入9395元，按可比口径计算比上年增长11.2%；农民年人均纯收入3256元，增长8.4%。城镇居民家庭恩格尔系数为43.5%；农村居民家庭恩格尔系数为53.4%，城乡居民生活质量进一步提高。城镇居民人均住房面积21.99平方米，比上年增长4.2 %；农村居民人均住房面积22.05平方米，增长1.1%。

（九）安全生产

事故死亡人数明显下降，安全生产成效显著。2006年，全省发生各类伤亡事故2900起，比上年下降11.0%；死亡（失踪）527人，下降19.1%；直接经济损失2629.05万元，下降20.3%。在各类伤亡事故中，交通道路发生事故1398起，下降5.5%；死亡人数427人，下降14.1%；直接经济损失600.58万元，下降5.9%。城乡发生火灾事故1418起，下降14.9%；死亡人数7人，下降53.3%；直接经济损失675.86万元，下降9.9%。亿元GDP生产安全事故死亡人数0.52人，下降28.8%。

二、改革开放

（一）体制改革

行政体制改革进一步深化，国企改革取得新的突破。成立省工业经济与信息产业局，进一步完善行政管理体制和监督体制；省政务中心挂牌运作，不断增强政府行政效能。组建海南路桥投资公司，通过资本市场运作政府投资。加快国有经济退市改革，完成海南高速公路股权分置，推进9家省属总公司整体退出市场，40%国有中小企业完成改制。在澄迈、临高、屯昌、白沙等市县实施林权改革试点，为全省林权改革探索经验。

（二）对外开放

对外贸易出口大幅增长，对内对外交流合作不断扩大。2006年，全省对外贸易进出口总值28.46亿美元，比上年增长9.8%。其中，出口总值13.76亿美元，增长34.5%；进口总值14.70亿美元，下降6.3%。在出口总值中，对香港出口4.91亿美元，增长52.8%；对日本出口1.34亿美元，增长21.6%；对美国出口2.08亿美元，增长44.9%；对欧盟出口1.35亿美元，下降2.0%；对东盟出口1.21亿美元，增长72.2%。全省实际利用外资总额7.93亿美元，比上年增长12.1%。其中，国外借款额0.44亿美元，增长89.7%；外商直接投资7.49亿美元，增长9.5%。新签利用外资协议合同数193宗，增长10.9%，新签协议合同规定外商投资额10.86亿美元，增长2.2倍。主办或协办经贸洽谈活动40场次，促成合作项目60个。全年对外承包工程和劳务合作合同金额307.00万美元，对外承包工程和劳务合作完成营业额246.00万美元。

三、社会发展

（一）劳动就业

劳动就业规模继续扩大，经济增长有效增加就业岗位。2006年末，全部在岗职工人数73.91万人，比上年增长1.8%。全年城镇新增就业人数8.51万人，增长1.3%。城镇登记失业率3.6%。

（二）教育事业

优先发展教育得到体现，教育事业较快发展。坚持优先发展教育，继续实施农村义务教育"两补一免"政策，加大困难大学生救助力度，完成农村中小学38.25万平方米D级危房改造，较好地解决了高考移民问题，给海南考生增加了8000多个上大学的机会。全力推进桂林洋高校园区建设，不断扩大高等教育规模。2006年，全省普通高等学校在校学生9.01万人，比上年增长28.8%；普通中等专业学校在校生6.76万人，比上年增长12.1%；高中在校学生13.79万人，增长16.8%；初中在校学生47.53万人，比上年增长2.0%；小学在校学生104.72万人，比上年下降0.9%。适龄儿童入学率99.8%，毛入学率97.7%。

（三）文化、卫生和体育事业

文化体制改革稳步推进，文化产业稳步发展。加快文化产业发展，努力打造新的产业特色，文化基础进一步夯实，文化事业和文化产业呈现新的景象。省博物馆等重点文化设施项目顺利推进，省图书馆即将投入使用，双向交互有线电视数字化项目已在海口、三亚部分小区试点。实施文化精品战略，大型民族舞剧《黄道婆》荣膺了第三届全国少数民族文艺会演大奖和组织奖。儋州调声、临高人偶剧、盅盘舞、黎族传统乐器鼻箫等乡土文化节隆重举行和纷纷登台，出版了《教育大百科全书》、《黎族传统织锦》等。省电影公司、省新华书店等文化单位通过体制改革，进一步增强了内部活力和市场竞争力。2006年，全省共有艺术表演团体21个，文化艺术馆21个，档案馆30个，图书馆20个，报纸20种，杂志41种。全年出版报纸23520万份，比上年减少9.5%；出版杂志1059万册，比上年减少12.2%。全省村村通广播电视工程稳步推进，全省广播、电视综合人口覆盖率为96.1%和95.0%。年末有线电视用户达66.00万户。

卫生事业取得较大成绩，公共卫生体系不断完善。2006年，全省有262个乡镇卫生院完成"一无三配套"改造，占85.1%。一批医疗设施正在加紧建设，农民就医条件日趋改善；新型农村合作医疗参合人数达421.60万人，参合率为86.03%，比全国规定时间提前两年基本实现了新型农村合作医疗制度。全省共有卫生机构（含诊所、卫生室）2337个，病床位2.02万张；各类卫生技术人员38199人，比上年增长2.7%。其中，执业医师(含执业助理医师)12195人，注册护士11508人。全省共有疾病预防控制中心（卫生防疫站）28个、农村乡（镇）卫生院312个。

体育事业取得新的成就，全民健身活动蓬勃发展。2006年，在各项世界性体育运动比赛中，获得金、银、铜牌3枚；在亚洲运动会比赛中，获得金牌2枚，首次在亚运会上实现金牌零的突破；获得银牌10枚，获得铜牌1枚；在全国性体育运动会比赛中，获得金牌29枚，获得银牌33枚，获得铜牌22枚。环岛国际公路自行车赛的成功举办，扩大了海南在海内外的影响。

（四）社会保障

社会保障事业继续发展，社会救济体系不断完善。2006年，全省共有城镇基本养老保险人数（不含离退休人员）94.00万人，比上年增长11.4%；城镇基本医疗保险参保人数（含退休人员）90.96万人，增长4.3%；工伤保险参保人数71.54万人，增长3.8%；城镇失业保险参保人数59.13万人，增长4.2%。年末全省抚恤、补助各类优抚对象2.48万人，比上年下降1.0%；城镇各种社区服务设施284个；城镇社区服务中心4个。农村社会保障工作不断完善，全省农村符合低保条件的对象全部纳入低保范围。年底全省农村低保人数达15.3万人。

四、可持续发展

（一）人口

人口再生产步入良性轨道，人口控制取得显著成效。完善和落实计划生育导向机制，人口再生产步入"低出生、低死亡、低增长"的良性发展轨道。2006年末，全省常住人口为835.88万人，比上年增加7.88万人。人口出生率为14.59‰，人口死亡率为5.73‰，人口自然增长率为8.86‰，比上年下降0.07个千分点。

（二）环境保护

生态环境建设力度加大，生态省建设取得新进展。划定全省饮用水资源保护区，加大"三边"建设力度，加强城市污水治理设施建设和环境污染防治工作，积极推进文明生态村、镇和城市三级人居环境创建工程，全省生态环境得到有效的保护和恢复。2006年，全省造林面积3.12万公顷，其中人工造林面积2.38万公顷，更新造林面积0.74万公顷；森林覆盖率达55.6%，比上年提高0.1个百分点；尖峰岭、蓝洋、吊罗山、七仙岭、火山口、黎母山、霸王岭被列为国家级森林公园。全省城市（镇）环境空气质量优良，主要污染物二氧化硫、二氧化氮含量符合国家环境空气质量一级标准，总悬浮颗粒物、可吸入颗粒物仅对个别市镇环境空气质量有轻微影响。全省地表水环境质量总体保持良好，80.7%的监测河段和82.4%的监测湖库达到或优于国家地表水Ⅲ类标准。全省近岸海域水质状况总体保持良好，一、二类海水占82.2%，绝大部分监测海域水质处于清洁状态。86.7%的监测海域符合水环境管理目标要求。年末全省共有环境监测站20个。其中国家一级环境监测站1个，国家二级环境监测站3个，国家三级环境监测站16个。环境监测人员316人。年末全省共有自然保护区69个，其中国家级自然保护区8个，省级自然保护区25个。自然保护区面积281.37万公顷，其中国家级自然保护区面积8.52万公顷，省级自然保护区面积263.55万公顷。列入国家一级野生保护动物有15种；列入国家二级野生保护动物有87种。列入国家一级保护植物有7种；列入国家二级保护植物有41种。

（三）科学技术

科技创新取得新成果，经济增长技术含量明显增强。2006年，全省取得重大科技成果115项，比上年增长36.9%；组织实施国家科技支撑计划项目5项，"863"计划项目4项，国家火炬计划项目7项，国家星火计划项目20项，国家自然科学基金项目36项。全年共申请专利538项，其中获得专利授权248项。全年科技经费支出15.74亿元，比上年增长21.1%。全年新增农业科技110服务站（点）177个，受益农民超过60万人。

Survey of Hainan Economic and Social Development for Year 2006

In 2006, Hainan Provincial Party Committee and Hainan Provincial People's Government highly uphold great banner of Deng Xiaoping theory and important thoughts of "three representatives" with scientific development concept as guidance, led Hainan people of all ethnic groups to seriously implement a series of significant strategies such as national macro-control, actively and reliably implemented the development strategy of "big companies and large projects", further conducted adjustment and optimization on industrial structure and put great efforts to transform the mode of economic growth. Good operation status has been observed for the economy of whole province with such characteristics as increased speed, optimized structure, increased benefit, reinforced vitality and stable price. New developments have been achieved in respect of deepened reform, opening to the outside world as well as exchanges and cooperation. Speedy developments have been observed in all social undertakings such as culture, education, health, sports and social security. New progress has been realized in respect of planned birth, environmental protection and construction of ecological province, urban and rural residents have got practical benefits form economic and social development. In summary, a good beginning for the Eleventh Five-year Plan Period has been achieved and a firm step has been taken to construct harmonic Hainan.

The major problems existing in economic and social development are that no essential changes have been observed in respect of weak agriculture infrastructure and level of modern agriculture is still low. The urban development and rural development is not coordinated with apparent features of "dual economy". "Three low and one small"(low level of industrialization, low level of urbanization, low level of urban and rural income and small economic aggregate) are still major contradictions existing in current economic development. There still exists great difference between the increasing demand for public products by urban and rural residents and the supplying capacity of government finance. Extensive economic growth has not got essentially transformed. The level of opening to the outside world needs to get further increased.

Part One Economic Development

I. Economic Aggregate

1. Accelerated economic growth is observed as a whole and comprehensive strength is apparently enhanced

In 2006,show that the GDP of whole province is 105.285 billion yuan with an increase of 12.5% over the previous year and 2.3% increase of the growth rate. Since GDP growth rate entered into two digit growth platform after getting out the shadow of "real estate bubble" in 2003, this is the highest increase of GDP growth rate since 1994 and the object of exceeding 100 billion yuan in terms of GDP has been realized one year ahead, of which, the added value of the first industry is 34.448 billion yuan (an increase of 9.1%), the added value of the secondary industry is 28.786 billion yuan (an increase of 19.8%) and the added values of the tertiary industry is 42.051 billion yuan (an increase of 11.0%). GDP per capita is 12654 yuan in terms of permanent population which is equivalent to about 1617 USD on the basis of average exchange rate in current year (an increase of 11.3%).

2. Industrial structure gets further adjusted and optimized, new industries and modern service industry get greatly developed

In 2006, the proportion of the first industry to the GDP of whole province is decreased from 32.97% last year to 32.72% and the contribution to economic growth by the first industry is 24.4%; the proportion of the secondary industry to the GDP of whole province is increased from 26.06% to 27.34% and the contribution to economic growth by the secondary industry is 38.8%; the proportion of the tertiary industry to the GDP of whole province is decreased from 40.97% to 39.94%. In terms of the internal structures of the industries, the advantageous agriculture in the first industry get speedy development, the contribution to the growth of agricultural economy by fishing sector, livestock industry, melons and vegetables as well as fruits is up to 80.8%. The proportion of high and new industries of the secondary industry gets apparently increased, the contribution to economic growth made by the production value of the above designated size industries such as petroleum processing, fertilizer, automobile manufacture, medicine and rotary kilns cement reaches 77.5%, technology and knowledge content existing in economic growth gets apparently increased. Exciting progress is observed for modern service sector of tertiary industry. New changes are observed for the structure of tourist source, the increase of overseas tourists is 38.0% faster than the increase of domestic tourists. Real estate market develops rationally in the process of macro-control and the sales area is larger than completed construction area. Finance environment gets further improved, the asset quality gets apparently improved and the inventory aggregate of foreign currency and local currency deposited in financial institutions increases in the same pace. Exhibition industry is still making progress and a lot of international large-scale conferences such as annual conference for Boao Forum for Asia, Agricultural Cooperation Forum over Straits, Southeast Seas Conference and Minister Conference as well as the First World Hainan Youth Congress have successfully been organized.

3. Prosperity index for macro-economy gets increased, economic operation get further improved in respect of quality and effectiveness.

In 2006, the enterpriser confidence index, which reflects the operation quality of macro-economy, is recorded as 134.1 with an increase of

9.6% over the previous year, which falls in relative prosperous interval for continuous four years. The enterprise prosperity index, which reflects the operation status of micro-entities, is recorded as 131.7 with an increase of 5.2%. The production and operation status of enterprises keeps improved and expected production confidence gets apparently enhanced. Total financial revenue of whole province is 17.988 billion yuan with an increase of 24.3% over the previous year, of which, local financial revenue is 10.235 billion yuan with an increase of 20.6%, which represents that target of exceeding 10 billion yuan of local financial revenue is realized one year ahead of schedule. Of the local financial revenue, general budgetary revenue accounts for 8.181 billion yuan with an increase of 19.1% over the previous year; fund revenue accounts for 2.054 billion yuan with an increase of 26.7% over the previous year; total tax revenue accounts for 13.921 billion yuan with an increase of 25.2%. Of all kinds of taxes, enterprise income tax increases by 26.2%, value added tax increases by 7.8%, business tax increases by 21.3%, individual income tax increases by 11.1% and real estate tax increases by 18.2%. The value added tax and consumption tax submitted to central government is 5.469 billion yuan with an increase of 37.7% and income tax submitted to central government is 1.438 billion yuan with an increase of 18.9%. Comprehensive index of economic effectiveness for 420 above designated scale industrial enterprises under statistical monitoring is 205.65% with an increase of 9.4% over the previous year and this index is the highest since statistical system of comprehensive index of economic effectiveness for industrial enterprises was established in 1997. Total realized profit is 4.150 billion yuan with an increase of 21.9%.

II. Farming, Forestry, Animal Husbandry and Fishery

Internal structure of agriculture keeps adjusted and optimized, rapid development is observed for agricultural production. Greater efforts are put to support agriculture and firmly push forward the construction of new socialist countryside to speed up the development of agriculture and rural economy. In 2006, the added value of agriculture of whole province is 34.448 billion yuan with an increase of 9.1% over the previous year, and the increase rate is increased by 3.1%. Advantageous agriculture such as fishery, animal husbandry, melons, vegetables and fruits keeps rapid development and its proportion to agriculture gets apparently increased, advantageous agriculture has become a dominant force leading rapid growth of agricultural economy. The production of aquatic products is 1.66 million tons with an increase of 10.7%; product of meats is 0.6831 million tons with an increase of 6.6%; production of melons and vegetables is 4.0039 million tons with an increase of 10.2%; production of fruits is 1.8785 million tons with an increase of 15.6%. The contribution to the growth of agricultural economy made by the four advantageous sectors, namely fishery, anima husbandry, melons and vegetables, fruits, is up to 80.8%. Agricultural benefits get apparently increased with adjustment of structure adjustment and price increase of agricultural products.

Table 1 Production of Major Agricultural Products

Name of Product	Unit	Actual Production in 2006	Increase or Decrease over the Last Year
Grain	10,000 ton	186.61	22.0
Sugarcane	10,000 ton	361.46	42.5
Oil Seeds	10,000 ton	8.96	5.1
Melons and Vegetables	10,000 ton	400.39	10.2
Fruits	10,000 ton	187.85	15.6
Of which: Banana	10,000 ton	108.63	19.0
Pineapple	10,000 ton	21.14	4.3
Mango	10,000 ton	26.24	17.8
Litchi	10,000 ton	8.85	25.9
Longan	10,000 ton	2.03	29.4
Citrus and Oranges	10,000 ton	2.66	34.9
Guava	10,000 ton	5.94	-5.6
Dried Rubber	10,000 ton	24.75	-0.1
Coconut	100 million	2.14	-10.8
Pepper	10,000 ton	3.14	0.9
Betel Nut	10,000 ton	7.48	16.3
Total Production of Meats	10,000 ton	68.31	6.6
Of which, production of pork, beef and mutton	10,000 ton	45.48	7.9
Production of poultry meat	10,000 ton	21.34	4.6
Production of Poultry Eggs	10,000 ton	2.61	-1.4
Total Production of Aquatic Products	10,000 ton	166.03	10.7
Of which, production of sea products	10,000 ton	138.03	8.6
Production of fresh water products	10,000 ton	28.00	22.0

III Industry and Building Sector

1. Industry "short leg" is apparently prolonged and industry becomes "locomotive" of pulling economic growth

The effects of "big companies and large projects" get further obvious, a group of large projects such as 8 million ton refinery, 0.6 million methane, 1.1 million ton fine iron powder, 80 thousand ton vinyl benzene, 150 thousand automobile engine are put into operation one by one to produce immediate benefits. Such new industries as petroleum processing, fertilizer, paper pulp, automobile manufacturing, medicine and rotary kilns cement have become new highlights of industrial growth to effectively push rapid development of industrial economy. In 2006, the added value of industry is 21.755 billion yuan with an increase of 24.1% over the previous year, and the increase rate is increased by 7.1%. Industry has become the "locomotive" of the economic growth of whole province as its contribution to economic growth is up to 33.6%. The proportion of industrial production value to gross domestic production is increased from 19.07% in the previous year to 20.66% with an increase of 1.6%, of which, added value realized by above designated size industries is 19.766 billion yuan with an increase of 26.5%. Of all the above designated industries, the added value realized by state owned holding enterprises is 10.164 billion yuan with an increase of 14.6%. In terms of light industry and heavy industry, the added value realized by heavy industry is 13.785 billion yuan with an increase of 36.8%; the added value realized by light industry is 5.981 billion yuan with an increase of 11.4%. In terms of economy type, the added value realized by state owned enterprises is 4.137 billion yuan with an increase of 8.5%; the added value realized by collective enterprises is 40 million yuan with an increase of 23.7%; the added value realized by cooperative stock enterprises is 7 million yuan with an increase of 24.9%; the added value realized by stockholding enterprises 7.916 billion yuan with an increase of 9.3%; the added value realized by the enterprises invested by foreign businessmen as well as enterprises from Hong Kong, Macao and Taiwan is 7.019 billion yuan with an increase of 66.7%; the added value realized by other types of industries is 0.647 billion yuan with an increase of 12.6%. The export value of industrial products is 4.605 billion yuan with an increase of 74.0%. The ration of sales to production is 96.8% and rapid development is observed for a group of industrial products meeting market demands.

Table 2 Production of Major Industrial Products

Name of Product	Unit	Actual Production in 2006	Increase or Decrease over the Last Year
Electricity Generation	100 million kWh	94.85	16.9
Production of Crude Iron Ore	10,000 ton	402.22	-4.5
Processing Quantity of Crude Oil	10,000 ton	179.86	1282.4
Steel (Steel Products)	10,000 ton	14.15	-4.8
Cement	10,000 ton	577.54	36.6
Artificial Board	10,000 m^3	17.81	-4.1
Automobile	10,000 set	8.36	14.4
Motor Cycle	10,000 set	13.37	98.2
Plastics Products	10,000 ton	2.12	9.7
Chemical Fiber	10,000 ton	5.59	21.1
Clothing	10,000 set	22.79	-8.6
Mixed and Blended Feed	10,000 ton	79.01	7.5
Sugar	10,000 ton	20.29	-22.6
Crude Salt	10,000 ton	18.25	9.4
Cigarette	10,000 Case	65.51	11.0
Canned Food	10,000 ton	13.67	10.3
Beverage without Alcohol	10,000 ton	27.70	0.9
Beverage Wine	10,000 ton	16.90	15.1
Of which: Beer	10,000 ton	14.05	17.3
Machine Made Board and paper Board	10,000 ton	1.36	7.0
Painting	10,000 ton	0.46	21.2
Nitrogen Fertilizer	10,000 ton	63.91	2.7
Phosphate Fertilizer	10,000 ton	0.36	-17.0
Polyester Chip	10,000 ton	23.79	457.1
Natural Crude Oil	10,000 ton	11.09	10.2
Natural Gas	10,000 m^3	20501	23.7
Paper Pulp	10,000 ton	103.65	32.8
LPG	10,000 ton	14.66	

2. Building sector is steadily developing

In 2006, the added value realized by building sector is 7.031 billion yuan with an increase of 9.3% in terms of comparable price. The construction area of housing and building is 7.8043 million square meters with an increase of 12.7% over the previous year. The completed construction of housing and building is 3.1497 million square meters with an increase of 53.2% over the previous year. Total amount of profit realized by building enterprises is 150 million yuan with a decrease of 42.1% over the previous year.

IV. Investment on Fixed Assets and Real Estate Development

Investment on fixed assets keeps stable increase. In 2006,total amount of the investment on fixed assets by whole society of whole province is 42.601 billion yuan with an increase of 12.3% over the previous year, of which, urban investment on fixed assets is 39.700 billion yuan with an increase of 13.1%; rural investment on fixed assets is 2.901 billion yuan with an increase of 3.9%. Of the urban investment on fixed assets, the investment made by the first industry is 1.460 billion yuan with an increase of 5.2%; the investment made the secondary industry is 10.877 billion yuan with a decrease of 15.6%; the investment made the tertiary industry is 27.363 billion yuan with an increase of 39.3%. The number of construction projects of whole province is 1493 with an increase of 5.2% over the previous year, of which, the number of new construction projects is 992 with an increase of 8.6%.

Large-scale projects are under smooth construction. In 2006, investment realized by investment projects, whose single investment is more than 15 million yuan, is 26.140 billion yuan which accounts for 61.4% of total investment on fixed assets of whole society. A group of large-scale projects such as 8 million ton refinery, 150 thousand automobile engine, 1.1 million ton fine iron powder, 0.6 million methane, 80 thousand ton vinyl benzene and Yuiehai western circular railway are put into operation or close to putting into operation, other projects such as Fuyao glass, Huaneng "big for small" power generation, Haikou round-city highway, the second phase expension of Phoenix Airport and Shenzhou Peninsula are steadily progressing.

The real estate market operates healthily. In 2006, the added value realized by real estate sector is 3.429 billion yuan with an increase of 0.3% over the previous year. Investment on real estate development is 8.926 billion yuan with an increase of 26.0%, of which, investment on commodity housing is 6.794billion yuan with an increase of 11.8%. The construction area of housing is 9.952 million square meters with an increase of8.0%. the completed construction area is 1.259million square meters and sales area is 2.034 million square meters.

Private investment becomes more and more active. In 2006, the realized fund for urban investment on fixed assets is45.794 billion yuan with an increase of 3.1% over the previous year. Investment vitality is apparently enhanced as the fund realization rate is 115.4%. Of the realized investment on fixed assets, state budgetary fund and bond is 3.106 billion yuan (6.7%), utilized foreign investment is 6.759 billion yuan and its proportion is increased from 6.1% in the previous year to 14.7% with an increase of 168.5%, self-raised fund is 14.866 billion yuan and its proportion is increased from 30.1% in the previous year to 32.5% with an increase of 18.6%. Private investment becomes more and more active and vitality of economic growth is apparently enhanced.

V Consumption Market and Price

Consumption market keeps highly marketable and upgrading of consumption structure is speeding. A group of famous retail enterprise such as Carrefour and RT-Mart enter into Hainan. The rapid development of chain retail sector makes consumption market become more active and prosperous. In 2006, the added value realized by wholesale, retail, accommodation and catering is12.218 billion yuan with an increase of 12.3% over the previous year and increase rate is increased by 1.8%. Total retail amount of social consumptions of whole province is up to 30.830 billion yuan with an increase of 14.8%, of which, retail amount of urban consumption is 24.358 billion yuan with an increase of 15.5% over the previous year and retail amount of rural consumption is 6.472 billion yuan with an increase of 12.4%. In terms of sectors, retail amount of wholesale and retail is 24.114 billion yuan with an increase of 15.3%, retail amount of accommodation and catering is 5.533 billion yuan with an increase of 13.2% and retail amount of other sectors is 1.183 billion yuan with an increase of 11.8%. Such consumption hotspot as housing, automobile, tourism and communication continues being hotter and the upgrade of consumption structure is speeded up.

Market price keep stable and economic operation environment is good. In 2006, total resident consumption price level increases by 1.5% and keeps at a low level for continuous 22 months. A good development status characteristic of high economic growth and low price increase has been realized to create stable environment for stable, rapid and healthy economy development. Urban resident consumption price increases by 1.2% and rural resident consumption price increases by 2.3%. In terms of category, price of residence category increases by 7.7%, price of food category increases by 2.3%, price of transportation and communication category increases by 1.2%, price of family equipment/article and maintenance service increases by 1.1%, price of wine and cigarette category increases by 0.5%, price of clothing category decreases by 4.2%, price of medical healthcare and personal articles decreases by 1.2%, price of articles of entertainment, education and culture as well as service category decreases by 1.0%. In whole year retail price of commodities increases by 1.3%, ex-works price of industrial products increases by 0.8%, price of raw material, fuel and power increases by 1.5%, price of fixed assets investment increase by 1.0% and price of agricultural production materials increases by 0.7%.

VI Transportation, Post, Communication and Tourism

New progress has been made in respect of trial operation of opening flight right and transportation keeps rapid growth. In 2006 two new inter-continent flight directly from Hainan to Russian are opened. There are 30 international flights and a modern land, ocean and air transportation system has been basically formed. See Table 3 for major transportation turnover and port throughput.

Table 3 Transportation Turnover and Port Throughput

	Unit	Actual Production in 2006	Increase or Decrease over the Last Year
1. Goods Turnover	100 million tonnage kilometer	612.82	32.9
Railway	100 million tonnage kilometer	10.96	55.2
Highway	100 million tonnage kilometer	66.07	9.3
Water Transportation	100 million tonnage kilometer	520.21	33.0
Civil Aviation	100 million tonnage kilometer	2.87	23.7
2. Passenger Turnover	100 million person kilometer	283.52	31.7
Railway	100 million person kilometer	1.84	50.8
Highway	100 million person kilometer	117.59	8.1
Water Transportation	100 million person kilometer	2.25	55.2
Civil Aviation	100 million person kilometer	161.84	55.8
3. Port Throughput			
Goods Throughput	10000 ton	5444	44.3
Of which, Ex-port Goods	10000 ton	2922.29	59.2
Passenger Throughput	10000 person	1709.73	6.9

Rapid growth is observed for post business, significant progress is achieved for telecommunication. In 2006, the post business volume is 472 million yuan with an increase of 15.4% over the previous year and the telecommunication business volume is 9.304 billion yuan with an increase of 31.1%. The number of fixed phone households of whole province at yearend is 2.4901 million with an increase of 8.3%, of which, the number of urban phone households is 1.7972 million with an increase of 5.7%, the number of rural phone households is 0.6929 million with an increase of 14.9%. The number of mobile phone household at yearend is 2.3989 million with an increase of 17.1% and the number of internet user at yearend is 0.4714 million with an increase of 11.4%.

Significant effects are achieved in respect of rectification of tourism market and adjustment of tourism structure with apparent increase of tourism benefits. Great efforts are put to rectify "four blacks"(namely black agency, black guide, black vehicle and black hotel). Decision on Further Enhancing Supervision and Regulation on Tourism Market is issued by NPC Standing Committee of Hainan Province and long-term supervision and regulation system has been basically formed on the basis of achieving progress in rectifying "four blacks" existing in tourism market. In 2006, the added value realized by tourism sector is 6.486 billion yuan with an increase of 12.6% over the previous year and increase rate is increased by 0.3%. Total number of overnight tourists for whole year is 16.0502 million person-times with an increase of 5.8%, of which, overseas tourists account for 0.6169 million person-times with an increase of 42.8% and domestic tourists account for 15.4333 million person-times with an increase of 4.80%. Total tourism revenue is 14.143 billion yuan with an increase of 13.1%, of which, overseas tourism revenue is 1.786 billion yuan with an increase of 78.4% and domestic tourism revenue is 12.357 billion yuan with an increase of 7.9%. The occupancy rate of tourism hotels is 52.5%. There are 261star hotels at yearend for whole province with an increase of 38 hotels over the year beginning, of which, five-star hotels account for 13, four-star hotels account for 50 and three- star hotels account for 115.

VII Finance, Security and Insurance Sector

Financial environment gets apparently improved and credit aggregate keeps stable growth. At the end of 2006, the foreign currency and local currency deposit balance of financial institutions in whole province is 156.030 billion yuan with an increase of 19.8% over the previous year, of which, the deposit balance of enterprises and institutions is 53.821 billion yuan with an increase of 30.8% over the previous year, balance of saving deposit of urban and rural residents is 81.218 billion yuan with an increase of 12.5% over the previous year. At the yearend the balance of foreign currency an local currency loans is 112.334 billion yuan with an increase of 12.8%, of which, shore-term loan is 24.713 billion yuan with an increase of 2.7% over the previous yearend, mid-term and long-term loan is 82.487 billion yuan with an increase of 17.5% over the previous yearend.

Capital market tends to be active and stock sector is under speedy development. In 2006, total market value of 20 items of listed A-shares for whole province is 54.587 billion yuan with an increase of 109.0% over the previous year. Transaction volume of shares (including fund) realized by stock business departments is 96.604 billion yuan with an increase of 187.4%. The transaction quantity of futures is 542.43 million with an increase of 62.4%, transaction volume of futures is 270.545 billion yuan with an increase of 97.0%.

Insurance business continues its expansion with apparently enhanced consciousness of risk prevention. In 2006, total amount of the insurances covered by insurance institutions is amounted to 827.554 billion yuan with an increase of 60.0% over the previous year. The realized premium income is 1.772 billion yuan with an increase of 18.5%, of which, the premium income of property insurances is 699million yuan with an increase of 23.7%, the premium income of life insurances is 940 million yuan with an increase of 15.1%, the premium of health insurances and accidental injury insurances is 133 million yuan with an increase of 17.8%. Claims and payments for whole year is amounted to 426 million yuan with an increase of 9.6% over the previous year, of which, claims and payments for property insurances is 272 million yuan with a decrease of 6.5%, claims and payments for life insurances is 128 million yuan with an increase of 82.3% and claims and payments for health insurances and accidental injury insurances is 25 million yuan with a decrease of 7.4%.

VIII People's Life

Rapid income growth is observed for urban and rural residents and people get benefits from economic growth. Greater efforts are put on the basis of economic development to actively expand urban employment, enhance transfer of rural labors, timely realize direct subsidy for grain, improve security system for low–income residents and take care of the life of weak groups so that people can get benefits from economic and social development. In 2006, average annual salary of staff and workers for whole province is 15890 yuan with an increase of 10.2%. Average disposable income per capita for urban residents is 9395 yuan with an increase of 11.20% over the previous year in terms of comparable price. Pure income per capita for peasants is 3256 yuan with an increase of 8.4%. The living quality of urban and rural residents gets further improved as the Engel's index for urban residents is 43.5% and the Engle's index for rural residents is 53.4%. Average housing area per capita for urban residents is 21.99 square meters with an increase of 4.2% over the previous year and average housing area per capita for rural residents is 22.05 square meters with an increase of 1.1%.

Ⅸ Safe Production

The number of fatality caused by accidents gets apparently decreased and significant progress is observed for safe production. In 2006, the number of all kinds of injury and fatal accidents occurred in whole province is 2900 with a decrease of 11.0%, the number of fatality (missing) is 527 persons with decrease of 19.1%, direct economic loss is amounted to 26.2905 million yuan with a decrease of 20.3%. Of all kinds of injury and fatal accidents, the number of traffic accidents is 1398 with a decrease of 5.5%, the number of fatality is 427 persons with a decrease of 14.1%, direct economic loss is 6.0058 million yuan with a decrease of 5.9%. The number of fire accidents in whole province is 1418 with a decrease of 14.9%, the number of fatality is 7 persons with decrease of 53.3%, direct economic loss is 6.7586 million yuan with a decrease of 9.9%. The number of fatality caused by safety accidents per 100 million yuan GDP is 0.52 person with a decrease of 28.8%.

Part Two Reform and Opening

I System Reform

Reform on administrative system gets further deepened and new breakthrough is made in respect of reforms on state owned enterprises. Hainan Provincial Industrial Economy and Information Industry Bureau to further improve administrative management system and supervision mechanism. Hainan Provincial Center for Governmental Affairs to continuously enhance government's administrative function. Hainan Road and Bridge Investment Corp. is founded to operate governmental investment through capital market. Reform of exiting from stock market by state economy is speeded up, separate placement of stock right is accomplished for Hainan Express Highway, great efforts are put to push 9 provincial general corporation to exit from market and system reforms are accomplished for 40% of medium and small state owned enterprises. Trial reforms on forest right are conducted in such city and county as Chengmai, Linggao, Dunchang and Baisha to accumulate experience for whole province.

II. Opening to the Outside World

Foreign trade export is greatly increased, domestic and foreign exchanges and cooperation get continuously expanded. In 2006, total volume of import and export of whole province is 2.846 billion USD with an increase of 9.8% over the previous year, of which, total export is amounted to 1.376 billion USD with an increase of 34.5% and total import is amounted to 1.470 billion USD with a decrease of 6.3%. Of total export volumes, the export to Hong Kong is amounted to 491 million USD with an increase of 52.8%, the export to Japan is amounted to 134 million USD with an increase of 21.6%, the export to USA is amounted to 208 million USD with an increase of 44.9%, the export to EU is amounted 135 million USD with a decrease of 2.0% and the export to ASEAN is amounted to 121 million USD with an increase of 72.2%. The actually used foreign fund for whole province is 793 million USD with an increase of 12.1%, of which, foreign loan is amounted to 44 million USD with an increase of 89.7% and foreign direct investment is amounted to 749 million USD with an increase of 9.5%. 193 items of new contracts and agreements are signed to use foreign investment with an increase of 10.9% and foreign investment under the newly signed agreements and contracts is amounted to 1.086 billion USD with an increase of 220%. Economy and trade negotiations are hold for 40 times as sponsor or co–sponsor to cause signing of 60 cooperation projects. Total amount of foreign contracting projects and labor cooperation contracts is up to 3.0700 million USD and the business volume accomplished by the foreign contracting projects and labor cooperation contracts is amounted to 2.46 million USD.

Part Three Social Development

I Labor Employment

The scale of labor employment continues its expansion and economic growth effectively promotes the increase of employment posts. At the end of 2006, total number of staff on duty is 0.7391million with an increase of 1.8%. The number of newly increased employed persons for whole year is 85,100 with an increase of 1.3%. The registered urban unemployment rate is 3.6%.

II Education Undertaking

Taking education development as priority is implemented and rapid development is observed for education undertaking. Strategy of taking education development is insisted, policy of "exemption of textbook fee, exemption of incidental expenses and subsidy for accommodation and living expenses" is implemented, greater efforts are put to accomplish the renovation of Grade D dangerous school building for rural primary and middle schools with total area of 0.3825 million square meters. Problem of immigrants for taking part in the examination of higher education institutions is properly solved to increase more than 8000 enrollment opportunities for Hainan students. Great efforts are put to fully promote the construction of higher education institution garden in Guilinyang to continuously expand the scale of higher education. In 2006, the students studying in common higher education institutions is 90,100 persons with an increase of 28.8% over the previous year; the students studying in common secondary specialized schools is 67600 persons with an increase of12.1% over the previous year; the students studying in senior middle schools is 0.1379 million persons with an increase of 16.8%; the students studying in junior middle schools is 0.4753 million persons with an increase of 2.0% over the previous year; the students studying in primary schools is 1.0472 million persons with a decrease of 0.9%. The enrollment rate is 99.8% and gross enrollment rate is 97.7% for school age children.

III Culture, Health and Sports Undertaking

Reforms on cultural system are steadily progressing and cultural sector is steadily developing. Development of cultural sector is speeded up, great efforts are put to create new culture features, cultural foundation is further firmed and new situations are observed for cultural undertaking and cultural sector. Key cultural facility projects such as provincial museum is under smooth construction, provincial library is to be put into operation soon and trial operations are conducted in some residence areas of Haikou and Sanya to extend mutual interactive cable TV digitalization project. Fine cultural product strategy is implemented, large-scale national dance drama Huangdaopo is awarded with performance prize and organization prize in the Third National Minority Performance Festival. Lots of local cultural festivals such as Danzhou song, Linggao puppet show and plate dance, vertical bamboo nose flute (traditional music instrument of Li minority) are organized and performed. Education Encyclopedia, Traditional Li Brocade are published. Such cultural agencies as provincial film corporation and provincial bookstore further enhance their internal vitality and market competitiveness. In 2006, there are21 artistic performance organizations, 21 artistic museums, 30 archive establishments, 20 libraries, 20 newspaper and 41magzines.235.20 million copies of newspapers are published in whole year with a decrease of 9.5% over the previous year; 10.59 million volumes of journals are published with a decrease of 12.2%. Broadcast and TV to Each Village Project is under steady implementation, comprehensive population coverage of broadcast and TV for whole province is 96.1% and 95.0% respectively. The number of cable TV users at yearend reaches 0.66 million households.

Great progress is realized in respect of health undertaking and public health system gets further improved. 262 village and town clinics (85.1% of total) have accomplished renovation to realize no dangerous building, availability of business building, availability of specialized equipment and availability of technical staff. A group of medical facilities are under construction and medical conditions for peasants get further improved. Up to 4.2160 million persons (86.03% of total) take part in new type of rural cooperative medical service and new type of rural cooperative medical service system is basically established two years ahead of the deadline as specified by state. There are 2337 medical organizations (including clinics and medical room) in whole province and 20200 hospital bed. The number of all kinds of medical and technical personnel is 38199persons with an increase of 2.7% over the previous year, of which, practicing doctors (including practicing assistant doctors) account for 12195 persons and registered nurses account for 11508 persons. In whole province there are 28 disease prevention control centers (epidemic prevention stations) and 312 rural medical stations at level of village and town.

New achievements are realized for sports undertaking and nationwide exercise activities become more and more active. In 2006, 3 items of gold medal, silver medal and bronze medal are awarded in world sports competitions; 2 items of gold medals, 10 items of silver medals and 1 item of bronze medal are awarded in Asian games which realizes a breakthrough of zero gold medal in Asian game for the first time; 29 items of gold medals, 33 items of silver medals and 22 bronze medals are awarded in national sports games. Successful organization of international round-island highway bicycle competition expands influences of Hainan in China and abroad.

IV Social Security

Social security undertaking gets continued development and social relief system gets further improved. In 2006, the number of people covered by urban basic aged insurance (not including retired staff) is 0.94 million persons with an increase of 11.4%; the number of people covered by urban basic medical insurance (not including retired staff) is 0.9096 million persons with an increase of 4.3%; the number of people covered by on-job injury insurance (not including retired staff) is 0.7154 million persons with an increase of 3.8%; the number of people covered by urban unemployment insurance (not including retired staff) is 0.5913 million persons with an increase of 4.2%. At the yearend the number of all sorts of specially cared people who receives compensations and subsidies in whole province is 24,800 persons with a decrease of 1.0%. There are 284 items of community service facilities and 4 items of service centers of all sorts in urban area. Rural social security work gets further improved and all of the people who are qualified to enjoy social security for low-income people are covered by social security for low-income people. At yearend the number of rural population covered by social security for low-income people is up to 0.153 million persons.

Part Four Continued Development

I Population

Population reproduction enters into favorable spiral orbit and significant achievements are realized in population control. Birth-control oriented mechanism is improved and implemented, population reproduction enters into favorable spiral orbit characteristic of "low birth, low death and low increase". At the end of 2006, permanent population of whole province is 8.3588 million persons with an increase of 78,800 persons over the previous year. Population birth rate is 1.459% and population fatality rate is 0.573%. Natural population increase rate is 0.886% with a decrease of 0.007%.

II Environment Protection

Construction of ecological environment is further enhanced and new progress is achieved in the construction of ecological province. Protection zones for drinking water resources are determined, great efforts are put to enhance the construction at roadside, riverside and seaside, construction of urban waste water treatment facilities and prevention of environmental pollution, human living environment construction project at level of civilized ecological village, town and city is under active construction and ecological environment of whole province gets effectively protected and recovered. In 2006, forestation area for whole province is 31200 ha, of which, artificial forestation area accounts for 23800 ha, reproduced and renovated forestation area accounts for 7400 ha. Forest coverage is up to 55.6% with an increase of 0.1%. Jianfeng Mountain, Lanyang, Diaoluo Mountain, Qixian Mountain, crater, Limu Mountain, Bawang Mountain are listed as national forest parks. All of the cities and towns in whole province enjoy excellent environmental air quality, major pollutants such as sulphur dioxide and nitrogen dioxide satisfy national standard for Class I environmental air, total suspension particles and inhalant particles possess light influences only on the environmental air of individual cities and towns. The environmental quality of surface water keeps good as a whole and 80.7% of the monitored river sections and 82.4% of the monitored lakes and reservoirs reach or surpass national standard for Class III surface water. Offshore water quality keeps good as a whole, Category I and Category II seawater account for 82.2% of total and the greatest majority of monitored sea keep clean. At yearend there are 20 environment monitoring stations, of which, there are 1 Grade I national environment monitoring station, 3 Grade II national environment monitoring stations and 16 Grade III national environment monitoring stations. The number of monitoring staff is up to 316 persons. At yearend there are 69 natural protection zones, of which, there are 8 natural protection zones at state level and 25 natural protection zones at province level. The area of natural protection zones is 2.8137 million ha, of which, the area of natural protection zones at state level accounts for 85,200 ha and the area of natural protection zones at province level accounts for 2.6355 million ha. 15 kinds of animals are listed as Grade I protected wild animal at state level and 87 kinds of animals are listed as Grade II protected wild animal at state level. 7 kinds of plants are listed as Grade I protected plant at state level and 41 kinds of plants are listed as Grade II protected plants at state level.

III Science and Technology

New progress is made in respect of scientific and technological creation and technology content of economic growth gets apparently increased. In 2006 the whole province accomplished 115 items of significant scientific and technological progress with an increase of 36.9% over the previous year. The whole province organized the implementation of 5 items of scientific research projects funded by state supporting plan for science and technology, 4 items of projects under 863 program, 7 items of projects under state torch program, 20 items of state star-spark and 36 items of projected funded by National Fund for Natural Science. 538 items of patents are applied for whole year, of which, 248 items are awarded with patent right. Total scientific and technological expenditure is amounted to 1.574 billion yuan with an increase of 21.1%. The number of newly established 110 service stations for agricultural technology is 177 and more than 0.6 million peasant get benefits from these stations.

资料整理:李 诚 唐忠民

Arranged by Licheng Tangzhongmin

1. 综 合
GENERAL SURVEY

1－1 行政区划
Administrative Divisions

单位:个 (Unit)

市 县	City and County	地级市 Cities at Prefectural Level	县级市 Cities at Country Level	县 Counties	民族自治县 Minority Nanat-ionality Autono-mous County	市辖区数 Districts Under the Jurisdiction of Cities	乡(镇) Township (Town)
全省总计	**Total**	2	6	4	6	4	200
海口市	Haikou	1				4	23
三亚市	Sanya	1					5
五指山市	Wuzhishan		1				7
文昌市	Wenchang		1				16
琼海市	Qionghai		1				12
万宁市	Wanning		1				12
定安县	Dingan			1			10
屯昌县	Tunchang			1			8
澄迈县	Chengmai			1			10
临高县	Lingao			1			11
儋州市	Danzhou		1				17
东方市	Dongfang		1				10
乐东黎族自治县	Ledong Li Nationality Autonomous County				1		11
琼中黎族苗族自治县	Qiongzhong Li and Miao Nationality Autonomous County				1		10
保亭黎族苗族自治县	Baoting Li and Miao Nationality Autonomous County				1		9
陵水黎族自治县	Lingshui Li Nationality Autonomous County				1		11
白沙黎族自治县	Baisha Li Nationality Autonomous County				1		11
昌江黎族自治县	Changjiang Li Nationality Autonomous County				1		7

注:海南省还管辖西、南、中沙群岛及其海域,群岛设立办事处驻西沙永兴岛。

a)Hainan provice government also dominate the west,south and middle sang isle and its maritime spance.the office is buit up in the isle and stationed in west sand Yong-Xing Island.a

综合 GENERAL SURVEY

1－2 自然资源
Natural Resources

项 目	Item	数量 Amount
土地资源和海洋	**Land Resources and Ocean**	
土地面积(平方公里)	Land Area(sp.km)	35354
海洋面积（万平方公里）	Area of Sea(10 000 sp.km)	200
海岸线长度（公里）	Length of Sea Coastline(km)	1928
岛屿个数（个）	Number of Islands(unit)	280
岛屿面积（平方公里）	Area of Island(sp.km)	930.00
气侯	**Climate**	
年降雨量(毫米)	Precipitation (mm)	961—2439
年平均气温(摄氏度)	Average Temperature(°C)	22.8—25.8
年日照时数(小时)	Hours of Sunshine(hour)	1832—2558
水利资源	**Water Resources**	
独流入海河流(条)	Nuberm of Rivers	154
水力资源理论蕴藏量(万千瓦)	Hydrpower Resources(100 million kw)	103.88
#可开发量	Developable Resources	89.77
淡水总面积(万公顷)	Freshwater Area(10 000 Hectares)	13.7
矿产资源	**Mineral Resources**	
铁矿石(保有储量)(万吨)	Iron Ore(Ensured Reserves)(10 000 ton)	23940.1
煤(保有储量)(万吨)	Coal(Ensured Reserves)(10 000 ton)	16660.4
森林资源		
活立木蓄积量(万立方米)	Tontal Standing Stock Volume(100 million cu.m)	11559.6
森林面积(万亩)	Forest Area(10000 hectares)	2827
森林覆盖率(%)	Forest-covorage Rate(%)	56.7
红树林(万亩)		5.9
野生植物(种)		4600
野生动物(种)		574

1－3 土地状况
Land Characteristics

项 目	Item	面积（万公顷） Area(10 000 Hectarea)	占总面积（%） Percentage to Total Area
土地面积	**Land Area**	353.54	100.0
耕地总资源	Cultivated Land Resources	83.72	23.7
常用耕地	Cultivated Land	41.62	11.8
按地形分类	**By Topographic Feature**		
山地	Mountains	86.1	25.4
丘陵	Hills	45.1	13.3
台地	Tableland	110.5	32.6
阶地平原	Plains	95.3	28.1
其他	Others	2.1	0.6

1－4 主要河流
Major Rivers

名称	River	发源地点	Source	长度（公里）Length(km)	集水面积（平方公里）Drainage Area(sp.km)
南渡江	Handu River	白沙县南峰山	Nanfeng Mountain in Baisha County	331	7176
昌化江	Changhua River	琼中县五指山	Wuzhi Mountain in Qiongzhong County	230	5070
万泉河	Wanquan River	琼中县五指山	Wuzhi Mountain in Qiongzhong County	163	3683
陵水河	Lingshui River	保亭县峨隆岭	Elong Mountain in Baoting County	76	1121
珠碧江	Zhubi River	白沙县南高岭	Nangao Mountain in Baisha County	86	1101
宁远河	Ningyuan River	保亭县甘蔗山	Ganzhe Mountain in Baoting County	90	986
望楼河	Wanglou River	乐东县尖峰岭	Jianfeng Mountain in Ledong County	83	827
文澜河	Wenlan River	儋州市马鞍岭	Maan Mountain in Danzhou City	71	795
藤桥河	Tengqiao River	保亭县峨月岭	Eyue Mountain in Baoting County	58	705
北门江	Beijiang River	儋州市马岭排	Malingpai Mountain in Danzhou City	62	653
太阳河	Taiyang River	琼中县长沙岭	Changsha Mountain in Qiongzhong County	83	576
春江	Chun River	儋州市高石岭	Gaoshi Mountain in Danzhou City	54	550
文教河	Wenjiao River	海口市大坡乡文德头村	Wendetou Village Dapo Township Haikou City	56	522

1－5 主要山脉情况
Major Mountain Ranges

名称	Mountains Range	山峰高程（米）Height of Mountain Perk(m)
五指山	Wuzhi Mountain	1867
霸王岭	Bawang Mountain	1560
莺歌岭	Yingge Mountain	1811
尖峰岭	Jianfeng Mountain	1412
吊罗山	Diaoluo Mountain	1519
黎母山	Limu Mountain	1411

1－6 大型水库概况
Large-scale Reservoir Survey

库 名 Reservoir	集水面积（平方公里）Catchment Area (sq.km)	库容 Storage Capacity		设计灌溉面积（万公顷）Design Irrigated Area (10 000 hectares)
		总库容（亿立方米）Total Storage Capacity (100 million cu.m)	正常库容(亿立方米) Normal Storage Capacity (100 million cu.m)	
大广坝 Da Guang Ba	3498	17.10	15.00	6.73
松 涛 Song Tao	1440	33.40	26.00	14.5
万 宁 Wan Ning	429	1.52	0.72	0.8
长 茅 Chang Mao	256	1.44	1.11	1.2
石 碌 Shi Lu	354	1.41	0.99	1
牛路岭 Niu Lu Ling	1236	7.79	5.30	发电 electric powre

1－7 主要矿产资源
Main Mineral Resources

等 级 Grade	矿 种 Mineral
Ⅰ Ⅰ	铁、钛、石灰石、石英沙、石油、天然气 Iron Ore,Titanium,Limestone,Quartz,Petroleum,Natural Gas,
Ⅱ Ⅱ	铜、锌、铅、钴、铝、磷、粘土、褐煤、油页岩、钼 Copper,Zinz,Lead,Cobalt,Aluminium,Phosphorus,Clay,Coal,Oil Shale,Quartz,Molybdenum
Ⅲ Ⅲ	石云岩、石英岩、耐火粘土、沸石、石墨、锰 Qurtzite,Refractory Clay,Boil,Graphite,Manganese
其他 Others	锡、钨、金、银、重晶石、硅藻土、黄铁矿、花岗岩板材、地下水、石粒、泥炭 Stannum,Wolfram,Gold,Silver,Heavy Spar,Diatomite,Pyrite,Granite(cantain Potassium),Rock,Peat

1－8 法人单位数和产业活动单位数
Institutional Unit and Establishments

单位:个 (Unit)

行业	Sector	法人单位数 Institutional Unit	单产业法人单位 Single Sector Unit	多产业法人单位 Multi-sector Unit	产业活动单位数 Establishments Unit	多产业法人所属的产业活动单位 Establishments of Multi-sector Institutional Unit
总计	**Total**	**27729**	**26274**	**1455**	**36893**	**10619**
农、林、牧、渔业	**Farming,Forestry,Animal Husbandry and Fishery**	**1831**	**1725**	**106**	**2071**	**346**
农业	Farming	1104	1092	12	1137	45
林业	Forestry	248	164	84	278	114
畜牧业	Animal Husbandry	89	87	2	91	4
渔业	Fishery	210	210		213	3
农、林、牧、渔服务业	Agricultural Services	180	172	8	352	180
采矿业	**Mining and Quarrying**	**180**	**175**	**5**	**193**	**18**
煤炭开采和洗选业	Coal Mining and Dressing					
石油和天然气开采业	Mining of Oil and Natural Gas	2	2		2	
黑色金属矿采选业	Mining and Dressing of Ferrous Metals	16	13	3	18	5
有色金属矿采选业	Mining and Dressing of Nonferrous Metals	78	78		78	
非金属矿采选业	Mining and Dressing of Nonmetal Minerals	74	72	2	85	13
其他采矿业	Others	10	10		10	
制造业	**Manufacturing**	**2126**	**2068**	**58**	**2286**	**218**
农副食品加工业	Agriculture and Non-Staple Food Processing	257	242	15	360	118
食品制造业	Food Production	157	151	6	167	16
饮料制造业	Beverages	107	105	2	109	4
烟草制品业	Tobacco	1	1		1	
纺织业	Textiles	27	26	1	27	1
纺织服装、鞋、帽制造业	Garments,Shoses and Hats	72	66	6	73	7
皮革、毛皮、羽毛(绒)及其制品业	Leather, Furs, Down and Related Products	8	8		8	7
木材加工及木、竹、藤、棕、草制品业	Timber Processing, Bamboo, Cane, Palm Fiber and Straw Products	143	142	1	149	
家具制造业	Furniture Manufacturing	90	88	2	91	3
造纸及纸制品业	Papermaking and Paper Products	62	62		63	1
印刷业和记录媒介的复制	Printing and Record Medium Reproduction	124	123	1	127	4
文教体育用品制造业	Cultural, Educational and Sports Goods					
石油加工、炼焦及核燃料加工业	Petroleum Processing, Coking and Nucleus Fuel Processing	6	6		6	
化学原料及化学制品制造业	Raw Chemical Materials and Chemical Products	147	141	6	148	7
医药制造业	Medical and Pharmaceutical Products	111	108	3	113	5
化学纤维制造业	Chemical Fiber	6	6		6	

本表按法人单位及其产业活动单位统计,含法人单位在外省的产业活动单位。(1-8)
Note: The form is based on impersonal entity and its industrial activity units, including the industrial activity units in other provinces.

1-8 续 1(continued 1)

行　业	Sector	法人单位数 Institutional Unit	单产业法人单位 Single Sector Unit	多产业法人单位 Multi-sector Unit	产业活动单位数 Establishments Unit	多产业法人所属的产业活动单位 Establishments of Multi-sector Institutional Unit
橡胶制品业	Rubber Products	24	23	1	25	2
塑料制品业	Plastic Products	95	95		100	5
非金属矿物制品业	Nonmetal Mineral Products	217	217		218	1
黑色金属冶炼及压延加工业	Smelting and Pressing of Ferrous Metals	14	14		14	
有色金属冶炼及压延加工业	Smelting and Pressing of Nonferrous Metals	11	11		11	
金属制品业	Metal Products	78	77	1	81	4
通用设备制造业	Ordinary Machinery	28	28		32	4
专用设备制造业	Equipment for Special Purposes	46	40	6	50	10
交通运输设备制造业	Transport Equipment	154	149	5	163	14
电气机械及器材制造业	Electric Equipment and Machinery	55	54	1	56	2
通信设备、计算机及其他电子设备制造业	Telecommunications Equipment,Computer and Other Electronic Equipment	32	31	1	32	1
仪器仪表及文化、办公用机械制造业	Instruments, Meters, Cultural and Office Machinery	4	4		4	
工艺品及其他制造业	Handicraft Article and Other Manufacturing	46	46		48	2
废弃资源和废旧材料回收加工业	Recovery and Processing of Discarded Resoures and Waste Materials	4	4		4	
电力、煤气及水的生产和供应业	**Production and Supply of Electric Power,Gas and Water**	**244**	**240**	**4**	**305**	**65**
电力、热力的生产和供应业	Production and Supply of Electric Power, Steam and Hot Water	147	144	3	198	54
燃气生产和供应业	Production and Supply of Gas	25	24	1	26	2
水的生产和供应业	Production and Supply of Tap Water	72	72		81	9
建筑业	**Construction**	**1144**	**1138**	**6**	**1269**	**131**
房屋和土木工程建筑业	House and Civil Engineering	263	258	5	378	120
建筑安装业	Installation	216	215	1	219	4
建筑装饰业	Decoration	540	540		544	4
其他建筑业	Others	125	125		128	3
交通运输、仓储和邮政业	**Transport, Storage, Postal Services**	**476**	**422**	**54**	**1249**	**827**
铁路运输业	Railway Transport	2	2		2	
道路运输业	Way Transport	190	169	21	561	392
城市公共交通业	Public Traffic in City	56	52	4	58	6
水上运输业	Waterway Transport	74	67	7	81	14
航空运输业	Air Transport	12	11	1	13	2
管道运输业	Pipeline Transport					
装卸搬运和其他运输服务业	Load and Unload Transport and Others Transport	104	99	5	124	25
仓储业	Storage	18	18		20	2
邮政业	Postal	20	4	16	390	386
信息传输、计算机服务和软件业	**Information Transmission,Computer Services and Software**	**464**	**453**	**11**	**496**	**43**
电信和其他信息传输服务业	Telecommunications and Other Information Transmission	64	57	7	92	35
计算机服务业	Computer Services	252	250	2	255	5
软件业	Software	148	146	2	149	3
批发和零售业	**Wholesale & Retail Trade**	**5804**	**5501**	**303**	**7194**	**1693**

1-8 续 2(continued 2)

行业	Sector	法人单位数 Institutional Unit	单产业法人单位 Single Sector Unit	多产业法人单位 Multi-sector Unit	产业活动单位数 Establishments Unit	多产业法人所属的产业活动单位 Establishments of Multi-sector Institutional Unit
批发业	Wholesale Trade	2845	2756	89	3072	316
零售业	Retail Trade	2959	2745	214	4122	1377
住宿和餐饮业	**Hotels and Catering Trade**	948	876	72	1190	314
住宿业	Hotels	709	653	56	799	146
餐饮业	Catering Trade	239	223	16	391	168
金融业	**Finance**	163	113	50	862	749
银行业	Banking	54	16	38	688	672
证券业	Stock	13	10	3	24	14
保险业	Insurance	25	16	9	77	61
其他金融活动	Other Finance Activities	71	71		73	2
房地产业	**Real Estate**	1904	1889	15	1952	63
房地产业	Real Estate	1904	1889	15	1952	63
租赁和商务服务业	**Rent and Business Affair Services**	1888	1845	43	2097	252
租赁业	Rent	84	84		86	2
商务服务业	Business Affair Services	1804	1761	43	2011	250
科学研究、技术服务和地质勘查业	**Scientific Research, Polytechnic Services and Geological Prospecting**	760	727	33	1064	337
研究与试验发展	R&D	146	143	3	168	25
专业技术服务业	Profesional Technology Services	435	425	10	501	76
科技交流和推广服务业	Scientific and Technological Interchange and Popularization Services	158	138	20	372	234
地质勘查业	Geological Prospecting	21	21		23	2
水利、环境和公共设施管理业	**Water Conservancy, Environmental and Public Installations Management Services**	256	229	27	379	150
水利管理业	Water Conservancy Management	87	75	12	133	58
环境管理业	Environmental Management	68	61	7	130	69
公共设施管理业	Public Installations Management Services	101	93	8	116	23
居民服务和其他服务业	**Resident Services and Other Social Services**	341	332	9	370	38
居民服务业	Resident Services	179	172	7	199	27
其他服务业	Other Social Services	162	160	2	171	11
教育	**Education**	2464	2243	221	4596	2353
教育	Education	2464	2243	221	4596	2353
卫生、社会保障和社会福利业	**Health Care,Social Security and Social Welfare**	668	657	11	928	271
卫生	Health Care	576	565	11	755	190
社会保障业	Social Security	25	25		65	40
社会福利业	Social Welfare	67	67		108	41
文化、体育和娱乐业	**Culture,Sports and Recreational Services**	460	445	15	650	205
新闻出版业	News Publishing House	60	58	2	63	5
广播、电视、电影和音像业	Radio, Television, Film and Audiovisual	68	59	9	156	97
文化艺术业	Culture and Arts	183	181	2	246	65
体育	Sports	34	33	1	36	3
娱乐业	Recreational Services	115	114	1	149	35
公共管理和社会组织	**Public Management and Social Organizations**	5608	5196	412	7742	2546
中国共产党机关	The Communist Party of China	174	157	17	184	27
国家机构	State Institution	1792	1413	379	3805	2392
人民政协和民主党派	People's Political Consultative Conference and Democratic Parties	41	41		41	
群众团体、社会团体和宗教组织	Mass Organization,Social Organizations and Religion Organizations	666	651	15	776	125
基层群众自治组织	Mass Autonomy Organization at the Grass-roots	2935	2934	1	2936	2
国际组织	**International Organization**					
国际组织	International Organization					

1－9 各市县法人单位数和产业活动单位数
Institutional Unit and Establishments by City and County

单位:个 (Unit)

市县	City and County	法人单位数 Institutaional Unit	单产业法人单位 Single Sector Unit	多产业法人单位 Multi-sector Unit	产业活动单位数 Establishments Unit	多产业法人所属的产业活动单位 Establishments of Multi-sector Institutional Unit
总计	**Total**	**27729**	**26274**	**1455**	**36893**	**10619**
海口市	Haikou	15282	14909	373	16424	1515
三亚市	Sanya	1641	1529	112	2150	621
五指山市	Wuzhishan	382	358	24	497	139
文昌市	Wenchang	1085	945	140	2337	1392
琼海市	Qionghai	1191	1165	26	1434	269
万宁市	Wanning	772	728	44	1268	540
定安县	Dingan	452	413	39	823	410
屯昌县	Tunchang	473	424	49	842	418
澄迈县	Chengmai	788	682	106	1346	664
临高县	Lingao	618	569	49	925	356
儋州市	Danzhou	972	929	43	1430	501
东方市	Dongfang	572	536	36	933	397
乐东县	Ledong	768	697	71	1227	530
琼中县	Qiongzhong	368	320	48	764	444
保亭县	Baoting	356	328	28	528	200
陵水县	Lingshui	439	409	30	820	411
白沙县	Baisha	368	305	63	697	392
昌江县	Changjiang	449	387	62	807	420
农垦	Land Reclamation	413	310	103	1249	939
洋浦	Yangpu	340	331	9	354	23

1－10 经济和社会发展主要指标
Major Indicators For National Economy

指　　标	Item	2004	2005	2006
人口与就业	Population and Employment			
年底常住人口(万人)	Year–End Permanents(10 000 persons)	817.83	828.00	835.88
年底户籍人口(万人)	Year–End Registered(10 000 persons)	805.88	819.03	833.44
从业人员数(万人)	Employment(10 000 persons)	371.1	382.53	391.96
#职工人数	Staff and Workers	72.53	72.63	73.91
生产总值(当年价)(亿元)	Gross Domestic Product(100 million yuan)	790.12	905.03	1052.85
第一产业	Primary Industry	287.3	300.75	344.48
第二产业	Secondary Industry	201.17	230.53	287.86
第三产业	Tertiary Industry	301.65	373.75	420.51
人均生产总值(元)	Per Capita GDP(yuan)	9704	10998	12654
农业	Agricuture			
农业总产值(当年价)(亿元)	Gross Ouput Value of Agricuture(100 million yuan)	452.92	475.88	543.9
粮　　食(万吨)	Grain(10 000 tons)	196.57	153	186.61
#谷　　物	Rice	156.9	116.04	150.09
油　　料(万吨)	Oil Plants(10 000 tons)	9.08	8.53	8.96
糖　　蔗(万吨)	Sugarcane(10 000 tons)	417.89	253.65	361.46
瓜　　菜(万吨)	Melon and Vegetable(10 000 tons)	412.8	363.39	400.39
水　　果(万吨)	Fruit(10 000 tons)(10 000 tons)	143.45	152.53	187.85
茶　　叶(万吨)	Tea(10 000 tons)	0.13	0.1	0.14
橡　　胶(干胶)(万吨)	Rubber(Dry Rubber)(10 000 tons)	32.98	24.78	24.75
椰　　子(万个)	Coconut(10 000 units)	24188	24007	21360
槟　　榔(吨)	Areca(tons)	62763	64338	21360
胡　　椒(吨)	Pepper(tons)	32551	31119	74808
腰　　果(吨)	Cashew(tons)	616	388	417
猪牛羊肉(万吨)	Supply of Pork,Beef and Mutton(10 000 tons)	38.95	42.15	45.48
水产品(万吨)	Aqutic Products(10 000 tons)	135.85	150	166.04
造林面积(万公顷)	Afforestation Area(10 000 hectares)	3.54	3.24	2.38
工业	Industry			
工业总产值(当年价)(亿元)	Gross Ouput Value of Industry(100 million yuan)	384.66	473.02	668.1
#轻工业	Light industry	164.52	192.84	225.15
重工业	Heavy Industry	220.15	280.18	442.95
发电量(亿千瓦时)	Electricity(10 000 kwh)	66.47	81.64	94.85

注:工业总产值为规模以上工业企业总产值。常住人口是指根据人口变动情况抽样调查的推算数据。
a)Gross output Value of industry is above sale industrial enterprise gross output value.The residents refer to calculated datas in accordance with the spot check result of the population alleration.

1-10 续 1(continued 1)

指　　标	Item	2004	2005	2006
铁 矿 石(万吨)	Iron Ore(10 000 tons)	473.6	285.65	402.22
钢　　材(万吨)	Steel Products(10 000 tons)	17.55	14.86	14.15
水　　泥(万吨)	Cement(10 000 tons)	418.7	442.55	577.54
人 造 板(万平方米)	Arificial Wooden Board(10 000 cu.m)	22.52	18.55	17.81
汽　　车(辆)	Motor Vvehicles	66954	73086	83636
摩 托 车(万辆)	Motorcicles(10 000)	12.11	6.74	13.37
轮胎外胎(万条)	Tires(10 000)			
化学肥料(折纯)(万吨)	Chemical Pesticides(100%)(10 000 tons)	65.01	62.65	64.27
#氮肥(折纯)	Nitrogen(100%)	64.61	62.21	63.91
合成纤维聚合物(万吨)	Synthetic Fiber(10 000tons)	5.47	4.27	23.79
化学纤维(吨)	Chemical Fibers(ton)	55667	46136	55859
布(万米)	Cloth(10 000 m)			
毛　　毯(万条)	woollen Blanket(10 000)	80.13	99.8	
食　　糖(万吨)	Sugar(10 000 tons)	45.8	26.22	20.29
原　　盐(万吨)	Salt(10 000 tons)	8.39	16.69	18.25
卷　　烟(万箱)	Cigarettes(10 000 Cases)	11.8	11.8	13.1
罐　　头(吨)	Canned Food(ton)	120265	138362	136725
软饮料(吨)	Soft Drink(ton)	261868	276183	276961
啤　　酒(吨)	Beer(ton)	87712	119870	140546
机制纸及纸板(万吨)	Paperboard(10 000 tons)	9547	12722	13610
运输邮电业	**Transportation,Post and Telecommunication**			
货物周转量(万吨公里)	Freight Ton-Kilometers(10 000 ton-km)	2322216	4609661	6128228
铁　　路	Railways	53973	70610	109628
公　　路	Highways	569888	604535	660653
水　　路	Waterways	1684877	3911304	5202102
民　　航	Civil Aviation	13478	23212	28698
旅客周转量(万人公里)	Passenger-Kilometers(10 000 passenger-km)	2064499	2153365	2835220
铁　　路	Railways	1992	12230	18379
公　　路	Highways	1054801	1087647	1175911

1-10 续 2(continued 2)

指　标	Item	2004	2005	2006
水　运	Waterways	15930	14465	22517
民　航	Civil Aviation	991776	1039023	1618413
沿海港口货物吞吐量(万吨)	Valume of Freight in Coastal Ports(10 000 tons)	2986	3066	3744
进　口	Import	1373	1410	1921
出　口	Export	1613	1656	1821
邮电业务总量(万元)	Telecommucation Services(10 000 yuan)	623520	750741	977651
固定资产投资	**Investment in Fixed Assets**			
全社会固定资产投资总额 (亿元)	Total Investment in Fixed Assets(100 million yuan)	325.28	379.43	426.01
全社会新增固定资产(亿元)	Total Newly Increased Fixed Assets (100 million yuan)	213.7	173.82	219.46
固定资产交付使用率(%)	Rate of Fixed Assets Transferred and in Use(%)	65.7	45.8	51.5
全社会竣工房屋建筑面积(万平方米)	Total Foor Space Completed of Buildings(10 000 sq.m)	665.8	1664.16	688.17
#住　宅	Residendial Housing	513.7	1271.65	420.76
国内商业	**Domestic Trade**			
社会消费品零售总额(亿元)	Total Retail Sales of Consumer Goods(100 million yuan)	219.23	268.55	308.3
城　镇	Town	167.55	210.96	243.58
乡　村	Rural	51.68	57.6	64.72
利用外资	**Utilization of Foreign Capital**			
对外签订协议合同项目(宗)	Number of Projects in the Signed Agreements and Contracts	171	174	193
#客商直接投资	Direct Investment by Foreigh Capital	169	174	191
对外签订协议合同金额 (万美元)	Total Amount of Foreign Capital to Be Utilized through the Signed Agreements and Contracts(USD 10 000)	74335	34211	108602
#客商直接投资	Direct Investment by Foreigh Capital	70285	34211	105112
实际利用外资(万美元)	Total Amount of Foreigh Capital Actually used (USD 10 000)	66998	70711	79259
#客商直接投资	Direct Investment by Foreigh Capital	64343	68401	74878
对外经济贸易	**Foreigh Trade and Economic Cooperation**			
进出口总额(万美元)	Total Imports and exports (USD 10 000)	340168	259175	284607
进　口	Import	230916	156921	147045
出　口	Export	109252	102254	137562

1-10 续 3(continued 3)

指　标	Item	2004	2005	2006
旅　游	Tourism			
接待旅游人数(万人次)	Number of Tourists Received by Tourist Hotels(10 000 persens)	1402.88	1516.47	1605.02
#境外游客	Foreign Tourists	30.86	43.19	61.69
国际旅游收入(万美元)	Earnings from International Tourism(USD10 000)	8160	12846	22912
财政金融	Government Finance and Banking			
地方财政收入(万元)	Local Financial Revenue(10 000yuan)	692965	848930	1023508
地方财政支出(万元)	Local Financial Expenditure(10 000yuan)	1407414	1675759	1961130
全社会存款年末余额（亿元）	Total Year-end Deposits of Financial Institutions (100 million yuan)	1159.31	1302.29	1560.3
#国家银行	National Banks	976.2	1085.7	1293.37
全社会贷款年末余额（亿元）	Total Year-end Loans of Financial Institutions(100 million yuan)	920.55	996.32	1123.34
#国家银行	National Banks	803.83	860.48	940.16
物价总指数(以上年为100)	Price Indices			
商品零售价格指数(%)	General Reatail Price Index(%)	103.4	100.9	101.3
居民消费价格指数(%)	General Consumer Price Index(%)	104.4	101.5	101.5
农业生产资料价格指数(%)	Price Index of Agriculture Means of Production(%)	111.3	108.9	100.7
教　育	Education			
在校学生数	Student Enrollment			
高等学校(人)	Regular Institutions of Higher Education(persens)	57450	69984	90138
中等专业学校(含中师、技工学校)(人)	Specialized Secondary Schools (persens)	52200	60317	67628
普通中学(万人)	Regular Secondary Schools(10 000 persens)	54.17	58.44	61.33
小　学(万人)	Primary Schools(10 000 persens)	100.18	105.68	104.72
卫生	Heath Care			
卫生机构病床数(张)	Number of Beds in Heath Institutions (unit)	18394	18873	20227
卫生技术人员数(人)	Number of Medical Technical personnel(persens)	25890	26230	26639
人民生活	Pepople's Livelihood			
职工工资总额(亿元)	Total Wages(100 million yuan)	91.32	104.19	116.84
职工平均工资(元)	Annual Average Wage(yuan)	12652	14417	15890
城镇居民人均可支配收入(元)	Per Capita Annual Disposable Income of Urban Residents(yuan)	7736	8124	9395
农民人均纯收入(元)	Per Capita Annual Net Income of Rural Residents(yuan)	2818	3004	3256
城乡居民储蓄存款余额（亿元）	Savings Deposit of Urban and Rural Residents(100 million yuan)	615.92	697.57	790.56

1－11 经济发展主要比例关系
Major Proportions of Economy Development

单位:% (%)

指　标	Item	2004	2005	2006
从业人员中三次产业比例	Industrial Structure of Employment			
第一产业	Primary Industry	57.26	55.37	54.79
第二产业	Secondary Industry	10.01	9.94	9.92
第三产业	Tertiary Industry	32.73	34.69	35.29
生产总值中三次产业比例	Industrial Structure of GDP			
第一产业	Primary Industry	34.00	32.97	32.72
第二产业	Secondary Industry	25.08	26.06	27.34
第三产业	Tertiary Industry	40.91	40.97	39.94
农业总产值内部比例	Internal Structure of Agricultural Gross Output Value			
种植业及其他农业	Plainting and Other Farming	42.53	39.83	41.51
林　业	Forestry	13.2	12.38	12.96
牧　业	Animal Husbandry	18.52	20.01	18.26
渔　业	Fishery	25.75	27.78	27.27
社会消费品零售总额内部构成	Internal Structure of Total Retail Sales of Consumer Goods			
城　市	Urban	78.35	78.55	79.01
乡　村	Rural	21.65	21.45	20.99
全社会固定资产投资中资金来源比例	Structure of Source of Funds in Total Investment in Assets			
国家预算内资金	State Budgetary Appropriations	5.15	7.90	6.63
国内贷款	Domestic Loans	23.88	33.56	19.82
股票债券	Stocks and Bonds	0.54	0.14	0.06
利用外资	Foreign Investment	5.71	6.24	13.88
自筹资金	Fundraising	52.32	32.69	35.82
其他投资	Others	12.4	19.47	23.79

1-11 续(continued)

指　　标	Item	2004	2005	2006
全社会固定资产投资比例	Structure of Total Investment in Assets			
城镇投资	urban investment	62.99	89.41	93.19
农村非农户	rural non-farmers	5.49	1.90	1.90
城乡个人	Individuals	17.21	8.69	4.91
固定资产投资中按经济类型分的投资比例	Structure in Fixed Assets by Ownership			
内资	Domestic Funded		90.02	87.41
港澳台商	Enterprises Funded by Entrepreneurs from Hong Kong,Macao and Taiwan		3.49	6.17
外商	Foreign Funded Enterprises		6.13	5.91
个体经营	Indinvidual Business		0.36	0.51
财政收入相当于国内生产总值比例	Proportion of Total Financial Revenue to GDP	8.77	9.38	9.72
财政支出内部比例	Internal Stucture of Government Expenditures			
基建拨款	Expenditures for Capital Construction	10.61	10.44	9.57
文教卫生科学事业费	Expenditure for Cultrue, Education, Science and Health Care	18.99	20.73	20.47
行政经费	Expenditure for Gvernment Administration	8.82	8.94	8.69
支援农业生产拨款	Expenditures for Supporting Agricultural Production	7.36	7.34	6.04
基金支出	Expenditure for Fund Budgetary	9.62	9.75	11
其他支出	Others	44.59	42.82	44.23
货运量中各种运输方式比例	Structure of Volume of Cargo Transportion by Various Means			
铁　　路	Railways	3.85	4.64	8.15
公　　路	Highways	77.52	71.19	62.83
水　　运	Waterways	18.56	24.07	28.68
民　　航	Civil Aviation	0.07	0.10	0.34
客运量中各种运输方式比例	Structure of Volume of Passenger Transportion by Various Means			
铁　　路	Railways	0.04	0.10	0.19
公　　路	Highways	95.81	95.28	93.94
水　　运	Waterways	1.77	1.92	2.83
民　　航	Civil Aviation	2.38	2.70	3.04

资料整理: 蔡智芬　陈　敏　陈灿宇

Arranged by Caizhifeng Chengmin Chengcanyu

2. 经济核算

NATIONAL ACCOUNTS

全省生产总值构成（%）

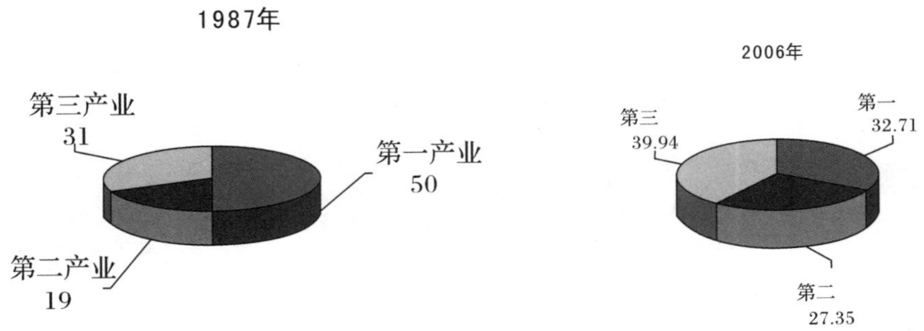

历年生产总值增长率（%）

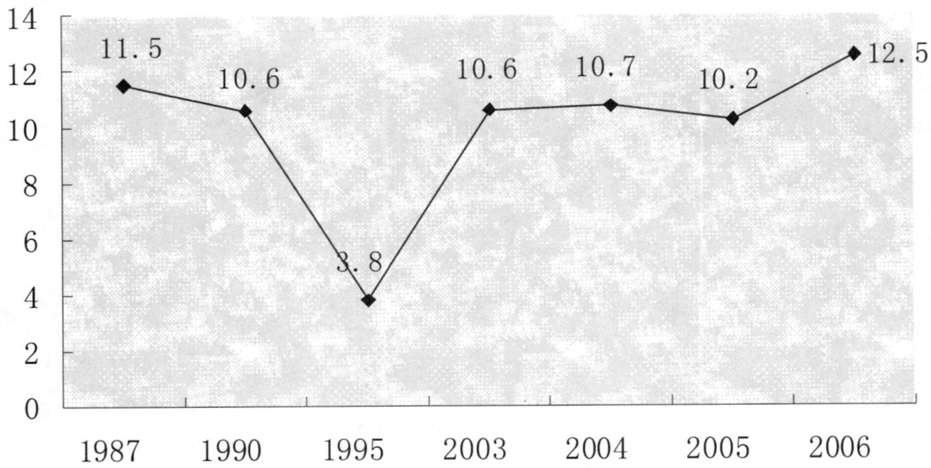

历年生产总值（亿元）

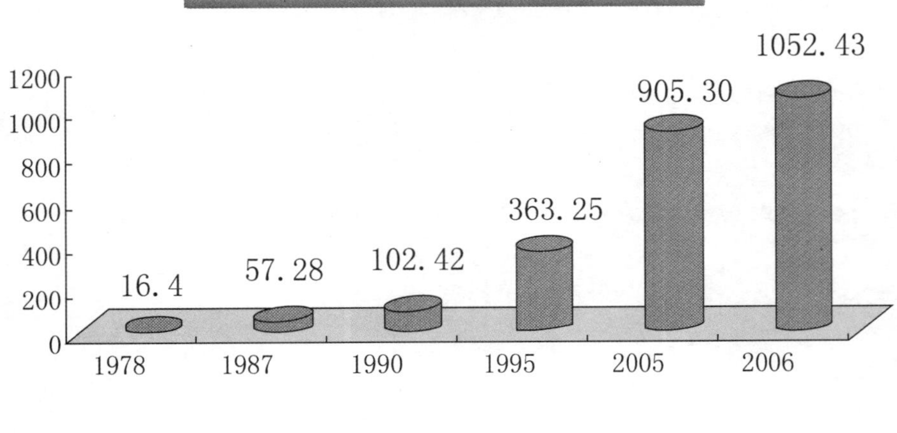

2－1 生产总值和构成

Gross Domestic Product and Composition

年 份 Year	生产总值 Gross Domestic Product	第一产业 Primary Industry	第二产业 Secondary Industry	第三产业 Tertiary Industry	人均生产总值(元) Per Capita GDP(yuan)
绝对数(亿元) Absolute Amount(100 million yuan)					
1982	28.86	17.25	4.04	7.57	510
1983	31.12	18.45	4.47	8.20	540
1984	37.18	20.48	6.68	10.02	636
1985	43.26	21.80	9.30	12.16	729
1986	48.03	24.05	9.92	14.06	798
1987	57.28	28.63	10.91	17.74	925
1988	77.00	38.46	14.19	24.35	1220
1989	91.32	42.64	18.29	30.39	1420
1990	102.42	45.71	20.19	36.52	1562
1991	120.52	49.80	24.71	46.01	1804
1992	184.92	53.59	38.27	93.06	2719
1993	260.41	76.82	66.08	117.50	3755
1994	331.98	106.12	83.32	142.54	4702
1995	363.25	128.90	78.48	155.87	5063
1996	389.68	141.15	81.52	167.01	5346
1997	411.16	148.52	83.13	179.51	5567
1998	442.13	156.05	91.41	194.66	5912
1999	476.67	172.62	96.02	208.04	6294
2000	526.82	192.00	103.97	230.85	6798
2001	579.17	196.78	133.84	248.56	7315
2002	642.73	222.89	148.88	270.96	8041
2003	713.96	244.29	175.82	293.85	8849
2004	819.66	278.76	205.60	335.30	10067
2005	905.03	300.75	230.53	373.75	10998
2006	1052.85	344.48	287.86	420.51	12654
构成(%) Composition					
1982	100	59.77	14.00	26.23	
1983	100	59.29	14.36	26.35	
1984	100	55.08	17.97	26.95	
1985	100	50.39	21.50	28.11	
1986	100	50.07	20.65	29.28	
1987	100	49.99	19.04	30.97	
1988	100	49.95	18.43	31.62	
1989	100	46.69	20.03	33.28	
1990	100	44.63	19.72	35.65	
1991	100	41.32	20.50	38.18	
1992	100	28.98	20.69	50.33	
1993	100	29.50	25.38	45.12	
1994	100	31.96	25.10	42.94	
1995	100	35.48	21.61	42.91	
1996	100	36.22	20.92	42.86	
1997	100	36.12	20.22	43.66	
1998	100	35.29	20.68	44.03	
1999	100	36.21	20.14	43.65	
2000	100	36.44	19.74	43.82	
2001	100	33.97	23.11	42.92	
2002	100	34.68	23.16	42.16	
2003	100	34.21	24.63	41.16	
2004	100	34.01	25.08	40.91	
2005	100	32.97	26.06	40.97	
2006	100	32.72	27.34	39.94	

注:本表按当年价格计算;从 1987 年起按 2004 年经济普查数据进行修订;从 2001 年起含中海油工业增加值,构成按同口径计算。
Note:Data in this table are calculated at current prices; and from the year 1987 on the data are revised on the basis of economic consus 2004, the value indudes the value-added of CNOOC to calculate on the same path since 2001.

2－2 生产总值指数
Indices of Gross Domestic Product

年份 Year	生产总值 Gross Domestic Product	第一产业 Primary Industry	第二产业 Secondary Industry	第三产业 Tertiary Industry	人均生产总值 Per Capita GDP
指数（以上年为 100） Indices(preceding year=100)					
1982	123.6	125.4	110.4	127.5	123.7
1983	105.8	104.8	108.4	106.7	109.3
1984	116.9	109.2	143.6	119.5	117.4
1985	112.0	102.4	133.8	117.0	112.9
1986	108.7	111.2	101.8	109.6	107.3
1987	111.5	109.2	109.8	116.7	109.5
1988	109.7	103.8	119.6	112.5	107.6
1989	105.7	103.1	113.1	104.4	103.8
1990	110.6	109.2	110.5	112.7	108.5
1991	114.9	108.7	120.1	119.7	112.7
1992	141.5	110.0	137.5	179.4	139.0
1993	120.6	110.5	150.1	115.1	118.2
1994	111.3	112.9	117.1	106.9	109.3
1995	103.8	111.5	94.3	104.0	102.1
1996	104.7	105.4	102.2	105.5	103.0
1997	106.8	107.6	105.6	106.9	105.4
1998	108.5	108.3	109.0	108.3	107.1
1999	108.5	110.8	108.0	107.0	107.1
2000	109.0	110.2	107.7	108.8	106.6
2001	109.1	109.7	108.8	108.7	106.8
2002	109.6	109.1	112.9	108.5	108.5
2003	110.6	109.0	119.5	107.8	109.6
2004	110.7	108.0	115.9	110.3	109.7
2005	110.2	106.0	116.9	110.2	109.1
2006	112.5	109.1	119.8	111.0	111.3
指数（1978=100） Indices(1978=100)					
1982	146.6	159.9	91.9	167.4	154.3
1983	155.1	167.6	99.7	178.6	168.6
1984	181.3	183.0	143.1	213.4	198.0
1985	203.1	187.4	191.5	249.7	223.5
1986	220.7	208.4	194.9	273.7	239.8
1987	246.1	227.6	214.1	319.3	262.7
1988	269.9	236.2	256.0	359.2	282.6
1989	285.4	243.5	289.7	375.0	293.3
1990	315.6	265.9	320.0	422.5	318.1
1991	362.6	289.1	384.2	506.0	358.6
1992	513.0	318.0	528.4	907.9	498.4
1993	618.5	351.4	792.9	1044.7	589.2
1994	688.1	396.7	928.4	1116.9	643.9
1995	714.0	442.3	875.7	1162.0	657.5
1996	747.5	466.2	895.2	1226.0	677.5
1997	798.5	501.7	945.7	1310.2	714.3
1998	866.0	543.3	1030.8	1418.7	765.0
1999	939.4	602.0	1112.8	1517.8	819.5
2000	1024.2	663.4	1198.7	1651.5	873.2
2001	1117.2	727.7	1304.7	1794.6	932.2
2002	1224.2	793.9	1472.6	1946.8	1011.8
2003	1354.0	865.4	1759.5	2098.6	1108.7
2004	1498.7	934.6	2039.4	2314.1	1216.2
2005	1651.6	990.7	2384.1	2550.2	1326.5
2006	1858.1	1080.9	2856.1	2830.7	1476.4

注：本表按可比价格计算。
The indices in this table are calculated at comparable prices.

2－3 生产总值构成要素
Structure of Gross Domestic Product

单位:亿元 (100 million yuan)

行业	Sector	增加值 Value-Added	劳动者报酬 Compensation of Employees	生产税净额 Net Taxes on Production	固定资产折旧 Depreciation of Fixed Assets	营业盈余 Operating Surplus
生产总值	**Gross Domestic Product**	**1052.85**	**502.66**	**121.10**	**162.54**	**266.55**
第一产业	Primary Industry	344.48	268.17	0.01	25.41	50.89
第二产业	Secondary Industry	287.86	75.93	65.74	40.20	105.99
工业	Industury	217.55	41.02	56.76	37.50	82.27
建筑业	Construction	70.31	34.91	8.98	2.70	23.72
第三产业	Tertiary Industry	420.51	158.56	55.35	96.93	109.67
交通运输、仓储和邮政业	Transport, Storage, Postal Services	73.81	16.72	8.80	20.55	27.74
铁路运输业	Railway Transport	2.82	1.02	0.09	2.38	-0.67
道路运输业	Way Transport	15.15	3.89	1.36	3.89	6.01
城市公共交通业	Public Traffic in City	1.79	0.47	0.18	0.51	0.63
水上运输业	Waterway Transport	20.72	2.73	2.09	2.62	13.28
航空运输业	Air Transport	27.84	5.40	4.54	10.29	7.61
管道运输业	Pipeline Transport	0.00	0.00	0.00	0.00	0.00
装卸搬运和其他运输服务业	Load and Unload Transport and Others Transport	2.79	0.56	0.30	0.33	1.60
仓储业	Storage	0.07	0.06	0.01	0.03	-0.03
邮政业	Postal	2.63	2.59	0.23	0.50	-0.69
信息传输、计算机服务和软件业	Information Transmission, Computer Services and Software	26.55	5.16	1.63	13.52	6.24
电信和其他信息传输服务业	Telecommunications and Other Information Transmission	24.67	3.96	1.40	13.11	6.20
计算机服务业	Computer Services	1.40	0.79	0.13	0.29	0.19
软件业	Software	0.48	0.41	0.10	0.12	-0.15
批发和零售业	Wholesale & Retail Trade	104.10	15.69	28.44	5.87	54.10
批发业	Wholesale Trade	52.99	8.46	22.22	3.65	18.66
零售业	Retail Trade	51.11	7.23	6.22	2.22	35.44
住宿和餐饮业	Hotels and Catering Trade	30.67	11.18	5.18	6.97	7.34
住宿业	Hotels	12.59	7.01	2.72	6.16	-3.30
餐饮业	Catering Trade	18.08	4.17	2.46	0.81	10.64
金融业	Finance	13.76	10.59	3.78	1.48	-2.09
银行业	Banking	10.02	8.07	2.18	1.09	-1.32
证券业	Stock	1.74	0.56	1.12	0.20	-0.14
保险业	Insurance	1.51	1.57	0.37	0.14	-0.57
其他金融活动	Other Finance Activities	0.49	0.39	0.11	0.05	-0.06

2-3 续(continued)

行业	Sector	增加值 Value-Added	劳动者报酬 Compensation of Employees	生产税净额 Net Taxes on Production	固定资产折旧 Depreciation of Fixed Assets	营业盈余 Operating Surplus
房地产业	Real Estate	34.41	5.66	3.42	29.03	-3.70
房地产开发经营业	Real Estate Development and Operation	4.81	2.99	2.61	1.58	-2.37
物业管理业	Real Estate Owners Management	2.88	1.92	0.37	0.81	-0.22
房地产中介服务业	Real Estate Intermediary Services	0.24	0.17	0.07	0.03	-0.03
其他房地产活动	other Real Estate Activities	0.48	0.58	0.37	0.61	-1.08
居民自有住房服务业	owned housing services of household	26.00	0.00	0.00	26.00	0.00
租赁和商务服务业	Rent and Business Affair Services	14.37	5.53	1.08	4.48	3.28
租赁业	Rent	0.39	0.09	0.04	0.28	-0.02
商务服务业	Business Affair Services	13.98	5.44	1.04	4.20	3.30
科学研究、技术服务和地质勘查业	Scientific Research, Polytechnic Services and Geological Prospecting	7.93	5.14	0.66	1.00	1.13
研究与试验发展	Research and Develoment	1.88	1.53	0.02	0.26	0.07
专业技术服务业	Profesional Technology Services	4.88	2.66	0.61	0.65	0.96
科技交流和推广服务业	Scientific and Technological Interchange and Popularization Services	0.70	0.58	0.01	0.07	0.04
地质勘查业	Geological Prospecting	0.47	0.37	0.02	0.02	0.06
水利、环境和公共设施管理业	Water Conservancy, Environmental and Public Installations Management Services	6.23	3.50	0.38	1.71	0.64
水利管理业	Water Conservancy Management	1.08	0.70	0.02	0.52	-0.16
环境管理业	Environmental Management	1.38	1.27	0.01	0.37	-0.27
公共设施管理业	Public Installations Management Services	3.77	1.53	0.35	0.82	1.07
居民服务和其他服务业	Resident Services and Other Social Services	13.38	3.62	0.85	0.67	8.24
居民服务业	Resident Services	8.26	2.52	0.45	0.38	4.91
其他服务业	Other Social Services	5.12	1.10	0.40	0.29	3.33
教育	Education	30.04	24.70	0.09	3.46	1.80
卫生、社会保障和社会福利业	Health Care,Social Security and Social Welfare	15.69	11.19	0.12	1.43	2.95
卫生	Health Care	14.48	10.30	0.12	1.31	2.75
社会保障业	Social Security	0.17	0.14	0.00	0.02	0.01
社会福利业	Social Welfare	1.04	0.75	0.00	0.10	0.19
文化、体育和娱乐业	Culture,Sports and Recreational Services	8.40	3.57	0.79	2.04	2.00
新闻出版业	News Publishing House	3.62	1.01	0.21	0.46	1.94
广播、电视、电影和音像业	Radio, Television, Film and Audiovisual	1.48	1.03	0.08	0.14	0.23
文化艺术业	Culture and Arts	0.85	0.68	0.03	0.12	0.02
体育	Sports	0.08	0.12	0.02	0.17	-0.23
娱乐业	Recreational Services	2.37	0.73	0.45	1.15	0.04
公共管理和社会组织	Public Management and Social Organizations	41.17	36.31	0.14	4.72	0.00

2－4 生产总值主要行业构成
Composition of Gross Domestic Product by Sector

年 份 Year	生产总值 Gross Domestic Product	农业 Agriculture	工业 Industury	建筑业 Construction	运输邮电业 Transport, Post and Telecommunication Services	商业饮食业 Wholesale, Retail rade& Catering Services	金融保险业 Finance and Insurance	房地产业 Real Estate	其他服务业 Other Social Services
绝对数（亿元） Absolute Amount (100 million yuan)									
1982	28.86	17.25	3.07	0.97	0.94	3.06	0.81	0.48	2.28
1983	31.12	18.45	3.53	0.94	0.97	3.34	0.95	0.51	2.43
1984	37.18	20.48	4.70	1.98	1.29	4.01	1.44	0.53	2.75
1985	43.26	21.80	5.88	3.42	2.15	4.16	1.79	0.55	3.51
1986	48.03	24.05	6.67	3.25	2.57	4.59	2.03	0.65	4.22
1987	57.28	28.63	7.73	3.18	3.26	5.74	2.30	0.98	5.46
1988	77.00	38.46	10.04	4.16	4.07	8.66	3.25	1.17	7.18
1989	91.32	42.64	11.70	6.59	4.87	10.27	3.43	1.43	10.39
1990	102.42	45.71	13.17	7.03	6.21	11.41	3.96	1.65	13.28
1991	120.52	49.80	15.23	9.48	8.01	15.15	4.43	2.48	15.94
1992	184.92	53.59	20.97	17.29	11.35	29.56	6.12	20.57	25.46
1993	260.41	76.82	35.58	30.50	16.61	39.13	7.58	20.43	33.75
1994	331.98	106.12	44.57	38.76	21.93	48.36	8.05	17.20	46.99
1995	363.25	128.90	44.04	34.44	26.35	52.47	8.25	13.69	55.11
1996	389.68	141.15	49.20	32.32	29.91	55.23	8.35	11.28	62.24
1997	411.16	148.52	52.05	31.08	34.57	58.93	8.58	11.30	66.13
1998	442.13	156.05	59.10	32.32	43.76	61.90	8.78	12.91	67.31
1999	476.67	172.62	63.37	32.65	46.94	64.88	8.98	14.62	72.62
2000	526.82	192.00	70.46	33.51	52.45	70.30	9.27	16.62	82.20
2001	579.17	196.78	97.85	35.98	57.13	74.08	9.75	18.81	88.78
2002	642.73	222.89	111.42	37.46	61.97	78.65	10.08	21.45	98.82
2003	713.96	244.29	132.25	43.56	66.54	85.64	10.68	25.14	105.85
2004	819.66	278.76	151.56	54.04	77.00	96.50	11.56	30.64	119.60
2005	905.03	300.75	166.62	63.91	87.32	107.57	12.44	33.61	132.81
2006	1052.85	344.48	217.55	70.31	96.69	122.18	13.76	34.41	153.47
构成（%） Composition									
1982	100	59.77	10.64	3.36	3.26	10.60	2.81	1.66	7.90
1983	100	59.29	11.34	3.02	3.12	10.73	3.05	1.64	7.81
1984	100	55.08	12.64	5.33	3.47	10.78	3.87	1.43	7.40
1985	100	50.39	13.59	7.91	4.97	9.62	4.14	1.27	8.11
1986	100	50.07	13.89	6.77	5.35	9.56	4.23	1.35	8.78
1987	100	49.99	13.49	5.55	5.68	10.02	4.02	1.71	9.54
1988	100	49.95	13.04	5.40	5.29	11.25	4.22	1.52	9.33
1989	100	46.69	12.81	7.21	5.34	11.25	3.76	1.56	11.38
1990	100	44.63	12.86	6.86	6.07	11.14	3.87	1.61	12.96
1991	100	41.32	12.64	7.86	6.65	12.57	3.67	2.06	13.23
1992	100	28.98	11.34	9.35	6.14	15.99	3.31	11.12	13.77
1993	100	29.50	13.66	11.71	6.38	15.03	2.91	7.85	12.96
1994	100	31.97	13.42	11.67	6.61	14.57	2.43	5.18	14.15
1995	100	35.49	12.13	9.48	7.25	14.44	2.27	3.77	15.17
1996	100	36.22	12.63	8.30	7.68	14.17	2.14	2.89	15.97
1997	100	36.12	12.66	7.56	8.41	14.33	2.09	2.75	16.08
1998	100	35.29	13.37	7.31	9.90	14.00	1.99	2.92	15.22
1999	100	36.21	13.29	6.85	9.85	13.61	1.88	3.07	15.24
2000	100	36.44	13.38	6.36	9.96	13.34	1.76	3.16	15.60
2001	100	33.97	16.89	6.21	9.86	12.79	1.68	3.25	15.33
2002	100	34.68	17.33	5.83	9.64	12.24	1.57	3.34	15.37
2003	100	34.22	18.52	6.10	9.32	11.99	1.50	3.52	14.83
2004	100	34.01	18.49	6.59	9.40	11.77	1.41	3.74	14.59
2005	100	32.96	19.07	7.00	9.57	11.79	1.36	3.69	14.56
2006	100	32.72	20.66	6.68	9.18	11.60	1.31	3.27	14.58

注：本表按当年价格计算；从 1987 年起按 2004 年经济普查数据进行修订；从 2001 年起含中海油工业增加值，构成按同口径计算。
Note:Data in this table are calculated at current prices; and from the year 1987 on the data are revised on the basis of economic consus 2004, the value indudes the value-added of CNOOC to calculate on the same path since 2001.

2－5 生产总值主要行业指数
Indices of Gross Domestic Product by Sector

年 份 Year	生产总值 Gross Domestic Product	农业 Agriculture	工业 Industury	建筑业 Construction	运输邮电业 Transport, Post and Telecommunication Services	商业饮食业 Wholesale, Retail rade& Catering Services	金融保险业 Finance and Insurance	房地产业 Real Estate	其他服务业 Other Social Services
指数(以上年为 100) Indices(preceding year=100)									
1982	123.6	125.4	106.5	123.6	138.2	128.4	201.5	106.9	112.5
1983	105.8	104.8	112.6	94.5	103.1	107.2	114.4	104.3	106.8
1984	116.9	109.2	128.4	200.6	128.2	117.9	145.3	103.9	110.2
1985	112.0	102.4	123.9	157.8	156.9	103.7	115.6	103.8	112.5
1986	108.7	111.2	105.8	95.0	117.2	105.7	111.4	111.1	108.6
1987	111.5	109.2	115.4	98.4	121.8	120.3	119.6	109.2	109.4
1988	109.7	103.8	123.2	110.9	106.1	116.5	120.5	107.5	108.6
1989	105.7	103.1	105.2	134.4	110.0	96.8	104.3	106.2	110.2
1990	110.6	109.2	110.0	111.5	107.2	110.3	116.5	110.9	117.1
1991	114.9	108.7	120.0	120.2	118.3	122.5	117.7	132.5	117.1
1992	141.5	110.0	131.8	148.2	137.6	180.6	166.8	574.3	146.4
1993	120.6	110.5	138.5	169.3	121.0	108.7	124.2	123.0	112.0
1994	111.3	112.9	114.0	121.3	113.1	112.2	108.2	82.6	112.5
1995	103.8	111.5	94.1	94.6	105.8	103.8	108.1	88.4	108.9
1996	104.7	105.4	106.1	97.3	110.0	107.0	104.2	90.5	107.8
1997	106.8	107.6	109.2	100.7	113.7	107.9	102.8	100.8	105.8
1998	108.5	108.3	109.6	108.1	113.6	108.6	105.6	113.1	104.7
1999	108.5	110.8	109.5	105.6	109.8	107.2	106.2	104.6	106.2
2000	109.0	110.2	110.0	104.1	111.2	108.5	106.6	109.5	108.3
2001	109.1	109.7	110.3	105.8	110.6	108.1	104.2	107.2	108.7
2002	109.6	109.1	115.9	106.2	109.2	108.2	104.1	107.8	108.9
2003	110.6	109.0	123.2	110.6	109.0	108.3	106.8	108.5	106.5
2004	110.7	108.0	116.7	113.8	115.3	108.8	103.1	108.1	109.4
2005	110.2	106.0	117.0	116.4	113.2	110.5	105.2	108.0	109.2
2006	112.5	109.1	124.1	109.3	110.3	112.3	109.5	101.2	113.1
指数（1978=100） Indices(1978=100)									
1982	146.6	159.9	84.5	126.4	161.9	185.9	280.7	131.0	179.1
1983	155.1	167.6	95.2	119.4	166.9	199.3	321.1	136.7	191.3
1984	181.3	183.0	122.2	239.6	213.9	234.9	466.6	142.0	210.8
1985	203.1	187.4	151.4	378.0	335.7	243.6	539.4	147.4	237.1
1986	220.7	208.4	160.2	359.1	393.4	257.5	600.9	163.8	237.1
1987	246.1	227.6	184.9	353.4	479.2	309.8	718.7	178.9	259.3
1988	269.9	236.2	227.8	391.9	508.4	360.9	866.0	192.3	281.6
1989	285.4	243.5	239.6	526.7	559.2	349.3	903.2	204.2	310.3
1990	315.6	265.9	263.6	587.2	599.5	385.3	1052.3	226.5	363.4
1991	362.6	289.1	316.3	705.9	709.2	472.0	1238.5	300.1	425.4
1992	513.0	318.0	416.9	1046.1	975.9	852.5	2065.9	1723.3	622.8
1993	618.5	351.4	577.3	1771.0	1180.8	926.6	2565.8	2119.6	697.5
1994	688.1	396.7	658.2	2148.3	1335.5	1039.7	2776.2	1750.8	784.7
1995	714.0	442.3	619.3	2032.3	1412.9	1079.2	3001.1	1547.7	854.5
1996	747.5	466.2	657.1	1977.4	1554.2	1154.7	3127.1	1400.7	921.1
1997	798.5	501.7	717.6	1991.2	1767.2	1245.9	3214.7	1411.9	974.5
1998	866.0	543.3	786.5	2152.5	2007.5	1353.1	3394.7	1596.9	1020.6
1999	939.4	602.0	861.2	2273.1	2204.2	1450.5	3605.2	1670.3	1083.9
2000	1024.2	663.4	947.3	2366.2	2451.1	1573.8	3843.1	1829.0	1174.0
2001	1117.2	727.7	1044.9	2503.5	2710.9	1701.3	4004.5	1960.7	1276.4
2002	1224.2	793.9	1211.0	2658.7	2960.3	1840.8	4168.7	2113.6	1389.5
2003	1354.0	865.4	1491.9	2940.5	3226.7	1993.6	4452.2	2293.3	1480.5
2004	1498.7	934.6	1741.1	3346.3	3720.4	2169.0	4590.2	2479.0	1619.2
2005	1651.6	990.7	2037.1	3895.1	4211.5	2396.8	4828.9	2677.3	1768.2
2006	1858.1	1080.9	2528.0	4257.4	4645.3	2691.6	5287.6	2709.5	1999.8

2－6 2006 年生产总值分行业比较
Gross Domestic Product by Sector

行 业	Sector	绝对数(亿元)Absolute Amount(100 million yuan)		构 成(%) Composition		2006 年比 2005 年增长 (%) Increase Rate in 2006over2005(%)
		2005	2006	2005	2006	
生产总值	**Gross DomesticProduct**	**905.03**	**1052.85**	**100.00**	**100.00**	**12.5**
第一产业	Primary Industry	300.75	344.48	32.97	32.72	9.1
第二产业	Secondary Industry	230.53	287.86	26.06	27.34	19.8
工业	Industury	166.62	217.55	19.06	20.66	24.1
建筑业	Construction	63.91	70.31	7.01	6.68	9.3
第三产业	Tertiary Industry	373.75	420.51	40.97	39.94	11.0
交通运输、仓储和邮政业	Transport, Storage, Postal Services	64.34	73.81	7.05	7.01	10.3
铁路运输业	Railway Transport	2.49	2.82	0.27	0.27	8.0
道路运输业	Way Transport	13.14	15.15	1.44	1.44	10.0
城市公共交通业	Public Traffic in City	1.49	1.79	0.16	0.17	15.8
水上运输业	Waterway Transport	17.65	20.72	1.93	1.97	12.0
航空运输业	Air Transport	24.17	27.84	2.65	2.64	9.9
管道运输业	Pipeline Transport	0.00	0.00	0.00	0.00	0.0
装卸搬运和其他运输服务业	Load and Unload Transport and Others Transport	2.74	2.79	0.30	0.26	1.1
仓储业	Storage	0.06	0.07	0.01	0.01	10.5
邮政业	Postal	2.59	2.63	0.28	0.25	13.1
信息传输、计算机服务和软件业	Information Transmission, Computer Services and Software	23.77	26.55	2.61	2.52	13.8
电信和其他信息传输服务业	Telecommunications and Other Information Transmission	22.98	24.67	2.52	2.34	10.5
计算机服务业	Computer Services	0.47	1.40	0.05	0.13	148.7
软件业	Software	0.32	0.48	0.04	0.05	50.0
批发和零售业	Wholesale & Retail Trade	91.67	104.10	10.05	9.89	12.1
批发业	Wholesale Trade	44.47	52.99	4.87	5.03	17.6
零售业	Retail Trade	47.20	51.11	5.17	4.85	6.9
住宿和餐饮业	Hotels and Catering Trade	27.55	30.67	3.02	2.91	11.7
住宿业	Hotels	11.65	12.59	1.28	1.20	9.2
餐饮业	Catering Trade	15.90	18.08	1.74	1.72	13.5
金融业	Finance	12.44	13.76	1.36	1.31	9.5
银行业	Banking	9.26	10.02	1.02	0.95	7.1
证券业	Stock	1.25	1.74	0.14	0.17	38.8
保险业	Insurance	1.45	1.51	0.16	0.14	2.7
其他金融活动	Other Finance Activities	0.48	0.49	0.05	0.05	0.0

注:绝对数按当年价格计算,增长速度按可比价格计算。
Note:Due to be calculated on the same path for the value which includes the data of CNOOC,the absolution data is calculdateed at current prices,the growth speed is calculated at comparable price.

2-6 续(continued)

行　　业	Sector	绝对数(亿元) Absolute Amount(100 million yuan)		构　成(%) Composition		2006 年比 2005 年增长 (%) Increase Rate in 2006over2005(%)
		2005	2006	2005	2006	
房地产业	Real Estate	33.61	34.41	3.68	3.27	1.2
房地产开发经营业	Real Estate Development and Operation	6.55	4.81	0.72	0.46	-29.3
物业管理业	Real Estate Owners Management	2.48	2.88	0.27	0.27	16.1
房地产中介服务业	Real Estate Intermediary Services	0.21	0.24	0.02	0.02	9.5
其他房地产活动	other Real Estate Activities	0.42	0.48	0.05	0.05	14.3
居民自有住房服务业	owned housing services of household	23.95	26.00	2.63	2.47	7.7
租赁和商务服务业	Rent and Business Affair Services	12.62	14.37	1.38	1.36	11.4
租赁业	Rent	0.36	0.39	0.04	0.04	8.3
商务服务业	Business Affair Services	12.25	13.98	1.34	1.33	11.6
科学研究、技术服务和地质勘查业	Scientific Research, Polytechnic Services and Geological Prospecting	6.62	7.93	0.73	0.75	18.7
研究与试验发展	Research and Develoment	1.67	1.88	0.18	0.18	11.4
专业技术服务业	Profesional Technology Services	4.01	4.88	0.44	0.46	20.7
科技交流和推广服务业	Scientific and Technological Interchange and Popularization Services	0.50	0.70	0.05	0.07	38.0
地质勘查业	Geological Prospecting	0.44	0.47	0.05	0.04	6.8
水利、环境和公共设施管理业	Water Conservancy, Environmental and Public Installations Management Services	5.63	6.23	0.62	0.59	9.4
水利管理业	Water Conservancy Management	0.99	1.08	0.11	0.10	8.1
环境管理业	Environmental Management	1.26	1.38	0.14	0.13	7.9
公共设施管理业	Public Installations Management Services	3.38	3.77	0.37	0.36	10.4
居民服务和其他服务业	Resident Services and Other Social Services	11.53	13.38	1.26	1.27	14.3
居民服务业	Resident Services	7.24	8.26	0.79	0.78	12.4
其他服务业	Other Social Services	4.29	5.12	0.47	0.49	17.5
教育	Education	26.99	30.04	2.96	2.85	9.9
卫生、社会保障和社会福利业	Health Care, Social Security and Social Welfare	13.50	15.69	1.48	1.49	17.5
卫生	Health Care	12.51	14.48	1.37	1.38	17.1
社会保障业	Social Security	0.14	0.17	0.02	0.02	21.4
社会福利业	Social Welfare	0.84	1.04	0.09	0.10	22.6
文化、体育和娱乐业	Culture,Sports and Recreational Services	7.43	8.40	0.81	0.80	14.6
新闻出版业	News Publishing House	3.06	3.62	0.34	0.34	19.6
广播、电视、电影和音像业	Radio, Television, Film and Audiovisual	1.36	1.48	0.15	0.14	10.3
文化艺术业	Culture and Arts	0.75	0.85	0.08	0.08	14.7
体育	Sports	0.06	0.08	0.01	0.01	33.3
娱乐业	Recreational Services	2.19	2.37	0.24	0.23	9.6
公共管理和社会组织	Public Management and Social Organizations	36.07	41.17	3.95	3.91	12.5

2－7 支出法生产总值
Gross Domestic Product by Expenditure Approach

单位:亿元　　100 million yuan

年份 Year	支出法生产总值 Gross Domestic Product by Expenditure Approach	最终消费 Final Consumption Expenditure	居民消费 Households Consumption Expenditure	农村居民 Rural Households	城镇居民 Urban Households	政府消费 Government Consumption Expenditure
1984	42.15	26.13	23.37	17.18	6.19	2.76
1985	54.19	31.58	28.05	20.59	7.46	3.53
1986	63.06	36.81	32.70	24.06	8.64	4.11
1987	57.28	39.80	35.62	25.53	10.09	4.19
1988	77.00	50.18	44.58	31.26	13.33	5.59
1989	91.32	57.67	49.29	33.50	15.80	8.38
1990	102.42	62.25	51.65	33.49	18.16	10.60
1991	120.52	70.13	55.61	31.94	23.66	14.52
1992	184.92	90.19	69.30	35.03	34.27	20.89
1993	260.41	125.21	94.49	49.36	45.13	30.72
1994	331.98	150.27	118.10	54.37	63.73	32.16
1995	363.25	178.88	143.00	66.77	76.22	35.88
1996	389.68	212.63	170.39	79.52	90.86	42.24
1997	411.16	228.39	179.58	82.21	97.37	48.80
1998	442.13	245.61	190.83	85.42	105.41	54.78
1999	476.67	258.66	197.11	86.57	110.54	61.55
2000	526.82	290.73	220.82	97.79	123.03	69.91
2001	558.41	310.47	235.21	99.80	135.41	75.26
2002	621.97	347.56	258.43	106.76	151.67	89.13
2003	693.20	378.65	281.13	108.53	172.61	97.51
2004	798.90	428.25	313.21	116.73	196.48	115.04
2005	894.57	468.71	341.06	126.43	214.63	127.65
2006	1052.85	547.33	394.02	142.36	251.66	153.31

年份 Year	资本形成总额 Gross Capital Formation	固定资本形成总额 Gross Fixed Capital Formation	存货增加 Changes in Inventories	资本形成率(%) Capital Formation Rate(%)	最终消费率(%) Final Consumption Rate(%)
1984	16.02	10.43	5.59	38.01	61.99
1985	22.61	16.37	6.24	41.72	58.28
1986	26.25	18.63	7.62	41.63	58.37
1987	26.49	20.92	5.57	46.25	69.49
1988	36.78	22.92	13.85	47.76	65.16
1989	44.68	29.06	15.62	48.92	63.15
1990	58.67	42.14	16.53	57.28	60.78
1991	67.16	50.90	16.26	55.72	58.19
1992	125.15	105.09	20.06	67.68	48.77
1993	172.23	145.40	26.83	66.14	48.08
1994	225.08	199.26	25.82	67.80	45.26
1995	220.21	193.64	26.57	60.62	49.24
1996	188.90	168.29	20.61	48.48	54.56
1997	188.95	163.39	25.56	45.96	55.55
1998	203.91	163.39	29.23	46.12	55.55
1999	225.24	189.32	35.92	47.25	54.26
2000	242.25	197.99	44.26	45.98	55.18
2001	255.55	208.18	47.37	45.76	55.60
2002	279.81	227.50	52.31	44.99	55.88
2003	317.63	265.55	52.08	45.82	54.62
2004	369.36	311.05	58.31	46.23	53.60
2005	424.33	363.37	60.96	47.43	52.40
2006	497.36	423.88	73.48	47.24	51.99

注:本表按当年价格计算。
Note:Data in this table are calculated at current prices.

2－8 各市县生产总值
Gross Domestic Product by City and County

单位:万元 (10 000 yuan)

地　区	Region	生产总值 Gross Domestic Product	第一产业 Primary Industry	第二产业 Secondary Industry	第三产业 Tertiary Industry	人均生产总值(元) Per Capita GDP(yuan)
全辖区	**Total Region**					
海口市	HaiKou	3620565	298481	1073193	2248890	24286
三亚市	SanYa	1092608	255130	413671	423807	21090
五指山市	WuZhiShan	69090	24266	8103	36721	6198
文昌市	WenChang	632114	317093	123826	191195	11604
琼海市	QiongHai	566348	321301	62576	182470	12136
万宁市	WanNing	468963	189457	87068	192438	8213
定安县	DingAn	200776	100765	28679	71332	6332
屯昌县	TunChang	183510	109757	15815	57938	6618
澄迈县	ChengMai	500900	178990	233277	88633	9825
临高县	LinGao	421914	320475	25889	75550	9661
儋州市	DanZhou	814853	496879	106674	211300	8627
东方市	DongFang	451799	149453	204192	98154	11353
乐东县	LeDong	293339	198510	18914	75915	5963
琼中县	QiongZhong	124650	83081	11368	30201	5913
保亭县	BaoTing	101578	60651	6768	34159	6277
陵水县	LingShui	218159	134956	16332	66871	6384
白沙县	BaiSha	128291	91287	10679	26325	6864
昌江县	ChangJiag	302270	96062	150701	55507	12473
洋　浦	YangPu	438676	17676	299884	121116	106994
不含农垦	**Out of Land Reclamat-ion and Cultivation**					
海口市	HaiKou	3501246	259459	1021223	2220564	24833
三亚市	SanYa	1023367	204127	410412	408828	22760
五指山市	WuZhiShan	64245	20452	7941	35852	6175
文昌市	WenChang	616356	305129	123519	187708	11919
琼海市	QiongHai	536315	297054	60881	178380	12810
万宁市	WanNing	436317	164479	86043	185795	8912
定安县	DingAn	185832	88305	28262	69265	6761
屯昌县	TunChang	146810	78679	15026	53105	6809
澄迈县	ChengMai	462926	146420	232610	83896	11321
临高县	LinGao	396241	300665	25542	70034	10573
儋州市	DanZhou	718257	427595	96128	194534	9237
东方市	DongFang	436877	135931	204029	96917	11606
乐东县	LeDong	249421	160098	18171	71152	5551
琼中县	QiongZhong	70909	37958	8862	24089	5278
保亭县	BaoTing	68158	32925	6188	29045	6253
陵水县	LingShui	205850	127553	16031	62266	6586
白沙县	BaiSha	75736	45671	9026	21039	5880
昌江县	ChangJiag	290577	86996	149884	53697	12647
农　垦	Nongken	706225	507009	77946	121270	6704
洋　浦	YangPu	438676	17676	299884	121116	106994

注:本表按当年价格计算。
Data in value terms in this table are calculated at current prices.

2－9 各市县生产总值构成
Composition of Gross Domestic Product by City and County

单位:% (%)

地 区	Region	生产总值 Gross DomesticProduct	第一产业 Primary Industry	第二产业 Secondary Industry	第三产业 Tertiary Industry
全 辖 区	**Total Region**				
海 口 市	HaiKou	100	8.3	29.6	62.1
三 亚 市	SanYa	100	23.3	37.9	38.8
五指山市	WuZhiShan	100	35.1	11.7	53.2
文 昌 市	WenChang	100	50.2	19.6	30.2
琼 海 市	QiongHai	100	56.7	11.1	32.2
万 宁 市	WanNing	100	40.4	18.6	41.0
定 安 县	DingAn	100	50.2	14.3	35.5
屯 昌 县	TunChang	100	59.8	8.6	31.6
澄 迈 县	ChengMai	100	35.7	46.6	17.7
临 高 县	LinGao	100	76.0	6.1	17.9
儋 州 市	DanZhou	100	61.0	13.1	25.9
东 方 市	DongFang	100	33.1	45.2	21.7
乐 东 县	LeDong	100	67.7	6.4	25.9
琼 中 县	QiongZhong	100	66.7	9.1	24.2
保 亭 县	BaoTing	100	59.7	6.7	33.6
陵 水 县	LingShui	100	61.9	7.5	30.6
白 沙 县	BaiSha	100	71.2	8.3	20.5
昌 江 县	ChangJiag	100	31.8	49.8	18.4
洋 浦	YangPu	100	4.0	68.4	27.6
不含农垦	**Out of Land Reclamat-ion and Cultivation**				
海 口 市	HaiKou	100	7.4	29.2	63.4
三 亚 市	SanYa	100	19.9	40.1	40.0
五指山市	WuZhiShan	100	31.8	12.4	55.8
文 昌 市	WenChang	100	49.5	20.0	30.5
琼 海 市	QiongHai	100	55.4	11.3	33.3
万 宁 市	WanNing	100	37.7	19.7	42.6
定 安 县	DingAn	100	47.5	15.2	37.3
屯 昌 县	TunChang	100	53.6	10.2	36.2
澄 迈 县	ChengMai	100	31.6	50.3	18.1
临 高 县	LinGao	100	75.9	6.4	17.7
儋 州 市	DanZhou	100	59.5	13.4	27.1
东 方 市	DongFang	100	31.1	46.7	22.2
乐 东 县	LeDong	100	64.2	7.3	28.5
琼 中 县	QiongZhong	100	53.5	12.5	34.0
保 亭 县	BaoTing	100	48.3	9.1	42.6
陵 水 县	LingShui	100	62.0	7.8	30.2
白 沙 县	BaiSha	100	60.3	11.9	27.8
昌 江 县	ChangJiag	100	29.9	51.6	18.5
农 垦	Nongken	100	71.8	11.0	17.2
洋 浦	YangPu	100	4.0	68.4	27.6

注:本表按当年价格计算。
Data in value terms in this table are calculated at current prices.

2－10 各市县生产总值指数

Indices of Gross Domestic Product by City and County

单位:%　　（以上年为 100）　　（%）

地区	Region	生产总值 Gross Domestic Product	第一产业 Primary Industry	第二产业 Secondary Industry	第三产业 Tertiary Industry	人均生产总值（元） Per Capita GDP(yuan)
全辖区	**Total Region**					
海口市	HaiKou	112.9	108.8	115.8	112.2	110.0
三亚市	SanYa	114.5	112.4	118.8	113.3	112.6
五指山市	WuZhiShan	110.5	112.9	112.7	108.5	109.8
文昌市	WenChang	113.8	113.8	116.8	112.1	113.1
琼海市	QiongHai	108.6	106.5	112.9	110.7	107.3
万宁市	WanNing	111.7	108.8	117.0	112.2	110.5
定安县	DingAn	112.7	112.3	122.3	109.9	112.1
屯昌县	TunChang	109.7	111.0	98.0	111.3	107.8
澄迈县	ChengMai	118.3	106.7	136.3	104.7	117.0
临高县	LinGao	106.2	105.7	107.3	107.8	104.1
儋州市	DanZhou	109.8	108.9	109.5	112.2	107.0
东方市	DongFang	112.0	109.7	113.4	112.5	109.7
乐东县	LeDong	113.1	116.3	107.2	107.2	111.9
琼中县	QiongZhong	112.1	113.7	106.7	110.4	110.5
保亭县	BaoTing	113.3	113.5	102.6	115.4	112.1
陵水县	LingShui	114.5	111.2	143.3	115.2	112.5
白沙县	BaiSha	110.6	112.7	100.3	108.3	109.6
昌江县	ChangJiag	115.1	111.5	118.3	112.6	113.0
洋浦	YangPu	136.5	103.3	155.1	109.7	135.2
不含农垦	**Out of Land Reclamat- ion and Cultivation**					
海口市	HaiKou	112.8	108.6	115.2	112.3	109.6
三亚市	SanYa	114.7	112.9	119.6	112.9	112.5
五指山市	WuZhiShan	108.5	108.5	111.7	107.7	107.7
文昌市	WenChang	114.1	114.1	116.9	112.4	113.3
琼海市	QiongHai	107.6	104.7	112.5	110.7	106.2
万宁市	WanNing	113.2	112.5	117.4	111.8	111.8
定安县	DingAn	112.8	112.5	122.1	109.8	112.1
屯昌县	TunChang	108.6	110.1	98.7	109.9	106.4
澄迈县	ChengMai	119.6	107.5	136.4	104.6	117.1
临高县	LinGao	106.5	105.8	110.3	108.2	103.6
儋州市	DanZhou	111.0	110.5	110.2	112.6	106.9
东方市	DongFang	111.6	108.2	113.5	112.3	109.3
乐东县	LeDong	112.1	114.5	109.2	107.9	110.6
琼中县	QiongZhong	109.4	110.1	113.3	107.0	107.6
保亭县	BaoTing	110.8	108.6	109.2	113.5	108.6
陵水县	LingShui	115.1	111.2	144.0	116.9	112.9
白沙县	BaiSha	113.1	116.9	107.7	108.1	111.7
昌江县	ChangJiag	115.2	110.3	119.2	112.3	112.9
农垦	Nongken	110.0	108.7	115.0	112.0	111.5
洋浦	YangPu	136.5	103.3	155.1	109.7	135.2

注:本表按可比价格计算。
The indices in this table are calculated at comparable prices.

主要统计指标解释

国内生产总值(GDP) 指一个国家(或地区)所有常住单位在一定时期内生产活动的最终成果。国内生产总值有三种表现形态,即价值形态、收入形态和产品形态。从价值形态看,它是所有常住单位在一定时期内生产的全部货物和服务价值超过同期中间投入的全部非固定资产货物和服务价值的差额,即所有常住单位的增加值之和;从收入形态看,它是所有常住单位在一定时期内创造并分配给常住单位和非常住单位的初次收入分配之和;从产品形态看,它是所有常住单位在一定时期内最终使用的货物和服务价值与货物和服务净出口价值之和。在实际核算中,国内生产总值有三种计算方法,即生产法、收入法和支出法。三种方法分别从不同的方面反映国内生产总值及其构成。

国民生产总值(GNP) 指一个国家(或地区)所有常住单位在一定时期内收入初次分配的最终结果。一国常住单位从事生产活动所创造的增加值在初次分配中主要分配给该国的常住单位,但也有一部分以生产税及进口税(扣除生产和进口补贴)、劳动者报酬和财产收入等形式分配给非常住单位;同时,国外生产所创造的增加值也有一部分以生产税及进口税(扣除生产和进口补贴)、劳动者报酬和财产收入等形式分配给该国的常住单位,从而产生了国民生产总值的概念。它等于国内生产总值加上来自国外的净要素收入。与国内生产总值不同,国民生产总值是个收入概念,而国内生产总值是个生产概念。

国民生产总值与国内生产总值的区别:国民生产总值是按国民原则计算;国内生产总值是按国土原则计算。两者的差别在于:前者包括本国居民在外国从事投资、服务所取得的收入,不包括外国居民在本国从事投资、服务所取得的收入。后者则与此相反。因掌握的资料有限,本省只计算国内生产总值。

三次产业 是根据社会生产活动历史发展的顺序对产业结构的划分,产品直接取自自然界的部门称为第一产业,对初级产品进行再加工的部门称为第二产业,为生产和消费提供各种服务的部门称为第三产业。它是世界上较为通用的产业结构分类,但各国的划分不尽一致。

我国的三次产业划分是:

第一产业:农业(包括种植业、林业、牧业和渔业)。

第二产业:工业(包括采掘业,制造业,电力、煤气及水的生产和供应业)和建筑业。

第三产业:除第一、第二产业以外的其他各业。由于第三产业包括的行业多、范围广,根据我国的实际情况,第三产业可分为两大部分;一是流通部门,二是服务部门。具体又可分为四个层次:

第一层次:流通部门,包括交通运输、仓储及邮电通信业,批发和零售贸易、餐饮业。

第二层次:为生产和生活服务的部门,包括金融、保险业,地质勘查业、水利管理业,房地产业,社会服务业,农、林、牧、渔服务业,交通运输辅助业,综合技术服务业等。

第三层次:为提高科学文化水平和居民素质服务的部门,包括教育、文化艺术及广播电影电视业,卫生、体育和社会福利业,科学研究业等。

第四层次:为社会公共需要服务的部门,包括国家机关、政党机关和社会团体以及军队、警察等。

当年价格 是指报告期的实际价格,如工业品的出厂价格,农产品的收购价格,商业的零售价格等。按当年价格计算,是指一些以货币表现的物量指标,如社会总产值、工农业总产值、国民收入、国内生产总值等,按照当年的实际价格计算总量。用当年价格计算的数字,反映当年的实际情况,使国民经济各项指标互相衔接,便于考察当年社会经济效益,便于对生产、流通、分配、消费之间进行综合平衡。

按当年价格计算的价值指标,因包括不同年份的价格变动因素,不同年份之间不能直接对比,在对比时应该使用按可比价格计算的数字。

可比价格 指计算各种总量指标所采用的扣除了价格变动因素的价格,可进行不同时期总量指标的对比。按可比价格计算总量指标有两种方法:一种是直接用产品产量乘某一年的不变价格计算;另一种是用价格指数进行缩减。

不变价格 指以同类产品某年的平均价格作为固定价格,用于计算各年的产品价值。按不变价格计算的产品价值消除了价格变动因素,不同时期对比可以反映生产的发展速度。新中国成立后,随着工农业产品价格水平的变化,国家统计局先后五次制定了全国统一的工业产品不变价格和农业产品不变价格。从1952年到1957年使用1952年工(农)业产品不变价格,从1957年到1970年使用1957年不变价格,从1971年到1980年使用1970年不变价格,从1981年到1990年使用1980年不变价格,从1991年开始使用1990年不变价格。

支出法国内生产总值 指一个国家(或地区)所有常住单位在一定时期内用于最终消费、资本形成总额,以及货物和服务的净出口总额,它反映本期生产的国内生产总值的使用及构成。

最终消费 指常住单位在一定时期内对于货物和服务的全部最终消费支出,也就是常住单位为满足物质、文化和精神生活的需要,从本国经济领土和国外购买的货物和服务的支出;不包括非常住单位在本国经济领土内的消费支出。最终消费分为居民消费和政府消费。

居民消费 指常住住户对货物和服务的全部最终消费支出。居民消费按市场价格计算,即按居民支付的购买者价格计算。购买者价格是购买者取得货物所支付的价格，包括购买者支付的运输和商业费用。居民消费除了直接以货币形式购买货物和服务的消费之外，还包括以其他方式获得的货物和服务的消费支出，即所谓的虚拟消费支出。居民虚拟消费支出包括以下几种类型：单位以实物报酬及实物转移的形式提供给劳动者的货物和服务；住户生产并由本住户消费了的货物和服务，其中的服务仅指住户的自有住房服务；金融机构提供的金融媒介服务；保险公司提供的保险服务。

政府消费 指政府部门为全社会提供公共服务的消费支出和免费或以较低价格向住户提供的货物和服务的净支出。前者等于政府服务的产出价值减去政府单位所获得的经营收入的价值，政府服务的产出价值等于它的经常性业务支出加上固定资产折旧；后者等于政府部门免费或以较低价格向住户提供的货物和服务的市场价值减去向住户收取的价值。

资本形成总额 指常住单位在一定时期内获得的减去处置的固定资产加存货的变动，包括固定资本形成总额和存货增加。固定资本形成总额 指常住单位购置、转入和自产自用的固定资产，扣除固定资产的销售和转出后的价值，分有形固定资产形成总额和无形固定资产形成总额。有形固定资产形成总额包括一定时期内完成的建筑工程、安装工程和设备工器具购置（减处置）价值，以及土地改良、新增役、种、奶、毛、娱乐用牲畜和新增经济林木价值。无形固定资产形成总额包括矿藏的勘探、计算机软件、娱乐和文学艺术品原件等获得减处置。

存货增加 指常住单位存货实物量变动的市场价值，即期末价值减期初价值的差额。存货增加可以是正值，也可以是负值；正值表示存货上升，负值表示存货下降。它包括生产单位购进的原材料、燃料和储备物资等存货，以及生产单位生产的产成品、在制品等存货等。

货物和服务净出口 指货物和服务出口减货物和服务进口的差额。出口包括常住单位向非常住单位出售或无偿转让的各种货物和服务的价值；进口包括常住单位从非常住单位购买或无偿得到的各种货物和服务的价值。由于服务活动的提供与使用同时发生，因此服务的进出口业务并不发生出入境现象，一般把常住单位从国外得到的服务作为进口，非常住单位从本国得到的服务作为出口。货物的出口和进口都按离岸价格计算。

劳动者报酬 指劳动者因从事生产活动所获得的全部报酬。包括劳动者获得的各种形式的工资、奖金和津贴，既包括货币形式的，也包括实物形式的；还包括劳动者所享受的公费医疗和医药卫生费、上下班交通补贴和单位支付的社会保险费等。对于个体经济来说，其所有者所获得的劳动报酬和经营利润不易区分，这两部分统一作为劳动者报酬处理。

生产税净额 指生产税减生产补贴后的余额。生产税指政府对生产单位生产、销售和从事经营活动以及因从事生产活动使用某些生产要素（如固定资产、土地、劳动力）所征收的各种税、附加费和规费。生产补贴与生产税相反，指政府对生产单位的单方面收入转移，因此视为负生产税，包括政策亏损补贴、粮食系统价格补贴、外贸企业出口退税收入等。

固定资产折旧 指一定时期内为弥补固定资产损耗按照核定的固定资产折旧率提取的固定资产折旧，或按国民经济核算统一规定的折旧率虚拟计算的固定资产折旧。它反映了固定资产在当期生产中的转移价值。各类企业和企业化管理的事业单位的固定资产折旧是指实际计提并计入成本费中的折旧费；不计提折旧的政府机关、非企业化管理的事业单位和居民住房的固定资产折旧是按照统一规定的折旧率和固定资产原值计算的虚拟折旧。原则上，固定资产折旧应按固定资产的重置价值计算，但是目前我国尚不具备对全社会固定资产进行重估价的基础，所以暂时只能采用上述办法。

营业盈余 指常住单位创造的增加值扣除劳动者报酬、生产税净额和固定资产折旧后的余额。它相当于企业的营业利润加上生产补贴，但要扣除从利润中开支的工资和福利等。

Explanatory Note on Main Statistical Indicators

Gross National Product (GNP) refers to the final result of the primary distribution of the income created by all the resident units of a country (or a region) during a certain period of time. The value-added created by the resident units of a country engaged in production activities is mainly distributed to the resident units of that country while a part of it is distributed to the non-resident units in the form of production tax and import duties (minus subsidies to production and import), remuneration for the labourers and property income. At the meantime, a part of the value-added created abroad is distributed to the resident units of the country in the form of production tax and import duties (minus subsidies to production and import), remuneration for the labourers and property income. Thus the concept of gross national product is formed, which equals to gross domestic product plus net factor income from abroad. Unlike gross domestic product which is a concept of production, gross national product is a concept of income.

Gross Domestic Product (GDP) refers to the final products of all resident units in a country (or a region) during a certain period of time. Gross domestic product is expressed in three different forms, i.e. value, income, and products respectively. The form of value refers to the total value of all products and services produced by all resident units during a certain period of time minus total value of intimidate input of materials and services of the nature of non-fixed assets or the summation of the value-added of all resident units; the form of income includes all the income created by all resident units and distributed primarily to all resident and non-resident units; the form of products refers to the value of all final goods and services for final use by all resident units plus the value of net exports of goods and services during a given period of time. In the practice of national accounting, gross domestic product is calculated with three approaches, i.e. production approach, income approach, and expenditure approach, which reflect gross domestic product and its composition from different aspects.

Three Industries Industry structure has been classified according to the historical sequence of development. Primary industry refers to extraction of natural resources; secondary industry involves processing of primary products; and tertiary industry provides services of various kinds for production and consumption. The above classification is universal although it varies to some extent form country to country. Industry in China comprises:

Primary industry: agriculture (including farming, forestry, animal husbandry and fishery).

Secondary industry: industry (including mining and quarrying, manufacturing, production and supply of electricity, water and gas) and construction.

Tertiary industry: all other industries not included in primary or secondary industry.

Due to the fact that tertiary industry involves in a large variety of industries in China, it is divided into two sectors: circulation sector and service sector and further into four levels:

The first level: circulation sector, including transportation, storage, postal and telecommunications, wholesale and retail trade, and catering trade.

The second level: service sector providing services for production and consumption, including banking, insurance, geological survey, water conservancy management, real estates, service for residents, service for agriculture, forestry, animal husbandry, fishery, subsidiary services for transportation and communications, comprehensive technical services, etc.

The third level: service sector for upgrading scientific, educational and cultural level of the people, including education, culture and arts, broadcasting, movies, television, public health, sports, social welfare and scientific research, etc.

The fourth level: sector providing services for public needs, including government agencies, political parties, social organizations, military and police service.

Comparable Prices refer to prices that are used to remove the factors of price change in calculating economic aggregates, so as to facilitate comparison of aggregates over time. Two methods are used for calculating economic aggregates at comparable prices: 1. Multiplying the output of products by their constant prices of certain year; 2. Deflation of data at current prices by relevant price index.

Constant Price refers to the average price of a given product in certain year, which is used for comparison of output value over time. As the output value at constant prices removes the factor of price changes, it reflects the trend of production development over time. Since 1949, with the changes in general price level, National Bureau of Statistics has issued nationally unified constant prices five times: the 1952 constant prices for 1949-1957; the 1957 constant prices for 1957-1971; the 1970 constant prices for 1971-1981; the 1980 constant prices for 1981-1990; and the 1990 constant prices have been used since 1991.

GDP Calculated with Expenditure Approach refers to total expenditure on final consumption, total capital formation an l net export of goods and services by resident units of a country in a certain period of time. It reflects the composition of GDP by its use.

Households Consumption refers to the total expenditure of resident households on the final consumption of goods and services. The households consumption is calculated at market prices, namely the purchasers prices which the households pay; the purchasers prices of goods are the prices the households pay when they obtain the goods, including the transport and commercial expenses paid by the households. In addition to the consumption of goods and services bought by the households directly with money, the expenditure on goods and services obtained by the households in other ways, i.e. the so-called imputed expenditure on consumption, is also included in the households consumption. The imputation expenditure of the households on consumption includes the following types: (a) the goods and services provided to the households by the units in the form of payment in kind and transfer in kind; (b) the goods and services produced and consumed by the households themselves, in which the services refer only to the services provided by the residential buildings owned by the households; (c) the services of financial intermediary provided by the financial institutions; (d) the insurance services provided by the insurance companies.

Government Consumption refers to the expenditure on the consumption of the public services provided by the government to the whole society and the net expenditure on the goods and services provided by the government to the households at free charge or lower prices. The former equals to the output value of the government services minus the value of operating income obtained by the government departments. (The output value of the government services equals to its current operating expenditure plus depreciation of fixed assets). The latter equals to the market value of the goods and services provided by the government free of charge or at low prices to the households minus the value received by the government from the households.

Total Capital Formation refers to the fixed assets acquired minus those disposed and the change in inventory, including the total fixed assets formation and the increase in inventory.

Total Fixed Capital Formation refers to the value of fixed assets purchased, transferred in by the resident units and those produced and used by themselves deducting the value of fixed assets sold and transferred out. It can be classified into total tangible assets formation and total intangible assets formation. The total tangible assets formation include the value of the construction projects, installation projects completed and the equipment, apparatus and instruments purchased as well as the value of land improved, the value of draught animals, breeding stock, milk, wool and recreational animals and the newly increased economic forest in a certain period. The total intangible assets formation includes the prospecting of minerals, the acquisition of computer software, the originals of recreational works and works of literature and arts minus the disposal of them.

Increase in Inventory refers to the market value of the change in inventory, i.e. the difference of value between the beginning and the end of the period. The increase in inventory can be positive or negative. A positive value indicates the increase in inventory while a negative value indicates the decrease in stock. The inventory includes the raw materials, fuels and reserve materials purchased by the production units as well as the inventory of finished products, semi-finished products, work-in-progress, etc.

Net Export of Goods and Services refers to the difference of the exports of goods and services minus the imports of goods and services. The imports include the value of various goods and services sold or gratuitously transferred by the resident units to the non-resident units. The imports include the value of various goods and services purchased or gratuitously acquired by the resident units from the non-resident units. Because the provision of services and the use of them happen simultaneously, the import and export of services do not appear to have the phenomena of crossing the border of the country. The acquisition of services by the resident units from abroad is usually treated as import while the acquisition of services by non-resident units in this country is usually treated as export. The export and import of goods are calculated at FOB.

Labourers Remuneration refers to the whole payment of various forms earned by the labourers from the productive activities they are engaged in. It includes wages, bonuses and allowances the labourers earned in monetary form and in kind. It also includes the free medical services provided to the labourers and the medicine expenses, traffic subsidies and social insurance fee paid by the labourers working units for them. As the individual economy is concerned, since the labourers remuneration is not easily distinguished from the operating profit, both are treated as labourers remuneration.

Net Taxes on Production refers to the residual of the taxes on production minus the subsidies on production. The taxes on production refers to the various taxes, extra charges and fees levied on the production units on their production, sale and business activities as well as on some factors of production, such as fixed assets, land and labour force, used in the production activities they are engaged in. In contrast to the taxes on production, the subsidies on production refer to the unilateral transfer of part of the governments revenue to the production units and is therefore regarded as negative taxes on production. They include subsidies on the loss due to implementation of government policies, price subsidies to the grain institutions, foreign trade corporations receipts from drawback, etc.

Depreciation of Fixed Assets refers to the depreciation of fixed assets of a given period, drawn in accordance with the stipulated depreciation rate for the purpose of compensating the wear loss of the fixed assets or the depreciation of fixed assets calculated in a fictitious way in accordance with the stipulated unified depreciation rate in the national economic accounting system. It reflects the value of transfer of the fixed assets in the production of the current period. The depreciation of fixed assets in various enterprises and institutions managed as enterprises refers to the depreciation expenses actually drawn and calculated as part of the cost. In government agencies and institutions not managed as enterprises which do not draw the depreciation expenses, as well as for the houses of residents, the depreciation of fixed assets is the imputed depreciation, which is calculated in accordance with the stipulated unified depreciation rate. In principle, the depreciation of fixed assets should be calculated on the basis of the re-purchased value of the fixed assets. However, there is no actual condition to re-evaluate all the fixed assets in China. Therefore, the above-mentioned methods are temporarily adopted at present.

Operating Surplus refers to the balance of the value added created by the resident units deducting the labourers remuneration, net taxes on production and the depreciation of fixed assets. It is equivalent to the business profit of the enterprises plus subsidies on production, but the wages and welfare expenses paid from the profits should be deducted

资料整理: 柯景华　陈翠青
Arranged by Kejinghua　Chengcuiqing

3. 人口和就业
POPULATION AND EMPLOYMENT

全省总人口（万人）（户籍人口）

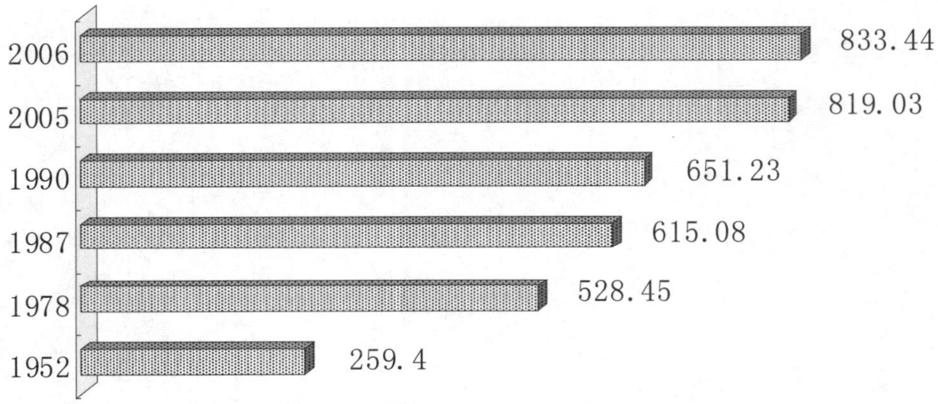

人口自然增长率（‰）

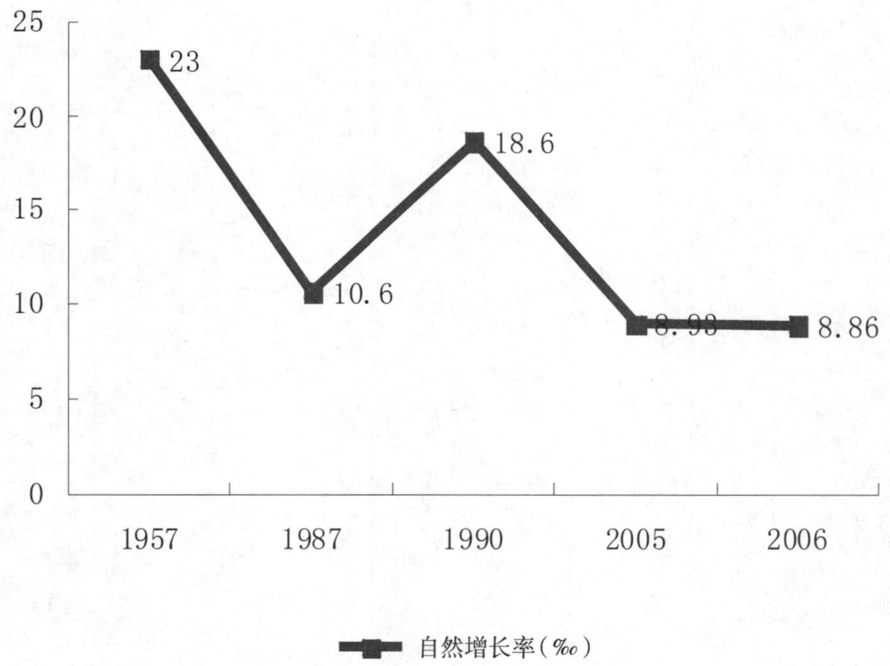

从业人员（按三次产业分）（万人）

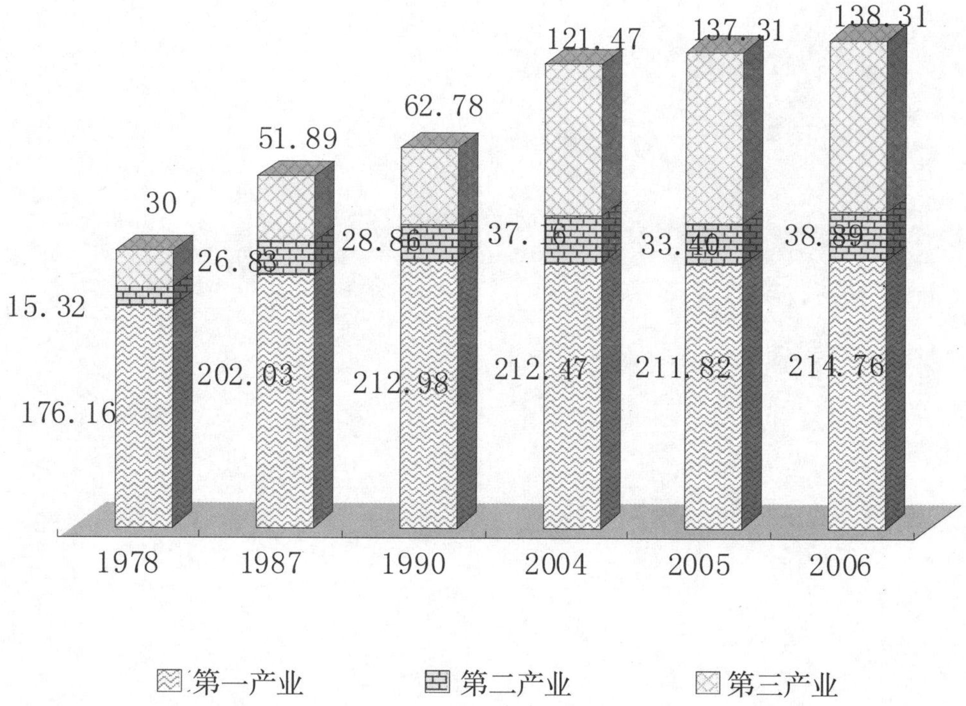

职工平均工资（元）

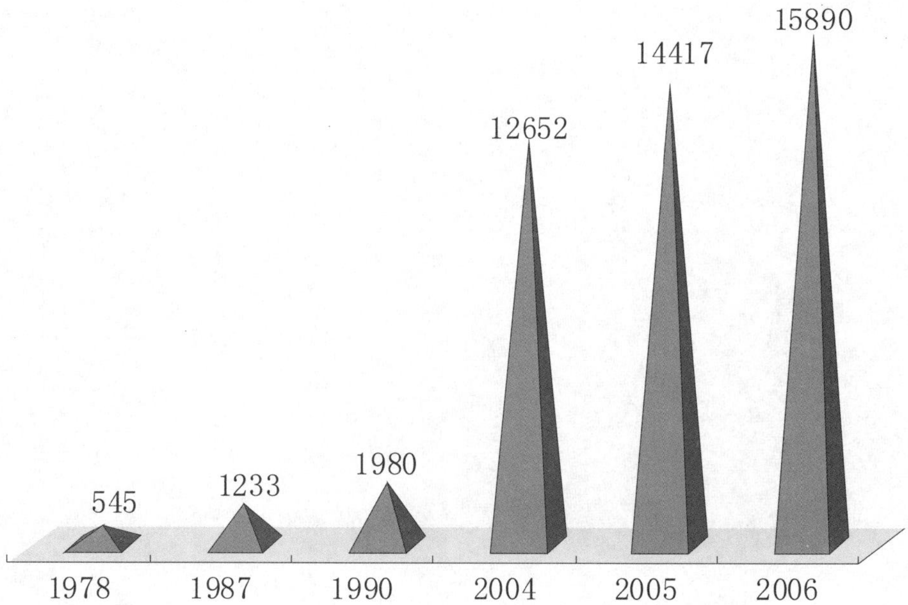

3－1 全省人口数及构成
Population and It's ComposItion

单位:万人　　（户籍人口）(Registered population)　　(10 000 persons)

年 份 Year	总户数（万户） Total Family Households (10 000 households)	总人口 Total Population	按性别分 By Sex 男 Male	女 Female	按农业、非农业分 By Agriculture and Non-Agriculture 农业人口 Agriculture Population	非农人口 Non-Agriculture Population
1952	66.06	259.40	126.84	132.56	239.28	20.12
1957	69.51	290.81	145.39	145.42	253.99	36.82
1962	76.20	335.18	184.21	150.97	287.91	47.27
1965	83.65	365.79	186.21	179.58	313.57	52.22
1970	98.81	428.89	218.11	210.78	374.84	54.05
1971	108.14	454.50	323.38	131.12	393.92	60.58
1973	100.96	479.49	245.30	234.19	414.69	64.80
1974	101.83	487.77	249.40	238.37	420.88	66.89
1975	103.34	496.82	253.73	243.09	427.36	69.46
1976	106.75	505.15	259.14	246.01	433.91	71.24
1977	110.33	516.36	264.32	252.04	442.38	73.98
1978	114.13	528.45	270.42	258.03	451.08	77.37
1979	115.76	540.30	276.53	263.77	458.86	81.44
1980	117.81	552.53	280.36	272.17	466.24	86.29
1981	117.68	560.77	287.09	273.68	469.76	91.01
1982	116.90	571.38	293.26	278.12	477.11	94.27
1983	120.09	580.66	298.83	281.83	482.79	97.87
1984	124.98	589.31	303.58	285.73	485.35	103.96
1985	127.26	597.51	313.08	284.43	485.50	112.01
1986	132.33	605.63	313.08	292.55	489.30	116.33
1987	136.87	615.08	318.23	296.85	493.49	121.59
1988	143.95	627.49	325.03	302.46	500.82	126.67
1989	147.73	638.79	331.63	307.16	506.20	132.59
1990	150.39	651.23	338.40	312.83	514.62	136.61
1991	155.39	661.50	344.38	317.12	520.68	140.82
1992	158.22	671.32	350.05	321.27	524.83	146.49
1993	161.01	681.78	355.70	326.08	530.36	151.42
1994	163.27	691.39	360.66	330.73	533.26	158.13
1995	166.62	702.42	367.78	334.64	537.36	165.06
1996	170.76	714.06	373.20	340.86	540.25	173.81
1997	174.84	724.53	379.36	345.17	543.07	181.46
1998	178.21	733.31	384.91	348.40	547.19	186.12
1999	181.39	743.21	390.07	353.14	554.09	189.12
2000	182.61	760.94	399.54	361.40	564.07	196.87
2001	185.67	769.50	403.71	365.79	567.19	202.31
2002	188.52	778.89	409.16	369.73	570.43	208.46
2003	191.29	790.26	415.21	375.05	574.90	215.36
2004	197.70	805.88	422.70	383.18	501.15	304.53
2005	202.79	819.03	428.67	390.37	505.30	313.73
2006	215.57	833.44	435.59	397.85	512.07	321.36

3－2 各市县总人口

Total Population by City and County

单位:人(年末户籍人口) (Registered population at Year-End) (person)

市县	City and County	总户数(户) Total Family Households (households)	总人口 Total Population	按性别分 By Sex 男 Male	女 Female	按农业、非农业分 By Agriculture and Non-Agriculture 农业人口 Agriculture Population	非农人口 Non-Agriculture Population
总计	Total	2155664	8334358	4355868	3978490	5120747	3213611
海口市	Haikou	439037	1508612	773466	735146	610894	897718
三亚市	Sanya	128116	524170	269082	255088	262938	261232
五指山市	Wuzhishan	36892	111393	57949	53444	56441	54952
文昌市	Wenchang	145542	549776	278515	271261	430246	119530
琼海市	Qionghai	129166	469912	245848	224064	326690	143222
万宁市	Wanning	158209	575155	302274	272881	404470	170685
定安县	Dingan	86864	317781	167753	150028	226460	91321
屯昌县	Dunchang	72521	281169	149923	131246	180407	100762
澄迈县	Chengmai	125650	511264	277665	233599	336704	174560
临高县	Lingao	107456	445848	235017	210831	318456	127392
儋州市	Danzhou	211931	989147	518565	470582	590746	398401
东方市	Dongfang	100522	402902	212621	190281	293834	109068
乐东县	Ledong	115606	493248	257072	236176	358757	134491
琼中县	Qiongzhong	63731	212678	114385	98293	114435	98243
保亭县	Baoting	44011	163339	84732	78607	87197	76142
陵水县	Lingshui	80068	346249	182200	164049	259868	86381
白沙县	Baisha	47993	188102	100558	87544	106096	82006
昌江县	Changjiang	64140	243367	128039	115328	156108	87259
西沙群岛	Xisha	209	246	204	42		246

3－3 各市县民族人口
Population for Nationality by City and County

单位:人 (2006 年末户籍人口) (Registered population at Year-End) (person)

市 县	City and County	汉族 Han Nationality	少数民族 Minority Nationalities	黎族 Li Nationality	苗族 Miao Nationality	壮族 Zhuang Nationality	回族 Hui Nationality	其他 Others	占总人口比重% % to Total
总 计	**Total**	**6885464**	**1448894**	**1319130**	**68427**	**34400**	**10736**	**16201**	**17.38**
海 口 市	Haikou	1482864	25748	13771	1148	2761	1590	6478	1.71
三 亚 市	Sanya	304809	219361	205052	3533	1736	7716	1324	41.85
五指山市	Wuzhishan	38328	73065	66656	5358	407	125	519	65.59
文 昌 市	Wenchang	547402	2374	1726	125	304	31	188	0.43
琼 海 市	Qionghai	454205	15707	3753	10040	1568	23	323	3.34
万 宁 市	Wanning	480994	94161	83525	6907	2501	70	1158	16.37
定 安 县	Dingan	312303	5478	1786	2451	927	5	309	1.72
屯 昌 县	Dunchang	253043	28126	15236	9294	3121	21	454	10.00
澄 迈 县	Chengmai	505908	5356	3861	513	810	24	148	1.05
临 高 县	Lingao	445130	718	474	50	103	8	83	0.16
儋 州 市	Danzhou	912736	76411	67924	2675	3929	347	1536	7.72
东 方 市	Dongfang	318256	84646	82999	1041	352	32	222	21.01
乐 东 县	Ledong	302771	190477	186031	2492	1664	24	266	38.62
琼 中 县	Qiongzhong	89255	123423	101964	13428	6756	73	1202	58.03
保 亭 县	Baoting	55940	107399	96763	6515	3353	48	720	65.75
陵 水 县	Lingshui	157192	189057	187459	695	621	22	260	54.60
白 沙 县	aisha	72624	115478	110148	1914	2702	17	697	61.39
昌 江 县	Changjiang	151458	91909	90002	248	785	560	314	37.77
西沙群岛	Xishaa	246							

3－4 人口变动抽样调查主要指标
Main Indicators of Sample Survey on Population Change

指　　标	Item	2003	2004	2005	2006
总人口(万人)	Total Population(10 000 persons)	810.52	817.83	828.00	835.88
自然增长情况	Condition of Natural Growth				
出生率(‰)	Birth Rate(‰)	14.68	14.77	14.65	14.59
死亡率(‰)	Death Rate(‰)	5.52	5.79	5.72	5.73
自然增长率(‰)	Natural Growth Rate(‰)	9.16	8.98	8.93	8.86
各年龄段占的比率(%)	PoPu Lation by Age Group				
0—14岁	0-14	24.1	23.9	23.69	22.35
15—64岁	15-65	68.08	68.58	67.77	68.96
65岁及以上	65 and Over	7.82	7.52	8.54	8.69
性别比(%)	Sex Radio(%)	113.33	113.5	110.46	110.22
家庭户平均每户人数(人)	Per Household Persons	3.98	4.16	3.83	3.94
年龄构成指数	Composition of Age Ratio				
总负担系数(%)	Total Dependency Ratio(%)	46.88	45.81	47.56	45.01
负担少年儿童系数(%)	Dependency Ratio of Children(%)	35.39	34.85	34.96	32.42
负担老年系数(%)	Dependency Ratio of the Aged(%)	11.49	10.96	12.60	12.59
孩次构成情况	Composition of Birth Order				
一孩率(%)	1st Birth Rate(%)	62.04	58.66	53.70	50.41
二孩率(%)	2nd Birth Rate(%)	27.76	33.19	36.84	41.56
三孩率(%)	3rd Birth Rate(%)	10.2	8.15	9.45	8.02
育龄妇女生育情况	Fertility of Women on Childbearing Age				
一般生育率(‰)	Ordinary Fertility Rate(‰)	44.62	45.2	46.80	48.89
总和生育率	Total Fertility	1.49	1.43	1.61	1.69

注:孩次构成情况中三孩率为三孩及以上孩次率;2005年数据为1%人口抽样调查数据。
a) 3rd birth rate of composition of birth orde refers to the 3rd rate and above the 3rd birth rate.

3－5 主要年份全部从业人员年末总人数
Total Number of Employed Persons at the Year–end in Major Years

单位：万人 (10 000 persons)

年份 Year	从业人员 Employment	国有单位 State–owned Units	城镇集体单位 Urban Collective–owned Units	其他经济类型单位 Units of Other Types of Ownership	城镇私营单位 Urban Private Enterprises	城镇个体 Urban Seif–employed Individuals	农村劳动者 Rural Labourers
1962	149.59	26.42	3.98			0.66	118.53
1965	156.81	33.02	4.33				119.46
1970	184.54	52.24	4.99				127.31
1971	192.81	57.28	5.14				130.39
1972	196.63	58.58	5.29				132.76
1973	199.89	58.57	5.44				135.88
1974	202.48	59.10	5.08				138.30
1975	202.02	60.42	5.39				136.21
1976	204.02	62.59	5.28			0.10	136.05
1977	218.00	70.56	9.59			0.09	137.76
1978	221.48	75.08	6.27			0.40	139.73
1979	226.23	77.41	6.60			0.71	141.51
1980	231.45	78.52	6.69			1.32	144.92
1981	242.46	85.05	6.69			2.18	148.54
1982	247.06	87.73	6.93			1.56	150.84
1983	253.09	89.34	6.72			2.06	154.97
1984	259.17	87.31	6.56	0.08		2.92	159.30
1985	268.40	89.93	9.27	0.41		4.54	164.25
1986	275.65	91.91	9.33	0.49		4.75	169.17
1987	280.75	91.66	9.11	0.57		5.56	173.85
1988	291.95	93.67	9.08	0.73		7.53	180.94
1989	298.35	94.80	8.83	1.13		7.64	185.95
1990	304.62	96.36	8.94	1.54		7.68	190.10
1991	318.13	99.24	8.54	2.34	3.24	9.66	195.11
1992	322.49	100.26	8.96	3.38	4.19	9.51	196.19
1993	333.33	98.84	9.41	4.19	9.95	12.40	198.54
1994	355.56	96.86	8.53	5.55	11.24	11.98	201.40
1995	334.49	94.08	8.43	5.82	11.96	11.35	202.85
1996	333.30	88.91	8.49	6.81	10.52	12.50	206.07
1997	341.65	87.71	8.35	8.06	11.05	16.75	209.73
1998	326.70	71.65	4.97	7.87	12.08	18.36	211.77
1999	326.77	68.83	4.63	8.23	13.68	16.27	215.13
2000	334.55	66.86	4.38	8.24	11.39	19.70	223.98
2001	338.39	63.58	4.42	8.48	9.91	22.47	229.53
2002	349.89	60.23	4.18	10.46	18.48	23.01	233.53
2003	360.34	58.66	4.05	10.83	23.87	22.66	240.27
2004	371.10	58.11	3.87	12.61	23.31	23.16	250.04
2005	382.53	57.93	4.07	12.71	25.02	26.78	256.01
2006	391.96	56.89	3.84	14.81	26.86	29.69	259.87

3－6 按三次产业分的从业人员及构成

Number of Employed Persons and Composition by Three Industry

年份 地区 Year Region	从业人员(万人) Employment (10 000 persons)				构成(%) Composition(%)		
		第一产业 Primary Industry	第二产业 Secondary Industry	第三产业 Tertiary Industry	第一产业 Primary Industry	第二产业 Secondary Industry	第三产业 Tertiary Industry
1978	221.48	176.16	15.32	30.00	79.54	6.92	13.54
1979	226.23	179.79	15.83	30.61	79.47	7.00	13.53
1980	231.45	183.93	16.71	30.81	79.47	7.22	13.31
1985	268.40	197.47	24.46	46.47	73.57	9.11	17.32
1986	275.65	200.29	27.01	48.35	72.66	9.80	17.54
1987	280.75	202.03	26.83	51.89	71.96	9.56	18.48
1988	291.95	207.23	26.99	57.73	70.98	9.24	19.78
1989	298.35	210.18	29.26	58.91	70.45	9.81	19.74
1990	304.62	212.98	28.86	62.78	69.92	9.47	20.61
1991	318.13	217.68	30.92	69.53	68.42	9.72	21.86
1992	322.49	215.29	34.23	72.97	66.76	10.61	22.63
1993	333.33	208.86	38.49	85.98	62.65	11.55	25.80
1994	335.56	204.52	40.09	90.95	60.95	11.95	27.10
1995	334.49	203.92	39.06	91.51	60.96	11.68	27.36
1996	333.30	201.53	39.22	92.56	60.46	11.77	27.77
1997	341.64	202.56	38.89	100.19	59.29	11.38	29.33
1998	326.70	198.05	32.85	95.80	60.62	10.06	29.32
1999	326.77	198.4	31.65	96.72	60.71	9.69	29.6
2000	334.55	203.60	31.15	99.80	60.86	9.31	29.83
2001	338.39	203.75	30.51	104.13	60.21	9.02	30.77
2002	349.89	205.59	33.24	111.06	58.76	9.5	31.74
2003	360.34	210.71	35.41	114.21	58.47	9.83	31.7
2004	371.10	212.47	37.16	121.47	57.26	10.01	32.73
2005	382.53	211.82	38.02	132.69	55.37	9.94	34.69
2006	391.96	214.76	38.89	138.31	54.79	9.92	35.29
按市县分(人)							
海口市 Haikou	949989	214542	168128	567319	22.58	17.70	59.72
三亚市 Sanya	242662	121261	15218	106183	49.97	6.27	43.76
五指山市 Wuzhishan	44479	24342	1975	18162	54.73	4.44	40.83
文昌市 Wenchang	228388	135777	25556	67055	59.45	11.19	29.36
琼海市 Qionghai	192580	118794	16855	56931	61.69	8.75	29.56
万宁市 Wanning	200245	116930	17348	65967	58.39	8.66	32.94
定安县 Dingan	130825	86002	10842	33981	65.74	8.29	25.97
屯昌县 Tunchang	98299	64303	6407	27589	65.42	6.52	28.07
澄迈县 Chengmai	213063	128290	23981	60792	60.21	11.26	28.53
临高县 Lingao	206615	142533	13473	50609	68.99	6.52	24.49
儋州市 Danzhou	349092	231139	26314	91639	66.21	7.54	26.25
东方市 Dongfang	197196	143683	12410	41103	72.86	6.29	20.84
乐东县 Ledong	236882	151618	18295	66969	64.01	7.72	28.27
琼中县 Qiongzhong	68722	44268	2231	22223	64.42	3.25	32.34
保亭县 Baoting	60293	38609	2523	19161	64.03	4.18	31.78
陵水县 Lingshui	148579	104623	6379	37577	70.42	4.29	25.29
白沙县 Baisha	69410	57290	2481	9639	82.54	3.57	13.89
昌江县 Changjiang	104033	67207	11394	25432	64.60	10.95	24.45
洋浦 Yangpu	6976		3809	3167		54.60	45.40
农垦 Land Reclamation	166927	156384	3322	7221	93.68	1.99	4.33
总后 Zonghou	4045			4045			100.00
西沙 Xisha	276			276			100.00

3－7 各市县从业人员年末总人数

Total Number of Employed Persons at the Year-end by City and County

单位:人 (person)

地区	Region	从业人员 Employment	国有单位 State-owned Units	城镇集体单位 Urban Collective-owned Units	其他经济类型单位 Units of Other Types of Ownership	城镇私营单位 Urban Private Enterprises	城镇个体 Urban Seif-employed Individuals	农村劳动者 Rural Labourers
总计	Total	3919576	568937	38408	148084	268569	296897	2598681
海口市	Haikou	949989	158358	12584	94764	215814	147199	321270
三亚市	Sanya	242662	29437	2063	19587	15886	20753	154936
五指山市	Wuzhishan	44479	8127	114	779	1804	4608	29047
文昌市	Wenchang	228388	16736	4852	3313	1341	7492	194654
琼海市	Qionghai	192580	15082	640	2427	2970	9389	162072
万宁市	Wanning	200245	17122	2506	2533	2978	14314	160792
定安县	Dingan	130825	8649	925	3086	1269	6934	109962
屯昌县	Tunchang	98299	9258	2851	375	1090	5713	79012
澄迈县	Chengmai	213063	18781	2915	6537	2629	4416	177785
临高县	Lingao	206615	10972	1821	1565	2257	15414	174586
儋州市	Danzhou	349092	27576	2440	885	8938	23610	285643
东方市	Dongfang	197196	13506	728	5211	1400	6700	169651
乐东县	Ledong	236882	15411	1465	88	445	5784	213689
琼中县	Qiongzhong	68722	7923	922	475	2203	8456	48743
保亭县	Baoting	60293	5984	199	179	2277	4263	47391
陵水县	Lingshui	148579	9739	416	714	161	5871	131678
白沙县	Baisha	69410	7477	524	48	117	2502	58742
昌江县	Changjiang	104033	14517	443	1576	4990	3479	79028
洋浦	Yangpu	6976	3034		3942			
农垦	Land Reclamation	166927	166927					
总后	Zonghou	4045	4045					
西沙	Xisha	276	276					

3-8 各市县城镇单位从业人员按执行会计制度分组
Number of Employed Persons at the Year-end by Sector

单位:人 (person)

地 区	Region	从业人员年末人数 Employment	企业 Enterprises	事业 Institutions	机关 Agencies& Organizations
总 计	Total	755429	494731	179754	80944
海口市	Haikou	265706	180382	56074	29250
三亚市	Sanya	51087	35063	11015	5009
五指山市	Wuzhishan	9020	2747	4688	1585
文昌市	Wenchang	24901	12026	9160	3715
琼海市	Qionghai	18149	8338	7299	2512
万宁市	Wanning	22161	10639	7952	3570
定安县	Dingan	12660	5154	5813	1693
屯昌县	Tunchang	12484	4891	4271	3322
澄迈县	Chengmai	28233	16824	7809	3600
临高县	Lingao	14358	4854	5818	3686
儋州市	Danzhou	30901	8780	18546	3575
东方市	Dongfang	19445	9071	7507	2867
乐东县	Ledong	16964	6870	7244	2850
琼中县	Qiongzhong	9320	3988	3734	1598
保亭县	Baoting	6362	1918	2829	1615
陵水县	Lingshui	10869	3464	2406	4999
白沙县	Baisha	8049	2680	3440	1929
昌江县	Changjiang	16536	10244	3812	2480
洋浦	Yangpu	6976	5258	1164	554
农垦	Land Reclamation	166927	161540	5128	259
总后	Zonghou	4045		4045	
西沙	Xisha	276			276

说明:本部份资料不包括私营经济和个体劳动者。下同。
a)The materials of statistic for Labor-wages in this year do not include the urban private units.(the same below)

3－9　各市县分行业城镇单位从业人员年末人数

Number of Employed Persons in Urban Units at the Year-end by Sector and Region

单位：人　　(person)

地区	Region	从业人员 Employment	农、林、牧、渔业 Farming, Forestry, Animal Husbandry and Fishery	采矿业 Mining and Quarrying	制造业 Manufacturing	电力、煤气及水的生产和供应业 Production and Supply of Electric Power, Gas and Water	建筑业 Construction	交通运输仓储及邮电通信业 Transport, Storage, Postal Services	信息传输、计算机服务和软件业 Information Transmission, Computer Services and Software	批发和零售业 Wholesale & Retail Trade Services	住宿和餐饮业 Hotels and Catering Trade
总计	**Total**	**755429**	**184917**	**8346**	**68796**	**20696**	**55749**	**41254**	**8251**	**27648**	**34007**
海口市	Haikou	265706	2234	361	35774	6394	42901	23852	5713	14447	10859
三亚市	Sanya	51087	946	230	2347	1381	2928	4862	331	2335	14785
五指山市	Wuzhishan	9020	49		535	644	19	418	47	447	347
文昌市	Wenchang	24901	936	231	3244	970	2553	886	93	1407	893
琼海市	Qionghai	18149	1514	49	1166	1035	154	770	105	696	2300
万宁市	Wanning	22161	3696	66	281	12	2021	618	814	356	2479
定安县	Dingan	12660	614		1790	559	526	561	135	316	477
屯昌县	Tunchang	12484	634		889	449	1176	523	61	925	56
澄迈县	Chengmai	28233	6525	28	4625	2937	546	905	81	1322	241
临高县	Lingao	14358	443	198	1869	423	536	125	79	746	46
儋州市	Danzhou	30901	3853	60	1696	1674	697	1018	137	684	240
东方市	Dongfang	19445	2383	406	2065	577	381	2461	74	372	436
乐东县	Ledong	16964	522	1299	1335	941	483	721	55	1344	
琼中县	Qiongzhong	9320	1575		466	352	366	664	94	413	115
保亭县	Baoting	6362	593		177	429		449	31	411	9
陵水县	Lingshui	10869	61	6	920	611	55	820	47	263	16
白沙县	Baisha	8049	1029		682	359	188	421	86	406	63
昌江县	Changjiang	16536	926	5412	2072	765	135	218	123	459	59
洋浦	Yangpu	6976			3625	184		909	57	15	184
农垦	Land Reclamation	166927	156384		3238		84	53	88	284	402
总后	Zonghou	4045									
西沙	Xisha	276									

表 3-9 续(continued)

地区 Region	金融 Finance	房地产业 Real Estate Trade	租赁和商务服务业 Rent and Business Affair Services	科学研究、技术服务和地质勘查业 Scientific Research, Polytechnic Services and Geological Prospecting	水利、环境和公共设施管理业 Water Conservancy, Environmental Protection and Public Installations Management Services	居民服务和其他服务业 Resident Services and Other Social Services	教育 Education	卫生、社会保障和社会福利业 Health Care, Social Security and Social Welfare	文化、体育和娱乐业 Culture, Sports and Recreational Services	公共管理和社会组织 Public Management and Social Organizations
总计 Total	**17199**	**15788**	**14477**	**16046**	**19404**	**776**	**87749**	**31898**	**12376**	**90052**
海口市 Haikou	8087	12785	8795	8229	7053	676	27511	11971	6396	31668
三亚市 Sanya	1481	1332	717	596	3808	22	4517	1979	1365	5125
五指山市 Wuzhishan	252	31	202	98	242	13	2648	854	154	2020
文昌市 Wenchang	834	372	263	459	450	11	5551	1630	116	4002
琼海市 Qionghai	761	61	59	214	541		4768	1234	118	2604
万宁市 Wanning	744	35	355	958		5	3089	1179	1878	3575
定安县 Dingan	304	41	608	38	792		3279	797	31	1792
屯昌县 Tunchang	533	104	63	94	526		2420	626	128	3277
澄迈县 Chengmai	573	97	276	25	544		4495	939	244	3830
临高县 Lingao	484	33	351	113	602		3603	1126	84	3497
儋州市 Danzhou	744	355	366	3625	1548		8305	1562	271	4066
东方市 Dongfang	452	42	208	131	861		4084	1262	383	2867
乐东县 Ledong	405	46	500	60	218		4556	1109	114	3256
琼中县 Qiongzhong	277	13	170	88	587		1944	486	73	1637
保亭县 Baoting	124	14	103	62	212		1702	357	36	1653
陵水县 Lingshui	379	20	627	162	727		9	951	46	5149
白沙县 Baisha	189		159	60	170	7	1700	433	91	2006
昌江县 Changjiang	345		26	83	253	42	2156	540	151	2771
洋浦 Yangpu	231	28	92		270			85	656	640
农垦 Land Reclamation		379	537	951			1412	2778	41	296
总后 Zonghou										4045
西沙 Xisha										276

3－10 分行业城镇单位女性从业人员年末人数

Number of Employed Persons in Urban Units at the Year-end by Sector、by Female and Region

单位：人 (person)

地区 Region	从业人员 Employment	农、林、牧、渔业 Farming, Forestry, Animal Husbandry and Fishery	采矿业 Mining and Quarrying	制造业 Manufacturing	电力、煤气及水的生产和供应业 Production and Supply of Electric Power,Gas and Water	建筑业 Construction	交通运输仓储及邮电通信业 Transport, Storage, Postal Services	信息传输、计算机服务和软件业 Information Transmission, Computer Services and Software	批发和零售业 Wholesale & Retail Trade Services	住宿和餐饮业 Hotels and Catering Trade
总计 Total	**283574**	**80428**	**2498**	**29920**	**6180**	**5566**	**12707**	**2814**	**10667**	**17826**
海口市 Haikou	93477	845	72	17583	2398	3465	7175	2142	6013	5993
三亚市 Sanya	20797	330	61	969	502	281	1561	119	915	7438
五指山市 Wuzhishan	3219	8		277	238	3	130	19	161	157
文昌市 Wenchang	8750	325	44	1417	276	509	253	29	334	487
琼海市 Qionghai	7427	868	14	494	222	20	228	26	192	1153
万宁市 Wanning	7824	1693	9	119	3	357	218	114	88	1181
定安县 Dingan	4793	160		1130	173	96	193	42	106	255
屯昌县 Tunchang	4265	231		250	148	280	198	18	388	35
澄迈县 Chengmai	7351	1600	10	1073	190	34	286	30	381	167
临高县 Lingao	4061	126	35	523	109	91	34	23	78	35
儋州市 Danzhou	10520	1477	10	789	478	110	381	35	252	159
东方市 Dongfang	6376	640	116	746	156	115	578	16	139	283
乐东县 Ledong	5825	166	396	393	435	105	263	10	735	
琼中县 Qiongzhong	3227	461		191	168	48	272	30	136	78
保亭县 Baoting	2649	264		96	138		183	9	197	6
陵水县 Lingshui	4138	24	1	506	171	5	325	9	105	11
白沙县 Baisha	2808	329		204	116	19	145	27	177	48
昌江县 Changjiang	5465	262	1730	794	231	6	84	47	182	43
洋浦 Yangpu	2103			862	28		187	20	2	93
农垦 Land Reclamation	75613	70619		1504		22	13	49	86	204
总后 Zonghou	2821									
西沙 Xisha	65									

表 3-10 续(continued)

地 区 Region	金 融 Finance	房地产业 Real Estate Trade	租赁和商务服务业 Rent and Business Affair Services	科学研究、技术服务和地质勘查业 Scientific Research, Polytechnic Services and Geological Prospecting	水利、环境和公共设施管理业 Water Conservancy, Environmental Protection and Public Installations Management Services	居民服务和其他服务业 Resident Services and Other Social Services	教育 Education	卫生、社会保障和社会福利业 Health Care, Social Security and Social Welfare	文化、体育和娱乐业 Culture, Sports and Recreational Services	公共管理和社会组织 Public Management and Social Organizations
总 计 Total	**6165**	**5036**	**4159**	**5187**	**9572**	**284**	**36413**	**18779**	**4732**	**24641**
海口市 Haikou	3035	3981	2301	2441	3568	249	13804	7305	2653	8454
三亚市 Sanya	673	511	300	136	1828	9	2320	1139	439	1266
五指山市 Wuzhishan	79	11	80	34	118	5	1065	292	72	470
文昌市 Wenchang	277	88	91	150	205	5	2438	877	43	902
琼海市 Qionghai	247	15	15	48	430		1984	898	38	535
万宁市 Wanning	215	3	100	457		2	1413	636	504	712
定安县 Dingan	90	7	224	9	356		1159	445	12	336
屯昌县 Tunchang	183	39	35	34	285		884	285	50	922
澄迈县 Chengmai	185	27	13	8	303		1469	510	77	988
临高县 Lingao	139	8	115	26	186		993	686	23	831
儋州市 Danzhou	213	129	69	1214	690		2524	983	120	887
东方市 Dongfang	141	22	68	62	405		1398	766	136	589
乐东县 Ledong	145	10	196	21	68		1560	522	41	759
琼中县 Qiongzhong	87	3	80	20	263		620	286	32	452
保亭县 Baoting	41	5	48	20	150		812	240	10	430
陵水县 Lingshui	140	7	148	36	292		1	608	14	1735
白沙县 Baisha	59		91	26	78	2	631	256	39	561
昌江县 Changjiang	130		6	14	108	12	658	318	76	764
洋浦 Yangpu	86	10	40		239			57	342	137
农垦 Land Reclamation		160	139	431			680	1670	11	25
总后 Zonghou										2821
西沙 Xisha										65

3－11 分行业城镇单位使用农村劳动力年末人数
Number of Employed Persons at the Year-end by Sector

单位:人 (person)

地区 Region	从业人员 Employment	农、林、牧、渔业 Farming, Forestry, Animal Husbandry and Fishery	采矿业 Mining and Quarrying	制造业 Manufacturing	电力、煤气及水的生产和供应业 Production and Supply of Electric Power, Gas and Water	建筑业 Construction	交通运输仓储及邮电通信业 Transport, Storage, Postal Services	信息传输、计算机服务和软件业 Information Transmission, Computer Services and Software	批发和零售业 Wholesale & Retail Trade Services	住宿和餐饮业 Hotels and Catering Trade
总计 Total	53505	1792	81	12829	688	22768	1393	22	435	5861
海口市 Haikou	32913	436		6621		19152	483	1	374	1724
三亚市 Sanya	4197	24		571	135	58	134		27	2786
五指山市 Wuzhishan	283						73		5	39
文昌市 Wenchang	2829	55	65	993	317	885	42		16	205
琼海市 Qionghai	1072	7	4	366						332
万宁市 Wanning	1729			14		955				611
定安县 Dingan	1189			649		178				
屯昌县 Tunchang	805			164	147	420	70			
澄迈县 Chengmai	440	16		45		227	135			
临高县 Lingao	973	131		555		182			1	
儋州市 Danzhou	1391	7		849		315	91			18
东方市 Dongfang	1481	897	12	290		159	21			90
乐东县 Ledong	52	5		5			19		6	
琼中县 Qiongzhong	339	44		18	69		102		2	
保亭县 Baoting	20				20					
陵水县 Lingshui	538			477						
白沙县 Baisha	367	113		115		112			4	3
昌江县 Changjiang	954	16		673		125		21		
洋浦 Yangpu	872			331			223			
农垦 Land Reclamation	187	41		93						53
总后 Zonghou	874									
西沙 Xisha										

表 3-11 续 continued

地　区　Region	金　融 Finance	房地产业 Real Estate Trade	租赁和商务服务业 Rent and Business Affair Services	科学研究、技术服务和地质勘查业 Scientific Research, Polytechnic Services and Geological Prospecting	水利、环境和公共设施管理业 Water Conservancy, Environmental Protection and Public Installations Management Services	居民服务和其他服务业 Resident Services and Other Social Services	教育 Education	卫生、社会保障和社会福利业 Health Care, Social Security and Social Welfare	文化、体育和娱乐业 Culture, Sports and Recreational Services	公共管理和社会组织 Public Management and Social Organizations
总　计 Total	**88**	**1699**	**190**	**664**	**1473**	**28**	**618**	**561**	**549**	**1766**
海口市 Haikou	6	1512	102	528	430	28	209	455	443	409
三亚市 Sanya		171			145		15		60	71
五指山市 Wuzhishan			8				52	2	2	102
文昌市 Wenchang		16			50		102	45		38
琼海市 Qionghai				31	300		24			8
万宁市 Wanning			39	95				12		3
定安县 Dingan			40		114		208			
屯昌县 Tunchang										4
澄迈县 Chengmai							3	3	11	
临高县 Lingao					7			3		94
儋州市 Danzhou				9	81		1	11	9	
东方市 Dongfang							4	4		4
乐东县 Ledong					3					14
琼中县 Qiongzhong	67				27			2		8
保亭县 Baoting										
陵水县 Lingshui	15				46					
白沙县 Baisha			1	1					14	4
昌江县 Changjiang								22		97
洋　浦 Yangpu					270			2	10	36
农　垦 Land Reclamation										
总　后 Zonghou										874
西　沙 Xisha										

3－12 单位从业人员变动情况
Changes of Employed Persons of Units

单位：人 (person)

项目	Item	本年增加人数 Number of Persons in Increaed	农村招收 Recruited from Rural Area	从城镇招收 Recruited from Urban Area	录用的退伍军人 Employment of Demobilized Soldiers	录用的大、中专、技工学校毕业生 Employment of Graduates from Universties Specialized Secondary Schools and Technical Training Schools	调入人数 Number of Persons Transferred into		其他 Others
								由外省调入 From Outside Hainan	
总计	**Total**	**147547**	**12531**	**11815**	**1549**	**13175**	**97725**	**1931**	**10752**
按类型分	**Grouped by Category**								
国有单位	State-owned Units	123105	4344	5692	796	7632	96292	1644	8349
城镇集体单位	Urban Collective-owned Units	1969	924	291	61	267	163	1	263
其他单位	Units of Others	22473	7263	5832	692	5276	1270	286	2140
按行业分	**By Sector**								
农、林、牧、渔业	Farming,Forestry,Animal Husbandry and Fishery	99444	690	3142	207	603	90617	114	4185
采矿业	Mining	164	12	13	7	25	40		67
制造业	Manufacturing	7808	4042	718	86	1671	114	62	1177
电力、燃气及水的生产和供应业	Production and Supply of Electric Power,Gas and Water	1006	564	39	3	181	119	10	100
建筑业	Construction	5964	2725	244	53	313	1168	1133	1461
交通运输、仓储和邮政业	Transport, Storage, Postal Services	3614	171	673	65	1353	751	105	601
信息传输、计算机服务和软件业	Information Transmission,Computer Services and Software	593	8	103	1	148	206	43	127
批发和零售业	Wholesale & Retail Trade Services	1516	136	573	84	455	129	59	139
住宿和餐饮业	Hotels and Catering Services	7761	2502	2581	344	1809	66	30	459
金融业	Finance	715	4	126	2	226	307	23	50
房地产业	Real Estate	1861	493	586	149	230	169	4	234
租赁和商务服务业	Rent and Business Affair Services	1609	119	1000	14	157	114	9	205
科学研究、技术服务和地质勘查业	Scientific Research, Polytechnic Services and Geological Prospecting	1138	260	218	17	326	101	4	216
水利、环境和公共设施管理业	Water Conservancy,Environmental Protection and Public Installations Management Services	1484	235	726	80	170	156	9	117
居民服务和其他服务业	Resident Services and Other Social Services	26	4	4		8	10		
教育	Education	5729	65	165	63	3165	1602	239	669
卫生、社会保障和社会福利业	Health Care,Social Security and Social Welfare	1969	33	256	24	1121	180	22	355
文化、体育和娱乐业	Culture,Sports and Recreational Services	843	118	317	16	213	61	13	118
公共管理和社会组织	Public Management and Social Organizations	4303	350	331	334	1001	1815	52	472

表 3-12 续(continued)

项　目	Item	本年减少人数 Number of Persons in Decreaed	离休退休退职 Retire and Resigned	开除除名辞退 Expelled and Discharge	终止解除合同 Contract Terminated	离开本单位仍保留劳动关系的职工 Left and Kept the Ralationship	死亡 Death	调出人数 Number of Persons Transferred out	调到外省 To Outside Hainan	其他 Others
总　计	**Total**	**135811**	**12682**	**4285**	**14326**	**11529**	**898**	**85391**	**893**	**6700**
按类型分	**Grouped by Category**									
国有单位	State-owned Units	118458	10475	1620	5428	10921	811	84456	574	4747
城镇集体单位	Urban Collective-owned Units	1802	557	139	705	92	51	51		207
其他单位	Units of Others	15551	1650	2526	8193	516	36	884	319	1746
按行业分	**By Sector**									
农、林、牧、渔业	Farming,Forestry,Animal Husbandry and Fishery	97358	5636	344	2097	7740	383	79405	14	1753
采矿业	Mining	2562	206	12	63	2142	27	46		66
制造业	Manufacturing	6343	1670	674	2487	757	33	180	24	542
电力、燃气及水的生产和供应业	Production and Supply of Electric Power,Gas and Water	654	271	10	28	111	23	136	4	75
建筑业	Construction	4388	208	815	1107	32	20	467	426	1739
交通运输、仓储和邮政业	Transport, Storage, Postal Services	2105	546	150	716	169	41	404	214	79
信息传输、计算机服务和软件业	Information Transmission, Computer Services and Software	333	25	9	121	15	1	62	4	100
批发和零售业	Wholesale & Retail Trade Services	1895	553	72	782	173	40	153	53	122
住宿和餐饮业	Hotels and Catering Services	7521	213	1541	4355	18	12	129	5	1253
金融业	Finance	904	100	47	329	51	16	335	18	26
房地产业	Real Estate	1197	145	206	590	20	9	58	9	169
租赁和商务服务业	Rent and Business Affair Services	535	108	28	83	32	23	127	7	134
科学研究、技术服务和地质勘查业	Scientific Research, Polytechnic Services and Geological Prospecting	1229	240	94	151	39	12	645	13	48
水利、环境和公共设施管理业	Water Conservancy,Environmental Protection and Public Installations Management Services	727	161	69	417	14	18	30		18
居民服务和其他服务业	Resident Services and Other Social Services	23	13	2	5	2		1		
教育	Education	3649	1259	97	277	42	74	157	63	323
卫生、社会保障和社会福利业	Health Care, Social Security and Social Welfare	811	354	27	85	43	34	166	8	102
文化、体育和娱乐业	Culture,Sports and Recreational Services	626	161	42	218	91	13	51	4	50
公共管理和社会组织	Public Management and Social Organizations	2951	813	46	415	38	119	1419	27	101

3－13 历年城镇注册经济单位职工年末人数
Total Number of Staff and Workers at the Year-end

单位:万人
(10 000 persons)

年 份 Year	全部职工年末人数 Total Number of Staff and Workers at the Year-end	女 性 Female	国有单位 State-owned Units	城镇集体单位 Urban Collective-owned Units	其他经济类型单位 Units of Other Types of Ownership
1957	13.06		13.06		
1962	31.15		26.42	4.73	
1965	37.48		33.02	4.46	
1970	57.23		52.24	4.99	
1971	62.42		57.28	5.14	
1972	63.87		58.58	5.29	
1973	64.01		58.57	5.44	
1974	64.18		59.10	5.08	
1975	65.81		60.42	5.39	
1976	67.87		62.59	5.28	
1977	80.15		70.58	9.59	
1978	79.84		73.62	6.22	
1979	82.53		76.15	6.38	
1980	84.13	33.21	77.53	6.60	
1981	91.13	36.85	84.50	6.63	
1982	94.05	37.76	87.16	6.89	
1983	94.63	38.29	87.96	6.67	
1984	95.45	38.99	85.87	9.50	0.08
1985	97.99	35.62	88.35	9.23	0.41
1990	105.64	43.08	95.19	8.91	1.54
1991	108.06	43.54	97.22	8.50	2.34
1992	111.85	43.62	99.64	8.94	3.27
1993	111.06	43.74	97.74	9.14	4.18
1994	109.10	42.35	95.14	8.46	5.50
1995	106.92	41.34	92.78	8.36	5.78
1996	102.82	40.61	87.68	8.37	6.77
1997	102.65	40.57	86.48	8.25	7.92
1998	83.27	33.49	70.66	4.93	7.68
1999	80.39	32.49	67.83	4.55	8.01
2000	77.79	32.06	65.45	4.28	8.06
2001	74.69	30.27	62.01	4.32	8.36
2002	73.11	29.49	58.84	4.08	10.19
2003	71.64	28.73	57.26	3.89	10.49
2004	72.53	28.75	56.67	3.71	12.15
2005	72.63	28.54	56.61	3.80	12.22
2006	73.91	28.36	55.78	3.68	14.45

注:1999 年以后的女性人数为从业人员数中的女性。
a)unit:people.The female members in 1999 refer to employee.

2007 74.79 28.20

3－14 历年分行业城镇注册经济单位在岗职工年末人数(全部)
Total Number of Staff and Workers at the Year-end by Sector

单位:人 (person)

行业	Sector	2003	2004	2005	2006
总计	**Total**	**716392**	**725276**	**726338**	**739157**
农、林、牧、渔业	Farming,Forestry,Animal Husbandry and Fishery	202061	187029	181208	182956
采矿业	Mining	11414	10708	10840	8261
制造业	Manufacturing	67490	69558	68942	67461
电力、燃气及水的生产和供应业	Production and Supply of Electric Power, Gas and Water	18625	18465	18686	19912
建筑业	Construction	42812	49858	49320	52747
交通运输、仓储和邮政业	Transport, Storage, Postal Services	34859	40823	41218	40314
信息传输、计算机服务和软件业	Information Transmission, Computer Services and Software	6220	6915	8990	8012
批发和零售业	Wholesale & Retail Trade Services	32143	28119	27477	27185
住宿和餐饮业	Hotels and Catering Services	30540	31255	30663	33669
金融业	Finance	17993	17516	17174	16674
房地产业	Real Estate	10481	13822	13762	15424
租赁和商务服务业	Rent and Business Affair Services	10038	11882	13007	15602
科学研究、技术服务和地质勘查业	Scientific Research, Polytechnic Services and Geological Prospecting	13961	14251	14346	14034
水利、环境和公共设施管理业	Water Conservancy, Environmental Protection and Public Installations Management Services	15693	18953	20109	18781
居民服务和其他服务业	Resident Services and Other Social Services	380	605	688	765
教育	Education	81571	84227	86738	85844
卫生、社会保障和社会福利业	Health Care, Social Security and Social Welfare	27868	27920	28898	30761
文化、体育和娱乐业	Culture,Sports and Recreational Services	11762	12053	12230	12241
公共管理和社会组织	Public Management and Social Organizations	80481	81317	82042	88514

3－15 各市县城镇注册经济单位在岗职工年末人数
Total Number of Staff and Workers at the Year-end by City and County

单位：人 (person)

地区	Region	在岗职工年末人数 Total Number of Staff and Workers at the Year-end	专业技术人员 Technical Personnel	女性 Female	国有单位 State-owned Units	城镇集体单位 Urban Collective-owned Units	其他经济类型单位 Units of Other Types of Ownership
总　计	**Total**	**739157**	**184791**	**73620**	**557780**	**36789**	**144588**
海口市	Haikou	260914	70720	29411	155135	12313	93466
三亚市	Sanya	50232	10408	3872	28834	1960	19438
五指山市	Wuzhishan	8537	2853	1181	7645	114	778
文昌市	Wenchang	24479	7764	3299	16368	4814	3297
琼海市	Qionghai	17705	6777	2942	14858	640	2207
万宁市	Wanning	21349	5736	2499	16316	2506	2527
定安县	Dingan	11682	4563	1677	8510	904	2268
屯昌县	Tunchang	11604	3332	1191	8889	2340	375
澄迈县	Chengmai	27949	5135	1528	18603	2812	6534
临高县	Lingao	13352	4922	1530	10131	1658	1563
儋州市	Danzhou	29533	10406	3392	26412	2254	867
东方市	Dongfang	18218	6458	2261	13107	707	4404
乐东县	Ledong	16201	4542	1486	14669	1465	67
琼中县	Qiongzhong	8494	2407	971	7142	877	475
保亭县	Baoting	6320	1581	898	5942	199	179
陵水县	Lingshui	10623	3959	1884	9493	416	714
白沙县	Baisha	7557	2237	835	7123	386	48
昌江县	Changjiang	16460	4853	1668	14471	424	1565
洋　浦	Yangpu	6803	1574	676	2987		3816
农　垦	Land Reclamation	166841	24205	10159	166841		
总　后	Zonghou	4033	295	255	4033		
西　沙	Xisha	271	64	5	271		

3-16 城镇单位分行业各市县在岗职工年末人数(全部)
Total Number of Staff and Workers at the Year-end by City and County

单位:人 (person)

项目	Item	从业人员 Employment	农、林、牧、渔业 Farming, Forestry, Animal Husbandry and Fishery	采矿业 Mining and Quarrying	制造业 Manufacturing	电力、煤气及水的生产和供应业 Production and Supply of Electric Power,Gas and Water	建筑业 Construction	交通运输仓储及邮电通信业 Transport, Storage, Postal Services	信息传输、计算机服务和软件业 Information Transmission, Computer Services and Software	批发和零售业 Wholesale & Retail Trade Services	住宿和餐饮业 Hotels and Catering Trade
总计	Total	739157	182956	8261	67461	19912	52747	40314	8012	27185	33669
海口市	Haikou	260914	2173	341	35283	6130	41498	23814	5685	14257	10728
三亚市	Sanya	50232	940	230	2342	1380	2896	4639	331	2302	14680
五指山市	Wuzhishan	8537	49		532	556	19	391	47	444	345
文昌市	Wenchang	24479	936	229	3228	970	2550	886	93	1399	885
琼海市	Qionghai	17705	1514	31	1162	820	154	770	105	688	2297
万宁市	Wanning	21349	3696	66	281	12	2021	618	614	356	2403
定安县	Dingan	11682	614		1446	559	61	541	130	313	477
屯昌县	Tunchang	11604	588		887	449	683	464	61	748	56
澄迈县	Chengmai	27949	6396	28	4617	2937	518	905	81	1322	241
临高县	Lingao	13352	431	198	1867	423	382	125	79	745	46
儋州市	Danzhou	29533	3649	60	1678	1671	432	625	137	681	236
东方市	Dongfang	18218	1608	390	2018	577	360	2461	74	372	427
乐东县	Ledong	16201	443	1296	1086	941	483	721	55	1340	
琼中县	Qiongzhong	8494	1154		462	270	366	573	94	381	115
保亭县	Baoting	6320	593		177	429		409	31	411	9
陵水县	Lingshui	10623	61	6	920	502	55	811	47	263	16
白沙县	Baisha	7557	803		680	359	50	381	82	406	63
昌江县	Changjiang	16460	925	5386	2059	743	135	218	121	459	59
洋浦	Yangpu	6803			3499	184		909	57	15	184
农垦	Land Reclamation	166841	156383		3237		84	53	88	283	402
总后	Zonghou	4033									
西沙	Xisha	271									

3-16 续(continued)

项 目	Item	金融业 Finance	房地产业 Real Estate	租赁和商务服务业 Rent and Business Affair Services	科学研究、技术服务和地质勘查业 Scientific Research, Polytechnic Services and Geological Prospecting	水利、环境和公共设施管理业 Water Conservancy, Environmental Protection and Public Installations Management Services	居民服务和其他服务业 Resident Services and Other Social Services	教育 Education	卫生、社会保障和社会福利业 Health Care, Social Security and Social Welfare	文化、体育和娱乐业 Culture, Sports and Recreational Services	公共管理和社会组织 Public Management and Social Organizations
总 计	**Total**	**16674**	**15424**	**14034**	**15602**	**18781**	**765**	**85844**	**30761**	**12241**	**88514**
海口市	Haikou	8075	12496	8702	7942	6800	666	27065	11646	6307	31306
三亚市	Sanya	1266	1317	713	511	3772	21	4502	1950	1363	5077
五指山市	Wuzhishan	252	31	202	98	242	13	2507	795	154	1860
文昌市	Wenchang	832	371	259	458	450	11	5218	1589	116	3999
琼海市	Qionghai	748	61	59	207	541		4620	1233	117	2578
万宁市	Wanning	565	35	355	958		5	3080	843	1878	3563
定安县	Dingan	304	41	603	38	792		3229	764	31	1739
屯昌县	Tunchang	460	103	63	92	526		2420	617	127	3260
澄迈县	Chengmai	573	97	276	25	497		4495	889	244	3808
临高县	Lingao	482	33	204	113	396		3533	1081	64	3150
儋州市	Danzhou	735	302	362	3612	1536		7947	1537	271	4062
东方市	Dongfang	452	42	208	131	857		3946	1228	379	2688
乐东县	Ledong	397	42	494	43	204		4416	1054	114	3072
琼中县	Qiongzhong	266	13	161	62	550		1938	440	67	1582
保亭县	Baoting	124	14	103	62	212		1702	357	36	1651
陵水县	Lingshui	378	20	517	162	713		9	951	46	5146
白沙县	Baisha	189		107	60	170	7	1678	433	90	1999
昌江县	Changjiang	345		26	83	253	42	2150	535	151	2770
洋 浦	Yangpu	231	28	92		270			85	645	604
农 垦	Land Reclamation		378	528	945			1389	2734	41	296
总 后	Zonghou										4033
西 沙	Xisha										271

3－17 城镇单位分行业职工人数

Number of Staff and Workers in State-owned Units by Sector

单位:人 (person)

项目	Item	在岗职工年末人数 Number of Staff and Workers at the Year-end	专业技术人员 Technical Personnel	在岗职工平均人数 Average Person	离开本单位仍保留劳动关系的职工平均人数 Remain Labour Ralationship	内部退养职工 Staff and Workers of Interior Resigned
总计	Total	739157	184791	735307	113707	20866
按企业、事业、机关分组	Grouped by Enterprises, Institutions and Agencies & Organizations					
企业	Enterprises	485190	76892	485107	108271	18624
事业	Institutions	174481	103504	171384	4076	1154
机关	Agencies & Organizations	79486	4395	78816	1360	1088
按国民经济行业分组	Grouped by Sector					
农、林、牧、渔业	Farming, Forestry, Animal Husbandry and Fishery	182956	21899	187293	46438	6227
农业	Farming	13206	1797	13279	12590	238
林业	Forestry	163482	18600	167888	33463	5960
畜牧业	Animal Husbandry	440	68	439	124	6
渔业	Fishery	2063	462	1967	149	14
农、林、牧、渔服务业	Agricultural Services	3765	972	3720	112	9
采矿业	Mining and Quarrying	8261	1789	9873	2396	618
制造业	Manufacturing	67461	8563	65308	14816	1463
电力、燃气及水的生产和供应业	Production and Supply of Electricity, Gas and Water	19912	2704	19920	3914	2887
建筑业	Construction	52747	6644	51067	2171	113
房屋和土木工程建筑业	House and Civil Engineering	45280	5422	43799	1932	85
建筑安装业	Installation	1769	501	1764	219	10
建筑装饰业	Decoration	5597	681	5403	6	6
其他建筑业	Others	101	40	101	14	12
交通运输、仓储和邮政业	Transport, Storage, Postal Services	40314	8643	39816	6979	2698
铁路运输业	Railway Transport	3560	516	3508	183	113
道路运输业	Way Transport	11422	949	11610	1311	370
城市公共交通业	Public Traffic in City	2172	59	2142	1084	21
水上运输业	Waterway Transport	7770	1612	7671	3122	1529
航空运输业	Air Transport	10133	4861	9861	136	136
管道运输业	Pipeline Transport					
装卸搬运和其他运输服务业	Load and Unload Transport and Others Transport	1777	179	1733	156	43
仓储业	Storage	441	48	414	493	1
邮政业	Postal	3039	419	2877	494	485

3-17 续 1（continued 1）

项 目	Item	在岗职工年末人数 Number of Staff and Workers at the Year-end	专业技术人员 Technical Personnel	在岗职工平均人数 Average Person	离开本单位仍保留劳动关系的职工平均人数 Remain Labour Ralationship	内部退养职工 Staff and Workers of Interior Resigned
信息传输、计算机服务和软件业	Information Transmission, Computer Services and Software	8012	4052	7927	1340	592
电信和其他信息传输服务业	Telecommunications and Other Information Transmission	6929	3761	6815	678	592
计算机服务业	Computer Services	505	89	553	574	
软件业	Software	578	202	559	88	
批发和零售业	Wholesale & Retail Trade	27185	3967	27164	22338	868
批发业	Wholesale Trade	16461	2890	16652	10873	577
零售业	Retail Trade	10724	1077	10512	11465	291
住宿和餐饮业	Hotels and Catering Trade	33669	2937	33314	2064	201
住宿业	Hotels	30129	2660	29782	1270	201
餐饮业	Catering Trade	3540	277	3532	794	
金融业	Finance	16674	7534	16786	2143	1848
银行业	Banking	14753	7119	14922	2122	1838
证券业	Stock	267	119	268	13	2
保险业	Insurance	1471	250	1405	4	4
其他金融活动	Other Finance Activities	183	46	191	4	4
房地产业	Real Estate	15424	2936	15062	1281	333
房地产开发经营	Real Estate Development and Operation	8392	1877	8306	780	233
物业管理	Real Estate Owners Management	6052	844	5775	496	100
房地产中介服务	Real Estate Intermediary Services	301	88	306		
租赁和商务服务业	Rent and Business Affair Services	14034	2845	13603	2565	860
租赁业	Rent	452	108	455	5	
商务服务业	Business Affair Services	13582	2737	13148	2560	860
科学研究、技术服务和地质勘查业	Scientific Research, Polytechnic Services and Geological Prospecting	15602	5737	15269	759	110
研究与试验发展	Research and Develoment	7179	1420	7168	569	79
自然科学研究与试验发展	Natural Science	97	33	96	3	
工程和技术研究与试验发展	Engineering and Technical Science	365	187	366	32	26
农业科学研究与试验发展	Agriculture Science	5511	1038	5503	526	47
医学研究与试验发展	Medical Science	42	32	40		
社会人文科学研究与试验发展	Humanities and Social Science	1164	130	1163	8	6
专业技术服务	Profesional Technology Services	6283	3428	6168	94	29
业气象服务	Meteorology Services	437	205	435	14	14

3-17 续 2（continued 2）

项 目	Item	在岗职工年末人数 Number of Staff and Workers at the Year-end	专业技术人员 Technical Personnel	在岗职工平均人数 Average Person	离开本单位仍保留劳动关系的职工平均人数 Remain Labour Ralationship	内部退养职工 Staff and Workers of Interior Resigned
地震服务	Seimology Services	69	29	69		
海洋服务	Ocean Services	152	28	144		
测绘服务	Survey Services	254	78	250	2	
技术检测	Technology Test	1045	533	1025	22	8
环境监测	Monitoring of Environment	144	99	141		
工程技术与规划管理	Project Technology and Programme Management	3996	2411	3916	53	4
科技交流和推广服务业	Scientific and Technological Interchange and Popularization Services	1402	590	1193	12	2
地质勘查业	Geological Prospecting	738	299	740	84	
水利、环境和公共设施管理业	Water Conservancy, Environmental and Public Installations Management Services	18781	1204	18301	470	123
水利管理业	Water Conservancy Management	4131	234	4126	428	100
环境管理业	Environmental Management	9832	245	9512	27	12
公共设施管理业	Public Installations Management Services	4818	725	4663	15	11
居民服务和其他服务业	Resident Services and Other Social Services	765	265	760	47	14
居民服务业	Resident Services	565	186	552		
其他服务业	Other Social Services	200	79	208	47	14
教育	Education	85844	71523	83852	383	141
初等教育	Elementary Education	41374	37757	40387	107	37
中等教育	Secondary Education	33595	26160	32903	146	46
高等教育	Higher Education	6503	4411	6245	64	42
卫生、社会保障和社会福利业	Health Care, Social Security and Social Welfare	30761	20757	30016	644	249
卫生	Health Care	29702	20594	28957	623	243
社会保障业	Social Security	505	87	507	5	3
社会福利业	Social Welfare	554	76	552	16	3
文化、体育和娱乐业	Culture,Sports and Recreational Services	12241	4870	12199	751	165
新闻出版社	News Publishing House	3588	1253	3566	91	80
广播、电视、电影和音像业	Radio, Television, Film and Audiovisual	4278	2449	4346	460	28
文化艺术业	Culture and Arts	2056	982	2044	197	56
体育	Sports	269	102	265	1	
娱乐业	Recreational Services	2050	84	1978	2	1
公共管理和社会组织	Public Management and Social Organizations	88514	5922	87777	2208	1356
中国共产党机关	The Communist Party of China	4059	38	3993	51	44
国家机构	State Institution	78229	5442	77626	1342	1081
人民政协和民主党派	People' s Political Consultative Conference and Democratic Parties	483	5	474	5	4
群众社团、社会团体和宗教组织	Mass Organization, Social Organizations and Religion Organizations	5743	437	5684	810	227

3－18 国有单位分行业职工人数
Number of Staff and Workers in State-owned Units by Sector

单位：人　　　　(person)

项 目	Item	在岗职工年末人数 Number of Staff and Workers at the Year-end	专业技术人员 Technical Personnel	在岗职工平均人数 Average Person	离开本单位仍保留劳动关系的职工平均人数 Remain Labour Ralationship	内部退养职工 Staff and Workers of Interior Resigned
总　计	Total	55780	151522	559472	93287	17729
按隶属关系分	Grouped by Administrative Relationship					
中　央	Central	32718	10998	32487	2919	2065
省、自治区、直辖市	Provine, Autonomous Region, Municipality	293117	51217	298162	59745	11379
地　区	Region	60189	18459	59023	10389	2044
县及县以下	at and below County	169785	70444	167868	20183	2228
其他	Others	1971	404	1932	51	13
按企业、事业、机关分组	Grouped by Enterprises, Institutions and Agencies & Organizations					
企　业	Enterprises	312649	48067	318007	88780	15540
地　方	Local	291769	38847	297281	86734	13784
事　业	Institutions	166543	99129	163547	3151	1101
地　方	Local	156469	96964	153522	2320	866
机　关	Agencies & Organizations	78588	4326	77918	1356	1088
地　方	Local	74853	4309	74250	1263	1001
按国民经济行业分组	Grouped by Sector					
农、林、牧、渔业	Farming,Forestry,Animal Husbandry and Fishery	180349	21593	184803	46424	6227
农　业	Farming	11519	1572	11603	12576	238
林　业	Forestry	163186	18587	167592	33463	5960
畜牧业	Animal Husbandry	338	59	336	124	6
渔　业	Fishery	1655	431	1660	149	14
农、林、牧、渔服务业	Agricultural Services	3651	944	3612	112	9
采矿业	Mining and Quarrying	8010	1756	9615	2396	618
制造业	Manufacturing	16678	2700	16695	9355	635
电力、燃气及水的生产和供应业	Production and Supply of Electricity, Gas and Water	13138	1603	13156	3324	2325
建筑业	Construction	33379	3886	32464	1811	71
房屋和土木工程建筑业	House and Civil Engineering	27917	3022	27171	1587	58
建筑安装业	Installation	998	335	1002	210	1
建筑装饰业	Decoration	4373	492	4200	0	0
其他建筑业	Others	91	37	91	14	12
交通运输、仓储和邮政业	Transport, Storage, Postal Services	24213	3471	24059	4819	2220
铁路运输业	Railway Transport	155	35	155	0	0
道路运输业	Way Transport	10838	837	10960	844	365
城市公共交通业	Public Traffic in City	1195	30	1209	508	2
水上运输业	Waterway Transport	3863	946	3902	2301	1301
航空运输业	Air Transport	3165	1037	3038	23	23

3-18 续 1（continued 1）

项 目	Item	在岗职工年末人数 Number of Staff and Workers at the Year-end	专业技术人员 Technical Personnel	在岗职工平均人数 Average Person	离开本单位仍保留劳动关系的职工平均人数 Remain Labour Ralationship	内部退养职工 Staff and Workers of Interior Resigned
管道运输业	Pipeline Transport	0	0	0	0	0
装卸搬运和其他运输服务业	Load and Unload Transport and Others Transport	1713	153	1672	156	43
仓储业	Storage	305	30	306	493	1
邮政业	Postal	2979	403	2817	494	485
信息传输、计算机服务和软件业	Information Transmission, Computer Services and Software	5602	3113	5525	987	424
电信和其他信息传输服务业	Telecommunications and Other Information Transmission	5027	3098	4950	508	424
计算机服务业	Computer Services	339	12	339	465	0
软件业	Software	236	3	236	14	
批发和零售业	Wholesale & Retail Trade	12737	2058	12956	13680	712
批发业	Wholesale Trade	8410	1681	8641	7605	446
零售业	Retail Trade	4327	377	4315	6075	266
住宿和餐饮业	Hotels and Catering Trade	8338	670	8468	1505	128
住宿业	Hotels	8036	657	8135	1083	128
餐饮业	Catering Trade	302	13	333	422	0
金融业	Finance	8402	4597	8523	1319	1151
银行业	Banking	7561	4349	7675	1298	1141
证券业	Stock	59	36	61	13	2
保险业	Insurance	624	175	619	4	4
其他金融活动	Other Finance Activities	158	37	168	4	4
房地产业	Real Estate	4882	755	4900	1010	280
房地产开发经营	Real Estate Development and Operation	2927	528	2935	704	213
物业管理	Real Estate Owners Management	1364	156	1377	301	67
房地产中介服务	Real Estate Intermediary Services	200	25	201	0	0
租赁和商务服务业	Rent and Business Affair Services	7120	2016	7131	1640	812
租赁业	Rent	215	22	215	5	
商务服务业	Business Affair Services	6905	1994	6916	1635	812
科学研究、技术服务和地质勘查业	Scientific Research, Polytechnic Services and Geological Prospecting	12667	4443	12579	758	110
研究与试验发展	Research and Develoment	6617	1373	6595	569	79
自然科学研究与试验发展	Natural Science	73	26	72	3	0
工程和技术研究与试验发展	Engineering and Technical Science	310	165	310	32	26
农业科学研究与试验发展	Agriculture Science	5493	1034	5485	526	47
医学研究与试验发展	Medical Science	39	29	37	0	0
社会人文科学研究与试验发展	Humanities and Social Science	702	119	691	8	6
专业技术服务业	Profesional Technology Services	4861	2541	4797	93	29
气象服务	Meteorology Services	385	200	384	14	14

3-18 续 2（continued 2）

项 目	Item	在岗职工年末人数 Number of Staff and Workers at the Year-end	专业技术人员 Technical Personnel	在岗职工平均人数 Average Person	离开本单位仍保留劳动关系的职工平均人数 Remain Labour Ralationship	内部退养职工 Staff and Workers of Interior Resigned
地震服务	Seimology Services	69	29	69	0	0
海洋服务	Ocean Services	136	12	128	0	0
测绘服务	Survey Services	254	78	250	2	0
技术检测	Technology Test	886	443	876	22	8
环境监测	Monitoring of Environment	144	99	141	0	0
工程技术与规划管理	Project Technology and Programme Management	2824	1638	2782	52	4
科技交流和推广服务业	Scientific and Technological Interchange and Popularization Services	492	230	486	12	2
地质勘查业	Geological Prospecting	697	299	701	84	0
水利、环境和公共设施管理业	Water Conservancy, Environmental and Public Installations Management Services	16194	790	15825	466	123
水利管理业	Water Conservancy Management	3798	202	3793	428	100
环境管理业	Environmental Management	9390	205	9067	27	12
公共设施管理业	Public Installations Management Services	3006	383	2965	11	11
居民服务和其他服务业	Resident Services and Other Social Services	367	85	368	12	12
居民服务业	Resident Services	236	43	235	0	0
其他服务业	Other Social Services	131	42	133	12	12
教育	Education	82214	69866	80262	356	136
初等教育	Elementary Education	40937	37570	39952	107	37
中等教育	Secondary Education	30916	24874	30232	121	41
高等教育	Higher Education	6428	4407	6173	64	42
卫生、社会保障和社会福利业	Health Care, Social Security and Social Welfare	26413	17633	25754	485	242
卫生	Health Care	25372	17473	24710	464	236
社会保障业	Social Security	505	87	507	5	3
社会福利业	Social Welfare	536	73	537	16	3
文化、体育和娱乐业	Culture,Sports and Recreational Services	9562	4654	9592	732	147
新闻出版社	News Publishing House	2991	1120	2975	73	62
广播、电视、电影和音像业	Radio, Television, Film and Audiovisual	4268	2444	4336	460	28
文化艺术业	Culture and Arts	1975	981	1953	197	56
体育	Sports	242	97	242	1	0
娱乐业	Recreational Services	86	12	86	1	1
公共管理和社会组织	Public Management and Social Organizations	87515	5833	86797	2208	1356
中国共产党机关	The Communist Party of China	4059	38	3993	51	44
国家机构	State Institution	77349	5373	76746	1342	1081
人民政协和民主党派	People' s Political Consultative Conference and Democratic Parties	483	5	474	5	4
群众社团、社会团体和宗教组织	Mass Organization, Social Organizations and Religion Organizations	5624	417	5584	810	227

3－19 各市县城镇注册经济单位在岗职工年末人数

Total Number of Staff and Workers at the Year-end in State-owned Units by City and County

单位:人 (person)

地区	Region	在岗职工年末人数 Total Number of Staff and Workers at the Year-end	农、林、牧、渔业 Farming, Forestry, Animal Husbandry and Fishery	采矿业 Mining and Quarrying	制造业 Manufacturing	电力、煤气及水的生产和供应业 Production and Supply of Electric Power,Gas and Water	建筑业 Construction	交通运输仓储及邮电通信业 Transport, Storage, Postal Services	信息传输、计算机服务和软件业 Information Transmission, Computer Services and Software	批发和零售业 Wholesale & Retail Trade Services	住宿和餐饮业 Hotels and Catering Trade
总计	**Total**	**739157**	**182956**	**8261**	**67461**	**19912**	**52747**	**40314**	**8012**	**27185**	**33669**
海口市	Haikou	260914	2173	341	35283	6130	41498	23814	5685	14257	10728
三亚市	Sanya	50232	940	230	2342	1380	2896	4639	331	2302	14680
五指山市	Wuzhishan	8537	49		532	556	19	391	47	444	345
文昌市	Wenchang	24479	936	229	3228	970	2550	886	93	1399	885
琼海市	Qionghai	17705	1514	31	1162	820	154	770	105	688	2297
万宁市	Wanning	21349	3696	66	281	12	2021	618	614	356	2403
定安县	Dingan	11682	614		1446	559	61	541	130	313	477
屯昌县	Tunchang	11604	588		887	449	683	464	61	748	56
澄迈县	Chengmai	27949	6396	28	4617	2937	518	905	81	1322	241
临高县	Lingao	13352	431	198	1867	423	382	125	79	745	46
儋州市	Danzhou	29533	3649	60	1678	1671	432	625	137	681	236
东方市	Dongfang	18218	1608	390	2018	577	360	2461	74	372	427
乐东县	Ledong	16201	443	1296	1086	941	483	721	55	1340	
琼中县	Qiongzhong	8494	1154		462	270	366	573	94	381	115
保亭县	Baoting	6320	593		177	429		409	31	411	9
陵水县	Lingshui	10623	61	6	920	502	55	811	47	263	16
白沙县	Baisha	7557	803		680	359	50	381	82	406	63
昌江县	Changjiang	16460	925	5386	2059	743	135	218	121	459	59
洋浦	Yangpu	6803			3499	184		909	57	15	184
农垦	Land Reclamation	166841	156383		3237		84	53	88	283	402
总后	Zonghou	4033									
西沙	Xisha	271									

3-19 续 (continued)

地 区 Region	金 融 Finance	房地产业 Real Estate Trade	租赁和商务服务业 Rent and Business Affair Services	科学研究、技术服务和地质勘查业 Scientific Research, Polytechnic Services and Geological Prospecting	水利、环境和公共设施管理业 Water Conservancy, Environmental Protection and Public Installations Management Services	居民服务和其他服务业 Resident Services and Other Social Services	教育 Education	卫生、社会保障和社会福利业 Health Care, Social Security and Social Welfare	文化、体育和娱乐业 Culture, Sports and Recreational Services	公共管理和社会组织 Public Management and Social Organizations
总 计 Total	**16674**	**15424**	**14034**	**15602**	**18781**	**765**	**85844**	**30761**	**12241**	**88514**
海口市 Haikou	8075	12496	8702	7942	6800	666	27065	11646	6307	31306
三亚市 Sanya	1266	1317	713	511	3772	21	4502	1950	1363	5077
五指山市 Wuzhishan	252	31	202	98	242	13	2507	795	154	1860
文昌市 Wenchang	832	371	259	458	450	11	5218	1589	116	3999
琼海市 Qionghai	748	61	59	207	541		4620	1233	117	2578
万宁市 Wanning	565	35	355	958		5	3080	843	1878	3563
定安县 Dingan	304	41	603	38	792		3229	764	31	1739
屯昌县 Tunchang	460	103	63	92	526		2420	617	127	3260
澄迈县 Chengmai	573	97	276	25	497		4495	889	244	3808
临高县 Lingao	482	33	204	113	396		3533	1081	64	3150
儋州市 Danzhou	735	302	362	3612	1536		7947	1537	271	4062
东方市 Dongfang	452	42	208	131	857		3946	1228	379	2688
乐东县 Ledong	397	42	494	43	204		4416	1054	114	3072
琼中县 Qiongzhong	266	13	161	62	550		1938	440	67	1582
保亭县 Baoting	124	14	103	62	212		1702	357	36	1651
陵水县 Lingshui	378	20	517	162	713		9	951	46	5146
白沙县 Baisha	189		107	60	170	7	1678	433	90	1999
昌江县 Changjiang	345		26	83	253	42	2150	535	151	2770
洋浦 Yangpu	231	28	92		270			85	645	604
农垦 Land Reclamation		378	528	945			1389	2734	41	296
总后 Zonghou										4033
西沙 Xisha										271

3－20 分行业各市县城镇国有经济单位在岗职工年末人数

Total Number of Staff and Workers at the Year-end in State-owned Units by City and County

单位：人 (person)

地区 Region	在岗职工年末人数 Total Number of Staff and Workers at the Year-end	农、林、牧、渔业 Farming, Forestry, Animal Husbandry and Fishery	采矿业 Mining and Quarrying	制造业 Manufacturing	电力、煤气及水的生产和供应业 Production and Supply of Electric Power, Gas and Water	建筑业 Construction	交通运输仓储及邮电通信业 Transport, Storage, Postal Services	信息传输、计算机服务和软件业 Information Transmission, Computer Services and Software	批发和零售业 Wholesale & Retail Trade Services	住宿和餐饮业 Hotels and Catering Trade
总计 Total	**557780**	**180349**	**8010**	**16678**	**13138**	**33379**	**24213**	**5602**	**12737**	**8338**
海口市 Haikou	155135	1323	299	5833	3579	30860	11721	3337	5296	2668
三亚市 Sanya	28834	653	230	1102	713	2194	2954	331	1120	2766
五指山市 Wuzhishan	7645	49		182	537	10	347	37	377	113
文昌市 Wenchang	16368	779	89	1230	935		833	88	525	96
琼海市 Qionghai	14858	1514	31	886	500	4	767	105	552	586
万宁市 Wanning	16316	3696	38	58			618	582	174	635
定安县 Dingan	8510	614		165	485		541	115	313	97
屯昌县 Tunchang	8889	248		340	449		464	61	647	56
澄迈县 Chengmai	18603	6105		249	781		897	81	635	141
临高县 Lingao	10131	226	198	244	423	9	125	79	201	30
儋州市 Danzhou	26412	3649	60	453	1611	80	434	137	379	236
东方市 Dongfang	13107	1348	390	205	228		631	74	191	243
乐东县 Ledong	14669	345	1296	1024	941		721	55	626	
琼中县 Qiongzhong	7142	1071		111	270		557	94	192	111
保亭县 Baoting	5942	593		171	252		409	31	299	9
陵水县 Lingshui	9493	61	6	151	502		661	47	251	16
白沙县 Baisha	7123	767		616	359	3	381	82	202	54
昌江县 Changjiang	14471	925	5373	421	475	135	190	121	459	59
洋浦 Yangpu	2987				98		909	57	15	20
农垦 Land Reclamation	166841	156383		3237		84	53	88	283	402
总后 Zonghou	4033									
西沙 Xisha	271									

3-20 续（continued）

地 区 Region	金 融 Finance	房地产业 Real Estate Trade	租赁和商务服务业 Rent and Business Affair Services	科学研究、技术服务和地质勘查业 Scientific Research, Polytechnic Services and Geological Prospecting	水利、环境和公共设施管理业 Water Conservancy, Environmental Protection and Public Installations Management Services	居民服务和其他服务业 Resident Services and Other Social Services	教育 Education	卫生、社会保障和社会福利业 Health Care, Social Security and Social Welfare	文化、体育和娱乐业 Culture, Sports and Recreational Services	公共管理和社会组织 Public Management and Social Organizations
总 计 Total	**8402**	**4882**	**7120**	**12667**	**16194**	**367**	**82214**	**26413**	**9562**	**87515**
海口市 Haikou	2147	3122	3105	5724	6117	321	23808	9790	4898	31187
三亚市 Sanya	1052	247	498	490	2867	21	4376	1950	193	5077
五指山市 Wuzhishan	192	23	109	98	242	13	2507	795	154	1860
文昌市 Wenchang	532	359	96	260	450		5218	763	116	3999
琼海市 Qionghai	534	61	37	207	541		4620	1218	117	2578
万宁市 Wanning	348	35	297	466		5	3080	843	1878	3563
定安县 Dingan	211	41	101	38	397		3178	444	31	1739
屯昌县 Tunchang	329	70	63	92	526		2420	617	127	2380
澄迈县 Chengmai	336	85	264	19	234		4376	448	144	3808
临高县 Lingao	310	27	189	113	396		3533	814	64	3150
儋州市 Danzhou	519	302	333	3612	1482		7878	914	271	4062
东方市 Dongfang	330	42	196	131	857		3946	1228	379	2688
乐东县 Ledong	241	42	475	43	204		4416	1054	114	3072
琼中县 Qiongzhong	266	13	79	62	289		1938	440	67	1582
保亭县 Baoting	67		91	62	212		1702	357	36	1651
陵水县 Lingshui	274	20	503	162	687		9	951	46	5146
白沙县 Baisha	138		92	60	170	7	1670	433	90	1999
昌江县 Changjiang	345		26	83	253		2150	535	151	2770
洋 浦 Yangpu	231	15	38		270			85	645	604
农 垦 Land Reclamation		378	528	945			1389	2734	41	296
总 后 Zonghou										4033
西 沙 Xisha										271

3-21 分行业各市县城镇集体经济单位在岗职工年末人数

Number of Staff and Workers at the Year-end in Urban Collective-owned Units by City and County

单位:人 (person)

地 区	Region	在岗职工年末人数 Total Number of Staff and Workers at the Year-end	农、林、牧、渔业 Farming, Forestry, Animal Husbandry and Fishery	采矿业 Mining and Quarrying	制造业 Manufacturing	电力、煤气及水的生产和供应业 Production and Supply of Electric Power, Gas and Water	建筑业 Construction	交通运输仓储及邮电通信业 Transport, Storage, Postal Services	信息传输、计算机服务和软件业 Information Transmission, Computer Services and Software	批发和零售业 Wholesale & Retail Trade Services	住宿和餐饮业 Hotels and Catering Trade
总 计	**Total**	**36789**	**772**		**3451**	**241**	**13813**	**620**	**53**	**5552**	**1618**
海口市	Haikou	12313	7		1134		5200	220	16	1370	744
三亚市	Sanya	1960	46		60		651	40		241	554
五指山市	Wuzhishan	114					9			45	
文昌市	Wenchang	4814			262		2550		5	839	
琼海市	Qionghai	640			41		150	3		136	74
万宁市	Wanning	2506			139		2021		32	67	30
定安县	Dingan	904			114						58
屯昌县	Tunchang	2340	334		178		683			101	
澄迈县	Chengmai	2812	10		563	10	518			579	100
临高县	Lingao	1658	176		95		373			538	16
儋州市	Danzhou	2254			412	60	352	191		302	
东方市	Dongfang	707			16		360			168	29
乐东县	Ledong	1465	98		17		483			708	
琼中县	Qiongzhong	877	83		39		366	16		146	4
保亭县	Baoting	199			6	12				112	
陵水县	Lingshui	416			60		50	150		12	
白沙县	Baisha	386	18		50		47			188	9
昌江县	Changjiang	424			265	159					

3-21 续（continued）

地区	Region	金融 Finance	房地产业 Real Estate Trade	租赁和商务服务业 Rent and Business Affair Services	科学研究、技术服务和地质勘查业 Scientific Research, Polytechnic Services and Geological Prospecting	水利、环境和公共设施管理业 Water Conservancy, Environmental Protection and Public Installations Management Services	居民服务和其他服务业 Resident Services and Other Social Services	教育 Education	卫生、社会保障和社会福利业 Health Care, Social Security and Social Welfare	文化、体育和娱乐业 Culture, Sports and Recreational Services	公共管理和社会组织 Public Management and Social Organizations
总计	**Total**	**2794**	**673**	**1092**	**142**	**433**	**44**	**101**	**4156**	**339**	**895**
海口市	Haikou	484	563	459	142	3	33	24	1685	214	15
三亚市	Sanya	196	68	64						40	
五指山市	Wuzhishan	60									
文昌市	Wenchang	300	3	18			11		826		
琼海市	Qionghai	214		22							
万宁市	Wanning	217									
定安县	Dingan	93		319					320		
屯昌县	Tunchang	131	33								880
澄迈县	Chengmai	237		12		263			435	85	
临高县	Lingao	172	6	15					267		
儋州市	Danzhou	216		29				69	623		
东方市	Dongfang	122		12							
乐东县	Ledong	140		19							
琼中县	Qiongzhong			82		141					
保亭县	Baoting	57		12							
陵水县	Lingshui	104		14		26					
白沙县	Baisha	51		15							
昌江县	Changjiang										

3－22 分行业各市县城镇其他经济单位在岗职工年末人数
Number of Staff and Workers at the Year-end in Units of Other Types of Ownership by City and County

单位：人 (person)

地区	Region	在岗职工年末人数 Total Number of Staff and Workers at the Year-end	农、林、牧、渔业 Farming, Forestry, Animal Husbandry and Fishery	采矿业 Mining and Quarrying	制造业 Manufacturing	电力、煤气及水的生产和供应业 Production and Supply of Electric Power,Gas and Water	建筑业 Construction	交通运输仓储及邮电通信业 Transport, Storage, Postal Services	信息传输、计算机服务和软件业 Information Transmission, Computer Services and Software	批发和零售业 Wholesale & Retail Trade Services	住宿和餐饮业 Hotels and Catering Trade
总计	**Total**	**144588**	**1835**	**251**	**47332**	**6533**	**5555**	**15481**	**2357**	**8896**	**23713**
海口市	Haikou	93466	843	42	28316	2551	5438	11873	2332	7591	7316
三亚市	Sanya	19438	241		1180	667	51	1645		941	11360
五指山市	Wuzhishan	778			350	19		44	10	22	232
文昌市	Wenchang	3297	157	140	1736	35		53		35	789
琼海市	Qionghai	2207			235	320					1637
万宁市	Wanning	2527		28	84	12				115	1738
定安县	Dingan	2268			1167	74	61		15		322
屯昌县	Tunchang	375	6		369						
澄迈县	Chengmai	6534	281	28	3805	2146		8		108	
临高县	Lingao	1563	29		1528					6	
儋州市	Danzhou	867			813						
东方市	Dongfang	4404	260		1797	349		1830		13	155
乐东县	Ledong	67			45					6	
琼中县	Qiongzhong	475			312					43	
保亭县	Baoting	179				165					
陵水县	Lingshui	714			709		5				
白沙县	Baisha	48	18		14					16	
昌江县	Changjiang	1565		13	1373	109		28			
洋浦	Yangpu	3816			3499	86					164

3-22 续（continued）

地区	Region	金融 Finance	房地产业 Real Estate Trade	租赁和商务服务业 Rent and Business Affair Services	科学研究、技术服务和地质勘查业 Scientific Research, Polytechnic Services and Geological Prospecting	水利、环境和公共设施管理业 Water Conservancy, Environmental Protection and Public Installations Management Services	居民服务和其他服务业 Resident Services and Other Social Services	教育 Education	卫生、社会保障和社会福利业 Health Care, Social Security and Social Welfare	文化、体育和娱乐业 Culture, Sports and Recreational Services	公共管理和社会组织 Public Management and Social Organizations
总　　计	**Total**	**5478**	**9869**	**5822**	**2793**	**2154**	**354**	**3529**	**192**	**2340**	**104**
海口市	Haikou	5444	8811	5138	2076	680	312	3233	171	1195	104
三亚市	Sanya	18	1002	151	21	905		126		1130	
五指山市	Wuzhishan		8	93							
文昌市	Wenchang		9	145	198						
琼海市	Qionghai								15		
万宁市	Wanning			58	492						
定安县	Dingan			183		395		51			
屯昌县	Tunchang										
澄迈县	Chengmai		12		6			119	6	15	
临高县	Lingao										
儋州市	Danzhou					54					
东方市	Dongfang										
乐东县	Ledong	16									
琼中县	Qiongzhong					120					
保亭县	Baoting		14								
陵水县	Lingshui										
白沙县	Baisha										
昌江县	Changjiang						42				
洋　浦	Yangpu		13	54							

3－23 各市县分行业城镇单位从业人员年劳动报酬(全部)

Number of Employed Persons at the Year-end by Sector

单位:千元 (1000 yuan)

地区 Region	从业人员劳动报酬 Total Number of Staff and Workers at the Year-end	农、林、牧、渔业 Farming, Forestry, Animal Husbandry and Fishery	采矿业 Mining and Quarrying	制造业 Manufacturing	电力、煤气及水的生产和供应业 Production and Supply of Electric Power,Gas and Water	建筑业 Construction	交通运输仓储及邮电通信业 Transport, Storage, Postal Services	信息传输、计算机服务和软件业 Information Transmission, Computer Services and Software	批发和零售业 Wholesale & Retail Trade Services	住宿和餐饮业 Hotels and Catering Trade
总计 Total	**11927133**	**1355590**	**166405**	**1029589**	**492488**	**679661**	**1012171**	**348072**	**342521**	**411854**
海口市 Haikou	5672526	25928	3471	571212	174015	558754	657329	291822	230026	127708
三亚市 Sanya	933222	11160	2436	23282	43632	36471	142927	10811	35714	201862
五指山市 Wuzhishan	139686	654		3236	10850	156	7486	1577	3338	3099
文昌市 Wenchang	368587	8839	2390	29718	13074	23249	18682	4458	10155	7533
琼海市 Qionghai	270894	10038	630	13713	19936	584	11249	1663	10189	27307
万宁市 Wanning	322188	34617	603	2225	156	20093	8811	9738	3022	26037
定安县 Dingan	170360	6023		13563	12717	2715	9334	2402	4584	3658
屯昌县 Tunchang	145322	4179		3227	11059	9577	5165	769	4519	353
澄迈县 Chengmai	379776	36980	1384	59514	92202	1701	12963	1390	8700	1741
临高县 Lingao	171426	2835	1250	15082	4293	3885	3403	2961	1099	451
儋州市 Danzhou	406406	23492	380	15170	23870	8433	12061	2796	9486	1768
东方市 Dongfang	339484	14523	3347	68179	11175	4760	45427	2918	2643	3471
乐东县 Ledong	222815	3258	12728	8937	18421	2079	11424	1897	3709	
琼中县 Qiongzhong	125025	12036		3124	10271	3683	10171	2819	2298	701
保亭县 Baoting	90794	8373		788	7895		6514	891	1422	36
陵水县 Lingshui	160882	564	14	8478	12431	147	12412	2076	3279	110
白沙县 Baisha	104426	9410		3373	4700	1015	6789	1377	1717	409
昌江县 Changjiang	311092	9148	137772	24286	16351	1176	3315	2456	2556	276
洋浦 Yangpu	220797			136876	5440		26113	1459	130	1740
农垦 Land Reclamation	1308109	1133533		25606		1183	596	1792	3935	3594
总后 Zonghou	57997									
西沙 Xisha	5319									

3-23 续（continued）

地 区 Region	金融 Finance	房地产业 Real Estate Trade	租赁和商务服务业 Rent and Business Affair Services	科学研究、技术服务和地质勘查业 Scientific Research, Polytechnic Services and Geological Prospecting	水利、环境和公共设施管理业 Water Conservancy, Environmental Protection and Public Installations Management Services	居民服务和其他服务业 Resident Services and Other Social Services	教育 Education	卫生、社会保障和社会福利业 Health Care, Social Security and Social Welfare	文化、体育和娱乐业 Culture, Sports and Recreational Services	公共管理和社会组织 Public Management and Social Organizations
总 计 Total	**581120**	**254033**	**231622**	**261191**	**225565**	**12273**	**1763695**	**638763**	**250895**	**1869625**
海口市 Haikou	370637	202411	158270	159764	102416	10702		301817	147834	878766
三亚市 Sanya	45461	29833	12978	10977	54989	728	699644	37462	17842	128629
五指山市 Wuzhishan	4176	515	2501	1574	2825	19	86028	13309	2643	32403
文昌市 Wenchang	19024	4731	5114	11661	3619	101	49325	25421	1947	75162
琼海市 Qionghai	17043	891	594	5612	5648		103709	21728	1650	43193
万宁市 Wanning	14655	630	4479	8906		50	79226	18918	39698	61733
定安县 Dingan	7879	469	4709	482	7525		67817	8909	438	30844
屯昌县 Tunchang	8608	948	341	1298	3445		54109	9905	1095	36368
澄迈县 Chengmai	11816	962	1886	273	4044		44466	13895	2044	53237
临高县 Lingao	7172	464	3270	961	2473		75044	13067	819	50045
儋州市 Danzhou	16974	3758	4381	44315	12694		57896	25589	3139	63987
东方市 Dongfang	9149	476	2418	1514	5267		134113	20826	9404	49194
乐东县 Ledong	9133	613	4398	1004	2265		84793	14331	1428	53931
琼中县 Qiongzhong	7253	186	2038	910	5695		73259	8035	804	28055
保亭县 Baoting	2274	201	852	854	1571		26946	4248	348	24557
陵水县 Lingshui	5491	275	6094	1806	4732		29970	9379	448	93000
白沙县 Baisha	5324		1543	823	1535	66	146	7224	984	30581
昌江县 Changjiang	9683		245	1149	3202	607	27556	9692	1514	48203
洋 浦 Yangpu	9368	1024	2029		1620		39461	1490	16050	17458
农 垦 Land Reclamation		5646	13482	7308				73518	766	6963
总 后 Zonghou							30187			57997
西 沙 Xisha										5319

3－24 分行业城镇注册经济单位从业人员劳动报酬

Payment for Labour of Employed Persons by Sector

行业	Sector	劳动报酬（万元）Payment for Labour (10 000 yuan)	国有单位 State-owned Units	城镇集体单位 Urban Collective-owned Units	其他各种经济单位 Units of Other Types of Ownership	平均劳动报酬（元）Payment for Labour (yuan)	国有单位 State-owned Units	城镇集体单位 Urban Collective-owned Units	其他各种经济单位 Units of Other Types of Ownership
总计	Total	**1192713**	**871848**	**36487**	**284378**	**15843**	**15254**	**9604**	**19848**
农、林、牧、渔业	Farming, Forestry, Animal Husbandry and Fishery	135559	132711	464	2384	7157	7137	5642	9046
工业	Industry	168848	63993	3217	101638	17335	15812	8833	19070
采矿业	Mining	16640	16185	0	455	16699	16691	0	16993
制造业	Manufacturing	102959	16998	2929	83032	15438	9978	8628	17948
电力、燃气及水的生产和供应业	Production and Supply of Electric Power,Gas and Water	49249	30810	288	18151	23741	22430	11668	26847
建筑业	Construction	67966	47458	13396	7112	12511	13881	9172	12861
交通运输、仓储和邮政业	Transport, Storage, Postal Services	101217	53494	756	46967	24626	21466	11478	30256
信息传输、计算机服务和软件业	Information Transmission, Computer Services and Software	34807	23110	49	11648	42635	40233	9245	49211
批发和零售业	Wholesale & Retail Trade Services	34252	16748	3485	14019	12405	12654	6180	16047
住宿和餐饮业	Hotels and Catering Trade	41185	9238	1801	30146	12241	10764	10817	219
金融业	Finance	58112	28377	3537	26198	33667	31558	12319	48534
房地产业	Real Estate	25403	7218	851	17334	16476	14376	13618	17738
租赁和商务服务业	Rent and Business Affair Services	23162	12717	959	9486	16560	17058	8726	17460
科学研究、技术服务和地质勘查业	Scientific Research, Polytechnic Services and Geological Prospecting	26119	21087	373	4659	16647	16340	21819	17822
水利、环境和公共设施管理业	Water Conservancy, Environmental Protection and Public Installations Management Services	22557	19614	401	2542	11881	11945	8363	12186
居民服务和其他服务业	Resident Services and Other Social Services	1227	679	70	478	15918	18305	15130	13520
教育	Education	176370	169538	116	6716	20560	20651	10464	18777
卫生、社会保障和社会福利业	Health Care,Social Security and Social Welfare	63876	57124	6448	304	20305	21155	15122	15958
文化、体育和娱乐业	Culture,Sports and Recreational Services	25090	21968	506	2616	20302	22569	14667	11476
公共管理和社会组织	Public Management and Social Organizations	186963	186774	58	131	20905	21117	648	13768

3－25 各市县城镇注册经济单位从业人员劳动报酬
Payment for Labour of Employed Persons by Sector

地区	Region	劳动报酬（千元）Payment for Labour (1000 yuan)	国有单位 State-owned Units	城镇集体单位 Urban Collective-owned Units	其他各种经济单位 Units of Other Types of Ownership	平均劳动报酬（元）Average Payment for Labour	国有单位 State-owned Units	城镇集体单位 Urban Collective-owned Units	其他各种经济单位 Units of Other Types of Ownership
总计	**Total**	**11927133**	**8718480**	**364865**	**2843788**	**15843**	**15254**	**9604**	**19848**
海口市	Haikou	5672526	3542913	155966	1973647	21737	22630	12673	21431
三亚市	Sanya	933222	619779	26694	286749	18583	21235	12877	15125
五指山市	Wuzhishan	139686	131702	944	7040	15301	15995	8281	9014
文昌市	Wenchang	368587	289884	44057	34646	15022	17549	9196	10740
琼海市	Qionghai	270894	231115	5656	34123	14906	15298	8838	14071
万宁市	Wanning	322188	269843	25643	26702	15158	16559	10257	10859
定安县	Dingan	170360	138569	6831	24960	13594	15906	7385	8622
屯昌县	Tunchang	145322	129616	14534	1172	11992	14198	5287	4883
澄迈县	Chengmai	379776	221633	19562	138581	13393	11761	6573	21199
临高县	Lingao	171426	147216	10011	14199	12303	13500	5608	11414
儋州市	Danzhou	406406	375709	22009	8688	13213	13679	9155	9784
东方市	Dongfang	339484	215274	7371	116839	17059	15820	9168	21290
乐东县	Ledong	222815	215737	5714	1364	13122	13985	3898	15500
琼中县	Qiongzhong	125025	113743	7282	4000	13649	14671	7881	8282
保亭县	Baoting	90794	84769	961	5064	14247	14107	4829	30691
陵水县	Lingshui	160882	149929	3420	7533	14917	15493	8182	10917
白沙县	Baisha	104426	101020	2986	420	13378	13869	6300	8750
昌江县	Changjiang	311092	292583	5224	13285	17615	18157	11792	12034
洋浦	Yangpu	220797	76021		144776	34355	25674		41770
农垦	Land Reclamation	1308109	1308109			7629	7629		
总后	Zonghou	57997	57997			14449	14449		
西沙	Xisha	5319	5319			19272	19272		

人口和就业 POPULATION AND EMPLOYMENT

3－26 各市县单位从业人员平均劳动报酬按会计制度分组(全部)
Average labor reward of persons employed in units of various cities and counties grouped by accounting system (all)

单位:元 (yuan)

地区	Region	从业人员平均劳动报酬 Earnings of Employed ersons	企业 Enterprises	事业 Institutions	机关 Agencies & Organizations
总计	**Total**	**15843**	**13882**	**18851**	**21312**
海口市	Haikou	21737	19707	24790	28425
三亚市	Sanya	18583	17774	18075	25231
五指山市	Wuzhishan	15301	11165	17201	17243
文昌市	Wenchang	15022	11500	18022	19090
琼海市	Qionghai	14906	13300	16183	16550
万宁市	Wanning	15158	10679	20785	17231
定安县	Dingan	13594	11432	14377	17319
屯昌县	Tunchang	11992	9309	15607	11102
澄迈县	Chengmai	13393	12818	14348	14023
临高县	Lingao	12303	8938	13817	14051
儋州市	Danzhou	13213	11688	13401	16006
东方市	Dongfang	17059	16313	18015	17010
乐东县	Ledong	13122	9672	14684	17503
琼中县	Qiongzhong	13649	11371	14605	17163
保亭县	Baoting	14247	12604	15015	14834
陵水县	Lingshui	14917	13203	10370	18300
白沙县	Baisha	13378	10179	14593	15363
昌江县	Changjiang	17615	17781	16980	17834
洋浦	Yangpu	34355	38580	19555	29122
农垦	Land Reclamation	7629	7083	24749	23137
总后	Zonghou	14449		14449	
西沙	Xisha	19272			19272

3－27 主要年份全部职工工资总额和平均工资
Total Wages and Average Wage of Staff and Workers in Major Years

年 份 Year	工资总额（万元）Total Wages (10 000 yuan)	国有单位 State-owned Units	城镇集体单位 Urban Collective-owned Units	其他各种经济单位 Units of Other Types of Ownership	平均工资（元）Average Wage (yuan)	国有单位 State-owned Units	城镇集体单位 Urban Collective-owned Units	其他各种经济单位 Units of Other Types of Ownership
1957	7160	7160			548	548		
1962	14477	14477			548	548		
1965	17282	17282			523	523		
1970	22872	22872			496	496		
1971	25387	25387			464	464		
1972	28438	28438			491	491		
1973	30658	30658			523	523		
1974	37105	34316	2789		578	583	532	
1975	35580	32731	2849		547	548	534	
1976	37833	34870	2963		566	567	439	
1977	42660	37915	4745		576	569	600	
1978	43576	39960	3616		545	554	574	
1979	50023	46324	3699		616	618	570	
1980	56888	52804	4084		692	697	638	
1981	62308	58337	3971		728	736	623	
1982	72132	67670	4462		790	799	671	
1983	75423	71043	4380		812	823	673	
1984	86964	79241	7658	65	929	940	830	1155
1985	97401	88621	8324	456	1020	1029	925	1329
1986	114202	105001	8515	686	1168	1190	943	1401
1987	122089	112713	8524	852	1233	1259	959	1417
1988	140367	129129	10069	1169	1399	1421	1141	1740
1989	168152	153969	11341	2842	1640	1658	1321	2655
1990	205810	187582	13497	4731	1980	2002	1549	3232
1991	232123	209803	14682	7638	2194	2198	1793	3530
1992	301790	269183	19763	12844	2720	2715	2282	1093
1993	385512	329098	29387	27027	3501	3387	3308	6658
1994	485782	414329	33265	38188	4058	4124	4086	7460
1995	569860	485955	38116	45789	5340	5230	4632	8214
1996	561205	471766	34286	55153	5476	5365	4222	8579
1997	580859	474729	34165	71965	5664	5468	4208	9462
1998	522554	425762	24742	72050	6248	5970	5020	9750
1999	552774	448027	25545	79202	6865	6586	5672	9913
2000	574995	467433	25159	82403	7408	7146	5919	10352
2001	623576	505589	26764	91223	8321	8102	6207	11091
2002	699965	555859	27157	116949	9480	9368	6615	11247
2003	754498	596934	27650	129914	10397	10305	7029	12130
2004	913157	717529	29891	165737	12652	12664	8121	14005
2005	1041882	814634	32618	194630	14417	14427	8640	16185
2006	1168412	861472	34956	271984	15890	15398	9580	19518

说明:从 1999 年以后,职工资料为在岗职工的资料。
Note: the data of workers and staff are the on-job ones since 1999.

3－28 主要年份城镇注册经济单位职工平均工资及指数
Average Wage of Staff and Workers and Related Indices

年 份 Year	职工平均工资(元) Average Wage (yuan)	国有单位 State-owned Units	城镇集体单位 Urban Collective-owned Units	其他各种经济单位 Units of Other Types of Ownership	职工实际工资指数(%)(1978=100) Average Real Wage Indices of Staff and Workers	国有单位 State-owned Units	城镇集体单位 Urban Collective-owned Units	其他各种经济单位 Units of Other Types of Ownership
1978	545	554	574		100.0	100.0	100.0	
1979	616	618	570		111.8	110.3	98.3	
1980	692	697	638		117.6	116.6	103.1	
1981	728	736	623		116.3	115.6	94.5	
1982	790	799	671		121.6	120.9	98.1	
1983	812	823	673		123.9	123.6	97.5	
1984	929	940	830	1155	138.1	137.5	117.2	100.0
1985	1020	1029	925	1329	134.1	133.1	115.4	101.7
1986	1168	1190	943	1401	147.5	147.8	113.1	103.1
1987	1233	1259	959	1417	141.8	142.5	104.7	94.9
1988	1399	1421	1141	1740	125.6	125.5	97.3	91.0
1989	1640	1658	1321	2655	114.7	114.1	87.7	108.1
1990	1980	2002	1549	3232	135.7	134.9	100.8	128.9
1997	2194	2198	1793	3530	144.6	142.6	112.2	135.5
1992	2720	2715	2282	4093	165.0	162.1	131.5	144.5
1993	3501	3387	3308	6658	172.3	163.9	154.6	190.7
1994	4485	4124	4086	7460	174.2	157.5	150.7	168.6
1995	5340	5230	4632	8214	182.7	176.0	150.5	163.6
1996	5476	5365	4222	8579	179.6	173.1	131.5	163.8
1997	5664	5468	4208	9462	190.7	181.1	135.6	186.9
1998	6248	5970	5020	9750	221.4	215.2	165.6	190.5
1999	6865	6586	5672	9913	242.7	229.1	190.4	204.1
2000	7408	7146	5919	10352	257.6	244.5	195.4	230.2
2001	8321	8102	6207	11091	292.7	280.6	207.3	223.7
2002	9480	9368	6615	11247	325.4	316.4	215.6	228.1
2003	10397	10305	7029	12130	356.6	347.7	228.9	243.5
2004	12652	12664	8121	14005	415.7	409.3	253.3	269.3
2005	14417	14427	8640	16185	475.1	467.7	270.3	298.5
2006	15890	15398	9580	19518	506.9	483.1	290.1	354.8

注:从 1999 年以后,工资资料为在岗职工。
Note: the data of workers and staff are the on-job ones since 1999.

3－29 各市县单位在岗职工平均工资按会计制度分组(全部)
Average wage of staff and workers in units of various cities and counties grouped by accounting system (all)

单位:元 (yuan)

地区	Region	在岗职工平均工资 Earnings of Employed Persons	企业 Enterprises	事业 Institutions	机关 Agencies & Organizations
总计	Total	15890	13801	19177	21599
海口市	Haikou	21815	19713	24995	28621
三亚市	Sanya	18467	17552	18082	25587
五指山市	Wuzhishan	15788	11269	18034	17455
文昌市	Wenchang	15132	11479	18483	19095
琼海市	Qionghai	15007	13284	16394	16636
万宁市	Wanning	15449	10847	21382	17271
定安县	Dingan	14221	12448	14542	17641
屯昌县	Tunchang	12468	10161	15622	11128
澄迈县	Chengmai	13489	12834	14673	14065
临高县	Lingao	12870	8822	14568	15565
儋州市	Danzhou	13504	11932	13731	16007
东方市	Dongfang	18006	17999	18119	17722
乐东县	Ledong	13501	10019	15010	18180
琼中县	Qiongzhong	14129	11606	15361	17542
保亭县	Baoting	14276	12666	15015	14838
陵水县	Lingshui	15440	13617	11163	18402
白沙县	Baisha	13673	10270	15180	15382
昌江县	Changjiang	17669	17855	17009	17840
洋浦	Yangpu	27525	29118	19676	30708
农垦	Land Reclamation	7623	7083	24851	23137
总后	Zonghou	14446		14446	
西沙	Xisha	19364			19364

3－30 各市县在岗职工工资总额和平均工资

Total Wages and Average Wage of Staff and Workers by City and county

地区	Region	工资总额(千元) Total Wages (1000 yuan)	国有单位 State-owned Units	城镇集体单位 Urban Collective-owned Units	其他各种经济单位 Units of Other Types of Ownership	平均工资(元) Average Wage (yuan)	国有单位 State-owned Units	城镇集体单位 Urban Collective-owned Units	其他各种经济单位 Units of Other Types of Ownership
总计	**Total**	**11684117**	**8614718**	**349561**	**2719838**	**15890**	**15398**	**9580**	**19518**
海口市	Haikou	5579362	3500965	150961	1927436	21815	22896	12516	21231
三亚市	Sanya	911583	611110	25229	275244	18467	21388	12807	14624
五指山市	Wuzhishan	134937	126975	944	7018	15788	16585	8281	9032
文昌市	Wenchang	364451	286719	43518	34214	15132	17783	9164	10652
琼海市	Qionghai	266032	229218	5656	31158	15007	15402	8838	14131
万宁市	Wanning	315828	263513	25643	26672	15449	17012	10257	10873
定安县	Dingan	164551	137715	6736	20100	14221	16064	7451	9599
屯昌县	Tunchang	140900	128239	11489	1172	12468	14535	5134	4883
澄迈县	Chengmai	378704	220906	19236	138562	13489	11833	6693	21206
临高县	Lingao	166653	144055	8430	14168	12870	14341	5072	11407
儋州市	Danzhou	396888	368411	20014	8463	13504	14011	8987	9728
东方市	Dongfang	324831	210286	7058	107487	18006	16152	9049	25345
乐东县	Ledong	218651	211736	5685	1230	13501	14438	3886	18358
琼中县	Qiongzhong	120137	109150	6987	4000	14129	15285	7949	8282
保亭县	Baoting	90410	84385	961	5064	14276	14137	4829	30691
陵水县	Lingshui	156411	145458	3420	7533	15440	16080	8182	11311
白沙县	Baisha	101245	98347	2478	420	13673	14108	6420	8750
昌江县	Changjiang	310618	292285	5116	13217	17669	18196	12066	12092
洋浦	Yangpu	172391	75711		96680	27525	25982		28868
农垦	Land Reclamation	1306454	1306454			7623	7623		
总后	Zonghou	57813	57813			14446	14446		
西沙	Xisha	5267	5267			19364	19364		

3－31 各市县分行业城镇单位在岗职工工资总额(全部)
Number of Employed Persons at the Year-end by Sector

单位:千元 (1000 yuan)

地 区 Region	在岗职工 Employment	农、林、牧、渔业 Farming, Forestry, Animal Husbandry and Fishery	采矿业 Mining and Quarrying	制造业 Manufacturing	电力、煤气及水的生产和供应业 Production and Supply of Electric Power,Gas and Water	建筑业 Construction	交通运输仓储及邮电通信业 Transport, Storage, Postal Services	信息传输、计算机服务和软件业 Information Transmission, Computer Services and Software	批发和零售业 Wholesale & Retail Trade Services	住宿和餐饮业 Hotels and Catering Trade
总 计 Total	**11684117**	**1343897**	**165851**	**950791**	**485340**	**647906**	**997695**	**345781**	**338331**	**396845**
海口市 Haikou	5579362	24857	3414	545924	172586	537593	654476	291101	226663	123780
三亚市 Sanya	911583	11049	2436	23246	43512	36127	140383	10811	35407	191867
五指山市 Wuzhishan	134937	654		3225	9508	156	7164	1577	3321	3097
文昌市 Wenchang	364451	8839	2382	29284	13074	23151	18682	4458	10109	7467
琼海市 Qionghai	266032	10038	465	13599	17620	584	11249	1663	10099	26739
万宁市 Wanning	315828	34617	603	2225	156	20093	8811	8298	3022	25663
定安县 Dingan	164551	6023		10754	12717	881	9238	2310	4541	3658
屯昌县 Tunchang	140900	4069		3212	11059	6592	4740	769	4407	353
澄迈县 Chengmai	378704	36548	1384	59475	92202	1544	12963	1390	8700	1741
临高县 Lingao	166653	2761	1250	15051	4293	2359	3403	2961	1097	451
儋州市 Danzhou	396888	23122	380	14945	23833	5633	9190	2796	9452	1745
东方市 Dongfang	324831	9199	3194	66951	11175	4447	42263	2918	2638	3418
乐东县 Ledong	218651	2950	12706	8571	18421	2050	11424	1897	3694	
琼中县 Qiongzhong	120137	9861		3109	9022	3683	9984	2819	2161	701
保亭县 Baoting	90410	8373		788	7895		6152	891	1422	36
陵水县 Lingshui	156411	564	14	8478	11903	147	11360	2076	3279	110
白沙县 Baisha	101245	7718		3368	4700	507	6189	1359	1717	409
昌江县 Changjiang	310618	9129	137623	24206	16224	1176	3315	2436	2556	276
洋 浦 Yangpu	172391			88780	5440		26113	1459	130	1740
农 垦 Land Reclamation	1306454	1133526		25600		1183	596	1792	3916	3594
总 后 Zonghou	57813									
西 沙 Xisha	5267									

3-31 续（continued）

地 区 Region	金 融 Finance	房地产业 Real Estate Trade	租赁和商务服务业 Rent and Business Affair Services	科学研究、技术服务和地质勘查业 Scientific Research, Polytechnic Services and Geological Prospecting	水利、环境和公共设施管理业 Water Conservancy, Environmental Protection and Public Installations Management Services	居民服务和其他服务业 Resident Services and Other Social Services	教育 Education	卫生、社会保障和社会福利业 Health Care, Social Security and Social Welfare	文化、体育和娱乐业 Culture, Sports and Recreational Services	公共管理和社会组织 Public Management and Social Organizations
总 计 Total	**574235**	**248572**	**228137**	**254242**	**222049**	**11819**	**1744783**	**621653**	**248768**	**1857422**
海口市 Haikou	370228	197665	156904	154620	100663	10279	692486	295101	146340	874682
三亚市 Sanya	41667	29481	12948	9920	54163	697	85713	36918	17618	127620
五指山市 Wuzhishan	4176	515	2501	1556	2773	19	48184	12602	2643	31266
文昌市 Wenchang	18949	4722	5048	11659	3619	101	101101	24734	1947	75125
琼海市 Qionghai	16657	891	594	5526	5648		78283	21722	1646	43009
万宁市 Wanning	13312	630	4479	8906		50	67713	15883	39698	61669
定安县 Dingan	7879	469	4577	482	7525		53834	8708	438	30517
屯昌县 Tunchang	8284	938	341	1293	3445		44466	9619	1090	36223
澄迈县 Chengmai	11816	962	1886	273	3997		75044	13614	2044	53121
临高县 Lingao	7158	464	2618	961	2303		57709	12474	691	48649
儋州市 Danzhou	16796	3470	4357	44111	12658		132203	25151	3139	63907
东方市 Dongfang	9087	476	2418	1514	5081		82558	20335	9275	47884
乐东县 Ledong	9043	586	4366	955	2165		71929	13717	1414	52763
琼中县 Qiongzhong	7074	186	1996	877	5432		26909	7771	755	27797
保亭县 Baoting	2274	201	852	854	1571		29970	4248	348	24535
陵水县 Lingshui	5460	275	5251	1806	4649		146	7767	448	92678
白沙县 Baisha	5324		1356	823	1535	66	27459	7224	981	30510
昌江县 Changjiang	9683		245	1149	3202	607	39422	9656	1514	48199
洋 浦 Yangpu	9368	1024	2029		1620			1490	15973	17225
农 垦 Land Reclamation		5617	13371	6957			29654	72919	766	6963
总 后 Zonghou										57813
西 沙 Xisha										5267

3－32 各市县分行业城镇单位在岗职工平均工资(全部)

Number of Employed Persons at the Year-end by Sector

单位:元 (yuan)

地 区 Region	在岗职工 Employment	农、林、牧、渔业 Farming, Forestry, Animal Husbandry and Fishery	采矿业 Mining and Quarrying	制造业 Manufacturing	电力、煤气及水的生产和供应业 Production and Supply of Electric Power,Gas and Water	建筑业 Construction	交通运输仓储及邮电通信业 Transport, Storage, Postal Services	信息传输、计算机服务和软件业 Information Transmission, Computer Services and Software	批发和零售业 Wholesale & Retail Trade Services	住宿和餐饮业 Hotels and Catering Trade
总 计 Total	**15890**	**7175**	**16798**	**14559**	**24364**	**12687**	**25058**	**43621**	**12455**	**11912**
海口市 Haikou	21815	11747	9726	15497	28270	13494	27836	51964	15969	11439
三亚市 Sanya	18467	11717	11491	10914	31439	12479	30518	33471	15715	13396
五指山市 Wuzhishan	15788	12824		6062	14903	8211	18464	33553	7480	8977
文昌市 Wenchang	15132	9433	10357	9443	13395	9231	21181	47426	7109	8485
琼海市 Qionghai	15007	6527	15000	11703	21567	3792	14477	15838	14765	11651
万宁市 Wanning	15449	9386	9277	8150	13000	9942	14166	13427	8394	11038
定安县 Dingan	14221	9842		8272	22872	14443	15448	17907	14508	8040
屯昌县 Tunchang	12468	6920		4942	24908	9652	10216	12607	5892	6304
澄迈县 Chengmai	13489	5714	49429	12882	31393	2981	14214	17160	6378	7224
临高县 Lingao	12870	6406	6313	9717	10149	6175	27224	36556	1471	9804
儋州市 Danzhou	13504	6300	6333	8901	14444	12949	14681	19417	13920	7457
东方市 Dongfang	18006	6754	8005	32095	19267	11581	17992	37896	6870	7366
乐东县 Ledong	13501	6629	9699	7988	19660	4271	15933	34491	2757	
琼中县 Qiongzhong	14129	8364		6587	34567	10063	17577	29989	5570	6149
保亭县 Baoting	14276	14096		4452	19024		14896	27000	3460	4000
陵水县 Lingshui	15440	9246	2333	9722	23711	2673	15167	44170	12420	6875
白沙县 Baisha	13673	9807		6135	13202	10140	16244	16573	4229	6492
昌江县 Changjiang	17669	9859	19708	15320	21836	8711	15347	20132	5569	4600
洋 浦 Yangpu	27525			29032	29565		30329	32422	8667	11013
农 垦 Land Reclamation	7623	7042		7948		14427	10643	20364	13503	8787
总 后 Zonghou	14446									
西 沙 Xisha	19364									

3-32 续(continued)

地 区 Region	金 融 Finance	房地产业 Real Estate Trade	租赁和商务服务业 Rent and Business Affair Services	科学研究、技术服务和地质勘查业 Scientific Research, Polytechnic Services and Geological Prospecting	水利、环境和公共设施管理业 Water Conservancy, Environmental Protection and Public Installations Management Services	居民服务和其他服务业 Resident Services and Other Social Services	教育 Education	卫生、社会保障和社会福利业 Health Care, Social Security and Social Welfare	文化、体育和娱乐业 Culture, Sports and Recreational Services	公共管理和社会组织 Public Management and Social Organizations
总 计 Total	**34209**	**16503**	**16771**	**16651**	**12133**	**15551**	**20808**	**20711**	**20392**	**21161**
海口市 Haikou	45963	16282	19095	20350	15361	15527	26319	25884	23527	28369
三亚市 Sanya	32809	22678	18288	19413	14762	33190	19060	19298	12611	25448
五指山市 Wuzhishan	16506	14714	12381	16208	11750	1462	19460	16095	17162	17039
文昌市 Wenchang	22451	12866	19341	26318	8244	10100	20040	15937	16500	18899
琼海市 Qionghai	22209	14607	10068	26440	10498		17003	17447	13949	16670
万宁市 Wanning	22834	18000	12761	9239		10000	31004	18819	20665	17265
定安县 Dingan	24777	11439	7540	12684	9685		16667	11398	14129	17528
屯昌县 Tunchang	18009	9107	5413	14054	6702		18504	16194	8583	11142
澄迈县 Chengmai	18434	9918	6833	10920	8042		16651	15418	8377	13935
临高县 Lingao	14851	14061	12709	8504	5743		16574	11937	10797	15483
儋州市 Danzhou	22852	11567	12136	12155	8262		16813	16846	11669	15842
东方市 Dongfang	20104	10818	11143	11557	6211		20573	16876	24866	17722
乐东县 Ledong	22164	13952	8820	22209	10613		16262	13164	12855	17181
琼中县 Qiongzhong	26297	14308	12475	14617	9841		13950	17906	11269	17627
保亭县 Baoting	18339	14357	8272	13774	7307		17485	11800	9667	14843
陵水县 Lingshui	14677	13750	10157	11080	7012		16222	11096	9739	18287
白沙县 Baisha	27303		8528	13949	9029	9429	16713	16645	13080	15339
昌江县 Changjiang	28148		9800	13843	12656	14452	18276	18150	9895	17413
洋 浦 Yangpu	40554	36571	22054		6000			17326	25154	28708
农 垦 Land Reclamation		14440	25420	7323			21772	26947	18683	24346
总 后 Zonghou										14446
西 沙 Xisha										19364

3－33 分行业城镇注册经济单位在岗职工工资总额和平均工资
Total Wages and Average Wage of Staff and Workers by Sector

行业	Sector	在岗职工 Staff and Workers	国有单位 State-owned Units	城镇集体单位 Urban Collective-owned Units	其他经济类型单位 Other Types of Ownership Units
工资总额（千元）	**Total Wages(1000 yuan)**	**11684117**	**8614718**	**349561**	**2719838**
农、林、牧、渔业	Farming,Forestry,Animal Husbandry and Fishery	1343897	1321641	4319	17937
采矿业	Mining	165851	161406		4445
制造业	Manufacturing	950791	169120	28805	752866
电力、燃气及水的生产和供应业	Production and Supply of Electric Power, Gas and Water	485340	303714	2854	178772
建筑业	Construction	647906	454025	125978	67903
交通运输、仓储和邮政业	Transport, Storage, Postal Services	997695	527309	6660	463726
信息传输、计算机服务和软件业	Information Transmission, Computer Services and Software	345781	229323	484	115974
批发和零售业	Wholesale & Retail Trade Services	338331	166140	34388	137803
住宿和餐饮业	Hotels and Catering Services	396845	91590	17997	287258
金融业	Finance	574235	277239	35358	261638
房地产业	Real Estate	248572	71370	8108	169094
租赁和商务服务业	Rent and Business Affair Services	228137	124728	9495	93914
科学研究、技术服务和地质勘查业	Scientific Research, Polytechnic Services and Geological Prospecting	254242	206099	3122	45021
水利、环境和公共设施管理业	Water Conservancy,Environmental Protection and Public Installations Management Services	222049	193526	3967	24556
居民服务和其他服务业	Resident Services and Other Social Services	11819	6724	508	4587
教育	Education	1744783	1678949	1139	64695
卫生、社会保障和社会福利业	Health Care, Social Security and Social Welfare	621653	557927	60793	2933
文化、体育和娱乐业	Culture,Sports and Recreational Services	248768	218254	5006	25508
公共管理和社会组织	Public Management and Social Organizations	1857422	1855634	580	1208
平均工资(元)	**Average Wage(yuan)**	**15890**	**15398**	**9580**	**19518**
农、林、牧、渔业	Farming,Forestry,Animal Husbandry and Fishery	7175	7152	5573	10459
采矿业	Mining	16798	16787		17229
制造业	Manufacturing	14559	10130	8684	16621
电力、燃气及水的生产和供应业	Production and Supply of Electric Power, Gas and Water	24364	23086	11842	27406
建筑业	Construction	12687	13985	9228	13712
交通运输、仓储和邮政业	Transport, Storage, Postal Services	25058	21917	10812	30627
信息传输、计算机服务和软件业	Information Transmission, Computer Services and Software	43621	41506	9490	49330
批发和零售业	Wholesale & Retail Trade Services	12455	12823	6164	15970
住宿和餐饮业	Hotels and Catering Services	11912	10816	10829	251
金融业	Finance	34209	32528	12320	48514
房地产业	Real Estate	16503	14565	13513	17684
租赁和商务服务业	Rent and Business Affair Services	16771	17491	8719	17446
科学研究、技术服务和地质勘查业	Scientific Research, Polytechnic Services and Geological Prospecting	16651	16384	21095	1007
水利、环境和公共设施管理业	Water Conservancy, Environmental Protection and Public Installations Management Services	12133	12229	9162	12020
居民服务和其他服务业	Resident Services and Other Social Services	15551	18272	11814	13143
教育	Education	20808	20918	11277	18543
卫生、社会保障和社会福利业	Health Care, Social Security and Social Welfare	20711	21664	14922	15601
文化、体育和娱乐业	Culture,Sports and Recreational Services	20392	22754	14595	11267
公共管理和社会组织	Public Management and Social Organizations	21161	21379	648	14212

3－34 工业、建筑企业职工人数和工资总额
Number of Staff and Workers and Total Wages in Industry and Construction

行　业	Sector	在岗职工人数（人）Number of Staff and Workers (person)	工资总额（万元）Total Wages (10 000 yuan)
总　　计	**Total**	148381	224988.8
工　　业	**Industry**	95634	160198.2
按经济类型分	**Grouped by Ownership**		
国有单位	State-owned Units	37826	63424.0
城镇集体单位	Urban Collective-owned Units	3692	3165.9
其他经济类型单位	Units of Other Types of Ownership	54116	93608.3
按行业分	**Grouped by sector**		
采掘业	**Mining and Quarrying**	8261	16585.1
煤炭开采和洗选业	Coal Mining and Dressing	254	182.4
石油和天然气开采业	Mining of Oil and Natural Gas	78	201.2
黑色金属矿采选业	Mining and Dressing of Ferrous Metals	5387	13768.9
有色金属矿采选业	Mining and Dressing of Nonferrous Metals	423	514.0
非金属矿采选业	Mining and Dressing of Nonmetal Minerals	2108	1889.6
其他采矿业	Other Mining	11	29.0
制造业	**Manufacturing**	67461	95079.1
农副食品加工业	Agriculture and Non-Staple Food Processing	11669	10090.6
食品制造业	Food Production	2750	2464.9
饮料制造业	Beverages	5535	9038.8
烟草制品业	Tobacco	531	2950.5
纺织业	Textiles	1639	1754.5
纺织服装、鞋、帽制造业	Garments,Shoses and Hats	5134	6121.9
皮革、毛皮、羽毛（绒）及其制品业	Leather, Furs, Down and Related Products	133	227.7
木材加工及木、竹、藤、棕、草制品业	Timber Processing, Bamboo, Cane, Palm Fiber and Straw Products	1417	1537.4
家具制造业	Furniture Manufacturing	673	887.2
造纸及纸制品业	Papermaking and Paper Products	4787	9388.2
印刷业和记录媒介的复制	Printing and Record Medium Reproduction	2039	2233.0
文教体育用品制造业	Cultural, Educational and Sports Goods		

3-34 续(continued)

行 业	Sector	在岗职工人数(人) Number of Staff and Workers (person)	工资总额(万元) Total Wages (10 000 yuan)
石油加工、炼焦及核燃料加工业	Petroleum Processing, Coking and Nucleus Fuel Processing	620	1976.5
化学原料及化学制品制造业	Raw Chemical Materials and Chemical Products	3986	9352.6
医药制造业	Medical and Pharmaceutical Products	6017	7803.8
化学纤维制造业	Chemical Fiber	1149	1342.3
橡胶制品业	Rubber Products	1696	1523.9
塑料制品业	Plastic Products	1142	1376.4
非金属矿物制品业	Nonmetal Mineral Products	4499	5869.8
黑色金属冶炼及压延加工业	Smelting and Pressing of Ferrous Metals	509	829.7
有色金属冶炼及压延加工业	Smelting and Pressing of Nonferrous Metals	62	70.1
金属制品业	Metal Products	1178	1949.3
通用设备制造业	Ordinary Machinery	124	92.8
专用设备制造业	Equipment for Special Purposes	1202	1366.1
交通运输设备制造业	Transport Equipment	5843	8546.5
电气机械及器材制造业	Electric Equipment and Machinery	1658	3722.6
通信设备、计算机及其他电子设备制造业	Telecommunications Equipment, Computer and Other Electronic Equipment	936	2084.6
仪器仪表及文化、办公用机械制造业	Instruments, Meters, Cultural and Office Machinery	68	20.9
工艺品及其他制造业	Handicraft Article and Other Manufacturing	428	400.1
废弃资源和废旧材料回收加工业	Recovery and Processing of Discarded Resoures and Waste Materials	37	56.4
电力、煤气及水的生产和供应业	**Production and Supply of Electric Power,Gas and Water**	**19912**	**48534.0**
电力、蒸汽、热水的生产和供应业	Production and Supply of Electric Power, Steam and Hot Water	14714	40308.0
煤气生产和供应业	Production and Supply of Gas	477	1288.5
自来水的生产和供应业	Production and Supply of Tap Water	4721	6937.5
建筑业	**Construction**	**52747**	**64790.6**
按经济类型分	**Grouped by Ownership**		
国有单位	State-owned Units	33379	45402.5
城镇集体单位	Urban Collective-owned Units	13813	12597.8
其他经济类型单位	Units of Other Types of Ownership	5555	6790.3

3－35 历年分行业单位在岗职工工资总额和平均工资
Total Wages and Average Wage of Staff and Workers by Sector

行业	Sector	2003	2004	2005	2006
工资总额（万元）	**Total Wages (1000 yuan)**	**754498**	**913157**	**1041882**	**1168412**
农、林、牧、渔业	Farming,Forestry,Animal Husbandry and Fishery	97555	117653	116418	1343897
采矿业	Mining	9719	12065	16765	165851
制造业	Manufacturing	70019	82112	87239	950791
电力、燃气及水的生产和供应业	Production and Supply of Electric Power, Gas and Water	29918	32269	35171	485340
建筑业	Construction	40661	51524	55816	647906
交通运输、仓储和邮政业	Transport, Storage, Postal Services	54397	70252	88985	997695
信息传输、计算机服务和软件业	Information Transmission, Computer Services and Software	17791	26772	41585	345781
批发和零售业	Wholesale & Retail Trade Services	28893	28180	30834	338331
住宿和餐饮业	Hotels and Catering Services	25729	31450	32826	396845
金融业	Finance	37768	45512	48746	574235
房地产业	Real Estate	13045	19136	21388	248572
租赁和商务服务业	Rent and Business Affair Services	10846	15310	19517	228137
科学研究、技术服务和地质勘查业	Scientific Research, Polytechnic Services and Geological Prospecting	16139	19406	21546	254242
水利、环境和公共设施管理业	Water Conservancy,Environmental Protection and Public Installations Management Services	14791	20055	23821	222049
居民服务和其他服务业	Resident Services and Other Social Services	473	807	1022	11819
教育	Education	108428	133913	160133	1744783
卫生、社会保障和社会福利业	Health Care,Social Security and Social Welfare	42490	49057	56207	621653
文化、体育和娱乐业	Culture,Sports and Recreational Services	16913	19289	21921	248768
公共管理和社会组织	Public Management and Social Organizations	118923	138395	161942	1857422
平均工资（元）	**Average Wage（yuan）**	**10397**	**12652**	**14417**	**15890**
农、林、牧、渔业	Farming,Forestry,Animal Husbandry and Fishery	4762	6206	6338	7175
采矿业	Mining	8264	11150	15337	16798
制造业	Manufacturing	9929	12068	12833	14559
电力、燃气及水的生产和供应业	Production and Supply of Electric Power, Gas and Water	15928	17624	18829	24364
建筑业	Construction	9190	10845	12082	12687
交通运输、仓储和邮政业	Transport, Storage, Postal Services	15571	17503	21504	25058
信息传输、计算机服务和软件业	Information Transmission, Computer Services and Software	27898	37486	44996	43621
批发和零售业	Wholesale & Retail Trade Services	8810	9943	11199	12455
住宿和餐饮业	Hotels and Catering Services	8352	10184	10869	11912
金融业	Finance	19979	25724	28094	34209
房地产业	Real Estate	12017	13942	15625	16503
租赁和商务服务业	Rent and Business Affair Services	10607	12691	15144	16771
科学研究、技术服务和地质勘查业	Scientific Research, Polytechnic Services and Geological Prospecting	11709	13758	15174	16651
水利、环境和公共设施管理业	Water Conservancy,Environmental Protection and Public Installations Management Services	9465	10693	11918	12133
居民服务和其他服务业	Resident Services and Other Social Services	12538	13259	16075	15551
教育	Education	13353	16036	18665	20808
卫生、社会保障和社会福利业	Health Care,Social Security and Social Welfare	15329	17712	19642	20711
文化、体育和娱乐业	Culture,Sports and Recreational Services	14726	16219	18082	20392
公共管理和社会组织	Public Management and Social Organizations	14785	17099	19854	21161

3－36 历年分行业国有单位在岗职工工资总额和平均工资

Total Wages and Average Wage of Staff and Workers in State-owned Units by Sectora

行 业	Sector	2003	2004	2005	2006
工资总额（万元）	**Total Wages（10000 yuan）**	**596934**	**717529**	**814634**	**861472**
农、林、牧、渔业	Farming,Forestry,Animal Husbandry and Fishery	95443	115449	114346	132164
采矿业	Mining	9202	11343	15785	16141
制造业	Manufacturing	22934	25174	26173	16912
电力、燃气及水的生产和供应业	Production and Supply of Electric Power, Gas and Water	16325	17134	19052	30371
建筑业	Construction	28159	37414	39938	45403
交通运输、仓储和邮政业	Transport, Storage, Postal Services	40260	47312	52421	52731
信息传输、计算机服务和软件业	Information Transmission, Computer Services and Software	9784	18795	31566	22932
批发和零售业	Wholesale & Retail Trade Services	16315	15427	17765	16614
住宿和餐饮业	Hotels and Catering Services	7256	9479	8402	9159
金融业	Finance	32392	40083	42457	27724
房地产业	Real Estate	5572	6708	7579	7137
租赁和商务服务业	Rent and Business Affair Services	7550	9316	10848	12473
科学研究、技术服务和地质勘查业	Scientific Research, Polytechnic Services and Geological Prospecting	14756	16954	19088	20610
水利、环境和公共设施管理业	Water Conservancy,Environmental Protection and Public Installations Management Services	13590	17933	21808	19353
居民服务和其他服务业	Resident Services and Other Social Services	347	446	578	672
教育	Education	105935	129948	155591	167895
卫生、社会保障和社会福利业	Health Care, Social Security and Social Welfare	38160	44427	50590	55793
文化、体育和娱乐业	Culture,Sports and Recreational Services	14898	16514	18836	21825
公共管理和社会组织	Public Management and Social Organizations	118056	137673	161811	185563
平均工资(元)	**Average Wage(yuan)**	**10305**	**12664**	**14427**	**15398**
农、林、牧、渔业	Farming,Forestry,Animal Husbandry and Fishery	4725	6183	6311	7152
采矿业	Mining	8224	11088	15612	16787
制造业	Manufacturing	8962	11308	11601	10130
电力、燃气及水的生产和供应业	Production and Supply of Electric Power, Gas and Water	12368	14469	16022	23086
建筑业	Construction	10274	12284	14228	13985
交通运输、仓储和邮政业	Transport, Storage, Postal Services	15617	17222	19262	21917
信息传输、计算机服务和软件业	Information Transmission, Computer Services and Software	29686	39761	47798	41506
批发和零售业	Wholesale & Retail Trade Services	9236	10499	12940	12823
住宿和餐饮业	Hotels and Catering Services	7743	10377	10306	10816
金融业	Finance	22275	29181	31609	32528
房地产业	Real Estate	11600	12500	14636	14565
租赁和商务服务业	Rent and Business Affair Services	11691	13072	14973	17491
科学研究、技术服务和地质勘查业	Scientific Research, Polytechnic Services and Geological Prospecting	11724	13541	15113	16384
水利、环境和公共设施管理业	Water Conservancy,Environmental Protection and Public Installations Management Services	9655	10910	12169	12229
居民服务和其他服务业	Resident Services and Other Social Services	18381	16646	20654	18272
教育	Education	13394	16048	18750	20918
卫生、社会保障和社会福利业	Health Care,Social Security and Social Welfare	16053	18653	20587	21664
文化、体育和娱乐业	Culture,Sports and Recreational Services	16223	18045	20025	22754
公共管理和社会组织	Public Management and Social Organizations	14937	17281	19852	21379

3－37 历年分行业城镇集体单位在岗职工工资总额和平均工资

Total Wages and Average Wage of Staff and Workers in Urban Collective-owned Units by Sector

行业	Sector	2003	2004	2005	2006
工资总额（万元）	**Total Wages**	**27650**	**29891**	**32618**	**34956**
农、林、牧、渔业	Farming,Forestry,Animal Husbandry and Fishery	343	416	426	432
采矿业	Mining	354	498	546	
制造业	Manufacturing	2914	2784	3516	2880
电力、燃气及水的生产和供应业	Production and Supply of Electric Power, Gas and Water	49	176	177	285
建筑业	Construction	7504	9238	9331	12598
交通运输、仓储和邮政业	Transport, Storage, Postal Services	606	721	727	666
信息传输、计算机服务和软件业	Information Transmission, Computer Services and Software	13	18	24	48
批发和零售业	Wholesale & Retail Trade Services	3782	3713	4023	3439
住宿和餐饮业	Hotels and Catering Services	1382	1599	1847	1800
金融业	Finance	3193	3128	3393	3536
房地产业	Real Estate	814	852	829	811
租赁和商务服务业	Rent and Business Affair Services	671	781	1132	949
科学研究、技术服务和地质勘查业	Scientific Research, Polytechnic Services and Geological Prospecting	54	82	126	312
水利、环境和公共设施管理业	Water Conservancy,Environmental Protection and Public Installations Management Services	291	367	385	397
居民服务和其他服务业	Resident Services and Other Social Services	21	25	26	51
教育	Education	512	186	191	114
卫生、社会保障和社会福利业	Health Care, Social Security and Social Welfare	4160	4469	5400	6079
文化、体育和娱乐业	Culture,Sports and Recreational Services	120	116	394	501
公共管理和社会组织	Public Management and Social Organizations	867	722	125	58
平均工资（元）	**Average Wage**	**7029**	**8121**	**8640**	**9580**
农、林、牧、渔业	Farming,Forestry,Animal Husbandry and Fishery	4518	5716	5552	5573
采矿业	Mining	8679	12396	13726	
制造业	Manufacturing	6533	6522	7912	8684
电力、燃气及水的生产和供应业	Production and Supply of Electric Power, Gas and Water	4450	7397	7468	11842
建筑业	Construction	6101	7829	7503	9228
交通运输、仓储和邮政业	Transport, Storage, Postal Services	7744	8929	9506	10812
信息传输、计算机服务和软件业	Information Transmission, Computer Services and Software	4267	3894	4175	9490
批发和零售业	Wholesale & Retail Trade Services	4989	5580	5836	6164
住宿和餐饮业	Hotels and Catering Services	7479	9897	10940	10829
金融业	Finance	9710	10841	11753	12320
房地产业	Real Estate	10861	10811	11238	13513
租赁和商务服务业	Rent and Business Affair Services	9533	10887	7612	8719
科学研究、技术服务和地质勘查业	Scientific Research, Polytechnic Services and Geological Prospecting	12810	18977	20387	21095
水利、环境和公共设施管理业	Water Conservancy,Environmental Protection and Public Installations Management Services	6550	8559	8796	9162
居民服务和其他服务业	Resident Services and Other Social Services	7429	10000	10115	11814
教育	Education	12967	10831	9052	11277
卫生、社会保障和社会福利业	Health Care, Social Security and Social Welfare	10827	11883	13868	14922
文化、体育和娱乐业	Culture,Sports and Recreational Services	7186	7503	14658	14595
公共管理和社会组织	Public Management and Social Organizations	6191	5678	22764	648

3-38 历年分行业其他经济类型单位在岗职工工资总额和平均工资
Total Wages and Average Wage of Staff and Workers in Other Types of OwnershipUnits by Sector

行　　业	Sector	2003	2004	2005	2006
工资总额(万元)	**Total Wages**	129914	165737	194630	271984
农、林、牧、渔业	Farming,Forestry,Animal Husbandry and Fishery	1769	1788	1646	1794
采矿业	Mining	163	224	434	445
制造业	Manufacturing	44172	54154	57550	75287
电力、燃气及水的生产和供应业	Production and Supply of Electric Power, Gas and Water	13544	14959	15942	17877
建筑业	Construction	4999	4872	6547	6790
交通运输、仓储和邮政业	Transport, Storage, Postal Services	13531	22219	35837	46372
信息传输、计算机服务和软件业	Information Transmission, Computer Services and Software	7993	7959	9995	11597
批发和零售业	Wholesale & Retail Trade Services	8795	9040	9046	13780
住宿和餐饮业	Hotels and Catering Services	17091	20372	22577	28726
金融业	Finance	2182	2301	2896	26164
房地产业	Real Estate	6658	11576	12980	16909
租赁和商务服务业	Rent and Business Affair Services	2625	5213	7537	9391
科学研究、技术服务和地质勘查业	Scientific Research, Polytechnic Services and Geological Prospecting	1330	2370	2332	4502
水利、环境和公共设施管理业	Water Conservancy,Environmental Protection and Public Installations Management Services	910	1755	1628	2456
居民服务和其他服务业	Resident Services and Other Social Services	105	336	418	459
教育	Education	1981	3779	4351	6470
卫生、社会保障和社会福利业	Health Care, Social Security and Social Welfare	171	161	217	293
文化、体育和娱乐业	Culture,Sports and Recreational Services	1895	2659	2691	2551
公共管理和社会组织	Public Management and Social Organizations			6	121
平均工资(元)	**Average Wage**	12130	14005	16185	19518
农、林、牧、渔业	Farming,Forestry,Animal Husbandry and Fishery	8499	8386	9450	10459
采矿业	Mining	9939	11899	10270	17229
制造业	Manufacturing	10915	13046	14045	16621
电力、燃气及水的生产和供应业	Production and Supply of Electric Power, Gas and Water	24739	24015	24335	27406
建筑业	Construction	11016	9275	11504	13712
交通运输、仓储和邮政业	Transport, Storage, Postal Services	16160	18737	26742	30627
信息传输、计算机服务和软件业	Information Transmission, Computer Services and Software	26200	33612	38728	49330
批发和零售业	Wholesale & Retail Trade Services	11646	12922	13093	15970
住宿和餐饮业	Hotels and Catering Services	8726	10119	298	251
金融业	Finance	20338	21481	28066	48514
房地产业	Real Estate	12558	15290	16701	17684
租赁和商务服务业	Rent and Business Affair Services	8569	12353	18138	17446
科学研究、技术服务和地质勘查业	Scientific Research, Polytechnic Services and Geological Prospecting	11513	15371	581	1007
水利、环境和公共设施管理业	Water Conservancy,Environmental Protection and Public Installations Management Services	8220	9289	9996	12020
居民服务和其他服务业	Resident Services and Other Social Services	6531	10646	12661	13143
教育	Education	11571	15981	16746	18543
卫生、社会保障和社会福利业	Health Care, Social Security and Social Welfare	16257	13619	14735	15601
文化、体育和娱乐业	Culture,Sports and Recreational Services	8874	10280	10992	11267
公共管理和社会组织	Public Management and Social Organizations			12000	14212

主要统计指标解释

总人口数 是指一定时点、一定地区范围内的有生命的个人的总和。年度统计的年末人口数是指每年 12 月 31 日 24 时的人口数，是在公安部门户籍登记的基础上取得的。普查人口数则是通过逐户逐人调查取得，调查标准时点为年中即 7 月 1 日零点正，包括常住县、市县户口在本县市的人口，常住本县市一年以上户口在外县的人口，住本县市面上不满一年离开户口登记地一年以上人口，住本县、市人口待定的人口，原住本县市现在国外工作或学习暂无户口的人口。

市镇人口和乡村人口 市人口指地级以上辖区的全部人口和县级市的街道人口，镇人口指县级和县所辖的居委会人口。本《年鉴》镇人口按照全省的城镇比例计算取得。

出生率(又称粗出生率) 指在一定时期内(通常为一年)平均每千人所出生的人数的比率，一般用千分率表示。计算公式为：

出生率 = 年出生人数 / 年平均人数×1000‰

式中：出生人数指活产婴儿，即胎儿脱离母体时(不管怀孕月数)，有过呼吸或其他生命现象。年平均人数指年初、年底人口数的平均数，也可用年中人口数代替。

死亡率(又称粗死亡率) 指在一定时期内(通常为一年)一定地区的死亡人数与同期平均人数(或期中人数)之比，一般用千分率表示。计算公式为：

死亡率 = 年死亡人数 / 年平均人数×1000‰

人口自然增长率 指在一定时期内(通常为一年)人口自然增加数(出生人数减死亡人数)与该时期内平均人数(或期中人数)之比，一般用千分率表示。计算公式为：

人口自然增长率 =（本年出生人数 - 本年死亡人数）/ 年平均人数×1000‰= 人口出生率 - 人口死亡率

性别比 人口中男性人数与女性人数之比。通常用每 100 名女性人口相对应的男性人口数来表示。

一孩率 指当年出生人数中第一个孩子所占的比例。

二孩率 指当年出生人数中第二个孩子所占的比例。

三孩率 指当年出生人数中第三及以上孩子所占的比例。

一般生育率 指当年每千名 15-49 岁育龄妇女生育的活产婴儿总数。

总和生育率 指当年各年龄别妇女生育率的合计数，说明每名妇女按某年的年龄别生育率度过育龄期，平均每个妇女在育龄期生育的子女数。

总负担系数 指被抚养人口（0-14 岁和 65 岁以上人口）与 15-64 岁人口的比例。计算公式为：

总负担系数 = 被抚养人口 /15-64 岁人口×100%

负担老年系数 指老年人口（65 岁以上人口）与 15-64 岁人口的比例。计算公式为：

负担老年系数 = 老年人口 /15-64 岁人口×100%

负担少年系数 指少年儿童与 15-64 岁人口的比例。计算公式为：

负担少年系数 = 少年儿童人口 /15-64 岁人口×100%

从业人员 指从事一定社会劳动并取得劳动报酬或经营收入的人员，包括在岗职工、再就业的离退休人员、私营业主、个体户主、私营和个体就业人员、乡镇企业就业人员、农村就业人员、其他就业人员（包括民办教师、宗教职业者、现役军人等）。这一指标反映了一定时期内全部劳动力资源的实际利用情况，是研究我国基本国情国力的重要指标。

各单位的从业人员 指在各级国家机关、政党机关、社会团体及企业、事业单位中工作，取得工资或其他形式的劳动报酬的全部人员。包括在岗职工、再就业的离退休人员、民办教师以及在各单位中工作的外方人员和港澳台方人员、兼职人员、借用的外单位人员和第二职业者。不包括离开本单位仍保留劳动关系的职工。各单位的从业人员反映了各单位实际参加生产或工作的全部劳动力。

城镇私营和个体就业人员 城镇私营就业人员指在工商管理部门注册登记，其经营地址设在县城关镇（含城关镇）以上的私营企业就业人员；包括私营企业投资者和雇工。城镇个体就业人员指在工商管理部门注册登记，并持有城镇户口或在城镇长期居住，经批准从事个体工商经营的就业人员；包括个体经营者和在个体工商户劳动的家庭帮工和雇工。

职工 指在国有经济、城镇集体经济、联营经济、股份制经济、外商和港、澳、台投资经济、其他经济单位及其附属机构工作，并由其支付工资的各类人员，不包括返聘的离退休人员、民办教师、在国有经济单位工作的外方人员和港、澳、台人员（1998 年以后的数据均为在岗职工数据，其他相关指标如职工工资总额，职工平均工资等指标也从 1998 年按此口径进行了相应调整）。

国有单位职工 指在国有经济单位及其附属机构工作，并由其支付工资的各类人员。

城镇集体单位职工 指在城镇集体经济单位及其管理部门工作，并由其支付工资的各类人员。

其他单位职工 指在联营经济、股份制经济、外商投资经济、港、澳、台投资经济单位工作，并由其支付工资的各类人员。

在岗职工 指在本单位工作并由单位支付工资的人员，以及有工作岗位，但由于学习、病伤产假等原因暂未工作，仍由单位支付工资的人员。

职工工资总额 指各单位在一定时期内直接支付给本单位全部职工的劳动报酬总额。工资总额的计算原则应以直接支付给职工的全部劳动报酬为根据。各单位支付给职工的劳动报酬以及其他根据有关规定支付的工资,不论是计入成本的还是不计入成本的,不论是按国家规定列入计征奖金税项目的,还是未列入计征奖金税项目的,不论是以货币形式支付的还是以实物形式支付的,均包括在工资总额内。

职工平均工资 指企业、事业、机关单位的职工在一定时期内平均每人所得的货币工资额。它表明一定时期职工工资收入的高低程度,是反映职工工资水平的主要指标。计算公式为:

职工平均工资 = 报告期实际支付的全部职工工资总额 / 报告期全部职工平均人数

Explanatory Note on Main Statistical Indicators

Total Population refers to the total number of people alive at a certain point of time within a given area.

The annual statistics on total population is taken at midnight, the 3lst of December, not including residents in Taiwan province, Chinese compatriots in Hong Kong and Macao and overseas Chinese.

Urban Population and Rural Population

The first definition (by the administrative system):

Urban Population refers to total population under the jurisdiction of city and the population of towns under the jurisdiction of counties.

Rural Population refers to total population of townships under the jurisdiction of counties.

The second definition (by the permanent residence):

Urban Population refers to total population of districts under the jurisdiction of a city with district establishment, the population of street committees under the jurisdiction of a city without district establishment, population of resident-committees of towns under the jurisdiction of a city without district establishment, and the of resident-committees of towns under the jurisdiction of a county.

Rural Population refers to total population except urban population.

The most recent definition of urban/rural population are classified according to the Regulation of Statistics Classification on Urban and Rural Population (Draft), formulated by the National Bureau of Statistics in 1999.

Data on urban/rural population for the 1982 population census are based on the first definition, data for the 1990 population census are based on the second definition, and data for the 2000 population census are based on the Regulation of Statistics Classification on Urban and Rural Population (Draft), formulated by the National Bureau of Statistics in 1999. Urban/rural population for other years between the censuses are adjusted in accordance with the 1990 and 2000 population census data.

Birth Rate or (Crude Birth Rate) refers to the ratio of the number of births to the average population (or mid-period population) during a certain period of time (usually a year) which is often expressed in ‰. Birth rate in the chapter refers to annual birth rate. The following formula is used:

Birth Rate = Number of Births/Average Number of Population×1000‰

Number of births refers to live births i.e. the births when babies had showed any vital phenomena regardless of the length of pregnancy.

Annual Average Number of Population is the average of the number of population at the beginning of the year and that at the end of the year. Sometimes it is substituted for with the mid year population.

Death Rate (or Crude Death Rate) refers to the ratio of the number of deaths to the average population (or mid-period population) during a certain period of time (usually a year) which is often expressed in ‰. Death rate in the chapter refers to annual death rate. The following formula is used:

Death Rate= Number of Deaths/Annual Average Number of Population×1000‰

Natural Growth Rate of Population refers to the ratio of natural increase in population (number of births minus number of deaths) in a certain period of time (usually a year) to the average population (or mid-period population) of the same period which is often expressed in ‰. The following formulas are applied:

Natural Growth of Population = (Number of Births-Number of Deaths)/Average Number of Population×1000‰

Natural Growth Rate of Population = Birth Rate-Death Rate

Total Dependency Ratio refers to the ratio of number of dependents to the total population aged 15-64, the number of dependents being population aged 0-14 and population aged 65 and over. The total dependency ratio is calculated as follows:

Total Dependency Ratio = Number of Dependents/Population Aged 15-64×100%

The Aged Dependency Ratio refers to the ratio of the number of the aged population to the total population aged 15-64, the aged being population aged 65 and over. The aged dependency ratio is calculated as follows:

The Aged Dependency Ratio = Number of the Aged Population/ Population Aged 15–64×100%

The Juvenile and Children Dependency Ratio refers to the ratio of the number of the juvenile and children to the total population aged 15–64, the juvenile and children being population aged 0–14. The juvenile and children dependency ratio is calculated as follows:

The Juvenile and Children Dependency Ratio = Number of Juvenile and Children/ Population Aged 15–64×100%

Employed Persons refer to the persons who are engaged in social working and receive remuneration payment or earn business income, including total staff and workers, re–employed retirees, employers of private enterprises, self–employed workers, employees in private enterprises and individual economy, employees in township enterprises, employed persons in the rural areas, and other employed persons (including teachers in the schools run by the local people, people engaged in religious profession and the servicemen, etc.). This indicator reflects the actual utilization of total labour force during a certain period of time and is often used for the research on China's economic situation and national power.

Persons Employed in Various Units refer to all the persons working in government agencies of various levels, political and party organizations, social organizations, enterprises and institutions, and receiving wages or other forms of payment. They include fully–employed staff and workers, re–employed retirees, teachers in schools run by the local people, foreigners and Chinese compatriots from Hong Kong, Macao, and Taiwan working in various units, part–time employees, employees of other units working temporarily at current posts, and employees holding the second job, but exclude staff and workers who have left their working units while keeping their labour contract (employment relation) unchanged. This indicator reflects the total number of laborers actually engaged in production or other operations in various units.

Persons Employed in Private Enterprises and Self–Employed Individuals in Urban Areas Persons employed in private enterprises refer to the persons employed in the private enterprises which have been registered at the departments of industrial and commercial administration and are situated at a county town (i.e. a town where the county government is located) for business operation or at urban areas with the level higher than a county town. The self–employed individuals in urban areas refer to persons who hold the certificates of residence in urban areas or have resided in the urban areas for a long time and have been registered at the departments of industrial and commercial administration and approved to be engaged in individual industrial or commercial business, including self–employed persons as well as helpers and hired labourers who work in the individual households engaged in industrial or commercial business.

Staff and Workers refer to the persons who work in (and receive payment therefrom) enterprises and institutions of state ownership, collective ownership, joint ownership, share holding, foreign ownership, and ownership by entrepreneurs from Hong Kong, Macao, and Taiwan, and other types of ownership and their affiliated units, excluding the retired persons invited to work in the units again, teachers in the schools run by the local people and foreigners and persons coming from Hong Kong, Macao and Taiwan and working in the state–owned economic units. (Number of staff and workers in this yearbook include only fully employed staff and workers, excluding those who have left their working units while keeping their labour contract/employment relation unchanged).

Staff and Workers in State–owned Economic Units refer to the persons who work in the state–owned economic units or their attached units and are listed in their payrolls.

Staff and Workers of Collective Owned Units in Urban Areas refer to the persons who work in collective owned units in urban areas and their administration departments and receive payment therefrom.

Staff and Workers in Units of Other types of Ownership refer to those who work in (and receive payment therefrom) enterprises and institutions of joint ownership, share holding, foreign ownership, and ownership by entrepreneurs from Hong Kong, Macao, and Taiwan.

Fully Employed Staff and Workers refer to persons who work in, and receive wages from their working units, as well as persons who have their work posts, but are temporarily absent from work for reasons of study or on sick, injury or maternal leave and still receive wages from their working units.

Total Wages of Staff and Workers refer to the total remuneration payment to staff and workers in various units during a certain period of time. The calculation of total wages is based on the total remuneration payment to the staff and workers. Therefore, all the wages and salaries and other payments to staff and workers are included in the total wages regardless of their sources, category, and forms (in kind or cash). (Total wages of staff and workers in this yearbook include only total wages of fully employed staff and workers, excluding the living allowances distributed to those who have left their working units while keeping their labour contract/employment relation unchanged).

Average Wage of Staff and Workers refers to the average wage in money terms per person during a certain period of time for staff and workers in enterprises, institutions, and government agencies, which reflects the general level of wage income during a certain period of time and is calculated as follows:

Average Wage of Staff and Workers = Total Wages of Staff and Workers at the Report/Average Number of Staff and Workers at the Report Period

资料整理: 吴慎安　蔡世沐
Arranged by Wushengan Caishimu

4. 固定资产和房地产开发投资

INVESTMENT IN FIXED ASSETS AND REAL ESTATE DEVELOPMENT

全社会固定资产投资总额（亿元）

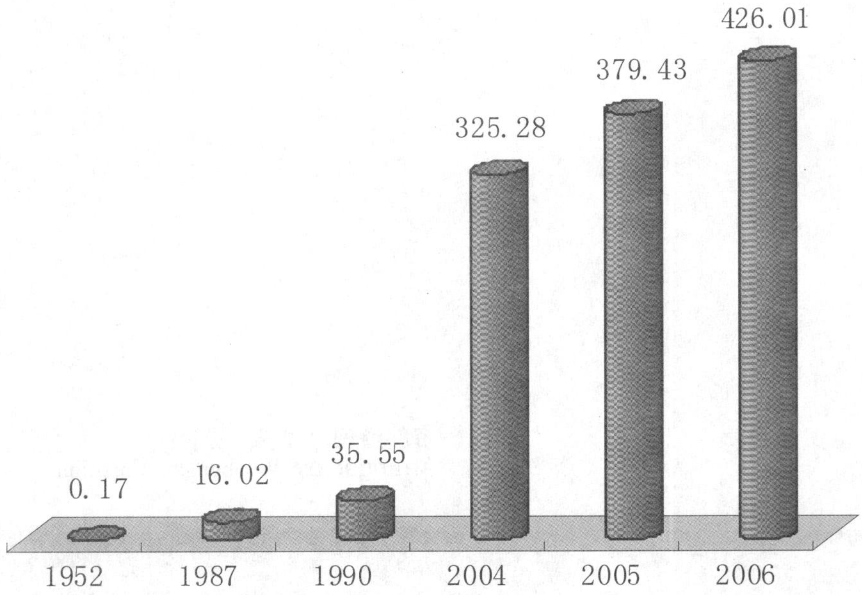

全社会固定资产投资构成（%）

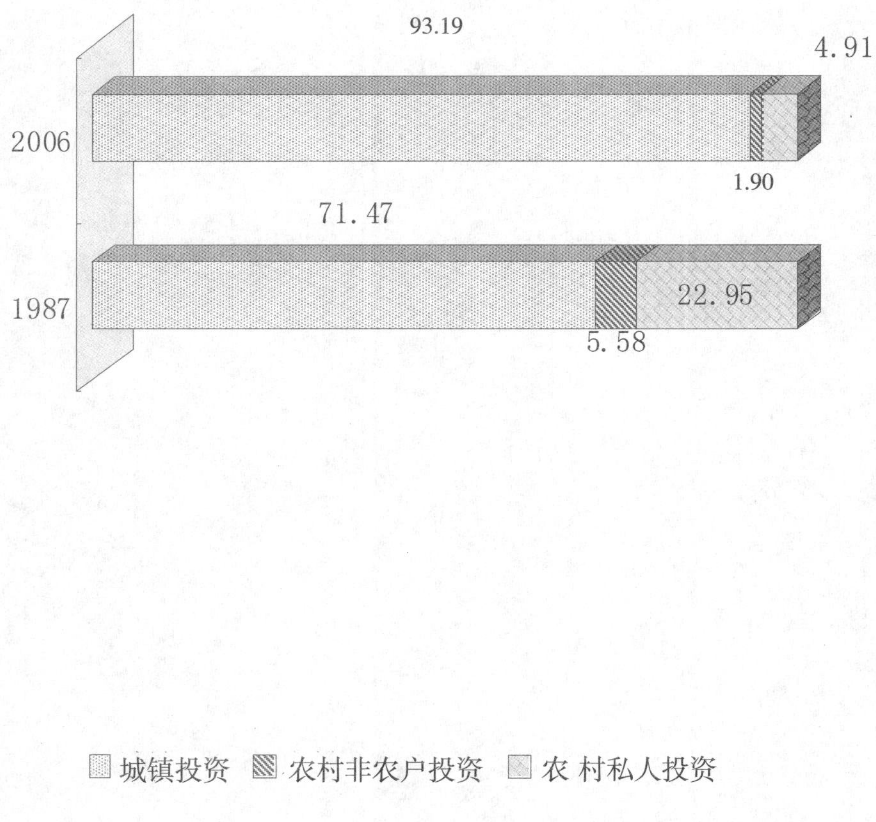

4-1 主要年份全社会固定资产投资
Total Investment in Fixed Assets in Major Years

单位:万元 (10000 yuan)

年 份 Year	固定资产投资总额 Investment in Fixed Assets	城镇投资 urban investment	房地产 Real Estate Development	农村非农户 rural non-farmers	农村私人 Rural
1952	1674	1674			
1978	33544	33544			
1979	32150	32150			
1980	34725	34725			
1981	47716	35830			11886
1982	58257	45289			12968
1983	63150	49575		1709	11866
1984	98274	79591		3522	15161
1985	153082	127284		7356	18442
1986	160028	132095		6283	21650
1987	160187	117247		8938	34002
1988	201399	158560		10942	31897
1989	288080	248677		8808	30595
1990	355508	315460	41380	9711	30337
1991	456303	413972	108645	13269	29062
1992	870451	803815	302192	17223	49513
1993	1882492	1785760	573317	32175	64557
1994	2202491	2075348	572054	44805	82338
1995	1980665	1864603	389024	19849	96213
1996	1859322	1736562	169837	18267	104493
1997	1678308	1511759	79926	45858	120691
1998	1833360	1650119	102398	36379	146862
1999	1901322	1678675	61994	51532	162146
2000	1934508	1695626	103372	62194	176688
2001	2064328	1821681	171111	59811	182836
2002	2257707	2019264	201112	60440	178003
2003	2763400	2488423	366131	78618	196359
2004	3252811	2997412	559917	51620	203779
2005	3794284	3515116	708494	72222	206946
2006	4260137	3970009	892554	81027	209101
"一五时期" The "First Five-year Plan" Period	30357	30357			
"二五时期" The "Second Five-year Plan" Period	63797	63797			
"三年调整时期" Three Year Adjustment Period	32311	32311			
"三五时期" The "Third Five-year Plan" Period	54328	54328			
"四五时期" The "Fourth Five-year Plan" Period	100998	100998			
"五五时期" The "Fifth Five-year Plan" Period	152668	967923			
"六五时期" The "Sixth Five-year Plan" Period	420479	337569		12587	70323
"七五时期" The "Seventh Five-year Plan" Period	1165202	972039	41380	44682	148481
"八五时期" The "Eighth Five-year Plan" Period	7392402	6943498	1945682	127211	321683
"九五时期" The "Ninth Five-year Plan" Period	9206820	8272741	517527	214230	710880
"十五时期" The "Tenth Five-year Plan" Period	14132530	12841896	2006765	322711	967923

4－2 按各种分组分的全社会固定资产投资额
Total Investment in Fixed Assets

单位:万元 (10000 yuan)

指 标	Item	总 计 Total	城镇投资 urban investment	房地产 Real Estate Development	农村非农户 rural non-farmers
固定资产投资额	**Investment in Fixed Assets**	**4260137**	**3970009**	**892554**	**81027**
按资金来源分	**Grouped by Source of Funds**				
国家投资	State Budgetary Appropriation	282616	266714		15177
国内贷款	Domestic Loans	844570	836095	67443	1268
债 券	Bond	2627	2604		
利用外资	Foreign Investment	591164	585992	151169	29
自筹投资	Fundraising	1526181	1288777	241054	48370
其他投资	Others	1012979	989827	432888	16183
按构成分	**Grouped by Use of Funds**				
建安工程	Construction and Installation	2590341	2316831	664062	64409
设备工具器具购置	Purchase of Equipment and Instruments	1046535	1042033	9782	4502
其 他	Others	623261	611145	218710	12116
按隶属关系分	**By Administrative Relationship**				
中央项目	Central Government	696156	696156	2369	
省属项目	Provincial	1089984	1089714	141423	270
地(市)属项目	Prefecture and Municipalities	1015542	1007253	392980	8289
县(市)属项目	Counties	424737	378321	38286	46416
其他项目	Others	1033718	798565	317496	26052
按建设性质分	**Grouped by Type of Construction**				
新 建	New Construction	2940086	2700050		30935
扩 建	Expansion	481930	449902		32028
改 建	Reconstruction	364087	347930		16157
建设项目(个)	**Number of Construction Projects(Unit)**				
施工项目	Projects Under Construction	1493	1338		155
本年新开工	Projects Newly Started This Year	1132	992		140

4-3 按经济类型分全社会固定资产投资额
Total Investment By Ownership

单位:万元 (10000 yuan)

指标	Item	总计 Total	其中:地方 Local	城镇投资 urban investment	其中:地方 Local	房地产开发 Real Estate Development	其中:地方 Local	农村非农户 rural non-farmers	其中:地方 Local
总计	**Total**	4260137	3563981	3970009	3273853	892554	890185	81027	81027
内资	**Domestic Funded**	3723838	3027682	3440394	2744238	630632	628263	74343	74343
国有	State-owned	1481225	924639	1429778	873192	5876	5876	51447	51447
集体	Collective-owned	13410	13410	9724	9724	1388	1388	3686	3686
股份合作	Cooperative Enterprises	28333	28323	27183	27173	22262	22252	1150	1150
国有联营	State Joint Ownership Enterprises	6554	6554	6554	6554	1764	1764		
集体联营	Collective Joint Ownership Enterprises	1210	1210	1210	1210	10	10		
其他联营	Joint Ownership Enterprises of Others	710	710	710	710				
股份有限公司	Share Holding Enterprises	653610	522744	651410	520544	30663	30663	2200	2200
私营	Private Enterprises	183153	183153	169282	169282	147157	147157	13871	13871
其他	Other Enterprises	1355633	1346939	1144543	1135849	421512	419153	1989	1989
港澳台商投资	**Enterprises Funded by Entrepreneurs from Hong Kong, Macao and Taiwan**	262934	262934	262889	262889	227087	227087	45	45
合资经营	Jointly Owned	38696	38696	38696	38696	22497	22497		
合作经营	Cooperative Management	8568	8568	8568	8568	8068	8068		
独资	Exclusive Investment	200740	200740	200695	200695	182592	182592	45	45
股份有限	Share Holding Enterprises	14930	14930	14930	14930	13930	13930		
外商投资	**Foreign Funded Enterprises**	251872	251872	251872	251872	34835	34835		
合资经营	Jointly Owned	77356	77356	77356	77356	25420	25420		
合作经营	Cooperative Management	4723	4723	4723	4723				
独资	Exclusive Investment	165523	165523	165523	165523	6408	6408		
股份有限	Share Holding Enterprises	4270	4270	4270	4270	3007	3007		
个体经营	**individual business**	21493	21493	14854	14854			6639	6639

4－4 主要年份全社会新增固定资产
Total Newly Increased Fixed Assets in Major Year

年 份 Year	新增固定资产(万元) Newly Increased Fixed Assets (10 000 yuan)	房地产 Real Estate Development	固定资产交付使用率(%) Rate of Fixed Assets Put into Use (%)
1978	22406		66.8
1979	22494		70.0
1980	27949		80.5
1981	38060		79.8
1982	48498		83.2
1983	44947		71.2
1984	73165		74.5
1985	114797		75.0
1986	130697		81.7
1987	146045		91.5
1988	143292		71.1
1989	203489		70.6
1990	296653	22953	83.4
1991	355971	52632	78.0
1992	558056	132255	64.1
1993	699207	77023	37.1
1994	1490207	192254	67.7
1995	1347016	119457	68.0
1996	1572488	149719	84.6
1997	1272129	83190	92.2
1998	1222709	30471	66.7
1999	1471814	45470	77.4
2000	1417062	72792	73.3
2001	1465555	111757	71.0
2002	1633425	108510	73.3
2003	1826577	213079	66.1
2004	2137048	215998	65.7
2005	1738236	368676	45.8
2006	2194602	224680	51.5

4－5 主要年份国有单位固定资产投资资金来源构成

Investment in Fixed Assets of State-owned Units by Source of Funds in Major Year

单位：万元 (10 000 yuan)

年 份 Year	固定资产投资总额 Investment in Fixed Assets	国家投资 State Budgetary Appropriation	国内贷款 Domestic Loans	债券 Bond	利用外资 Foreign Investment	自筹投资 Fundraising	其他投资 Others
1990	304969	32823	60263		42085	127903	41895
1991	405693	34716	135623		26385	143164	65805
1992	788916	37436	231553		100491	347672	71764
1993	1752926	47009	402608	67555	196112	657059	382583
1994	2031306	46534	516303	5648	268714	935758	258349
1995	1778995	35535	328925	93765	553754	503177	263839
1996	1680248	44537	277441	31000	473535	677481	176254
1997	1448067	41940	248793	22953	323791	683769	126821
1998	1546078	113828	271920	14615	323303	710274	112138
1999	1258866	114111	309864	34266	217405	459939	123281
2000	1322314	116745	225320	25849	258471	568427	127502
2001	1385695	120106	133304	14202	186240	746435	185408
2002	1573017	113257	224941	23595	243818	800666	166740
2003	1935713	118078	292293	7743	284550	886557	346492
2004	2582229	173599	817768	19358	200505	1166442	204557
2005	1644549	106895	484062	2117	100635	501175	449665
2006	1641825	113803	340090	1058	238049	540921	407904
按时期分（亿元）							
"一五时期" The "First Five-year Plan" Period	3.04	3.04					
"二五时期" The "Second Five-year Plan" Period	6.38	6.38					
"三年调整时期" Three Year Adjustment Period	3.23	3.06				0.17	
"三五时期" The "Third Five-year Plan" Period	5.43	4.55				0.88	
"四五时期" The "Fourth Five-year Plan" Period	10.1	7.8				2.3	
"五五时期" The "Fifth Five-year Plan" Period	15.26	10.31			0.02	4.84	0.09
"六五时期" The "Sixth Five-year Plan" Period	33.49	8.93	9.48		1.4	12.47	1.21
"七五时期" The "Seventh Five-year Plan" Period	93.22	13.58	21.32		9.64	39.32	
"八五时期" The "Eighth Five-year Plan" Period	675.78	20.12	161.5	16.7	114.55	258.68	104.23
"九五时期" The "Ninth Five-year Plan" Period	725.56	43.12	133.33	12.87	159.65	309.99	66.6
"十五时期" The "Tenth Five-year Plan" Period	912.12	63.19	195.24	6.70	101.57	410.13	135.29

4－6 按国民经济行业分的固定资产投资额
Investment in Fixed Assets by Sector

单位:万元 (10 000 yuan)

行 业	Sector	总 计 Total	城镇投资 urban investment	房地产 Real Estate Development	农村非农户 rural non-farmers
总 计	**Total**	4051036	3970009	892554	81027
农、林、牧、渔业	**Farming, Forestry, Animal Husbandry and Fishery**	173686	145985		27701
农 业	Farming	27396	17809		9587
林 业	Forestry	91159	88800		2359
畜牧业	Animal Husbandry	3349	2949		400
渔 业	Fishery	30992	18321		12671
农、林、牧、渔服务业	Agricultural Services	20790	18106		2684
采矿业	**Mining and Quarrying**	32092	32042		50
煤炭开采和洗选业	Coal Mining and Dressing				
石油和天然气开采业	Mining of Oil and Natural Gas	7542	7542		
黑色金属矿采选业	Mining and Dressing of Ferrous Metals	14102	14102		
有色金属矿采选业	Mining and Dressing of Nonferrous Metals	6140	6140		
非金属矿采选业	Mining and Dressing of Nonmetal Minerals	4258	4258		
其他采矿业	Others	50			50
制造业	**Manufacturing**	828703	826568		2135
农副食品加工业	Agriculture and Non-Staple Food Processing	28543	27643		900
食品制造业	Food Production	606	506		
饮料制造业	Beverages	977	977		
烟草制品业	Tobacco				
纺织业	Textiles	307	307		
纺织服装、鞋、帽制造业	Garments,Shoses and Hats				
皮革、毛皮、羽毛(绒)及其制品业	Leather, Furs, Down and Related Products				
木材加工及木、竹、藤、棕、草制品业	Timber Processing, Bamboo, Cane, Palm Fiber and Straw Products	7585	7585		
家具制造业	Furniture Manufacturing	1808	1808		
造纸及纸制品业	Papermaking and Paper Products	73975	73975		
印刷业和记录媒介的复制	Printing and Record Medium Reproduction	589	589		
文教体育用品制造业	Cultural, Educational and Sports Goods				
石油加工、炼焦及核燃料加工业	Petroleum Processing, Coking and Nucleus Fuel Processing	383294	383294		
化学原料及化学制品制造业	Raw Chemical Materials and Chemical Products	125839	125839		
医药制造业	Medical and Pharmaceutical Products	19832	19832		
化学纤维制造业	Chemical Fiber		145		
橡胶制品业	Rubber Products	2647	2647		
塑料制品业	Plastic Products				
非金属矿物制品业	Nonmetal Mineral Products	52693	51543		1150
黑色金属冶炼及压延加工业	Smelting and Pressing of Ferrous Metals	28000	28000		
有色金属冶炼及压延加工业	Smelting and Pressing of Nonferrous Metals	4513	4513		
金属制品业	Metal Products	3727	3727		
通用设备制造业	Ordinary Machinery	340	340		
专用设备制造业	Equipment for Special Purposes	3600	3600		

4-6 续 1(continued1)

行 业	Sector	总 计 Total	城镇投资 urban investment	房地产 Real Estate Development	农村非农户 rural non-farmers
交通运输设备制造业	Transport Equipment	77236	77236		
电气机械及器材制造业	Electric Equipment and Machinery	6604	6604		
通信设备、计算机及其他电子设备制造业	Telecommunications Equipment, Computer and Other Electronic Equipment	4855	4770		85
仪器仪表及文化、办公用机械制造业	Instruments, Meters, Cultural and Office Machinery				
工艺品及其他制造业	Handicraft Article and Other Manufacturing	1133	1133		
废弃资源和废旧材料回收加工业	Recovery and Processing of Discarded Resoures and Waste Materials				
电力、燃气及水的生产和供应业	**Production and Supply of Electric Power, Gas and Water**	**218684**	**216884**		**1800**
电力、热力的生产和供应业	Production and Supply of Electric Power, Steam and Hot Water	185767	185767		270
燃气生产和供应业	Production and Supply of Gas	5421	5421		
水的生产和供应业	Production and Supply of Tap Water	27496	27496		1530
建筑业	**Construction**	**12544**	**12303**		**241**
房屋和土木工程建筑业	House and Civil Engineering	10404	10163		241
建筑安装业	Installation	1200	1200		
建筑装饰业	Decoration				
其他建筑业	Others	940	940		
交通运输、仓储和邮政业	**Transport, Storage, Postal Services**	**744951**	**725557**		**19394**
铁路运输业	Railway Transport	27300	27300		
道路运输业	Way Transport	228749	209603		19146
城市公共交通业	Public Traffic in City	705	705		
水上运输业	Waterway Transport	80527	80527		
航空运输业	Air Transport	402354	402354		
管道运输业	Pipeline Transport				
装卸搬运和其他运输服务业	Load and Unload Transport and Others Transport	248			248
仓储业	Storage	741	741		
邮政业	Postal	4327	4327		
信息传输、计算机服务和软件业	**Information Transmission,Computer Services and Software**	**151911**	**151911**		
电信和其他信息传输服务业	Telecommunications and Other Information Transmission	151911	151911		
计算机服务业	Computer Services				
软件业	Software				
批发和零售业	**Wholesale & Retail Trade**	**29345**	**28829**		**516**
批发业	Wholesale Trade	11252	11142		110
零售业	Retail Trade	18093	17687		406
住宿和餐饮业	**Hotels and Catering Trade**	**210240**	**206183**		**4057**
住宿业	Hotels	208744	204687		4057
餐饮业	Catering Trade	1496	1496		
金融业	**Finance**	**15759**	**15759**		
银行业	Banking	15696	15696		
证券业	Stock				
保险业	Insurance	9631	9631		
其他金融活动	Other Finance Activities	63	63		

4-6 续 2(continued2)

行 业	Sector	总 计 Total	城镇投资 urban investment	房地产 Real Estate Development	农村非农户 rural non-farmers
房地产业	**Real Estate**	**907089**	**907089**	**892554**	
房地产业	Real Estate	907089	907089	892554	
租赁和商务服务业	**Rent and Business Affair Services**	**16846**	**15346**		**1500**
租赁业	Rent				
商务服务业	Business Affair Services	16846	15346		1500
科学研究、技术服务和地质勘查业	**Scientific Research, Polytechnic Services and Geological Prospecting**	**12907**	**12584**		**323**
研究与试验发展	R&D	10624	10624		
专业技术服务业	Profesional Technology Services	1501	1501		
科技交流和推广服务业	Scientific and Technological Interchange and Popularization Services	782	459		323
地质勘查业	Geological Prospecting				
水利、环境和公共设施管理业	**Water Conservancy, Environmental and Public Installations Management Services**	**243089**	**236737**		**6352**
水利管理业	Water Conservancy Management	77278	72339		4939
环境管理业	Environmental Management	9387	9157		230
公共设施管理业	Public Installations Management Services	156424	155241		1183
居民服务和其他服务业	**Resident Services and Other Social Services**	4607	4263		344
居民服务业	Resident Services	1065	1065		
其他服务业	Other Social Services	3542	3198		344
教育	**Education**	**191129**	**189577**		**1552**
教 育	Education	191129	189577		1552
卫生、社会保障和社会福利业	**Health Care, Social Security and Social Welfare**	**46146**	**46146**		
卫 生	Health Care	46146	46146		
社会保障业	Social Security				
社会福利业	Social Welfare				
文化、体育和娱乐业	**Culture,Sports and Recreational Services**	**82194**	**79591**		**2603**
新闻出版业	News Publishing House				
广播、电视、电影和音像业	Radio, Television, Film and Audiovisual	5918	5918		
文化艺术业	Culture and Arts	7447	6944		503
体 育	Sports	5596	5596		
娱乐业	Recreational Services	63233	61133		2100
公共管理和社会组织	**Public Management and Social Organizations**	**127923**	**115464**		**12459**
中国共产党机关	The Communist Party of China	3847	3847		
国家机构	State Institution	122794	110578		12216
人民政协和民主党派	People' s Political Consultative Conference and Democratic Parties				
群众团体、社会团体和宗教组织	Mass Organization, Social Organizations and Religion Organizations	1039	1039		
基层群众自治组织	Mass Autonomy Organization at the Grass-roots	243			243
国际组织	**International Organization**				
国际组织	International Organization				

4-7 各市县全社会固定资产投资额
Total Investment in Fixed Assets in Major Years by City and County

单位:万元 (10 000 yuan)

市县	City and County	总计 Total	城镇投资 urban investment	房地产 Real Estate Development	农村非农户 rural non-farmers	农村私人 Rural Individuals
总计	**Total**	**4260137**	**3970009**	**892554**	**81027**	**209101**
海口市	HaiKou	1574390	1545787	504730	6900	21703
三亚市	SanYa	686486	668817	296556	2787	14882
五指山市	WuZhiShan	14925	12869	1060	147	1909
文昌市	WenChang	210893	138461	44434	13343	59089
琼海市	QiongHai	100021	82368	30408	5000	12653
万宁市	WanNing	146717	108189		4200	34328
定安县	DingAn	41213	32652			8561
屯昌县	TunChang	22028	18886			3142
澄迈县	ChengMai	207116	199643	804	1475	5998
临高县	LinGao	35189	21953		3747	9489
儋州市	DanZhou	170222	113283		31043	25896
东方市	DongFang	138195	134694		2151	1350
乐东县	LeDong	36751	20856		489	15406
琼中县	QiongZhong	25968	21400		2453	2115
保亭县	BaoTing	17484	15334	2659		2150
陵水县	LingShui	47551	37022		1895	8634
白沙县	BaiSha	22537	18069		1107	3361
昌江县	ChangJiag	81836	74981	610	4290	2565
农垦	NongKen	173267	173267	11293		
洋浦	YangPu	531478	531478			

4-7 续(continued)

市 县	City and County	固定资产投资额 Investment in Fixed Assets	按构成分 Grouped by Use of Funds			按登记注册类型分 Grouped by Type of Register			
			建筑工程 Construction	安装工程 Installation	设备工具购置 Purchase of Equipment and Instruments	内资 Domestic Funded	港澳台 Enterprises with funds Hong Kong, Macao and Taiwan	外商投资 Foreign Funded	其他 Others
总 计	**Total**	**4260137**	**2265655**	**324686**	**1046535**	**3723838**	**262934**	**251872**	**21493**
海口市	HaiKou	1574390	667902	90142	595142	1265036	194574	114665	115
三亚市	SanYa	686486	556274	15355	21706	634338	42423	9725	
五指山市	WuZhiShan	14925	13054	586	553	14416		263	246
文昌市	WenChang	210893	170522	4368	13703	181650	18478	5100	5665
琼海市	QiongHai	100021	83121		2000	100021			
万宁市	WanNing	146717	122757	6850	1396	136865	5503	4049	300
定安县	DingAn	41213	29738	3471	3859	37212	956	1900	1145
屯昌县	TunChang	22028	14775	354	5626	20705			1323
澄迈县	ChengMai	207116	76731	34094	44545	169116		38000	
临高县	LinGao	35189	23549	2409	4243	30768		340	4081
儋州市	DanZhou	170222	112704	36658	17176	164003		1221	4998
东方市	DongFang	138195	77074	14543	38050	138195			
乐东县	LeDong	36751	28682	990	5353	36151			600
琼中县	QiongZhong	25968	18436	6289	957	24968	1000		
保亭县	BaoTing	17484	16122			17484			
陵水县	LingShui	47551	35706	2830	5112	41257		3550	2744
白沙县	BaiSha	22537	21062	200	1275	22261			276
昌江县	ChangJiag	81836	31015	13673	15978	81836			
农 垦	NongKen	173267	107674	5123	16014	173267			
洋 浦	YangPu	531478	82887	86733	253847	458419		73059	

4－8 各市县按行业分的固定资产投资额

Investment in Fixed Assets by Sector by City and County

单位:万元 (10 000 yuan)

市 县	City and County	总 计 Total	农、林、牧、渔业 Farming, Forestry, Animal Husbandry and Fishery	采矿业 Mining and Quarrying	制造业 Manufac-turing	电力、煤气及水的生产和供应业 Production and Supply of Electric Power,Gas and Water	建筑业 Construction	交通运输仓储及邮电通信业 Transport, Storage, Postal Services
总 计	**Total**	**4051036**	**173686**	**32092**	**828703**	**218684**	**12544**	**744951**
海口市	HaiKou	1552687	1608	1679	103103	15739	2186	474806
三亚市	SanYa	671604	16727		10443	14973		72758
五指山市	WuZhiShan	13016	123			1131		4667
文昌市	WenChang	151804	15246	1590	5126	12370	80	28782
琼海市	QiongHai	87368				9850	1500	15510
万宁市	WanNing	112389	1000		4691	1680	300	16647
定安县	DingAn	32652	2062		5648	250	1229	4897
屯昌县	TunChang	18886	2014	315	5275	826	856	1225
澄迈县	ChengMai	201118		6363	44364	111250		6707
临高县	LinGao	25700	5477			1297	472	6445
儋州市	DanZhou	144326	21330	6713	29081	17384	805	21336
东方市	DongFang	136845	2790		91507	1301		14979
乐东县	LeDong	21345		4700		8514	241	1246
琼中县	QiongZhong	23853	375		723	9283		6973
保亭县	BaoTing	15334	625			470	450	2145
陵水县	LingShui	38917	7119	430	390	3334	3945	4997
白沙县	BaiSha	19176	300		2310		80	8090
昌江县	ChangJiag	79271	8480	10302	25833	9032		10245
农 垦	NongKen	173267	88410		7412		400	5315
洋 浦	YangPu	531478			492797			37181

4-8 续 1(continued 1)

市 县	City and County	信息传输、计算机服务和软件业 Information Transmission, Computer Services and Software	批发和零售业 Wholesale & Retail Trade Services	住宿和餐饮业 Hotels and Catering Trade	金 融 Finance	房 地 产 业 Real Estate Trade	租赁和商务服务业 Rent and Business Affair Services	科学研究、技术服务和地质勘查业 Scientific Research, Polytechnic Services and Geological Prospecting
总 计	**Total**	**151911**	**29345**	**210240**	**15759**	**907089**	**16846**	**12907**
海 口 市	HaiKou	136417	6920	11482	13622	506666	129	5838
三 亚 市	SanYa	900	6500	123721	2047	300506		3250
五指山市	WuZhiShan	263	130	846	90	1060		
文 昌 市	WenChang	275	467	4177		44434	11570	277
琼 海 市	QiongHai			27100		30408		
万 宁 市	WanNing		2550	17547				
定 安 县	DingAn	329		1145			93	
屯 昌 县	TunChang	2900		52		200		182
澄 迈 县	ChengMai	1010		10476		2494	1833	
临 高 县	LinGao	340		550				
儋 州 市	DanZhou	7440	5020	5760			1500	2029
东 方 市	DongFang		3600					
乐 东 县	LeDong	300	50				108	822
琼 中 县	QiongZhong	1248					113	323
保 亭 县	BaoTing		200	2550		2659		
陵 水 县	LingShui		1154	2894		1178	1500	
白 沙 县	BaiSha	489	376			720		96
昌 江 县	ChangJiag		1685	1940		610		90
农 垦	NongKen		693			16154		
洋 浦	YangPu							

4-8 续 2(continued 2)

市 县	City and County	水利、环境和公共设施管理业 Water Conservancy, Environmental Protection and Public Installations Management Services	居民服务和其他服务业 Resident Services and Other Social Services	教育 Education	卫生、社会保障和社会福利业 Health Care, Social Security and Social Welfare	文化、体育和娱乐业 Culture, Sports and Recreational Services	公共管理和社会组织 Public Management and Social Organizations	国际组织 International Organization
总 计	**Total**	**243089**	**4607**	**191129**	**46146**	**82194**	**127923**	
海口市	HaiKou	105367		84497	30939	9028	42661	
三亚市	SanYa	72985		20504	4928	15599	5763	
五指山市	WuZhiShan	2247		1165	160		1134	
文昌市	WenChang	847	4357	6625		2397	13184	
琼海市	QiongHai					3000		
万宁市	WanNing	10200		7821		49503	450	
定安县	DingAn	10876		535	86		5502	
屯昌县	TunChang	2102		833			2106	
澄迈县	ChengMai	8292		2023	3637		2669	
临高县	LinGao	371	250	5842	248	1765	2643	
儋州市	DanZhou	6392		3719	370		15447	
东方市	DongFang	9792			500		12376	
乐东县	LeDong	560		3957		156	691	
琼中县	QiongZhong						4815	
保亭县	BaoTing	2775		1556		412	1483	
陵水县	LingShui	3913		771	713	214	6365	
白沙县	BaiSha	3870		2429			416	
昌江县	ChangJiag	2500		1004			7550	
农 垦	NongKen			47839	4565	120	1168	
洋 浦	YangPu						1500	

4－9 按构成分的各市县固定资产投资及交付使用率

Investment in Fixed Assets and Rate of Fixed Assets Put into Use by Use of Funds by City andCounty

单位:万元 (10 000 yuan)

市县	City and County	合计 Total	按构成分 Grouped by Use of Funds 建筑工程 Construction	安装工程 Installation	设备工器具购置 Purchase of Equipment and Instruments	其他费用 Others	新增固定资产 Newly Increased Fixed Assets	固定资产交付使用率(%) Rate of Fixed Assets Put into Use(%)
总计	**Total**	**4260137**	**2265655**	**324686**	**1046535**	**623261**	**2194602**	**51.5**
海口市	HaiKou	1574390	667902	90142	595142	221204	914672	58.1
三亚市	SanYa	686486	556274	15355	21706	93151	355383	51.8
五指山市	WuZhiShan	14925	13054	586	553	732	12440	83.4
文昌市	WenChang	210893	170522	4368	13703	22282	133654	63.4
琼海市	QiongHai	100021	83121		2000	14900	38653	38.6
万宁市	WanNing	146717	122757	6850	1396	15714	35799	24.4
定安县	DingAn	41213	29738	3471	3859	4145	38141	92.5
屯昌县	TunChang	22028	14775	354	5626	1273	25537	115.9
澄迈县	ChengMai	207116	76731	34094	44545	51746	152609	73.7
临高县	LinGao	35189	23549	2409	4243	4988	29870	84.9
儋州市	DanZhou	170222	112704	36658	17176	3684	98186	57.7
东方市	DongFang	138195	77074	14543	38050	8528	1350	1.0
乐东县	LeDong	36751	28682	990	5353	1726	15795	43.0
琼中县	QiongZhong	25968	18436	6289	957	286	42264	162.8
保亭县	BaoTing	17484	16122			1362	11673	66.8
陵水县	LingShui	47551	35706	2830	5112	3903	26066	54.8
白沙县	BaiSha	22537	21062	200	1275		15047	66.8
昌江县	ChangJiag	81836	31015	13673	15978	21170	79002	96.5
农垦	NongKen	173267	107674	5123	16014	44456	173942	100.4
洋浦	YangPu	531478	82887	86733	253847	108011	18649	3.5

4－10 各市县固定资产财务拨款及新增固定资产
Investment in Fixed Assets by sector by City and County

单位:万元 (10 000 yuan)

市 县	City and County	财务拨款额 Financial Appropriation	国家预算内资金 State Budgetary Appropriation	国内贷款 Domestic Loans	债券 Bond	利用外资 Foreign Investment	自筹资金 Fundraising	其他投资 Others
总 计	**Total**	**4871239**	**323156**	**965721**	**3004**	**675965**	**1745106**	**1158287**
海口市	HaiKou	1939770	28653	235021		626030	509511	540555
三亚市	SanYa	805493	90977	62382		3425	465040	183669
五指山市	WuZhiShan	16314	5592	2296		48	4318	4060
文昌市	WenChang	214070	17678	5172	537	24970	115546	50167
琼海市	QiongHai	100021	16690	1400			81931	
万宁市	WanNing	148830	32357	38773		11884	59774	6042
定安县	DingAn	60095	9213	22190		1775	19010	7907
屯昌县	TunChang	22028	7555	322			13464	687
澄迈县	ChengMai	269974	4217	108605		1941	103649	51562
临高县	LinGao	38492	7325	3640		2579	16461	8487
儋州市	DanZhou	170222	14132	25666			126395	4029
东方市	DongFang	138195	17383	82243			25061	13508
乐东县	LeDong	36751	6256	1228			26900	2367
琼中县	QiongZhong	25968	11300			41	10121	4506
保亭县	BaoTing	18723	7584	900	400		9289	550
陵水县	LingShui	50161	14507	905	2067		28173	4509
白沙县	BaiSha	22537	11123	700		589	8474	1651
昌江县	ChangJiag	82240	7972	2400		30	69194	2644
农 垦	NongKen	183267	10842	6441		2653	50504	112827
洋 浦	YangPu	552218	1800	365437			26421	158560

4-10 续(continued)

市 县	City and County	新增固定资产 Newly Increased Fixed Assets	城镇投资 urban investment	房地产开发 Real Estate Development	农村非农户 rural non-farmers	农村私人 Rural Individuals
总 计	Total	2194602	1934553	224680	50948	209101
海口市	HaiKou	914672	886611	155825	6358	21703
三亚市	SanYa	355383	337714	40575	2787	14882
五指山市	WuZhiShan	12440	10384		147	1909
文昌市	WenChang	133654	66705	6166	7860	59089
琼海市	QiongHai	38653	21000	4000	5000	12653
万宁市	WanNing	35799	1471			34328
定安县	DingAn	38141	29580			8561
屯昌县	TunChang	25537	22395			3142
澄迈县	ChengMai	152609	146381		230	5998
临高县	LinGao	29870	16516		3865	9489
儋州市	DanZhou	98186	57813		14477	25896
东方市	DongFang	1350				1350
乐东县	LeDong	15795	389			15406
琼中县	QiongZhong	42264	37696		2453	2115
保亭县	BaoTing	11673	9523	1322		2150
陵水县	LingShui	26066	14882		2550	8634
白沙县	BaiSha	15047	10645		1041	3361
昌江县	ChangJiag	79002	72257	1550	4180	2565
农 垦	NongKen	173942	173942	15242		
洋 浦	YangPu	18649	18649			

4－11 各市县按行业分的城镇固定资产投资额
Investment in Fixed Assets by Sector by City and County

单位:万元 (10 000 yuan)

市 县	City and County	总 计 Total	农、林、牧、渔业 Farming, Forestry, Animal Husbandry and Fishery	采矿业 Mining and Quarrying	制造业 Manufac-turing	电力、煤气及水的生产和供应业 Production and Supply of Electric Power,Gas and Water	建筑业 Construction	交通运输仓储及邮电通信业 Transport, Storage, Postal Services
总 计	**Total**	**3970009**	**145985**	**32042**	**826568**	**216884**	**12303**	**725557**
海口市	HaiKou	1545787	125	1679	103103	15739	2186	472653
三亚市	SanYa	668817	16727		10443	14973		72758
五指山市	WuZhiShan	12869	123			1131		4667
文昌市	WenChang	138461	10283	1540	3691	12100	80	28782
琼海市	QiongHai	82368				9850	1500	10510
万宁市	WanNing	108189	1000		4691	1680	300	12447
定安县	DingAn	32652	2062		5648	250	1229	4897
屯昌县	TunChang	18886	2014	315	5275	826	856	1225
澄迈县	ChengMai	199643		6363	44364	111250		6707
临高县	LinGao	21953	2151			1297	472	6445
儋州市	DanZhou	113283	9601	6713	29081	15854	805	13603
东方市	DongFang	134694	1290		91507	1301		14979
乐东县	LeDong	20856		4700		8514		998
琼中县	QiongZhong	21400			723	9283		6973
保亭县	BaoTing	15334	625			470	450	2145
陵水县	LingShui	37022	7084	430	390	3334	3945	4997
白沙县	BaiSha	18069	300		1610		80	8030
昌江县	ChangJiag	74981	4190	10302	25833	9032		10245
农 垦	NongKen	173267	88410		7412		400	5315
洋 浦	YangPu	531478			492797			37181

4-11 续 1(continued 1)

市 县	City and County	信息传输、计算机服务和软件业 Information Transmission, Computer Services and Software	批发和零售业 Wholesale & Retail Trade Services	住宿和餐饮业 Hotels and Catering Trade	金 融 Finance	房 地 产 业 Real Estate Trade	租赁和商务服务业 Rent and Business Affair Services	科学研究、技术服务和地质勘查业 Scientific Research, Polytechnic Services and Geological Prospecting
总 计	**Total**	**151911**	**28829**	**206183**	**15759**	**907089**	**15346**	**12584**
海口市	HaiKou	136417	6810	11482	13622	506666	129	5838
三亚市	SanYa	900	6500	123721	2047	300506		3250
五指山市	WuZhiShan	263	130	846	90	1060		
文昌市	WenChang	275	432	600		44434	11570	277
琼海市	QiongHai			27100		30408		
万宁市	WanNing		2550	17547				
定安县	DingAn	329		1145			93	
屯昌县	TunChang	2900		52		200		182
澄迈县	ChengMai	1010		10476		2494	1833	
临高县	LinGao	340		320				
儋州市	DanZhou	7440	4925	5760			1500	2029
东方市	DongFang		3600					
乐东县	LeDong	300	50				108	822
琼中县	QiongZhong	1248					113	
保亭县	BaoTing		200	2550		2659		
陵水县	LingShui		1154	2644		1178		
白沙县	BaiSha	489	100			720		96
昌江县	ChangJiag		1685	1940		610		90
农 垦	NongKen		693			16154		
洋 浦	YangPu							

4-11 续 2(continued 2)

市 县	City and County	水利、环境和公共设施管理业 Water Conservancy, Environmental Protection and Public Installations Management Services	居民服务和其他服务业 Resident Services and Other Social Services	教育 Education	卫生、社会保障和社会福利业 Health Care,Social Security and Social Welfare	文化、体育和娱乐业 Culture, Sports and Recreational Services	公共管理和社会组织 Public Management and Social Organizations	国际组织 International Organization
总 计	**Total**	**236737**	**4263**	**189577**	**46146**	**79591**	**115464**	
海口市	HaiKou	103003		84319	30939	8525	42552	
三亚市	SanYa	72985		19504	4928	15599	3976	
五指山市	WuZhiShan	2180		1165	160		1054	
文昌市	WenChang	744	4013	6251		297	13092	
琼海市	QiongHai					3000		
万宁市	WanNing	10200		7821		49503	450	
定安县	DingAn	10876		535	86		5502	
屯昌县	TunChang	2102		833			2106	
澄迈县	ChengMai	8062		2023	3637		1424	
临高县	LinGao	371	250	5842	248	1765	2452	
儋州市	DanZhou	2804		3719	370		9079	
东方市	DongFang	9792			500		11725	
乐东县	LeDong	560		3957		156	691	
琼中县	QiongZhong						3060	
保亭县	BaoTing	2775		1565		412	1483	
陵水县	LingShui	3913		771	713	214	6255	
白沙县	BaiSha	3870		2429			345	
昌江县	ChangJiag	2500		1004			7550	
农 垦	NongKen			47839	4565	120	1168	
洋 浦	YangPu						1500	

4－12 各市县城镇投资施工及投产项目个数和新增固定资产
Number of Capital Construction Projects under Construction and Put into Use and Newly Increased Fixed Assets by City and County

市 县	City and County	施工项目(个) Number of Projects Under Construction (Unit)	全部建成投产项目(个) Number of Projects Completed and Put into Use(Unit)	项目建成投产率(%) Rate of Projects Completed and Put into Use(%)	投资额(万元) Investment (10 000 yuan)	新增固定资产(万元) Newly Increased Fixed Assets (10 000 yuan)	固定资产交付使用率(%) Rate of Fixed Assets Put into Use(%)
总 计	Total	1338	617	46.1	3970009	1934553	48.7
海口市	HaiKou	211	54	25.6	1545787	886611	57.4
三亚市	SanYa	86	38	44.2	668817	337714	50.5
五指山市	WuZhiShan	67	42	62.7	12869	10384	80.7
文昌市	WenChang	144	90	62.5	138461	66705	48.2
琼海市	QiongHai	10		0.0	82368	21000	25.5
万宁市	WanNing	58		0.0	108189	1471	1.4
定安县	DingAn	44	30	68.2	32652	29580	90.6
屯昌县	TunChang	48	44	91.7	18886	22395	118.6
澄迈县	ChengMai	145	29	20.0	199643	146381	73.3
临高县	LinGao	24	12	50.0	21953	16516	75.2
儋州市	DanZhou	57	36	63.2	113283	57813	51.0
东方市	DongFang	39		0.0	134694		0.0
乐东县	LeDong	34	2	5.9	20856	389	1.9
琼中县	QiongZhong	18		0.0	21400	37696	176.1
保亭县	BaoTing	31	21	67.7	15334	9523	62.1
陵水县	LingShui	48	3	6.3	37022	14882	40.2
白沙县	BaiSha	26	6	23.1	18069	10645	58.9
昌江县	ChangJiag	54	41	75.9	74981	72257	96.4
农 垦	NongKen	187	169	90.4	173267	173942	100.4
洋 浦	YangPu	7		0.0	531478	18649	3.5

4－13 各市县按构成分的城镇投资额

Investment in Capital Construction by by Use of Funds by City and County

单位:万元 (10 000 yuan)

市县	City and County	城镇投资额 urban investment	按构成分 Grouped by Use of Funds			
			建筑工程 Construction	安装工程 Installation	设备工器具购置 Purchase of Equipment and Instruments	其他费用 Others
总计	Total	3970009	1994028	322803	1042033	611145
海口市	HaiKou	1545787	640724	89935	595092	220036
三亚市	SanYa	668817	538772	15323	21601	93121
五指山市	WuZhiShan	12869	10998	586	553	732
文昌市	WenChang	138461	103798	4213	12681	17769
琼海市	QiongHai	82368	65468		2000	14900
万宁市	WanNing	108189	84229	6850	1396	15714
定安县	DingAn	32652	21177	3471	3859	4145
屯昌县	TunChang	18886	11633	354	5626	1273
澄迈县	ChengMai	199643	69258	34094	44545	51746
临高县	LinGao	21953	13449	1898	1618	4988
儋州市	DanZhou	113283	58790	35998	16926	1569
东方市	DongFang	134694	73573	14543	38050	8528
乐东县	LeDong	20856	12787	990	5353	1726
琼中县	QiongZhong	21400	13918	6289	907	286
保亭县	BaoTing	15334	13972			1362
陵水县	LingShui	37022	25677	2530	4912	3903
白沙县	BaiSha	18069	16794	200	1075	
昌江县	ChangJiag	74981	28450	13673	15978	16880
农垦	NongKen	173267	107674	5123	16014	44456
洋浦	YangPu	531478	82887	86733	253847	108011

4－14 各市县城镇投资财务拨款
Financial Appropriation in Capital Construction by City and County

单位:万元 (10 000 yuan)

市 县	City and County	财务拨款额 Financial Appropriation	国家预算内资金 State Budgetary Appropriation	国内贷款 Domestic Loans	债券 Bond	利用外资 Foreign Investment	自筹资金 Fundraising	其他投资 Others
总 计	**Total**	**4579360**	**307651**	**964426**	**3004**	**675935**	**1486590**	**1141754**
海口市	HaiKou	1911276	28653	235021		626030	481134	540438
三亚市	SanYa	787824	89977	62382		3425	449671	182369
五指山市	WuZhiShan	14258	5520	2296		48	2409	3985
文昌市	WenChang	139938	16261	5172	537	24940	49990	43038
琼海市	QiongHai	82368	11690	1400			69278	
万宁市	WanNing	110302	28157	38773		11884	25446	6042
定安县	DingAn	51534	9213	22190		1775	10449	7907
屯昌县	TunChang	18886	7555	322			10322	687
澄迈县	ChengMai	262501	4217	108605		1941	96293	51445
临高县	LinGao	25256	7260	3640		2579	6781	4996
儋州市	DanZhou	113283	12108	25466			73065	2644
东方市	DongFang	134694	16732	82243			23711	12008
乐东县	LeDong	20856	6015	1228			11246	2367
琼中县	QiongZhong	21400	10465			41	7341	3553
保亭县	BaoTing	16573	7584	900	400		7139	550
陵水县	LingShui	39472	14507	510	2067		18039	4349
白沙县	BaiSha	18069	11123			589	5012	1345
昌江县	ChangJiag	75385	7972	2400		30	62339	2644
农 垦	NongKen	183267	10842	6441		2653	50504	112827
洋 浦	YangPu	552218	1800	365437			26421	158560

4－15 房地产开发投资和新增固定资产
Investment in Real Estate Development and Newly Increased Fixed Assets

指　标	Item	2004	2005	2006
本年完成投资额(万元)	Investment Completed This Year	559917	708494	892554
按资金来源分	Grouped by Source of Funds			
国家投资	State Budgetary Appropriation	1397		
国内贷款	Domestic Loans	53380	56398	98214
债券	Bond			
利用外资	Foreign Investment	8096	10194	220142
自筹投资	Fundraising	284081	234169	351038
其他投资	Others	212963	407733	630397
按构成分	Grouped by Use of Funds			
建安工程	Construction and Installation	423043	551437	664062
设备工具器具购置	Purchase of Equipment and Instruments	12251	16386	9782
其 他	Others	124623	140671	218710
新增固定资产(万元)	Newly Increased Fixed Assets (10 000 yuan)	215998	368676	224680
房屋建筑面积(万平方米)	Floor Space of Buildings (10000 sq.m)			
施工面积	Floor Space under Construction	684	921.1	995.2
竣工面积	Floor Space Completed	105.3	187.1	125.9
#住 宅	Residential Buildings	100.1	172.1	93.8
商品房销售额(万元)	Sales of Commercial Houses (10 000 yuan)	302438	729458	770477
商品房销售面积(万平方米)	Floor Space of Selling House (10 000 sq.m)	125.8	249.4	203.4

4－16 按各种经济类型分的房地产开发投资及新增固定资产
Investment in Real Estate Development and Newly Increased Fixed Assets

指　标	Item	房地产开发投资 Investment in Real Estate Development	国有经济 State-owned Units	集体经济 Collective-owned Units	其他经济 Others
本年完成投资额(万元)	**Investment Completed This Year**	**892554**	**86924**	**70753**	**734877**
商品房建设投资	Construction of Commercial house	679426	82262	68832	528332
土地开发投资	Land Development	191055	3519	162	187374
按构成分	Grouped by Use of Funds				
建筑工程	Construction	626835	60879	66384	499572
安装工程	Installation	37227	5135	2475	29617
设备工器具购买	Purchase of Equipment and Instruments	9782	800	860	8122
其他费用	Others	218710	20110	1034	197566
土地购置费	Land Purchased	165325	10167		155158
按工程用途分	Grouped by Purpose				0
住宅	Residential Buildings	632158	71597	63334	497227
90平方米以下住房	common housing	228995	37955	14927	176113
经济适用房	Economical Houses	52848	6184		46664
别墅、高档公寓	Villas and Good Apartments	220182	20850	27941	171391
办公楼	Office Buildings	10135	360	1017	8758
商业营业用房	Houses for Business Use	76618	5218	6077	65323
其他	Others	173643	9749	325	163569
本年新增固定资产(万元)	Newly Increased Fixed Assets This Year(10 000 yuan)	224680	29849	30472	164359
本年完成开发土地面积(万平方米)	Area of Land Developed This Year (10 000 sq.m)	100.27	16.27		84.00
待开发土地面积(万平方米)	Area of Lanaiting for Development (10 000 sq.m)	185.04	91.3		93.78
本年购置土地面积(万平方米)	Area of Land Purchased This Year (10 000 sq.m)	408.41	100.7		307.67

4－17 房地产开发房屋建筑面积及造价

Floor Space of Buildings and their Cost in Real Estate Development

年份 市县	Year City and County	施工房屋面积(万平方米) Floor Space under Construction (10 000 sq.m)	竣工房屋面积(万平方米) Floor Space Completed (10 000 sq.m)	竣工率(%) Rate of Floor Completed (%)	竣工房屋价值(万元) Value of Building Completed (10 000 yuan)	竣工房屋造价(元/平方米) Cost of Building Completed (10 000 sq.m)
1990		86.7	29.0	33.5		
1991		187.8	50.1	26.7		
1992		503.9	106.1	21.1		
1993		745.6	68.7	9.2		
1994		826.8	78.7	9.5		
1995		696.2	68.7	9.9	92334	1349
1996		313.1	58.1	18.6	119275	2051
1997		164.5	42.9	26.1	70941	1654
1998		147.6	24.9	16.9	28756	1154
1999		123.1	28.6	23.2	40494	1416
2000		138.7	36.0	26.0	54601	1517
2001		264.9	62.5	23.6	97709	1563
2002		272.8	54.4	19.9	98893	1818
2003		459.1	115.0	25.0	192314	1672
2004		683.9	105.3	15.4	201173	1910
2005		921.1	187.1	20.3	345378	1846
2006		995.2	125.9	12.7	187806	1491
海口市	Haikou	710.9	80.2	11.3	126964	1583
三亚市	SanYa	212.3	20.7	9.8	36736	1775
五指山市	wuzhishan	4.4				
文昌市	WenChang	15.5	2.8	18.1	5992	2140
琼海市	QiongHai	21.1				
澄迈县	ChengMai	1.4				
儋州市	Danzhou					
保亭县	BaoTing	2.3	2.0	87.0	1322	661
昌江县	ChangJiag	2.6	1.5	57.7	1550	1033
农垦	Nongken	24.7	18.8	76.1	15242	811

4-17 续(continued)

指标	Item	施工面积(万平方米) Floor Space under Construction (10 000 sq.m)	新开工 Projects Newly Started This Year	竣工房屋 Building Completed 面积(万平米) Floor Space (10 000 sq.m)	竣工房屋 Building Completed 价值(万元) Value (10 000 yuan)	房屋实际销售(万平方米) actual selling areas of housing (10000 sq.m)	房屋预售面积(万平方米) advance selling areas of housing (10000 sq.m)	空置面积(万平方米) Empty Space of Commercial Houses (10 000 sq.m)
合计	Total	995.2	294.9	125.9	187806	65.1	138.3	68.8
住宅	Residential Buildings	826.8	263.1	93.8	131288	62.1	131.6	40.5
别墅.高档公寓	Villas and Good Apartments	220.8	69.1	6.2	473	3.4	33.1	1.8
经济适用房	Economical Houses	57.1	24.2	20.7	14020	3.7	3.5	2.7
办公楼	Office Buildings	22.3	6.4	2.0	3782	0.3	0.6	1.7
商业营业用房	Houses for Business Use	111.8	18.2	25.3	45646	2.4	6.1	21.6
其他	Others	34.3	7.2	4.7	7090	0.3	0.1	5.0

4－18 房地产开发经济效益
Economic Returns of Real Estate Development

单位:万元 (10 000 yuan)

指　标	Item	2003	2005	2006
资本金合计	Total Capital	484964	815064	932358
年末资产负债情况	Liabilities to Assets at The Year-end			
资产总计	Total Assets	1702798	3511069	5366981
固定资产累计折旧	Accumulative Depreciation of Fixed Assets	34023	67317	80656
# 本年折旧	Depreciation of This Year	3780	9285	14186
负债总计	TotalLiabilities	1347173	3240784	3970588
所有者权益	Creditors Equity	355625	270285	1396393
损益情况	Profit and Loss			
经营收入总计	Total Revenue	230178	440257	700268
土地转让收入	Land Transferred	10530	23820	64236
商品房屋销售收入	Commercial Houses Sold	181920	391083	608309
房屋出租收入	Houses Leased	2451	773	392
经营成本	Business Coat	196320	361376	518422
销售费用	Sales expenses	10245	20321	40719
经营税金及附加	Business Tax and Extra Charges	11061	2520	40577
管理费用及财务费用	Management expenses and financial expenses	32396	83569	92319
投资收益及营业外收入	Investment profit and non-business revenue	8357	10827	19009
利润总额	Total Profits	-11898	-43961	22760

4－19 按隶属及经济类型分的房地产开发经济效益

Economic Returns of Real Estate Development by Administrative Relationship and Ownership

单位:万元 (10 000 yuan)

指标	Item	总计 Total	按隶属关系分 by Administrative Relationship		按经济类型分 Grouped by Ownership		
			中央 Central Government	地方 Local	国有 State-owned Units	集体 Collective-owned Units	其他 Others
资本金合计	**Total Capital**	932358	7896	924462	121593	86657	724108
年末资产负债情况	**Liabilities to Assets at The Year-end**						
资产总计	Total Assets	5366981	46442	5320539	811385	613113	3942483
固定资产累计折旧	Accumulative Depreciation of Fixed Assets	80656	2578	78078	21721	15289	43646
#本年折旧	Depreciation of This Year	14186	102	14084	2362	2075	9749
负债总计	TotalLiabilities	3970588	33749	3936839	546760	407194	3016634
所有者权益	Creditors Equity	1396393	12693	1383700	264625	205919	925849
损益情况	Profit and Loss						
经营收入总计	Total Revenue	700268	10325	689943	94095	73760	532413
土地转让收入	Land Transferred	64236	2400	61836	4823		59413
商品房屋销售收入	Commercial Houses Sold	608309	7383	600926	83175	62477	462657
房屋出租收入	Houses Leased	392	2	390	240	2	150
经营成本	Business Coat	518422	6226	512196	76700	52706	389016
销售费用	Sales expenses	40719	673	40046	2954	2032	35733
经营税金及附加	Business Tax and Extra Charges	40577	541	40036	5453	3483	31641
管理费用及财务费用	Management expenses and financial expenses	92319	1610	90709	9237	11848	71234
投资收益及营业外收入	Investment profit and non-business revenue	19009	23	18986	11849	156	7004
营业外支出	Expenditure Non-business	6884	29	6855	160	179	6545
利润总额	Total Profits	22760	1398	21362	11953	4046	6761

4－20 按构成分的各市县房地产开发投资额

Investment in Real Estate Development by Use of Funds by City and County

单位:万元 (10 000 yuan)

市 县	City and County	投资额 Investment in Real Estate Development	按构成分 Grouped by Use of Funds: 建筑工程 Construction	安装工程 Installation	设备工具购置 Purchase of Equipment and Instruments	其他费用 Others
总 计	**Total**	**892554**	**626835**	**37227**	**9782**	**218710**
海口市	HaiKou	504730	305267	29106	6520	163837
三亚市	SanYa	296556	245796	6127	2820	41813
五指山市	Wuzhishan	1060	739			321
文昌市	WenChang	44434	36495	1969	442	5528
琼海市	QiongHai	30408	25408			5000
澄迈县	ChengMai	804	804			
保亭县	BaoTing	2659	1930			729
昌江县	ChangJiag	610	560	25		25
农 垦	NongKen	11293	9836			1457

4－21 各市县房地产开发投资财务拨款

Financial Appropriation in Real Estate Development by City and County

单位:万元 (10 000 yuan)

市 县	City and County	拨款合计 Financial Appropriation	国家预算内资金 State Budgetary Appropriation	国内贷款 Domestic Loans	债券 Bond	利用外资 Foreign Investment	自筹资金 Fundraising	其他投资 Others
总 计	**Total**	**1034969**		**82386**		**14892**	**342075**	**595616**
海口市	HaiKou	850513		69650		196248	137203	447412
三亚市	SanYa	356248		28564		2500	159480	165704
五指山市	Wuzhishan	1100					542	558
文昌市	WenChang	44452				21394	18550	4508
琼海市	QiongHai	30408					30408	
澄迈县	ChengMai	804					636	168
保亭县	BaoTing	3959					3609	350
昌江县	ChangJiag	1014					610	404
农 垦	NongKen	11293						11293

4－22 各市县农村非农户投资额

Investment of Rural Collective-ownerd Units by City and County

单位:万元 (10 000 yuan)

市 县	City and County	施工项目个数 Number of Projects Under Construction	投资额 Investment of Rural Collective-ownerd Units	按行业分 Grouped by Sector					
				建筑工程 Construction	农林牧渔业 Farming, Forestry, Animal Husbandry and Fishery	工业 Industry	交通运输业 Transport, Storage, Postal and Telecommunication Services	贸易餐饮业 Wholesale & Retail Trade and Catering Services	文教卫生社会福利业 Health Care, Sports and Social Welfare
总　计	**Total**	**155**	**81027**	**62526**	**27701**	**3985**	**19394**	**516**	**4155**
海口市	HaiKou	37	6900	5475	1483	439	2153	110	681
三亚市	SanYa	3	2787	2620					1000
五指山市	WuZhiShan	2	147	147					
文昌市	WenChang	29	13343	7635	4963	1755		35	2474
琼海市	QiongHai	1	5000	5000			5000		
万宁市	WanNing	1	4200	4200			4200		
定安县	DingAn								
屯昌县	TunChang								
澄迈县	ChengMai	3	1475	1475					
临高县	LinGao	6	3747	611	3326				
儋州市	DanZhou	49	31043	28018	11729	1530	7733	95	
东方市	DongFang	2	2151	2151	1500				
乐东县	LeDong	2	489	489			248		
琼中县	QiongZhong	7	2453	2403	375				
保亭县	BaoTing								
陵水县	LingShui	2	1895	1395	35			250	
白沙县	BaiSha	5	1107	907		700	60	276	
昌江县	ChangJiag	6	4290		4290				
农　垦	NongKen								
洋　浦	YangPu								

4-22 续 (continued)

市 县 City and County	投资额按资金来源分 Grouped by Source of Funds				本年新增固定资产 Newly Increased Fixed Assets This Year	施工面积(平方米) Floor Space of under Construction (sq.m)	竣工面积(平方米) Floor Space of Completed (sq.m)	
	国家资金 State Budgetary Appropriation	国内贷款 Domestic Loans	自筹资金 Fundraising	其他 Others				住宅 Residential Buildings
总 计 Total	15177	1268	48370	16212	50948	201467	115654	69602
海口市 HaiKou			6781	119	6358	11350	9670	
三亚市 SanYa	1000		487	1300	3500	43033	43033	
五指山市 WuZhiShan	72			75				
文昌市 WenChang	1257		5736	6350	20318	32864	8130	5490
琼海市 QiongHai	5000				5000			
万宁市 WanNing	4200							
定安县 DingAn								
屯昌县 TunChang								
澄迈县 ChengMai			1358	117	230	13272		
临高县 LinGao	65		191	3491	3865	5860	5860	3240
儋州市 DanZhou	2024	200	27434	1385	8563	7112	7112	4398
东方市 DongFang	651			1500		9823		
乐东县 LeDong	241		248					
琼中县 QiongZhong	835		665	953	2453	2955	2955	
保亭县 BaoTing								
陵水县 LingShui		364	1383	148	2550	8720	6920	4870
白沙县 BaiSha		700	101	306	2572	2700	2700	
昌江县 ChangJiag			4290		4180			
农 垦 NongKen								
洋 浦 YangPu								

4－23 各市县农村私人固定资产投资
Individual Investment in Fixed Assets in Rural Areas by City and County

市县	City and County	投资额(万元) Individual Investment in Fixed Assets (10 000 yuan)	生产性器具购置及其他投资(万元) Purchase of Productive Fixed Assets (10 000 yuan)	全年竣工房屋间数(间) Number of Buildings Completed	竣工房屋建筑面积(平方米) Floor Space of Buildings Completed (sq.m)	住宅 Residential Buildings	竣工房屋价值(万元) Value of Buildings Completed (10 000 yuan)	住宅 Residential Buildings
总计	**Total**	**209101**	**44908**	**56994**	**2397440**	**2096835**	**117548**	**109552**
海口市	HaiKou	21703	2231	3454	274017	271210	13556	12705
三亚市	SanYa	14882	5329	11273	176462	172888	9032	8898
五指山市	WuZhiShan	1909	212	654	43158	43158	1697	1697
文昌市	WenChang	59089	3139	17468	279492	247015	18167	16056
琼海市	QiongHai	12653	6132	1832	180757	180757	12653	12653
万宁市	WanNing	34328	3689	2318	295036	264854	16227	14566
定安县	DingAn	8561	698	1334	118770	110730	4912	4668
屯昌县	TunChang	3142	250	597	51939	48418	2258	2094
澄迈县	ChengMai	5998	1028	1165	102553	92500	3956	3584
临高县	LinGao	9489	3120	3339	131027	118132	5020	4243
儋州市	DanZhou	25896	13421	5560	164460	15930	6578	6361
东方市	DongFang	1350		212	12300	12300	1350	1350
乐东县	LeDong	15406	2838	2402	262410	230858	12123	11423
琼中县	QiongZhong	2115	78	643	51440	51440	1354	1354
保亭县	BaoTing	2150	600	450	4085	4085	1550	1550
陵水县	LingShui	8634	1045	2034	101745	95623	2644	2485
白沙县	BaiSha	3361	604	1102	121308	113000	2757	2235
昌江县	ChangJiag	2565	494	1157	26481	23937	1714	1630
农垦	NongKen							
洋浦	YangPu							

4－24 各市县全社会施工房屋建筑面积
Total Floor Space of Building under Construction by City and County

单位:万平方米 （10 000 sq.m）

市 县	City and County	施工面积 Floor Space of under Construction	城镇投资 urban investment	房地产开发 Real Estate Development	农村非农户 rural non-farmers	农村私人 Rural Individuals
总计	Total	1978.72	1718.83	995.17	20.15	239.74
海口市	HaiKou	983.10	954.56	710.92	1.14	27.40
三亚市	SanYa	355.05	333.74	212.30	3.66	17.65
五指山市	WuZhiShan	18.21	13.78	4.35	0.11	4.32
文昌市	WenChang	86.28	52.76	15.54	5.57	27.95
琼海市	QiongHai	64.03	45.95	21.11		18.08
万宁市	WanNing	44.50	15.00			29.50
定安县	DingAn	25.26	13.38			11.88
屯昌县	TunChang	10.46	5.27			5.19
澄迈县	ChengMai	51.28	39.70	1.38	1.33	10.25
临高县	LinGao	41.10	27.41		0.59	13.10
儋州市	DanZhou	31.72	14.56		0.71	16.45
东方市	DongFang	16.88	14.67		0.98	1.23
乐东县	LeDong	35.20	8.96			26.24
琼中县	QiongZhong	7.04	1.60		0.30	5.14
保亭县	BaoTing	7.94	7.53	2.33		0.41
陵水县	LingShui	19.92	8.88		0.87	10.17
白沙县	BaiSha	15.06	2.54		0.39	12.13
昌江县	ChangJiag	21.89	19.24	2.55		2.65
农垦	NongKen	139.30	139.30	24.69		
洋浦	YangPu					

4-24 续(continued)

市 县	City and County	住宅 Residential Buildings	城镇投资 urban investment	房地产开发 Real Estate Development	农村非农户 rural non-farmers	农村私人 Rural Individuals
总计	HaiKou	1241.71	1023.42	826.80	8.61	209.68
海口市	SanYa	624.68	597.56	555.83		27.12
三亚市	WuZhiShan	236.42	217.08	205.35	2.05	17.29
五指山市	WenChang	15.07	10.64	4.35	0.11	4.32
文昌市	QiongHai	58.60	32.81	13.25	1.09	24.70
琼海市	WanNing	55.49	37.41	21.11		18.08
万宁市	DingAn	31.39	4.90			26.49
定安县	TunChang	14.65	3.58			11.07
屯昌县	ChengMai	6.30	1.46			4.84
澄迈县	LinGao	13.27	3.05	1.38	0.97	9.25
临高县		16.75	4.62		0.32	11.81
儋州市	DanZhou	4.31	2.28		0.44	1.59
东方市	DongFang	9.28	7.75		0.30	1.23
乐东县	LeDong	26.30	3.21			23.09
琼中县	QiongZhong	5.79	0.65			5.14
保亭县	BaoTing	2.82	2.41	1.29		0.41
陵水县	LingShui	16.16	6.11		0.49	9.56
白沙县	BaiSha	12.08	0.78			11.30
昌江县	ChangJiag	11.03	8.64	2.55		2.39
农垦	NongKen	78.47	78.47	21.70		
洋浦	YangPu					

4－25 各市县全社会竣工房屋建筑面积
Total Floor Space of Building Completed by City and County

单位:万平方米 (10 000 sq.m)

市 县	City and County	竣工面积 Floor Space of Completed	城镇投资 urban investment	房地产开发 Real Estate Development	农村非农户 rural non-farmers	农村私人 Rural Individuals
总 计	Total	688.17	436.86	125.92	11.57	239.74
海口市	HaiKou	161.64	133.27	80.22	0.97	27.40
三亚市	SanYa	95.73	74.42	20.66	3.66	17.65
五指山市	WuZhiShan	8.81	4.38		0.11	4.32
文昌市	WenChang	52.89	23.68	2.76	1.26	27.95
琼海市	QiongHai	18.08				18.08
万宁市	WanNing	29.50				29.50
定安县	DingAn	20.05	8.17			11.88
屯昌县	TunChang	10.00	4.81			5.19
澄迈县	ChengMai	15.13	4.88			10.25
临高县	LinGao	38.04	24.35		0.59	13.10
儋州市	DanZhou	33.94	13.50		3.99	16.45
东方市	DongFang	1.23				1.23
乐东县	LeDong	26.67	0.43			26.24
琼中县	QiongZhong	7.04	1.60		0.30	5.14
保亭县	BaoTing	4.33	3.92	2.03		0.41
陵水县	LingShui	13.21	2.35		0.69	10.17
白沙县	BaiSha	12.62	0.49			12.13
昌江县	ChangJiag	13.48	10.83	1.47		2.65
农 垦	NongKen	125.79	125.79	18.77		
洋 浦	YangPu					

4-25 续(continued)

市 县	City and County	住 宅 Residential Buildings	城镇投资 urban investment	房地产开发 Real Estate Development	农村非农户 rural non-farmers	农村私人 Rural Individuals
总 计	Total	420.76	204.12	93.84	6.96	209.68
海口市	HaiKou	97.32	70.20	54.49		27.12
三亚市	SanYa	43.36	24.02	18.36	2.05	17.29
五指山市	WuZhiShan	6.81	2.38		0.11	4.32
文昌市	WenChang	38.99	13.49	0.16	0.80	24.70
琼海市	QiongHai	18.08				18.08
万宁市	WanNing	26.49				26.49
定安县	DingAn	14.63	3.56			11.07
屯昌县	TunChang	6.29	1.45			4.84
澄迈县	ChengMai	9.59	0.34			9.25
临高县	LinGao	16.60	4.47		0.32	11.81
儋州市	DanZhou	7.02	2.23		3.20	1.59
东方市	DongFang	1.23				1.23
乐东县	LeDong	23.35	0.26			23.09
琼中县	QiongZhong	5.79	0.65			5.14
保亭县	BaoTing	1.86	1.45	1.00		0.41
陵水县	LingShui	11.36	1.31		0.49	9.56
白沙县	BaiSha	11.48	0.18			11.30
昌江县	ChangJiag	9.94	7.55	1.47		2.39
农 垦	NongKen	70.60	70.60	16.98		
洋 浦	YangPu					

主要统计指标解释

全社会固定资产投资 固定资产投资是社会固定资产再生产的主要手段。通过建造和购置固定资产的活动,国民经济不断采用先进技术装备,建立新兴部门,进一步调整经济结构和生产力的地区分布,增强经济实力,为改善人民物质文化生活创造物质条件。这对我国的社会主义现代化建设具有重要意义。

固定资产投资额 是以货币表现的建造和购置固定资产活动的工作量,它是反映固定资产投资规模、速度、比例关系和使用方向的综合性指标。全社会固定资产投资按经济类型可分为国有、集体、个体、联营、股份制、外商、港澳台商、其他等。按照管理渠道,全社会固定资产投资总额分为基本建设、更新改造、房地产开发投资和其他固定资产投资四个部分。

城镇固定资产投资 指城镇各种登记注册类型的企业、事业、行政单位及个体户进行的计划总投资50万元及50万元以上的建设项目投资。县城及以上区域内发生的投资,县及县以上各级政府及主管部门直接领导、管理的建设项目和企事业单位的投资均为城镇固定资产投资。

农村固定资产投资 指发生在农村区域范围内的非农户固定资产投资项目完成的投资。不包括县及县以上各级政府及主管部门直接领导、管理的建设项目和企事业单位的投资。

基本建设投资 基本建设指企业、事业、行政单位以扩大生产能力或工程效益为主要目的的新建、扩建工程及有关工作。其综合范围为总投资50万元以上(含50万元,下同)的基本建设项目。具体包括:(1)列入中央和各级地方本年基本建设计划的建设项目,以及虽未列入本年基本建设计划,但使用以前年度基建计划内结转投资(包括利用基建库存设备材料)在本年继续施工的建设项目;(2)本年基本建设计划内投资与更新改造计划内投资结合安排的新建项目和新增生产能力(或工程效益)达到大中型项目标准的扩建项目,以及为改变生产力布局而进行的全厂性迁建项目;(3)国有单位既未列入基建计划,也未列入更新改造计划的总投资在50万元以上的新建、扩建、恢复项目和为改变生产力布局而进行的全厂性迁建项目,以及行政、事业单位增建业务用房和行政单位增建生活福利设施的项目。

更新改造投资 更新改造指企业、事业单位对原有设施进行固定资产更新和技术改造,以及相应配套的工程和有关工作(不包括大修理和维护工程)。其综合范围为总投资50万元以上的更新改造项目。具体包括:(1)列入中央和各级地方本年更新改造计划的投资单位(项目)和虽未列入本年更新改造计划,但使用上年更新改造计划内结转的投资在本年继续施工的项目;(2)本年更新改造计划内投资与基本建设计划内投资结合安排的对企、事业单位原有设施进行技术改造或更新的项目和增建主要生产车间、分厂等其新增生产能力(或工程效益)未达到大中型项目标准的项目,以及由于城市环境保护和安全生产的需要而进行的迁建工程;(3)国有企、事业单位既未列入基建计划也未列入更新改造计划,总投资在50万元以上的属于改建或更新改造性质的项目,以及由于城市环境保护和安全生产的需要而进行的迁建工程。

房地产开发投资 指房地产开发公司、商品房建设公司及其他房地产开发法人单位和附属于其他法人单位实际从事房地产开发或经营的活动单位统一开发的包括统代建、拆迁还建的住宅、厂房、仓库、饭店、宾馆、度假村、写字楼、办公楼等房屋建筑物和配套的服务设施,土地开发工程(如道路、给水、排水、供电、供热、通讯、平整场地等基础设施工程)的投资;不包括单纯的土地交易活动。

其他固定资产投资 指全社会固定资产投资中未列入基本建设、更新改造和房地产开发投资的建造和购置固定资产的活动。具体包括:

(1)国有单位按规定不纳入基本建设计划和更新改造计划管理,计划总投资(或实际需要总投资)在50万元以上的以下工程:①用油田维护费和石油开发基金进行的油田维护和开发工程;②煤炭、铁矿、森工等采掘采伐业用维简费进行的开拓延伸工程;③交通部门用公路养路费对原有公路、桥梁进行改建的工程;④商业部门用简易建筑费建造的仓库工程。

(2)城镇集体固定资产投资:指所有隶属城市、县城和经国务院及省、自治区、直辖市批准建制的镇领导的集体单位(乡镇企业局管理的除外)建造和购置固定资产计划总投资(或实际需要总投资)在50万元以上的项目。

(3)除上述以外的其他各种企、事业单位、个体建造和购置固定资产总投资在50万元以上的、未列入基本建设计划和更新改造计划的项目。

固定资产投资的资金来源 根据固定资产投资的资金来源不同,分为国家预算内资金、国内贷款、利用外资、自筹资金和其他资金来源。

(1)国家预算内资金:指中央财政和地方财政中由国家统筹安排的基本建设拨款和更新改造拨款,以及中央财政安排的专项拨款中用于基本建设的资金和基本建设拨款改贷款的资金等。

(2)国内贷款:指报告期内企、事业单位向银行及非银行金融机构借入的用于固定资产投资的各种国内借款。包括银行利用自有资金及吸收的存款发放的贷款、上级主管部门拨入的国内贷款、国家专项贷款(包括煤代油贷款、劳改煤矿专项贷款等)、地方财政专项资金安排的贷款、国内储备贷款、周转贷款等。

(3)利用外资:指报告期内收到的用于固定资产投资的国外资金,包括统借统还、自借自还的国外贷款,中外合资项目中的外资,以及对外发行债券和股票等。国家统借统还的外资指由我国政府出面同外国政府、团体或金融组织签订贷款协议、并负责偿还本息的国外贷款。

（4）自筹资金：指建设单位报告期内收到的，用于进行固定资产投资的上级主管部门、地方和企、事业单位自筹资金。

（5）其他资金来源：指报告期内收到的除以上各种拨款、借款、自筹资金以外其他用于固定资产投资的资金。

固定资产投资按国民经济行业分 建设项目归哪个行业，按其建成投产后的主要产品或主要用途及社会经济活动性质来确定。基本建设按建设项目划分国民经济行业，更新改造、国有单位其他固定资产投资及城镇集体投资根据整个企业、事业单位所属的行业来划分。一般情况下，一个建设项目或一个企业、事业单位只能属于一种国民经济行业。为了更准确地反映国民经济各行业之间的比例关系，联合企业（总厂）所属分厂属于不同行业的，原则上按分厂划分行业。

固定资产投资按建设性质分 建设项目的性质一般分为新建、扩建、改建、迁建、恢复。基本建设按建设项目划分建设性质，更新改造、国有单位其他固定资产投资及城镇集体投资等按整个企业、事业单位的建设情况确定建设性质，房地产开发单位、农村投资、城镇工矿区私人建房等投资不划分建设性质。

⑴新建：一般是指从无到有、"平地起家"新开始建设的单位。有的单位原有的基础很小，经过建设后其新增加的固定资产价值超过原有固定资产价值(原值)三倍以上的也算新建。

⑵扩建：一般是指为扩大原有产品的生产能力，在厂内或其他地点增建主要生产车间(或主要工程)、独立的生产线或分厂的企业；事业单位和行政单位在原单位增建业务用房(如学校增建教学用房、医院增建门诊部或病床用房、行政机关增建办公楼等)也作为扩建。

⑶改建：一般是指现有企业、事业单位为了技术进步，提高产品质量，增加花色品种，促进产品升级换代，降低消耗和成本，加强资源综合利用和三废治理、劳保安全等，采用新技术、新工艺、新设备、新材料等对现有设施、工艺条件进行技术改造或更新(包括相应配套的辅助性生产、生活福利设施)。有的企业为充分发挥现有生产能力，进行填平补齐而增建不增加本单位主要产品生产能力的车间等，也属于改建。

固定资产投资按构成分 固定资产投资活动按其工作内容和实现方式分为建筑安装工程，设备、工具、器具购置，其他费用三个部分。

⑴建筑安装工程(建筑安装工作量)：指各种房屋、建筑物的建造工程和各种设备、装置的安装工程。包括各种房屋建造工程，各种用途设备基础和各种工业窑炉的砌筑工程；为施工而进行的各种准备工作和临时工程以及完工后的清理工作等；铁路、道路的铺设，矿井的开凿及石油管道的架设等；水利工程；防空地下建筑等特殊工程；以及各种机械设备的安装工程；为测定安装工程质量，对设备进行的试运工作。在安装工程中，不包括被安装设备本身的价值。

⑵设备、工具、器具购置：指购置或自制达到固定资产标准的设备、工具、器具的价值，固定资产的标准按财务部门规定。新建单位、扩建单位的新建车间按照设计和计划要求购置或自制的全部设备、工具、器具，不论是否达到固定资产标准均计入"设备、工具、器具购置"中。

⑶其他费用：指在固定资产建造和购置过程中发生的，除建筑安装工程和设备、工具、器具购置以外的各种应摊入固定资产的费用。

施工项目 指报告期内曾进行建筑或安装工程施工活动的建设项目，包括报告期内新开工项目、报告期以前开工跨入报告期继续施工的项目以及报告期施过工并在报告期内全部建成投产或停缓建的项目。

全部建成投产项目 工业项目是指设计文件规定形成生产能力的主体工程及其相应配套的辅助设施全部建成，经负荷试运转，证明具备生产设计规定合格产品的条件，并经过验收鉴定合格或达到竣工验收标准，与生产性工程配套的生活福利设施可以满足近期正常生产的需要，正式移交生产的建设项目。非工业项目是指设计文件规定的主体工程和相应的配套工程全部建成，能够发挥设计规定的全部效益，经验收鉴定合格或达到竣工验收标准，正式移交使用的建设项目。

新增生产能力 指通过固定资产投资活动而增加的设计能力或工程效益，它是用实物形态表示的固定资产投资的成果。新增生产能力的计算，是以能独立发挥生产能力或工程效益的单项工程(或项目)为对象。当单项工程(或项目)建成，经有关部门鉴定合格，正式移交投入生产，即可计算新增生产能力。

新增生产能力或工程效益有以下几种表现形式：

⑴以建设项目或单项工程建成后的年产能力表示，如煤炭开采、石油开采等。

⑵以建设项目或单项工程建成后处理原料的能力表示，如选矿工程的年处理矿石能力、洗煤厂年洗原煤能力等。

⑶以新增的主要设备数量或容量表示，如棉纺锭锭数、发电机组容量等。

⑷以建筑物容积、容量、面积或长度表示，如水库容量、铁路公路里程等。

新增生产能力的数量一般按设计能力计算。设计能力是指设计文件中规定的在正常情况下能够达到的生产能力，而不论投产后的实际产量如何。以设备数量、建筑物容积、面积、长度等表示的新增生产能力或工程效益，则按建成的实际数量计算。

新增固定资产 指通过投资活动所形成的新的固定资产价值，包括已经建成投入生产或交付使用的工程价值和达到固定资产标准的设备、工具、器具的价值及有关应摊入的费用。它是以价值形式表示的固定资产投资成果的综合性指标，可以综合反映不同时期、不同部门、不同地区的固定资产投资成果。

固定资产交付使用率 指一定时期新增固定资产与同期完成投资额的比率。它是反映各个时期固定资产动用速度，衡量建设过程中投资效果的一个综合性指标。

施工面积 指报告期内施工的全部房屋建筑面积。包括本期新开工的面积、上期跨入本期继续施工的房屋面积、上期停缓建在本期恢复施工的房屋面积、本期竣工的房屋面积及本期施工后又停缓建的房屋面积。

竣工面积 指在报告期内房屋建筑按照设计要求已全部完工，达到住人和使用条件，经验收鉴定合格，正式移交使用单位的建筑面积。

Explanatory Note on Main Statistical Indicators

Total Investment in Fixed Assets in the Whole Country Total investment in fixed assets refers to the volume of activities in construction and purchases of fixed assets in monetary terms. It is a comprehensive indicator which shows the size, pace, proportional relations and use orientation of the investment in fixed assets. Total investment in fixed assets in the whole country includes, by registration type of ownership, the investment by the state-owned units, collective units, individuals, joint ownership units, share-holding units, as well as investment by businessmen from foreign countries and from Hong Kong, Macau and Taiwan, and by other units. According to China's current management system, the investment in fixed assets in the whole country is classified into the following four parts: investment in capital construction, investment in innovation, investment in real estates development and other investment in fixed assets.

Investment in Capital Construction Capital construction refers to the new construction projects or extension projects and the related activities of the enterprises, institutions or administrative units mainly for the purpose of expanding production capacity or improving project efficiency covering only projects each with a total investment of 500,000 RMB yuan and over. It includes: (1) projects listed in the capital construction plan of the current year of the central government and the local governments at various levels as well as the projects, though not listed in the capital construction plan of the current year, but continued to be constructed in this year, using the investment listed in the plan of capital construction of previous years and carried forward to this year (also using the equipment and materials kept in stock of the capital construction); (2) new construction projects arranged both in the plan of capital construction and the plan of innovation; extension projects with the newly increased production capacity (or project efficiency) up to the standard of a large and medium-sized project; and the projects of moving the whole factory to a new site so as to improve the distribution of productive forces; (3) new construction projects, extension projects or restoration projects with the total investment of 500,000 RMB yuan and over by the state-owned units, though listed neither in the plan of capital construction nor in the plan of innovation; the projects in the state-owned units of moving the whole factory to a new site so as to improve the distribution of productive forces; and the projects of building additional business houses by the administrative units and institutions and building welfare facilities by the administrative units.

Investment in Innovation Innovation refers to the renewal of fixed assets and technological innovation of the original facilities by the enterprises and institutions as well as the corresponding supplementary projects and the related activities (excluding major overhaul and maintenance projects) covering only projects each with a total investment of 500,000 RMB yuan and over. It includes: (1) projects listed in the innovation plan of the current year of the central government and the local governments at various levels as well as the projects, though not listed in the innovation plan of the current year, but continued to be constructed in this year, using the investment listed in the plan of innovation of previous years and carried forward to this year; (2) projects of technological innovation or renewal of the original facilities, arranged both in the plan of innovation and in the plan of capital construction; extension projects (main workshops or a branch of the factory) with the newly increased production capacity (or project efficiency) not up to the standard of a large and medium-sized project; and the projects of moving the whole factory to a new site so as to meet the requirements of urban environmental protection or safe production; (3) projects of reconstruction or technological innovation with the total investment of 500,000 RMB yuan and over by the state-owned units, though listed neither in the plan of capital construction nor in the plan of innovation; the projects in the state-owned units of moving the whole factory to a new site so as to meet the requirements of urban environmental protection or safe production.

Investment in Real Estate Development It includes the investment by the real estate development companies, commercial buildings construction companies and other real estate development units of various types of ownership in the construction of house buildings, such as residential buildings, factory buildings, warehouses, hotels, guesthouses, holiday villages, office buildings, and the complementary service facilities and land development projects, such as roads, water supply, water drainage, power supply, heating, telecommunications, land leveling and other projects of infrastructure. It excludes the activities in simple land transactions.

Other Investment in Fixed Assets refers to the construction and purchases of fixed assets not listed in the investment in capital construction, investment in innovation and investment in real estate development. It includes:

A) The following projects of the state-owned units with the total planned (or actually needed) investment of 500,000 yuan and over, which are not included in the plan of capital construction and the plan of innovation: (1) projects of oil fields maintenance and exploitation with the oil fields maintenance funds and petroleum development funds; (2) opening and extending projects with the maintenance funds in coal, ore and other mining enterprises and logging enterprises; (3) project of reconstruction of the original highways and bridges with the highway maintenance funds in the department of communication; (4) projects of construction of warehouses with the funds of simple construction in the commercial department.

B) The investment in fixed assets by urban collective units: refer to projects of construction and purchases of fixed assets with the planned total investment of 500,000 yuan and over by all collective units in cities and county towns and in townships which are approved by the State Council or provincial governments, excluding investment by collective units under township enterprise administration offices.

C) The projects of construction and purchases of fixed assets by the enterprises, institutions or individuals other than those mentioned above with total investment of 500,000 yuan and over, which are not included in the plan of capital construction and the plan of innovation.

Private Investment in House Construction in Urban Areas, Industrial and Mining Areas and Individual Investment in Rural Areas The private house construction in the urban areas and industrial and mining areas includes all the private house construction under the jurisdiction of cities, counties, towns and industrial and mining areas, no matter whether the owner of the house is registered as the permanent resident in the locality or not. The individual investment in the rural areas includes the investment in house construction and purchase of productive fixed assets by the individuals in the rural areas.

Sources of Funds for Investment in Fixed Assets state budgetary appropriation, domestic loans, foreign investment, self-raised funds, and others.

(1)State budgetary appropriation refers to appropriation in the budget of the central and local governments earmarked for capital construction and for innovation projects, and the special appropriation from the budget of the central government for capital construction and for the transfer fund to banks to be issued as loans for capital construction projects.

(2)Domestic loans refer to various funds borrowed by enterprises and institutions from banks and non-bank financial institutions during the reference period for the purpose of investment in fixed assets, including loans issued by banks from their self-owned funds and deposit, loans appropriated by higher responsible authorities, special loans by government (including loan for replacing petroleum with coal, special loan for reform-through-labour coal mines), loans arranged by local government from special funds, domestic reserve loan, and working loan, etc..

(3) Foreign Investment refers to foreign funds received during the reference period for the purpose of investment in fixed assets, including foreign funds borrowed and managed by the government, by individual units, foreign fund in joint venture program, and issue of bonds and stocks at the international financial markets. The foreign funds borrowed and managed by the government refer to foreign loans borrowed by the government from foreign governments, organizations, or financial institutions under official agreements signed by both parties, under which government is responsible for the repayment of both the principal and interests of the foreign loans.

(4)Self-raised funds refer to funds received by construction enterprises from their higher responsible authorities, local governments, or raised by enterprises or institutions themselves for the purpose of investment in fixed assets during the reference period.

(5) Others refer to funds received during the reference period which are not included in the above-mentioned sources.

Investment in Fixed Assets by Sector The classification of construction projects by sector is determined by the major products or the purpose of the projects when they are put into production or use, and by the nature of their social economic activities. The investment in capital construction is classified by construction projects, while investment in innovation, other investment by state-owned units and urban collective units are classified according to the sector which the whole enterprise or institution belongs to. In general, one project or one enterprise or institution can only belong to one sector. In order to reflect more accurately the proportions among various sectors, the branch factories of integrated complex are classified into different sectors according to their economic activities.

Investment in Fixed Assets by Type of Construction The construction projects in general can be classified by the type of construction into new construction, expansion, reconstruction and moving away. In capital construction, the type of construction is determined by the condition of the project. In investment in innovation, in other investment by state-owned units and investment by collective-owned units, the type of construction is determined by the condition of the whole enterprise or institutions. Investment by type of construction is not applied to investment by real-estate development units, investment in rural areas and investment in housing by urban individuals.

(1)New construction in general refers to newly constructed units. In the case in which the value of the original fixed assets is quite small, and the value of newly added fixed assets exceeds the original ones by three times, the expansion construction is considered as new construction.

(2)Expansion refers to construction of new major production workshop or independent production line within a factory or in other locations, or construction of a branch factory so as to increase the production capacity of the original products. Newly constructed business houses in institutions and administrative organizations (such as the newly constructed teaching buildings in schools, clinics or bed building in hospitals, and office buildings in administrative agencies, etc.) are also classified as expansion.

(3) Reconstruction refers to technical innovation and transformation of the existing equipment and technical conditions undertaken by enterprises and institutions for the purposes of technological advancement, improvement in product quality, enlarging variety of products, promoting new generation of products, reducing production consumption and cost, promoting comprehensive utilization of resources,

strengthening treatment of waste gas, waste water and solid wastes, and safety in production, etc. through application of new technologies and techniques, use of new equipment and new materials (including accessory facilities for production or for living and welfare purposes). Construction of new workshops for improving existing production capacity rather than increasing production capacity is also considered as reconstruction.

Investment in Fixed Assets by Structure refers to the three major parts of investment activities, i.e. construction and installation, purchase of equipment and instrument, and other expenses.

(1) Construction and installation (work volume of construction and installation) refers to the construction of various houses and buildings and installation of various kinds of equipment and instruments, including construction of various houses, equipment foundations and industrial kilns and stoves, preparation works for project construction, and clearing up works post project construction, pavement of railways and roads, drilling of mines and putting up of oil pipes, construction of projects of water conservancy, construction of underground air-raid shelters and construction of other special projects, installation of various machinery equipment, testing operation for pre-testing the quality of installation projects. The value of equipment installed is not included in the value of installation projects.

(2)Purchase of equipment and instruments refers to the total value of equipment, tools, and vessels purchased or self-produced which come up to standards for fixed assets. Equipment, tools and vessels purchased or self-produced for new workshops by newly established or expanded units are categorized as "purchase of equipment and instruments" no matter whether they come up to the standards for fixed assets or not.

(3)Other expenses refer to expenses occurring during the construction or purchase of fixed assets other than construction, installation or purchase of equipment and instruments.

Projects under Construction refer to projects having construction and installation activities undertaken in the reference period, including projects started in the reference period, or continued from the previous period, or completed and put into production or suspended in the reference period.

Projects Completed and Put into Use Industrial projects refer to the major projects and accessory facilities completed which result in forming production capacity and have been checked and accepted while the living and welfare facilities have been completed and can ensure normal production and formally put into production. Non-industrial projects refer to the major projects and accessory facilities completed which possess the designed capacity and have been checked, accepted and formally put into production.

Newly Increased Production Capacity refers to the increase of designed capacity and project efficiency through investment in fixed assets, which reflects the accomplishment of investment in fixed assets in kind. The calculation of newly increased production capacity is based on individual project which operates independently and efficiently. When an individual project is completed and checked and accepted and put into production, it is counted as newly increased production capacity.

The newly increased production capacity and project efficiency are usually expressed in one of the following forms:

(1)annual production capacity, such as extraction of coal and petroleum;

(2)raw material processing capacity, such as ore dressing capacity of ore dressing projects, the dressing capacity of a coal washery;

(3)number or capacity of major equipment increased, such as the number of cotton spindles increased and the capacity of generating sets increased;

(4)physical measures of construction, such as volume, capacity, area, and length, for instance, the capacity of reservoirs, the length of railways or highways.

Newly increased production capacity in terms of quantity is calculated in designed capacity in general, which refers to the production capacity of a project under normal conditions designed in construction documents regardless of the actual output.

Newly Increased Fixed Assets refer to the newly increased value of fixed assets through investment, including the value of projects completed and put into production, the value of equipment, tools, and vessels considered as fixed assets, as well as the relevant expenses as investment in fixed assets. This is a comprehensive indicator of investment in fixed assets, reflecting the achievements of investment in fixed assets in different periods, different sectors, and different regions.

Floor Space under Construction refers to total floor space of all buildings under construction during the reference period, including floor space of newly started buildings during the reference period, floor space of construction extended from the previous period to the current period, floor space of construction suspended during the previous period and resumed in the current period, floor space of construction completed in the current period, and floor space of construction started and then suspended in the current period.

Floor Space of Buildings Completed refers to the floor space of buildings completed in the reference period, which have come up to the designed standards and have been put into use.

中共海南省委组织部

1、扎实开展全省第三批保持共产党员先进性教育活动。上半年，加大创建生态文明村力度，提高综合创建水平，实施调整经济结构2000例计划，促进农民增收，加强农村阵地建设，巩固党在农村执政基础，加强农村基层党风廉政建设，努力打造海南农村先进性教育活动特色。

2、突出抓好市县、乡镇换届考察工作。7月召开全省换届工作会议，9月派出9个考察组顺利完成18个市县72个领导班子（包括法、检系统）近500名班子成员和近200名拟提拔干部的考察工作。

3、精心组织部机关保持共产党员先进性教育活动。上半年，以“坚持公道正派，加强能力建设，永葆共产党员先进性”主题实践活动为载体，突出“围绕一个目标、抓好双示教育、加强三种培训、开展四项活动”的活动特点，群众满意度测评达到100%。

4、举办农村党支部书记专题培训示范班。5月、6月115名“村官”参加2期示范班学习，省委领导罗保铭、于迅、周文彰、方晓宇参加开班仪式或结业典礼。

5、加大干部人事制度改革力度。8月印发《海南省市县（市、区）党政领导班子和领导干部综合考核评价实施办法（试行）》，9月出台《中共海南省委关于党员领导干部述职述廉的实施办法》等五个法规性文件，并全面运用到换届考察工作中。

6、积极推进《公务员法》实施工作。7月出台我省实施《公务员法》“1+5”配套文件，召开全省实施《公务员法》动员大会，认真做好六大机关公务员登记审批工作，全年新招录省直党群机关和法检两院系统343名公务员。

7、认真落实《海南省教育人才智力扶持中部和少数民族地区实施办法》和《海南省卫生人才智力扶持中部和少数民族地区实施办法》。10月正式启动“双五百”人才工程项目，开展顶岗支教和师资培训工作，加大中部和少数民族地区人才智力扶持力度。

8、自身建设取得好成绩。部机关党委被评为2004-2006年度省直机关先进基层党组织，部办公室被评为2006年度省直机关后勤管理工作先进集体，积极开展丰富多彩的文体活动，获得2006年省直机关“树荣辱观、唱正气歌”歌咏比赛二等奖等多项荣誉。

全省组织部长会议在海口召开

全省换届工作会议在海口召开

省领导在定安调研

部机关在临高角开展先进性见行动主题实践活动

获得省直机关“树荣辱观、唱正气歌”歌咏比赛二等奖

海南省 财经领导小组办公室

海南省财经领导小组办公室于2003年5月组建成立，是海南省财经领导小组下设办事机构。

主要职责：

一是研究我省经济发展战略、经济建设的发展规划和产业发展方针；提出我省经济建设和改革开放的决策思路。

二是负责省财经领导小组会议有关服务工作，包括准备会议文件，整理会议纪要，督促与协调会议决定事项的落实工作。

三是了解掌握并及时向省委反映我省国民经济建设和改革开放中的重要情况和问题。

四是组织开展重要经济问题的调查研究。包括为省委领导同志调查研究提供服务，召开必要的会议，吸取有关部门和市县的意见，提出政策建设等。

五是参与筹备省委有关经济工作重要会议并起草有关文件。

六是承办海南省财经领导小组交办的其他事项。

①省财经领导小组办公室主任裴真主持工作

②省财经领导小组全体会议

③省财经领导小组办公室工作人员深入基层调研

海南省财政国库支付局

求真务实 开拓创新 规范政府会计管理

海南省财政国库支付局（省直单位会计管理中心）成立于2000年12月，隶属海南省财政厅，主要承担省直单位的国库集中支付、会计委派集中核算和工资统发三项财政管理制度改革工作。几年来，在省委、省政府和省财政厅的领导下，以构建公共财政体制为己任，以科学发展观为统领，以提升总体服务质量为主线，牢固树立发展、创新和服务意识，依法行政、依法理财，在规范财政资金管理、提高财政资金使用效益、提升省直单位财政财务管理水平等方面取得了显著成效，基本建成了具有海南特色的从预算编制、指标管理到集中支付、会计核算等，各业务环节紧密相扣、首尾呼应的公共财政支出管理新模式。通过及时提供真实、完整、准确的财务会计信息，为政府部门经济决策服务。在抓好业务工作的同时，支付局领导班子注重干部队伍建设，深入开展创建学习型机关活动，建设富有鲜明业务特色的组织文化，努力打造一支会想、会写、会算、会讲、会做的财会干部队伍。支付局秉承“诚信为本、操守为重、坚持准则、不做假账”的会计职业道德，将单位“满意不满意”作为衡量工作的重要标准，主动提供服务，以优质高效的服务促进改革的深化。2004年，支付局第一、第九核算站被团省委授予“海南省青年文明号”，局合唱团在第七届中国（海口）合唱节中获铜奖；2005年，第一核算站被团中央授予“全国青年文明号”；2006年，局党总支被省委、省直机关工委评为先进基层党组织。

目前，省本级527家预算单位全部实行了国库集中支付，其中，185家单位实行了公务卡制度。集中支付资金包括所有纳入预算管理的资金，以及纳入财政专户管理的预算外事业性收费资金、彩票公益金及发行经费。纳入会计委派集中核算的单位共242家，基本覆盖了省本级驻海口地区的全部单位；省本级驻市县的133家单位实施会计网络核算集中监管。全省工资网络统发人数达到15万人，其中省本级实行工资统发单位共315家，统发人数21690人，年发放工资额22亿元。

省财政国库支付局领导班子。中为局长（主任）方光荣

召开全省会计委派工作座谈会

举办业务知识竞赛

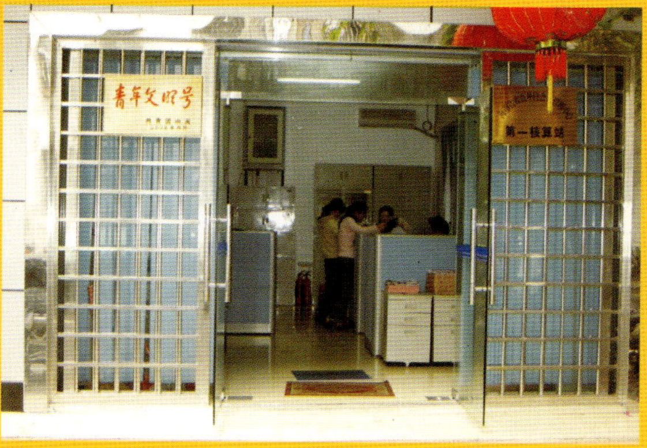

荣获“全国青年文明号”的第一核算站

海南省公安厅

厅长：贾东军

2006年是海南省全面实施“十一五”规划的开局之年，也是省公安厅新领导班子励精图治的第一年，面对错综复杂的斗争形势和繁重艰巨的公安保卫任务，省公安厅在省委、省政府和公安部的正确领导下，团结带领全省各级公安机关，紧紧围绕全省工作大局，始终坚持以科学发展观统领公安工作和队伍建设，以“创建平安海南，构建和谐社会”为目标，以“三基”（抓基层、打基础、苦练基本功）工程建设为重点，全面推进公安工作和队伍正规化建设，为维护全省社会政治稳定和治安形势的持续稳定，有力促进我省社会经济又好又快发展作出了积极贡献。

始终把维护社会政治稳定置于工作首位。全省各级公安机关坚持稳定压倒一切的方针，不断增强政权意识，国家安全意识，突出维稳工作的重要位置。严密防范、严厉打击境内外敌对势力、敌对分子的各种渗透破坏活动，加强侦察深挖，开展专项斗争。积极稳妥地处置群体性事件，全年全省各级公安机关共成功处置因人民内部矛盾引发的各类群体性事件461起，涉及上访人员24380人次。

大力推进“三基”工程建设。我省各级公安机关把“三基”工程建设作为今年工作的重中之重，精心谋划，周密组织，抓点带面，严格考评。省委、省政府、市县党委政府和省有关部门加大对公安基层基础建设的投入力度，基层警务保障条件进一步改善，全省共投入“三基”工程建设经费达1.9亿元。全省基层

海南省公安厅厅长贾东军（左一）在中国禁毒志愿者汽车万里行海南站活动发车仪式上

厅长贾东军视察海南省安康医院

威武的武装警察

一线和实战单位的警力达到7364名，占市县公安机关总警力的88%。科技强警取得新进展，我省“金盾工程”一期建设任务已圆满完成，“三台合一”建设提前一年半完成任务，全省建设了街面监控探头1230个，提高了城市交通和治安防控的能力。全省公安机关掀起了苦练基本功的热潮，把苦练基本功作为加强基层公安机关经常性工作和提高战斗力的根本性措施来抓，开展了多层次、多形式的练兵活动。

坚持不懈地严厉打击各类刑事犯罪活动。全省各级公安机关毫不动摇地坚持严打方针，切实起到“打一伙，保一片，铲一批，稳一方”的效果。针对突发性严重刑事犯罪组织专项斗争。我厅坚持以打黑除恶、侦破命案和打击“两抢一盗”专项行动为重点，严厉打击各类严重刑事犯罪活动。今年全省共破获各类刑事案件7956起，共查处治安案件14441起，共破获市场经济案件152起，共查处各类毒品案件5402起，有力地打击了犯罪分子的嚣张气焰。

进一步规范公安行政管理工作。从人民群众最关心的问题入手，进一步改进户籍管理、治安管理、交通管理、出入境管理、边防管理、消防管理，不断推出便民利民措施，更好地服务经济社会发展大局。

全面加强公安队伍正规化建设。我省各级公安机关以“三基”工程建设、社会主义法治理念和社会主义荣辱观教育为契机，全面推进队伍的正规化建设。切实抓好干部队伍建设，落实公安机关党风廉政建设责任制。持续组织开展“规范执法行为，促进执法公正”专项整改活动，深入推进执法质量考核评议工作，有效地提高了民警的执法水平，促进了严格、公正、文明执法。

以“无毒岛”为目标，加大禁毒工作力度

“三基”工程建设中，公安民警在苦练基本功

整装待发的海南省公安特警

公安民警在进行反恐演习

消防队员正在营救演习

海南省政府国有资

海南省国有企业改革暨产权转让信息发布会

海南省政府国有资产监督管理委员会，成立于2003年10月，为省政府直属正厅级特设机构，代表省政府履行出资人职责。根据省委决定，省国资委成立党委，履行省委规定的职责。省国资委的监管范围为省政府履行出资人职责的国有及国有控股、国有参股企业的国有资产。

2006年，在省委、省政府的正确领导下，我委以科学发展观统领全局，全面加快国有企业改革重组和发展，促进国有经济布局结构调整和整体效益的提高，实现了“十一五”规划第一年开好局，省属重点监管企业全年实现销售收入53.49亿元，比上年增长10.1%，实现利润总额4.37亿元，超额完成了预算任务。

我们认真贯彻省委、省政府的决策部署，编制了《海南省省属国有经济布局结构调整和发展十一五规划纲要》，加强对重点企业发展的规划引导，促进国有经济布局结构调整。

全省加快推进国有企业改革发展暨国有资产监督管理工作会议

重点企业改制和资产重组取得新进展。加快了海南钢铁公司、省汽车运输总公司引进战略投资者改制重组的步伐。两公司的改制重组方案正在报省政府常务会议审议。积极协调推进国有控股上市公司股权分置改革。圆满解决了困扰多年的东线高速公路投资补偿欠款问题。

发挥国有资本的引导和带动作用，促进了重点工程建设。海钢公司完成了总投资近2亿元的110万吨选矿项目，并与省外大企业签署了锆钛矿资源开采和深加工合作项目的框架协议，协议总投资达14亿元。省水利电力公司基本完成了大广坝二期工程项目的开工准备，并引进华能集团合作共同开发建设。

省发展控股有限公司参与完成了西环铁路提速改造工程，正在积极推进东环铁路项目的建设。海南高速公路股份有限公司承担了全省高速公路养护任务，正在加快三亚六道湾渔港建设。省路桥投资建设有限公司完成

省国资系统理论研讨会

省国资委领导听取有关人员汇报工作

产监督管理委员会

了三亚雅亮大桥主体工程施工任务。省林业总公司积极开展花卉基地和交易市场项目的前期工作。海南有线公司100万户数字化有线电视网络工程等项目也正在推进中。

全面推进中小国有企业改制和关闭破产，劣势企业有序退出取得新突破。省国资委与省财政厅联合省政府申请同意，省政府于2005、2006年共安排国企改革专项资金1.66亿元，其中用于职工安置资金1.45亿元。2006年完成了192家省属企业整合重组、改制关闭或落实职工安置工作，安置职工1.23万人，9家行业总公司基本完成了改制退出。国资委成立以来累计已有247家省属企业完成了整合重组、改制关闭或已落实职工安置工作，改革面超过40%，涉及资产总额65.9亿元，负债总额62.1亿元，安置职工1.72万人，其中0.77万人实现了再就业，职工安置费用约5.05亿元。利用省政府建立的省属国有企业改革专项资金，资助优先解决下岗职工社保接续问题，使多年来难以推进的困难企业改制关闭破产有了重大突破。

积极做好不良金融债务重组工作、规范资产处置和产权交易。海南联合资产管理公司以较低价格完成对长城公司海口办共53.08亿元两个债权包的回购。海南产交所受理产权交易业务150宗，成交71宗，成交金额20628万元，比资产评估值增值25.9%。

企业党的建设、领导班子建设和党风廉政建设迈出新步伐。落实党建工作目标责任制，进一步理顺企业党组织的领导关系和党员管理关系。先后组织省国资系统企业党组织开展了“回头看”工作、宣传学习贯彻社会主义荣辱观、“共产党员先进性见行动”活动等，评比表彰了12个“四好”领导班子、29个党建工作全覆盖先进基层党组织、15名党员优秀企业家等，努力建立加强和改进基层党组织建设、保持共产党员先进性教育的长效机制。今年以来，调整充实企业领导班子，提高人员素质。并与省委组织部联合对20家企业的领导班子及其成员进行了年度考核评价。

积极抓好企业党风建设和反腐倡廉工作。与省监察厅联合开展省属企业“效能监察年”活动，取得初步成效。19家企业共立项74项，增加经济效益5400多万元，避免经济损失550多万元，提出监察建议139条，建章立制85项。组织对59家省属重点企业和中央驻琼企业党风廉政建设工作情况逐一进行了调研检查，加强具体指导，使省属国有企业党风廉政建设薄弱的局面得到了基本扭转。

海南省国税局

认真开展社会主义荣辱观教育，教育和引导干部职工“知荣辱、树新风”

全面部署全省国税系统信息化建设工作，努力推进税收管理现代化

2006年，海南省国税系统在海南省委、省政府和国家税务总局的正确领导下，以邓小平理论和“三个代表”重要思想为指导，以科学发展观统领全局，在改革中谋发展，在创新中求突破，税收征管质量和效率明显提高，税收管理体制和机制不断完善，干部队伍综合素质和执法水平进一步提升，各项工作跃上了新台阶。特别是组织收入工作在2005年高增长基数的基础上，再次实现税收收入总量、计划考核收入和增值税直接收入“三个突破”，分别完成84.4亿元、61.3亿元和41.1亿元，比上年增长30.3%、15.1%和8.5%，创下了历史新高。

依法治税是税收工作的永恒主题。2006年，海南国税系统继续坚持聚财为国、执法为民，认真贯彻执行各项税收政策，大力整顿和规范税收秩序，努力规范执法行为，奏响了一首雄浑的依法治税之歌。

万事以人为本，治税必先治队。海南国税系统坚持以促进人的全面发展为目标，大力推进税收文化建设和税收道德建设，分级分类地组织开展大规模、全

特邀省内外专家学者共同探讨经济社会发展及其政策变化对税收工作的影响，研究国税工作如何更好地服务于我省经济和社会发展的大局

中纪委领导到我局检查指导工作，参观我省国税系统“三个文明”建设图片展

召开三年一度的“三个文明”建设工作会议，全面回顾过去三年全系统“三个文明”建设的成绩，确定未来三年全省国税工作的指导思想、奋斗目标和工作任务

方位的教育培训活动，干部队伍的综合素质显著提升，精神面貌焕然一新。在勤奋、团结、廉洁、开拓、求实的海南国税精神的引领下，全系统广大干部职工立足平凡岗位，挥洒激情，倾注智慧，用赤诚和信念维护了税法尊严，用青春和汗水捍卫了共和国的血脉。一年来，先后有多个单位和个人荣获中央和省级表彰。其中：文昌市国税局办税服务厅获国家级“青年文明号”荣誉称号。全系统有9个单位获省级“青年文明号”荣誉称号，1人被评为“海南省杰出青年卫士”，4人被评为“海南省优秀青年卫士”，2人被评为“海南省杰出青年岗位能手”，13人被评为“海南省优秀青年岗位能手”。

基础不牢，地动山摇。一年来，海南国税系统认真贯彻落实科学化、精细化管理的工作要求，积极投身税收信息化建设大潮，深入开展税收分析，全面实施税源分类管理，努力推进纳税服务体系建设。全系统凝心聚力打基础，向管理要税收，向管理要效率，向管理要形象，为完成各项税收工作任务提供了坚实保障。

一分耕耘，一分收获。在新的一年里，海南国税人将以饱满的热情、昂扬的斗志，扎实工作，竭诚奉献，奋发进取，按照“五个构建，三个确保”的总体要求，不断推进海南国税事业持续、快速、和谐发展，为促进经济社会全面协调发展作出新的更大的贡献。

全面推行公开招标办法，努力提高全省国税系统政府采购工作透明度

加强计算机业务培训，提高全系统干部职工的计算机应用水平

开展丰富多彩的文体活动，丰富干部职工业余文化生活，促进国税文化建设

海南省

2006 年，全省农业系统按照我省社会主义新农村建设的总体思路和阶段性任务要求，抓好各项重点工作的落实，促进了农业经济快速健康发展。

农业厅肖杰厅长(中)参加神农大丰公司临高制种基地建成典礼

农业经济和农民收入同步较快增长。全省农业增加值达到 344.48 亿元，同比增长 9.1%，农民人均纯收入达到 3256 元，同比增长 8.4%，超出“十一五”规划年均递增 6% 的目标。

——农村经济结构调整取得显著成效。积极实施农村经济结构调整增收 2000 例计划，示范村农民人均增收 534 元，同比增长 15%。渔业、畜牧业、瓜菜、水果等优势产业快速发展，四大优势产业对农业经济增长的贡献率达 80.8%。种植业结构调整取得重大突破，瓜菜、水果产值占种植业产值比重达 72.28%。全省香蕉下水田新种面积达 13 万亩，推广甘蔗下水田 15 万亩。全省设施大棚栽培面积突破 5 万亩，西甜瓜下水田 3 万亩。全省瓜菜塑盘和营养袋育苗面积占育苗总面积 60% 以上。积极发展制种产业，全省早造制种面积 11 万亩，生产杂交稻种子 477.7 万公斤，全年推广超级稻 10 万亩。

南繁育种基地

—— 主要农产品快速发展。加快畜牧业生产方式转变，全省建立 177 个养殖专业村，新增规模养殖户 1 万户。生猪出栏 50 头以上和肉鸡出栏 2000 只以上规模的比例分别达 37.2% 和 75.2%，实现增加值 57.31 亿元，增长 6.9%，肉类总产量 68.31 万吨，增长 6.6%。粮食 185.61 万吨、糖料 361.46 万吨、瓜菜 400.39 万吨、水果 187.86 万吨，同比分别增长 21.31%、42.51%、10.2%、15.6%。橡胶受上年强台风“达维”影响，产量 24.75 万吨，同比减少 0.1%。

农产品出岛出口稳步发展。2006 年瓜果菜出岛总量 371.6 万吨，总产值达 106.4 亿元，同比分别增长 8.3%、46.3%。其中冬季瓜菜出岛 230.6 万吨、产值达 55.7 亿元，同比分别增长 18.2%、54.1%，实现了产量、效益超历史的目标。水果出岛 141 万吨，产值 50.6 亿元，增长了 38.6%。全年农产品出口总额 2.58 亿美元，占全省出口总额 18.7%，水产品占农产品出口总额 82%。热带水果出口额 415.4 万美元，全年生猪出岛 38 万头，同比增长 82%；文昌鸡出岛量 2000 万只，同比增长 66.7%，其中出口港澳市场 31 万只，同比增长 210%，创汇 1643 万港元。

特色瓜菜

——农业科技推广和农民培训力度加大。积极实施农业科技入户、新型农民培训、测土配方施肥等科技工程，引进推广农作物和畜禽优良 220 多个，良种覆盖率达 85%，先进实用技术入户率 80%，推广测土配方施肥面积达 140 万亩，耕种收综合机械化水平达到 22.4%。组织开展农业实用技术培训和农村劳动转移培训，培训农民 83 万人次，完成阳光工程主体培训 3.45 万人，转移率为 86.3%, 带动全省农村劳动力转移 8.5 万人。

——农业安全保障能力不断增强。加强农产品基地认证和产品认证，2006 年全省累计认定无公害生产基地 205 个，面积 268.2 万亩，124 个企业的 204 个农产品被批准使用无公害农产品标志，有效使用绿色食品标志的有 27 个产品。组织编制和实施 37 个农业标

农业厅

高效热带水果

高效热带水果

准化项目。2006 年抽检 2000 多个农产品样品，农产品抽检达标率为 95.6%。组织开展农资打假、放心农资下乡进村及毒鼠强专项整治等活动，深入开展春秋动物防疫行动，确保我省重大疫病“零”发生。加强三叶草斑潜蝇、稻飞虱、黄龙病等防控工作，东亚飞蝗防控面积 95 万亩，确保“控制位、不蔓延”。

——农产品保鲜加工取得新进展。全省乡镇企业农产品加工规模企业新增 13 家，达到 75 家，实现增加值 4.8 亿元，同比增长 11.4%。抓好果蔬冷藏保鲜加工，年内新建、扩建冷藏保鲜项目 16 个，新增冷藏保鲜能力 2 万吨。

——农业市场化、产业化进程加快。成功举办 2006 年“海交会”，成交总金额达 105.72 亿元人民币和 1.86 亿美元，成交金额比 2005 年“冬交会”增长 34.9%。进一步健全农产品市场体系，巩固国内 100 个大城市销地市场，开发一批具消费潜力的中等市场，扩大优势农产品出口。加快农业产业化进程，至 2006 年底，全省农业产业化经济组织 1582 个，龙头企业 244 家，联接农户 34.35 万户。各类农民专业合作经济组织 769 家，带动农户 15.88 万户。

——农村沼气建设取得明显成效。抓好“四个一”沼气工程（一个猪场、一个果园、一个学校、一个村庄各建一个大中型沼气池）试点示范，取得良好效果。新建农村沼气池 3.63 万个。举办沼气技术培训班，年内培训人员 5 万人次，取得职业技能资格证书的沼气技工达 2656 人。

——农村经营管理和农业法制建设得到加强。制定《海南省实施〈农村土地承包法〉办法》，加强农民负担监督管理。开展村级债务债权摸底清查工作，制止发生新的乡村债务。完善农业地方法规体系，不断规范农业行政许可管理，继续推进农业综合执法体制改革。

蓬勃发展的生态畜牧业

中国最大的天然橡胶生产基地

海南省农垦总局

海南农垦创建于1952年1月，是我国三大直属垦区之一。

海南农垦拥有国有土地1280万亩，占海南陆地面积的1/4；人口达100万人，占海南全省总人口的1/8；年实现国内生产总值70多亿元。

海南农垦地处北纬18度至20度之间，在北纬18度以北地区大面积种植天然橡胶的成功，是海南农垦对我国作出的历史性贡献。海南垦区主要经营天然橡胶种植与初加工，在全岛18个市县分布着92个国营农场和橡胶（热作）研究所，其中95%的农业单位都是以种植天然橡胶为主。垦区现拥有天然橡胶总面积381万亩，最高年产量达23万吨，约占全国产量的一半，是我国最大的天然橡胶生产基地。海南农垦在天然橡胶生产方面，总结和积累出了一套在自然环境远不如其他主要产胶国家条件下，具有中国特色的橡胶管理和种植与采割技术的先进经验，使天然橡胶亩产达到70公斤以上，达到世界平均水平。海南农垦不但雄踞中国最大的天然橡胶生产基地的显赫地位，而且还是我国最大的热带作物生产基地。经过三代农垦人的艰苦努力，海南农垦目前已建成集农工商旅运等综合经营的大型农业企业集团。

海南农垦创建50多年来，已累计向国家上缴利税60多亿元，国家投资回收率达143.9%，而且还积累固定资产现值100亿元。

垦区花园式的农场场部

农垦人酒店外景

海南农垦已建成全国最大的天然橡胶生产基地

海南省商务厅

彭瑞林厅长陪同省领导在第三届“珠洽会”上视察海南展馆

海南省商务厅于2003年6月挂牌成立，是负责全省对外贸易、利用外资、对内对外经济技术合作、内贸市场建设与监管的经济综合管理部门。下属省政府采购中心、省散装水泥推广办等4个事业单位。

2006年，省商务厅认真贯彻落实省委科学发展观，着眼于用好国际国内两个市场、两种资源，加大对内对外开放力度，加快开放型经济发展步伐，取得积极成效。

一、积极发展对外贸易，外贸出口创历史新高

全年，外贸进出口达28.50亿美元，同比增长10%；其中出口达13.8亿美元，同比增长35.3%，创历史新高。

二、抓好投资促进工作，利用外资呈现良好势头

全年，合同利用外资10.51亿美元，同比增长3倍：外商直接投资7.49亿美元，同比增长9.5 %，创近十年新高。

三、积极融入区域经济合作，大力宣传推介海南

在昆明举办的第三届“珠洽会”上，与云南省签定了旅游合作协议书。在第十届（深圳）中国国际高新技术投资洽谈会上，共达成投资意向15个，金额15.86亿元。在2006年中国（天津）全国商品交易会暨投资洽谈会上，进一步密切与“京津冀经济圈”的经贸合作。在“广交会”上，我省与境外客商共签定出口合同2亿多美元，在第三届中国东盟博览会上，签订了800万美元的出口合同。

与此同时，省商务厅努力打造海南投资贸易平台，协助省农业厅成功举办了“海交会”，共签订订单1237份，总成交金额105.72亿元人民币和1.86亿美元。

在新的一年，省商务厅将以进一步扩大开放和夯实商务发展基础为主线，重点抓好以下工作：一是调整出口产品结构，转变外贸增长方式；二是拓展利用外资领域，提高利用外资质量；三是发挥我省区位优势，积极参与区域经济合作；四是建设现代市场体系，积极扩大消费，不断推动海南特区的经济发展。

彭瑞林厅长在第三届“东盟博览会”上接受记者采访

商务部领导在海南调研

海南省 信访局

海南省信访局局长：卓连存

海南省信访工作会议

海南省信访局为省政府办公厅内设机构，副厅级单位，下设办信综合处、来访接待处、督查调研处，编制人员19名。主要职能：贯彻落实党中央、国务院和省委、省政府关于信访工作的方针、政策和规定；处理群众来信，接待群众来访，收集信访信息，及时、准确地向省委、省政府领导同志反映来信中提出的重要建议、意见和问题；开展调查研究，综合分析信访信息和形势，预测发展趋势，提出建议；办理中央有关部门和省委、省政府领导批办的信访事项；协调处理群众集体来省上访和异常、突发事件；担负省处理信访突出问题及群体性事件联席会议办公室日常工作和省信访督查专员的管理工作。

近年来，在省委、省政府领导的高度重视和大力支持下，省信访局各项工作取得了较大的进步。

一是信访工作大格局初步形成。在全省的市、县和乡（镇）三级政府和省直14个职能厅局设立了信访工作机构，成立了信访工作领导小组，并按照“属地管理、分级负责，谁主管、谁负责，依法及时就地解决问题与疏导教育相结合”的信访工作原则，积极构建统一领导、统筹兼顾，各负其责、齐抓共管的的信访工作大格局。

二是信访渠道规范畅通。开设了《省长电子信箱》、《网上信访》；推行律师参与接访，对上访群众进行疏导、分流；向社会公布了信访方式方法以及查询信访事项处理进展及结果等相关事项；积极引导群众依法上访，反映合理诉求。按照《信访条例》要求，建立“畅通、务实、高效、有序”的信访秩序。2006年全局办理群众来信6911封，接待群众来访13882人（次）。

三是信访工作机制不断健全。在各市县建立和完善了领导信访接待日制度、领导批阅人民来信制度、领导包案制度以及领导下访制度，并建立了信访工作责任制。做到“小事不出村、中事不出乡镇、大事不出县，矛盾不上交”。

四是督查督办工作进一步加强。实行首办责任制，在“事要解决”上下功夫；发挥信访督查专员作用，加强跟踪督办，提高案件办结率。2006年信访案件结案率达90%，受到省委、省政府主要领导表扬。

五是加强处理信访突出问题及群体性事件工作。注重加强矛盾纠纷的排查化解工作和信访突出问题及群体性事件的处理工作，坚持从源头抓起，做到发现得早，化解得了，控制得住，处理得好。

六是信访工作人员素质得到提高。按照国家信访局要求，积极开展“创学习型机关，建高素质队伍”活动，认真学习胡锦涛总书记等中央领导关于信访工作的重要批示精神，进一步增强信访工作人员的服务意识和宗旨意识，做到外树形象，内强素质，不断更新观念，开拓创新，推动信访工作，为构建和谐海南、平安海南作出更大的贡献。

认真学习，努力建立“畅通、务实、高效、有序”的信访新秩序

海南省信访局综合处的同志正在研究工作

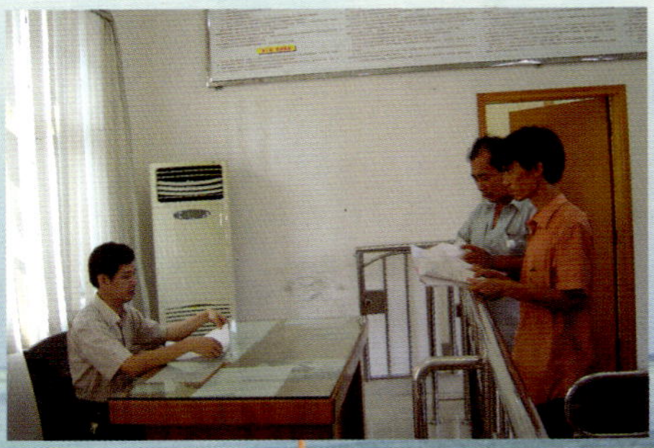

信访局工作人员接待来访群众

前进中的海南省审计厅

2006年，全省各级审计机关在审计署和省委、省政府的正确领导下，认真履行审计监督职能，各项工作取得显著成绩。全省共完成审计项目653个，查出违纪违规金额15.2亿元，其中应归还原渠道资金1.46亿元，已归还6088万元；应减少财政拨款1.04亿元，已减少财政拨款9039万元；应上交财政2.58亿元，已上交财政1.47亿元。移交审计案件4宗。提交工作报告和审计信息603篇，其中被各级领导批示和各媒体采用364篇，不少审计建议被有关单位采纳，已成为规范管理的重要措施。特别是，审计署李金华审计长，刘家义、余效明副审计长和中国审计学会会长翟熙贵先后到我省调研，对我省倡导审计新理念，稳妥、规范推行审计公开，构建具有海南特色的审计业务格局等工作给予充分肯定。我省的不少审计理念以及经验做法在全国审计界发生了很大的影响，呈现审计思路更加清晰、审计重点更加突出、审计公开更加规范和理性、审计整改更加有效、审计管理更加严格、审计和被审计的关系更加协调等六个特点。

①省政府主要领导在听取审计工作汇报

②符兴厅长向省人大做工作报告

③审计署主要领导来琼指导工作

④全国首届审计职工运动会

⑤审计厅文化艺术演出活动

海南省民族宗教事务厅

2006年，我厅坚持以“三个代表”重要思想为指导，深入贯彻党的十六大和十六届五中、六中全会精神以及中央民族工作会议和宗教工作座谈会精神，紧紧围绕省委、省政府的中心工作，认真落实《海南省国民经济和社会发展十一个五年规划》，为促进全省各民族共同团结奋斗、共同繁荣发展、维护社会稳定、构建和谐海南发挥了应有的职能作用。

一、坚持科学的发展观，努力促进少数民族和民族地区的经济社会加快发展；

二、加大工作力度，做好教育危房改造和全省民族地区民房改造工作；

三、认真贯彻民族区域自治法，加强民族团结，促进民族关系健康发展；

四、积极协调有关部门，努力促进民族地区教育科技事业发展；

五、大力宣传和弘扬民族文化，推动民族体育事业的发展；

六、整顿民族风情旅游点（区），组织各民族风情旅游点（区）开展评A活动；

七、依法加强对宗教事务的管理；

八、积极配合省委巡视组的工作，加强机关建设，全面提高全厅依法行政的能力。

①刘明哲厅长在2006年海南三亚黎族苗族传统“三月三”节上致辞。

②2006年9月29日，省民宗厅在海口召开全省民宗系统“四五”普法总结表彰大会暨“五五”普法动员大会。图为受国家民委表彰的我省先进集体代表在表彰大会上领奖。

③逢年过节，省民宗厅领导亲自给贫困的少数民族群众送温暖。

④省民宗厅刘明哲厅长率先垂范，亲自下基层开展调查研究，为少数民族群众排忧解难。图为刘明哲厅长与厅联手扶贫单位——琼中什运乡的干部商讨扶贫工作。

⑤2006年4月12日，我省唯一的道教活动场所——定安玉蟾宫举行开光仪式。图为省民宗厅与省道教协会（筹）在海口召开新闻发布会。

⑥2006年9月，省民宗厅会同省文体厅在三亚、五指山两市举办海南省第三届少数民族传统体育运动会。图为五指山市主会场的开幕式。

海南省人口和计划生育局

省领导与基层计生干部座谈

国家人口计生委领导在海南视察人口和计划生育工作

2006年是“十一五”时期的开局之年，为开创“十一五”时期人口和计划生育工作的新局面，我局认真贯彻落实国家人口计生委《全面深化综合改革建立和完善工作新机制的指导意见》精神，积极推进人口和计划生育综合改革，不断探索建立工作新机制，紧紧围绕“稳定低生育水平、改善人口结构”的中心任务，开展各项工作。

省领导在省人口计生局局长周公卒的陪同下深入基层调研指导人口计生工作

一是完善人口和计划生育目标管理责任制，将人口自然增长率、出生人口性别比列为“一票否决”指标，并首次把省直相关部门纳入目标管理考核范畴；

二是逐步完善和落实利益导向机制，今年我省享受国家农村部分计划生育家庭奖励扶助的对象有6456人，全省用于奖励扶助资金共352.46万元。今年，我省开展实施国家“少生快富”工程，兑现符合“少生快富”工程范围的计划生育家庭1400户，每户奖励3000元，共计经费420万元；

三是进一步推动综合治理出生人口性别比偏高问题工作深入开展，加强部门联合执法力度，开展全省巡回督查工作，依法打击非法胎儿性别鉴定和非法终止妊娠行为。以“关爱女孩”行动为载体，推动综合治理出生人口性别比偏高问题工作的开展；

四是大力倡导科学、文明、进步的婚育新风，以开展社会主义新农村建设的有利契机，推动计划生育村（居）民自治工作；

五是正确把握流动人口计划生育工作的新问题新情况，将流动人口纳入属地化管理、市民化服务，充分发挥各有关单位的作用，将计划生育工作纳入社会治安综合治理和平安建设工作当中，并将其有机地结合起来；

六是深入开展以技术服务为重点的计划生育优质服务，启动“关爱妇女生殖健康行动”，引进“中国中西部地区生殖健康家庭保健服务能力建设项目，提高育龄群众的自我保健能力和生殖健康水平。加强县乡两级计划生育服务网络建设，今年共投入270万元对市县服务站（所）进行改扩建。

周公卒局长为获得“全国农村部分计划生育家庭奖励扶助制度和‘少生快富’工程试点工作先进单位”颁奖

海南省水务局

局长：王扬俊

海南省水务局是主管全省水务工作的省政府直属机构。自从实行水务一体化以来，在省委省政府的直接领导下，在水利部的大力支持下，海南省水务局统筹城乡水务发展规划，根据海南经济社会发展需求，优化配置水资源，为构建和谐社会和新农村建设提供水利支撑，为海南经济社会全面发展提供水资源保障。特别是2006年，水利投资持续增加，前期工作得到加强，重点项目建设进展顺利，城乡供水协调发展，病险水库除险加固步伐加快，水利改革进一步深化，水利信息化程度得到提高，灌区续建配套和节水改造工程取得新的进展，实现“十一五”良好开局。至今年12月初止，省级以上财政投入水利资金33163.49万元，其中：中央下达投资计划21560万元，省级下达投资计划11603.49万元。大隆水库已提前10个月完成年度施工计划。完成病险水库安全加固6宗；新建供水项目8个，扩建供水项目4个，管网改造工程5个。完成各类饮水工程安全工程881宗，完成投资6288万元，解决27.20万人饮水安全问题；15座水电站已建成投产，合计装机25940千瓦。

2007年是实施国民经济和社会发展第十一个五年规划的重要一年。我局要认真学习贯彻党的十六届六中全会精神，继续贯彻落实省委五届一次全会、全省经济工作会议、农村工作会议和全国水利厅局长会议精神，以科学发展观统领水务工作全局，以建设社会主义和谐社会为着力点，继续抓好水利前期工作，积极推进重点水利项目建设，全力作好防风防汛防旱工作，抓好城乡饮水安全工程建设，抓好灌区续建配套和节水改造工程，深化水管体制及水价改革，加强水行政执法和水资源管理工作，扎实推进全省大中型水库移民后期扶持工作，切实推动海南又快又好发展。

海南省水环境监测中心实验室

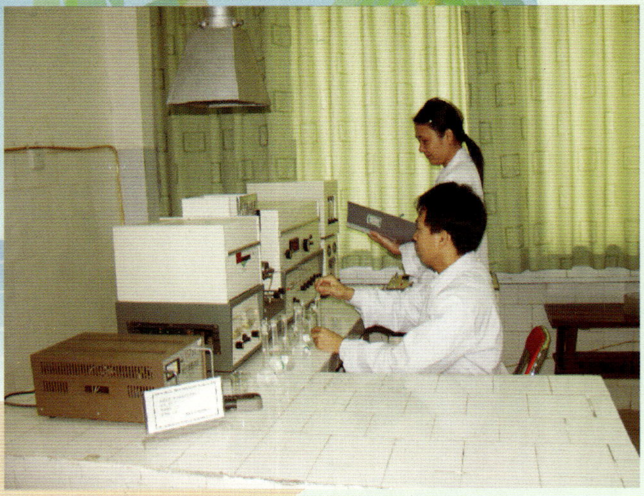

水环境监测中心工作人员进行水质分析

海南省水文水资源勘测局

局长：韩香丰

先进性教育活动中的局领导班子

海南省水文水资源勘测局隶属海南省水务局，是具有行政管理职能的全额拨款正处级事业单位，挂牌机构：“海南省水环境监测中心”、“海南省水土保持监测总站”。

主要工作职责：负责全省水文行业管理和全省水资源开发利用和保护规划；负责全省实时水文信息的收集、处理、分析与预报；参与水资源论证和编制水土保持方案；负责有关水事纠纷、涉水案件裁决所需水文资料的审定；承担水环境监测、水土保持监测；担负全省取水许可初审、取水许可证发放及年度审验，收取水资源费、水土保持设施补偿费和水土流失防治费等。

近几年来，我局获市厅级以上先进集体12个，先进个人6个，其中获得“海南省直属机关2000～2001年度文明单位”、“2004-2005年度省直单位按比例安排残疾人就业工作先进单位”称号，下属加积水文站2004年被授予“全国文明水文站”称号，周亚诗同志2005年被水利部、人事部授予“全国水利系统先进工作者”荣誉称号等。

“十一五”期间，我省水文将运用现代先进技术，开展水文数据信息、水情信息、水资源信息、水环境监测信息和办公自动化等应用服务系统的基础设施建设和软件开发，努力提高支撑能力和工作水平，强化为各级政府的决策服务、社会公众的生活服务、经济发展的专业服务和重要工程的建设服务能力，基本实现水文服务的自动化，为保障经济社会的可持续发展提供可靠支撑。

资质证书

办公地址

海南省教育厅

海南省教育厅与中共海南省教育工作委员会合署办公，是主管教育事业和语言文字工作的省政府组成部门。2006年是教育事业不平凡的一年。全省教育系统全面贯彻落实科学发展观，各项工作都取得了新成绩，实现了“十一五”教育工作的良好开局。一是教育特别是基础教育始终被放到优先发展的位置，各级政府抓教育的意识明显增强，尊师重教的社会氛围正在形成。二是继续实行农村义务教育“两免一补”政策，加大对贫困家庭学生的资助力度。投入3.8亿元实行“两免一补”，受惠学生达252.3万人；投入1200多万元，对1.07万名困难中职学校学生和大学生予以资助，努力使每个孩子都能上得起学。三是实行“集中资金、集中项目、集中区域”打歼灭战，中小学危房改造工程成为继“两基”攻坚之后，投入最多、办学条件改善幅度最大的“民心工程”、“德政工程”，列入计划的38.26万平方米农村中小学D级危房全部改造完毕，使海南成为全国中西部地区第一个彻底消除中小学D级危房的省份。四是推进农村中小学现代远程教育工程，使之覆盖全省78%的农村中小学校，初步实现优质教育资源共享，农村中小学面貌发生了很大变化。五是采取有力措施，较好地解决了“高考移民”问题，增加了8000多个海南考生上大学的机会，减少了社会不稳定因素。六是职业教育加快发展，办学思想进一步明确，中等职业学校招生人数达3.3万，比上年增长16%,在校生规模达7.2万人。七是推进桂林洋高校区建设，扩大了高校发展的空间。高等教育规模不断扩大，教育教学质量不断提高。八是基础教育课程改革取得显著成效，中等学校、高校招生考试改革和素质教育进一步推进。九是深入贯彻中央2004年8号文件和16号文件，中小学生思想道德建设和大学生思想政治教育得到加强。总结推广省工业学校教师陶海林和海南师范学院学生张九精的典型经验，他们的感人事迹在学校、在琼州大地，乃至在全国都产生了极大反响，有力推动学生德育工作和师德建设。

省领导在全省中小学危房改造攻坚总结表彰大会上作重要讲话

省领导出席全省2006年度教育工作会议

省领导在桂林洋高校调研

第13届中学生运动会开幕式

厅机关干部参加省直工委组织的树荣辱观唱正气歌合唱比赛荣获一等奖

海南省考试局

省领导（左）、省教育厅副厅长史贻云（中）在省考试局局长郑万发（右）的陪同下莅临高考录取现场指导工作

2006年，海南省考试局在省委、省政府和省教育厅的领导下，认真贯彻落实国家和省各项考试政策、法规，铁腕扼制“高考移民”，扎实推进招生“阳光工程”，确保招生考试的公平公正；各类教育考试及各项社会考试稳步发展，考试信息化管理水平继续提高，较好地完成了全年的各项工作任务。全年共完成了18项考试（考查）工作任务，其中全国性考试15项，省级考试（考查）3项，接受委托考试12次。考试项目比2005年增加3项，即增加了高校英语应用能力考试、高职（专科）升本科考试、全国中小学教师教育技术水平考试。考查项目比2005年减少1项，即普通高中实验操作考查。

2006年全省普通高校招生工作会议

【招生考试信息工作】

2006年，省考试局信息中心加强了硬件方面的建设，新购进12台刀片服务器，有效地提高了填（补）报志愿程序后台数据库的效率。一年来共采集了25万名考生的报名、体检、志愿等考试信息，评阅了近60万份答卷，向高校传输了6万个考生电子档案；通过我局网站向社会发布了150多条招生考试信息。

完善的设备为考务管理信息化的发展奠定了坚实的基础

网上录取现场

海南省邮政局

海南邮政业务发展态势良好。图为在2006年海交会上，海南邮政物流公司签订20000多吨农副产品和3000多吨药品的全国运输、配送协议

2006年4月30日，海南省邮政局荣获“全国五一劳动奖状”。图为文兴元局长代表海南省邮政局上台领奖

2006年，海南邮政事业在新的发展平台上取得了新的成绩。业务收入持续较快增长，成本结构不断优化，经济效益稳步提高，和谐发展取得成效。

截至12月底，全省邮政部门从业人员为5750人，其中：在岗职工年末人数为2725人；聘用工年末人数为82人；劳务工年末人数2943人。邮政局所726处，其中电子化局所213处，城市邮政支局所152处，农村邮政支局所311处，代办所50处；局所服务面积74.17平方公里/处；全省邮政总固定资产98797万元，固定资产原值106441万元。全年邮政业务总量完成4.7亿元，比上年增长15.37%；业务收入完成4.2亿元，完成年计划的103.25%，比上年增长9.78%；收支差额完成国家邮政局下达的计划任务。全省邮政部门连续两年实现“三无”目标，即：无发生重大责任事故、无发生资金案件、无发生重大新闻曝光事件。2006年4月，海南省邮政局获得全国“五一”劳动奖状。

进一步完善跨年度业务奖励政策，邮储、新邮预订、报刊流转额等都超额完成了跨年度目标任务。认真开展“6+1”（6个劳动竞赛加一个岗位培训练功比赛）劳动竞赛，较好地调动了广大干部职工为企业创收的主观能动性。中国邮政贺卡业务收入比上年增长200%。全省“单证照”、“录取通知书”、“思乡月”等专项营销成绩突出，国际速递收入实现正增长，物流业务收入比去年增长24.4%。

组织开展社会主义荣辱观和“爱心邮路”的宣传教育活动，努力形成“知荣辱、树新风、建和谐”的良好局风。突出做好各种层次的业务培训和岗位培训，提高了干部职工队伍的整体素质。推进企业服务形象工程和网点标准化改造，建成一批标准化网点和电子化支局，进一步提升了企业形象。

海南邮政不断提高服务质量。图为洋浦开发区邮政局营业员在营业厅帮助用户包装包裹

海南省邮政局注重企业文化建设。图为3月28日晚在海口人大会堂举办的“舞动二十年，唱响一百亿”邮政储蓄文艺晚会

市县局

海口气象局

东方气象局

昌江气象局

白沙气象局

屯昌气象局

琼海气象局

陵水气象局

海南省气象局

党组书记、局长：吴岩峻

职责范围：制定本省气象事业发展规划、计划并负责组织实施；负责重要气象设施建设项目的审查；对气象活动进行指导、监督和行业管理。负责全省气象台站布局调整；组织管理全省气象探测资料；依法保护气象探测环境，组织、协调本省涉外气象活动。负责全省重大灾害性天气跨地区、跨部门的联合监测、预报工作，制订气象灾害防御措施，负责管理本省公众气象预报、灾害性天气警报以及农业气象预报、城市环境气象预报、火险气象等级预报等专业气象预报。管理、指导和组织人工影响天气作业；组织管理雷电灾害防御、制定本省防雷减灾管理规定、雷电灾害的研究、监测、预报、预警、灾情调查与鉴定，会同有关部门对防雷工程的专业设计、施工以及防雷装置的检查工作进行指导和监督。会同市县政府对市县气象部门进行统一领导和管理。承办省委、省政府和中国气象局交办的其他工作。

取得成就：在省委省政府和中国气象局的关心支持下，在气象部门广大干部职工的共同努力下，海南气象事业取得了快速发展。建立了比较完备的气象信息网络系统，卫星通信网和地面通信网互为备份，确保了各类气象信息的及时传送。建立了中短期天气预报、气候与气候预测、农业气象、人工增雨、雷电防御等气象业务服务系统。建立了由卫星、雷达、地面观测、高空探测、闪电定位等现代化大气综合观测网。基本组成了由天气预报、气候预测、人工影响天气、干旱监测与预报、雷电防御、农业气象与生态、气候资源开发利用等构成的气象服务体系，气象服务领域涉及我省工业、农业、渔业、商业、电力、交通、运输、建筑、林业、水利、海洋、盐业、环保、旅游、航空、保险等多个行业和部门。近年来，随着科学技术和经济社会的发展，防雷装置检测和工程专业设计、重大社会活动、海上救助、军事演习、突发公共事件紧急响应等气象保障服务得到迅速发展。全省气象部门在编人员488人，本科以上学历的人数占在编人员总数39%，正研究员3人，高级职称44人，队伍素质有了明显提高。

省气象局办公大楼

海口多普勒天气雷达

参加全国气象行业文艺汇演获二等奖

前景规划：到2010年，通过建立地面、海洋无空白监测网络系统，精细、定量无缝隙预报系统，立体、综合无障碍预警系统，大力提升海南气象灾害的监测、预报、预警能力，使海南气象防灾减灾体系的总体水平跨入全国先进行列。到2020年，建成结构完善、布局科学、功能先进的气象现代化体系，气象科技水平和服务质量全面提升，整体实力处于全国前列。

海南省国土环境资源厅

国土厅厅长：林诗銮

海南省国土环境资源厅是省政府主管全省土地、环境保护和矿产资源工作的职能部门。2006年，该厅国土环境资源管理工作取得了较好成绩，为促进我省社会经济又好又快地发展做出了新贡献。

大力组织推进生态省建设工作，认真履行生态办职责，召开了生态省建设暨全省环境保护大会，成功举办了“2006中国·海南生态省建设论坛”，加强落实督办，使生态省建设年度工作计划落到实处。积极运用土地政策参与宏观调控，把好土地供应“闸门”，提高土地节约集约利用水平。积极为重点建设项目提供征地和用地服务，促进重点工程建设。大力推进土地市场的健康发展。加大闲置建设用土处置力度，全年共处置118宗1302.48公顷的闲置建设用地，并纳入了政府土地储备管理，提高了政府调控土地市场的能力。严格落实耕地保护制度和“占一补一”制度，从严控制建设占用耕地，加强项目耕地占补平衡工作检查，落实耕地补充工作，本年度补充耕地面积达895.99公顷，实现耕地占补平衡有余，连续8年实现耕地占补平衡。加大土地开发整理，加快9个国家投资土地开发整理项目的建设，预计新增耕地1454.79公顷，各项目工程已达到竣工验收条件。制定颁布了《海南省土地储备整理管理办法》。加大对新建项目的环境管理，积极推行循环经济和清洁生产，从严把好新建项目环评审批和竣工收关，对项目违反环境保护的行为进行严厉查处。加强污染防治，以饮水安全和三大流域治理为重点，加强水污染防治。三大流域环境综合整治工作取得了显著成效，得到了省人大检查组的充分肯定。认真做好城市环境综合整治定量考核及环境保护目标责任制工作，对全省8个城市“城考”工作进行了督促检查。加强对排污单位的现场检查，全年检查排污企业1653家次，对108家存在环境违法行为的企业进行了处罚，较好地遏制了污染反弹。开展淘汰消耗臭氧层物质工作，我省荣获国家环保总局授予的保护臭氧层示范省称号。加强矿产资源管理，推进矿业市场建设，大力推行矿权的招、拍、挂，矿产资源得到合理利用和优化配置。建立和完善相关的整顿和规范矿产资源开发秩序工作的相关制度，切实抓好“三查”工作。我省治乱工作取得较好成效，全省非法采矿已基本得到遏制。我省的整顿工作得到了国务院整顿和规范矿产资源开发秩序检查验收组的充分肯定。开展矿山生态环境保护和恢复，完善矿山环境恢复治理保证金制度。加强汛期地质灾害防治工作，做好地质灾害气象预警预报，开展地质灾害危险性评估，全省建设项目地质灾害危险性评估备案的有108项。加强地质遗迹保护管理，完成了海口石山火山群国家地质公园揭碑开园工作，联合国科教文组织也批准了中国雷琼世界地质公园。加大宣传教育工作，围绕国土环境资源重大节日开展了丰富多彩的宣传活动，深入开展“完善体制提高素质”活动，全系统管理人员素质迅速提高。加强党风廉政建设，全面推进教育、制度、监督和预防工作。开展文体活动，创建了和谐“大家庭”，展示了全系统精神风貌。

海南省民政厅

2006年我省各级民政部门求真务实，开拓创新，在调节社会利益、化解社会矛盾、促进社会公平、维护社会稳定等方面发挥了重要的基础作用。一是社会救助体系建设不断完善，城乡困难群众基本生活得到较好保障。二是基层自治组织建设取得新进展，较好地保障了人民群众的民主权利。三是进一步完善优抚对象抚恤补助制度，重点优抚对象住房、就医等困难得到较好解决。四是加强对民间组织的培育和监管，推动了我省经济社会的协调发展。五是社会福利社会化稳步推进，社会弱势群体的合法权益进一步得到保障。

2007年，我省民政工作以邓小平理论和“三个代表”重要思想为指导，以科学发展观为统领，加强分类指导，注重整体推进，实现重点突破，全面开创我省民政工作新局面！大力推进社会救助体系建设，切实保障社会弱势群体的合法权益。完善和落实优抚安置政策，做好拥军优属工作，巩固和发展新型的军政军民关系。加大培育发展行业协会和农村专业经济协会的力度，促进我省经济社会协调发展。改革发展社会专项行政事务，不断提升专项社会行政事务管理和公共服务的质量和水平。发展慈善事业，培育全民慈善意识。

海南慈善总会、海南省福彩中心积极向农村社区捐赠图书

我省隆重召开拥军优属拥政爱民会议

海南省委老干部局

全省老干部工作者双先表彰大会

2006年，我省各级组织部门、老干部工作部门坚持以邓小平理论和“三个代表”重要思想为指导，树立和落实科学发展观，坚持以人为本，服务为先，紧扣主线，稳步推进，老干部工作取得了明显成效。

老干部的政治待遇得到较好落实。各级党委及有关部门认真做好巩固和扩大老干部党员先进性教育活动成果工作，逐步完善了离退休干部党支部“三会一课”、集中学习、报告工作、党员管理、联系党员等制度。老干部的政治生活丰富多彩，队伍思想稳定，在构建和谐海南中发挥了积极的作用。

离休干部的生活待遇得到保障。各市县各部门认真贯彻落实中办厅字[2005]12号文件精神，省委办公厅、省政府办公厅出台《关于做好省属国有改制和破产企业离休干部管理服务工作的实施意见》，各市县也相应出台了管理办法，切实把国有改制和破产企业离休干部各项待遇落实好。进一步完善“三个机制”，加强督查力度，积极解决离休干部“两费”落实过程中遇到的新问题。

老干部的精神文化生活更加丰富。各级老干部工作部门及时传达学习2006年全国老干部活动中心、老年大学工作座谈会精神，争取政府和有关部门加大投入，进一步改善老干部活动场所基础设施，积极开展有益老干部身心健康的各种文体娱乐和学习活动，丰富了老干部的精神文化生活。

调研、宣传工作取得了新成果。各级老干部工作部门主动深入基层开展调查研究，对新形势下老干部工作的热点、难点问题认真进行研讨，取得了不少实践成果，为党委（党组）科学决策和制定政策提供了依据；充分利用各种宣传手段，大力宣传党的老干部政策，宣传老干部的丰功伟绩，宣传全国、全省老干部工作先进集体和先进工作者的典型事迹，营造了尊重老干部、重视老干部工作的浓厚舆论氛围。

老干部工作部门的自身建设不断加强。省委老干部局机关和下属各单位从实际出发，突出行业特点，扎实搞好先进性教育活动。各级工作部门认真巩固和拓展先进性教育活动的成果，建立健全保持共产党员先进性的长效机制。

省领导看望老干部

组织老干部活动

2007年我省老干部工作总的要求是：按照全国老干部工作先进集体和先进工作者表彰大会及全国老干部局长会议的要求，围绕落实好老干部的政治待遇、生活待遇和发挥好老干部作用三大重点工作，进一步加强离退休干部党支部建设、“三个机制”建设、活动学习阵地建设和老干部工作部门自身建设，与时俱进，求真务实，努力开创我省老干部工作的新局面。

中共海南省西南中沙群岛工作委员会
海南省西南中沙群岛办事处

2006年以来，在省委和省政府的正确领导下，工委、办事处认真贯彻落实党的十六大和十六届五中、六中全会精神，以“三个代表”重要思想为指导，紧紧围绕年初确定的工作任务和目标：坚持以捍卫国家主权和海洋权益为中心，以军政军民团结、军民共建为基础，以开放促开发、以开发保主权为基本工作思路，进一步加大改革创新力度；强化内部管理，充分调动广大干部职工的积极性和创造性，转变思想，开拓创新，真抓实干，与时俱进，整体推进，重点突破，努力做好各项工作。一、以落实重大项目为重点，加强项目建设的跟踪服务；二、加强内部管理，促进各项工作协调发展；三、节支创收，确保经营任务按计划完成；四、以“三个代表”为指导，加强党的建设；五、与时俱进，提高精神文明建设水准；六、加强海域管理，加大渔业执法力度；七、不断加强民兵队伍建设。

①谭显坤同志在琼沙3号轮首航仪式上讲话

②省领导参加琼沙3号轮西沙永兴岛首航仪式

③2007年工委扩大会议暨2006年度总结表彰大会

海南省扶贫开发领导小组办公室

全省联手扶贫现场会代表在省纪委联手扶贫五指山市毛道乡卫生院参观学习

全省扶贫开发理论研讨会在保亭县召开

全省贫困地区劳动力转移培训现场会在乐东县召开

2006年，全省扶贫开发工作坚持以“三个代表”重要思想为指导，认真贯彻落实党的十六届五中、六中全会精神，用科学发展观统领扶贫开发工作，用新农村建设推动扶贫开发工作，用构建和谐社会促进扶贫开发工作，实行“三集中”扶贫新机制，整合扶贫资金，强化整村推进扶贫，强化劳动力转移培训，强化产业化扶贫，促使扶贫工作进村入户，有力地推进贫困地区经济社会快速发展。

贫困地区经济不断增强，贫困人口逐步减少。全省11个国家、省扶贫开发工作重点市县的国内生产总值219.10亿元，增长11.5%；农民人均纯收入达到2724元，比上年增加200元，增长7.9%。全省基本实现贫困人口减少1.2万人、低收入人口减少3.5万人的目标。

产业结构得到调整优化，支柱产业进一步发展壮大。全省利用财政扶贫资金扶持12.48万贫困农民种植和管理各种热带经济作物15.47万亩，扶持2.84万贫困农民饲养猪1.15万头、兔1.50万只、鸡6.70万只等。

基础设施建设力度加大，生产生活条件有了明显改善。全省利用财政扶贫资金扶持97个贫困村整村推进建设，修建乡村道路176公里、建桥25座、涵洞103个，建饮水工程56宗，打井88眼，解决14.03万人交通难、4.99万人饮卫生水难问题；建水利工程11宗，解决1.86万亩耕地灌溉问题；建设中小学校危房校舍及灾区民房等，建筑面积3.40万m^2，改善1.18万名师生教学条件。

科技扶贫与培训不断增强，劳动者素质进一步提高。全省利用财政扶贫资金举办各种培训班451期，培训贫困农民4.32万人次。其中，举办劳动力转移培训班122期，培训1.30万人，转移就业1.24万人；举办实用技术培训班276期，培训2.71万人次；举办贫困地区中小学教师脱产培训班2期，培训530人，以及选派海师269名大学生到贫困地区顶岗支教。

社会帮扶力度加大，联手扶贫成效显著。136个省直联手扶贫单位共派出干部408人次轮流常驻帮扶点，投入资金和物资折款合计2323.44万元，实施扶贫项目113个，扶持种植各种经济作物0.86万亩，饲养家禽家畜1.02万头（只），修建乡村道路15公里，拉电12公里，打饮水井21眼，解决1.75万人行路难、0.6万人用电难、0.8万人饮水难问题，修建渠道10.5公里，浇灌面积1206亩，修建学校15所，扶持学生1357人，举办培训班103期，培训贫困农民0.83万人次，发放图书资料2.4万册等等。

保亭黎族苗族自治县什玲镇大田村槟榔扶贫种植基地

五指山市毛阳镇方满整村推进扶贫村掠影

海南省农业综合开发办公室

财政厅副厅长兼省农综办主任：曾德运

我省农业综合开发办公室的主要职能范围是：贯彻执行国家农业综合开发方针政策，负责拟定农业综合开发地方性管理办法（细则）及项目管理、资金管理、财务管理制度，编制农业综合开发计划，统筹安排和管理中央财政和地方财政配套的农业综合开发资金，组织检查农业综合开发项目的执行情况，验收农业综合开发工程，落实工程管护措施等。

农业综合开发项目管理分为：土地治理项目和产业化经营项目两类，土地治理项目建设的目的是改善农业生产基础条件，提高农业综合开发生产能力，包括在项目区范围内实施的农业、林业、农田水利、科技示范推广等措施；产业化经营项目主要是通过对农业龙头企业的扶持，带动农民增加收入。产业化经营项目分为：种植养殖业基地、农副产品加工、流通设施三类项目。

海南省自1989年实施农业综合开发，通过实施农业综合开发，改善了我省落后的农业生产条件，促进了农业结构调整，提高农业综合开发生产能力和综合效益，也为我省改造传统农业，发展现代农业，开辟了一条新的道路，对拉动全省农业和农村经济的发展发挥了重要的作用。近年来，我省农业综合开发工作深入贯彻落实科学发展观，围绕建设社会主义新农村，较大幅度增加农业综合开发投入，以粮食生产大县为重点，加强中低田的改造，改善农业基本条件，发展农业产业化经营，提高农业综合开发生产能力，促进农民增收。据统计，2004-2006年，我省共投入资金66525万元，其中中央财政资金47810万元，地方财政配套资金18715万元，农民投工投劳1148万个。完成建设标准农田100个，面积54万亩。共开挖排灌渠道737公里，硬化排灌渠道4163公里，修整机耕路1503条，长1637公里，配套田间建筑物17.4万座，铺设草坪754万平方米。扶持产业化经营项目27个，其中种植业项目5个，养殖业项目5个，农副产品加工项目14个，产地批发市场项目3个。发展种植业4228亩，水产养殖700亩，建设加工厂房21946平方米，产地批发市场流通设施面积25992平方米，冷库3980平方米。

今后，我省农业综合开发工作，在省委、省政府的正确领导下，在国家农业综合开发办公室的指导下，牢固树立为农民群众谋利益的思想，进一步落实科学发展观，紧紧围绕建设社会主义新农村、发展现代农业的思路，继续加大农业基础设施建设，把项目区农田建成“旱能灌、涝能排、渠相连、路相通、配套建筑物齐全”的标准农田，为发展现代农业夯实基础。同时，加大对农业产业化龙头企业的扶持，推进农业产业化经营，促进农业和农村经济结构的战略性调整，提高农业综合效益。

农业综合开发项目区文昌市无公害生产基地

农业综合开发项目区文昌市农民培训基地

文昌市产业化经营项目海南永青绿色农业食品加工有限公司果蔬加工车间

农业综合开发支持新农村建设。图为三亚市凤凰镇槟榔村结合农田综合整治，配套建设道路一角

农业综合开发加强中低产田改造，实行山、水、田、林、路综合治理。图为三亚市凤凰镇槟榔田洋农业综合开发项目区

农村环境，得到改善，昔日贫困落后村变成今日文明生态村。图为三亚市凤凰镇槟榔村新貌

海南省招商办

2006厦洽会期间，省招商办陪同省领导会见广东美国商会代表

海南省人民政府招商办公室主任冯鸣

一、省招商办工作职能

（一）制定和实施全省招商引资中长期规划与年度计划。

（二）建立对外招商引资工作的信息网络及联系渠道；策划和包装招商项目。

（三）策划、组织、牵头和协调全省重大招商引资活动和经贸洽谈活动。

（四）负责引进重点招商项目，协调落实建设条件，做好跟踪服务，促进项目建设。

二、2006年大事纪要

1、举办和参与的重大招商活动

⑴在海口举办“港澳台侨与内地企业领袖峰会暨海南新型工业发展论坛推介会”，港澳台近百家企业代表参会。

⑵举办福耀杯高尔夫赛事，以球会友，加强与国内外玻璃加工企业的交流和联系。

⑶组织省政府代表团和企业参加第三届泛珠三角区域论坛暨经贸洽谈会，签署了23个合作项目，金额达62.1亿元。

⑷参加第二届“津洽会”，组织召开海南省介绍会。

2、积极引进大企业大项目

福耀集团70万吨浮法玻璃项目开工。PX项目、大甲醇项目、商业石油储备等项目前期进展顺利。中信泰富开发万宁神州半岛、7家大公司联合开发三亚海棠湾、雅居乐地产公司投资陵水清水湾、新加坡PRM公司修造船厂等项目进程加快。中国华能与省政府签署加强能源合作协议。引进香港名源发展公司投资建设生命科学研究教育基地。

2006年全省招商专业会议

3、签约项目履约取得新进展

截止2006年底，近几年组织签约的243项目中，项目履约率达77%。其中竣工投产或执行合同项目70个，完成投资96.94亿元；在建项目44个，完成投资46.08亿元；正在开展前期工作的项目72个；其余57个项目正在逐步落实土地和规划设计等事宜。

主任：吴亚明

海南省财政投资评审中心

评审中心为隶属省财政厅的正处级事业单位。内设综合部、稽核部、业务部3个科级机构。

工作任务和职责范围：

根据财政部门的委托，对财政性资金投资项目的工程概算、预（结）算和竣工财务决算进行审查，实施对财政性基本建设资金使用的监督管理和建设项目绩效评价等。具体是：

1、对我省建设项目预（结）算、竣工决算评审；

2、在编制年度部门预算期间，对部门项目预算进行评审；

3、受财政部委托，对中央投资在我省或外省的大型项目预（结）算、竣工决算评审；

4、受财政部和省财政厅委托，参加财政投资项目的专项监督检查。

评审工作开展情况：

评审工作开展几年来已取得了明显的成效，为财政资金管理提供了强有力的技术支撑。截止2006年底，共评审和核查各类项目277个，金额达297.7亿元，审查发现不合理资金约10.7亿元，审减财政资金6.3亿元。

2006年，中心出具的《湖南衡枣高速公路预算评审报告》被评为全国财政系统投资评审优秀评审报告。中心主任吴亚明同志荣获全国财政系统投资评审工作先进个人称号。

评审工作成效主要体现在以下几方面：

1、为财政部门科学合理的安排资金提供了技术支持。

2、为财政部门批复项目决（结）算提供了技术支持。

3、争取国家资金，支持我省经济建设，发挥了积极作用。

4、为财政部门加强建设项目资金管理、提高财政资金使用效益提供了技术支持。

舒畅的办公环境

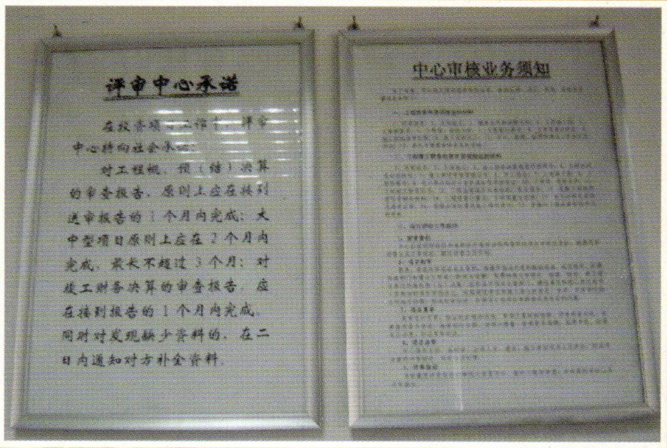

在投资项目工作中，中心向社会的承诺

海南省财政信息中心

海南省财政信息中心主任：吉兆民

2006年9月全省财政系统金财工程建设工作会议在海口召开

全省财政数据中心机房

省财政信息中心开发部办公环境

海南省财政信息中心于1989年组建，具有法人代表资格，属省财政厅处室管理的正处级事业单位，经费实行全额预算单位管理，编制8人。

工作职责：负责制订全省财政系统信息化的规划；负责全省财政系统广域网和厅机关局域网建设和管理；负责指导市县财政部门信息化建设实施；承担财政业务应用信息系统开发和数据处理；承担财政系统应用软件的技术评审和推广应用；承担信息资源开发、数据库建设和信息服务；负责计算机网络系统的安全保密工作；承担财政系统信息技术培训工作。

2000年以来，在厅党组的正确领导下，财政信息化建设紧紧围绕财政改革全面推进，以实现财政管理科学化为目标，以“十五”期间重大财政改革为契机，建成了财政部-省财政厅-市县财政局-乡镇财政所三级骨干通信网络，开发和应用了部门预算编制、预算执行、非税收入和工资统发等四大应用系统，有力地支撑了部门预算编制、国库集中收付、政府采购、工资统一发放和收支两条线等重大财政改革。2005年又成功开发了海南省政府财政管理信息系统（GFMIS），该系统支撑了现行财政管理所有主体业务，具有自主知识产权，达到了当前国外政府财政管理信息系统先进水平，得到财政部充分肯定。财政信息化建设不仅确立了信息中心在财政管理和改革中不可或缺的基础保障地位，也锻炼和培养了一支既熟悉业务又精通计算机技术的队伍，为我省“十一五”期间高起点财政信息化建设创造了的良好条件。由于成绩突出，2005年被省信息化建设领导小组评为“海南省信息化先进单位”；2006年被省直机关工委评为2004-2006年度“海南省精神文明先进单位”；2007年6月，被海南省委、省政府评为“2003-2006年度海南省文明单位。”

今后三年，我省财政信息化建设将以全面提高财政管理水平为目标，以政府收支分类改革为契机，以建立科学、合理的业务管理流程为主线，全面推进我省政府财政管理信息系统的建设。至2009年，按照大集中的模式，建成覆盖省、市县、乡镇三级政府，覆盖同级部门与预算单位，覆盖全部财政资金，融合管理与技术、服务便捷、运行安全的政府财政管理信息系统。

海南省地质矿产勘查开发局

省领导、国土资源部领导到海南地矿局标本室参观

中国地质调查局领导来到我局指导地质工作

海南省地质矿产勘查开发局（前身为地矿部中南地质局410勘探队）成立于1953年，现为海南省政府直属的正厅级事业单位。主要职能是贯彻执行国家和本省有关地质矿产勘查开发工作的法律法规，指导、协调并从事国家基础性、公益性、战略性地质和矿产勘查；实施矿业开发、工程勘察施工等工作。

海南省地矿局现有职工1827人，各类专业技术人员902人，其中高级职称139人（教授级19人），中级职称315人。所属有海南省地质调查院、海南省水文地质工程地质勘察院（国家综合甲级勘察资质单位）、海南省地质测试研究中心（国家级计量认证单位）、海南省地质环境监测总站等十三家下属事业单位。

进岛五十三年以来，该地勘队伍开展艰苦细致的地质找矿和科研等工作，取得了丰硕的找矿成果，全省共发现各类矿产88种；经评价有工业储量的矿产66种。发现矿点372处，大型矿床49处，矿产资源储量潜在总值为2558.亿元以上。累计向国家提交各类地质报告1000多份，获国家科技进步奖1项，部找矿成果奖5项，省部级科技进步奖18项，省部级优秀工程勘察奖6项，省科技成果转化一等奖1项，为国家和海南省的经济建设，提供了一大批矿产资源和基础地质资料。

近年来，该局坚持树立和落实科学发展观，围绕“资源与环境”两大主题，充分利用“两种资源，两个市场”，不断加强国内外矿产资源勘查开发工作，积极为海南省地方经济建设提供科技与人才服务。

省环境资源厅厅长林诗銮(右一)、省地矿局局长廖正伟(中)、省环境资源厅副厅长丁式江（右一）到我局共商海南地矿事业的发展

海南省最大的金矿——抱伦矿区远景

局长廖正伟（右二）、局总工廖香俊（右一）深入矿山第一线实地考察工作

农业厅肖杰厅长在企业调研

农业厅肖杰厅长在养蜂专业户考察

2006年各级畜牧兽医部门努力克服国内外高致病性禽流感疫情、饲料原料价格上涨及生猪市场价格波动等因素给畜牧业带来的冲击和影响，坚持把畜牧业作为发展农村经济、增加农民收入的首要任务，调整优化畜牧业结构布局，大力发展外向型畜牧业，加快推进进出口基地建设，提升产业化经营水平，引导生产方式转变，培育新的经济增长点，使全省畜牧业保持了持续发展的良好势头。2006年畜牧业产值（现行价，下同）99.3亿元，同比增长7.12%；畜牧业增加值57.31亿元，增长6.9%；肉类总产量68.31万吨，增长6.6%，为“十一五”畜牧业发展打下良好的基础。

生产持续增长。在品种改良、规模化发展、“沼气+养猪”、“果园+养猪”及“百头万户”等措施推动下，特别是在市场价格促进下，生猪存栏量、出栏量仍然保持较大幅度增长。2006年全省生猪存栏量373.3万头，增长6.30%；生猪出栏480.22万头，增长8.60%；猪肉产量达41.1万吨，增长6%。养禽业缓慢恢复生产，进入第三季度养禽业高迅发展。家禽存栏量4127.77万只，增长2.00%；出栏量13424.90万只，增长6.40%；禽肉产量达21.34万吨，增长12%。牛存栏量138.61万头，羊存栏量92.95万只，牛、羊出栏量分别为34.55万头与100.10万只，增长4.0%和3.0%。

结构布局逐步优化。畜产品结构不断优化，在肉类总产量中，猪肉比重为64%，比1980年下降30个百分点。与此同时，禽肉比重达21.7%，牛羊肉比重为11.8%，正向节粮型畜牧业生产结构转变。在生产布局方面，区位优势逐渐凸显，资源配置进一步优化。畜牧生产区域集中度明显提高，优势区域布局初步形成。

规模化饲养水平提高。畜禽生产的规模比例大幅度提高。工厂化饲养与养殖小区蓬勃兴起。全省已建立177个养殖专业村、新建13个畜禽养殖小区，新增规模养殖户1万户。2006年生猪出栏50头以上规模比例达37.2%，蛋鸡存栏500只以上规模比例68.2%，肉鸡出栏2000只以上规模比例75.2%。

饲料工业稳步发展。全省饲料产品总产量达到108万吨，同比增长8%。全省拥有规模饲料生产企业近39家，年产10万吨以上的饲料企

海南无疫区建设新闻发布会

春防工作现场会

业8家。饲料生产结构日趋合理，在稳定配合饲料生产的同时，不断加快浓缩饲料、添加剂预混合饲料生产。

畜产品出岛、出口重大突破。年内畜牧业出岛、出口取得了新的成就，生猪外销38万头，同比增长82%；文昌鸡外销1800万只，同比增长66.7%；肉牛达3.5万头，增长12.5%。更为可贵的是生猪和文昌鸡出口实现了历史以来零的突破：出口香港生猪7000多头，文昌鸡30.6万只，总创汇额2129万港币。

畜禽品种资源调查认证及地方品种标准制订成绩显著。2006年3月成立了省畜禽遗传资源调查领导小组，各市县也相应成立了畜禽遗传资源调查机构。到2006年底已完成文昌鸡、嘉积鸭、文昌猪、屯昌猪、临高猪、五指山猪、海南黄牛、兴隆水牛、黑山羊资源调查报告。完成了五指山猪、文昌鸡、黑山羊、嘉积鸭标准制定。

畜牧业对农业和农村经济的支撑能力增强。2006年畜牧业总产值近100亿元，占农业总产值的比重达19%，逐步成为农业和农村经济的重要产业，带动了种植业、饲料工业、畜产品加工业、兽药、食品、制革等相关产业发展，产值超过30亿元。畜牧业吸纳的劳动力近15万人。畜牧业在农民增收中的作用日益重要，目前农民现金收入中来自畜牧业的收入占30%，文昌、琼海等一些畜牧业主产市县超过50%。

无疫区建设迈上新台阶。成立18个防疫工作督导小组、4个业务指导小组、1个宣传小组，到全省18个市县201个乡镇进行督导。通过实施“集中免疫行动”、“疫情监测行动”和“强化检疫监管行动”，强化养殖场（户）的防疫措施、规范动物防疫和检疫监督工作，有效控制重大动物疫病和人畜共患病。在春秋两季开展高致病禽流感、口蹄疫集中强制免疫会战，明确集中免疫时间，规定疫苗使用品种和免疫程序，结合日常补免工作，严格做到“五统一”和“五不漏”，确保强制免疫取得实效。完善了检疫、补免、无害化处理和微机登记等监督手段，严格施行24小时值班制度，对过往的动物、动物产品实行严格监督检查，对发现染疫、疑似染疫动物和动物产品进行严格处理，严防外疫传入，实现重大动物疫病零发生，捍卫无疫区成果。

全省畜牧兽医年终总结工作大会

农业厅副厅长、省畜牧兽医局局长朱清敏在实验室考察

农业厅副厅长、省畜牧兽医局局长朱清敏同志在企业调研

林下养鸡

海南省乡镇企业管理局

农业部乡企局领导到加工企业调研

潘孝平副局长

省乡镇企业局领导到包装企业调研

乡镇企业以农为本，贴近农业，服务农民，扎根农村，是农民就业增收的重要渠道、新农村建设的重要力量、构建和谐社会的重要基础。海南乡镇企业坚持以邓小平理论和“三个代表”重要思想为指导，全面落实科学发展观，大力发展农产品加工业，注重企业的各项经济管理，2006年实现增加值615773万元，同比增长9.5%，其中工业增加值299083万元，同比增长11.1%；营业收入2211053万元，同比增长8.1%；出口产品交货值43005万元，同比增长153%；利润总额192782万元，同比增长9.3%；上缴税金71900万元，同比增长12.8%。

海南乡镇企业第一产业稳定发展，大力发展热带高效农业，增加值5.16亿元；第二产业是海南乡镇企业发展的主体部分，主要围绕热带水果、瓜菜、淡海水产品和畜禽产品为主要原料发展起来的具有海南特色的农产品加工业和与之配套的冷藏、保鲜、包装、运输、服务业，实现增加值51044万元；第三产业增加值的36.7%左右，主要是一些小商品、饮食业、旅游业、交通运输业和涉农服务业。海南乡镇企业的快速发展，促进了农村剩余劳动力的有效转移，促进了县域经济发展，为当地财政税收增长做出一定贡献。

海南乡镇企业是农民增收的重要途径。2006年乡镇企业支付劳动者工资22.01亿元，占全省农民人均纯收入的13.2%。乡镇企业在建设社会主义新农村、捐资助学、扶老帮困、修路架桥、生态文明村建设等公益事业中也发挥了重要作用。

80年代农民要脱贫，着力发展乡镇企业；90年代农民致富，依靠发展乡镇企业；21世纪农民要奔小康生活，仍然离不开乡镇企业。

海南儋州新潮包装实业有限公司

海南儋州新潮包装实业有限公司始建于1995年，地处儋州市内，位于那大中兴大道，水陆交通十分便捷。公司是我省一家具有相当规模大的纸箱，彩盒包装企业。本公司纸箱机械设备齐全，专业化程度高,加工经验丰富，具有雄厚的技术实力，先进的检测手段，完整的管理体系，是我省纸箱、彩盒行业的后起之秀。

我公司产品种类多，版面时尚，能满足不同用户的需求，本着“精益求精”、“独占熬头”的精神，我公司积极推行全面的质量管理工作。产品外观美观大方，工艺严谨细致，价格合理以及完善的售后服务，多年来深受各地用户的一致好评。

公司以振兴我省纸箱行业为己任，竭诚与广大用户合作，将以不断提高产品质量和更完善的售后服务满足用户的需要。

地址：海南儋州市中兴大街西

电话：23861233
23861432

传真：23861035

海南新大食品有限公司

海南新大食品有限公司创办于1997年，是一家集食品研发、生产、销售为一体的食品生产企业，主要从事海南热带农副产品深加工特色食品生产企业。位于海口市美兰新市区，交通运输方便，具有区位优势。

公司现已成功开发出四大系列产品：热带水果罐头系列、高纤维椰果罐头系列、水产品罐头系列、热带果汁饮料系列，48个品种，是目前海南一家从事海南热带水果等农副产品深加工企业。公司生产“椰牛”、“椰神”、“新大”牌系列产品，经国家卫生部门、技术监督部门验证，均完全达到国家食品卫生标准，并于2006年8月6日通过ISO9001：2000国际质量管理体系认证。

公司年生产各类食品15000多吨，从业职工240人,总资产1000多万,年产值3000万元。拥有国内目前较先进的罐头、饮料，全自动化生产线。带动1300户农民种植热带水果，解决农村富余劳动力5000多人，培训农民3200多人次，走出了一条公司加农户符合国家发展产业政策的道路，2006年获得海南新型工业十佳杰出开拓企业的称号。

國際綠色產品證書
INTERNATIONAL GREEN PRODUCT'S CERTIFICATION
NO:CN20060105
海南新大食品有限公司
新大牌果蔬罐頭
符合GIA“國際綠色產品”標準
Hainan Xinda Food Co.,LTD
Xinda Fruits and Vegetables Can
國際綠色產業協會

2004年度
海口市十大农业龙头企业
海口市人民政府
二○○五年二月

海口十大农业龙头企业

海南省农业产业化
优秀龙头企业
海南省农业厅
二○○五年十一月

海南省重点龙头企业

海南省农业产业化
重点龙头企业
海南省人民政府
二○○五年三月

优秀龙头企业

坚持以科学发展观统领全局　不断推进科协工作创新发展

海南省科学技术协会

海南省科学技术协会（简称海南省科协，英文名称Hainan Association for Science & Technology，英文简称HAST）是中共海南省委领导下的人民团体，是党和政府联系科学技术工作者的桥梁和纽带，是中国科学技术协会的地方组织，是政协海南省委员会的组成单位，是海南省科技工作者之家，是推动海南省科学技术事业发展的重要力量。

省科协副主席黄俊忠接受记者采访

海南省科协的主要任务是：开展学术交流，活跃学术思想，促进学科发展，推动自主创新；组织科学技术工作者为建立以企业为主体的技术创新体系、全面提升企业的自主创新能力作贡献；依照《中华人民共和国科学技术普及法》，弘扬科学精神，普及科学知识，传播科学思想和科学方法；捍卫科学尊严，推广先进技术，开展青少年科学技术教育活动，提高全民科学素质；反映科学技术工作者的建议、意见和诉求，维护科学技术工作者的合法权益；促进学术道德建设和学风建设；组织科学技术工作者参与国家科学技术政策、法规制定和国家事务的政治协商、科学决策、民主监督工作；表彰奖励优秀科学技术工作者，举荐人才；开展科学论证、咨询服务，提出政策建议，促进科学技术成果的转化；接受委托承担项目评估、成果鉴定，参与技术标准制定、专业技术资格评审和认证等任务；开展民间国际科学技术交流活动，促进国际科学技术合作，发展同国外的科学技术团体和科学技术工作者的友好交往；开展继续教育和培训工作。

组织科技沙龙活动

海南省科协按照中国科协提出的“三服务一加强”的要求积极开展各项工作：

——贯彻落实科学发展观，推动科技与经济相结合，为经济社会发展服务；

——全面实施《全民科学素质行动计划纲要》，推动公民科学素质建设，为提高全民科学素质服务；

——认真履行党和政府联系科技工作者的桥梁和纽带职责，推动学术交流和创新人才成长，为科技工作者服务；

——加强自身建设，增强科协服务能力。

举办科技论坛

农民盼来了专家组

海南省实施“全民科学素质行动计划纲要”动员大会

开展国际学术交流

美丽三亚　浪漫天涯

中国最佳魅力城市

在浩瀚的中国南海之滨，椰香飘逸的海南岛南端，有一个美丽而神奇的地方，她凝聚了阳光、海水、沙滩、气候、森林、动物、温泉、岩洞、风情、田园等十大风景资源和浓厚的历史文化底蕴，她就是中国最佳魅力城市三亚。在这块肥沃的土地上，人才荟萃，民风淳朴，物阜民丰，经济发展迅速。以美丽迷人的热带自然海滨风光，悠久独特的历史文化和浓郁多彩的民族风情驰名海内外。一张名片“美丽三亚、浪漫天涯”彰显着三亚特有的魅力。

三亚市沿海而建，美丽有活力，环保和谐，环岛高速公路东线西线在这里交会。至海口 285 公里，交通通讯发达。凤凰国际机场为国际友人提供着便利。农业综合开发、生态环境建设、旅游资源开发、高新技术的开发为三亚经济腾飞提供更多的机遇和挑战。

这座“中国最佳人居环境城市”，碧海、青山、高楼、雕塑、巨石、礁盘和谐一体，宛若七彩交融的丹青画屏，椰林、波涛、渔帆、鸥燕、云层辉映点衬，构成南国特有的椰风海韵。

一首“请到天涯海角来”更是唱出了三亚的独特魅力，“天涯海角”已经成为海南和三亚旅游的标志和代名词。作为中国优秀旅游城市，千百年的积淀，使三亚承载了丰富深刻的文化内涵，“天涯”、“海角”和“南天一柱”巨石，雄峙南海之

省领导为欢乐节敲响平安祥和的钟声

市委书记江泽林（中）、市长陆志远慰问基层党员、干部

项目“卓达 东方巴哈马”二期开工奠基

充满魅力的三亚

三亚

滨，笑傲惊涛骇浪。人们心中的“天涯情节”使国内外游人慕名而来到这块圣地。天涯海角、亚龙湾、南山、大东海、鹿回头、小洞天、三亚湾、黎族风情园、海天自然景区等重要景点尽兴游览，足可圆你心中天涯之梦。尤其站在“南海情山”鹿回头半岛至高点，观海，看日出日落，更令人心旷神怡，艺术效果、灯光五彩斑斓，将三亚夜空装扮成人间仙境。108 米高的海上观音，一体三面，是慈悲、智慧、虔诚的象征，是佛教界、学术界、文化界的交流。江泽民主席游览三亚景区后挥笔写下“碧海连天运、琼崖尽是春”的佳句。

随着三亚的发展与建设，三亚不再是海南的三亚，而是世界的三亚，她的实力、活力、魅力深深吸引着世人的目光，一年一度盛大的天涯海角国际婚庆节和新丝路中国模特大赛，又使这里成为情侣们表达忠贞爱情的圣殿和展示美丽风采的舞台，世界小姐总决赛等众多国际赛事更是拉近了三亚和世界的距离。一座新兴的国际化热带滨海旅游城市正屹立在世界的东方。

国家5A级南山文化旅游区海上观音

重点项目三亚凤凰岛投资签约仪式

重大招商项目

天涯海角

琼海——恬静 温馨 浪漫 宜居的家园

The best Inhabitant and Envivanment of Qionghai

万泉河漂流

市委书记祝春荣（中）、市长符宣朝视察建设工地

琼海，美丽而富有魅力的城市，被誉为海南省东海岸的明珠。充满传奇的红色娘子军、风光旖旎的万泉河、殊惊世界的博鳌亚洲论坛，构架起琼海的与众不同。红色的历程、蓝色的诱惑、绿色的魅力，张扬出琼海光彩四射。

琼海市基础设施良好，交通通讯发达。由嘉积、博鳌、官塘三大人口、建筑组团构成的大琼海，在21世纪初推进城市化进程中崛起为海南第三大城市。琼海倍受胡锦涛、江泽民、温家宝、朱镕基、贾庆林、曾庆红等党和国家领导人的关怀与重视。他们亲临琼海，向亚洲乃至世界发出热情的邀请，琼海聚集了四海群贤，也聚拢了天下目光。

琼海，历史悠久、人杰地灵、物阜民丰，文化发达，是著名的侨乡、温泉之乡。在这块美丽而神奇的土地上，资源丰富、社会安定、民风高尚、环境良好，是国内外投资商的乐园与天堂。琼海到处是春潮涌、人气旺、商机多、气象新。

站在新世纪改革开放的新潮头，琼海人民牢牢把握历史发展的新机遇，把琼海创建成中国优秀旅游城市，全国双拥模范城。今天，琼海人坚持以人为本的科学发展观，朝着实现中等城市、海南岛东商贸中心城市的目标跨步迈进。

琼海素有爱商的热心、亲商的威望，助商的诚恳，兴商的能力。琼海将竭诚奉献真情！迎接四方客商八面宾朋前来旅游观光、投资置业，共同创造美好的未来！

全国无公害瓜果菜生产示范基地市

胡椒基地

新天久公司生产鲜鱼片车间

博鳌亚洲论坛会址

锦绣博鳌

迷人的琼海夜色

官塘度假村

红色娘子军

恬静、温馨、浪漫、宜居的家园

东方

崛起的现代化滨海工业城市

市委书记王河山（右一）视察抗旱情况

东方市地处海南省西南部，西临北部湾，北距海口 210 公里，南距三亚 150 多公里，土地总面积 2256 平方公里，全市总人口 40 万。属热带季风海洋性气候区，旱湿两季分明，降雨量偏小，日照充足，蒸发量大。

东方境内海岸线长 84.4 公里，市政府所在地依托八所港而建，八所港是国家一类口岸，是海南省对外开放较早的重要贸易口岸和深水天然良港。环岛高速公路、粤海铁路西环线及海榆西线公路横贯境内，东方市附近海域油气资源丰富，区位优势、交通优势和资源优势明显。

近年来，东方市以科学发展观统领全局，紧紧抓住发展这个执政兴市第一要务和历史机遇，统筹城乡互动协调发展，全面构建和谐东方，全力打造海南西部现代化滨海工业城市。

经济实力不断增强。按照“以工业化带动城市化，进而推进农业产业化”的发展思路，东方市着力解决经济社会发展中存在的城市化水平滞后、第三产业发展滞后、发展观念滞后问题，以及工业化发展与不完善的城市基础设施不协调，落后的观念与东方发展进程不协调，东方的区位、产业优势与农民收入、非农收入不协调问题，经济实力得到增强。2006 年全市生产总值达 43.6 亿元，比 2002 年增长 67.9%，年均递增 13.9%；产业结构不断优化，三次产业比重由 2002 年 38.5：36.4：25.1 调整到 31.2：46.8：22.0；工业产值超过农业产值，工业成为东方经济发展的重要支柱；地方财政收入 1.7890 亿元，比 2002 年增长 72.2%，年均递增 14.6%。

城市基础设施不断完善。近年来，东方市加快城市基础设施建设步伐，相继改造建设市区中心大道，实现了市区与化工城的对接，建成了滨海大道、东府路、人民北路、东风路，总长度 8.6 公里；万福隆商城、日供水 10 万吨自来水供水工程建成；6.2 公里长的货运大道已建成通车；工业大道等项目正加紧建设。城市供水、供电、供气、通信、排水排污等设施基本配套，为城区的加速发展奠定了良好的基础。

新农村建设稳步推进。针对干旱少雨的实际，东方市大力加强农田水利基本建设，2003 年以来，硬化水渠 300 多公里，为农业发展奠定了基础。同时，大力推进农业产业结构调整，香蕉、芒果、海淡水养殖、冬季瓜菜等有了较大发展，初步形成了“一带三区”农业

和谐、环保市区

市长谭灯耀（右二）视察海防林

由市委书记带领的考察团到三亚考察学习

产业新格局。2006 年，全市农民人均收入 3291 元，比 2002 年增长 33.0%，年均递增 7.4%。建立了农业科技“110”服务中心，广泛开展科技推广工作，连续三年被省评为农业科技进步先进市。建立了畜牧疫病防治、蝗虫防治等机构，建成了“无规定动物疫病区”。乡村道路建设不断改善，乡镇通了柏油路，村级道路建设也有了进一步加强。实施城乡一体化供水，初步解决了城区周边 25 个村庄群众饮用自来水问题。大力推进文明生态村建设，涌现出了高排、冲俄等一批省级文明生态村。植树造林取得新成绩，被评为全国绿化先进单位。

此外，近年来还先后被评为全国团建先进市、全国妇联系统先进集体、全省社区建设示范市、全省双拥模范城、全省模范组织部、全省民政工作先进市县、执行党风廉政建设责任制优秀单位、全省科技进步先进市、全省无毒市等。

按照“十一五”规划，东方市将以东方工业区的建设为契机，大力发展临港经济，着力实施新型工业化战略、农业产业化战略、城市现代化战略，着力构架南海油气产业开发供给基地平台和海南西部物流平台，全面协调发展社会各项事业，全面建设社会主义新农村，把东方建设成为海南西部现代化滨海工业城市。

重点企业富岛二期

吊装化肥出口美国

东方1-1平台

大广坝水利水电二期工程开工仪式

塑编项目

跨越式发展的万宁市

胡光辉书记视察劳动技能培训

市长邓泽永在重点项目签字仪式

市领导到神州半岛考察

万宁市重点项目签字仪式

万宁市位于海南省东南部，北距省会海口130公里，南距三亚100余公里，海榆东线高速公路横穿全境。全市陆地面积1883.5平方公里，海岸线长109公里，海域面积约2500平方公里。全市12个镇，5个国营农场，1个华侨农场，总人口57.52万人。此外，还有30多万华侨和港澳台胞，是海南省著名的侨乡之一。

万宁市拥有着丰富的物产，风光遍地。地处热带季风气候，气候温和，雨量充沛，年平均气温23° C至25° C，年降雨量达2200至2400毫米，是发展热带作物的理想基地，现主产橡胶、胡椒、椰子、槟榔、菠萝、咖啡等，是海南最大的南药生产基地，素有“天然药圃”、“南药宝库”之称。有天造地设的自然旅游资源，拥有“海南第一山”东山岭，驰名中外的兴隆温泉、兴隆热带植物园、兴隆热带花园；拥有正在开发的神州半岛、石梅湾、日月湾等10多处滨海港湾。还有丰富的矿产资源，其中钛矿储量约占全国的43%。改革开发以来，万宁市蕴藏的巨大发展潜力和商机，已成为海内外投资开发的一方热土，形成了旅游、热作、海洋水产和养殖等为支柱产业，展望出商机无限，引人注目的发展前景。

2006年万宁市委、市政府确定为“项目推进年”，围绕“打造旅游强市、推进城镇化和发展资源加工业”三个重点，大力推进“9+1”工程项目

重点企业纸箱厂

海南第一山－东山岭

万宁南燕湾高尔夫球会

建设，使全市经济发展步入快车道。全市完成地区生产总值（不含农垦）436317万元，增长13.2%。其中第一产业完成164479万元，增长12.5%，第二产业完成86043万元，增长17.4%，第三产业完成185795万元，增长11.8%，工业完成增加值48368万元，增长15.5%，全社会固定资产投资完成146717万元，增长28.5%，社会消费品零售额完成150100万元，增长14.3%，旅游接待过夜人数268万人次，增长0.3%，旅游总收入78360万元，增长4.8%，地方财政收入完成16598万元，增长23.3%，城镇居民人均可支配收入7868元，增长14%，农民人均纯收入3635元，增长9.1%。

目前香港中信泰富、中信国安和华润三大财团正在紧锣密鼓地开发神州半岛、博鳌二期（万宁区）和石梅湾，这标志着万宁新一轮开发建设的热潮已经到来。勤劳朴素、热情好客的万宁人竭诚欢迎海内外各界人士前来万宁观光、投资、开发，共同描绘互利蓝图。

兴隆康乐园五星级酒店

马来西亚引进新品种菠萝蜜

特色农产品——白茄子

特色农产品

特色农产品

万杰公司生产车间

五指山市

省领导视察五指山市花卉基地

省领导在李江华书记、黄坚市长的陪同下视察五指山市水岸别墅

五指山市位于海南岛中南部五指山腹地，东与保亭县、北与琼中县、西与乐东县和白沙县、南与三亚市接壤。面积 1128.98 平方公里，人口 11 万人，其中少数民族占 66%。市政府驻地冲山镇。矿产资源主要有大理石、花岗岩、金砂、银汞、石墨等。森林资源丰富，有多片热带雨林，珍贵树种 150 多种，药用植物 1000 多种。有大小河流 120 条，常年流量 13 亿立方米；有中小型水库 16 座，总库容量 800 多万立方米。旅游资源独特，五指山被国际旅游组织列为 A 级旅游点，是登山、探险、猎奇、观光、疗养和避暑的旅游胜地。近几年来，五指山市先后荣获“全国民族团结进步模范单位”、“全国双拥模范城”、“全国文化先进市”、“全国造林绿化百佳市”、“全国园林绿化优秀城市”、“全国林业生态建设先进市”等荣誉称号。

2003 年至 2006 年这四年中，五指山市紧紧围绕建设生态型精品五指山和热带雨林山地花园旅游城市的目标，注重用改革和发展的办法解决前进中的问题，胜利完成“十五”计划。国民经济快速发展，2006 年比 2002 年全市生产总值增长 33.6 %，年递增 7.5%。城市居民收入进一步

五指山市传达省第五次党代会精神干部大会

外地游客纷纷到五指山购房安家

提高，2006 年城镇居民人均可支配收入 5430 元，比上年增长 9.0%，农民人均纯收入 2216 元，比上年增长 7.0%。四年累计农民人均纯收入增长 20.4%，年递增 4.7%。农村经济结构进一步调整优化。2006 年全市已种植橡胶树 10.6 万亩，比四年前增加 2.7 万亩。热带水果达户均 1 亩。新种植竹藤、南药合计 5 万亩，2006 年农业增加值 2.1 亿元，比上年增长 9%。旅游业转型升级，欧盟项目步行街、雨林栈道、大峡谷探险漂流、蝴蝶生态牧场、观山点、水满上村黎族农家乐、热带雨林漂流项目等一批旅游精品相继建成并投入运营。扩大招商引资，大力发展非公有经济成效显著。2006 年度，五指山冠军国际足球训练基地项目已在我办办理工商注册手续；海南中时富森林旅游业开发有限公司在五指山景区完成了调查工作，同时完成了五指山景区西区规划纲要编制；海航集团与我市签订了开发建设五指山山地高尔夫球场项目的协议。目前，全市拥有非公有制外来投资大、中、小企业 330 家，2006 年地方财政收入的税收中，非公有制企业和个体户贡献大，占 70.6%。

在今后的五年中，五指山市的经济的社会发展将进入新的阶段。主要是加快推进“一市三地”建设，精心实施“八个一”工程和“一区两路三个组团”战略；大力调整优化产业结构，努力打造产业特色；充分利用热带雨林绿色旅游、红色旅游、民族风情文化旅游、水资源丰富和中部地区文化教育的中心地位及优良的人居环境等资源，狠抓投资环境建设，加大招商引资力度，大力发展非公有制经济，重点发展旅游业，不断壮大第三产业；加快社会事业发展，着力解决民生问题；不断加大对农业和农村的投入，扎实稳步地推进新农村建设。

李江华书记在第二届人民代表大会上听取报告

黄坚市长在第二届人民代表大会第一次会议上作政府工作报告

五指山南圣镇什兰文明生态村

从2007年春季开学起，五指山市免除全市中小学校学生作业本费、在五指山中学高中阶段就读学生的学杂费、在市职业技术学校就读学生的全部费用。图为市一小中海油教学大楼

我省首个利用欧盟资金建设的旅游项目——南圣河步行街

海南岛北部的一颗明珠 澄迈县

中共澄迈县委书记 张作荣

中共澄迈县委副书记、县政府县长杨思涛

澄迈县是海南文化古县之一，原名苟中县，自西汉元封元年（公元前 110 年）置县至今已有两千余年的悠久历史。

澄迈县位于海南岛的西北部，毗邻省会海口市，与雷州半岛隔海相望。全县辖 10 个镇，境内有 6 个国营农场和 2 个省直属农（林）场，总人口 50 万人。全县土地总面积 2067.6 平方公里，可利用土地面积占 95.99%，自然条件十分优越，资源丰富，气候温和，雨量充沛，年均气温 23.7 摄氏度，年均日照为 2060.5 小时，年均降雨量 1765 毫米。

澄迈区位优势明显。海榆中、西干线及环岛西线高速公路和西环铁路穿越境内，北部港口码头成群，水陆交通便捷，电信畅通。北部沿海有港湾 15 处，已建成六大码头，年吞吐能力达 800 多万吨，并设有国家一类对外开放口岸；粤海铁路南站货运编组站设在老城开发区内，年物流总量达 700 万吨以上，境内建有目前海南省最大的火力发电厂马村电厂。

近几年来，澄迈县坚持改革开放，发展经济的方针，制定了“一县一点一地”（新兴工业强

老城开发区全貌

澄迈县瓜菜生产基地

县、琼北旅游新热点、热带高效农业基地）的经济发展目标，按照“依托中心城市，加快发展澄迈；服务中心城市，不断提高澄迈；融入中心城市，缩小发展落差”的努力方向，实施“突出龙头、提升中心、拓展两翼、带动腹地、科学发展”的县域总体发展战略，进一步优化经济结构，切实转变增长方式，在创新中加快澄迈的经济发展，在和谐中促进澄迈的社会全面进步。2006 年全县生产总值完成 46.33 亿元，比上年增长 19.8%。其中第一产业增长 8.1%，第二产业增长 36.4%，第三产业增长 4.6%。全县经济产业结构不断优化，三次产业结构为 31∶51∶18，第二产业占全县经济主体地位。固定资产投资 20.51 亿元，比上年增长 24.0%。全口径财政收入突破 6 亿元大关，达到 6.21 亿元，比上年增长 26.6%。农村居民人均纯收入 3678 元，增长 9.2%。

几年来，澄迈县先后荣获中国 50 家投资环境诚信安全区、中国果菜十强县、中国果菜无公害科技示范县和中国科普示范县等殊荣。

海南中海油气海湾精细化工厂

盈滨半岛金色海湾度假村

绿地广场

新兴工业区 昌江

县委书记关进平、县长吉明江陪同省发改厅厅长林回福考察棋子湾旅游、核电项目

县长吉明江（右一）会见南国超市投资项目代表

中国芒果之乡昌江黎族自治县位于海南的西北部，依山面海。县人民政府驻石碌镇，距省会海口市196公里，距洋浦开发区100公里，距三亚220公里，距八所港50公里。县内公路四通八达，海榆西线公路、环岛高速公路、粤海铁路贯穿全境，水利、电力、通讯等基础设施完善。昌江属典型的热带季风气候区，年平均气温24.3摄氏度，全年无冬，四季如春，日照充足，年平均降水量为1676毫米，生态环境好，土地肥沃，水源充足，发展名特优水果，反季节瓜菜等热带高效农业具有得天独厚的条件。

昌江资源丰富，开发利用潜力很大。主要港口有昌化港、海尾港、新港和沙鱼塘。昌化港是昌江主要通商港口，昌化渔港是一个天然渔港，也是华南四大渔场之一；石碌铁矿是亚洲第一富铁矿，最高品位达68%，泥下石灰岩矿储量十分丰富，是制作水泥的优质原料。境内有猕猴岭、雅加大岭、霸王岭等原始森林。野生动物有、坡鹿、野猿、黑熊。昌江旅游资源开发潜力巨大，被国外旅游专家誉为“万亩沙漠落海南”的棋子湾，被海南省定为第八大旅游圈，是岛西的旅游中心，县内主要旅游景点有霸王岭（人类祖先之一，黑冠长臂猿栖息的地方）、石碌水库、皇帝

重点企业

昌江华盛水泥厂

国投海岛水泥厂

海钢公司林立的厂房

黎族自治县

洞、赵鼎墓等一百多个。

昌江立足本地自然资源，充分发挥区域优势。确定“两条腿（工业和农业）走路，四个轮子（旅游业、海洋渔业、畜牧业、服务业）齐驱动”的发展思路，高举工业牌，精心打造西部工业走廊。打造海南省农业两大品牌（即“昌香”牌芒果和香水菠萝），是海南“香蕉大县”和“香水菠萝生产基地县”，曾获“全国高产优质高效农业（芒果）标准化示范县”称号，是全国著名的“芒果之乡”，目前，与全国各地的客商建立长期的热带高效农业产品销售网络，形成“产、供、销”一条龙服务体系。

昌江社会发展日新月异，文明之花处处开放。县城主要街道整齐干净，灯火辉煌，鲜花斗妍，草木成荫，县城绿化覆盖率达42%，曾获“全国城镇园林绿化先进单位”和“环境卫生整治先进市县”。“投资者是上帝”是全县人民的共识，以人为本，让投资者发财，寻求共赢是我们工作的出发点和落脚点，为客商提供更优惠政策和更优质服务将成为全县人民不懈努力的目标。

昌江热忱欢迎国内外的朋友和社会各界人士到昌江来旅游观光、投资开发。热情好客的昌江人民邀请你跟我们共同描绘明日蓝图！

海尾镇繁忙的新港码头

欢送农村富余劳动力外出务工

县城石碌环城路

特色农产品

新农村建筑

省领导在县委书记陈健春(右)县长王雄(左)的陪同下视察陵水河建设情况

省领导考察陵水县重点项目建设情况

省领导视察分界洲岛

陵水县三大重点项目竣工典礼

陵水

陵水黎族自治县位于海南岛东南部，介于东经109° 45′ --110° 8′、北纬18° 27′之间，至西北于保亭和琼中县毗邻，西南与三亚市接壤，东南临南海、南北长40公里，东西宽32公里，面积1128平方公里。全县辖11个乡镇、116个行政村，602个自然村，总人口34.6万人，黎族及少数民族人口占总人口56.7%，汉族人口占43.3%。椰林镇是县委县政府的所在地。

我县地处热带，气候温和，光照充足，素有“天然温室”和“绿色聚宝盆”之称，是我省重点的热作基地、南繁育种基地、反季节瓜菜生产基地和海水养殖基地。土地肥沃、田洋面积较大、灌溉条件较好，拥有国家一级的天然渔港新村港和黎安港。港湾面积4.8万亩，其中可养面积3万亩，海域、港湾鱼类200多种。以水产品为依托，发展了一批鱼制品加工业。全县农副产品加工业67家，藤竹制品和小鱼干是我县的品牌。

我县旅游资料丰富，自然景观、人文景观皆有，民俗风情浓郁，具有阳光、海水、沙滩、绿色、空气五大旅游要素，拥有河流、港湾、湖泊、岛屿、气候、森林、动植物多样、温泉、黎苗及疍家民族风情十大风景区，特别是有“三湾、三岛、一山、一水、二湖（三湾：香水湾、土福湾、清水湾；三岛：南湾猴岛、分界洲岛、椰子岛；一山：吊罗山国家森林公园；一水：田仔高峰温泉；两湖：新村泻湖、黎安泻湖；南湾猴岛旅游区是全国最大的中华猕猴保护区。陵水靠近兴隆、毗邻三亚市，处在海南东线黄金旅游线上，交通便捷，三亚凤凰国际机场距我县县城85公里，三亚市各旅游景点均在此距离范围之内，行程约1小时。

陵水是国家扶贫开发重点县，不仅享受海南经济特区优惠政策，少数民族地区政策，还享受比照西部发展政策，这些优惠政策对陵水积极寻求上级在资金、技术、项目等方面的扶持，加快发展陵水经济起着重要的作用。

县委、县政府结合陵水实际，在县委第十二次代表大会上和县十三届人民代表大会第一次会议上明确提

黎族自治县

分界洲岛生态景区

香水湾度假酒店

枫果山瀑布

出：“三做一加”发展思路，即做精农业，做大海洋渔业，做强旅游业，加快发展资源型加工业。围绕发展思路，调整产业结构，着力打造旅游、农业和高新技术三大产业特色。“十一五”规划提出今后五年我县经济社会发展的主要预期目标是：全县生产总值年均递增13%左右，到2010年，达到38亿元左右，人均生产总值突破10000元；财政收入突破亿元大关；固定资产投资累计达30亿元；农民人均纯收入年均增幅不低于10%，达到3520元；城镇居民人均可支配收入年均增幅不低于8%，达到7880元；人口自然增长率控制在7.3‰以内；各项社会事业协调发展，构建和谐陵水取得新的进步。

2006年，全县生产总值20.5亿元，同比增长15.1%，财政收入6188万元，同比增长32.1%，全社会固定资产投资5亿，同比增长45.9%，农民人均纯收2498元，同比增长9.0%，城镇居民可支配收入6367元，按同口径增长13.5%，各项主要指标增长率高于全省的平均水平。

2006年全县17个重点项目，已开工项目14个，计划投资18.1亿，已完成5.6亿元，日产3万吨自来水厂，陵水旧桥改造、陵河防洪提（上段）三大项目相继竣工，大大改善了陵水的投资环境。

按照“沿河建城”的城市建设规划，实施新城区建设工程，高水平、高规格建设文化体育公园广场，珍珠花园、商务大厦、滚水坝、水乡大观园等一批公共建设和房地产项目，城市建成区面积由7.8公里扩展到16.3平方公里，精心打造“水在城中、城在林中、人在绿中”的花园式美丽新陵水。

南湾猴岛景区

新兴工业富县、海洋渔业强县、高效农业稳县、文化旅游活县

解放公园一角

临高县

建设中的新盈港

海南临高化工实业有限公司

神农大丰

临高县位于海南岛西北部，东邻澄迈县，西南与儋州市接壤，北濒琼州海峡。陆地面积 1317平方公里。人口45万。辖11个镇、171个村（居）委会、733个自然村，境内有2个国营农场。县委、县政府驻临城镇。临高县自然资源和土地资源丰富，地势平坦，土壤肥沃，雨量充沛，具有得天独厚的农业发展条件，盛产水稻、橡胶、糖蔗、荔枝、香蕉等多种农作物，制种业发达，是全省第二大制种基地，临高乳猪、多文空心菜等优良农产品驰名省内外。海岸线长71公里，11处港湾，有金牌、新盈、调楼、黄龙等天然优良港口，浅海滩涂面积5333公顷，发展海水养殖条件优越，海洋捕捞业发达，是全省重要的渔业生产县。旅游资源有临高角、高山岭、桐乡夏荫、孔庙、多文岭、百仞滩、冼太夫人庙等，其中临高角是海南重点开发的滨海旅游区之一。

临高实施“新兴工业富县、海洋渔业强县、高效农业稳县、文化旅游活县”发展战略，统筹发展“三沿一中心”区域经济。沿海重点发展新兴工业、海洋渔业和旅游业；沿文澜江重点发展商住地产业；沿高速公路、粤海铁路重点发展高效农业、农副产品加工业和物流业；以临城镇为中心，重点发展商住、贸易、服务业。目前正采取以商引商等方式积极对外招商引资，以首届文化节为契机，开展招商项目推介活动，主要推介金牌

临高县城区

木偶戏

港重油改质、临高角滨海公园、临城地表水厂等19个项目，各地客商对临高的项目非常感兴趣，纷纷致函要求到临高考察、投资，临高涌起了新一轮的招商热潮。新加坡钻井平台建造项目由省政府与新加坡PRM公司签署合作意向书；海南路桥公司投资1亿元兴建临城至临高角市政大道；神农大丰公司投资2300万元建设水稻制种基地；海南名角公司投资2700万元兴建的临高角解放公园，已竣工开放，现又投资4600万元建设临高角滨海公园；与海南盛澜置业有限公司合作，将从金牌港至文澜江建立一个中国乃至亚洲一流的大型退休养老社区。2006年，临高提出建设全国渔业强县战略目标、工作思路和措施。全县渔港布局规划通过评审，并与业主签订了合作建设合同；新盈港、武莲港已进场施工；全省首次修造的两艘1000吨位补给船已投入使用；与大连市长海县缔结友好县，合作底播养殖。

临高风土人情独特，2003年被国家文化部命名为“中国民间艺术之乡”， 2006年国务院决定临高人偶戏为国家级非物质文化遗产。近年来获得多项国家级、省级荣誉，被评为全国粮食生产先进县，冬季农田水利基本建设二等奖，全国第五次人口普查国家级先进单位，全国第一次经济普查国家级先进单位，全省统计基层建设先进单位，全国全民健身周先进单位等。

渔业船队

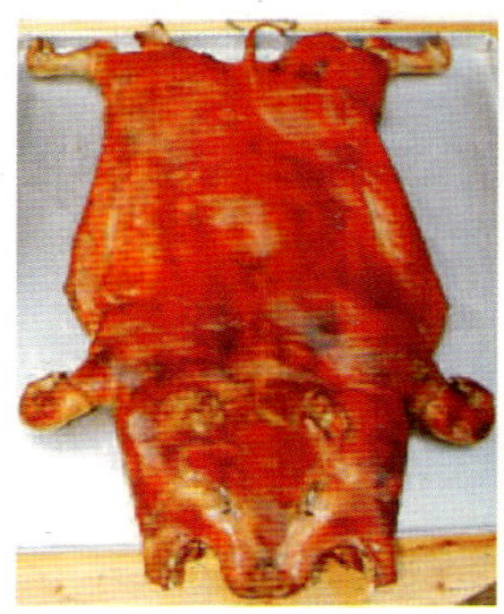
特色食品烧乳猪

临高灯塔

魅力定安

县委书记孙颖（左）考察工业项目

县委副书记、县长杨树岷（左二）考察农副产品加工项目

定安县在南丽湖畔召开的旅游发展研讨暨旅游推介会

定安县北邻海口市，距海口中心城区仅32公里，土地总面积1189平方公里，下辖10个镇，有4个国营农林场，总人口32万。属热带海洋气候湿润区，四季温和，风光秀丽，景色迷人，被誉为琼北旅游的明珠。2006年，全县GDP 185490万元，增长12.8%；其中，第一产业增加值87963万元，增长12.5%；第二产业增加值28262万元，增长22.1%；第三产业增加值69265万元，增长9.8%。地方财政一般预算收入6151万元，增长13.45%。农民人均纯收入2862元，增长9.4%，城镇居民可支配收入7215元，增长16.4%。

定安人杰地灵，民风淳朴，先后养育了明代奏考回琼的礼部尚书王弘诲，海南唯一的探花张岳崧等历史名人，享有“一里三进士”“父子进士”“公孙举人”的美称。“一湖十景”（南丽湖、文笔峰、母瑞山、海南热带飞禽世界、万嘉果农庄、见龙塔、定安古城、王弘诲故居、张岳崧故居、江滨公园、岭尾文明生态村）旅游精品突出，古色、绿色、红色“三色”旅游发展脉络清晰。定安初步形成了以南丽湖风景区为核心，以文笔峰道家文化苑为龙头，带动母瑞山红色旅游景区及绿色生态旅游发展的旅游新格局，成为琼北休闲度假旅游胜地。

定安县凭借得天独厚的区位优势、环境优势、资源优势、产业优势，实施“两区一城一调整”战略，开发以塔岭工业园为龙头的农副产品加工和生态药业等新兴工业产业链；以南

丽湖风景名胜区开发为重点的旅游服务业，以定城为主的北部瓜菜板块，以雷鸣、龙湖为主的中部养殖板块，以岭口、翰林为主的南部热带高效作物板块等三大经济板块；建设了罗非鱼、樱桃鸭、四季鹅、三元杂交猪等四大基地；培植出了瓜菜、胡椒、槟榔、圣女果和火龙果等五大特色农业；创建了农副产品加工业；形成了以果蔬、橡胶以及南药为龙头的热带高效农业等三大产业链优势。特别是塔岭工业园被批准为全国绿色农业示范区建设单位和海南省唯一的农产品加工示范区，园区投资势头火热。目前，已落户园区的农产品加工企业和医药企业达48家。

优良的投资环境，引来商贾云集，投资开发方兴未艾，成为一片投资的热土。善良勤劳，淳朴好客的定安人民竭诚欢迎各方宾朋商贾前来参观考察，投资开发，共谋发达富裕的大计，共绘互利繁荣的宏图，共创和谐美好的明天。

2006年海交会签约仪式

定安县的热带花卉—红掌

落户海南省塔岭农副产品加工示范区和生态药业园区的工业企业

琼北著名旅游景点文笔峰道家文化苑

风光秀丽的南丽湖

江河之源　绿橙之乡

琼中黎族苗族自治县

中共琼中县委书记董宪曾(左三)

琼中县人民政府县长伍学云

在美丽、富饶的海南岛腹地，有这样一个地方：巍峨的五指山在这里巍然耸立，清澈的万泉河在这里起源，这里就是被人们喻为海南“江河之源、绿橙之乡”的琼中黎族苗族自治县。

琼中的历史，可以追溯到2000多年前。西汉时期，琼中隶属珠崖郡；唐贞观元年为岭南道琼山县所管辖；到元朝时分属琼山、定安、乐会和万安军。直到1948年3月，琼中县的名称才正式设立，1987年12月改称琼中黎族苗族自治县。

琼中位于海南岛的中部，五指山北麓，周边与九个市县毗邻。全县辖10个乡镇、2个县属林场和1个县属农场，境内有15个国营农（林、茶、牧）场，总人口20.36万人。全县土地总面积2693.1平方公里，自然条件十分优越，处热带海洋季风气候区北缘，夏长无酷暑，冬短无严寒，年均气温22.8摄氏度，年均日照1741.1小时，年均降雨量2444毫米，为海南降雨量最多的县份。

琼中地理位置独特，资源优势十分明显。东靠琼海和万宁，西连白沙和儋州，南接陵水、保亭和五指山，北邻屯昌和澄迈。琼中北距省会海口市137公里，南至三亚市165公里，海榆中线贯穿全境，陆路交通十分便捷，是海南中部交通枢纽。热带农业资源得天独厚，是闻名遐迩的琼中绿橙的故乡，橡胶、槟榔、黎母山鸡、七彩山鸡、灵芝、蜂蜜等是琼中的特色产业；黎苗风情浓郁，生态环境综合指数居全国第四位，旅游资源独具特色，主要景点有落差300多米堪称海南第一瀑布的百花瀑布、仕阶摩崖石刻群、长兴大飞瀑、黎母山国家森林公园、白沙起义纪念园、琼纵一大旧址等等，自然景观与文化古迹交相辉映；南药资源丰富，可入药的野生植物有2千多种，较珍贵的药材有沉香、灵芝、

琼中灵芝

琼中蜂蜜

槟榔、益智等，全县种植槟榔、益智等南药8万亩；水能资源丰富，境内有大小河溪241条，蕴藏量约 10.83万千瓦，尚有8.61万千瓦待开发；地下矿藏储藏量大，品位高，主要有金、银、铜、水晶等14种。

近几年来，琼中县坚持改革开放，发展经济的方针，确立了“三个六”工作思路：坚持六大原则（即坚持以人为本、可持续发展、统筹兼顾、富民利民、民族团结、政府主导）；做好六个统筹（即统筹好经济社会、城乡、区域、人与自然、改革与发展、保护与开发的关系）；实现六大突破（即经济结构调整、提升二三产业比重、稳农兴工活商，新农村建设，城镇化建设，山区生态民族旅游业发展，增加财政收入，发展农村教育六方面的工作有新的重大突破），全力推进琼中经济社会又好又快发展。2006年全县生产总值完成 71005 万元，比上年增长 9.5 %。 其中第一产业增长10.2%，第二产业增长13.3%，第三产业增长7.0%，全县经济产业结构不断优化，三次产业结构为55.6:17.9:26.5，第一次产业仍然占全县经济主体地位。固定资产投资26173亿元，比上年增长16.53%。全口径财政收入3679万元，比上年增长13.3%。农民人均纯收入1871元，增长7.6%。

琼中在发展的过程中获得了骄人的成绩。几年来，琼中县先后荣获中国科普示范县、中国民族团结进步先进县、中国城市环境综合治理优秀县城、中国残疾工作先进县、中国经济林建设先进县和海南省科技进步先进县以及海南省政府授予的“无毒市县”等殊荣。

“十一五” 时期，琼中人民将迈上全面建设小康社会的新征程。在县委、县政府的领导下，琼中各族人民以党中央、国务院和海南省委、省政府加快少数民族地区、贫困地区、中部山区和革命老区发展为契机，大力推进琼中经济社会发展取得新的飞跃，逐步使琼中向海南中部市县经济发展的前列迈进。

不久的将来，琼中将是一幅人与自然和谐发展，经济与社会共同进步的动人画卷。

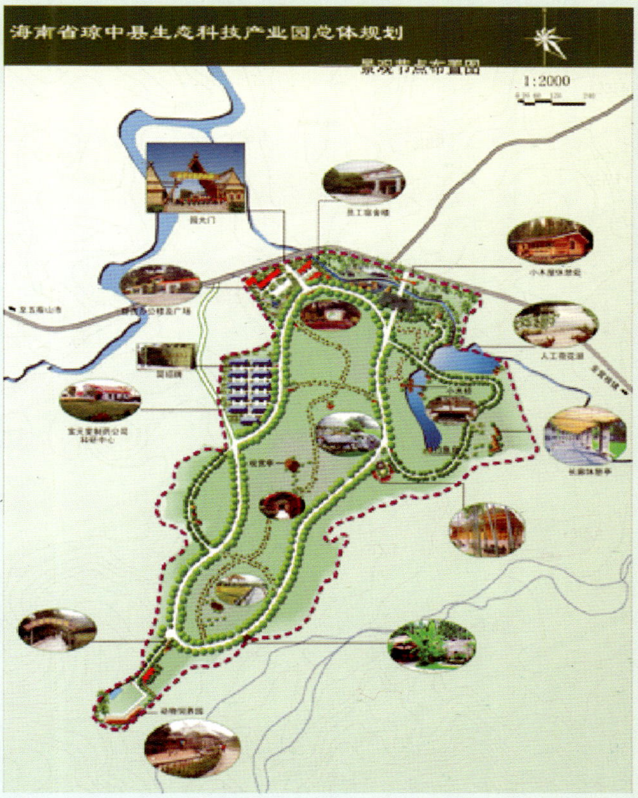

琼中县生态产业园总体规划图

琼中绿橙，无公害食品认证，海南第一个地理标志商标

万众齐聚县民族文化广场庆祝黎族苗族传统节日“三月三”

海南省文化体制改革工作领导小组办公室

中共海南省委常委会于2006年5月11日决定成立“海南省文化体制改革工作领导小组”，省委副书记（现兼任省政府省长）罗保铭任组长，省委常委、宣传部长周文彰，省政府副省长符桂花任副组长。领导小组在省委宣传部设办公室，主要职责是：在省委、省政府和省文化体制改革工作领导小组的领导下，根据中央关于深化文化体制改革，加快文化事业和文化产业发展的决策部署，协调各方力量，指导推动我省文化体制改革与文化发展工作，并提供相应的服务。办公室负责人由省委宣传部、省文化广电出版体育厅、省政府国有资产监督管理委员会的领导同志担任，办公室内设文秘综合组、政策调研组、省直改革指导组、市县改革指导组，工作人员从省委宣传部、省文体厅及相关文化单位抽调。

①2006年9月25日，中共海南省委副书记、海南省文化体制改革工作领导小组组长罗保铭在全省文化体制改革与文化发展工作会议上代表省委省政府作主旨讲话。

②2006年9月26日，中共海南省委常委、宣传部部长、海南省文化体制改革工作领导小组副组长周文彰在全省文化体制改革与文化发展工作会议上作总结讲话。

③2006年5月18日，中共海南省委宣传部常务副部长、海南省文化体制改革工作领导小组成员兼办公室主任张松林率团出席第二届中国（深圳）国际文化产业博览交易会。图为张松林与海南省文化广电出版体育厅厅长徐庄（右1）、副厅长朱寒松（左1）在博览会开幕式上。

联系电话：

文 秘 综 合 组0898-65333867

政 策 调 研 组0898-65342822

省直改革指导组0898-65339395

市县改革指导组0898-65331674

传　真：0898-65325823，65226386

电邮地址：hnggb2005@126.com

资料整理: 林静云　俞祥初
Arranged by Linjingyun Yuxiangchu

5. 能源和环境

ENERGY AND ENVIRONMENT PROTECTION

能源终端消费量（万吨标准煤）

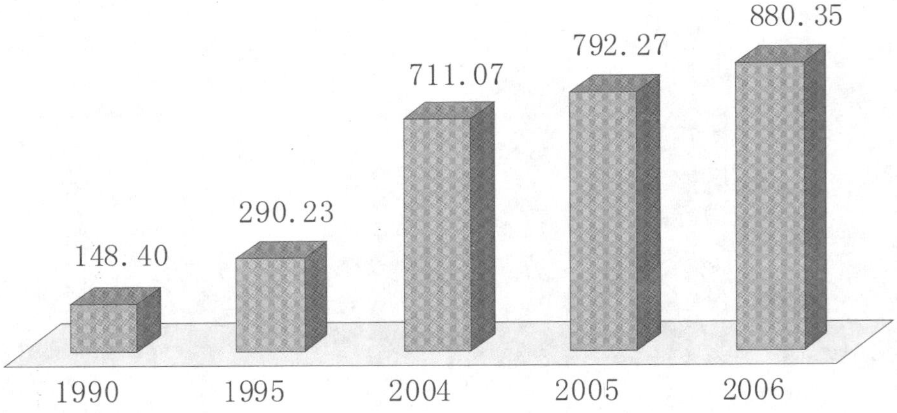

能源消费弹性系数

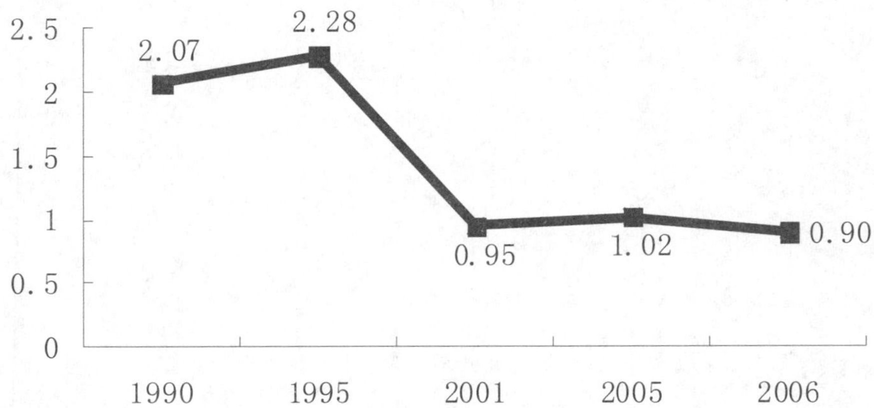

平均每人生活消费能源（千克标准煤/人）

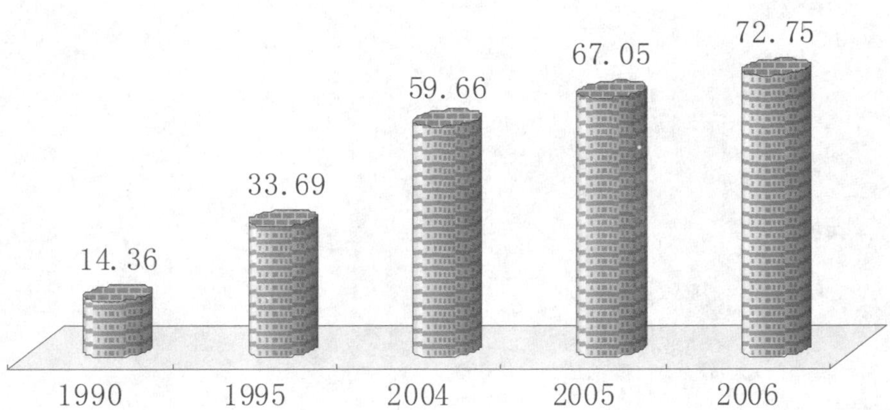

5－1 综合能源平衡表
Overall Energy Balance Sheet

单位:万吨标准煤 (10 000 tons of SCE)

项　目	Item	2004	2005	2006
可供消费的能源总量	**Total Energy Available for Consumption**	**371.35**	**172.13**	**386.25**
一次能源生产量	Primary Energy Output	41.21	59.19	81.65
回收能	Recovery of Energy	20.68	29.12	54.00
外省调入量	Quantity of Fold	504.09	362.45	382.12
进口量	Imports	99.41	110.79	438.90
本省调出量(一)	Allocation			-182.34
出口量(一)	Exports (-)	-296.29	-394.74	-330.01
年初末库存差额	Stock Changes in the Year	2.25	5.32	-58.07
能源消费总量	**Energy Consumption**	**742.48**	**819.05**	**910.91**
在总量中	Consumption by Sector			
第一产业	(Ⅰ)Primary Industry	49.25	53.22	63.58
农、林、牧、渔业	Farming,Forestry,Animal Husbandry,Fishery	49.25	53.22	63.58
第二产业	(Ⅱ) Secondary Industry	595.12	486.58	523.65
工　业	Industry	584.00	474.81	510.98
轻工业	Light Industry	60.44	126.96	77.83
重工业	Heavy Industry	519.55	347.84	433.15
建筑业	Construction	11.11	11.77	12.67
第三产业	(Ⅲ) Tertiary Industry	256.26	196.94	262.87
交通运输、仓储及邮电通讯业	Transport, Storage, Post and Telecommunication Services	136.42	135.93	156.81
批发和零售贸易业、餐饮业	Wholesale and Retail Trade and Catering Services	36.78	27.01	40.20
其他	Others	83.07	34.00	65.86
生活消费	(Ⅳ)Residential Consumption	48.08	55.52	60.81
在总量中	Consumption by Usage			
终端消费	Final Consumption	711.07	792.27	880.38
#工　业	Industry	584.00	474.81	483.13
加工转换损失量	Losses in Processing and Transformation	1.00	1.00	4.11
损失量	Other Losses	11.60	25.51	26.43
#运输和输配损失	Losses in Transmission	11.60	25.51	26.43
平衡差	**Balance**	**-371.13**	**-646.92**	**-524.66**

注:1、村办工业包括在工业中(下同)。
2、电力按等价热值折算,因此加工转换损失量中不包括发电损失量。

a)Data on industry include the data of village-run industry. (The sane as in the following tables).

b)Electric power and heat are converted on the basic of equal caloric value. Therefore, losses in processing and transformation exclude losses in power generation and heating.

5－2 煤炭平衡表
Coal Balance Sheet

单位:万吨 (10 000 tons)

项　目	Item	2004	2005	2006
可供总量	**Total Energy Available for Consumption**	**480.47**	**341.6**	**331.72**
生产量	Output			
外省调入量	Quantity of Fold	408.33	261.29	244.30
进口量	Imports	66.14	71.03	88.17
本省调出量(－)	Allocation			
年初末库存差额	Stock Changes in the Year	6.00	9.28	−0.75
消费量	**Energy Consumption**	**480.47**	**341.6**	**332.23**
在消费量中	Consumption by Sector			
第一产业	(Ⅰ)Primary Industry	4.55	4.56	
农、林、牧、渔业	Farming,Forestry,Animal Husbandry,Fishery	4.55	4.56	
第二产业	(Ⅱ) Secondary Industry	272.61	326.01	327.97
工　业	Industry	272.61	326.01	327.97
轻工业	Light Industry		37.15	21.51
重工业	Heavy Industry		288.86	306.46
建筑业	Construction			
第三产业	(Ⅲ) Tertiary Industry	11.52	11.03	1.16
交通运输、仓储及邮电通讯业	Transport, Storage, Post and Telecommunication Services	6.10	5.60	
批发和零售贸易业、餐饮业	Wholesale and Retail Trade and Catering Services	5.42	5.43	0.86
其他	Others			0.30
生活消费	(Ⅳ)Residential Consumption			3.10
在消费量中	Consumption by Usage			
终端消费	Final Consumption	288.68	111.45	76.50
#工　业	Industry	272.61	95.86	72.24
中间消费(用于加工转换)	Intermediate Consumption (Consumed in Transformation)	188.61	228.95	255.73
#发　电	Power Generation	188.61	228.95	255.73
加工转换损失量	Losses in Processing and Transformation			
损失量	Other Losses	3.18	1.20	
#运输和输配损失	Losses in Transmission	3.18	1.20	
平衡差	**Balance**			−0.51

注:生产量为原煤产量。
a)Data on output refer to the output of raw coal.

5－3 石油平衡表
Petroleum Balance Sheet

单位:万吨 (10 000 tons)

项　目	Item	2004	2005	2006
可供总量	**Total Energy Available for Consumption**	**180.54**	**168.52**	**225.69**
生产量	Output			11.09
回收能	Recovery of Energy			7.86
外省调入量	Quantity of Fold	146.03	118.59	130.09
进口量	Imports	35.79	40.77	262.09
本省调出量(－)	Allocation			122.67
出口量(－)	Exports (–)			22.66
年初末库存差额	Stock Changes in the Year	–1.28	–0.94	–40.11
消费量	**Energy Consumption**	**181.24**	**165.26**	**218.43**
在消费量中	Consumption by Sector			
第一产业	(Ⅰ)Primary Industry	23.00	26.05	32.00
农、林、牧、渔业	Farming,Forestry,Animal Husbandry,Fishery	23.00	23.05	32.00
第二产业	(Ⅱ) Secondary Industry	27.63	29.14	50.76
工　业	Industry	21.72	22.54	43.74
轻工业	Light Industry	1.94	8.91	5.43
重工业	Heavy Industry	19.78	13.63	38.31
建筑业	Construction	5.91	6.60	7.02
第三产业	(Ⅲ) Tertiary Industry	122.43	102.67	124.35
交通运输、仓储及邮电通讯业	Transport, Storage, Post and Telecommunication Services	87.72	87.44	102.34
批发和零售贸易业、餐饮业	Wholesale and Retail Trade and Catering Services	4.30	4.35	10.00
其他	Others	30.50	10.88	12.01
生活消费	(Ⅳ)Residential Consumption	7.56	8.58	11.32
在消费量中	Consumption by Usage			
终端消费	Final Consumption	180.62	163.44	194.67
#工　业	Industry	21.72	22.54	21.85
中间消费(用于加工转换)	Intermediate Consumption (Consumed in Transformation)		1.50	21.89
#发　电	Power Generation	0.06	0.14	1.99
炼油损失量	Losses in Petvoleum Refining			10.10
损失量	Other Losses	0.20	0.20	1.87
#运输和输配损失	Losses in Transmission	0.20	0.20	1.87
平衡差	**Balance**		**3.26**	**7.26**

5－4 电力平衡表
Electricity Balance Sheet

单位:亿千瓦小时 (100 million kwh)

项 目	Item	2004	2005	2006
可供总量	**Total Energy Available for Consumption**	**68.66**	**82.04**	**98.78**
生产量	Output	68.66	82.04	94.54
水电	Hydropower	11.77	10.50	13.70
火电	Thermal Power	56.89	71.54	85.08
消费量	**Energy Consumption**	**68.66**	**81.61**	**97.66**
在消费量中	Consumption by Sector			
第一产业	(Ⅰ)Primary Industry	3.70	4.62	5.37
农、林、牧、渔业	Farming,Forestry,Animal Husbandry,Fishery	3.70	4.62	5.37
第二产业	(Ⅱ) Secondary Industry	35.04	44.73	55.91
工业	Industry	34.31	44.14	55.15
轻工业	Light Industry	5.60	13.47	16.64
重工业	Heavy Industry	28.71	30.67	38.51
建筑业	Construction	0.73	0.60	0.76
第三产业	(Ⅲ) Tertiary Industry	17.18	20.43	23.70
交通运输、仓储及邮电通讯业	Transport, Storage, Post and Telecommunication Services	1.80	1.35	1.46
批发和零售贸易业、餐饮业	Wholesale and Retail Trade and Catering Services	4.22	5.96	7.03
其他	Others	11.16	13.12	15.21
生活消费	(Ⅳ)Residential Consumption	10.16	11.60	12.69
在消费量中	Consumption by Usage			
终端消费	Final Consumption	66.08	74.71	90.14
#工业	Industry	34.31	44.14	47.62
输配电损失量	Losses in Transmission	2.58	6.90	7.52
平衡差	**Balance**			**1.12**

5－5 能源生产总量及构成
Total Production of Energy and Its Composition

年 份 Year	能源生产总量 (万吨标准煤) Total Energy Production (10 000 tons of SCE)	占能源生产总量的比重(%) As Percentage of Total Energy Production			
		原 煤 Coal	水 电 Hydro-power	天然气 Natural Gas	原油 Crude Oil
1991	29.39	3.60	96.40		
1992	31.98	3.60	96.40		
1993	26.23	3.50	96.50		
1994	42.53	3.30	96.70		
1995	46.53	2.20	97.80		
1996	49.61	2.50	97.50		
1997	57.55	1.90	98.10		
1998	38.50	2.80	97.20		
1999	36.03		100.00		
200	54.04		100.00		
2001	61.41		100.00		
2003	50.49		100.00		
2004	41.21		100.00		
2005	59.19		62.63	37.30	0.07
2006	81.65		52.98	27.62	19.40

注:电力折算标准煤的系用当年平均发电煤耗计算。下表同。
a)The coefficient for conversion of electric power into SCE (standard coal equivalent) is calculated on the basic of the data on the average coal consumption in generating electric power in the same year. The same as in the following tables.

5－6 能源消费总量及构成
Total Consumption of Energy and Its Composition

年 份 Year	能源消费总量 (万吨标准煤) Total Energy Consumption (10 000 tons of SCE)	占能源消费总量的比重(%) As Percentage of Total Energy Consumption			
		煤 炭 Coal	石 油 Crude Oil	天然气 Natural Gas	水 电 Hydro-power
1991	178.87	36.20	29.40		15.80
1992	214.58	39.10	27.30		14.40
1993	241.75	39.40	35.20		10.80
1994	278.71	35.80	38.20		14.70
1995	309.33	38.80	40.60		15.10
1996	352.08	30.30	47.50	8.20	14.00
1997	390.26	25.40	44.20	15.90	14.50
1998	409.26	29.80	44.40	16.60	9.20
1999	430.60	29.60	46.10	14.40	9.90
2000	479.95	28.50	46.80	13.40	11.30
2001	520.44	27.30	45.60	15.30	11.80
2003	683.74	28.90	47.10	18.20	5.80
2004	742.48	29.20	45.70	19.50	5.60
2005	819.05	29.80	29.64	34.05	4.50
2006	910.91	27.99	34.11	28.95	4.75

5－7 能源生产弹性系数
Elasticity Ratio of Energy Production

年 份 Year	能源生产比上年增长(%) Growth Rate of Energy Production over Preceding Year (%)	电力生产比上年增长(%) Growth Rate of Electricity Production over Preceding Year(%)	国内生产总值比上年增长(%) Growth Rate of Gross Domestic Product(GDP) over Preceding Year(%)	能源生产弹性系数 Elasticity Ratio of Energy Production	电力生产弹性系数 Elasticity Ratio of Electricity Production
1991	-9.50	17.90	14.90		1.20
1992	8.80	20.20	41.50	0.22	0.50
1993	-18.00	24.80	20.60		1.20
1994	62.10	17.40	11.30	5.50	1.54
1995	9.40	8.80	3.80	2.47	2.13
1996	6.60	4.10	4.70	1.40	0.87
1997	16.00	5.50	6.80	2.35	0.81
1998	-33.10	6.00	8.50		0.71
1999	-6.40	5.30	8.50		0.62
2000	49.99	38.67	9.00	5.55	3.19
2001	13.64	6.20	9.10	1.50	0.68
2004	-18.40	14.90	10.70		1.39
2005	43.63	19.49	10.10	4.32	1.93
2006	37.95	21.60	12.50	3.04	1.73

注:国内生产总值增长速度按可价格计算。下表同。
a)The growth rates of GDP are calculated at comparable prices. The same as in the following tables.

5－8 能源消费弹性系数
Elasticity Ratio of Energy Consumption

年 份 Year	能源消费比上年增长(%) Growth Rate of Energy Consumption over Preceding Year(%)	电力消费比上年增长(%) Growth Rate of Electricity Consumption over Preceding Year(%)	国内生产总值比上年增长(%) Growth Rate of Gross Domestic Product(GDP) over Preceding Year(%)	能源消费弹性系数 Elasticity Ratio of Energy Consumption	电力消费弹性系数 Elasticity Ratio of Electricity Consumption
1991	12.70	17.90	14.90	0.85	1.20
1992	20.00	20.20	41.50	0.50	0.50
1993	15.00	24.80	20.60	0.72	1.19
1994	14.20	17.40	11.30	1.19	1.46
1995	9.80	10.40	3.80	2.28	2.42
1996	13.80	4.10	4.70	2.88	0.85
1997	10.80	5.50	6.80	1.61	0.82
1998	4.87	6.00	8.50	0.59	0.72
1999	5.21	5.30	8.50	0.61	0.62
2000	11.46	9.25	9.00	1.30	1.05
2001	8.43	6.20	9.10	0.95	0.70
2004	8.60	14.90	10.70	0.83	1.43
2005	10.33	19.49	10.10	1.02	1.93
2006	11.22	20.06	12.50	0.90	1.60

5－9 平均每天各种能源消费量
Average Daily Energy Consumption by Variety

能源品种	Item	2000	2001	2003	2004	2005	2006
合计（万吨标准煤）	Total (10 000 tons of SCE)	1.32	1.43	1.87	2.03	2.24	2.50
煤炭（万吨）	Coal (10 000 tons of SCE)	0.52	0.55	1.19	1.32	0.94	0.91
汽油（万吨）	Gasoline (10 000 tons of SCE)	0.09	0.09	0.08	0.09	0.11	0.09
煤油（万吨）	Kerosene (10 000 tons of SCE)	0.08	0.08	0.14	0.15	0.17	0.18
柴油（万吨）	Diesel Oil(10 000 tons of SCE)	0.13	0.13	0.14	0.15	0.11	0.17
液化石油气（万吨）	Liquefied Petroleum Gas (10 000 tons)	0.04	0.05	0.02	0.01	0.01	0.02
天然气（亿立方米）	Natural Gas (100 million cu.m)	0.02	0.02	0.05	0.07	0.06	0.07
电力（亿千瓦小时）	Electricity (100 million kwh)	0.12	0.12	0.16	0.19	0.23	0.27

5－10 每人年平均生活用能源
Annual Average Per Capita Energy Consumption for Non-Production Purpose

年份 Year	平均每人生活消费能源（千克标准煤） Annual Average Non-productive Consumption per Capita(Kg of SCE)	煤炭（千克） Coal (kg)	电力（千瓦小时） Electricity (kwh)	煤油（千克） Kerosene (kg)	液化石油气（千克） Liquefied Petroleum Gas (kg)
1990	14.36	6.57	12.40	1.83	1.13
1991	14.84	6.87	13.41	1.49	1.95
1992	17.65	6.35	15.91	2.03	2.04
1993	27.11	5.17	23.21	2.50	5.91
1994	27.44	4.95	22.87	2.62	5.42
1995	33.69	0.36	30.71	1.59	9.83
1996	42.01	0.89	49.94	1.56	9.88
1997	53.36	0.31	72.15	1.40	11.90
1998	53.51	0.45	73.37	0.70	12.59
1999	54.00	0.28	75.62	0.69	13.28
2000	54.39	0.57	76.62	0.68	12.29
2001	61.70	0.42	89.92	0.48	12.98
2003	56.10	0.48	98.07		7.91
2004	59.66		126.07		5.30
2005	67.05		140.10		6.36
2006	72.75	3.71	151.82		6.52

5－11 能源加工转换效率
Efficiency of Energy Conversion

年 份 Year	总效率 Total Efficiency	#发 电 Electricity Generation
1991	31.82	31.82
1992	28.67	28.67
1993	32.01	32.01
1994	29.91	29.91
1995	30.00	30.00
1996	31.06	30.87
1997	32.84	32.31
1998	34.14	33.45
1999	38.15	36.03
2000	38.85	33.30
2001	35.28	32.39
2003	41.87	35.29
2004	40.43	35.10
2005	38.29	34.81
2006	70.92	38.92

5－12 分品种生活能源年消费量
Average Annual Energy Consumption for Non-Production Purposes by Variety

能源品种	Item	2000	2001	2003	2004	2005	2006
合计（万吨标准煤）	Total (10 000 tons of SCE)	41.39	47.48	44.06	48.08	55.52	60.81
煤炭（万吨）	Coal (10 000 tons of SCE)	0.43	0.32	0.38			3.10
煤油（万吨）	Kerosene (10 000 tons of SCE)	0.52	0.37				
液化石油气（万吨）	Liquefied Petroleum Gas (10 000 tons)	9.35	9.99	6.25	4.27	5.27	5.45
电力（亿千瓦小时）	Electricity (100 million kwh)	5.83	6.92	8.5	10.16	11.6	12.69

5－13 能源平衡表(实物量)

Energy Balance Province (Physicat Quantity)

指 标	Item	煤合计 Total Coal (万吨) (10000 tons)	原煤 Coal (万吨) (10000 tons)	煤制品 Briquettes (万吨) (10000 tons)	焦炭 Coke (万吨) (10000 tons)	石油合计 Total Oil (万吨) (10000 tons)	原油 Crude Oil (万吨) (10000 tons)	汽油 Gasoline (万吨) (10000 tons)	煤油 Kerosene (万吨) (10000 tons)
可供本地区消费的能源量	**Energy Quantity for Local Consumption**	331.72	327.42	4.30	18.65	225.69	228.59	−31.00	62.45
年初库存量	Inventory at the Year Beginning	10.93	10.93		1.30	3.83	1.28	0.01	0.98
一次能源生产量	One－time Energy Production Quantity					11.09	11.09		
回收能	Recovered Energy					7.86			
外省调入量	Energy Allocated from Other Provinces (Autonomous Regions and Cities)	244.30	240.00	4.30	18.34	130.09	21.02	29.50	64.50
进口量	Imported Energy	88.17	88.17			262.09	225.30		
我轮.机在外国加油量	Oil Filling of Chinese Ships and Planes in Foreign Countries								
本省调出量(－)	Energy Allocated to the Provinc (Autonomous Region and City) (－)					−122.67		−34.30	−1.29
出口量(－)	Export Volume(－)					−22.66		−22.58	
外轮.机在我国加油量(－)	Oil Filling of Foreign Ships and Planes in China								
年初末库存差额	Inventory at Year End (－)	−11.68	−11.68		−0.99	−43.94	−30.10	−3.63	−1.74
加工转换投入(－)产出(＋)量	**Quantity of Processing Transformation Input (－) and Output (＋)**	−255.73	−255.73			−21.89	−226.24	65.68	3.43
火力发电	Thermal Generation	−255.73	−255.73			−1.99			
供 热	Heat Supply					−9.80			
煤炭洗选	Coal Washing								
炼 焦	Coking								
炼 油	Oil Refining					−10.10	−226.24	65.68	3.43
制 气	Gas Production								
其中:焦炭再投入量(－)	Of which, Quantity of Re－inputted Coke (－)								
煤制品加工	Processing of Coal Products								
损 失 量	**Loss Quantity**					1.87	1.74	0.06	0.03
其中：运输和输配损失	Of which, Transport and Distribution Loss					1.87	1.74	0.06	0.03
终端消费量	**Terminal Consumption**	76.50	72.20	4.30	18.65	194.65	2.12	33.28	65.89
第一产业	1. First Industry					32.00			
农、林、牧、渔业	Agriculture, Forestry, Livestock and Fishing Industry					32.00			
第二产业	2. Secondary Industry	72.24	72.20	0.04	18.65	28.87	2.12	3.74	0.02
工 业	Industry	72.24	72.20	0.04	18.65	21.85	2.12	1.02	0.02
#用作原料.材料	# Used for Raw Material and Material	4.41	4.41		16.00	0.16			
建筑业	Building Industry					7.02		2.72	0.00
第三产业	3. Tertiary Industry	1.16		1.16		122.48		23.69	65.87
交通运输、仓储及邮电通讯业	Transport, Warehouse and Post					100.47		8.25	65.87
批发和零售贸易业、餐饮业	Wholesale, Retail, Lodging and Catering	0.86		0.86		10.00		5.20	
其他	Others	0.30		0.30		12.01		10.24	
生活消费	4. Living Consumption	3.10		3.10		11.32		5.87	
城 镇	Urban Consumption	2.30		2.30		10.00		4.55	
乡 村	Rural Consumption	0.80		0.80		1.32		1.32	
平衡差额(＋、－)	**Balanced Difference (＋－)**	−0.51	−0.51			7.26	−1.51	1.32	−0.04
消费量合计	**Total Consumption**	332.23	327.93	4.30	18.65	218.43	230.10	33.36	65.92

5-13 续(continued)

指　标	Item	柴油 Diesel Oil (万吨) (10000 tons)	燃料油 Fuel Oil (万吨) (10000 tons)	液化石油气 Liquefied Petroleum Gas (万吨) (10000tons)	炼厂干气 Refinery (万吨) (10000 tons)	天然气 Natural Gas 亿立方米 (100million cu.m)	其它石油制品 Other Petroleum Products (万吨) (10000 tons)	热力 (万百万千焦) Heat (10billion kilo-joule)	电力 Electricity 亿千瓦时 (100 milliom kwh)	其它能源 Other Energy 万吨标煤 (10000 tons of SCE)
可供本地区消费的能源量	**I. Energy Quantity for Local Consumption**	**-30.99**	**-1.00**	**-11.00**		**-24.92**	**8.64**	**0.00**	**13.70**	**43.01**
年初库存量	Inventory at the Year Beginning	0.64	0.84				0.08			0.01
一次能源生产量	One-time Energy Production Quantity					2.05			13.70	
回收能	Recovered Energy						7.86			43.00
外省(区、市)调入量	Energy Allocated from Other Provinces (Autonomous Regions and Cities)	10.58	3.37	0.38			0.74			
进口量	Imported Energy	35.00		1.75			0.04			
我轮．机在外国加油量	Oil Filling of Chinese Ships and Planes in Foreign Countries									
本省(区、市)调出量(-)	Energy Allocated to the Provinc (Autonomous Region and City) (-)	-71.61	-3.10	-12.37						
出口量(-)	Export Volume(-)					-26.97	-0.08			
外轮．机在我国加油量(-)	Oil Filling of Foreign Ships and Planes in China									
年末库存量(-)	Inventory at Year End (-)	-5.60	-2.11	-0.76						
加工转换投入(-)产出(+)量	**II. Quantity of Processing Transformation Input (-) and Output (+)**	**93.74**	**13.60**	**14.85**	**4.99**	**-7.68**	**8.06**	**203.54**	**85.08**	**-0.19**
火力发电	Thermal Generation	-0.86	-1.13	0.00		-7.54			85.08	-0.19
供　热	Heat Supply	-0.10	-0.69	0.00	-1.15	-0.14	-7.86	203.54		
煤炭洗选	Coal Washing									
炼　焦	Coking									
炼　油	Oil Refining	94.70	15.42	14.85	6.14		15.92			
制　气	Gas Production									
其中:焦炭再投入量(-)	Of which, Quantity of Re-inputted Coke (-)									
煤制品加工	Processing of Coal Products									
损失量	**III. Loss Quantity**	0.03		0.01					7.52	
其中:运输和输配损失	Of which, Transport and Distribution Loss	0.03		0.01					7.52	
终端消费量	**IV. Terminal Consumption**	61.92	9.46	8.88	5.15	16.29	7.95	187.66	90.14	42.81
第一产业	1. First Industry	32.00							5.37	
农、林、牧、渔业	Agriculture, Forestry, Livestock and Fishing Industry	32.00							5.37	
第二产业	2. Secondary Industry	8.80	0.96	0.13	5.15	15.82	7.95	187.66	48.38	42.81
工　业	Industry	4.50	0.96	0.13	5.15	15.82	7.95	187.66	47.62	42.81
#用作原料、材料	# Used for Raw Material and Material				0.16				0.00	3.10
建筑业	Building Industry	4.30							0.76	
第三产业	3. Tertiary Industry	21.12	8.50	3.30		0.39			23.70	
交通运输.仓储和邮政业	Transport, Warehouse and Post	17.85	8.50			0.21			1.46	
批发、零售业和住宿、餐饮业	Wholesale, Retail, Lodging and Catering	1.50		3.30		0.18			7.03	
其他	Others	1.77							15.21	
生活消费	4. Living Consumption			5.45		0.08			12.69	
城　镇	Urban Consumption			5.45		0.08			7.25	
乡　村	Rural Consumption								5.44	
平衡差额(+、-)	**V. Balanced Difference (+-)**	**0.80**	**3.14**	**-5.04**	**-0.16**	**-48.89**	**8.75**	**15.88**	**1.12**	**0.01**
消费量合计	**VI. Total Consumption**	**62.91**	**11.28**	**8.89**	**6.30**	**23.97**	**15.81**	**187.66**	**97.66**	**43.00**

5－14 能源平衡表(标准量)
Energy Balance Province (Standard Quantity)

指 标	Item	煤合计 Total Coal (万吨) (10000 tons)	原煤 Coal	煤制品 Briquettes	焦炭 Coke	石油合计 Total Oil (万吨) (10000 ton)	原油 Crude Oil	汽油 Gasoline
可供本地区消费的能源量	**I. Energy Quantity for Local Consumption**	236.49	233.88	2.61	18.12	319.49	326.56	−45.61
年初库存量	1. Inventory at the Year Beginning	7.81	7.81		1.26	5.53	1.83	0.01
一次能源生产量	2. One-time Energy Production Quantity					15.84	15.84	
回收能	3. Recovered Energy					11.00		
外省(区、市)调入量	4. Energy Allocated from Other Provinces (Autonomous Regions and Cities)	174.04	171.43	2.61	17.82	190.26	30.03	43.41
进口量	5. Imported Energy	62.98	62.98			375.92	321.86	
我轮．机在外国加油量	6. Oil Filling of Chinese Ships and Planes in Foreign Countries							
本省(区、市)调出量(－)	7. Energy Allocated to the Province (Autonomous Region and City) (－)					−182.34		−50.47
出口量(−)	8. Export Volume(−)					−33.34		−33.22
外轮．机在我国加油量(−)	9. Oil Filling of Foreign Ships and Planes in China							
年末库存量(−)	10. Inventory at Year End (−)	−8.34	−8.34		−0.96	−63.38	−43.00	−5.34
加工转换投入(−)产出(+)量	**II. Quantity of Processing Transformation Input (−) and Output (+)**	−182.67	−182.67			−20.92	−323.21	96.64
火力发电	1. Thermal Generation	−182.67	−182.67			−2.87		
供热	2. Heat Supply					−13.94		
煤炭洗选	2. Coal Washing							
炼焦	3. Coking							
炼油	4. Oil Refining					−4.11	−323.21	96.64
制气	5. Gas Production							
其中:焦炭再投入量(−)	Of which, Quantity of Re－inputted Coke (−)							
煤制品加工	7. Processing of Coal Products							
损失量	**III. Loss Quantity**					2.68	2.49	0.09
其中:运输和输配损失	Of which, Transport and Distribution Loss					2.68	2.49	0.09
终端消费量	**IV. Terminal Consumption**	54.18	51.57	2.61	18.12	287.16	3.03	49.00
第一产业	1. First Industry					46.63		
农、林、牧、渔业	(1) Agriculture, Forestry, Livestock and Fishing Industry					46.63		
第二产业	2. Secondary Industry	51.60	51.57	0.02	18.12	42.20	3.03	5.50
工业	(1) Industry	51.60	51.57	0.02	18.12	31.93	3.03	1.50
#用作原料、材料	# Used for Raw Material and Material	3.15	3.15		15.54	0.25		
建筑业	(2) Building Industry					10.27		4.00
第三产业	3. Tertiary Industry	0.70		0.70		180.35		39.86
交通运输、仓储和邮政业	(1) Transport, Warehouse and Post					147.21		12.14
批发、零售业和住宿、餐饮业	(2) Wholesale, Retail, Lodging and Catering	0.52		0.52		15.49		7.65
其他	(3) Others	0.18		0.18		17.65		15.07
生活消费	4. Living Consumption	1.88		1.88		17.98		8.64
城镇	(1) Urban Consumption	1.40		1.40		16.04		6.69
乡村	(2) Rural Consumption	0.49		0.49		1.94		1.94
平衡差额(+、−)	**V. Balanced Difference (+−)**	−0.36	−0.36			8.74	−2.16	1.94
消费量合计	**VI. Total Consumption**							

5-14 续 1(continued1)

指标	Item	煤油 Kerosene	柴油 Diesel Oil	燃料油 Fuel Oil	液化石油气 Liquefied Petroleum Gas	炼厂干气 Refinery	天然气 Natural Gas	其它石油制品 Other Oil
可供本地区消费的能源量	**I. Energy Quantity for Local Consumption**	91.89	-45.16	-1.43	-18.86	0.00	-274.12	12.10
年初库存量	1. Inventory at the Year Beginning	1.44	0.93	1.20				0.11
一次能源生产量	2. One-time Energy Production Quantity						22.55	
回收能	3. Recovered Energy							11.00
外省(区、市)调入量	4. Energy Allocated from Other Provinces (Autonomous Regions and Cities)	94.91	15.42	4.81	0.65			1.04
进口量	5. Imported Energy		51.00		3.00			0.06
我轮、机在外国加油量	6. Oil Filling of Chinese Ships and Planes in Foreign Countries							
本省(区、市)调出量(-)	7. Energy Allocated to the Province (Autonomous Region and City) (-)	-1.90	-104.34	-4.43	-21.21			
出口量(-)	8. Export Volume(-)						-296.67	-0.11
外轮.机在我国加油量(-)	9. Oil Filling of Foreign Ships and Planes in China						0.00	
年末库存量(-)	10. Inventory at Year End (-)	-2.56	-8.16	-3.01	-1.30		0.00	
加工转换投入(-)产出(+)量	**II. Quantity of Processing Transformation Input (-) and Output (+)**	5.05	136.59	19.43	25.46	7.84	-84.48	11.28
火力发电	1. Thermal Generation		-1.25	-1.61		0.00	-82.94	
供热	2. Heat Supply		-0.15	-0.99		-1.81	-1.54	-11.00
煤炭洗选	2. Coal Washing							
炼焦	3. Coking							
炼油	4. Oil Refining	5.05	137.99	22.03	25.46	9.65		22.29
制气	5. Gas Production							
其中:焦炭再投入量(-)	Of which, Quantity of Re-inputted Coke (-)							
煤制品加工	7. Processing of Coal Products							
损失量	**III. Loss Quantity**	0.04	0.04		0.02			
其中:运输和输配损失	Of which, Transport and Distribution Loss	0.04	0.04		0.02			
终端消费量	**IV. Terminal Consumption**	96.95	90.22	13.51	15.22	8.09	179.19	11.13
第一产业	1. First Industry		46.63					
农、林、牧、渔业	(1) Agriculture, Forestry, Livestock and Fishing Industry		46.63					
第二产业	2. Secondary Industry	0.03	12.82	1.37	0.22	8.09	174.02	11.13
工业	(1) Industry	0.03	6.56	1.37	0.22	8.09	174.02	11.13
#用作原料、材料	# Used for Raw Material and Material					0.25		
建筑业	(2) Building Industry	0.00	6.27					
第三产业	3. Tertiary Industry	96.92	30.77	12.14	5.66		4.29	
交通运输、仓储和邮政业	(1) Transport, Warehouse and Post	96.92	26.01	12.14			2.31	
批发、零售业和住宿、餐饮业	(2) Wholesale, Retail, Lodging and Catering		2.19		5.66		1.98	
其他	(3) Others		2.58					
生活消费	4. Living Consumption				9.34		0.88	
城镇	(1) Urban Consumption				9.34		0.88	
乡村	(2) Rural Consumption							
平衡差额(+、-)	**V. Balanced Difference (+-)**	-0.06	1.17	4.49	-8.64	-0.25	-537.79	12.25
消费量合计	**VI. Total Consumption**							

5-14 续 2(continued2)

指 标	Item	热力(万百万千焦) Heat(10 bilion kilo-joule) 当量值 Equivalent Value	热力 等价值 Equaled Value	电 力(万吨标准煤) Electric Power (10,000 Ton Standard Coal) 当量值 Equivalent Value	电力 等价值 Equaled Value	其它能源 Other Energies	合计 Total (当量值) Equivalent Value	合计 Total (等价值) Equaled Value
可供本地区消费的能源量	**I. Energy Quantity for Local Consumption**			**16.84**	**43.26**	**43.01**	**359.82**	**386.25**
年初库存量	1. Inventory at the Year Beginning					0.01	14.61	14.61
一次能源生产量	2. One-time Energy Production Quantity			16.84	43.26		55.23	81.65
回收能	3. Recovered Energy					43.00	54.00	54.00
外省(区、市)调入量	4. Energy Allocated from Other Provinces (Autonomous Regions and Cities)						382.12	382.12
进口量	5. Imported Energy						438.90	438.90
我轮.机在外国加油量	6. Oil Filling of Chinese Ships and Planes in Foreign Countries							
本省(区、市)调出量(-)	7. Energy Allocated to the Province (Autonomous Region and City) (-)						-182.34	-182.34
出口量(-)	8. Export Volume(-)						-330.01	-330.01
外轮.机在我国加油量(-)	9. Oil Filling of Foreign Ships and Planes in China							
年末库存量(-)	10. Inventory at Year End (-)						-72.68	-72.68
加工转换投入(-)产出(+)量	**II. Quantity of Processing Transformation Input (-) and Output (+)**	**6.94**	**15.48**	**104.56**	**268.67**	**-0.19**	**-176.75**	**-4.11**
火力发电	1. Thermal Generation			104.56	268.67	-0.19	-164.10	
供 热	2. Heat Supply	6.94	15.48				-8.54	
煤炭洗选	2. Coal Washing							
炼 焦	3. Coking							
炼 油	4. Oil Refining						-4.11	-4.11
制 气	5. Gas Production							
其中:焦炭再投入量(-)	Of which, Quantity of Re-inputted Coke (-)							
煤制品加工	7. Processing of Coal Products							
损失量	**III. Loss Quantity**			**9.24**	**23.75**		**11.92**	**26.43**
其中:运输和输配损失	Of which, Transport and Distribution Loss			9.24	23.75		11.92	26.43
终端消费量	**IV. Terminal Consumption**	**6.4**	**14.27**	**110.78**	**284.64**	**42.81**	**698.64**	**880.38**
第一产业	1. First Industry			6.60	16.96		53.23	63.58
农、林、牧、渔业	(1) Agriculture, Forestry, Livestock and Fishing Industry			6.60	16.96		53.23	63.58
第二产业	2. Secondary Industry	6.4	14.27	59.46	152.77	42.81	394.60	495.79
工 业	(1) Industry	6.4	14.27	58.52	150.37	42.81	383.40	483.13
#用作原料、材料	# Used for Raw Material and Material					3.10	22.04	22.04
建筑业	(2) Building Industry			0.93	2.40		11.20	12.67
第三产业	3. Tertiary Industry			29.13	74.84		214.47	260.19
交通运输、仓储和邮政业	(1) Transport, Warehouse and Post			1.79	4.61		151.32	154.13
批发、零售业和住宿、餐饮业	(2) Wholesale, Retail, Lodging and Catering			8.64	22.20		26.64	40.20
其他	(3) Others			18.69	48.03		36.52	65.86
生活消费	4. Living Consumption			15.60	40.07		36.34	60.81
城 镇	(1) Urban Consumption			8.91	22.89		27.22	41.21
乡 村	(2) Rural Consumption			6.69	17.18		9.11	19.61
平衡差额(+、-)	**V. Balanced Difference (+-)**	0.54	1.21	**1.38**	**3.54**	**0.01**	**-527.49**	**-524.66**
消费量合计	**VI. Total Consumption**						**887.31**	**910.91**

5－15　电力收支情况表
Electricity Generation and Consumption

指　标	Item	用户个数 User Number	用户用电装接容量（千瓦）Consumption and Installed Capacity(kW)	电　量（万千瓦时）Electricity Consumption (10000 kW.h) 本年累计 Accumulation this Year	去年同期累计 Accumulation for the Same Period of Last Year
收入电量总计	**Total Electricity Generation**			**987383.21**	**821511.55**
本地区发电量（6000千瓦及以上）	1. Local Electricity Generation (6000kW and above)			945421.42	793238.83
6000以下电厂上网电量	2. Electricity Transmitted by Power Plants below 6000 kW			41961.79	28272.71
由外省及国外（外电力系统）输入电量	2. Electricity transmitted from Other Provinces and Foreign Countries (Other Electric Systems)				
全社会用电量总计	**Total Electricity Consumption of Whole Society**	**1638498**	**5757921.41**	**976759.06**	**813560.77**
农、林、牧、渔业	1. Agriculture, Forestry, Livestock and Fishing Industry	12471	296235.88	53707.24	46171
工业	2. Industry	12113	1839724.49	551490.79	441393.79
建筑业	3. Building Industry	1246	100697.2	7621.77	5954.07
交通运输、仓储、邮政业	4. Transport, Warehouse and Post	1459	122159.32	14637.04	13724.36
信息传输、计算机服务和软件业	5. Information Transmission, Computer Service and Software	2448	86804.89	15769.68	14406.55
商业、住宿和餐饮业	6. Commerce, Lodging and Catering	44368	477765.62	70329.89	59617.88
金融、房地产、商务及居民服务业	7. Finance, Real Estate, Business and Resident Service	9045	885093.45	76214.2	61896.57
公共事业及管理组织	8. Public Undertaking and Administrative Organization	8670	437382.23	60081.39	54519.78
城乡居民生活用电	**Living Electricity Consumption by Urban and Rural Residents**	**1546678**	**1512058.33**	**126907.06**	**115876.77**
其中：城镇	Of which, Urban Residents	362536	728618.12	72458.39	68528.61
乡村	Rural Residents	1184142	783440.21	54448.67	47348.16
其中：全社会净用电量总计	Of which, Total Net Electricity Consumption of Whole Society			828705.21	682708.4
向外省（外电力系统）输出电量合计	Total Electricity Exported to Other provinces (Other Electric Systems)				
支出电量总计	**Total Electricity Consumption**				

5－16 全社会用电分类表
Classification Table of Electricity Consumption for Whole Society

指 标	Item	用户个数 User Number	用户用电装接容量（千瓦） Consumption and Installed Capacity(kW)	用电量（万千瓦时） Electricity Consumption (10000kw.h) 本年累计 Accumulation this Year	去年同期累计 Accumulation for the Same Period of Last Year	年增长% Annual Growth(%)
全社会用电量总计	**Total Electricity Consumption of Whole Society**	**1638498**	**5757921.41**	**976759.07**	**813560.77**	**20.06**
全行业用电	Electricity Consumption of Three Industries	91820	4245863.08	849852	697683.99	21.81
第一产业	First Industry	12471	296235.88	53707.24	46171	16.32
第二产业	Secondary Industry	13359	1940421.69	559112.55	447347.87	24.98
第三产业	Tertiary Industry	65990	2009205.51	237032.21	204165.12	16.10
城乡居民生活用电	Electricity Consumption of Urban and Rural Residents	1546678	1512058.33	126907.06	115876.77	9.52
城镇居民	Urban Residents	362536	728618.12	72458.39	68528.61	5.73
乡村居民	Rural Residents	1184142	783440.21	54448.67	47348.16	15.00
各行业用电分类	**Electricity Consumption of All Sectors**	**91820**	**4245863.08**	**849852**	**697683.99**	**21.81**
农、林、牧、渔业	I. Agriculture, Forestry, Livestock and Fishing Industry	12471	296235.88	53707.24	46171	16.32
农业	Agriculture	2529	49869.67	8320.4	6100.76	36.38
林业	Forestry	379	9931	1305.66	1458.46	-10.48
畜牧业	Livestock Industry	576	8046.84	2223.63	2115.5	5.11
渔业	Fishing Industry	6972	148599.35	29441.88	26044.07	13.05
农、林、牧、渔服务业	Service Sector for griculture, Forestry, Livestock and Fishing Industry	2015	79789.02	12415.67	10452.21	18.79
其中：排灌	Of which, Irrigation	1128	35795.08	4561.52	3543.18	28.74

能源和环境 energyandenvironmentprotection

5-16 续 1(continued 1)

指 标	Item	用户个数 User Number	用户用电装接容量（千瓦）Consumption and Installed Capacity(kW)	用电量（万千瓦时）Electricity Consumption (10000kw.h) 本年累计 Accumulation this Year	去年同期累计 Accumulation for the Same Period of Last Year	年增长% Annual Growth (%)
工业	Enterprises	12113	1839724.49	551490.79	441393.79	24.94
轻工业	Light Industry	7484	553253.09	166421.98	134731.05	23.52
重工业	Heavy Industry	4629	1286471.4	385068.81	306662.74	25.57
采矿业	Mining Industries	1153	244775	48812.73	42179	15.73
煤炭开采和洗选业	Coal Mining and Dressing	1	535.5	12.28	8.82	39.23
石油和天然气开采业	Petroleum and Natural Gas Production	16	2198.5	254.04	56.16	352.35
黑色金属矿采选业	Ferrous Metals Mining and Dressing	37	65620	11000.98	13198.5	-16.65
有色金属矿采选业	Nonferrous Metals Mining and Dressing	583	135018	30805.94	22905.34	34.49
非金属矿采选业	Nonmetal Minerals Mining and Dressing	460	36403	5759.11	5128.05	12.31
其他采矿业	Other Mining Industries	56	5000	980.37	882.12	11.14
制造业	Production Industries	10444	1511586.48	343849.91	258524.35	33.00
食品、饮料和烟草制造业	Food Beverage and Tobacco Production Industries	4995	207743.49	32922.5	27260.28	20.77
其中:农副食品加工业	Farm Products and Non-staple Foodstuffs Processing Industry	2976	72384.27	16171.36	11280.43	43.36
纺织业	Textile Industry	85	27613	4675.49	5322.84	-12.16
服装鞋帽、皮革羽绒及其制品业	Manufacturing of Garments, Shoes and Hats	144	4446	925.68	973.13	-4.88
木材加工及制品和家具制造业	Timber Processing, Bamboo, Cane, Palm Fiber and Straw Products	1273	87787.73	11045.91	10925.3	1.10
其中:轻工业	Light Industry	273	16405.71	2136.19	1584.42	34.82
造纸及纸制品业	Papermaking and Paper Products	130	99392	88218.61	68804.32	28.22
印刷业和记录媒介的复制	Printing and Copying of Recording Mediums	189	11380.74	2153.86	2055.36	4.79
文体用品制造业	Manufacturing of Cultural, Educational and Sports Goods	13	1500	100.36	207.3	-51.59
石油加工、炼焦及核燃料加工业	Petroleum Processing, Coking and Nuclear Fuel Processing	25	331554	31449.65	3093.74	916.56
化学原料及化学制品制造业	Production of Raw Chemical Materials and Chemical Products	172	121603.5	29369.76	26246.37	11.90
其中:轻工业	Light Industry	14	1260	353.15	256.18	37.85
氯碱	chlor-alkali	0	0	0	0	0.00
电石	carbide	1	630	88.58	138.7	-36.14
黄磷	phosphor	0	0	0	0	0.00
肥料制造	#Production of Chemical Fertilizers	54	110447	27608.02	24960.14	10.61
医药制造业	Production of Pharmaceutical Products	216	51467.75	5406.17	5053.64	6.98
化学纤维制造业	Manufacturing of Chemical Fiber	40	49005	14634.41	9956.35	46.99

5-16 续 2(continued 2)

指 标	Item	用户个数 User Number	用户用电装接容量（千瓦） Consumption and Installed Capacity(kW)	用电量（万千瓦时） Electricity Consumption (10000kw.h)		年增长% Annual Growth (%)
				本年累计 Accumulation this Year	去年同期累计 Accumulation for the Same Period of Last Year	
橡胶和塑料制品业	Manufacturing of Rubber Products	362	44810.5	7715.62	6539.08	17.99
其中:轻工业	Light Industry	125	7605	1928.11	1429.72	34.86
非金属矿物制品业	Manufacturing of Nonmetal Mineral Products	801	209499.5	59776.61	49337.53	21.16
其中:轻工业	Light Industry	64	5010	1026.08	1190.36	-13.80
水泥制造	Manufacturing of Cements Products	1656	136947.12	49732.15	40221.25	23.65
黑色金属冶炼及压延加工业	Smelting and Pressing of Ferrous Metals	222	80951	23263.39	16284	42.86
其中:铁合金冶炼	Among which: iron alloy smelting	0	0	36.35	78.92	-53.94
有色金属冶炼及压延加工业	Smelting and Pressing of Nonferrous Metals	83	30238	3806.46	3007.42	26.57
其中:铝冶炼	Among which: Aluminum alloy	3	2500	1365.89	1486.78	-8.13
金属制品业	Metal Products	462	42110.3	6675.53	6255.75	6.71
其中:轻工业	Light Industry	142	7208.5	324.72	224.59	44.58
通用及专用设备制造业	Manufacturing of General and Exclusive Equipments	74	13398	3749.51	3057.73	22.62
其中:轻工业	Light Industry	16	1240	160.76	146.23	9.94
交通运输、电气、电子设备制造业	Manufacturing of Transport Equipments	210	68012.67	11050.33	8573.39	28.89
其中:轻工业	Light Industry	45	2186.67	402.03	736.88	-45.44
交通运输设备制造业	Manufacturing of Transport Equipments	43	40752	4980.11	4682.74	6.35
工艺品及其他制造业	Manufacturing of Handicrafts and Others	765	24071	6303.91	5024.91	25.45
废弃资源和废旧材料回收加工业	Recovery and Processing of Discarded Resources and Waste Materials	183	4742.3	606.15	545.9	11.04
电力、燃气及水的生产和供应业	Production and Supply of Electric Power and Thermal Power and Water	515	83413.01	158828.14	140690.44	12.89
电力、热力的生产和供应业	Production and Supply of Electric Power and Thermal Power	1	6300	148051.03	130852.37	13.14
其中:电厂生产全部耗用电量	Among which: all power consumption generated by the power plant	0	0	72809.76	62529.92	16.44
线路损失电量	system loss electric quantity	0	0	75244.1	68322.45	10.13
抽水蓄能抽水耗用电量	Power consumption from pumped storage	16	200	0	0	0
燃气生产和供应业	Production and Supply of Gas	67	6624.68	682.45	331.66	105.77
水的生产和供应业	Production and Supply of Water	449	70698.33	10094.66	9506.42	6.19
其中:轻工业	Light Industry	308	38201.23	4749.97	4504.54	5.45
建筑业	Construction	1246	100697.2	7621.77	5954.07	28.01

5-16 续 3(continued 3)

指 标	Item	用户个数 User Number	用户用电装接容量（千瓦）Consumption and Installed Capacity(kW)	用电量（万千瓦时）Electricity Consumption (10000kw.h)		年增长% Annual Growth (%)
				本年累计 Accumulation this Year	去年同期累计 Accumulation for the Same Period of Last Year	
交通运输、仓储、邮政业	Transport, Storage, Postal Services	1459	122159.32	14637.04	13724.36	6.65
交通运输业	Transport, Storage	425	96042.5	11172.23	9835.15	13.59
其中:城市公共交通	Public Traffic in City	111	36907	2993.59	2944.24	1.68
管道运输业	Pipeline Transport	19	2150	168.62	189.19	-10.87
电气化铁路	Railway Transport	0	0	0	0	0.00
仓储业	Storage	154	12921.8	1399.26	1720.88	-18.69
邮政业	Postal	880	13195.02	2065.55	2168.32	-4.74
信息传输、计算机服务和软件业	Information Transmission, Computer Services and Software	2448	86804.89	15769.68	14406.55	9.46
电信和其他信息传输服务业	Telecommunications and Other Information Transmission	1864	76908.1	15012.01	13967.37	7.48
计算机服务和软件业	Computer Services and Software	584	9896.79	757.67	439.18	72.52
商业、住宿和餐饮业	Hotels and Catering Trade	44368	477765.62	70329.89	59617.88	17.97
批发和零售业	Wholesale Retail Trade	23352	156577.02	20922.95	18816.82	11.19
住宿和餐饮业	Hotels andCatering Trade	21016	321178.6	49406.94	40801.06	21.09
金融、房地产、商务及居民服务业	Finance Real Estate Rent and Business Affair Services	9045	885093.45	76214.2	61896.57	23.13
金融业	Finance	794	58345.16	6433.1	5710.97	12.64
房地产业	Real Estate	2348	636150	43050.95	35168.75	22.41
租赁和商务服务、居民服务和其它服务业	Rent and Business Affair Services Resident Services and Other Social Services	5903	190598.29	26730.15	21016.85	27.18
公共事业及管理组织	Public Management and Social Organizations	8670	437382.23	60081.39	54519.78	10.20
科学研究、技术服务和地质勘查业	Scientific Research, Polytechnic Services and Geological Prospecting	215	14558	1489.39	1415.48	5.22
其中:地质勘查业	Geological Prospecting	28	649	55.33	45.08	22.74
水利、环境和公共实施管理业	Water Conservancy, Environmental and Public Installations Management Services	1707	64338.26	7777.15	6856.66	13.42
其中:水利管理业	Water Conservancy Management	52	2662.5	197.87	392.63	-49.60
公共照明	Public Installations Management Services	1435	58877.79	6788.48	5896.45	15.13
教育、文化、体育和娱乐业	Education Culture, Sports and Recreational Services	3273	127014.15	17298.68	15229.99	13.58
其中:教育	Education	1982	74436.23	11226.31	9897.71	13.42
卫生、社会保障和社会福利业	Health Care, Social Security and Social Welfare	1031	44574.78	7996.55	7396.53	8.11
公共管理和社会组织、国际组织	Public Management and Social Organizations International Organization	2444	186897.04	25519.64	23621.1	8.04
输(售)出量	Total Electricity Consumption					
全社会净用电量总计	Total net power consumption	1638498	5757921.41	976759.07	813560.77	20.06

5－17 工业企业污染治理情况
Treatment of Pollution by Industry Enterprises

项 目	Item	2001	2002	2003	2004	2005	2006
污染治理项目本年完成投资(万元)	Investements of Pollution Treated(10 000 yuan)	1685.8	76294.7	2699.0	1921.2	27866.4	54012.2
#治理废水	Treatment of Waste Water	1232.7	20954.9	2214.5	1032.1	11527.6	30040.6
治理废气	Treatment of Waste Gas	331.0	94351.9	295.5	627.1	6608	4971.4
治理固体废物	Treatment of Solid Waste	0.1	11696.4		262	2351.1	7744.5
治理噪声	Noise Abatement	7.0					10.0
其 他	Others	1					925.0
本年竣工项目数(个)	Number of Projects Completed (unit)	39		28	27	27	43
#治理废水	Treatment of Waste Water	27		12	15	15	32
治理废气	Treatment of Waste Gas	9		13	11	8	6
治理固体废物	Treatment of Solid Waste	1			1	2	1
治理噪声	Noise Abatement	1					
本年竣工项目新增处理能力	Nemly Added Design Capacity form Projects Completed						
治理废水(吨/日)	Waste Water(ton/day)	24860		16563	6241	9731	34513
治理废气(万标立米/时)	Waste Gas(10000cu.m/h)	8.66		2.88	19.1	12.17	55
治理固体废物(吨/年)	Waste Residue(ton/year)	1			1	40	

5－18 工业“三废”排放及处理情况

Discharge and Disposal of Waste Water,Waste Gas and Solid Wastes by Industrial Enterprises

单位:人 (person)

项 目	Item	2000	2001	2002	2003	2004	2005	2006
废水(万吨)	**Waste Water(10 000tons)**							
工业废水排放总量	Total Volume of Industrial Waste Water Discharged	7063.92	7000.96	6776.14	7181.15	6566.77	7188.84	7350.7
直接排入海的	Discharged Directly to Sea	2940.56		2707.90	1845.41	2463.86	3717.56	4100:5
工业废水排放达标量	Volume of Treated Industrial Waste Water Up to the Discharge Standards	6133.69	6539.91	6453.23	6740.74	6259.12	6814.57	6956.17
废气	**Waste Gas**							
工业废气排放总量(万立方米)	Total Volume of Industrial Waste Gas Emission(10 000cu.m)	4340000	13644.96	5280993	5325058	6343805	9101908	8597485
燃料燃烧过程废气排放量(万立方米)	Volume of Waste Gas in the Process of Fuel Burning(10 000cu.m)	2257600		2905653	2938916	3416944	5522068	5654788
生产工艺过程中废气排放量(万立方米)	Volume of Waste Gas from the Process of Production(10 000cu.m)	2082400		2375340	2386142	2926861	3579840	2943297
工业二氧化硫排放量(吨)	Volume of Industrial Sulphur Dioxide Emission(ton)	20177	19282.88	21616.76	22441.94	21942.01	21825.47	23286.3
工业二氧化硫去除量(吨)	Volume of Industrial Sulphur Dioxide Removed(ton)			4521.72	4526.96	4363.11	1260.84	9640.0
工业烟尘排放量(吨)	Volume of Industrial Soot Emission(ton)	18077	9025.2	10475.51	10825.97	9983.88	10225.03	10229.1
工业烟尘去除量(吨)	Volume of Industrial Soot Removed(ton)			348392.37	334963.76	472439.91	510415.54	611868.8
工业粉尘排放量(吨)	Volume of Industrial Dust Emission(ton)	13469	12666.57	12458.1	12592.16	1014.42	10642.81	1021901
废物(万吨)	**Waste Residue(10 000tons)**							
工业固体废物产生量	Volume of Industrial Solid Wastes Produced	94.89	74.53	83.83	90.94	105.42	126.80	146.9
工业固体废物综合利用量	Volume of Industrial Solid Wastes Utilized in a Comprehensive Way	53.65	38.62	64.11	65.22	71.12	86.63	113.3
工业固体废物贮存量	Volume of Industrial Solid Wastes Accumulated	32.92	16.11	13.44	30.54	32.89	38.27	33.9
工业固体废物处置量	Volume of Industrial Solid Wastes Treated	8.94	19.80	6.32	19.13	1.83	0.8	0.2
汇总工业企业单位数(个)	Number of Industrial Enterprises (unit)	286		294	285	296	281	246
工业总产值(按90年不变价计)(万元)	Gross Otput Value of Industrial (10 000 yuan)	3767500		1992820.2	2584570.4	2969039.4	3337390.3	5580563.4
三废综合利用产品产值(万元)	Output Value of Products Made from Comprehensive Utilization of Waste Water, Waste Gas and Solid Wastes(10 000 yuan)	1148.8		2301.9	1402.7	5243.5	14738.3	12714.2
工业锅炉(台)	Industrial Boiler (set)	451		199	201	196	188	177
蒸吨	Steam tons	1259.3		3428.7	3497.4	3807.7	5340.7	8439
# 烟尘排放达标的	Soot Discharge Standardized	430		169	176	180	172	161
蒸吨	Steam tons	874.3		3290.7	3383.4	3644.6	5282.7	8351
工业炉窑数(座)	Industrial Stove(set)	240		289	279	281	255	209
# 烟尘排放达标的	Soot Discharge Standardized	194		188	188	252	230	179

主要统计指标解释

能源生产总量 指一定时期内全省一次能源生产量的总和，是观察全省能源生产水平、规模、构成和发展速度的总量指标。一次能源生产量包括原煤，原油，天然气，水电、核能及其他动力能（如风能、地热能等）发电量，不包括低热值燃料生产量、生物质能、太阳能等的利用和由一次能源加工转换而成的二次能源产量。

能源消费总量 指一定时期内全省物质生产部门、非物质生产部门和生活消费的各种能源的总和，是观察能源消费水平、构成和增长速度的总量指标。能源消费总量包括原煤和原油及其制品、天然气、电力，不包括低热值燃料、生物质能和太阳能等的利用。能源消费总量分为终端能源消费量、能源加工转换损失量和损失量三部分。

（1）终端能源消费量：指一定时期内全省生产和生活消费的各种能源在扣除了用于加工转换二次能源消费量和损失量以后的数量。

（2）能源加工转换损失量：指一定时期内全省投入加工转换的各种能源数量之和与产出各种能源产品之和的差额，是观察能源在加工转换过程中损失量变化的指标。

（3）能源损失量：指一定时期内能源在输送、分配、储存过程中发生的损失和由客观原因造成的各种损失量，不包括各种气体能源放空、放散量。

能源生产弹性系数 是研究能源生产增长速度与国民经济增长速度之间关系的指标。计算公式为：

能源生产弹性系数 = 能源生产总量年平均增长速度 / 国民经济年平均增长速度

国民经济年平均增长速度，可根据不同的目的或需要，用国民生产总值、国内生产总值等指标来计算，本年鉴是采用国内生产总值指标计算的。

电力生产弹性系数 是研究电力生产增长速度与国民经济增长速度之间关系的指标。一般来说，电力的发展应当快于国民经济的发展，也就是说电力应超前发展。计算公式为：

电力生产弹性系数 = 电力生产总量年平均增长速度 / 国民经济年平均增长速度

能源消费弹性系数 是反映能源消费增长速度与国民经济增长速度之间比例关系的指标。计算公式为：

能源消费弹性系数 = 能源消费量年平均增长速度 / 国民经济年平均增长速度

电力消费弹性系数 反映电力消费增长速度与国民经济增长速度之间比例关系的指标。计算公式为：

电力消费弹性系数 = 电力消费年平均增长速度 / 国民经济年平均增长速度

能源加工转换效率 指一定时期内能源经过加工、转换后，产出的各种能源产品的数量与同期内投入加工转换的各种能源数量的比率。它是观察能源加工转换装置和生产工艺先进与落后、管理水平高低等的重要指标。计算公式为：

能源加工转换效率 = 能源加工、转换产出量 / 能源加工、转换投入量×100%

工业废水排放量 指经过企业厂区所有排放口排到企业外部的工业废水量。包括生产废水 、外排的直接冷却水、超标排放的矿井地下水和与工业废水混排的厂区生活污水，不包括外排的间接冷却水(清污不分流的间接冷却水应计算在内)。

工业废水排放达标量 指各项指标都达到国家或地方排放标准的外排工业废水量，包括未经处理外排达标和经过处理后外排达标两部分(国家排放标准见 GB8978-88)。

工业废水处理量 指报告期内各种水治理设施实际处理的工业废水量，包括处理后外排和处理后回用的工业废水量和虽经处理但未达到国家或地方排放标准的废水量。如车间和厂排 放口均有治理设施，并对同一废水分级处理时，不应重复计算工业废水处理量。

工业废气排放量 指企业厂区内燃料燃烧和生产工艺过程中产生 的各种排入空气的含有污染物的气体总量，按标准状态［273K，101325Pa］计算。

工业二氧化硫排放量指企业在燃料燃烧和生产工艺过程中排入大气的二氧化硫数量。

工业粉尘排放量 指企业在生产工艺过程中排放的颗粒物重量，如钢铁企业的耐火材料粉尘、焦化企业的筛焦系统粉尘、烧结机的粉尘、石灰窑的粉尘、建材企业的水泥粉尘等。不包括电厂排入大气的烟尘。

工业固体废物产生量 指企业在生产过程中产生的固体状、半固体状和高浓度液体状废弃物的总量、包括危险废物、冶炼废渣、粉煤灰、炉渣、煤矸石、尾矿、放射性废物和其他废物等；不包括矿山开采的剥离废石和掘进废石(煤矸石和呈酸性或碱性的废石除外)。酸性或 碱性废石指采掘的废石其流经水、雨淋水的 PH 值小于 4 或 PH 值大于 10.5 者。

工业固体废物综合利用量 指通过回收、加工、循环、交换等方式，从固体废物中提取或 者使其转化为可以利用的资源、能源和其他原材料的固体废物量(包括当年利用往年的工业 固体废物累计贮存量)，如用作农业肥料、生产建筑材料、筑路等。综合利用量由原产生固体废物的单位统计。

工业固体废物贮存量 指以综合利用或处置为目的，将固体废物暂时贮存或堆存在专设的贮存设施或专设的集中堆存场所内的数量。专设的固体废物贮存场所或贮存设施必须有防扩散、防流失、防渗漏、防止污染大气、水体的措施。

工业固体废物处置量 指将固体废物焚烧或者最终置于符合环境保护规定要求的场所，并不再回取的工业固体废物量(包括当年处置往年的工业固体废物累计贮存量)。处置方法有填 埋(其中危险废物应安全填埋)、焚烧、专业贮存场(库)封场处理、深层灌注、回填矿井等。

工业固体废物排放量 指将所产生的固体废物排到固体废物污染 防治设施、场所以外的数量、不包括矿山开采的剥离废石和掘进废石(煤矸石和呈酸性或碱性的废石除外)。

Explanatory Note on Main Statistical Indicators

Total Energy Production refers to the total production of primary energy by all energy producing enterprises in the country in a given period of time. It is a comprehensive indicator to show the capacity, scale, composition and development of energy production of the country. The production of primary energy includes that of coal, crude oil, natural gas, hydro-power and electricity generated by nuclear energy and other means such as wind power and geothermal power. However, it excludes the production of fuels of low calorific value, bio-energy, solar energy and the secondary energy converted from the primary energy.

Total Domestic Energy Consumption refers to the total consumption of energy of various kinds by material production sectors, non material production sectors and households in the country in a given period of time. It is a comprehensive indicator to show the scale, composition and development of energy consumption. The total energy consumption includes that of coal, crude oil and their products, natural gas and electricity, However, it excludes the consumption of fuel of low calorific value, bio-energy and solar energy. Total domestic energy consumption can be divided into three parts:

(1)Final Energy Consumption: It refers to the total energy consumption by material production sectors, non material production sectors and households in the country (region) in a given period of time, but excludes the consumption in conversion of the primary energy into the secondary energy and the loss in the process of energy conversion.

(2)Loss During the Process of Energy Conversion: It refers to the total input of various kinds of energy for conversion, minus the total output of various kinds of energy in the country in a given period of time. It is an indicator to show the loss that occurs during the process of energy conversion.

(3)Loss: It refers to the total of the loss of energy during the course of energy transport, distribution and storage and the loss caused by any objective reason in a given period of time. The loss of various kinds of gas due to gas discharges and stocktaking is excluded.

Elasticity Ratio of Energy Production is an indicator to show the relationship between the growth rate of energy production and the growth rate of the national economy. The formula is:

Elasticity Ratio of Energy Production = Average Annual Growth Rate of Energy Production Average Annual Growth Rate of National Economy

The average annual growth rate of the national economy can be shown by the gross national product, gross domestic product and other indicators, depending upon the purposes or needs. The gross domestic product is used in calculation of the ratio in this chapter.

Elasticity Ratio of Electricity Production is an indicator to show the relationship between the growth rate of electricity production and the growth rate of the national economy. Generally speaking, the growth rate of electricity production should be higher than that of the national economy.

Its formula is:

Elasticity Ratio of Electricity Production = Average Annual Growth Rate of Electricity Production Average Annual Growth Rate of National Economy

Elasticity Ratio of Energy Consumption is an indicator to show the relationship between the growth rate of energy consumption and the growth rate of the national economy. The formula is:

Elasticity Ratio of Energy Consumption = Average Annual Growth Rate of Energy Consumption Average Annual Growth Rate of National Economy

Elasticity Ratio of Electricity Consumption is an indicator to show the relationship between the growth rate of electricity consumption and the growth rate of the national economy. The formula is:

Elasticity Ratio of Electricity Consumption = Average Annual Growth Rate of Electricity Average Annual Growth Rate of National Economy

Efficiency of Energy Processing and Conversion refers to the ratio of the total output of energy products of various kinds after processing and conversion and the total input of energy of various kinds for processing and conversion in the same reference period. It is an important indicator to show the current conditions of energy processing and conversion equipment, production technique and management. The formula is:

Efficiency of Energy Processing & Conversion = Output of Energy After Processing & Conversion / Input of Energy for Processing & Conversion×100%

Volume of Industrial Waste Water Discharged refers to the volume of industrial waste water discharged, through all outlets, to the outside of industrial enterprises, including waste water produced, direct-cooling water, underground water from mines that does not meet the standard of discharge, and the domestic sewage mixed up with industrial waste water when discharged, but excluding discharged indirect-cooling water.

Volume of Waste Water up to the Standard for Discharge refers to the volume of discharged industrial waste water that, with or without treatment, has come up to the national or local standards for discharge.

Volume of Treated Industrial Waste Water refers to the volume of industrial waste water after being treated and purified through various water treatment facilities in the reference period, including the volume discharged or recovered after being treated. The volume of waste water that fails to meet the national or local standards after treatment is also included. If there are treatment facilities both at the outlets of workshops and at the outlets of the factory, and the same volume of waste water has been treated twice, duplication should be avoided in the calculation of the volume of treated industrial waste water.

Volume of Waste Industrial Gas Emission refers to waste gas emitted from burning of fuels and from production process in the area of the factory, and is measured by 10000 standard cubic meters each year under normal condition.

Volume of Industrial Sulphur Dioxide Discharged refers to the volume of sulphur dioxide discharged to the air in the process of fuel burning or in the production process.

Volume of Industrial Soot Discharged refers to the volume of solid soot in the smoke discharged in the process of fuel burning in the area of the factory.

Industrial Dust Discharged refers to the total weight of solid dust discharged by industrial enterprises in the production process, such as dust of refractory materials from iron plants, dust from coke-screening system or from sintering machines of coking plants, dust from lime kilns, cement dust from building material enterprises, etc., but excluding smoke and dust discharged by power plants.

Volume of Industrial Solid Wastes Produced refers to the total volume of solid, semi-solid or high concentration liquid residue produced by industrial enterprises in their production process, including dangerous wastes, residues from melting, slag, powdered coal ash, gangue, chemical residues, tailings, radioactive residues and other residues, but excluding stripped or dug stones in mining (except gangue and acid or alkali stones which are stones washed or soaked by water with a pH value smaller than 4 or larger than 10.5)

Volume of Industrial Solid Wastes Utilized in a Comprehensive Way refers to the volume of solid wastes from which useful materials can be extracted or which can be changed to be utilizable resources, energy or other materials, including the volume of industrial solid wastes stored up in the previous years and utilized in the current year, such as the solid wastes utilized as fertilizers, building materials, for making roads or for other purpose. Statistical data on utilization of industrial solid wastes are collected by solid wastes producing units.

Volume of Industrial Stored up Solid Wastes refers to the volume of industrial solid wastes temporarily stored up or piled with special facilities or piled in the special sites for the purpose of utilization or treatment in future. The special facilities or special sites for storing up solid wastes should have the measures against spreading or being washed away to other places, permeating the soil or causing air pollution or water contamination.

Volume of Industrial Solid Wastes Treated refers to solid wastes disposed of in a non-recoverable place that meet the requirement of environmental protection, such as burying (The dangerous wastes should be buried safely), burning, piling in designated sites, pouring water into the deep strata, filling of old mines, etc. (including treatment of solid wastes piled up in the previous years).

Volume of Industrial Solid Wastes Discharged refers to the volume of industrial solid wastes produced and discharged at the places outside the special facilities or special sites for preventing against pollution, excluding stripped or dug stones in mining (except gangue and acid or alkali waste stones).

资料整理: 罗　玲

Arranged by Luoling

6. 财　　政

GOVERNMENT FINANCE

地方财政收入（亿元）

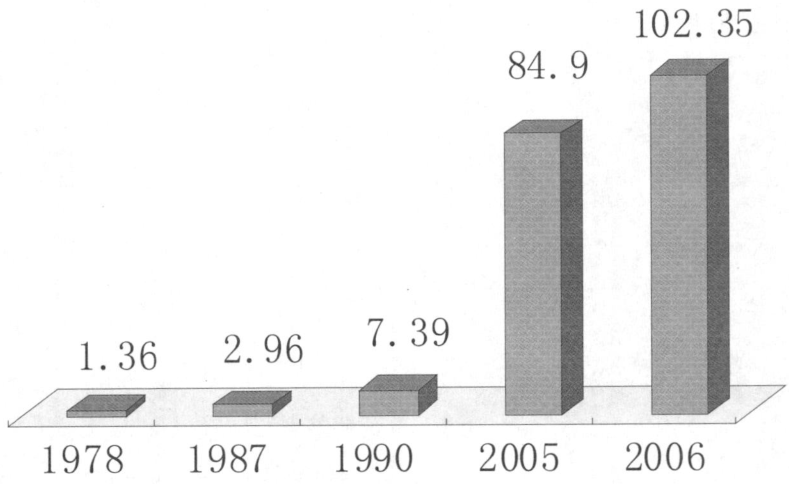

地方财政支出（亿元）

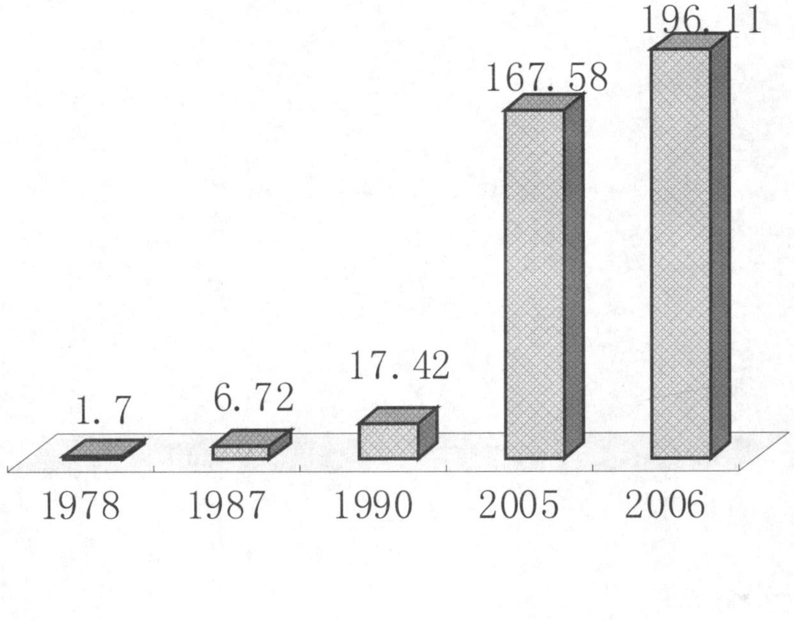

6－1 历年地方财政收入
Revenue of Local Covernment in Various Years

单位：万元 (10000yuan)

年份 Year	地方财政收入 Local Financial Revenue	各项税收 Various Taxes	工商税收 Industrial and Commercial Tax	企业所得税 Enterprise Income Tax	农业四税 4 Agricultural Taxes	国有资产经营收益 Operational Income of State-owned Assets	国有企业计划亏损补贴 Subsidies to Loss-suffering State-owned Enterprises	其他收入 Other Revenue	基金收入 Fund Revenue
1982	12770	13620	12053		1567	-1034		184	
1983	16177	16479	14424		1273	-499		197	
1984	30548	30012	27914		2098	-357		893	
1985	31613	40817	36443		2337	201		1299	
1986	21894	31872	25237		3496	91	-7699	1630	
1987	29588	35068	29239		4055	137	-6701	1084	
1988	48236	51059	37573	6097	7389	1853	-7666	2990	
1989	62481	61479	50448	5522	5509	3434	-9506	7074	
1990	73894	64378	52373	4898	7107	5858	-8212	11870	
1991	93064	84409	67077	7457	9875	5323	-11539	14871	
1992	149728	136335	109218	11591	15526	5192	-14478	22679	
1993	291219	260568	211989	29920	18659	3553	-14052	41150	
1993*	230260	189609	151030	29920	18659	3553	-14052	51150	
1994	275316	242430	173889	33643	34898	1902	-5886	70513	
1995	285339	248086	184895	21400	41791	877	-7045	43421	
1996	307034	259198	197651	22451	39096	1635	-4303	50504	
1997	316485	250504	198604	17388	34512	1356	-3170	60008	7787
1998	364870	272409	214350	18098	39961	3862	-6099	66547	28151
1999	420666	291712	218787	27836	45089	7739	-4131	66121	59225
2000	449084	315156	240048	24774	50334	9035	-5136	72940	57089
2001	495924	350854	263775	43037	44042	13727	-3129	76204	58268
2002	518324	363797	282405	32958	48434	12887		85701	55939
2003	615971	405425	324585	26044	54796	14978		92802	102766
2004	692965	446747	382886	33856	30005	21785		101826	122607
2005	848930	545149	476585	45265	23299	24816		116837	193486
2006	1023508	657533	561843	57109	38581	37109		123497	205369

注：1.工商税收 1985 年以前仅包括产品税、增值税和营业税，1985 年起包括城市维护建设税等其他税种。 2.农业四税从 1985 年起包括农林特产税、耕地占用税和契税。 3.从 1994 年起按税制改革新口径统计，1993 年有 * 符号数为按 1994 年新口径调整数。

Note: 1.Industrial and commercial tax only included product tax、value - added tax and business tax before 1985 ,since 1985it included tax on urban maintenance and construction etc.

2.4 Agricultural Taxes included the tax on special agricultural products、the tax on the use of cultivated land and the contract tax since 1985.

6-2 历年地方财政支出
Expenditure of Local Government in Various Years

单位:万元 (10000yuan)

年份 Year	地方财政支出 Local Financial Expenditures	基本建设拨款 Appropriation for Capital Construction	支援农业拨款 Appropriation for Supporting Agricultural	科教文卫事业费 Operating Expenses for Culture, Education Science & Health Care	教育 Educatin	行政管理费 Expenditure For Government Administration	其他支出 Others	基金支出 Found Expenditures
1982	25874	1631	3691	9811	6422	4839	5902	
1983	31847	1523	4173	11407	7172	6325	8419	
1984	45283	4057	4621	14216	8452	10469	11920	
1985	58994	13606	5260	16865	10886	7128	14326	
1986	66305	7761	5546	21666	14706	8540	20797	
1987	67221	4689	5674	22328	14721	9734	22639	
1988	92475	12549	7976	28502	18923	10973	32475	
1989	138090	24651	14220	36108	23608	14374	48737	
1990	174247	34821	16908	44627	27385	17859	60032	
1991	193876	36063	18475	48580	29308	21667	69091	
1992	253642	42773	24634	61291	35613	28853	96091	
1993	385215	80688	31103	78285	46715	43459	151680	
1994	400117	65293	37633	104728	62705	55716	136747	
1995	423860	60800	39358	113452	68897	61308	154347	
1996	451649	49070	40587	111384	68779	61265	189343	
1997	484809	51760	35099	113436	69689	58951	219162	6401
1998	575132	71157	42795	122075	77749	60295	252744	26066
1999	625993	70892	43191	130117	84937	61949	261682	58162
2000	705387	78697	47419	144639	96278	64798	305640	64194
2001	845763	101717	55353	164256	111541	78448	384809	61180
2002	984520	113012	60296	200493	141259	93086	455687	61946
2003	1151756	134463	70151	221395	147959	105078	522897	97772
2004	1407414	149311	103559	267330	179249	124176	627630	135408
2005	1675759	174881	122951	347344	242088	149745	717500	163338
2006	1961130	187708	118418	401449	278479	170519	867272	215764

6-3 国税税收收入
Revenue of National Tax Bureau

单位:万元 (10000yuan)

指标	Item	2004	2005	2006
收入合计	**Total Revenue**	**540733**	**647871**	**844366**
其中:中央收入	Central Revenue	441636	523441	702205
地方收入	Local Revenue	99097	124430	142161
税收收入	Taxes Revenue	426500	518531	622716
国内增值税	Domestic Value-added Tax	326191	390821	421089
国内消费税	Domestic Consumption Tax	54119	59247	77078
中央营业税	Central Business Tax	29	-8	-3
外资企业、外国企业所得税	Income Tax of Enterprises With Sole Foreign funds and Foreign Enterprises	9785	12692	21676
企业所得税	Enterprise Income Tax	20547	37727	51318
其中:中央收入	Central Revenue	13272	23298	31743
地方收入	Local Revenue	7275	14429	19575
储蓄存款利息所得个人所得税	Individual Income Tax of Int. of City & Town Deposits, Share-holding Enterprises and Joint Ownership Enterprises	15829	18052	21194
海关代征	Tax Levied by The Customs	114233	103562	221650
其中:增值税	Value-added Tax	114183	103497	221611
消费税	Consumption Tax	50	65	39
出口退税	**Tax of Export Rebate**	**-67136**	**-57900**	**-57734**
其中:退增值税	Value-added Tax	-58211	-46127	-47876
退消费税	Consumption Tax	-25	-73	-124

6－4 地方财政用于文教、卫生、科学支出
Expenditure of Local Government For Education、Sanitation and Sciences

单位：万元 (10000 yuan)

指 标	Item	2004	2005	2006
总 计	**Total**	**267330**	**347344**	**401449**
文教卫生支出	**Expenditure for Operating Expenses of Culture,Education and Public Health**	**262423**	**341942**	**394773**
文化事业费	Expenditure for Operating Expenses of Culture	4697	5749	8598
文物事业费	Expenditure for Operating Expenses of Culture Relic	788	775	1175
教育支出	Expenditure for Operating Expenses of Education	179249	242088	278479
党政群干部训练事业费	Expenditure for Operating Expenses of Training of Cadres of Government	2024	2379	2699
医疗卫生支出	Expenditure for Operating Expenses of Public Health	54270	65191	76109
体育事业费	Expenditure for Operating Expenses of Sports	3268	3053	3624
广播电影电视事业费	Expenditure for Operating Expenses of Broadcast, film and TV	6187	9109	8576
计划生育事业费	Expenditure for Operating Expenses of Family Planning	8962	10689	11422
科学支出	**Expenditure for Operating Expenses of Science**	**4907**	**5402**	**6676**
自然科学支出	Expenditure for Operating Expenses of Natural Science	3780	4278	4873
社会科学支出	Expenditure for Operating Expenses of Social Science	188	261	484
其他	Others	939	863	1319
文教卫科占总支出(%)	**Percentage to Total Expenditure**	**19.0**	**20.7**	**20.5**

6－5 地方财政用于社会福利支出
Expenditure of Local Government for Social Welfare

单位:万元 (10000 yuan)

指 标	Item	2004	2005	2006
总 计	Total	35194	48268	58206
抚恤	Pensions for Handicapped and Bereaved Families	6591	9682	10702
烈军属复退军人生活补贴	Expenditure for the Subsidies to the Military Martyrs Dependents and the Demobilized Army Men	2591	3816	4722
优抚事业单位经费	Operaing Expenses of Consoling Institutions	1482	1133	1865
退伍军人安置费	Expenditure for Settling Down the Demobilized Army Men	3050	4608	7150
军队安置离退休人员费用	Expenditure for Settling Down the Retired Army Men	2835	3359	4205
农村及其他社会救济	Social Relief Fonds of Rural Areas and Other	3283	4667	10035
农村社会救济费	Social Relief Funds of Rural Areas	2596	3360	5847
其他	Other	687	1307	3335
自然灾害救济事业费	Orperating Expenses for Providing Relief to the Areas of Natural Calamity	3984	9756	5972
其他民政事业费	Others	1970	1578	4802
特大自然灾害补助费	Subsidies on the Reconstruction After the Particularly Severe Natural Calamities	2977	7051	5059

6－6 财政收支决算平衡表

Balance Sheet of Actual Budget of Government Revenue and Expenditure

单位:万元 (10000 yuan)

指 标	Item	2004	2005	2006
财政总收入	**Total Financial Revenue**	1708569	2020385	2420516
地方财政收入	**Local Financial Revenue**	692965	848930	1023508
一般预算收入	**General Budgetary Revenue**	570358	686802	818138
工商税收类	Industrial and Commercial Taxes	382886	476585	561843
#增值税	Value-added Tax	69873	97395	104951
营业税	Business Tax	190337	236794	287308
农业四税	4 Agricultural Taxes	30005	23299	38581
#农业特产税	Tax on Special Agricultural Products	5624	30	31
企业所得税	Enterprise Income Tax	33856	45265	57109
国有资产经营收益	Operational Income of State-owned Assets	21785	24816	37109
罚没及行政收费	Penalty and Fee Collection	75002	82405	82607
专项收入	Special Revenue	18440	21133	23674
其他收入	Other Revenue	8384	12002	12318
基金收入	**Fund Budgetary Revenue**	122607	162128	205369
#文教部门基金收入	Fund Revenue of Department of Culture and Education	2136	2891	3445
中央补助收入(包括基金补助)	Subsidy Revenue of Central Government (Including the fund subsidy)	772580	875653	1059671
#原体制补助	The Substance System Subsidy	17105	17105	17105
专项补助	Special Subsidy	306425	339897	379742
国债转贷收入	the Income of Crown Debt Onlet	2720	3300	7705
国债转贷资金上年结余	the Fund Balance of Crown Debt Onlet Last Year	26497	12820	11180
上年结余收入(包括基金结余)	the Income of Balance of Last Year (Including Fund Balance)	234626	283475	328738
调入其他资金(包括基金)	Other Fund Transferred (including the fund)	8398	12327	8599

注:1."国有企业所得税"从1994年起,含集体企业所得税。
2.1997年的"其他收入"指基金预算中的"其他"收入。

1.The income tax levied on state-owned enterprises included the income tax levied on collective-owned enterprises since 1994.
2.Other revenue refers to other revenue of fund budgetary in 1997.

6-6 续 (continued)

指 标	Item	2004	2005	2006
财政总支出	**Expenditure of Financial Expenditures**	**1425094**	**1691647**	**1977824**
地方财政支出	**Expenditure of Local Financial Expenditures**	**1407414**	**1675759**	**1961130**
一般预算支出	**Expenditure for General Budgetary Expenditures**	**1272006**	**1512421**	**1745366**
基本建设支出	Expenditure for Capital Construction	149311	174881	187708
企业挖潜改造资金	Technical Updates and Transformation	3390	4969	4294
地质勘探费	Exenditure for Geological Prospection	3474	3724	3611
科技三项费用	New Products Promotion Funds	5229	7497	10212
支援农村生产支出	Expenditure for supporting rural production	103559	122951	118418
工业交通部门事业费	Expenditure for Operating Expenses of Department of Industry and Transportation	5699	8399	9581
流通部门事业费	Expenditure for Operating Expenses of Department of Commerce	1068	1223	1471
城市维护费	City Maintenance	44324	55480	61549
文教支出	Expenditure for Operating Expenses of Culture Education	208153	276751	318664
医疗卫生支出	Public Health	54270	65191	76109
科学支出	Expenditure for Operating Expenses of Science	4907	5402	6676
税务等部门事业费	Expenditure for Operating Expenses of Department of Tax ,etc.	73589	87570	94043
抚恤和社会福利救济费	Expenditure for Pensions and Social Welfare and Relief Funds	35194	48268	58206
行政管理费	Expenditure for Government Administration	124176	149745	170519
外交外事支出	Expenditure for Armed Police and Foreign Affairs	1558	1731	1645
行政事业单位离退休经费	Expenditure for Retired Persons in Administrative Department	56553	62623	65377
社会保障补助支出	Expenditure for Social Security Subsidies	114568	117149	138928
公检法司支出	Expenditure for Public Security Agency,Procuratorial Agency,Court of Justice	83182	102942	119658
政策性补贴支出	Expenditure for Price Subsidies	14373	11385	42310
支援不发达地区支出	Expenditure for Supporting Under-developed Areas	25995	25504	35960
海域开发建设和场地使用支出	Expenditure for Developing Land and Sea Area	668	803	915
专项支出	Special Expenditure	15480	17558	22898
其他支出	Others	136838	139792	168596
基金预算支出	**appropriation Fund**	**135408**	**163338**	**215764**
上解中央支出	Exeenditure of Funds Transference to Centre	15361	13577	14310
增设预算周转金	Budgetary Working Funs	2000		
国债转贷收入安排的支出	expenditure Arranging from the Income of Crown Debt Onlet	16397	4940	8330
国债转贷收入结余	the Balance of the Income of Crown Debt Onlet	12820	11180	9925
调出资金(包括基金调出)	Capital Transferred (including fund transferred)	2319	2311	2384
年终滚存结余(包括基金结余)	Rolling eposits Balance year-end	283475	328738	442692
#省本级	Provincial	216239	253755	282422
净结余	Net Balance	63357	57612	107262

6－7 预算外资金收支决算
Actual Budget of Extra-budgetary Revenue and Expenditure

单位:万元 (10000 yuan)

指 标	Item	2004	2005	2006
预算外资金收入总计	**Total Extra-budgetary Revenue**	**170180**	**192323**	**243282**
本年财政预算外收入	The Year Financial Extra-budgetary Revenue	137493	154715	182566
行政事业单位收入	Revenue of Administrative Department	107423	119924	146312
乡镇自筹、统筹资金	Revenue Form Fundraising Programs of Township Governments		62	45
基金和附加收入	Funds and Extra Revenue	4306	1543	1315
主管部门集中收入	Concentrated Income of The Competent Department	862	162	41
其他收入	Other Revenue	24902	33024	34853
上年滚存结余	Rolling deposits Balance Last Year	32687	37608	60716
预算外资金支出总计	**Total Extra-budgetary Expenditure**	**170180**	**192323**	**243282**
本年预算外资金支出	Current Year Extra－budgetary Expenditure	133944	134402	162913
基本建设支出	Capital Construction	60	169	819
城市维护支出	Urban Maintenance Expenses	10703		
行政事业支出	Expenditure of Administrative and Institutional Units	108358	104352	135723
乡镇统筹支出	Expenditure by Township Governments		96	45
其他支出	Other Expenditure	14823	29785	26326
政府调剂资金	Funds Relieved by Government	77	1701	5889
年终结余	Surplus Year-end	36159	56220	74480

注:地方财政预算外收支,从1993年起不含国有企业部分。
Note:The extra-budgetary expenditure of local government do not include extra-budgetary expenditure of state-owned enterprises since 1993.

6－8 各市县地方财政收支
Revenue and Expenditure of Local Government By Region

单位:万元 (10000 yuan)

市县 Region	财政收入 Financial Revenue	工商税收 Industrial and Commercial Taxes	个人所得税 Personal Income Tax	城市维护建设税	财政支出 Financial Expenditures	基本建设支出 Capital Construction	支援农业拨款 Appropriation for Supporting Agricultural	教育事业费 Education
总计 Total	**617050**	**209244**	**16519**	**37559**	**1267406**	**51319**	**94294**	**223514**
海口市 Haikou	262984	53835	4912	21838	377159	18486	13849	48623
三亚市 Sanya	100947	47682	2202	3584	125427	14396	12128	19485
五指山市 Wuzhishan	3490	1371	217	116	25261	260	3310	3865
文昌市 Wenchang	22724	7952	1015	633	65767		5924	14797
琼海市 Qionghai	23348	10506	875	957	53722		4928	11614
万宁市 Wanning	16598	5418	575	757	53793		5195	12798
定安县 Dingan	7131	2497	255	375	33360		3366	9283
屯昌县 Tunchang	4562	933	146	102	27324	10	2902	6460
澄迈县 Chengmai	27285	10541	857	1945	63512		5989	13292
临高县 Lingao	5931	2088	306	285	42741		3438	9858
儋州市 Danzhou	20701	5548	908	799	69985	1369	7208	17418
东方市 Dongfang	17890	5485	585	550	53801	2033	4577	10096
乐东县 Ledong	5339	2032	316	201	49440	1842	4582	12104
琼中县 Qiongzhong	3679	1320	239	139	29792		3129	5066
保亭县 Baoting	3579	950	193	88	26108		2843	5028
陵水县 Lingshui	6188	2123	271	193	36116		3389	8173
白沙县 Baisha	3556	1453	210	141	28386		2916	5187
昌江县 Changjiang	21904	5521	694	1120	42494	2941	4475	7131
洋浦 Yangpu	59214	41989	1743	3736	63218	10000	146	3236

说明:工商税收包括增值税、营业税两项。支援农业拨款包括农业支出、林业支出、水利和气象支出。

Note: Industrial and commercial taxes include value-added tax and business tax.

Appropriation for supporting agricultural includes supporting agricultural production expenditure and operating expenses of the departments of farming forestry,water and meteorology.

6－9 各市县主要年份地方财政收支

Revenue and Expenditure of Local Government By Region in Major Year

单位:万元 (10000 yuan)

市 县	Region	2004	2005	2006
收入合计	**Total Revenue**	**411858**	**499336**	**617050**
海口市	Haikou	174330	216777	262984
三亚市	Sanya	53782	73120	100947
五指山市	Wuzhishan	3192	2953	3490
文昌市	Wenchang	15225	17305	22724
琼海市	Qionghai	20506	20332	23348
万宁市	Wanning	12953	13470	16598
定安县	Dingan	5688	5704	7131
屯昌县	Tunchang	4188	4134	4562
澄迈县	Chengmai	17042	19308	27285
临高县	Lingao	6290	4936	5931
儋州市	Danzhou	15638	17558	20701
东方市	Dongfang	15564	17173	17890
乐东县	Ledong	5595	4078	5339
琼中县	Qiongzhong	3536	3273	3679
保亭县	Baoting	3017	3050	3579
陵水县	Lingshui	4452	4721	6188
白沙县	Baisha	3466	3110	3556
昌江县	Changjiang	17092	18246	21904
支出合计	**Total Expenditure**	**868614**	**1055755**	**1267406**
海口市	Haikou	286396	324721	377159
三亚市	Sanya	74480	96974	125427
五指山市	Wuzhishan	16916	19308	25261
文昌市	Wenchang	44632	53746	65767
琼海市	Qionghai	41791	48753	53722
万宁市	Wanning	34349	45138	53793
定安县	Dingan	25548	30795	33360
屯昌县	Tunchang	19858	25174	27324
澄迈县	Chengmai	36471	50382	63512
临高县	Lingao	28062	33272	42741
儋州市	Danzhou	42728	54087	69985
东方市	Dongfang	35402	42324	53801
乐东县	Ledong	33630	40616	49440
琼中县	Qiongzhong	20099	25257	29792
保亭县	Baoting	17721	20951	26108
陵水县	Lingshui	24252	29133	36116
白沙县	Baisha	21327	24451	28386
昌江县	Changjiang	20626	37884	42494

说明:收入合计和支出合计数中包括洋浦开发区的数字。
Note: The datas in the table do not include the expenditure of Yangpu

6－10 各市县地方财政收入相当于生产总值比重

Local Government Revenue as Percentage to Gross Domestic Product by Region

单位：%　　(percent)

市 县	Region	2004	2005	2006
海口市	Haikou	5.7	7.0	7.3
三亚市	Sanya	11.0	9.9	9.2
五指山市	Wuzhishan	4.3	4.9	5.1
文昌市	Wenchang	3.0	3.2	3.6
琼海市	Qionghai	3.6	4.0	4.1
万宁市	Wanning	3.0	3.3	3.5
定安县	Dingan	3.7	3.3	3.6
屯昌县	Tunchang	2.5	2.6	2.5
澄迈县	Chengmai	4.7	4.7	5.4
临高县	Lingao	1.9	1.3	1.4
儋州市	Danzhou	2.0	2.4	2.5
东方市	Dongfang	4.3	4.3	4.0
乐东县	Ledong	2.1	1.7	1.8
琼中县	Qiongzhong	3.3	3.1	3.0
保亭县	Baoting	3.6	3.6	3.5
陵水县	Lingshui	2.6	2.6	2.8
白沙县	Baisha	3.2	2.9	2.8
昌江县	Changjiang	7.3	6.9	7.2

6－11 各市县财政一般预算收支平衡表

Balance Sheet of General Budgetary Revenue and Expenditure of Local Government by Region

单位：万元 (10000 yuan)

市 县	Region	收入总计 Total Revenue	本年收入 Current Year Revenue	税返补助 the Subsidy of Tax Returned	原体制补助 Original System Subsidy	专项补助 Special Subsidy	上年结余 Balance of Last Year	其 他 Others
总 计	**Total**	**1351203**	**536504**	**92041**	**44695**	**216926**	**63620**	**397417**
海口市	Haikou	342875	211288	40393	27135	24821	2438	36800
三亚市	Sanya	150413	97338	6179	768	13518	12604	20006
五指山市	Wuzhishan	28508	3168	717	804	9466	1041	13312
文昌市	Wenchang	65862	19298	4469	1069	13746	132	27148
琼海市	Qionghai	59663	21784	5416	717	11176	2875	17695
万宁市	Wanning	55916	14856	1655	701	12095	424	26185
定安县	Dingan	37513	6151	1996	763	8412	73	20118
屯昌县	Tunchang	32077	4181	826	956	7580	82	18452
澄迈县	Chengmai	63030	20555	7800	1561	9986	2967	20161
临高县	Lingao	50080	5385	2459	1668	13257	3054	24257
儋州市	Danzhou	75951	18787	5439	750	16509	1886	32580
东方市	Dongfang	58418	14223	2787	1521	10900	9298	19689
乐东县	Ledong	58017	4493	1635	1666	13175	4740	32308
琼中县	Qiongzhong	38443	3519	681	804	9595	4590	19254
保亭县	Baoting	28523	2263	599	861	9286	645	14869
陵水县	Lingshui	48947	6073	1061	1664	12730	5735	21684
白沙县	Baisha	38082	3420	1220	730	9767	4168	18777
昌江县	Changjiang	54059	20902	4083	557	9382	6176	12959
洋 浦	Yangpu	64826	58820	2626		1525	692	1163

6–11 续（continued）

市 县	Region	支出总计 Total Expenditure	本年支出 Current Year Expenditure	原体制上解 Original system Expenditure	专项上解 Special Expenditure	其 他 Others	年终结余 Surplus Year-end	净结余 Net Balance
总 计	**Total**	**1209929**	**1177655**		**14071**	**18203**	**141274**	**67243**
海口市	Haikou	334625	322454		2464	9707	8250	1571
三亚市	Sanya	129462	123275		2951	3236	20951	17385
五指山市	Wuzhishan	25229	24860		369		3279	19
文昌市	Wenchang	62798	62112		675	11	3064	1376
琼海市	Qionghai	53891	52549		192	1150	5772	2399
万宁市	Wanning	50515	50418		94	3	5401	241
定安县	Dingan	32678	32437		236	5	4835	3932
屯昌县	Tunchang	27184	26330		54	800	4893	15
澄迈县	Chengmai	56980	56417		358	205	6050	3218
临高县	Lingao	41667	41391		276		8413	4947
儋州市	Danzhou	67610	67056		167	387	8341	881
东方市	Dongfang	49675	48264		157	1254	8743	6914
乐东县	Ledong	49160	48476		183	501	8857	2951
琼中县	Qiongzhong	29804	29428		76	300	8639	5748
保亭县	Baoting	24360	24195		98	67	4163	2851
陵水县	Lingshui	36466	35658		305	503	12481	10817
白沙县	Baisha	28214	28111		103		9868	2116
昌江县	Changjiang	41636	41323		313		12423	3011
洋 浦	Yangpu	67975	62901		5000	74	–3149	–3149

6－12 各市县财政基金预算收支平衡表

Balance Sheet of Fund Budgetary Revenue and Expenditure of Local Government by Region

单位：万元 (10000 yuan)

市 县	Region	收入合计 Total Revenue	本年收入 Current Year Revenue	文教部门基金 Fund Revenue of Department of Culture and Education	农业部门基金 Fund Revenue of Agricultural Department	土地有偿使用收入 Revenue of Compensable Use of Land	其 他 Others
总 计	Total	109064	80546	394	1275	78497	380
海口市	Haikou	57556	51696		90	51467	139
三亚市	Sanya	7125	3609		147	3352	110
五指山市	Wuzhishan	655	322		10	305	7
文昌市	Wenchang	5048	3426		154	3257	15
琼海市	Qionghai	3346	1564		42	1521	1
万宁市	Wanning	4104	1742		189	1541	12
定安县	Dingan	1547	980		98	873	9
屯昌县	Tunchang	1625	381		64	312	5
澄迈县	Chengmai	8415	6730		105	6618	7
临高县	Lingao	1729	546		39	496	11
儋州市	Danzhou	3335	1914		91	1800	23
东方市	Dongfang	6029	3667		22	3641	4
乐东县	Ledong	1764	846		1	840	5
琼中县	Qiongzhong	585	160		45	108	7
保亭县	Baoting	2236	1316		54	1259	3
陵水县	Lingshui	947	115		3	102	10
白沙县	Baisha	506	136		90	44	2
昌江县	Changjiang	1628	1002		31	961	10
洋 浦	Yangpu	884	394	394			

6-12续(continued)

市 县	Region	支出合计 Total Expenditure	本年支出 Expenditure Year Revenue	文教部门基金 Fund Expenditure of Department of Culture and Education	农业部门基金 Fund Expenditure of Agricultural Department	土地有偿使用支出 Expenditure of Compensable Use of Land	其 他 Others
总 计	Total	90068	89751	279	4292	82816	2364
海口市	Haikou	55005	54705		569	54136	
三亚市	Sanya	2152	2152		215	1562	375
五指山市	Wuzhishan	401	401		102	248	51
文昌市	Wenchang	3655	3655		481	2991	183
琼海市	Qionghai	1173	1173		315	703	155
万宁市	Wanning	3375	3375		964	2249	162
定安县	Dingan	923	923		43	778	102
屯昌县	Tunchang	994	994		44	888	62
澄迈县	Chengmai	7095	7095		151	6865	79
临高县	Lingao	1350	1350		236	976	138
儋州市	Danzhou	2935	2929		161	2562	206
东方市	Dongfang	5537	5537		153	5233	151
乐东县	Ledong	964	964		189	637	138
琼中县	Qiongzhong	375	364		126	133	105
保亭县	Baoting	1913	1913		48	1766	99
陵水县	Lingshui	458	458		173	107	178
白沙县	Baisha	275	275		166	57	52
昌江县	Changjiang	1171	1171		156	915	100
洋 浦	Yangpu	317	317	279	0	10	28

主要统计指标解释

财政收入 指国家财政参与社会产品分配所取得的收入，是实现国家职能的财力保证。财政收入所包括的内容几经变化，目前主要包括：

(1)各项税收：包括增值税、营业税、消费税、土地增值税、城市维护建设税、资源税、城市土地使用税、印花税、个人所得税、企业所得税、关税、农牧业税和耕地占用税等。

(2)专项收入：包括征收排污费收入、征收城市水资源费收入、教育费附加收入等。

(3)其他收入：包括基本建设贷款归还收入、基本建设收入、捐赠收入等。

(4)国有企业计划亏损补贴：这项为负收入，冲减财政收入。

财政支出 国家财政将筹集起来的资金进行分配使用，以满足经济建设和各项事业的需要，主要包括：

(1)基本建设支出：指按国家有关规定，属于基本建设范围内的基本建设有偿使用、拨款、资本金支出以及经国家批准对专项和政策性基建投资贷款，在部门的基建投资额中统筹支付的贴息支出。

(2)企业挖潜改造资金：指国家预算内拨给的用于企业挖潜、革新和改造方面的资金。包括各部门企业挖潜改造资金和企业挖潜改造贷款资金，为农业服务的县办"五小"企业技术改造补助，挖潜改造贷款利息支出。

(3)地质勘探费用：指国家预算用于地质勘探单位的勘探工作费用，包括地质勘探管理机构及其事业单位经费、地质勘探经费。

(4)科技三项费用：指国家预算用于科技支出的费用，包括新产品试制费、中间试验费、重要科学研究补助费。

(5)支援农村生产支出：指国家财政支援农村集体(户)各项生产的支出。包括对农村举办的小型农田水利和打井、喷灌等的补助费，对农村水土保持措施的补助费，对农村举办的小水电站的补助费，特大抗旱的补助费，农村开荒补助费，扶持乡镇企业资金，农村农技推广和植保补助费，农村草场和畜禽保护补助费，农村造林和林木保护补助费，农村水产补助费，发展粮食生产专项资金。

(6)农林水利气象等部门的事业费用：指国家财政用于农垦、农场、农业、畜牧、农机、林业、森工、水利、水产、气象、乡镇企业的技术推广、良种推广(示范)、动植物(畜禽、森林)保护、水质监测、勘探设计、资源调查、干部训练等项费用，园艺特产场补助费，中等专业学校经费，飞播牧草试验补助费，营林机构、气象机构经费，渔政费以及农业管理事业费等。

(7)工业交通商业等部门的事业费：指国家预算支付给工交商各部门用于事业发展的经费，包括勘探设计费、中等专业学校经费、技术学校经费、干部训练费。

(8)文教科学卫生事业费：指国家预算用于文化、出版、文物、教育、卫生、中医、公费医疗、体育、档案、地震、海洋、通讯、电影电视、计划生育、党政群干部训练、自然科学、社会科学、科协等项事业的经费支出和高技术研究专项经费。主要包括工资、补助工资、福利费、离退休费、助学金、公务费、设备购置费、修缮费、业务费、差额补助费。

(9)抚恤和社会福利救济费：指国家预算用于抚恤和社会福利救济事业的经费。包括由民政部门开支的烈士家属和牺牲病残人员家属的一次性、定期抚恤金，革命伤残人员的抚恤金，各种伤残补助费，烈军属、复员退伍军人生活补助费，退伍军人安置费，优抚事业单位经费，烈士纪念建筑物管理、维修费，自然灾害救济事业费和特大自然灾害灾后重建补助费等。

(10)国防支出：指国家预算用于国防建设和保卫国家安全的支出，包括国防费、国防科研事业费、民兵建设以及专项工程支出等。

(11)行政管理费：包括行政管理支出，党派团体补助支出，外交支出，公安安全支出，司法支出，法院支出，检察院支出和公检法办案费用补助。

(12)价格补贴支出：指经国家批准，由国家财政拨给的政策性补贴支出。主要包括粮食加价款，粮、棉、油差价补贴，棉花收购价外奖励款，副食品风险基金，市镇居民的肉食价格补贴，平抑市价肉食、蔬菜价差补贴等以及经国家批准的教材课本、报刊新闻纸等价格补贴。

中央财政收入和地方财政收入 指按财政体制划分的中央本级收入和地方本级收入。1994 年分税制财政体制以后，属于中央财政的收入包括关税、海关代征消费税和增值税，消费税，中央企业所得税，地方银行和外资银行及非银行金融企业所得税，铁道、银行总行、保险总公司等集中缴纳的营业税、所得税、利润和城市维护建设税，增值税的 75%部分，证券交易税(印花税)50%部分和海洋石油资源税。属于地方财政的收入包括营业税，地方企业所得税，个人所得税，城镇土地使用税，固定资产投资方向调节税，城镇维护建设税，房产税，车船使用税，印花税，屠宰税，农牧业税，农业特产税，耕地占用税，契税，增值税 25%部分，证券交易税(印花税)50%部分和除海洋石油资源税以外的其他资源税。

中央财政支出和地方财政支出 指根据政府在经济和社会活动中的不同职责，划分中央和地方政府的责权，按照政府的责权划分确定的支出。中央财政支出包括国防支出，武装警察部队支出，中央级行政管理费和各项事业费，重点建设支出以及中央政府调整国民经济结构、协调地区发展、实施宏观调控的支出。地方财政支出主要包括地方行政管理和各项事业费，地方统筹的基本建设、技术改造支出，支援农村生产支出，城市维护和建设经费，价格补贴支出等。

预算外资金收支 预算外资金指国家机关、事业单位和社会团体为履行或代行政府职能,依据国家法律、法规和具有法律效力的规章而收取、提取和安排使用的未纳入国家预算管理的各种财政性资金。其范围主要包括:法律、法规规定的行政事业性收费、基金和附加收入等;国务院或省级人民政府及其财政、计划(物价)部门审批的行政事业性收费;国务院及财政部审批建立的基金、附加收入等;主管部门所属单位集中上缴资金;用于乡镇政府开支的乡自筹和乡统筹资金;其他未纳入预算管理的财政性资金。社会保障基金在国家财政尚未建立社会管理。部门和单位的预算外收入必须上缴同级财政专户,支出由同级财政按预算外资金收支计划和单位财务收支计划统筹安排,从财政专户中拨付,实行收支两条线管理。

Explanatory Note on Main Statistical Indicators

Government Revenue refers to the revenue of the government finance by means of participating in the distribution of the social products, which is the financial resources for ensuring the government to function. The contents of government revenue have been changed several times. Now it includes the following main items:

(1) Various tax revenues, including value added tax, business tax, consumption tax, land value added tax, tax on city maintenance and construction, resources tax, tax on use of urban land, stamp tax, personal income tax, enterprise income tax, tariff, tax on agriculture and animal husbandry and tax on occupancy of cultivated land, etc.

(2) Special revenues,including revenue collected from imposing fee on sewage treatment, revenue collected from imposing fee on urban water resources, and extra–charges for education, etc.

(3) Other revenues, including revenue from the repayment of capital construction loan, revenue from capital construction projects, and donations and grants.

(4) Planned subsidies for the losses of the state–owned enterprises.This is an item of negative revenue, used to eat up part of the government revenue.

Government Expenditure refers to the distribution and use of the funds the government finance has raised, so as to meet the needs of economic construction and various causes. It includes the following main items:

(1) Expenditure for capital construction: It refers to the non–gratuitous use and appropriation of funds for capital construction in the range of capital construction, outlay of capital as well as the loans on capital construction approved by the government for special purpose or policy purpose and the expenditure with discount paid in an overall way within the amount of the funds appropriated to the departments for capital construction.

(2) Innovation funds of the enterprises: They refer to the funds appropriated from the government budget for the enterprises to tap the latent power, upgrade the technology and carry out innovation, including the innovation fund of the departments, loan of the enterprises for innovation, subsidies on the innovation of the small fertilizer plant, small cement plant, small coal mines, small machinery plant and small steel plant, the expenditure of interest for the loan for innovation.

(3) Geological prospecting expenses: They refer to the expenses appropriated from the government budget to the geological prospecting units for the expenditure of the prospecting work, including the expenditures of the administrative agencies for geological prospecting and their institutional units as well as the geological prospecting expenditure.

(4) expenditures for science and technology promotion: They refer to the expenses appropriated from the government budget for the scientific and technological expenditure, including new products development expenditure, expenditure for intermediate trial and subsidies on important scientific researches.

(5) Expenditure for supporting rural production: It refers to the expenditures appropriated from the government budget for supporting the various expenditures of the rural collective units or households for production, including the subsidies to the small water conservancy projects and well drilling, sprinkling irrigation projects run by the villages; subsidies on the rural water and soil conserving measures; subsidies to the small power stations run by the villages; subsidies to the expenditure for fighting against particularly severe draughts; subsidies on the rural waste land exclamation; fund for supporting the township enterprises; subsidies to the expenditure for popularization of the agricultural technologies and plant protection in the rural areas; subsidies to the expenditure for the protection of grasslands and cattle and fowls; subsidies on afforestation and forest protection in rural areas; subsidies on the rural aquatic products industry; special fund for developing grain production.

(6) Operating expenses of the departments of farming, forestry, water conservancy and meteorology etc.: They refer to the expenses appropriated from the government budget for the expenditures of agricultural exclamation, farms, agriculture, animal husbandry, agricultural machinery, forestry, timber industry, water conservancy, aquatic products industry, meteorology, technology popularization in township enterprises, popularization (demonstration) of improved varieties, plant (cattle and fowls, forest) protection, water quality monitoring, prospecting and designing, resources investigation, cadres training, subsidies to horticulture gardens, expenditure of specialized secondary schools, subsidies on the experiments of sowing herbage seeds by flights, expenditures of afforestation agencies and meteorology agencies, expenses for fishery administration and operating expenses for agricultural administration, etc.

(7) Operating expenses of the departments of industry, transport and commerce: They refer to the expenses appropriated from the government budget to the departments of industry, transport and commerce for the expenditure of business development, including expenses for prospecting and designing, expenditures of specialized secondary schools, expenditures of the technical training schools and

expenditures for cadres training, etc.

(8) Operating expenses of the departments of culture, education, science and public health: They refer to the expenses appropriated from the government budget for the expenditures of the causes of culture, publication, cultural relics, education, public health, traditional Chinese medical science, free medical services, sports, archives, earthquake, ocean, communications, broadcasting, film and television, family planning; expenditure for training of cadres of government, party and mass organization; expenditures for natural sciences, social sciences, associations for science and technology and the special expenditure for the high-tech researches. They include mainly wages, extra wages, welfare funds, pension for the retirees, stipend, expenses for official business, expenses for equipment purchases, expenses for repairs, business expenses and subsidies to the units which are unable to support their expenditures by their own earnings.

(9) Pension for the disabled or for the families of the bereaved and relief funds for social welfare: They refer to the funds appropriated from the government budget for the expenditures of pension for the disabled or for the families of the bereaved and relief funds for social welfare, including the lump-sum or regular pension paid by the departments of civil affairs to the members of martyrs families and families of those who died for the public interest, pension to the revolutionary disabled, subsidies for permanent disability of various kinds, subsidies to the military martyrs dependents and the demobilized servicemen, expenditure for settling down the demobilized servicemen, operating expenses of the consoling institutions, expenses for management and repair of the commemorative buildings for the martyrs, the expenses managed by the departments of civil affairs for the retirees and those who have quitted their work, expenses for social relief in rural and urban areas, operating expenses for providing relief to the areas of natural calamity and subsidies on the reconstruction after the particularly severe natural calamities, etc.

(10) Expenditures for national defence: They refer to the funds appropriated from the government budget for the expenditures for building up national defence and safeguarding national security, including expenses of national defence, expenses of scientific researches on national defence, expenses for building up peoples militia and expenditure for special projects, etc.

(11) Administrative expenses: They include expenditure for administration, subsidies to the parties and mass organizations, diplomatic expenditure, expenditure for public security, judicial expenditure, law court expenditure, procuratorial expenditure and subsidies to the expenses for treating the cases by the public security departments, procuratorial organs and law courts.

(12) Expenditure for price subsidies: It refers to the expenditure appropriated, with the approval of the government, from the government budget for the policy subsidies to price adjustment, including the fund for the increase of grain prices, the subsidies to the difference between the selling prices and purchasing prices of grains, cotton and edible oil, awards in addition to the purchasing prices of cotton, risk fund for non-staple food, subsidies on the prices of meat and meat products, subsidies on the price difference for curbing the high market prices of meat, meat products and vegetables and the subsidies approved by the government on the prices of textbooks and newsprint of newspapers and periodicals.

Revenue of the central government and revenue of the local governments: In accordance with the classification of the structure of the government finance in 1994 on the basis of the classification of channels for collection of tax revenues, the revenue of the central government and the revenue of the local governments have different coverage. The revenue of the central government includes tariff, consumption tax and value added tax levied by the customs, consumption tax, income tax of the enterprises subordinate to the central government, income taxes of the local banks, foreign-funded banks and non-bank financial institutions, business tax, income tax and profits of railways, head offices of banks, head office of insurance company , which are handed over to the government in a centralized way, tax on city maintenance and construction, 75% of the value added tax, tax on ocean petroleum resources, 50% of the tax on stock dealing (stamp tax). The revenue of the local governments includes business tax, income tax of the enterprises subordinate to the local government, personal income tax, tax on the use of urban land, tax on the adjustment of the investment in fixed assets, tax on town maintenance and construction, tax on real estates, tax on the use of vehicles and ships, stamp tax, slaughter tax, tax on agriculture and animal husbandry, tax on special agricultural products, tax on the occupancy of cultivated land, contract tax, 25% of the value added tax, 50% of the tax on stock dealing (stamp tax) and tax on resources other than the ocean petroleum resources.

Expenditure of the central government and expenditure of the local governments: according to the different functions of the central government and local governments in the economic and social activities, the rights of affairs administration are classified between the central government and local governments; and the classification of the expenditure between the central government and local governments are made on the basis of the classification of the rights of affairs administration between them. The expenditure of the central government includes the expenditure for national defence, expenditure for armed police forces, the administrative expenses and various operating expenses at the level of central government, expenditure for key projects and the expenditure of the central government for adjusting the national economic structure, coordinating the development among different regions and exercising the macro-economic regulation and control. The expenditure of the local governments includes mainly the administrative expenses and various operating expenses at the level of local governments, the expenditure for capital construction and technological innovation with the funds raised by the local government, expenditure for supporting rural production, expenditure for city maintenance and construction and expenditure for price subsidies, etc.

Extra–budgetary revenue and expenditure Extra–budgetary fund refers to financial fund of various types not covered by the regular government budgetary management, which is collected, allocated or arranged by government agencies, institutions and social organizations while performing duties delegated to them or on behalf of the government in accordance with laws, rules and regulations. It mainly covers following items: administrative and institutional fees, funds and extra charges that are stipulated by laws and regulations; administrative and institutional fees approved by the State Council and provincial governments and their financial and planning (price management) departments; funds and extra charges established by the State Council and the Ministry of Finance; funds turned over to competent departments by their subordinate institutions; self–raised and collected funds by township governments for their own expenditure; and other financial funds that are not covered in budgetary management. Social security funds are treated as extra–budget fund and managed for its exclusive use, given the circumstance that separate government budgetary system for social security is yet to be designed. Special accounts are opened by the financial departments in banks for the management of revenue and expenditure of extra–budgetary fund. Extra–budgetary revenue and expenditure is managed separately, namely, revenue of institutions and departments must enter into the special accounts of the financial departments at the same administrative level, and their extra–budgetary expenditure is arranged in line with the extra–budget plans and appropriated from these accounts.

资料整理:郑 路 辜武陆
Arranged by Zhenglu Guwulu

7. 物价指数
PRICE INDICES

商品零售价格指数（%）
（以上年为100）

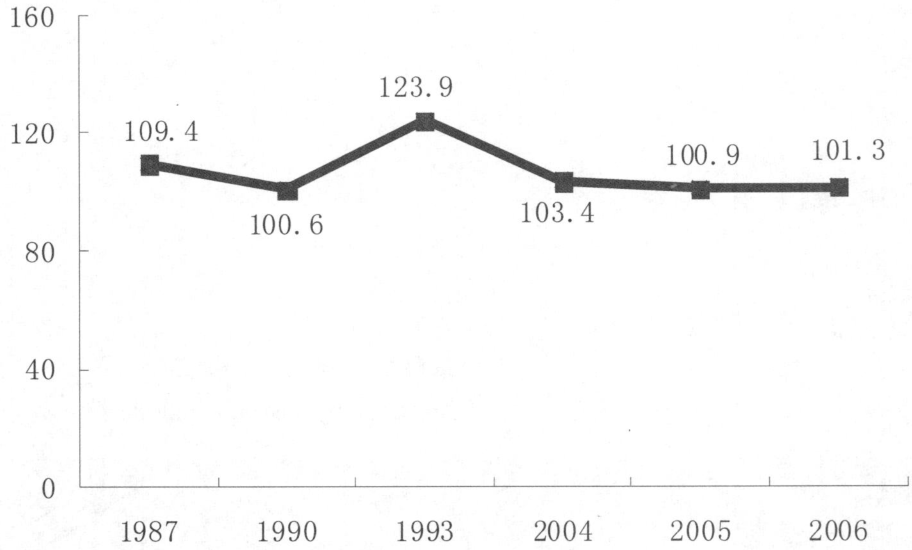

居民消费价格指数（%）
（以上年为100）

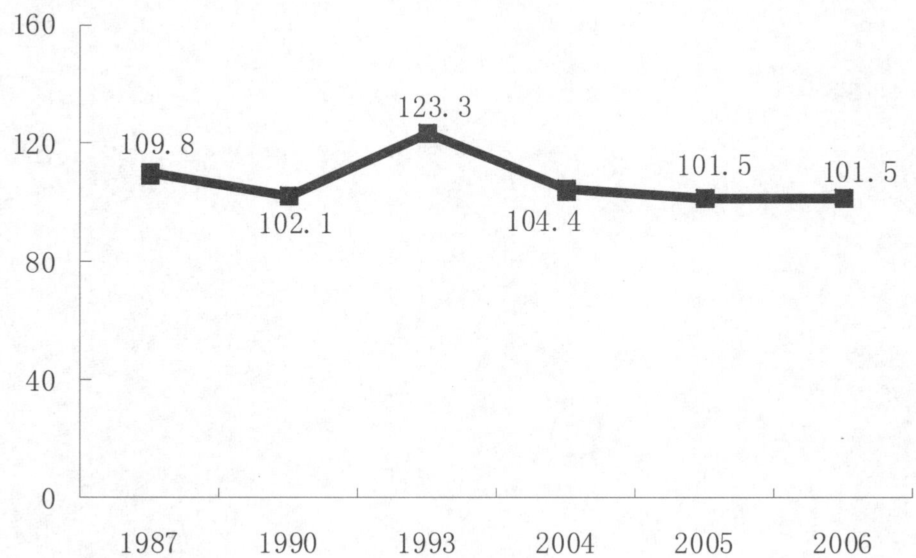

7－1 全省各种物价总指数
General Price Indices

(上年＝100) (preceding year=100)

年 份 Year	商品零售价格指数 General Retail Price Index	城 市 Urban Areas	农 村 Rural Areas	农业生产资料价格总指数 General Price Indices of Agricultural Means of Production
1979	102.0	100.9	103.0	103.6
1980	107.2	108.3	103.1	108.9
1981	107.5	106.4	108.6	109.2
1982	104.5	105.5	103.4	106.1
1983	100.9	99.9	101.9	102.5
1984	99.3	98.3	100.3	97.6
1985	112.8	113.9	111.6	105.4
1986	103.8	102.7	104.8	105.0
1987	109.4	109.5	109.3	105.4
1988	127.8	129.8	124.9	118.9
1989	126.8	127.5	124.9	124.6
1990	100.6	97.7	106.4	109.1
1991	103.1	103.6	102.9	100.6
1992	108.7	109.1	102.5	100.7
1993	123.9	124.2	119.1	130.4
1994	121.6	121.2	122.9	138.2
1995	111.3	108.7	115.5	115.7
1996	102.3	102.7	101.4	106.8
1997	99.3	99.6	99.1	100.3
1998	96.5	96.3	96.8	98.4
1999	96.6	98.0	95.2	97.1
2000	99.9	101.0	99.0	98.0
2001	97.7	97.6	97.8	99.5
2002	98.4	99.0	97.7	101.7
2003	100.4	100.2	100.8	104.8
2004	103.4	103.0	103.8	111.3
2005	100.9	100.4	101.5	108.9
2006	101.3	100.6	102.3	100.7

(1978=100)

年 份 Year	商品零售价格指数 General Retail Price Index	城 市 Urban Areas	农 村 Rural Areas	农业生产资料价格总指数 General Price Indices of Agricultural Means of Production
1978	100.0	100.0	100.0	100.0
1979	102.0	100.9	103.0	103.6
1980	109.3	109.3	109.3	112.8
1981	117.3	116.3	118.7	123.2
1982	122.8	122.7	122.7	130.7
1983	123.9	122.5	125.0	134.0
1984	123.1	120.5	125.4	130.8
1985	138.9	137.2	140.0	137.8
1986	144.2	140.9	146.7	144.7
1987	157.8	154.3	160.3	152.5
1988	201.7	200.3	200.3	181.4
1989	255.8	255.3	250.1	226.0
1990	257.3	249.5	266.1	246.5
1991	265.3	258.5	273.8	248.0
1992	288.4	282.0	280.7	249.8
1993	357.3	350.2	334.3	325.7
1994	434.5	424.4	410.9	450.1
1995	483.6	461.4	474.5	520.8
1996	494.7	473.8	481.2	556.2
1997	491.2	471.9	476.9	557.9
1998	474.0	454.4	461.6	549.0
1999	457.9	445.3	439.4	533.1
2000	457.4	449.8	435.0	522.4
2001	446.9	439.0	425.4	519.8
2002	439.7	434.6	415.6	528.6
2003	441.5	435.5	418.9	554.0
2004	456.5	448.6	434.8	616.6
2005	460.6	450.4	441.3	671.5
2006	466.6	453.1	451.5	676.2

7-1 续(continued) (上年 =100) (preceding year=100)

年 份 Year	居民消费价格指数 General Consumer Price Index	城 市 Urban Areas	农 村 Rural Areas	消费品指数 Consumer Goods Index	服务项目指数 Services Index
1979	101.0	100.3	101.7	100.8	102.8
1980	106.8	107.5	106.1	106.6	108.7
1981	106.5	105.8	107.2	106.3	108.4
1982	103.8	104.5	103.1	103.6	105.7
1983	100.8	100.1	101.5	100.6	102.6
1984	102.7	102.0	103.4	104.5	104.5
1985	113.1	116.1	106.2	112.9	115.2
1986	104.1	103.7	105.1	103.7	108.9
1987	109.8	109.8	109.8	110.0	107.9
1988	128.1	129.3	126.4	128.6	122.6
1989	128.4	126.3	127.5	126.9	141.0
1990	102.1	99.6	108.1	100.0	122.2
1991	103.9	104.0	103.6	103.3	108.2
1992	108.7	109.0	103.4	108.8	107.9
1993	123.3	123.7	116.5	123.8	119.7
1994	126.7	125.6	128.2	125.6	137.4
1995	113.5	110.6	118.4	111.9	120.4
1996	104.3	104.8	103.7	103.6	107.6
1997	100.8	101.5	100.3	99.8	112.1
1998	97.3	97.6	96.6	96.8	102.1
1999	98.3	99.1	97.3	97.2	108.4
2000	101.1	101.5	100.2	93.6	113.4
2001	98.5	98.8	98.3	98.1	99.8
2002	99.5	99.0	100.2	98.1	104.5
2003	100.1	99.4	100.9	100.9	97.2
2004	104.4	103.2	106.4	105.5	100.4
2005	101.5	101.3	101.7	101.1	103.0
2006	101.5	101.2	102.3	101.8	100.8

(1978=100)

年 份 Year	居民消费价格指数 General Consumer Price Index	城 市 Urban Areas	农 村 Rural Areas	消费品指数 Consumer Goods Index	服务项目指数 Services Index
1978	100.0	100.0	100.0	100.0	100.0
1979	101.1	100.3	101.7	100.8	102.8
1980	107.9	107.8	107.9	107.5	111.7
1981	114.9	114.1	115.7	114.2	121.1
1982	119.2	119.2	119.3	118.2	128.0
1983	120.2	119.3	121.1	119.0	131.4
1984	123.4	121.7	125.2	124.4	137.3
1985	139.6	141.3	132.9	140.4	158.1
1986	145.3	146.5	139.8	145.6	172.2
1987	159.5	160.9	153.5	160.2	185.8
1988	204.3	208.0	194.0	206.0	227.8
1989	262.3	262.8	247.4	261.5	321.2
1990	267.8	261.7	267.4	261.5	392.5
1991	278.3	272.2	277.0	270.1	424.7
1992	302.4	296.7	286.5	293.8	458.3
1993	372.9	367.0	333.7	363.8	548.5
1994	472.5	460.9	427.8	456.9	753.7
1995	536.3	507.0	506.6	507.2	907.5
1996	559.4	531.4	525.3	525.4	976.4
1997	563.9	539.4	526.9	524.3	1094.5
1998	548.7	526.5	509.0	507.5	1117.5
1999	539.4	521.8	495.3	493.3	1211.4
2000	545.3	529.6	496.3	461.7	1373.7
2001	537.1	523.2	487.9	452.9	1371.0
2002	534.4	518.0	488.9	444.3	1432.7
2003	534.9	514.9	493.3	448.3	1392.6
2004	558.4	531.4	524.9	473.0	1398.2
2005	566.8	538.3	533.8	478.2	1440.1
2006	575.3	544.8	546.1	486.8	1451.6

7-2 商品零售价格分类指数
Retail Price Indices by Category of Commodities

(上年=100) (preceding year=100)

项 目	Item	2004	2005	2006
商品零售价格指数	General Retail Price Index	103.4	100.9	101.3
食品	Food	109.7	102.4	102.6
粮　食	Grain	113.0	100.1	103.7
油　脂	Oil or Fat	105.3	98.7	99.7
肉禽及其制品	Meal, Poultry andRelated Products	122.8	100.9	98.7
蛋	Eggs	111.2	105.6	98.4
水产品	Aquatic Products	108.8	104.6	104.7
调味品	Condiments	98.9	101.7	104.4
食　糖	Sugar	108.9	116.8	133.0
鲜　菜	Fresh Vegetables	104.3	112.2	101.3
干菜及菜制品	Dried Vegetables	101.2	96.5	103.7
鲜瓜果	Fresh Fruits	105.6	95.1	124.6
干(坚)果	Dried Fruits	109.5	100.5	98.1
液体乳及乳制品	Milk and Its Products	101.6	99.5	100.9
其他食品	Other Food	100.5	102.6	102.0
饮料、烟酒	Beverages, Tobacco and Liquor	99.5	100.9	100.9
饮　料	Beverages	96.4	99.5	100.7
烟　草	Tobacco	99.8	101.3	100.1
酒	Liquor	100.6	101.0	101.0
服装、鞋帽	Garments, Shoes and Hats	98.5	96.6	96.1
服　装	Garments	98.5	95.5	95.5
鞋	Shoes	98.8	100.1	94.9
纺织品	Textiles	102.8	98.0	99.4
棉　布	Cotton Cloth	99.5	101.0	100.0
棉混纺布	Blend Cloth	100.9	99.0	100.0
化纤布	Chemical Fiber Cloth	101.0	100.0	99.8
家用电器及音像器材	Household Appliances,Music and Video Equipment	96.6	97.0	95.3
日用品	Articles for Daily Use	99.6	100.7	102.3
体育娱乐用品	Sports and Recreation Articles	99.6	99.8	98.9
化妆品	Cosmetics	101.7	100.9	100.0
金银珠宝	Gold,Silver and Jewelry	113.7	105.0	116.5
中西药品及医疗保健用品	Traditional Chinese and Western Medicines and Health	99.8	97.4	99.2
中药材及中成药	Traditional Chinese Medicine Materials and Medicines	97.2	95.9	99.1
西　药	Western Medicine	101.5	98.5	99.6
医疗器具及用品	Medical Apparatus and Articles	102.8	98.8	97.4
书报杂志及电子出版物	Book, Newspapers,Magazines and Electronic Publications	99.4	99.4	99.2
燃料	Fuels	106.9	113.4	114.6
建筑材料及五金电料	Building Materials and Hardware	106.3	106.6	106.7

7－3 分城乡商品零售价格指数
Retail Price Indices of Commodities by Urban and Rural

(上年=100) (preceding year=100)

项 目	Item	全省 Total	城市 Urban Areas	农村 Rural Areas	海口市 Haikou	文昌市 Wenchang	琼中县 Qiongzhong
商品零售价格指数	General Retail Price Index	101.3	100.6	102.3	100.6	103.0	102.2
食品	Food	102.6	102.5	102.7	102.5	103.2	101.0
粮 食	Grain	103.7	102.2	105.8	102.3	106.1	103.1
油 脂	Oil or Fat	99.7	100.4	99.0	100.4	100.6	104.2
肉禽及其制品	Meal, Poultry andRelated Products	98.7	98.3	99.1	98.2	99.2	97.9
蛋	Eggs	98.4	95.7	103.8	95.7	104.8	92.0
水产品	Aquatic Products	104.7	104.1	105.6	104.3	107.1	98.8
调味品	Condiments	104.4	104.0	105.0	104.2	105.2	100.1
糖	Sugar	117.6	118.8	116.6	116.9	118.3	99.9
鲜 菜	Fresh Vegetables	101.3	104.3	96.4	104.3	95.6	103.5
干菜及菜制品	Dried Vegetables	103.7	108.7	99.3	108.7	99.3	98.5
鲜瓜果	Fresh Fruits	124.6	125.4	123.4	125.4	123.6	120.6
干(坚)果	Dried Fruits	98.1	99.8	96.4	99.8	96.6	92.8
液体乳及乳制品	Milk and Its Products	100.9	101.5	99.3	101.7	99.2	101.2
其他食品类	Other Food	102.0	101.7	102.4	101.7	102.5	100.8
饮料烟酒	Beverages, Tobacco and Liquor	100.9	100.4	101.6	100.4	101.8	100.2
饮 料	Beverages	100.7	102.0	99.0	102.0	98.7	100.7
烟 草	Tobacco	100.1	100.4	99.7	100.4	99.8	100.2
酒	Liquor	101.0	99.7	102.9	99.8	103.3	100.0
服装、鞋帽	Garments, Shoes and Hats	96.1	94.5	100.5	95.0	99.6	110.0
服 装	Garments	95.5	93.6	100.5	94.3	99.2	114.2
鞋	Shoes	94.9	93.5	100.4	93.5	100.4	100.0
纺织品	Textiles	99.4	99.2	99.7	98.3	100.0	96.8
衣着材料	Clothing Material	99.9	100.0	99.7	100.0	99.7	100.0
床上用品	Goods in Bed	99.1	98.8	99.7	97.3	100.1	95.7
家用电器及音像器材	Household Appliances,Music and Video Equipment	95.3	92.8	99.8	92.9	99.9	100.5
文化办公用品	Stationery	97.3	96.7	98.3	96.5	98.3	100.0
日用品类	Articles for Daily Use	102.3	102.7	101.6	102.8	101.8	99.4
体育娱乐用品	Cultural and Sports Goods	98.9	98.6	100.1	98.6	100.1	100.0
交通、通信用品	Transportation and Communications Goods	92.2	94.4	90.0	94.2	89.9	100.2
家 具	Fumitures	103.5	101.2	107.8	101.2	108.8	100.0
化妆品	Cosmetics	100.0	100.0	100.0	100.0	100.0	100.1
金银珠宝	Gold,Silver and Jewelry	116.5	116.4	116.8	117.2	115.7	131.8
中、西药品及医疗保健	Traditional Chinese and Western Medicines and Health	99.2	99.0	99.7	99.1	100.0	98.1
中药材及中成药	Traditional Chinese Medicine Materials and Medicines	99.1	98.6	100.2	98.6	99.9	103.1
西 药	Western Medicine	99.6	99.6	99.7	99.8	100.4	94.2
医疗器具及用品	Medical Apparatus and Articles	97.4	96.9	99.7	96.9	100.0	95.5
书报杂志及电子出版物	Book, Newspapers, Magazines and Electronic Publications	99.2	98.5	100.1	98.0	100.2	101.2
燃料	Fuels	114.6	114.2	114.8	113.5	114.9	114.7
建筑材料及五金电料	Building Materials and Hardware	106.7	103.4	110.7	103.0	119.8	102.3

7－4 居民消费价格分类指数
Consumer Price Indices by Category

(上年 =100) (preceding year=100)

项 目	Item	2004	2005	2006
居民消费价格指数	**General Consumer Price Index**	104.4	101.5	101.5
食 品	**Food**	111.0	101.7	102.3
粮 食	Grain	115.4	100.7	102.1
油 脂	Oil or Fat	107.7	95.3	100.1
肉禽及其制品	Meal, Poultry and Their Products	123.7	100.8	98.6
水产品	Aquatic Products	109.0	104.0	105.2
菜	Vegetables	105.1	108.6	103.0
糖	Carbohydrate	106.5	107.3	118.7
鲜瓜果	Fresh Fruits	107.0	95.5	124.9
干(坚)果	Dried Fruits	109.4	101.2	98.7
糕 点	Cake	99.8	101.4	100.8
液体乳及乳制品	Milk and Its Products	102.4	100.1	100.7
烟酒及用品	**Tobacco;Liquor and Articles**	100.5	101.2	100.5
衣 着	**Clothing**	98.8	97.0	95.8
服 装	Garments	98.6	96.0	95.7
衣着材料	Clothing Material	100.8	99.8	99.9
棉 布	Cotton Cloth	99.2	101.8	100.0
棉混纺布	Blend Cloth	101.8	98.3	100.0
化纤布	Chemical Fiber Cloth	101.7	100.0	99.8
鞋	Shoes	98.6	99.6	94.9
家庭设备用品及维修服务	**Household Facilities Articles and Services**	100.3	100.7	101.1
家 具	Furniture	99.1	100.8	103.0
家庭设备	Household Facilities	98.4	100.0	99.6
家庭日用杂品	Daily Use Household Articles	101.1	101.2	100.8
医疗保健和个人用品	**Health Cares & Personal Articles**	99.7	99.7	98.8
医疗保健	Medical Appliances and Articles	100.2	99.0	97.2
中药材及中成药	Traditional Chinese Medicine	97.4	95.0	98.8
西 药	Western Medicine	98.5	99.0	99.4
交通和通信	**Transportation and Communication**	99.6	100.5	101.2
交 通	Transportation	100.5	102.0	104.8
通 信	Telecommunication	98.4	98.3	96.8
娱乐教育文化用品及服务	**Recreation, Education and Culture Articles and Services**	97.9	101.1	99.0
文娱用耐用消费品及服务	Durable Consumer Goods for Recreational Use and Services	92.8	93.8	91.9
教 育	Education	99.6	104.2	101.3
居 住	**Residence**	101.9	105.9	107.7
建房及装修材料	Building and Building Decoration Materials	106.0	105.2	110.6
自有住房	Private Housing	100.1	105.1	107.0
水、电、燃料	Water, Electricity and Fuels	100.7	106.7	107.0

7－5 城乡居民消费价格指数
Consumer Price Indices of Residents by Urban and Rural Areas

项目	Item	以1985年价格为100 (1985=100) 全省 Total	城镇 Urban	农村 Rural	以1987年价格为100 (1987=100) 全省 Total	城镇 Urban	农村 Rural	以1993年价格为100 (1993=100) 全省 Total	城镇 Urban	农村 Rural
居民消费价格指数	General Consumer Price Index	406.5	383.5	404.5	355.5	337.8	356.2	156.6	151.0	166.4
食品	Food	481.1	452.8	469.1	413.0	388.6	402.8	161.8	154.4	173.7
粮食	Grain	813.3	716.3	952.1	705.0	670.0	799.4	180.9	183.6	195.1
油脂	Oil or Fat	560.0	573.0	581.0	523.6	535.8	543.1	139.7	133.0	150.5
肉禽及其制品	Meal, Poultry and Their Products	308.3	313.6		259.9	264.4		149.9	132.3	167.4
水产品	Aquatic Products	457.3	401.2	603.3	354.6	311.2	406.8	150.1	146.4	153.6
鲜菜	Fresh Vegetables	495.7	486.5	0.0	482.9	474.0	0.0	201.5	197.8	196.6
烟草	Tobacco	243.7	215.8	278.7	229.8	210.5	250.8	94.7	83.9	106.4
其他食品类	Other Food	300.8	278.5	347.2	262.0	242.6	302.4	138.3	134.7	152.8
衣着	Clothing	206.9	197.0	229.7	191.3	182.3	215.7	117.6	112.4	128.7
棉布	Cotton Cloth	295.5	305.8	326.7	275.9	287.7	295.5	138.2	144.8	143.3
化纤布	Chemical Fiber Cloth	235.9	335.7	184.4	233.4	332.0	182.4	178.8	263.2	132.6
家庭设备用品及维修服务	Household Facilities Articles and Services	212.9	196.1	277.9	197.3	188.0	219.3	131.2	128.9	134.5
耐用消费品	Durable Consumer Goods	207.3	202.0	221.4	185.4	180.7	198.1	105.3	103.6	111.5
家庭日用杂品	Daily Use Household Articles	384.9	379.8	356.9	317.3	312.5	275.1	171.4	172.1	164.9
医疗保健和个人用品	Health Cares & Personal Articles	288.6	262.4	337.8	270.0	243.5	313.6	145.9	129.6	176.5
中药材及中成药	Traditional Chinese Medicine	285.2	247.6	332.8	273.0	237.0	318.4	132.1	112.9	163.0
西药	Western Medicine	213.1	208.6	234.3	192.9	188.9	212.3	122.8	121.6	135.0
交通和通信	Transportation and Communication	255.1	236.8	220.0	182.5	172.7	115.7	77.0	71.3	67.6
娱乐教育文化用品及服务	Recreation, Education and Culture Articles and Services	165.1	200.0	183.9	151.4	161.7	159.6	119.1	124.7	122.6
文娱用耐用消费品及服务	Durable Consumer Goods for Recreational Use and Services	62.9	73.3	66.3	59.2	69.3	62.7	51.8	57.5	55.0
居住	Residence	386.6	389.4	439.5	361.7	364.6	410.9	217.1	213.9	213.6
自有住房	Private Housing	337.5	256.8	542.3	321.8	244.9	517.2	235.1	189.7	281.8
水、电、燃料	Water, Electricity and Fuels	410.3	469.6	358.4	380.5	436.8	331.8	205.6	227.6	166.6

7-5 续 1 (上年 =100)(continued1)

(preceding year=100)

项 目	Item	全省 Total	城市 Urban Areas	农村 Rural Areas	海口市 Haikou	文昌市 Wenchang	琼中县 Qiongzhong
居民消费价格指数	**General Consumer Price Index**	**101.5**	**101.2**	**102.3**	**101.3**	**102.7**	**101.2**
食 品	**Food**	**102.3**	**102.3**	**102.2**	**102.6**	**103.0**	**100.3**
粮 食	Grain	102.1	101.1	105.0	101.1	105.4	103.2
淀 粉	Starches	104.4	106.5	98.3	106.5	98.5	97.5
干豆类及豆制品	Bean and Its Products	101.6	101.9	101.2	101.9	101.7	101.1
油 脂	Oil or Fat	100.1	100.4	99.7	100.4	98.8	104.8
肉禽及其制品	Meal, Poultry and Their Products	98.6	98.2	99.3	98.6	99.6	98.0
蛋	Eggs	98.2	96.1	101.4	96.1	104.9	91.8
水产品	Aquatic Products	105.2	104.6	106.2	104.2	108.2	98.8
菜	Vegetables	103.0	104.7	98.3	104.9	96.7	104.3
鲜 菜	Fresh Vegetables	102.6	104.3	97.2	104.3	95.6	103.5
干菜及菜制品	Dried Vegetables	105.8	108.7	99.2	108.7	99.3	98.5
调味品	Condiments	104.9	105.0	104.6	104.5	106.0	100.3
糖	Carbohydrate	118.7	120.3	116.7	121.5	119.2	99.9
食 糖	Sugar	133.7	137.7	128.2	137.7	131.8	100.1
糖 果	Candy	104.1	104.4	103.7	104.4	104.3	100.0
茶及饮料	Liquor and Beverages	102.5	102.1	103.1	101.8	103.4	100.5
干鲜瓜果	Dried and Fresh Melons and Fruits	122.6	123.4	119.7	122.8	119.0	117.8
鲜瓜果	Fresh Fruits	124.9	125.4	123.1	125.4	123.6	120.6
干(坚)果	Dried Fruits	98.7	99.8	96.2	99.8	96.6	92.8
糕点饼干	Cake and Biscuit	100.8	99.9	103.2	99.9	103.6	101.2
液体乳及乳制品	Milk and Its Products	100.7	101.4	99.7	101.3	99.3	101.2
在外用膳食品	Catering Trade	100.2	100.0	101.2	100.0	101.5	100.0
其他食品	Other Food	102.0	101.7	102.3	101.7	102.5	100.8
烟酒及用品	**Tobacco, Liquor and Article**	**100.5**	**100.1**	**101.0**	**100.1**	**101.3**	**100.1**
烟 草	Tobacco	100.1	100.4	99.8	100.4	99.8	100.2
酒	Liquor	101.0	99.6	102.5	99.8	103.6	100.0
衣 着	**Clothing**	**95.8**	**93.9**	**101.6**	**93.9**	**99.6**	**110.4**
服 装	Garments	95.7	93.6	102.0	93.7	99.2	114.2
衣着材料	Clothing Material	99.9	100.0	99.8	100.0	99.8	100.0
棉 布	Cotton Cloth	100.0	100.0	100.0	100.0	100.0	100.0

7-5 续 2 (上年 =100)(continued2) (preceding year=100)

项 目	Item	全省 Total	城市 Urban Areas	农村 Rural Areas	海口市 Haikou	文昌市 Wenchang	琼中县 Qiongzhong
棉混纺布	Blend Cloth	100.0	100.0	100.0	100.0	100.0	100.0
化纤布	Chemical Fiber Cloth	99.8	100.0	99.4	100.0	99.3	100.0
鞋袜帽	Footgear and Hats	95.5	93.9	100.6	93.8	100.8	100.0
鞋	Shoes	94.9	93.5	100.4	93.5	100.5	100.0
袜子	Socks and Stockings	100.8	100.0	101.8	100.0	102.2	100.0
帽子	Hats	100.0	100.0	100.0	100.0	100.0	100.0
家庭设备用品及维修服务	**Household Facilities Articles and Services**	**101.1**	**100.3**	**103.2**	**100.2**	**104.3**	**98.9**
耐用消费品	Durable Consumer Goods	101.3	99.7	104.8	99.8	105.8	100.2
家具	Furniture	103.0	100.8	106.4	100.8	107.9	100.0
家庭设备	Household Facilities	99.6	99.0	101.9	99.3	102.2	100.8
室内装饰品	Interior Decorations	98.6	98.9	97.5	98.9	97.2	100.0
床上用品	Bed Articles	99.1	99.1	99.0	98.6	99.9	95.7
家庭日用杂品	Daily Use Household Articles	100.8	100.0	102.7	100.0	103.9	98.3
医疗保健和个人用品	**Medicine and Medical Articles**	**98.8**	**98.1**	**100.6**	**98.0**	**101.2**	**98.7**
医疗器具及用品	Medical Appliances and Articles	98.5	96.9	99.4	96.9	100.0	95.5
中药材及中成药	Traditional Chinese Medicine	98.8	98.5	100.5	98.3	99.9	103.2
西药	Western Medicine	99.4	99.6	99.0	99.6	100.3	94.2
交通和通信	**Transportation and Communication**	**101.2**	**101.8**	**99.8**	**101.7**	**99.0**	**102.6**
交通	Means of Transportation	104.8	105.1	104.4	105.6	103.8	106.0
通信	Telecommunication	96.8	98.3	92.3	98.4	90.1	97.4
娱乐教育文化用品及服务	**Recreation, Education and Culture Articles and Services**	**99.0**	**98.4**	**100.3**	**99.2**	**100.7**	**99.3**
文娱用耐用消费品及服务	Durable Consumer Goods for Recreational Use and Services	91.9	90.1	97.5	91.1	97.2	99.9
教育	Education	101.3	101.3	101.2	101.7	101.5	100.2
文化娱乐	Cultural and Recreational Articles	99.3	99.6	98.7	99.5	99.8	95.6
书报杂志	Newspapers and Magazines	99.1	98.8	99.7	98.8	99.6	100.0
居住	**Residence**	**107.7**	**107.0**	**109.4**	**106.3**	**110.3**	**105.5**
建房及装修材料	Building Decoration Materials	110.6	103.7	113.9	103.8	115.9	104.8
租房	Rent	100.1	99.9	100.7	99.9	101.0	100.0
自有住房	Private Housing	107.0	107.5	102.0	107.2	102.0	102.6
水、电、燃料	Water, Electricity and Fuels	107.0	107.8	104.2	107.1	103.3	107.9

7－6 农业生产资料价格指数
Price Indices of Agricultural Means of Production

(上年=100) (preceding year=100)

项目	Item	全省 Total	农村 Rural Areas	文昌市 Wenchang	琼中县 Qiongzhong
农业生产资料价格指数	Price Indices of Agricultural Means of Production	100.7	100.7	100.7	101.4
农用手工工具	Small Farm Tools	101.9	101.9	101.5	105.1
饲料	Forage	100.9	100.9	101.0	99.2
幼禽家畜	Young Livestock and Fowls	75.9	75.9	74.4	85.8
半机械化农具	Semimechanized Farm Implements	103.5	103.5	103.5	103.5
机械化农具	Mechanized Farm Implements	100.1	100.1	100.1	100.0
化学肥料	Chemecal Fertilizer	102.8	102.8	102.4	107.1
农药及农药械	Pesticide and Its Appliances	99.8	99.8	100.1	98.2
化学农药	Chemecal Pesticide	99.7	99.7	100.0	98.0
农药器械	Chemecal Pesticide Appliances	100.5	100.5	100.6	100.0
农用机油	Oil for Farm Machinery	116.7	116.7	116.7	116.4
其他农业生产资料	Others	110.1	110.1	112.4	103.9

7－7 主要消费品零售价格指数
Retail Price Indice of Main Consumer Goods

(上年＝100) (preceding year=100)

项 目	Item	2004	2005	2006
植物油制品	Edible Vegetable Oil (kg)	108.8	98.6	97.6
肉禽及其制品	Meal, Poultry andRelated Products	122.8	100.9	98.7
蛋	Eggs	111.2	105.6	98.4
水产品	Aquatic Products	108.8	104.6	104.7
鲜 菜	Fresh Vegetables	104.3	112.2	101.3
干菜及菜制品	Dried Vegetables	101.2	96.5	103.7
调味品	Condiments	98.9	101.7	104.4
食 糖	Sugar	108.9	116.8	133.0
糖 果	Candy	107.0	99.1	104.1
鲜瓜果	Fresh Fruits	105.6	95.1	124.6
干（坚）果	Dried Fruits	109.5	100.5	98.1
糕 点	Cake	97.7	99.5	101.8
液体乳及乳制品	Milk and Its Products	101.6	99.5	100.9
烟 草	Tobacco	99.8	101.3	100.1
酒	Liquor	100.6	101.0	101.0
茶 叶	Tea	100.0	101.6	107.6
棉 布	Cotton Cloth	99.5	101.0	100.0
服 装	Garments	98.5	95.5	95.5
鞋	Shoes	98.8	100.1	94.9
棉混纺布	Blend Cloth	100.9	99.0	100.0
化纤布	Chemical Fiber Cloth	101.0	100.0	99.8
日用杂品	Sundries for Daily Use	101.5	99.6	102.1
家 具	Furniture	98.8	100.5	103.5
中药材及中成药	Traditional Chinese Medicine Materials and Medicines	97.2	95.9	99.1
西 药	Western Medicine and Medical Articles	101.5	98.5	99.6

7-7 续(continued)

项 目	Item	以1987年价格为100 (1987=100)			以1998年价格为100 (1998=100)		
		全省 Total	城镇 Urban	农村 Rural	全省 Total	城镇 Urban	农村 Rural
植物油制品	Edible Vegetable Oil (kg)	473.5	518.0	443.8	95.5	94.5	90.6
肉禽及其制品	Meal, Poultry andRelated Products	235.2	243.8		113.3	106.9	120.8
水产品	Aquatic Products	352.8	343.9	450.0	120.2	115.5	124.0
鲜 菜	Fresh Vegetables	469.8	440.8		127.6	125.6	130.4
干菜及菜制品	Dried Vegetables	281.6	263.6	308.0	101.8	112.0	95.0
调味品	Condiments	238.6	206.0	317.1	97.6	93.6	103.7
食 糖	Sugar	320.4	326.6	376.3	123.1	135.9	114.0
鲜瓜果	Fresh Fruits	270.2	281.3		125.6	134.1	114.9
干(坚)果	Dried Fruits	254.6	243.9	257.3	84.5	84.9	85.0
糖 果	Candy	376.0	342.1	390.1	101.5	94.3	116.9
糕 点	Cake	424.7	432.6	333.0	97.7	98.9	97.4
液体乳及乳制品	Milk and Its Products	243.3	214.6	278.7	85.9	83.4	91.6
烟 草	Tobacco	295.5	264.9	303.3	88.5	90.6	85.7
酒	Liquor	233.3	179.7	249.9	105.8	88.5	112.7
茶 叶	Tea	212.3	128.4	343.9	99.0	87.1	115.3
服 装	Garments	150.1	148.5	180.3	85.7	83.1	92.0
鞋	Shoes	340.4	288.5	395.2	103.7	107.6	102.1
棉 布	Cotton Cloth	280.8	269.4	287.7	89.6	85.5	91.2
棉混纺布	Blend Cloth	364.8	423.8	348.2	104.5	109.1	97.5
化纤布	Chemical Fiber Cloth	274.8	327.2	192.6	118.9	137.9	104.7
日用杂品	Sundries for Daily Use	311.9	288.2	346.6	105.5	106.2	104.6
家 具	Furniture	175.9	144.9	231.6	90.0	88.3	94.9
中药材及中成药	Traditional Chinese Medicine Materials and Medicines	267.9	228.7	297.7	104.2	96.0	113.9
西 药	Western Medicine and Medical Article	236.4	213.8	244.1	101.9	92.7	109.7

主要统计指标解释

商品零售价格指数 是反映城乡商品零售价格变动趋势的一种经济指数。零售物价的调整变动直接影响到城乡居民的生活支出和国家的财政收入,影响居民购买力和市场供需平衡,影响消费与积累的比例。因此,计算零售价格指数,可以从一个侧面对上述经济活动进行观察和分析。

居民消费价格指数 是反映一定时期内城乡居民所购买的生活消费品价格和服务项目价格变动趋势和程度的相对数,是对城市居民消费价格指数和农村居民消费价格指数进行综合汇总计算的结果。利用居民消费价格指数,可以观察和分析消费品的零售价格和服务价格变动对城乡居民实际生活费支出的影响程度。

城市居民消费价格指数 是反映城市居民家庭所购买的生活消费品价格和服务项目价格变动趋势和程度的相对数。城市居民消费价格指数可以观察和分析消费品的零售价格和服务项目价格变动对职工货币工资的影响，作为研究职工生活和确定工资政策的依据。

农村居民消费价格指数 是反映农村居民家庭所购买的生活消费品价格和服务项目价格变动趋势和程度的相对数。农村居民消费价格指数可以观察农村消费品的零售价格和服务项目价格变动对农村居民生活消费支出的影响，直接反映农民生活水平的实际变化情况,为分析和研究农村居民生活问题提供依据。

Explanatory Note on Main Statistical Indicators

Retail Price Index reflects the general change in retail prices of commodities. The change and adjustment in retail prices directly affect the living expenditure of urban and rural residents, government revenue, purchasing power of residents and the equilibrium of market supply and demand, and the ratio of consumption to accumulation. Therefore, the calculation of retail price index is useful to analyze the changes of the above economic activities.

Consumer Price Index reflects the trend and degree of changes in prices of consumer goods and services purchased by urban and rural residents, and is a composite index derived from the urban consumer price index and the rural consumer price index. Consumer price index can be used to analyze the impact of consumer price change on actual expenditure for living cost of urban and rural residents.

Urban Consumer Price Index reflects the trend and degree of changes in prices of consumer goods and services purchased by urban households. It can be used to observe and analyze the impact of price changes in consumer goods and services on money wages of staff and workers, and provide basis for policy making concerning the living cost and wages of staff and workers.

Rural Consumer Price Index reflects the trend and degree of changes in prices of consumer goods and services purchased by rural households. It can be used to observe the impact of change in retail prices of consumer goods and service prices in rural areas on living expenditure of rural households, and to show the changes in the living standard of peasants. It provides basis for analysis and research on condition of life in rural areas.

资料整理:叶 薇 黄 怡
Arranged by Yewei huangyi

8. 居民生活
PEOPLE' S LIVELHOOD

城乡居民储蓄存款余额（亿元）

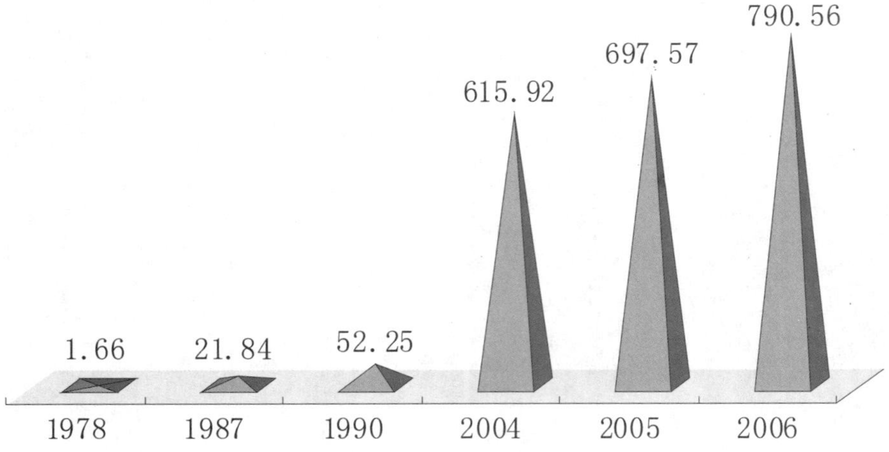

城乡居民人均可支配收入（元）

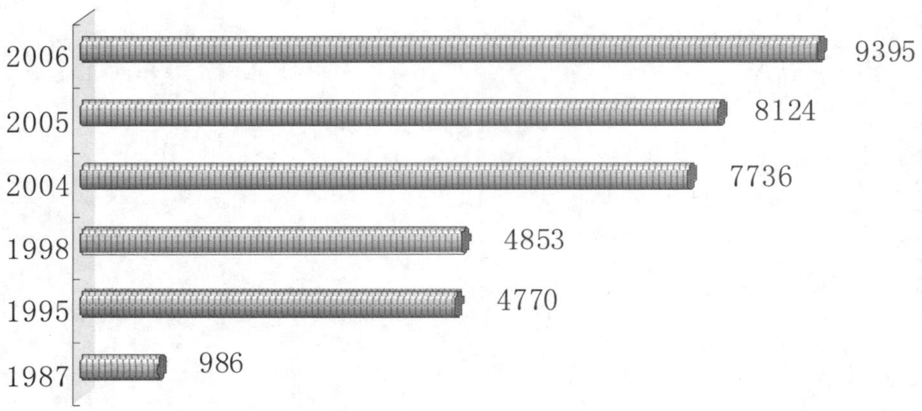

农民人均纯收入（元）

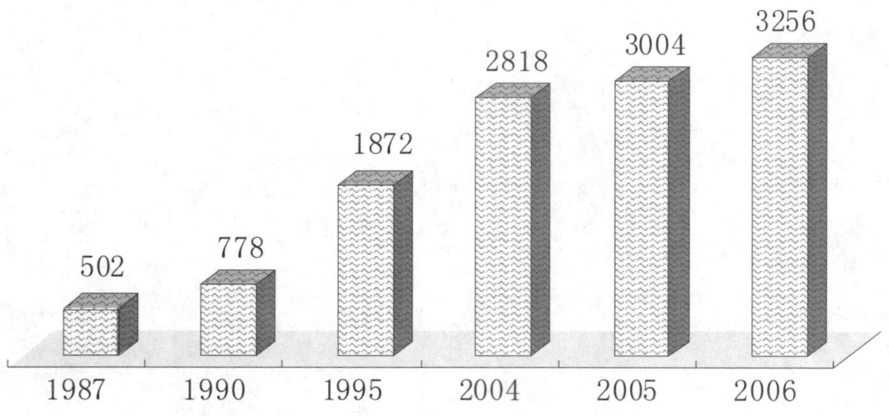

8－1 人民物质文化生活情况
People's Material and Cultural Life

项 目	Item	2004	2005	2006
就　业	**Employment**			
每一农村劳动力负担人口(人)	Number of Dependents per Rural Laborer (persons)	1.55	1.57	1.55
每一城镇就业者负担人口(人)	Number of Dependents per Urban Employee(persons)	2.17	2.31	2.24
收　入	**Income of Rural and Urban Residents**			
农村居民家庭人均纯收入(元)	Annual Per Capita Net Income of Rural Residents(yuan)	2818	3004	3256
城镇居民家庭人均可支配收入(元)	Annual Per Capita Disposable Income of Urban Residents(yuan)	7736	8124	9395
职工年平均工资(元)	Annual Average Wages of Staff and Workers (yuan)	12652	14417	15890
消费水平	**Annual Per Capita Consumption (yuan)**			
全部居民(元)	All Residents	3847	4144	4736
农民(元)	Rural Residents	2261	2419	2792
非农业居民(元)	Urban Residents	6596	7019	7688
储　蓄	**Savings**			
城乡居民年底储蓄存款余额(亿元)	Balance of Savings Deposit of Rural and Urban Residents (year-end) (100 million yuan)	615.92	697.57	790.56
平均每人储蓄存款余额(元)	Per Capita Balance of Saving Deposit (yuan)	7642.8	8517.03	9485.55
住　房(平方米)	**Per Capita Floor Space of Residential Buildings(sq.m)**			
农村人均住房面积	Rural Areas (Net)	19.48	21.82	22.05
城镇人均住房面积	Urban Areas (Gross)	18.55	21.10	21.99
文化教育卫生	**Culture,Education and Public Health**			
城镇每百户有彩色电视机(台)	Number of Color TV Sets per 100 Households in Urban Areas	118.51	118.69	124.22
农村每百户有电视机(台)	Number of TV Sets per 100 Households in Rural Areas	85.42	80.83	87.5
学龄儿童入学率(%)	Enrollment Ratio of School-Age Children (%)	99.32	99.79	99.81
每万人口中在校大学生(人)	Number of University Students per 10 000 Persons (person)	71	85	108
每万人口中在校中学生(人)	Number of Secondary School Students per 10 000 Persons(person)	662	706	734
每万人口中在校小学生(人)	Number of Primary School Students per 10 000 Persons(person)	1225	1276	1253
每万人中有医生人数(人)	Number of Hospital Beds per 10 000 Persons (person)	15	14	15
每万人中有医院病床位(张)	Number of Hospital Beds per 10 000 Persons	23	22	24.00

8－2 城乡居民家庭人均收入及指数

Per Capita Annual Income and Index of Urban and Rural Households

年份 Year	农村居民家庭人均纯收入(元) Annual Per Capita Net Income of Rural Residents (yuan)	指数(1987=100) Index	城镇居民家庭人均可支配收入(元) Annual Per Capita Disposable Income of Urban Residents(yuan)	指数(1987=100) Index	城镇居民家庭恩格尔系数(%) Engle Coefficient of Urban Households (%)	农村居民家庭恩格尔系数(%) Engle Coefficient of Rural Households (%)	职工平均工资(元) Annual Average Wages of Staff and Workers (yuan)	指数(1987=100) Index
1987	502	100.0	986	100.0		61.0	1233	100.0
1988	609	121.3	1196	121.3	64.0	57.8	1399	113.5
1989	696	138.6	1367	138.6	62.9	56.9	1640	133.0
1990	778	155.0	1650	167.3	60.7	63.3	1980	160.6
1991	790	157.4	1799	182.5	62.1	60.6	2194	177.9
1992	892	177.7	2318	235.1	60.9	62.9	2720	220.6
1993	1031	205.4	3072	311.6	61.8	52.6	3501	283.9
1994	1274	253.8	3920	397.6	60.5	56.6	4058	329.2
1995	1520	302.8	4770	483.8	59.3	59.7	5340	433.1
1996	1748	347.8	4926	499.6	58.6	57.1	5476	444.1
1997	1819	362.4	4850	491.9	57.0	53.8	5664	459.4
1998	1966	391.6	4853	449.2	55.0	61.6	6248	506.7
1999	2119	422.1	5338	541.4	51.2	54.1	6865	556.8
2000	2231	444.4	5358	543.4	49.3	56.9	7408	600.8
2001	2285	455.2	5839	592.2	46.3	59.0	8321	674.8
2002	2423	482.7	6823	692.0	45.4	59.1	9480	768.8
2003	2588	515.5	7259	736.2	44.8	57.6	10397	843.2
2004	2818	561.4	7736	784.6	46.9	58.9	12652	1026.1
2005	3004	598.4	8124	823.9	47.6	57.6	14417	1169.2
2006	3256	648.6	9395	952.8	43.5	53.4	15890	1288.7

8－3 城乡居民储蓄存款余额

Savings Deposit in Urban and Rural Areas

年份 Year	城乡居民储蓄存款余额(万元) Balance of Savings Deposit of Rural and Urban Residents (10 000 yuan)	城镇 Urban	农村 Rural	城乡居民储蓄存款人均余额(元) Per Capita Balance of Saving Deposit of Rural and Urban Residents(yuan)	城镇 Urban	农村 Rural
1987	218371	160171	58200	355.0	1570.9	113.4
1988	299822	230862	68960	367.9	2165.5	132.4
1989	375937	302913	73024	474.2	2694.2	138.7
1990	522494	428434	94060	802.3	3620.7	176.5
1991	687361	570831	116530	1039.1	4672.8	216.1
1992	1127517	961425	166092	1679.6	7597.2	304.9
1993	1840167	1559101	281066	2699.1	11240.0	517.6
1994	2329142	1990673	338469	3368.8	14137.3	614.7
1995	2794077	2429174	364903	3977.8	16587.1	656.3
1996	3271283	2863752	407531	4581.2	18333.9	738.1
1997	3626146	3175942	450204	5004.8	18660.1	819.9
1998	3855237	3377784	477453	5257.3	19105.1	864.8
1999	3983884	3485812	498072	5360.4	19089.9	896.5
2000	4047376	3550268	497108	5138.9	18904.5	881.1
2001	4273277	3780777	492500	5584.4	19650.6	859.5
2002	4840769	4279136	561633	6252.6	21215.3	980.7
2004	6159162	5461655	697507	7642.8	17934.7	1391.8
2005	6975744	6219155	756589	8517.1	19823.3	1497.3
2006	7905634	7034669	870965	9485.6	21890.3	1700.87

8－4 城镇居民家庭基本情况
Basic Conditions of Urban Households

项　目	Item	2004	2005	2006
调查户数(户)	Number of Households Surveyed (household)	300	600	600
平均每户家庭人口数(人)	Average Household Size (person)	3.53	3.60	3.51
平均每户就业人口数(人)	Average Number of Employed Persons per Household (persons)	1.63	1.56	1.57
平均每户就业面(%)	Percentage of Employment per Household(%)	46.18	43.33	44.70
平均每一就业者负担人数(人)	Number of Persons Supported by Each Employee (person)	2.17	2.31	2.24
平均每人全年家庭总收入(元)	Per Capita Annual Total Income of Household(yuan)	8122	8670	10082
#可支配收入	Disposable Income	7736	8124	9395
平均每一就业者全年实际收入(元)	Per Each Employee Annual Real Income (yuan)	12888	15648	17340
平均每人全年总支出(元)	Per Capita Annual Total Expenditures(yuan)	7346	7932	9066
#消费性支出	Living Expenditures for Consumption(yuan)	5802	5928	7128
平均每户年末手存现金(元)	Hold Cash per Household at the Year-end(yuan)	2194	1723	1476
平均每人居住面积(平方米)	Per Capita Floor Space of Residential Buildings(sq.m)	18.55	21.10	21.99

8-4 续 (continued)

项　目	Item	最低收入户 Lowest Income Households (first decile)	困难户 Poor Households (first five percent)	低收入户 Low Income Households (second decile)	中等偏下户 Lower Middle Income Households (second quintile)	中等收入户 Middle Income Households (third quintile)	中等偏上户 Upper Middle Income Households (fourth quintile)	高收入户 High Income Households (ninth decile)	最高收入户 Highest Income Households (tenth decile)
调查户数(户)	Number of Households Surveyed (household)	60	30	60	120	120	120	60	60
比重(%)	Proportion(%)	10	5	10	20	20	20	10	10
平均每户家庭人口数(人)	Average Household Size (person)	4.34	4.58	3.97	3.95	3.43	3.38	2.85	2.44
平均每户就业人口数(人)	Average Number of Employed Persons per Household (persons)	1.19	1.14	1.37	1.68	1.63	1.78	1.57	1.44
平均每户就业面(%)	Percentage of Employment per Household (%)	27.42	24.89	34.51	42.53	47.52	52.66	55.09	59.02
平均每一就业者负担人数(人)	Number of Persons Supported by Each Employee (person)	3.65	4.02	2.90	2.35	2.10	1.90	1.82	1.69
平均每人全年家庭总收入(元)	Per Capita Annual Total Income of Household (yuan)	2885.61	2416.04	4549.87	6389.46	9225.02	13004.07	18154.74	28801.97
#可支配收入	Disposable Income	2775.91	2339.73	4389.29	6064.97	8655.41	12171.80	16834.51	25870.16
平均每人每月可支配收入(元)	Per Capita Annual Total Expenditures(yuan)	231.33	194.98	365.77	505.41	721.28	1014.32	1402.88	2155.85
平均每人年家庭总支出(元)		2602.55	2323.67	4223.60	5428.07	8163.40	11459.28	13972.73	30483.30
#消费性支出	Living Expenditures for Consumption(yuan)	2413.93	2149.50	3715.47	4649.84	6476.98	8913.23	10799.33	21740.29
平均每人每月消费性支出(元)		201.16	179.13	309.62	387.49	539.75	742.77	899.94	1811.69
平均每一就业者全年实际收入(元)	Per Each Employee Annual Real Income (yuan)								
平均每户年末手存现金(元)	Hold Cash per Household at the Year-end(yuan)	1294.25	1219.27	1232.98	1216.93	1448.64	1690.50	1833.81	1747.83

8－5 城镇居民家庭年人均收入来源及构成

Per Capital Incom in Urban Residents by Source and Composition

项 目	Item	2004	2005	2006	06比05增长(%)
家庭总收入(元)	Total Income of Household	8121.77	8670.05	10081.70	11.8
工薪收入	Wages Income	5599.20	6071.04	6954.45	10.2
工资及补贴收入	Wages and Subsidy Income	5231.16	5693.38	6531.75	9.9
其他劳动收入	Part-time Income	368.04	377.66	422.70	15.8
经营净收入	Net Income of Management	261.99	661.65	727.12	10.2
财产性收入	Property Income	267.81	198.16	231.24	9.5
利息收入	Interest Income	6.20	5.12	17.64	213.9
股息与红利收入	Dividend and Bonus Income	38.27	17.66	39.93	94.5
其他投资收入	Other Inventment Income	107.54	99.88	68.96	-36.5
出租房屋收入	Income of Houses to Let	111.55	68.84	95.44	36.4
其他财产性收入	Others	3.88	6.30	5.76	4.7
转移性收入	Transfer Income	1992.78	1739.20	2168.90	18.0
养老金或离退休金	Old-age Pensions, Pensions for Termination and Retirement Pensions	1457.47	1217.93	1451.99	12.4
社会救济收入	Social Relief Income	8.96	6.40	8.31	32.3
保险收入	Insurance Income	10.15	20.39	16.72	11.2
赡养收入	Support Income	152.17	132.13	164.86	11.7
捐赠收入	Donation Income	192.47	180.11	266.99	44.6
亲友搭伙费	Expenses of	51.99	51.83	76.30	36.4
提取住房公积金	Accumulation Fund of Housing	26.04	8.46	16.25	90.3
记帐补贴	Keep Accounts Subsidy	58.30	60.77	66.10	8.8
其他转移性收入	Others	32.00	61.17	58.50	-9.4
收入构成(%)	Composition of Income(%)	100	100	100	---
工薪收入	Wages Income	68.94	70.02	68.98	---
经营净收入	Net Income of Management	3.23	7.63	7.21	---
财产性收入	Property Income	3.30	2.29	2.29	---
转移性收入	Transfer Income	24.54	20.06	21.51	---

注:(1)城市住户调查从2002年起,国家采用新的指标体系,本表数据用新的指标体系计算得到.
Since 2002,the stat has used a new index system for urban househol survey and the data in this table is calculated from it

(2)此表中的2006年与2005年相比增速按同比口径计算.
The growth speed is calculated at comparable price

8-5 续 1 (continued1)

项目	Item	最低收入户 Lowest Income Households (first decile)	困难户 Poor Households (first five percent)	低收入户 Low Income Households (second decile)	中等偏下户 Lower Middle Income Households (second quintile)	中等收入户 Middle Income Households (third quintile)	中等偏上户 Upper Middle Income Households (fourth quintile)	高收入户 High Income Households (ninth decile)	最高收入户 Highest Income Households (tenth decile)
家庭总收入(元)	**Total Income of Household**	2885.61	2416.04	4549.87	6389.46	9225.02	13004.07	18154.74	28801.97
工薪收入	Wages Income	1603.48	1218.44	2709.58	4522.71	5906.24	9637.08	13144.63	19651.70
工资及补贴收入	Wages and Subsidy Income	1143.69	851.04	2183.20	4049.54	5604.18	9290.38	12601.91	19228.85
其他劳动收入	Part-time Income	459.79	367.41	526.38	473.17	302.07	346.70	542.73	422.86
经营净收入	Net Income of Management	533.69	533.04	585.36	596.54	1033.97	716.73	318.82	1371.74
财产性收入	Property Income	53.01	39.35	88.04	128.37	236.87	225.70	671.43	591.66
利息收入	Interest Income	0.00	0.00	0.74	2.28	5.85	28.85	17.24	129.76
股息与红利收入	Dividend and Bonus Income	0.00	0.00	18.47	6.52	69.57	39.46	130.10	63.76
其他投资收入	Other Inventment Income	2.24	2.20	15.14	36.19	66.25	89.39	258.67	108.91
出租房屋收入	Income of Houses to Let	41.85	20.89	53.68	76.20	90.73	64.68	223.26	266.21
其他财产性收入	Others	8.92	16.25	0.00	7.18	4.46	2.33	14.70	7.90
转移性收入	Transfer Income	695.43	625.20	1166.89	1141.83	2047.94	2424.56	4019.86	7186.86
养老金或离退休金	Old-age Pensions, Pensions for Termination andRetirement Pensions	448.98	385.44	804.62	805.01	1427.84	1737.04	2819.96	4048.49
社会救济收入	Social Relief Income	39.96	50.44	0.00	8.01	4.43	4.28	0.00	0.00
保险收入	Insurance Income	0.00	0.00	14.95	11.92	38.04	15.71	21.46	1.24
赡养收入	Support Income	44.31	75.34	131.70	76.53	168.43	84.63	395.28	647.71
捐赠收入	Donation Income	84.05	57.82	136.82	146.26	171.46	209.93	351.40	1518.20
亲友搭伙费	Expenses of	16.12	4.02	13.25	29.29	89.58	108.51	88.25	300.47
提取住房公积金	Accumulation Fund of Housing	0.00	0.00	0.00	0.00	3.24	51.67	18.13	62.97
记帐补贴	Keep Accounts Subsidy	54.59	52.14	59.79	57.14	68.68	66.68	82.46	97.37
其他转移性收入	Others	7.43	0.00	5.75	7.67	76.25	92.28	115.46	191.27
收入构成(%)	**Composition of Income(%)**	100	100	100	100	100	100	100	100
工薪收入	Wages Income	55.57	50.43	59.55	70.78	64.02	74.11	72.40	68.23
经营净收入	Net Income of Management	18.49	22.06	12.87	9.34	11.21	5.51	1.76	4.76
财产性收入	Property Income	1.84	1.63	1.94	2.01	2.57	1.74	3.70	2.05
转移性收入	Transfer Income	24.10	25.88	25.65	17.87	22.20	18.64	22.14	24.95

8-5 续 2 (continued2)

项 目	Item	海口市 Haikou	三亚市 Sanya	文昌市 Wenchang	东方市 Dongfang	乐东县 Ledong	琼中县 Qiongzhong
家庭总收入(元)	**Total Income of Household**	**11474.82**	**10035.84**	**9012.80**	**8719.50**	**7196.04**	**7940.40**
工薪收入	Wages Income	7870.41	6290.13	5761.89	6483.48	5989.96	6279.20
工资及补贴收入	Wages and Subsidy Income	7437.20	6124.56	5048.87	5744.44	5644.90	6149.18
其他劳动收入	Part-time Income	433.21	165.57	713.02	739.04	345.06	130.02
经营净收入	Net Income of Management	552.41	1544.87	702.19	409.89	339.33	283.18
财产性收入	Property Income	233.48	371.85	231.54	171.77	41.04	62.92
利息收入	Interest Income	29.33	5.04	20.09	12.80	0.00	7.25
股息与红利收入	Dividend and Bonus Income	83.92	0.00	0.87	5.85	23.83	0.00
其他投资收入	Other Inventment Income	45.28	137.97	86.01	72.26	16.39	22.72
出租房屋收入	Income of Houses to Let	59.71	222.72	121.85	74.47	0.00	32.96
其他财产性收入	Others	7.71	6.11	0.00	6.38	0.81	0.00
转移性收入	Transfer Income	2818.51	1828.99	2317.18	1654.36	825.72	1315.10
养老金或离退休金	Old-age Pensions,Pensions for Termination andRetirement Pensions	1952.16	1275.91	1489.60	929.92	375.71	1046.96
社会救济收入	Social Relief Income	4.87	10.43	0.00	22.15	0.00	13.59
保险收入	Insurance Income	0.00	0.00	1.25	0.00	199.51	0.00
赡养收入	Support Income	230.05	135.22	179.16	101.06	61.93	33.84
捐赠收入	Donation Income	324.58	238.52	153.71	338.83	66.18	117.09
亲友搭伙费	Expenses of	110.43	71.50	28.82	31.92	49.78	30.60
提取住房公积金	Accumulation Fund of Housing	33.46	0.00	21.75	0.00	0.00	0.00
记帐补贴	Keep Accounts Subsidy	69.37	66.44	40.78	63.72	70.93	71.21
其他转移性收入	Others	45.46	30.96	87.67	166.76	1.69	1.80
附:人均可支配收入	Appended: Annual Per Capita Disposable Income	10712.23	9416.18	8496.00	8013.02	6672.17	7170.71
收入构成(%)	**Composition of Income**	**100**	**100**	**100**	**100**	**100**	**100**
工薪收入	Wages Income	68.59	62.68	63.93	74.36	83.24	79.08
经营净收入	Net Income of Management	4.81	15.39	7.79	4.70	4.72	3.57
财产性收入	Property Income	2.03	3.71	2.57	1.97	0.57	0.79
转移性收入	Transfer Income	24.56	18.22	25.71	18.97	11.47	16.56

8－6 城镇居民家庭人均年可支配收入和消费性支出
Annual Per Capita Disposable Income and Living Expenditures in Urban Households

单位:元 yuan

项　目	Item	2004	2005	2006	06比05增长(%)
人均可支配收入	**Annual Per Capita Disposable Income**	**7736**	**8124**	**9395**	**11.2**
最低收入户	Lowest Income Households (first decile)	2308	2636	2776	4.3
#困难户	Poor Households (first five percent)	1973	2119	2340	6.7
低收入户	Low Income Households (second decile)	3478	3816	4389	15.0
中等偏下户	Lower Middle Income Households (second quintile)	5299	5355	6065	13.5
中等收入户	Middle Income Households (third quintile)	7774	7875	8655	10.0
中等偏上户	Upper Middle Income Households (fourth quintile)	10396	11012	12172	10.1
高收入户	High Income Households (ninth decile)	14132	15576	16835	8.1
最高收入户	Highest Income Households (tenth decile)	21550	23636	25870	9.7
人均消费性支出	**Total Per Capita Living Expenditures**	**5802**	**5928**	**7128**	**14.5**
最低收入户	Lowest Income Households (first decile)	2446	2397	2414	-1.1
#困难户	Poor Households (first five percent)	2120	2040	2150	1.2
低收入户	Low Income Households (second decile)	3114	3150	3715	12.9
中等偏下户	Lower Middle Income Households (second quintile)	4459	4055	4650	12.6
中等收入户	Middle Income Households (third quintile)	5896	6183	6477	3.2
中等偏上户	Upper Middle Income Households (fourth quintile)	6850	7631	8913	14.6
高收入户	High Income Households (ninth decile)	11703	10606	10799	1.0
最高收入户	Highest Income Households (tenth decile)	13176	15464	21740	39.8

注:(1)城市住户调查从2002年起,国家采用新的指标体系,本表数据用新的指标体系计算得到.
Since 2002,the stat has used a new index system for urban househol survey and the data in this table is calculated from it
(2)此表中的2006年与2005年相比增速按同比口径计算.
The growth speed is calculated at comparable price

8－7 城镇居民家庭人均消费性支出及构成
Per Capita Annual Living Expenditure of Urban Residents and Composition

项　目	Item	2004	2005	2006	06比05增长(%)
消费性支出(元)	**Total Living Expenditures**	**5802.04**	**5927.98**	**7127.61**	**14.5**
食　品	Food	2722.91	2819.64	3098.48	6.6
#粮　食	Grain	199.52	193.87	192.95	0.2
油　脂	Oil and Fats	79.68	88.48	87.74	-0.4
肉禽及其制品	Meat, Poultry and Related Products	769.07	810.02	823.87	1.0
蛋　类	Eggs	27.86	35.10	35.57	-1.6
水产品	Aquatic Products	384.98	398.99	434.20	8.0
菜　类	Vegetables	240.79	268.91	291.55	6.6
烟　草	Tobacco	69.43	93.96	104.33	6.0
酒和饮料	Liquor and Beverages	55.99	61.76	66.18	5.5
干鲜瓜果	Dried and Fresh Melons and Fruits	141.10	145.14	176.07	12.1
奶及奶制品	Milk and Dairy Products	85.01	69.49	83.90	12.3
衣　着	Clothing	300.17	309.47	375.43	15.2
#服　装	Garments	233.19	242.39	288.53	13.7
衣着材料	Clothing Materials	1.55	0.54	0.68	1.5
家庭设备用品及服务	Household Facilities, Articles and Services	302.41	304.06	405.39	25.7
#日用耐用消费品	Durable Consumer Goods	134.21	118.47	168.05	33.1
医疗保健	Medicine and Medical Services	350.17	351.07	369.26	-1.3
交通与通讯	Transport, Post and Communication Services	701.89	728.13	1154.79	49.7
娱乐教育文化服务	Recreation, Education and Cultural Services	686.34	651.81	791.20	12.5
文娱耐用消费品	Durable Consumer Goods for Recreational Use	159.99	162.67	206.56	19.2
文化娱乐	Recreation	153.72	142.20	145.38	-0.8
教　育	Aducation	372.63	346.94	439.26	14.6
居　住	Residence	564.86	585.25	743.95	18.0
杂项商品与服务	Miscellaneous Commodities and Services	173.28	178.54	189.10	-1.3
消费性支出构成(%)	**Composition of Living Expenditures(%)**	100	100	100	---
食　品	Food	46.9	47.6	43.5	---
衣　着	Clothing	5.2	5.2	5.3	---
家庭设备用品及服务	Household Facilities, Articles and Services	5.2	5.1	5.7	---
医疗保健	Medicine and Medical Services	6.0	5.9	5.2	---
交通与通讯	Transport, Post and Communication Services	12.1	12.3	16.2	---
娱乐教育文化服务	Recreation, Education and Cultural Services	11.8	11.0	11.1	---
居　住	Residence	9.7	9.9	10.4	---
杂项商品与服务	Miscellaneous Commodities and Services	3.1	3.0	2.7	---

注: 此表中的2006年与2005年相比增速按同比口径计算
The growth speed is calculated at comparable price

8-7 续 1(continued1)

项　目	Item	最低收入户 Lowest Income Households (first decile)	困难户 Poor Households (first five percent)	低收入户 Low Income Households (second decile)	中等偏下户 Lower Middle Income Households (second quintile)	中等收入户 Middle Income Households (third quintile)	中等偏上户 Upper Middle Income Households (fourth quintile)	高收入户 High Income Households (ninth decile)	最高收入户 Highest Income Households (tenth decile)
消费性支出(元)	Total Living Expenditures	2413.93	2149.50	3715.47	4649.84	6476.98	8913.23	10799.33	21740.29
食　品	Food	1475.46	1352.08	2098.48	2465.68	3133.96	3856.68	4364.18	6003.52
#粮　食	Grain	173.00	174.57	173.79	171.92	193.94	210.80	225.86	237.58
油　脂	Oil and Fats	70.48	66.53	79.67	86.35	82.54	101.64	105.16	92.41
肉禽及其制品	Meat, Poultry and Related Products	464.68	419.35	644.96	758.32	884.77	992.85	990.52	1137.52
蛋　类	Eggs	15.26	12.37	23.27	29.00	38.86	39.22	60.10	64.70
水 产 品	Aquatic Products	207.57	217.68	299.30	366.63	459.71	547.48	584.34	718.58
菜　类	Vegetables	209.11	190.85	255.67	262.20	296.58	328.81	359.10	395.19
烟　草	Tobacco	18.87	17.93	74.18	75.40	116.61	112.40	135.03	304.39
酒和饮料	Liquor and Beverages	9.69	6.55	35.04	42.50	72.69	87.59	109.00	166.40
干鲜瓜果	Dried and Fresh Melons and Fruits	44.30	25.92	82.07	118.61	178.67	257.02	293.62	384.08
奶及奶制品	Milk and Dairy Products	20.76	31.38	27.75	52.41	63.90	144.33	168.63	182.78
衣　着	Clothing	71.26	61.08	140.35	237.70	342.67	527.69	636.93	1117.32
#服　装	Garments	57.30	50.92	108.67	184.05	266.42	390.11	489.20	881.92
衣着材料	Clothing Materials	0.35	0.00	0.00	0.21	0.78	0.63	1.62	2.65
家庭设备用品及服务	Household Facilities, Articles and Services	99.97	126.62	163.32	174.63	294.16	574.43	651.35	1654.17
#日用耐用消费品	Durable Consumer Goods	26.74	45.76	60.31	47.79	97.51	274.53	270.84	772.26
医疗保健	Medicine and Medical Services	86.74	34.71	94.98	201.87	379.56	476.01	706.94	1146.54
交通与通讯	Transport, Post and Communication Services	126.95	104.10	358.22	477.40	749.59	1183.23	1904.12	6650.70
娱乐教育文化服务	Recreation, Education and Cultural Services	213.95	177.54	397.22	473.53	706.57	1009.43	1291.21	2540.95
文娱耐用消费品	Durable Consumer Goods for Recreational Use	38.94	26.92	55.13	90.51	151.16	328.25	335.98	802.09
文化娱乐	Recreation	13.92	8.32	38.64	56.95	126.17	139.00	244.56	793.42
教　育	Aducation	161.09	142.30	303.45	326.06	429.24	542.17	710.67	945.44
居　住	Residence	299.32	262.20	396.30	508.52	714.40	1033.97	936.79	1935.43
杂项商品与服务	Miscellaneous Commodities and Services	40.28	31.18	66.61	110.51	156.07	251.79	307.81	691.66
消费性支出构成(%)	Composition of Living Expenditures(%)	100	100	100	100	100	100	100	100
食　品	Food	61.1	62.9	56.5	53.0	48.4	43.3	40.4	27.6
衣　着	Clothing	2.5	2.8	3.8	5.1	5.3	5.9	5.9	5.1
家庭设备用品及服务	Household Facilities, Articles and Services	4.1	5.9	4.4	3.8	4.5	6.4	6.0	7.6
医疗保健	Medicine and Medical Services	3.6	1.6	2.6	4.3	5.9	5.3	6.5	5.3
交通与通讯	Transport, Post and Communication Services	5.3	4.8	9.6	10.3	11.6	13.3	17.6	30.6
娱乐教育文化服务	Recreation, Education and Cultural Services	8.9	8.3	10.7	10.2	10.9	11.3	12.0	11.7
居　住	Residence	12.4	12.2	10.7	10.9	11.0	11.6	8.7	8.9
杂项商品与服务	Miscellaneous Commodities and Services	1.7	1.5	1.8	2.4	2.4	2.8	2.9	3.2

8-7 续 2(continued 2)

项　目	Item	海口市 Haikou	三亚市 Sanya	文昌市 Wenchang	东方市 Dongfang	乐东县 Ledong	琼中县 Qiongzhong
消费性支出(元)	**Total Living Expenditures**	**8103.39**	**7295.03**	**5900.17**	**6533.44**	**4561.20**	**5107.97**
食　品	Food	3506.42	3093.73	2811.88	2608.41	2391.67	2438.47
#粮　食	Grain	186.11	218.25	202.38	177.17	183.09	196.73
油　脂	Oil and Fats	81.37	97.62	86.88	108.72	53.87	96.88
肉禽及其制品	Meat, Poultry and Related Products	851.00	823.22	745.81	762.23	833.70	881.52
蛋　类	Eggs	37.41	44.92	14.40	31.05	27.58	35.31
水产品	Aquatic Products	437.34	517.34	458.41	402.32	334.51	228.65
菜　类	Vegetables	301.56	310.51	259.46	294.04	224.18	263.92
烟　草	Tobacco	131.83	74.95	113.60	89.33	66.06	79.87
酒和饮料	Liquor and Beverages	70.58	87.97	48.16	38.20	56.57	57.98
干鲜瓜果	Dried and Fresh Melons and Fruits	231.19	158.96	146.39	92.73	111.29	165.93
奶及奶制品	Milk and Dairy Products	101.39	97.88	85.51	38.41	50.78	54.53
衣　着	Clothing	423.13	420.07	357.13	240.35	296.08	320.21
#服　装	Garments	318.67	328.08	267.14	193.34	239.41	244.33
衣着材料	Clothing Materials	1.00	0.88	0.00	0.11	0.00	0.78
家庭设备用品及服务	Household Facilities, Articles and Services	478.22	408.04	300.06	365.66	248.67	240.39
#日用耐用消费品	Durable Consumer Goods	214.21	133.83	111.49	175.52	73.51	106.85
医疗保健	Medicine and Medical Services	458.22	321.16	288.73	265.87	262.94	406.66
交通与通讯	Transport, Post and Communication Services	1223.59	1189.35	774.22	1628.21	470.23	444.52
娱乐教育文化服务	Recreation, Education and Cultural Services	883.44	927.85	586.05	630.03	487.13	633.60
文娱耐用消费品	Durable Consumer Goods for Recreational Use	240.88	162.44	173.16	217.95	133.27	234.68
文化娱乐	Recreation	154.80	178.93	88.84	139.17	64.72	150.15
教　育	Aducation	487.77	586.48	324.05	272.91	289.13	248.77
居　住	Residence	914.86	754.09	533.89	626.72	322.31	482.15
杂项商品与服务	Miscellaneous Commodities and Services	215.51	180.73	248.22	168.19	82.16	141.96
消费性支出构成(%)	**Composition of Living Expenditures(%)**	**100**	**100**	**100**	**100**	**100**	**100**
食　品	Food	43.3	42.4	47.7	39.9	52.4	47.7
衣　着	Clothing	5.2	5.8	6.1	3.7	6.5	6.3
家庭设备用品及服务	Household Facilities, Articles and Services	5.9	5.6	5.1	5.6	5.5	4.7
医疗保健	Medicine and Medical Services	5.7	4.4	4.9	4.1	5.8	8.0
交通与通讯	Transport, Post and Communication Services	15.1	16.3	13.1	24.9	10.3	8.7
娱乐教育文化服务	Recreation, Education and Cultural Services	10.9	12.7	9.9	9.6	10.7	12.4
居　住	Residence	11.3	10.3	9.0	9.6	7.1	9.4
杂项商品与服务	Miscellaneous Commodities and Services	2.7	2.5	4.2	2.6	1.8	2.8

8－8 城镇居民家庭人均年购买主要消费品
Per Capita Annual Purchases of Major Consumer Goods in Urban Households

项 目	Item	2004	2005	2006
粮 食(公斤)	Grain (kg)	64.86	61.97	60.16
食用植物油(公斤)	Edible Vegetable Oil (kg)	7.61	8.13	8.19
鲜 菜(公斤)	Fresh Vegetables (kg)	100.98	100.43	101.68
猪 肉(公斤)	Pork (kg)	24.83	25.92	26.68
牛 羊 肉(公斤)	Beef and Mutton (kg)	2.33	2.87	2.87
家 禽(公斤)	Poultry (kg)	15.08	16.49	16.94
鲜 蛋(公斤)	Fresh Eggs (kg)	2.89	3.89	3.62
鱼(公斤)	Fish (kg)	23.60	26.69	26.12
食 糖(公斤)	Sugar (kg)			
卷 烟(盒)	Cigarettes (pack)			
白 酒(公斤)	Liquor (kg)	1.24	0.78	0.67
啤 酒(公斤)	Beer (kg)	0.67	0.87	0.92
茶 叶(公斤)	Tea(kg)	0.07	0.09	0.10
鲜 瓜(公斤)	Fresh Melons (kg)	5.65	5.45	5.94
鲜 果(公斤)	Fresh Fruits (kg)	30.34	26.92	28.50
干 果(公斤)	Dried Fruits(kg)	0.10	0.14	0.18
糖 果(公斤)	Candy(kg)			
糕 点(公斤)	Cake (kg)	2.88	2.70	2.70
鲜 奶(公斤)	Fresh Milk(kg)	3.19	2.83	3.96
各种服装(件)	Clothing(piece)	6.08	4.83	5.16
各种鞋类(双)	Shoes(pair)	1.84	1.59	1.81
肥 皂(块)	Soap(piece)			
洗 衣 粉(公斤)	Laundry Detergent(kg)			
煤 炭(公斤)	Coal (kg)	12.02	10.32	7.46
液化石油气(公斤)	Liquefied Petroleum Gas(kg)	32.20	28.31	25.70

8-7 续 1(continued1)

项 目	Item	最低收入户 Lowest Income Households (first decile)	困难户 Poor Households (first five percent)	低收入户 Low Income Households (second decile)	中等偏下户 Lower Middle Income Households (second quintile)	中等收入户 Middle Income Households (third quintile)	中等偏上户 Upper Middle Income Households (fourth quintile)	高收入户 High Income Households (ninth decile)	最高收入户 Highest Income Households (tenth decile)
粮 食(公斤)	Grain (kg)	59.96	60.05	57.36	56.16	60.36	62.80	64.25	65.59
食用植物油(公斤)	Edible Vegetable Oil (kg)	6.38	5.69	7.44	8.04	7.74	9.59	9.57	8.94
鲜 菜(公斤)	Fresh Vegetables (kg)	82.12	80.33	95.66	93.99	103.93	113.01	111.30	122.21
猪 肉(公斤)	Pork (kg)	18.97	16.99	21.81	25.54	27.55	30.88	29.79	34.50
牛 羊 肉(公斤)	Beef and Mutton (kg)	1.05	0.84	2.70	2.49	3.43	3.48	3.10	3.97
家 禽(公斤)	Poultry (kg)	10.53	9.83	14.31	16.28	18.48	20.13	17.95	20.57
鲜 蛋(公斤)	Fresh Eggs (kg)	1.60	1.30	2.41	2.77	4.12	4.01	6.00	6.58
鱼(公斤)	Fish (kg)	19.72	22.47	23.18	25.09	28.46	27.92	30.50	28.92
白 酒(公斤)	Liquor (kg)	0.40	0.12	0.84	0.69	0.82	0.64	0.44	0.66
啤 酒(公斤)	Beer (kg)	0.17	0.14	0.67	0.98	1.05	0.89	1.20	1.81
茶 叶(公斤)	Tea(kg)	0.00	0.00	0.09	0.06	0.13	0.13	0.12	0.19
鲜 瓜(公斤)	Fresh Melons (kg)	2.31	1.18	2.79	3.68	6.11	8.58	8.82	13.87
鲜 果(公斤)	Fresh Fruits (kg)	9.33	5.38	14.55	21.23	31.24	39.53	44.09	52.79
干 果(公斤)	Dried Fruits(kg)	0.05	0.01	0.15	0.07	0.15	0.28	0.28	0.52
糕 点(公斤)	Cake (kg)	0.64	0.53	1.70	2.44	2.48	3.84	3.52	5.43
鲜 奶(公斤)	Fresh Milk(kg)	0.12	0.07	1.21	2.14	2.76	6.75	10.60	9.20
男士服装(件)	Men's Clothing (piece)	0.59	0.48	0.98	1.16	1.67	2.48	2.33	3.46
女士服装(件)	Women's Clothing (piece)	0.64	0.50	1.21	1.83	2.30	2.81	3.42	5.71
童 装(件)	Children's Clothing (piece)	0.54	0.46	0.62	1.28	1.43	1.29	1.53	1.80
各种鞋类(双)	Shoes(pair)	0.64	0.48	1.09	1.57	1.92	2.51	2.40	2.93
煤 炭(公斤)	Coal (kg)	24.07	24.54	12.66	5.92	2.75	0.00	14.24	0.00
液化石油气(公斤)	Liquefied Petroleum Gas(kg)	17.23	14.36	21.78	24.54	29.34	30.38	30.39	22.32

8-9 城镇居民家庭每百户主要耐用消费品年购买量和拥有量
Number of Major Durable Consumer Goods Purchases and Owned Per 100 Urban Households

项 目	Item	2004	2005	2006	06比05增长(%)
每百户年购买量	**Number of Purchases Per 100 Households**				
摩托车(辆)	Motorcycle	1.80	1.56	0.84	-36.4
自行车(辆)	Bicycle	7.20	5.28	4.92	-12.8
家用汽车(辆)	Automobile	0.24	0.12	1.44	1100.0
电风扇(台)	Electric Fan	7.80	8.64	10.32	22.9
洗衣机(台)	Washing Machine	3.60	1.80	2.76	43.8
电冰箱(台)	Refrigerator	2.40	2.16	2.40	5.3
彩色电视机(台)	Color Television Set	3.24	4.32	4.32	2.9
影碟机(台)	Video Disc Player	3.36	2.40	3.72	29.9
家用电脑	Computer	5.04	3.00	4.56	35.7
录音机(台)	Tape Recorder	2.28	3.24	1.92	-50.0
微波炉	Oven	2.76	0.84	1.80	85.7
空调器(台)	Air Conditioner	6.24	3.24	3.60	3.4
普通电话	Telephone	4.92	4.56	6.36	32.5
移动电话	Hand Telephone	14.88	15.60	17.16	6.7
每百户年拥有量	**Number of Owned Per 100 Households**				
成套家具(套)	Composite Furniture (set)	18.66	59.11	57.76	6.0
摩托车(辆)	Motorcycle	67.54	55.43	54.11	-0.7
自行车(辆)	Bicycle	111.95	70.09	72.35	1.9
家用汽车(辆)	Automobile	2.25	3.52	5.01	25.3
洗衣机(台)	Washing Machine	80.51	56.33	61.81	4.2
电风扇(台)	Electric Fan	193.05	182.12	190.59	4.2
电冰箱(台)	Refrigerator	71.41	67.00	71.63	2.3
冰柜	Freezer	2.03	4.95	5.30	12.5
彩色电视机(台)	Color Television Set	118.51	118.69	124.22	4.7
影碟机(台)	Video Disc Player	58.68	68.49	69.97	1.3
录音机(台)	Tape Recorder	48.75	27.05	29.67	1.9
录放象机(台)	Video-recorder	11.11	10.48	10.04	-7.8
家用电脑	Computer	18.96	26.21	33.45	15.7
组合音响	Hi-Fi Stereo Component System	25.06	23.89	26.24	7.9
照相机(架)	Camera	21.53	21.93	24.64	3.8
微波炉	Oven	20.63	20.74	24.70	9.8
空调器(台)	Air Conditioner	36.20	45.80	55.54	8.5
电炊具	Electric Cooking Appliances	149.19	127.50	140.44	7.4
淋浴热水器	Shower	79.46	69.48	75.27	5.3
排油烟机	Smoke Absorber	55.85	53.53	56.23	1.1
消毒碗柜	Disinfected Cupboard(unit)	50.99	52.19	53.95	2.1
饮水机	Water Cooler(unit)	19.51	30.46	32.84	11.5
普通电话	Telephone	95.55	97.32	98.28	0.4
移动电话	Hand Telephone	85.40	128.37	141.13	8.2

注:此表中的2006年与2005年相比增速按同比口径计算.
The growth speed is calculated at comparable price

8-10 按收入等级分的城镇居民家庭每百户耐用消费品拥有量

Number of Durable Consumer Goods Owned Per 100 Urban Households at Year-end by Level of Income

项 目	Item	最低收入户 Lowest Income Households (first decile)	困难户 Poor Households (first five percent)	低收入户 Low Income Households (second decile)	中等偏下户 Lower Middle Income Households (second quintile)	中等收入户 Middle Income Households (third quintile)	中等偏上户 Upper Middle Income Households (fourth quintile)	高收入户 High Income Households (ninth decile)	最高收入户 Highest Income Households (tenth decile)
成套家具(套)	Composite Furniture (set)	35.73	43.51	48.40	53.35	51.72	65.95	73.49	78.11
摩 托 车(辆)	Motorcycle	33.60	27.84	47.32	46.90	58.10	70.10	68.02	42.44
自 行 车(辆)	Bicycle	65.04	73.30	77.60	76.89	78.76	79.17	55.36	56.08
家用汽车(辆)	Automobile	0.00	0.00	0.00	5.09	3.82	4.53	4.60	18.75
洗 衣 机(台)	Washing Machine	34.79	26.85	39.77	46.22	65.70	73.49	83.32	89.85
电 风 扇(台)	Electric Fan	137.38	126.62	156.49	184.08	189.81	216.15	211.93	221.46
电 冰 箱(台)	Refrigerator	39.17	30.50	52.06	57.31	78.04	82.33	90.51	99.40
冰柜	Freezer	2.92	0.00	3.73	2.99	8.76	8.26	1.30	5.17
彩色电视机(台)	Color Television Set	94.47	73.25	106.68	120.44	123.28	134.80	140.11	144.31
影 碟 机(台)	Video Disc Player	32.52	26.36	52.32	55.88	76.68	89.70	74.88	96.15
录 音 机(台)	Tape Recorder	14.27	5.61	16.10	24.22	29.74	44.35	26.69	44.01
录放象机(台)	Video-recorder	4.49	0.00	2.73	7.43	14.38	11.57	5.85	20.84
家用电脑	Computer	5.30	4.13	5.15	15.37	27.69	49.95	64.95	74.05
组合音响	Hi-Fi Stereo Component System	12.19	10.23	15.95	11.95	25.38	29.70	46.19	53.90
照 相 机(架)	Camera	0.00	0.00	11.36	8.34	21.40	33.15	45.61	63.67
微波炉	Oven	4.71	0.00	10.69	11.63	18.57	36.00	43.54	56.05
空 调 器(台)	Air Conditioner	16.65	11.28	16.14	24.48	48.99	73.25	89.81	140.34
电炊具	Electric Cooking Appliances	96.68	82.37	119.60	125.02	143.44	164.18	159.71	163.93
淋浴热水器	Shower	33.22	19.28	59.23	58.02	78.87	94.11	99.95	98.47
排油烟机	Smoke Absorber	20.82	16.26	38.39	38.19	60.66	69.56	85.47	80.87
消毒碗柜	Disinfected Cupboard(unit)	26.91	20.76	35.72	39.80	59.15	67.68	73.95	70.14
饮水机	Water Cooler(unit)	9.21	3.02	19.43	28.29	37.09	40.68	36.19	51.80
普通电话	Telephone	73.10	67.22	93.59	97.63	99.87	110.44	101.56	98.87
移动电话	Hand Telephone	48.63	45.16	75.02	128.21	138.57	195.90	184.44	181.14

8－11 农村居民家庭基本情况
Basic Conditions of Rural Households

项 目	Item	2004	2005	2006
调查户数(户)	Number of Households Surveyed(household)	720	720	720
调查户常住人口(人)	Number of Permanent Residents in the Households Surveyed	3776	3641	3626
6岁以下儿童(人)	Children under Six	222	264	240
7—15岁人口(人)	Age 7-15	722	701	622
16—60岁人口(人)	Age 16-60	2575	2449	2524
61岁以上人口(人)	Age 61 and Obove	257	227	240
#在校人口(人)	Population Enrollment	933	940	918
15—17岁人口(人)	Age 15-17	334	288	306
平均每户常住人口(人)	Average Number of Permanent Residents per Household	5.24	5.06	5.04
调查户整半劳动力(人)	Number of Able-bodied and Semi-able-bodied Laborers ofHouseholds Surveyed	2435	2313	2338
文盲、半文盲(人)	Illiteracy and Semiliterate	146	158	169
小学程度(人)	Primary School	538	535	471
初中程度(人)	Junior Secondary School	1317	1187	1272
高中程度(人)	Senior Secondary	360	362	360
中专程度(人)	Secondary Technical	54	53	48
大专程度(人)	Junior College and Above	20	18	18
平均每户整半劳动力(人)	Average Number of Able-bodied and Semi-able- bodied Laborers per Household	3.38	3.21	3.25
平均每个劳动力负担人口(人)	Average Number of Persons Supported by a Laborer	1.55	1.57	1.55

8－12 农村居民家庭人均纯收入
Per Capita Annual Net Income of Rural Households

单位:元 yuan

市 县	City and County	2004	2005	2006
全省人均纯收入	Per Capital Annual Net Income	2818	3004	3256
海口市	HaiKou	3572	3829	4154
三亚市	SanYa	3157	3377	3723
五指山市	WuZhiShan	1982	2071	2220
文昌市	WenChang	3554	3799	4133
琼海市	QiongHai	3287	3205	3490
万宁市	WanNing	3096	3331	3635
定安县	DingAn	2479	2617	2862
屯昌县	TunChang	2470	2639	2865
澄迈县	ChengMai	3177	3368	3678
临高县	LinGao	2768	2823	2950
儋州市	DanZhou	3136	3381	3674
东方市	DongFang	2879	3076	3291
乐东县	LeDong	2442	2590	2813
琼中县	QiongZhong	1775	1739	1871
保亭县	BaoTing	1673	1783	1942
陵水县	LingShui	2123	2291	2498
白沙县	BaiSha	1999	1760	1982
昌江县	ChangJiag	2246	2437	2663

8－13 农村居民家庭人均总收入及构成
Per Capita Total Income and and Composition of Rural Households

项　目	Item	2004	2005	2006
全年人均总收入(元)	**Per Capital Total Income(yuan)**	3708.2	4129.93	4507.13
家庭经营收入	Household Business Income	3119.6	3434.22	3688.14
第一产业收入	Primary Industry Income	2766	3017.34	3234.8
第二产业收入	Secondary Industry Income	77.4	85.26	127.21
第三产业收入	Tertiary Industry Income	276.2	331.62	326.13
务工及工资性收入	Labour servies and Wages Income	403.1	473.06	555.72
转移性收入	Transfer Income	125.0	167.08	213.83
财产性收入	Property Income	60.5	55.58	49.44
全年人均总收入构成(%)	**Composition of Per Capital Total Income(%)**	100	100	100
家庭经营收入	Household Business Income	84.1	83.2	81.8
第一产业收入	Primary Industry Income	74.6	73.1	71.8
第二产业收入	Secondary Industry Income	2.1	2.1	2.8
第三产业收入	Tertiary Industry Income	7.4	8.0	7.2
务工及工资性收入	Labour servies and Wages Income	10.9	11.5	12.3
转移性收入	Transfer Income	3.4	4.0	4.7
财产性收入	Property Income	1.6	1.3	1.1

8－14 农村居民家庭人均总支出及构成
Per Capita Total Expenditure and Composition of Rural Households

项 目	Item	2004	2005	2006
全年人均总支出(元)	**Per Capital Total Expenditure(yuan)**	**2671.2**	**3127.2**	**3495.24**
家庭经营费用	Expenditure for Household Business	789.02	984.9	1100.78
税 金	Expenditure for Tax	8.99	4.61	1.55
生活消费支出	Expenditure for Consumption	1745.92	1969.09	2232.19
食 品	Food	1028.45	1134.75	1191.09
衣 着	Clothing	58.79	66.35	75.15
居 住	Residence	134	146	252.34
医疗保健	Medicines and Medical Services	86.57	93	110.92
家庭设备用品及服务	Household Facilities, Articles and Services	83.16	92.28	87.86
文教娱乐用品及服务	Cultural, Educational and Recreational Articles and Services	164.42	198.7	238.47
交通通信及其它	Transport and Communication Services and Others	133.77	178	205.68
全年人均总支出构成(%)	**Composition of Per Capital Total Expenditure(%)**	**100**	**100**	**100**
家庭经营费用	Expenditure for Household Business	29.54	31.49	31.49
税 金	Expenditure for Tax	0.34	0.15	0.04
生活消费支出	Expenditure for Consumption	65.36	62.97	63.86
食 品	Food	38.50	36.29	34.08
衣 着	Clothing	2.20	2.12	2.15
居 住	Residence	5.02	4.67	7.22
医疗保健	Medicines and Medical Services	3.24	2.97	3.17
家庭设备用品及服务	Household Facilities, Articles and Services	3.11	2.95	2.51
文教娱乐用品及服务	Cultural,Educational and Recreational Articles and Services	6.16	6.35	6.82
交通通信及其它	Transport and Communication Services and Others	5.01	5.69	5.88

8－15 农村居民家庭人均现金收入及构成
Per Capita Cash Income and Composition of Rural Households

项　目	Item	2004	2005	2006
全年人均现金收入(元)	**Per Capital Cash Income(yuan)**	3095.99	3603.35	3912.51
家庭经营收入	Household Business Income	2507.96	2908.37	3095.95
第一产业收入	Primary Industry Income	2154.47	2491.49	2645.48
第二产业收入	Secondary Industry Income	77.37	85.26	127.21
第三产业收入	Tertiary Industry Income	276.12	331.62	323.27
务工及工资性收入	Labour servies and Wages Income	403.06	473.01	555.12
转移性收入	Transfer Income	124.43	166.4	212.01
财产性收入	Property Income	60.54	55.58	49.44
全年人均现金收入构成(%)	**Composition of Per Capital Cash Income(%)**	100	100	100
家庭经营收入	Household Business Income	81.01	80.71	79.13
第一产业收入	Primary Industry Income	69.59	69.14	67.62
第二产业收入	Secondary Industry Income	2.50	2.37	3.25
第三产业收入	Tertiary Industry Income	8.92	9.20	8.26
务工及工资性收入	Labour servies and Wages Income	13.02	13.13	14.19
转移性收入	Transfer Income	4.02	4.62	5.42
财产性收入	Property Income	1.96	1.54	1.26

8－16 农村居民家庭人均现金支出及构成
Per Capita Expenditure in Cash and Composition of Rural Households

项 目	Item	2004	2005	2006
全年人均现金支出(元)	**Per Capital Cash Expenditure(yuan)**	**2143.31**	**2609.9**	**2953.4**
家庭经营费用	Expenditure for Household Business	715.01	913.03	1032.14
税 金	Expenditure for Tax	5.71	4.6	1.55
生活消费支出	Expenditure for Consumption	1295.67	1523.85	1759.26
食 品	Food	614.82	719.64	768.24
衣 着	Clothing	58.96	66.35	75.15
居 住	Residence	97.4	115.88	202.27
医疗保健	Medicines and Medical Services	86.57	93	110.92
家庭设备用品及服务	Household Facilities,Articles and Services	83.16	92.28	87.85
文教娱乐用品及服务	Cultural, Educational and Recreational Articles and Services	164.42	198.7	238.47
交通通信及其它	Transport and Communication Services and Others	133.77	178	205.68
其他借贷性现金支出	Others of Credit Expenditure	346.38	230.48	297.56
全年人均现金支出构成(%)	**Composition of Per Capital Cash Expenditure(%)**	**100**	**100**	**100**
家庭经营费用	Expenditure for Household Business	33.36	34.98	34.95
税 金	Expenditure for Tax	0.27	0.18	0.05
生活消费支出	Expenditure for Consumption	60.45	58.39	59.57
食 品	Food	28.69	27.57	26.01
衣 着	Clothing	2.75	2.54	2.54
居 住	Residence	4.54	4.44	6.85
医疗保健	Medicines and Medical Services	4.04	3.56	3.76
家庭设备用品及服务	Household Facilities,Articles and Services	3.88	3.54	2.97
文教娱乐用品及服务	Cultural, Educational and Recreational Articles and Services	7.67	7.61	8.07
交通通信及其它	Transport and Communication Services and Others	6.24	6.82	6.96
其他借贷性现金支出	Others of Credit Expenditure			

8－17 农村居民家庭人均主要消费品生产、出售和消费量
Per Capita Output ,Sales and Consumption of Major Consumer Goods in Rural Households

项 目	Item	2004	2005	2006
人均生产量	Per Capita OutPut			
粮 食(公斤)	Grain(kg)	392.82	302.54	338.38
油 料(公斤)	Oilseed(kg)	12.57	13.13	15.83
水 果(公斤)	Fruits(kg)	132.15	159.56	187.99
瓜 菜(公斤)	Melon and Vegetables(kg)	287.06	445.18	450.1
猪 肉(公斤)	Pork(kg)	22.79	35.04	33.84
牛 肉(公斤)	Beef(kg)	2.48	2.3	2.54
羊 肉(公斤)	Mutton(kg)	0.49	0.68	1.01
家 禽(公斤)	Poultry(kg)	12.64	9.31	9.37
蛋 类(公斤)	Eggs(kg)	9.4	0.33	0.41
人均出售量	Per Capita Sales			
粮 食(公斤)	Grain(kg)	92.21	60.05	77.94
油 料(公斤)	Oilseed(kg)	8.82	7.61	11.17
水 果(公斤)	Fruits(kg)	113.05	153.23	173.46
瓜 菜(公斤)	Melon and Vegetables(kg)	254.61	405.03	406.75
生 猪(公斤)	Pork(kg)	21.11	33.05	30.37
牛(公斤)	Beef(kg)	2.37	2.26	2.42
羊(公斤)	Mutton(kg)	0.47	0.63	0.81
家 禽(公斤)	Poultry(kg)	4.77	4.47	4.4
蛋 类(公斤)	Eggs(kg)	9.08	0.03	0.04
水产品(公斤)	Aquatic Product(kg)	58.19	72.76	50.89
人均消费量	Per Capita Consumption			
粮 食(公斤)	Grain (kg)	207.78	189.72	209.03
蔬 菜(公斤)	Vegetables (kg)	67.44	71.19	63.68
动物油(公斤)	Animal Oil(kg)	2.67	2.94	2.55
植物油(公斤)	Edible Vegetable Oil (kg)	1.59	1.4	1.45
猪 肉(公斤)	Pork (kg)	12.5	17.84	17.5
牛羊肉(公斤)	Beef and Mutton (kg)	0.76	0.65	1.09
家禽肉(公斤)	Poultry (kg)	9.09	10.02	10.05
蛋 品(公斤)	Eggs and Related Products(kg)	1.28	1.23	1.47
水产品(公斤)	Aquatic Product(kg)	16.16	15.07	15.16
食 糖(公斤)	Sugar(kg)	1.23	1.1	1.07
香 烟(盒)	Cigarettes (packs)	14.3	14.1	14.5
酒 类(公斤)	Liquor(kg)	4.29	4.82	5.01
水 果(公斤)	Fruits(kg)	8.05	6.54	6.75
茶 叶(公斤)	Tea(kg)	0.06	0.11	0.07

8－18 农村居民家庭住房情况
Housing Conditions of Rural Households

项　目	Item	2004	2005	2006
平均每人新建房屋面积(平方米)	Per Capita Floor Space of Newly-Buit Houses (sq.m)	0.45	0.76	0.65
砖木结构面积	Brick and Wood Structure	0.26	0.34	0.31
钢筋结构面积	Reinforced Concrete Structure	0.19	0.42	0.34
平均每人新建房屋价值(元)	Per Capita Value of Newly-Buit Houses (yuan)	144.36	350	260.91
平均每人新建生活用房面积(平方米)	Per Capita Floor Space of Newly-Buit Living Houses (sq.m)	0.45	0.76	0.65
年末人均生活用房面积(平方米)	Per Capita Living Floor Space at the Year-end(sq.m)	19.48	21.82	22.05
砖木结构面积	Brick and Wood Structure	14.49	16.18	16.13
钢筋结构面积	Reinforced Concrete Structure	4.4	5.48	5.85
年末人均使用房屋价值(元)	Per Capita Value of Houses at the Year-end(yuan)	4432.59	5884.19	6149.06

8－19 农村居民家庭每百户耐用消费品、生产性固定资产拥有量
Number of Durable Consumer Goods and Productive Fixed Assets Owned Per 100 Rural Households

项 目	Item	2004	2005	2006
年末耐用品拥有量	Number of Durable Consumer Goods Owned at the Year-end			
大型家具(件)	Large Furniture(unit)	237.92	195.42	189.17
洗衣机(台)	Washing Machine (set)	8.19	3.89	5.83
电风扇(台)	Electric Fan (set)	121.03	125.28	132.36
电冰箱(台)	Refrigerator(set)	10.14	7.36	7.92
空调机(台)	Air Conditioner (unit)	0.69	0.42	0.83
抽油烟机(台)	Exhaust Fan(unit)	0.69	0.97	0.56
吸尘器(台)	Dust Catcher(unit)	0.14	0.14	0.14
微波炉(台)	Oven (unit)	1.11	4.03	7.22
热水器(台)	Shower (unit)	13.33	13.33	14.44
自行车(辆)	Bicycle(unit)	51.53	48.06	43.61
摩托车(辆)	Motorcycle(unit)	76.11	77.22	85.28
汽车(生活用)(辆)	Automobile(unit)	0.69	1.39	0.83
电话机(部)	Telephone Set(set)	36.25	43.75	51.53
移动电话(部)	Hand Telephone(set)	32.78	49.31	58.19
寻呼机(部)	Beef-pager(unit)	7.50	1.94	0.69
彩色电视机(台)	Color Television Set(set)	76.53	77.36	85.14
黑白电视机(台)	Black and White TV Set(set)	8.89	3.47	2.36
录放像机(台)	Videorecorder(set)	7.08	8.06	7.22
摄像机(台)	Pickup Camera(set)	0.97	0.28	0.83
影碟机(台)	Video Disc Player (set)	25.14	28.47	31.67
组合音箱(台)	Hi-Fi Stereo Component System(set)	15.14	16.11	17.64
收音机(台)	Radio(set)	18.61	11.39	8.61
照相机(架)	Camera(set)	1.67	1.53	0.56
家用计算机(台)	Computer(set)	2.92	1.53	1.11
中高档乐器(件)	Medium and High Gade Musical Instrument(unit)	0.14	0.00	0.00
年末生产性固定资产	Productive Fixed Assets at the End of Year			
汽车(部)	Automobile(unit)	0.83	0.49	0.63
小型和手扶拖拉机(部)	Small and Walking Tractor	7.85	9.03	9.31
机动脱粒机(台)	Motordriven Thresher	10.66	13.69	13.61
农用动力机械(台)	Engine Rural	19.65	18.61	18.75
胶轮大车(辆)	Cars with Rubber Tyres	3.61	1.39	1.25
水泵(台)	Pumps	19.39	24.35	22.40
役畜(头)	Draught Animals	74.22	59.15	57.69
产品畜(头)	Commodity Animals	70.42	49.86	50.28
年末生产性固定资产原值(元)	Original Value of Productive Fixed Assets at the End of Year	547183.75	749218.33	746941.46

主要统计指标解释

城镇居民家庭就业人口 指从事社会劳动并取得劳动报酬或经营收入的人口。不论在全民所有制、集体所有制单位工作或从事个体劳动，不论有固定性职业或临时性职业都是就业人口。“就业人口”“包括全民所有制职工”、“集体所有制职工”、“其他所有制职工”、“个体经营者”、“离退休再就业人员”、“其他就业售人员”七项。

城镇居民家庭可支配收入 指被调查的城镇居民家庭在支付个人所得税、记帐补贴、家庭副业生产支出后所余下的实际收入。

城镇居民家庭消费性支出 指被调查的城镇居民家庭用于日常生活的全部支出，包括购买商品支出和文化生活、服务等非商品性支出。不包括罚没、丢失款和缴纳的各种税款(如个人所得税、牌照税、房产税等)，也不包括个体劳动者生产经营过程中发生的各项费用。

农村住户整半劳动力 整劳动力指男子 18--50 周岁，女子 18--45 周岁，半劳动力指男子 16--17 周岁和 51--60 周岁，女子 16--17 周岁和 46--50 周岁的同时具有劳动能力的人，在劳动年龄之内，但丧失劳动能力的人，不算劳动力；在劳动年龄之外，但能经常参加劳动，能顶上一个整或半劳动力的，也算作劳动力。

农村居民家庭纯收入 指农村常住居民家庭总收入中，扣除从事生产和非生产经营费用支出、缴纳税款和上交承包集体任务金额以后剩余的，可直接用于进行生产性、非生产性建设投资、生活消费和积蓄的那一部分收入。农村居民家庭纯收入包括从事生产性和非生产性的经营收入，取自在外人口寄回带回和国家财政救济、各种补贴等非经营性收入；既包括货币收入，又包括自产自用的实物收入。但不包括向银行、信用社和向亲友借款等属于借贷性的收入。

农村居民家庭生活消费支出 指农村常住居民家庭年内用于日常生活的全部开支。它是用来反映和研究农民家庭实际生活消费水平高低的重要指标。农民家庭生活消费支出，包括用于吃、穿、住、烧、用等生活消费品开支和文化、生活服务费用开支两大部分。

恩格尔系数 指食物支出金额在消费性总支出金额中所占的比例。计算公式为：

恩格尔系数 = 食品支出金额 / 消费性总支出金额 *100%

Explanatory Note on Main Statistical Indicators

Employed Population in Urban Households refers to urban residents engaged in certain work and receiving payment for their labor or income from their business operation, including those who work in state-owned or collective units, joint ventures, foreign-owned units and private units with permanent or temporary jobs. The self - employed individuals and reemployed retirees are also basic data for calculating employment rate and dependency ratio.

Disposable Income of Urban Households refers to the actual income of the sample households which can be used for daily expenses, i.e., total income minus personal income tax, sample household subsidy and expenditure on household sideline production.

Expenditure for Consumption of Urban Households refers to total expenditure of the sample households for consumption in daily life, including expenditure for various commodities and expenses for non-commodity items such as culture and service, etc. ,but excluding fines and confiscation, loss, tax payments (such as income tax, license tax, real estates tax, etc.) and various expenses by individual laborers for business purposes.

Able - bodied and Semi - able-bodied Laborers of Rural Households refer to permanent residents of rural households who are able to work and actually engaged in social labor, which are one factor of production and sources of rural household income. According to the relevant regulations, male aged 18-50, female aged 18-45 is considered as able-bodied laborers; male aged 16-17 and 51-60, female aged 16-17 and 46-55 are considered as semi - able-bodied laborers. Those who are nor in the above age range but able to work and actually engaged in social labor are also considered as able - bodied or semi - able-bodied laborers, while those who are within the above age range but unable to work are not counted as able - bodied or semi - able-bodied laborers.

Net Income of Rural Households refers to the total income of the permanent residents of the rural households during a year after the deduction of the expenses for productive and non-productive business operation, the payment for taxes and the payment for collective units for their contracted tasks, which can then be spent for investments in productive and non-productive construction, for consumption in daily life and for savings deposit. It is a comprehensive indicator to show the actual level of the income of the peasants household. The net income of the rural households includes not only the income from the productive and non-productive business operation, but also the income from the non-business operation, such as the money remitted or brought back by the members of the household who are in other places, the government relief payment and various subsidies. It includes not only the money income, but also the income in kind. But the income from borrowing from banks, friends and relatives is excluded.

Expenditure of Rural Households for Consumption refers to total expenses of rural households on daily life, including expenses on food, clothing, housing, fuel, articles for daily use, and expenses on cultural life and services. This indicator is used to show the actual consumption level of peasants.

Engel Coefficient refers to the percentage of expenditure on food in the total consunmption expenditure, using the follow-ing formula:

Engel Coefficient=(expenditure on food/ total consunmption expenditure)*100%

资料整理：蔡展能　李少云　朱　珊　周文喜　陈文科
Arranged by Caizhanneng Lishaoyun Zhushan Zhouwenxi Chenwenke

9. 农业和农村经济
AGRLCULTURE AND RURAL ECONOMY

农业总产值（亿元）
（当年价）

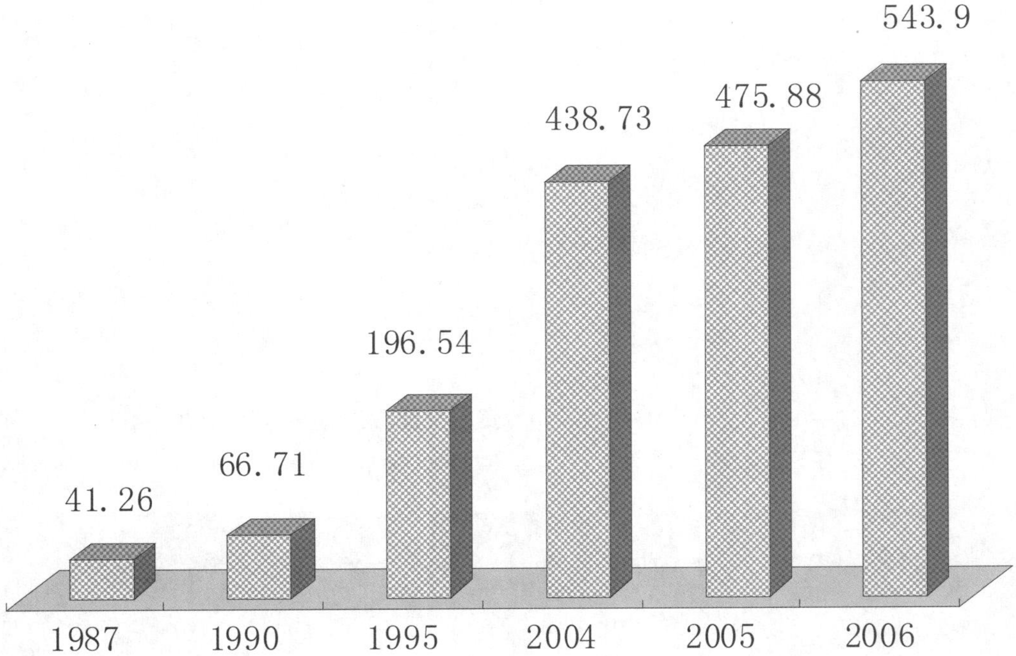

农业总产值构成（%）

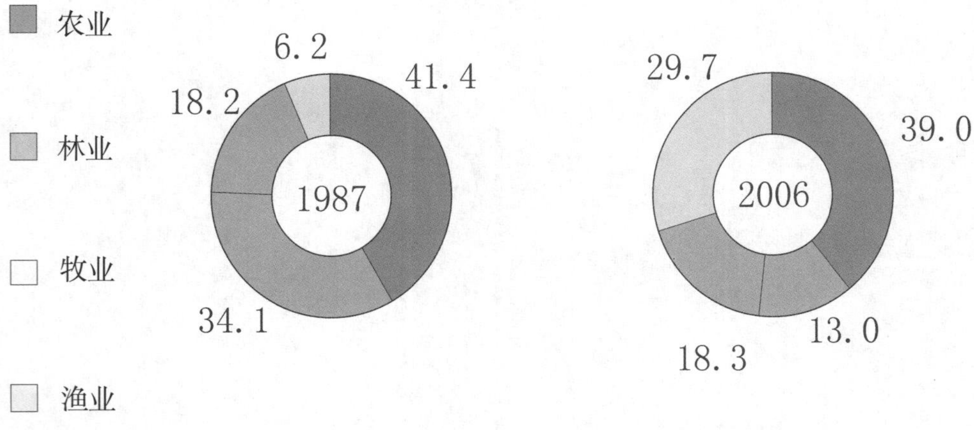

9－1 农村基层组织情况
Conditions of Rural Grassroots Unit

项　目	Item	2003	2004	2005	2006
农村基层组织情况	**Conditions of Rural Grassroots Units**				
乡镇政府个数(个)	Number of Township and Town Govvernments(unit)	200	200	200	
乡政府	Number of Township	20	20	20	
民族乡	Number of Minority Nationalities Township	20	20	20	
镇政府	Number of Town Govvernments	180	180	180	
民族镇	Number of Minority Nationalities Town Govvernments	43	48	49	
黎族镇	Town Govvernments of Li Nationality				
村民委员会(个)	Number of Villagers' Committees(unit)	2633	2624	2615	
民族村委会	Number of Minority Nationalities Villagers Committees	706	701	705	
村民小组(个)	Number of Villagers Groups(unit)	25761	25892	25907	
自然村(个)	Villages(unit)	18693	18645	18605	
民族自然村	Minority Nationalities Villages	3609	3601	3621	
乡镇户数(万户)	**Number of Rural Households (10,000 Households)**	**108.73**	**110.88**	**112.58**	
农业户	Agricultural Households	98.48	100.89		
民族户	Minority Nationalities Households	19.99	20.71	21.09	
黎族户	Households of Li Nationality	19.04	19.40	19.77	
苗族户	Households of Miao Nationality	0.84	0.85	0.89	
乡镇人口(万人)	**Rural Population(10,000 persons)**	**511.44**	**519.61**	**525.6**	
农业人口	Agricultural Population	472.69	478.17	484.19	
民族人口	Minority Nationalities Population	104.25	106.29	107.8	
黎族人口	Population of Li Nationality	99.11	100.86	102.09	
苗族人口	Population of Miao Nationality	4.61	4.73	4.89	

9－2 各市县农村基层组织情况
Grassroots Unit of Rural Areas by City and County

(2005)

市 县	Cities and Counties	乡镇政府(个) Number of Township and Town Govvernments (unit)	镇政府 Town Govvernments	村民委员会(个) Villagers' Committees (unit)	村民小组(个) Villagers' Groups (unit)	乡(镇)总户数(户) Number of Rural Households (Household)	农业户 Agricultural Households	乡(镇)总人口(人) Total Population of Rural	农业人口 Agricultural Population	农村家庭从业人员(人) Numers of Rural Laborers	#女 Female
全省总计	**Total**	**200**	**180**	**2615**	**25907**	**1125811**	**1020108**	**5256031**	**4841944**	**2560114**	**1234474**
海口市	Haikou	23	23	250	2747	153092	129546	646648	575025	312397	156771
三亚市	Sanya	5	5	108	948	54890	49461	284459	258401	152262	73747
五指山市	Wuzhishan	7	4	59	329	12114	12070	55341	54883	28829	14119
文昌市	Wenchang	16	16	255	3985	104966	100078	445276	424441	196744	98353
琼海市	Qionghai	12	12	190	2690	85228	79524	337739	319330	168661	84939
万宁市	Wanning	12	12	207	2121	81026	75937	396402	388474	158587	82099
定安县	Dingan	10	10	109	1668	57088	50739	246569	222865	112712	56765
屯昌县	Tunchang	8	8	119	1172	44217	36474	194794	147606	75826	37378
澄迈县	Chengmai	10	10	165	1002	75726	62374	340875	300167	167115	75608
临高县	Lingao	11	11	153	901	68741	65511	326166	307587	169377	74759
儋州市	Danzhou	17	17	218	1972	102766	89630	561708	488050	281977	131098
东方市	Dongfang	10	8	185	1579	62085	59985	312811	302585	167640	82143
乐东县	Ledong	11	11	172	1518	82576	73425	402782	364571	207063	96557
琼中县	Qiongzhong	10	7	99	623	19536	19485	95652	95467	48356	25052
保亭县	Baoting	9	6	61	467	16088	15684	83729	82569	46696	21468
陵水县	Linshui	11	9	114	1104	54972	50875	268601	249948	130586	62191
白沙县	Baisha	11	4	74	439	19567	19363	97914	96895	56986	25677
昌江县	Changjiang	7	7	77	580	31133	29947	158565	153080	78300	35750

9–2 续(continued)

市 县	Cities and Counties	民族乡镇(个) Number of Minority Nationality Township and Town Govvernments (unit)	民族村委会(个) Number of Minority Nationality Villagers Committees (unit)	民族自然村(个) Number of Minority Nationality Villages (unit)	乡镇民族户数(户) Number of Minority Nationality Households (Household)	黎族 Li	苗黎 Miao	乡镇民族人口(人) Minority Nationality Population (person)	黎族 Li	苗黎 Miao
全省总计	**Total**	**69**	**705**	**3621**	**210877**	**197720**	**8876**	**1077970**	**1020865**	**48937**
海口市	Haikou									
三亚市	Sanya	3	63	445	30376	28412	637	167156	155652	3221
五指山市	Wuzhishan	7	59	299	11818	10972	831	53795	49419	4376
文昌市	Wenchang									
琼海市	Qionghai	1	6	27	1306	67	1239	9750	2705	7029
万宁市	Wanning	3	39	264	9421	8240	1142	51754	45188	6532
定安县	Dingan									
屯昌县	Tunchang	1	4	20	1442	983	439	9642	6998	2642
澄迈县	Chengmai		1	1	39		39	279		279
临高县	Lingao									
儋州市	Danzhou	3	18	79	9089	8662	391	44546	42325	2123
东方市	Dongfang	5	77	122	16284	16112	172	78112	76738	917
乐东县	Ledong	6	102	463	33140	32689	421	172489	170436	2701
琼中县	Qiongzhong	10	99	512	17679	15567	2112	90616	79685	10931
保亭县	Baoting	9	61	641	15079	13983	1048	79439	73452	5933
陵水县	Linshui	6	628	470	31755	28652	99	150376	149793	583
白沙县	Baisha	11	74	378	17711	17711	252	89055	87744	1390
昌江县	Changjiang	4	40	108	15723	15656	53	80886	80660	275

9－3 各市县乡镇劳动力
Rural Labor Force by City and County

单位：人 (2005) (person)

市 县	Cities and Counties	乡镇劳动力总数 Total Number of Villages and Town Labor Force	劳动年龄内的人口数 Population in the Age of Labor Force	劳动年龄内上学的学生数 Students in School in the Age of Labor Force	不足劳动年龄而参加劳动的人口数 Pupulation of Taking Part in Working but Lacking of the Age of Working	超过劳动年龄而参加劳动的人口数 Pupulation of Taking Part in Working but Surpassing of the Age of Working	劳动年龄内丧失劳动能力的人口数 Population in the Age of Labor Force but Losing Working Ability
全省总计	Total	2737274	2504542	120701	102318	178081	47667
海口市	Haikou	334671	304175	17820	11548	25147	6199
三亚市	Sanya	154165	150207	1670	2715	1582	339
五指山市	Wuzhishan	30692	28178	1863	1757	1505	748
文昌市	Wenchang	210376	189109	6000	5184	19772	3689
琼海市	Qionghai	176067	158257	5017	5964	15388	3542
万宁市	Wanning	183804	173050	8258	5953	9081	4280
定安县	Dingan	116940	105189	4228	4761	9574	2584
屯昌县	Tunchang	82006	74525	2514	2858	6183	1560
澄迈县	Chengmai	180786	163209	8542	6677	14808	3708
临高县	Lingao	186445	167090	11314	9469	14678	4792
儋州市	Danzhou	298726	279038	12199	9034	14434	3780
东方市	Dongfang	178888	161686	10685	9443	11446	3687
乐东县	Ledong	225718	206000	13496	9870	12578	2730
琼中县	Qiongzhong	50441	44632	1564	2649	4241	1081
保亭县	Baoting	48857	46214	2161	1814	1256	427
陵水县	Linshui	136966	124833	5777	5466	8866	2199
白沙县	Baisha	61242	53789	4256	4406	4197	1150
昌江县	Changjiang	80484	75361	3337	2750	3545	1172
洋浦	Yangpu						

9－4　农村家庭从业人员
Number of Rural Laborers

单位:万人　　(10 000 persons)

指　标	Item	2003	2004	2005	2006
农村家庭从业人员	Number of Rural Laborers	240.27	250.05	256.01	
按性别分	By sex				
男	Male	124.25	128.99	132.56	
女	Female	116.02	121.05	123.45	
按产业分	By Industry				
第一产业	The first industry	187.25	190.76	193.39	
第二产业	The second industry	16.33	16.71	17.89	
第三产业	The third industry	36.69	42.58	44.73	
按行业分	By Profession				
农　业	Farming	187.25	190.76	193.39	
工　业	Industry	8.28	8.59	9.24	
建筑业	Construction	8.05	8.12	8.65	
交通运输业和邮电业	Transportation,Post	6.3	6.36	6.75	
商业、饮食、物资供销仓储业	Wholesale, Retail, Storage and Catering Trades	11.05	17.22	18.58	
其它	Others	19.34	18.99	19.4	

9－5 各市县农村家庭从业人员
Number of Rural Laborers by City and County

单位:人 (2005) (person)

市县	Cities and Counties	农村家庭从业人员 Numers of Rural Laborers	农业 Farming	工业 Industry	建筑业 Construction	交通运输邮电业 Transportation, Post Transportation, Post	商业、饮食、物资供销仓储业 Wholesale, Retail,Storage and Catering Trades	其他 Others
全省总计	**Total**	**2560114**	**1933906**	**92399**	**86521**	**67536**	**185768**	**193984**
海口市	Haikou	575025	206444	21455	16989	8993	26218	294926
三亚市	Sanya	152262	118239	3326	1739	4218	14580	10160
五指山市	Wuzhishan	288299	24111	191	222	184	391	3730
文昌市	Wenchang	196744	136289	7427	11059	5637	11815	24517
琼海市	Qionghai	168661	122048	6099	8321	4783	13576	13834
万宁市	Wanning	158587	111681	7518	6657	4253	11653	16825
定安县	Dingan	112712	87523	2860	5046	2261	7124	7898
屯昌县	Tunchang	75826	61102	1655	1872	1521	3389	6287
澄迈县	Chengmai	167115	114457	8859	5541	7365	12908	17985
临高县	Lingao	169377	137851	4936	4760	4518	23039	–5727
儋州市	Danzhou	281977	224369	10864	9274	7794	14037	15639
东方市	Dongfang	167640	139625	4808	3790	3767	7948	7702
乐东县	Ledong	207063	146411	7785	5924	7842	21950	17151
琼中县	Qiongzhong	48356	42354	518	84	65	1361	3974
保亭县	Baoting	46696	37458	715	725	235	1250	6313
陵水县	Linshui	130586	103695	1672	3043	2546	10748	8882
白沙县	Baisha	56986	54579	768	424	69	882	264
昌江县	Changjiang	78300	65670	943	1051	1485	2899	6252
洋浦	Yangpu							

9－6 历年年末耕地面积
Cultivated Area at the Year-end

年 份 Year	耕地总面积（公顷）Cultivated Area (hectares)	水旱田 Paddy Fields and Dry land			旱 地 Dry Fields	人均占有耕地面积（公顷/人）Per Capita Cultivated Area (hectare/person)	#农业人口人均耕地（公顷/人）Per Capita Cultivated Area (by Agriculture Population) (hectare/person)
			水 田 Paddy Fields	旱 田 Dry land			
1952	344 714	266 447	108 473	157 974	78 267	0.1 327	0.1440
1957	396 960	283 760	134 440	149 320	113 200	0.1 367	0.1560
1962	399 466	255 773	129 933	125 840	143 693	0.1 167	0.1387
1965	393 767	254 400	140 840	113 560	139 367	0.1 073	0.1253
1970	393 687	257 447	165 594	91 853	136 240	0.0 920	0.1053
1971	407 720	264 720	177 200	87 520	143 000	0.0 900	0.1033
1972	417 967	269 493	185 413	84 080	148 474	0.0 893	0.1040
1973	425 214	271 447	191 680	79 767	153 767	0.0 887	0.1027
1974	434 974	274 334	199 867	74 467	160 640	0.0 893	0.1033
1975	435 827	274 740	204 707	70 033	161 087	0.0 893	0.1033
1976	447 667	275 013	207 873	67 140	172 667	0.0 887	0.1020
1977	450 550	273 967	207 567	66 400	176 253	0.0 873	0.1020
1978	453 260	275 073	208 947	66 126	178 187	0.0 860	0.1007
1979	448 467	273 647	208 000	65 647	174 820	0.0 833	0.0973
1980	446 020	271 613	205 347	66 266	174 407	0.3 807	0.0953
1981	439 133	267 033	199 873	67 160	172 100	0.0 780	0.0933
1982	440 393	265 440	200 093	65 347	174 953	0.0 773	0.0920
1983	441 353	264 220	199 107	65 133	177 133	0.0 760	0.0913
1984	438 793	262 446	197 093	65 353	176 347	0.0 747	0.0907
1985	436 033	259 520	194 327	65 193	176 513	0.0 727	0.0900
1986	433 947	258 500	194 680	63 820	175 447	0.0 713	0.0887
1987	431 701	256 174	192 187	63 987	175 527	0.0 700	0.0873
1988	431 587	255 907	191 040	64 867	175 680	0.0 687	0.0860
1989	433 560	256 353	191 200	65 153	177 207	0.0 680	0.0853
1990	435 067	255 327	191 847	63 480	179 740	0.0 667	0.0847
1991	437 286	255 093	191 100	63 993	182 193	0.0 660	0.1013
1992	435 660	254 493	190 380	64 133	181 167	0.0 647	0.1000
1993	431 427	250 707	188 253	62 453	180 720	0.0 633	0.0813
1994	428 690	248 331	187 113	61 213	180 359	0.0 620	0.0807
1995	429 185	248 215	186 341	61 874	180 970	0.0 612	0.0798
1996	429 327	246 793	183 969	62 824	182 534	0.0 600	0.0795
1997	426 796	243 420	184 122	59 298	183 376	0.0 588	0.0736
1998	427 852	242 568	183 615	58 922	185 284	0.0 583	0.0782
1999	429 599	241 939	183 359	58 580	187 660	0.0 578	0.0775
2000	433 181	240 653	182 541	58 112	192 528	0.0 569	0.0764
2001	425888	234455	177429	57026	191433	0.0 553	0.0 751
2002	423336	234329	177737	56592	189007	0.0 544	0.0 742
2003	418185	218948	166393	52555	199237	0.0529	0.0727
2004	417765	219616	166339	53277	198149	0.05184	0.08727
2005	416178	221556	166725	54830	194623	0.0792	0.0860
2006							

9－10 农业现代化情况
Agricultural Modernization

指 标	Item	2003	2004	2005	2006
农村电气化	Electric Situation of Rural Areas				
乡村办水电站(个)	Number of Hydropower Station in Rural Areas(unit)	57	40	38	
发电能力(千瓦)	Generating Capacity (kw)	83532	87353	83993	
农村用电量(万千瓦时)	Electricity Consumed in Rural Areas (10,000 kwh)	29850	33111	38452.25	
化肥施用量(实物量)(万吨)	Consumption of Chemical Fertillzer (10 000tons)	86.08	126	93.6	
氮 肥	Nitrogenous Fertilizer	25.93	27.54	20.35	
磷 肥	Phosphate Fertilizer	20.6	53.97	10.18	
钾 肥	Potash Fertilizer	8.19	9.55	35.19	
复 合 肥	Compound Fertilizer	31.36	35.2	0.96	
化学农药使用量(万吨)	Consumption of Pesticide(10 000tons)	1.34	1.56	1.81	
农田水利有效灌溉面积(公顷)	Effective Irrigated Area (hectares)	177274	169822	168266	
旱涝保收面积(公顷)	Area With Stable Yieds Despite Drought or waterlogging (hectares)	104359	92312.8	92271	

9－11 各市县农业机械总动力

Total Power of Agriculture Machinery by City and County

单位：千瓦 (2005) (kw)

市 县	Cities and Counties	农业机械总动力 Total Power of Agricultural Machinery	柴油发动机动力	汽油发动机动力	电动机动力	其他机械动力
全省总计	Total	2682069	2204830.8	236276.1	143970	96992.5
海口市	Haikou	232482	187442	22834	12691	9515
三亚市	Sanya	160756	112213	8329	960	39254
五指山市	Wuzhishan	43127	13103	2202	1267	26555
文昌市	Wenchang	212291	198096	11024	3171	
琼海市	Qionghai	193721	178940.1	6852.4	4524	3404.5
万宁市	Wanning	87328	81249	3933	1316	830
定安县	Dingan	45608	41354	2532	1722	
屯昌县	Tunchang	34226	27575.4	5593.6	1057	
澄迈县	Chengmai	162483.4	126673.3	24519.1	4047	7244
临高县	Lingao	360269	285650	8457	66058	104
儋州市	Danzhou	312625	288161	17917	6547	
东方市	Dongfang	137952	122708	10409	2067	2768
乐东县	Ledong	208536	168610	34400	3903	1623
琼中县	Qiongzhong	41975	34911		7064	
保亭县	Baoting	16447	16259		188	
陵水县	Linshui	66467	59293	5042	2132	
白沙县	Baisha	18986	16422		2564	
昌江县	Changjiang	85291	79359	3259	1399	1274
农垦系统	Nongken	261499	166812	68973	21293	4421
洋浦	Yangpu					

9－12 各市县农业机械拥有量
Possession of Agriculture Machinery by City and County

(2005)

市县	Cities and Counties	耕作机械 Machinery for Plough		排灌机械 Machinery for Agricultural Drainage and Irrigation			收获机械 Machinery for Harvesters	
		大中型拖拉机(台) Large and Medium Agricultural Tractors(unit)	手扶拖拉机(台) Walking Tractors (unit)	柴油机(台) Diesel Engines (unit)	电动机(台) Electric Motors (unit)	农用水泵(台) Pumps (unit)	机动收割机(台) Machinery for Combine Harvesters (unit)	机动脱粒机(台) Motorized Threshing Harvesters (unit)
全省总计	**Total**	**3931**		**93649**	**4472**	**62661**	**66**	**38543**
海口市	Haikou	199		6082	1184	5956	7	2843
三亚市	Sanya	178		8282	113	8908		364
五指山市	Wuzhishan	68		303	33	341		
文昌市	Wenchang	589		5838	465	5594	16	1423
琼海市	Qionghai	249		5078	406	6242	1	14189
万宁市	Wanning	166		3258	427	2322		
定安县	Dingan	52		2786	254	1905	2	5873
屯昌县	Tunchang	56		623	18	263	6	376
澄迈县	Chengmai	236		8798	190	4323	5	3611
临高县	Lingao	225			457			6732
儋州市	Danzhou	556		2623	81	2608		624
东方市	Dongfang	74		13609	107	9694	2	233
乐东县	Ledong	208		24582	113	8417		354
琼中县	Qiongzhong	298		466	18	102		
保亭县	Baoting	13		832	94	304		438
陵水县	Linshui	49		1832	3	1514	2	280
白沙县	Baisha	5		366	396			572
昌江县	Changjiang	137		5130	61	3772	4	388
农垦系统	System of farm	573		3161	448		21	243
洋浦	Yangpu							

9－12 续(continued)

市县	Cities and Counties	畜牧机械 Machinery for Animal Husbandry	植保机械 Machinery for Plant Protection	渔用机动船 Machinery for Fishery		运输机械 Machinery for Transport		其它农业机械 Other Machinery for Agriculture Use
		粉碎机(台) Fodder Grinders (unit)	机动喷雾(粉)机(台) Motorized Sprayers(unit)	艘 unit	吨 ton	农用载重汽车(辆) Trucks for Agricultural Use(unit)	农用运输车(辆) Transport Trucks for agriculture Use(unit)	推土机(台) Bulldozers (unit)
全省总计	**Total**			**19935**			**25581**	
海口市	Haikou			1470			5077	
三亚市	Sanya			2258			2441	
五指山市	Wuzhishan						409	
文昌市	Wenchang			2346			1603	
琼海市	Qionghai			738			2149	
万宁市	Wanning			1290			1019	
定安县	Dingan			2			1657	
屯昌县	Tunchang						996	
澄迈县	Chengmai			1033			1605	
临高县	Lingao			3073			1542	
儋州市	Danzhou			3339			1294	
东方市	Dongfang			509			1412	
乐东县	Ledong			883			1754	
琼中县	Qiongzhong						404	
保亭县	Baoting						302	
陵水县	Linshui			2324			1150	
白沙县	Baisha			5			328	
昌江县	Changjiang			494			439	
农垦系统	System of farm			171				
洋浦	Yangpu							

9－13 各市县农业现代化情况

Situation of Agriculture Modernization by City and County

(2005)

市县	Cities and Counties	化肥施用实物量(吨) Consumption of Chemical Fertillzer(tons) 合计 Total	氮肥 Nitrogenous Fertilizer	磷肥 Phosphate Fertilizer	钾肥 Potash Fertilizer	复合肥 Compound Fertilizer
全省总计	**Total**	**936043.72**	**278809.87**	**203530.83**	**101837.64**	**351865.38**
海口市	Haikou	73335	22442	22002	10500	18391
三亚市	Sanya	32992	11152	6761	4728	10351
五指山市	Wuzhishan	2456	1161	586	79	630
文昌市	Wenchang	71336	21061	15234	9945	25096
琼海市	Qionghai	100304.7	25001.2	30540.8	13354.8	31407.9
万宁市	Wanning	40389.1	12366.5	9572	6678.6	11772
定安县	Dingan	37114	10093	11572	4970	10479
屯昌县	Tunchang	20171	7084	7095	1750	4242
澄迈县	Chengmai	52742.2	16651.8	14097.2	8351.7	13641.5
临高县	Lingao	52883	18017	15415	8302	11149
儋州市	Danzhou	49103	18173	16472	4419	10039
东方市	Dongfang	22264	7391	4077	2809	7987
乐东县	Ledong	71608	31353	12336	9211	18708
琼中县	Qiongzhong	6906.52	2522.37	2489.13	345.64	1549.38
保亭县	Baoting	7202.2	2476	1979.7	747.9	1998.6
陵水县	Linshui	25541	7480	6432	4444	7185
白沙县	Baisha	11766	5187	3003	669	2907
昌江县	Changjiang	34769	18349	4854	862	10704
农垦系统	Nongken	223161	40849	19013	9671	153628
洋浦	Yangpu					

9-13 续(continued)

市县	Cities and Counties	农药使用量(吨) Consumption of Pesticide (10 000tons)	农田有效灌溉面积(公顷) Effective Irrigated Area (hectares)	机电灌溉面积 Mechanical and Electrical Irrigation	旱涝保收面积(公顷) Area With Stable Yieds Despite Drought or waterlogging (hectares)	农村用电量(万千瓦时) Electricity Consumed in Rural Area (10 000 kwh)
全省总计	**Total**	**18100.58**	**168266.10**	**23498.88**	**92271.00**	**38452**
海口市	Haikou	498	15893.50	4440.47	6493.40	6567
三亚市	Sanya	520	6954.33	375.27	5238.40	1462
五指山市	Wuzhishan	85	1881.60	199.67	541.80	126
文昌市	Wenchang	2254.5	11369.00	2098.93	5994.27	15369
琼海市	Qionghai	946	12031.05	1989.12	8648.13	2800
万宁市	Wanning	1534.5	9454.53	1026.60	5944.73	1790
定安县	Dingan	208.3	7491.67	726.40	5199.13	1204
屯昌县	Tunchang	163	3581.00	87.87	2199.47	415
澄迈县	Chengmai	526.3	11348.54	1818.09	3588.13	995
临高县	Lingao	461	9014.87	328.00	7030.33	1226
儋州市	Danzhou	249	13450.53	2057.27	8180.00	1641
东方市	Dongfang	325	10597.60	2341.53	8187.40	627
乐东县	Ledong	985	13700.13	201.00	9309.93	1613
琼中县	Qiongzhong	213.59	358.73	4.67	2608.67	406
保亭县	Baoting	155.09	3593.93	32.27	2305.80	210
陵水县	Linshui	335	8478.87	391.07	520.13	960
白沙县	Baisha	249	3064.53	24.33	1575.00	203
昌江县	Changjiang	147.3	6702.80	916.33	4918.73	838
农垦系统	Nongken	8245	16105.47	4440.00	3787.53	10
洋浦	Yangpu					

9－14 农村外出从业人员
Number of Rural Outgo Laborers

单位：人　　(persons)

指　标	Item	2004	2005	2006
期内外出从业的劳动力人数	I. Number of Outgoing Labor during the Term	259609	302478	
其中：男性劳动力	of which: Male Labor	134153	148085	
受过专业劳动技能培训	Labor who Received Professional Labor Skill Training	40749	41419	
当年外出劳动力	Outgoing Labor in Current Year	82863	86884	
外出劳动力的文化程度	II. Education Level of Outgoing Labor	259609	302478	
不识字或识字很少	Illiteracy or Know few Words	6218	7459	
小学程度	Primary School	37953	41515	
初中程度	Junior Middle School	142098	169099	
高中程度	Senior Middle School	50864	56229	
中专	Technical Secondary School	14488	19314	
大专及以上	Junior College or above	7988	8862	
外出劳动力的年龄结构	III. Age Structure of Outing Labors	259609	302478	
16-22 岁	16- 22 Years Old	66057	82279	
23-25 岁	23-25 Years Old	85521	97587	
26-30 岁	26-30 Years Old	56833	63868	
31-40 岁	31-40 Years Old	30220	35884	
41-50 岁	41-50 Years Old	13178	16363	
50 岁以上	Older than 50 Years Old	5189	5303	
劳动力外出方式	IV. Mode of Labor Outgoing	259609	302478	
政府或单位组织	Organized by Government or Agencies	15524	27458	
亲戚朋友介绍	Introduced by Relatives and Friends	104236	121738	
自发	Self Arranged	102104	13259	
其他	Others	37745	40023	
外出劳动力就业的产业分布	V. Industry Profile of Outgoing Labor Employment	259609	302478	
第一产业	First Industry	26794	30542	
第二产业	Secondary Industry	78358	92156	
#工业从业	# Industry	48547	56497	
建筑业从业	Construction	29811	35659	
第三产业	Tertiary Industry	154457	179780	
#批发与零售业	# Wholesale and Retail	44622	54491	
住宿和餐饮业从业	Accommodation and Catering	77146	105284	
外出从业地区	VI. Region Profile of Outgoing Labors	259609	302478	
县内乡外	Outside Village and Inside County	93142	109852	
省内县外	Outside County and Inside Province	109627	118456	
国内省外	Outside Province and Inside China	55047	72464	
国外	Outside China	1793	1706	
补充资料：	Supplementary Data:			
本乡内劳动力转移人数	Number of Labor Transfer in the Village	58790	58423	
#第一产业转第二产业	# From the First Industry to Secondary Industry	23434	22754	
第一产业转第三产业	From the First Industry to Tertiary Industry	36807	35053	

9－15 历年农业总产值
Gross Output Value of Farming

单位：万元 (10,000 yuan)

年 份 Year	总 计 Total	农 业 Farming	林 业 Forestry	牧 业 Animal Husbandry	渔 业 Fishery
（按 1970 年不变价格计算） By the 1970's constant price					
1952	25724	19287	1589	3652	1196
1957	36381	25651	4218	3877	2635
1962	39960	22086	9550	6637	1687
1965	50630	33116	11439	3800	2275
1970	60792	35644	18110	5065	1973
1971	79614	39129	33514	4855	2116
1972	80856	43759	29312	5323	2462
1973	80014	41706	29600	6248	2460
1974	86605	48651	28134	7034	2786
1975	94570	49915	33094	7893	3668
1976	101736	50952	38735	8318	3731
1977	103915	49604	42856	7731	3724
1978	95612	39152	46023	8462	1975
1979	100329	42214	48622	7700	1793
1980	102432	40236	52208	8429	1559
1981	122056	48893	57655	11823	3685
（按 1980 年不变价格计算） By the 1980's constant price					
1981	136392	54635	64427	13212	4118
1982	175421	73840	77734	19409	4438
1983	178641	76277	84799	21693	4872
1984	218458	91129	96837	24136	6356
1985	222225	88022	98811	28748	6644
1986	245783	97676	108437	31558	8112
1987	263766	100208	122918	31090	9550
1988	266851	100767	121979	33492	10613
1989	273408	110232	115467	35221	12488
1990	299427	119867	124013	39658	15889
（按 1990 年不变价格计算） By the 1990's constant price					
1990	603140	277635	176470	79553	69482
1991	670114	293374	205759	87362	83619
1992	768695	331611	232942	100091	104051
1993	819624	348606	247339	94136	129543
1994	962678	375496	280952	138449	167781
1995	1087941	414740	310625	161040	201536
1996	1140081	449026	297108	169259	224688
1997	1261306	495660	336708	182201	246737
1998	1374723	540733	351108	209238	273644
1999	1566337	615418	387269	229703	333947
2000	1730872	674746	393662	258645	403819
2001	1943625	773100	416468	297179	478358
2002	2070544	753274	445612	326414	545244
2002*	2007265	770169	355062	287245	547068
2003	2178585	826568	382857	307216	616791
2004	2369918	879192	411309	345814	682338
2005	2455822	869651	397319	382414	745725
2006	2666233	1017480	370770	400899	802062

注：2002*－2006 年农林牧渔总产值按国家新的计算方法
a)The table is composed on the basis of new state calculation methods since 2002*
　2002*－2006 年的农业总产值不含家庭经营性工业
Gross output value of farming in the year of 2002* and 2003－2006 is not including family industry

9－16 农林牧渔业总产值及指数

Gross Output Value and Indices of Farming, Forestry, Animal Husbandry and Fishery

单位:万元

指 标	Item	2005 产值 Value	2005 指数 Indices 上年=100	2006 产值 Value	2006 指数 Indices 上年=100
农林牧渔业总产值	**Total**	**4758846.8**	**6.7**	**5438994.8**	**9.4**
农业产值	**Gross Output Value of Farming**	**1796344.4**	**5.8**	**2146044.0**	**11.1**
谷物及其他作物	Rice and Other Plants	471934.7	-13.3	547592.4	12.5
其中:谷 物	Rice	194671.4		246244.7	
豆 类	Bean	7371.0		7281.9	
油 料	Oil anticipates	29784.1		33332.3	
糖 蔗	Sugarcane	67197.6		98590.9	
蔬菜园艺作物	Vegetables and Horticultue Plant	673367.3	8.6	788967.9	6.4
其中：蔬菜类	Vegetables	626168.2		749427.4	
水果、坚果、饮料和香料作物	Fruit, Nut, Beverage and Perfume Plant	643006.7	20.9	804779.6	15.8
其中:水果、坚果	Fruit,Nut	640399.5		801732.6	
中药材	Chinese Medicinal Materials	8035.7	41.2	4704.2	-52.0
林业产值	**Gross Output Value of Forestry**	**589276.0**	**-8.4**	**705016.3**	**4.7**
林木的培育和种植	Cultivating and Planting of Forest Tree	71114.3	2.9	97649.7	37.3
竹木采运	Lumbering and Transportation of Timber and Bamboo	101773.3	108.9	58606.4	-43.6
林产品	Forestry Products	416388.4	-21.6	548760.2	10.9
牧业产值	**Gross Output Value of Animal Husbandry**	**952114.5**	**15.0**	**993117.9**	**7.1**
牲畜饲养	Rearing of Livestock	87466.7	29.6	89016.9	-1.3
猪的饲养	Rearing of Pigs	477277.8	6.8	506325.4	7.0
#肉猪	Hogs	458266.2		487254.4	
家禽饲养	Rearing of Birds	361266.4	22.8	368075.3	8.9
#肉禽	Birds for Meat	339126.3		345864.5	
渔业产值	**Gross Output Value of Fishery**	**1321823.8**	**8.6**	**1483085.4**	**10.8**
海水产品	Seawater Aquatic Products	1167579.8	8.3	1289267.4	8.4
#养殖	Cultured	122187.1		122096.3	
淡水产品	Freshwater Aquatic Products	154244.1	10.3	193818.0	29.0
#养殖	Cultured	60020.7		105053.0	
农业服务业	**Agricultural Services**	**99288.1**	**28.2**	**111731.2**	**10.9**
家庭兼营工业	**Family industry**	**129425.1**	**-8.8**	**126120.0**	**-2.6**

注:绝对数按当年价格计算,指数按可比价格计算

a)Data in value terms in this table are calculated at current prices,indices are calculated at constant price

2005-2006 年农林牧渔总产值按国家新的计算方法且不含家庭经营性工业

a)The table is composed on the basis of new state calculation methods since 2005and 2005-2006 is not including family industry

9-16 续(continued)

指 标	Item	2004	2005	2006
农林牧渔业总产值	**Total**	**4387282.75**	**4758846.8**	**5438994.75**
农业产值	**Gross Output Value of Farming**	**1709181.79**	**1796344.41**	**2146044.01**
谷物及其他作物	Rice and Other Plants	527754.74	471934.71	547592.38
其中:谷 物	Rice	238829.81	194671.38	246244.71
豆 类	Bean	9191.51	7371.04	7281.88
油 料	Oil anticipates	30686.01	29784.1	33332.28
糖 蔗	Sugarcane	86300.3	67197.6	98590.91
蔬菜园艺作物	Vegetables and Horticultue Plant	640609.24	673367.32	788967.86
其中:蔬菜类	Vegetables	597262.7	626168.2	749427.44
水果、坚果、饮料和香料作物	Fruit,Nut,Beverage and Perfume Plant	535396.5	643006.73	804779.62
其中:水果、坚果	Fruit,Nut	526283.69	640399.53	801732.62
中药材	Chinese Medicinal Materials	5421.3	8035.7	4704.15
林业产值	**Gross Output Value of Forestry**	**597917.5**	**589275.98**	**705016.27**
林木的培育和种植	Cultivating and Planting of Forest Tree	61101.81	71114.25	97649.65
竹木采运	Lumbering and Transportation of Timber and Bamboo	49027.44	101773.29	58606.41
林产品	Forestry Products	487788.3	416388.4	548760.21
牧业产值	**Gross Output Value of Animal Husbandry**	**838720.55**	**952114.46**	**993117.91**
牲畜饲养	Rearing of Livestock	65808.22	87466.68	89016.86
猪的饲养	Rearing of Pigs	475749.43	477277.75	506325.36
# 肉猪	Hogs	456532.9	458266.2	487254.39
家禽饲养	Rearing of Birds	281304.08	361266.4	368075.28
# 肉禽	Birds for Meat	259845.5	339126.3	345864.54
渔业产值	**Gross Output Value of Fishery**	**1166270.6**	**1321823.83**	**1483085.36**
海水产品	Seawater Aquatic Products	1030183.51	1167579.76	1289267.35
# 养 殖	Cultured	199267.04	122187.09	122096.25
淡水产品	Freshwater Aquatic Products	136087.1	154244.1	193818.01
# 养 殖	Cultured	69632.76	60020.74	105052.97
农业服务业	**Agricultural Services**	**75192.3**	**99288.1**	**111731.2**
家庭兼营工业	**Family industry**	**141934.81**	**129425.08**	**126120.02**

注:按当年价格计算。
a)Data in value terms in this table are calculated at current prices。
2004-2006 年农林牧渔总产值按国家新的计算方法
a)The table is composed on the basis of new state calculation methods since 2004-2006
2004-2006 年的农业总产值不含家庭经营性工业
Gross output value of farming in the year of 2004-2006 is not including family industry

9－17 农林牧渔业总产值及构成

Gross Output Value of Farming, Forestry, Animal Husbandry and Fishery and Its Composition

单位：万元　　(10,000 yuan)

指 标	Item	2002	2003	2004	2005	2006
农林牧渔业总产值	Total	3377691	3798508	4387283	4758847	5438995
农业产值	Gross Output Value of Farming	1395017	1525721	1709182	1796344	2146044
林业产值	Gross Output Value of Forestry	416994	533321	597918	589276	705016
牧业产值	Gross Output Value of Animal Husbandry	584895	647685	838721	952114	993118
渔业产值	Gross Output Value of Fishery	925727	1031098	1166271	1321824	1483085
海水产品	Seawater Aquatic Products	818794	914553	1030184	1167580	1289267
淡水产品	Freshwater Aquatic Products	106933	116545	136087	154244	193818
农业服务业	Agricultural Services	55058	60683	75192	99288	111731
家庭兼营性工业	Family industry	159128	158270	141935	129425	126120
比 重(%)	Specific (%)					
农业产值	Gross Output Value of Farming	41.30	40.17	38.96	37.75	39.46
林业产值	Gross Output Value of Forestry	12.35	14.04	13.63	12.38	12.96
牧业产值	Gross Output Value of Animal Husbandry	17.32	17.05	19.12	20.01	18.26
渔业产值	Gross Output Value of Fishery	27.41	27.14	26.58	27.78	27.27
海水产品	Seawater Aquatic Products	24.24	24.08	23.48	24.53	23.70
淡水产品	Freshwater Aquatic Products	3.17	3.07	3.10	3.24	3.56
农业服务业	Agricultural Services	1.63	1.60	1.71	2.09	2.05

注：按当年价格计算。
a)Data in value terms in this table are calculated at current prices。
2002-2006 年农林牧渔总产值按国家新的计算方法
a)The table is composed on the basis of new state calculation methods since 2002-2006

9－18 农林牧渔业增加值及指数

Gross Output Value of Farming, Forestry, Animal Husbandry and Fishery and Its Composition

单位：万元　　(10,000 yuan)

	Item	2002	2003	2004	2005	2006
增加值	Total					
农林牧渔业增加值	Added Value of Farming, Forestry, Animal Husbandry and Fishery	2228905	2442878	2787639	3007523	3444859
农业增加值	Added Value of Farming	934238	993720	1101173	1156730	1381247
林业增加值	Added Value of Forestry	283473	363831	413457	407479	487490
牧业增加值	Added Value ofAnimal Husbandry	349559	383339	486169	549478	573136
渔业增加值	Added Value of Fishery	632044	671167	748823	844947	947969
农业服务业	Agricultural Services	29591	30819	38018	48889	55017
指 数(%)	indices (%)					
农林牧渔业增加值	Added Value of Farming, Forestry, Animal Husbandry and Fishery	109.1	109.0	108.85	106.14	109.06
农业增加值	Added Value of Farming	103.1	107.5	106.36	105.57	111.17
林业增加值	Added Value of Forestry	115.3	111.3	108.25	91.42	102.30
牧业增加值	Added Value of Animal Husbandry	117.9	109.0	111.01	114.84	106.91
渔业增加值	Added Value of Fishery	112.1	110.6	111.23	108.50	110.73
农业服务业	Agricultural Services		100.1	117.39	124.85	110.87

注：增加值按当年价格计算；指数按可比价格计算，上年为 100
a)Data in value terms in this table are calculated at current prices。

9－19 各市县农林牧渔业总产值

Gross Output Value of Farming, Forestry, Animal Husbandry and Fishery of City and County

单位:万元 (10,000 yuan)

市县	Cities and Counties	农业总产值 Total	农业 Farming	林业 Forestry	牧业 Animal Husbandry	渔业 Fishery
		(按1990年不变价格计算) By the 1990's Constant Price				
海口市	Haikou	218506.06	100288.28	14395.98	67700.8	29721
三亚市	Sanya	148207.06	59255.93	3843.3	17278.03	61299.8
五指山市	Wuzhishan	18426.71	9241.02	5470.78	2972.89	684.02
文昌市	Wenchang	228716.23	64250.57	22026.08	47013	90832.08
琼海市	Qionghai	204980.71	73711.58	32594.74	34812.52	44245.98
万宁市	Wanning	136091.97	39611.61	14158.87	19692.16	59490.83
定安县	Dingan	65910.56	34584.98	6526.62	19151.39	2158.57
屯昌县	Tunchang	64659.8	32558.59	9179.29	15582.03	3693.89
澄迈县	Chengmai	120478.43	50771.32	14766.05	20422.52	32789.18
临高县	Lingao	205069.44	48115.95	6106.87	18406.57	129730.05
儋州市	Danzhou	347485.14	76666.76	15340.66	39723.17	212341.05
东方市	Dongfang	90397.77	60176.08	4564.63	13437.72	10492.34
乐东县	Ledong	134288.37	101817.58	5312.84	12116.01	13229.54
琼中县	Qiongzhong	32932.42	18537.29	7234.97	4901.69	1210.22
保亭县	Baoting	27178.81	15182.8	4991.87	2560.17	1140.97
陵水县	Linshui	92568.39	38925.16	4531.78	6862.05	36710.02
白沙县	Baisha	47174.64	26095.71	13429.45	5620.51	1725.47
昌江县	Changjiang	69559.33	35753.73	2209.06	9568.66	19864.88
农垦系统	System of Farm	399611.62	131854.35	184086.44	42842.26	37028.57
洋浦	Yangpu	13989.33	80.58	0	234.78	13673.97
		(按当年价格计算) By Current Price				
海口市	Haikou	433396.04	183092.48	23827.58	160055.18	52420.8
三亚市	Sanya	315992.07	156601.93	7117.22	34302.82	110455.6
五指山市	Wuzhishan	32038.35	15992.98	8386.44	6477.73	1123.2
文昌市	Wenchang	478482.5	158707.84	29643.69	138933.3	146102.61
琼海市	Qionghai	474728.2	214420.51	50382.48	102547.04	81112.66
万宁市	Wanning	259171.85	97248.79	25126.14	49645.92	83549.4
定安县	Dingan	142760.28	73635.59	11038.31	47206.06	3176.87
屯昌县	Tunchang	129696.77	66383.27	15071.75	36673.31	5494.97
澄迈县	Chengmai	231260.1	110709.62	23639.8	50269.73	43452.11
临高县	Lingao	483730.31	91862.69	11432.19	41333.52	335191.91
儋州市	Danzhou	660494.7	178723.79	31669.71	91725.65	352714.55
东方市	Dongfang	216932.95	144789.48	6634.77	32241.6	30255.1
乐东县	Ledong	255606.73	179911.81	10148.85	31661	31585.07
琼中县	Qiongzhong	59049.76	31535.73	12387.85	11457.49	1864.36
保亭县	Baoting	50801.3	27472.2	9143.76	7762.04	1660.8
陵水县	Linshui	207313.14	99042.56	6810.65	16519.67	76068.62
白沙县	Baisha	72099.9	35423.83	19217.48	13410.89	3139.5
昌江县	Changjiang	143614.13	65411.08	3218.4	21058.73	51484.82
农垦系统	System of Farm	763111.06	214793.03	400119.2	100133.63	43505.2
洋浦	Yangpu	29251.75	162.46	0	472.8	28616.49

9－20 农林牧渔业总产值、中间消耗和增加值

Gross Output Value, Middle Material Consumption and Added Value of Farming, Forestry,Animal Husbandry and Fishery

单位:万元 (10,000 yuan)

市 县	Cities and Counties	农林牧渔业总产值 Gross Output Value	农林牧渔业中间消耗 Middle Material Consumption	农林牧渔业增加值 Value added	占总产值比重(%) Percentage to Output Value	
					中间消耗 Middle Material Consumption	增加值 Value added
1991		705108	207100	498008	29.4	70.6
1992		804869	268986	535883	33.4	66.6
1993		1110173	341941	768232	30.8	69.2
1994		1584676	523504	1061172	33.0	67.0
1995		1887905	598901	1289004	31.7	68.3
1996		2079391	667854	1411537	32.1	67.9
1997		2163255	678097	1485158	31.3	68.7
1998		2335922	775433	1560489	33.2	66.8
1999		2668748	942580	1726168	35.3	64.7
2000		2975338	1055334	1920004	35.5	64.5
2001		3077589	1109799	1967790	36.1	63.9
2002		3377691	1148786	2228905	34.0	66.0
2003		3798508	1355630	2442878	35.7	64.3
2004		4387283	1599644	2787639	36.5	63.5
2005		4758847	1751324	3007523	36.8	63.2
2006		5438995	1994136	3444859	36.7	63.3
海口市	Haikou	433396	173937	259459	40.1	59.9
三亚市	Sanya	315992	111865	204127	35.4	64.6
五指山市	Wuzhishan	32038	11586	20452	36.2	63.8
文昌市	Wenchang	478483	173353	305129	36.2	63.8
琼海市	Qionghai	474728	177674	297054	37.4	62.6
万宁市	Wanning	259172	94693	164479	36.5	63.5
定安县	Dingan	142760	54456	88305	38.1	61.9
屯昌县	Tunchang	129697	51018	78679	39.3	60.7
澄迈县	Chengmai	231260	84840	146420	36.7	63.3
临高县	Lingao	483730	183065	300665	37.8	62.2
儋州市	Danzhou	660495	232900	427595	35.3	64.7
东方市	Dongfang	216933	81002	135931	37.3	62.7
乐东县	Ledong	255607	95509	160098	37.4	62.6
琼中县	Qiongzhong	59050	21092	37958	35.7	64.3
保亭县	Baoting	50801	17876	32925	35.2	64.8
陵水县	Linshui	207313	79760	127553	38.5	61.5
白沙县	Baisha	72100	26428	45671	36.7	63.3
昌江县	Changjiang	143614	56618	86996	39.4	60.6
农垦系统	System of Farm	763111	264669	498442	34.7	65.3
洋浦	Yangpu	29252	11575	17676	39.6	60.4

注:1991-2006 年农林牧渔总产值按国家新的计算方法。
1991-2006 年农林牧渔总产值、增加值不含家庭经营工业。
a)The table is composed on the basis of new state calculation methods since 2002
Gross output value of farming in the year of 1991-2006 is not including famlly industry

9－21 各市县农林牧渔业增加值
Value added of Farming, Forestry, Animal Husbandry and Fishery

单位:万元　(10,000 yuan)

市 县	Cities and Counties	合 计 Total	农 业 Farming	林 业 Forestry	牧 业 Animal Husbandry	渔 业 Fishery
农林牧渔业增加值	Value added					
海口市	Haikou	259459	117573	15671	87190	32779
三亚市	Sanya	204127	102197	4896	19646	72666
五指山市	Wuzhishan	20452	10084	5649	3978	714
文昌市	Wenchang	305129	103533	19433	87392	92331
琼海市	Qionghai	297054	139317	34840	58325	51853
万宁市	Wanning	164479	64010	17492	28856	52434
定安县	Dingan	88305	47318	7302	27537	1966
屯昌县	Tunchang	78679	42614	9782	19743	3465
澄迈县	Chengmai	146420	71418	15746	29335	28363
临高县	Lingao	300665	55881	7136	20217	215722
儋州市	Danzhou	427595	116770	21937	51863	234294
东方市	Dongfang	135931	91059	4617	18830	20017
乐东县	Ledong	160098	115244	5890	18874	18985
琼中县	Qiongzhong	37958	20282	8133	7608	1054
保亭县	Baoting	32925	18750	6193	4594	956
陵水县	Linshui	127553	63094	4244	9515	46308
白沙县	Baisha	45671	23123	12601	7443	2074
昌江县	Changjiang	86996	38197	2075	12193	33350
农垦系统	System of Farm	498442	134606	284743	51497	25385
洋浦	Yangpu	17676	98	0	262	17316
农林牧渔业中间消耗	Middle Material Consumption					
海口市	Haikou	173937	65519	8156	72865	19642
三亚市	Sanya	111865	54405	2221	14656	37790
五指山市	Wuzhishan	11586	5909	2737	2500	409
文昌市	Wenchang	173353	55174	10211	51541	53772
琼海市	Qionghai	177674	75104	15543	44222	29260
万宁市	Wanning	94693	33239	7634	20790	31115
定安县	Dingan	54456	26317	3736	19669	1210
屯昌县	Tunchang	51018	23770	5290	16931	2030
澄迈县	Chengmai	84840	39291	7894	20934	15090
临高县	Lingao	183065	35982	4296	21117	119470
儋州市	Danzhou	232900	61953	9733	39863	118420
东方市	Dongfang	81002	53730	2018	13411	10238
乐东县	Ledong	95509	64668	4259	12787	12600
琼中县	Qiongzhong	21092	11254	4255	3850	810
保亭县	Baoting	17876	8722	2951	3168	705
陵水县	Linshui	79760	35948	2567	7005	29761
白沙县	Baisha	26428	12301	6617	5968	1066
昌江县	Changjiang	56618	27214	1144	8865	18135
农垦系统	System of Farm	264669	80187	115376	48637	18120
洋浦	Yangpu	11575	64	0	211	11301

9－22 人均主要农产品产量
Per Capita Output of Major Farm Products

单位:公斤/人 (kg/person)

年 份	year	粮 食 Grain	稻 谷 Rice	油 料 Oil-bearing Crops	糖 蔗 Sugarcane	猪牛羊肉 Pork,Beef and Mutton	猪 肉 Pork	水产品 Aquatic Products
1978		216	180	5	113	8	8	13
1980		210	181	4	119	8	8	11
1985		204	179	6	679	16	15	15
1987		185	187	7	425	17	16	18
1990		259	221	7	550	19	17	26
1991		277	236	7	586	20	18	30
1992		303	252	8	646	23	21	38
1993		293	240	9	560	26	24	48
1994		296	240	10	570	26	23	56
1995		307	246	11	443	30	26	62
1996		290	229	11	424	31	27	67
1997		309	246	11	477	32	29	71
1998		314	246	13	482	35	31	82
1999		312	237	13	518	33	29	95
2000		279	215	13	445	35	31	109
2001		270	208	13	443	38	33	124
2002		261	201	13	481	41	37	140
2003		248	191	12	509	44	39	156
2004		244	189	11	519	48	43	169
2005		185	134	10	306	51	46	181
2006		224	174	11	437	55	50	200
海口市	Haikou	92	74	3	130	50	48	34
三亚市	Sanya	126	106	3	0	41	37	175
五指山市	Wuzhishan	261	193	7	0	31	27	17
文昌市	Wenchang	288	190	24	9	32	28	269
琼海市	Qionghai	260	214	4	1	59	55	190
万宁市	Wanning	160	124	4	0	44	41	110
定安县	Dingan	266	218	17	596	76	70	18
屯昌县	Tunchang	298	243	17	326	80	71	33
澄迈县	Chengmai	233	195	5	254	52	45	110
临高县	Lingao	267	210	4	1303	47	43	1016
儋州市	Danzhou	211	138	19	1333	53	47	423
东方市	Dongfang	255	201	20	61	47	41	106
乐东县	Ledong	313	261	23	1	37	29	86
琼中县	Qiongzhong	298	236	8	4	43	36	16
保亭县	Baoting	175	163	4	0	27	23	17
陵水县	Linshui	285	234	9	0	27	25	284
白沙县	Baisha	285	188	4	2031	52	44	25
昌江县	Changjiang	231	168	8	1771	56	45	269
农垦系统	Nongken	133	110	6	455	57	52	38
洋 浦	Yangpu							

9－23 农作物播种面积和复种指数
Sown Area and Multiple Crop Index of Crops

年份 Year	总播种面积（公顷）Total Sown Area (hectare)	粮食作物 Grain Crops		经济作物 Economical Crops		复种指数（%）Multiple Crop Index (%)
		播种面积（公顷）Sown Area (hectare)	占总播种面积 Percentage of Grain Crops to Total Sown Area (%)	播种面积（公顷）Sown Area (hectare)	占总播种面积 Percentage of Grain Crops to Total Sown Area (%)	
1952	553640	522547	94.40	17300	3.10	190.60
1957	752647	684560	94.10	49660	6.60	189.60
1962	704993	641727	91.00	59460	8.40	176.50
1965	690527	569780	82.50	81480	11.80	175.40
1970	728187	616893	87.40	89633	12.30	175.00
1975	909007	690033	75.90	129253	14.20	205.40
1978	796433	642093	80.60	120833	15.00	175.00
1980	696313	575440	82.60	91233	13.10	156.00
1981	678647	551393	81.00	96693	14.00	155.00
1982	706760	549293	77.70	122160	17.00	160.00
1983	710560	542146	76.00	133113	19.00	164.00
1984	715880	532320	74.40	141600	20.20	163.00
1985	739887	507900	68.60	188267	25.40	170.00
1986	754607	516726	68.50	186393	24.70	174.00
1987	760193	509520	67.00	190493	25.10	175.80
1988	740380	496940	67.10	177000	23.90	171.60
1989	789587	539887	68.40	175093	22.20	182.10
1990	821253	560573	68.30	176580	21.50	188.80
1991	829467	561747	67.70	179280	21.60	189.70
1992	868307	577700	66.50	186260	21.50	198.90
1993	846160	550173	65.00	175200	20.70	195.20
1994	844108	549420	65.09	167197	19.81	196.28
1995	870064	559376	64.29	170575	19.60	202.72
1996	890779	559314	62.79	166821	18.73	207.48
1997	914513	577197	63.11	177992	19.46	214.55
1998	937573	576954	61.54	177109	18.89	219.13
1999	931756	567702	60.93	180008	19.32	216.89
2000	909539	545634	59.99	168862	18.57	209.97
2001	893928	526872	58.94	164471	18.40	209.90
2002	900987	522287	57.97	164454	18.25	212.83
2003	876170	495229	56.52	160355	18.30	209.05
2004	862309	482303	55.93	161116	18.68	206.41
2005	782095	423751	66.97	137798	17.62	187.92
2006	821150	444547	54.14	153226	18.66	

9－24 主要农作物播种面积
Sown Areas of Major Farm Crops

单位:公顷 (hectare)

年份 Year	粮食作物 Grain Crops	谷物 Cereal	水稻 Rice	早造 Early Season Rice	晚造 Late Season Rice	旱粮 Dry Rice	蕃薯 Tubers	大豆 Beans	经济作物 Economical Crops
1952	522547	421747	394980	144087	250893	26767	100800	2927	17300
1957	684560	517020	463860	157207	306660	53160	167540	4993	49660
1962	541727	472267	394867	141207	253660	77400	169460	2927	59460
1965	569780	437733	408920	157873	251047	28813	132047	3740	81480
1970	616893	456180	406773	161380	245393	49407	160713	4107	89633
1971	672427	513594	464067	198707	265360	49527	158833	4633	77704
1972	674021	523174	476814	207647	269167	46360	150847	5027	98619
1973	692360	524787	488807	216967	271840	35980	167573	5533	105549
1974	721087	533894	500634	224747	275887	33260	187193	6240	110484
1975	690033	521993	500773	226193	274580	21220	168040	5467	129253
1976	673453	521960	501927	228360	273567	20033	151493	6273	139801
1977	690880	513573	496553	225840	270713	17020	177307	5240	124687
1978	642093	486173	464613	194347	270266	21560	155920	5060	120833
1979	601973	479660	457333	203487	253847	22327	122313	6193	99230
1980	575440	462220	433027	184647	248380	29193	113220	6893	91233
1981	551393	446973	421166	183713	237453	25807	104420	7180	96693
1982	549293	444546	421613	185353	236260	22933	104747	7853	122160
1983	542146	441233	424093	188793	235300	17140	100913	7133	133113
1984	532320	437533	419027	185800	233227	18506	94787	6753	141600
1985	507900	412607	395200	175873	219327	17407	95293	6907	188267
1986	516726	419253	403240	180547	222693	16013	97473	7140	186393
1987	509520	404740	387667	176807	210860	17073	104780	7000	190493
1988	496940	387473	367640	160787	206853	19833	109467	6960	177000
1989	539887	426327	403800	178467	225333	22527	113560	7427	175093
1990	560573	437680	414347	186293	228054	23333	122893	6880	176580
1991	561747	434660	411340	184883	226457	23320	127087	7360	179280
1992	577700	442667	413793	185973	227820	28874	135033	7727	186260
1993	550473	409920	390373	176493	213880	19547	140253	8347	175200
1994	549420	407880	387093	168306	218787	20787	141539	7649	167197
1995	559376	415867	393620	175543	218077	22247	143509	7394	170575
1996	559314	414024	390470	176254	214216	23584	145261	7970	166821
1997	577197	414788	396678	175806	215568	26462	143750	8568	177992
1998	576954	413322	388452	173685	214767	24870	146149	9792	177109
1999	567702	409583	385295	170489	214806	24288	140988	8757	180008
2000	545634	397000	373684	166948	206736	23316	131687	9367	168862
2001	526872	382072	359903	160174	199729	22169	128118	8796	164471
2002	522287	379539	359477	159285	200192	20061	126968	8824	164454
2003	495229	362386	344287	154572	189715	18099	118453	7828	160355
2004	482304	354478	340475	150839	187761	15083	114115	6685	161116
2005	423751	306192	290485	115550	173315	15707	105968	5423	137798
2006	444547	334327	318912	139334	178457	15415	99682	5262	153226

9-24 续(continued)

年 份 Year	油料 Oil-bearing Crops	花生 Peanuts	芝麻 Sesames	糖蔗 Sugarcane	黄红麻 Jute and Ambary Hemp	土烟 Flue-Cured Tobacco	其它作物 Other Crops	蔬 菜 Vegetables	瓜 类 Melon
1952	11840	10107	1733	4480	113	427	10867		
1957	36673	26200	10473	11667	133	580	13433		
1962	30620	20887	9733	8067	287	953	880		
1965	51000	43273	7727	23227	193	500	35527		
1970	47193	37713	9480	27980	207	313	17367		
1971	42740	33007	9733	26807	187	220	18500		
1972	58633	47780	10853	33300	253	173	24450		
1973	63653	51420	12233	35513	733	200	28530		
1974	66013	43346	22667	36587	2927	247	37620		
1975	67140	52973	14167	49673	1920	233	84253		
1976	70247	52607	17640	56607	3253	280	48302		
1977	64953	51706	13247	42240	2687	307	35670		
1978	63347	44707	18640	31787	2760	373	28447		
1979	52940	39227	13713	25580	953	260	27300		
1980	46340	34240	12100	25607	393	247	22747	17167	1740
1981	450102	32947	12173	33047	287	180	23380	17020	1793
1982	51400	39073	12327	49933	267	247	27360	20873	2313
1983	47500	37193	10307	66393	180	200	28167	21940	2700
1984	44040	36893	7147	78533	140	213	35207	23293	3493
1985	44600	37533	7067	115700	287	213	36800	27347	4407
1986	47200	40640	6560	99013	233	253	44353	32207	6620
1987	46333	39066	7267	83293	447	213	53180	37767	9913
1988	43553	36666	6887	71653	193	213	59480	43753	10113
1989	42960	36320	6640	75193	180	233	66847	50313	11247
1990	45033	38420	6613	83953	227	280	77213	57033	15547
1991	43820	37107	6713	92953	280	380	81073	62233	13473
1992	47293	40593	6700	97387	333	733	96620	73073	17393
1993	48493	42067	6426	83147	460	793	106887	82667	18347
1994	48793	72877	5916	67299	248	533	119842	95350	18315
1995	51168	45576	5592	67359	250	414	132719	105995	19452
1996	51311	45953	5358	68075	243	420	148058	118569	21456
1997	52160	46876	5284	70871			163112	134496	21547
1998	55885	50381	5501	72387	789	359	175807	147068	17788
1999	53703	48510	5193	72847	703	201	175908	147260	19998
2000	54141	48868	5253	61770	697	205	173473	148860	15591
2001	54569	48965	5114	60783	352	200	192378	161007	17438
2002	53450	49173	4277	64950	179	237	190111	160697	18134
2003	49749	45468	4283	69094	206	122	190861	161857	19695
2004	47410	43881	3529	69901	228	98	514389	161002	21098
2005	44478	41343	3135	50251	174	45	50445	172427	21506
2006	42901	40403	2488	61700	176	43	49299	184215	172427

9－25 主要农作物总产量
Yield of Major Farm Crops

单位:万吨 (10,000 tons)

年 份 Year	粮食总产量 Yield of Grain	谷 物 Cereal	水 稻 Rice	早 造 Early Season Rice	晚 造 Late Season Rice	旱 粮 Dry Rice	蕃 薯 Tubers	大 豆 Beans
1952	56.92	48.04	46.63	16.21	30.42	1.41	8.88	0.10
1957	81.88	65.32	62.73	20.10	42.63	2.59	16.56	0.22
1962	63.53	54.62	51.53	15.37	36.16	3.09	8.91	0.11
1965	91.34	81.46	80.05	32.43	47.62	1.41	9.88	0.15
1970	98.40	81.00	78.08	34.05	44.03	2.92	17.40	0.15
1971	123.27	108.71	102.00	47.53	54.47	6.71	14.56	0.22
1972	130.08	114.61	106.19	49.37	56.82	8.42	15.47	0.20
1973	125.03	109.13	105.94	57.17	48.77	3.19	15.9	0.21
1974	145.75	127.36	125.42	62.99	62.43	1.94	18.39	0.22
1975	152.01	135.98	131.40	66.57	64.83	4.58	19.03	0.26
1976	151.26	137.19	135.15	76.98	58.17	2.04	14.07	0.23
1977	154.10	137.03	135.65	70.31	65.34	1.38	17.07	0.17
1978	114.29	97.18	95.25	49.87	46.38	1.93	17.11	0.21
1979	123.77	109.76	107.48	49.81	57.67	2.28	14.01	0.33
1980	115.89	102.69	99.96	47.77	52.19	2.73	13.20	0.33
1981	121.61	108.30	105.73	52.19	53.54	2.57	13.31	0.38
1982	132.53	119.35	117.18	56.30	60.88	2.17	13.18	0.50
1983	132.08	119.67	118.15	59.17	58.98	1.52	12.41	0.46
1984	140.94	128.7	126.87	62.81	64.06	1.83	12.24	0.43
1985	121.70	108.80	107.10	53.99	53.11	1.70	12.90	0.45
1986	138.08	123.61	122.14	61.92	60.22	1.47	14.47	0.48
1987	133.50	116.77	114.95	57.18	57.77	1.82	16.73	0.50
1988	119.81	103.21	101.00	52.21	48.79	2.21	16.60	0.52
1989	151.21	133.09	130.09	69.28	60.81	3.00	18.12	0.59
1990	168.99	147.84	144.23	70.53	73.70	3.61	21.15	0.58
1991	183.44	160.27	156.37	74.22	82.15	3.90	23.17	0.70
1992	203.65	175.02	169.33	80.68	88.65	5.69	28.63	0.82
1993	199.99	167.37	163.28	76.33	86.95	3.16	32.62	0.90
1994	204.65	169.80	165.31	74.04	91.27	4.49	34.85	0.87
1995	215.46	178.11	173.07	79.02	94.05	5.04	37.35	0.93
1996	206.99	168.56	162.35	81.44	80.91	5.71	38.43	0.97
1997	223.09	181.53	176.73	84.65	90.89	6.19	38.89	1.21
1998	230.12	185.97	179.10	83.47	95.63	6.87	41.43	1.58
1999	231.80	187.31	180.48	83.19	97.29	6.83	41.56	1.40
2000	212.24	169.05	162.34	82.06	80.28	6.71	40.22	1.67
2001	207.62	165.84	159.21	77.35	81.86	6.63	38.84	1.56
2002	203.33	161.45	155.37	73.98	81.39	6.08	38.89	1.57
2003	195.85	155.36	149.92	72.37	77.55	5.44	37.47	1.61
2004	196.57	156.9	152.13	72.33	79.31	5.25	36.78	1.3
2005	153	116.04	110.56	51.36	58.82	5.49	34.77	0.99
2006	186.61	150.09	144.39	68.34	75.78	5.70	33.36	1.05

9-25 续(continued)

年 份 Year	油 料 Oil-bearing Crops	花 生 Peanuts	芝 麻 Sesames	糖 蔗 Sugarcane	黄红麻 Jute and Ambary Hemp	土 烟 Flue-Cured Tobacco	蔬 菜 Vegetables	瓜 类 Melon
1952	0.83	0.77	0.06	14.88	0.01	0.02		
1957	1.56	1.30	0.26	35.65	0.01	0.03		
1962	1.06	0.89	0.17	11.95	0.02	0.03		
1965	2.10	1.96	0.14	53.58	0.02	0.02		
1970	1.85	1.65	0.20	57.03	0.02	0.10		
1971	1.61	1.51	0.10	48.93	0.02	0.10		
1972	2.57	2.39	0.18	67.84	0.03	0.01		
1973	2.22	1.90	0.32	61.10	0.06	0.01		
1974	2.54	2.29	0.25	69.33	0.22	0.01		
1975	3.16	2.85	0.31	102.17	0.16	0.01		
1976	3.38	3.10	0.28	105.42	0.24	0.01		
1977	2.43	2.23	0.20	64.04	0.19	0.02		
1978	2.84	2.56	0.28	59.78	0.23	0.02		
1979	2.40	2.10	0.30	60.45	0.10	0.02		
1980	2.21	1.96	0.25	65.93	0.04	0.01	14.64	1.44
1981	2.38	2.08	0.30	99.54	0.04	0.01	14.64	1.70
1982	3.50	3.21	0.29	182.70	0.06	0.01	17.18	1.95
1983	3.37	3.13	0.24	234.96	0.03	0.01	18.49	2.14
1984	3.88	3.66	0.22	283.99	0.02	0.01	22.68	3.56
1985	3.67	3.46	0.21	405.70	0.05	0.01	24.59	4.29
1986	4.31	4.07	0.24	322.52	0.06	0.02	30.77	8.87
1987	4.44	4.14	0.30	261.4	0.07	0.02	40.24	12.29
1988	4.24	3.92	0.32	243.41	0.05	0.01	45.00	13.03
1989	4.50	4.25	0.25	274.23	0.04	0.05	53.17	15.27
1990	4.54	4.30	0.24	358.31	0.07	0.02	59.18	21.02
1991	4.67	4.39	0.28	387.48	0.09	0.04	66.67	20.23
1992	5.67	5.34	0.33	433.97	0.10	0.06	78.60	28.82
1993	6.21	5.87	0.35	359.91	0.11	0.07	95.93	30.54
1994	6.63	6.31	0.32	294.14	0.08	0.04	110.98	28.29
1995	7.60	7.26	0.34	311.27		0.03	132.74	30.63
1996	8.00	7.67	0.32	302.5	0.05	0.03	156.79	35.31
1997	8.42	8.02	0.4	347.84			184.78	38.44
1998	9.50	9.11	0.39	353.74	0.29	0.01	223.16	34.44
1999	9.60	9.22	0.38	384.61	0.30	0.02	255.23	41.07
2000	10.09	9.52	0.42	338.86	0.29	0.02	267.06	36.97
2001	10.30	9.69	0.43	340.69	0.16	0.05	275.81	43.97
2002	10.04	9.72	0.32	374.79	0.10	0.10	279.42	43.65
2003	9.62	9.28	0.34	402.08	0.12	0.01	298.39	45.43
2004	9.08	8.80	0.28	417.89	0.12	0.08	313.94	47.19
2005	8.53	8.35	0.18	253.65	0.09		312.16	51.23
2006	8.96	8.76	0.20	361.46	0.09		341.01	59.38

9－26 主要农作物单位面积产量
Yield of Major Farm Crops Per Hectare

单位:公斤/公顷 (kg/hectare)

年份 Year	粮食 Grain	水稻 Rice	蕃薯 Tubers	糖蔗 Sugarcane	油料 Oil-bearing Crops	花生 Peanuts	芝麻 Sesames
1952	1095	1185	870	33210	705	765	345
1957	1200	1425	990	30555	420	480	2595
1962	990	1305	525	14820	345	420	180
1965	1605	1950	750	23070	405	450	195
1970	1590	1920	1080	20385	390	435	210
1975	2205	2625	1125	20565	465	540	210
1978	1785	2055	1095	18000	450	525	1695
1980	2010	2295	1170	25500	480	570	210
1981	2205	2505	1275	30120	525	630	240
1982	2415	2775	1260	36585	690	825	240
1983	2430	2790	1230	35385	720	840	225
1984	2640	3015	1290	36165	885	990	315
1985	2400	2715	1350	35100	825	915	300
1986	2670	3030	1485	32580	915	1005	360
1987	2625	2970	1590	31380	960	1065	420
1988	2415	2745	1515	33975	975	1065	465
1989	2805	3225	1590	36750	1050	1170	375
1990	3015	3480	1725	42675	1005	1125	360
1991	3270	3795	1830	41685	1065	1185	420
1992	3525	4095	2160	44565	1200	1320	495
1993	3630	4185	1725	43290	1275	1395	540
1994	3720	4275	2520	4376	1350	1350	540
1995	3851	4370	2602	46210	1485	1593	606
1996	3701	4158	2646	44437	1558	1670	604
1997	3906	4516	2705	49081	1614	1711	749
1998	3989	4611	2835	48867	1700	1808	717
1999	4083	4684	2947	52795	1788	1900	740
2000	3890	4344	3055	54858	1863	1949	791
2001	3941	4424	3032	56050	1888	1979	841
2002	3893	4322	3063	57704	1878	1977	746
2003	3955	4354	3164	58193	1933	2042	775
2004	4075	4468	3223	59783	1917	2006	808
2005	3611	3806	3282	50476	1918	2019	584
2006	4198	4528	3346	58583	2089	2168	804

9－27 各市县农作物播种面积
Sown Area of Crops by City and County

市县	Cities and Counties	农作物总播种面积（公顷）Sown Areas of Farm Crops (hectare)	粮食 Grain	豆类 Soybeans	甘蔗 Sugarcane	蔬菜 Vegetables	占总播种面积(%) Percentage to Total Sown Areas(%) 粮食 Grain	豆类 Soybeans	甘蔗 Sugarcane	蔬菜 Vegetables
全省总计	TOTAL	821150	444547	10525	66447	184215	54.14	1.28	8.09	22.43
海口市	Haikou	82900	41894	904	4398	22594	50.54	1.09	5.31	27.25
三亚市	Sanya	30867	16175	517	48	9578	52.40	1.67	0.15	31.03
五指山市	Wuzhishan	9405	5651	316	163	1802	60.08	3.36	1.73	19.16
文昌市	Wenchang	74043	44227	46	391	16288	59.73	0.06	0.53	22.00
琼海市	Qionghai	45655	28178	435	553	13644	61.72	0.95	1.21	29.89
万宁市	Wanning	33197	20880	517	577	6881	62.90	1.56	1.74	20.73
定安县	Dingan	36459	21324	954	2416	6541	58.49	2.62	6.63	17.94
屯昌县	Tunchang	38238	20698	1219	2157	8451	54.13	3.19	5.64	22.10
澄迈县	Chengmai	45525	25865	434	2766	12150	56.82	0.95	6.08	26.69
临高县	Lingao	43962	24776	103	8162	9453	56.36	0.23	18.57	21.50
儋州市	Danzhou	89244	41305	1760	21625	15571	46.28	1.97	24.23	17.45
东方市	Dongfang	45090	25298	394	649	11152	56.11	0.87	1.44	24.73
乐东县	Ledong	60689	35274	1778	188	13626	58.12	2.93	0.31	22.45
琼中县	Qiongzhong	19617	11156	396	525	2263	56.87	2.02	2.68	11.54
保亭县	Baoting	11083	6788	26	17	3717	61.25	0.23	0.15	33.54
陵水县	Linshui	40350	23317	14	190	10780	57.79	0.03	0.47	26.72
白沙县	Baisha	24796	10859	201	6477	2799	43.79	0.81	26.12	11.29
昌江县	Changjiang	30381	13059	43	7814	6823	42.98	0.14	25.72	22.46
农垦系统	Farms	59582	27815	469	7302	15032	46.68	0.79	12.25	25.23
洋浦	Yangpu	67	9	0	32	26	12.96	0.00	48.16	38.88

9－28 各市县主要农作物面积和产量
Area and Output of Main Crops by City and County

市县	Cities and Counties	粮食作物 Grain Crops 播种面积(公顷) Sown Area (hectare)	粮食作物 Grain Crops 总产量(吨) Total Output (ton)	谷物 Cereal 播种面积(公顷) Sown Area (hectare)	谷物 Cereal 总产量(吨) Total Output (ton)	水稻 Rice 播种面积(公顷) Sown Area (hectare)	水稻 Rice 总产量(吨) Total Output (ton)
全省总计	**TOTAL**	**444547**	**1856103**	**334327**	**1500896**	**318912**	**1443864**
海口市	Haikou	41894	158981	30727	129597	30361	128081
三亚市	Sanya	16175	65780	13178	59039	11941	55688
五指山市	Wuzhishan	5651	27391	4529	23298	3591	20331
文昌市	Wenchang	44227	159588	33208	106134	33001	105023
琼海市	Qionghai	28178	123358	23884	104913	23070	101633
万宁市	Wanning	20880	88963	16347	70137	16096	68698
定安县	Dingan	21324	82503	16701	71265	16362	67564
屯昌县	Tunchang	20698	80698	13757	66751	13485	65670
澄迈县	Chengmai	25865	112170	21112	95274	20841	93694
临高县	Lingao	24776	111435	17567	88022	17494	87775
儋州市	Danzhou	41305	190794	24697	131225	23454	125111
东方市	Dongfang	25298	103917	19061	86389	17743	81878
乐东县	Ledong	35274	145729	28270	129804	25162	121466
琼中县	Qiongzhong	11156	53327	9064	44704	8220	42186
保亭县	Baoting	6788	26074	6236	25108	5954	24310
陵水县	Linshui	23317	94283	16666	81089	15933	77444
白沙县	Baisha	10859	48702	7767	38287	5816	32113
昌江县	Changjiang	13059	56086	9268	42863	8744	40917
农垦系统	Nongken	27815	126272	22280	106943	21633	104228
洋浦	Yangpu	9	54	9	54	9	54

9－27 续1(continued 1)

市县	Cities and Counties	早造水稻 Early Season Rice 播种面积(公顷) Sown Area (hectare)	早造水稻 Early Season Rice 总产量(吨) Total Output (ton)	晚造水稻 Late Season Rice 播种面积(公顷) Sown Area (hectare)	晚造水稻 Late Season Rice 总产量(吨) Total Output (ton)	蕃薯 Tubers 播种面积(公顷) Sown Area (hectare)	蕃薯 Tubers 总产量(吨) Total Output (ton)
全省总计	**Total**	**139334**	**683358**	**178457**	**757804**	**99682**	**333577**
海口市	Haikou	13447	60901	16763	66805	10263	28058
三亚市	Sanya	5455	29237	6485	26451	2480	5991
五指山市	Wuzhishan	1655	10803	1800	9227	806	3346
文昌市	Wenchang	12825	42802	20174	62214	10974	53415
琼海市	Qionghai	10722	51792	12334	49791	3847	16414
万宁市	Wanning	6576	30606	9520	38092	4017	17703
定安县	Dingan	6684	29428	9602	37812	3669	9882
屯昌县	Tunchang	6475	32412	6978	33184	5723	12065
澄迈县	Chengmai	9604	46912	11237	46782	4319	15818
临高县	Lingao	8658	51140	8831	36628	7106	23169
儋州市	Danzhou	10046	54024	13409	71087	14848	55840
东方市	Dongfang	7987	41353	9602	40210	5843	16805
乐东县	Ledong	9691	52296	15307	68760	5225	12279
琼中县	Qiongzhong	4025	22078	4031	19794	1696	7995
保亭县	Baoting	2497	10697	3455	13608	526	902
陵水县	Linshui	6073	29681	9860	47763	6637	13129
白沙县	Baisha	2731	15727	2951	16091	2891	9990
昌江县	Changjiang	3828	19716	4890	21113	3748	13120
农垦系统	Nongken	10354	51754	11219	52338	5066	17656
洋浦	Yangpu	0	0	9	54	0	0

9-28 续 2(continued 2)

市 县	Cities and Counties	大 豆 Beans		甘 蔗 Sugarcane		糖蔗 Sugarcane		油 料 Oil-bearing Crops	
		播种面积(公顷) Sown Area (hectare)	总产量(吨) Total Output (ton)	播种面积(公顷) Sown Area (hectare)	总产量(吨) Total Output (ton)	播种面积(公顷) Sown Area (hectare)	总产量(吨) Total Output (ton)	播种面积(公顷) Sown Area (hectare)	总产量(吨) Total Output (ton)
全省总计	**Total**	**5262**	**10527**	**66447**	**3855463**	**61700**	**3614631**	**42901**	**89621**
海 口 市	Haikou	851	1268	4398	242460	3998	225005	4573	5334
三 亚 市	Sanya	154	245	48	973	0	0	754	1579
五指山市	Wuzhishan	0	0	163	2828	0	0	253	703
文 昌 市	Wenchang	46	39	391	16561	100	5229	6625	13207
琼 海 市	Qionghai	167	480	553	40369	3	250	1379	2017.12
万 宁 市	Wanning	124	266	577	37115	0	0	1005	2448
定 安 县	Dingan	729	1052	2416	196143	2247	185115	3062	5382.8
屯 昌 县	Tunchang	892	1334	2157	126153	1505	88103	3110	4647
澄 迈 县	Chengmai	383	974	2766	148177	2310	122261	1583	2637.75
临 高 县	Lingao	87	222	8162	548881	8092	544012	913	1499
儋 州 市	Danzhou	853	2199	21625	1212875	21508	1205009	5557	17407
东 方 市	Dongfang	0	0	649	25446	629	24847	3407	8274
乐 东 县	Ledong	506	1084	188	9844	17	598	4151	10802
琼 中 县	Qiongzhong	180	261	525	12119	37	785	809	1505.1
保 亭 县	Baoting	7	9	17	262	0	0	349	591.33
陵 水 县	Linshui	0	0	190	4907	0	0	1348	3123
白 沙 县	Baisha	0	0	6477	349300	6433	346949	235	642
昌 江 县	Changjiang	0	0	7814	431583	7797	430658	914	1841
农垦系统	Nongken	283	1094	7302	444637	6992	430980	2877	5981
洋 浦	Yangpu	0	0	32	4830	32	4830	0	0

9-27 续 3(continued 3)

市 县	Cities and Counties	花 生 Peanuts		芝 麻 Sesames		蔬 菜 Vegetables		瓜 类 Melon	
		播种面积(公顷) Sown Area (hectare)	总产量(吨) Total Output (ton)	播种面积(公顷) Sown Area (hectare)	总产量(吨) Total Output (ton)	播种面积(公顷) Sown Area (hectare)	总产量(吨) Total Output (ton)	播种面积(公顷) Sown Area (hectare)	总产量(吨) Total Output (ton)
全省总计	**Total**	**40403**	**87563**	**2488**	**2025**	**184215**	**3410065**	**24310**	**593795**
海 口 市	Haikou	2827	3871	1746	1463	22594	418903	1042	33840
三 亚 市	Sanya	754	1579	0	0	9578	311542	2616	75413
五指山市	Wuzhishan	253	703	0	0	1802	12180	0	0
文 昌 市	Wenchang	6625	13207	0	0	16288	364620	6028	154427
琼 海 市	Qionghai	1379	2017	0	0	13644	411425	944	32616
万 宁 市	Wanning	1005	2448	0	0	6881	160880	2783	61402
定 安 县	Dingan	2949	5273	113	109.8	6541	115059	516	17940
屯 昌 县	Tunchang	3110	4647	0	0	8451	118547	264	5810
澄 迈 县	Chengmai	1234	2358	349	280	12150	283094	617	15161
临 高 县	Lingao	690	1386	224	113	9453	172802	144	2559
儋 州 市	Danzhou	5523	17336	24	38	15571	330358	369	17311
东 方 市	Dongfang	3407	8274	0	0	11152	177481	2295	63909
乐 东 县	Ledong	4151	10802	0	0	13626	290674	2650	62617
琼 中 县	Qiongzhong	809	1505	0	0	2263	14807	84	375
保 亭 县	Baoting	349	591	0	0	3717	69671	0	0
陵 水 县	Linshui	1348	3123	0	0	10780	163474	3668	93827
白 沙 县	Baisha	235	642	0	0	2799	26574	97	1679
昌 江 县	Changjiang	914	1841	0	0	6823	114013	306	5456
农垦系统	Nongken	2843	5960	34	21	15032	275310	793	10843
洋 浦	Yangpu	0	0	0	0	26	259	0	54

注：瓜菜全省合计数为抽样调查数，分市县数为全面调查数。

a)The sum number in Provices of melon is auording to the result spot Chech.The dispant cities and counties numberis auording to theresult of orerall check.

9－29 瓜菜生产情况
Production of Melons and Vegetables

项 目	Item	播种面积(公顷) Sown Area(hectare)	单产(公斤/公顷) Per Unit Area Yield(kg/hectare)	总产量(吨) Total Output(ton)
蔬菜、瓜菜	Vegetables,Melons	208525	19201	4003860
蔬菜	Vegetables	184215	18511	3410065
瓜类	Melons	24310	24425	593795
分品种瓜菜	Sorts			
椒 类	Chili	34801	25125	874387
苦 瓜	Bitter Gourd	12484	24900	310847
丝 瓜	Towel Gourd	5169	20145	104138
长豆角	Fresh Kidney Beans	12296	24360	299521
四季豆	Kidney Beans	6407	18510	118599
长 茄	Eggplant	7814	25050	195729
冬 瓜	White Gourd	7830	53835	421514
青 瓜	Cucumber	12300	33225	408674
其它蔬菜	Others	85114	7950	676656
西 瓜	Watermelon	18525	27720	513509
甜 瓜	Muskmelon	1420	22260	31617
蜜 瓜	Mi Melon	1180	16950	20003
其它果用瓜	Others	3185	9000	28666

9－30 水果、茶叶面积和产量
Area and Output of Fruit and Tea

年份 市县	Year Cities and Counties	水果 Fruit				茶叶 Tea		
		年末面积（公顷）Area at the Year-end (hectare)	当年新种 Newly Grown Area at This Courrent Year	收获面积 Harvest Area	总产量（吨）Total Output (ton)	年末面积（公顷）Area at the Year-end (hectare)	收获面积 Harvest Area	总产量（吨）Total Output (ton)
1987		43607	9647	15600	147155	71600	4980	5807
1990		36700	2013	18253	152831	7627	6280	7782
1991		34207	3273	16860	138380	7807	6460	6113
1992		36967	5120	19193	153958	7960	6613	6941
1993		49113	13713	21307	194010	7540	6547	6323
1994		65087	17573	27860	282103	7007	6407	5362
1995		81227	19834	33526	360496	5835	5351	3769
1996		89861	16794	36606	361641	6134	5155	3776
1997		100552	16888	40062	398893	5135	3546	3122
1998		106217	18359	42195	566279	4838	4223	3001
1999		130671	29639	53757	759555	3368	2809	2353
2000		139231	38288	64106	1063269	3298	2541	2239
2001		148086	33028	80659	1436354	2954	2263	1945
2002		157430	30868	86887	1390840	2947	2054	1359
2003		159161	26549	89217	1480544	1927	1350	1276
2004		163814	25873	96316	1434490	1895	1454	1338
2005		163401	23397	103660	1525256	1489	1349	950
2006		169743	26557	114543	1878502	1428	1330	1150
海口市	Haikou	19426	2499	9859	174843	0	0	0
三亚市	Sanya	13197	1247	9127	133682	0	0	0
五指山市	Wuzhishan	3854	1	1961	14162	125	88	22
文昌市	Wenchang	5604	1326	3911	81472	0	0	0
琼海市	Qionghai	9010	2732	6015	142683	0	0	0
万宁市	Wanning	5744	1180	3528	79687	0	0	0
定安县	Dingan	3267	412	2087	31241	0	0	0
屯昌县	Tunchang	3223	352	1865	23415	0	0	0
澄迈县	Chengmai	6872	2138	4653	107397	36	36	19
临高县	Lingao	5778	1488	4654	108608	0	0	0
儋州市	Danzhou	4697	811	3099	55781	0	0	0
东方市	Dongfang	14964	3841	10510	191109	0	0	0
乐东县	Ledong	14140	4682	10884	268151	0	0	0
琼中县	Qiongzhong	5321	73	2186	20749	0	0	0
保亭县	Baoting	1957	84	1081	6653	0	0	0
陵水县	Linshui	6038	107	4088	44698	0	0	0
白沙县	Baisha	2305	148	1422	14722	0	0	0
昌江县	Changjiang	8179	536	6641	103171	0	0	0
农垦系统	System of Farm	36168	2901	26971	276279	1267	1206	1109
洋浦	Yangpu	0	0	0	0	0	0	0

9-30 续 1(continued 1)

年份 市县	Year Cities and Counties	菠萝 Pineapple 年末面积(公顷) Area at the Year-end (hectare)	当年新种 Newly Grown	收获面积 Harvest Area	总产量(吨) Total Output (ton)	荔枝 Litchi 年末面积(公顷) Area at the Year-end (hectare)	当年新种 Newly Grown	收获面积 Harvest Area	总产量(吨) Total Output (ton)
1987		20587	6027	7653	76153	3807	127	173	1033
1990		11440	680	8287	77177	4053	40	820	4622
1991		8660	453	6307	58751	4120	147	433	1987
1992		8240	1493	5333	57946	4507	380	1580	4017
1993		8313	1813	4887	54735	5767	1300	613	2941
1994		9867	2180	5307	61405	6887	1080	1440	4397
1995		10825	2348	5980	82288	8570	1775	904	3115
1996		12102	3036	6943	92320	10803	2237	1929	4152
1997		12666	3411	7020	113458	13496	2460	1437	6143
1998		14733	6039	6416	157743	15645	2020	1350	4290
1999		19378	7171	8174	192323	18570	2795	3139	14141
2000		19153	5040	9919	238853	20475	3139	3249	10376
2001		15994	4086	10744	262884	25374	5019	4218	13403
2002		14490	3503	9131	227681	31770	5900	8683	29560
2003		13182	4279	8153	224013	32223	1691	9951	35782
2004		12548	4026	7490	203097	32382	815	14661	62758
2005		11815	4361	7240	202648	31523	542	16664	70337.5
2006		12833	4351	7501	211386	30328	384	19354	88532
海口市	Haikou	1694	416	1017	22680	5037	57	1911	9213
三亚市	Sanya	1	0	1	40	254	16	117	865
五指山市	Wuzhishan	8	0	7	42	555	0	172	453
文昌市	Wenchang	694	338	492	16327	1697	115	1172	9679
琼海市	Qionghai	3358	1660	1809	60117	1804	16	1382	9229
万宁市	Wanning	3785	1096	1848	66516	853	4	802	4799
定安县	Dingan	579	217	271	8672	1282	10	858	5010
屯昌县	Tunchang	475	193	326	9216	1076	76	470	1358
澄迈县	Chengmai	253	20	230	4479	1415	35	1010	4277
临高县	Lingao	0	0	3	52	1125	0	908	3338
儋州市	Danzhou	19	4	16	416	1735	20	1171	8748
东方县	Dongfang	111	0	124	2700	20	0	20	115
乐东县	Ledong	0	0	0	0	223	12	141	1116
琼中县	Qiongzhong	356	4	317	2180	746	0	188	582
保亭县	Baoting	15	0	11	29	577	1	188	711
陵水县	Linshui	72	0	72	1324	1630	0	848	4260
白沙县	Baisha	24	18	18	187	466	0	317	1559
昌江县	Changjiang	367	8	311	6191	26	0	19	64
农垦系统	System of Farm	1023	378	627	10217	9807	23	7659	23155
洋浦	Yangpu	0	0	0	0	0	0	0	0

9-30 续 2(continued 2)

年 份 市 县	Year Cities and Counties	柑桔橙 Citrus and Orange				香 蕉 Banana			
		年末面积 (公顷) Area at the Year-end (hectare)	当年新种 Newly Grown	收获面积 Harvest Area	总产量 (吨) Total Output (ton)	年末面积 (公顷) Area at the Year-end (hectare)	当年新种 Newly Grown	收获面积 Harvest Area	总产量 (吨) Total Output (ton)
1987		2707	340	660	3845	9613	1793	5727	52304
1990		2873	67	1140	4299	7780	573	5273	52188
1991		2567	27	1193	4746	7713	640	5473	55334
1992		2520	73	1580	6654	9133	1807	6067	61751
1993		2573	173	1627	10371	14193	5540	7320	89970
1994		2553	187	1627	10483	17393	4420	10400	156257
1995		2524	123	1547	11002	19141	3792	13013	191089
1996		2503	71	1568	10020	18171	4214	13258	177032
1997		2434	122	1609	9221	18957	4135	14209	188479
1998		2217	81	1452	10921	17343	5148	12082	265466
1999		2110	137	1403	11219	27138	12821	13993	358241
2000		2226	331	1208	13742	32980	22672	20439	600274
2001		2568	364	1232	14866	34142	16885	32994	912569
2002		2573	164	1379	18398	34076	13347	28540	853678
2003		2471	384	1211	14549	30807	13417	26914	841935
2004		3081	604	1387	23861	34919	16499	24130	733341
2005		3673	581	1607	19747.78	37331	15733	28056	913257
2006		3614	127	1820	26640.39	46036	20341	32994	1086296
海口市	Haikou	673	11	411	4851	5833	1859	3778	109418
三亚市	Sanya	1	0	1	4	1855	997	1755	67091
五指山市	Wuzhishan	0	0	0	0	1349	1	970	11484
文昌市	Wenchang	127	6	94	2612	1667	766	1145	34120
琼海市	Qionghai	130	25	97	1185	1495	921	934	29655
万宁市	Wanning	16	0	9	65	354	75	397	4812
定安县	Dingan	142	0	131	1149	411	170	252	7962
屯昌县	Tunchang	104	2	88	653	562	42	364	6031
澄迈县	Chengmai	43	0	24	288	4160	2050	2835	91699
临高县	Lingao	0	0	0	0	3382	1488	2811	87246
儋州市	Danzhou	36	1	5	56	1236	706	681	27720
东方市	Dongfang	0	0	0	0	6790	3755	3265	130252
乐东县	Ledong	0	0	0	0	6490	4580	5426	239514
琼中县	Qiongzhong	1597	36	537	9950	544	25	382	4628
保亭县	Baoting	0	0	0	0	201	48	172	3383
陵水县	Linshui	30	0	30	60	877	0	824	15887
白沙县	Baisha	1	0	1	9	582	124	380	7301
昌江县	Changjiang	0	0	0	0	2276	497	2006	72403
农垦系统	System of Farm	716	45	392	5758	5972	2238	4619	135690
洋浦	Yangpu	0	0	0	0	0	0	0	0

9-30 续 3(continued 3)

年 份 市 县	Year Cities and Counties	龙眼 Longan				芒果 Mango			
		年末面积(公顷) Area at the Year-end (hectare)	当年新种 Newly Grown	收获面积 Harvest Area	总产量(吨) Total Output (ton)	年末面积(公顷) Area at the Year-end (hectare)	当年新种 Newly Grown	收获面积 Harvest Area	总产量(吨) Total Output (ton)
1987		1307	33	87	477	2720	1327	280	1641
1990		1360	13	187	649	5220	467	873	3241
1991		1387	13	213	615	5813	567	1360	4749
1992		1247	33	200	682	7073	1040	2087	6795
1993		1480	200	213	717	11420	3520	3253	10686
1994		2527	1227	273	864	18673	6960	4747	14685
1995		5268	2800	261	695	27075	8397	7081	28626
1996		7634	2619	423	749	30681	3885	7843	35859
1997		8985	1591	280	920	34946	3263	10781	36891
1998		9412	636	365	892	36344	2627	14919	67511
1999		9672	358	1073	2615	38156	2773	18911	100517
2000		9829	1064	1621	3644	36076	2406	19455	101220
2001		9684	807	1025	2708	38907	3220	21050	108604
2002		12530	1864	2690	6407	42146	4241	25920	139898
2003		12451	1377	3045	7162	46726	2977	26559	180730
2004		12876	732	3852	11918	47603	1737	30856	196284
2005		12314	420	4521	15654	47105	785	32682	222685
2006		11795	194	4981	20250	46169	441	35227	262400
海口市	Haikou	1019	4	237	769	170	3	106	1007
三亚市	Sanya	193	35	76	733	9963	172	6594	54193
五指山市	Wuzhishan	894	0	191	512	895	0	511	1037
文昌市	Wenchang	232	6	153	1396	38	1	23	244
琼海市	Qionghai	65	0	27	161	34	0	30	372
万宁市	Wanning	319	5	72	453	138	0	181	681
定安县	Dingan	255	4	83	440	33	0	24	278
屯昌县	Tunchang	128	4	57	189	148	0	87	859
澄迈县	Chengmai	473	0	181	700	80	0	65	732
临高县	Lingao	623	0	382	1597	135	0	98	534
儋州市	Danzhou	350	26	161	1358	783	26	674	12216
东方市	Dongfang	261	0	173	852	7666	0	6592	44615
乐东县	Ledong	869	35	377	1383	6070	52	4579	22412
琼中县	Qiongzhong	1603	0	507	1842	182	0	57	202
保亭县	Baoting	433	16	164	701	325	4	234	1621
陵水县	Linshui	90	0	47	712	2517	107	1609	13421
白沙县	Baisha	689	0	250	845	420	0	336	3378
昌江县	Changjiang	110	0	24	110	4895	0	3844	21706
农垦系统	System of Farm	3190	60	1817	5498	11678	76	9585	82893
洋浦	Yangpu	0	0	0	0	0	0	0	0

9－31 热带作物年末面积
Area of Tropical Crops at the Year-End

单位:公顷 (hectares)

年 份 Year	热带作物总面积 Total Area	橡胶 Rubber	椰子 Coconut	胡椒 Pepper	香茅 Lemongrass	咖啡 Coffee	槟榔 Betel nut	腰果 Cashew nut
1952	25220	18327	5513		87	47	1053	
1957	73347	47367	9800	27	11487	1040	1560	
1962	123307	79533	9733	107	5800	887	1040	1600
1965	167420	102233	13173	813	30180	227	773	473
1970	263300	222580	15207	4467	7560	73	1107	313
1971	259607	220373	14280	4207	8313	100	1113	313
1972	251620	209760	13347	3767	9920	180	1167	347
1973	244520	207400	11860	2433	11927	193	1140	1833
1974	241473	201367	11147	1853	16660	280	1313	3973
1975	246793	202207	10653	1693	17373	300	1580	9327
1976	246160	202620	10413	1813	16753	313	1247	10213
1977	241333	201373	9847	1740	13120	287	987	11047
1978	246367	205153	9793	2433	11480	347	967	12993
1979	256440	213593	10513	3460	10927	393	940	13387
1980	269620	228147	11607	4500	9533	553	1120	11587
1981	287280	245267	13387	5147	9027	1027	987	9913
1982	311673	266573	14547	4800	10180	1280	1193	9733
1983	324967	279393	15147	3800	9100	1300	1867	10607
1984	341000	296427	15780	3660	6053	1280	2640	11427
1985	355593	310207	16667	4587	4047	1660	3313	10713
1986	382273	328980	18433	8080	3540	3940	5893	9207
1987	422727	347287	19553	11733	7640	14080	8180	9447
1988	442120	356873	20453	13040	9800	15853	8740	11640
1989	442880	364093	21047	13133	7753	11593	9647	10427
1990	441533	369320	21127	12607	4993	8393	10113	9773
1991	441580	374187	21693	11587	2780	5307	11100	9673
1992	447293	377107	25333	11107	2033	3920	11840	9800
1993	442520	373187	26593	9967	1460	3007	12460	9613
1994	439165	368251	27464	10234	1647	2373	13160	9625
1995	441603	367945	28761	10763	1742	2114	15214	8789
1996	437851	367198	28549	11176	1365	1365	16556	8327
1997	446670	370544	29268	11991	473	1130	22103	7835
1998	452016	371115	29285	13381	425	999	25955	7479
1999	464828	372653	38201	17524	171	761	26242	6981
2000	472281	369841	44426	22792	95	682	26944	5272
2001	478244	369904	46872	24228	422	559	29855	3720
2002	481403	368855	45727	25374	372	495	35050	3160
2003	499298	379794	44893	25397	325	427	42944	2749
2004	511320	391259	42258	25220	240	371	46747	2280
2005	511470	393011	42875	22971	25	237	47714	1780
2006	526155	402156	43073	22924	19	193	53065	1740

9－32 主要热带作物产品产量
Output of Main Tropical Crops Products

单位：吨 (ton)

年份 Year	橡胶 Rubber	椰子(万个) Coconut (10 000 unit)	胡椒 Pepper	香茅 Lemongrass	咖啡 Coffee	槟榔 Betel nut	腰果 Cashew nut
1952	426	1312		1	9	1185	
1957	750	1649		563	45	905	
1962	5016	2292	38	127	82	2423	3
1965	13969	2497	5	1389	63	1501	3
1970	38037	3117	917	592	6	787	34
1971	40841	1580	328	402	15	724	34
1972	36699	2604	1522	661	8	563	1
1973	37653	1805	801	610	17	827	27
1974	33207	1347	546	789	22	573	67
1975	44989	1770	328	885	13	587	64
1976	55661	1824	297	895	37	495	89
1977	63977	1647	344	726	27	290	145
1978	67719	2065	509	490	32	422	150
1979	71289	2470	837	501	40	488	153
1980	70326	2523	784	491	56	579	179
1981	79445	2896	1274	690	53	773	234
1982	95794	3361	1933	940	105	980	260
1983	107601	3197	1704	1400	105	1185	345
1984	125353	3864	1430	699	118	1567	550
1985	126266	4571	2852	394	180	2150	500
1986	138262	5405	3383	420	350	1880	820
1987	158239	6547	3054	645	430	2378	701
1988	156478	6127	3800	924	642	2382	976
1989	145407	6662	3891	835	849	3028	863
1990	156747	6840	5492	515	777	3860	485
1991	172659	8145	7971	287	797	5539	567
1992	187256	8707	7265	233	839	8371	608
1993	198673	9780	7200	194	735	10995	738
1994	231552	10270	9504	229	602	11938	918
1995	260384	11613	8175	233	581	15673	960
1996	225793	12671	11754	619	619	18749	1224
1997	269991	14768	10084	53	491	22631	1562
1998	280369	16083	14003	53	485	27691	1363
1999	294501	17122	16816	12	371	32065	1545
2000	280880	19166	18093	4	419	35598	1177
2001	279228	21844	21747	19	388	41889	1115
2002	303070	22625	25131	33	420	49753	1036
2003	316041	22959	27889	41	266	55015	1208
2004	329796	24188	32551	544	276	62763	616
2005	247775	24007	31119	70	283	64338	388
2006	247505	21360	31404	9	256	74808	417

9－33 各市县热带作物年末面积
Area of Tropical Crops at the Year-end by City and County

单位:公顷 (hectares)

市 县	Cities and Counties	2003	2004	2005	2006
全省总计	**Total**	**499298**	**511320**	**511470**	**526155**
海口市	Haikou	13377	13237	13408	14463
三亚市	Sanya	9076	9279	8761	8895
五指山市	Wuzhishan	6888	7572	7822	8411
文昌市	Wenchang	27520	27081	25835	26533
琼海市	Qionghai	37723	38955	31910	35631
万宁市	Wanning	14249	14611	14157	14750
定安县	Dingan	9794	11431	12146	12887
屯昌县	Tunchang	13153	13779	12238	13596
澄迈县	Chengmai	7999	8771	10007	11857
临高县	Lingao	5301	6016	6146	7517
儋州市	Danzhou	19239	20003	21722	24174
东方市	Dongfang	3184	3340	3244	3610
乐东县	Ledong	12852	12880	12961	13754
琼中县	Qiongzhong	17835	19622	18616	20272
保亭县	Baoting	8989	9651	9818	10021
陵水县	Linshui	9993	8009	10565	10718
白沙县	Baisha	14748	15502	15137	16219
昌江县	Changjiang	4681	4751	5292	5503
农垦系统	System of Farm	262697	266830	271684	267345

9－34 各市县主要热带作物面积和产量
Area and Output of Main Tropical Crops by City and County

年份 市县	Year Cities and Counties	橡胶 Rubber				椰子 Coconut			
		年末面积（公顷）Area at the Year-end (hectare)	新种面积 Newly Grown Area at This Courrent Year	收获面积 Harvest Area	总产量（吨）Total Output (ton)	年末面积（公顷）Area at the Year-end (hectare)	新种面积 Newly Grown Area at This Courrent Year	收获面积 Harvest Area	总产量（万个）Total Output (1000 unit)
1978		205153		95826	67719	9793			2065
1980		228147		102473	70326	11607			2523
1985		310207	16426	148487	126266	16667	1007	8487	4571
1987		347287	15787	162487	158239	19553	1813	9227	6547
1990		369320	8986	190037	156747	21127	571	11284	6840
1991		374187	8940	201347	172659	21693	987	12106	8145
1992		377107	10080	217727	187256	25333	3186	13656	8707
1993		373187	6617	218099	198673	26593	2263	13602	9780
1994		368251	5087	229025	231552	27464	1610	n	10270
1995		367945	6760	244162	260384	28761	1706	15382	1613
1996		367198	7731	246054	225793	28549	1970	15730	12671
1997		370544	9650	257149	269991	29268	1078	16799	14768
1998		371115	9807	263730	280369	29285	1653	16189	16083
1999		372653	11560	269728	294501	38201	9171	18046	17122
2000		369841	9575	271716	280880	44426	7250	19598	19166
2001		369904	11267	272058	279228	46872	4189	21793	21844
2002		368855	9441	275788	303070	45727	2097	22493	22625
2003		379794	16546	281612	316041	44893	1091	23627	23170
2004		391259	14739	287417	329796	42258	625	23991	24188
2005		393011	16992	292541	247775	42875	275	24896	24007
2006		402156	21395	291414	247505	43073	521	24866	21360
海口市	Haikou	9199	482	6051	6091	2311	2	1190	1260
三亚市	Sanya	3046	214	1968	3558	2968	51	1838	2676
五指山市	Wuzhishan	7066	628	3256	3344	274	0	150	121
文昌市	Wenchang	5261	276	4337	3779	15338	254	9510	5070
琼海市	Qionghai	13789	2509	9661	11049	6253	139	4291	3788
万宁市	Wanning	6662	178	5010	4075	2089	0	1413	709
定安县	Dingan	7431	453	3605	3529	1119	13	591	534
屯昌县	Tunchang	8678	1289	5418	5591	437	7	192	309
澄迈县	Chengmai	10208	1592	5349	6813	323	1	224	194
临高县	Lingao	7302	1262	3122	3265	88	0	19	24
儋州市	Danzhou	23132	2777	12586	14528	732	6	266	358
东方市	Dongfang	1472	271	729	482	533	0	210	322
乐东县	Ledong	9742	1435	7295	4462	1032	3	837	2022
琼中县	Qiongzhong	13885	1262	4937	5459	907	0	268	70
保亭县	Baoting	6541	116	4604	3835	877	31	569	503
陵水县	Linshui	1644	40	666	756	5530	7	1793	2008
白沙县	Baisha	15463	1111	7169	8063	52	1	31	31
昌江县	Changjiang	3014	217	317	418	246	0	144	102
农垦系统	System of Farm	248624	5283	205335	158408	1964	4	1332	1258

9-34 续 1(continued1)

年份 市县	Year Cities and Counties	咖啡 Coffee 年末面积(公顷) Area at the Year-end (hectare)	咖啡 Coffee 新种面积 Newly Grown Area at This Courrent Year	咖啡 Coffee 收获面积 Harvest Area	咖啡 Coffee 总产量(吨) Total Output (ton)	槟榔 Betel nut 年末面积(公顷) Area at the Year-end (hectare)	槟榔 Betel nut 新种面积 Newly Grown Area at This Courrent Year	槟榔 Betel nut 收获面积 Harvest Area	槟榔 Betel nut 总产量(吨) Total Output (ton)
1978		347			32	967			422
1980		553			56	1120			579
1985		1660	533	453	180	3313	620	487	2150
1987		14080	10153	767	430	8180	2833	693	2378
1990		8393	74	1936	777	10113	829	1549	3860
1991		5307	47	1787	797	11100	1193	2113	3539
1992		3920	88	1755	839	11840	1002	3651	8371
1993		3007	39	1367	735	12460	657	4646	15673
1994		2373	9	1071	602	13160	681	5565	11938
1995		2114	21	975	581	15214	1836	7378	15673
1996		1365	10	882	619	16556	2492	7972	18749
1997		1130	22	728	491	22103	5119	9290	22631
1998		999	3	651	485	25955	3772	10888	27691
1999		761	29	508	371	26242	1676	11337	32065
2000		773	53	570	419	26944	1958	12597	35598
2001		559	2	404	388	29855	3316	13924	41889
2002		495	7	348	420	35050	6211	15263	49753
2003		427	2	283	266	42944	8638	16610	55015
2004		371	9	283	276	46747	4286	18545	62763
2005		237	14	198	283	47714	3649	20785	64338
2006		193		165	256	53065	5108	23285	74808
海口市	Haikou	51		49	20	945	56	307	1033
三亚市	Sanya	0		0	0	2882	98	1867	8137
五指山市	Wuzhishan	0		0	0	941	50	253	924
文昌市	Wenchang	59		45	42	826	315	289	1769
琼海市	Qionghai	0		0	0	8830	1314	4377	13970
万宁市	Wanning	40		31	10	4124	433	2650	7078
定安县	Dingan	0		0	0	3452	272	1126	5131
屯昌县	Tunchang	0		0	0	4217	308	2014	4793
澄迈县	Chengmai	26		23	140	884	142	198	762
临高县	Lingao	0		0	0	5	0	1	1
儋州市	Danzhou	0		0	0	264	213	14	19
东方市	Dongfang	0		0	0	10	0	8	49
乐东县	Ledong	0		0	0	2765	137	2081	7654
琼中县	Qiongzhong	0		0	0	5417	413	1056	3345.4
保亭县	Baoting	0		0	0	2603	99	1163	5743.7
陵水县	Linshui	0		0	0	3449	64	1678	4386
白沙县	Baisha	0		0	0	703	50	153	603
昌江县	Changjiang	0		0	0	3	0	2	2
农垦系统	System of Farm	17		17	44	10747	1143	4047	9408

9-34 续 2(continued 2)

年 份 市 县	Year Cities and Counties	胡椒 Pepper				香茅 Lemongrass			
		年末面积(公顷) Area at the Year-end (hectare)	新种面积 Newly Grown Area at This Courrent Year	收获面积 Harvest Area	总产量(吨) Total Output (ton)	年末面积(公顷) Area at the Year-end (hectare)	新种面积 Newly Grown Area at This Courrent Year	收获面积 Harvest Area	总产量(吨) Total Output (ton)
1978		2433			509	11480			490
1980		4500			784	9533			494
1985		4587	1147	2507	2852	4047	820	3513	394
1987		11733	3493	3533	3054	7640	4607	3653	645
1990		12607	291	6576	5492	4993	634	4323	515
1991		11587	267	7753	7911	2780	240	2473	207
1992		11107	230	8147	7265	2033	140	1723	233
1993		9967	195	7637	7200	1460	248	1254	194
1994		10234	447	8074	9504	1647	485	1214	229
1995		10763	808	8132	8175	1742	416	1358	233
1996		11176	932	8227	11754	1365	10	882	619
1997		11991	1437	8377	10084	473	44	457	53
1998		13381	2161	8423	14003	381	55	278	50
1999		17524	4390	9271	16816	171		161	12
2000		22792	5366	10498	18093	95		101	4
2001		24228	2922	11956	21747	422	251	374	18
2002		25374	1399	13568	25131	372	9	359	33
2003		25397	1027	15354	27889	325	37	309	41
2004		25221	724	16806	32551	240	8	240	544
2005		22971	400	17735	31119	25		25	71
2006		22924	473	16747	31404	19		19	9
海口市	Haikou	1958	64	1162	1858				
三亚市	Sanya	0	0	0	0				
五指山市	Wuzhishan	129	0	98	203				
文昌市	Wenchang	5049	37	3577	7252				
琼海市	Qionghai	6741	275	5110	8444.5	19		19	9
万宁市	Wanning	1836	27	1271	2516				
定安县	Dingan	885	13	638	1150.4				
屯昌县	Tunchang	264	0	124	392				
澄迈县	Chengmai	416	0	272	859.6				
临高县	Lingao	123	0	89	117				
儋州市	Danzhou	38	0	36	55				
东方市	Dongfang	0	0	0	0				
乐东县	Ledong	0	0	0	0				
琼中县	Qiongzhong	11	1	7	10.4				
保亭县	Baoting	0	0	0	0				
陵水县	Linshui	0	0	0	0				
白沙县	Baisha	0	0	0	0				
昌江县	Changjiang	0	0	0	0				
农垦系统	System of Farm	5475	54	4364	8546				

9-34 续 3(continued 3)

年份 市县	Year Cities and Counties	腰果 Cashew nut				剑麻 Sisal Hemp			
		年末面积(公顷) Area at the Year-end (hectare)	新种面积 Newly Grown Area at This Courrent Year	收获面积 Harvest Area	总产量(吨) Total Output (ton)	年末面积(公顷) Area at the Year-end (hectare)	新种面积 Newly Grown Area at This Courrent Year	收获面积 Harvest Area	总产量(吨) Total Output (ton)
1978		12993			150				
1980		11587			179				
1985		10713			500				
1987		9447	914	6030	701	955	185	526	1178
1990		9773	113	5275	485	2080	201	807	1248
1991		9673	80	5387	567	2404	538	817	1255
1992		9800	357	5331	608	3326	1544	1158	1557
1993		9613	161	5129	738	3404	545	1182	1626
1994		9625	164	4766	918	3601	116	1247	1588
1995		8789	146	4911	960	3567	37	1683	2225
1996		8327	73	5782	1224	3425	16	1897	2529
1997		7835	116	6035	1562	3296	137	2274	4286
1998		7479	39	6176	1363	3317	84	2315	4019
1999		6981	46	5633	1545	2266	50	1862	2957
2000		5272	31	3178	1177	2215	41	1817	5104
2001		3720	72	2284	1115	2683	176	1802	6102
2002		3160	40	2727	1036	2363	220	1780	6790
2003		2749	114	2518	1208	2760	265	1805	4561
2004		2281	47	2070	616	2942	379	1833	6853
2005		1780		1538	388	2849	80	1675	5640
2006		1740		1622	417	2978	116	1714	6471
海口市	Haikou	0		0	0	0	0	0	0
三亚市	Sanya	0		0	0	0	0	0	0
五指山市	Wuzhishan	0		0	0	0	0	0	0
文昌市	Wenchang	0		0	0	0	0	0	0
琼海市	Qionghai	0		0	0	0	0	0	0
万宁市	Wanning	0		0	0	0	0	0	0
定安县	Dingan	0		0	0	0	0	0	0
屯昌县	Tunchang	0		0	0	0	0	0	0
澄迈县	Chengmai	0		0	0	0	0	0	0
临高县	Lingao	0		0	0	0	0	0	0
儋州市	Danzhou	0		0	0	0	0	0	0
东方市	Dongfang	93		60	132	1503	68	877	4136
乐东县	Ledong	215		165	93	0	0	0	0
琼中县	Qiongzhong	0		0	0	53	0	0	0
保亭县	Baoting	0		0	0	0	0	0	0
陵水县	Linshui	95		95	61	0	0	0	0
白沙县	Baisha	0		0	0	0	0	0	0
昌江县	Changjiang	1334		1301	131	905	33	486	1575
农垦系统	System of Farm	3		0	0	516	14	351	760

9－35 南药面积和产量
Area and Output of South-drugs

年份 市县	Year Cities and Counties	槟榔 Betel Nut		益智 Yizhi		砂仁 Sharen		巴戟 Baji	
		年末面积（公顷）Area at the Year-end (hectare)	总产量（吨）Total Output (ton)	年末面积（公顷）Area at the Year-end (hectare)	总产量（吨）Total Output (ton)	年末面积（公顷）Area at the Year-end (hectare)	总产量（吨）Total Output (ton)	年末面积（公顷）Area at the Year-end (hectare)	总产量（吨）Total Output (ton)
1978		966	422						
1980									
1985									
1987		8180	2378	25147	1371	227	5	27	1
1990		10113	3860	13827	1070	87	23	7	
1991		11100	5539	9093	3791	87	19	33	3
1992		11840	8371	6620	1875	107	33	20	
1993		12460	10995	7893	2221	73	28		
1994		13160	11938	4953	1836	100	36		
1995		15214	15673	2746	4799	100	38		8
1996		16556	18749	2926	1212	106	57		
1997		22103	22631	2450	1517	164	338		
1998		25955	27691	2817	1825	285	204		
1999		26242	32065	3834	2494	270	208		
2000		26944	35598	2855	3805	285	219		
2001		29855	41889	3783	3460	341	304		
2002		35050	49753	3845	4154	240	230	29	35
2003		42944	55015	3034	4713	448	2045		
2004		46747	62763	3559	3801	220	197		
2005		47714	64338	3668	5223	311	246		
2006		53065	74808	2995	2906	223	217		
海口市	Haikou	945	1033	0	0	0	0		
三亚市	Sanya	2882	8137	0	0	0	0		
五指山市	Wuzhishan	941	924	302	669	11	10		
文昌市	Wenchang	826	1769	0	0	0	0		
琼海市	Qionghai	8830	13970	7	8	0	0		
万宁市	Wanning	4124	7078	171	312	0	0		
定安县	Dingan	3452	5131	0	0	0	0		
屯昌县	Tunchang	4217	4793	0	0	0	0		
澄迈县	Chengmai	884	762	0	0	0	0		
临高县	Lingao	5	1	0	0	0	0		
儋州市	Danzhou	264	19	20	131	0	0		
东方市	Dongfang	10	49	0	0	0	0		
乐东县	Ledong	2765	7654	0	0	0	0		
琼中县	Qiongzhong	5417	3345.4	2322	1656	0	0		
保亭县	Baoting	2603	5743.7	30	0	0	0		
陵水县	Linshui	3449	4386	0	0	0	0		
白沙县	Baisha	703	603	72	63	212	207		
昌江县	Changjiang	3	2	0	0	0	0		
农垦系统	System of Farm	10747	9408	73	67	0	0		

9－36 造林面积
Afforestation Area

单位:公顷 (hectares)

项 目	Item	2004	2005	2006
当年造林总面积	Total Afforestation Area of the Current Year	35393	32379	23762
中央丰产林	High Yield Forest			
用材林	Timber Forest	6497	23118	15771
经济林	Economic Forest	5977	3243	1304
防护林	Shelter-forest	22530	5754	6531
薪炭林	Charcoal Forest	296	217	
其它林	Other Forest	93	45	156

9－37 各市县造林面积
Afforestation Area by City and County

单位:公顷 (hectares)

市 县	Cities and Counties	用材林 Timber Forest	经济林 Economic Forest	防护林 Shelter-forest	薪炭林 Charcoal Forest	特种林 Special Use Forest
全省总计	**Total**	**15771**	**1304**	**6531**	**0**	**156**
海 口 市	Haikou	158	116	237		
三 亚 市	Sanya	419		52		
五指山市	Wuzhishan	353	56			
文 昌 市	Wenchang	1342	146	469		26
琼 海 市	Qionghai	165	94			
万 宁 市	Wanning	611	42	150		
定 安 县	Dingan	527	255			24
屯 昌 县	Tunchang	440		266		
澄 迈 县	Chengmai	3	10	1724		
临 高 县	Lingao	270	407	1372		7
儋 州 市	Danzhou	3964		267		99
东 方 县	Dongfang	2325		83		
乐 东 县	Ledong	562		1170		
琼 中 县	Qiongzhong	297		40		
保 亭 县	Baoting	136				
陵 水 县	Linshui	37		139		
白 沙 县	Baisha	689	43	252		
昌 江 县	Changjiang	3055		208		
农垦系统	System of Farm	418	135	102		

9－38 牲畜、家禽饲养头数
Number of livestock and Poultry

单位:万头 (10,000 heads)

年份 市县	Year Cities and Counties	牛年末存栏量 Number of Cattle and Buffaloes in Stock (Year-end)	黄牛 Oxes	水牛 Buffaloes	奶牛 Dairy Cattle	牛年内出栏量 Number of Slaughtered Cattle and Buffaloes of the Current Year	山羊年底存栏量 Goat in stock (Year-end)	山羊年内出栏量 Number of Slaughtered Goat of the Current Year
1978		83.87	35.30	48.35	0.22	2.11	23.94	2.85
1987		91.01	34.90	55.97	0.14	5.89	26.50	9.73
1990		101.17	37.56	63.49	0.12	7.59	31.71	12.25
1991		104.41	38.57	65.73	0.11	7.95	33.81	15.42
1992		110.19	40.40	69.72	0.07	9.92	37.08	19.06
1993		113.99	41.72	72.16	0.11	12.68	43.07	22.74
1994		117.37	42.57	74.73	0.07	13.18	49.04	28.87
1995		121.20	44.15	76.98	0.07	15.65	53.53	33.38
1996		123.60	45.06	78.38	0.16	16.98	57.23	35.62
1997		122.62	45.16	77.40	0.06	15.47	65.98	43.78
1998		127.23	47.09	80.12	0.02	17.08	78.82	53.08
1999		138.36	55.54	82.79	0.03	21.18	91.08	67.70
2000		144.93	57.67	87.21	0.05	22.79	92.48	72.14
2001		150.21	58.77	91.41	0.03	25.82	96.95	83.96
2002		149.46	58.22	91.22	0.02	28.56	94.81	90.15
2003		147.04	57.79	89.21	0.04	30.48	93.86	92.43
2004		147.03	58.32	88.67	0.05	31.88	90.13	95.02
2005		142.99	58.62	84.27	0.10	33.11	88.87	97.62
2006		138.61	57.04	81.50	0.07	34.55	92.95	100.10
海口市	Haikou	10.91	4.40	6.48	0.03	2.55	8.65	14.90
三亚市	Sanya	7.77	1.99	5.78		1.84	4.39	3.47
五指山市	Wuzhishan	2.29	1.06	1.23		0.49	0.10	0.15
文昌市	Wenchang	6.23	2.56	3.67		1.48	3.98	3.94
琼海市	Qionghai	3.30	0.84	2.46		1.54	2.41	3.65
万宁市	Wanning	4.52	1.28	3.24		1.24	2.72	3.32
定安县	Dingan	6.85	2.71	4.14		2.33	2.08	3.22
屯昌县	Tunchang	6.47	0.61	5.86		2.11	2.12	2.39
澄迈县	Chengmai	8.18	3.03	5.12	0.03	2.80	3.10	3.43
临高县	Lingao	8.65	4.84	3.81		1.48	2.98	4.08
儋州市	Danzhou	14.56	7.97	6.59		3.13	19.87	17.90
东方市	Dongfang	11.89	7.47	4.42		2.40	4.53	3.50
乐东县	Ledong	11.72	5.42	6.3		2.99	7.45	8.00
琼中县	Qiongzhong	4.69	0.97	3.72		1.35	0.43	0.47
保亭县	Baoting	2.29	0.25	2.04		0.50	1.21	1.43
陵水县	Linshui	6.03	1.89	4.14		0.69	2.66	2.43
白沙县	Baisha	3.48	0.41	3.07		1.21	0.71	0.71
昌江县	Changjiang	6.41	3.75	2.66		2.46	4.51	5.04
农垦系统	System of Farm	12.37	5.59	6.77	0.01	1.96	19.05	18.07
洋浦	Yangpu							

注:全省数包含洋浦的数据,历年数为经过调整的与农业普查衔接的数据,后同。

a)The datas in the past has been adjusted and Linked up the agricultureal generral check datas.The f lowing is the same

9-38 续(continued)

年 份 市 县	Year Cities and Counties	猪年末存栏量 Fattened Pigs in Stock (Year-end)	能繁殖母猪 Breeding Sow	猪全年饲养量 Number of Pigs Raised This Year	年内出栏肥猪 Number of Slaughtered Fattened Hogs of the Current Year	家禽年内出栏量（万只） Number of Slaughtered Poultry of the Current Year	鸡 Chicken	鸭 Duck	鹅 Goose
1978		203.08	21.61	258.04	54.96	91			
1987		217.73	15.38	325.45	105.54	1011.29	560.7	391.95	58.64
1990		222.99	15.82	343.33	118.11	1421.81	816.82	555.32	49.67
1991		225.55	16.16	353.59	125.78	1632.44	961.03	615.76	55.65
1992		234.91	15.57	380.38	143.12	1887.37	1131.58	694.15	61.64
1993		235.92	17.27	398.80	160.52	2926.78	1972.33	868.88	85.57
1994		232.07	17.67	402.25	167.86	3826.18	2648.53	1065.15	112.50
1995		236.72	20.39	425.97	186.88	4370.72	3012.35	1224.93	133.44
1996		242.44	19.29	440.73	195.87	4443.73	3042.87	1232.11	168.75
1997		236.68	19.61	459.67	220.62	4853.03	3263.08	1347.60	242.35
1998		256.51	19.16	493.77	234.69	5259.95	3559.29	1539.69	160.97
1999		282.64	28.25	543.80	258.33	7406.66	4926.97	2249.61	230.08
2000		306.67	37.98	585.60	278.93	8496.68	5592.17	2601.96	302.55
2001		329.42	31.76	636.99	307.57	9364.93	6026.09	3006.05	332.79
2002		334.27	35.3	674.64	340.37	10112.50	6556.64	3215.34	340.52
2003		327.83	35.52	694.20	366.37	10425.98	6844.08	3249.84	332.06
2004		347.28	37.72	759.87	412.59	11476.09	7766.41	3316.25	393.43
2005		363.92	37.98	807.48	443.56	12939.17	8805.52	3699.78	433.87
2006		373.29	39.13	853.51	480.22	13424.91	9197.72	3794.92	432.27
海 口 市	Haikou	64.55	4.29	155.94	91.39	1060.86	658.43	354.76	47.67
三 亚 市	Sanya	13.89	1.08	40.96	27.07	352.68	183.07	161.94	7.67
五指山市	Wuzhishan	2.73	0.39	6.56	3.83	31.38	22.59	7.02	1.77
文 昌 市	Wenchang	9.99	1.00	27.65	17.66	3932.39	3265.78	628.45	38.15
琼 海 市	Qionghai	13.70	1.13	40.02	26.32	2137.83	1820.64	247.37	69.82
万 宁 市	Wanning	17.19	1.67	46.03	28.84	616.72	196.12	407.14	13.46
定 安 县	Dingan	16.88	2.49	39.63	22.75	599.48	204.33	296.42	98.74
屯 昌 县	Tunchang	16.25	1.86	36.14	19.89	310.07	115.12	186.00	8.95
澄 迈 县	Chengmai	22.16	2.49	47.00	24.84	486.25	111.52	344.15	30.58
临 高 县	Lingao	36.02	4.59	54.11	18.09	423.25	247.21	155.37	20.67
儋 州 市	Danzhou	43.47	4.08	99.03	55.56	1352.35	1023.15	307.30	21.90
东 方 县	Dongfang	24.09	4.44	48.40	24.31	215.68	73.65	139.34	2.69
乐 东 县	Ledong	17.59	2.15	35.73	18.14	238.52	129.84	94.13	14.55
琼 中 县	Qiongzhong	5.05	0.33	12.36	7.31	53.60	33.61	15.89	4.10
保 亭 县	Baoting	4.64	0.98	9.34	4.70	45.48	33.19	11.28	1.01
陵 水 县	Linshui	11.16	0.97	24.94	13.78	129.39	71.22	52.04	6.13
白 沙 县	Baisha	6.21	0.32	16.19	9.98	106.52	72.75	30.92	2.85
昌 江 县	Changjiang	11.41	2.24	26.40	14.99	107.48	84.52	17.40	5.56
农垦系统	System of Farm	35.90	2.63	85.89	49.99	1224.00	850.00	338.00	36.00
洋 浦	Yangpu	0.41		1.19	0.78	0.98	0.98		

9－39 畜产品产量

Output of Livestock Products

单位:吨 (ton)

年份 市县	Year Cities and Counties	肉类总产量 Total output of Meat	猪牛羊肉 Pork, beef and mutton output	猪肉 Pork	牛肉 Beef	羊肉 mutton	禽肉 Meat of Poultry	牛奶产量 Cow Milk Output	禽蛋产量 Poultry eggs output	蜂蜜产量 Honey output
1987		107405	107405	99093	6472	1840	22272		10013	
1990		125381	105377	97829	6322	1226	20004	646	11612	154
1991		140846	115436	106105	7809	1522	25410	692	12186	193
1992		165976	135272	123700	9612	1960	30704	528	13923	247
1993		203012	155196	141203	11526	2467	47816	578	17350	289
1994		218301	155799	140140	12644	3015	62502	454	17573	556
1995		255147	179877	162091	14056	3730	75270	518	22040	433
1996		266576	191937	169191	17107	5639	74639	361	22311	589
1997		293799	206028	185362	16088	4578	87771	205	22188	684
1998		335799	228340	201825	17210	9305	104305	227	24413	311
1999		361440	242320	214235	18303	9782	115180	315	24155	370
2000		397346	264670	234240	20515	9915	128367	320	28704	398
2001		442546	292492	257303	23697	11492	142620	335	31347	654
2002		496846	322711	284608	25690	12413	158486	365	31108	456
2003		525714	345722	306083	27079	12560	164676	604	25912	524
2004		587229	389518	348263	28503	12752	182322	1009	26784	832
2005		640870	421526	378629	29599	13298	204070	1140	26516	718
2006		683104	454812	410432	30525	13855	213448	940	26136	829
海 口 市	Haikou	107783	87059	82544	2312	2203	18468	778	6616	232
三 亚 市	Sanya	26569	21414	19453	1382	579	4726		876	4
五指山市	Wuzhishan	4054	3307	2872	412	23	520		63	21
文 昌 市	Wenchang	77148	17597	15659	1329	609	59355		2527	28
琼 海 市	Qionghai	61882	28035	25995	1505	535	33527	0.5	2042	3
万 宁 市	Wanning	36797	24530	23055	1132	343	12190		1130	1
定 安 县	Dingan	32948	23691	21759	1628	304	9043		1121	39
屯 昌 县	Tunchang	27632	21637	19269	2089	279	5287		1394	56
澄 迈 县	Chengmai	35753	25020	21862	2688	470	9347	103.5	1504	60
临 高 县	Lingao	29688	19822	18001	1328	493	6274		533	5
儋 州 市	Danzhou	70806	48349	42785	2877	2687	20324	58	1869	117
东 方 市	Dongfang	24282	19204	16897	1853	454	4436		1963	
乐 东 县	Ledong	21257	17138	13603	2509	1026	3595		1120	17
琼 中 县	Qiongzhong	9090	7744	6411	1278	55	947		109	49
保 亭 县	Baoting	4957	4087	3433	475	179	734		155	1
陵 水 县	Linshui	11966	9001	8269	487	245	2237		343	
白 沙 县	Baisha	10421	8878	7590	1185	103	1543		44	
昌 江 县	Changjiang	15624	13521	10994	2091	436	1685		582	65
农垦系统	System of Farm	73943	54289	49492	1965	2832	19196		2145	131
洋 浦	Yangpu	504	489	489			14			

9－40 渔业生产情况
Condition on Fishery

年份 Year	水产品总产量(吨) Total Aquatic Products (ton)	海洋捕捞 Catching in Ocean	海水养殖 Seawater Aquatic	淡水捕捞 Catching in Freshwater	淡水养殖 Freshwater Aquatic	水产养殖面积(公顷) Total Cultured Area(hectare)	海水养殖 Seawater Aquatic	淡水养殖 Freshwater Aquatic
1952	30645	30645						
1957	69547	68617			930	2200	173	2027
1962	63282	61872	210	704	496	3800	1127	2673
1965	77986	75606	260	1082	1038	7380	627	6753
1970	75963	73138	130	1141	1554	27580	187	27393
1971	77782	75837	130	589	1226	29593	380	29213
1972	92821	89311	250	669	2591	33787	1047	32740
1973	81099	77899	140	862	2198	38680	540	38140
1974	91341	88071	235	800	2235	36480	753	35727
1975	123956	120311	425	600	2620	35547	1027	34520
1976	123511	119568	345	554	3044	31954	1107	30847
1977	113249	109179	390	500	3180	31067	1420	29647
1978	64070	63671	445	274	2680	27740	987	26753
1979	58259	55042	275	387	2555	29700	833	28867
1980	59073	55696	456	344	2577	27720	680	27040
1981	64451	60384	318	628	3121	30200	800	29400
1982	66396	61527	374	620	3875	31727	1247	30480
1983	75428	69056	575	727	5070	34320	1567	32753
1984	82041	73312	713	966	7050	35553	1840	33713
1985	90008	75806	1795	956	11451	35027	2560	32467
1986	99798	85837	1920	1174	10867	33726	2893	30833
1987	112126	96339	3036	1424	11327	35520	3960	31560
1988	128269	106128	3130	1483	17528	37386	3893	33493
1989	148828	126317	3628	1837	17046	35747	3707	32040
1990	167464	141351	4204	2558	19351	36953	3713	33240
1991	198787	167280	5199	2626	23682	37940	3780	34160
1992	257361	217290	7371	3723	28977	39700	3993	35707
1993	329755	276915	10831	4992	37017	40334	4767	35567
1994	387416	313896	16474	5894	51152	43160	5795	37365
1995	432509	340580	14773	7831	69325	47837	6931	40906
1996	475705	370315	22050	9278	74062	49813	7594	42219
1997	522689	396391	29874	9976	86448	51404	8483	42921
1998	597676	440578	44459	13124	99515	54049	10620	43429
1999	707119	511008	59954	18349	117808	57181	13070	44111
2000	830642	598853	77007	20108	134674	59584	14526	45058
2001	955778	691178	104486	20604	139510	60633	15851	44782
2002	1092951	789122	129499	22566	151764	61865	16434	45431
2003	1230690	895610	149518	22670	162892	62180	16770	45410
2004	1358484	990365	160155	24788	183176	63517	17717	45800
2005	1500129	1079799	190762	24255	205313	64373	18094	46279
2006	1660391	1165104	215246	24727	255314	69987	19164	50823

9－41 各市县水产养殖面积
Breeding Area of Aquatic Products by City and County

单位:公顷 (hectare)

市县	Cities and Counties	海水养殖面积 Area of Seawater Aquatic	鱼类 Fish	#虾蟹类 Shrimps, Prawns and Crabs	贝类 Shellfish	藻类 Seaweed	淡水养殖面积 Area of Freshwater Aquatic
全省总计	**Total**	**19164**	**1665**	**13291**	**1993**	**2108**	**50763**
海口市	Haikou	2038	126	1352	359	201	3612
三亚市	Sanya	1225	7	737	215	235	979
五指山市	Wuzhishan						233
文昌市	Wenchang	2830	367	2237	65	84	7591
琼海市	Qionghai	901	107	525	3	266	3316
万宁市	Wanning	1463	49	1349		65	2866
定安县	Dingan						2333
屯昌县	Tunchang						2050
澄迈县	Chengmai	1077	107	390	163	417	2435
临高县	Lingao	1327	540	425	322	41	1509
儋州市	Danzhou	3894		3231	534	128	12653
东方市	Dongfang	961	13	677	104	167	1526
乐东县	Ledong	882	147	717		18	1665
琼中县	Qiongzhong						608
保亭县	Baoting						635
陵水县	Linshui	1018	115	504	11	388	320
白沙县	Baisha						462
昌江县	Changjiang	394	28	268		98	2237
洋浦	Yangpu	10	10				
农垦系统	System of Farm	1144	48	879	217		3733

9－42 各市县水产品总产量
Gross Output of Aquatic Products by City and County

单位:吨 (ton)

市 县	Cities and Counties	2004	2005	2006
全省总计	Total	1358484	1500129	1660391
海口市	Haikou	50341	54999	59628
三亚市	Sanya	77282	82725	91501
五指山市	Wuzhishan	1728	1749	1807
文昌市	Wenchang	95972	114441	148637
琼海市	Qionghai	73961	81026	90110
万宁市	Wanning	47849	53599	61088
定安县	Dingan	4074	4286	5600
屯昌县	Tunchang	6752	7745	9030
澄迈县	Chengmai	43000	46939	52800
临高县	Lingao	366862	401188	424143
儋州市	Danzhou	314616	348732	382799
东方市	Dongfang	32981	37813	43007
乐东县	Ledong	35306	37502	40006
琼中县	Qiongzhong	2483	2675	2936
保亭县	Baoting	2113	2192	2501
陵水县	Linshui	77974	84639	94200
白沙县	Baisha	3250	3640	4186
昌江县	Changjiang	55083	60018	65308
农垦系统	System of Farm	31137	34395	36051
洋 浦	Yangpu	35720	39826	45053

说明:表中数字差额为省直属企业数据。
a)The margin part is the statistic of the enterprise dire ctly under the province

9-42 续 1(continued 1)

市 县	Cities and Counties	水产品总产量 Total Aquatic Products	按海、淡水分 By sea water and freshwater					
			海水产品 Seawater Aquatic Products	海水捕捞 Seawater Aquatic Products Caught	海水养殖 Seawater Aquatic Products Cultured	淡水产品 Freshwater Aquatic Products	淡水捕捞 Seawater Aquatic Products Cultured	淡水养殖 Freshwater Aquatic Products Cultured
全省总计	Total	1660391	1380350	1165104	215246	280041	24727	255314
海口市	Haikou	59628	41223	26387	14836	18405	1360	17045
三亚市	Sanya	91501	86825	74409	12416	4676	212	4464
五指山市	Wuzhishan	1807				1807	393	1414
文昌市	Wenchang	148637	62570	35780	26790	86067	1203	84864
琼海市	Qionghai	90110	59730	51450	8280	30380	3601	26779
万宁市	Wanning	61088	49890	25578	24312	11198	1248	9950
定安县	Dingan	5600				5600	265	5335
屯昌县	Tunchang	9030				9030	340	8690
澄迈县	Chengmai	52800	42407	32838	9569	10393	1287	9106
临高县	Lingao	424143	419362	389281	30081	4781	1018	3763
儋州市	Danzhou	382799	345699	300343	45356	37100	5946	31154
东方县	Dongfang	43007	37714	29696	8018	5293	56	5237
乐东县	Ledong	40006	30800	22139	8661	9206	2758	6448
琼中县	Qiongzhong	2936				2936	527	2409
保亭县	Baoting	2501				2501	122	2379
陵水县	Linshui	94200	93091	80808	12283	1109		1109
白沙县	Baisha	4186				4186	1047	3139
昌江县	Changjiang	65308	57873	51858	6015	7435	2953	4482
洋浦	Yangpu	45053	45053	44259	794			
农垦系统	System of Farm	36051	8113	278	7835	27938	391	27547

9-41 续 2(continued 2)

市 县	Cities and Counties	按品类分类 By Category						
		鱼类 Fresh	虾蟹类 Shrimps, Prawns and Crabs	海养对虾 Prawn	贝类 Shellfish	藻类 Seaweed	江蓠 Gracilaria Confervoides	其它 Others
全省总计	Total	1272798	205175	123186	19838	30342	10848	132238
海口市	Haikou	36907	8768	6618	1533	6590	20	5830
三亚市	Sanya	74890	10107	7943	929	2086	1895	3489
五指山市	Wuzhishan	1733	7					67
文昌市	Wenchang	118820	22489	19020	614	1070	880	5644
琼海市	Qionghai	62177	7184	6490	210	300	300	20239
万宁市	Wanning	35569	23095	20332		273		2151
定安县	Dingan	5535	55					10
屯昌县	Tunchang	8741	42					247
澄迈县	Chengmai	31009	7365	1967	663	6175		7588
临高县	Lingao	364528	32788	7539	5388	280	110	21159
儋州市	Danzhou	279096	49475	27809	8322	4074	15	41832
东方县	Dongfang	31193	8722	5180	561	1737		794
乐东县	Ledong	20122	16868	7343		129		2887
琼中县	Qiongzhong	2834	21					81
保亭县	Baoting	2493						8
陵水县	Linshui	82090	3968	3401	9	6128	6128	2005
白沙县	Baisha	4075	111					0
昌江县	Changjiang	46039	5987	4248		1500	1500	11782
洋浦	Yangpu	39078	1466					4509
农垦系统	System of Farm	25869	6657	5296	1609			1916

主要统计指标解释

农林牧渔业总产值 指以货币表现的农、林、牧、渔业全部产品的总量,它反映一定时期内农业生产总规模和总成果。农业总产值的计算方法通常是按农林牧渔业产品及其副产品的产量分别乘以各自单位产品价格求得;少数生产周期较长,当年没有产品或产品产量不易统计的,则采用间接方法匡算其产值;然后将四业产品产值相加即为农业总产值。1957 年以前的农业总产值中包括了厩肥和农民自给性手工业(如农民自制衣服、鞋、袜,自己从事粮食初步加工等)。1958 年及以后的农业总产值,林业中增加了村及村以下竹木采伐产值;牧业中取消了厩肥产值;副业中取消了农民自给性手工业产值,增加了村及村以下办的工业产值;渔业中增加了海洋捕捞水产品产值。1980 年及以后的农业总产值,在副业中增加了农民家庭兼营工业商品部分的产值。从 1984 年起村及村以下工业产值划归工业。从 1993 年起取消副业,将野生动物的捕猎划入牧业、野生植物采集和农民家庭兼营商品性工业划归农业。

粮食产量 指全社会的产量。包括国有经济经营的、集体统一经营的和农民家庭经营的粮食产量,还包括工矿企业办的农场和其他生产单位的产量。粮食除包括稻谷、小麦、玉米、高粱、谷子及其他杂粮外,还包括薯类和豆类。其产量计算方法,豆类按去豆荚后的干豆计算;薯类(包括甘薯和马铃薯,不包括芋头和木薯)1963 年以前按每 4 公斤鲜薯折 1 公斤粮食计算,从 1964 年开始改为按 5 公斤鲜薯折 1 公斤粮食计算。城市郊区作为蔬菜的薯类(如马铃薯等)按鲜品计算,并且不作粮食统计。其他粮食一律按脱粒后的原粮计算。

油料产量 指全部油料作物的生产量。包括花生、油菜籽、芝麻、向日葵籽、胡麻籽(亚麻籽)和其他油料。不包括大豆、木本油料和野生油料。花生以带壳干花生计算。

水产品产量 指人工养殖的水产品和天然生长的水产品的捕捞量。包括海水的鱼类、虾蟹类、贝类和藻类以及内陆水域的鱼类、虾蟹类和贝类,不包括淡水生植物。

猪、牛、羊肉产量 指当年出栏并已屠宰、除去头蹄下水后带骨肉(即胴体重)的重量。

期初(末)畜禽存栏头(只)数 指报告期初(末)农村各种合作经济组织和国营农场、农民个人、机关、团体、学校、工矿企业、部队等单位以及城镇居民饲养的大牲畜、猪、羊、家禽等畜禽的存栏数。

耕地面积 指可以用来种植农作物、经常进行耕锄的田地,包括熟地、当年新开荒地、连续撂荒未满三年的耕地和当年的休闲地(轮歇地),还包括以种植农作物为主并附带种植桑树、茶树、果树和其他林木的土地,以及沿海、沿湖地区已围垦利用的"海涂"、"湖田"等面积。不包括属于专业性的桑园、茶园、果园、果木苗圃、林地、芦苇地、天然或人工草地面积。

农作物播种面积 指实际播种或移植有农作物的面积。凡是实际种植有农作物的面积,不论种植在耕地上还是种植在非耕地上,均包括在农作物播种面积中。在播种季节基本结束后,因遭灾而重新改种和补种的农作物面积,也包括在内。

有效灌溉面积 指具有一定的水源,地块比较平整,灌溉工程或设备已经配套,在一般年景下当年能够进行正常灌溉的耕地面积。

农用化肥施用量 指本年内实际用于农业生产的化肥数量,包括氮肥、磷肥、钾肥和复合肥。化肥施用量要求按折纯量计算数量。折纯量是指把氮肥、磷肥、钾肥分别按含氮、含五氧化二磷、含氧化钾的百分之一百成份进行折算后的数量。复合肥按其所含主要成分折算。

农业机械总动力 指主要用于农、林、牧、渔业的各种动力机械的动力总和。包括耕作机械、排灌机械、收获机械、农用运输机械、植物保护机械、牧业机械、林业机械、渔业机械和其他农业机械〔内燃机按引擎马力折成瓦(特)计算、电动机按功率折成瓦(特)计算〕。不包括专门用于乡、镇、村、组办工业、基本建设、非农业运输、科学试验和教学等非农业生产方面用的动力机械与作业机械。

农林牧渔业劳动力 指全社会直接参加农林牧渔业生产活动的劳动力。

Explanatory Note on Main Statistical Indicators

Gross Output Value of Farming, Forestry, Animal Husbandry and Fishery refers to the total value of products of farming, forestry, animal husbandry and fishery, which reflects the total scale and result of agricultural production during a given period. Gross output value of agriculture is obtained by first multiplying the output of each product or by product by its price, resulting in the output value of each single item. For a small number of products, annual output of which is not available or difficult to get due to the long production growing process involved, the output value is estimated through an indirect approach. The sum of output value of all products of farming, forestry, animal husbandry, and fishery is then equal to the gross output value of agriculture. Prior to 1957, Chinas gross agricultural output value included barnyard manure and handicraft products for self consumption (clothes, shoes, stockings, and initial grain processing undertaken by peasants). Since 1958, cutting and felling of bamboo and trees by villages and other cooperative organizations under villages have been included in forestry; value of barnyard manure has been excluded from animal husbandry; self consumed handicrafts has been excluded from sideline occupations, while the output value of industries run by villages and cooperative organizations under village had been included in sideline occupations and the output value of fish catches by motor fishing boats has been added to fishery. Since 1980, the value of handicraft products made for sale by individuals in households had been added to sideline occupations. Since 1984, industries run by villages and under villages have been included in the sector of industry. Since 1993, the subdivision of sideline occupations has been canceled, and the hunting of wild animals has been classified into animal husbandry, and the gathering of wild plants and commodity industry run by rural household have been included in farming. The first agriculture census of China in 1996 revealed some discrepancy between the production of animal products from the annual reports and that from the census. Efforts were made by the Rural Socio-economic Survey Organization of NBS to adjust the output value of animal husbandry to make the figures from the annual reports consistent with the census data.

Grain Output refers to the grain production in the whole country including grains produced by state farms, collective units, industrial enterprises and mines. Grain includes rice, wheat, corn, sorghum, millet and other miscellaneous grains as well as tubers and beans. Output of beans refers to dry beans without pods. The output of tubers (sweet potatoes and potatoes, not including taros and cassava) was converted into that of grain at the ratio 4:1, i.e. 4 kilograms of fresh tubers was equivalent to 1 kilogram of grain up to 1963. Since 1964 the ratio for conversion has been 5:1. Tubers supplied as vegetables (such as potatoes) in cities and suburbs are calculated as fresh vegetables and their output is not included in the output of grain. Output of all other grains refers to husked grain.

Cotton Output refers to the cotton production in the whole country including cotton sown in spring and in autumn. Output is measured as the weight of ginned cotton.

Output of Oil-bearing Crops refers to the total production of oil bearing crops of various kinds, including peanuts, (dry, in shell) rapeseeds, sesame, sunflower seeds, flax seeds, and other oil bearing crops. Soybeans, oil-bearing woody plants, and wild oil-bearing crops are not included.

Output of Aquatic Products refers to catches of both artificially cultured and naturally grown aquatic products, including fish, shrimps, crabs and shellfish in sea and inland water as well as seaweed. Freshwater plants are not included.

Output of Pork, Beef, and Mutton refers to the meat of slaughtered hogs, cattle, sheep and goats with head, feet, and offal taken away.

Number of Livestock or Poultry in Stock at Beginning (or End) refers to the total number of large animals, pigs, sheep, fowls, etc. raised by rural cooperative organizations, state farms, rural individuals, government agencies, schools, industrial and mining enterprises, army, and urban residents at the beginning (or end) of the reference period.

Cultivated Area (Area under Cultivated) refers to farmland which is plowed constantly for growing crops, including cultivated land, newly cultivated land in the current year, farmland left without cultivation for less than three years and fallow land in the current year, rotation land of grass and crops, farmland with some fruit trees, mulberry trees and other trees and cultivated seashore land, lake land and etc. the land of mulberry fields, tea plantations, orchards, nurseries of young plants, forestland, reed land, natural and man-made grassland and other land are not included in cultivated land.

Sown Area of Crops refers to area of land sown or transplanted with crops regardless of being in cultivated area or non cultivated area. Area of land re-sown due to natural disasters is also included.

Irrigated Area refers to areas that are effectively irrigated, i.e. level land which has water source and complete sets of irrigation facilities to lift and move adequate water for irrigation purpose under normal conditions. Under normal conditions, irrigated area is the sum of watered fields and irrigated fields where irrigation systems or equipment have been installed for regular irrigation purpose.

Consumption of Chemical Fertilizers in Agriculture refers to the quantity of chemical fertilizers applied in agriculture in the year, including nitrogenous fertilizer, phosphate fertilizer, potash fertilizer, and compound fertilizer. The consumption of chemical fertilizers is required in calculation to convert the gross weight into weight containing 100% effective component (e.g. 100% nitrogen content in nitrogenous fertilizer, 100% phosphorous pentoxide contents in phosphate fertilizer, 100% potassium oxide contents in potash fertilizer). Compound fertilizer is converted with its major component.

Total Power of Farm Machinery refers to total mechanical power of machinery used in farming, forestry, animal husbandry, and fishery, including ploughing, irrigation and drainage, harvesting, transport, plant protection, stock breeding, forestry and fishery. The power of internal combustion engines is required to convert horsepower into watts and the power of electric motors is required to be converted into watts. Machinery employed for non agricultural purposes, such as the machines used in township run and village-run industry, construction, non agricultural transport, scientific experiments and teaching, is excluded.

Labour Force Engaged in Farming, Forestry, Animal Husbandry and Fishery refers to the total laborers who are directly engaged in production of farming, forestry, animal husbandry and fishery.

资料整理: 吴声波 林明学
Arranged by Wushengbo Linmingxue

10. 工 业
INDUSTRY

工业总产值（亿元）（规模以上工业）

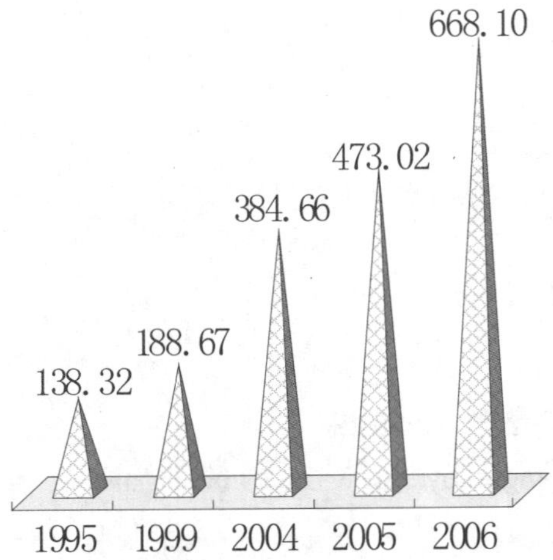

铁矿石（万吨）

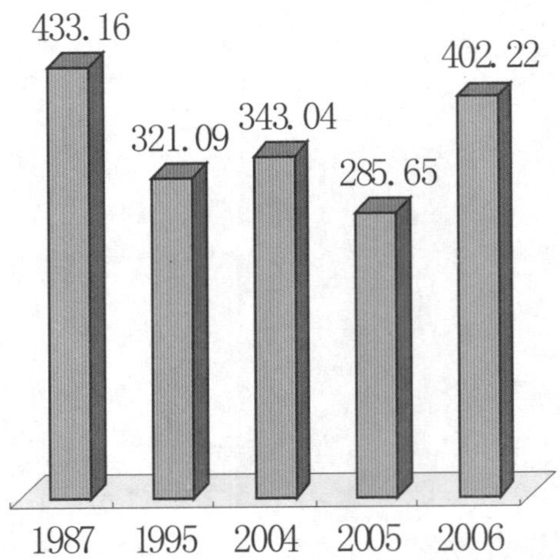

汽车（辆）

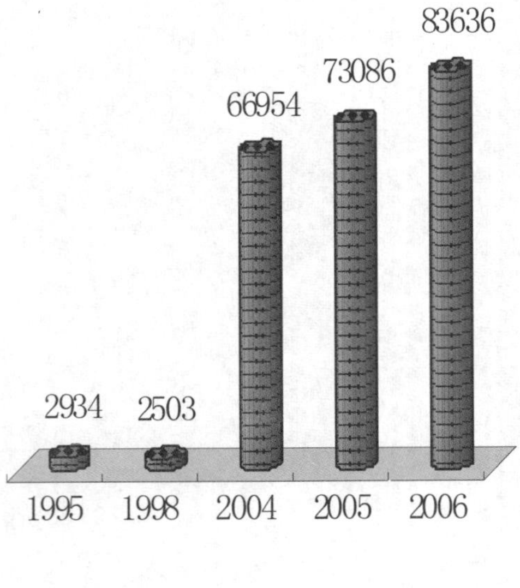

化肥（万吨）

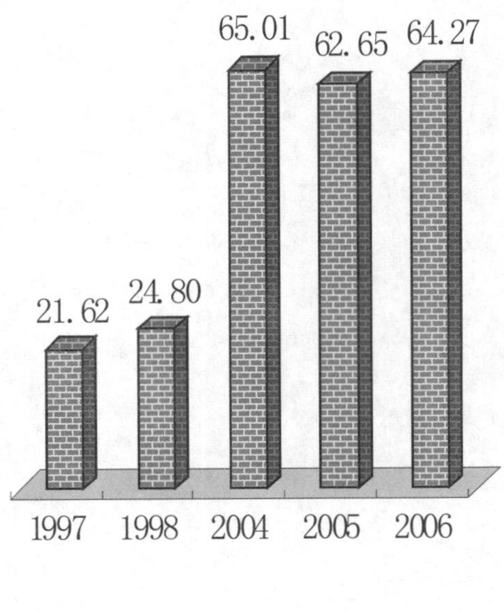

10－1 全部工业企业单位数
Number of All Industrial Enterprises

单位:个 (unit)

年份 地区	Year Region	总计 Total	按规模分 Grouped by Designed Size Industry 规模以上工业 Above Designed Size Industry	规模以下工业 Below Designed Size Industry
按年份分				
1991		14431	1572	12859
1992		13858	1634	12224
1993		18745	1810	16935
1994		20851	1803	19048
1995		17880	1895	15985
1996		20323	1793	18530
1997		15718	1805	13913
1998		19888	640	19248
1999		21109	579	20530
2000		20771	597	20174
2001		21365	589	20776
2002		21408	601	20807
2003		21427	620	20807
2004		19202	596	18606
2005		19252	646	18606
2006		19236	630	18606
海口市	Haikou	3675	221	3454
三亚市	SanYa	703	24	679
五指山市	WuZhiShan	132	12	120
文昌市	WenChang	1745	44	1701
琼海市	QionHai	1098	19	1079
万宁市	WanNing	2063	36	2027
定安县	DingAn	561	19	542
屯昌县	TunChan	813	14	799
澄迈县	ChengMai	890	40	850
临高县	LinGao	1214	13	1201
儋州市	DanZhou	2271	31	2240
东方市	DongFang	978	11	967
乐东县	LeDong	912	11	901
琼中县	QiongZhong	88	11	77
保亭县	BaoTing	360	7	353
陵水县	LingShui	192	8	184
白沙县	BaiSha	363	10	353
昌江县	ChangJiang	396	27	369
农垦	Land Reclamation and Cultivation System	633	48	585
洋浦	YangPu Develop District	149	24	125

注:“规模以上”与“规模以下”工业之分:全部国有及年销售收入500万元以上(包括500万元)非国有工业企业列入规模以上工业统计,其余列入规模以下(含个体)工业统计。从1998年起执行,下同。本表中的“规模以上工业”,1997年以前为乡及乡以上企业,“规模以下工业”,1997年以前为农村村办、城乡合作及个体工业。

a)Above designed size industry refer to all state-owned industrial enterprises and the non-state-owned industrial with an annual sales income of over 5 million yuan.Other is below designed size industry. (the same below)

10－2 各市、县规模以上工业企业单位数

Number of Above Designed Size Industrial Enterprises by City and County

单位:个 (unit)

年份 地区	Year Region	总计 Total	大中型企业 Large& Medical -sized Industrial Enterprises	国有控股企业 State-holding Enterprises	按轻重工业分 Grouped by Light & Heavy Industry 轻工业 Light Industry	重工业 Heavy Industry	按企业经济组织类型分 Grouped by Economic Organizational Category 国有企业 State-owned Industry	集体企业 Collective -owned Industry	股份合作企业 Cooperative Enterprises	股份制企业 Share Holding Enterprises	外商及港澳台投资 Enterprises with Funds from Hong Kong,Macao and Taiwan	其他经济 Other Enterprises
1998		640	124	486	341	299	409	29	8	53	101	40
1999		579	120	428	316	263	343	25	10	64	92	45
2000		597	118	402	319	278	320	24	11	80	98	64
2001		589	129	372	325	264	295	23	8	110	94	59
2002		601	129	354	347	254	275	25	9	135	94	63
2003		620	56	346	323	297	270	22	7	160	97	64
2004		596	71	255	310	286	196	9	1	257	90	43
2005		646	73	299	333	313	230	16	7	224	102	67
2006		630	67	272	322	308	209	11	2	237	107	64
海口市	Haikou	221	28	85	140	81	52	0	0	96	61	12
三亚市	SanYa	24	3	8	13	11	4	0	0	12	4	4
五指山市	WuZhiShan	12	1	9	4	8	9	0	0	3	0	0
文昌市	WenChang	44	0	11	19	25	8	2	0	12	10	12
琼海市	QionHai	19	2	8	11	8	6	0	0	5	4	4
万宁市	WanNing	36	0	16	14	22	15	0	0	5	2	14
定安县	DingAn	19	1	7	13	6	7	0	0	8	4	0
屯昌县	TunChan	14	1	12	5	9	12	1	0	1	0	0
澄迈县	ChengMai	40	3	9	20	20	4	0	0	27	5	4
临高县	LinGao	13	1	5	5	8	5	2	0	5	1	0
儋州市	DanZhou	31	5	7	14	17	7	2	0	17	2	3
东方市	DongFang	11	3	8	3	8	5	0	0	3	1	2
乐东县	LeDong	11	1	10	4	7	9	0	0	2	0	0
琼中县	QiongZhong	11	0	8	6	5	8	0	0	0	1	2
保亭县	BaoTing	7	0	6	3	4	6	0	0	1	0	0
陵水县	LingShui	8	1	7	4	4	7	1	0	0	0	0
白沙县	BaiSha	10	2	7	5	5	7	0	0	3	0	0
昌江县	ChangJiang	27	5	12	5	22	7	3	1	16	0	0
农垦	Land Reclamation and Cultivation System	48	8	33	21	27	29			8	7	4
洋浦	YangPu Develop District	24	2	4	13	11	2		1	13	5	3

工业 INDUSTRY

10－3 全部工业总产值
All Industrial Enterprises Gross Output Value

单位:万元 (当年价)Current Prices (10 000 yuan)

年 份 Year	工业总产值 Gross Industrial Output Value	按经济类型分 Grouped by Economic Category		
		国有经济 State-owned Economy	集体经济 Collective-owned Economy	其他类型经济 Other Economy
1985	165067	136119	15150	13798
1986	177186	144820	16484	15882
1987	215463	163565	15891	36007
1988	312461	233559	19691	59211
1989	389642	288862	22553	78227
1990	443189	335585	21988	85616
1991	566876	402864	29714	134298
1992	762529	541931	38982	181616
1993	1282709	742095	64200	476414
1994	1647525	824301	102043	721181
1995	1978805	787572	85438	1105795
(按新规定计算) Bynew state calculation metholld				
1995	1768092	705211	78046	984835
1996	2159908	712517	103498	1343893
1997	2310449	814768	115079	1380602
1998	2485801	612844	131102	1741855
1999	2547041	541609	45742	1959690
2000	2656097	622347	38539	1995211
2001	2831193	715401	47319	2068473
2002	3320361	959553	53430	2307378
2003	3997050	1340071	47916	2609063
2004	4778935	566076	22440	4190419
2005	5485227	836570	25178	4623479
2006	7437765	858700	18348	6560717

注:从 2004 年开始工业生产速度采用工业生产指数紧缩法计算,表中 04 及 05 年的工业总产值已经紧缩为可比价格。2004 年数据重新采用经济普查数。

Note: The increase rate of Industrial Production is calculated on the method of Reduced Industrial Production Index, the Gross Industrial Output Value in 2004 and 2005 in this table have already reduced to comparable prices. However, data in 2004 are reus

10－4 全部工业总产值构成

The Constitute of All Industrial Enterprises Gross Output Value

单位：%

年 份 Year	工业总产值 Gross Industrial Output Value	按经济类型分 Grouped by Economic Category		
		国有经济 State-owned Economy	集体经济 Collective-owned Economy	其他类型经济 Other Economy
1952	100	19		81.0
1957	100	76.5	23.1	0.4
1962	100	77	22.6	0.4
1965	100	83.8	16.2	0
1970	100	84	16	0
1975	100	84.1	15.9	0
1978	100	82.6	17.4	0
1980	100	82.3	17.7	0
1981	100	83	16.9	0.1
1985	100	80.1	10.4	9.4
1987	100	71.1	7.6	21.2
1988	100	71.4	7	21.5
1989	100	67.3	7.2	25.5
1990	100	75.2	5.1	19.7
1991	100	70.4	5.3	24.2
1992	100	69.8	5.2	25.0
1993	100	54.8	5.4	39.8
1994	100	46.2	7	46.9
1995	100	35	5	60.0
1996	100	29.9	5	65.1
1997	100	33.7	4.6	61.7
1998	100	23.7	5.5	70.8
1999	100	21.8	4.2	74.1
2000	100	20.9	3	76.2
2001	100	22.4	2.8	74.8
2002	100	26.0	2.7	71.3
2003	100	33.0	2.1	64.9
2004	100	12.3	0.5	87.2
2005	100	15.6	0.8	83.6
2006	100	11.5	0.02	88.5

注：本表按可比价格计算。
a)The tabel is calculated at constant prices.

10－5 全部工业总产值指数
The Index of All Industrial Enterprises Gross Output Value

单位:%　　（以上年为100）　　(%)

年份 Year	工业总产值 Gross Industrial Output Value	按经济类型分 Grouped by Economic Category		
		国有经济 State-owned Economy	集体经济 Collective-owned Economy	其他类型经济 Other Economy
1952	124.4			
1957	110.4	109.5	119.1	
1962	79.2	77.6	85.2	
1965	109.9	107.7	129.6	
1970	116.7	116.5	117.6	
1975	118.1	117.3	122.8	
1980	93.0	91.8	99.1	
1981	97.6	98.2	94.5	
1985	131.2	119.6	116.7	3383.3
1987	124.2	111.7	88.9	258.2
1988	125.1	125.7	115.2	126.7
1989	104.9	98.8	107.0	124.2
1990	114.5	116.4	97.6	114.2
1991	122.5	114.7	127.6	150.8
1992	134.2	138.3	130.9	138.5
1993	143.2	112.4	149.3	227.7
1994	113.7	95.8	146.9	133.9
1995	114.9	87.0	80.5	147.6
1996	116.8	99.6	116.7	126.8
1997	110.6	124.8	102.1	104.7
1998	108.8	76.5	131.1	124.8
1999	107.7	98.9	81.3	112.7
2000	106.1	101.8	75.2	109.1
2001	110.9	119.3	104.3	108.9
2002	119.7	138.8	114.7	114.1
2003	118.1	149.4	94.5	107.5
2004	114.8	42.9	26.3	154.2
2005	120.1	151.8	187.1	115.3
2006	134.5	101.8	72.3	140.8

注:本表按可比价格计算
a)The tabel is calculated at negotiable prices.

10－6 按各种分组的规模以上工业产销情况

Proportion of Products Sold above Designated Size Industrial Enterprises

单位:万元 (10000 yuan)

类 别	Item	企业单位数(个) Number of Enterprises	工业总产值(当年价格) Gross Industrial Output Value (At Constant Prices)	新产品产值 New Products Value	工业销售产值(当年价格) Sales Revenue (At Current Prices)	出口交货值 Delivery Value of Industry	产品销售率(%) Proportion of Products Sold
总　计	Total	633	6680960	39229	6468361	460515	96.8
按经济类型分:	Grouped by Economic Category						
国有企业	State-owned Industy	209	858700	496	837644	20325	97.5
中央企业	Gentral	5	15024		14852		98.9
集体企业	Collective-owned Industry	11	18348		16476		89.8
股份合作企业	Cooperative Enterprises	2	2785		2785		100
股份制企业	Share Holding Enterprises	239	3117524	19207	3008192	126694	96.5
外商及港澳台投资企业	Enterprises with Funds from Hong Kong ,Macao and Taiwan	108	2460789	19526	2387925	299155	97
其他经济类型企业	Other Economy	64	222814	0	215340	14341	96.6
按轻重工业分:	Grouped by Light & Heavy Industry						
在总计中:轻工业	Of the Total:Light Industry	322	2251482	17825	2196269	268264	97.5
重工业	Heavy Industry	311	4429478	21404	4272092	192251	96.4
按企业规模分:	Grouped by Size of Enterprises						
大型企业	Large-sized	4	2219479		2124682	108377	95.7
中型企业	Medium-sized	63	1618697	17437	1604729	141639	99.1
小型企业	Small-sized	566	2842784	21792	2738950	210499	96.3
在总计中: 国有控股企业	Of the Total:State-owned and State-holding Enterprises	273	3020725	14354	2940415	32278	97.3
按行业分	By Sector						
石油和天然气开采业	Petroleum and Natural Gas Extraction	2	329453		329268		99.9
天然原油和天然气开采	Production of Petroleum and Natural Gas	2	329453		329268		99.9
黑色金属矿采选业	Ferrous Metals Mining and Dressing	10	138644		133242		96.1
铁矿采选业	Iron Ore Mining and Dressing	10	138644		133242		96.1
有色金属矿采选业	Nonferrous Metals Mining and Dressing	19	47782		47461		99.3
常用有色金属矿采选	General Nonferrous Metals Mining and Dressing	15	29601		29347		99.1
其他常用有色金属矿采选	Other General Nonferrous Metals Mining and Dressing	15	29601		29347		99.1
贵金属矿采选	Precious Metals Mining and Dressing	1	1305		1305		100.0
金矿采选	Gold Mining and Dressing	1	1305		1305		100.0
稀有稀土金属矿采选	Rare Earth Metal Mining and Dressing	3	16876		16809		99.6
其他稀有金属矿采选	Other Rare Earth Metal Mining and Dressing	3	16876		16809		99.6
非金属矿采选业	Nonmetal Mining and Dressing	9	20614		18039	778	87.5
采盐业	Salt Mining	4	6203		4185	333	67.5
石棉及其他非金属矿采选	Asbestos and Other Nonmetal Mining and Dressing	5	14411		13853	445	96.1
其他非金属矿采选	Other Nonmetal Mining and Dressing	4	13341		12784		95.8
农副食品加工业	Processing of Farm Products and Non-staple Foodstuffs	79	493481	344	464927	162991	94.2
谷物磨制	Grain Milling	2	2466		1962		79.6
饲料加工	Feed Processing	9	160772		154599		96.2
制糖业	Sugar Production	19	77285		74246		96.1
屠宰及肉类加工	Slaughtering and Meats Processing	1	68		68		100.0
畜禽屠宰	Stock and Poultry Slaughtering	1	68		68		100.0

10-6 续 1(continued1)

类 别	Item	企业单位数(个) Number of Enterprises	工业总产值(当年价格) Gross Industrial Output Value (At Constant Prices)	新产品产值 New Products Value	工业销售产值(当年价格) Sales Revenue (At Current Prices)	出口交货值 Delivery Value of Industry	产品销售率(%) Proportion of Products Sold
水产品加工	Aquatic Products Processing	37	240048	237	223489	161839	93.1
水产品冷冻加工	Freezing and Processing of Aquatic Products	26	206763		192444	161602	93.1
鱼糜制品及水产品干腌制加工	Production of Dried Preservation and Processing of Fish Products and Aquatic Products	1	2458		2315		94.2
水产饲料制造	Production of Aquatic Feeds	3	21259	237	20972		98.6
鱼油提取及制品的制造	Extraction of Fish Oil and Production of Fish Oil Products	2	1232		1220		99.0
其他水产品加工	Processing of Other Aquatic Products	5	8337		6539	237	78.4
蔬菜、水果和坚果加工	Processing of Vegetables, Fruits and Nut fruits	3	2614		2104	1152	80.5
其他农副食品加工	Processing of Other Farms Products and Non-staple Foodstuffs	8	10230	108	8458		82.7
淀粉及淀粉制品的制造	Production of Starches and Starch Products	7	9609	108	7815		81.3
食品制造业	Food Production Industry	24	146717	118	164202	2328	111.9
焙烤食品制造	Production of Baked Foods	2	1291		1218		94.4
糕点、面包制造	Production of Cakes and Breads	1	807		739		91.5
饼干及其他焙烤食品制造	Production of Biscuits and Other Baked Foods	1	484		480		99.1
糖果、巧克力及蜜饯制造	Production of Candies, Chocolates and Preserved Fruits	4	4186		4009		95.8
糖果、巧克力制造	Production of Candies and Chocolates	3	3443		3281		95.3
方便食品制造	Production of Instant Foods	2	6235		6235		100.0
方便面及其他方便食品制造	Production of Instant Noodles and Other Instant foods	2	6235		6235		100.0
液体乳及乳制品制造	Production of Liquid Milk and Milk Products	3	3308		3227		97.6
罐头制造	Production of Canned Food	1	95079	118	89317		93.9
蔬菜、水果罐头制造	Production of Canned Vegetables and Fruits	1	95079	118	89317		93.9
其他食品制造	Production of Other Foods	12	36618		60197	2328	164.4
营养、保健食品制造	Production of Nutrition and Health Foods	4	26177		49384		188.7
冷冻饮品及食用冰制造	Production of Frozen Drinks and Edible Ice	2	548		549		100.1
盐加工	Salt Processing	1	1619		1619		100.0
食品及饲料添加剂制造	Production of Food and Feed Additives	1	2719		2789		102.6
其他未列明的食品制造	Production of Other Unlisted Foods	4	5555		5857	2328	105.4
饮料制造业	Beverage Production Industry	23	242623	257	238430	3132	98.3
酒精制造	Alcohol Production	1	905		905		100.0
酒的制造	Wine Production	4	159430		156469	1135	98.1
白酒制造	Production of White Wine	1	14935		14313		95.8
啤酒制造	Production of Beer	1	50111		50086	1135	99.9
其他酒制造	Production of Other Wines	2	94384		92071		97.5
软饮料制造	Production of Soft Beverage	12	76861	257	76022	1997	98.9
碳酸饮料制造	Production of Carbonate Beverage	1	18670		17995		96.4
瓶(罐)装饮用水制造	Production of Bottled (Canned) Drinking Water	3	16758		16673		99.5
果菜汁及果菜汁饮料制造	Production of Fruit/Vegetable Juices and Fruit/Vegetable Juice Beverages	4	29650	257	29361	1997	99.0
固体饮料制造	Production of Solid Beverages	3	4064		4073		100.2
茶饮料及其他软饮料制造	Production of Tea Beverages and Other Soft Beverages	1	7718		7920		102.6
精制茶加工	Fine Tea Processing	6	5428		5035	161	92.7
烟草制品业	Tobacco Product Industry	1	71392		69041		96.7

10-6 续 2(comtinued2)

类 别	Item	企业单位数(个) Number of Enterprises	工业总产值(当年价格) Gross Industrial Output Value (At Constant Prices)	新产品产值 New Products Value	工业销售产值(当年价格) Sales Revenue (At Current Prices)	出口交货值 Delivery Value of Industry	产品销售率(%) Proportion of Products Sold
卷烟制造	Tobacco Processing Industry	1	71392		69041	161	96.7
纺织业	Textile Industry	9	100780		98694	51520	97.9
棉、化纤纺织及印染精加工	Spinning, Weaving, Printing, Dyeing and Fine Processing of Cotton and Chemical Fiber						0.0
棉、化纤印染精加工	Printing Dyeing and Fine Processing of Cotton and Chemical Fiber						0.0
麻纺织	Hemp Spinning and Weaving	1	905		1209		133.7
丝绢纺织及精加工	Spinning, Weaving and Fine Processing of Tiffany	1	2009		2079		103.5
绢纺和丝织加工	Spinning and Weaving of Silk	1	2009		2079		103.5
纺织制成品制造	Production of Silk Products	2	32721		30155	12152	92.2
毛制品制造	Production of Wool Products	1	8176		8042	7722	98.4
无纺布制造	Production of Non-woven Fabric	1	24545		22113	4430	90.1
针织品、编织品及其制品制造	Production of Knitting and Weaving Products	5	65145		65250	39368	100.2
棉、化纤针织品及编织品制造	Knitting Products and Weaving Products of Cotton and Chemical Fabric	3	63130		63268	39368	100.2
毛针织品及编织品制造	Wool Knitting and Weaving Products	2	2015		1982		98.4
纺织服装、鞋、帽制造业	Manufacturing of Garments, Shoes and Hats	2	41		12		29.8
纺织服装制造	Manufacturing of Garments	2	41		12		29.8
皮革、毛皮、羽毛(绒)及其制品业	Manufacturing of Leather, Furs, Down and their Products	3	2195		1993		90.8
皮革制品制造	Manufacturing of Leather Products	1	1823		1676		91.9
皮箱、包(袋)制造	Manufacturing of Leather Suitcases and Bags	1	1823		1676		91.9
皮手套及皮装饰制品制造	Manufacturing of Leather Gloves and Leather Decoration Products						0.0
其他皮革制品制造	Manufacturing of Other Leather Products						0.0
羽毛(绒)加工及制品制造	Furs, Down and Related Products	2	372		318		85.4
羽毛(绒)加工	Furs and Down Processing	2	372		318		85.4
木材加工及木、竹、藤、棕、草制	Timber Processing, Bamboo, Cane, Palm Fiber and Straw Products	31	61475		64339	4009	104.7
锯材、木片加工	Saw Timber and Wood Chip Processing	19	30846		33511		108.6
锯材加工	Saw Timber Processing	8	4045		4102		101.4
木片加工	Wood Chip Processing	11	26801		29409		109.7
人造板制造	Artificial Board Manufacturing Industry	6	21139		21479		101.6
胶合板制造	Manufacturing of Glued Boards	3	4223		5078		120.3
纤维板制造	Manufacturing of Fiber Board	2	15920		15492		97.3
木制品制造	Manufacturing of Wood Products	6	9490		9350		98.5
软木制品及其他木制品制造	Manufacturing of Soft Wood Products and Other Wood Products	6	9490		9350		98.5
家具制造业	Furniture Manufacturing Industry	14	47360		45108		95.2
木质家具制造	Wooden Furniture Manufacturing Industry	13	47360		45108		95.2
其他家具制造	Manufacturing of Other Furniture	1					0.0
造纸及纸制品业	Papermaking and Paper Products	16	528512		528012		99.9
纸浆制造	Paper Pulp Manufacturing	1	508993		508993		100.0
造纸	Papermaking	4	6728		6342		94.3
机制纸及纸板制造	Manufacturing of Machine-made Paper and Paper Boards	4	6728		6342		94.3
纸制品制造	Manufacturing of Paper Products	11	12791		12676		99.1
纸和纸板容器的制造	Manufacturing of Paper and Paper Containers	9	10741		10598		98.7

10-6 续 3(continued3)

类 别	Item	企业单位数(个) Number of Enterprises	工业总产值(当年价格) Gross Industrial Output Value (At Constant Prices)	新产品产值 New Products Value	工 业销售产值(当年价格) Sales Revenue (At Current Prices)	出口交货值 Delivery Value of Industry	产品销售率(%) Proportion of Products Sold
其他纸制品制造	Manufacturing of Other Paper Products	2	2050		2078		101.4
印刷业和记录媒介的复制	Printing Industry, Copying of Record Mediums	27	37620		36787		97.8
印刷	Printing	25	36603		35770		97.7
书、报、刊印刷	Printing of Books, Newspapers and Journals	18	11919		11615		97.4
本册印制	Printing of Excise Books	2	915		1009		110.3
包装装潢及其他印刷	Packing Decoration and Other Printing	5	23769		23146		97.4
记录媒介的复制	Copying of Record Mediums	2	1017		1017		100.0
石油加工、炼焦及核燃料加工业	Petroleum Processing, Coking and Nuclear Fuel Processing	3	896318		832881	108377	92.9
精炼石油产品的制造	Production of Refined Petroleum Products	3	896318		832881	108377	92.9
原油加工及石油制品制造	Crude Oil Processing and Petroleum Products	3	896318		832881	108377	92.9
化学原料及化学制品制造业	Raw Chemical Materials and Chemical Products	51	576461		559966	11792	97.1
基础化学原料制造	Production of Basic Chemical Raw materials	5	4286		4262		99.4
有机化学原料制造	Production of Organic Chemical Raw Materials	2	1500		1532		102.1
肥料制造	Chemical Fertilizer Products	11	272931		270171	11792	99.0
氮肥制造	Production of Nitrogen Fertilizers Products	3	260539		258108	11792	99.1
复混肥料制造	Production of Compound Fertilizer	7	11010		10547		95.8
农药制造	Production of Agricultural Pesticides	1	8307		8086		97.3
化学农药制造	Production of Agricultural Chemical Pesticides	1	8307		8086		97.3
涂料、油墨、颜料及类似产品制造	Production of Coatings, Inks, Paints and Similar Products	2	5103		5527		108.3
涂料制造	Production of Coatings	2	5103		5527		108.3
合成材料制造	Production of Synthetic Materials	2	224410		220917		98.4
合成纤维单(聚合)体的制造	Production of Synthetic Fiber Monomer and Polymer	2	224410		220917		98.4
专用化学产品制造	Production of Exclusive Chemical Products	15	17852		14428		80.8
化学试剂和助剂制造	Production of Chemical Reagents and Auxiliaries	2	2952		2117		71.7
专项化学用品制造	Production of Exclusive Chemical Products	2	687		989		144.1
林产化学产品制造	Production of Forestry Chemical Products	5	4037		4172		103.4
炸药及火工产品制造	Production of Explosives and Blasting Products	5	10097		7068		70.0
其他专用化学产品制造	Production of Other Exclusive Chemical Products	1	80		81		101.3
日用化学产品制造	Production of Daily Chemical Products	15	43572		36575		83.9
肥皂及合成洗涤剂制造	Production of Soaps and Synthetic Detergents	2	1566		707		45.1
化妆品制造	Production of Cosmetic	5	31659		23518		74.3
口腔清洁用品制造	Production of Mouth Cleaning Products	1	631		736		116.7
香料、香精制造	Production of Perfumes and Perfumery Compounds	7	9717		11615		119.5
其他日用化学产品制造	Production of Other Daily Chemical Products						
医药制造业	Production of Pharmaceutical Products	52	314849	17025	296288	389	94.1
化学药品原药制造	Production of Chemical Medicine Products	2	889	0	921	8	103.5
化学药品制剂制造	Production of Chemical Medicines and Preparations	34	261921	16186	241634		92.3
中药饮片加工	Processing of Prepared Chinese Herbal Medicine	2	14889		15173		101.9
中成药制造	Production of Traditional Chinese Patent Medicine	9	24968		25376		101.6
生物、生化制品的制造	Production of Biological and Biochemical Products	3	7272	839	9151		125.8

10-6 续(continued4)

类 别	Item	企业单位数(个) Number of Enterprises	工业总产值(当年价格) Gross Industrial Output Value (At Constant Prices)	新产品产值 New Products Value	工业销售产值(当年价格) Sales Revenue (At Current Prices)	出口交货值 Delivery Value of Industry	产品销售率(%) Proportion of Products Sold
卫生材料及医药用品制造	Production of Sanitation Materials and Medical Products	2	4910		4033	381	82.1
化学纤维制造业	Chemical Fiber Manufacturing	3	69365		68103		98.2
合成纤维制造	Synthetic Chemical Fiber Manufacturing	3	69365		68103		98.2
涤纶纤维制造	Polyester Fiber Manufacturing	3	69365		68103		98.2
橡胶制品业	Manufacturing of Rubber Products	4	30167		29403		97.5
日用及医用橡胶制品制造	Manufacturing of Daily and Medical Rubber Products	2	1298		1225		94.4
其他橡胶制品制造	Manufacturing of Other Rubber Products	2	28869		28178		97.6
塑料制品业	Manufacturing of Plastic Products	21	47639		47204	10900	99.1
塑料薄膜制造	Manufacturing of Plastic Film	5	21391		21625	2818	101.1
塑料板、管、型材的制造	Manufacturing of Plastic Boards, Pipes and Profiles	2	2359		2417	2416	102.5
塑料丝、绳及编织品的制造	Manufacturing of Plastic Threads, Ropes and Weaving Products	4	8369		8557	30	102.3
泡沫塑料制造	Manufacturing of Foamy Plastics	3	2802		2983		106.4
塑料包装箱及容器制造	Manufacturing of Plastic Packing Cases and Containers	6	12499		11410	5636	91.3
日用塑料制造	Manufacturing of Daily Plastics	1	220		212		96.4
日用塑料杂品制造	Manufacturing of Miscellaneous Daily Plastic Products	1	220		212		96.4
非金属矿物制品业	Production of Nonmetal Mineral Products	42	192088		180763	2991	94.1
水泥、石灰和石膏的制造	Production of Cements, Limes and Gypsums	23	153005		144000	2991	94.1
水泥制造	Production of Cement Products	23	153005		144000	2991	94.1
水泥及石膏制品制造	Production of Cements and Gypsum Products	11	35458		33409		94.2
水泥制品制造	Production of Cement Products	10	34893		32916		94.3
砖瓦、石材及其他建筑材料制造	Production of Bricks, Tiles, Stone Materials and Other Building Materials	4	1522		1383		90.9
粘土砖瓦及建筑砌块制造	Production of of Clay Bricks, Tiles and Building Blocks	4	1522		1383		90.9
陶瓷制品制造	Production of Ceramics Products	1	6		6		96.7
日用陶瓷制品制造	Production of Daily Ceramics Products	1	6		6		96.7
耐火材料制品制造	Production of Fire-proof Products	1					0.0
耐火陶瓷制品及其他耐火材料制造	Production of Fire-proof Ceramics Products and Other Fire-proof Materials	1					0.0
石墨及其他非金属矿物制品制造	Production of Graphite and Other Nonmetal Mineral Products	2	2096		1966		93.8
其他非金属矿物制品制造	Production of Nonmetal Mineral Products	2	2096		1966		93.8
黑色金属冶炼及压延加工业	Smelting and Pressing of Ferrous Metals	7	94944	9509	83869		88.3
炼铁	Iron Smelting Industry	1	10345		6358		61.5
炼钢	Steel Smelting	1	37124		30546		82.3
钢压延加工	Steel Pressing and Processing	5	47475	9509	46966		98.9
有色金属冶炼及压延加工业	Smelting and Pressing of Nonferrous Metals	3	15474		15300		98.9
常用有色金属冶炼	Smelting of General Nonferrous Metals	1	1821		1493		82.0
镍钴冶炼	Smelting of Nickel and Cobalt	1	1821		1493		82.0
贵金属冶炼	Smelting of Precious Metals	1	11720		11720		100.0
其他贵金属冶炼	Smelting of Other Precious Metals	1	11720		11720		100.0
稀有稀土金属冶炼	Smelting of Rare Earth Metals	1	1934		2087		107.9
钨钼冶炼	Smelting of Tungsten and Molybdenum	1	1934		2087		107.9
金属制品业	Manufacturing of Metal Products	10	160069	834	162831	12678	101.7

10-6 续 5(continued5)

类 别	Item	企业单位数(个) Number of Enterprises	工业总产值(当年价格) Gross Industrial Output Value (At Constant Prices)	新产品产值 New Products Value	工业销售产值(当年价格) Sales Revenue (At Current Prices)	出口交货值 Delivery Value of Industry	产品销售率(%) Proportion of Products Sold
结构性金属制品制造	Manufacturing of Structural Metal Products	3	1328		637		48.0
金属门窗制造	Manufacturing of Metal Doors and Windows	3	1328		637		48.0
集装箱及金属包装容器制造	Manufacturing of Containers and Metal Packaging Containers	4	51906		51900		100.0
金属包装容器制造	Manufacturing of Metal Packaging Containers	4	51906		51900		100.0
金属丝绳及其制品的制造	Manufacturing of Metal Threads, Ropes and their Products	1	834	834	691	691	82.9
建筑、安全用金属制品制造	Manufacturing of Building and Safety Metal Products	1	55		55		100.0
建筑、家具用金属配件制造	Manufacturing of Building and Furniture Metal Fittings	1	55		55		100.0
金属表面处理及热处理加工	Metal Surface Treatment and Heat Processing	1	105947		109549	11987	103.4
通用设备制造业	Manufacturing of General Equipments	4	4578	122	4296		93.8
泵、阀门、压缩机及类似机械的制造	Manufacturing of Pumps, Valves, Compressors and Similar Machineries	1	12		11		89.9
泵及真空设备制造	Manufacturing of Pumps and Vacuum Equipments	1	12		11		89.9
轴承、齿轮、传动和驱动部件的制造	Manufacturing of Shafts, Gears, Transmission and Driving Parts	1	3441		3165		92.0
齿轮、传动和驱动部件制造	Manufacturing of Gears, Transmission and Driving Parts	1	3441		3165		92.0
金属铸、锻加工	Metal Casting and Forging	2	1126		1121		99.6
钢铁铸件制造	Iron and Steel Forging	2	1126		1121		99.6
专用设备制造业	Manufacturing of Exclusive Equipments	8	19043		18268	255	95.9
化工、木材、非金属加工专用设备	Manufacturing of Exclusive Equipments for Chemical Processing, Timber Processing and Nonmetal Processing	3	1543		1619		104.9
橡胶加工专用设备制造	Manufacturing of Exclusive Rubber Processing Equipments	2	1493		1579		105.8
木材加工机械制造	Manufacturing of Timber Processing Machineries	1	50		40		79.8
食品、饮料、烟草及饲料生产专用设备制造	Manufacturing of Exclusive Equipments for the production of Foods, Beverages, Tobaccos and Feeds	1	866		827		95.5

10-6 续 6(continued6)

类 别	Item	企业单位数(个) Number of Enterprises	工业总产值(当年价格) Gross Industrial Output Value (At Constant Prices)	新产品产值 New Products Value	工业销售产值(当年价格) Sales Revenue (At Current Prices)	出口交货值 Delivery Value of Industry	产品销售率(%) Proportion of Products Sold
食品、饮料、烟草工业专用设备制造	Manufacturing of Exclusive Equipments for the production of Foods, Beverages, Tobaccos	1	866		827		95.5
农、林、牧、渔专用机械制造	Manufacturing of Exclusive Machineries for Agriculture, Forestry, Livestock Farming and Fishing	2	13809		13228	255	95.8
拖拉机制造	Manufacturing of Tractors	1	13683		13102	255	95.8
其他农林牧渔业机械制造及机械修理	Manufacturing of Other Exclusive Machineries for Agriculture, Forestry, Livestock Farming and Fishing as well as Machinery Repair	1	126		126		100.0
环保、社会公共安全及其他专用设备制造	Manufacturing of Exclusive Equipments for Environmental Protection, Social Public Security and Other Purposes	2	2825		2593		91.8
环境污染防治专用设备制造	Manufacturing of Exclusive Equipments for Treatment of Environmental Pollution	1	2705		2592		95.8
水资源专用机械制造	Manufacturing of Exclusive Equipments for Water Resources	1	120		1		1.2
交通运输设备制造业	Manufacturing of Transport Equipments	44	1014602	81	980078	11	96.6
汽车制造	Automobile Manufacturing	32	938827		904540		96.3
汽车整车制造	Manufacturing of Complete Vehicles	1	771174		740292		96.0
汽车零部件及配件制造	Manufacturing of Automobile Parts and Fittings	18	162003		158585		97.9
汽车修理	Automobile Repair	13	5650		5664		100.2
摩托车制造	Motorcycle Manufacturing	8	65178	81	64959	11	99.7
摩托车整车制造	Manufacturing of Complete Motorcycle	1	56935		56897		99.9
摩托车零部件及配件制造	Manufacturing of Motorcycle Parts and Fittings	7	8243	81	8062	11	97.8
船舶及浮动装置制造	Manufacturing of Ships and Floating Facilities	2	10452		10452		100.0
船舶修理及拆船	Ship Repair and Ship-breaking	2	10452		10452		100.0
交通器材及其他交通运输设备制造	Manufacturing of Transport Facilities and Other Transport Equipments	2	145		127		87.7
交通管理用金属标志及设施制造	Manufacturing of Metal Marks and Facilities for Transport Management	2	145		127		87.7
电气机械及器材制造业	Manufacturing of Electric Equipments and Facilities	10	143390	10822	139152	22585	97.0

10-6 续 7(continued7)

类 别	Item	企业单位数(个) Number of Enterprises	工业总产值(当年价格) Gross Industrial Output Value (At Constant Prices)	新产品产值 New Products Value	工业销售产值(当年价格) Sales Revenue (At Current Prices)	出口交货值 Delivery Value of Industry	产品销售率(%) Proportion of Products Sold
输配电及控制设备制造	Manufacturing of Equipments for Electric Transmission, Distribution and Control	4	91207	10822	92473	1100	101.4
变压器、整流器和电感器制造	Manufacturing of Transformers, Rectifiers and Inductors	2	87352	10822	88586	1100	101.4
配电开关控制设备制造	Manufacturing of Distribution Switch Board Control Equipments	2	3856		3887		100.8
电线、电缆、光缆及电工器材制造	Manufacturing of Electric Wire, Cable, Optical Cable and Electric Equipment	4	48560		43223	21485	89.0
电线电缆制造	Manufacturing of Electric Wire and Cable	3	23146		17484		75.5
光纤、光缆制造	Manufacturing of Optical Wire and Cable	1	25414		25739	21485	101.3
电池制造	Manufacturing of Batteries	2	3623		3456		95.4
通信设备、计算机及其他电子设备	Manufacturing of Communication Equipments, Computers and Other Electronic Equipments	6	59550	118	43201	27531	72.5
通信设备制造	Manufacturing of Communication Equipments	2	25668	118	9319		36.3
移动通信及终端设备制造	Manufacturing of Mobile Communication Equipments and Terminal Equipments	1	25				0.0
电子器件制造	Manufacturing of Electronic Devices	3	7240		7240	889	100.0
半导体分立器件制造	Manufacturing of Semiconductor Devices	1	151		151		100.0
光电子器件及其他电子器件制造	Manufacturing of Optoelectronic Devices and Other Electronic Devices	2	7089		7089	889	100.0
电子元件制造	Manufacturing of Electronic Devices	1	26642		26642	26642	100.0
印制电路板制造	Manufacturing of Printed Circuit Boards	1	26642		26642	26642	100.0
仪器仪表及文化、办公用机械制造	Manufacturing of Instruments, Meters, Cultural and Office Machinery	2	303		303		100.1
通用仪器仪表制造	Manufacturingof General Instruments and Meters	1	15		12		79.2
工业自动控制系统装置制造	Manufacturing of Industrial Automatic Control Systems and Facilities	1	15		12		79.2
电工仪器仪表制造	Manufacturingof Electric Instruments and Meters						0.0
钟表与计时仪器制造	Manufacturing of Clocks, Watches and Timing Devices	1	287		291		101.2
工艺品及其他制造业	Manufacturing of Handicrafts and Others	4	19875		19042		95.8
工艺美术品制造	Manufacturing of Handicrafts and Artistic Works	4	19875		19042		95.8
珠宝首饰及有关物品的制造	Manufacturing of Jewels and Related Articles	4	19875		19042		95.8
煤制品制造	Production of Coal Products						
电力、热力的生产和供应业	Production and Supply of Electric Power and Thermal Power	59	660294		658556		99.7
电力生产	Electric Power Production	36	251414		249697		99.3
火力发电	Thermal Power Generation	4	224327		222804		99.3
水力发电	Hydraulic Power Generation	31	26052		25858		99.3
其他能源发电	Other Energy Power	1	1035		1035		100.0
电力供应	Supply of Electric Power	23	408880		408859		100.0
燃气生产和供应业	Production and Supply of Gas	5	56569		55458		98.0
水的生产和供应业	Production and Supply of Water	23	36695		33847		92.2
自来水的生产和供应	Production and Supply of Tap Water	23	36695		33847		92.2

10－7 分市县规模以上工业增加值

Value-added of above Designated Size Industrial Enterprises by City and County

单位：万元 (10000 yuan)

地 区	Region	2001	2002	2003	2004	2005	2006	2006年比2005年增长(%)
总 计	**Total**	758051	882400	1074275	1348547	1484686	1976585	26.5
海口市	Haikou	268266	370117	473170	526778	570429	743830	21.2
三亚市	Sanya	232239	233187	237330	250027	181426	260088	16.3
五指山市	Wuzhishan	3510	4490	4028	3403	3682	3660	7.3
文昌市	Wenchang	11585	19482	19470	23333	25456	34895	9.3
琼海市	Qionghai	16352	18508	15586	23443	25268	24492	8.8
万宁市	Wanning	6493	8804	14393	18999	18084	17511	12.3
定安县	Dingan	3630	4428	7092	7128	10927	14182	28.8
屯昌县	Tunchang	1047	1377	1372	2612	3324	3152	15.8
澄迈县	Chengmai	72198	88498	94312	116536	136975	198571	38.5
临高县	Lingao	5047	5313	5215	12068	12341	14221	8.3
儋州市	Danzhou	22600	29557	22844	36186	42474	40257	21.7
东方市	Dongfang	41413	53320	65025	137590	147477	169747	16.2
乐东县	Ledong	5115	4732	4685	3175	3874	7400	23.2
琼中县	Qiongzhong	1108	1363	1692	1308	1780	2168	34.6
保亭县	Baoting	1545	1471	937	1403	1224	1769	36.1
陵水县	Lingshui	2320	3031	1467	3477	3418	3833	20.0
白沙县	Baisha	3012	2982	3002	3441	2601	2650	-5.2
昌江县	Changjiang	25680	26072	41984	98522	119756	136614	19.5
农 垦	Land Reclamation	42421	43709	38274	43577	36368	49785	4.6
洋 浦	Yangpu	3728	21009	22396	35541	137802	247759	73.6

注：1、本表绝对数按现价计算，增长速度按可比价格计算。
Note: In this table, value is calculated at current prices and the increase rate is calculated at comparable prices.

10－8 各市县规模以上工业总产值

Gross Industrial Output Value of All Above Designed Size Industry by City and County

单位：万元 (10000 yuan)

市县	City and County	合计 Total	大中型 Large& Medical -sized Industrial Enterprises	国有控股企业 State-holding Enterprises	按轻、重分 Grouped by Light & Heavy Industry: 轻工业 Light Industry	重工业 Heavy Industry	按类型分 Grouped by Category: 国有企业 State-owned Industy	集体企业 Collective -owned Industry	股份合作企业 Cooperative Enterprises	股份制企业 Share Holding Enterprises	外商及港澳台投资 Enterprises with Funds from Hong Kong,Macao and Taiwan	其他经济 Other Economy
全省	**Total**	**6680960**	**3838176**	**3020725**	**2251482**	**4429478**	**858700**	**18348**	**2785**	**3117524**	**2460789**	**222814**
海口市	Haikou	2836658	1658404	1742325	1107362	1729297	243424			1964653	593484	35098
三亚市	SanYa	423508	34233	86219	57709	365798	10872			126455	277358	8823
五指山市	WuZhiShan	14244	4972	5625	5884	8360	5625			8619		
文昌市	WenChang	115570		46830	22551	93019	39446	4114		26228	31393	14390
琼海市	QionHai	83919	19247	28978	45892	38027	12283			39485	17446	14705
万宁市	WanNing	70362		26752	21199	49163	24920			13225	3200	29018
定安县	DingAn	32817	2844	6861	25939	6879	6861			21876	4080	
屯昌县	TunChan	12372	805	8222	2032	10340	8222	980		3170		
澄迈县	ChengMai	577709	194108	321454	170735	406974	17672			489912	44574	25550
临高县	LinGao	44437	10734	7764	18584	25853	7764	8296		27674	703	
儋州市	DanZhou	202406	21713	70476	45149	157257	70476	1255		114301	3227	13147
东方市	DongFang	296791	223507	283661	7482	289309	110243			127679	48297	10572
乐东县	LeDong	16354	4715	16354	375	15979	16310			44		
琼中县	QiongZhong	10692		3957	4515	6177	3957				2956	3779
保亭县	BaoTing	5314		3541	215	5099	3541			1773		
陵水县	LingShui	16536	8176	15722	9117	7419	15722	813				
白沙县	BaiSha	14659	10180	8628	11300	3359	8628	0		6031		
昌江县	ChangJiang	258304	181455	178529	18050	240255	166386	2890	236	88792		
农垦	Land Reclamation	179909	118308	70643	142765	37144	64046			24468	89028	2367
洋浦	YangPu	1468401	1344775	88186	534629	933771	22302		2549	33140	1345044	65366

10－9 各市县规模以上工业销售产值

Sales Revenue of All Above Designed Size Industry by City and County

单位:万元 (10000 yuan)

市县	City and County	工业销售产值(当年价格) Sales Revenue (At Current Prices)	轻工业 Light Industry	重工业 Heavy Industry	出口交货值 Delivery Value of Industry	国有控股企业 State-holding Enterprises	大中型工业企业 Large & Medical-sized Industrial Enterprises	国有企业 State-owned Industy
全省	Total	6468361	2196269	4272092	39229	2940415	3729411	497541
海口市	Haikou	2767198	1094718	1672480	28420	1671944	1628922 32343 4270	175873
三亚市	SanYa	420109	54240	365869		84194	18971	10291
五指山市	WuZhiShan	13523	5207	8316		5583	2802 805	
文昌市	WenChang	116988	23081	93908		50173	192433 10734	
琼海市	QionHai	80624	42888	37735	122	28710	19235 228949 3167	3165
万宁市	WanNing	68395	19762	48632		26144		
定安县	DingAn	27066	20220	6846		6895	8042 9750	
屯昌县	TunChan	11995	2018	9977		7934	168695 116826 1283467	805
澄迈县	ChengMai	559143	157632	401511	9746	319748		
临高县	LinGao	44844	18988	25855		7686		
儋州市	DanZhou	185154	38052	147102		69836		252
东方市	DongFang	292598	5957	286642		280834		108597
乐东县	LeDong	14806	375	14431		14806		3167
琼中县	QiongZhong	10072	3906	6167		3888		
保亭县	BaoTing	5320	215	5104		3421		
陵水县	LingShui	16260	8886	7375		15544		8042
白沙县	BaiSha	14229	10870	3359		8481		4967
昌江县	ChangJiang	239765	16015	223750		176828		140086
农垦	Land Reclamation	177095	140065	37030		71105		42296
洋浦	YangPu	1403177	533174	870004	941	86662		

10-9 续(continued)

市 县 City and County	工业销售产值(当年价格) Sales Revenue (At Current Prices)	按类型分 Grouped by Category					
		国有企业 State-owned Industy	集体企业 Collective-owned Industry	股份合作企业 Cooperative Enterprises	股份制企业 Share Holding Enterprises	外商及港澳台投资 Enterprises with Funds from Hong Kong ,Macao and Taiwan	其他经济 Other Economy
全　省 Total	**6468361**	**837644**	**16476**	**2785**	**3008192**	**2387925**	**215340**
海口市 Haikou	2767198	225323			1909437	596941	35498
三亚市 SanYa	420109	10886			124673	273277	11273
五指山市 WuZhiShan	13523	5583			7940		
文昌市 WenChang	116988	41111	1877		28531	31933	13537
琼海市 QionHai	80624	12101			37452	17300	13770
万宁市 WanNing	68395	24345			12902	3263	27885
定安县 DingAn	27066	6895			17017	3154	
屯昌县 TunChan	11995	7934	975		3086		
澄迈县 ChengMai	559143	17450	0		476508	43893	21292
临高县 LinGao	44844	7686	8559		27976	623	0
儋州市 DanZhou	185154	69836	1155		97615	3976	12573
东方市 DongFang	292598	111370			130672	40425	10132
乐东县 LeDong	14806	14762			44		
琼中县 QiongZhong	10072	3888			0	2956	3229
保亭县 BaoTing	5320	3421			1899		
陵水县 LingShui	16260	15544	717				
白沙县 BaiSha	14229	8481	0		5748		
昌江县 ChangJiang	239765	164151	3195	236	72184		
农　垦 Land Reclamation	177095	64577			23586	86476	2456
洋　浦 YangPu	1403177	22302		2549	30924	1283708	63695

10－10 各市县规模以上工业产销率

Proportion of Products Sold above Designated Industrial Enterprises by City and County

单位:万元 (10000 yuan)

市县	City and County	工业总产值(当年价格) Gross Industrial Output Value (At Constant Pric	工业销售产值(当年价格) Sales Revenue (At Current Prices)	产品销售率% Proportion of Products Sold(%)
总 计	**Total**	**6680960**	**6468361**	**96.8**
海口市	Haikou	2836658	2767198	97.6
三亚市	Sanya	423508	420109	99.2
五指山市	Wuzhishan	14244	13523	94.9
文昌市	Wenchang	115570	116988	101.2
琼海市	Qionghai	83919	80624	96.1
万宁市	Wanning	70362	68395	97.2
定安县	Dingan	32817	27066	82.5
屯昌县	Tunchang	12372	11995	97.0
澄迈县	Chengmai	577709	559143	96.8
临高县	Lingao	44437	44844	100.9
儋州市	Danzhou	202406	185154	91.5
东方市	Dongfang	296791	292598	98.6
乐东县	Ledong	16354	14806	90.5
琼中县	Qiongzhong	10692	10072	94.2
保亭县	Baoting	5314	5320	100.1
陵水县	Lingshui	16536	16260	98.3
白沙县	Baisha	14659	14229	97.1
昌江县	Changjiang	258304	239765	92.8
农 垦	Land Reclamation	179909	177095	98.4
洋 浦	Yangpu	1468401	1403177	95.6

10－11 主要工业产品产量
Output of Major Industrial Products

产品名称	Item	2005	2006
天然原油(吨)	Crude Petroleum Oil(ton)	100678	110909
天然气(万立方米)	Natural Gsa(100million cu.m)	16567	20501
铁矿石(原矿)(吨)	Iron Mineral (raw mineral)(ton)	4212035	4022192
铁矿石(成品矿)(吨)	Iron Mineral (Finished Product)(ton)	2856548	2810551
原　盐(吨)	Salt(ton)	166888	182492
发电量(万千瓦小时)	Electricity(millionkwh)	811102.07	948487.58
#火　电	Thermal-electricity	724626.48	850766.02
水　电	Hydropower	83668.39 1933	94556.56 0.00
小麦粉(吨)	wheat flour (ton)	262204.51	202928.27
糖(吨)	Sugar(ton)	734714.22	790069.64
配混合饲料(吨)	Forage(ton)	485	698
糖　果(吨)	Candy(ton)	3179	2963
乳制品(吨)	Dairy products (ton)	123935	136725
罐　头(吨)	Canned Food(ton)	7546	6857
发酵酒精千升)	Fermentable Liquor(kiloliter)	146894	168997
饮料酒(千升)	Alcohol Beverage(kiloliter)	8019	7238
#白　酒	Liquor(kiloliter)	119870	140546
啤　酒	Beer (kiloliter)	274425	276961
软饮料(吨)	Soft Beverage(ton)	57689	54808
碳酸饮料(吨)	Carbonic acid drinks (ton)	32318	36460
果汁及果汁饮料(吨)	beverage(ton)	3179	2963
液体乳	Milk(ton)	751	982
精制茶(吨)	Tea(ton)	168167	171222
瓶(罐)装饮用水	Pootable Water in Bottles(can)(ton)	590000	655146
卷　烟(万支)	Cigarettes(10000pieces)	46144	55859
化学纤维(吨)	Chemical Fiber(ton)	46144	55859
合成纤维	Synthetic Fiber(ton)		

10-11 续 1(continued1)

产品名称	Item	2005	2006
丝织品(万米)	Silk(10000m)	594.00	528.00
服　装(万件)	Garment(10 000 Pieces)	24.93	22.79
人造板(立方米)	Artificial Board(cu.m)	185630	178062
家　具(件)	Furniture(Pieces)	881144	887837
纸浆(吨)	paper pulp (ton)	780831	1036548
机制纸及纸板(吨)	Machine-made Paper and Paperboard (ton)	12722	13610
纸 制 品(吨)	Pappe-made Product(ton)	19311	21196
原油加工量(吨)	volume of processed crude oil (ton)	130113	1798647
汽油	gasoline		656795
柴油	diesel oil		946968
硫酸(折合 100%)(吨)	Sulfuric Acid (100%)(ton)	12678	10049
合 成 氨(吨)	Synthetic Ammonia(ton)	784239	792253
农用化学肥料总计(吨)	Chemical Fertilizers(ton)	626458	642705
氮肥(折合 100%)(吨)	Nitrogen Fertilizers (100%)	622060	639056
#尿 素	Carbamide	622060	639056
磷肥(折合 100%)	Phosphate Fertilizers (100%)	4398	3649
纯苯(吨)	benzene(ton)		9359
精甲醇(吨)	extracted methanol(ton)		149534
油　漆(吨)	Oil Paint(ton)	3818	4627
聚丙烯树酯(吨)	polypropylene colophony(ton)		58978
合成纤维聚合物(吨)	Synthetic Fiber(ton)	42697	237877
聚　脂	Slices or Chips of Polyethylene Terephthalate	42697	237877
肥　皂(吨)	Soap(ton)	582	508
合成洗涤剂(吨)	Synthetic Detergents(ton)	1387	1432
香精(吨)	Fragrance (ton)	637	287
牙膏(自然支)(万支)	Toothpaste(10 000 units)	451	524
中 成 药(吨)	Traditional Chinese Medicine (ton)	384	363
塑料制品(吨)	Plastic Products(ton)	19303	21182
#塑料薄膜	Plastic Membrane	7446	8904
塑料编织袋(万吨)	plastic knitted sacks (10000 tons)	5199	6400

10-11 续 2(continued2)

产品名称	Item	2005	2006
水泥熟料(吨)	cement clinker (ton)	3248869	4430451
水 泥(吨)	Cement(ton)	4227402	5775364
商品混凝土(立方米)	commercial concrete (cu.m)	204496	367168
砖(万块)	Brick(10 000 units)	7857	5636
日用陶瓷(吨)	Household Ceramics(ton)	5	4
耐火材料制品(吨)	Refractory Material(ton)	170	
生 铁(吨)	Pig Iron(ton)	60032	133366
钢 (吨)	Steel(ton)	2183	2178
钢材(吨)	Steel Products(ton)	148569	141486
钢筋	corrugated steel bar	51363	72007
盘条(线材)	wire rod	8305	7112
冷轧薄板	Steel sheet	88901	62367
铁合金(吨)		0	20689
黄金(千克)		135.70	85.00
泵(液体泵)(台)	pump(set)	121	119
小型拖拉机(台)	Mini-tractors(set)	7311	7924
汽 车(辆)	Motor Vehicles(set)	73086	83636
#公路客车	Buses	14271	15726
轿车	Cars	58815	67910
摩托车(辆)	Motorcycles(units)	67434	133661
变压器(千伏安)	Transformer(kva)	4175632	4666961
电力电缆(公里)	Electric Cable(kilo)	33380	12263
通信电缆(公里)	Communicative Cable(kilo)	10188	4294
光缆(芯千米)	cable (core km)	93659	503772
钢芯铝绞线(吨)	Aluminium Stand Wire with Steel(ton)	937	925
原电池及原电池组(折R20标准只)(万只)	Batteries and the battery (standard unit for R20) (10000 units)	1616.72	1092.48
半导体分立器件(万只)	semiconductor separation devices (10000 units)	2.67	5.85

10－12 规模以上工业企业主要财务指标
Main Indicators on Finance of above Designated Size Industrial Enterprises

类 别	Item	企业单位数（个）Number of Enterprises (unit)	亏损企业 Number of Loss Making Industrial Enterprises	工业总产值（当年价格）Gross Industrial Output Value (At Current Prices)	工业销售产值(当年价格) Sales Revenue (At Current Prices)
总 计	Total	595	238	6402592	6220817
按注册登记类型分	Grouped by Economic Category				
国有企业	State-owned Industy	181	93	732856	736588
集体企业	Collective-owned Industry	10	5	13327	10744
股份合作企业	Cooperative Enterprises	2	0	7504	7664
股份制企业	Share Holding Enterprises	127	45	1225142	1193097
外商投资企业	Foreign Funded Enterprises	53	15	2007963	1941523
港澳台商投资企业	Enterprises with Funds from Hong Kong ,Macao and Taiwan	49	19	233774	234312
其他经济类型企业	Other Economy	173	61	2182025	2096889
按轻重工业分	Grouped by Light & Heavy Industry				
轻工业	Light Industry	303	122	2249035	2192685
重工业	Heavy Industry	292	116	4153557	4028133
按企业规模分	Grouped by Size of Enterprises				
大型企业	Large-sized	0	0	0	0
中型企业	Medium-sized	82	15	4257327	4122166
小型企业	Small-sized	513	223	2145265	2098652
在总计中:国有控股企业	Of the Total:State-owned and State-holding Enterprises	284	129	2973010	2909622
按工业行业分	Grouped by Industrial Sector:				
煤炭开采和洗选业	Coal Mining and Dressing	0	0	0	0
石油和天然气开采业	Petroleum and Natural Gas Extraction	1	0	69452	69268
黑色金属矿采选业	Ferrous Metals Mining and Dressing	8	3	138644	158144
#铁矿采选	Iron Ore Mining and Dressing	8	3	138644	158144
有色金属矿采选业	Nonferrous Metals Mining and Dressing	20	5	48559	47894
非金属矿采选业	Nonmetal Minerals Mining and Dressing	10	4	27531	24929
#采盐	Salt Mining and Dressing	4	1	6203	4158
其他采矿业	Other Mining Industries	0	0	0	0
农副食品加工业	Farm Products and Non-staple Foodstuffs Processing Industry	75	29	492116	462259
#制糖	Carbohydrate Processing	17	7	75691	71294
水产品加工	Aquatic Products Processing	35	13	236242	219596
食品制造业	Food Manufacturing	24	5	174682	191246
#制糖	Carbohydrate Processing	2	0	1291	1218
水产品加工	Aquatic Products Processing	3	0	124701	118012
饮料制造业	Beverage Manufacturing	22	7	214570	211368
#酒精制造	Liquor Manufacturing	1	0	905	905
酒的制造	Alcohol Production	3	0	159430	156469

10-12 续 1(continued1)

类 别	Item	企业单位数(个) Number of Enterprises (unit)	亏损企业 Number of Loss Making Industrial Enterprises	工业总产值(当年价格) Gross Industrial Output Value (At Current Prices)	工业销售产值(当年价格) Sales Revenue (At Current Prices)
软饮料制造	Soft Beverage Manufacturing	13	5	51863	51819
精制茶加工	Fine Tea Processing	5	2	2373	2175
烟草制品业	Tobacco Manufacturing	1	0	71392	69041
#卷烟制造	Cigarettes Manufacturing	1	0	71392	69041
纺织业	Textile Industry	9	4	102063	98977
#棉、化纤纺织及印染精加工	# Spinning, Weaving, Printing, Dyeing and Fine Processing of Cotton and Chemical Fiber				
毛纺织和染整精加工	Wool Textile and Dyeing, Finishing and Fine Processing	0	0	0	0
针织品、编织品及其制品制造	Manufacturing of Knitting Products and Weaving Products	5	2	66429	65511
纺织服装、鞋、帽制造业	Manufacturing of Garments, Shoes and Hats	2	2	135	118
#纺织服装制造	# Manufacturing of Garments	2	2	135	118
皮革、毛皮、羽毛(绒)及其制品业	Leather, Furs, Down and Related Products	1		1823	1696
#皮革制品制造	Leather Products	1	0	1823	1696
木材加工及木、竹、藤、棕、草制品业	Timber Processing, Bamboo, Cane, Palm Fiber and Straw Products	30	11	59768	62542
#锯材、木片加工	Timber Processing	19	6	32557	35135
人造板制造	Artificial Wooden Products	6	3	21139	21479
家具制造业	Furniture Manufacturing	13	5	49649	48190
#木质家具制造	Wooden Furniture Manufacturing	13	5	49649	48190
造纸及纸制品业	Papermaking and Paper Products	15	6	532602	531211
#纸浆制造	#Paper Pulp Production	1	0	508993	508993
造纸	Papermaking	4	1	6728	6342
印刷业和记录媒介的复制	Printing and Copying of Recording Mediums	26	12	39002	38176
#印刷	Printing	23	10	37804	36979
文教体育用品制造业	Cultural, Educational and Sports Goods	0	0	0	0
#文化用品制造	Cultural Goods	0	0	0	0
体育用品制造	Sports Goods	0	0	0	0
石油加工、炼焦及核燃料加工业	Petroleum Processing, Coking and Nuclear Fuel Processing	3	1	896318	832881
#精炼石油产品的制造	#Production of Refined Petroleum Products	3	1	896318	832881
化学原料及化学制品制造业	Raw Chemical Materials and Chemical Products	44	18	576461	568883
#肥料制造	Chemical Fertilizer Products	11	2	272931	278043
#氮肥制造	Nitrogenous Fertilizer Products	2	0	212242	217683
农药制造	Agricultural Chemicals Products	1	0	8322	8074
日用化学产品制造	Production of Daily Chemical Products	12	3	43417	37565
医药制造业	Medical and Pharmaceutical Products	51	19	315851	297484
#化学药品原药制造	# Production of Chemical Medicine Products	4	3	2857	2617
化学药品制剂制造	Production of Chemical Medicines and Preparations	34	11	282014	263939
中成药制造	Production of Traditional Chinese Patent Medicine	9	4	14767	16118
兽用药品制造	Production of Animal Medicines	0	0	0	0
化学纤维制造业	Chemical Fiber	3	3	69365	68103
#合成纤维制造	# Manufacturing of Synthetic Chemical Fiber	3	3	69365	68103
橡胶制品业	Rubber Products	4	0	30004	28729

10-12 续 2(continued2)

类 别	Item	企业单位数(个) Number of Enterprises (unit)	亏损企业 Number of Loss Making Industrial Enterprises	工业总产值(当年价格) Gross Industrial Output Value (At Current Prices)	工业销售产值(当年价格) Sales Revenue (At Current Prices)
# 轮胎制造	Tire Manufacturing	0	0	0	0
塑料制品业	Plastic Products	18	7	39197	39242
# 塑料薄膜制造	Plastic Membrane	5	2	20476	21328
非金属矿物制品业	Nonmetal Mineral Products	35	19	170190	158373
# 水泥、石灰和石膏的制造	#Production of Cements, Limes and Gypsums	17	10	138024	128298
水泥及石膏制品制造	Production of Cements and Gypsum Products	9	4	28541	26491
砖瓦、石材及其他建筑材料制造	Production of Tiles, Stone Materials and Other Architectural Material Products	4	2	1522	1383
玻璃及玻璃制品制造	Glass and Glass Manufacturing	0	0	0	0
陶瓷制品制造	Ceramics Products	1	1	6	6
黑色金属冶炼及压延加工业	Smelting and Pressing of Ferrous Metals	7	4	94944	84837
# 炼铁	Iron Refine Products	0	0	0	0
钢压延加工	Steel Refine Products	5	2	47475	46966
有色金属冶炼及压延加工业	Smelting and Pressing of Nonferrous Metals	4	1	15662	15488
金属制品业	Metal Products	10	4	160073	162831
# 结构性金属制品制造	#Structural Metal Products	3	2	1328	637
集装箱及金属包装容器制造	Container and Metal Packaging Products	4		51906	51900
通用设备制造业	Manufacturing of General Equipments	3	2	4555	4278
专用设备制造业	Special Purpose Equipment	10	7	19250	18574
# 农、林、牧、渔专用机械制造	Manufacturing of Exclusive Machineries for Agriculture, Forestry, Livestock Farming and Fishing	5	3	15510	15008
交通运输设备制造业	Transport Equipment	40	18	1013191	978988
# 汽车制造	Automobile Manufacturing	29	9	937297	903473
摩托车制造	Motorcycle Manufacturing	8	7	65420	65041
电气机械及器材制造业	Electric Equipment and Machinery	10	4	143922	138639
# 电线、电缆、光缆及电工器材制造	# Manufacturing of Electric Wires, Cables, Optic Cables and Electrician Equipments	4	1	48560	43223
通信设备、计算机及其他电子设备制造业	Manufacturing of Communication Equipments, Computers and Other Electronic Equipments	6	2	59941	43593
# 通信设备制造	Telecommunications Equipment	2	1	25668	9319
家用视听设备制造	Household Audio-visual Equipment Manufacturing	0	0	0	0
仪器仪表及文化、办公用机械制造业	Instruments, Meters, Cultural and Office Machinery	2	2	332	372
工艺品及其他制造业	Industrial Arts and other Manufacturing	3	0	19561	18902
# 工艺美术品制造	Industrial Arts Manufacturing	3	0	19561	18902
废弃资源和废旧材料回收加工业	Recovery and Processing of Discarded Resoures and Weste Material				
电力、热力的生产和供应业	Production and Supply of Electric Power, Steam and Hot Water	57	22	657882	656099
# 电力生产	Electric Power Production	34	19	251941	250211
电力供应	Supply of Electric Power	23	3	405941	405888
燃气生产和供应业	Production and Supply of Gas	5	0	57047	55458
水的生产和供应业	Production and Supply of Water	23	12	36858	34006
# 自来水的生产和供应	Production and Supply of Tap Water	23	12	36858	34006
污水处理及其再生利用	Treatment and Reuse of Waste Water	0	0	0	0

10-12 续 3(continued3)

类 别	Item	出口交货值 Delivery Value of Industry	工业增加值(当年价格) Value-added of Industry (At Current Prices)	全部从业人员年平均人数(人) Annual Average Number of All Employees (person)	本年应付工资总额 Salaries and Wages Payable of Current Year
总 计	**Total**	457317		121964	218057
按注册登记类型分	**Grouped by Economic Category**				
国有企业	State-owned Industy	2331	291165	39356	68793
集体企业	Collective-owned Industry	0	3564	1310	1600
股份合作企业	Cooperative Enterprises	0	1649	252	369
股份制企业	Share Holding Enterprises	86193	448286	22658	40403
外商投资企业	Foreign Funded Enterprises	218137	475662	19273	47711
港澳台商投资企业	Enterprises with Funds from Hong Kong ,Macao and Taiwan	72118	70463	8721	13290
其他经济类型企业	Other Economy	78538	605037	30394	45892
按轻重工业分	**Grouped by Light & Heavy Industry**				
轻工业	Light Industry	267695	677265	63183	95328
重工业	Heavy Industry	189622	1218415	58781	122729
按企业规模分	**Grouped by Size of Enterprises**				
大型企业	Large-sized	0	0	0	0
中型企业	Medium-sized	342171	1176493	64330	135173
小型企业	Small-sized	115145	719278	57634	82884
在总计中:国有控股企业	Of the Total:State-owned and State-holding Enterprises	51794	1054393	61718	120555
按工业行业分	**Grouped by Industrial Sector:**				
煤炭开采和洗选业	Coal Mining and Dressing	0	0	0	0
石油和天然气开采业	Petroleum and Natural Gas Extraction	0	52672	31	203
黑色金属矿采选业	Ferrous Metals Mining and Dressing	0	93174	8809	17870
#铁矿采选	Iron Ore Mining and Dressing	0	93174	8809	17870
有色金属矿采选业	Nonferrous Metals Mining and Dressing	0	12553	1017	1392
非金属矿采选业	Nonmetal Minerals Mining and Dressing	778	12518	2808	2617
#采盐	Salt Mining and Dressing	333	4135	2102	1730
其他采矿业	Other Mining Industries	0	0	0	0
农副食品加工业	Farm Products and Non-staple Foodstuffs Processing Industry	162619	117137	20168	21325
#制糖	Carbohydrate Processing	0	26303	7815	6629
水产品加工	Aquatic Products Processing	161802	58145	10024	11774
食品制造业	Food Manufacturing	4659	44823	4664	7419
#制糖	Carbohydrate Processing	0	335	174	175
水产品加工	Aquatic Products Processing	2332	29191	2280	2620
饮料制造业	Beverage Manufacturing	1135	67035	3070	7463
#酒精制造	Liquor Manufacturing	0	104	53	24
酒的制造	Alcohol Production	1135	47480	1066	2461

10-12 续 4(continued4)

类 别	Item	出口交货值 Delivery Value of Industry	工业增加值(当年价格) Value-added of Industry (At Current Prices)	全部从业人员年平均人数(人) Annual Average Number of All Employees (person)	本年应付工资总额 Salaries and Wages Payable of Current Year
软饮料制造	Soft Beverage Manufacturing	0	18713	1638	3774
精制茶加工	Fine Tea Processing	0	738	313	1203
烟草制品业	Tobacco Manufacturing	161	49244	429	420
# 卷烟制造	Cigarettes Manufacturing	161	49244	429	420
纺织业	Textile Industry	51520	29858	7257	13086
# 棉、化纤纺织及印染精加工	# Spinning, Weaving, Printing, Dyeing and Fine Processing of Cotton and Chemical Fiber				
毛纺织和染整精加工	Wool Textile and Dyeing, Finishing and Fine Processing	0	0	0	0
针织品、编织品及其制品制造	Manufacturing of Knitting Products and Weaving Products	39368	20481	5738	11554
纺织服装、鞋、帽制造业	Manufacturing of Garments, Shoes and Hats	0	6	189	345
# 纺织服装制造	# Manufacturing of Garments	0	6	189	345
皮革、毛皮、羽毛(绒)及其制品业	Leather, Furs, Down and Related Products		405	195	285
# 皮革制品制造	Leather Products	0	405	195	285
木材加工及木、竹、藤、棕、草制品业	Timber Processing, Bamboo, Cane, Palm Fiber and Straw Products	1185	13164	3342	3222
# 锯材、木片加工	Timber Processing	0	6083	1768	1629
人造板制造	Artificial Wooden Products	0	5296	1084	1092
家具制造业	Furniture Manufacturing	40264	11292	3394	4193
# 木质家具制造	Wooden Furniture Manufacturing	40264	11292	3394	4193
造纸及纸制品业	Papermaking and Paper Products	5636	159099	4476	13603
# 纸浆制造	#Paper Pulp Production	0	151343	2353	10941
造纸	Papermaking	0	2789	355	551
印刷业和记录媒介的复制	Printing and Copying of Recording Mediums		16960	2325	3079
# 印刷	Printing	0	16474	2207	2935
文教体育用品制造业	Cultural, Educational and Sports Goods	0	0	0	0
# 文化用品制造	Cultural Goods	0	0	0	0
体育用品制造	Sports Goods	0	0	0	0
石油加工、炼焦及核燃料加工业	Petroleum Processing, Coking and Nuclear Fuel Processing	108377	139935	675	3812
# 精炼石油产品的制造	#Production of Refined Petroleum Products	108377	139935	675	3812
化学原料及化学制品制造业	Raw Chemical Materials and Chemical Products	14208	268147	4958	13906
# 肥料制造	Chemical Fertilizer Products	11792	203984	1585	8842
# 氮肥制造	Nitrogenous Fertilizer Products	0	157232	715	6655
农药制造	Agricultural Chemicals Products	0	2199	387	924
日用化学产品制造	Production of Daily Chemical Products	0	22026	630	843
医药制造业	Medical and Pharmaceutical Products	389	115586	6478	10770
# 化学药品原药制造	# Production of Chemical Medicine Products	8	842	196	292
化学药品制剂制造	Production of Chemical Medicines and Preparations	0	104290	5446	9486
中成药制造	Production of Traditional Chinese Patent Medicine	0	4859	448	550
兽用药品制造	Production of Animal Medicines	0	0	0	0
化学纤维制造业	Chemical Fiber	0	4873	774	1681
# 合成纤维制造	# Manufacturing of Synthetic Chemical Fiber	0	4873	774	1681
橡胶制品业	Rubber Products	0	7927	611	1078

10-12 续 5(continued5)

类 别	Item	出口交货值 Delivery Value of Industry	工业增加值(当年价格) Value-added of Industry (At Current Prices)	全部从业人员年平均人数(人) Annual Average Number of All Employees (person)	本年应付工资总额 Salaries and Wages Payable of Current Year
#轮胎制造	Tire Manufacturing	0	0	0	0
塑料制品业	Plastic Products	2818	10176	1321	1546
#塑料薄膜制造	Plastic Membrane	2818	5720	428	597
非金属矿物制品业	Nonmetal Mineral Products	0	56232	5797	6679
#水泥、石灰和石膏的制造	#Production of Cements, Limes and Gypsums		45838	4202	4538
水泥及石膏制品制造	Production of Cements and Gypsum Products	0	9399	868	1519
砖瓦、石材及其他建筑材料制造	Production of Tiles, Stone Materials and Other Architectural Material Products		251	476	332
玻璃及玻璃制品制造	Glass and Glass Manufacturing	0	0	0	0
陶瓷制品制造	Ceramics Products	0	2	20	10
黑色金属冶炼及压延加工业	Smelting and Pressing of Ferrous Metals		21959	2010	2639
#炼铁	Iron Refine Products	0	0	0	0
钢压延加工	Steel Refine Products	0	11295	968	1496
有色金属冶炼及压延加工业	Smelting and Pressing of Nonferrous Metals		4896	241	384
金属制品业	Metal Products	12678	22435	1515	2715
#结构性金属制品制造	#Structural Metal Products	0	406	125	123
集装箱及金属包装容器制造	Container and Metal Packaging Products		10772	1013	1362
通用设备制造业	Manufacturing of General Equipments	0	1634	677	626
专用设备制造业	Special Purpose Equipment	255	3812	1083	1177
#农、林、牧、渔专用机械制造	Manufacturing of Exclusive Machineries for Agriculture, Forestry, Livestock Farming and Fishing	255	3230	837	1003
交通运输设备制造业	Transport Equipment	11	240516	9544	18649
#汽车制造	Automobile Manufacturing	0	226619	6313	12271
摩托车制造	Motorcycle Manufacturing	11	10586	1869	3469
电气机械及器材制造业	Electric Equipment and Machinery	22585	32647	1976	4153
#电线、电缆、光缆及电工器材制造	# Manufacturing of Electric Wires, Cables, Optic Cables and Electrician Equipments	21485	10468	495	1586
通信设备、计算机及其他电子设备制造业	Manufacturing of Communication Equipments, Computers and Other Electronic Equipments	27922	22502	1470	3303
#通信设备制造	Telecommunications Equipment	0	12639	489	1931
家用视听设备制造	Household Audio-visual Equipment Manufacturing	0	0	0	0
仪器仪表及文化、办公用机械制造业	Instruments, Meters, Cultural and Office Machinery	115	61	268	140
工艺品及其他制造业	Industrial Arts and other Manufacturing	0	2686	310	544
#工艺美术品制造	Industrial Arts Manufacturing	0	2686	310	544
废弃资源和废旧材料回收加工业	Recovery and Processing of Discarded Resoures and Weste Material				
电力、热力的生产和供应业	Production and Supply of Electric Power, Steam and Hot Water		216604	14279	40828
#电力生产	Electric Power Production	0	91102	5977	13980
电力供应	Supply of Electric Power	0	125509	8302	26848
燃气生产和供应业	Production and Supply of Gas	0	23771	592	1839
水的生产和供应业	Production and Supply of Water	0	19243	5211	5064
#自来水的生产和供应	Production and Supply of Tap Water	0	19243	5211	5064
污水处理及其再生利用	Treatment and Reuse of Waste Water	0	0	0	0

10-12 续 6(continued6)

类 别	Item	本年应付福利费总额 Welfare Expenses Payable of Current Year	主营业务收入 Major Business Revenue	主营业务成本 Major Business Cost	主营业务税金及附加 Major Business Tax and Extra Charges
总 计	Total	25392	5984362	4602248	115269
按注册登记类型分	Grouped by Economic Category				
国有企业	State-owned Industy	8228	753480	421616	9673
集体企业	Collective-owned Industry	143	10450	9826	49
股份合作企业	Cooperative Enterprises	49	7552	6897	31
股份制企业	Share Holding Enterprises	5727	1196590	960502	6369
外商投资企业	Foreign Funded Enterprises	5440	1701601	1340480	26555
港澳台商投资企业	Enterprises with Funds from Hong Kong ,Macao and Taiwan	260	232473	168243	225
其他经济类型企业	Other Economy	5545	2082217	1694684	72367
按轻重工业分	Grouped by Light & Heavy Industry				
轻工业	Light Industry	11863	2125605	1560850	40002
重工业	Heavy Industry	13529	3858758	3041399	75267
按企业规模分	Grouped by Size of Enterprises				
大型企业	Large-sized	0	0	0	0
中型企业	Medium-sized	16150	3888930	2957601	104789
小型企业	Small-sized	9242	2095432	1644647	10479
在总计中:国有控股企业	Of the Total:State-owned and State-holding Enterprises	14800	2861439	2105249	80439
按工业行业分	Grouped by Industrial Sector:				
煤炭开采和洗选业	Coal Mining and Dressing	0	0	0	0
石油和天然气开采业	Petroleum and Natural Gas Extraction	5	69268	11890	1481
黑色金属矿采选业	Ferrous Metals Mining and Dressing	2299	146469	72995	5832
# 铁矿采选	Iron Ore Mining and Dressing	2299	146469	72995	5832
有色金属矿采选业	Nonferrous Metals Mining and Dressing	112	49582	43537	68
非金属矿采选业	Nonmetal Minerals Mining and Dressing	-19	28255	14085	429
# 采盐	Salt Mining and Dressing	305	4478	1889	205
其他采矿业	Other Mining Industries	0	0	0	0
农副食品加工业	Farm Products and Non-staple Foodstuffs Processing Industry	2454	478942	428590	848
# 制糖	Carbohydrate Processing	987	74300	55904	542
水产品加工	Aquatic Products Processing	1054	220837	200438	287
食品制造业	Food Manufacturing	498	187146	137273	1006
# 制糖	Carbohydrate Processing	0	1230	900	2
水产品加工	Aquatic Products Processing	322	114243	87905	680
饮料制造业	Beverage Manufacturing	641	249333	174617	6635
# 酒精制造	Liquor Manufacturing	0	905	795	50
酒的制造	Alcohol Production	300	190468	130631	6280

10-12 续 7(continued7)

类 别	Item	本年应付福利费总额 Welfare Expenses Payable of Current Year	主营业务收入 Major Business Revenue	主营业务成本 Major Business Cost	主营业务税金及附加 Major Business Tax and Extra Charges
软饮料制造	Soft Beverage Manufacturing	293	55017	40866	272
精制茶加工	Fine Tea Processing	47	2944	2325	33
烟草制品业	Tobacco Manufacturing	510	69041	31252	26076
#卷烟制造	Cigarettes Manufacturing	510	69041	31252	26076
纺织业	Textile Industry	2486	98386	69960	255
#棉、化纤纺织及印染精加工	# Spinning, Weaving, Printing, Dyeing and Fine Processing of Cotton and Chemical Fiber				
毛纺织和染整精加工	Wool Textile and Dyeing, Finishing and Fine Processing	0	0	0	0
针织品、编织品及其制品制造	Manufacturing of Knitting Products and Weaving Products	2282	67425	44148	200
纺织服装、鞋、帽制造业	Manufacturing of Garments, Shoes and Hats	49	1462	1347	31
#纺织服装制造	# Manufacturing of Garments	49	1462	1347	31
皮革、毛皮、羽毛(绒)及其制品业	Leather, Furs, Down and Related Products	10	2117	1073	16
#皮革制品制造	Leather Products	10	2117	1073	16
木材加工及木、竹、藤、棕、草制品业	Timber Processing, Bamboo, Cane, Palm Fiber and Straw Products	246	61610	55474	204
#锯材、木片加工	Timber Processing	117	34757	29435	102
人造板制造	Artificial Wooden Products	124	20924	21004	91
家具制造业	Furniture Manufacturing	649	46652	41512	529
#木质家具制造	Wooden Furniture Manufacturing	649	46652	41512	529
造纸及纸制品业	Papermaking and Paper Products	1530	423943	292734	49
#纸浆制造	#Paper Pulp Production	1403	401765	272084	0
造纸	Papermaking	62	6362	5871	26
印刷业和记录媒介的复制	Printing and Copying of Recording Mediums	457	34450	26682	147
#印刷	Printing	414	33252	25486	139
文教体育用品制造业	Cultural, Educational and Sports Goods	0	0	0	0
#文化用品制造	Cultural Goods	0	0	0	0
体育用品制造	Sports Goods	0	0	0	0
石油加工、炼焦及核燃料加工业	Petroleum Processing, Coking and Nuclear Fuel Processing	566	725494	668271	22108
#精炼石油产品的制造	#Production of Refined Petroleum Products	566	725494	668271	22108
化学原料及化学制品制造业	Raw Chemical Materials and Chemical Products	1542	542060	409145	769
#肥料制造	Chemical Fertilizer Products	1021	251092	145422	253
#氮肥制造	Nitrogenous Fertilizer Products	918	218976	127206	253
农药制造	Agricultural Chemicals Products	13	8123	5595	23
日用化学产品制造	Production of Daily Chemical Products	108	37493	20239	420
医药制造业	Medical and Pharmaceutical Products	1362	297940	155731	2072
#化学药品原药制造	# Production of Chemical Medicine Products	30	2497	2120	26
化学药品制剂制造	Production of Chemical Medicines and Preparations	1145	253971	125989	1805
中成药制造	Production of Traditional Chinese Patent Medicine	90	26798	21924	127
兽用药品制造	Production of Animal Medicines	0	0	0	0
化学纤维制造业	Chemical Fiber	189	68174	69637	40
#合成纤维制造	# Manufacturing of Synthetic Chemical Fiber	189	68174	69637	40
橡胶制品业	Rubber Products	44	28834	27078	87

10-12 续 8(continued8)

类 别	Item	本年应付福利费总额 Welfare Expenses Payable of Current Year	主营业务收入 Major Business Revenue	主营业务成本 Major Business Cost	主营业务税金及附加 Major Business Tax and Extra Charges
#轮胎制造	Tire Manufacturing	0	0	0	0
塑料制品业	Plastic Products	168	40107	34056	71
#塑料薄膜制造	Plastic Membrane	88	21902	17718	13
非金属矿物制品业	Nonmetal Mineral Products	724	153175	131559	956
#水泥、石灰和石膏的制造	#Production of Cements, Limes and Gypsums	554	124928	107656	729
水泥及石膏制品制造	Production of Cements and Gypsum Products	122	24391	20856	217
砖瓦、石材及其他建筑材料制造	Production of Tiles, Stone Materials and Other Architectural Material Products	15	1621	1207	3
玻璃及玻璃制品制造	Glass and Glass Manufacturing	0	0	0	0
陶瓷制品制造	Ceramics Products	0	6	5	0
黑色金属冶炼及压延加工业	Smelting and Pressing of Ferrous Metals	283	87723	85038	273
#炼铁	Iron Refine Products	0	0	0	0
钢压延加工	Steel Refine Products	125	49780	46972	218
有色金属冶炼及压延加工业	Smelting and Pressing of Nonferrous Metals	43	13280	12841	48
金属制品业	Metal Products	55	147686	129678	436
#结构性金属制品制造	#Structural Metal Products	12	604	538	21
集装箱及金属包装容器制造	Container and Metal Packaging Products	37	54974	48065	415
通用设备制造业	Manufacturing of General Equipments	24	4124	3592	24
专用设备制造业	Special Purpose Equipment	150	18414	15358	19
#农、林、牧、渔专用机械制造	Manufacturing of Exclusive Machineries for Agriculture, Forestry, Livestock Farming and Fishing	134	14858	12523	13
交通运输设备制造业	Transport Equipment	1331	940246	795026	39297
#汽车制造	Automobile Manufacturing	710	865546	728203	37702
摩托车制造	Motorcycle Manufacturing	254	65954	60491	1593
电气机械及器材制造业	Electric Equipment and Machinery	482	135804	109414	121
#电线、电缆、光缆及电工器材制造	# Manufacturing of Electric Wires, Cables, Optic Cables and Electrician Equipments	23	44966	40838	39
通信设备、计算机及其他电子设备制造业	Manufacturing of Communication Equipments, Computers and Other Electronic Equipments	280	56280	41934	44
#通信设备制造	Telecommunications Equipment	246	21710	15030	0
家用视听设备制造	Household Audio-visual Equipment Manufacturing	0	0	0	0
仪器仪表及文化、办公用机械制造业	Instruments, Meters, Cultural and Office Machinery		371	334	2
工艺品及其他制造业	Industrial Arts and other Manufacturing	18	19022	17278	29
#工艺美术品制造	Industrial Arts Manufacturing	18	19022	17278	29
废弃资源和废旧材料回收加工业	Recovery and Processing of Discarded Resoures and Weste Material				
电力、热力的生产和供应业	Production and Supply of Electric Power, Steam and Hot Water	5421	653455	422203	4354
#电力生产	Electric Power Production	2451	238918	213463	2246
电力供应	Supply of Electric Power	2970	414536	208740	2108
燃气生产和供应业	Production and Supply of Gas	223	79333	55171	693
水的生产和供应业	Production and Supply of Water	560	26189	15886	219
#自来水的生产和供应	Production and Supply of Tap Water	560	26189	15886	219
污水处理及其再生利用	Treatment and Reuse of Waste Water	0	0	0	0

10-12 续 9(continued9)

类别	Item	其他业务收入 Other Business Income	营业费用 Funds Expenses	管理费用 Administrative Expense	财务费用 Financal Expenses
总计	**Total**	**51718**	**229678**	**275714**	**114030**
按注册登记类型分	**Grouped by Economic Category**				
国有企业	State-owned Industy	9347	19835	63793	12403
集体企业	Collective-owned Industry	49	195	1004	143
股份合作企业	Cooperative Enterprises	1	67	106	62
股份制企业	Share Holding Enterprises	14226	53497	46292	15700
外商投资企业	Foreign Funded Enterprises	18039	74949	60402	62319
港澳台商投资企业	Enterprises with Funds from Hong Kong ,Macao and Taiwan	2199	20018	12900	1516
其他经济类型企业	Other Economy	7858	61117	91217	21888
按轻重工业分	**Grouped by Light & Heavy Industry**				
轻工业	Light Industry	15489	161931	136822	59599
重工业	Heavy Industry	36229	67747	138892	54431
按企业规模分	**Grouped by Size of Enterprises**				
大型企业	Large-sized	0	0	0	0
中型企业	Medium-sized	27080	137673	168209	87366
小型企业	Small-sized	24638	92005	107504	26665
在总计中:国有控股企业	Of the Total:State-owned and State-holding Enterprises	24655	58732	141197	43371
按工业行业分	**Grouped by Industrial Sector:**				
煤炭开采和洗选业	Coal Mining and Dressing	0	0	0	0
石油和天然气开采业	Petroleum and Natural Gas Extraction	0	905	2480	-205
黑色金属矿采选业	Ferrous Metals Mining and Dressing	3177	5991	20567	-196
#铁矿采选	Iron Ore Mining and Dressing	3177	5991	20567	-196
有色金属矿采选业	Nonferrous Metals Mining and Dressing	286	1797	1466	192
非金属矿采选业	Nonmetal Minerals Mining and Dressing	803	5932	2337	279
#采盐	Salt Mining and Dressing	728	1201	1251	252
其他采矿业	Other Mining Industries	0	0	0	0
农副食品加工业	Farm Products and Non-staple Foodstuffs Processing Industry	2934	8161	21532	4293
#制糖	Carbohydrate Processing	696	719	8406	257
水产品加工	Aquatic Products Processing	1769	4663	7235	2700
食品制造业	Food Manufacturing	2742	33409	10498	-424
#制糖	Carbohydrate Processing	27	179	79	2
水产品加工	Aquatic Products Processing	1709	18380	5403	-595
饮料制造业	Beverage Manufacturing	582	30080	26541	898
#酒精制造	Liquor Manufacturing	0	0	34	0
酒的制造	Alcohol Production	68	24303	22766	994

10-12 续 10(continued10)

类 别	Item	其他业务收入 Other Business Income	营业费用 Funds Expenses	管理费用 Administrative Expense	财务费用 Financal Expenses
软饮料制造	Soft Beverage Manufacturing	494	5611	3291	-188
精制茶加工	Fine Tea Processing	21	166	449	93
烟草制品业	Tobacco Manufacturing	163	447	4644	-175
#卷烟制造	Cigarettes Manufacturing	163	447	4644	-175
纺织业	Textile Industry	1415	12286	11300	1393
#棉、化纤纺织及印染精加工	# Spinning, Weaving, Printing, Dyeing and Fine Processing of Cotton and Chemical Fiber				
毛纺织和染整精加工	Wool Textile and Dyeing, Finishing and Fine Processing	0	0	0	0
针织品、编织品及其制品制造	Manufacturing of Knitting Products and Weaving Products	1225	10230	9035	262
纺织服装、鞋、帽制造业	Manufacturing of Garments, Shoes and Hats	9	12	282	0
#纺织服装制造	# Manufacturing of Garments	9	12	282	0
皮革、毛皮、羽毛(绒)及其制品业	Leather, Furs, Down and Related Products		868	138	3
#皮革制品制造	Leather Products	0	868	138	3
木材加工及木、竹、藤、棕、草制品业	Timber Processing, Bamboo, Cane, Palm Fiber and Straw Products	29	2506	2630	705
#锯材、木片加工	Timber Processing	6	1434	1071	155
人造板制造	Artificial Wooden Products	8	898	1316	484
家具制造业	Furniture Manufacturing	0	1563	1839	471
#木质家具制造	Wooden Furniture Manufacturing	0	1563	1839	471
造纸及纸制品业	Papermaking and Paper Products	1635	21537	10546	45786
#纸浆制造	#Paper Pulp Production	1033	20881	9364	45681
造纸	Papermaking	8	37	187	41
印刷业和记录媒介的复制	Printing and Copying of Recording Mediums	337	1270	3083	162
#印刷	Printing	337	1262	2802	61
文教体育用品制造业	Cultural, Educational and Sports Goods	0	0	0	0
#文化用品制造	Cultural Goods	0	0	0	0
体育用品制造	Sports Goods	0	0	0	0
石油加工、炼焦及核燃料加工业	Petroleum Processing, Coking and Nuclear Fuel Processing	8877	1362	4435	14374
#精炼石油产品的制造	#Production of Refined Petroleum Products	8877	1362	4435	14374
化学原料及化学制品制造业	Raw Chemical Materials and Chemical Products	10206	11050	15881	7283
#肥料制造	Chemical Fertilizer Products	7012	2408	5843	1245
#氮肥制造	Nitrogenous Fertilizer Products	7012	1336	4852	946
农药制造	Agricultural Chemicals Products	0	1068	1124	107
日用化学产品制造	Production of Daily Chemical Products	29	2714	3905	-13
医药制造业	Medical and Pharmaceutical Products	1403	45170	30565	1622
#化学药品原药制造	# Production of Chemical Medicine Products	1	115	360	0
化学药品制剂制造	Production of Chemical Medicines and Preparations	1401	40615	25107	2788
中成药制造	Production of Traditional Chinese Patent Medicine	0	2333	2013	-1169
兽用药品制造	Production of Animal Medicines	0	0	0	0
化学纤维制造业	Chemical Fiber	214	572	1769	2708
#合成纤维制造	# Manufacturing of Synthetic Chemical Fiber	214	572	1769	2708
橡胶制品业	Rubber Products	5	260	1022	39

10-12 续 11(continued11)

类 别	Item	其他业务收入 Other Business Income	营业费用 Funds Expenses	管理费用 Administrative Expense	财务费用 Financal Expenses
#轮胎制造	Tire Manufacturing	0	0	0	0
塑料制品业	Plastic Products	780	1142	1714	192
#塑料薄膜制造	Plastic Membrane	336	918	1082	76
非金属矿物制品业	Nonmetal Mineral Products	745	8918	9353	2242
#水泥、石灰和石膏的制造	#Production of Cements, Limes and Gypsums	694	8545	7213	1766
水泥及石膏制品制造	Production of Cements and Gypsum Products	21	235	1464	316
砖瓦、石材及其他建筑材料制造	Production of Tiles, Stone Materials and Other Architectural Material Products	23	109	411	102
玻璃及玻璃制品制造	Glass and Glass Manufacturing	0	0	0	0
陶瓷制品制造	Ceramics Products	0	0	2	0
黑色金属冶炼及压延加工业	Smelting and Pressing of Ferrous Metals	563	474	2532	201
#炼铁	Iron Refine Products	0	0	0	0
钢压延加工	Steel Refine Products	529	207	1599	136
有色金属冶炼及压延加工业	Smelting and Pressing of Nonferrous Metals		96	344	
金属制品业	Metal Products	795	5995	3902	27
#结构性金属制品制造	#Structural Metal Products	49	19	154	0
集装箱及金属包装容器制造	Container and Metal Packaging Products	308	2426	2263	70
通用设备制造业	Manufacturing of General Equipments	124	168	163	226
专用设备制造业	Special Purpose Equipment	22	788	1364	57
#农、林、牧、渔专用机械制造	Manufacturing of Exclusive Machineries for Agriculture, Forestry, Livestock Farming and Fishing	19	506	1073	56
交通运输设备制造业	Transport Equipment	5972	3408	42115	4248
#汽车制造	Automobile Manufacturing	2872	3026	36713	4279
摩托车制造	Motorcycle Manufacturing	3016	382	3325	-11
电气机械及器材制造业	Electric Equipment and Machinery	4739	11664	6455	639
#电线、电缆、光缆及电工器材制造	# Manufacturing of Electric Wires, Cables, Optic Cables and Electrician Equipments	2829	2395	3246	287
通信设备、计算机及其他电子设备制造业	Manufacturing of Communication Equipments, Computers and Other Electronic Equipments	283	2040	5140	209
#通信设备制造	Telecommunications Equipment	243	1156	4067	-65
家用视听设备制造	Household Audio-visual Equipment Manufacturing	0	0	0	0
仪器仪表及文化、办公用机械制造业	Instruments, Meters, Cultural and Office Machinery			55	
工艺品及其他制造业	Industrial Arts and other Manufacturing	0	436	339	55
#工艺美术品制造	Industrial Arts Manufacturing	0	436	339	55
废弃资源和废旧材料回收加工业	Recovery and Processing of Discarded Resoures and Weste Material				
电力、热力的生产和供应业	Production and Supply of Electric Power, Steam and Hot Water	900	554	20647	22278
#电力生产	Electric Power Production	809	227	3697	16186
电力供应	Supply of Electric Power	91	327	16950	6092
燃气生产和供应业	Production and Supply of Gas	1355	6586	3105	1879
水的生产和供应业	Production and Supply of Water	625	2231	4930	2570
#自来水的生产和供应	Production and Supply of Tap Water	625	2231	4930	2570
污水处理及其再生利用	Treatment and Reuse of Waste Water	0	0	0	0

10-12 续 12(continued12)

类 别	Item	利息支出 Interest Expenses	利润总额 Total Profits	亏损企业亏损总额 Total Deficit of Loss Making Industrial Enterprises	利税总额 Total Profits and Taxes	本年应交增值税 Value Added Tax Payable
总 计	**Total**	106468	600036	115884	1019031	303727
按注册登记类型分	**Grouped by Economic Category**					
国有企业	State-owned Industy	7459	207788	17929	265002	47541
集体企业	Collective-owned Industry	147	-715	816	23	689
股份合作企业	Cooperative Enterprises	61	599	0	925	295
股份制企业	Share Holding Enterprises	14254	123732	13818	193057	62957
外商投资企业	Foreign Funded Enterprises	61444	92832	50305	203342	83954
港澳台商投资企业	Enterprises with Funds from Hong Kong ,Macao and Taiwan	1570	29142	1918	43455	14088
其他经济类型企业	Other Economy	21534	146657	31099	313227	94203
按轻重工业分	**Grouped by Light & Heavy Industry**					
轻工业	Light Industry	58943	176992	30590	339140	122146
重工业	Heavy Industry	47525	423044	85294	679891	181581
按企业规模分	**Grouped by Size of Enterprises**					
大型企业	Large-sized	0	0	0	0	0
中型企业	Medium-sized	80299	396015	61176	697754	196950
小型企业	Small-sized	26169	204020	54708	321277	106777
在总计中:国有控股企业	Of the Total:State-owned and State-holding Enterprises	36549	428992	49630	660750	151319
按工业行业分	**Grouped by Industrial Sector:**					
煤炭开采和洗选业	Coal Mining and Dressing	0	0	0	0	0
石油和天然气开采业	Petroleum and Natural Gas Extraction	0	45995	0	53763	6287
黑色金属矿采选业	Ferrous Metals Mining and Dressing	-232	40840	1893	60969	14298
#铁矿采选	Iron Ore Mining and Dressing	-232	40840	1893	60969	14298
有色金属矿采选业	Nonferrous Metals Mining and Dressing	126	494	400	2688	2125
非金属矿采选业	Nonmetal Minerals Mining and Dressing	270	5312	432	8493	2751
#采盐	Salt Mining and Dressing	260	165	5	1071	702
其他采矿业	Other Mining Industries	0	0	0	0	0
农副食品加工业	Farm Products and Non-staple Foodstuffs Processing Industry	2846	15524	8634	34988	18616
#制糖	Carbohydrate Processing	553	8395	4329	15839	6901
水产品加工	Aquatic Products Processing	1409	4544	2294	9283	4451
食品制造业	Food Manufacturing	186	6891	244	19754	11856
#制糖	Carbohydrate Processing	0	18	0	68	48
水产品加工	Aquatic Products Processing	10	4039	0	11823	7104
饮料制造业	Beverage Manufacturing	1569	10974	991	30690	13080
#酒精制造	Liquor Manufacturing	0	25	0	90	15
酒的制造	Alcohol Production	1515	5327	0	21431	9824

10-12 续 13(continued13)

类 别	Item	利息支出 Interest Expenses	利润总额 Total Profits	亏损企业亏损总额 Total Deficit of Loss Making Industrial Enterprises	利税总额 Total Profits and Taxes	本年应交增值税 Value Added Tax Payable
软饮料制造	Soft Beverage Manufacturing	-34	5603	727	8982	3107
精制茶加工	Fine Tea Processing	88	20	264	187	134
烟草制品业	Tobacco Manufacturing	-175	7717	0	41183	7390
#卷烟制造	Cigarettes Manufacturing	-175	7717	0	41183	7390
纺织业	Textile Industry	1088	2671	2207	3795	869
#棉、化纤纺织及印染精加工	# Spinning, Weaving, Printing, Dyeing and Fine Processing of Cotton and Chemical Fiber					
毛纺织和染整精加工	Wool Textile and Dyeing, Finishing and Fine Processing	0	0	0	0	0
针织品、编织品及其制品制造	Manufacturing of Knitting Products and Weaving Products	36	4078	199	4687	409
纺织服装、鞋、帽制造业	Manufacturing of Garments, Shoes and Hats	0	-203	203	-163	9
#纺织服装制造	# Manufacturing of Garments	0	-203	203	-163	9
皮革、毛皮、羽毛(绒)及其制品业	Leather, Furs, Down and Related Products		34		248	198
#皮革制品制造	Leather Products	0	34	0	248	198
木材加工及木、竹、藤、棕、草制品业	Timber Processing, Bamboo, Cane, Palm Fiber and Straw Products	552	-1364	3377	820	1980
#锯材、木片加工	Timber Processing	121	654	755	1505	749
人造板制造	Artificial Wooden Products	389	-2110	2529	-938	1082
家具制造业	Furniture Manufacturing	367	559	192	2237	1149
#木质家具制造	Wooden Furniture Manufacturing	367	559	192	2237	1149
造纸及纸制品业	Papermaking and Paper Products	45129	61503	998	93702	32151
#纸浆制造	#Paper Pulp Production	45050	61950	0	93557	31607
造纸	Papermaking	42	132	62	347	190
印刷业和记录媒介的复制	Printing and Copying of Recording Mediums	164	2112	2089	4214	1955
#印刷	Printing	63	2409	1791	4323	1775
文教体育用品制造业	Cultural, Educational and Sports Goods	0	0	0	0	0
#文化用品制造	Cultural Goods	0	0	0	0	0
体育用品制造	Sports Goods	0	0	0	0	0
石油加工、炼焦及核燃料加工业	Petroleum Processing, Coking and Nuclear Fuel Processing	14582	-42062	45264	8872	28827
#精炼石油产品的制造	#Production of Refined Petroleum Products	14582	-42062	45264	8872	28827
化学原料及化学制品制造业	Raw Chemical Materials and Chemical Products	6831	103343	13993	125844	21732
#肥料制造	Chemical Fertilizer Products	1115	106419	333	123998	17325
#氮肥制造	Nitrogenous Fertilizer Products	635	94263	0	106603	12087
农药制造	Agricultural Chemicals Products	107	206	0	435	206
日用化学产品制造	Production of Daily Chemical Products	50	9001	308	11924	2503
医药制造业	Medical and Pharmaceutical Products	2716	67686	3083	97564	27806
#化学药品原药制造	# Production of Chemical Medicine Products	0	-95	180	44	113
化学药品制剂制造	Production of Chemical Medicines and Preparations	2680	62600	2461	89349	24945
中成药制造	Production of Traditional Chinese Patent Medicine	25	255	211	1423	1042
兽用药品制造	Production of Animal Medicines	0	0	0	0	0
化学纤维制造业	Chemical Fiber	2707	-6393	6393	-5950	403
#合成纤维制造	# Manufacturing of Synthetic Chemical Fiber	2707	-6393	6393	-5950	403
橡胶制品业	Rubber Products	36	360	0	543	96

10-12 续 14(continued14)

类 别	Item	利息支出 Interest Expenses	利润总额 Total Profits	亏损企业亏损总额 Total Deficit of Loss Making Industrial Enterprises	利税总额 Total Profits and Taxes	本年应交增值税 Value Added Tax Payable
#轮胎制造	Tire Manufacturing	0	0	0	0	0
塑料制品业	Plastic Products	276	2728	578	4789	1990
#塑料薄膜制造	Plastic Membrane	164	2202	156	3534	1319
非金属矿物制品业	Nonmetal Mineral Products	1184	674	3976	11096	9466
#水泥、石灰和石膏的制造	#Production of Cements, Limes and Gypsums	755	-599	3377	8203	8073
水泥及石膏制品制造	Production of Cements and Gypsum Products	302	1445	180	2952	1290
砖瓦、石材及其他建筑材料制造	Production of Tiles, Stone Materials and Other Architectural Material Products	103	-196	276	-194	0
玻璃及玻璃制品制造	Glass and Glass Manufacturing	0	0	0	0	0
陶瓷制品制造	Ceramics Products	0	-1	1	-1	0
黑色金属冶炼及压延加工业	Smelting and Pressing of Ferrous Metals	125	-653	1781	2619	3000
#炼铁	Iron Refine Products	0	0	0	0	0
钢压延加工	Steel Refine Products	73	779	348	3435	2438
有色金属冶炼及压延加工业	Smelting and Pressing of Nonferrous Metals	2	89	54	326	189
金属制品业	Metal Products	352	8334	118	14041	5271
#结构性金属制品制造	#Structural Metal Products	0	-87	87	-27	39
集装箱及金属包装容器制造	Container and Metal Packaging Products	85	2148	0	4861	2298
通用设备制造业	Manufacturing of General Equipments	226	-900	903	-549	326
专用设备制造业	Special Purpose Equipment	55	665	206	874	189
#农、林、牧、渔专用机械制造	Manufacturing of Exclusive Machineries for Agriculture, Forestry, Livestock Farming and Fishing	55	530	181	612	69
交通运输设备制造业	Transport Equipment	2445	64445	3624	134041	30300
#汽车制造	Automobile Manufacturing	2467	66473	1160	132684	28509
摩托车制造	Motorcycle Manufacturing	-1	-2300	2312	1067	1774
电气机械及器材制造业	Electric Equipment and Machinery	330	14211	668	18385	4053
#电线、电缆、光缆及电工器材制造	# Manufacturing of Electric Wires, Cables, Optic Cables and Electrician Equipments	9	6041	2	6774	695
通信设备、计算机及其他电子设备制造业	Manufacturing of Communication Equipments, Computers and Other Electronic Equipments	143	6292	19	8326	1990
#通信设备制造	Telecommunications Equipment	-61	1546	18	1546	0
家用视听设备制造	Household Audio-visual Equipment Manufacturing	0	0	0	0	0
仪器仪表及文化、办公用机械制造业	Instruments, Meters, Cultural and Office Machinery	0	-15	15	1	15
工艺品及其他制造业	Industrial Arts and other Manufacturing	32	933	0	1311	349
#工艺美术品制造	Industrial Arts Manufacturing	32	933	0	1311	349
废弃资源和废旧材料回收加工业	Recovery and Processing of Discarded Resoures and Weste Material	0	0	0	0	0
电力、热力的生产和供应业	Production and Supply of Electric Power, Steam and Hot Water	18573	166717	11251	219564	48493
#电力生产	Electric Power Production	17479	664	7778	27861	24950
电力供应	Supply of Electric Power	1094	166053	3473	191703	23542
燃气生产和供应业	Production and Supply of Gas	1930	14068	0	17963	3201
水的生产和供应业	Production and Supply of Water	2034	452	2299	1990	1318
#自来水的生产和供应	Production and Supply of Tap Water	2034	452	2299	1990	1318
污水处理及其再生利用	Treatment and Reuse of Waste Water	0	0	0	0	0

10-12 续 15(continued15)

类 别	Item	固定资产原价 Original Value of Fixed Assets	固定资产净值年均余额 Annual Average Balance of Fixed Assets	流动资产年平均余额 Annual Average Balance of Circulating Funds	流动资产合计 Total Circulating Funds
总 计	**Total**	6528083	4742118	3033149	3393295
按注册登记类型分	**Grouped by Economic Category**				
国有企业	State-owned Industy	1488348	978993	270734	393270
集体企业	Collective-owned Industry	16874	8188	11004	11119
股份合作企业	Cooperative Enterprises	1691	1767	1689	1871
股份制企业	Share Holding Enterprises	1413443	841084	632020	649141
外商投资企业	Foreign Funded Enterprises	2199384	1992996	945427	1008792
港澳台商投资企业	Enterprises with Funds from Hong Kong ,Macao and Taiwan	125367	73385	149728	173931
其他经济类型企业	Other Economy	1282976	845704	1022547	1155171
按轻重工业分	**Grouped by Light & Heavy Industry**				
轻工业	Light Industry	2105525	1533563	1538701	1622664
重工业	Heavy Industry	4422557	3208555	1494448	1770631
按企业规模分	**Grouped by Size of Enterprises**				
大型企业	Large-sized	0	0	0	0
中型企业	Medium-sized	4477406	3348877	1916490	2199983
小型企业	Small-sized	2050677	1393241	1116660	1193312
在总计中:国有控股企业	Of the Total:State-owned and State-holding Enterprises	3789750	2404105	1297259	1520982
按工业行业分	**Grouped by Industrial Sector:**				
煤炭开采和洗选业	Coal Mining and Dressing	0	0	0	0
石油和天然气开采业	Petroleum and Natural Gas Extraction	63171	41213	13254	14037
黑色金属矿采选业	Ferrous Metals Mining and Dressing	266404	181319	29373	133985
#铁矿采选	Iron Ore Mining and Dressing	266404	181319	29373	133985
有色金属矿采选业	Nonferrous Metals Mining and Dressing	9112	5257	9362	7931
非金属矿采选业	Nonmetal Minerals Mining and Dressing	24617	16231	20403	24175
#采盐	Salt Mining and Dressing	10450	5509	7819	7370
其他采矿业	Other Mining Industries	0	0	0	0
农副食品加工业	Farm Products and Non-staple Foodstuffs Processing Industry	208031	133153	237030	255022
#制糖	Carbohydrate Processing	93891	55729	73035	76361
水产品加工	Aquatic Products Processing	67258	39927	95240	112586
食品制造业	Food Manufacturing	108599	38463	113457	116230
#制糖	Carbohydrate Processing	353	143	452	315
水产品加工	Aquatic Products Processing	72604	20766	67052	68152
饮料制造业	Beverage Manufacturing	140485	82883	158180	152101
#酒精制造	Liquor Manufacturing	152	152	291	296
酒的制造	Alcohol Production	95794	66750	114454	105148

10-12 续 16(continued16)

类 别	Item	固定资产原价 Original Value of Fixed Assets	固定资产净值年均余额 Annual Average Balance of Fixed Assets	流动资产年平均余额 Annual Average Balance of Circulating Funds	流动资产合计 Total Circulating Funds
软饮料制造	Soft Beverage Manufacturing	39101	14041	41534	45193
精制茶加工	Fine Tea Processing	5437	1939	1901	1464
烟草制品业	Tobacco Manufacturing	36576	17690	35970	37044
#卷烟制造	Cigarettes Manufacturing	36576	17690	35970	37044
纺织业	Textile Industry	111170	65866	80097	78007
#棉、化纤纺织及印染精加工	# Spinning, Weaving, Printing, Dyeing and Fine Processing of Cotton and Chemical Fiber				
毛纺织和染整精加工	Wool Textile and Dyeing, Finishing and Fine Processing	0	0	0	0
针织品、编织品及其制品制造	Manufacturing of Knitting Products and Weaving Products	17198	7123	35530	34456
纺织服装、鞋、帽制造业	Manufacturing of Garments, Shoes and Hats	1026	646	1177	1242
#纺织服装制造	# Manufacturing of Garments	1026	646	1177	1242
皮革、毛皮、羽毛(绒)及其制品业	Leather, Furs, Down and Related Products	525	141	1390	1411
#皮革制品制造	Leather Products	525	141	1390	1411
木材加工及木、竹、藤、棕、草制品业	Timber Processing, Bamboo, Cane, Palm Fiber and Straw Products	50775	31730	24214	25515
#锯材、木片加工	Timber Processing	11439	8547	13752	15048
人造板制造	Artificial Wooden Products	38463	22753	7742	7707
家具制造业	Furniture Manufacturing	25123	13963	31803	35577
#木质家具制造	Wooden Furniture Manufacturing	25123	13963	31803	35577
造纸及纸制品业	Papermaking and Paper Products	825522	765858	409322	447942
#纸浆制造	#Paper Pulp Production	814907	760674	390763	428593
造纸	Papermaking	3666	2264	5576	5505
印刷业和记录媒介的复制	Printing and Copying of Recording Mediums	57603	31344	27922	28553
#印刷	Printing	46351	24124	26083	26709
文教体育用品制造业	Cultural, Educational and Sports Goods	0	0	0	0
#文化用品制造	Cultural Goods	0	0	0	0
体育用品制造	Sports Goods	0	0	0	0
石油加工、炼焦及核燃料加工业	Petroleum Processing, Coking and Nuclear Fuel Processing	1023848	995619	213799	212443
#精炼石油产品的制造	#Production of Refined Petroleum Products	1023848	995619	213799	212443
化学原料及化学制品制造业	Raw Chemical Materials and Chemical Products	686926	449010	234731	254605
#肥料制造	Chemical Fertilizer Products	529733	327388	156145	170027
#氮肥制造	Nitrogenous Fertilizer Products	414109	269618	123725	123725
农药制造	Agricultural Chemicals Products	2279	2036	6339	6639
日用化学产品制造	Production of Daily Chemical Products	5493	3121	19954	21077
医药制造业	Medical and Pharmaceutical Products	183635	119715	328975	348442
#化学药品原药制造	# Production of Chemical Medicine Products	3238	1948	3128	3350
化学药品制剂制造	Production of Chemical Medicines and Preparations	160486	102750	259100	277196
中成药制造	Production of Traditional Chinese Patent Medicine	11016	8264	47066	48056
兽用药品制造	Production of Animal Medicines	0	0	0	0
化学纤维制造业	Chemical Fiber	114733	60472	22373	19835
#合成纤维制造	# Manufacturing of Synthetic Chemical Fiber	114733	60472	22373	19835
橡胶制品业	Rubber Products	4159	3355	5261	5396

10-12 续 17(continued17)

类 别	Item	固定资产原价 Original Value of Fixed Assets	固定资产净值年均余额 Annual Average Balance of Fixed Assets	流动资产年平均余额 Annual Average Balance of Circulating Funds	流动资产合计 Total Circulating Funds
#轮胎制造	Tire Manufacturing	0	0	0	0
塑料制品业	Plastic Products	20323	12717	26624	26011
#塑料薄膜制造	Plastic Membrane	5339	3484	10761	10559
非金属矿物制品业	Nonmetal Mineral Products	204671	135640	67826	71516
#水泥、石灰和石膏的制造	#Production of Cements, Limes and Gypsums	175827	117431	43680	49063
水泥及石膏制品制造	Production of Cements and Gypsum Products	16684	11056	19114	17284
砖瓦、石材及其他建筑材料制造	Production of Tiles, Stone Materials and Other Architectural Material Products	7402	4729	3134	3370
玻璃及玻璃制品制造	Glass and Glass Manufacturing	0	0	0	0
陶瓷制品制造	Ceramics Products	805	560	39	39
黑色金属冶炼及压延加工业	Smelting and Pressing of Ferrous Metals	58953	46411	55622	67215
#炼铁	Iron Refine Products	0	0	0	0
钢压延加工	Steel Refine Products	46535	25520	28926	29118
有色金属冶炼及压延加工业	Smelting and Pressing of Nonferrous Metals	3834	2942	5221	4660
金属制品业	Metal Products	70095	37723	57933	54759
#结构性金属制品制造	#Structural Metal Products	1576	1262	707	715
集装箱及金属包装容器制造	Container and Metal Packaging Products	23451	6084	23824	21171
通用设备制造业	Manufacturing of General Equipments	6537	2610	6533	6250
专用设备制造业	Special Purpose Equipment	5863	3365	6560	7457
#农、林、牧、渔专用机械制造	Manufacturing of Exclusive Machineries for Agriculture, Forestry, Livestock Farming and Fishing	2976	1384	3266	4390
交通运输设备制造业	Transport Equipment	264257	145489	458898	572961
#汽车制造	Automobile Manufacturing	192875	107401	429974	543689
摩托车制造	Motorcycle Manufacturing	57893	31005	18862	20052
电气机械及器材制造业	Electric Equipment and Machinery	34262	21406	72192	79910
#电线、电缆、光缆及电工器材制造	# Manufacturing of Electric Wires, Cables, Optic Cables and Electrician Equipments	11225	9116	17177	20025
通信设备、计算机及其他电子设备制造业	Manufacturing of Communication Equipments, Computers and Other Electronic Equipments	26372	15497	25962	58922
#通信设备制造	Telecommunications Equipment	2563	997	13826	43775
家用视听设备制造	Household Audio-visual Equipment Manufacturing	0	0	0	0
仪器仪表及文化、办公用机械制造业	Instruments, Meters, Cultural and Office Machinery	1179	772	828	828
工艺品及其他制造业	Industrial Arts and other Manufacturing	771	436	10019	10584
#工艺美术品制造	Industrial Arts Manufacturing	771	436	10019	10584
废弃资源和废旧材料回收加工业	Recovery and Processing of Discarded Resoures and Weste Material				
电力、热力的生产和供应业	Production and Supply of Electric Power, Steam and Hot Water	1566152	1025770	185360	169048
#电力生产	Electric Power Production	918397	559993	107830	101450
电力供应	Supply of Electric Power	647755	465777	77530	67599
燃气生产和供应业	Production and Supply of Gas	107722	75498	30435	29979
水的生产和供应业	Production and Supply of Water	215054	161914	25047	33706
#自来水的生产和供应	Production and Supply of Tap Water	215054	161914	25047	33706
污水处理及其再生利用	Treatment and Reuse of Waste Water	0	0	0	0

10-12 续 18(continued18)

类 别	Item	应收帐款净额 Net Accounts Receivable	产成品存货 Stock up Sales	资产总计 Total Property	负债合计 Total Liabilities	流动负债合计 Total Circulating Liabilities
总 计	**Total**	**754289**	**348870**	**9611482**	**5814834**	**2947346**
按注册登记类型分	**Grouped by Economic Category**					
国有企业	State-owned Industy	60334	18585	1708881	1211985	404814
集体企业	Collective-owned Industry	2252	2488	27360	17469	13926
股份合作企业	Cooperative Enterprises	508	507	3797	2518	1018
股份制企业	Share Holding Enterprises	150527	72446	1823305	927642	577541
外商投资企业	Foreign Funded Enterprises	280455	116077	3374790	2241051	864724
港澳台商投资企业	Enterprises with Funds from Hong Kong ,Macao and Taiwan	53381	19971	292865	143351	124357
其他经济类型企业	Other Economy	206831	118796	2380484	1270817	960967
按轻重工业分	**Grouped by Light & Heavy Industry**					
轻工业	Light Industry	418233	172912	3776935	2182279	1283632
重工业	Heavy Industry	336056	175957	5834547	3632554	1663715
按企业规模分	**Grouped by Size of Enterprises**					
大型企业	Large-sized	0	0	0	0	0
中型企业	Medium-sized	432836	241836	6521983	4122804	1831475
小型企业	Small-sized	321453	107034	3089499	1692030	1115872
在总计中:国有控股企业	Of the Total:State-owned and State-holding Enterprises	190769	117695	4833183	2871551	1448820
按工业行业分	**Grouped by Industrial Sector:**					
煤炭开采和洗选业	Coal Mining and Dressing	0	0	0	0	0
石油和天然气开采业	Petroleum and Natural Gas Extraction	485	185	82268	6787	6787
黑色金属矿采选业	Ferrous Metals Mining and Dressing	6853	10459	360407	66442	66438
#铁矿采选	Iron Ore Mining and Dressing	6853	10459	360407	66442	66438
有色金属矿采选业	Nonferrous Metals Mining and Dressing	2762	1654	15933	13125	11999
非金属矿采选业	Nonmetal Minerals Mining and Dressing	3345	2109	60434	31979	21393
#采盐	Salt Mining and Dressing	2066	991	25916	17247	16414
其他采矿业	Other Mining Industries	0	0	0	0	0
农副食品加工业	Farm Products and Non-staple Foodstuffs Processing Industry	76476	47607	457131	247048	227593
#制糖	Carbohydrate Processing	15835	12514	160160	87555	81609
水产品加工	Aquatic Products Processing	45173	29868	176678	92614	85350
食品制造业	Food Manufacturing	16792	14105	183849	103853	101864
#制糖	Carbohydrate Processing	23	8	650	340	249
水产品加工	Aquatic Products Processing	2784	10664	105797	61410	61410
饮料制造业	Beverage Manufacturing	36413	14634	258787	102676	98504
#酒精制造	Liquor Manufacturing	0	0	448	978	901
酒的制造	Alcohol Production	28928	10741	184476	62844	62844

10-12 续 19(continued19)

类 别	Item	应收帐款净额 Net Accounts Receivable	产成品存货 Stock up Sales	资产总计 Total Property	负债合计 Total Liabilities	流动负债合计 Total Circulating Liabilities
软饮料制造	Soft Beverage Manufacturing	6931	3886	68063	34411	31292
精制茶加工	Fine Tea Processing	554	7	5800	4444	3468
烟草制品业	Tobacco Manufacturing	732	1689	63196	21680	20547
#卷烟制造	Cigarettes Manufacturing	732	1689	63196	21680	20547
纺织业	Textile Industry	18511	16650	187855	153571	75937
#棉、化纤纺织及印染精加工	# Spinning, Weaving, Printing, Dyeing and Fine Processing of Cotton and Chemical Fiber					
毛纺织和染整精加工	Wool Textile and Dyeing, Finishing and Fine Processing	0	0	0	0	0
针织品、编织品及其制品制造	Manufacturing of Knitting Products and Weaving Products	11470	7499	42344	15145	14248
纺织服装、鞋、帽制造业	Manufacturing of Garments, Shoes and Hats	136	125	2424	1748	1748
#纺织服装制造	# Manufacturing of Garments	136	125	2424	1748	1748
皮革、毛皮、羽毛(绒)及其制品业	Leather, Furs, Down and Related Products	195	191	1592	930	904
#皮革制品制造	Leather Products	195	191	1592	930	904
木材加工及木、竹、藤、棕、草制品业	Timber Processing, Bamboo, Cane, Palm Fiber and Straw Products	9254	5310	64159	27187	19951
#锯材、木片加工	Timber Processing	6345	3328	29861	15905	12733
人造板制造	Artificial Wooden Products	2599	1709	30716	9412	5822
家具制造业	Furniture Manufacturing	7380	5710	52676	25176	20972
#木质家具制造	Wooden Furniture Manufacturing	7380	5710	52676	25176	20972
造纸及纸制品业	Papermaking and Paper Products	111544	23030	1479220	1012998	386636
#纸浆制造	#Paper Pulp Production	103997	21241	1451432	999198	373911
造纸	Papermaking	1309	840	8555	2773	2305
印刷业和记录媒介的复制	Printing and Copying of Recording Mediums	8945	1838	73063	35647	22944
#印刷	Printing	8704	1702	62571	31105	19879
文教体育用品制造业	Cultural, Educational and Sports Goods	0	0	0	0	0
#文化用品制造	Cultural Goods	0	0	0	0	0
体育用品制造	Sports Goods	0	0	0	0	0
石油加工、炼焦及核燃料加工业	Petroleum Processing, Coking and Nuclear Fuel Processing	43249	63140	1220769	964961	264961
#精炼石油产品的制造	#Production of Refined Petroleum Products	43249	63140	1220769	964961	264961
化学原料及化学制品制造业	Raw Chemical Materials and Chemical Products	42598	15907	789482	348867	214685
#肥料制造	Chemical Fertilizer Products	28454	2701	565450	185814	111085
#氮肥制造	Nitrogenous Fertilizer Products	9198	3	402618	88924	67008
农药制造	Agricultural Chemicals Products	865	1563	10386	2958	2913
日用化学产品制造	Production of Daily Chemical Products	6058	3799	29146	8923	6494
医药制造业	Medical and Pharmaceutical Products	120445	23280	596027	207907	175597
#化学药品原药制造	# Production of Chemical Medicine Products	785	440	6978	2702	2507
化学药品制剂制造	Production of Chemical Medicines and Preparations	96842	20756	501505	174743	143591
中成药制造	Production of Traditional Chinese Patent Medicine	15469	1470	58436	22770	22007
兽用药品制造	Production of Animal Medicines	0	0	0	0	0
化学纤维制造业	Chemical Fiber	3856	7380	75788	53244	37230
#合成纤维制造	# Manufacturing of Synthetic Chemical Fiber	3856	7380	75788	53244	37230
橡胶制品业	Rubber Products	1176	2122	9679	5578	4858

10-12 续 20(continued20)

类 别	Item	应收帐款净额 Net Accounts Receivable	产成品存货 Stock up Sales	资产总计 Total Property	负债合计 Total Liabilities	流动负债合计 Total Circulating Liabilities
# 轮胎制造	Tire Manufacturing	0	0	0	0	0
塑料制品业	Plastic Products	9268	3877	40831	22119	19812
# 塑料薄膜制造	Plastic Membrane	4138	1274	15295	5981	5981
非金属矿物制品业	Nonmetal Mineral Products	22479	3365	246228	107446	67441
# 水泥、石灰和石膏的制造	#Production of Cements, Limes and Gypsums	11712	1658	202485	83046	49785
水泥及石膏制品制造	Production of Cements and Gypsum Products	9209	1629	29683	15258	12395
砖瓦、石材及其他建筑材料制造	Production of Tiles, Stone Materials and Other Architectural Material Products	1314	42	9556	4552	2062
玻璃及玻璃制品制造	Glass and Glass Manufacturing	0	0	0	0	0
陶瓷制品制造	Ceramics Products	16	1	700	342	298
黑色金属冶炼及压延加工业	Smelting and Pressing of Ferrous Metals	19208	9941	124235	119858	67290
# 炼铁	Iron Refine Products	0	0	0	0	0
钢压延加工	Steel Refine Products	975	5142	57445	81507	28939
有色金属冶炼及压延加工业	Smelting and Pressing of Nonferrous Metals	205	1252	8328	4977	4888
金属制品业	Metal Products	16999	3899	101605	45064	27821
# 结构性金属制品制造	#Structural Metal Products	102	8	1952	436	376
集装箱及金属包装容器制造	Container and Metal Packaging Products	9358	794	35794	9749	8604
通用设备制造业	Manufacturing of General Equipments	1313	2394	10688	8572	8367
专用设备制造业	Special Purpose Equipment	1497	690	14716	8686	7913
# 农、林、牧、渔专用机械制造	Manufacturing of Exclusive Machineries for Agriculture, Forestry, Livestock Farming and Fishing	489	471	8990	6628	5963
交通运输设备制造业	Transport Equipment	54430	49573	868353	572767	508946
# 汽车制造	Automobile Manufacturing	50306	46472	787901	509453	447095
摩托车制造	Motorcycle Manufacturing	1716	2814	62093	56739	56658
电气机械及器材制造业	Electric Equipment and Machinery	36306	7230	121603	46778	45900
# 电线、电缆、光缆及电工器材制造	# Manufacturing of Electric Wires, Cables, Optic Cables and Electrician Equipments	10810	1055	44455	6517	6517
通信设备、计算机及其他电子设备制造业	Manufacturing of Communication Equipments, Computers and Other Electronic Equipments	11847	1300	78470	50237	49387
# 通信设备制造	Telecommunications Equipment	3566	758	44996	37957	37276
家用视听设备制造	Household Audio-visual Equipment Manufacturing	0	0	0	0	0
仪器仪表及文化、办公用机械制造业	Instruments, Meters, Cultural and Office Machinery	37	162	1766	975	924
工艺品及其他制造业	Industrial Arts and other Manufacturing	1825	7095	13715	3778	3778
# 工艺美术品制造	Industrial Arts Manufacturing	1825	7095	13715	3778	3778
废弃资源和废旧材料回收加工业	Recovery and Processing of Discarded Resoures and Weste Material					
电力、热力的生产和供应业	Production and Supply of Electric Power, Steam and Hot Water	60687	7	1539531	1194597	290629
# 电力生产	Electric Power Production	33990	6	831766	514460	229586
电力供应	Supply of Electric Power	26698	1	707765	680137	61043
燃气生产和供应业	Production and Supply of Gas	3537	961	191289	68057	32658
水的生产和供应业	Production and Supply of Water	3503	1	215384	129520	30046
# 自来水的生产和供应	Production and Supply of Tap Water	3503	1	215384	129520	30046
污水处理及其再生利用	Treatment and Reuse of Waste Water	0	0	0	0	0

10-12 续 21(continued21)

类 别	Item	长期负债合计 Total Long-period Liabilities	所有者权益合计 Creditors' Equity	实收资本 Total Capital Hold	国家资本 Nation Capital
总 计	**Total**	**2824018**	**3796648**	**3065726**	**872317**
按注册登记类型分	**Grouped by Economic Category**				
国有企业	State-owned Industy	803924	496896	443855	418302
集体企业	Collective-owned Industry	3543	9891	8993	371
股份合作企业	Cooperative Enterprises	1500	1279	1372	0
股份制企业	Share Holding Enterprises	344507	895663	681733	281932
外商投资企业	Foreign Funded Enterprises	1376317	1133739	1124812	12561
港澳台商投资企业	Enterprises with Funds from Hong Kong ,Macao and Taiwan	10323	149514	100339	1227
其他经济类型企业	Other Economy	283904	1109666	704623	157924
按轻重工业分	**Grouped by Light & Heavy Industry**				
轻工业	Light Industry	887501	1594656	1197526	148302
重工业	Heavy Industry	1936517	2201993	1868200	724014
按企业规模分	**Grouped by Size of Enterprises**				
大型企业	Large-sized	0	0	0	0
中型企业	Medium-sized	2273360	2399179	2005846	441081
小型企业	Small-sized	550658	1397469	1059880	431236
在总计中:国有控股企业	Of the Total:State-owned and State-holding Enterprises	1401511	1961631	1600289	863574
按工业行业分	**Grouped by Industrial Sector:**				
煤炭开采和洗选业	Coal Mining and Dressing	0	0	0	0
石油和天然气开采业	Petroleum and Natural Gas Extraction	0	75481	5000	0
黑色金属矿采选业	Ferrous Metals Mining and Dressing	4	293965	182299	177642
#铁矿采选	Iron Ore Mining and Dressing	4	293965	182299	177642
有色金属矿采选业	Nonferrous Metals Mining and Dressing	1126	2808	5323	988
非金属矿采选业	Nonmetal Minerals Mining and Dressing	2077	28455	24504	8953
#采盐	Salt Mining and Dressing	832	8669	8953	8953
其他采矿业	Other Mining Industries	0	0	0	0
农副食品加工业	Farm Products and Non-staple Foodstuffs Processing Industry	15271	210083	118763	9799
#制糖	Carbohydrate Processing	3594	72606	19284	2526
水产品加工	Aquatic Products Processing	7264	84064	50943	0
食品制造业	Food Manufacturing	1948	79996	36627	9020
#制糖	Carbohydrate Processing	91	310	224	0
水产品加工	Aquatic Products Processing	0	44386	14355	8499
饮料制造业	Beverage Manufacturing	4172	156111	142332	8818
#酒精制造	Liquor Manufacturing	77	-530	0	0
酒的制造	Alcohol Production	0	121632	121321	2385

10-12 续 22(continued22)

类　别	Item	长期负债合计 Total Long-period Liabilities	所有者权益合计 Creditors' Equity	实收资本 Total Capital Hold	国家资本 Nation Capital
软饮料制造	Soft Beverage Manufacturing	3119	33652	18529	4312
精制茶加工	Fine Tea Processing	976	1356	2482	2122
烟草制品业	Tobacco Manufacturing	1133	41516	20616	0
#卷烟制造	Cigarettes Manufacturing	1133	41516	20616	0
纺织业	Textile Industry	77633	34285	46163	1052
#棉、化纤纺织及印染精加工	# Spinning, Weaving, Printing, Dyeing and Fine Processing of Cotton and Chemical Fiber				
毛纺织和染整精加工	Wool Textile and Dyeing, Finishing and Fine Processing	0	0	0	0
针织品、编织品及其制品制造	Manufacturing of Knitting Products and Weaving Products	897	27199	9866	756
纺织服装、鞋、帽制造业	Manufacturing of Garments, Shoes and Hats	0	676	619	519
#纺织服装制造	# Manufacturing of Garments	0	676	619	519
皮革、毛皮、羽毛(绒)及其制品业	Leather, Furs, Down and Related Products	26	663	565	
#皮革制品制造	Leather Products	26	663	565	0
木材加工及木、竹、藤、棕、草制品业	Timber Processing, Bamboo, Cane, Palm Fiber and Straw Products	2117	36972	38248	23129
#锯材、木片加工	Timber Processing	200	13956	11788	2804
人造板制造	Artificial Wooden Products	1605	21304	25548	20235
家具制造业	Furniture Manufacturing	4007	27501	30770	609
#木质家具制造	Wooden Furniture Manufacturing	4007	27501	30770	609
造纸及纸制品业	Papermaking and Paper Products	625755	466223	447575	753
#纸浆制造	#Paper Pulp Production	625286	452235	440688	0
造纸	Papermaking	468	5782	1297	516
印刷业和记录媒介的复制	Printing and Copying of Recording Mediums	11163	37416	24985	9311
#印刷	Printing	9687	31467	18225	9151
文教体育用品制造业	Cultural, Educational and Sports Goods	0	0	0	0
#文化用品制造	Cultural Goods	0	0	0	0
体育用品制造	Sports Goods	0	0	0	0
石油加工、炼焦及核燃料加工业	Petroleum Processing, Coking and Nuclear Fuel Processing	700000	255809	400700	
#精炼石油产品的制造	#Production of Refined Petroleum Products	700000	255809	400700	0
化学原料及化学制品制造业	Raw Chemical Materials and Chemical Products	131780	440614	385649	263875
#肥料制造	Chemical Fertilizer Products	74729	379636	314062	261292
#氮肥制造	Nitrogenous Fertilizer Products	21916	313694	260237	260237
农药制造	Agricultural Chemicals Products	45	7428	7354	0
日用化学产品制造	Production of Daily Chemical Products	47	20223	9971	620
医药制造业	Medical and Pharmaceutical Products	31478	388120	142807	19209
#化学药品原药制造	# Production of Chemical Medicine Products	0	4276	4378	0
化学药品制剂制造	Production of Chemical Medicines and Preparations	30515	326762	120683	19162
中成药制造	Production of Traditional Chinese Patent Medicine	763	35666	11046	47
兽用药品制造	Production of Animal Medicines	0	0	0	0
化学纤维制造业	Chemical Fiber	16015	22543	57681	13135
#合成纤维制造	# Manufacturing of Synthetic Chemical Fiber	16015	22543	57681	13135
橡胶制品业	Rubber Products	720	4101	3480	2650

10-12 续 23(continued23)

类 别	Item	长期负债合计 Total Long-period Liabilities	所有者权益合计 Creditors' Equity	实收资本 Total Capital Hold	国家资本 Nation Capital
#轮胎制造	Tire Manufacturing	0	0	0	0
塑料制品业	Plastic Products	2307	18712	13598	3402
#塑料薄膜制造	Plastic Membrane	0	9314	3041	0
非金属矿物制品业	Nonmetal Mineral Products	23285	138782	107975	61955
#水泥、石灰和石膏的制造	#Production of Cements, Limes and Gypsums	16860	119439	90544	55179
水泥及石膏制品制造	Production of Cements and Gypsum Products	2589	14425	10513	1917
砖瓦、石材及其他建筑材料制造	Production of Tiles, Stone Materials and Other Architectural Material Products	2490	5005	4157	2376
玻璃及玻璃制品制造	Glass and Glass Manufacturing	0	0	0	0
陶瓷制品制造	Ceramics Products	0	358	308	308
黑色金属冶炼及压延加工业	Smelting and Pressing of Ferrous Metals	52567	4377	26750	
#炼铁	Iron Refine Products	0	0	0	0
钢压延加工	Steel Refine Products	52567	-24062	14750	0
有色金属冶炼及压延加工业	Smelting and Pressing of Nonferrous Metals		3352	4902	600
金属制品业	Metal Products	17243	56540	24589	2422
#结构性金属制品制造	#Structural Metal Products	60	1516	1078	520
集装箱及金属包装容器制造	Container and Metal Packaging Products	1146	26045	5907	1193
通用设备制造业	Manufacturing of General Equipments	205	2116	768	130
专用设备制造业	Special Purpose Equipment	774	6030	3351	1893
#农、林、牧、渔专用机械制造	Manufacturing of Exclusive Machineries for Agriculture, Forestry, Livestock Farming and Fishing	666	2362	1660	1390
交通运输设备制造业	Transport Equipment	62937	295586	165161	10231
#汽车制造	Automobile Manufacturing	62043	278449	150335	2024
摩托车制造	Motorcycle Manufacturing	81	5354	9258	2639
电气机械及器材制造业	Electric Equipment and Machinery	877	74826	41280	6666
#电线、电缆、光缆及电工器材制造	# Manufacturing of Electric Wires, Cables, Optic Cables and Electrician Equipments		37938	23145	
通信设备、计算机及其他电子设备制造业	Manufacturing of Communication Equipments, Computers and Other Electronic Equipments	285	28233	16823	1719
#通信设备制造	Telecommunications Equipment	115	7039	1541	1541
家用视听设备制造	Household Audio-visual Equipment Manufacturing	0	0	0	0
仪器仪表及文化、办公用机械制造业	Instruments, Meters, Cultural and Office Machinery		791	935	110
工艺品及其他制造业	Industrial Arts and other Manufacturing	0	9938	4406	0
#工艺美术品制造	Industrial Arts Manufacturing	0	9938	4406	0
废弃资源和废旧材料回收加工业	Recovery and Processing of Discarded Resoures and Weste Material				
电力、热力的生产和供应业	Production and Supply of Electric Power, Steam and Hot Water	903398	344934	360122	140940
#电力生产	Electric Power Production	284350	317306	287313	69140
电力供应	Supply of Electric Power	619049	27627	72808	71800
燃气生产和供应业	Production and Supply of Gas	35399	123232	84600	22600
水的生产和供应业	Production and Supply of Water	98317	85864	95760	70187
#自来水的生产和供应	Production and Supply of Tap Water	98317	85864	95760	70187
污水处理及其再生利用	Treatment and Reuse of Waste Water	0	0	0	0

10－13 规模以上工业企业主要经济效益指标
Main Indicators on Economic Benefit of Above Designed Size Industrial Enterprises

类 别	Item	企业亏损面(%) Ratio of Loss Making Industrial Enterprises	工业增加值率(%) Ratio of Value-added of Industry	总资产贡献率(%) Ratio of Assets to Industrial Output Value	资产负债率(%) Assets-Liability Ratio
总 计	**Total**	40.00	29.61	11.71	60.50
按注册登记类型分	**Grouped by Economic Category**				
国有企业	State-owned Industy	51.38	39.73	15.94	70.92
集体企业	Collective-owned Industry	50.00	26.74	0.62	63.85
股份合作企业	Cooperative Enterprises	0.00	21.97	25.97	66.32
股份制企业	Share Holding Enterprises	35.43	36.59	11.37	50.88
外商投资企业	Foreign Funded Enterprises	28.30	23.69	7.85	66.41
港澳台商投资企业	Enterprises with Funds from Hong Kong ,Macao and Taiwan	38.78	30.14	15.37	48.95
其他经济类型企业	Other Economy	35.26	27.73	14.06	53.38
按轻重工业分	**Grouped by Light & Heavy Industry**				
轻工业	Light Industry	40.26	30.11	10.54	57.78
重工业	Heavy Industry	39.73	29.33	12.47	62.26
按企业规模分	**Grouped by Size of Enterprises**				
大型企业	Large-sized	0.00	0.00	0.00	0.00
中型企业	Medium-sized	18.29	27.63	11.93	63.21
小型企业	Small-sized	43.47	33.53	11.25	54.77
在总计中:国有控股企业	Of the Total:State－owned and State－holding Enterprises	45.42	35.47	14.43	59.41
按工业行业分	**Grouped by Industrial Sector:**				
煤炭开采和洗选业	Coal Mining and Dressing	0.00	0.00	0.00	0.00
石油和天然气开采业	Petroleum and Natural Gas Extraction	0.00	75.84	65.35	8.25
黑色金属矿采选业	Ferrous Metals Mining and Dressing	37.50	67.20	16.85	18.44
#铁矿采选	Iron Ore Mining and Dressing	37.50	67.20	16.85	18.44
有色金属矿采选业	Nonferrous Metals Mining and Dressing	25.00	25.85	17.66	82.38
非金属矿采选业	Nonmetal Minerals Mining and Dressing	40.00	45.47	14.50	52.92
#采盐	Salt Mining and Dressing	25.00	66.66	5.14	66.55
其他采矿业	Other Mining Industries	0.00	0.00	0.00	0.00
农副食品加工业	Farm Products and Non-staple Foodstuffs Processing Industry	38.67	23.80	8.28	54.04
#制糖	Carbohydrate Processing	41.18	34.75	10.23	54.67
水产品加工	Aquatic Products Processing	37.14	24.61	6.05	52.42
食品制造业	Food Manufacturing	20.83	25.66	10.85	56.49
#制糖	Carbohydrate Processing	0.00	25.95	10.46	52.31
水产品加工	Aquatic Products Processing	0.00	23.41	11.18	58.05
饮料制造业	Beverage Manufacturing	31.82	31.24	12.47	39.68
#酒精制造	Liquor Manufacturing	0.00	11.49	20.09	218.30
酒的制造	Alcohol Production	0.00	29.78	12.44	34.07
软饮料制造	Soft Beverage Manufacturing	38.46	36.08	13.15	50.56
精制茶加工	Fine Tea Processing	40.00	31.10	4.74	76.62
烟草制品业	Tobacco Manufacturing	0.00	68.98	64.89	34.31
#卷烟制造	Cigarettes Manufacturing	0.00	68.98	64.89	34.31
纺织业	Textile Industry	44.44	29.25	2.60	81.75
#棉、化纤纺织及印染精加工	#Spinning, Weaving, Printing, Dyeing and Fine Processing of Cotton and Chemical Fiber				
毛纺织和染整精加工	Wool Textile and Dyeing, Finishing and Fine Processing	0.00	0.00	0.00	0.00

10-13 续 1(continued1)

类 别	Item	企业亏损面(%) Ratio of Loss Making Industrial Enterprises	工业增加值率(%) Ratio of Value-added of Industry	总资产贡献率(%) Ratio of Assets to Industrial Output Value	资产负债率(%) Assets-Liability Ratio
针织品、编织品及其制品制造	Manufacturing of Knitting Products and Weaving Products	40.00	30.83	11.15	35.77
纺织服装、鞋、帽制造业	Manufacturing of Garments, Shoes and Hats	100.00	4.44	-6.72	72.11
#纺织服装制造	# Manufacturing of Garments	100.00	4.44	-6.72	72.11
皮革、毛皮、羽毛(绒)及其制品业	Leather, Furs, Down and Related Products		22.22	15.58	58.42
#皮革制品制造	Leather Products	0.00	22.22	15.58	58.42
木材加工及木、竹、藤、棕、草制品业	Timber Processing, Bamboo, Cane, Palm Fiber and Straw Products	36.67	22.03	2.14	42.37
#锯材、木片加工	Timber Processing	31.58	18.68	5.45	53.26
人造板制造	Artificial Wooden Products	50.00	25.05	-1.78	30.64
家具制造业	Furniture Manufacturing	38.46	22.74	4.94	47.79
#木质家具制造	Wooden Furniture Manufacturing	38.46	22.74	4.94	47.79
造纸及纸制品业	Papermaking and Paper Products	40.00	29.87	9.39	68.48
#纸浆制造	#Paper Pulp Production	0.00	29.73	9.55	68.84
造纸	Papermaking	25.00	41.45	4.56	32.41
印刷业和记录媒介的复制	Printing and Copying of Recording Mediums	46.15	43.48	5.99	48.79
#印刷	Printing	43.48	43.58	7.01	49.71
文教体育用品制造业	Cultural, Educational and Sports Goods	0.00	0.00	0.00	0.00
#文化用品制造	Cultural Goods	0.00	0.00	0.00	0.00
体育用品制造	Sports Goods	0.00	0.00	0.00	0.00
石油加工、炼焦及核燃料加工业	Petroleum Processing, Coking and Nuclear Fuel Processing	33.33	15.61	1.92	79.05
#精炼石油产品的制造	#Production of Refined Petroleum Products	33.33	15.61	1.92	79.05
化学原料及化学制品制造业	Raw Chemical Materials and Chemical Products	40.91	46.52	16.81	44.19
#肥料制造	Chemical Fertilizer Products	18.18	74.74	22.13	32.86
#氮肥制造	Nitrogenous Fertilizer Products	0.00	74.08	26.64	22.09
农药制造	Agricultural Chemicals Products	0.00	26.42	5.22	28.48
日用化学产品制造	Production of Daily Chemical Products	25.00	50.73	41.08	30.61
医药制造业	Medical and Pharmaceutical Products	37.25	36.60	16.82	34.88
#化学药品原药制造	# Production of Chemical Medicine Products	75.00	29.47	0.63	38.72
化学药品制剂制造	Production of Chemical Medicines and Preparations	32.35	36.98	18.35	34.84
中成药制造	Production of Traditional Chinese Patent Medicine	44.44	32.90	2.48	38.97
兽用药品制造	Production of Animal Medicines	0.00	0.00	0.00	0.00
化学纤维制造业	Chemical Fiber	100.00	7.03	-4.28	70.25
#合成纤维制造	# Manufacturing of Synthetic Chemical Fiber	100.00	7.03	-4.28	70.25
橡胶制品业	Rubber Products	0.00	26.42	5.98	57.63
#轮胎制造	Tire Manufacturing	0.00	0.00	0.00	0.00
塑料制品业	Plastic Products	38.89	25.96	12.40	54.17
#塑料薄膜制造	Plastic Membrane	40.00	27.94	24.18	39.10
非金属矿物制品业	Nonmetal Mineral Products	54.29	33.04	4.99	43.64

10-13 续 2(continued2)

类　别	Item	企业亏损面(%) Ratio of Loss Making Industrial Enterprises	工业增加值率(%) Ratio of Value-added of Industry	总资产贡献率(%) Ratio of Assets to Industrial Output Value	资产负债率(%) Assets-Liability Ratio
#水泥、石灰和石膏的制造	#Production of Cements, Limes and Gypsums	58.82	33.21	4.42	41.01
水泥及石膏制品制造	Production of Cements and Gypsum Products	44.44	32.93	10.96	51.40
砖瓦、石材及其他建筑材料制造	Production of Tiles, Stone Materials and Other Architectural Material Products	50.00	16.49	-0.94	47.63
玻璃及玻璃制品制造	Glass and Glass Manufacturing	0.00	0.00	0.00	0.00
陶瓷制品制造	Ceramics Products	100.00	33.33	-0.14	48.86
黑色金属冶炼及压延加工业	Smelting and Pressing of Ferrous Metals	57.14	23.13	2.21	96.48
#炼铁	Iron Refine Products	0.00	0.00	0.00	0.00
钢压延加工	Steel Refine Products	40.00	23.79	6.11	141.89
有色金属冶炼及压延加工业	Smelting and Pressing of Nonferrous Metals	25.00	31.26	3.94	59.76
金属制品业	Metal Products	40.00	14.02	14.17	44.35
#结构性金属制品制造	#Structural Metal Products	66.67	30.57	-1.38	22.34
集装箱及金属包装容器制造	Container and Metal Packaging Products		20.75	13.82	27.24
通用设备制造业	Manufacturing of General Equipments	66.67	35.87	-3.03	80.20
专用设备制造业	Special Purpose Equipment	70.00	19.80	6.31	59.02
#农、林、牧、渔专用机械制造	Manufacturing of Exclusive Machineries for Agriculture, Forestry, Livestock Farming and Fishing	60.00	20.83	7.42	73.73
交通运输设备制造业	Transport Equipment	45.00	23.74	15.72	65.96
#汽车制造	Automobile Manufacturing	31.03	24.18	17.15	64.66
摩托车制造	Motorcycle Manufacturing	87.50	16.18	1.72	91.38
电气机械及器材制造业	Electric Equipment and Machinery	40.00	22.68	15.39	38.47
#电线、电缆、光缆及电工器材制造	# Manufacturing of Electric Wires, Cables, Optic Cables and Electrician Equipments	25.00	21.56	15.26	14.66
通信设备、计算机及其他电子设备制造业	Manufacturing of Communication Equipments, Computers and Other Electronic Equipments	33.33	37.54	10.79	64.02
#通信设备制造	Telecommunications Equipment	50.00	49.24	3.30	84.36
家用视听设备制造	Household Audio-visual Equipment Manufacturing	0.00	0.00	0.00	0.00
仪器仪表及文化、办公用机械制造业	Instruments, Meters, Cultural and Office Machinery	100.00	18.37	0.11	55.21
工艺品及其他制造业	Industrial Arts and other Manufacturing	0.00	13.73	9.79	27.55
#工艺美术品制造	Industrial Arts Manufacturing	0.00	13.73	9.79	27.55
废弃资源和废旧材料回收加工业	Recovery and Processing of Discarded Resoures and Weste Material				
电力、热力的生产和供应业	Production and Supply of Electric Power, Steam and Hot Water	38.60	32.92	15.47	77.59
#电力生产	Electric Power Production	55.88	36.16	5.45	61.85
电力供应	Supply of Electric Power	13.04	30.92	27.24	96.10
燃气生产和供应业	Production and Supply of Gas	0.00	41.67	10.40	35.58
水的生产和供应业	Production and Supply of Water	52.17	52.21	1.87	60.13
#自来水的生产和供应	Production and Supply of Tap Water	52.17	52.21	1.87	60.13
污水处理及其再生利用	Treatment and Reuse of Waste Water	0.00	0.00	0.00	0.00

10-13 续 3(continued3)

类 别	Item	流动资产周转次数(次) Number of Times of Annual of Turnover Circulating Funds	工业成本费用利润率(%) Ratio of Profits to Industrial Cost	全员劳动生产率(元/人) Overall Labor Productivity	产品销售率(%) Proportion of Products Sold(%)
总 计	**Total**	1.97	11.49	15.54	97.16
按注册登记类型分	**Grouped by Economic Category**				
国有企业	State-owned Industy	2.78	40.14	7.40	100.51
集体企业	Collective-owned Industry	0.95	-6.40	2.72	80.62
股份合作企业	Cooperative Enterprises	4.47	8.40	6.54	102.13
股份制企业	Share Holding Enterprises	1.89	11.50	19.78	97.38
外商投资企业	Foreign Funded Enterprises	1.80	6.04	24.68	96.69
港澳台商投资企业	Enterprises with Funds from Hong Kong ,Macao and Taiwan	1.55	14.38	8.08	100.23
其他经济类型企业	Other Economy	2.04	7.85	19.91	96.10
按轻重工业分	**Grouped by Light & Heavy Industry**				
轻工业	Light Industry	1.38	9.22	10.72	97.49
重工业	Heavy Industry	2.58	12.81	20.73	96.98
按企业规模分	**Grouped by Size of Enterprises**				
大型企业	Large-sized	0.00	0.00	0.00	0.00
中型企业	Medium-sized	2.03	11.82	18.29	96.83
小型企业	Small-sized	1.88	10.91	12.48	97.83
在总计中:国有控股企业	Of the Total:State-owned and State-holding Enterprises	2.21	18.27	17.08	97.87
按工业行业分	**Grouped by Industrial Sector:**				
煤炭开采和洗选业	Coal Mining and Dressing	0.00	0.00	0.00	0.00
石油和天然气开采业	Petroleum and Natural Gas Extraction	5.23	305.21	1699.10	99.74
黑色金属矿采选业	Ferrous Metals Mining and Dressing	4.99	41.10	10.58	114.06
#铁矿采选	Iron Ore Mining and Dressing	4.99	41.10	10.58	114.06
有色金属矿采选业	Nonferrous Metals Mining and Dressing	5.30	1.05	12.34	98.63
非金属矿采选业	Nonmetal Minerals Mining and Dressing	1.38	23.47	4.46	90.55
#采盐	Salt Mining and Dressing	0.57	3.59	1.97	67.03
其他采矿业	Other Mining Industries	0.00	0.00	0.00	0.00
农副食品加工业	Farm Products and Non-staple Foodstuffs Processing Industry	2.02	3.36	5.81	93.93
#制糖	Carbohydrate Processing	1.02	12.86	3.37	94.19
水产品加工	Aquatic Products Processing	2.32	2.11	5.80	92.95
食品制造业	Food Manufacturing	1.65	3.81	9.61	109.48
#制糖	Carbohydrate Processing	2.72	1.55	1.93	94.35
水产品加工	Aquatic Products Processing	1.70	3.64	12.80	94.64
饮料制造业	Beverage Manufacturing	1.58	4.73	21.84	98.51
#酒精制造	Liquor Manufacturing	3.11	3.02	1.96	100.00
酒的制造	Alcohol Production	1.66	2.98	44.54	98.14
软饮料制造	Soft Beverage Manufacturing	1.32	11.30	11.42	99.92
精制茶加工	Fine Tea Processing	1.55	0.66	2.36	91.66
烟草制品业	Tobacco Manufacturing	1.92	21.34	114.79	96.71
#卷烟制造	Cigarettes Manufacturing	1.92	21.34	114.79	96.71
纺织业	Textile Industry	1.23	2.81	4.11	96.98
#棉、化纤纺织及印染精加工	#Spinning, Weaving, Printing, Dyeing and Fine Processing of Cotton and Chemical Fiber				
毛纺织和染整精加工	Wool Textile and Dyeing, Finishing and Fine Processing	0.00	0.00	0.00	0.00

10-13 续 4(continued4)

类 别	Item	流动资产周转次数(次) Number of Times of Annual of Turnover Circulating Funds	工业成本费用利润率(%) Ratio of Profits to Industrial Cost	全员劳动生产率(元/人) Overall Labor Productivity	产品销售率(%) Proportion of Products Sold(%)
针织品、编织品及其制品制造	Manufacturing of Knitting Products and Weaving Products	1.90	6.40	3.57	98.62
纺织服装、鞋、帽制造业	Manufacturing of Garments, Shoes and Hats	1.24	-12.37	0.03	87.41
#纺织服装制造	# Manufacturing of Garments	1.24	-12.37	0.03	87.41
皮革、毛皮、羽毛(绒)及其制品业	Leather, Furs, Down and Related Products	1.52	1.63	2.08	93.03
#皮革制品制造	Leather Products	1.52	1.63	2.08	93.03
木材加工及木、竹、藤、棕、草制品业	Timber Processing, Bamboo, Cane, Palm Fiber and Straw Products	2.54	-2.22	3.94	104.64
#锯材、木片加工	Timber Processing	2.53	2.04	3.44	107.92
人造板制造	Artificial Wooden Products	2.70	-8.90	4.89	101.61
家具制造业	Furniture Manufacturing	1.47	1.23	3.33	97.06
#木质家具制造	Wooden Furniture Manufacturing	1.47	1.23	3.33	97.06
造纸及纸制品业	Papermaking and Paper Products	1.04	16.60	35.54	99.74
#纸浆制造	#Paper Pulp Production	1.03	17.80	64.32	100.00
造纸	Papermaking	1.14	2.15	7.86	94.26
印刷业和记录媒介的复制	Printing and Copying of Recording Mediums	1.23	6.77	7.29	97.88
#印刷	Printing	1.27	8.14	7.46	97.82
文教体育用品制造业	Cultural, Educational and Sports Goods	0.00	0.00	0.00	0.00
#文化用品制造	Cultural Goods	0.00	0.00	0.00	0.00
体育用品制造	Sports Goods	0.00	0.00	0.00	0.00
石油加工、炼焦及核燃料加工业	Petroleum Processing, Coking and Nuclear Fuel Processing	3.39	-6.11	207.31	92.92
#精炼石油产品的制造	#Production of Refined Petroleum Products	3.39	-6.11	207.31	92.92
化学原料及化学制品制造业	Raw Chemical Materials and Chemical Products	2.31	23.31	54.08	98.69
#肥料制造	Chemical Fertilizer Products	1.61	68.69	128.70	101.87
#氮肥制造	Nitrogenous Fertilizer Products	1.77	70.17	219.90	102.56
农药制造	Agricultural Chemicals Products	1.28	2.61	5.68	97.02
日用化学产品制造	Production of Daily Chemical Products	1.88	33.53	34.96	86.52
医药制造业	Medical and Pharmaceutical Products	0.91	29.04	17.84	94.18
#化学药品原药制造	# Production of Chemical Medicine Products	0.80	-3.66	4.30	91.60
化学药品制剂制造	Production of Chemical Medicines and Preparations	0.98	32.19	19.15	93.59
中成药制造	Production of Traditional Chinese Patent Medicine	0.57	1.02	10.85	109.15
兽用药品制造	Production of Animal Medicines	0.00	0.00	0.00	0.00
化学纤维制造业	Chemical Fiber	3.05	-8.56	6.30	98.18
#合成纤维制造	# Manufacturing of Synthetic Chemical Fiber	3.05	-8.56	6.30	98.18
橡胶制品业	Rubber Products	5.48	1.27	12.97	95.75
#轮胎制造	Tire Manufacturing	0.00	0.00	0.00	0.00
塑料制品业	Plastic Products	1.51	7.35	7.70	100.11
#塑料薄膜制造	Plastic Membrane	2.04	11.12	13.36	104.16
非金属矿物制品业	Nonmetal Mineral Products	2.26	0.44	9.70	93.06

10-13 续 5(continued5)

类 别	Item	流动资产周转次数(次) Number of Times of Annual of Turnover Circulating Funds	工业成本费用利润率(%) Ratio of Profits to Industrial Cost	全员劳动生产率(元/人) Overall Labor Productivity	产品销售率(%) Proportion of Products Sold(%)
#水泥、石灰和石膏的制造	#Production of Cements, Limes and Gypsums	2.86	-0.48	10.91	92.95
水泥及石膏制品制造	Production of Cements and Gypsum Products	1.28	6.32	10.83	92.82
砖瓦、石材及其他建筑材料制造	Production of Tiles, Stone Materials and Other Architectural Material Products	0.52	-10.72	0.53	90.87
玻璃及玻璃制品制造	Glass and Glass Manufacturing	0.00	0.00	0.00	0.00
陶瓷制品制造	Ceramics Products	0.15	-14.29	0.10	100.00
黑色金属冶炼及压延加工业	Smelting and Pressing of Ferrous Metals	1.58	-0.74	10.92	89.35
#炼铁	Iron Refine Products	0.00	0.00	0.00	0.00
钢压延加工	Steel Refine Products	1.72	1.59	11.67	98.93
有色金属冶炼及压延加工业	Smelting and Pressing of Nonferrous Metals	2.54	0.67	20.32	98.89
金属制品业	Metal Products	2.55	5.97	14.81	101.72
#结构性金属制品制造	#Structural Metal Products	0.85	-12.24	3.25	47.97
集装箱及金属包装容器制造	Container and Metal Packaging Products	2.31	4.07	10.63	99.99
通用设备制造业	Manufacturing of General Equipments	0.63	-21.69	2.41	93.92
专用设备制造业	Special Purpose Equipment	2.81	3.79	3.52	96.49
#农、林、牧、渔专用机械制造	Manufacturing of Exclusive Machineries for Agriculture, Forestry, Livestock Farming and Fishing	4.55	3.74	3.86	96.76
交通运输设备制造业	Transport Equipment	2.05	7.63	25.20	96.62
#汽车制造	Automobile Manufacturing	2.01	8.61	35.90	96.39
摩托车制造	Motorcycle Manufacturing	3.50	-3.58	5.66	99.42
电气机械及器材制造业	Electric Equipment and Machinery	1.88	11.09	16.52	96.33
#电线、电缆、光缆及电工器材制造	# Manufacturing of Electric Wires, Cables, Optic Cables and Electrician Equipments	2.62	12.92	21.15	89.01
通信设备、计算机及其他电子设备制造业	Manufacturing of Communication Equipments, Computers and Other Electronic Equipments	2.17	12.76	15.31	72.73
#通信设备制造	Telecommunications Equipment	1.57	7.66	25.85	36.31
家用视听设备制造	Household Audio-visual Equipment Manufacturing	0.00	0.00	0.00	0.00
仪器仪表及文化、办公用机械制造业	Instruments, Meters, Cultural and Office Machinery	0.45	-3.86	0.23	112.05
工艺品及其他制造业	Industrial Arts and other Manufacturing	1.90	5.15	8.66	96.63
#工艺美术品制造	Industrial Arts Manufacturing	1.90	5.15	8.66	96.63
废弃资源和废旧材料回收加工业	Recovery and Processing of Discarded Resoures and Weste Material				
电力、热力的生产和供应业	Production and Supply of Electric Power, Steam and Hot Water	3.53	35.80	15.17	99.73
#电力生产	Electric Power Production	2.22	0.28	15.24	99.31
电力供应	Supply of Electric Power	5.35	71.54	15.12	99.99
燃气生产和供应业	Production and Supply of Gas	2.61	21.08	40.15	97.21
水的生产和供应业	Production and Supply of Water	1.05	1.76	3.69	92.26
#自来水的生产和供应	Production and Supply of Tap Water	1.05	1.76	3.69	92.26
污水处理及其再生利用	Treatment and Reuse of Waste Water	0.00	0.00	0.00	0.00

10-13 续 6(continued6)

类 别	Item	每百元销售收入实现的利润(元) Actual Net Profit Per 100 Sales Revenue	每百元销售收入实现的利税(元) Actual Gross Profit Per 100 Sales Revenue	平均每一职工创造的利润(元) Average Net Profit Per Employee's Output	平均每一职工创造的利税(元) Average Gross Profit Per Employee's Output
总 计	**Total**	**9.65**	**16.38**	**4.92**	**8.36**
按注册登记类型分	**Grouped by Economic Category**				
国有企业	State-owned Industy	28.21	35.98	5.28	6.73
集体企业	Collective-owned Industry	-6.65	0.21	-0.55	0.02
股份合作企业	Cooperative Enterprises	7.82	12.07	2.38	3.67
股份制企业	Share Holding Enterprises	10.37	16.18	5.46	8.52
外商投资企业	Foreign Funded Enterprises	4.78	10.47	4.82	10.55
港澳台商投资企业	Enterprises with Funds from Hong Kong ,Macao and Taiwan	12.44	18.55	3.34	4.98
其他经济类型企业	Other Economy	6.99	14.94	4.83	10.31
按轻重工业分	**Grouped by Light & Heavy Industry**				
轻工业	Light Industry	8.07	15.47	2.80	5.37
重工业	Heavy Industry	10.50	16.88	7.20	11.57
按企业规模分	**Grouped by Size of Enterprises**				
大型企业	Large-sized	0.00	0.00	0.00	0.00
中型企业	Medium-sized	9.61	16.93	6.16	10.85
小型企业	Small-sized	9.72	15.31	3.54	5.57
在总计中:国有控股企业	Of the Total:State-owned and State-holding Enterprises	14.74	22.71	6.95	10.71
按工业行业分	**Grouped by Industrial Sector:**				
煤炭开采和洗选业	Coal Mining and Dressing	0.00	0.00	0.00	0.00
石油和天然气开采业	Petroleum and Natural Gas Extraction	66.40	77.62	1483.71	1734.29
黑色金属矿采选业	Ferrous Metals Mining and Dressing	25.82	38.55	4.64	6.92
#铁矿采选	Iron Ore Mining and Dressing	25.82	38.55	4.64	6.92
有色金属矿采选业	Nonferrous Metals Mining and Dressing	1.03	5.61	0.49	2.64
非金属矿采选业	Nonmetal Minerals Mining and Dressing	21.31	34.07	1.89	3.02
#采盐	Salt Mining and Dressing	3.97	25.76	0.08	0.51
其他采矿业	Other Mining Industries	0.00	0.00	0.00	0.00
农副食品加工业	Farm Products and Non-staple Foodstuffs Processing Industry	3.36	7.57	0.77	1.73
#制糖	Carbohydrate Processing	11.78	22.22	1.07	2.03
水产品加工	Aquatic Products Processing	2.07	4.23	0.45	0.93
食品制造业	Food Manufacturing	3.60	10.33	1.48	4.24
#制糖	Carbohydrate Processing	1.48	5.58	0.10	0.39
水产品加工	Aquatic Products Processing	3.42	10.02	1.77	5.19
饮料制造业	Beverage Manufacturing	5.19	14.52	3.57	10.00
#酒精制造	Liquor Manufacturing	2.76	9.94	0.47	1.70
酒的制造	Alcohol Production	3.40	13.70	5.00	20.10
软饮料制造	Soft Beverage Manufacturing	10.81	17.33	3.42	5.48
精制茶加工	Fine Tea Processing	0.92	8.60	0.06	0.60
烟草制品业	Tobacco Manufacturing	11.18	59.65	17.99	96.00
#卷烟制造	Cigarettes Manufacturing	11.18	59.65	17.99	96.00
纺织业	Textile Industry	2.70	3.83	0.37	0.52
#棉、化纤纺织及印染精加工	#Spinning, Weaving, Printing, Dyeing and Fine Processing of Cotton and Chemical Fiber				
毛纺织和染整精加工	Wool Textile and Dyeing, Finishing and Fine Processing	0.00	0.00	0.00	0.00

10-13 续 7(continued7)

类 别	Item	每百元销售收入实现的利润(元) Actual Net Profit Per 100 Sales Revenue	每百元销售收入实现的利税(元) Actual Gross Profit Per 100 Sales Revenue	平均每一职工创造的利润(元) Average Net Profit Per Employee's Output	平均每一职工创造的利税(元) Average Gross Profit Per Employee's Output
针织品、编织品及其制品制造	Manufacturing of Knitting Products and Weaving Products	6.22	7.15	0.71	0.82
纺织服装、鞋、帽制造业	Manufacturing of Garments, Shoes and Hats	-172.03	-138.14	-1.07	-0.86
#纺织服装制造	# Manufacturing of Garments	-172.03	-138.14	-1.07	-0.86
皮革、毛皮、羽毛(绒)及其制品业	Leather, Furs, Down and Related Products	2.00	14.62	0.17	1.27
#皮革制品制造	Leather Products	2.00	14.62	0.17	1.27
木材加工及木、竹、藤、棕、草制品业	Timber Processing, Bamboo, Cane, Palm Fiber and Straw Products	-2.18	1.31	-0.41	0.25
#锯材、木片加工	Timber Processing	1.86	4.28	0.37	0.85
人造板制造	Artificial Wooden Products	-9.82	-4.37	-1.95	-0.87
家具制造业	Furniture Manufacturing	1.16	4.64	0.16	0.66
#木质家具制造	Wooden Furniture Manufacturing	1.16	4.64	0.16	0.66
造纸及纸制品业	Papermaking and Paper Products	11.58	17.64	13.74	20.93
#纸浆制造	#Paper Pulp Production	12.17	18.38	26.33	39.76
造纸	Papermaking	2.08	5.47	0.37	0.98
印刷业和记录媒介的复制	Printing and Copying of Recording Mediums	5.53	11.04	0.91	1.81
#印刷	Printing	6.51	11.69	1.09	1.96
文教体育用品制造业	Cultural, Educational and Sports Goods	0.00	0.00	0.00	0.00
#文化用品制造	Cultural Goods	0.00	0.00	0.00	0.00
体育用品制造	Sports Goods	0.00	0.00	0.00	0.00
石油加工、炼焦及核燃料加工业	Petroleum Processing, Coking and Nuclear Fuel Processing	-5.05	1.07	-62.31	13.14
#精炼石油产品的制造	#Production of Refined Petroleum Products	-5.05	1.07	-62.31	13.14
化学原料及化学制品制造业	Raw Chemical Materials and Chemical Products	18.17	22.12	20.84	25.38
#肥料制造	Chemical Fertilizer Products	38.27	44.60	67.14	78.23
#氮肥制造	Nitrogenous Fertilizer Products	43.30	48.97	131.84	149.10
农药制造	Agricultural Chemicals Products	2.55	5.39	0.53	1.12
日用化学产品制造	Production of Daily Chemical Products	23.96	31.74	14.29	18.93
医药制造业	Medical and Pharmaceutical Products	22.75	32.80	10.45	15.06
#化学药品原药制造	# Production of Chemical Medicine Products	-3.63	1.68	-0.48	0.22
化学药品制剂制造	Production of Chemical Medicines and Preparations	23.72	33.85	11.49	16.41
中成药制造	Production of Traditional Chinese Patent Medicine	1.58	8.83	0.57	3.18
兽用药品制造	Production of Animal Medicines	0.00	0.00	0.00	0.00
化学纤维制造业	Chemical Fiber	-9.39	-8.74	-8.26	-7.69
#合成纤维制造	# Manufacturing of Synthetic Chemical Fiber	-9.39	-8.74	-8.26	-7.69
橡胶制品业	Rubber Products	1.25	1.89	0.59	0.89
#轮胎制造	Tire Manufacturing	0.00	0.00	0.00	0.00
塑料制品业	Plastic Products	6.95	12.20	2.07	3.63
#塑料薄膜制造	Plastic Membrane	10.32	16.57	5.14	8.26
非金属矿物制品业	Nonmetal Mineral Products	0.43	7.01	0.12	1.91

10-13 续 8(continued8)

类 别	Item	每百元销售收入实现的利润(元) Actual Net Profit Per 100 Sales Revenue	每百元销售收入实现的利税(元) Actual Gross Profit Per 100 Sales Revenue	平均每一职工创造的利润(元) Average Net Profit Per Employee's Output	平均每一职工创造的利税(元) Average Gross Profit Per Employee's Output
#水泥、石灰和石膏的制造	#Production of Cements, Limes and Gypsums	-0.47	6.39	-0.14	1.95
水泥及石膏制品制造	Production of Cements and Gypsum Products	5.45	11.14	1.66	3.40
砖瓦、石材及其他建筑材料制造	Production of Tiles, Stone Materials and Other Architectural Material Products	-14.17	-14.03	-0.41	-0.41
玻璃及玻璃制品制造	Glass and Glass Manufacturing	0.00	0.00	0.00	0.00
陶瓷制品制造	Ceramics Products	-16.67	-16.67	-0.05	-0.05
黑色金属冶炼及压延加工业	Smelting and Pressing of Ferrous Metals	-0.77	3.09	-0.32	1.30
#炼铁	Iron Refine Products	0.00	0.00	0.00	0.00
钢压延加工	Steel Refine Products	1.66	7.31	0.80	3.55
有色金属冶炼及压延加工业	Smelting and Pressing of Nonferrous Metals	0.57	2.10	0.37	1.35
金属制品业	Metal Products	5.12	8.62	5.50	9.27
#结构性金属制品制造	#Structural Metal Products	-13.66	-4.24	-0.70	-0.22
集装箱及金属包装容器制造	Container and Metal Packaging Products	4.14	9.37	2.12	4.80
通用设备制造业	Manufacturing of General Equipments	-21.04	-12.83	-1.33	-0.81
专用设备制造业	Special Purpose Equipment	3.58	4.71	0.61	0.81
#农、林、牧、渔专用机械制造	Manufacturing of Exclusive Machineries for Agriculture, Forestry, Livestock Farming and Fishing	3.53	4.08	0.63	0.73
交通运输设备制造业	Transport Equipment	6.58	13.69	6.75	14.04
#汽车制造	Automobile Manufacturing	7.36	14.69	10.53	21.02
摩托车制造	Motorcycle Manufacturing	-3.54	1.64	-1.23	0.57
电气机械及器材制造业	Electric Equipment and Machinery	10.25	13.26	7.19	9.30
#电线、电缆、光缆及电工器材制造	# Manufacturing of Electric Wires, Cables, Optic Cables and Electrician Equipments	13.98	15.67	12.20	13.68
通信设备、计算机及其他电子设备制造业	Manufacturing of Communication Equipments, Computers and Other Electronic Equipments	14.43	19.10	4.28	5.66
#通信设备制造	Telecommunications Equipment	16.59	16.59	3.16	3.16
家用视听设备制造	Household Audio-visual Equipment Manufacturing	0.00	0.00	0.00	0.00
仪器仪表及文化、办公用机械制造业	Instruments, Meters, Cultural and Office Machinery	-4.03	0.27	-0.06	
工艺品及其他制造业	Industrial Arts and other Manufacturing	4.94	6.94	3.01	4.23
#工艺美术品制造	Industrial Arts Manufacturing	4.94	6.94	3.01	4.23
废弃资源和废旧材料回收加工业	Recovery and Processing of Discarded Resoures and Weste Material				
电力、热力的生产和供应业	Production and Supply of Electric Power, Steam and Hot Water	25.41	33.47	11.68	15.38
#电力生产	Electric Power Production	0.27	11.14	0.11	4.66
电力供应	Supply of Electric Power	40.91	47.23	20.00	23.09
燃气生产和供应业	Production and Supply of Gas	25.37	32.39	23.76	30.34
水的生产和供应业	Production and Supply of Water	1.33	5.85	0.09	0.38
#自来水的生产和供应	Production and Supply of Tap Water	1.33	5.85	0.09	0.38
污水处理及其再生利用	Treatment and Reuse of Waste Water	0.00	0.00 a	0.00	0.00

10-13 续 9(continued9)

类 别	Item	平均每一职工负债额(元) Average Liabilities Per Employee	每百元固定资产原价实现的产值(元) Output Per 100 Yuan Original Value of Fixed Assets	每百元固定资产原价实现的利税(元) Actual Gross Profit Per 100 Yuan Original Value of Fixed Assets	平均每一职工占用的固定资产(元) Average Fixed Assets Employed Per Employee
总 计	Total	47.68	98.08	15.61	38.88
按注册登记类型分	Grouped by Economic Category				
国有企业	State-owned Industy	30.80	49.24	17.81	24.88
集体企业	Collective-owned Industry	13.34	78.98	0.14	6.25
股份合作企业	Cooperative Enterprises	9.99	443.76	54.70	7.01
股份制企业	Share Holding Enterprises	40.94	86.68	13.66	37.12
外商投资企业	Foreign Funded Enterprises	116.28	91.30	9.25	103.41
港澳台商投资企业	Enterprises with Funds from Hong Kong ,Macao and Taiwan	16.44	186.47	34.66	8.41
其他经济类型企业	Other Economy	41.81	170.08	24.41	27.82
按轻重工业分	Grouped by Light & Heavy Industry				
轻工业	Light Industry	34.54	106.82	16.11	24.27
重工业	Heavy Industry	61.80	93.92	15.37	54.58
按企业规模分	Grouped by Size of Enterprises				
大型企业	Large-sized	0.00	0.00	0.00	0.00
中型企业	Medium-sized	64.09	95.08	15.58	52.06
小型企业	Small-sized	29.36	104.61	15.67	24.17
在总计中:国有控股企业	Of the Total:State-owned and State-holding Enterprises	46.53	78.45	17.44	38.95
按工业行业分	Grouped by Industrial Sector:				
煤炭开采和洗选业	Coal Mining and Dressing	0.00	0.00	0.00	0.00
石油和天然气开采业	Petroleum and Natural Gas Extraction	218.94	109.94	85.11	1329.45
黑色金属矿采选业	Ferrous Metals Mining and Dressing	7.54	52.04	22.89	20.58
#铁矿采选	Iron Ore Mining and Dressing	7.54	52.04	22.89	20.58
有色金属矿采选业	Nonferrous Metals Mining and Dressing	12.91	532.91	29.50	5.17
非金属矿采选业	Nonmetal Minerals Mining and Dressing	11.39	111.84	34.50	5.78
#采盐	Salt Mining and Dressing	8.21	59.36	10.25	2.62
其他采矿业	Other Mining Industries	0.00	0.00	0.00	0.00
农副食品加工业	Farm Products and Non-staple Foodstuffs Processing Industry	12.25	236.56	16.82	6.60
#制糖	Carbohydrate Processing	11.20	80.62	16.87	7.13
水产品加工	Aquatic Products Processing	9.24	351.25	13.80	3.98
食品制造业	Food Manufacturing	22.27	160.85	18.19	8.25
#制糖	Carbohydrate Processing	1.95	365.72	19.26	0.82
水产品加工	Aquatic Products Processing	26.93	171.75	16.28	9.11
饮料制造业	Beverage Manufacturing	33.44	152.74	21.85	27.00
#酒精制造	Liquor Manufacturing	18.45	595.39	59.21	2.87
酒的制造	Alcohol Production	58.95	166.43	22.37	62.62
软饮料制造	Soft Beverage Manufacturing	21.01	132.64	22.97	8.57
精制茶加工	Fine Tea Processing	14.20	43.65	3.44	6.19
烟草制品业	Tobacco Manufacturing	50.54	195.19	112.60	41.24
#卷烟制造	Cigarettes Manufacturing	50.54	195.19	112.60	41.24
纺织业	Textile Industry	21.16	91.81	3.41	9.08
#棉、化纤纺织及印染精加工	#Spinning, Weaving, Printing, Dyeing and Fine Processing of Cotton and Chemical Fiber				
毛纺织和染整精加工	Wool Textile and Dyeing, Finishing and Fine Processing	0.00	0.00	0.00	0.00

10-13 续 10(continued10)

类 别	Item	平均每一职工负债额(元) Average Liabilities Per Employee	每百元固定资产原价实现的产值(元) Output Per 100 Yuan Original Value of Fixed Assets	每百元固定资产原价实现的利税(元) Actual Gross Profit Per 100 Yuan Original Value of Fixed Assets	平均每一职工占用的固定资产(元) Average Fixed Assets Employed Per Employee
针织品、编织品及其制品制造	Manufacturing of Knitting Products and Weaving Products	2.64	386.26	27.25	1.24
纺织服装、鞋、帽制造业	Manufacturing of Garments, Shoes and Hats	9.25	13.16	-15.89	3.42
#纺织服装制造	# Manufacturing of Garments	9.25	13.16	-15.89	3.42
皮革、毛皮、羽毛(绒)及其制品业	Leather, Furs, Down and Related Products	4.77	347.24	47.24	0.72
#皮革制品制造	Leather Products	4.77	347.24	47.24	0.72
木材加工及木、竹、藤、棕、草制品业	Timber Processing, Bamboo, Cane, Palm Fiber and Straw Products	8.13	117.71	1.61	9.49
#锯材、木片加工	Timber Processing	9.00	284.61	13.16	4.83
人造板制造	Artificial Wooden Products	8.68	54.96	-2.44	20.99
家具制造业	Furniture Manufacturing	7.42	197.62	8.90	4.11
#木质家具制造	Wooden Furniture Manufacturing	7.42	197.62	8.90	4.11
造纸及纸制品业	Papermaking and Paper Products	226.32	64.52	11.35	171.10
#纸浆制造	#Paper Pulp Production	424.65	62.46	11.48	323.28
造纸	Papermaking	7.81	183.52	9.47	6.38
印刷业和记录媒介的复制	Printing and Copying of Recording Mediums	15.33	67.71	7.32	13.48
#印刷	Printing	14.09	81.56	9.33	10.93
文教体育用品制造业	Cultural, Educational and Sports Goods	0.00	0.00	0.00	0.00
#文化用品制造	Cultural Goods	0.00	0.00	0.00	0.00
体育用品制造	Sports Goods	0.00	0.00	0.00	0.00
石油加工、炼焦及核燃料加工业	Petroleum Processing, Coking and Nuclear Fuel Processing	1429.57	87.54	0.87	1474.99
#精炼石油产品的制造	#Production of Refined Petroleum Products	1429.57	87.54	0.87	1474.99
化学原料及化学制品制造业	Raw Chemical Materials and Chemical Products	70.36	83.92	18.32	90.56
#肥料制造	Chemical Fertilizer Products	117.23	51.52	23.41	206.55
#氮肥制造	Nitrogenous Fertilizer Products	124.37	51.25	25.74	377.09
农药制造	Agricultural Chemicals Products	7.64	365.16	19.09	5.26
日用化学产品制造	Production of Daily Chemical Products	14.16	790.41	217.08	4.95
医药制造业	Medical and Pharmaceutical Products	32.09	172.00	53.13	18.48
#化学药品原药制造	# Production of Chemical Medicine Products	13.79	88.23	1.36	9.94
化学药品制剂制造	Production of Chemical Medicines and Preparations	32.09	175.72	55.67	18.87
中成药制造	Production of Traditional Chinese Patent Medicine	50.83	134.05	12.92	18.45
兽用药品制造	Production of Animal Medicines	0.00	0.00	0.00	0.00
化学纤维制造业	Chemical Fiber	68.79	60.46	-5.19	78.13
#合成纤维制造	# Manufacturing of Synthetic Chemical Fiber	68.79	60.46	-5.19	78.13
橡胶制品业	Rubber Products	9.13	721.42	13.06	5.49
#轮胎制造	Tire Manufacturing	0.00	0.00	0.00	0.00
塑料制品业	Plastic Products	16.74	192.87	23.56	9.63
#塑料薄膜制造	Plastic Membrane	13.97	383.52	66.19	8.14
非金属矿物制品业	Nonmetal Mineral Products	18.53	83.15	5.42	23.40

10-13 续 11(continued11)

类别	Item	平均每一职工负债额(元) Average Liabilities Per Employee	每百元固定资产原价实现的产值(元) Output Per 100 Yuan Original Value of Fixed Assets	每百元固定资产原价实现的利税(元) Actual Gross Profit Per 100 Yuan Original Value of Fixed Assets	平均每一职工占用的固定资产(元) Average Fixed Assets Employed Per Employee
#水泥、石灰和石膏的制造	#Production of Cements, Limes and Gypsums	19.76	78.50	4.67	27.95
水泥及石膏制品制造	Production of Cements and Gypsum Products	17.58	171.07	17.69	12.74
砖瓦、石材及其他建筑材料制造	Production of Tiles, Stone Materials and Other Architectural Material Products	9.56	20.56	-2.62	9.93
玻璃及玻璃制品制造	Glass and Glass Manufacturing	0.00	0.00	0.00	0.00
陶瓷制品制造	Ceramics Products	17.10	0.75	-0.12	28.00
黑色金属冶炼及压延加工业	Smelting and Pressing of Ferrous Metals	59.63	161.05	4.44	23.09
#炼铁	Iron Refine Products	0.00	0.00	0.00	0.00
钢压延加工	Steel Refine Products	84.20	102.02	7.38	26.36
有色金属冶炼及压延加工业	Smelting and Pressing of Nonferrous Metals	20.65	408.50	8.50	12.21
金属制品业	Metal Products	29.75	228.37	20.03	24.90
#结构性金属制品制造	#Structural Metal Products	3.49	84.26	-1.71	10.10
集装箱及金属包装容器制造	Container and Metal Packaging Products	9.62	221.34	20.73	6.01
通用设备制造业	Manufacturing of General Equipments	12.66	69.68	-8.40	3.86
专用设备制造业	Special Purpose Equipment	8.02	328.33	14.91	3.11
#农、林、牧、渔专用机械制造	Manufacturing of Exclusive Machineries for Agriculture, Forestry, Livestock Farming and Fishing	7.92	521.17	20.56	1.65
交通运输设备制造业	Transport Equipment	60.01	383.41	50.72	15.24
#汽车制造	Automobile Manufacturing	80.70	485.96	68.79	17.01
摩托车制造	Motorcycle Manufacturing	30.36	113.00	1.84	16.59
电气机械及器材制造业	Electric Equipment and Machinery	23.67	420.06	53.66	10.83
#电线、电缆、光缆及电工器材制造	# Manufacturing of Electric Wires, Cables, Optic Cables and Electrician Equipments	13.17	432.61	60.35	18.42
通信设备、计算机及其他电子设备制造业	Manufacturing of Communication Equipments, Computers and Other Electronic Equipments	34.17	227.29	31.57	10.54
#通信设备制造	Telecommunications Equipment	77.62	1001.48	60.32	2.04
家用视听设备制造	Household Audio-visual Equipment Manufacturing	0.00	0.00	0.00	0.00
仪器仪表及文化、办公用机械制造业	Instruments, Meters, Cultural and Office Machinery	3.64	28.16	0.08	2.88
工艺品及其他制造业	Industrial Arts and other Manufacturing	12.19	2537.09	170.04	1.41
#工艺美术品制造	Industrial Arts Manufacturing	12.19	2537.09	170.04	1.41
废弃资源和废旧材料回收加工业	Recovery and Processing of Discarded Resoures and Weste Material				
电力、热力的生产和供应业	Production and Supply of Electric Power, Steam and Hot Water	83.66	42.01	14.02	71.84
#电力生产	Electric Power Production	86.07	27.43	3.03	93.69
电力供应	Supply of Electric Power	81.92	62.67	29.59	56.10
燃气生产和供应业	Production and Supply of Gas	114.96	52.96	16.68	127.53
水的生产和供应业	Production and Supply of Water	24.86	17.14	0.93	31.07
#自来水的生产和供应	Production and Supply of Tap Water	24.86	17.14	0.93	31.07
污水处理及其再生利用	Treatment and Reuse of Waste Water	0.00	0.00	0.00	0.00

10－14 各市县规模以上工业企业主要财务指标

Main Indicators on Finance of above Designated Size Industrial Enterprises by City and County

地区	Region	企业单位数(个) Number of Enterprises (unit)	亏损企业 Number of Loss Making Industrial Enterprises	工业总产值(当年价格) Gross Industrial Output Value (At Current Prices)	工业销售产值(当年价格) Sales Revenue (At Current Prices)	出口交货值 Delivery Value of Industry	工业增加值(当年价格) Value-added of Industry (At Current Prices)
总　计	**Total**	**595**	**238**	**6402592**	**6220817**	**457317**	
海口市	Haikou	217	83	2838869	2769914	194925	739822
三亚市	Sanya	21	4	163507	160109	21677	53525
五指山市	Wuzhishan	11	6	14198	13477	0	3573
文昌市	Wenchang	41	16	115570	116988	7680	37162
琼海市	Qionghai	18	9	84815	81493	17826	27214
万宁市	Wanning	36	8	70362	68824	0	19147
定安县	Dingan	15	5	29102	23769	5461	12011
屯昌县	Tunchang	14	8	12372	11995	0	3267
澄迈县	Chengmai	36	14	563207	542759	30445	205056
临高县	Lingao	13	7	44437	44844	0	13890
儋州市	Danzhou	31	11	203140	185703	5471	54660
东方市	Dongfang	11	2	296791	300470	15053	213664
乐东县	Ledong	9	7	16354	14779	253	7400
琼中县	Qiongzhong	11	6	10692	10072	0	3066
保亭县	Baoting	5	2	5314	5320	0	2493
陵水县	Lingshui	8	5	16536	16260	7722	4181
白沙县	Baisha	9	5	14659	14229	0	3653
昌江县	Changjiang	26	14	258304	262668	0	137665
农　垦	Land Reclamation	46	20	179780	176996	41620	36650
洋　浦	Yangpu	17	6	1464584	1400149	109183	317586

10-14 续 1(continued1)

地区	Region	全部从业人员年平均人数(人) Annual Average Number of All Employees (person)	本年应付工资总额 Salaries and Wages Payable of Current Year	本年应付福利费总额 Welfare Expenses Payable of Current Year	主营业务收入 Major Business Revenue	主营业务成本 Major Business Cost	主营业务税金及附加 Major Business Tax and Extra Charges
总计	**Total**	**121964**	**218057**	**25392**	**5984362**	**4602248**	**115269**
海口市	Haikou	44053	78277	9272	2806113	2169045	75169
三亚市	Sanya	6088	12585	1194	160626	139448	937
五指山市	Wuzhishan	1396	1729	227	13177	12844	45
文昌市	Wenchang	4166	7079	144	121483	100572	646
琼海市	Qionghai	3832	6823	480	77127	61550	271
万宁市	Wanning	2732	4108	449	68053	49917	309
定安县	Dingan	1851	2682	179	24385	20065	110
屯昌县	Tunchang	941	1538	242	11782	10099	21
澄迈县	Chengmai	8074	16738	2454	535529	415622	4412
临高县	Lingao	2080	2409	157	44488	33141	312
儋州市	Danzhou	8746	10637	1121	191746	118578	832
东方市	Dongfang	2830	11590	1776	272199	165857	581
乐东县	Ledong	2517	2841	467	13062	10316	229
琼中县	Qiongzhong	1165	1448	140	10072	8012	36
保亭县	Baoting	557	847	108	5196	3849	34
陵水县	Lingshui	1557	1850	246	16126	13708	75
白沙县	Baisha	1220	1010	357	14340	12355	164
昌江县	Changjiang	13633	24637	3093	250143	144824	6231
农垦	Land Reclamation	10354	12846	1147	184119	154703	2660
洋浦	Yangpu	4172	16384	2138	1164596	957743	22195

10-14 续 2(continued2)

地 区	Region	其他业务收入 Other Business Income	营业费用 Funds Expenses	管理费用 Administrative Expense	财务费用 Financal Expenses	利息支出 Interest Expenses	利润总额 Total Profits
总 计	Total	51718	229678	275714	114030	106468	600036
海口市	Haikou	20764	145771	149441	20723	19803	268745
三亚市	Sanya	627	5572	7946	2964	746	4739
五指山市	Wuzhishan	18	99	2020	1662	1585	-3514
文昌市	Wenchang	1034	6465	4542	1901	483	7184
琼海市	Qionghai	635	1743	3548	1815	1051	4006
万宁市	Wanning	394	2168	10750	553	54	761
定安县	Dingan	78	557	2135	582	704	1048
屯昌县	Tunchang	7	12	326	-7	3	561
澄迈县	Chengmai	2417	15949	17067	8796	8539	67003
临高县	Lingao	191	265	1893	18	0	1918
儋州市	Danzhou	483	1648	8901	497	474	60552
东方市	Dongfang	7017	2741	6043	4369	4325	102823
乐东县	Ledong	315	956	1066	554	234	-91
琼中县	Qiongzhong	2	213	566	114	98	720
保亭县	Baoting	11	32	343	29	32	929
陵水县	Lingshui	167	705	1417	129	26	57
白沙县	Baisha	3	221	673	71	76	623
昌江县	Changjiang	3932	10432	27027	1687	623	52490
农 垦	Land Reclamation	3314	11129	12813	1677	1362	1828
洋 浦	Yangpu	10309	23003	17202	65899	66252	27653

10-14 续 3(continued3)

地 区	Region	亏损企业亏损总额 Total Deficit of Loss Making Industrial Enterprises	利税总额 Total Profits and Taxes	本年应交增值税 Value Added Tax Payable	固定资产原价 Original Value of Fixed Assets	固定资产净值年均余额 Annual Average Balance of Fixed Assets	流动资产年平均余额 Annual Average Balance of Circulating Funds
总 计	**Total**	**115884**	**1019031**	**303727**	**6528083**	**4742118**	**3033149**
海口市	Haikou	29278	459100	115186	1439083	837097	1457193
三亚市	Sanya	2057	15155	9480	233927	148888	61335
五指山市	Wuzhishan	3726	-2329	1140	52724	30609	3494
文昌市	Wenchang	1350	13982	6152	149274	113883	41287
琼海市	Qionghai	4075	8681	4404	144075	76264	49834
万宁市	Wanning	202	4256	3186	59164	43352	17049
定安县	Dingan	431	2366	1208	29192	20004	15854
屯昌县	Tunchang	119	993	411	22281	17868	5435
澄迈县	Chengmai	2238	106784	35369	599184	367726	244926
临高县	Lingao	2500	5270	3040	33977	23394	20246
儋州市	Danzhou	4204	68928	7543	157317	121551	88465
东方市	Dongfang	4375	123646	20242	740047	456447	174612
乐东县	Ledong	328	1190	1052	36117	21294	7377
琼中县	Qiongzhong	227	1334	578	14142	11097	4464
保亭县	Baoting	132	1239	277	11898	7577	2258
陵水县	Lingshui	125	569	437	48159	41878	7273
白沙县	Baisha	61	2021	1234	32259	24937	8058
昌江县	Changjiang	4075	77671	18951	459029	300481	84758
农 垦	Land Reclamation	6964	14907	10419	162405	86994	94570
洋 浦	Yangpu	49418	113268	63420	2103830	1990779	644662

10-14 续 4(continued4)

地 区	Region	流动资产合计 Total Circulating Funds	应收帐款净额 Net Accounts Receivable	产成品存货 Stock up Sales	资产总计 Total Property	负债合计 Total Liabilities	流动负债合计 Total Circulating Liabilities
总 计	**Total**	**3393295**	**754289**	**348870**	**9611482**	**5814834**	**2947346**
海口市	Haikou	1623852	348536	147211	2948915	1614122	1208358
三亚市	Sanya	53864	16507	8018	244819	177190	77472
五指山市	Wuzhishan	7258	1948	515	57112	41448	7307
文昌市	Wenchang	50998	13808	6511	187801	138488	34105
琼海市	Qionghai	59137	16250	6215	171911	159590	75984
万宁市	Wanning	17837	4628	4709	85817	68303	14033
定安县	Dingan	16378	1526	4266	45479	28027	13823
屯昌县	Tunchang	5453	1114	334	26955	19006	5553
澄迈县	Chengmai	249488	50688	26409	840645	504333	251865
临高县	Lingao	21502	3425	822	54747	36517	20275
儋州市	Danzhou	99616	33674	17834	283044	201623	93669
东方市	Dongfang	184278	34168	3065	740423	260588	126962
乐东县	Ledong	7834	2144	1036	37394	36526	13546
琼中县	Qiongzhong	5153	1344	359	17369	9615	5409
保亭县	Baoting	2426	566	22	13622	10177	2332
陵水县	Lingshui	6963	1848	817	52530	51915	5808
白沙县	Baisha	4901	849	2217	33833	20548	9198
昌江县	Changjiang	193687	24648	17056	592675	182643	115827
农 垦	Land Reclamation	97735	28810	12479	221366	144228	131708
洋 浦	Yangpu	684934	167809	88976	2955024	2109947	734113

10-14 续 5(continued5)

地 区	Region	长期负债合计 Total Long-period Liabilities	所有者权益合计 Creditors' Equity	实收资本 Total Capital Hold	国家资本 Nation Capital
总 计	**Total**	**2824018**	**3796648**	**3065726**	**872317**
海口市	Haikou	395690	1334793	860630	153248
三亚市	Sanya	98718	67629	37952	14831
五指山市	Wuzhishan	34141	15664	7556	2926
文昌市	Wenchang	90435	49313	31352	2226
琼海市	Qionghai	83322	12321	34666	7578
万宁市	Wanning	54080	17514	50903	45510
定安县	Dingan	14203	17452	11697	3001
屯昌县	Tunchang	13364	7949	8981	2314
澄迈县	Chengmai	252004	336312	223194	957
临高县	Lingao	16242	18230	8840	573
儋州市	Danzhou	107944	81421	30874	3530
东方市	Dongfang	133625	479835	412235	262391
乐东县	Ledong	22980	868	12653	12578
琼中县	Qiongzhong	4206	7754	8441	6687
保亭县	Baoting	7845	3445	3385	2385
陵水县	Lingshui	46107	615	4980	919
白沙县	Baisha	11350	13285	4002	1876
昌江县	Changjiang	51456	410031	270433	234849
农垦	Land Reclamation	10473	77138	75279	36525
洋浦	Yangpu	1375834	845077	967675	77413

10－15 各市县规模以上工业企业主要经济效益指标

Main Indicators on Economic Benefit of Above Designed Size Industrial Enterprises by City and County

地区	Region	企业亏损面(%) Ratio of Loss Making Industrial Enterprises	工业增加值率(%) Ratio of Value-added of Industry	总资产贡献率(%) Ratio of Assets to Industrial Output Value	资产负债率(%) Assets-Liability Ratio	流动资产周转次数(次) Number of Times of Annual of Turnover Circulating Funds	工业成本费用利润率(%) Ratio of Profits to Industrial Cost	全员劳动生产率(元/人) Overall Labor Productivity	产品销售率(%) Proportion of Products Sold(%)
总　　计	**Total**	**40.00**	**29.61**	**11.71**	**60.50**	**1.97**	**11.49**	**15.54**	**97.16**
海口市	Haikou	38.25	26.06	16.24	54.74	1.93	10.81	16.79	97.57
三亚市	Sanya	19.05	32.74	6.50	72.38	2.62	3.04	8.79	97.92
五指山市	Wuzhishan	54.55	25.17	-1.30	72.57	3.77	-21.14	2.56	94.92
文昌市	Wenchang	39.02	32.16	7.70	73.74	2.94	6.33	8.92	101.23
琼海市	Qionghai	50.00	32.09	5.66	92.83	1.55	5.83	7.10	96.08
万宁市	Wanning	22.22	27.21	5.02	79.59	3.99	1.20	7.01	97.81
定安县	Dingan	33.33	41.27	6.75	61.63	1.54	4.49	6.49	81.67
屯昌县	Tunchang	57.14	26.41	3.70	70.51	2.17	5.38	3.47	96.95
澄迈县	Chengmai	38.89	36.41	13.72	59.99	2.19	14.65	25.40	96.37
临高县	Lingao	53.85	31.26	9.63	66.70	2.20	5.43	6.68	100.92
儋州市	Danzhou	35.48	26.91	24.52	71.23	2.17	46.71	6.25	91.42
东方市	Dongfang	18.18	71.99	17.28	35.19	1.56	57.44	75.50	101.24
乐东县	Ledong	77.78	45.25	3.81	97.68	1.77	-0.71	2.94	90.37
琼中县	Qiongzhong	54.55	28.68	8.24	55.36	2.26	8.09	2.63	94.20
保亭县	Baoting	40.00	46.91	9.34	74.71	2.30	21.84	4.48	100.11
陵水县	Lingshui	62.50	25.28	1.13	98.83	2.22	0.36	2.69	98.33
白沙县	Baisha	55.56	24.92	6.20	60.73	1.78	4.68	2.99	97.07
昌江县	Changjiang	53.85	53.30	13.21	30.82	2.95	28.53	10.10	101.69
农　　垦	Land Reclamation	43.48	20.39	7.35	65.15	1.95	1.01	3.54	98.45
洋　　浦	Yangpu	35.29	21.68	6.08	71.40	1.81	2.60	76.12	95.60

10-15 续 1(continued1)

地 区	Region	每百元销售收入实现的利润(元) Actual Net Profit Per 100 Sales Revenue	每百元销售收入实现的利税(元) Actual Gross Profit Per 100 Sales Revenue	平均每一职工创造的利润(元) Average Net Profit Per Employee's Output	平均每一职工创造的利税(元) Average Gross Profit Per Employee's Output	平均每一职工负债额(元) Average Liabilities Per Employee	每百元固定资产原价实现的产值(元) Output Per 100 Yuan Original Value of Fixed Assets	每百元固定资产原价实现的利税(元) Actual Gross Profit Per 100 Yuan Original Value of Fixed Assets	平均每一职工占用的固定资产(元) Average Fixed Assets Employed Per Employee
总 计	**Total**	**9.65**	**16.38**	**4.92**	**8.36**	**47.68**	**98.08**	**15.61**	**38.88**
海口市	Haikou	9.70	16.57	6.10	10.42	36.64	197.27	31.90	19.00
三亚市	Sanya	2.96	9.47	0.78	2.49	29.10	69.90	6.48	24.46
五指山市	Wuzhishan	-26.07	-17.28	-2.52	-1.67	29.69	26.93	-4.42	21.93
文昌市	Wenchang	6.14	11.95	1.72	3.36	33.24	77.42	9.37	27.34
琼海市	Qionghai	4.92	10.65	1.05	2.27	41.65	58.87	6.03	19.90
万宁市	Wanning	1.11	6.18	0.28	1.56	25.00	118.93	7.19	15.87
定安县	Dingan	4.41	9.95	0.57	1.28	15.14	99.69	8.10	10.81
屯昌县	Tunchang	4.68	8.28	0.60	1.06	20.20	55.53	4.46	18.99
澄迈县	Chengmai	12.34	19.67	8.30	13.23	62.46	94.00	17.82	45.54
临高县	Lingao	4.28	11.75	0.92	2.53	17.56	130.79	15.51	11.25
儋州市	Danzhou	32.61	37.12	6.92	7.88	23.05	129.13	43.81	13.90
东方市	Dongfang	34.22	41.15	36.33	43.69	92.08	40.10	16.71	161.29
乐东县	Ledong	-0.62	8.05	-0.04	0.47	14.51	45.28	3.29	8.46
琼中县	Qiongzhong	7.15	13.24	0.62	1.15	8.25	75.60	9.43	9.53
保亭县	Baoting	17.46	23.29	1.67	2.22	18.27	44.66	10.41	13.60
陵水县	Lingshui	0.35	3.50	0.04	0.37	33.34	34.34	1.18	26.90
白沙县	Baisha	4.38	14.20	0.51	1.66	16.84	45.44	6.26	20.44
昌江县	Changjiang	19.98	29.57	3.85	5.70	13.40	56.27	16.92	22.04
农 垦	Land Reclamation	1.03	8.42	0.18	1.44	13.93	110.70	9.18	8.40
洋 浦	Yangpu	1.98	8.09	6.63	27.15	505.74	69.62	5.38	477.18

主要统计指标解释

工业 指从事自然资源的开采,对采掘品和农产品进行加工和再加工的物质生产部门。具体包括:(1)对自然资源的开采,如采矿、晒盐、森林采伐等(但不包括禽兽捕猎和水产捕捞);(2)对农副产品的加工、再加工,如粮油加工、食品加工、轧花、缫丝、纺织、制革等;(3)对采掘品的加工、再加工,如炼铁、炼钢、化工生产、石油加工、机器制造、木材加工等,以及电力、自来水、煤气的生产和供应等;(4)对工业品的修理、翻新,如机器设备的修理、交通运输工具(包括小卧车)的修理等。
1984年以前农村的村及村以下办工业归属农业,1984年以后划归工业。

工业统计调查单位 工业统计调查单位分为两类:独立核算法人工业企业和工业活动单位。

(1)独立核算法人工业企业 是指从事工业生产经营活动的单位。独立核算法人工业企业应同时具备以下条件:①依法成立,有自己的名称、组织机构和场所,能够承担民事责任;②独立拥有和使用资产,承担负债,有权与其他单位签订合同;③独立核算盈亏,并能够编制资产负债表。

(2)工业活动单位 是指在一个场所从事一种或主要从事一种工业生产活动的经济单位。它包括独立核算工业企业按主营业务活动(即工业生产活动)划分的主营业务活动单位和非工业企业所属的工业生产活动单位(即原非独立核算工业生产单位)。工业活动单位,一般应同时具备以下三个条件:①具有一个场所,从事一种或主要从事一种工业活动;②单独组织工业生产、经营或业务活动;③单独核算收入和支出。

本年鉴中涉及的企业登记注册类型:

(1)国有及国有控股企业 指国有企业加上国有控股企业。国有企业(即过去的全民所有制工业或国营工业)是指企业全部资产归国家所有,并按《中华人民共和国企业法人登记管理条例》规定登记注册的非公司制的经济组织。包括国有企业、国有独资公司和国有联营企业。1957年以前的公私合营和私营工业,后均改造为国营工业,1992年改为国有工业,这部分工业的资料不单独分列时,均包括在国有企业内。国有控股企业是对混合所有制经济的企业进行的"国有控股"分类。它是指这些企业的全部资产中国有资产(股份)相对其他所有者中的任何一个所有者占资(股)最多的企业。该分组反映了国有经济控股情况。

(2)集体企业 指企业资产归集体所有,并按《中华人民共和国企业法人登记管理条例》规定登记注册的经济组织。是社会主义公有制经济的组成部分。包括城乡所有使用集体投资举办的企业,以及部分个人通过集资自愿放弃所有权并依法经工商行政管理机关认定为集体所有制的企业。

(3)股份合作企业 指以合作制为基础,由企业职工共同出资入股,吸收一定比例的社会资产投资组建,实行自主经营,自负盈亏,共同劳动,民主管理,按劳分配与按股分红相结合的一种集体经济组织。

(4)联营企业 指两个及两个以上相同或不同所有制性质的企业法人或事业单位法人,按自愿、平等、互利的原则,共同投资组成的经济组织。联营企业包括:

国有联营企业指国有企业与国有企业间的联营;

集体联营企业指集体企业与集体企业间的联营;

国有与集体联营企业指国有企业与集体企业间的联营。

(5)有限责任公司 指根据《中华人民共和国公司登记管理条例》规定登记注册,由两个以上,五十个以下的股东共同出资,每个股东以其所认缴的出资额对公司承担有限责任,公司以其全部资产对其债务承担责任的经济组织。
有限责任公司包括国有独资公司以及其他有限责任公司。

(6)股份有限公司 指根据《中华人民共和国企业法人登记管理条例》规定登记注册,其全部注册资本由等额股份构成并通过发行股票筹集资本,股东以其认购的股份对公司承担有限责任,公司以其全部资产对其债务承担责任的经济组织。

(7)私营企业 指由自然人投资设立或由自然人控股,以雇佣劳动为基础的营利性经济组织。包括按照《公司法》、《合伙企业法》、《私营企业暂行条例》规定登记注册的私营有限责任公司、私营股份有限公司、私营合伙企业和私营独资企业。

(8)港、澳、台商投资企业 指企业注册登记类型中的港、澳、台资合资、合作、独资经营企业和股份有限公司之和。

(9)外商投资企业 指企业注册登记类型中的中外合资、合作经营企业、外资企业和外商投资股份有限公司之和。
"三资"企业系指港、澳、台商投资企业和外资企业的简称。

轻工业 指主要提供生活消费品和制作手工工具的工业。按其所使用的原料不同,可分为两大类:(1)以农产品为原料的轻工业,是指直接或间接以农产品为基本原料的轻工业。主要包括食品制造、饮料制造、烟草加工、纺织、缝纫、皮革和毛皮制作、造纸以及印刷等工业;(2)以非农产品为原料的轻工业,是指以工业品为原料的轻工业。主要包括文教体育用品、化学药品制造、合成纤维制造、日用化学制品、日用玻璃制品、日用金属制品、手工工具制造、医疗器械制造、文化和办公用机械制造等工业。
重工业 是指为国民经济各部门提供物质技术基础的主要生产资料的工业。按其生产性质和产品用途,可以分为下列三类:(1)采掘(伐)工业,是指对自然资源的开采,包括石油开采、煤炭开采、金属矿开采、非金属矿开采和木材采伐等工业;(2)原材料工业,指向国民经济各部门提供基本材料、动力和燃料的工业。包括金属冶炼及加工、炼焦及焦炭、化学、化工原料、水泥、人造板以及电力、石油和煤炭加工等工业;(3)加工工业,是指对工业原材料进行再加工制造的工业。包括装备国民经济各部门的机械设备制造工业、金属结构、水泥制品等工业，以及为农业提供的生产资料如化肥、农药等工业。

根据上述划分原则，修理业中以重工业产品为修理作业对象的划为重工业，反之划为轻工业。

工业总产值 是以货币表现的工业企业在一定时期内生产的已出售或可供出售工业产品总量，它反映一定时间内工业生产的总规模和总水平。它包括：在本企业内不再进行加工，经检验、包装入库（规定不需包装的产品除外）的成品价值，对外加工费收入，自制半成品、在产品期末初差额价值。工业总产值采用"工厂法"计算，即以工业企业作为一个整体，按企业工业生产活动的最终成果来计算，企业内部不允许重复计算，不能把企业内部各个车间（分厂）生产的成果相加。但在企业之间、行业之间、地区之间存在着重复计算。

轻重工业总产值的划分是按"工厂法"计算的，即一个工业企业生产的主要产品性质属于轻工业，则该企业的全部总产值作为轻工业总产值；如它的主要产品性质属于重工业，则该企业的全部总产值作为重工业总产值。

工业增加值 是指工业行业在报告期内以货币表现的工业生产活动的最终成果。

实收资本 指企业实际收到的投资人投入的资本。按投资主体可分为国家资本、集体资本、法人资本、个人资本、港澳台资本和外商资本等。

资产合计 指企业拥有或控制的能以货币计量的经济资源。包括各种财产、债权和其他权利。资产按其流动性划分为流动资产、长期投资、固定资产、无形及递延资产和其他资产。

（1）流动资产 指企业可以在一年内或者超过一年的一个生产周期内变现或耗用的资产合计。包括现金及各种存款、短期投资、应收及预付款项、存货等。

（2）固定资产 指企业固定资产净值、固定资产清理、在建工程、待处理固定资产损失所占用的资金合计。

（3）无形资产 指企业长期使用而没有实物形态的资产。包括专利权、非专利技术、商标权、著作权、土地使用权、商誉等。

负债合计 指企业承担的能以货币计量，将以资产或劳务偿付的债务。负债一般按偿还期长短分为流动负债和长期负债、递延税项等。

（1）流动负债 指企业在一年内或者超过一年的一个营业周期内需要偿还的债务合计，其中包括短期借款、应付及预收款项、应付工资、应交税金和应交利润等。

（2）长期负债 指企业在一年以上或者超过一年的一个营业周期以上需要偿还的债务合计，其中包括长期借款、应付债务、长期应付款项等。

所有者权益 指企业投资人对企业净资产的所有权。企业净资产等于企业全部资产减去全部负债后的余额，其中包括投资者对企业的最初投入，以及资本公积金、盈余公积金和未分配利润，对股份制企业即为股东权益。

固定资产原价 指企业在建造、购置、安装、改建、扩建、技术改造某项固定资产时所支出的全部货币总额。它一般包括买价、包装费、运杂费和安装费等。

固定资产净值 是指固定资产原价减去历年已提折旧额后的净额。

流动资产 是指可以在一年或者超过一年的一个营业周期内变现或者耗用的资产，包括现金及各种存款、短期投资、应收及预付货款、存货等。

产品销售收入 指企业销售产品和提供劳务等主要经营业务取得的收入总额。

产品销售成本 指企业销售产品和提供劳务等主要经营业务的实际成本。

产品销售税金及附加 指企业销售产品和提供工业性劳务等主要经营业务应负担的城市维护建设税、消费税、资源税和教育费附加。

产品销售利润 指企业销售产品和提供工业性劳务等主要经营业务收入扣除其成本、费用、税金后的利润。

利润总额 指企业实现的利润。

应交增值税 指企业在报告期内应交纳的增值税额。

总资产贡献率 反映企业全部资产的获利能力，是企业经营业绩和管理水平的集中体现，是评价和考核企业盈利能力的核心指标。计算公式为：

总资产贡献率 =(利润总额 + 税金总额 + 利息支出)/ 平均资产总额×100%

资产负债率 该指标既反映企业经营风险的大小，也反映企业利用债权人提供的资金从事经营活动的能力。计算公式为：

资产负债率 = 负债总额 / 资产总额×100%

工业成本费用利润率 指在一定时期内实现的利润与成本费用之比，是反映工业生产成本及费用投入的经济效益指标，同时也是反映降低成本的经济效益的指标。计算公式为：

工业成本费用利润率(%)= 利润总额 / 成本及费用总额×100%

工业增加值率 指在一定时期内工业增加值占同期工业总产值的比重，反映降低中间消耗的经济效益。计算公式为：

工业增加值率(%)= 工业增加值(现价)/ 工业总产值×100%

流动资产周转次数 指在一定时期内流动资产完成的周转次数，反映流动资产的周转速度。计算公式为：

流动资产周转次数 = 产品销售收入 / 全部流动资产平均余额

产品销售率 指报告期工业销售产值与同期全部工业总产值之比，是反映工业产品已实现销售的程度，分析工业产销衔接情况，研究工业产品满足社会需求程度的指标。计算公式为:

产品销售率(%)= 工业销售产值 / 工业总产值(现价) ×100%

全员劳动生产率 指根据产品的价值量指标计算的平均每一个就业人员在单位时间内的产品生产量。是考核企业经济活动的重要指标，是企业生产技术水平、经营管理水平、职工技术熟练程度和劳动积极性的综合表现。目前我国的全员劳动生产率是将工业企业的工业增加值除以同一时期全部就业人员的平均人数来计算的。计算公式为:

全员劳动生产率 = 工业增加值 / 全部就业人员平均人数

Explanatory Note on Main Statistical Indicators

Industry refers to the material production sector which is engaged in extraction of natural resources and processing and reprocessing of minerals and agricultural products, including (1) extraction of natural resources, such as mining, salt production, logging (but not including hunting and fishing); (2) processing and reprocessing of farm and sideline produces, such as rice husking, flour milling, wine making, oil pressing, cotton ginning, silk reeling, spinning and weaving, and leather making; (3) manufacture of industrial products, such as steel making, iron smelting, chemicals manufacturing, petroleum processing, machine building, timber processing; water and gas production and electricity generation and supply; (4)repairing of industrial products such as the repairing of machinery and means of transport (including cars).

Prior to 1984, the rural industry run by villages and cooperative organizations under village was classified into agriculture. Since 1984, it has been grouped into industry.

Units of Industrial Statistics and Inquiry: They are classified into two categories (1) corporate industrial enterprises with independent accounting system (2) industrial establishments.

(1) **Corporate industrial enterprises with independent accounting system** refer to enterprises engaging in industrial production activities, which meet the following requirements: ①They are established legally, having their own names, organizations, location, able to take civil liability; ②They possess and use their assets independently, assume liabilities, and are entitled to sign contracts with other units; ③They are financially independent and compile their own balance sheets.

(2) **Industrial establishments** refer to economic units which located in one single place and engaged entirely or primarily in one kind of industrial activity, including financially independent industrial enterprises and units engaged in industrial activities under the non industrial enterprises (or financially dependent). Industrial establishments generally meet the following requirements: ① They have each one location and are engaged in one kind of industrial activity each; ② They operate and manage their industrial production activities separately;③ They have accounts of income and expenditures separately.

(1) **State-owned Enterprises** refer to industrial enterprises where the means of production or income are owned by the state. Joint state-private industries and private industries, which existed before 1957, have been transformed into state industries. Statistics on these enterprises has been included in the state-owned industries since 1957 when separation of data was no longer necessary.

(2) **Collective-owned Enterprises** refer to industrial enterprises where the means of production are owned collectively, including urban and rural enterprises invested by collectives and some enterprises which were formerly owned privately but have been registered in industrial and commercial administration agency as collective units through raising fund from the public.

(3) **Share-holding Cooperative Enterprises** refer to economic units set up on cooperative basis, with funding partly from members of the enterprise and partly from outside investment, where the operation and management is decided by the members who also participate in the production, and the distribution of income is based both on work (labour input) and on shares (capital input).

(4) **Joint-operation enterprises** refer to economic units that are established by joint investment by two or more corporate enterprises or institutions of the same or different types of ownership on voluntary, equal and mutual-beneficial basis. They include:

a) state-owned joint-operation enterprises (joint operation between state-owned enterprises);

b) collective joint-operation enterprises (joint operation between collective enterprises; and

c) state-collective joint-operation enterprises (joint operation between state and collective enterprises).

(5) **Limited Liability Corporations** refer to economic units registered in accordance with the Regulation of the People's Republic of China on the Management of Registration of Corporations, with capitals from 2 to 49 investors, each investor bears limited liability to the corporation depending on his/her holding of shares, and the corporation bears liability to its debt to the maximum of its total assets.

(6) **Share-holding Corporations Ltd.** refer to economic units registered in accordance with the Regulation of the People's Republic of China on the Management of Registration of Corporate Enterprises, with total registered capitals divided into equal shares and raised through issuing stocks. Each investor bears limited liability to the corporation depending on the holding of shares, and the corporation bears liability to its debt to the maximum of its total assets.

(7) **Private Enterprises** refer to economic units invested or controlled (by holding the majority of the shares) by natural persons who hire labours for profit-making activities. Included in this category are private limited liability corporations, private share-holding corporations Ltd., private partnership enterprises and private sole investment enterprises registered in accordance with the Corporation Law, Partnership Enterprise Law and Tentative Regulation on Private Enterprises.

(8) **Enterprises with Funds form Hong Kong, Macao and Taiwan** refers to all industrial enterprises registered as the joint-venture,

cooperative, sole (exclusive) investment industrial enterprises and limited liability corporations with funds from Hong Kong, Macao and Taiwan.

(9) **Foreign Funded Enterprises** refers to all industrial enterprises registered as the joint-venture, cooperative, sole (exclusive) investment industrial enterprises and limited liability corporations with foreign funds.

Light Industry refers to the industry that produces consumer goods and hand tools. It consists of two categories, depending on the materials used:

(1)Industries using farm products as raw materials. These are branches of light industry which directly or indirectly use farm products as basic raw materials, including the manufacture of food and beverages, tobacco processing, textile, clothing, fur and leather manufacturing, paper making, printing, etc.

(2)Industries using non farm products as raw materials. These are branches of light industry which use manufactured goods as raw materials, including the manufacture of cultural, educational articles and sports goods, chemicals, synthetic fiber, chemical products for daily use, glass products for daily use, metal products for daily use, hand tools, medical apparatus and instruments, and the manufacture of cultural and clerical machinery.

Heavy Industry refers to the industry which produces capital goods, and provides various sectors of the national economy with necessary material and technical basis. It consists of the following three branches according to the purpose of production or the use of products:

(1)Mining, quarrying and logging industry refers to the industry that extracts natural resources, including extraction of petroleum, coal, metal and non-metal ores and logging.

(2)Raw materials industry refers to the industry that provides various sectors of the national economy with raw materials, fuels and power. It includes smelting and processing of metals, coking and coke chemistry, chemical materials and building materials such as cement, plywood, and power, petroleum refining and coal dressing.

(3)Manufacturing industry refers to the industry that processes raw materials. It includes machine building industry which equips sectors of the national economy, industries of metal structure and cement products, industries producing means of agricultural production, such as chemical fertilizers and pesticides. According to the above principle of classification, the repairing trades which are engaged primarily in repairing products of heavy industry are classified into heavy industry while these engaged in repairing products of light industry are classified into light industry.

Gross Industrial Output Value is the total volume of industrial products sold or available for sale in value terms which reflects the total achievements and overall scale of industrial production during a given period. It includes the value of the finished products, which are not to be further processed in the enterprises and have been inspected, packed and put in storage, the value of industrial services rendered to other units, and the changes in the value of the semi-finished products and products in process between the beginning and closing of the period. The gross industrial output value is calculated with "factory method". No double calculations are to be made within the same enterprise. However, double counting does occur among different enterprises.

Output value of light and heavy industries is based on the "factory" method. If the major products of an industrial enterprise are classified as light industry products, the entire gross output value of that enterprise is classified into the light industry; the same principle applies to heavy industry.

Value-added of Industry refers to the final results of industrial production of the industrial trade in money terms during the reference period.

Capital Obtained refers to capital actually received by the enterprise from investors. It can be further classified by investors as state capital, collective capital, corporate capital, individual capital, capital from Hong Kong, Macau and Taiwan and foreign capital.

Total Assets refer to all economic resources, owned or controlled by enterprises, that could be measured in monetary terms, including properties, creditors equity and other economic rights of all forms. Classified by the degree of equitability, total assets include circulating assets, long term investment, fixed assets, intangible assets and deferred assets, and other assets.

(1)**Circulating assets (working capital)** refer to assets which can be cashed in or spent or consumed in an operating cycle of one year or over one year, including cash, all kinds of deposits, short term investment, receivables, advance payment, stock, etc.

(2)**Fixed assets** refer to the net value of fixed assets, clearance of fixed assets, project under construction, fixed assets losses in suspense. These are corporations' fund holdings.

(3)**Intangible assets** refer to the assets without material form used by enterprises over a long time, such as patents, non-patent technologies, trade marks, copyright, land use right, business reputation, etc.

Total Liabilities refer to the debts, measured in monetary terms, that enterprises are responsible for repayment in the form of cash, assets or labour. Classified by terms of repayment, liability include liquid liabilities and long–term liabilities.

(1) **Liquid liabilities (also called quick liabilities or immediate liabilities)** refer to enterprises' total debt payable within an operating cycle of one year or over one year, including short term loans, payable and advance payments, wages payable, taxes payable and profit payable, etc.

(2) **Long term liabilities** refers to total debt payable within an operating cycle of one year or over one year, including long–term loans, payable liabilities, long–term payable, etc.

Creditors' Equity refers to investors ownership of net assets of the enterprise. It is equal to the total assets of the enterprise minus its total liabilities, including the primary input from investors, capital accumulation fund, surplus accumulation fund and undistributed profit. It is the shareholder's equity in share–holding companies.

Original Value of Fixed Assets refers to the original value of all fixed assets owned by industrial enterprises, calculated at the cost paid at the time of purchase, installation, reconstruction, expansion, and technical innovation and transformation of the said assets, which includes expenses on purchase, package, transportation, and installation, etc.

Net Value of Fixed Assets is obtained by deducting depreciation over years from the original value of fixed assets.

Working Capital (Circulating Assets) refers to assets which can be cashed in or spent or consumed in an operating cycle of one year or over one year, which includes cash, various deposits, short term investment, and receivable payments, and advance payments, stock, etc.

Sales Revenue of Industrial Products refers to the revenue from the sales of products by industrial enterprises and the revenue from services provided and etc.

Sales Cost of Industrial Products refers to the actual cost of products of industrial enterprises and industrial services provided, etc..

Tax and Extra Charges on Sales of Products refer to the tax on city maintenance and construction, consumption tax, resources tax and extra charges for education, which should be borne by the enterprises in selling products and providing industrial services.

Sales Profit of Products refers to the profit gained by the enterprises by deducting cost, charges and taxes from the business income of the enterprises obtained in selling products and providing industrial services.

Total Profits refer to the profits gained by the enterprises.

Value–added Tax Payable refers to the amount of the value added tax which should be paid by the enterprises in the reporting period.

Ratio of Profits, Taxes and Interests to Average Assets reflects the profit–making capability of all assets of the enterprise and is a key indicator manifesting the performance and management and evaluating the profit–making potential of the enterprise. It is calculated as follows:

Ratio of profits, taxes and interests to average assets (%) = [(Total profits+total Taxes+interest payment) / average assets]×100%

Ratio of Debts to Assets reflect both the operation risk and the capability of the enterprise in making use of the capital from the creditors. It is calculated as follows:

Ratio of debts to assets (%) = (Total debts / total assets)×100%

Ratio of Profits to Total Industrial Costs refers to the ratio of profits realized in a given period to the total costs in the same period, which reflects the economic efficiency of input cost and is calculated as follows:

Ratio of Profits to Total Industrial Cost(%)=(Total Profits/ Total Costs)×100%

Value–added Rate of Industry refers to the ratio of value added of industry in a given period to the gross output value in the same period, which reflects the economic efficiency of cutting down the intermediate input and is calculated as follows:

Value–added Rate of Industry(%)=[Value–added of Industry (at current prices)] / [Gross Output Value (at Current Prices)]×100%

Turnover of Working Capital refers to the number of times of turnover of working capital in a given period of time, which reflects the speed of the turnover of working capital and is calculated as follows:

Turnover of Working Capital(%)=(Sales Revenue of Products) / (Average Balance of Total Working Capital)×100%

Ratio of Sales to Gross Output Value refers to the sales of industrial products to the gross industrial output value during the reference period, and is important in reflecting the linkage between production and sales and the extent of the needs of the society that has been met by the supply of industrial products. It is calculated as follows:

Ratio of Sales to Gross Output Value=[Industrial sales / Gross industrial output value (at current prices)] ×100%

Overall Labour Productivity of Industrial Enterprises refers to the average output per employed person in industrial enterprises in value terms. At present, the value added and the average number of staff and workers of an industrial enterprises in a given period are used to calculate the overall labour productivity. The formula used is:

Overall Labour Productivity=(Value Added of Industry) / (Average Number of Staff and Workers)

资料整理: 邱育任
Arranged by Qiuyuren

11. 建筑业
CONSTRUCTION

建筑业总产值（亿元）

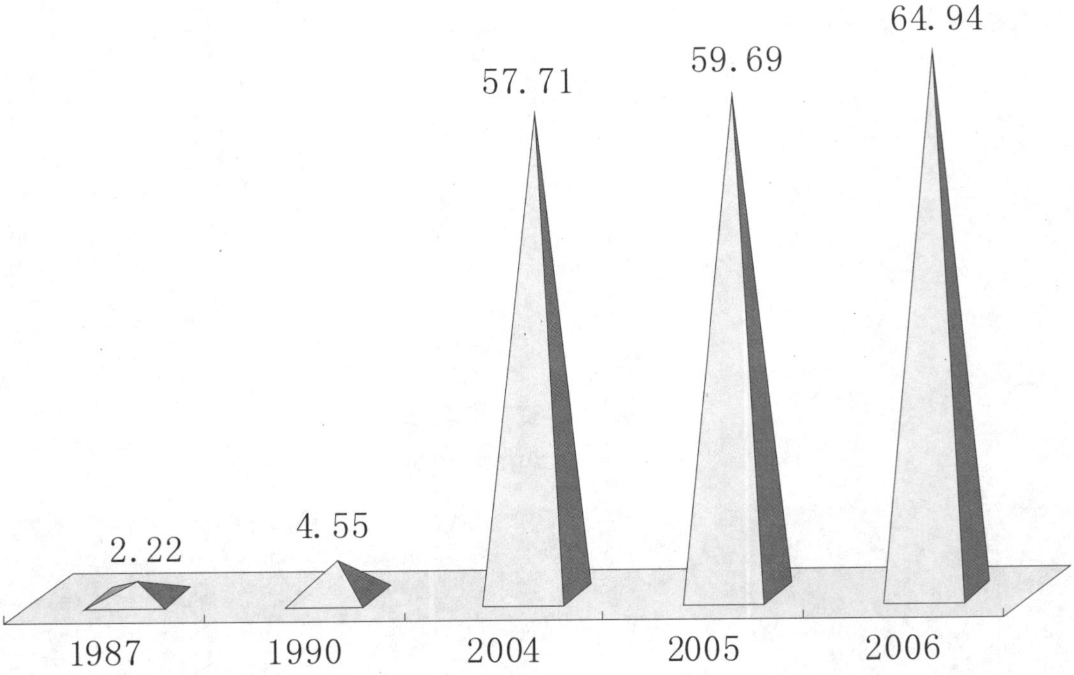

建筑业增加值（亿元）

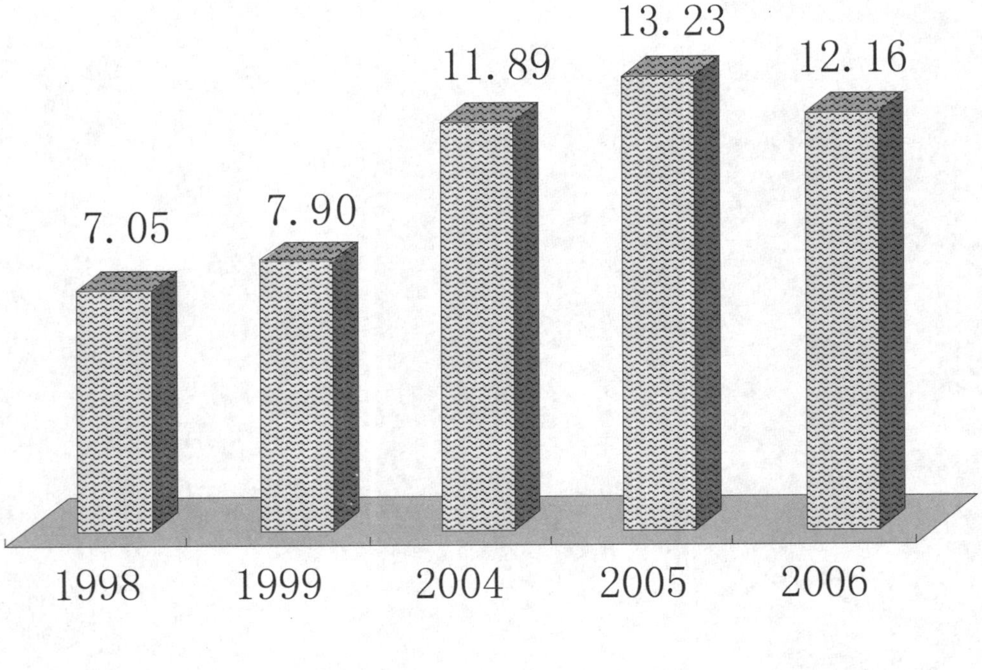

11－1 建筑业主要经济指标
Major Economic Indicators of Construction

项　目	Item	2004	2005	2006
企业单位数(个)	Number of Enterprises(unit)	152	154	148
企业从业人员(万人)	Number of Staff and Workers(10 000 persons)	7.19	6.68	7.25
建筑业总产值(万元)	Gross output Value of Contruction(10,000 yuan)	577077	596925	649436
竣工产值(万元)	Output Value of Building Completed(10,000 yuan)	332082	314656	484717
增加值(万元)	Value-added of Construction(10,000 yuan)	118927	132325	121596
房屋建筑施工面积(万平方米)	Floor Space of Buildings Under Contruction (10 000 sq.m)	636.46	692.38	780.43
房屋建筑竣工面积(万平方米)	Floor Space of Buildings Completed (10 000 sq.m)	213.07	205.56	314.97
#住宅	Residence	126.85	114.41	185.10
房屋建筑面积竣工率(%)	Rate of Floor Space of Buildings Completed(%)	37.3	29.6	40.4
年末固定资产原值(万元)	Original Value of Fixed Assets at the Year-end(10,000 yuan)	246594	179881	183306
年末固定资产净值(万元)	Year-end Fixed Assets Net Worth (10,000 yuan)	235075	154421	155557
年末流动资产(万元)	Year-end Current Assets(10,000 yuan)	376066	405580	437958
#流动资金	Flowing Funds	329915	351754	380365
利润总额(万元)	Total Profits(10,000 yuan)	26957	25871	14976
利税总额(万元)	Total Pre-tax Profits(10,000 yuan)	38667	44171	34915
产值利润率(%)	Ratio of Profit to Gross Output Value(%)	2.9	4.3	2.3

注:本表统计范围是全省所有具有资质等级独立核算的总承包和专业承包企业。2003 年以后企业单位数大幅度减少，其主要原因是国家实行新的建筑业资质管理办法，省外部分驻琼法人建筑企业失去法人资格,按建筑业统计属地原则,这部分不可统计在我省范围内。

a)It is all always contracting and professional contracting enterprise with independent accounting of qualification gradeses of the whole province that this form counts the range . Enterprises counted and reduced by a large margin after 2003, the main rea

11－2 各市县按登记注册类型分的建筑业企业单位数
Number of Construction Enterprises by Registration Status and City and County

单位:个 (unit)

市 县	Cities and Counties	合计 Total	内资企业 Domestic Funded	国有 State-owned	集体 Collectice-owned	港澳台商投资企业 Funded from Hongkong, Macao and Taiwan	港澳台商独资企业 Solely Owned	外商投资企业 Foreign Funded	外商独资企业 Solely Owned
总 计	Total	148	143	43	32			5	2
海口市	Haikou	105	100	31	9			5	2
三亚市	Sanya	4	4	3					
五指山市	Wuzhishan	1	1	1					
文昌市	Wenchang	2	2		2				
琼海市	Qionghai	7	7		7				
万宁市	Wanning	5	5		5				
定安县	Dingan	1	1						
屯昌县	Tunchang	3	3	1	2				
澄迈县	Chengmai	1	1		1				
临高县	Lingao	3	3						
儋州市	Danzhou	5	5	2	2				
东方市	Dongfang	3	3		2				
乐东县	Ledong	1	1		1				
琼中县	Qiongzhong								
保亭县	Baoting								
陵水县	Linshui								
白沙县	Baisha	1	1		1				
昌江县	Changjiang	1	1	1					
农 垦	Land Redamation	5	5	4					

11－3 各市县按登记注册类型分的建筑业企业从业人员
Employment of Construction Enterprises by Registration Status and City and County

单位:人 (Person)

市县	Cities and Counties	合计 Total	内资企业 Domestic Funded	国有 State-owned	集体 Collectice-owned	港澳台商投资企业 Funded from Hongkong, Macao and Taiwan	港澳台商独资企业 Solely Owned	外商投资企业 Foreign Funded	外商独资企业 Solely Owned
总计	**Total**	**72470**	**72232**	**41509**	**13996**			**238**	**10**
海口市	Haikou	54498	54260	35315	4763			238	10
三亚市	Sanya	1097	1097	917					
五指山市	Wuzhishan	180	180	180					
文昌市	Wenchang	2103	2103		2103				
琼海市	Qionghai	2997	2997		2997				
万宁市	Wanning	2305	2305		2305				
定安县	Dingan	540	540						
屯昌县	Tunchang	873	873	410	463				
澄迈县	Chengmai	220	220		220				
临高县	Lingao	685	685						
儋州市	Danzhou	1270	1270	360	260				
东方市	Dongfang	511	511		221				
乐东县	Ledong	483	483		483				
琼中县	Qiongzhong								
保亭县	Baoting								
陵水县	Linshui								
白沙县	Baisha	181	181		181				
昌江县	Changjiang	773	773	773					
农垦	Land Redamation	3754	3754	3554					

11－4 各市县建筑业总产值
Gross Output Value of Construction by City and County

单位:万元 (10000 yuan)

市 县	Cities and Counties	建筑业总产值 Total Output Value	建筑工程产值 Output Value of Construction	安装工程产值 Output Value of Installation	其它产值 Others	竣工产值 Output Value of Completed Construction
总 计	**Total**	**649436**	**580158**	**54721**	**14557**	**484717**
海口市	Haikou	543360	481322	50246	11792	397268
三亚市	Sanya	7762	7762			5437
五指山市	Wuzhishan	2020	2020			2020
文昌市	Wenchang	11445	11300	145		8335
琼海市	Qionghai	16221	13921	2230	70	14483
万宁市	Wanning	20336	17758	1000	1578	16755
定安县	Dingan	1602	1602			1563
屯昌县	Tunchang	3011	2761		250	3095
澄迈县	Chengmai	1077	1077			1177
临高县	Lingao	3421	3114		307	2849
儋州市	Danzhou	6361	5890	361	110	5952
东方市	Dongfang	6402	5581	679	142	6836
乐东县	Ledong	2101	2101			1890
琼中县	Qiongzhong					
保亭县	Baoting					
陵水县	Lingshui					
白沙县	Baisha	2418	2410		8	2418
昌江县	Changjiang	1509	1372	14	123	1504
农 垦	Land Redamation	20391	20168	45	178	13136

11－5 各市县建筑业增加值
Added Valueand of Construction by City and County

单位:万元 (10 000 yuan)

市 县	Cities and Counties	建筑业增加值 Value-added of Construction	营业利润 Profits of Project Settle Accounts	工程结算税金及附加 Taxes and Extra Charges on Project Settle Accounts	管理费用中的税金 Taxes in Management Expenses	主营业务应付工资 Wages Payable	主营业务应付福利费 Welfare Expenses Payable	本年提取固定资产折旧 Depreciation of Fixed Assets	其他 Others
总 计	**Total**	**121596**	**16250**	**18805**	**1133**	**70865**	**7136**	**5092**	**2315**
海口市	Haikou	98170	14923	15379	703	55524	5785	4459	1397
三亚市	Sanya	829	-400	341	11	737	62	77	2
五指山市	Wuzhishan	424	-20	115	…	207	26	62	34
文昌市	Wenchang	3520	686	343	30	1609	212	15	625
琼海市	Qionghai	2102	142	465	3	1478	1	12	1
万宁市	Wanning	3562	325	678	101	2323	53	75	7
定安县	Dingan	355	23	52	38	224	11	5	1
屯昌县	Tunchang	1243	11	116	3	973	113	27	1
澄迈县	Chengmai	148	9	50	…	65		25	
临高县	Lingao	854	236	281	78	158	8	44	48
儋州市	Danzhou	1881	111	374	58	1013	83	139	104
东方市	Dongfang	1415	120	108	84	906	123	62	12
乐东县	Ledong	318	-1	108	…	208		3	
琼中县	Qiongzhong								
保亭县	Baoting								
陵水县	Lingshui								
白沙县	Baisha	268	-95	14	14	320		15	…
昌江县	Changjiang	277	3	48	2	145	15	21	43
农 垦	Land Redamation	6230	178	334	8	4976	643	51	40

11－6 建筑业企业财务状况
Financial Codition of Construction Enterprises

单位:万元 (10 000 yuan)

项　目	Item	总 计 Total	# 国有及国有控股 Eterprises With Controlling Share Hold by the State	内资企业 Domestic Funded	港澳台商投资企业 Funded from Hongkong, Macao and Taiwan	外商投资企业 Foreign Funded
年初存货		65857	10994	65744		113
流动资产合计	Total Circulating Funds	437958	136835	434030		3927
长期投资	Total Long-term Investment	13516	3385	13516		
固定资产合计	Total fixed assets	172985	41136	170576		2409
固定资产原价合计	Total Original Value of Fixed Assets	183306	46372	180376		2931
累计折旧	Total Depreciation	27749	11120	27227		522
在建工程	Under Construction	15396	5285	15396		
无形及递延资产合计	Total Intangible and Deferred Assetses	16826	7307	16826		
资产总计	Total Assets	642201	189109	635865		6336
流动负债合计	Liquid Liabilities	252615	99329	250941		1674
长期负债合计	Long-term Liabilities	112268	28219	112268		
所有者权益合计	Total Creditors' Equity	277318	61561	272656		4662
工程结算收入	Revenue of Project Settlement Accounts	562253	312638	556964		5289
工程结算成本	Costs of Project Settlement Accounts	491054	280564	487079		3976
工程结算税金及附加	Taxes and Extra Charges on Project Settlement Accounts	18805	10307	18631		175
工程结算利润	Profits of Project Settlement Accounts	37798	13169	36782		1017
其他业务收入	Income of Other Business	1238	791	1238		
其他业务利润	Profits of Other Business	924	601	924		
经营费用	Business Expenses	14595	8598	14473		122
管理费用	Management Expenses	19972	8766	19076		897
财务费用	Financial Expenses	2500	9	2507		
营业利润	Profits of Business	16250	4994	16123		127
利润总额	Total Profits	14976	4540	14873		104
应交所得税	Income Taxes Payable	2737	1166	2720		18
应付利润	Profits Payable	9333	2402	9252		81
本年应付工资	Wages Payable this Year	70865	40502	70561		304
本年应付福利费	Welfare Expenses Payable this Year	7136	4641	7107		29

11－7 各市县建筑业主要财务指标
Main Finance Indicators of Construction

单位:万元 (10 000 yuan)

市 县	Cities and Counties	资产总计 Total Assets	流动资产 Circulating Funds	长期投资 Long-term Investment	固定资产 Fixed Assets	无形及递延资产年末合计 Total Intangible and Deferred Assetses	其他 Others	负债合计 Total Liabilities
总 计	Total	642201	437958	13516	172985	16826	916	364883
海口市	Haikou	545434	372882	13443	143978	14242	890	301598
三亚市	Sanya	10264	7797	38	2269	160		6878
五指山市	Wuzhishan	2335	801		1534			221
文昌市	Wenchang	17015	16071		925	19		11096
琼海市	Qionghai	18257	14173		3779	280	25	12865
万宁市	Wanning	7670	3662		3807	200	1	3395
定安县	Dingan	922	37		842	43		80
屯昌县	Tunchang	5287	3722		965	600		3116
澄迈县	Chengmai	848	183		664			39
临高县	Lingao	5296	2050		3246			2437
儋州市	Danzhou	12206	3605		7419	1182		7403
东方市	Dongfang	4887	3230	36	1621			3476
乐东县	Ledong	161	141		20			146
琼中县	Qiongzhong							
保亭县	Baoting							
陵水县	Lingshui							
白沙县	Baisha	685	4		581	101		2
昌江县	Changjiang	1164	1011		153			195
农 垦	Land Redamation	9771	8589		1182			11937

11-7 续 1(continued 1)

市 县	Cities and Counties	所有者权益 Total Creditors' Equity	企业总收入 Total Income of Enterprises	工程结算收入 Revenue of Project Settlement Accounts	工程结算成本 Costs of Project Settlement Accounts	工程结算税金及附加 Taxes and Extra Charges on Project Settlement Accounts	工程结算利润 Profits of Project Settlement Accounts	其他业务收入 Income of Other Business
总 计	Total	277318	563491	562253	491054	18805	37798	1238
海口市	Haikou	243836	481541	480800	419916	15379	32854	742
三亚市	Sanya	3386	9417	9417	8440	341	166	
五指山市	Wuzhishan	2114	2020	2020	1717	115	188	
文昌市	Wenchang	5919	10623	10585	9262	343	937	38
琼海市	Qionghai	5392	9065	9065	8142	465	331	
万宁市	Wanning	4275	12091	12091	10373	678	657	
定安县	Dingan	842	1602	1602	1288	52	231	
屯昌县	Tunchang	2171	3100	3095	2803	116	148	5
澄迈县	Chengmai	809	1270	1270	950	50	72	
临高县	Lingao	2860	3551	3542	2556	281	545	9
儋州市	Danzhou	4803	6369	6350	5093	374	690	20
东方市	Dongfang	1411	3662	3562	3112	108	195	100
乐东县	Ledong	15	2101	2101	1878	108	38	
琼中县	Qiongzhong							
保亭县	Baoting							
陵水县	Lingshui							
白沙县	Baisha	683	2418	2418	2207	14	124	
昌江县	Changjiang	969	1676	1501	1532	48		175
农 垦	Land Redamation		12985	12835	11785	334	704	150

11-7 续 1(continued 2)

市县	Cities and Counties	经营费用 Business Expenses	管理费用 Management Expenses	财务费用 Finance Expenses	营业利润 Profits of Business	利润总额 Total Profits	利税总额 Total Pre-tax Profits	产值利润率(%) Ratio of Profit to Gross Output Value(%)
总计	**Total**	**14595**	**19972**	**2500**	**16250**	**14976**	**34915**	**2.3**
海口市	Haikou	12650	16161	2210	14923	13904	29985	2.6
三亚市	Sanya	471	567					
五指山市	Wuzhishan	…	208				95	
文昌市	Wenchang	43	274	15	686	524	897	4.6
琼海市	Qionghai	127	123	66	142	142	610	0.9
万宁市	Wanning	383	286	47	325	153	932	0.8
定安县	Dingan	32	192	15	23	23	113	1.4
屯昌县	Tunchang	28	142	1	11	10	129	0.3
澄迈县	Chengmai	199	60	3	9	9	58	0.8
临高县	Lingao	160	229	89	236	236	594	6.9
儋州市	Danzhou	194	573	22	111	96	527	1.5
东方市	Dongfang	148	168	7	120	98	291	1.5
乐东县	Ledong	77	39			1	109	0.1
琼中县	Qiongzhong							
保亭县	Baoting							
陵水县	Lingshui							
白沙县	Baisha	73	219				28	
昌江县	Changjiang	…	88		3	3	53	0.2
农垦	Land Redamation	12	645	27	178	204	546	1.0

11-8 各市县建筑业职工人数及劳动生产率

Number of Staff and Workers and Overall Labor Productivity by City and County

市县	Cities and Counties	计算劳动生产率的平均人数(人) Average Nmber of Staff and Workers (persons)	劳动生产率 Overall Labor Productivity				产值工资率(%) Ratio of Wages to Gross Output Value(%)
			按企业总收入计算(元/人) In Terms of Total Income of Enterprises (yuan/person)	按总产值计算(元/人) In Terms of Gross output Value(yuan/person)	按增加值计算(元/人) In Terms of Value-added(yuan/person)	按房屋竣工面积计算(平方米/人) In Terms of Floor Space of Buildings Completed (sq.m/person)	
总计	**Total**	**73732**	**76424**	**88081**	**16492**	**43**	**10.9**
海口市	Haikou	57542	83685	94428	17061	39	10.2
三亚市	Sanya	685	137480	113318	12108	56	9.5
五指山市	Wuzhishan	280	72132	72132	15136	95	10.2
文昌市	Wenchang	2098	50632	54550	16777	60	14.1
琼海市	Qionghai	2597	34907	62461	8094	89	9.1
万宁市	Wanning	1936	62453	105040	18398	51	11.4
定安县	Dingan	420	38143	38143	8448	43	14.0
屯昌县	Tunchang	720	43060	41822	17269	25	32.3
澄迈县	Chengmai	220	57727	48941	6741	76	6.0
临高县	Lingao	634	56006	53959	13462	80	4.6
儋州市	Danzhou	1218	52291	52225	15444	69	15.9
东方市	Dongfang	630	58125	101614	22456		14.1
乐东县	Ledong	484	43409	43409	6574	39	9.9
琼中县	Qiongzhong						
保亭县	Baoting						
陵水县	Lingshui						
白沙县	Baisha	175	138154	138154	15320	162.8	13.2
昌江县	Changjiang	332	50491	45461	8340	4.9	9.6
农垦	Land Redamation	3761	34524	54217	16564	40.8	24.4

11－9 各市县房屋建筑完成情况
Floor Space of Buildings by City and County

市　县	Cities and Counties	房屋建筑面积(平方米)Floor Space of Building				房屋竣工价值(万元) Value of Building Completed (10000 yuan)
		施工面积 Floor Space of Buildings Under Contruction	本年新开工 Floor Space of Stared This Year	竣工面积 Floor Space of Buildings Completed	房屋建筑面积竣工率(%) Percentage of Floor Space of Buildings Completed	
总　计	**Total**	**7804303**	**3966062**	**3149697**	**40.4**	**290071**
海口市	Haikou	6459817	3125738	2238675	34.7	225272
三亚市	Sanya	38272	21109	38272	100	2957
五指山市	Wuzhishan	26672		26672	100	2019
文昌市	Wenchang	165728	151911	125912	76	8335
琼海市	Qionghai	265366	109031	231638	87.3	14483
万宁市	Wanning	155818	151418	98784	63.4	7686
定安县	Dingan	34060	29080	17860	52.4	1432
屯昌县	Tunchang	25360	19849	17964	70.8	1187
澄迈县	Chengmai	18828	9078	16690	88.6	1060
临高县	Lingao	70095	22876	50864	72.6	2823
儋州市	Danzhou	87517	41295	83982	96	5264
东方市	Dongfang	83121	37119			
乐东县	Ledong	37264	34364	18684	50.1	1890
琼中县	Qiongzhong					
保亭县	Baoting					
陵水县	Lingshui					
白沙县	Baisha	30672	7980	28487	92.9	2418
昌江县	Changjiang	2332	1718	1622	69.6	277
农　垦	Land Redamation	303381	203496	153591	50.6	12968

11–9 续 1(continued 1)

市　县	Cities and Counties	竣工面积按用途分 By Use					
		厂房、仓库 Factory Buildings	住　宅 Residential Buildings	办公用房 Official Buildings	批发和零售用房 Wholesale and Retail Buildings	住宿和餐饮用房 Hotels and Catering Buildings	居民服务业用房 Commercial and Residential ServiceBuildings
总　计	**Total**	**91448**	**1851045**	**230150**	**189740**	**70678**	**28778**
海口市	Haikou	62665	1452171	148647	124553	61622	2000
三亚市	Sanya	900	37372				
五指山市	Wuzhishan			26672			
文昌市	Wenchang	2051	92424	4899			
琼海市	Qionghai	25056	84942	4760	63100	5119	26778
万宁市	Wanning		63820	4288			
定安县	Dingan		6800	480		1500	
屯昌县	Tunchang	400	1015	4060	87	2437	
澄迈县	Chengmai		11900	400			
临高县	Lingao			1188			
儋州市	Danzhou		9800	5930			
东方市	Dongfang						
乐东县	Ledong		4320	2480			
琼中县	Qiongzhong						
保亭县	Baoting						
陵水县	Lingshui						
白沙县	Baisha		6256	21236			
昌江县	Changjiang	376					
农　垦	Land Redamation		80225	5110	2000		

11-9 续 2(continued 2)

市 县	Cities and Counties	教育用房 Culture and Education Buildings	文化、体育娱乐用房	卫生医疗用房 Medical Treatment Buildings	科研用房 Scientific Research Buildings	其他用房 Other Buildings
总 计	**Total**	**344162**	**103325**	**52011**	**17033**	**171327**
海口市	Haikou	184042	82865	25849	10235	84026
三亚市	Sanya					
五指山市	Wuzhishan					
文昌市	Wenchang			630		25908
琼海市	Qionghai	15629	335	4998	921	
万宁市	Wanning	20576		2630		7470
定安县	Dingan	2380		1500		5200
屯昌县	Tunchang	7105	1000	1260	600	
澄迈县	Chengmai	2857				1533
临高县	Lingao	12470	18000	3617		15589
儋州市	Danzhou	44518		10339	5277	8118
东方市	Dongfang					
乐东县	Ledong	11884				
琼中县	Qiongzhong					
保亭县	Baoting					
陵水县	Lingshui					
白沙县	Baisha	595	400			
昌江县	Changjiang			1188		58
农 垦	Land Redamation	42106	725			23425

11－10 各市县建筑业企业技术装备情况

Number and Power of Machinery and Equipment of Construction Enterprises by City and County

市 县	Cities and Counties	总台数(台) Total number of Machinery and Equipment (set)	净 值 (万元) Net Value (10 000yuan)	总功率 (千瓦) Total Power(kw)	施工机械功率 Power of Construction Machines	技术装备率 (元/人) Value of Machines per Laborer (yuan/person)	动力装备率 (千瓦/人) Power of Machines per Laborer (kw/person)
总 计	**Total**	**20569**	**34378**	**664654**	**664654**	**4744**	**9.2**
海口市	Haikou	11881	25425	251905	251905	4665	4.6
三亚市	Sanya	3596	82	317784	317784	748	289.7
五指山市	Wuzhishan	18	5	60	60	278	0.3
文昌市	Wenchang	630	588	980	980	2796	0.5
琼海市	Qionghai	676	3048	26672	26672	10170	8.9
万宁市	Wanning	1490	2484	26476	26476	10777	11.5
定安县	Dingan	136	473	330	330	8759	0.6
屯昌县	Tunchang	693	705	11050	11050	8078	12.7
澄迈县	Chengmai	150	397	2700	2700	18064	12.3
临高县	Lingao	362	398	4212	4212	5809	6.1
儋州市	Danzhou	375	110	8283	8283	862	6.5
东方市	Dongfang	212	318	1768	1768	6221	3.5
乐东县	Ledong	5	18	200	200	362	0.4
琼中县	Qiongzhong						
保亭县	Baoting						
陵水县	Lingshui						
白沙县	Baisha	84	136	1802	1802	7514	10
昌江县	Changjiang	180	26	7920	7920	332	10.2
农 垦	Land Redamation	81	166	2512	2512	442	0.7

主要统计指标解释

建筑业总产值(即自行完成施工产值) 是以货币表现的建筑安装企业在一定时期内生产的建筑业产品的总和。建筑业总产值包括:

⑴建筑工程产值:指列入建筑工程预算内的各种工程价值。

⑵设备安装工程产值:指设备安装工程价值,不包括被安装设备本身价值。

⑶房屋、构筑物修理产值:指房屋、构筑物修理所完成的价值,但不包括被修理房屋、构筑物本身的价值和生产设备的修理价值。

⑷非标准设备制造产值:指加工制造没有定型的、非标准的生产设备的加工费和原材料价值,以及附属加工厂为本企业承建工程制作的非标准设备的价值。

建筑业增加值 指建筑业企业在报告期内以货币表现的建筑业生产经营活动的最终成果。目前建筑业增加值采用分配法(收入法)计算,即从收入的角度出发,根据生产要素在生产过程中应得的收入份额计算。具体计算公式为:

建筑业增加值 = 本年提取的固定资产折旧 + 应付工资 + 应付福利费 + 管理费用中的劳动待业保险金、税金 + 工程结算税金及附加 + 工程结算利润

房屋建筑施工面积 指在报告期内施工的全部房屋建筑面积,包括本期新开工的房屋面积、上期施工跨入本期继续施工的房屋面积、上期停缓建在本期恢复施工的房屋面积、本期竣工的房屋面积及本期施工后又停缓建的房屋面积。

房屋建筑竣工面积 指在报告期内房屋建筑按照设计要求全部完工,达到了住人和使用条件,经验收鉴定合格,正式移交使用单位的房屋建筑面积。

自有机械设备年末总台数 指归本企业所有,属于本企业固定资产的生产性机械设备年末总台数。包括施工机械、生产设备、运输设备以及其他设备。

自有机械设备年末总功率 指本企业自有施工机械、生产设备、运输设备以及其他设备等列为在册固定资产的生产性机械设备年末总功率,按设定能力或查定能力计算。包括机械本身的动力和为该机械服务的单独动力设备,如电动机等。计算单位用千瓦,动力换算可按 1 马力 =0.735 千瓦折合成千瓦数。电焊机、变压器、锅炉不计算动力。

工程结算收入 指企业承包工程实现的工程价款结算收入,以及向发包单位收取的除工程价款以外的按规定列作营业收入的各种款项,如临时设施费、劳动保险费、施工机械调迁费等以及向发包单位收取的各种索赔款。

工程结算利润 指已结算工程实现的利润,如亏损以 "-" 号表示。计算公式为:

工程结算利润 = 工程结算收入 - 工程结算成本 - 工程结算税金及附加

企业总收入 指与企业生产经营直接有关的各项收入,包括工程结算收入和其他业务收入。计算公式为:

企业总收入 = 工程结算收入 + 其他业务收入

Explanatory Note on Main Statistical Indicators

Gross Output Value of Construction (Output Value of Projects Under Construction) refers to total of construction products, expressed in money terms, completed by construction and installation enterprises during a given period of time. It includes:

(1)Output value of construction projects, that is the value of projects covered by the project budgets;

(2)Output value of installation projects, that is the value of the installation of equipment, (excluding the value of the equipment to be installed);

(3)Output value of repair of buildings and structures, that is the value created through the repairs of buildings or structures, but does not include the value of buildings or structures being repaired and the value of the repair of production equipment;

(4)Output value of manufactured non-standard equipment, that is the value of non-standard production equipment (including raw materials and manufacturing cost) made for the construction project, and the equipment manufactured by subsidiary workshops.

Value-added of Construction refers to the final result of the activities of production and management of construction in monetary terms in the reference period. At present, the value-added of construction is calculated with the income approach. In other words, it is the sum of income of various production factors in the production process. The formula is as follows:

Value-added of construction=depreciation of fixed assets in the year+wages payable+welfare expenses payable+insurance premium and tax for waiting for employment in the administrative expenses+taxes and surcharges on project settlement+profit gained from project settlement.

Floor Space of Buildings Under Construction refers to floor space of buildings under construction during the reference period, including newly started buildings, buildings started earlier and continued during the reference period, and buildings suspended earlier but restarted during the reference period, buildings completed during the reference period, and buildings under construction and then suspended during the reference period.

Floor Space of Buildings Completed refers to the floor space of buildings that are completed in the reference period in accordance with the requirements of the design, up to the standard for putting them into use, and have been checked and accepted by concerned departments as qualified ones.

Total Number of Machinery and Equipment Owned by the End of Year refers to the number of machines and equipment owned by the enterprises, and listed as the fixed assets of the enterprises by the end of the year, including machinery and equipment for construction, production and transportation.

Total Power of Machinery and Equipment Owned by the End of Year refers to the total power of machinery and equipment owned by the enterprises, and listed as the fixed assets of the enterprises by the end of the year, including machinery and equipment for construction, production and transportation. The power of the machinery is calculated on basis of the designed or verified capacity, covering the power of the machinery/equipment and the separate power equipment serving the machinery/equipment (such as electric motors), but excluding welders, transformers and boilers. The unit used for the calculation of power is kilowatt, with horsepower converted to kilowatt by 1 horsepower=0.735 kilowatt.

Income from Settlement of Projects refers to the income received by the construction enterprise from the contracted project through settlement procedures, and other charges to the contractoree as operational costs in addition to the value of the project, such as temporary facility fee, labour insurance premium, moving cost of construction equipment, as well as various types of claims to the contractee.

Profit from Settlement of Projects refers to profit realized through settled projects. It is calculated with the following formula:

Profit from Settlement of Projects=Income from Settlement of Projects-Settled Cost-Settled Taxes and Other Cost

Total Revenue of Enterprises refers to the sum of income from production and operation of enterprises, including income from settlement of projects and other operational income, namely:

Total Revenue of Enterprises=Income from Settlement of Projects+Other Operational Income

资料整理: 李秀芳

Arranged by Lixiufang

12. 交通运输邮电通讯业

TRANSPORTATION,POSTAL AND TELECOMMUNICATIONS SERVICES

港口货物吞吐量（万吨）

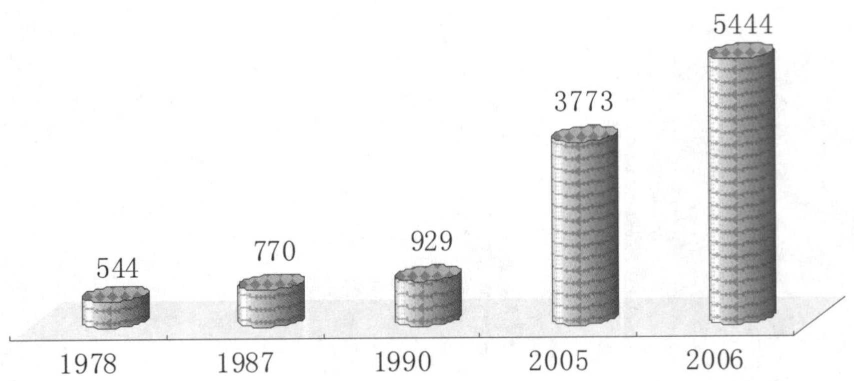

邮政通信业务总量（万元）

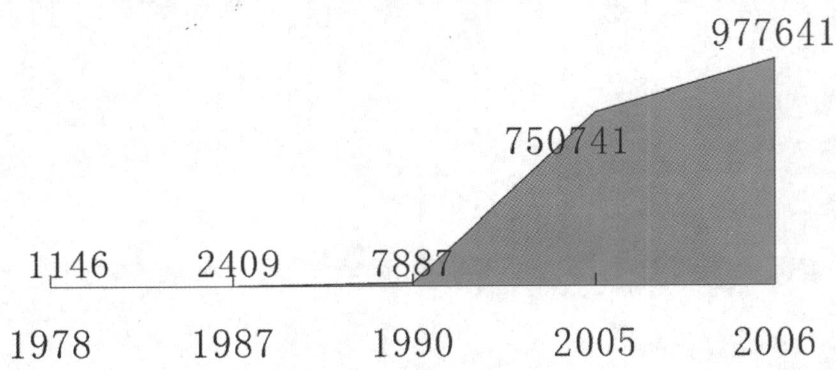

社会货物、旅客周转量

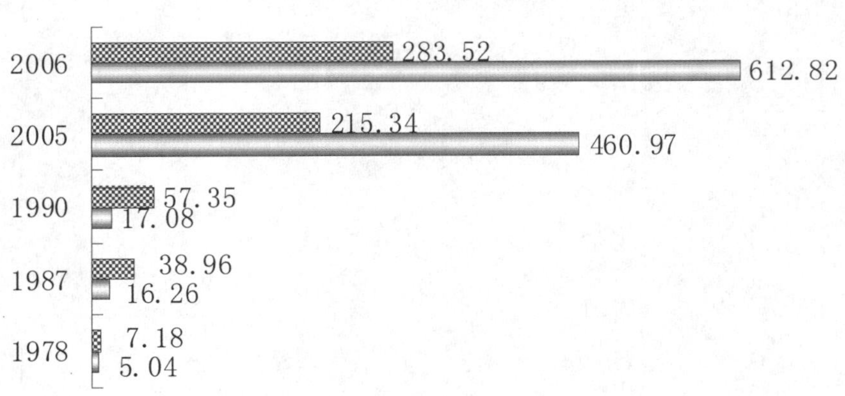

12－1 交通运输线路长度
Length of Transportation Routes

单位:公里 (km)

年 份 Year	公路通车里程 Length of Highways	铁路营业里程 Length of Railways in Operation	内河航道里程 Length of Navigable Inland Waterways	民航航线里程 Length of Civil Aviation Routes	国际航线 International Routes
1952	1412				
1957	3667				
1962	5113				
1965	5274	144	612		
1970	9409	144	612		
1975	10119	144	612		
1978	12641	144	556		
1979	14064	144	556		
1980	14110	214	338		
1985	12784	214	338		
1987	12794	214	338	5431	1647
1990	12902	214	338	19652	6536
1991	12922	214	338	24131	6536
1992	12937	214	338	48622	6536
1993	12937	214	338	62319	6536
1994	13014	214	338	82703	6536
1995	14808	214	338	127248	15444
1996	15165	214	403	154508	18702
1997	15246	214	414	152068	13269
1998	16920	214	414	201553	26006
1999	17317	214	414	316417	23171
2000	17401	214	414	399155	42503
2001	20667	214	414	240551	12144
2002	20876	214	414	477317	43299
2003	20877	214	434	306747	9082
2004	20873	705	343	540749	40673
2005	21162	361	343	770782	33757
2006	17577	579	343	1090212	87794

注:1、铁路营运里程含过海轮渡里程。
2、2006 年公路通车里程以交通部最新标准的口径计算。
a) The length of railways in operation is include of the length of ferrying.
b) The length of railways in 2006 is cacutated on the newest standard caliber which is promu lgated by the state trattic de partment

12－2 公路线路里程
Total Length of Highways

项　目	Item	总 计 Total	干线公路 Highways of Main Lines 总 计 Total	国 道 State Highway	省 道 Provincial Highway	县 道 County Highway	乡 道 Rural Highway	专用公路 Special Highway
公路通车里程（公里）	Length of Highways(km)	17577	3264	1289	1975	2823	5027	25
#:晴雨通车	Be Open to Traffic When Sunny or Rainy Day	9259	3264	1289	1975	2541	1641	4
等级路(公里)	Expressway and Class I to IV Highways(km)	8347	3108	1280	1828	2513	1440	4
#:高速公路	Expressway	625	625	249	376			
一级	First Class	189	173	59	114	8	3	
二级	Second Class	1237	1070	560	510	104	62	
三级	Third Class	1444	908	359	549	355	98	
四级	Fourth Class	4852	331	52	279	2047	1277	4
等外路(公里)	Highway Below Class IV(km)	9231	156	9	147	309	3588	21
有路面里程(公里)	Length of Road Surfaces(km)	5425	3144	1289	1855	1391	512	4
高级	Advanced & Second Advanced Road	4481	2302	757	1545	1344	480	4
次高级	Second advanced	944	842	532	310	47	32	
无路面里程(公里)	Length of No Road Surfaces (km)	12153	120		120	1431	4545	21
绿化里程(公里)	Length of Afforest Road(km)	15148	2094	1176	1728	2412	4235	19
养护里程(公里)	Length of Cultivate Road(km)	14672	3249	1289	1960	2608	3803	25
桥　梁(座)	Bridge(unit)	3561	1570	653	917	517	692	3
# 永久性	Perpetuity	3519	1570	653	917	512	672	3
桥梁长度(米)	Length of Bridge(m)	108982	60263	23647	36616	14467	16211	96
# 永久性	Perpetuity	107951	60263	23647	36616	14308	15740	96

12－3 全社会民用汽车拥有量
Total Number of Civil Motor Vehicles Owned

年份 Year	民用汽车总计(辆) Total Number(unit)	载客汽车 Passenger Vehicles		普通载货汽车 Ordinary Trucks		特种汽车 Special Motor Vehicles (辆)(unit)
		辆 (unit)	客位 Number of Seats	辆 (unit)	客位 Number of Seats	
1987	23896	8429	90483	14862	52610	605
1990	32121	15387	165202	16305	57721	420
1991	36600	18239	195825	17710	62694	651
1992	49201	26947	289354	21719	76887	535
1993	66659	35812	384546	29697	105129	1150
1994	86335	46861	411885	36940	137635	2534
1995	91269	52527	564998	36715	128801	2027
1996	98712	56065	602309	40215	169638	2432
1997	95074	54964	461965	38444	146310	634
1998	90620	50325	477454	38068	141193	504
1999	95934	53643	509064	33670	123357	596
2000	90069	52180	473628	36541	104389	1132
2001	82750	49449	418440	22123	78952	1429
2002	109777	62506	632170	30392	108462	1813
2003	125770	77664	840443	49147	123345	1959
2004	145548	88887	961757	54397	135993	2264
2005	173430	105433	1138676	56084	140210	
2006	202004	125627	1356772	58584	146460	

注:民用汽车总计包括其它专用载货汽车。
a)Number of Civil Motor Vehicles Owned include Trucks.

12－4 社会货物运输量和周转量
Freight Traffic & freight Ton-Kilometers

年 份 Year	总 计 Total	铁 路 Railways	公 路 Highways	水 运 Waterways	民 航(吨) Civil Aviation (ton)
(货物运输量:万吨)(Freight Traffic:10 000 tons)					
1975	709	370	232	107	700
1978	714	386	222	106	400
1979	644	356	201	87	400
1980	1922	298	1611	83	400
1985	3486	405	3022	59	700
1986	3601	415	3128	58	700
1987	3722	438	3216	68	1100
1988	4224	420	3661	143	2900
1989	4530	422	3941	167	2000
1990	4765	423	4115	227	4000
1991	5711	356	4929	425	5500
1992	6253	387	5393	472	7800
1993	8613	390	6968	1254	9000
1994	8735	346	6997	1390	20000
1995	10505	279	8256	1967	30000
1996	10975	252	8842	1877	40000
1997	11415	283	9116	2012	42220
1998	11630	286	9186	2153	46655
1999	11533	348	9049	2129	69340
2000	11304	331	8962	2002	90000
2001	10502	287	8190	2018	72572
2002	10498	288	8177	2025	79400
2003	11249	341	8797	2104	69401
2004	11824	455	9166	2195	74794
2005	13558	629	9652	3264	131899
2006	16417	1338	10314	4709	160763
(货物周转量:万吨公里)(Freight Ton-Kilometers:10 000 ton-km)					
1975	49809	18330	9380	22062	37
1978	50390	18550	9798	22021	21
1979	46333	17100	8938	20276	19
1980	87953	15436	50049	22449	19
1985	131999	20808	90979	20160	32
1986	128616	22048	88931	17600	37
1987	162541	23651	118752	20071	67
1988	155894	22839	104336	28515	204
1989	165224	23085	108778	33220	141
1990	170802	22297	112175	36094	236
1991	212497	19025	149373	43729	370
1992	1152027	20728	200921	929400	978
1993	1793404	22731	277160	1492385	1128
1994	2331985	20697	342859	1965433	2996
1995	2509302	17509	348344	2140099	3350
1996	2697179	14662	381856	2296117	4544
1997	2892786	15964	391614	2479846	5362
1998	3067272	16222	421853	2623165	6032
1999	3244281	20045	438097	2776990	9149
2000	3189774	19730	461477	2695903	12664
2001	2317396	17816	452542	1836134	10904
2002	2263521	18315	471396	1761616	12194
2003	2359930	21725	506391	1821294	10520
2004	2322216	53973	569888	1684877	13478
2005	4609661	70610	604535	3911304	23212
2006	6128228	109628	660653	5202102	28698

12－5 社会旅客运输量和周转量
Passenger Traffic & Passenger-kilometers

年份 Year	总计 Total	铁路 Railways	公路 Highways	水运 Waterways	民航(吨) Civil Aviation (ton)
(旅客运输量:万人)(Passenger Traffic:10 000 persons)					
1975	1145	80	1002	60	3
1978	1504	119	1296	85	4
1979	1717	126	1484	103	4
1980	2570	117	2320	128	5
1985	6057	75	5686	289	7
1986	6091	98	5732	249	12
1987	8952	100	8496	340	16
1988	13183	91	12528	537	27
1989	13680	75	13215	360	30
1990	15914	46	15371	455	42
1991	17133	44	16497	542	50
1992	17708	44	16838	758	68
1993	19010	55	18067	797	91
1994	18829	65	17781	830	153
1995	19667	54	18727	653	233
1996	19688	29	18754	637	268
1997	21296	27	20292	682	295
1998	21549	22	20633	544	350
1999	22085	17	21196	457	415
2000	23013	14	21930	537	532
2001	26711	12	25484	633	582
2002	27992	13	26766	613	600
2003	28083	13	26876	648	546
2004	31276	13	29966	555	742
2005	32933	33	31377	632	891
2006	36326	70	34126	1029	1101
(旅客周转量:万人公里)(Passenger-Kilometers:10 000 passenger-km)					
1975	53444	2973	47215	1471	1785
1978	71818	4533	63262	1978	2045
1979	82516	4820	73116	2460	2120
1980	104292	4368	94290	3204	2430
1985	236378	2678	222264	7986	3450
1986	239912	6066	222018	5770	6058
1987	389556	6695	369031	6785	7045
1988	429066	6501	391708	10675	20185
1989	442014	5410	408143	8337	20124
1990	573483	3541	536132	10888	22922
1991	633143	3514	574397	11400	43832
1992	684129	3627	594667	12907	72928
1993	758342	4777	632798	22487	98280
1994	849304	5642	629735	47453	166474
1995	937212	4794	665591	24266	242561
1996	1021380	2959	719396	17507	281518
1997	1111744	2963	783422	18574	306785
1998	1189441	2391	802417	17756	366877
1999	1256557	1801	782395	23112	449249
2000	1468769	1296	811786	25882	629805
2001	1600212	997	834657	23833	740725
2002	1730002	1103	921622	21943	785334
2003	1629661	1080	894204	18378	715999
2004	2064499	1992	1054801	15930	991776
2005	2153365	12230	1087647	14465	1039023
2006	2835220	18379	1175911	22517	1618413

12－6 各市县公路、水运运输量

Traffic of Highways&Waterways by City and County

单位：万吨、万人 (10 000 tons、10 000 persons)
单位：万吨公里、万人公里 (10 000 ton-km、10 000 person-km)

市县	Region	运输量 Freight Volume 合计 Total	公路 Highways	水运 Waterways	周转量 Rotation Volume 合计 Total	公路 Highways	水运 Waterways
货物运输	**Freight Traffic**	**16417**	**10314**	**4709**	**6207744**	**660653**	**5202102**
海口市	Haikou	7175	1542	4242	5434931	112631	5187724
三亚市	Sanya	915	896	17	86197	82776	1038
五指山市	Wuzhishan	42	42		2209	2209	
文昌市	Wenchang	244	229	15	34895	25876	9019
琼海市	Qionghai	388	388		47990	47990	
万宁市	Wanning	1438	1438		128728	128728	
定安县	Dingan	409	409		8486	8486	
屯昌县	Tunchang	198	198		9683	9683	
澄迈县	Chengmai	595	595		22875	22875	
临高县	Lingao	630	462	168	43005	11860	3115
儋州市	Danzhou	1870	1605	265	67761	66557	1204
东方市	Dongfang	1043	1043		21883	21883	
乐东县	Ledong	526	526		34790	34790	
琼中县	Qiongzhong	212	212		15913	15913	
保亭县	Baoting	54	54		9150	9150	
陵水县	Lingshui	72	72		7671	7671	
白沙县	Baisha	223	223		15236	15236	
昌江县	Changjiang	126	126		9629	9629	
洋浦区	Yangpu	257	255	2	26712	26710	2
旅客运输	**Passenger Traffic**	**36266**	**34126**	**1029**	**2716691**	**1175911**	**22517**
海口市	Haikou	15836	14478	410	1720004	404611	17983
三亚市	Sanya	1921	1596	162	352673	99618	2202
五指山市	Wuzhishan	142	142		12420	12420	
文昌市	Wenchang	1225	1185	40	71962	71898	64
琼海市	Qionghai	1076	900	176	47998	47802	196
万宁市	Wanning	3953	3953		122056	122056	
定安县	Dingan	1325	1325		26938	56938	
屯昌县	Tunchang	1160	1160		49569	49569	
澄迈县	Chengmai	929	929		40587	40587	
临高县	Lingao	618	618		28070	28070	
儋州市	Danzhou	1689	1641	48	63847	63655	192
东方市	Dongfang	984	984		47084	47084	
乐东县	Ledong	556	556		31950	31950	
琼中县	Qiongzhong	484	484		26418	26418	
保亭县	Baoting	411	411		7036	7036	
陵水县	Lingshui	3193	3016	177	41717	39853	1864
白沙县	Baisha	338	338		14733	14733	
昌江县	Changjiang	388	388		8892	8892	
洋浦区	Yangpu	38	22	16	2737	2721	16

12－7 旅客运输平均运距
Average Transport Distance of Passengers

单位:公里 (km)

年 份 Year	总 计 Total	铁 路 Railways	公 路 Highways	水 运 Waterways	民 航(吨) Civil Aviation (ton)
1975	47	37	47	25	595
1980	41	37	47	26	486
1983	38	35	40	23	
1985	39	38	39	27	493
1987	44	70	39	20	440
1988	33	71	43	23	748
1990	36	77	31	24	546
1991	40	80	35	21	877
1992	39	82	35	17	1072
1993	40	87	35	28	1080
1994	45	87	39	57	685
1995	50	88	37	41	1041
1996	52	102	38	27	1050
1997	54	110	38	27	1040
1998	55	109	39	33	1048
1999	57	106	37	51	1083
2000	63	93	37	48	1184
2001	60	83	33	38	1273
2002	62	85	34	36	1309
2003	58	83	33	28	1311
2004	66	153	35	29	1336
2005	65	370	34	22	1166
2006	78	262	34	22	1470

12－8 货物运输平均运距
Average Transport Distance of Freight

单位:公里 (km)

年 份 Year	总 计 Total	铁 路 Railways	公 路 Highways	水 运 Waterways	民 航(吨) Civil Aviation (ton)
1975	70	50	40	206	529
1980	44	52	31	270	475
1983	40	51	27	315	
1985	38	51	30	342	457
1987	44	54	37	295	609
1988	37	55	28	199	703
1990	36	53	27	159	590
1991	37	53	30	103	673
1992	184	54	37	1969	1254
1993	208	58	40	1190	1253
1994	267	59	49	1414	1498
1995	239	63	42	1220	1117
1996	246	58	43	1223	1292
1997	253	56	43	1233	1271
1998	264	57	46	1218	1293
1999	281	58	48	1304	1319
2000	282	60	51	1347	1407
2001	221	62	55	910	1504
2002	216	64	58	870	1536
2003	210	64	57	865	1516
2004	196	119	62	768	1802
2005	340	112	62	1198	1759
2006	373	82	64	1105	1785

12－9 铁路运输主要财务成本指标
Main Financial Indicators of Railway Transport

单位:万元 (10 000 yuan)

项 目	Item	2001	2002	2003	2004	2005	2006
运输总收入	Total Transport Revenue	3427	3386	4089	13469	34959	52506
客运收入	Revenue from Passenger Traffic	99	115	123	1066	9094	15685
货运收入	Revenue from Freight Traffic	3021	3271	3966	12359	13031	36025
行李包裹收入	Revenue from Luggage	13			19	50	20
其他收入	Other Revenue	294			25	12784	796
运输总支出	Total Transport Costs	6420	6873	7728	25503	50146	69274
工 资	Wages and Salaries	1783	2446	2188	6251	8384	15772
材 料	Materials	294	361	357	945	1454	1669
燃 料	Fuel	74	789	813	2499	4634	6593
电 力	Electricity	725	74	91	479	563	718
折 旧	Depreciation	610	765	591	3269	3095	12239
其 他	Other Costs	2934	2439	1115	12060	10389	32283
营业外收支净额	Non-operating Net Revenue or Expenditure	438	976	845	4245	-1290	540
应激税金	Taxes Payable	111	110	116	584	1149	1725
#应激营业税	Business Taxes Payable	111	82	104	511	1149	
实现利润	Profits	-1786	-2373	-2926	-17490	-17626	-18444
#建设基金	Construction Fund	582	589	647			

12－10 民用航空航线及飞机架数
Number of Civil Aviation Routes and Civil Aircrafts

项 目	Item	2001	2002	2003	2004	2005	2006
民用航空航线(条)	Number of Civil Aviation Routes(line)	6	291	240	340	391	422
国际航线	International Routes	6	9	2	10	12	19
国内航线	Domestic Routes				330	379	403
#地区航线	Regional Routes				4	4	4
民用航空航线里程(公里)	Length of Civil Aviation Routes(km)	236514	477317	306747	540749	804539	1079246
国际航线	International Routes	12144	43299	9082	40673	33757	87794
国内航线	Domestic Routes	224370	434018	297665	500076	770782	991452
#地区航线	Regional Routes	4037	4190	3660	3660	9660	13885
民用航班飞行机场(个)	Number of Civil Airports(unit)	2	2	2	2	2	2
#可降波音737以上机型	Number of civil airports can land Boeing 737 and above Boeing 737	2	2	2	2	2	2
民用飞机架数(架)	Number of Civil Aircraft(unit)	36	52	83	54	46	60
#波音757	Boeing 757	4	4	4	4	4	4
波音737	Boeing 737	19	27	42	27	24	35
波音767	Boeing 767		2	3	2	5	5
MD-82		4	5	5	8	14	12
D328		6	14	26	12	10	22
M23					0		
D84		3		3	1	1	

注:民用航线采用重复计算方法
a)Civil aviation routes are calculated at repetition.

12－11 民用航空运输量及通用飞行时间
Civil Aviation Traffic and Flying Time of General Aviation

指 标	Item	总计 Total	按航线 Aviation Routes 国际航线 International Routes	国内航线 Domestic Routes	地区航线 Regional Routes	按机形分 Aerotransport 波音737 Boeing 737	波音757 Boeing 757	波音767 Boeing 767	md-84
客运量(万人)	Passenger Traffic(10 000 persons)	1100.86	14.31	1073.84	12.71	601.5	92.27	121.18	7
旅客周转量(万人公里)	Passenger-tons(10 000 person-km)	1618413.24	65690.83	1463366.09	515592.82	840702.6	148248.59	249380.84	5817
货邮运量(吨)	Freight Traffic(Ton)	160763.4	3731.4	156895.9	136.1	76505.9	12023.3	49453.7	149
邮件	Mail	4918.5	100.7	4816.9	0.9	3024.5	207.4	1011.7	27
货物	Commodity	155844.9	3630.7	152079	135.2	73481.4	11815.9	48442	122
货邮周转量(万吨公里)	Freight Ton-kilometers(10 000 ton-km)	28698.18	2636.99	26052.71	8.48	11889.77	2165.62	10981.79	14
邮件	Mail	723.16	66.08	657.06	0.02	390.82	37.86	218.31	3
货物	Commodity	27975.02	2570.91	25395.65	8.46	11498.95	2127.76	10763.48	11
飞行班次(班次)	Number of Times Scheduled Form of Aircrafes(unit)	104619	1072	102081	1466	53631	6436	6236	1306
飞行公里(万公里)	Flight kilometre(10 000 km)	289703.61	504.94	13793.74	74.24	7087.2	969.67	1385.39	104
飞行时间(小时)	Flight Time(hr)	219094	6959	210145	1990	110849	14818	19811	2244

12－12 港口货物吞吐量
Volume of Freight Handled in Major Coastal Ports

单位:万吨 (10 000 tons)

年 份 Year	总 计 Total	海口港 Haikou	火车轮渡码头	三亚港 Sanya	八所港 Basuo	洋浦港 Yangpu	其他沿海小港 Other Ports
1971	509	67		44	328		70
1972	408	60		29	252		67
1973	473	67		37	306		63
1974	471	57		37	303		74
1975	514	76		31	302		105
1976	496	57		35	284		120
1977	539	76		42	285		136
1978	544	76		45	307		116
1979	533	83		41	305		104
1980	483	72		38	278		95
1981	483	79		33	284		87
1982	557	88		36	343		90
1983	628	109		39	372		108
1984	686	131		53	411		91
1985	624	171		77	288		88
1986	722	174		64	391		93
1987	770	198		64	405		103
1988	826	241		59	392		134
1989	895	256		63	410		166
1990	929	288		37	431		173
1991	886	321		37	350		178
1992	1040	413		39	376		212
1993	1307	580		65	384		278
1994	1459	699		79	355		326
1995	1252	469		43	275		465
1996	1407	537		31	265		574
1997	1424	486		30	336		572
1998	1474	470		33	358	44	569
1999	1682	674		27	380	42	559
2000	1976	808		48	378	46	696
2001	1982	888		71	342	60	621
2002	2309	1073		49	343	91	753
2003	2757	1329		61	425	114	828
2004	3602	1439		75	548	220	1320
2005	3773	2118		49	489	431	686
2006	5444	2173	1111	76	479	1016	589

12－13 主要港口货物、旅客吞吐量

Volume of Freight Handled in Major Coastal Ports by Type of Freight and Passenger

单位:万吨 (10 000 tons)

港口(货物)	Port(Type of Freight)	货物吞吐量 Volume of Freight	出口 Out-port	进口 In-port
总　计	**(Total)**	**3744**	**1821**	**1921**
按主要港口分	Major Coastal Ports			
海口港	HaiKuo	2173	1005	1168
八所港	BaSuo	479	423	56
三亚港	SanYa	76	26	50
洋浦港	YangPu	1016	367	647
海口新港	HaiKuo New Port			
按货物分类	Type of Freight			
煤炭	Coal	75.64	1.52	74.04
成品油	Petroleum	16.08	4.11	11.97
金属矿石	Metal Ores	423.45	332.83	90.6
钢铁	Steel and Iron	109.06	26.23	82.83
矿建材料	Mineral Building Materials	42.57	22.64	19.93
水泥	Cement	3.35	3.23	0.12
木材	Timber	92.8	29.03	63.77
非金属矿石	Nonmetal Ores	48.28	34.05	14.23
化肥及农药	Chemical Fertilizers and Pesticides	135.89	95.17	40.72
盐	Salt	14.95	8.57	6.38
粮食	Grain	111.7	7.42	104.29
机械设备及电器	Mechanical Equipment & Electric Device	861.32	386.73	474.6
化工原料及制品	Raw Chemical Materials and Chemical Products	132.06	79.04	53.01
有色金属	Nonferrous Metals	4.4	0.56	3.83
轻工医药产品	Light Industtry and Medical Products	89.81	57.43	32.38
农副产品	Agrcultural Products and By-products	677.49	389.52	287.98
其他	Others	158.23	115.65	42.58

12-13 续(Continued)

港口	Port	旅客吞吐量 Volume of Passenger (万人) (10 000 persons)	出口 Out-port	进口 In-port
总　计	**Total**	**493**	**262**	**230**
海口港	Haikuo	492	262	230
三亚港	Sanya	0.56	0.28	0.28

12－14 邮电通信网

Postal and Telecommunication Communication Network

年 份 Year	邮电局所 Number of Post and Telecommunication Offices （处）(unit)	设在农村 In Country	邮路总长度 Length of Postal Routes （公里） (km)	航空邮路 Airline Routes	农村投递路线总长 Length of Rural Delivery Routes （公里） (km)
1952	22		540		
1957		140	8100		
1962	222	196	6700		10801
1965	228	204	8200		
1970	312	288	11200		18155
1975	377	355	15200		27343
1978	385	359	16700		28076
1979	389	361	16300		28681
1980	393	365	14000		18750
1985	389	359	14400		23001
1986	351	356	13700		23845
1987	408	372	13143		23503
1988	406	344	14051	460	22685
1989	410	341	30342	20653	22429
1990	406	361	51381	42061	21014
1991	412	336	50937	41154	20990
1992	426	340	60698	51644	21394
1993	440	364	88752	82498	20800
1994	474	368	97955	87798	20312
1995	506	386	87007	78135	19701
1996	524	369	55107	46477	19291
1997	575	385	88656	79497	20474
1998	621	384	50198	39740	21745
1999	525	343	51028	40909	19838
2000	503	352	58029	46079	19732
2001	504	352	33942	22194	20353
2002	494	437	35873	23148	20296
2003	487	336	41939	25311	22858
2004	468	322	34831	20710	23108
2005	458	315	36498	22012	23172
2006	463	311	32414	20383	23645

12－15 各市县邮电局所和邮政车辆
Postal and Postal Car by City and County

市 县	Region	邮电局所 Number of Post and Telecommunication Offices (处)(unit)	提供邮政全功能服务的 Provide All Postal Services	汽车 Number of Motor Vehicles (辆) (unit)	摩托车 Number of Motorcycles (辆) (unit)
总 计	Total	463	427	452	209
海口市	Haikou	81	80	120	43
三亚市	Sanya	25	24	22	20
五指山市	Wuzhishan	12	8	5	17
文昌市	Wenchang	36	36	15	16
琼海市	Qionghai	28	28	18	55
万宁市	Wanning	22	19	15	5
定安县	Dingan	18	18	11	1
屯昌县	Tunchang	19	19	9	4
澄迈县	Chengmai	26	25	13	4
临高县	Lingao	15	15	5	3
儋州市	Danzhou	29	39	15	0
东方市	Dongfang	23	18	10	5
乐东县	Ledong	23	22	9	0
琼中县	Qiongzhong	20	20	8	13
保亭县	Baoting	15	11	8	3
陵水县	Lingshui	18	17	10	4
白沙县	Baisha	20	10	9	2
昌江县	Changjiang	18	16	8	0
洋 浦	Yangpu	2	2	5	3

12－16 邮政通信业务总量和电话总户数
Telecommunication Services and Telephone Subscribers

年 份 Year	通信业务总量 Business Volume of Post and Telecommunication Services (万元)(10 000 yuan)	邮政业务总量 Business Volume of Paid Services （万元）	固定电话总户数 Numbe of Telephone Subscribers （户） (Subscribers)	城 市 Numbe of Urban Telephone Subscribers	农 村 Numbe of Rural Telephone Subscribers
1976	630	394	10093	4547	5546
1977	787	376	10446	4742	5704
1978	779	367	10370	4814	5556
1979	780	367	10386	4996	5390
1980	791	380	9576	5088	4480
1981	1074	525	9053	5344	3709
1982	1077	535	9091	5528	3563
1983	1097	517	9276	5931	3345
1984	1222	556	10778	7236	3542
1985	1370	581	12298	8649	3649
1986	1449	597	13662	9901	3761
1987	1758	651	16685	12736	3949
1988	2746	879	22243	18053	4190
1989	3676	1050	30340	25900	4440
1990	5073	2814	40611	35924	4687
1991	15810	3538	57256	52278	4978
1992	27662	4558	84936	78849	6087
1993	54019	6549	135848	127838	8010
1994	86698	8579	237386	216558	20828
1995	104931	9377	280401	248770	31631
1996	125872	10895	341327	292629	48698
1997	161307	12399	386895	326007	60888
1998	185239	14257	434038	361181	72857
1999	229481	17470	527000	422000	105000
2000	310559	18957	690059	523601	166458
2001	322833	32848	1055097	726277	328820
2002	397037	32347	1373520	968516	405004
2003	430530	34509	1628063	1153666	474397
2004	586339	37181	1972932	1420975	551957
2005	709812	40929	2300167	1710769	589398
2006	930423	47218	2490114	1797233	692881

注：邮电业务总量 1971－1980 年按 1970 年不变价计算，1981－1990 年按 1980 年不变价计算，1991－1999 年按 1990 年不变价计算，1970 年不变价与 1980 年不变价换算系数为 2.091，1980 年不变价与 1990 年不变价换算系数为 3.04。

a):The business volume of post and telecommunication services between 1971 and 1980 were constant calculated at 1970's constantprices and that between 1981 and 1990 were calculated at 1980's prices and that between 1991and 1990 were calculated at 1990's constant prices. The conversion at constant price between 1970 and 1980 were 2.091 . The conversion at constant price between 1980 and 1990 were 3.04 。

12－17 邮政主要业务量
Business Volume of Post

年份 地区	Region	函件 Number of Letters (万件) (10 000 pec)	包裹 Package (万件) (10 000 pcs)	汇票 Draft (万张) (10 000)	邮政储蓄平均余额 Average Remaining Sum of Post Save (万元) (10 000 yuan)	特快传递 Pieces of Express Mail Services (万件) (10 000 pcs)	订销报纸累计份数 Newpapers Circulation (万份) (10 000 pcs)	订销杂志累计份数 Magazines Circulation (万份) (10 000 pcs)
1987		2969	38	207			12683	1208
1988		3345	39	205	1117			
1989		3473	39	196	1700			
1990		3438	41	192	3116	5.4	8295	686
1991		3659	41	200	13648	8.4	9134	811
1992		4257	46	235	19762	12.1	10842	926
1993		5384	58	341	50348	23.7	11231	949
1994		5689	58	435	91110	31.5	12905	924
1995		4998	68	353	141049	33	14322	1019
1996		4353	72	302	193611	39.2	16450	825
1997		3789	61	272	214021	39.9	14999	744
1998		3313	62	238	286248	42.3	14109	667
1999		3178	63	214	373788	50.1	13072	345
2000		2547	60	204	418177	47.1	12539	686
2001		3010	63.5	184.4	457930	62.9	12800	548
2002		2441	68.3	161.3	511013	70	12290	505
2003		2304	76	137	608736	64.8	12072	467
2004		1959	85	103	730994	95.7	9185	474
2005		2012	59	85	889905	108.1	9692	474
2006		1735	46	84	1082517	124	9772	471
海口市	Haikou	543	24	28	349497	40.9	3090	272
三亚市	Sanya	162	8	9	81210	11.1	1011	19
五指山市	Wuzhishan	15	1	2	13339	1.5	197	13
文昌市	Wenchang	49	1	4	75171	4.0	889	13
琼海市	Qionghai	47	2	5	66993	3.5	503	15
万宁市	Wanning	22	1	5	68574	2.4	389	10
定安县	Dingan	28	1	1	29495	0.9	309	5
屯昌县	Tunchang	16	1	1	24212	1.0	225	5
澄迈县	Chengmai	27	1	4	46501	1.8	457	15
临高县	Lingao	17	1	2	33464	1.1	257	7
儋州市	Danzhou	41	2	7	66659	3.8	712	22
东方市	Dongfang	21	1	3	40004	2.1	345	12
乐东县	Ledong	31	1	3	46983	1.7	276	12
琼中县	Qiongzhong	15	1	2	28268	1.0	170	6
保亭县	Baoting	10	0	2	21510	1.1	156	7
陵水县	Lingshui	16	1	2	25079	1.2	230	10
白沙县	Baisha	10	0	2	31197	0.9	204	6
昌江县	Changjiang	13	1	2	28255	1.9	265	16
洋浦	Yangpu	15	1	1	6105	2.3	88	6

12－18 电信主要业务量
Business Volume of Telecommunication Services

年 份 Year	移动电话用户 Number of Mobile Telephone Subscribers (户) (10 000 subscribers)	城市电话用户 Number of Local (urban) Telephone Subscribers (户) (10 000 subscribers)	住宅电话 Residential Telephone Subscribers (户) (10 000 subscribers)	公用电话 Public Telephone Subscribers (部) (10 000 subscribers)	农村电话用户 Number of Rural Telephone Subscribers (户) (10 000 subscribers)	长途电话 Number of Long Distance Telephone Calls (万分钟) (10 000)
1987			360	32	3949	236
1990		35924	4605	62	4687	643
1991		52278	13393	298	4978	1482
1992	1013	78849	24988	1063	6087	3117
1993	10385	127838	54720	3290	8010	7417
1994	19467	216558	129673	5387	20828	13033
1995	31090	248770	166384	10182	31631	11520
1996	52907	292629	181351	14159	48698	11732
1997	131029	326007	208618	18667	60888	12661
1998	194874	361181	230593	19206	72857	11722
1999	284828	422000	286000	33000	105000	9724
2000	478182	523601	468557	39479	166458	16009
2001	853822	726277	694297	31980	328820	7711
2002	1100672	968516	455648	32460	405004	6561
2003	1363023	1153666	899320	144047	474397	13290
2004	1660355	1420975	983326	177701	551957	20598
2005	2038712	1710769	553596	236593	589398	138882
2006	2398888	1797233	1703170	220335	692881	173353

12－19 邮电通信网及主要设备

Post and Telecommunications Communication Network and Its Main Facilities

单位:万吨 (10 000 tons)

年份 Year	长途业务电路 Number of Long-distance Telephone Lines（2M）()	长途自动交换机容量 Capacity of Long-distance Telephone Exchanges（路端）(line)	局用交换机容量 Capacity of Office Telephone Exchanges（门）(line)	移动交换机总容量 Capacity of Mobile Telephone Exchanges（万户）(10 000 subscribers)	城市电话 Number of (urban) Telephone Subscribers（户）	农村电话 Number of Rural Telephone Subscribers（户）
1987	323		25590		18433	10693
1988	571	0	37390		25063	11636
1989	633	0	41490		36075	12065
1990	865		64000		47900	12360
1991	1379		86700		72634	12939
1992	1876		109840		103619	13647
1993	5073		210970		175643	16377
1994	9604	13494	386488		265022	25910
1995	10343	27860	495048		355116	35375
1996	11331	38730	586470		382938	52617
1997	12373	42420	637944		396713	66261
1998	18346	42420	667888		430600	82538
1999	22032	38572	723851	55.5	580676	117495
2000	17317	69930	773648	112.5	781255	166458
2001	17317	55000	836181	121	726277	328820
2002	17258	66102	884814	139	968516	405004
2003	873	75296	969834	158	1153666	474397
2004	801	66196	928926	194	1420975	551957
2005	1828	66516	2794892	245	1710769	589398
2006	1848	72634	3102590	319	1797233	692881

12－20 邮电通信质量及服务水平

Level of Postal and Telecommunication Services

服务水平指标	Item	2001	2002	2003	2004	2005	2006
平均每百人订有报刊数(份)	Annual Average Number of Newspaper and Magazine Subscribed per 100 Persons(piece)	1682	1663	1550	1222	1256	1245
平均每百人拥有电话(户)	Number of Telephone Sets Owned per 100 Persons(unit)	13.26	32.15	38.4	47.6	53.06	59.04
已通电话的行政乡比重(%)	Percentage of Townships with Telephone Communication(%)	99	100	100	96.2	98.9	100

从 2006 年起无线寻呼用户和无线寻呼系统容量已取消
The volume of radio paging user and radio paging system has been removed since 2006.

主要统计指标解释

公路里程 指在一定时期内实际达到《公路工程[WTBZ]技术标准 JTJ01-88》规定的等级公路，并经公路主管部门正式验收交付使用的公路里程数。包括大中城市的郊区公路以及通过小城镇街道部分的公路里程和桥梁、渡口的长度，不包括大中城市的街道、厂矿、林区生产用道和农业生产用道的里程。两条或多条公路共同经由同一路段，只计算一次，不得重复计算里程长度。它是反映公路建设发展规模的重要指标，也是计算运输网密度等指标的基础资料。

内河航道里程 也称内河通航里程，指在一定时期内，能通航运输船舶及排筏的天然河流、湖泊水库、运河及通航渠道的长度。包括全年季节性通航累计三个月以上的航道，不包括仅供零散流放竹、木排的河道。它是反映内河水运网规模、水平和发展情况的主要指标。

民用航空航线里程 指民航运输定期班机飞行的航线长度的总和。航线长度按机场之间的距离计算，通常有两种计算方法：一是将每条航线长度相加称为重复计算航线里程；一是将两线或两条以上航线经过同一区段里程，只计算一次航线长度称为不重复计算航线里程。一般常用的是后者，它能确切反映民航运输网的规模，是表明民航事业为国民经济服务和方便人民生活程度的主要指标。

货(客)运量 指在一定时期内，各种运输工具实际运送的货物(旅客)数量。它是反映运输业为国民经济和人民生活服务的数量指标，也是制定和检查运输生产计划、研究运输发展规模和速度的重要指标。货运按吨计算，客运按人计算。货物不论运输距离长短、货物类别，均按实际重量统计。旅客不论行程远近或票价多少，均按一人一次客运量统计；半价票、小孩票也按一人统计。

货物(旅客)周转量 指在一定时期内，由各种运输工具运送的货物(旅客)数量与其相应运输距离的乘积之总和。它是反映运输业生产总成果的重要指标，也是编制和检查运输生产计划，计算运输效率、劳动生产率以及核算运输单位成本的主要基础资料。计算货物周转量通常按发出站与到达站之间的最短距离，也就是计费距离计算。计算公式为：

货物(旅客)周转量 =∑货物(旅客)运输量×运输距离

沿海主要港口货物吞吐量 指经水运进出沿海主要港区范围，并经过装卸的货物数量，包括邮件及办理托运手续的行李、包裹以及补给运输船舶的燃、物料和淡水。货物吞吐量按货物流向分为进口、出口吞吐量，按货物交流性质分为外贸货物吞吐量和国内贸易货物吞吐量。货物吞吐量的货类构成及其流向，是衡量港口生产能力大小的重要指标。

邮电业务总量 指以价值量形式表现的邮电通信企业为社会提供各类邮电通信服务的总数量。邮电业务量按专业分类包括函件、包件、汇票、报刊发行、邮政快件、特快专递、邮政储蓄、集邮、公众电报、用户电报、传真、长途电话、出租电路、市话无线寻呼、移动电话、分组交换数据通信、出租代维等。计算方法为各类产品乘以相应的平均单价(不变价)之和，再加上出租电路和设备、代用户维护电话交换机和线路等的服务收入。它综合反映了一定时期邮电业务发展的总成果，是研究邮电业务量构成和发展趋势的重要指标。计算公式为：

邮电业务总量 =∑(各类邮电业务量×不变单价)+ 出租代维及其他业务收入

无线寻呼用户 无线寻呼是指电话用户通过无线寻呼中心，在规定范围内向携带小型寻呼机的用户发出声音、数字或文字显示信息。在寻呼台办理登记手续携带小型寻呼机的用户，称为无线寻呼用户。

移动电话用户 是指通过移动电话交换机进入移动电话网、占用移动电话号码的电话用户。用户数量以报告期末在移动电话营业部门实际办理登记手续进入移动电话网的户数进行计算，一部移动电话统计为一户。

电话用户 指接入国家公众固定电话网，并按固定电话业务进行经营管理的电话用户。1997 年以前，电话用户分为市内电话用户和农村电话用户。“市内电话用户”是指接入县城及县以上城市的电话网上的电话用户；“农村电话用户”是指接入县邮电局农话台及县以下农村电话交换点，以县城为中心(除市话用户外)联通县、乡(镇)、行政村、村民小组的用户。从 1997 年起，电话用户数分组调整为以用户所在区域划分为“城市电话用户”和“乡村电话用户”，与过去的按市内电话和农村电话划分方法不同。而电话用户总数、电话机总部数统计范围不变。

城市电话用户 指直辖市、省辖市、地级市、县级市的市区、市郊区及县城(包括县人民政府所在地的县城关区或行政建制相当于县人民政府所在地的镇)范围内接入局用交换机的电话用户数，包括分布在农村地区的独立工矿区、林区、驻军等接入局用交换机的电话用户数。

乡村电话用户 指县城关区以下的集镇和农村接入局用交换机的电话用户数。

Explanatory Note on Main Statistical Indicators

Length of Highways refers to the length of highways which are built in conformity with the grades specified by the highway engineering standard formulated by the Ministry of Communications, and have been formally checked and accepted by the departments of highways and put into use. The length of highways includes that of the suburb highways at large and medium-sized cities, highways passing through streets at small cities and towns, and also the length of bridges and ferries. It does not include the length of streets in big and medium-sized cities and highways built for the production purpose at factories, mines, forest areas and agricultural areas. If two or more highways go the same section of the way, the length of the section is only calculated for once and no duplication is allowed. The length of highways is an important indicator to show the development of the highway construction and to provide essential information to calculate the transport network density.

Length of Navigable Inland Waterways an indicator reflecting the size and development of inland water network, it refers to the length of the natural rivers, lakes, reservoirs, canals, and ditches open to navigation during a given period, which enables the transport by ships and rafts. It includes the channels open to navigation for over an accumulative 3 months in a year, yet this does not include the river courses which are only used to float odd logs and bamboo rafts.

Length of Civil Aviation Routes refers to the length of all routes for regular civil aviation flights. There are usually two ways to calculate the distance between airports connected by the route length: One is to put the length of all air routes together, called duplicated calculation of the length of the routes; the other is not to allow the duplication in calculation when two or more routes passing the same section of aviation routes. The latter is usually used, as it can precisely show the size of the civil aviation network and indicate the extent of civil aviation serving the national economy and the people.

Freight (Passenger) Traffic refers to the volume of freight (passenger) transported with various means. Freight transport is calculated in tons and passenger traffic is calculated in the number of persons. Despite the type of freight and travelling distance, the freight transport is calculated in the actual weight of the goods: and despite the travelling distance and ticket price, the passenger traffic is calculated by the principle that one person can be counted only once in one travel. The passenger who travel with a half price ticket or a child ticket is also calculated as one person. The freight (passenger) traffic provides a quantitative measure to show how the transport industry serves the national economy and people, and is also an important indicator for planning the transport industry and for studying the development scale and speed of the transport industry.

Freight Ton-kilometers (Passenger-kilometers) refer to the sum of the products of the volume of transported cargo (passengers) multiplying by the transport distance, usually using ton-kilometer and passenger-kilometer as units for measurement. Normally, the shortest distance between the departure station and the destination station (i.e., the payable distance) is the basis to calculate the freight ton-kilometers. This is an important indicator to show the total results of the transport industry, to prepare and examine the transport plan and to measure the efficiency, the labour productivity and the unit cost of transport.

The formula is as follows:

Freight Ton-kilometers (Passenger-kilometers) = $\sum$ {Freight (Passenger) Traffic x Distance of Transportation}

Measuring unit: ton-kilometer (person-kilometer)

Volume of Freight Handled in Major Coastal Ports refers to the volume of cargo passing in and out the harbor area of the major coastal ports and having been loaded and unloaded. The volume includes that of the postal matters, registered luggage and fuels, materials and fresh water as supplies of the ships. The volume of freight handled may be classified by direction of flow as freight for import and freight for export, or by nature of cargo as freight for domestic trade and freight for foreign trade. As an important indicator, the volume of freight handled by type of cargo and by main flow direction reflects the production capacity of ports.

Business Volume of Post and Telecommunications refers to the total amount of post and telecommunications services, expressed in value terms, provided by the post and telecommunications departments for the society. Post and telecommunication services can be classified as letters, parcels, remittance, issue of newspapers and magazines, fast mail service, express mail service, savings deposits, stamps for collection, public and individual telegraph service, facsimiles, long-distance telephone service, leasing of telephone lines, urban paging service, mobile telephone service, data transfer and transmission, etc. The accounting approach is to multiply the service products of all types with their average unit price (constant price) to get sum of business value, plus income from other services such as leasing of telephone lines and equipment, maintenance of telephone switchboards and lines on behalf of customers. This indicator reflects the overall results of post and telecommunications service during a given period, and is important to study the composition of business service and the development of post and telecommunications service.

The formula is as follows:

Business Volume of Post and Telecommunications= $\sum$ (Transaction of Post and Telecommunication Service × Constant Price) + Income from Leasing, Maintenance and other Services

Subscribers of Wireless Paging Services Wireless paging service refers the service by which telephone users send audio, digital or character signals to persons carrying small-size pagers within the designated areas through wireless paging centers. The page carriers who have registered in paging centers are counted as paging subscribers.

Mobile Telephone Subscribers refer to the persons who own mobile telephone numbers and are connected with the mobile telephone communication network through the mobile telephone switchboards. The number of subscribers is calculated by the subscribers who have completed registration at mobile communication business centers and entered into the mobile telephone network. One mobile telephone is taken as a subscriber.

Telephone Subscribers refer to subscribers that are connected to the public line telephone network provided with telephone services. Before 1997, telephone subscribers were classified as city subscribers and village subscribers. City subscribers referred to those connected to city telephone networks in county towns and cities, while village subscribers referred to those connected to village telephone stations at and below counties. Since 1997, the classification of telephone subscribers was modified on the basis of physical location of the subscribers as "urban telephone subscribers" and "rural telephone subscribers", which is different from the previous classification of categorizing "local telephones" and "rural telephones", while the definition of total subscribers and total number of telephones remain unchanged.

Urban Telephone Subscribers refer to subscribers telephone subscribers, located at municipalities, cities under the jurisdiction of province, cities at prefectural level, downtown and suburb of city at county level town and county towns (including country towns where county government located, and towns of county level according to the administrative organizational system), that are connected to the public line telephone network, including rural mineral area, forest area, military area.

Rural Telephone Subscribers refer to telephone subscribers, located at towns under county town and country, that are connected to the public line telephone network.

省领导陪同中宣部、中央文明办领导参观文昌市生态村

省领导到保亭县农村指导工作

海南省文明办

认真贯彻落实中央1号文件和党的十六届五中全会精神，扎实推进文明生态村建设。到2006年底，全省文明生态村总数已达到6523个，占全省自然村总数的28.1%。认真开展社会主义荣辱观宣传教育活动和第四个“公民道德宣传日”活动，思想道德教育取得新的进展。进一步加大文明高效机关、文明安全社区、文明诚信企业、文明规范行业等品牌的创建力度。深入开展科教、文体、法律、卫生“四进社区”活动，有2个节目在全国“四进社区”文艺展演活动荣获金奖，4个社区被评为“全国文化先进社区”，2位同志被评为全国“社区文化优秀辅导员”。积极开展提升公民文明旅游素质活动。在全省范围内开展文明单位、精神文明建设先进个人评选活动，推动全省各地精神文明创建。做好中宣部、中央文明办资助贫困大学生推选工作。利用中宣部、中央文明办资助资金和省财政配套资金，建成23个乡镇宣传文化站和108个文明生态村宣传文化室。继续办好“海南文明生态村网”，建立“天涯农浓情”网站。组织好中央文明办“万村书库工程”，建立了150个农村图书室，发动机关、企业为农民送书、送报，开展“百部科教电影农村行”活动，为农村放映电影12454场。开展“电视进万家工程”，给少数民族和革命老区贫困农民赠送了10000台电视机，活跃农民精神文化生活。

2006年5月20日，社会主义新农村与文明生态村建设研讨会在海口召开

2007年2月12日，全国“电视进万家工程”赠送仪式在海南省保亭黎族苗族自治县举行

共青团海南省委

2006年，海南各级团组织在“区域有特色，全团创一流”的工作方针指引下，开创了基础建设更趋扎实、品牌项目渐成体系、重大活动精彩纷呈、服务领域延伸拓展、整体工作稳健推进的良好工作局面，共青团事业呈现出持续快速健康发展的蓬勃态势。

一是青少年思想政治教育活动有声有色。组建了海南志愿者艺术团，在海口、三亚举办了2场宣传社会主义荣辱观专场演出；编印了《海南省青少年社会主义荣辱观读本》10万册，在全省百万青少年中进行传阅接力大行动；开展了海南省青少年树立社会主义荣辱观网上大讨论，在青少年中掀起学习实践社会主义荣辱观的热潮。二是服务经济社会发展有新作为。开展了“咱们村里的年轻人”青年增收成才行动和“大学生来到咱村里”行动，启动了“青春建功新农村”行动，培训青年农民，促进农村青年转移就业，投资30多万元建设的10个“共青号”文明生态村项目已经完工。三是引导青年促进社会和谐有新举措。全省18个市县团委组建文化、消防、法律、卫生等各行业志愿服务队广泛开展志愿服务活动，拉开了全省青年大规模参与构建和谐海南的序幕。志愿者立法进程在加快，注册志愿者队伍在壮大，各市县志愿者组织开展了“邻居节”、“邻里互助名片”、“爱心超市”、“爱心门铃”、“社区义工”等和谐社区创建活动，掀起了社区志愿服务新高潮。四是服务区域协调工作有新发展。深入实施了大学生志愿服务中西部计划，招募选派了360名大学毕业生奔赴我省陵水、屯昌等12个市县76个乡镇的教育、卫生、农技、青年中心、基层检察院等领域127个服务单位从事12年志愿服务工作，为我省少数民族和贫困地区经济社会发展注入了生机与活力；继续抓好联手扶贫工作，全年直接投入合计45万元，帮扶项目3个，帮助引进人才37名，举办各类培训班6期，共培训干部群众2000多人次。五是服务青少年工作迈上新台阶。实施了“希望工程圆梦行动”，共筹集社会各界捐款686万元，资助贫困大学新生1148人；成立了海南省青少年维权中心，开通了12355服务热线，为青少年合法权益维护提供切实有效的服务。

省领导出席省第四次少代会时听取少先队员汇报

团中央领导、省领导在团省委书记唐剑光的陪同下视察三亚市河西区儋州社区青年中心

参加2006年“五四”群英表彰大会的青年共同宣誓：知荣明耻，我们先行

海南省供销合作联社

在发展现代农业推进社会主义新农村建设中实现体制创新

近年来，在省委省政府和总社的正确领导与支持下，海南省供销合作联社领导班子不断加强执政能力建设，以深化改革卸掉包袱推动合作经济发展，为海南现代农业发展服务为重点，因地制宜开展各项工作，取得了较好成效。该社坚持为农服务宗旨，不断加大为农服务、助农增收工作力度，大力组织兴办农村专业合作社，积极做好农业生产资料的组织供应和废旧物资回收、农产品购销工作，不断培育新的经济增长点，由供销社组织兴办的30多个农村专业合作社实现销售收入5470万元，助农增收2610万元，入社农民6298户，人均增收达300-6000元不等。同时，于2006年全面展开社属企业改制工作，通过控股、参股、重组等方式努力实现社属企业产权多元化，盘活存量资产，重新整合资源，力争2007年年内全面完成改制重组工作，至2008年初步建立起以化肥农资、农药专营、果菜运销、烟花爆竹、再生资源为主营业务的现代企业构架。

随着供销社“四项改造”工作的不断深化，该社全体干部职工坚信，在省委省政府、有关部门及各界有识之士的关心支持下，海南供销合作经济事业一定能够在发展海南现代农业推进社会主义新农村建设工作中实现又好又快的发展。

省社主任赵子导陪同全国政协副主席、总社理事会主任白立忱视察2005年冬交会展馆

省社领导陪同总社赵显人副主任检察海交会布展情况

基层供销社兴办的农产品种植基地

省社主任赵子导陪同省领导视察冬交会农资展馆

海南省人力资源开发局（就业局）

林志向局长（右一）向国务院两纲检查组介绍情况

下岗失业人员参加我局举办的公益性岗位招聘会

海南省人力资源开发局（海南省就业局）是隶属海南省人事劳动保障厅的副厅级事业单位，从事人力资源开发和就业服务工作。主要承担人才交流、人事代理、档案托管、劳动力市场、跨省就业、失业保险、境外就业、大中专毕业生就业指导服务、留学回国人员就业和创业、各类培训、职称考试、技能鉴定等管理和服务职能。现该局不仅具备了省级人事、劳动保障部门大部分的执行职能，而且实现人才、劳动力两市场统一贯通，和兼顾了教育口的大中专毕业生就业指导服务、留学回国人员就业和创业等工作。这种全国独有的体制和资源优势，有效促进了市场机制在人力资源配置中的基础性作用的充分发挥并为全省的社会经济发展提供坚实的人力资源保障。

海南省人力资源开发局（海南省就业局）现内设：综合处、就业指导处、职业技能鉴定（职称考试）处和人才管理服务处等四处，并下设海南省境外就业职业介绍所、海南省劳务管理所和海南省人力资源培训中心等事业单位。

近年来，该局认真贯彻落实胡锦涛总书记再就业服务体系要实现“制度化、专业化、社会化”的重要指示精神，按照“优质服务求生存、开拓创新谋发展”的发展理念，不断探索和完善就业、再就业服务运行机制，大力推进人力资源开发工作。2006年，共举办各类人才劳动力交流大会52届、进场求职者达116,000人次；开发了劳动保障协管员、劳动就业信息采集员等717个公益性岗位；组织各类人事考试、职业资格考试，报考人数达5.7万人次；完成农村劳动力转移就业8.5万人次；组织1108名下岗失业人员参加了技能培训和创业培训；对1400名农村劳动力进行了引导培训及政策培训。局集体和个人多次荣获国家人事部、劳动和社会保障部及省级有关部门表彰和奖励。

开展农民工权益保障政策咨询活动

人才劳动力交流大会

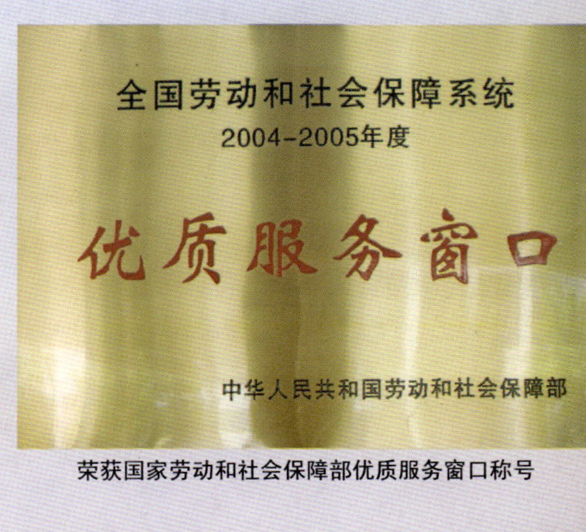

荣获国家劳动和社会保障部优质服务窗口称号

武警海南省警卫局

中国人民武装警察部队海南省警卫局（亦称海南省公安厅警卫局），系武警系列现役编制，正师级单位，隶属于海南省公安厅和公安部警卫局的双重领导，主要任务是担负来琼的党和国家领导人、重要外宾，以及在琼举办的重要会议、重大活动的安全警卫工作。1995年6月，由职业制人民警察转改为武警现役编制以来，按照公安部“抓管理、抓训练、抓基础”的要求，狠抓部队思想政治工作和正规化建设，部队建设取得了长足的进步。

2006年，出色完成了博鳌亚洲论坛年会、两岸农业合作论坛、海南省“两会”等一系列重大安全警卫任务，确保了贾庆林、曾庆红、李长春、罗干、李岚清等党和国家领导人及密克罗尼西亚总统乌鲁赛马尔、斯洛文尼亚总统德尔诺夫舍克、斯里兰卡总理维克勒马纳亚克、苏丹共和国总统巴希尔、塞舍尔共和国总统詹姆斯·米歇尔等重要外宾来琼期间的绝对安全，得到了各级领导的充分肯定和高度赞扬。在新的一年里，我局将在省委、省政府和省公安厅的领导下，在上级业务部门的指导和有关部门的密切配合下，全面落实公安部关于“抓基层、打基础、苦练基本功”的要求，大力加强队伍建设和业务建设，不断提高队伍的战斗力，圆满完成各项安全警卫任务，确保来琼的党和国家领导人、重要外宾以及在我省举办的重要会议、重大活动的绝对安全。

①警卫局党委书记、局长潘密

②部署博鳌亚洲论坛年会警卫工作

③开展忠诚卫士教育

④开展警卫战术红蓝对抗训练

⑤苦练“首发命中”基本功

⑥舍己救人，勇救驻地落水儿童

海南省公安厅出入境管理处

海南省公安厅出入境管理处负责对本省范围内的公安出入境管理业务的组织实施和监督指导，按照公安部有关出入境管理工作的部署，在中央事权的要求下，积极组织各项工作的贯彻落实，组织指挥重特大出入境违法犯罪案件的查处，承担制作签发出国境证件、因私出入境中介机构审批和管理以及特殊事项的出入境证件审批等实战任务。负责全省公安外事工作。

多年来，海南省公安厅出入境管理处，认真履行职责，充分发挥职能作用，在管理与服务方面与时俱进、开拓创新。在完成了大量的受理、审批、制证具体业务的同时，先后推出了一系列便民举措：2001 年在全国率先向农村市县推广凭身份证、户口簿按需申领护照便民措施；2003 年在全国首创在基层派出所中设置“外事民警”工作机制及境外人员临时住宿登记管理四级联网；2004 年在全国独创往来港澳探亲无审批便民措施；2005 年对离海口较远的境外人员较多的大型企业来省厅办理外国人签证证件、台胞签注证件，承诺 1 个工作日内完成（原为 5 个工作日）；2005 年将十二项往来港澳审批权下放海口、三亚、洋浦公安局，2006 年又将落地签证权下放口岸所在地公安局；2006 年 5 月 1 日起开始办理海口居民个人赴港澳地区旅游并推出海南省居民个人赴港澳地区旅游无审批机制。

据统计，自建省以来全省办理出入境证件逐年迅猛上升，1988 年全省的办证量仅有 11884 人次，至 2006 年全省办证量增至 143064 人次，增长了 12 倍。

公安部出入境管理局领导视察工作

与美国驻华使领馆官员会谈

海南省公安厅下放出入境证件审批权

2004年在全国独创往来港澳探亲无审批便民措施

2003年在全国率先向农村市县推广凭身份证、户口簿按需申领护照便民措施

海南省森林公安局在前进

岁末年初，2006年12月30日上午，海南省林业局党组书记、局长朱选成带领局党组领导班子成员，亲切慰问省森林公安局机关全体民警，深受民警们的热烈欢迎

海南省森林公安局始建于1982年，局机关内设有综合科、法制督察科、刑侦治安科、刑警大队、指挥中心和信访办，在岗民警31人。全省现有编制森林公安局25个、派出所共62个，民警719人，管护全省林地面积近3000万亩。

2006年我省森林公安机关在省林业局党组和国家林业局森林公安局及省公安厅的领导下，充分发挥森林公安哨兵、尖兵、排头兵的作用，在打击破坏森林资源违法犯罪活动、维护林区社会治安稳定、解决编制经费、狠抓三基建设及信访工作等方面，取得了较为显著的成绩，有效地保护了全省森林和野生动植物资源安全，维护了林区社会治安秩序稳定。二十五坡度以上毁林种植，三边毁林开垦、盗伐滥伐、非法占用林地等现象逐步得到遏制和取得良好效果。

从2005年12月至2006年11月份，全省各级森林公安机关共受理各类案件825起，查处706起；野生动物刑事案件立案8起，破案4起；森林行政案件受理588起，查处549起；野生动物行政案件受理34起，查处34起，收缴财物价值567.7943万元，缴获林木树木2216.66立方米，收缴野生动物13536只。各类罚款148.849万元，打击各类违法犯罪分子1258人；出动机动车3904辆次，出动警力11290人次。

今年来，我们坚决贯彻国家局和省林业局及公安厅的指示精神，紧紧围绕保护生态安全这个大局，牢牢掌握打击破坏森林资源斗争的主动权，始终坚持“三个第一”和“四个新字”上下功夫，“三个第一”即把打击与破案作为第一要务，把落实国办42号文件作为第一责任，把落实“三基”建设作为第一目标；“四个新字”即在应对新计划上要有新思路，在解决问题上要有新对策，在攻克难点、热点上要有新突破，在实际工作上要不断开创公安工作新局面。因此，全年工作注重围绕着“一督二打三整治四开展”的工作重点，取得了较好的成效。一督是挂牌督办案件，相继攻破大案要案；二打是领导重视，精心部署，全力开展好二次专项严打行动；三整治是集中力量进行三次整治活动，扩大打击破坏森林资源战果；四开展是积极开展四项活动，扎实有效地做好森林公安工作。

2006年7月30日上午，我局以命题的方式对局机关全体民警进行“八荣八耻”和社会主义法制理念的有关理论知识考试。图为省局黄守强局长正在监考中

先进单位代表坝王岭林区公安分局局长陈国雄在介绍先进经验

海南省森林公安局刑警大队的民警正在苦练基本功

海南省海防与口岸办公室

海南省海防与口岸办公室，由原省口岸管理办公室、省打击走私领导小组办公室与省海防委员会办公室合并成立，为省政府办公厅副厅级内设机构，内设海防管理处（打私管理处）、海港管理处和空港管理处等3个处级机构（琼编［2005］22号）。主要职责：负责制订本省海防管理与基础设施建设、口岸管理与建设和打击走私的法规规章、发展规划和实施细则并组织实施；负责本省海防委员会、打击走私领导小组办公室日常工作；负责本省海防、打击走私与口岸工作的综合管理和协调工作；负责组织验收和审查上报本省口岸的开放与关闭；组织协调开辟国际航线和临时航班（含包机），协助报批外国籍交通运输工具临时进出非开放口岸事宜；督促检查口岸查验单位按照各自的职责，对出入境人员、交通运输工具、货物和行李物品进行检查、检验、检疫、监管；指导监督本省各级口岸管理机构的工作。

2006年以来，我办认真贯彻省委、省政府关于“深化改革、扩大开放、加快发展”的指示精神，较好地完成了各项工作任务，有效地保证了海防基础设施建设、打击走私犯罪和口岸工作顺利进行。一、加强组织指导，海防安全和基础设施建设进展顺利；二、加强组织协调，打击走私工作成效明显；三、大力支持重点项目建设，洋浦港口岸扩大开放工作进展顺利；四、积极配合航权开放，空港航班服务保障力度明显增强；五、开展和谐口岸建设，全省口岸通关效率不断提高，环境明显改善。

海南省海防与口岸办主任：符元壮

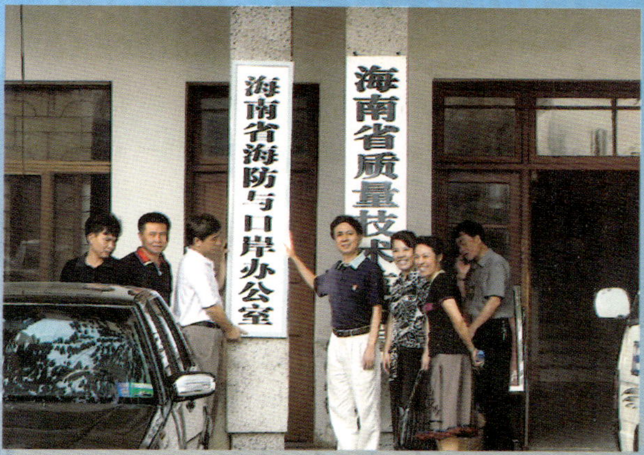

海南省海防与口岸办公室挂牌

为做好博鳌亚洲论坛年会通关服务保障，办领导与查验单位领导深入机场检查空港口岸通关环境

符元壮主任检查海防工作

海南省军供站站长：王平

军供站党总支在进行“党员先进性”教育

海南省军供站

海南省军供站是地方政府支援过往部队的组织机构。2006年，该站坚持以科学发展观为指导，以构筑和谐单位为己任，以争创一流服务为目标，整合队伍，强化素质教育，各项工作都有新的进展和突破。全站干部职工团结一致，思想同步，行动同拍，利益同享，工作勤奋，爱岗敬业，主人翁意识不断增强，福利待遇逐步提高。该站立足现有资源和条件，不断加强基础设施建设，努力改善站容站貌，军供保障能力不断提升，工作效率越来越高，服务质量越来越好。高标准、高质量、高速度完成了军供保障任务，得到了军地领导的充分肯定。分别被国家四部一局评为“军供站正规化建设先进单位”，被广州军区国防动员委员会评为“保障任务成绩突出先进单位”。

为了站容站貌和良好的工作环境，站领导积极带头，率领工作人员经常清扫环境卫生，整治卫生死角

站领导深入保障现场，认真检查供应质量，确保安全快捷

我站在军供保障任务中，视军人为亲人，热情服务，积极工作，受到有关部队称赞

民航海南安全监督管理办公室

2006年，我办工作以邓小平理论和“三个代表”重要思想为指导，认真贯彻落实党的十六届六中全会、民航总局和民航中南局工作会议精神，积极开展各项思想政治工作、安全监管工作，加强内部管理，较好地完成了各项任务，保证了辖区内飞行安全、空防安全和航空地面安全。截止11月底，共保障各类飞行8.47万架次，旅客吞吐量949.12万人次，货邮行吞吐量12.84万吨，安全飞行34.17万小时，加注燃油21.68万吨。主要工作情况：

一、大力抓好安全监管工作：按照民航总局、中南局安全工作会议的要求，我办在1月份就认真制定下发了《2006年航空安全监管工作实施方案》，有计划地开展各项监管工作，较好地实现了全年航空安全监管工作目标。在保证辖区各企事业单位完成正常航班运输任务的同时，还出色地完成了“博鳌亚洲论坛年会”、“两会”、“春运”、“五一”、“十一”黄金周、海南“三项重大活动”等专机、VIP重要运输飞行任务。截止11月20日，我办共下发《安全、运行监察结果通知单》97份，指出企业运行中存在的各类问题共279条，企业回执率100%，整改率100%，整改情况复查率100%。查处各类不安全事件11起，实施行政处罚1起。

二、大力加强航空运输市场监管。1、积极做好重大航空运输的保障和监管协调工作；2、落实日常监督检查制度；3、加强对辖区内的航班监管；4、加强对通用航空运营的监管；5、认真做好国防交通战备工作；6、积极做好消费者事务处理工作。

三、大力抓好培训工作。我办十分重视公务员的自身建设，加大法律法规知识和专业技术知识的培训力度，有效地提高了监察员的业务水平和工作能力。

四、认真做好思想政治工作。1、加强思想教育，不断提高政治素质；2、认真开好民主生活会，进一步增强团结；3、积极开展纪检监察工作，不断提高拒腐防变自觉性；4、大力加强工会工作，充分调动工作积极性。

海南省海洋监测预报中心

海南省海洋监测预报中心（以下简称“中心”）是海南省海洋与渔业厅下属的公益服务性事业单位，是国家海洋环境监测网、国家渔业环境监测网和海南省防灾减灾体系的成员单位，目前是全省唯一有权向社会公开发布海洋环境预报、海洋与渔业监测通报、公报和年报的单位，也是我省获得国家颁发的渔业污染事故调查资格证书的单位。“中心”拥有先进的分析测试仪器和设备，技术力量雄厚，拥有一批高、中级专业技术人才。

主任：王红心

“中心”的职责工作有：

1、负责组织实施海南省所辖海域海洋环境监测、渔业水域环境监测、海洋生物体监测、倾废监测、应急监测和巡航监测监视工作；

2、负责海南省管辖海域及附近海域的海洋环境日常预报和中长期预报，发布海洋环境灾害警报，进行海洋灾害统计和海洋信息资料管理。

除了核定的工作职责，“中心”提供对外专项服务工作，如海域使用论证、海洋环境预报专项服务、海洋监测专项服务等。目前为止，“中心”已经为多家涉海单位提供海洋环境监测和预报专项服务，并与其中的一些单位建立了长期的服务关系。

国家海洋局领导视察中心

技术人员在做实验

南海明灯——

中华人民共和国海南海事局
海口航标处

中华人民共和国海南海事局海口航标处，系海南海区沿海航标管理机构，主要负责海南海区除军用航标和渔业航标外沿海航标的总体规划，专用航标的建设审批和日常监管；以及海上干线公用航标和主要商港航标的维护管理、规划建设。近年来，海口航标处在交通部海事局和海南海事局的正确领导下，围绕“航运更安全、海洋更清洁”的主题，以建设“三个海事”（交通海事、阳光海事、数字海事）、实现“三个追求”（追求社会满意度最高、追求工作岗位业绩最优、追求职工归属感最强）为目标，大力实施科技兴标战略，不断加大新技术、新能源的引进和推广力度，强化航标行业监管职能，进一步调整完善辖区航标配布状况，有效地改善了辖区航标的助航效能，为海南航运业的健康发展提供了安全保障，截止2006年全处所辖航标达191座。2004年该处率先在全国沿海航标系统实现灯浮标能源100%太阳能化；在海口港秀英航道全部18座灯浮标上引进应用灯浮标同步闪和标牌号发光技术；对秀英、清澜、洋浦和八所等港口灯浮标的配布进行了调整，新增各类航标27座；成功引进并投入使用了国际最新助航设施AIS系统（船舶自动识别系统），进一步提高辖区助航设施科技含量；对辖区业主单位的133座专用航标进行有效地监管；2006年首度实现了海上灯浮标两年一度大保养，使辖区航标综合管理水平又向前迈进了一大步。

近年来，海口航标处始终坚持“两手抓，两手都要硬”的工作方针，一手抓业务发展，一手抓精神文明建设，两个文明建设取得了丰硕成果，1999年该处被授予全国海事系统文明达标单位称号，2003年被评为全国海事系统先进集体，2001-2004年连续四年被评为海南海事局先进单位。

雄关漫道臻如铁，而今迈步从头跃。面对昔日骄人成绩，海口航标处领导班子清醒地认识到，发展的道路尤如逆水行舟不进则退；在今后的工作中，全处干部职工要以科学发展观统领全局，协调航标各项工作发展，开拓创新、团结奋斗，为实现海南航标又好又快发展做出新的贡献。

处长：刘德珍

党总支书记：雷新国

团结奋进、开拓创新的领导班子

海上作业

张光亮总队长

省政府领导和国家海洋局领导出席省海监总队揭牌仪式

省海洋与渔业厅厅长李应济出席中国渔政46013船首航仪式

海南省 渔业监察总队

海南省渔业监察总队（中国海监海南省总队）成立于1997年1月28日，为依照公务员制度管理的正处级事业单位，隶属海南省海洋与渔业厅，共有人员78人，执法船只2艘，担负着海洋渔业行政执法，维权护渔巡航和渔业无线电通信管理等重要职责。

成立十年来，海南省渔业监察总队（中国海监海南省总队）坚持以邓小平理论，“三个代表”重要思想为指导，依法行政，执法为民，为维护我省海洋、渔业生产秩序，促进海洋经济发展做出较大贡献。

历年来，被授以多项荣誉称号：

2003年　被农业部评为“维权护渔先锋”

2004-2005　被农业部渔政指挥中心评为专属经济区渔政巡航先进单位

2004-2006　被省机关工委评为文明单位

2000-2006　被省直机关工委连续评为先进党支部

2006年春节期间慰问儋州特困渔民

张光亮总队长主持召开总队长办公会议

在三亚检查贩卖国家保护水生野生动物制品

海南省国土环境资源监察总队

2006年，在厅党组的领导下，总队加强对全省现场执法工作的指导和监督，按照省厅的部署，抓住工作重点，扎扎实实开展执法工作，取得了较好的成绩。全年，总队共出动769人次，现场检查企业298家次，采矿点183个次；受理、处理信访案件121宗，直接调查处理57宗，转交市县办理64宗，处理率100%；立案处理违法案件14宗，其中土地6宗，环保8宗，已结案8宗，行政处罚罚没款46.5646万元，其中土地罚没9.9246万元，环保罚没36.64万元。

2006年，总队被国家人事部、环保总局评为“全国环境保护系统先进单位”，被环保总局评为“全国环境政策法制工作先进集体”和“全国排污费征收工作二等奖”、“全国排污申报核定工作二等奖”，被省直机关工委评为“2004-2006年度文明单位”。

一、加强队伍政治、业务学习和能力建设，不断强化队伍服务意识和办案意识，执法人员综合素质有了较大的提高，执法硬件设备有了明显改善，全省队伍面貌焕然一新。

二、全面开展土地执法调研，掌握土地执法现状，加强土地动态巡查，严查土地违法行为，较好地打开了总队土地执法工作新局面，有力地配合了全省土地调控工作。

三、加大环保宣传力度，提高环境监控能力，组织环保专项行动，严查环境生态违法案件，做好排污申报工作，全省环境违法行为得到有效遏制，环境执法成效继续提高。

四、紧密配合规范矿产资源开发秩序专项行动，明查暗访，加强矿产资源监察，组织实施砂石粘土矿专项整治工作，进一步强化了执法队伍矿产资源监察职能，为维护全省矿业管理秩序做出了应有贡献。

五、严格执行《信访条例》各项制度，认真、及时做好来信来访受理、处理工作，解决了一大批老大难问题，为构建和谐社会做出了一定贡献，树立了“文明接访、执法为民”的良好形象。

六、按时、足额、规范征收排污费和矿产资源补偿费，强化收费执法监督，严查欠缴违法企业，较好地完成了征收任务。

总队领导陪同厅领导现场检查排污企业

吴开成总队长现场检查生态破坏现场

吴开成总队长现场检查违法采矿企业

周斌副总队长现场了解环境监测数据材料

总队全体人员

海南省建设项目规划设计研究院

党组书记、院长：张世有

海南省建设项目规划设计研究院（CPPD）是1992年经海南省委、省政府批准成立归省发展与改革厅领导的副厅级事业单位。主要从事工程咨询、城市规划设计、建筑工程设计、市政公用工程设计、公路工程设计、农业工程设计、建设项目环境影响评价、房地产与土地评估、造价咨询、招投标代理、工程监理、项目管理（代建）等业务。

经过十多年的发展，全院已获得工程咨询综合甲级、建筑行业建筑工程甲级、城市规划乙级等十三项执业资质。院下设十三个处室并附设九个子公司，现在职人员160人，拥有100多名专业理论水平高、实践经验丰富的高、中级专业技术人员和管理人员，类别齐全、专业结构合理，并建有由多学科、各专业的资深专家、教授、学者和企业家等近二百人组成的专家库，为提供高质量的咨询、工程设计等服务奠定了强有力的智力支持。办公设备先进，实现电脑化和网络化办公。是海南省唯一能提供建设项目一条龙服务、实力最雄厚的综合性规划设计研究院。

建院十余年来，业务成果累累。完成各类项目咨询、规划、设计、造价咨询、招投标代理、监理等1800项，投资总额2000多亿元，为政府部门和企业的投资决策提供科学依据，为海南省经济建设做出了积极的贡献。2003年3月荣获“海南省用户满意企业”称号，2001-2004年连续三年荣获“先进党组织”称号，2005年3月获海南省人才建设成果显著单位称号。

自来水厂设计项目

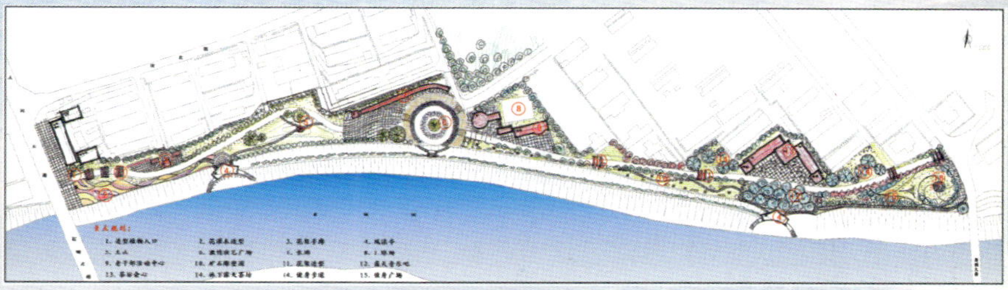

石碌河总平面规划图

吉欣花园设计项目

三星项目

海南省图书馆工程监理、造价咨询项目

地址：中国海南省海口市海府一横路七号美舍大厦9楼
邮编：570203
电话：0898-65361660（办公室） 0898-65365615（发展经营处）
传真：0898-65327510
网址：http://www.hainanbiz.com
E-mail:cppd@hainanbiz.com

院长：岳平

团结务实的领导班子

海南省环境科学研究院

海南省环境科学研究院于2002年12月在原海南省环境科学研究所和原海南省环境监测中心站的基础上合并组建，同时挂海南省环境监测中心站牌子。是海南省国土环境资源厅直属的公益性科学技术事业单位，为国家一级环境监测站，也是我省唯一的省级环境科学专业研究机构。主要负责全省环境监测，基础性、战略性、公益性环境科学研究等工作。拥有一支综合素质高、经验丰富的环境科研及监测队伍。现有在岗职工102人，其中各类专业技术人员83人，有博士研究生1名、硕士研究生14名；中级职称以上技术人员37人，高级职称以上17人。拥有包括原子吸收、气相色谱、气质联用仪、离子色谱、液相色谱、等离子发射光谱仪等价值约1200万元的各类环境科研、监测设备200多台套。可开展包括水质、空气、土壤、生物等环境要素中876项次的监测。拥有环境影响评价甲级资质、省级计量认证合格证、环境监理资质、丙级地质灾害评估资质等，具备开展环境监测、环境污染治理技术研究、环境及生态规划、环境及生态专项调查、环境影响评价、环境监理、绿色食品认证监测、清洁生产审核等能力。

在充分发挥海南省环境监测的技术中心、信息中心、网络中心、培训中心职能，组织和指导全省各级环境监测站开展全省环境质量监测、生态监测、污染源监测、建设项目“三同时”验收监测和环保设施竣工验收，定期发布全省环境质量、生态环境、污染源状况的同时，积极推进环境科研工作，并取得丰硕成果。近年来先后完成国家科技部软科学项目海南省可持续发展水资源战略研究，省重点科技项目高位池养殖废水治理技术研究、海南生态环境变迁研究，省科技项目海南岛资源与环境可持续性研究、海南水生态研究、海南省水利水电工程施工期环境监理研究，海南省生态环境现状调查、海南省地表水

技术人员在进行色谱实验分析

技术人员在进行原子吸收光谱实验分析

2006年院领导在指挥环境应急演练

水质监测采样

环境容量核定、海南省高位池生态环境影响调查及对策研究、海南省绿色国民经济核算和环境污染经济损失调查、海南岛水环境功能区划、海南省环境保护“十一五”规划、海南省水污染防治规划等国家级及省级科研课题、环境及生态规划、环境影响评价和专项调查项目共计200余项。获得省科技进步三等奖2项，国家环境保护总局质量报告书评比二、三等奖各1项，合作项目获省科技进步一等奖1项，获国家专利2项，在各类学术期刊发表科技论文60余篇。

近年来，省环境科学研究院先后和加拿大、英国、瑞典、挪威、日本、新加坡、泰国等开展了广泛的环境保护国际合作工作，先后有20多位技术人员赴国外考察、进修、学习和交流，进一步提高了环科院的整体科研水平。先后开展了海南中部少数民族地区饮用水源水质调查、铜鼓岭自然保护管理对策研究、海南省松涛水库流域水资源管理研究、铜鼓岭自然保护区生态保护利用研究、白沙城镇垃圾堆肥、松涛库区面源污染机理研究等项目。依托国际合作工作的开展，建立起了院遥感与地理信息系统实验室。

建设项目环境影响评价资格证书

单位名称：海南省环境科学研究院

评价机构：环境影响评价中心

证书等级：甲

证书编号：国环评证 甲字第 3001 号

有效期：2005年6月30日至2006年12月31日

中华人民共和国

计量认证合格证书

海南省环境监测中心站

国际合作项目研讨

科技论文在国家及省级期刊发表

海南有色长勘勘察院

三亚凤凰机场工程勘察（荣获海南省省优三等奖）

院长：李社青

海南有色长勘勘察院（原中国有色金属工业长沙勘察设计研究院海南分院）成立于1988年，是经建设部注册具有独立法人资格的甲级勘察院。

1992年被海南省人民政府授予“先进驻琼企业”荣誉称号，1993-1998年被海南省建设厅授予“免检单位”称号（后来未开展此项活动）；2000年海南省勘察协会换届，被省建设厅推选为海南省勘察协会副理事长单位，2001年李社青同志被海南省建设厅评为“海南省优秀勘察设计院院长”。十多年来，本院以长勘人的品德、长勘人的智慧、长勘人的勤劳与海南同呼吸共命运，洒下了无数辛勤的汗水，创下了有目共睹的业绩，为海南的开发、建设立下了汗马功劳。

院　长：李社青　总工：秦跃
地　址：海口市海秀大道顺发新村26栋
电　话：（0898）68916490　68912493
传　真：（0898）68925107
三亚经理部：（0898）88272726　88236953
三亚经理部经理：李海林　总工：谭寿林

海南省东方天然气化肥厂工程勘察（荣获海南省省优一等奖）

海南省“置地花园”工程勘测（荣获海南省省优三等奖）

海南省国土环境资源信息中心

海南省国土环境资源信息中心成立于一九九七年，是海南省国土环境资源厅直属正处级事业单位。承担土地、地质矿产和环境保护管理信息化建设、运行及维护。对外进行各种软件开发及信息系统集成，生产各种电子地图等空间数据。内设部门有办公室（财务部）、规划设计部、系统开发部、数据工程部、网络(客户服务)部。

设计开发了各种基于WEB技术、数据库技术和GIS技术的管理信息系统,包括“海南省12369环保信息系统”、“海南省农村土地产权登记数字化建库系统”、“海南省水环境功能区划管理信息系统”、“海南省国土环境资源厅办公自动化系统”、“海南省地质资料目录数据查询系统”、“政务服务网站信息发布管理系统”、“海南省农用地分等系统”、“海南省土地适宜性评价系统”、“海南省耕地占补平衡系统”、“建设项目数据管理地理信息系统”。

生产及建立各种属性数据库、空间数据库，结合信息中心开发的相关系统，可实现查询、统计、报表、打印、拓朴分析、影像图配准、地图编辑、代码库维护、用户权限维护等功能。包括“海南省级矿产资源规划空间数据库”、“海南省矿产资源储量空间数据库”、“海南省土壤分布空间数据库”、“海南省水文地质空间数据库”、“海南省地质地貌空间数据库”、“海南省环境质量空间数据库”、“海南省建设项目空间数据库”、“海南省农村土地产权空间数据库”、“海南省水环境功能区划空间数据库”等，并建立了大量的各种属性数据库。

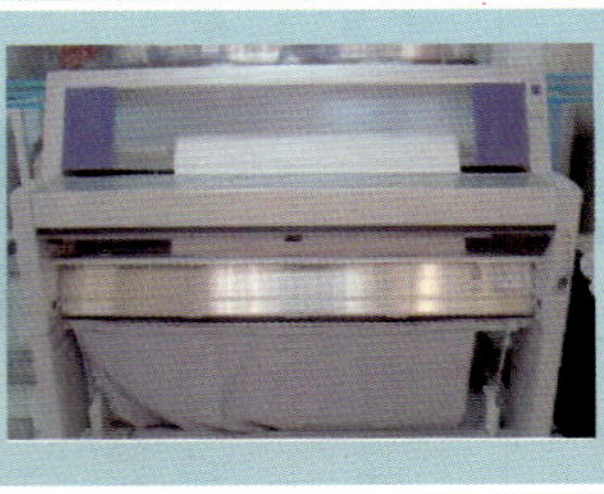

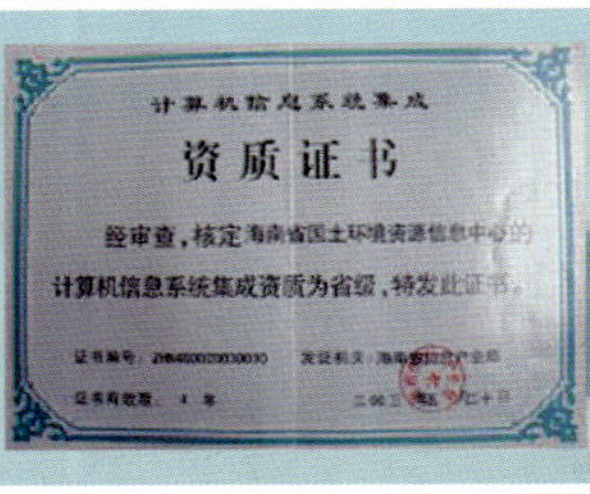

计算机信息系统集成

资质证书

经审查，核定海南省国土环境资源信息中心的计算机信息系统集成资质为省级，特发此证书。

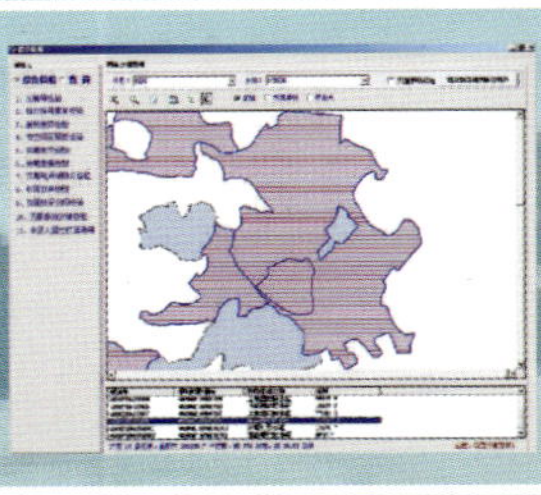

海南省土地开发整理中心

海南省土地开发整理中心从2003年正式开始成立运转，立足于建立一个服务国土环境资源基础业务的技术平台，逐步形成了以土地开发整理、土地调查评价、土地规划、土地测绘、土地数据库建设和重大项目征地服务等为主的业务体系，设立了土地整理部、土地勘测部、土地规划部、综合财务部、测绘队等内部机构。

中心围绕我省国土资源管理的各项重点工作开展基础业务和技术服务指导工作，近年来扎扎实实完成了全省后备资源调查、土地基础图件与现状数据更新、土地利用数据库建设、土地利用“十一五”规划、省级土地利用规划实施评价和修编前期工作、市县土地规划修编前期工作、全年征地统一年产值测算、地籍图编印、农村宅基地确权发证试点等一批技术性、基础性、公益性项目，并高效实施了国家、省和市县三级30多个土地开发整理项目的选址、踏勘、规划设计、预算编制和实施管理等工作，为我省国土资源事业的发展作出了积极贡献，在完成各类项目的同时，省整理中心也获得了全面的较快的发展：由成立之初的几张办公桌，到现在拥有600多平方米办公用房产权、3部工作用车、40多台计算机以及绘图仪、扫描仪、激光打印机、复印机、数码相机、投影仪、全站仪、电子经纬仪、GPS测绘仪等现代化办公设备和专业仪器；由成立之初的5人发展到现在40多人的专业队伍；并逐步建立了以集体会议制度、项目负责人制度、项目过程管理制度、项目考核与奖惩制度、质量控制制度、合同聘用与人才激励制度等一系列制度进行规范化管理的现代管理模式。

展望未来，中心将继续推动土地事业的健康发展，积极服务于我省国土资源管理工作，不断加强队伍建设和提高项目管理水平，扩大业务范围、开拓新的市场领域，打造我省整理中心的技术和质量品牌。

王业侨主任

群众赠送锦旗

万宁市礼纪镇土地整理项目后期效果图

部分文字成果

部分图件成果

中国通信服务
CHINA COMSERVICE

海南省通信产业

公司总经理包铁军

通信运营商的服务商

海南省通信产业服务有限公司是中国电信旗下第二家上市公司——中国通信服务股份有限公司的全资子公司，由海南省电信实业集团有限公司重组设立。公司2006年9月成立，注册资本7883万元，专业子公司七家。

公司定位为通信运营商的服务商，致力于为通信运营商、设备制造商、专用通信网及社会公众客户提供通信网络建设、外包服务、内容应用及其他等三大板块的一站式服务。公司产品及服务覆盖电信产业链各环节，是通信运营商不可或缺的合作伙伴。

公司拥有省内领先的资质、良好的客户合作关系、广泛的本地化服务网络、独具特色的一体化服务模式和具有丰富经验的服务团队。作为海南省内唯一一家为通信运营商提供综合支撑服务的企业，公司将以上市为新起点，牢牢把握3G业务契机，加快业务发展，持续为客户创造服务，为股东创造价值，成为运营商转型的最佳战略合作伙伴和服务于社会信息化的重要力量。

愿继续与社会各界精诚合作，实现共赢！

地址：海南省海口市海府路28号　邮编：570203
电话：（0898）65381608
传真：（0898）68381607
E-mail:hntic@hntic.com

海府路营业厅

一流的工程施工及维护

专业的技术服务

优秀的服务团队

服务有限公司

七家专业子公司
为客户提供一站式服务

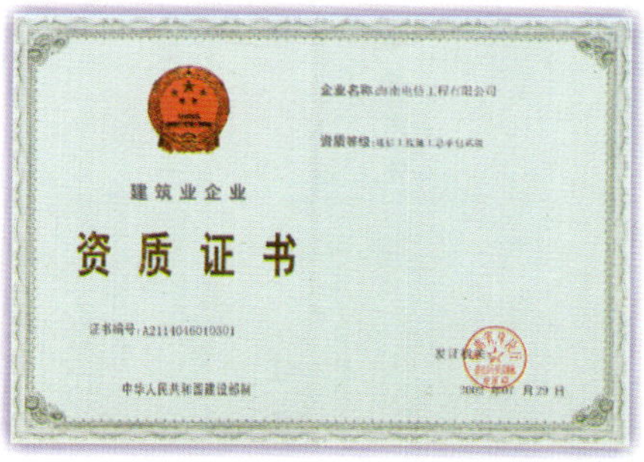

海南电信工程有限公司

省内唯一的通信工程施工总承包二级资质，提供通信工程建设、电信设备、基站的维护及维修等服务。

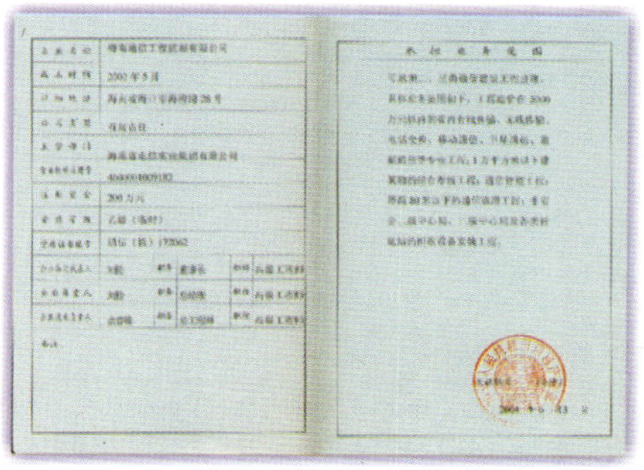

海南电信规划设计院有限公司

海南省通信及信息化咨询、设计行业的骨干企业，提供专业通信及信息化咨询、勘察、设计等服务。

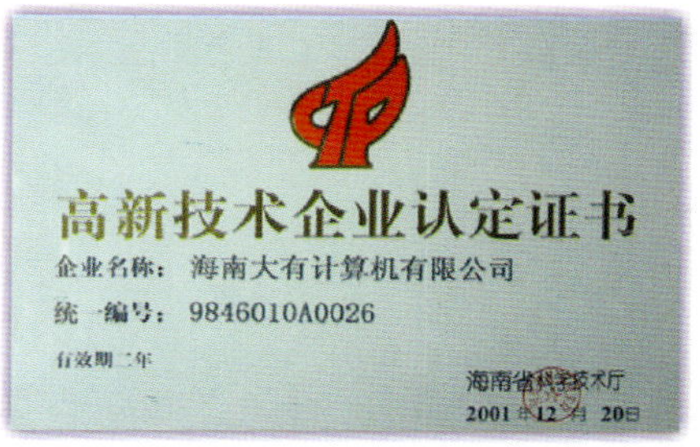

海南通信工程监理有限公司

省内唯一具有通信建设监理资质的企业，提供通信、土建工程监理及咨询、项目管理等服务。

海南大有计算机有限公司

海南省政府认定的第一批高新技术企业，提供软件开发、系统集成、技术服务、增值业务等服务。

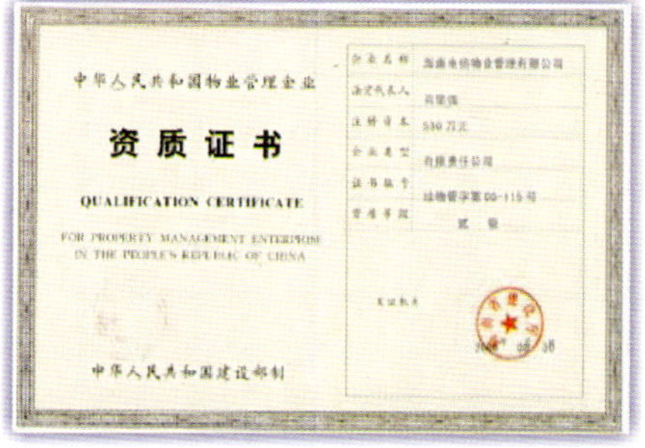

海南电信信息网络有限公司

增值业务内容提供商，提供企业信息门户、高附加值解决方案和总体顾问咨询、广告代理服务。

海南大有电信营销有限公司

海南通信运营商代营业务服务商，提供电信业务外包、终端产品销售及维修、物资采购等服务。

海南电信物业管理有限公司

国家物业管理企业二级资质，提供物业管理、水电设备、空调安装及维修、运营商资源管理等服务。

中国农业发展银行海南省分行

2006年，我行认真贯彻落实全国分行行长会议精神，围绕建设社会主义新农村这条主线，积极拓展业务，强化支农功能，狠抓经营管理，注重风险防范，深化内部改革，加强队伍建设，全行业务经营呈现出速度快、效益好、运行平稳、发展后劲较足等特点。在信贷规模扩大、贷款利率上调、清理财务挂帐、狠抓增收节支等措施的共同推动下，提前两年摘掉了亏损帽子，一举实现扭亏为盈。全面完成了总行下达的各项任务与考核指标：不良贷款比年初下降5876万元；不良贷款比例6.45%，比年初下降3.74个百分点；资产利润率0.19%，比上年提高212.34%；收入成本率44.68%，比上年下降25.6个百分点；人均利润1.53万元，比上年增加12.47万元；人均存款159.1万元，比上年增加16.8万元；人均中间业务收入1455元，比上年增加622元。

（一）实施“一体两翼”的业务经营思路，信贷支农开创了新局面。

--信贷投放较快增长，贷款规模稳步提高；
--商业性贷款占比明显提高，贷款结构进一步优化；
--贷款累放累收同步增加，信贷资金周转速度明显加快；
--信贷支农职能明显增强。我行信贷业务的迅猛增长，有力地支持了海南社会主义新农村建设。

（二）坚持制度与管理并重，信贷风险控制取得了新成效。

--抓制度和机制建设。顺利完成了县级支行贷款审批权限上收工作；
--抓信贷风险防范的基础管理。认真组织申请贷款企业的信用等级评定；
--抓好各项审计；
--成立了反洗钱工作领导小组和办事机构，明确岗位职责，建立了反洗钱内部控制制度。

中国农业发展银行海南省分行行长栗惠民（前排中）在海南翔泰渔业有限公司调研

（三）强化成本核算和效率观念，资产质量、经营效益、经营手段等有了新的提高。

--信贷资金营运效益不断提高；
--各项存款继续保持“双增”态势；
--财政补贴资金基本实现全额到位；
--中间业务起步较晚但发展势头良好；
--经营的信息化手段明显改善。

（四）深化班子建设和反腐倡廉，党的建设呈现出新气象。

--着力推进保持共产党员先进性长效机制建设；
--加强基层行后备干部管理；
--加强反腐倡廉制度建设；
--认真开展治理商业贿赂专项工作；
--认真落实党风廉政建设责任制。

海南农发行部分市县行行长信贷管理座谈会

民安保险（中国）有限公司
海南分公司

民安保险（中国）有限公司隶属于中国保险（控股）有限公司暨香港中国保险（集团）有限公司。公司于2004年5月10日经中国保险监督管理委员会批准，在原香港民安保险有限公司深圳分公司的基础上改建成为具有独立法人资格的全国性保险公司，是中国第一家获准由分公司改建为独资子公司的保险公司。

民安保险（中国）有限公司之母公司香港民安保险有限公司于1949年在香港注册成立。在香港众多保险公司中，民安保险是实力较强，信誉卓著，作风稳健，深具影响力的保险公司之一。

公司前台

从1988年进入海南的香港民安保险海口分公司，到2006年的民安保险（中国）海南分公司，我们凭借着总公司雄厚的实力及母公司先进的管理经验，坚持重管理、重服务、重信誉、重效益的宗旨，发扬“追求卓越、锐意创新”的企业精神，坚持“民安保险、诚信永远”的经营理念，以坚守法规，恪守诚信为己任，在海南逐渐赢得了市场的认可，与中石化集团、海航公司、中酒集团、第一投资、海南电网公司、中国工商银行、中国银行等都建立了长期稳定的业务关系，并且是海南省内首批可以经营交强险的保险公司之一。

民安保险（中国）海南分公司正迎来新的发展契机，我们将在秉承香港民安优质服务和高效管理的同时，继续以开拓进取来获得创新，以全方位的服务来赢得市场，在挑战中寻求更大发展，取得更大的成就。

创新理念　追求卓越

天安保险股份有限公司

分公司党委书记、总经理：赖运南

赖运南总经理向省消防总队防火部长周天赠书

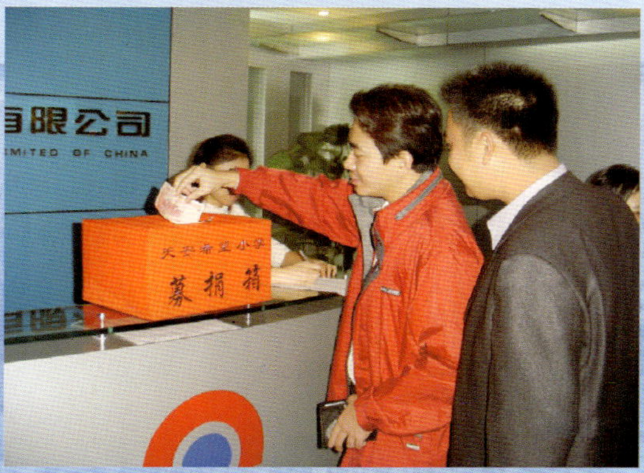

向社会献爱心

3．15消费日向社会承诺

天安保险股份有限公司是中国首家由企业出资组建的股份制商业保险公司，成立于1994年10月，总部设在上海。现注册资金为人民币10亿元。主要经营中国保险监督管理委员会核准的人民币、外币的各种财产保险、责任保险、信用保险、水险、意外伤害保险、健康保险、金融服务保险等业务，办理各种再保险、法定保险和资金运用保险等业务。2005年，公司实现保费收入64亿元，并05、06年连续光荣入榜中国企业500强和荣获了"十大行业百佳雇主企业奖"、"全国企业文化建设工作先进单位"、"中国企业诚信经营示范单位"、"2005年度最受信赖的财险公司"、"06年度上海现代服务业百强企业"等光荣称号。

公司现拥有800余家营业网点，机构遍布全国各地，具有完善和快捷的服务网络。公司还先后通过了ISO9002、ISO9001：2000国际质量体系认证和ISO14001环境管理体系认证。 公司不断推出符合市场需求的创新险种，形成了具有天安特色的，有较强市场竞争力的产品体系，并承保了一大批在国内外颇具影响力的重大项目，如上海黄浦江上四座著名大桥、上海地铁、南京长江二桥、江阴长江大桥、天津地铁等重大工程建设项目，参与共保了亚太卫星、中卫1号等航天保险。公司以"客户至上、服务社会、信誉为本、追求卓越"为宗旨，以诚取信，建立起一整套优质、高效的客服体系，赢得了客户的信赖和好评。天安保险股份有限公司始终以"化险为夷，补天爱人"作为自己的神圣使命，坚持以"更及时、更全面、更专业、更道德的服务，建设中国保险第一品牌"的经营理念，为天安客户提供专业的全程服务和周全完善的风险保障。

海南省分公司于2003年10月正式开业。根据海南保险行业协会提供数据显示，截至2005年12月天安保险股份有限公司海南省分公司实现保费收入4840.12万元， 市场份额为8.40%，位居海南省五家财产保险公司第三名，仅次于人保、太保，超过平安和香港民安，保费增幅排名第一。天安保险股份有限公司海南省分公司的稳健快速发展，为海南经济的发展起到了积极的作用，并为海南保险业所高度关注。

海南省分公司地址：海口市国贸路45号银通国际中心22层

电话：68555688　　传真：68559688

三亚公司地址：三亚市新风路创业大厦B座802室

电话：88366616　　传真：88366466

儋州公司地址：儋州市中兴大道嘉鑫大厦（华阳宾馆对面）二楼

电话：23334000　　传真：23334777

琼海公司地址：琼海市金海路172号隆达大厦二楼

电话：62922177　　传真：62922177

文昌机构地址：文清路

电话：63281206

五指山机构：琼南车管所内

电话：86639320

东方市营业机构地址：东方市东海路12号

电话：25513988

公司网址：

http://www.tianan-insurance.com

海口市委

组织部

部机关全体党员在母瑞山革命根据地纪念园接受革命传统教育

市委组织部对帮扶点龙华区市井村委会昌盛村的特困生结对帮扶

"三·八"节前夕，部机关全体女党员到部帮扶点慰问老党员

部机关党员在保持共产党员先进性教育活动中积极参加集中学习，认真做好学习笔记

部机关全体党员积极参加保持共产党员先进性教育义务劳动

部机关干部在军事日到部队接受军事训练，认真听取部队领导讲解有关军事知识

海口市中级人民法院

近几年，该院以邓小平理论和“三个代表”重要思想为指导，全面贯彻落实科学发展观，紧紧围绕依法治国方略，把握人民法院工作的时代特点，坚持“公正司法，一心为民”指导方针，坚持社会主义法治理念，坚持“公正与效率”工作主题，振奋精神，扎实工作，忠实履行法律赋予的神圣职责，充分发挥审判机关的职能作用，为海口市的经济社会全面发展和和谐社会建设作出了应有的贡献。该院在审判工作、队伍建设、司法改革、基层基础建设等各方面都取得了长足的发展。四年来，该院共受理各类诉讼案件18964件，审结18868件，每年结案率均达到98%以上；执行案件共收案1468件，结案1360件，执结涉案标的额35.4亿元。受案数、结案数、结案率均创历史新高。

院长屈建民在接访

该院牢记神圣职责，充分发挥法院审判职能，全力服务大局，维护稳定，构建和谐，促进发展。开展了打击“两抢一盗”、涉毒犯罪、打黑除恶等专项斗争；积极配合省、市的反腐倡廉工作，依法审理了一批职务犯罪大案要案。以解决纠纷、化解矛盾、促进和谐为工作目标，始终坚持 “能调则调，当判则判，判调结合，案结事了”的原则，平等保护当事人的合法权益，成功解决了大量民事纠纷。坚持维持与监督并举、支持与制约并重的原则，通过对具体行政行为的司法审查，维护公民、法人和其他组织的合法权益，支持和促进行政机关依法行政。大力加强执行工作，连续四年实现了当年执行结案高于执行收案，执行工作步入良性循环。高度重视申诉信访工作，做到了申诉案件有案必理，热情接待。形成了“一把手”亲自抓，分管院长直接抓，庭室领导具体抓，人人办信访的“大信访工作格局”，四年来没有发生因案件审理或信访处理不当而引发群体性上访事件，得到了省委、市委、人大和省高院的高度评价。

该院大力加强法官队伍建设，队伍的凝聚力、向心力得到增强了，司法能力和司法水平不断提高，法院正气得到树立和弘扬，法院面貌得到较大的改观。四年间涌现出一批先进集体和先进个人，陈援朝被海口市委授予 “模范共产党员”称号、被省委授予 “优秀共产党员”称号、被最高法院授予 “全国模范法官”称号，书记官处荣获“全国巾帼文明示范岗”称号、行政庭荣获“全国法院行政审判工作先进集体”、研究室荣获“全国法院调研工作先进集体”、法警支队荣获“全国法院司法警察先进集体”、甘文萍同志荣获“全国三八红旗手”荣誉称号等，共有26个集体、48个个人获得市级以上奖励。

公开宣判

法官依法耐心调处纷争

农民工数着法院为其执行回来的被拖欠的工钱喜笑颜开

海口市 秀英区

秀英区位于海口市西部，东起丘海大道，西与澄迈县接壤，南同定安县相连，北临琼州海峡。下辖长流、海秀、西秀、石山、永兴、东山6个镇和海秀、秀英2个街道办事处。面积511.5平方公里，常住人口31.6万人。境内资源丰富、交通便利。有绵延20公里的美丽的西海岸带状公园；有全省最大的港口海口港；是海口至三亚的环岛西线、中线公路的起点；粤海铁路海口火车客运站和货运南站在辖区内建成；有高新技术工业园和农副产品园区。假日海滩、海南热带野生动植物园、火山口主题公园等是市民度假休闲的好去处。名胜古迹有丘浚墓等。

“十五”时期，秀英区农业基础地位进一步巩固，新型工业化进程步伐加快，第三产业健康发展。2006年，全区生产总值48.8亿元，比2002年增长11.7%；人均生产总值15321元，比2002年均增长8.6%。财政收入4.48亿元，比2002年均增长22.8%。社会固定资产投资累计62.4亿元。加快发展生态农业和旅游观光农业，大力推行科技兴农，加快农村道路、饮水、沼气、“农网”改造。2006年，全区农业总产值达10亿元，比2002年均增长7.8%。骨干大企业、优势产业的支撑作用明显，形成了以制药化纤纺织和食品饮料为主的三大支柱产业结构。2006年，全区工业总产值达70亿元，比2002年均增长18.3%。房地产、运动休闲旅游度假产业健康发展，长信花园、黄金海岸、阳光西海岸等一批中高档商住小区陆续建成投入使用，美视、西海岸等高尔夫球场建成营业并顺利举办各种赛事，喜来登、凯莱等一批五星级国际著名大酒店顺利开业，石山火山群世界地质公园、海南热带野生动植物园、热带森林博览园等一大批景区、景点相继建成。新建了第一摩尔铜锣湾广场、义乌小商品南洋批发城、南海大道汽车交易一条街、爱华汽车广场、海南建材城、海口钢材交易市场等大型专业交易市场，现代综合服务业和物流业集聚效应初步显现。

秀英区今后五年的奋斗目标是：大力实施“优势产业战略、城市化发展战略、科教兴区战略、可持续发展战略”，实现由农业经济向工业经济，农村社会向城市社会的历史性转变。政府工作的目标是：初步建成以特色农业为基础，以港口为依托，以新型工业、商贸物流业、山海特色休闲度假旅游业为支柱产业，实现可持续发展的海口新型工业集聚区、临港经济中心区、行政中心城区和环北部湾热带滨海休闲度假旅游胜地。

火山口世界地质公园

西海岸带状公园

农业园区

海口药谷

粤海铁路海口火车站

海口港

西秀海湾

热带水果竞优赛

现代化养鸡场

琼台福地——

海口市琼山区

琼山区位于海口市中南部，东接美兰区和文昌市，南连定安县，西邻龙华区，北临美兰区。面积953.30平方公里，人口37万人，辖8个镇、1个街道办事处，区政府驻府城镇建国路。琼山历史悠久，文化底蕴深厚，是海口市的国家历史文化名城核心区。

正在紧张施工的绿色佳园“天上人间”居住小区现场

2006年，琼山区经济稳步攀升，全区生产总值达到30.66亿元，比上年增长（下同）11.8%；全社会固定资产投资完成9.12亿元，增长15%；社会消费品零售总额15亿元，增长13%；财政收入5.05亿元，增长19.8%；城镇居民人均可支配收入8428元，增长9%；农民人均纯收入3482元，年均递增8.7%。工业在全区国民经济中的主体地位突出，特色产业品牌逐步形成。新农村建设取得新进展，涌现出本立、昌文等一批省级示范村。社会各项事业取得新成果，基础教育工作通过省级评估，农业科技工作被评为全省科技进步先进区，新型农村合作医疗工作居省、市前列，全民健身活动连续三年获得全国先进单位称号，农村青年转移就业工作被评为全国先进单位。城区建设管理规范有序，成为优良的休闲、娱乐、宜居城区。

整治后的美舍河

“十一五”期间，琼山区将继续加大投入，奠定基础，突出产业特色，打造品牌，力争实现国民经济“三个翻番、三个突破”和社会事业“六个明显进步”，即地区生产总值、工业增加值、财政收入比2003年翻一番，城镇居民收入、农民人均纯收入和社会消费品零售总额有新的突破；教育科技、医疗卫生、计划生育、文化体育、社会保障和城镇化程度要在现有基础上取得新进步。

文明生态村道路

中国城

海南最大的综合文化休闲娱乐场，海南旅游风情演艺中心是海南省少有的顶级剧院，每天上演大型海南风情歌舞《天涯情》和法国红磨坊大型欧洲歌舞，演绎传统与现代文化相结合的“欢乐颂”，是游人文化娱乐的最佳去处。

农民收获的香蕉

红塔卷烟厂厂区

亚洲制药厂

绿色佳园生态住宅小区

琼山区政务大楼

海口市财政局

张美文局长

2007年海口市财政工作会议

2006年，在市委、市政府的正确领导和省财政厅的正确指导下，海口市财政局认真贯彻落实科学发展观，扎实推进各项财政工作，超额完成了全年的预算任务，财政工作实现了“十一五”的良好开局。全市财政总收入（来源地）跨越式增长，达到700，778万元，同比增长15.2%，突破了70亿元大关；全市地方财政总收入388，198万元，市本级地方财政总收入358，097万元。财政支出结构不断优化，财政保障能力不断增强，在积极支持经济发展的同时，对“三农”、教育、社会保障等方面倾斜力度不断加大，为逐步改善民生、构建和海口奠定了物质基础。2006年，市本级专项支出共投入支农资金3，976万元，同比增长45.4%。投入教育资金13，299万元，同比增长31%。发放城市低保金1，524万元，全年城市低保达到8.9万户次，22万人次，低保率达2.27%;发放农村低保金1，250万元，人均补差44.6元，全年农村低保达到17.8万户次，29万人次，低保率达4.2%；安排新型合作医疗资金1，000万元，提高对参合农民的补偿水平，全市有47.4万农民签订合同自愿参加了新型农村合作医疗，占应参合人数的95.05%。财政改革稳步推进，国库管理制度改革、政府收支分类改革、部门预算管理与改革、政府采购、财户管理等各项工作不断深入，财政管理制度不断完善，财政运行机制不断创新，财政管理水平得到进一步提高。财政监督力度加大，预算约束性逐步增长，财经纪律专项检查成效显著，财经秩序明显改善。抓好财政队伍自身建设，开展“三个方面、四个领域、一个环节”的反商业贿赂自查自纠和整改，制定完善教育奖励制度和荣誉优秀奖励制度等，搞好业务培训，促进财政事业和财政人的共同发展。

2005年度表彰大会

2006年度财政系统优秀工作者表彰现场

2007总结表彰大会

海口市政府国有资产监督管理委员会

2006年是“十一五”规划的开局之年，也是我市国资监管工作步入崭新阶段的一年。一年来，在市委、市政府的正确领导下，市国资委认真落实科学发展观，依法履行出资人的职责，以“监管、运营、发展”为主线，加强国有资产监管，优化国有经济布局和结构调整，积极推进国有企业改革，确保国有资产保值增值，主动认真地完成市委、市政府交办的其他工作事项。

目前，市属国有企业资产总额135亿元，负债总额94亿元，净资产总额40亿元；国有权益36亿元。列入市国资委监管的14家重点企业资产总额约120亿元，负债总额79亿元，净资产约40亿元，其中，国有资本权益约36亿元。重点企业2006年1-9月份实现利润总额约2454万元，监管企业运营效率有所提升。主要工作成绩：

一、国有经济战略性调整初步到位。以发展统领全局，抢抓机遇、致力探索，以新的思路，新的举措努力推动国有经济在全市经济社会发展中发挥更好的引领带动作用。完成了市属国有企业经济布局和结构调整，五年规划制定；对市自来水公司和污水处理厂实施重组，新成立了水务集团。正积极筹建城建集团、公交集团等集团公司，以及港航控股移交我市的产权管理相关工作。

二、国有企业改革取得突破性进展。基本完成椰树集团的改制工作；完成海南椰岛股份有限公司股权分置改革和市煤管总参股的民生燃气公司股权分置改革；完成泰华旅业国有股权整体转让后的国有资产收益催收等收尾工作；指导推进市长流开发建设总公司等开发区企业的改制工作；加快推进劣势企业推出步伐；指导各局、各区国有企业改制工作。

三、国有资产监管体系进一步完善。进一步加强国资监管制度建设；加强企业财务统计、分析，强化国有资产的日常监管；全面开展企业财务预算和负责人经营业绩考核工作；继续作好改制企业清产核资专项审计报告的审核工作；加强企业国有产权转让监督检查；抓好产权管理工作；加快行政事业单位资产处置工作。

四、国有企业党建和党风廉政建设工作得到加强。以加强企业领导班子建设为重点，不断提升国企党建工作水平；加强党风廉政建设和反腐败工作。

五、加强委领导班子思想作风建设和干部队伍建设。

六、解决遗留问题，做好信访工作，维护社会的稳定。

2007年，我委将继续围绕全市总体工作要求，加快优化国有经济结构布局和调整，进一步推进国资监管体系的建设，大力推进国有企业改革与发展。

海口市国资委王永书记和徐伟主任下企业调研

● 省领导亲临中心视察工作

● 省委组织部部长方晓宇陪同中组部领导视察工作

海口市政务服务中心

● 省领导参加中心启动仪式

● 中心领导下乡到永兴镇美德村调研

海口市政务服务中心于 2005年9月7日启动运行，是海口市政府各职能部门集中对社会提供政府服务的窗口，依法履行全市政府服务的组织、协调、监督、管理和服务职能，对外为办事群众提供统一的政务服务平台、对内为职能部门提供统一的协同办公平台，对上为党政领导、监察部门提供阳光监督平台。

目前，全市共有33家行政职能进驻“中心”，为社会提供339项行政许可服务事项。通过“阳光大厅、公正透明”的服务窗口，中心对行政许可服务进行透明化跟踪督办，确保服务申请人享受到公平、公正、公开、高效的政务服务。截止2006年12月止，共受理办件157325宗，平均每个工作日受理400宗，已审结149962宗，承诺期限内审结率高于99％。中心不断加大服务力度，便民、利民的各项服务新举措受到投资者，市民的广泛好评，共收到锦旗15面、匾牌3面、感谢信5封、留言表扬百余条。

2006年，在市委、市政府的正确领导和大力支持下，海口市政务服务中心以“三个代表”重要思想为指导，以胡锦涛同志“八荣八耻”为标杆，以

● 开拓创新、锐意进取的领导班子

阳光大厅 公正透明

二楼受理大厅

优质服务月活动动员大会

“规范、便民、廉洁、高效”为宗旨，进一步内强管理，外树形象，在机制创新、规范管理、服务优化、电子政务上狠下功夫，取得了较好的成效：

- 抓项目进驻，顺利完成第二批单位及项目进驻中心
- 抓项目管理，大力推进审批制度改革
- 抓制度建设，建立健全各项规章制度
- 抓优质服务，推出多项服务新举措
- 抓电子政务，不断提高信息化建设水平
- 抓队伍建设，将中心建设成为转变作风的示范窗口
- 抓媒体宣传，树立服务型政府良好形象

为进一步搞好中心建设，优化我市投资软环境，为企业和社会提供更优质的服务，2007年着重抓好以下几项工作：

- 发挥协调职能，确保中心正常运行
- 严格进行监督监察、保障中心规范运作
- 做好项目调整和完善工作、继续优化审批程序
- 加速电子政务建设、全面实现网上协同审批
- 大力加强机关建设、创造良好工作环境

海口市政务服务中心以“规范、便民、廉洁、高效”为基本工作原则，努力探索改革和实施行政审批制度，完善行政运行机制，提高行政效率，努力实现把中心构建成政府联系群众最密切的零距离通道，打造成最有影响力的政务服务平台，建设成椰城最靓丽的政务服务窗口的“三最”目标。

海口市信访局

市委书记陈辞（中）、秘书长蒙国海（右）、副秘书长、信访局局长王宁（左）在市长接待日与来访群众面对面交流

副市长徐唐先在市长接待日接待来访群众

市长接待日来访群众代表向市领导反映情况

海口市信访局为市政府办公厅内设机构，行政级别为副处级，我市专门从事信访工作的人员仅有16人。

群众信访活动的基本情况：随着改革的深化和经济的发展，群众集体上访、重复上访较以前增多。按照“属地管理，分级负责，谁主管、谁负责”的原则，2006年，我市受理人民群众来访9254件（次），上升41.9%。其中来信3560件，上升65.6%；来访5694人次，上升30.3%；集体上访179批4600人次，人数增加700人次，分别上升4%和17.9%，重复上访58批，1840人次，分别增长30.8%和52.3%。

市长接待日：自2005年5月18日开展市长接待日以来，陈辞市长、黄行光副市长、王路副市长、吴伟雄副市长、袁秀梅副市长、徐唐先常务副市长、刘庆声副市长就我市的投资环境、个体工商户在生产经营中存在的问题，教育事业发展与子女上学、城市管理、农村村务管理与村务公开、公交车管理、环境保护与生态建设、旅游市场管理和综合整治等八个方面，先后接待群众来访，使广大市民直接与市长对面交流，共同商讨如何解决我市在经济建设和社会发展中存在的问题，缩小了百姓与市长的距离，使百姓真正感受到市政府“人民利益无小事”的工作作风。

切实抓好《信访条例》的宣传培训和配套措施建设工作：一是切实抓好学习培训工作，二是切实抓好宣传工作，三是切实抓好《信访条例》配套措施的制定工作，四是切实加强基层信访工作。

2007年，我们将继续以邓小平理论为指导，深入贯彻十六大和十六届三中全会精神，努力实践“三个代表”，解放思想，转变观念，改进工作作风，积极探索，总结新时期信访工作的经验和工作方法，关注热点、跟踪焦点、解决难点，为我市的改革开放和经济建设创造良好的社会环境。

海口市审计局积极关注社会热点问题。图为审计人员在对医疗医药行业的收费情况进行审计

海口市审计局十分重视农村帮扶工作，先后筹集资金10多万元，帮助帮扶村修建文化室、硬化村道路。图为审计局局长孙芬在考察规划帮扶点的文明生态村建设蓝图

海口市审计局

海口市审计局成立于1983年12月，是海口市人民政府的职能部门，依法独立行使审计监督职能。

近年来，海口市审计工作在市委、市政府的领导和省审计厅的指导下，以“三个代表”重要思想和科学发展观为指导，紧紧围绕全市经济工作中心和建设和谐社会的目标，认真贯彻审计工作方针，依法履行审计监督职责；适应审计工作的转变，更新审计理念，努力探索新形势下的审计创新，调整工作思路，创新工作体制，形成以投资审计为重点的审计业务新格局；提高依法审计能力和审计工作质量，审计结论办理、审计整改取得明显成效；大力推进审计信息化建设，促进审计方式的变革，在创新中加快了海口审计工作的全面发展。有效地节约了国家建设资金，提高了政府投资效益。审计监督在促进加强宏观管理、推进依法行政、维护群众利益、促进廉政建设等方面发挥了积极作用。

海口市审计局积极参加文明生态村建设。图为审计人员就文明生态村建设给农村带来的变化向农民进行问卷调查

中小学危房改造工程建设的好坏，关系到师生的人身安危，为了保证改造资金的安全和效益，海口市审计展开了危改资金的审计调查。图为审计人员在实地审查危改校舍

局党组书记、局长潘泽和同志在机关作风建设动员大会上讲话

局党组成员在庆“七一”表彰暨文艺晚会上高唱《没有共产党就没有新中国》

海口市人事劳动保障局

海口市人事劳动保障局是市政府对全市人事、劳动和社会保障工作进行行政管理的职能部门。内设办公室、人事科、综合规划与政策法规科、专业技术人员管理科、公务员管理科、人才流动开发科（设军队转业干部安置办公室）、工资福利与离退休科、培训就业科、劳动保障监察科、劳动关系科、社会保险科等11个科级职能机构。下属4个副处级事业单位、6个正科级事业单位，分别是：市人力资源开发局、市社会保险事业局、市高级技工学校，市人事劳动仲裁院、市劳动保障监察支队、市农村养老保险办公室、市职业技术培训中心、市机关幼儿园、市人事劳动保障信息中心、市自主择业军队转业干部管理办公室。

海口市人事劳动保障局在市委、市政府的正确领导和海南省人事劳动保障厅的具体指导下，紧紧围绕全市中心工作，充分发挥人事劳动保障职能作用，奋力拼搏，使就业再就业人数不断增加，保障制度不断完善，维权更加有力，各项工作都取得了新进展,有力地促进了我市改革深化、经济发展和社会和谐稳定。先后被劳动和社会保障部评为“全国劳动保障系统先进集体”、“劳动保障宣传先进单位”，荣获劳动和社会保障部、公安部、人事部、国家工商总局“开展清理整顿劳动力市场秩序专项行动先进集体”；荣获劳动和社会保障部“开展贯彻实施《禁止使用童工规定》专项检查活动先进集体”；被市委、市政府评为“拥军优属先进单位”。市劳动争议仲裁委员会被劳动和社会保障部、全国总工会等评为“全国先进劳动争议仲裁委员会”；劳动争议仲裁委办公室被评为“全国劳动保障系统优质服务窗口单位”。

海口市第四届人才劳动力现场招聘会

为鼓励和帮助驻市随军未就业军属创业和实现再就业，市人事劳动保障部门每年都举办一至二次随军家属专场招牌会。图为招牌会现场

“民营企业招聘周”现场

“零就业”家庭招聘会现场

振奋精神 创新机制 真抓实干 努力开创城管行政执法工作新局面

海口市城市管理行政执法局

2006年是我市实施相对集中行政处罚权的开局之年。一年来，在市委、市政府的正确领导下，我们以“新体制、新模式、新标准、新队伍、新风貌”为目标，以实施综合执法为契机，切实加强队伍建设，狠抓环境综合整治，为海口市经济社会又好又快发展做出了积极贡献。

一、抓改制，组建新队伍，实施新体制。2006年9月13日，市、区城市管理行政执法局正式挂牌成立，新体制开始运作实施，是我市城市管理改革的一件大事。我局先后制定了九个工作方案、14项队伍管理制度，提出了全市“六个统一”的运作模式。组织竞争上岗，组建行政执法队伍。

二、抓创新，完善新机制，探索新路子。按照“五新”要求，探索新体制，完善新机制，开辟新路子。主动走访规划、建设、公安等部门，召开联席会议，共同探讨加强城市管理，做好综合执法工作的对策措施。建立计算机网络平台、制定并实施执法督察警示方案、开展市民体验城管执法活动、开展人力三轮车区域试点运营工作、启动市场化治理乱张贴的试点工作，取得了初步成效。

全体党员聆听海南党校葛教授讲党课

三、抓立法，出台新规章，保障新体制。市政府颁布实施了《海口市城市管理相对集中行政处罚权暂行办法》、《海口市三轮车管理暂行规定》，使相对集中行政处罚权有法可依。此外，我局制订了《海口市城市管理行政执法工作联席会议制度》、《海口市城市管理行政执法协作制度》、《海口市城市管理行政执法达标管理实施方案》、《海口市城市管理行政执法督察警示实施方案》等五项管理制度，以政府规范性文件发布实施，强化依法行政。

四、抓整治，美化市容市貌，彰显新成效。开展城市环境梳理行动，结合重大活动，突出重点整治占道经营、乱张贴、泥头车污染、噪声污染、乱设广告招牌、三轮车违法入市等行为。截止12月底，共查处各类违章1845283宗，教育纠正各类违章315020宗。经过集中整治，城市环境有一定改观。

五、抓互动，承办提案和投诉，推行新举措。充分发挥社会各界参与城管执法的积极性，招贤纳士，接受各界监督，共同管理好城市。一是壮大社会义务监督员队伍；二是认真处理信访和投诉工作；三是提供优质服务；四是加强部门互动，做好城管执法工作。

六、抓宣传，营造舆论氛围，促进城管工作。由于宣传声势大、舆论引导正确，市民对新体制给予支持，对新队伍寄予厚望。2006年11月，我局被国家建设部评为“全国城市管理先进集体”。

海口市环卫局

2006年，海口市环卫局全体干部职工在市委、市政府和局党组的正确领导下，以邓小平理论、“三个代表”重要思想为指针，不断加快环卫体制改革步伐，科学规划，合理发展，积极推进“生态海口”工程建设，促使环卫行业管理和各项建设迈上了新的台阶，城市环境卫生管理水平进一步提高。

积极开展党风廉政建设，深入开展以“八荣八耻”为主要内容的社会主义荣辱观和新党章教育活动。通过深入开展以“八荣八耻”为主要内容的社会主义荣辱观和新党章教育活动，不断增强干部职工的荣辱意识和执政理念，为我市环卫事业健康发展提供了强有力的政治保证。

科学规划，完善设施，进一步提高其社会服务功能。在市里和相关部门的大力支持下，相继新建和完善了一批环卫设施。今年。一是投资7300万元的白水塘大型垃圾转运站项目于2006年12月建成，与之相配套的小型垃圾转运收集站工程也抓紧进行；二是投资1500万元的颜春岭生活垃圾填埋场垃圾渗滤液处理厂改造工程已进入施工阶段，明年初可投入运行，届时我市生活垃圾处理全部达到无害化处理水平；三是投入1000万元，新增和更新了一批环卫机械设备，机械化清扫率达到20%；四是对市区内损坏的200多个果皮箱进行维修更换；五是泰华公厕及转运站已竣工验收并交付使用，对15座公厕进行维修，使我市公厕设施齐全，档次有所提高；六是龙塘垃圾中转站和两座公厕已先后建成并投入使用。

健全机制，强化管理，全面提高城区环境卫生质量。积极组织开展宣传教育活动，全面提高市民环卫意识。其次，开展环境卫生综合整治，不断提高市区环境卫生质量。

2006年，我局被国家建设部授予“全国城市市容环境卫生工作先进集体”称号和“时传祥奖”奖牌。颜春岭垃圾处理场被国家建设部评为“一级无害化垃圾卫生填埋场”。此外，在海口市“两湖四沟”清淤、为民办实事、社会宣传工作、人大政协提案办理等工作方面也受到上级表彰。

局领导班子精心描划发展前景：

认真落实科学发展观，精心描划发展新蓝图，努力开创大特区省会城市环卫事业新局面

王周兴局长赴北京喜领“全国城市市容环境卫生工作先进集体”称号和“时传祥奖”奖牌

2006年12月26日，海口市白水塘大型垃圾中转站落成投入使用

2006年12月14日，海口市对新增道路实行社会化承包管理。图为招标现场

海南省海口地方税务局

海口地税局坚持以提升干部职工素质为目标，以服务税收工作为主线，扎实抓好干部职工的教育培训工作。图为省地税局冯大安局长（左一）、该局吴连义局长巡视税管员考试现场

围绕税收中心工作，海口地税局大力拓展业务范围，不断创新信息化建设与服务工作，推进技术开发和项目管理。图为该局吴连义局长（右二）察看新购进的网络设备

2006年以来，在省地税局和海口市委、市政府的正确领导下，海口地税局认真贯彻落实党的十六大和十六届五中、六中全会精神，以“三个代表”重要思想为指导，以组织收入为中心，以征收管理为重点，以信息化建设为依托，树立和落实科学发展观，坚持依法治税，强化科学管理，优化纳税服务，加强队伍建设，完成了各项工作任务。

一、坚持应收尽收，全力完成税费收入任务。强化调研，周密计划；认真做好处置积压房地产转让环节减免税的审批工作；调整农业税征管重点，力争应收尽收；加强涉外税收征管，提高质量和效率，一是加强税源管理，夯实征管基础，二是开展全国企业税收资料调查工作和涉外企业所得税汇算清缴工作，进一步摸清税源，三是加强对双定业户的定税管理，及时征收零星税源，四是加强对涉外企业中外方高级、中级管理人员的个人所得税征管工作，五是进一步加强对外商投资房地产开发经营企业所得税和土地增值税的预征和清算。

二、大力实施科学化精细化管理，税收管理能力显著增强。强化重点税源监控；加强征管质量考核；加强房地产营业税、土地增值税的管理；开展房产税和城镇土地使用税税源清查；扎实抓好社保费征缴。

三、努力构建规范有效的税收执法机制，进一步提高执法水平。全面推行税收执法责任制；全面落实税收管理员制度；发挥稽查部门职能作用，进一步整顿和规范税收秩序；开展重大税务案件的审理工作；依法管票，以票控税。

四、改进和优化纳税服务，进一步营造和谐的税收工作环境。1、加强投资环境建设，营造和谐征纳关系。一是加强税企沟通，密切税企关系；二是改善办公场所，为纳税人提供舒适的办税环境；三是坚持以人为本，创建和谐征纳（缴费）关系，四是转变服务理念，为纳税（缴费）人排忧解难。2、加强政策研究和管理，认真落实税收优惠政策。3、借助新闻媒体，积极做好税收宣传工作。

五、整合规范信息资源，提高税收征管的科技含量。围绕税收中心工作，不断创新信息化建设与服务工作，推进技术开发和项目管理。认真做好“银税一体化系统”项目管理的验收工作；跟踪维护《车管所车船税征收软件》、《交管处公路运输税收征收系统》，完善《大厅即时办税信息查询系统》；跟踪做好《建安分局房产交易税收软件》项目管理；组织oracle数据库的培训；清理小型机生产系统的征管数据；配合深海鑫公司和各业务部门做好新征管大集中系统项目的测试工作；加强设备管理和技术支持，努力为基层服务。

六、坚持以人为本抓教育，干部队伍整体素质明显提升。以科学发展观为统领，大力加强思想政治建设；常抓不懈，切实加强党风廉政建设；加强学习培训，努力提高税务干部队伍素质；加强干部队伍管理和使用；加强党组织建设，充分发挥战斗堡垒作用。

今年4月是全国第16个税收宣传月，海口地税局紧紧围绕“依法诚信纳税，共建和谐社会”这一主题，精心组织了一系列富有成效的税收宣传活动。图为吴连义局长（左一）正在接受记者采访

海口地税局响应海口市委市政府号召，积极抓好扶贫帮困工作。图为吴连义局长（左一）到该局帮扶点龙华区新坡镇光荣村保礼村调研，并慰问村里的五保户

海口市人口和计划生育局

“十一五”以来，海口市人口和计划生育工作，在不断探索、创新中取得了显著成绩。人口出生率由2000年的12.84‰下降到2005年的10.30‰；人口自然增长率由2000年的9.71‰下降到2005年的7.31‰；计划生育率由2000年的87.99%提高到2002年的92.8%；符合法定生育率由2003年的90.2%提高到2005年的96.52%；出生人口性别比由2003年的129.85下降到2005年的112.18；全市已进入较为稳定的低生育水平时期。

近年来，海口市各级党委、政府把人口和计划生育工作摆在重要位置，始终坚持党政一把手亲自抓、负总责；坚持人口与发展综合决策；坚持“抓基层、打基础、求规范、上水平”的工作方针；坚持实行人口和计划生育工作目标管理责任制和“一票否决”制；坚持以人为本，积极推行避孕节育优质服务。以与时俱进的创新精神，积极推行人口与计划生育综合改革，探索以居住地为主，双向管理的属地管理模式和建立“依法管理、村（居）民自治、优质服务、政策推动、综合治理”的管理机制。在城市，建立以社区为主“属地管理、单位负责、居民自治、社区服务”和综合治理流动人口计划生育的工作机制以及企业法人代表责任制的管理模式；在农村，改镇包办为以村为主，改行政干预为村民自治，广泛建立了以村党支部为核心，村委会、计生协会和中心户长“三位一体”的计划生育村民自治体系。基本实现了计划生育工作“三为主”和“两个转变”的目标，人口生育率平稳下降，人口素质不断得到提高，人口再生产进入了低生育水平，促进了全市人口与经济、社会、资源、环境的协调发展。市、区连年完成人口计划，并取得了可喜的成果：海口市龙华区2000年被评为“全国计划生育协会先进单位”；2001年被评为“全国婚育新风进万家活动先进区”；2003年被评为“全国计生系统抗击非典先进集体”；2004年被评为“全国计划生育优质服务先进区”。美兰区2004年被评为“全国药具工作先进集体”；2005年被评为“全国计生协会先进单位”和“全国婚育新风进万家活动先进区”。海口市连续十二年被评为“全省人口与计划生育先进单位”称号；2003年被评为“全国人口和计划生育法制建设先进集体”；2003年被评为“全国计划生育协会先进单位”；2001年至2005年被评为《人口与计划生育》杂志全国基层宣传发行先进集体和《中国人口报》新闻宣传与发行先进单位。

上门为流动人口提供计划生育宣传，技术服务

街头宣传吸引市民踊跃参与

计划生育宣传进村入户到人

海口市 海洋与渔业局

海口市海洋与渔业局是市政府的组成部门。2006年，在市委市政府的正确领导和省海洋与渔业厅的具体指导下，我局认真贯彻党的十六届五、六中全会精神，认真贯彻省委省政府《关于加快海洋经济发展的决定》、《海口市社会经济第十一个五年发展纲要》和《海口市建设社会主义新农村的实施意见》，紧紧围绕渔业产业和海洋综合管理的目标任务，增加科技和资金投入，调整优化产业结构，加快发展罗非鱼精养产业.强化渔业生产安全、水产品质量安全和渔业资源保护的监管，初步建立起渔业生产安全管理机制和生产流程中水产品质量安全体系，生产秩序明显改善，渔业资源得到有效保护。加强海洋综合管理，养殖用海确权登记发证工作稳妥推进，渔业用海管理进一步规范；加大执法力度，查处多起违规行为；坚持海洋环境监测监视，及时处理2宗海洋赤潮事件，把赤潮造成的影响降低到最小，海洋生态环境保持良好。2006年水产品总产量完成59442吨，同比增长8.07%，占全年目标任务的102.49%，产值5.2421亿元，同比增长9.4%;水产品加工出口达到3.2万吨，创汇1.093亿美元，分别比2005年同比增长28%和52.3%；全年收缴海域使用金13833.34万元。协助国家海洋局、省、市政府成功举办了第一次国际性2006年东亚海大会和部长会议，得到国家海洋局和省政府领导高度赞扬。

局长、党组书记：郑道英

东寨港牡蛎吊养

三江水产养殖基地

水产品加工

海口市房产管理局

海口市房产管理局是海口市人民政府主管城镇房产管理的工作部门。主要职能是依法制定和组织实施房产管理规章，负责全市房屋产权登记发证、房屋交易、评估、测绘、租赁、直管公房、物业管理监察指导等工作。

2006年，海口市房产管理局以促进房地产健康发展为重点，搞好房地产业服务为宗旨，积极建设现代化房产管理信息网络，不断创新房产管理手段和方法，努力打造数字房产，提高房产管理水平。在全局干部职工的共同努力下，海口市房产管理局管理水平跨上新的台阶，一个规划化、法制化、科学化的房产管理已经形成。

今年，海口市房产管理局共办理房屋转让交易23849宗，成交面积301.3万平方米；房屋评估1432宗，评估面积17万平方米；房屋产权登记发证70940宗，发证面积1835.15万平方米，办理房产他项权利登记9723宗；受理房屋档案入库共70396宗，提供利用档案62616宗，现馆藏房屋档案达到39.3万宗，建筑面积约5917万平方米；办理房屋租赁监证1531宗，验租面积19.53万平方米；完成房产测绘项目692宗，测绘面积155万平方米。

海口市房产管理局积极开展帮扶工作。图为帮扶村给该局赠送锦旗“帮扶情永在、携助义长存”

海口市房产管理局响应党和政府“建设社会新农村”号召，图为该局领导向受旱的琼山区旧州镇联星村捐赠运水拖拉机一台

海口市房产管理局积极开展献爱心、送温暖活动。图为该局领导前往秀英区东山镇凤山村慰问“特困户”、“五保户”村民

创优质服务、努力打造“数字房产”，该局工作人员通过计算机进行数字化、信息化服务

海口市房产管理局工作人员走上街头，开展“走出机关、贴近市民、倾听呼声”活动

该局为帮扶秀英区东山镇凤山村捐款建设的村公路

中共海口市直属机关

工作委员会

2006年度，市直机关工委充分发挥党组织的战斗堡垒作用和共产党员的先锋模范作用，机关党的思想、组织、作风和制度建设都取得了新的成绩，为海口又好又快发展发挥了应有的作用。

(一)、扎实开展保持共产党员先进性教育活动。把先进性教育活动作为加强和改进机关党建工作的一项重要任务，开展了“做党的忠诚使者，为党的建设奋斗”为主题实践系列活动。(二)、思想理论建设持续深化。先后举办党务干部理论骨干培训班、市直机关干部理论培训暨《江泽民文选》辅导班。(三)、机关基层党组织建设取得明显成效。评选出54个开展“最佳党日”活动先进单位予以表彰；共发展党员978名，为538名预备党员按时办理了转正手续；“七一”期间表彰了50个先进基层党组织，100名优秀党员和50名优秀党务工作者；我委党支部被评为市先进基层党组织。(四)、机关作风建设得到加强。开展投资环境监督评议评价活动，召开各种座谈会52个，23个被评单位的平均满意率为83.3%，比去年提高23.2%。(五)、反腐倡廉工作扎实推进。开展以典型示范教育和警示教育为主要形式的廉政教育，今年共审理案件5件，办结率100%；受理群众来信11件，已办结10件，办结率90.9%。(六)、思想政治工作得到改进。开展机关思想政治工作“理论与实践”征文活动，共征集到论文40多篇。(七)、机关精神文明建设成效明显。组织开展了市直机关大众广播体操比赛、海口市领导干部“流动杯”篮球赛和市直机关处级干部乒乓球赛、建市80周年“热爱海口、奔向未来”万人长跑接力活动、“党旗颂”大型文艺晚会、市直机关美术书法摄影展、“中国(海口)冼太夫人节琼粤书画联展”等文体活动；组织市直机关“送温暖、献爱心”捐款活动，共收到捐款31万元；积极做好农村帮扶工作，为帮扶联系点三门坡镇青草自然村修道路、建水塔、建文化活动室、农民科技培训室、灯光球场和卫生垃圾池。

机关工委党员参观冯白驹故居

思想政治工作研讨暨征文颁奖会

建党85周年文艺晚会

突出热带滨海特色　展现椰城园林魅力

海口市园林局

绿在延伸

华海公园

海秀西路绿化

城市绿化

城市绿化

近年来，海口市紧紧围绕改善城市生态环境，努力发展园林绿化事业。五年共增加绿地面积1047公顷。目前，建成区绿地率达35.5%，绿化覆盖率39.5%，人均公共绿地8.3平方米。几年来，海口市先后获得了“全国园林绿化先进城市”、“全国造林绿化十佳城市”、“国家园林城市”等国家级荣誉称号。如今，海口市基本形成了以椰子树等棕榈科植物为主，配置常绿乔木和四季间隔开花的树木花卉，点、线、面相交映的总格局，初步展现“椰风海韵，热带风光，终年葱翠，四季常青”的园林绿化景观。

一、加强城市绿地系统规划，努力落实城市园林绿化“绿线”管制制度。在城市绿化工作中，突出“热带风光”和“滨海城市”特色，从整体布局、长远发展来考虑城市园林绿化设置，科学确定不同绿地控制指标及建设内容。根据国家、省实行城市“绿线”管制方法的要求，采取全市绿化普查，特别是作为重点部位的道路两侧、河岸、绿化隔离带、公园绿地、古树名木用地等用“绿线”加以划定保护。

二、坚持以人为本、可持续发展的原则，扎实打造园林绿化精品工程，多方位增加绿化投入。为把海口建设为国家生态园林城市和最理想的居住城市，坚持以人为本及可持续发展的原则，按照“打基础，抓管理，创精品，上档次”的要求，高品位、高水准地进行园林景观设计，大刀阔斧地绿化美化。近五年来，海口市多渠道筹措资金，保证绿化建设的投入，全市共投入园林绿化建设资金近10亿元。

三、建立完善的城市公园体系，切实加强城市公园的保护管理。出台《海口市关于加强城市公园绿地规划建设的意见》，正在制订《海口市公园管理办法》，建立完善的城市公园体系，确保公园绿地。目前全市共有各类公园13个，面积400多公顷。

四、广泛开展全民义务植树及先进单位创建活动，加强古树古木的保护。坚持大力开展园林绿化建设的宣传和教育，促进了义务植树的开展。开展了古树古木的普查，对上报的2088株古树进行挂牌保护。

五、加强园林绿化法规建设及绿化工程建设的监督管理，严格执法。结合实际，制订了《海口市城市绿化条例》，提供了法律依据和法律保障。加强护绿巡逻，仅去年，出动警力1284人次，车辆321次，共查处绿化案件30宗，制止破坏绿化案件达10多起。

六、加大苗木储备，促进园林科研发展。抓好新、特、优绿化花卉品种的引进和培育，培育出一大批较适合海口土壤气候条件的特性优良品种。目前，全市共有园林绿化苗圃14个，苗圃面积不断扩大。

海口市林业局

在市委、市政府的正确领导下，在省林业局的帮助指导下，我局深入贯彻落实党的十六大及十六届五、六中全会精神，努力实践“三个代表”重要思想，以林业生态建设为重点，大力调整林业产业结构，提升林业生产力，加大森林资源保护力度，提高全市人民的生态环保意识，有效地促进人与自然和谐发展，林业建设取得了新的进展。

主要工作任务完成情况

（一）造林绿化方面

全年造林总面积2300.2公顷。完成浆纸林造林1798.6公顷，占任务的135%。完成三边林建设1214.3公顷，其中海防林97.9公顷，路边林426.1公顷，城边林690.3公顷。完成海南珍贵乡土树种种植139.2公顷，占任务的104%。完成花卉种植面积277.2公顷，占任务的104%；

（二）全面加强林政资源管理工作

1、今年以来，报省林业局审批办理征占用林地8宗，征占用林地面积139.5公顷，应收取森林植被恢复费558.8万元，征（占）用林地审核率达100%；审批林木采伐申请88宗，共计14678.6立方米，征收育林基金23.9万元，采伐指标控制在省下达的指标范围（5万立方米）之内。

2、木材检查执法外出执勤1091车次，共检查木材流量达135000立方米，查处违法运输木材402宗；核发《野生动物运输证》649张，运输野生动物（主要是我省养殖的虎纹蛙）120万公斤；依法办理《海南省野生动物及其产品经营许可证》66家。查扣国家二级及省级保护动物35512只（绝大多数是我省养殖的虎纹蛙），经专业鉴定、检疫救护后放归大自然的野生动物8956只（条）；查获风景树、绿化苗木、古树1106株以及花梨木5350公斤。

3、今年以来，市森林公安局共出动警力 2163 人次，车辆 592辆次，查处各类林业案件81宗，处理违法犯罪分子9人（治安拘留2人、取保候审5人、逮捕2 人），扣押非法运输车辆38辆次，为国家和群众挽回经济损失450万余元。

（三）今年以来，全市共发生森林火灾5起，总计过火面积7.76公顷，受害森林面积1.3公顷，森林火灾受害率0.016‰，没有人员伤亡事故发生。在今年全省“三无创优”活动中，受到省森林防火指挥部的通报表彰。

（四）在有关部门的大力支持下，我局及各区农林局全力以赴，对我市的森林植物病虫害，特别是椰心叶甲虫害展开了全方位的防治，取得了明显的防治效果，有效扼制疫情进一步扩散。

（五）2006年，我市林业产业总产值约为21亿元。

省林业局领导视察我市花卉产业

局领导到帮扶村研究落实帮扶工作

营造乡村道路路边林

大力发展花卉产业

大力发展经济林

人与自然和谐相处

抓好森林防火设施设备建设

海口市森林公安局

海口市森林公安局于2006年6月正式挂牌成立，现有在职民警31人，下设新海林场、新民林场和东寨港国家级自然保护区三个基层派出所，负责全市23个乡镇、二个林场、一个保护区、120多万亩林地和130公里海防线长的林业管护。森林公安是国家林业部门和公安机关的重要组成部门，是具有武装性质的兼有刑事执法和行政执法的重要力量。其职能是打击一切破坏森林资源和野生动植物资源的违法犯罪行为，保护森林资源和野生动植物资源安全，维护林区社会治安稳定。在线长、面广、人少事多、经费严重不足的情况下，森林公安全体齐心协力，团结一致，依法治林，严厉打击破坏森林资源和野生动植物资源的违法犯罪活动，为构建和谐海口，打造生态海南做出了积极的贡献。2006年森林公安局共出动警力1580人次，车辆586辆次，查处各类案件81宗，其中刑事案件10宗，林业行政案件71宗；处理违法犯罪嫌疑人58人，逮捕5人，刑拘7人，治安拘留7人，没收木材156立方米，缴获野生动物15680只（条），为国家和群众挽回经济损失250万元。组建以来，森林公安被国家森林公安局授予二等功一次，三等功一次，队伍中先后有15人受到国家森林公安局、省森林公安局、市林业局等上级部门的嘉奖和表彰，其中3人荣立二等功，5人荣立三等功。今后森林公安全体民警将再接再厉，锐意进取，与时俱进，为保护海南生态安全和林业又好又快发展再立新功。

团结、务实、朝气蓬勃的领导班子

没收非法经营的野生动物

缴获非法运输的木材

海口市公安局交巡警支队

海口市交巡警支队在市委、市政府、市局的正确领导下，以“三个代表”重要思想与科学发展观为指导，以开展社会主义荣辱观、社会主义法治理念和《江泽民文选》等教育活动为主线，以创建平安和谐海口为目标，认真完成了交通治安管理和队伍建设等各项工作，并取得了突出成绩。据统计，2006年共查处各类交通违法50万人次，其中查扣违法机动车66368辆次，治安拘留163人，强制报废机动车9689辆。查处各类治安案件1355宗，抓获犯罪嫌疑人1864人。适用普通程序处理的交通事故510起，死亡89人，受伤658人，经济损失156万元，与去年同比，起数下降5.03%，死亡人数下降8.2%，死亡人数比目标控制数少31人。

一、通过交通整顿，有力促进交通事故稳步下降。先后通过“预防交通事故百日竞赛”、代号“春雷”大型交通综合整治、代号“蓝剑”摩托车专项整治，有效地减少交通违法行为，促进交通事故起数与死亡人数“两下降”。

全年交通整顿工作体现三个特点：一是各种交通整顿坚持绩效考核；二是警力资源合理使用；三是交通整顿突出“重点”。

二、以维护社会面稳定为中心，加强“两抢一盗”专项斗争与处突防范工作。据统计，2006年共查处“两抢”案件76宗118人，盗窃、扒窃案件681宗834人，涉毒538宗799人，其他案件61宗112人，缴获作案工具570件，赃款赃物341件（约人民币18万元）。与去年同比，“两抢”案件破获率上升29%。

三、坚持“警卫工作无小事”的原则，圆满完成交通安全警卫、保卫工作。全年支队共完成交通警卫工作471个，完成节假日、重要活动交通安全保卫169个。尤其是博鳌年会、“五·一”、“十·一”、“欢乐节”安保工作，周永康部长到海口调研的交通警卫工作。市领导对我交巡警支队执行保卫工作给予充分肯定。

四、启动交警指挥监控中心，交通管理科技含量明显提升。

省领导亲切慰问一线民警

交警指挥监控中心建成后，通过电视监视点、电子警察，对全市重要路口、重要路段、重要场所实时监控、现场抓拍、屏幕指挥，促进交巡警工作向科学化、智能化的方向迈进。

五、完善交通设施，提高道路硬件服务水平。积极参与交通设施与道路修建改造“三同步”，评审新改建道路30多条，确保新建道路交通设施覆盖率100%。

六、以“交通宣传五进”活动为载体，多形式开展全民交通普法工作。一是深入推进“五进”宣传工作（进乡镇、进行政村、进社区、进学校、进家庭）；二是加强运输单位及其驾驶人交通安全教育；三是开展未成年人交通安全教育活动；四是联合新闻媒体，拓宽与市民沟通交流的平台。

七、进一步完善服务窗口，提高便民服务质量。

2006年，支队全面贯彻落实公安部党委“抓基层、打基础、苦练基本功”的决定，“三基”工程建设、队伍正规化建设、规范执勤执法以及岗位大练兵活动，让这支队伍更富有战斗力和生命力，为“十一五”规划开了好头，为海口经济发展和社会稳定做出了突出贡献。

支队领导在深入“欢乐节”演出现场了解交通疏导和安全情况

海口市工业和招商局

陈小鹰局长

海口市工业和招商局成立于2007年3月，是主管全市工业和招商工作的正处级市政府直属机构，内设办公室、规划法规科、工业经济科、项目协调科、招商储备科、招商管理科6个科室及工业科学研究所1个下属单位。

海口市工业和招商局主要职责：贯彻执行党和国家及省政府有关工业、招商引资的方针政策；组织实施国家产业政策的监督、检查执行情况；研究拟定并组织实施全市工业经济发展和招商引资的中长期发展规划、年度计划和工业布局调整规划、工业结构调整方案；加强对工业产业行业的宏观指导和协调；指导资源节约和综合利用；指导、协调、促进全市中小企业的改革与发展；做好煤炭销售行业的管理及经营许可证的初审工作；组织国内外各类招商活动及有关工业方面的对外交流工作；承担全市投资环境形象宣传的策划、组织、推广活动；负责招商项目的包装、策划、宣传和对外发布；督查招商引资优惠政策的落实情况；承担全市招商信息化工作，提供招商信息咨询服务；负责全市外引内联重大项目的跟踪协调服务，及时了解项目进展情况，协调解决项目在建设生产中存在的问题。

我局将秉承“服务、创新、高效、廉洁”的理念，集社会各界之合力，全力做好海口市工业和招商工作。

海口市工业和招商网：www.hkgz.gov.cn

海口保税区

2006年，海口保税区在市委、市政府的正确领导下，着力打造环境、体制、产业和开发新优势，提升核心竞争力，实现经济质量与规模、效益与速度同步发展，物质文明、政治文明、精神文明建设迈上了新的台阶，促进了和谐园区建设。

2006年，全区完成工业总产值119.7亿元，同比增长25.7%；完成工业销售产值119.63亿元，同比增长28.75%；完成产品销售收入116.94亿元，同比增长27.58%；完成工业增加值26.13亿元，同比增长9.15%；完成利润总额9.79亿元，同比增长29.3%；完成财税收入11.2亿元，同比增长18.6%；进出口总额11.09亿美元，同比增长32.57%。

2006年，狮子岭飞地工业园招商引资的企业有23家，入园企业总投资13亿元，年税收3.5亿元。可安排就业人数4105人。海马二期的发动机厂、铸造厂等及14家配套厂总投资36亿元，预计新增产值达50亿元，可安排就业人数4500人。药谷二期招商引资企业12家，总投资15.6亿元，预计年产值25亿元，年利税5亿元。这些企业的入驻，为园区“十一五”期间健康、持续发展奠定了坚实的基础。

一汽海马汽车有限公司

三星光通信技术有限公司

海口保税区园区一角

中和药业有限公司

海口市道路交通运输管理处

局党组书记、局长吴淑楷参加我处“八荣八耻”演讲比赛

市直机关工委领导到我处视察工作

李文光处长在全市道路运输市场整治大会上做动员讲话

2006年，市道路交通运输管理处在市交通局的领导下，以邓小平理论、“三个代表”、“八荣八耻”重要思想和党的十六届四中、六中全会和省、市交通工作会议精神为指导思想，牢固树立科学发展观，围绕道路运输管理“改革、整治、规范、文明、和谐”这一主题，全处干部职工，在处领导班子的带领下，群策群力，奋勇拼搏，开拓进取，求真务实，扎实工作，较好地完成了2006年全年的工作任务。今年以来，我处运政服务大厅继续保持了“全国三八红旗集体”称号，处党总支被海口市机关工委评为先进基层党组织，2006年绿色通道工作被省交通厅评为先进单位。

一、加强领导班子建设，积极开展运管队伍思想政治教育，加强业务培训，强化运管队伍思想作风建设，努力打造省会城市良好形象的运管队伍。加强理论学习，积极开展形势教育活动；积极开展“八荣八耻”教育活动；加强运政窗口建设，立足岗位建功；讲政治、讲大局、统一思想，抓好班子建设。

二、按照市委市政府、市交通局关于交通运输综合整治的精神，加强市场监管，净化市场环境，规范市场秩序，以科学发展观，推进我市和谐交通建设。加强对运输市场的监管，整治道路运输市场环境，规范我市运输市场秩序，创造和谐交通运输环境，全年我处共出动执法人员18000多人次，查处各项违法违章运输14735件，使我市道路交通运输市场环境得到进一步净化，经营管理进一步规范，服务质量不断改善，经济效益、行业效益不断提高，运输安全得到进一步保障；积极做好公交、出租汽车行业的维稳工作；加强对货运市场的监管；进一步加强公交客运管理；专项整治非法售票点；进一步强化乡镇运管工作；加强营运驾驶员从业培训工作，建立从业培训长效监管机制；积极做好2006年陆上春运工作；基本完成2005年度营业性道路运输车辆审验工作；加强财务工作计划，严格财经纪律，完成税费征收工作；加强旅客投诉的处理，积极为群众排忧解难。

三、发扬艰苦奋斗，勇于拼搏的优良传统，狠抓内部管理和建设，全面推动各项工作。

四、在精神文明建设方面贯彻了“贵在坚持，重在建设”的方针，精神文明建设取得良好成效，宣传、信访、计生、社会治安综合治理取得比往年更好的成绩。

市六龙公交公司给我处赠送锦旗

稽查人员在路上执法

资料整理: 黄丹慧 邢春城
Arranged by Huangdanhui Xingchuncheng

13. 批发零售贸易和住宿餐饮业
WHOLESALE,RETAIL AND RESTAURANT

社会消费品零售总额（亿元）

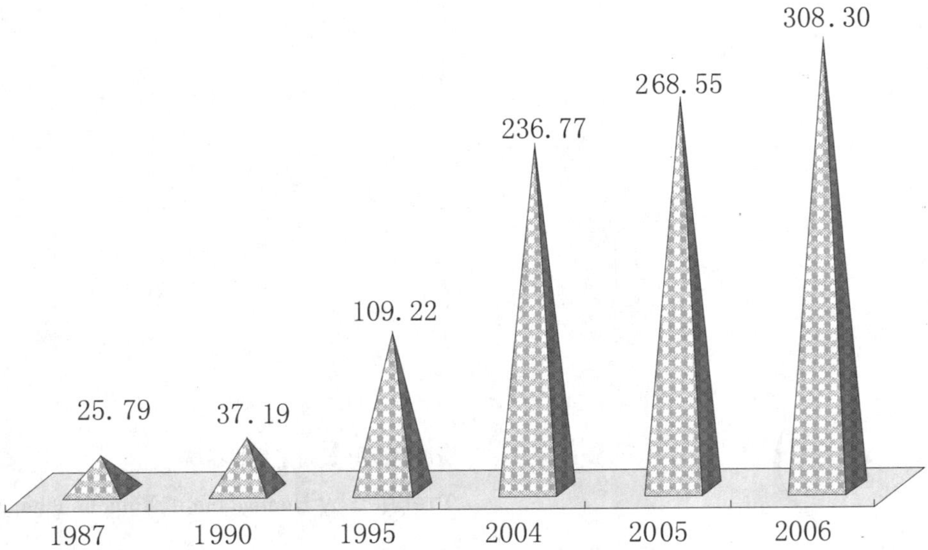

社会消费品零售总额构成（%）

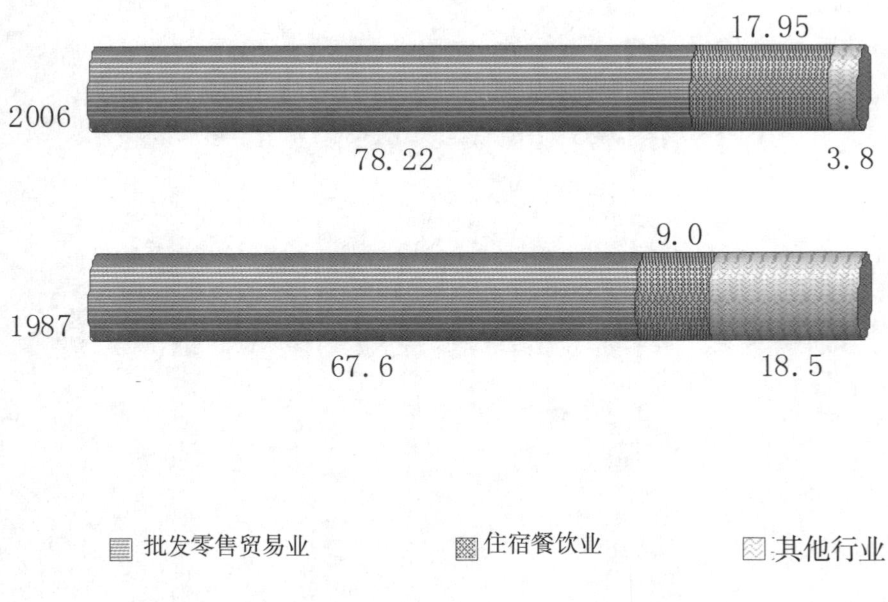

13－1 历年社会消费品零售总额
Total Retail Sales of Consumer Goods in Various Years

单位:万元 (10 000 yuan)

年 份 Year	社会消费品零售总额 Total Retail Sales of Consumer Goods	批发零售贸易业 Wholesale and Retail trade	住宿餐饮业 Hotel and Catering Trade	制造业 Manufacturing	其他行业 Others	农民对城市居民零售 Retail Sales of Peasantry to Urban Residents	按城乡分 By Urban and Rural 城镇 Urban	农村 Rural
1952	14292	11244	1050	1112	886	866	6227	8065
1957	24370	18946	2067	1561	1796	1614	10412	13958
1962	36792	28894	3697	1348	2853	2431	15867	20925
1965	40692	33618	2827	769	3478	2781	17981	22711
1970	47710	39881	2886	550	4393	3621	21711	25999
1975	69206	56563	4421	1576	6646	5394	32280	36926
1980	99323	79882	5980	3133	10328	8958	44703	54620
1981	110224	86256	6149	4795	13024	10235	49710	60514
1982	133610	100702	9640	5492	17776	13010	68788	64822
1983	146678	105941	10949	6388	23400	17972	82174	64504
1984	181578	135336	13208	7940	25094	17882	101767	79811
1985	215775	157638	16980	11547	29610	23037	129660	86115
1986	231599	160487	18032	11541	41539	31735	136931	94668
1987	257922	174314	23332	12594	47682	38044	151751	106171
1988	343223	224823	38156	17659	62585	48577	224456	118767
1989	376428	235268	39261	18169	83730	59301	261334	115094
1990	371865	240503	39737	16888	74737	61743	253578	118287
1991	419728	271748	46479	19380	82121	65964	294820	124908
1992	550179	344500	62862	31518	111299	73899	394343	155836
1993	727186	481419	85167	14668	145932	142260	567836	159350
1994	947393	560183	96466	36492	254252	159683	708232	239161
1995	1092190	648076	134928	34119	275067	183276	838195	253995
1996	1215705	684311	159872	32990	338532	237338	924903	290802
1997	1334090	754745	157665	35861	385819	303218	1019049	315041
1998	1447280	828288	179722	33823	405447	337423	1091508	355772
1999	1576565	932677	202062	38399	403427	335606	1182889	393676
2000	1724762	1039113	228847	44542	412260	352226	1283423	441339
2001	1874593	1132181	260497	49303	432612	363441	1400482	474111
2002	2043952	1253104	287498	52173	451177	368799	1522784	521168
2003	1916353	1505313	309937		101103		1447428	468925
2004	2367741	1858334	416918		92489		1855126	512615
2005	2685506	2090835	488904		105767		2109556	575950
2006	3082961	2411371	553330		118260		2435769	647192

注:从 2003 年起社会消费品零售总额中不包括制造业和农民对城市居民的零售额(下同)
Total Retail Sales of Consumer Goods is not including Retail Sales of Manufacturing and Retail Sales of Peasantry to Urban Residents Since 2003(the same below)

13-1 续(continued)

年 份 Year	社会消费品零售总额 Total Retail Sales of Consumer Goods	食品类 Food	衣着类 Clothing	日用品类 Articles for Daily Use	文化娱乐用品类 Cultural and recreational Articles	书报杂志类 Books, Newspapers and Magazines	药和医疗用品类 Medicines and Medical Appliances	燃料类 Fuels
1978								
1979	92855							
1980	99323	51151	17183	18077	4072	1192	4271	3377
1981	110224	56986	19399	20501	4409	1433	4850	2646
1982	133610	69477	22714	25252	5211	1871	5745	3340
1983	146678	76565	25082	27136	5867	1907	6601	3520
1984	181578	94965	30686	33955	7082	2179	8353	4358
1985	215775	113282	35602	41430	8199	1942	10573	4747
1986	231599	123442	37056	44004	9264	2316	11580	3937
1987	257922	145726	39978	45394	9285	2321	10317	4901
1988	343223	195637	53543	58691	12699	2746	15445	4462
1989	376428	219081	56841	63240	11293	3011	17692	5270
1990	371865	216054	56895	62845	10784	2603	17106	5578
1991	419728	245121	64638	70094	10493	3358	18888	7136
1992	550179	316982	85527	94131	12855	6124	25857	8703
1993	727186	420314	111987	122167	17452	8726	35632	10908
1994	947393	540961	144951	167089	24285	12316	42633	15158
1995	1092190	617087	157277	199870	28397	19659	52425	17475
1996	1215705	686873	175063	222473	31608	21882	58354	19452
1997	1334090	707067	220124	262816	54697	22679	38692	28015
1998	1447280	758585	217402	299556	60996	26051	49076	35614
1999	1576565	826350	236822	326315	66445	28378	53460	38795
2000	1724762	904027	259083	356989	72690	31046	58485	42442
2001	1874593	982560	281589	388001	79005	33743	63566	46129
2002	2043952	1071329	307029	423055	86143	36791	69309	50296
2003	1916353	1004449	287862	396644	80765	34494	64982	47157
2004	2367741	1241042	355666	490072	99788	42619	80288	58266
2005	2685506	1407596	403399	555842	113182	48338	91063	66086
2006	3082961	1615920	463102	638107	129933	55492	104540	75867

13－2 各市县社会消费品零售总额
Total Retail Sales of Consumer Goods By Region

单位:万元 (10 000 yuan)

年份 地区	Region	社会消费品零售总额 Total Retail Sales of Consumer Goods	批发零售贸易业 Wholesale and Retail trade	住宿餐饮业 Hotel and Catering Trade	其他行业 Others	按城乡分 By Urbars and Rural 城市 Urban	乡村 Rural
总计	Total	3082961	2411371	553330	118260	2435769	647192
海口市	Haikou	1613497	1334363	211489	67645	1613497	
三亚市	Sanya	239361	140331	91489	7541	172753	66608
五指山市	Wuzhishan	22003	14398	6572	1033	15708	6295
文昌市	Wenchang	153784	114903	36598	2283	63942	89842
琼海市	Qionghai	161272	111572	40936	8764	109887	51385
万宁市	Wanning	150100	116580	29195	4325	73321	76779
定安县	Dingan	52726	33308	16578	2840	22043	30683
屯昌县	Tunchang	48364	31162	14185	3017	27711	20653
澄迈县	Chengmai	75487	58448	10108	6931	42010	33477
临高县	Lingao	62906	53685	8058	1163	33331	29575
儋州市	Danzhou	156124	124746	30559	819	93798	62326
东方市	Dongfang	73909	60173	10196	3540	47795	26114
乐东县	Ledong	62477	49068	12440	969	29851	32626
琼中县	Qiongzhong	12996	8976	3058	962	7419	5577
保亭县	Baoting	18866	15073	3086	707	9893	8973
陵水县	Lingshui	26154	19746	4942	1466	19102	7052
白沙县	Baisha	15508	13126	1707	675	9681	5827
昌江县	Changjiang	31669	29033	1735	901	23823	7846
农垦系统	Nongken	90681	72417	15585	2679	5127	85554
洋浦	Yangpu	15077	10263	4814		15077	

13－3 限额以上批发零售贸易业商品购进、销售、库存总额

Total Purchases, Sales and Inventory of Wholesale and Retail Enterprises above Designatal Size

单位:万元 (10 000 yuan)

项 目	Item	法人企业(个) Institutional Unit	产业活动单位(个) Establishments Unit	年末从业人数(人) Employment	购进总额 Total Purchases	进口 Total Exports
总 计	**Total**	**297**	**446**	**17855**	**3671160.3**	**76671.1**
批发业	**Wholesale Trade**	**165**	**234**	**9567**	**3190827.4**	**71731.6**
其中:国有及国有控股	etc: State-owned and state-holding	37	96	5429	1597735.1	8142.9
按登记注册类型分组	**By Types of Registration**					
内资	Domestic Funded	160	195	9151	3064723.7	57530.0
国有	State-owned Enterprises	28	57	2748	752317.3	3061.2
集体	Collective-owned Enterprises	4	4	174	16126.3	2186.1
股份合作	Cooperative Enterprises					
有限责任公司	Limited-liability Companies	81	87	2881	1225930.3	49150.6
国有独资公司	State Sole Funded Corporations					
其他有限责任公司	Other Limited-liability Companies	81	87	2881	1225930.3	49150.6
股份有限公司	Share Holding Ltd. Companies	4	4	2299	628702.3	0.0
私营企业	Private Enterprises	36	36	861	393689.9	3132.1
私营独资	Private-funded Enterprises					
私营合伙	Private Partnership Enterprises					
私营有限责任公司	Private Limited-liability Companies	35	35	784	327052.2	3132.1
私营股份有限公司	Private Share Holding Ltd. Companies	1	1	77	66637.7	
其他	Other Enterprises	7	7	188	47957.6	0.0
港澳台商投资企业	Enterprises with Funds from Hong Kong Macao and Taiwan	3	7	264	68156.4	14201.6
港澳台商独资	Enterprises with Sole Investment	2	4	178	64517.4	14201.6
外商投资企业	Foreign Investment Enterprises	2	32	152	57947.3	
中外合资经营	Cooperative Enterprises	1	1	23	12469.3	
外资企业	Enterprises with Sole Foreign Investment	1	31	129	45478.0	
按国民经济行业分组	By Sector					
农畜产品批发业	Wholesale Trade for Live stock	1	1	6	9715.8	
食品、饮料及烟草制品批发业	Wholesale Trade for Food Beverages and Tobaccos Products	14	43	1993	666150.3	2971.0
米、面制品及食用油批发业	Wholesale Trade for Rice Flour and Edible Oil	6	19	594	44665.8	2971.0
烟草制品批发业	Wholesale Trade for Tobaccos Products	6	20	1263	612364.4	
纺织、服装及日用品批发业	Wholesale Trade for Textiles Garments Daily Sundry Articles	13	13	223	66248.5	136.1
服装批发业	Wholesale Trade for Garments	8	8	95	46634.0	136.1
文化、体育用品及器材批发业	Wholesale Trade for Culture Sports and Equipment	7	7	475	35284.1	
医药及医疗器材批发业	Wholesale Trade for Medicines and Medical Appliances	49	53	2530	246477.0	21821.9
矿产品、建材及化工产品批发业	Wholesale Trade for Mineral Products Building Materials and Chemical Products	53	85	3455	1407440.9	42904.3
煤炭及制品批发业	Wholesale Trade for Coal and Related Products	4	4	135	79268.7	
石油及制品批发业	Wholesale Trade for Petroleum and Related Products	13	13	2582	859684.4	29951.8
金属及金属矿批发业	Wholesale Trade for Metal and Metal Products	8	8	78	33942.3	169.8
建材批发业	Wholesale Trade for Building materials	6	8	115	18822.2	0.0
化肥批发业	Wholesale Trade for Chemical Fertilizer	6	36	319	72963.8	11984.9
机械设备、五金交电及电子产品批发业	Wholesale Trade or Machinery Equipment Hardware Transport Electric and Electronic Products	23	25	694	725459.1	3639.3
汽车、摩托车及零配件批发业	Wholesale Trade for Spare and Component Parts for Motor vehicles Motorcycles	4	4	153	666872.2	1527.7
家用电器批发业	Wholesale Trade for Household Appliances	2	4	156	16077.7	
计算机、软件及辅助设备批发业	Wholesale Trade for Computers Software and Supplementary Equipment	3	3	153	14141.6	
其他批发业	Others	5	7	191	34051.7	259.0

13-3 续 1(continued1)

项　目	Item	法人企业(个) Institutional Unit	产业活动单位(个) Establishments Unit	年末从业人数(人) Employment	购进总额 Total Purchases	进　口 Total Exports
零售业	**Retail Trade**	132	212	8288	480332.9	4939.5
其中:国有及国有控股	etc: State-owned and state-holding	17	34	1239	54059.2	
按登记注册类型分组	**By Types of Registration**					
内资	Domestic Funded	129	208	7768	456286.3	4939.5
国有	State-owned Enterprises	6	7	667	17628.9	
集体	Collective-owned Enterprises	2	2	20	2186.1	
有限责任公司	Limited-liability Companies	80	138	4514	230456.7	
其他有限责任公司	Other Limited-liability Companies	79	137	4510	230245.9	
股份有限公司	Share Holding Ltd. Companies	3	3	545	34817.8	37.5
私营企业	Private Enterprises	35	54	1748	157159.2	4902.0
私营合伙	Private Partnership Enterprises	2	2	26	3906.8	
私营有限责任公司	Private Limited-liability Companies	27	46	1247	141080.0	4902.0
私营股份有限公司	Private Share Holding Ltd. Companies	5	5	465	11093.6	
其他	Other Enterprises	3	4	274	14037.6	
港澳台商投资企业	Enterprises with Funds from Hong Kong Macao and Taiwan	2	2	54	15019.0	
港澳台商独资	Enterprises with Sole Investment	2	2	54	15019.0	
外商投资企业	Foreign Investment Enterprises	1	2	466	9027.6	
中外合作经营	Cooperative Enterprises		1	26	4449.0	
按国民经济行业分组	**By Sector**					
综合零售业	Comprehensive Retail Sale Trade	29	35	3210	109303.0	
百货零售业	Retail Sale Trade for Daily Use Article	25	27	2897	94914.0	
超级市场零售业	Retail Sale Trade for Suppmarkets	3	7	300	13617.6	
食品、饮料及烟草制品专门零售业	Retail Sale Trade for Food Beverages and Tobaccos Products	4	7	480	8778.3	
纺织、服装及日用品专门零售业	Retail Sale Trade for Textiles Garments Daily Sundry Articles	6	21	900	31530.2	
服装零售业	Retail sale Trade for Clothing	5	19	834	25568.5	
文化、体育用品及器材专门零售业	Retail Sale Trade for Culture Sports and Equipment	8	9	586	7270.5	
图书零售业	Retail Sale Trade for Books	2	2	197	3214.0	
医药及医疗器材专门零售业	Retail Sale Trade for Medicines and Medical Appliances	3	38	174	796.8	
药品零售业	Retail Sale Trade for Medicines	3	38	174	796.8	
汽车、摩托车、燃料及零配件专门零售业	Retail Sale Trade for Spare and Component Parts for Motor Vehicles Motorcycles and Fuels	55	61	1626	241555.4	4939.5
汽车零售业	Retail Sale Trade for Motor Vehicles	49	53	1449	233800.9	4939.5
机动车燃料零售业	Retail Sale Trade for Fuels for Motordriven Vehicles	6	8	177	7754.5	
家用电器及电子产品专门零售业	Retail Sale Trade for Electrical Household Applianses and Electronic Products	24	38	1268	77842.9	
家用电器零售业	Retail Sale Trade for Electrical Household Applianses	9	11	633	50439.4	
计算机、软件及辅助设备零售业	Retail Sale Trade for Computers Software and Supplementary Equipment	10	11	240	13279.4	
通讯设备零售业	Retail Sale Trade for Telecommunications	3	11	114	9858.8	
五金、家具及室内装修材料专门零售业	Hardware,Electrical Appliance Furniture and Interior Decoration Material	2	2	36	1803.7	
无店铺及其他零售业	Retail Sale Trade for No Shop and Others	1	1	8	1452.1	

13-3 续 2(continued2)

项 目	Item	销售总额 Total Sales	批发 Wholesale Trade	出口 Total Exports	零售 Retail Trade	年末库存总额 Inventory (year-end)
总计	**Total**	**4055784.3**	**3089450.5**	**195243.6**	**966333.8**	**209525.6**
批发业	**Wholesale Trade**	**3556166.6**	**3067196.9**	**195243.6**	**488969.7**	**137146.7**
其中:国有及国有控股	etc: State-owned and state-holding	1795078.1	1324128.4	43431.7	470949.7	70681.1
按登记注册类型分组	**By Types of Registration**					
内资	Domestic Funded	3407923.4	2921738.2	195243.6	486185.2	132366.9
国有	State-owned Enterprises	887370.1	880216.3	43431.7	7153.8	42700.7
集体	Collective-owned Enterprises	17390.4	17054.1		336.3	1695.0
股份合作	Cooperative Enterprises					
有限责任公司	Limited-liability Companies	1340363.6	1251654.8	100069.1	88708.8	55888.2
国有独资公司	State Sole Funded Corporations					
其他有限责任公司	Other Limited-liability Companies	1340363.6	1251654.8	100069.1	88708.8	55888.2
股份有限公司	Share Holding Ltd. Companies	682255.9	294806.3	2647.3	387449.6	16313.8
私营企业	Private Enterprises	429904.0	429145.0	26360.1	759.0	14302.7
私营独资	Private-funded Enterprises					
私营合伙	Private Partnership Enterprises					
私营有限责任公司	Private Limited-liability Companies	352275.3	351516.3	26360.1	759.0	14302.7
私营股份有限公司	Private Share Holding Ltd. Companies	77628.7	77628.7			
其他	Other Enterprises	50639.4	48861.7	22735.4	1777.7	1466.5
港澳台商投资企业	Enterprises with Funds from Hong Kong Macao and Taiwad	88677.0	85892.5		2784.5	4451.6
港澳台商独资	Enterprises with Sole Investment	79438.4	79438.4			4169.6
外商投资企业	Foreign Investment Enterprises	59566.2	59566.2			328.2
中外合作经营	Cooperative Enterprises					
外资企业	Enterprises with Sole Foreign Investment	46839.4	46839.4			
按国民经济行业分组	**By Sector**					
农畜产品批发业	Wholesale Trade for Live stock	10097.2	10097.2			37.2
食品、饮料及烟草制品批发业	Wholesale Trade for Food Beverages and Tobaccos Products	786580.1	783123.5		3456.6	30867.4
米、面制品及食用油批发业	Wholesale Trade for Rice Flour and Edible Oil	67831.9	67792.6		39.3	17948.9
烟草制品批发业	Wholesale Trade for Tobaccos Products	704164.5	700747.2		3417.3	12878.9
纺织、服装及日用品批发业	Wholesale Trade for Textiles Garments Daily Sundry Articles	85330.0	85330.0	68809.5		2027.9
服装批发业	Wholesale Trade for Garments	61826.9	61826.9	52903.9		1676.2
文化、体育用品及器材批发业	Wholesale Trade for Culture Sports and Equipment	41731.1	37773.6	10719.1	3957.5	6968.1
医药及医疗器材批发业	Wholesale Trade for Medicines and Medical Appliances	297465.0	297151.3	94.2	313.7	32068.6
矿产品、建材及化工产品批发业	Wholesale Trade for Mineral Products Building Materials and Chemical Products	1519437.8	1052630.3	78391.4	466807.5	48809.7
煤炭及制品批发业	Wholesale Trade for Coal and Related Products	94948.8	94948.8			919.3
石油及制品批发业	Wholesale Trade for Petroleum and Related Products	921599.7	458140.1	151.6	463459.6	31077.9
金属及金属矿批发业	Wholesale Trade for Metal and Metal Products	52122.1	52122.1	40112.1		3498.1
建材批发业	Wholesale Trade for Building materials	27392.2	24607.7	10668.8	2784.5	590.7
化肥批发业	Wholesale Trade for Chemical Fertilizer	73621.7	73621.7			4926.6
机械设备、五金交电及电子产品批发业	Wholesale Trade for Machinery Equipment Hardware Transport Electric and Electronic Products	781289.8	771305.8	24878.6	9984.0	15263.2
汽车、摩托车及零配件批发业	Wholesale Trade for Spare and Component Parts for Motor vehicles Motorcycles	710837.8	706830.1	5272.6	4007.7	10444.5
家用电器批发业	Wholesale Trade for Household Appliances	20492.7	20492.7	1024.9		1397.4
计算机、软件及辅助设备批发业	Wholesale Trade for Computers Software and Supplementary Equipment	18977.0	15898.1		3078.9	722.0
其他批发业	Others	34235.6	29785.2	12350.8	4450.4	1104.6

13-3 续 3(continued3)

项　目	Item	销售总额 Total Sales	批 发 Wholesale Trade	出 口 Total Exports	零 售 Retail Trade	年末库存总额 Inventory (year-end)
零售业	Retail Trade	499617.7	22253.6		477364.1	72378.9
其中:国有及国有控股	etc: State-owned and state-holding	56456.5	1690.8		54765.7	13676.3
按登记注册类型分组	By Types of Registration					
内资	Domestic Funded	469800.0	21180.6		448619.4	68118.8
国有	State-owned Enterprises	13505.8	1464.3		12041.5	10021.2
集体	Collective-owned Enterprises	2297.9			2297.9	92.1
有限责任公司	Limited-liability Companies	257488.7	7060.7		250428.0	23976.0
其他有限责任公司	Other Limited-liability Companies	257049.2	6834.2		250215.0	23976.0
股份有限公司	Share Holding Ltd. Companies	34973.2			34973.2	10723.4
私营企业	Private Enterprises	150472.9	12655.6		137817.3	19577.1
私营合伙	Private Partnership Enterprises	4136.6			4136.6	173.8
私营有限责任公司	Private Limited-liability Companies	139671.2	12655.6		127015.6	14681.6
私营股份有限公司	Private Share Holding Ltd. Companies	5741.1			5741.1	4566.9
其他	Other Enterprises	11061.5			11061.5	3729.0
港澳台商投资企业	Enterprises with Funds from Hong Kong Macao and Taiwan	20061.0	1073.0		18988.0	2125.8
港澳台商独资	Enterprises with Sole Investment	20061.0	1073.0		18988.0	2125.8
外商投资企业	Foreign Investment Enterprises	9756.7			9756.7	2134.3
中外合作经营	Cooperative Enterprises	6250.8			6250.8	356.3
按国民经济行业分组	By Sector					
综合零售业	Comprehensive Retail Sale Trade	103710.1			103710.1	33925.5
百货零售业	Retail Sale Trade for Daily Use Article	91778.4			91778.4	30788.5
超级市场零售业	Retail Sale Trade for Suppmarkets	10985.9			10985.9	2769.7
食品、饮料及烟草制品专门零售业	Retail Sale Trade for Food Beverages and Tobaccos Products	12008.1	1073.0		10935.1	985.8
纺织、服装及日用品专门零售业	Retail Sale Trade for Textiles Garments Daily Sundry Articles	31921.9			31921.9	2948.6
服装零售业	Retail sale Trade for Clothing	24158.4			24158.4	2481.5
文化、体育用品及器材专门零售业	Retail Sale Trade for Culture Sports and Equipment	9515.0	1464.3		8050.7	2501.8
图书零售业	Retail Sale Trade for Books	4429.5			4429.5	1307.0
医药及医疗器材专门零售业	Retail Sale Trade for Medicines and Medical Appliances	1385.6			1385.6	262.8
药品零售业	Retail Sale Trade for Medicines	1385.6			1385.6	262.8
汽车、摩托车、燃料及零配件专门零售业	Retail Sale Trade for Spare and Component Parts for Motor Vehicles Motorcycles and Fuels	258793.6	15041.3		243752.3	19993.8
汽车零售业	Retail Sale Trade for Motor Vehicles	247346.0	15041.3		232304.7	19776.4
机动车燃料零售业	Retail Sale Trade for Fuels for Motordriven Vehicles	11447.6			11447.6	217.4
家用电器及电子产品专门零售业	Retail Sale Trade for Electrical Household Applianses and Electronic Products	78633.7	4675.0		73958.7	11293.3
家用电器零售业	Retail Sale Trade for Electrical Household Applianses	49094.8	712.1		48382.7	8028.1
计算机、软件及辅助设备零售业	Retail Sale Trade for Computers Software and Supplementary Equipment	13701.4	253.5		13447.9	2003.2
通讯设备零售业	Retail Sale Trade for Telecommunications	9667.8	3709.4		5958.4	821.3
五金、家具及室内装修材料专门零售业	Hardware,Electrical Appliance Furniture and Interior Decoration Material	2149.5			2149.5	314.6
无店铺及其他零售业	Retail Sale Trade for No Shop and Others	1500.2			1500.2	152.7

13－4 星级住宿业和限额以上餐饮业经营情况

Operating Condition of Grade Lodgings Trade and Catering Trade above Desingnated Size

单位:万元 (10000 yuan)

项目	Item	法人企业(个) Institutional Unit	产业活动单位(个) Establishments Unit	从业人数(人) Employment	年末餐饮营业面积(万平方米) Business area of catering at the year-end (10000sq.m)	年末住宿和餐饮企业拥有床位数(万个) The beds of enterprises in catering services and hotel services at the year-end (10000 units)	年末住宿和餐饮企业拥有餐位数(万位) The seats of enterprises incatering services and hotel services at the year-end (10000 units)
总计	Total	296	350	42473	32.5	8.6	11.0
住宿业	Hotel Services	254	289	37597	22.0	8.6	8.2
其中:国有及国有控股	etc: State-owned and state-holding	93	105	14978	8.2	2.9	3.5
按登记注册类型分组	By Types of Registration						
内资	Domestic Funded	223	249	27833	16.2	7.2	6.2
国有	State-owned Enterprises	57	66	6787	3.2	1.4	1.4
集体	Collective-owned Enterprises	8	8	319	0.1	0.1	0.1
股份合作	Cooperative Enterprises	7	8	1010	1.5	1.0	0.5
联营企业	Joint Ownership Enterprises	8	8	786	0.4	0.2	0.2
国有联营	State Joint Ownership Enterprises	4	4	246	0.1	0.1	0.1
国有与集体联营	Collective Joint Ownership Enterprises	3	3	522	0.4	0.1	0.1
有限责任公司	Limited-liability Companies	54	63	9766	6.7	2.0	2.1
国有独资公司	State Sole Funded Corporations						
其他有限责任公司	Other Limited-liability Companies	54	63	9766	6.7	2.0	2.1
股份有限公司	Share Holding Ltd. Companies	20	20	2504	1.0	0.5	0.5
私营企业	Private Enterprises	65	70	6066	3.1	1.8	1.3
私营独资	Private-funded Enterprises	13	14	883	0.4	0.2	0.3
私营合伙	Private Partnership Enterprises	5	5	869	0.1	0.2	0.1
私营有限责任公司	Private Limited-liability Companies	42	46	4003	2.5	1.3	0.9
私营股份有限公司	Private Share Holding Ltd. Companies	5	5	311	0.1	0.1	0.1
其他	Other Enterprises	4	6	595	0.1	0.1	0.1
港澳台商投资企业	Enterprises with Funds from Hong Kong Macao and Taiwan	15	18	4311	2.4	0.6	0.9
与港澳台商合资经营	Joint-venture Enterprises	6	7	3144	1.6	0.4	0.6
与港澳台商合作经营	Cooperative Enterprises						
港澳台商独资	Enterprises with Sole Investment	8	10	1142	0.8	0.2	0.3
外商投资企业	Foreign Investment Enterprises	16	22	5453	3.4	0.7	1.1
中外合资经营	Joint-venture Enterprises	10	15	4142	2.4	0.5	0.8
中外合作经营	Cooperative Enterprises	1	1	104	0.3		
外资企业	Enterprises with Sole Foreign Investment	5	6	1207	0.8	0.2	0.2
按国民经济行业分组	By Sector						
旅游饭店	Tourism Hotel	247	282	37334	22.0	8.3	8.1
一般旅馆	General Hotel	7	7	263	0.1	0.3	0.1

13-4 续 1(continued1)

项 目	Item	营业额 turnover	客房收入 rooms income	餐费收入 meals income	商品销售收入 Sales Revenue	其他收入 other revenue
总 计	**Total**	**373335.1**	**189287.6**	**146899.0**	**5224.7**	**31923.8**
住宿业	**Hotel Services**	**320649.5**	**188740.7**	**97514.9**	**3984.4**	**30409.5**
其中:国有及国有控股	etc: State-owned and state-holding	154669.2	91786.4	49584.4	1083.7	12214.7
按登记注册类型分组	**By Types of Registration**					
内资	Domestic Funded	194146.8	113555.2	61209.2	2020.4	17362.0
国有	State-owned Enterprises	48588.3	29087.0	14833.2	371.6	4296.5
集体	Collective-owned Enterprises	1261.5	995.4	192.0		74.1
股份合作	Cooperative Enterprises	9521.4	6388.8	2778.5		354.1
联营企业	Joint Ownership Enterprises	20064.5	11322.1	5483.4	3.2	3255.8
国有联营	State Joint Ownership Enterprises	712.6	461.6	228.3		22.7
国有与集体联营	Collective Joint Ownership Enterprises	19256.7	10787.0	5247.6		3222.1
有限责任公司	Limited-liability Companies	71789.8	40588.2	24213.2	411.5	6576.9
国有独资公司	State Sole Funded Corporations					
其他有限责任公司	Other Limited-liability Companies	71789.8	40588.2	24213.2	411.5	6576.9
股份有限公司	Share Holding Ltd. Companies	14571.9	7919.5	5150.4	143.4	1358.6
私营企业	Private Enterprises	25222.6	15059.4	8155.4	1090.7	917.1
私营独资	Private-funded Enterprises	2591.7	1414.1	1084.6	34.6	58.4
私营合伙	Private Partnership Enterprises	2308.6	1382.1	853.6	14.9	58.0
私营有限责任公司	Private Limited-liability Companies	19295.4	11552.7	6006.3	1028.6	707.8
私营股份有限公司	Private Share Holding Ltd. Companies	1026.9	710.5	210.9	12.6	92.9
其他	Other Enterprises	3126.8	2194.8	403.1		528.9
港澳台商投资企业	Enterprises with Funds from Hong Kong Macao and Taiwan	50220.5	27886.0	14986.7	1354.4	5993.4
与港澳台商合资经营	Joint-venture Enterprises	35880.0	20749.6	11486.6	1081.7	2562.1
与港澳台商合作经营	Cooperative Enterprises	110.7	110.7			
港澳台商独资	Enterprises with Sole Investment	14229.8	7025.7	3500.1	272.7	3431.3
外商投资企业	Foreign Investment Enterprises	76282.2	47299.5	21319.0	609.6	7054.1
中外合资经营	Joint-venture Enterprises	57213.0	37095.2	17020.6	495.0	2602.2
中外合作经营	Cooperative Enterprises	472.5	310.0	145.4	2.8	14.3
外资企业	Enterprises with Sole Foreign Investment	18596.7	9894.3	4153.0	111.8	4437.6
按国民经济行业分组	**By Sector**					
旅游饭店	Tourism Hotel	319187.8	188205.4	97115.3	3980.2	29886.9
一般旅馆	General Hotel	1461.7	535.3	399.6	4.2	522.6

13-4 续 2(continued2)

项　目	Item	法人企业（个）Institutional Unit	产业活动单位（个）Establishments Unit	从业人数（个）Employment (unit)	年末餐饮营业面积(万平方米) Business area of catering at the year-end (10000sq.m)	年末住宿和餐饮企业拥有餐位数（万位）The seats of enterprises in catering services and hotel services at the year-end (10000 units)
餐饮业	Catering Services	42	61	4876	10.4	2.8
其中:国有及国有控股	etc: State-owned and state-holding	1	1	56	0.1	
按登记注册类型分组	By Types of Registration					
内资	Domestic Funded	37	49	3729	9.5	2.5
国有	State-owned Enterprises					
集体	Collective-owned Enterprises	1	1	106	0.1	
股份合作	Cooperative Enterprises	1	1	87	0.2	
有限责任公司	Limited-liability Companies	7	10	786	2.2	0.9
其他有限责任公司	Other Limited-liability Companies	7	10	786	2.2	0.9
股份有限公司	Share Holding Ltd. Companies	2	2	69	0.3	0.1
私营企业	Private Enterprises	20	29	2038	4.8	1.2
私营独资	Private-funded Enterprises	5	10	628	1.0	0.4
私营合伙	Private Partnership Enterprises	1	1	268	0.3	0.1
私营有限责任公司	Private Limited-liability Companies	12	14	916	3.2	0.6
私营股份有限公司	Private Share Holding Ltd. Companies	2	4	226	0.3	0.1
其他	Other Enterprises	6	6	643	1.9	0.2
港澳台商投资企业	Enterprises with Funds from Hong Kong Macao and Taiwan	3	6	296	0.5	0.1
港澳台商独资	Enterprises with Sole Investment	3	6	296	0.5	0.1
外商投资企业	Foreign Investment Enterprises	2	6	851	0.4	0.2
中外合资经营	Joint-venture Enterprises	1	1	127	0.1	
外资企业	Enterprises with Sole Foreign Investment	1	4	663	0.2	
按国民经济行业分组	By Sector					0.2
正餐服务业	Dinner	41	58	4267	10.2	2.7
快餐服务业	Fast Food	1	3	609	0.2	0.1
饮料及冷饮服务业	Beverages					

13-4 续 3(continued3)

项　目	Item	营业额	客房收入 rooms income	餐费收入 meals income	商品销售收入 Sales Revenue	其他收入 other revenue
餐饮业	Catering Services	52685.6	546.9	49384.1	1240.3	1514.3
其中:国有及国有控股	etc: State-owned and state-holding	449.4		449.4		
按登记注册类型分组	By Types of Registration					
内资	Domestic Funded	36742.0	546.9	34928.4	1240.3	26.4
国有	State-owned Enterprises					
集体	Collective-owned Enterprises	1011.5		1011.5		
股份合作	Cooperative Enterprises	624.6		624.6		
有限责任公司	Limited-liability Companies	5790.9		5769.0		21.9
其他有限责任公司	Other Limited-liability Companies	5790.9		5769.0		21.9
股份有限公司	Share Holding Ltd. Companies	1757.1	174.0	1582.8		0.3
私营企业	Private Enterprises	20563.8	372.9	19118.9	1072.0	
私营独资	Private-funded Enterprises	6529.1	372.9	6146.2	10.0	
私营合伙	Private Partnership Enterprises	2310.4		2310.4		
私营有限责任公司	Private Limited-liability Companies	8281.1		8281.1		
私营股份有限公司	Private Share Holding Ltd. Companies	3443.2		2381.2	1062.0	
其他	Other Enterprises	6994.1		6821.6	168.3	4.2
港澳台商投资企业	Enterprises with Funds from Hong Kong Macao and Taiwan	3388.2		3378.3		9.9
港澳台商独资	Enterprises with Sole Investment	3388.2		3378.3		9.9
外商投资企业	Foreign Investment Enterprises	12555.4		11077.4		1478.0
中外合资经营	Joint-venture Enterprises	2697.8		1219.8		1478.0
外资企业	Enterprises with Sole Foreign Investment	8914.7		8914.7		
按国民经济行业分组	By Sector					
正餐服务业	Dinner	45508.6	546.9	42207.1	1240.3	1514.3
快餐服务业	Fast Food	7177.0		7177.0		
饮料及冷饮服务业	Beverages					

13－5 限额以上批发和零售业企业财务状况

Financial Condition of Large-scale and Medium-scale Enter Prises in Wholesale ad Retail Trade

单位:万元 (10000 yuan)

项 目	Item	法人企业(个) Institutional Unit	产业活动单位(个) Establishments Unit	年末从业人数(人) Employment	购进总额 Total Purchases	进口 Total Exports
总 计	Total	297	136	1062504.8	195469.9	399386.0
批发业	Wholesale Trade	165	62	879377.3	137239.7	292081.2
其中:国有及国有控股	etc: State-owned and state-holding	37	7	333424.7	65515.4	269991.7
按登记注册类型分组	By Types of Registration					
内资	Domestic Funded	160	61	795851.6	132679.0	288538.9
国有	State-owned Enterprises	28	6	221149.3	37849.3	77475.5
集体	Collective-owned Enterprises	4	2	12620.8	1227.9	3328.1
股份合作	Cooperative Enterprises					
有限责任公司	Limited-liability Companies	81	37	405523.9	58731.5	52960.0
国有独资公司	State Sole Funded Corporations					
其他有限责任公司	Other Limited-liability Companies	81	81	81	81	81
股份有限公司	Share Holding Ltd. Companies	4	4	4	4	4
私营企业	Private Enterprises	36	36	36	36	36
私营独资	Private-funded Enterprises					
私营合伙	Private Partnership Enterprises					
私营有限责任公司	Private Limited-liability Companies	35	35	35	35	35
私营股份有限公司	Private Share Holding Ltd. Companies	1	1	1	1	1
其他	Other Enterprises	7	7	7	7	7
港澳台商投资企业	Enterprises with Funds from Hong Kong Macao and Taiwan	3	3	3	3	3
港澳台商独资	Enterprises with Sole Investment	2		31304.3	4169.6	495.4
按国民经济行业分组	By Sector					
农畜产品批发业	Wholesale Trade for Live stock	1		2183.5	37.4	19.4
食品、饮料及烟草制品批发业	Wholesale Trade for Food Beverages and Tobaccos Products	14	2	155330.9	28840.2	61597.2
米、面制品及食用油批发业	Wholesale Trade for Rice Flour and Edible Oil	6	2	51900.0	17945.6	11832.1
烟草制品批发业	Wholesale Trade for Tobaccos Products	6		101605.2	10786.5	49721.8
纺织、服装及日用品批发业	Wholesale Trade for Textiles Garments Daily Sundry Articles	13	9	32623.5	2185.0	2396.0
服装批发业	Wholesale Trade for Garments	8	5	25303.3	1766.5	1829.9
文化、体育用品及器材批发业	Wholesale Trade for Culture Sports and Equipment	7	1	13505.7	3444.1	7151.9
医药及医疗器材批发业	Wholesale Trade for Medicines and Medical Appliances	49	16	157356.5	31657.9	7317.1
矿产品、建材及化工产品批发业	Wholesale Trade for Mineral Products Building Materials and Chemical Products	53	20	264207.1	52055.2	207087.1
煤炭及制品批发业	Wholesale Trade for Coal and Related Products	4	1	34026.9	3632.2	1677.8
石油及制品批发业	Wholesale Trade for Petroleum and Related Products	13	3	86151.3	31383.6	195328.8
金属及金属矿批发业	Wholesale Trade for Metal and Metal Products	8	5	25237.6	3445.1	1587.1
建材批发业	Wholesale Trade for Building materials	6	4	7089.0	591.7	2307.8
化肥批发业	Wholesale Trade for Chemical Fertilizer	6	2	63787.6	4957.0	3633.5
机械设备、五金交电及电子产品批发业	Wholesale Trade for Machinery Equipment Hardware Transport Electric and Electronic Products	23	11	227111.0	17869.8	1431.8
汽车、摩托车及零配件批发业	Wholesale Trade for Spare and Component Parts for Motor vehicles Motorcycles	4	3	146543.0	9473.2	198.9
家用电器批发业	Wholesale Trade for Household Appliances	2	1	16331.0	1121.8	107.8
计算机、软件及辅助设备批发业	Wholesale Trade for Computers Software and Supplementary Equipment	3	1	6525.9	4930.1	69.0
其他批发业	Others	5	3	27059.1	1150.1	5080.7

13-5 续 1(continued1)

项　目	Item	企业数(个) Number of Enterprises (unit)	亏损企业数(个) Number of loss Making Industrial Enterprises(unit)	流动资产合计 Total Circulating Funds	存货 Inventory	固定资产原价 Original Value of Fixed Assets
零售业	**Retail Trade**	**132**	**74**	**183127.5**	**58230.2**	**107304.8**
其中:国有及国有控股	etc: State-owned and state-holding	17	10	47445.8	17812.7	18453.1
按登记注册类型分组	**By Types of Registration**					
内资	Domestic Funded	129	74	175437.3	54492.9	102726.8
国有	State-owned Enterprises	6	3	4434.5	1094.8	2335.1
集体	Collective-owned Enterprises	2	1	378.7	92.1	170.4
有限责任公司	Limited-liability Companies	80	47	111626.9	34086.9	44604.0
其他有限责任公司		79	46	111614.2	34086.9	44604.0
股份有限公司	Share Holding Ltd. Companies	3	2	7877.0	1658.7	39075.6
私营企业	Private Enterprises	35	19	45416.4	14439.6	12091.1
私营合伙	Private Partnership Enterprises	2		1538.4	138.1	20.2
私营有限责任公司	Private Limited-liability Companies	27	14	39606.6	12937.7	11818.9
私营股份有限公司	Private Share Holding Ltd. Companies	5	4	3225.1	1209.0	246.2
其他	Other Enterprises	3	2	5703.8	3120.8	4450.6
港澳台商投资企业	Enterprises with Funds from Hong Kong Macao and Taiwan	2		5407.2	2125.8	497.2
港澳台商独资	Enterprises with Sole Investment	2		5407.2	2125.8	497.2
按国民经济行业分组						
综合零售业	Comprehensive Retail Sale Trade	29	21	41161.5	10206.5	75442.8
百货零售业	Retail Sale Trade for Daily Use Article	25	17	34823.2	6865.3	70694.5
超级市场零售业	Retail Sale Trade for Suppmarkets	3	3	5663.8	2973.9	4712.9
食品、饮料及烟草制品专门零售业	Retail Sale Trade for Food Beverages and Tobaccos Products	4	2	3180.4	1077.3	1874.5
纺织、服装及日用品专门零售业	Retail Sale Trade for Textiles Garments Daily Sundry Articles	6	4	24236.8	13675.7	2838.6
服装零售业	Retail sale Trade for Clothing	5	3	23696.6	13564.9	2551.7
文化、体育用品及器材专门零售业	Retail Sale Trade for Culture Sports and Equipment	8	4	9408.2	2454.2	13036.3
图书零售业	Retail Sale Trade for Books	2	1	5529.0	1232.7	9193.3
医药及医疗器材专门零售业	Retail Sale Trade for Medicines and Medical Appliances	3	3	3172.5	827.4	225.4
药品零售业	Retail Sale Trade for Medicines	3	3	3172.5	827.4	225.4
汽车、摩托车、燃料及零配件专门零售业	Retail Sale Trade for Spare and Component Partsfor Motor Vehicles Motorcycles and Fuels	55	26	80458.8	21100.4	12860.2
汽车零售业	Retail Sale Trade for Motor Vehicles	49	24	77947.9	20918.6	8525.3
机动车燃料零售业	Retail Sale Trade for Fuels for Motordriven Vehicles	6	2	2510.9	181.8	4334.9
家用电器及电子产品专门零售业	Retail Sale Trade for Electrical Household Appliances and Electronic Products	24	13	20183.6	8421.4	862.6
家用电器零售业	Retail Sale Trade for Electrical Household Appliances	9	6	11713.6	5239.6	188.6
计算机、软件及辅助设备零售业	Retail Sale Trade for Computers Software and Supplementary Equipment	10	4	5282.8	2003.2	262.2
通讯设备零售业	Retail Sale Trade for Telecommunications	3	2	1871.3	871.8	46.1
五金、家具及室内装修材料专门零售业	Hardware, Electrical Appliance Furniture and Interior Decoration Material	2	1	873.0	314.6	148.0
无店铺及其他零售业	Retail Sale Trade for No Shop and Others	1		452.7	152.7	16.4

13-5 续 2(continued2)

项目	Item	累计折旧 Total depreciation Drawn Accumulated	本年折旧 Drawn Accumulated This Year	资产合计 Total Assets	负债合计 Total Liabilities	所有者权益合计 Total Greditors Equity
总计	**Total**	**105002.5**	**13499.4**	**1507501.6**	**962361.8**	**545139.8**
批发业	**Wholesale Trade**	**82781.6**	**8090.5**	**1217169.7**	**741928.1**	**475241.6**
其中:国有及国有控股	etc: State-owned and state-holding	75897.2	6603.1	617856.1	294329.8	323526.3
按登记注册类型分组	**By Types of Registration**					
内资	Domestic Funded	81657.8	8061.4	1129853.4	674476.8	455376.6
国有	State-owned Enterprises	21952.8	3216.0	336831.5	185114.9	151716.6
集体	Collective-owned Enterprises	664.0	-23.0	17855.5	12283.9	5571.6
股份合作	Cooperative Enterprises					
有限责任公司	Limited-liability Companies	20057.7	3012.6	472481.1	358309.1	114172.0
国有独资公司	State Sole Funded Corporations					
其他有限责任公司	Other Limited-liability Companies	20057.7	3012.6	472481.1	358309.1	114172.0
股份有限公司	Share Holding Ltd. Companies	37341.4	1279.2	172075.1	41267.3	130807.8
私营企业	Private Enterprises	1227.8	365.0	109973.1	60276.5	49696.6
私营独资	Private-funded Enterprises					
私营合伙	Private Partnership Enterprises					
私营有限责任公司	Private Limited-liability Companies	1061.1	365.0	80482.0	58765.7	21716.3
私营股份有限公司	Private Share Holding Ltd. Companies	166.7	0.0	29491.1	1510.8	27980.3
其他	Other Enterprises	414.1	211.6	20637.1	17225.1	3412.0
港澳台商投资企业	Enterprises with Funds from Hong Kong Macao and Taiwan	113.4	19.0	32784.3	17853.8	14930.5
港澳台商独资	Enterprises with Sole Investment	97.0	18.9	31789.5	16712.3	15077.2
按国民经济行业分组	**By Sector**					
农畜产品批发业	Wholesale Trade for Live stock	14.8	5.2	2240.1	1596.1	644.0
食品、饮料及烟草制品批发业	Wholesale Trade for Food Beverages and Tobaccos Products	17238.9	2433.9	245708.8	108193.0	137515.8
米、面制品及食用油批发业	Wholesale Trade for Rice Flour and Edible Oil	3722.5	278.0	63559.0	64877.6	-1318.6
烟草制品批发业	Wholesale Trade for Tobaccos Products	13481.2	2148.4	180316.0	41702.9	138613.1
纺织、服装及日用品批发业	Wholesale Trade for Textiles Garments Daily Sundry Articles	1345.9	243.4	36227.0	28519.0	7708.0
服装批发业	Wholesale Trade for Garments	1105.2	187.6	28538.9	22698.5	5840.4
文化、体育用品及器材批发业	Wholesale Trade for Culture Sports and Equipment	1319.2	379.8	19571.7	14867.2	4704.5
医药及医疗器材批发业	Wholesale Trade for Medicines and Medical Appliances	3566.0	806.4	177340.6	126331.9	51008.7
矿产品、建材及化工产品批发业	Wholesale Trade for Mineral Products Building Materials and Chemical Products	57611.5	3947.3	457324.6	218321.4	239003.2
煤炭及制品批发业	Wholesale Trade for Coal and Related Products	365.5	6.0	37720.4	5863.3	31857.1
石油及制品批发业	Wholesale Trade for Petroleum and Related Products	54432.9	3428.3	257309.4	79132.1	178177.3
金属及金属矿批发业	Wholesale Trade for Metal and Metal Products	689.9	103.3	28417.2	15969.4	12447.8
建材批发业	Wholesale Trade for Building materials	595.4	229.0	10078.2	10429.2	-351.0
化肥批发业	Wholesale Trade for Chemical Fertilizer	850.9	-15.2	69802.8	63351.8	6451.0
机械设备、五金交电及电子产品批发业	Wholesale Trade for Machinery Equipment Hardware Transport Electric and Electronic Products	562.7	158.8	232475.3	212642.4	19832.9
汽车、摩托车及零配件批发业	Wholesale Trade for Spare and Component Parts for Motor vehicles Motorcycles	133.5	34.6	148681.0	137529.5	11151.5
家用电器批发业	Wholesale Trade for Household Appliances	25.5	14.5	16415.8	15919.2	496.6
计算机、软件及辅助设备批发业	Wholesale Trade for Computers Software and Supplementary Equipment	27.1	6.1	6639.4	5807.3	832.1
其他批发业	Others	1122.6	115.7	46281.6	31457.1	14824.5

13-5 续 3(continued3)

项　目	Item	累计折旧 Total depreciation Drawn Accumulated	本年折旧 Drawn Accumulated This Year	资产合计 Total Assets	负债合计 Total Liabilities	所有者权益合计 Total Greditors Equity
零售业	**Retail Trade**	**22220.9**	**5408.9**	**290331.9**	**220433.7**	**69898.2**
其中:国有及国有控股	etc: State-owned and state-holding	4043.3	867.6	69112.9	59575.2	9537.7
按登记注册类型分组	**By Types of Registration**					
内资	Domestic Funded	21886.2	5332.2	278327.0	211134.8	67192.2
国有	State-owned Enterprises	357.6	42.5	6966.9	4965.0	2001.9
集体	Collective-owned Enterprises	91.7	18.9	526.1	276.0	250.1
有限责任公司	Limited-liability Companies	12190.3	3526.1	162450.0	122055.5	40394.5
其他有限责任公司	Other Limited-liability Companies	12190.3	3526.1	162437.3	121994.3	40443.0
股份有限公司	Share Holding Ltd. Companies	6753.8	966.3	40821.0	30023.3	10797.7
私营企业	Private Enterprises	2393.6	679.4	57290.7	43439.3	13851.4
私营合伙	Private Partnership Enterprises	11.6	3.8	2467.3	1399.2	1068.1
私营有限责任公司	Private Limited-liability Companies	2294.6	661.2	50178.9	38843.9	11335.0
私营股份有限公司	Private Share Holding Ltd. Companies	82.8	12.8	3597.0	3115.1	481.9
其他	Other Enterprises	99.2	99.0	10272.3	10375.7	-103.4
港澳台商投资企业	Enterprises with Funds from Hong Kong Macao and Taiwan	290.3	32.3	5664.0	3320.8	2343.2
港澳台商独资	Enterprises with Sole Investment	290.3	32.3	5664.0	3320.8	2343.2
按国民经济行业分组	**By Sector**					
综合零售业	Comprehensive Retail Sale Trade	14484.7	3434.4	110570.0	91251.9	19318.1
百货零售业	Retail Sale Trade for Daily Use Article	14250.1	3297.1	99491.9	80063.4	19428.5
超级市场零售业	Retail Sale Trade for Suppmarkets	207.9	133.3	10393.3	10380.5	12.8
食品、饮料及烟草制品专门零售业	Retail Sale Trade for Food Beverages and Tobaccos Products	340.1	51.2	4723.9	3121.9	1602.0
纺织、服装及日用品专门零售业	Retail Sale Trade for Textiles Garments Daily Sundry Articles	1389.4	175.3	25795.0	22597.2	3197.8
服装零售业	Retail sale Trade for Clothing	1107.9	174.7	25198.5	21912.4	3286.1
文化、体育用品及器材专门零售业	Retail Sale Trade for Culture Sports and Equipment	2548.5	527.4	21962.5	16224.8	5737.7
图书零售业	Retail Sale Trade for Books	1874.2	414.7	13571.3	13995.5	-424.2
医药及医疗器材专门零售业	Retail Sale Trade for Medicines and Medical Appliances	99.5	0.0	3358.4	4340.3	-981.9
药品零售业	Retail Sale Trade for Medicines	99.5	0.0	3358.4	4340.3	-981.9
汽车、摩托车、燃料及零配件专门零售业	Retail Sale Trade for Spare and Component Parts for Motor Vehicles Motorcycles and Fuels	2908.3	955.6	101020.9	65445.7	35575.2
汽车零售业	Retail Sale Trade for Motor Vehicles	2292.3	706.1	93549.9	62921.9	30628.0
机动车燃料零售业	Retail Sale Trade for Fuels for Motordriven Vehicles	616.0	249.5	7471.0	2523.8	4947.2
家用电器及电子产品专门零售业	Retail Sale Trade for Electrical Household Applianses and Electronic Products	432.3	261.9	21429.1	16487.3	4941.8
家用电器零售业	Retail Sale Trade for Electrical Household Applianses	78.3	28.8	12560.2	10609.9	1950.3
计算机、软件及辅助设备零售业	Retail Sale Trade for Computers Software and Supplementary Equipment	136.9	31.8	5436.1	3864.5	1571.6
通讯设备零售业	Retail Sale Trade for Telecommunications	18.4	8.7	1929.0	1067.6	861.4
五金、家具及室内装修材料专门零售业	Hardware,Electrical Appliance Furniture and Interior Decoration Material	13.5	1.0	1007.6	832.6	175.0
无店铺及其他零售业	Retail Sale Trade for No Shop and Others	4.6	2.1	464.5	132.0	332.5

13-5 续 4(continued4)

项 目	Item	实收资本 Capital Hold	国家资本 Nation Capital	集体资本 collective-owned capital	法人资本 institutional capital	个人资本 individual capital	港澳台资本 Hong Kong Macao and Taiwan capital
总 计	**Total**	**335669.4**	**157862.2**	**5262.8**	**88341.0**	**65702.8**	**12512.5**
批发业	**Wholesale Trade**	**256267.8**	**154358.1**	**3362.8**	**48517.3**	**37857.0**	**11051.2**
其中:国有及国有控股	etc: State-owned and state-holding	172880.0	150715.1		20842.4	201.1	
按登记注册类型分组	**By Types of Registration**						
内资	Domestic Funded	242403.7	154358.1	3362.8	46825.8	37857.0	
国有	State-owned Enterprises	31249.5	24019.2		7220.3	10.0	
集体	Collective-owned Enterprises	4314.1	3798.6	500.0		15.5	
股份合作	Cooperative Enterprises						
有限责任公司	Limited-liability Companies	60936.1	2475.0	2862.8	34209.3	21389.0	
国有独资公司	State Sole Funded Corporations						
其他有限责任公司	Other Limited-liability Companies	60936.1	2475.0	2862.8	34209.3	21389.0	
股份有限公司	Share Holding Ltd. Companies	127733.0	124065.3		3446.6	221.1	
私营企业	Private Enterprises	15923.0			897.0	15026.0	
私营独资	Private-funded Enterprises	14923.0			897.0	14026.0	
私营合伙	Private Partnership Enterprises	1000.0			0.0	1000.0	
私营有限责任公司	Private Limited-liability Companies	2248.0			1052.6	1195.4	
私营股份有限公司	Private Share Holding Ltd. Companies	11372.2			321.0		11051.2
其他	Other Enterprises	2248.0			1052.6	1195.4	0.0
港澳台商投资企业	Enterprises with Funds from Hong Kong Macao and Taiwan	11372.2			321.0		11051.2
港澳台商独资	Enterprises with Sole Investment	11051.2					11051.2
按国民经济行业分组	**By Sector**						
农畜产品批发业	Wholesale Trade for Live stock	500.0				500.0	
食品、饮料及烟草制品批发业	Wholesale Trade for Food Beverages and Tobaccos Products	21693.5	18310.0		3183.5	200.0	
米、面制品及食用油批发业	Wholesale Trade for Rice Flour and Edible Oil	3556.7	3496.7		60.0		
烟草制品批发业	Wholesale Trade for Tobaccos Products	17936.8	14813.3		3123.5		
纺织、服装及日用品批发业	Wholesale Trade for Textiles Garments Daily Sundry Articles	6420.0		200.0	2230.0	3990.0	
服装批发业	Wholesale Trade for Garments	4890.0		200.0	1890.0	2800.0	
文化、体育用品及器材批发业	Wholesale Trade for Culture Sports and Equipment	2722.7	2385.9		46.8	290.0	
医药及医疗器材批发业	Wholesale Trade for Medicines and Medical Appliances	38063.6	542.9	1827.7	6092.9	18548.9	11051.2
矿产品、建材及化工产品批发业	Wholesale Trade for Mineral Products Building Materials and Chemical Products	170965.0	131951.3	1105.1	25135.1	11652.1	
煤炭及制品批发业	Wholesale Trade for Coal and Related Products	3140.3	580.3			2560.0	
石油及制品批发业	Wholesale Trade for Petroleum and Related Products	145994.9	126865.3	500.0	16192.1	1316.1	
金属及金属矿批发业	Wholesale Trade for Metal and Metal Products	9453.0			6432.0	3021.0	
建材批发业	Wholesale Trade for Building materials	1748.7	387.7		1361.0		
化肥批发业	Wholesale Trade for Chemical Fertilizer	4748.1	3643.0	605.1	500.0		
机械设备、五金交电及电子产品批发业	Wholesale Trade for Machinery Equipment Hardware Transport Electric and Electronic Products	7499.0		230.0	4829.0	2440.0	
汽车、摩托车及零配件批发业	Wholesale Trade for Spare and Component Parts for Motor vehicles Motorcycles	2760.0			2000.0	760.0	
家用电器批发业	Wholesale Trade for Household Appliances	300.0			190.0	110.0	
计算机、软件及辅助设备批发业	Wholesale Trade for Computers Software and Supplementary Equipment	580.0			280.0	300.0	
其他批发业	Others	8404.0	1168.0		7000.0	236.0	

13-5 续 5(continued5)

项　目	Item	实收资本 Capital Hold	国家资本 Nation Capital	集体资本 collective-owned capital	法人资本 institutional capital	个人资本 individual capital	港澳台资本 Hong Kong Macao and Taiwan capital
零售业	**Retail Trade**	**79401.6**	**3504.1**	**1900.0**	**39823.7**	**27845.8**	**1461.3**
其中:国有及国有控股	etc: State-owned and state-holding	19402.1	3504.1		15873.0	25.0	
按登记注册类型分组	**By Types of Registration**						
内资	Domestic Funded	77624.4	3504.1	1900.0	39823.7	27845.8	
国有	State-owned Enterprises	1994.1	1994.1				
集体	Collective-owned Enterprises	138.0		100.0		38.0	
有限责任公司	Limited-liability Companies	48974.7	1510.0	800.0	21799.7	20314.2	
其他有限责任公司	Other Limited-liability Companies	48924.7	1510.0	800.0	21749.7	20314.2	
股份有限公司	Share Holding Ltd. Companies	8800.0			8800.0		
私营企业	Private Enterprises	17617.6		1000.0	9224.0	7393.6	
私营合伙	Private Partnership Enterprises	1020.6				1020.6	
私营有限责任公司	Private Limited-liability Companies	14147.0		1000.0	8424.0	4723.0	
私营股份有限公司	Private Share Holding Ltd. Companies	1450.0			800.0	650.0	
其他	Other Enterprises	100.0				100.0	
港澳台商投资企业	Enterprises with Funds from Hong Kong Macao and Taiwan	1461.3					1461.3
港澳台商独资	Enterprises with Sole Investment	1461.3					1461.3
按国民经济行业分组	**By Sector**						
综合零售业	Comprehensive Retail Sale Trade	25739.1	382.4		14175.2	6314.8	
百货零售业	Retail Sale Trade for Daily Use Article	25164.1	382.4		13950.2	5964.8	
超级市场零售业	Retail Sale Trade for Suppmarkets	475.0			125.0	350.0	
食品、饮料及烟草制品专门零售业	Retail Sale Trade for Food Beverages and Tobaccos Products	2073.0	1511.7		80.0	20.0	461.3
纺织、服装及日用品专门零售业	Retail Sale Trade for Textiles Garments Daily Sundry Articles	5830.0			5030.0	800.0	
服装零售业	Retail sale Trade for Clothing	5730.0			5030.0	700.0	
文化、体育用品及器材专门零售业	Retail Sale Trade for Culture Sports and Equipment	6931.5	100.0		6251.5	580.0	
图书零售业	Retail Sale Trade for Books	3288.0	100.0		3188.0		
医药及医疗器材专门零售业	Retail Sale Trade for Medicines and Medical Appliances	1708.0	1000.0			708.0	
药品零售业	Retail Sale Trade for Medicines	1708.0	1000.0			708.0	
汽车、摩托车、燃料及零配件专门零售业	Retail Sale Trade for Spare and Component Parts for Motor Vehicles Motorcycles and Fuels	32048.0	510.0	1800.0	12565.0	16173.0	1000.0
汽车零售业	Retail Sale Trade for Motor Vehicles	28218.0	510.0	1800.0	9535.0	15373.0	1000.0
机动车燃料零售业	Retail Sale Trade for Fuels for Motordriven Vehicles	3830.0			3030.0	800.0	
家用电器及电子产品专门零售业	Retail Sale Trade for Electrical Household Applianses and Electronic Products	4564.0		100.0	1572.0	2892.0	
家用电器零售业	Retail Sale Trade for Electrical Household Applianses	2211.0			711.0	1500.0	
计算机、软件及辅助设备零售业	Retail Sale Trade for Computers Software and Supplementary Equipment	1568.0			176.0	1392.0	
通讯设备零售业	Retail Sale Trade for Telecommunications	480.0			480.0		
五金、家具及室内装修材料专门零售业	Hardware,Electrical Appliance Furniture and Interior Decoration Material	200.0			150.0	50.0	
无店铺及其他零售业	Retail Sale Trade for No Shop and Others	308.0				308.0	

13-5 续 6(continued6)

项 目	Item	营业收入合计 Total Business Income	主营业务收入 Major Business Revenue	主营业务成本 Major Business Costs	主营业务税金及附加 Major Business Tax and Extra Charges	主营业务利润 Profits of Major Business
总 计	**Total**	**3777453.6**	**3766389.9**	**3421561.7**	**5094.6**	**288489.3**
批发业	**Wholesale Trade**	**3321703.0**	**3316722.8**	**3014478.1**	**3857.3**	**249256.0**
其中:国有及国有控股	etc: State-owned and state-holding	1692924.3	1688198.2	1498137.0	2391.3	143705.6
按登记注册类型分组	**By Types of Registration**					
内资	Domestic Funded	3197257.9	3192277.7	2899148.1	3887.0	240111.2
国有	State-owned Enterprises	784917.2	784721.0	655355.9	1579.0	83379.0
集体	Collective-owned Enterprises	17275.6	17275.6	16205.8	8.4	893.6
股份合作	Cooperative Enterprises					
有限责任公司	Limited-liability Companies	1238310.2	1238113.6	1151012.3	1449.8	83294.7
国有独资公司	State Sole Funded Corporations					
其他有限责任公司	Other Limited-liability Companies	1238310.2	1238113.6	1151012.3	1449.8	83294.7
股份有限公司	Share Holding Ltd. Companies	682870.0	678304.4	632100.9	604.5	45391.1
私营企业	Private Enterprises	426105.2	426083.4	398247.6	222.9	25814.8
私营独资	Private-funded Enterprises					
私营合伙	Private Partnership Enterprises					
私营有限责任公司	Private Limited-liability Companies	348476.5	348454.7	334567.1	122.2	11967.3
私营股份有限公司	Private Share Holding Ltd. Companies	77628.7	77628.7	63680.5	100.7	13847.5
其他	Other Enterprises	47779.7	47779.7	46225.6	22.4	1338.0
港澳台商投资企业	Enterprises with Funds from Hong Kong Macao and Taiwan	64336.3	64336.3	57521.0	-56.8	6872.1
港澳台商独资	Enterprises with Sole Investment	61551.8	61551.8	54691.6	-56.8	6917.0
按国民经济行业分组	**By Sector**					
农畜产品批发业	Wholesale Trade for Live stock	10097.2	10097.2	9861.3	1.6	234.3
食品、饮料及烟草制品批发业	Wholesale Trade for Food Beverages and Tobaccos Products	680994.6	680948.5	568983.4	1406.5	67160.1
米、面制品及食用油批发业	Wholesale Trade for Rice Flour and Edible Oil	67434.1	67388.6	66612.6	2.4	727.2
烟草制品批发业	Wholesale Trade for Tobaccos Products	608339.6	608339.0	497457.6	1398.8	66130.5
纺织、服装及日用品批发业	Wholesale Trade for Textiles Garments Daily Sundry Articles	85330.0	85330.0	81214.4	27.7	3661.8
服装批发业	Wholesale Trade for Garments	61826.9	61826.9	59163.5	23.5	2213.8
文化、体育用品及器材批发业	Wholesale Trade for Culture Sports and Equipment	38079.8	38079.8	27428.3	39.8	10126.8
医药及医疗器材批发业	Wholesale Trade for Medicines and Medical Appliances	276670.5	276575.6	234445.1	574.4	40431.2
矿产品、建材及化工产品批发业	Wholesale Trade for Mineral Products Building Materials and Chemical Products	1517998.6	1513197.3	1421921.2	1072.3	86693.2
煤炭及制品批发业	Wholesale Trade for Coal and Related Products	94422.4	94422.4	77823.7	132.5	16466.2
石油及制品批发业	Wholesale Trade for Petroleum and Related Products	923183.2	918574.4	858892.8	841.6	58467.8
金属及金属矿批发业	Wholesale Trade for Metal and Metal Products	51655.8	51655.8	46470.6	62.5	3460.0
建材批发业	Wholesale Trade for Building materials	27119.4	27064.2	26136.9	11.0	916.3
化肥批发业	Wholesale Trade for Chemical Fertilizer	73626.9	73621.7	70774.7	0.3	1896.0
机械设备、五金交电及电子产品批发业	Wholesale Trade for Machinery Equipment Hardware Transport Electric and Electronic Products	680246.0	680208.1	641239.9	724.5	38057.3
汽车、摩托车及零配件批发业	Wholesale Trade for Spare and Component Parts for Motor vehicles Motorcycles	623111.1	623111.0	590404.1	527.3	32044.5
家用电器批发业	Wholesale Trade for Household Appliances	12911.9	12911.9	11792.7	11.8	1107.4
计算机、软件及辅助设备批发业	Wholesale Trade for Computers Software and Supplementary Equipment	13318.4	13318.4	12785.0	10.2	523.2
其他批发业	Others	32286.3	32286.3	29384.5	10.5	2891.3

13-5 续 7(continued7)

项　目	Item	营业收入合计 Total Business Income	主营业务收入 Major Business Revenue	主营业务成本 Major Business Costs	主营业务税金及附加 Major Business Tax and Extra Charges	主营业务利润 Profits of Major Business
零售业	**Retail Trade**	**455750.6**	**449667.1**	**407083.6**	**1237.3**	**39233.3**
其中:国有及国有控股	etc: State-owned and state-holding	51654.8	51353.9	42810.0	356.0	8064.9
按登记注册类型分组	**By Types of Registration**					
内资	Domestic Funded	432673.8	426590.3	385487.5	1237.3	37752.6
国有	State-owned Enterprises	10770.4	10709.5	8818.3	224.2	1544.0
集体	Collective-owned Enterprises	2202.9	2198.5	2049.7	4.0	144.8
有限责任公司	Limited-liability Companies	251607.2	246459.3	224544.0	546.6	19701.1
其他有限责任公司	Other Limited-liability Companies	251167.7	246019.8	224109.7	545.7	19696.8
股份有限公司	Share Holding Ltd. Companies	25496.3	25491.4	19350.3	149.8	5806.2
私营企业	Private Enterprises	133074.3	132425.2	122432.6	181.4	9674.0
私营合伙	Private Partnership Enterprises	4136.6	4136.6	3982.6	4.4	149.6
私营有限责任公司	Private Limited-liability Companies	122889.4	122240.3	113533.8	152.2	8417.1
私营股份有限公司	Private Share Holding Ltd. Companies	5124.3	5124.3	4051.7	23.8	1048.8
其他	Other Enterprises	9522.7	9306.4	8292.6	131.3	882.5
港澳台商投资企业	Enterprises with Funds from Hong Kong Macao and Taiwan	20061.0	20061.0	19031.1		1029.9
港澳台商独资	Enterprises with Sole Investment	20061.0	20061.0	19031.1		1029.9
按国民经济行业分组	**By Sector**					
综合零售业	Comprehensive Retail Sale Trade	93091.2	89062.6	74814.0	488.9	12540.6
百货零售业	Retail Sale Trade for Daily Use Article	80818.9	77130.9	64454.8	353.8	11103.2
超级市场零售业	Retail Sale Trade for Suppmarkets	11326.5	10985.9	9784.5	132.1	1069.3
食品、饮料及烟草制品专门零售业	Retail Sale Trade for Food Beverages and Tobaccos Products	11881.5	11881.5	10698.7	205.7	977.1
纺织、服装及日用品专门零售业	Retail Sale Trade for Textiles Garments Daily Sundry Articles	22103.7	21512.0	17039.8	97.5	4144.3
服装零售业	Retail sale Trade for Clothing	20591.0	20351.0	16265.5	93.7	3991.8
文化、体育用品及器材专门零售业	Retail Sale Trade for Culture Sports and Equipment	7311.9	7307.0	4889.1	51.0	2181.8
图书零售业	Retail Sale Trade for Books	4198.6	4198.6	2895.6	15.6	1287.4
医药及医疗器材专门零售业	Retail Sale Trade for Medicines and Medical Appliances	1385.6	1385.6	1224.7	3.2	157.7
药品零售业	Retail Sale Trade for Medicines	1385.6	1385.6	1224.7	3.2	157.7
汽车、摩托车、燃料及零配件专门零售业	Retail Sale Trade for Spare and Component Parts for Motor Vehicles Motorcycles and Fuels	257724.4	256458.9	240412.9	262.1	15778.0
汽车零售业	Retail Sale Trade for Motor Vehicles	246276.8	245015.6	230844.0	223.0	13942.7
机动车燃料零售业	Retail Sale Trade for Fuels for Motordriven Vehicles	11447.6	11443.3	9568.9	39.1	1835.3
家用电器及电子产品专门零售业	Retail Sale Trade for Electrical Household Applianses and Electronic Products	58602.6	58409.8	54741.6	119.8	3127.8
家用电器零售业	Retail Sale Trade for Electrical Household Applianses	30485.1	30346.9	28605.4	21.5	1448.3
计算机、软件及辅助设备零售业	Retail Sale Trade for Computers Software and Supplementary Equipment	13819.8	13765.3	12722.9	46.6	911.1
通讯设备零售业	Retail Sale Trade for Telecommunications	9024.4	9024.4	8703.9	11.3	245.0
五金、家具及室内装修材料专门零售业	Hardware,Electrical Appliance Furniture and Interior Decoration Material	2149.5	2149.5	1896.3	7.3	245.9
无店铺及其他零售业	Retail Sale Trade for No Shop and Others	1500.2	1500.2	1366.5	1.8	80.1

13-5 续 8(continued8)

项　目	Item	其他业务利润 Profits of Other Business	营业费用 Business Cost	管理费用 Management Cost	税金 Tax	差旅费 travel cost	工会经费 labor union funds
总　计	**Total**	**20463.3**	**134418.4**	**82222.8**	**1747.8**	**4103.5**	**517.6**
批发业	**Wholesale Trade**	**3482.4**	**112292.2**	**57215.9**	**1302.9**	**3384.5**	**407.2**
其中:国有及国有控股	etc: State-owned and state-holding	2467.2	37944.8	38403.1	1049.3	1004.0	375.3
按登记注册类型分组	**By Types of Registration**						
内资	Domestic Funded	3482.4	108165.5	55695.2	1277.3	3328.2	405.8
国有	State-owned Enterprises	1538.1	13058.0	30136.8	622.3	739.3	314.6
集体	Collective-owned Enterprises	108.5	504.6	701.1	14.1	18.1	4.7
股份合作	Cooperative Enterprises		89.1	43.6	0.5	3.1	
有限责任公司	Limited-liability Companies	1569.4	60532.3	12899.0	240.2	1816.1	34.3
国有独资公司	State Sole Funded Corporations						
其他有限责任公司	Other Limited-liability Companies	1569.4	60532.3	12899.0	240.2	1816.1	34.3
股份有限公司	Share Holding Ltd. Companies	-111.2	17394.0	6882.0	344.2	204.2	47.3
私营企业	Private Enterprises	153.1	15654.3	4501.5	55.1	491.0	4.9
私营独资	Private-funded Enterprises						
私营合伙	Private Partnership Enterprises						
私营有限责任公司	Private Limited-liability Companies	96.0	8101.4	3239.8	30.0	389.8	1.9
私营股份有限公司	Private Share Holding Ltd. Companies	57.1	7552.9	1261.7	25.1	101.2	3.0
其他	Other Enterprises	224.5	1022.3	574.8	1.4	59.5	
港澳台商投资企业	Enterprises with Funds from Hong Kong Macao and Taiwan		2871.3	917.0	13.0	43.5	
港澳台商独资	Enterprises with Sole Investment		2840.8	714.8	13.0	43.5	
按国民经济行业分组	**By Sector**						
农畜产品批发业	Wholesale Trade for Live stock		36.3	40.9	0.3	3.1	
食品、饮料及烟草制品批发业	Wholesale Trade for Food Beverages and Tobaccos Products	889.7	8038.7	25029.8	515.7	430.6	279.4
米、面制品及食用油批发业	Wholesale Trade for Rice Flour and Edible Oil	623.7	930.1	1676.2	32.5	49.0	7.2
烟草制品批发业	Wholesale Trade for Tobaccos Products	200.5	6778.5	23337.2	483.2	378.1	272.2
纺织、服装及日用品批发业	Wholesale Trade for Textiles Garments Daily Sundry Articles	292.9	2970.5	1273.4	7.9	201.4	2.4
服装批发业	Wholesale Trade for Garments	175.1	1570.1	936.7	5.1	98.5	2.0
文化、体育用品及器材批发业	Wholesale Trade for Culture Sports and Equipment	182.4	2172.8	1828.5	60.6	11.5	13.9
医药及医疗器材批发业	Wholesale Trade for Medicines and Medical Appliances	42.3	24990.2	8481.7	103.3	1215.8	24.5
矿产品、建材及化工产品批发业	Wholesale Trade for Mineral Products Building Materials and Chemical Products	1484.8	42064.8	15902.5	586.0	881.1	68.0
煤炭及制品批发业	Wholesale Trade for Coal and Related Products	57.1	8715.9	1508.0	30.4	113.0	3.0
石油及制品批发业	Wholesale Trade for Petroleum and Related Products	141.5	22800.0	8757.4	459.0	435.3	56.5
金属及金属矿批发业	Wholesale Trade for Metal and Metal Products	0.0	2571.5	1469.4	14.5	197.2	0.1
建材批发业	Wholesale Trade for Building materials	63.8	798.2	825.3	2.2	20.6	1.2
化肥批发业	Wholesale Trade for Chemical Fertilizer	101.9	2010.9	1314.7	36.6	42.8	5.8
机械设备、五金交电及电子产品批发业	Wholesale Trade for Machinery Equipment Hardware Transport Electric and Electronic Products	320.5	30764.8	3083.2	8.5	532.6	0.8
汽车、摩托车及零配件批发业	Wholesale Trade for Spare and Component Parts for Motor vehicles Motorcycles	94.3	27533.4	1183.2	1.5	276.7	
家用电器批发业	Wholesale Trade for Household Appliances		927.5	28.4	0.3	4.3	
计算机、软件及辅助设备批发业	Wholesale Trade for Computers Software and Supplementary Equipment	110.1	291.9	305.0			
其他批发业	Others	269.8	1254.1	1575.9	20.6	108.4	18.2

13-5 续 9(continued9)

项 目	Item	其他业务利润 Profits of Other Business	营业费用 Business Cost	管理费用 Management Cost	税金 Tax	差旅费 travel cost	工会经费 labor union funds
零售业	**Retail Trade**	16980.9	22126.2	25006.9	444.9	719.0	110.4
其中:国有及国有控股	etc: State-owned and state-holding	445.8	2473.4	4909.8	155.5	144.9	39.4
按登记注册类型分组	**By Types of Registration**						
内资	Domestic Funded	16353.8	21407.1	23953.9	433.8	685.3	110.4
国有	State-owned Enterprises	240.6	380.2	1343.5	3.6	39.9	24.6
集体	Collective-owned Enterprises	6.8	108.1	64.0		5.2	
有限责任公司	Limited-liability Companies	5467.0	12566.9	14366.0	285.1	429.8	61.1
其他有限责任公司	Other Limited-liability Companies	5467.0	12559.3	14363.9	285.1	429.3	61.1
股份有限公司	Share Holding Ltd. Companies	9483.3	2168.3	2241.3	15.0	44.2	2.5
私营企业	Private Enterprises	503.9	4528.8	5905.4	130.1	166.2	22.2
私营合伙	Private Partnership Enterprises	51.9	47.0	75.8			
私营有限责任公司	Private Limited-liability Companies	312.6	3936.3	4650.4	130.1	146.6	16.0
私营股份有限公司	Private Share Holding Ltd. Companies	139.4	482.1	1177.6		19.6	6.2
其他	Other Enterprises	652.2	1654.8	33.7			
港澳台商投资企业	Enterprises with Funds from Hong Kong Macao and Taiwan	35.3	345.2	433.4	11.1	33.7	
港澳台商独资	Enterprises with Sole Investment	35.3	345.2	433.4	11.1	33.7	
按国民经济行业分组	**By Sector**						
综合零售业	Comprehensive Retail Sale Trade	14786.6	9802.6	10492.1	122.9	173.9	56.2
百货零售业	Retail Sale Trade for Daily Use Article	14005.4	7471.3	10422.4	122.9	170.4	55.3
超级市场零售业	Retail Sale Trade for Suppmarkets	776.5	2020.6	20.9			
食品、饮料及烟草制品专门零售业	Retail Sale Trade for Food Beverages and Tobaccos Products	52.0	404.0	460.6		61.7	5.2
纺织、服装及日用品专门零售业	Retail Sale Trade for Textiles Garments Daily Sundry Articles	385.3	894.4	3079.8	125.1	34.7	15.0
服装零售业	Retail sale Trade for Clothing	375.2	664.0	2844.2	125.1	34.7	15.0
文化、体育用品及器材专门零售业	Retail Sale Trade for Culture Sports and Equipment	-68.4	1545.8	1448.6	44.2	54.0	12.9
图书零售业	Retail Sale Trade for Books	-84.6	766.5	999.1	24.8	23.5	6.4
医药及医疗器材专门零售业	Retail Sale Trade for Medicines and Medical Appliances		491.5	147.6	0.2	6.3	0.5
药品零售业	Retail Sale Trade for Medicines		491.5	147.6	0.2	6.3	0.5
汽车、摩托车、燃料及零配件专门	Retail Sale Trade for Spare and Component Parts for Motor Vehicles Motorcycles and Fuels	766.9	6667.9	6449.7	141.5	276.9	8.9
汽车零售业	Retail Sale Trade for Motor Vehicles	715.4	5772.0	5972.5	127.9	244.2	8.1
机动车燃料零售业	Retail Sale Trade for Fuels for Motordriven Vehicles	51.5	895.9	477.2	13.6	32.7	0.8
家用电器及电子产品专门零售业	Retail Sale Trade for Electrical Household Applianses and Electronic Products	1058.5	2108.3	2777.6	11.0	71.1	11.7
家用电器零售业	Retail Sale Trade for Electrical Household Applianses	216.1	1132.4	1000.2	8.0	17.8	3.8
计算机、软件及辅助设备零售业	Retail Sale Trade for Computers Software and Supplementary Equipment	217.1	511.9	746.0	3.0	44.3	7.9
通讯设备零售业	Retail Sale Trade for Telecommunications	178.5	458.6	69.6		3.8	
五金、家具及室内装修材料专门零售业	Hardware, Electrical Appliance Furniture and Interior Decoration Material		160.0	82.6		8.8	
无店铺及其他零售业	Retail Sale Trade for No Shop and Others		51.7	68.3		31.6	

13-5 续 10(continued10)

项　目	Item	财务费用 Financial Cost	利息支出 Expenses of Interest	营业利润 Business Profits	利润总额 Total After-tax Profits	应交所得税 Income Tax Payable
总　计	**Total**	**9493.0**	**7453.9**	**137974.8**	**99348.2**	**19052.6**
批发业	**Wholesale Trade**	**6099.8**	**5572.6**	**128073.9**	**91846.7**	**17918.2**
其中:国有及国有控股	etc: State-owned and state-holding	3239.2	3547.6	110553.7	72249.3	13949.8
按登记注册类型分组	**By Types of Registration**					
内资	Domestic Funded	6175.9	5520.8	124500.4	88245.0	17333.6
国有	State-owned Enterprises	2574.8	2051.2	83558.3	43662.8	6969.0
集体	Collective-owned Enterprises	55.7	70.6	-91.5	-99.7	1.0
股份合作	Cooperative Enterprises					
有限责任公司	Limited-liability Companies	2056.4	2575.6	12730.6	14236.4	2751.5
国有独资公司	State Sole Funded Corporations					
其他有限责任公司	Other Limited-liability Companies	2056.4	2575.6	12730.6	14236.4	2751.5
股份有限公司	Share Holding Ltd. Companies	677.4	631.4	20534.4	22576.5	6155.1
私营企业	Private Enterprises	795.0	182.6	7626.1	7716.4	1415.3
私营独资	Private-funded Enterprises					
私营合伙	Private Partnership Enterprises					
私营有限责任公司	Private Limited-liability Companies	955.4	182.6	2375.6	2465.9	493.8
私营股份有限公司	Private Share Holding Ltd. Companies	-160.4		5250.5	5250.5	921.5
其他	Other Enterprises	16.6	9.4	142.5	152.6	41.7
港澳台商投资企业	Enterprises with Funds from Hong Kong Macao and Taiwan	-62.7	51.8	3146.5	3155.3	515.0
港澳台商独资	Enterprises with Sole Investment	-62.7	51.2	3424.1	3432.9	515.0
按国民经济行业分组	**By Sector**					
农畜产品批发业	Wholesale Trade for Live stock	10.7	5.4	146.4	146.3	22.0
食品、饮料及烟草制品批发业	Wholesale Trade for Food Beverages and Tobaccos Products	1471.7	1102.4	76908.1	41730.1	6380.4
米、面制品及食用油批发业	Wholesale Trade for Rice Flour and Edible Oil	1294.2	1027.8	-2503.2	-13.2	1.5
烟草制品批发业	Wholesale Trade for Tobaccos Products	167.8	75.1	79399.6	41731.6	6377.1
纺织、服装及日用品批发业	Wholesale Trade for Textiles Garments Daily Sundry Articles	224.3	140.5	-87.4	-49.2	63.7
服装批发业	Wholesale Trade for Garments	195.5	140.7	112.7	174.9	56.1
文化、体育用品及器材批发业	Wholesale Trade for Culture Sports and Equipment	913.4	14.0	6690.2	1194.7	196.5
医药及医疗器材批发业	Wholesale Trade for Medicines and Medical Appliances	717.7	836.6	7691.1	7946.4	1873.2
矿产品、建材及化工产品批发业	Wholesale Trade for Mineral Products Building Materials and Chemical Products	1090.4	1856.0	32944.5	35530.4	8550.6
煤炭及制品批发业	Wholesale Trade for Coal and Related Products	-156.6		6456.1	6494.5	1099.8
石油及制品批发业	Wholesale Trade for Petroleum and Related Products	765.0	1643.9	26666.4	28319.2	7016.9
金属及金属矿批发业	Wholesale Trade for Metal and Metal Products	107.5	109.7	974.3	1063.4	310.4
建材批发业	Wholesale Trade for Building materials	71.8	-0.1	-715.2	-657.9	3.2
化肥批发业	Wholesale Trade for Chemical Fertilizer	-19.6	1.3	-51.2	-55.7	40.4
机械设备、五金交电及电子产品批发业	Wholesale Trade for Machinery Equipment Hardware Transport Electric and Electronic Products	766.6	877.4	4354.9	5179.2	743.0
汽车、摩托车及零配件批发业	Wholesale Trade for Spare and Component Parts for Motor vehicles Motorcycles	-61.4		3618.7	3620.2	443.6
家用电器批发业	Wholesale Trade for Household Appliances	-18.5		170.0	170.1	58.0
计算机、软件及辅助设备批发业	Wholesale Trade for Computers Software and Supplementary Equipment	3.7	740.3	32.7	31.6	6.9
其他批发业	Others	905.0		-573.9	168.8	88.8

13-5 续 11(continued11)

项　目	Item	财务费用 Financial Cost	利息支出 Expenses of Interest	营业利润 Business Profits	利润总额 Total After-tax Profits	应交所得税 Income Tax Payable
零售业	**Retail Trade**	3393.2	1881.3	9900.9	7501.5	1134.4
其中:国有及国有控股	etc: State-owned and state-holding	850.5	814.7	606.9	-318.8	365.6
按登记注册类型分组	**By Types of Registration**					
内资	Domestic Funded	3503.1	1881.3	9455.3	7055.9	1005.5
国有	State-owned Enterprises	20.8		370.0	164.4	42.2
集体	Collective-owned Enterprises	-0.4		-20.1	-20.1	0.9
有限责任公司	Limited-liability Companies	1478.6	1270.1	-258.2	-1917.8	557.5
其他有限责任公司	Other Limited-liability Companies	1478.5	1270.0	-252.7	-1912.3	557.2
股份有限公司	Share Holding Ltd. Companies	1458.1	122.2	9606.9	9681.7	220.6
私营企业	Private Enterprises	540.0	489.0	-83.5	-692.5	184.3
私营合伙	Private Partnership Enterprises	14.8		63.9	1.0	
私营有限责任公司	Private Limited-liability Companies	509.0	489.0	68.2	-312.8	184.3
私营股份有限公司	Private Share Holding Ltd. Companies	16.3		-209.2	-373.7	
其他	Other Enterprises	6.0		-159.8	-159.8	
港澳台商投资企业	Enterprises with Funds from Hong Kong Macao and Taiwan	-111.9		398.5	398.5	59.6
港澳台商独资	Enterprises with Sole Investment	-111.9		398.5	398.5	59.6
按国民经济行业分组	**By Sector**					
综合零售业	Comprehensive Retail Sale Trade	2233.3	746.9	7414.8	6642.9	304.4
百货零售业	Retail Sale Trade for Daily Use Article	2202.3	746.9	7628.2	6857.4	304.4
超级市场零售业	Retail Sale Trade for Suppmarkets	6.0		-201.7	-201.7	
食品、饮料及烟草制品专门零售业	Retail Sale Trade for Food Beverages and Tobaccos Products	15.8		172.7	148.7	31.7
纺织、服装及日用品专门零售业	Retail Sale Trade for Textiles Garments Daily Sundry Articles	277.4	274.7	616.3	616.0	158.1
服装零售业	Retail sale Trade for Clothing	291.9	274.7	674.8	675.1	158.1
文化、体育用品及器材专门零售业	Retail Sale Trade for Culture Sports and Equipment	373.1	324.7	-1068.9	-1580.5	25.0
图书零售业	Retail Sale Trade for Books	312.8	310.6	-875.5	-954.9	10.5
医药及医疗器材专门零售业	Retail Sale Trade for Medicines and Medical Appliances	6.7		-377.1	-363.4	
药品零售业	Retail Sale Trade for Medicines	6.7		-377.1	-363.4	
汽车、摩托车、燃料及零配件专门零售业	Retail Sale Trade for Spare and Component Parts for Motor Vehicles Motorcycles and Fuels	452.2	534.2	3278.7	2268.5	588.9
汽车零售业	Retail Sale Trade for Motor Vehicles	432.6	515.1	2784.6	1732.7	500.9
机动车燃料零售业	Retail Sale Trade for Fuels for Motordriven Vehicles	19.6	19.1	494.1	535.8	88.0
家用电器及电子产品专门零售业	Retail Sale Trade for Electrical Household Applianses and Electronic Products	35.0	0.9	-151.1	-245.7	23.8
家用电器零售业	Retail Sale Trade for Electrical Household Applianses	29.0	0.8	-62.6	-198.3	9.3
计算机、软件及辅助设备零售业	Retail Sale Trade for Computers Software and Supplementary Equipment	2.5	0.1	-47.5	-5.6	10.0
通讯设备零售业	Retail Sale Trade for Telecommunications	4.2		-44.7	-45.9	
五金、家具及室内装修材料专门零售业	Hardware,Electrical Appliance Furniture and Interior Decoration Material	-0.4	-0.2	3.7	3.2	0.7
无店铺及其他零售业	Retail Sale Trade for No Shop and Others	0.1	0.1	11.8	11.8	1.8

13-5 续 12(continued12)

项　目	Item	劳动、失业保险费 labor、unemployment insurance	住房公积金和住房补贴 accumulation fund of housing and housing subsidy	本年应付工资总额 Current Year Accrued Wages	本年应付福利费总额 Ought Pay for Welfare	本年应交增值税 Value Added Tax Payable This Year
总　计	**Total**	**11820.0**	**1823.2**	**35733.3**	**5562.5**	**59383.4**
批发业	**Wholesale Trade**	**10607.6**	**1715.8**	**24589.3**	**3628.8**	**42968.1**
其中:国有及国有控股	etc: State-owned and state-holding	3081.4	1593.7	17669.4	2783.5	33301.9
按登记注册类型分组	**By Types of Registration**					
内资	Domestic Funded	10558.7	1701.2	23831.8	3604.0	41707.1
国有	State-owned Enterprises	2462.1	1247.4	13818.7	2297.4	15579.8
集体	Collective-owned Enterprises	16.0		213.6	31.4	78.0
股份合作	Cooperative Enterprises					
有限责任公司	Limited-liability Companies	7504.4	199.6	5453.5	750.3	6614.2
国有独资公司	State Sole Funded Corporations					
其他有限责任公司	Other Limited-liability Companies	7504.4	199.6	5453.5	750.3	6614.2
股份有限公司	Share Holding Ltd. Companies	470.7	252.6	2612.1	332.4	16515.8
私营企业	Private Enterprises	89.4	1.6	1478.5	160.5	2700.0
私营独资	Private-funded Enterprises					
私营合伙	Private Partnership Enterprises					
私营有限责任公司	Private Limited-liability Companies	75.3	1.6	1226.2	140.3	1693.2
私营股份有限公司	Private Share Holding Ltd. Companies	14.1		252.3	20.2	1006.8
其他	Other Enterprises	16.1		255.4	32.0	219.3
港澳台商投资企业	Enterprises with Funds from Hong Kong Macao and Taiwan	42.2	9.5	491.5	1.0	1192.9
港澳台商独资	Enterprises with Sole Investment	42.2	9.5	479.6	1.0	1071.9
按国民经济行业分组	**By Sector**					
农畜产品批发业	Wholesale Trade for Live stock	2.5		8.8	1.2	15.7
食品、饮料及烟草制品批发业	Wholesale Trade for Food Beverages and Tobaccos Products	2193.7	1212.0	11281.4	1910.9	13521.3
米、面制品及食用油批发业	Wholesale Trade for Rice Flour and Edible Oil	211.8	4.2	603.6	65.0	-19.5
烟草制品批发业	Wholesale Trade for Tobaccos Products	1979.1	1207.8	10618.8	1838.4	13476.2
纺织、服装及日用品批发业	Wholesale Trade for Textiles Garments Daily Sundry Articles	72.9	18.2	492.2	8.5	154.5
服装批发业	Wholesale Trade for Garments	36.1	9.0	308.0	-14.8	113.6
文化、体育用品及器材批发业	Wholesale Trade for Culture Sports and Equipment	80.2	7.7	882.9	244.4	546.1
医药及医疗器材批发业	Wholesale Trade for Medicines and Medical Appliances	435.2	104.4	4325.6	548.4	7448.2
矿产品、建材及化工产品批发业	Wholesale Trade for Mineral Products Building Materials and Chemical Products	7617.4	339.0	5826.1	711.1	20372.6
煤炭及制品批发业	Wholesale Trade for Coal and Related Products	19.0	0.0	375.9	26.4	1199.9
石油及制品批发业	Wholesale Trade for Petroleum and Related Products	600.6	304.9	3558.5	443.8	18293.8
金属及金属矿批发业	Wholesale Trade for Metal and Metal Products	10.1	1.6	710.3	78.1	109.7
建材批发业	Wholesale Trade for Building materials	43.5	0.4	167.9	33.2	627.5
化肥批发业	Wholesale Trade for Chemical Fertilizer	6869.0	0.9	501.2	42.6	0.0
机械设备、五金交电及电子产品批发业	Wholesale Trade for Machinery Equipment Hardware Transport Electric and Electronic Products	83.0	9.9	1359.2	163.4	738.0
汽车、摩托车及零配件批发业	Retail Sale Trade for Spare and Component Parts for Motor Vehicles Motorcycles and Fuels	13.3		412.6	45.2	329.0
家用电器批发业	Wholesale Trade for Household Appliances	16.6	24.6	227.6	30.4	117.7
计算机、软件及辅助设备批发业	Wholesale Trade for Computers Software and Supplementary Equipment	10.4		235.9	28.1	134.1
其他批发业	Others	122.7		413.1	40.9	171.7

13-5 续 13(continued13)

项 目	Item	劳动、失业保险费 labor、unemployment insurance	住房公积金和住房补贴 accumulation fund of housing and housing subsidy	本年应付工资总额 Current Year Accrued Wages	本年应付福利费总额 Ought Pay for Welfare	本年应交增值税 Value Added Tax Payable This Year
零售业	**Retail Trade**	**1212.4**	**107.4**	**11144.0**	**1933.7**	**16415.3**
其中:国有及国有控股	etc: State-owned and state-holding	201.3	101.4	3094.9	308.5	1202.0
按登记注册类型分组	**By Types of Registration**					
内资	Domestic Funded	1192.6	105.1	10901.9	1876.4	16117.7
国有	State-owned Enterprises	128.1	81.9	1782.8	125.1	307.2
集体	Collective-owned Enterprises			42.0	3.0	14.3
有限责任公司	Limited-liability Companies	614.1	23.2	6011.1	1162.7	9151.5
其他有限责任公司	Other Limited-liability Companies	613.9	23.2	6010.5	1162.6	9142.5
股份有限公司	Share Holding Ltd. Companies	332.1		883.8	246.4	4748.5
私营企业	Private Enterprises	102.5		2091.0	329.6	1505.4
私营合伙	Private Partnership Enterprises	0.0		24.0	2.8	15.8
私营有限责任公司	Private Limited-liability Companies	81.7		1574.6	257.9	1129.8
私营股份有限公司	Private Share Holding Ltd. Companies	18.3		475.9	66.4	350.1
其他	Other Enterprises	15.8		91.2	9.6	390.8
港澳台商投资企业	Enterprises with Funds from Hong Kong Macao and Taiwan	19.0	0.7	137.7	3.2	127.7
港澳台商独资	Enterprises with Sole Investment	19.0	0.7	137.7	3.2	127.7
按国民经济行业分组	**By Sector**					
综合零售业	Comprehensive Retail Sale Trade	818.1	27.1	4612.2	1049.9	7137.4
百货零售业	Retail Sale Trade for Daily Use Article	762.1	24.1	4383.0	1041.4	6656.9
超级市场零售业	Retail Sale Trade for Suppmarkets	46.3	0.0	186.7	8.5	442.7
食品、饮料及烟草制品专门零售业	Retail Sale Trade for Food Beverages and Tobaccos Products	106.1	12.1	776.3	107.1	262.6
纺织、服装及日用品专门零售业	Retail Sale Trade for Textiles Garments Daily Sundry Articles	57.0	5.6	804.8	120.4	900.8
服装零售业	Retail sale Trade for Clothing	57.0	5.6	741.3	103.3	865.2
文化、体育用品及器材专门零售业	Retail Sale Trade for Culture Sports and Equipment	47.9	48.0	919.3	120.3	243.2
图书零售业	Retail Sale Trade for Books	32.5	48.0	483.0	60.9	94.6
医药及医疗器材专门零售业	Retail Sale Trade for Medicines and Medical Appliances	4.3		106.9	9.5	6.0
药品零售业	Retail Sale Trade for Medicines	4.3		106.9	9.5	6.0
汽车、摩托车、燃料及零配件专门零售业	Retail Sale Trade for Spare and Component Parts for Motor Vehicles Motorcycles and Fuels	117.5	14.6	2618.5	382.2	7268.5
汽车零售业	Retail Sale Trade for Motor Vehicles	101.7	14.6	2341.8	362.7	7067.7
机动车燃料零售业	Retail Sale Trade for Fuels for Motordriven Vehicles	15.8		276.7	19.5	200.8
家用电器及电子产品专门零售业	Retail Sale Trade for Electrical Household Applianses and Electronic Products	54.9		1256.6	141.9	515.8
家用电器零售业	Retail Sale Trade for Electrical Household Applianses	12.9		369.1	44.7	204.7
计算机、软件及辅助设备零售业	Retail Sale Trade for Computers Software and Supplementary Equipment	42.0		370.0	48.3	170.3
通讯设备零售业	Retail Sale Trade for Telecommunications	0.0		138.3		53.5
五金、家具及室内装修材料专门零售业	Hardware,Electrical Appliance Furniture and Interior Decoration Material	6.6		39.3	1.0	62.4
无店铺及其他零售业	Retail Sale Trade for No Shop and Others			10.1	1.4	18.6

13－6 星级住宿业和限额以上餐饮企业财务状况

Finamial Indicator of Grade Lodgings Tracle and Catering Trail abore Desingnated size

单位:万元 (10000 yuan)

项　目	Item	企业数(个) Number of Enterprises (unit)	亏损企业数(个) Number of loss Making Industrial Enterprises	流动资产合计 Total Circulating Funds	存货 Inventory	固定资产原价 Original Value of Fixed Assets
总　计	Total	42	21	15630.9	1452.7	21324.0
其中:国有及国有控股	etc: State-owned and state-holding	1	1	72.1	52.4	1773.9
按登记注册类型分组	By Types of Registration					
内资	Domestic Funded	37	18	13817.5	1363.5	20413.2
国有	State-owned Enterprises					
集体	Collective-owned Enterprises	1		676.0		1840.8
股份合作	Cooperative Enterprises	1	1	1582.1	8.8	943.8
有限责任公司	Limited-liability Companies	7	4	2320.7	220.3	2774.7
其他有限责任公司	Other Limited-liability Companies	7	4	2320.7	220.3	2774.7
股份有限公司	Share Holding Ltd. Companies	2	2	629.7	55.9	651.8
私营企业	Private Enterprises	20	8	6789.8	572.4	8986.1
私营独资	Private-funded Enterprises	5	2	833.0	81.0	3633.6
私营合伙	Private Partnership Enterprises	1		744.2	39.2	1407.1
私营有限责任公司	Private Limited-liability Companies	12	5	4106.6	441.2	3191.3
私营股份有限公司	Private Share Holding Ltd. Companies	2	1	1106.0	11.0	754.1
其他	Other Enterprises	6	3	1819.2	506.1	5216.0
港澳台商投资企业	Enterprises with Funds from Hong Kong Macao and Taiwan	3	3	844.5	19.5	575.4
港澳台商独资	Enterprises with Sole Investment	3	3	844.5	19.5	575.4
外商投资企业	Foreign Investment Enterprises	2		968.9	69.7	335.4
中外合作经营	Cooperative Enterprises	1		918.9	64.7	235.4
外资企业	Enterprises with Sole Foreign Investment	1		50.0	5.0	100.0
按国民经济行业分组	By Sector					
正餐服务业	Dinner	41	20	15530.9	1382.7	21204.0
快餐服务业	Fast Food	1	1	100.0	70.0	120.0
饮料及冷饮服务业	Beverages					

13-6 续 1(continued1)

项 目	Item	累计折旧 Total depreciation Drawn Accumulated	本年折旧 Drawn Accumulated This Year	资产合计 Total Assets	负债合计 Total Liabilities	所有者权益合计 Total Greditors Equity
总 计	**Total**	**6210.2**	**1879.7**	**34732.8**	**15218.1**	**19514.7**
其中:国有及国有控股	etc: State-owned and state-holding	458.6	65.7	1387.4	500.1	887.3
按登记注册类型分组	**By Types of Registration**					
内资	Domestic Funded	5599.7	1757.7	32619.2	13575.3	19043.9
国有	State-owned Enterprises					
集体	Collective-owned Enterprises	1067.5	95.7	1449.2	14.6	1434.6
股份合作	Cooperative Enterprises	224.2	56.0	2568.4	1535.2	1033.2
有限责任公司	Limited-liability Companies	873.4	316.3	4274.3	2606.6	1667.7
其他有限责任公司	Other Limited-liability Companies	873.4	316.3	4274.3	2606.6	1667.7
股份有限公司	Share Holding Ltd. Companies	257.3	33.5	1070.9	787.8	283.1
私营企业	Private Enterprises	2409.0	1056.6	16522.6	6517.6	10005.0
私营独资	Private-funded Enterprises	500.6	183.9	4362.1	2271.1	2091.0
私营合伙	Private Partnership Enterprises	238.7	74.6	1912.6	409.0	1503.6
私营有限责任公司	Private Limited-liability Companies	1056.1	786.3	8381.4	3568.6	4812.8
私营股份有限公司	Private Share Holding Ltd. Companies	613.6	11.8	1866.5	268.9	1597.6
其他	Other Enterprises	768.3	199.6	6733.8	2113.5	4620.3
港澳台商投资企业	Enterprises with Funds from Hong Kong Macao and Taiwan	379.0	106.6	1040.9	727.7	313.2
港澳台商独资	Enterprises with Sole Investment	379.0	106.6	1040.9	727.7	313.2
外商投资企业	Foreign Investment Enterprises	231.5	15.4	1072.7	915.1	157.6
中外合作经营	Cooperative Enterprises	152.6	10.2	1001.6	915.1	86.5
外资企业	Enterprises with Sole Foreign Investment	78.9	5.2	71.1		71.1
按国民经济行业分组	**By Sector**					
正餐服务业	Dinner	6210.2	1879.7	34512.8	15068.1	19444.7
快餐服务业	Fast Food			220.0	150.0	70.0
饮料及冷饮服务业	Beverages					

13-6 续 2(continued2)

项 目	Item	实收资本 Capital Hold	国家资本 Nation Capital	集体资本 collective-owned capital	法人资本 institutional capital	个人资本 individual capital	港澳台资本 Hong Kong Macao and Taiwan capital
总 计	**Total**	**18017.1**	**1741.6**	**1385.6**	**7494.7**	**6713.6**	**469.1**
其中:国有及国有控股	etc: State-owned and state-holding	1741.6	1741.6				
按登记注册类型分组	**By Types of Registration**						
内资	Domestic Funded	17198.0	1741.6	1385.6	7357.2	6713.6	
国有	State-owned Enterprises						
集体	Collective-owned Enterprises	1280.6		1280.6			
股份合作	Cooperative Enterprises	1022.2			1022.2		
有限责任公司	Limited-liability Companies	1558.0			358.0	1200.0	
其他有限责任公司	Other Limited-liability Companies	1558.0			358.0	1200.0	
股份有限公司	Share Holding Ltd. Companies	200.0			0.0	200.0	
私营企业	Private Enterprises	7457.7		105.0	2827.0	4525.7	
私营独资	Private-funded Enterprises	1117.2			568.0	549.2	
私营合伙	Private Partnership Enterprises	1408.5			0.0	1408.5	
私营有限责任公司	Private Limited-liability Companies	3994.8		105.0	2259.0	1630.8	
私营股份有限公司	Private Share Holding Ltd. Companies	937.2				937.2	
其他	Other Enterprises	5679.5	1741.6		3150.0	787.9	
港澳台商投资企业	Enterprises with Funds from Hong Kong Macao and Taiwan	469.1					469.1
港澳台商独资	Enterprises with Sole Investment	469.1					469.1
外商投资企业	Foreign Investment Enterprises	350.0			137.5		
中外合作经营	Cooperative Enterprises	250.0			137.5		
外资企业	Enterprises with Sole Foreign Investment	100.0					
按国民经济行业分组	**By Sector**						
正餐服务业	Dinner	17917.1	1741.6	1385.6	7394.7	6713.6	469.1
快餐服务业	Fast Food	100.0			100.0		
饮料及冷饮服务业	Beverages						

13-6 续 3(continued3)

项　目	Item	营业收入合计 Total Business Income	主营业务收入 Major Business Revenue	主营业务成本 Major Business Costs	主营业务税金及附加 Major Business Tax and Extra Charges	主营业务利润 Profits of Major Business
总　计	**Total**	**39504.6**	**39465.4**	**21217.3**	**2411.8**	**14285.1**
其中:国有及国有控股	etc: State-owned and state-holding	469.0	460.2	437.6	7.9	14.5
按登记注册类型分组	**By Types of Registration**					
内资	Domestic Funded	34016.9	33987.6	18684.4	2141.3	11610.7
国有	State-owned Enterprises					
集体	Collective-owned Enterprises	1011.5	1011.5	440.9	96.9	473.7
股份合作	Cooperative Enterprises	624.6	624.6	316.9	106.9	200.8
有限责任公司	Limited-liability Companies	4844.4	4823.9	2565.1	268.6	1990.2
其他有限责任公司	Other Limited-liability Companies	4844.4	4823.9	2565.1	268.6	1990.2
股份有限公司	Share Holding Ltd. Companies	1757.1	1757.1	947.5	82.9	391.6
私营企业	Private Enterprises	18765.8	18765.8	10408.2	1163.7	5978.0
私营独资	Private-funded Enterprises	4458.6	4458.6	2860.2	245.8	862.7
私营合伙	Private Partnership Enterprises	2310.4	2310.4	1367.4	112.7	830.3
私营有限责任公司	Private Limited-liability Companies	8553.6	8553.6	4487.7	592.8	2747.3
私营股份有限公司	Private Share Holding Ltd. Companies	3443.2	3443.2	1692.9	212.4	1537.7
其他	Other Enterprises	7013.5	7004.7	4005.8	422.3	2576.4
港澳台商投资企业	Enterprises with Funds from Hong Kong Macao and Taiwan	2409.9	2400.0	953.9	134.7	1311.4
港澳台商独资	Enterprises with Sole Investment	2409.9	2400.0	953.9	134.7	1311.4
外商投资企业	Foreign Investment Enterprises	3077.8	3077.8	1579.0	135.8	1363.0
中外合作经营	Cooperative Enterprises	2697.8	2697.8	1319.0	135.8	1243.0
外资企业	Enterprises with Sole Foreign Investment	380.0	380.0	260.0		120.0
按国民经济行业分组	**By Sector**					
正餐服务业	Dinner	39324.6	39285.4	21147.3	2391.6	14195.3
快餐服务业	Fast Food	180.0	180.0	70.0	20.2	89.8
饮料及冷饮服务业	Beverages					

13-6 续 4(continued4)

项　目	Item	营业费用 Business Cost	管理费用 Management Cost	税金 Tax	差旅费 travel cost	工会经费 labor union funds
总　计	**Total**	12073.0	3175.5	104.2	49.0	4.8
其中:国有及国有控股	etc: State-owned and state-holding	156.4				
按登记注册类型分组	**By Types of Registration**					
内资	Domestic Funded	10280.0	2290.9	78.1	38.2	4.3
国有	State-owned Enterprises					
集体	Collective-owned Enterprises	308.0	40.7	3.9	3.2	
股份合作	Cooperative Enterprises	102.6	92.9			
有限责任公司	Limited-liability Companies	1643.4	448.3	1.9	1.8	0.6
其他有限责任公司	Other Limited-liability Companies	1643.4	448.3	1.9	1.8	0.6
股份有限公司	Share Holding Ltd. Companies	684.6	75.5		2.3	
私营企业	Private Enterprises	5220.5	1415.4	56.7	19.1	3.7
私营独资	Private-funded Enterprises	1024.3	146.6	52.9	8.5	2.9
私营合伙	Private Partnership Enterprises	466.0	229.3	1.8	1.1	
私营有限责任公司	Private Limited-liability Companies	2274.1	979.1	2.0	6.4	0.8
私营股份有限公司	Private Share Holding Ltd. Companies	1456.1	60.4		3.1	
其他	Other Enterprises	2320.9	218.1	15.6	11.8	
港澳台商投资企业	Enterprises with Funds from Hong Kong Macao and Taiwan	717.5	673.7		0.7	
港澳台商独资	Enterprises with Sole Investment	717.5	673.7		0.7	
外商投资企业	Foreign Investment Enterprises	1075.5	210.9	26.1	10.1	0.5
中外合作经营	Cooperative Enterprises	1039.5	186.8	4.0	9.1	0.5
外资企业	Enterprises with Sole Foreign Investment	36.0	24.1	22.1	1.0	
按国民经济行业分组	**By Sector**					
正餐服务业	Dinner	11953.2	3173.5	104.2	49.0	4.8
快餐服务业	Fast Food	119.8	2.0			
饮料及冷饮服务业	Beverages					

13-6 续 5(continued5)

项　目	Item	财务费用 Financial Cost	利息支出 Expenses of Interest	营业利润 Business Profits	利润总额 Total After-tax Profits	应交所得税 Income Tax Payable
总　计	**Total**	644.4	392.9	43.2	-124.0	277.2
其中:国有及国有控股	etc: State-owned and state-holding			-132.9	-132.9	
按登记注册类型分组	**By Types of Registration**					
内资	Domestic Funded	607.2	391.6	71.6	-56.0	271.1
国有	State-owned Enterprises					
集体	Collective-owned Enterprises	-0.2		125.2	125.2	
股份合作	Cooperative Enterprises	6.0		-0.7	-0.7	
有限责任公司	Limited-liability Companies	90.9	-0.3	-164.4	-158.9	42.7
其他有限责任公司	Other Limited-liability Companies	90.9	-0.3	-164.4	-158.9	42.7
股份有限公司	Share Holding Ltd. Companies	8.6		-38.5	-38.5	
私营企业	Private Enterprises	192.2	140.4	403.2	385.8	205.8
私营独资	Private-funded Enterprises	66.3	60.6	151.0	139.1	25.9
私营合伙	Private Partnership Enterprises	19.8		115.2	115.2	51.7
私营有限责任公司	Private Limited-liability Companies	105.1	79.8	116.8	111.3	128.2
私营股份有限公司	Private Share Holding Ltd. Companies	1.0		20.2	20.2	
其他	Other Enterprises	309.7	251.5	-253.2	-368.9	22.6
港澳台商投资企业	Enterprises with Funds from Hong Kong Macao and Taiwan	20.3	1.1	-88.1	-88.3	6.1
港澳台商独资	Enterprises with Sole Investment	20.3	1.1	-88.1	-88.3	6.1
外商投资企业	Foreign Investment Enterprises	16.9	0.2	59.7	20.3	
中外合作经营	Cooperative Enterprises	16.7				
外资企业	Enterprises with Sole Foreign Investment	0.2	0.2	59.7	20.3	
按国民经济行业分组	**By Sector**					
正餐服务业	Dinner	644.4	392.9	73.2	-94.0	277.2
快餐服务业	Fast Food			-30.0	-30.0	
饮料及冷饮服务业	Beverages					

13-6 续 6(continued6)

项　目	Item	其他业务利润 Profits of Other Business	劳动、失业保险费 labor、unemployment insurance	本年应付工资总额 Current Year Accrued Wages	本年应付福利费总额 Ought Pay for Welfare
总　计	Total	43.8	279.9	3989.1	114.2
其中:国有及国有控股	etc: State-owned and state-holding			66.1	
按登记注册类型分组	By Types of Registration				
内资	Domestic Funded	43.5	232.8	3489.1	101.0
国有	State-owned Enterprises	62.7			
集体	Collective-owned Enterprises		1.7	83.3	3.6
股份合作	Cooperative Enterprises		23.5	74.4	
有限责任公司	Limited-liability Companies	27.9	30.4	858.3	25.6
其他有限责任公司	Other Limited-liability Companies	27.9	30.4	858.3	25.6
股份有限公司	Share Holding Ltd. Companies	3.5	9.6	137.4	5.5
私营企业	Private Enterprises	2.0	142.7	1398.5	47.7
私营独资	Private-funded Enterprises		14.9	292.7	24.9
私营合伙	Private Partnership Enterprises		16.9	236.9	
私营有限责任公司	Private Limited-liability Companies	2.0	91.9	689.7	22.8
私营股份有限公司	Private Share Holding Ltd. Companies		19.0	179.2	
其他	Other Enterprises	10.1	24.9	937.2	18.6
港澳台商投资企业	Enterprises with Funds from Hong Kong Macao and Taiwan	0.3	4.3	278.9	13.2
港澳台商独资	Enterprises with Sole Investment	0.3	4.3	278.9	13.2
外商投资企业	Foreign Investment Enterprises		42.8	221.1	
中外合作经营	Cooperative Enterprises				
外资企业	Enterprises with Sole Foreign Investment		3.0	36.4	
按国民经济行业分组	By Sector				
正餐服务业	Dinner	41.8	279.9	3959.1	112.1
快餐服务业	Fast Food	2.0		30.0	2.1
饮料及冷饮服务业	Beverages				

主要统计指标解释

社会消费品零售总额 指国民经济各行业直接售给城乡居民和社会集团的消费品总额。它是反映各行业通过多种商品流通渠道向居民和社会集团供应的生活消费品总量，是研究国内零售市场变动情况、反映经济景气程度的重要指标。

社会消费品零售总额包括：⑴售给城乡居民作为生活用的商品和修建房屋用的建筑材料；⑵售给社会集团的各种办公用品和公用消费品；⑶售给机关、团体、学校、部队、企业、事业单位的职工食堂和旅店(招待所)附设专门供本店旅客食用，不对外营业的食堂的各种食品、燃料；企业、单位和国营农场直接售给本单位职工和职工食堂的自己生产的产品；⑷售给部队干部、战士生活用的粮食、副食品、衣着品、日用品、燃料；⑸售给来华的外国人、华侨、港澳台同胞的消费品；⑹居民自费购买的中、西药品、中药材及医疗用品；⑺报社、出版社直接售给居民和社会集团的报纸、图书、杂志，集邮公司出售的新、旧纪念邮票、特种邮票、首日封、集邮册、集邮工具等；⑻旧货寄售商店自购、自销部分的商品；⑼煤气公司、液化石油气站售给居民和社会集团的煤气灶具和罐装液化石油气；⑽农民售给非农业居民和社会集团的商品。不包括售给国民经济各部门企业、事业单位(包括国有经济的农场)生产经营用的各种原材料、燃料、设备、工具等和售给批发零售贸易业、餐饮业作为转卖用的商品，旧货寄售商店受托寄售卖出的商品，服务业的营业收入，邮局出售邮票的收入，自来水、电力、煤气生产(供应)单位的产品供应收入，也不包括农民之间的商品销售。

批发零售贸易业商品购、销、存总额 指各种登记注册类型的批发、零售贸易业企业（单位）以本企业（单位）为总体的商品购进、销售、库存总额。

商品购进总额 指从本企业（单位）以外的单位和个人购进（包括从境外直接进口）作为转卖或加工后转卖的商品总额。它反映批发零售贸易业从国内、国外市场上购进商品的总量。商品购进总额包括:（1）从工农业生产者购进的商品;（2）从出版社、报社的出版发行部门购进的图书、杂志和报纸;（3）从各种登记注册类型的批发零售贸易企业（单位）购进的商品;（4）从其他单位购进的商品，如从机关、团体、企业等单位购进的剩余物资，从餐饮业、服务业购进的商品，从海关、市场管理部门购进的缉私和没收的商品，从居民手中收购的废旧商品等;（5）从国（境）外直接进口的商品。不包括企业（单位）为自身经营用和未通过买卖行为而收入的商品以及销售退回、商品升溢等。

商品销售总额 指对本企业（单位）以外的单位和个人出售（包括对境外直接出口）的商品总额。它反映批发零售贸易业在国内市场上销售商品以及出口商品的总量。商品销售总额包括:（1）售给城乡居民和社会集团消费用的商品;（2）售给工业、农业、建筑业、运输邮电业、批发零售贸易业、餐饮业、服务业等作为生产、经营使用的商品;（3）售给批发零售贸易业作为转卖或加工后转卖的商品;（4）对国（境）外直接出口的商品。不包括出售本企业（单位）自用的废旧包装用品;未通过买卖行为付出的商品;经本单位介绍，由买卖双方直接结算，本单位只收取手续费的业务;购货退出的商品以及商品损耗和损失等。

批发零售贸易业库存 指报告期末各种登记注册类型的批发零售贸易企业（单位）已取得所有权的商品。它反映批发零售贸易企业（单位）的商品库存情况和对市场商品供应的保证程度。期末库存包括:（1）存放在批发零售贸易业经营单位（如门市部、批发站、经营处）仓库、货场、货柜和货架中的商品;（2）挑选、整理、包装中的商品;（3）已记入购进而尚未运到本单位的商品，即发货单或银行承兑凭证已到而货未到的部分;（4）寄放他处的商品，如因购货方拒绝承付而暂时存放在购货方的商品和已办完加工成品收回手续而未提回的商品;（5）委托其他单位代销（未作销售或调出）尚未售出的商品;（6）代其他单位购进尚未交付的商品。不包括所有权不属于本单位的商品、拨付除批发零售贸易业以外的其他行业所属独立核算加工厂等加工生产尚未收回成品的商品、代国家物资储备部门保管的商品等。

库存总额采用的计算价格是:农副产品采购单位按购进价计算;批发单位按进货价计算;零售单位按核算价格计算，即按什么价格核算就按什么价格计算。

消费品市场成交额 指从事消费品交易的商品市场的全部商品成交金额。消费品市场包括农副产品市场和工业消费品市场。

Explanatory Note on Main Statistical Indicators

Total Retail Sales of Consumer Goods refer to the sum of retail sales of consumer goods sold by all sectors of the national economy to urban and rural residents and social groups. This indicator is used to show the supply of consumers goods through various channels to households and institutions, and is very important for the study on changes at the domestic retail market, and on economic cycles.

The retail sales of consumer goods include: (1) commodities sold to urban and rural residents for their daily use and building materials sold to them for the construction or repair of houses; (2) office appliances and supplies sold to institutions; (3) food and fuels sold to canteens of institutions, enterprises, schools, military units and to canteens of hotels and hostels that only serve their guests, and commodities produced by enterprises, institutions or state farms and sold directly to their employees or their canteens; (4) grain and non-staple food, clothing, daily articles and fuels sold to military personnel; (5)consumer goods sold to foreigners, overseas Chinese, and Chinese compatriots from Taiwan, Hong Kong and Macao during their stay in the mainland of China; (6) Chinese and western medicines, herbs and medical facilities purchased by residents; (7) newspapers, books and magazines directly sold to residents and social groups by publishers, new and old commemorative stamps, special stamps, first–day covers, stamp albums and other stamp–collection articles sold by stamp companies; (8) consumer goods purchased and then sold by second–hand shops; (9) stoves and other heating facilities and liquefied gas sold by gas companies to households and institutions; and (10) commodities sold by farmers to non–agricultural residents and social groups. Excluded under this heading are: raw materials, fuels, equipment, tools sold to enterprises, institutions and state farms for production purpose; commodities sold to trade establishments for re–selling; commissioned sales at second–hand shops; operational income of urban public utilities; stamps sold at post offices; income of water, power, gas production and supply establishments from the supply of their products; and sales of commodities among farmers.

Purchase, Sales and Stock of Commodities by Wholesale and Retail Trade refer to the purchase, sales and stock of commodities by wholesale and retail establishments of different status of registration (excluding individual sellers).

Total Purchases of Commodities refer to the total value of purchases of commodities by the establishments from other establishments or individuals (including direct import from abroad) for the purpose of re–selling, either with or without further processing of the commodities purchased. This indicator is used to show the total value of purchases of commodities by wholesale and retail establishments from domestic and overseas markets. The total purchases include: (1) agricultural and industrial products purchased from producers; (2) books, magazines and newspapers purchased from distribution departments of the publishers; (3) commodities purchased from wholesale and retail establishments of different status of registration; (4) commodities purchased from other units, such as surplus materials purchased from government agencies, enterprises or institutions, commodities purchased from catering and service establishments, confiscated goods purchased from customs authorities or market management agencies, second–hand goods and wastes purchased from residents; and (5) commodities directly imported from abroad. Excluded are commodities purchased by establishments (units) for use in their own business operation, commodities obtained without buying or selling procedures, rejected commodities, etc.

Total Sales of Commodities refer to value of commodities sold by the establishments to other establishments and individuals (including direct export). This indicator is used to show the total value of sales of commodities at domestic markets and export. The total sales include: (1) commodities sold to urban and rural residents and social groups for their consumption; (2) commodities sold to establishments in industry, agriculture, construction, transportation, post and telecommunications, wholesale and retail trades, catering trade and public utility for their production and operation; (3) commodities sold to wholesale and retail establishments for re selling, with or without further processing; and (4)commodities for direct export to other countries. Excluded are selling of waste packaging materials used by the establishments (units) themselves, commodities transferred without buying or selling procedures, commission income from brokerage in transactions whose settlement is directly handled by buyers and sellers, rejected commodities in the purchase, loss in commodities, etc.

Commodity Stock of Wholesale and Retail Enterprises refers to total commodities possessed by wholesale and retail enterprises (units) of various types of registration status at the end of the reference period, which reflects the commodity stock level of various wholesale and retail enterprises and the potential for market supply. It includes: (1) commodities located in storage, garages, counters, and shelves of operating units (such as sale stores, wholesale centers, and operating offices) of wholesale and retail enterprises; (2) commodities in the process of selecting, sorting, and packing; (3)commodities not arrived but recorded as purchase in the account, i.e. commodities not arrived but payment receipts for the commodities from the sellers or the banks arrived; (4) commodities deposited in other places rather than places mentioned above, for instance: commodities in the hold of purchasers temporarily due to the refusal of payment and commodities not taken back after going through the formalities; (5) commodities entrusted to other units to sell but not sold yet; (6) commodities purchased for other units but not delivered yet. Commodities not included as stock are those not owned by the enterprises (units), those allocated to financially independent factories rather than wholesale and retail enterprises for processing but not taken back yet, and finally those put in stock by wholesale and retail enterprises on behalf of the state material reserves units.

For the calculation of the value of commodities stock, the value is calculated at purchasing prices in agricultural goods purchasing units and wholesale units, and at the accounting prices in retail units.

Volume of Transaction at Free Markets for Consumer Goods refers to the value of transaction of all goods at the free trade markets for consumer goods, where markets include both free markets for farm and sideline products and for manufactured consumer goods.

资料整理: 李芙蓉　孟莉
Arranged by Lifurong Mengli

14. 旅游业
TOURISM

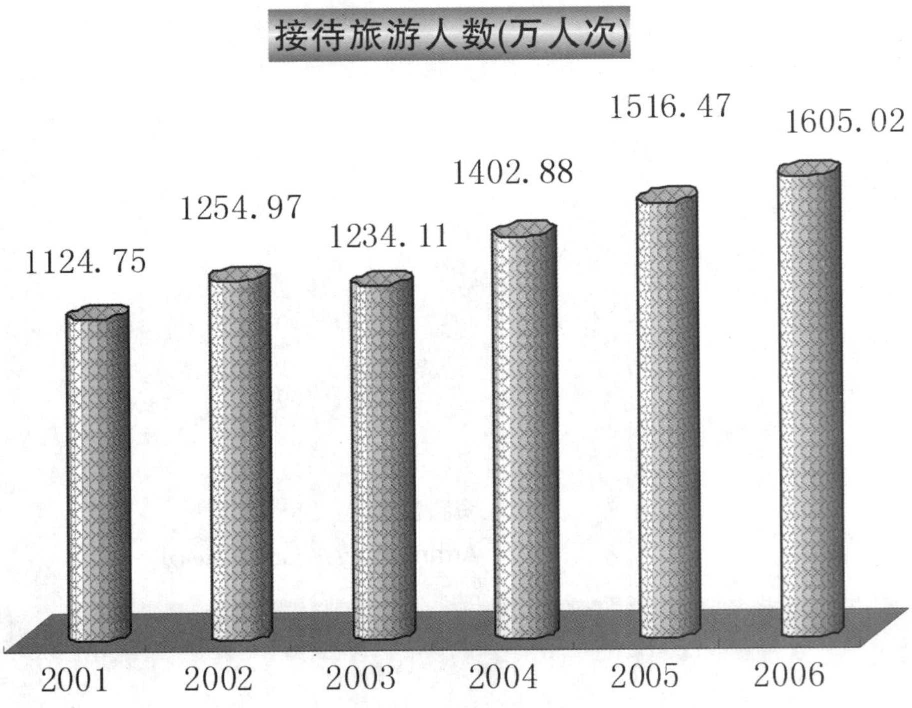
接待旅游人数(万人次)
1124.75
1254.97
1234.11
1402.88
1516.47
1605.02
2001
2002
2003
2004
2005
2006

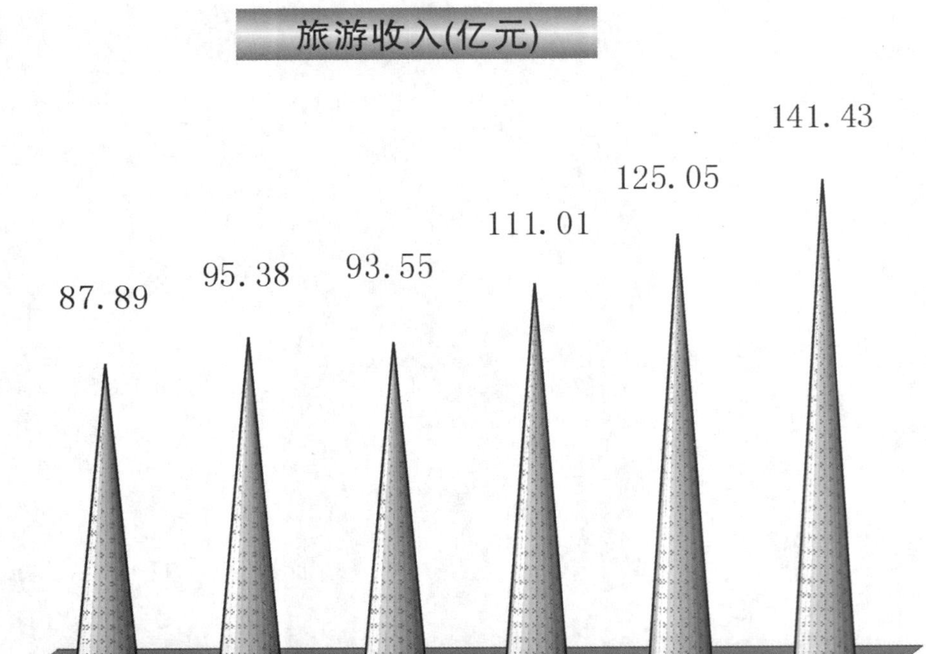
旅游收入(亿元)
87.89
95.38
93.55
111.01
125.05
141.43
2001
2002
2003
2004
2005
2006

14－1 旅游饭店设施和旅行社情况
Utilization of Installation of Tourism Hotel and Travel Agencies

项　目	Item	2004	2005	2006
旅游饭店总数(个)	Hotels of Tourism(unit)	326	364	387
客房总数(间)	Total Rooms(unit)	44439	48388	53977
床位总数(张)	Total Bets(unit)	83438	89396	98623
客房开房率(%)	Room Occupancy Rate	54.3	53.6	52.5
旅行社总数(个)	Total Number of Travel Agencies(unit)	158	158	158
国际社	International Travel Agencies	40	40	43
国内社	Domestic Travel Agencies	118	118	115

14－2 口岸出入境人数
Persons of Entry and Outbound Through Ports

单位：人次　　(person－time)

项　目	Item	2004	2005	2006
入境人数	**Personnal of Entry Through Ports**	**167162**	**194277**	**235267**
境外游客	Total Number of International Tourists Arrival to China	134637	180807	217570
外国人	Foreigners	57822	87986	136606
华侨	Overseas Chinese	480	503	367
港澳同胞	Compatriots from Hong Kong and Macao	52182	61873	54807
台湾同胞	Compatriots from Taiwan	24153	30445	25790
境内游客	Total Number of Domestic Tourists	32525	13470	17697
出境人数	**Total Number of Tourists Outbound**	**159051**	**191774**	**297423**
境外游客	Total Number of International Tourists Arrival to China	133868	177534	277694
外国人	Foreigners	58491	90659	127470
华侨	Overseas Chinese	930	1165	588
港澳同胞	Compatriots from Hong Kong and Macao	51032	55868	120222
台湾同胞	Compatriots from Taiwan	23415	29842	29414
境内游客	Total Number of Domestic Tourists	25183	14240	19729

14－3 旅游人数及旅游收入
Total Number of Tourists and Receipts of Tourism

项 目	Item	2004	2005	2006
接待旅游人数合计(人次)	**Total Number of Tourists**	**14028802**	**15164735**	**16050241**
旅游饭店接待人数	Received by Tourist Hotels	10821103	11844929	12585053
境外游客	Total Number of International Tourists Arrival to China	308638	431907	616932
外国人	Foreigners	183845	269400	465750
华侨	Overseas Chinese			
港澳同胞	Compatriots from Hong Kong and Macao	81093	106749	99468
台湾同胞	Compatriots from Taiwan	43700	55758	51714
境内游客	Total Number of Domestic Tourists	10512465	11413022	11968121
一般旅馆接待人数	Number of Tourists Receired by without Tourist Hotels	3207699	3319806	3465188
接待外国人按国别分	**by Country**			
日 本	Japan	17650	27635	38291
新加坡	Singapore	11147	16481	21272
泰 国	Thailand	5263	7564	7359
美 国	United States	9086	15033	19006
韩 国	South Korea	36542	54742	132623
英 国	United Kingdom	5276	5249	6461
俄罗斯	Russia	10551	29259	85543
德 国	Germany	4680	9710	12654
马来西亚	Ma Laysia	9914	25396	15438
澳大利亚	Australia	2369	5755	5980
其 他	Others	71367	72576	121123
旅游收入(亿元)	Receipts of Tourism	111.01	125.05	141.43
国内旅游收入(亿元)	Domestic Tourism Receipts	104.24	114.56	123.57
国际旅游收入(万美元)	International Tourism Receipts	8160.17	12845.77	22912.28

注："旅游收入"和"一般旅馆接待人数"采用抽样调查推算。
Note: Data in this tablc are Froni the Sampling Survey

14－4 各市县旅游饭店设施
Installation of Tourism Hotel by City and County

市 县	City and County	饭店数(家) Total Number of Hotel(unit)	客房数(间) Rooms(unit)	床位数(张) Beds(unit)	客房开房率(%) Room Occupancy Rate
全省合计	**Total**	**387**	**53977**	**98623**	**52.49**
海口市	Haikou	96	14401	25698	57.31
三亚市	Sanya	138	22754	41550	53.2
五指山市	Wuzhishan	6	510	971	46.66
文昌市	Wenchang	10	996	1885	45.2
琼海市	Qionghai	26	2977	5077	54.0
万宁市	Wanning	45	6934	13709	45.36
定安县	Dingan	6	783	1486	33.5
屯昌县	Tunchang	6	173	320	48.41
澄迈县	Chengmai	2		510	26.02
临高县	lingao	3	105	206	68.2
儋州市	Danzhou	15	1202	2251	57.74
东方市	Dongfang	5	300	567	59.58
乐东县	Ledong	7	232	416	26.15
琼中县	Qiongzhong	1	80	148	53.2
保亭县	Baoting	5	397	672	55.08
陵水县	Lingshui	13	1563	2731	40.0
白沙县	Baisha				
昌江县	Changjiang	3	225	426	58.91

14－5 各市县按等级分星级饭店数

Number of Tourist Hotels By City and County

市 县	City and County	星级饭店数(家) Total Number of Tourist Hotel(unit)	五星级 Five-Stars	四星级 Four-Stars	三星级 Three-Stars	二星级 Two-Stars	一星级 One-Stars
全省合计	**Total**	**261**	**13**	**50**	**115**	**71**	**12**
海口市	Haikou	77	4	15	33	25	
三亚市	Sanya	88	7	20	29	25	7
五指山市	Wuzhishan	6			4	1	1
文昌市	Wenchang	6			4	2	
琼海市	Qionghai	21	1	4	10	4	2
万宁市	Wanning	44	1	9	26	8	
定安县	Dingan	1			1		
屯昌县	Tunchang						
澄迈县	Chengmai						
临高县	lingao						
儋州市	Danzhou	8			6	1	1
东方市	Dongfang	4		1	1	2	
乐东县	Ledong						
琼中县	Qiongzhong	1				1	
保亭县	Baoting	1				1	
陵水县	Lingshui	3		1	1	1	
白沙县	Baisha						
昌江县	Changjiang	1					1

14－6 各市县按规模分星级饭店数
Number of Tourist Hotels by Capacity ancl Regions

市 县	City and County	星级饭店数(家) Total Number of Tourist Hotel(unit)	客房 300 间以上 with 300 Rooms and Ovor	客房 200~299 间 with 200-299 Rooms	客房 100~199 间 with 100-199 Rooms	客房 99 间以下 with Less than 100 Rooms
全省合计	**Total**	**261**	**20**	**33**	**98**	**110**
海口市	Haikou	77	7	11	31	28
三亚市	Sanya	88	8	14	34	32
五指山市	Wuzhishan	6			2	4
文昌市	Wenchang	6			2	4
琼海市	Qionghai	21	1		7	13
万宁市	Wanning	44	4	7	17	16
定安县	Dingan	1		1		
屯昌县	Tunchang					
澄迈县	Chengmai					
临高县	lingao					
儋州市	Danzhou	8			3	5
东方市	Dongfang	4				4
乐东县	Ledong					
琼中县	Qiongzhong	1				1
保亭县	Baoting	1				1
陵水县	Lingshui	3			2	1
白沙县	Baisha					
昌江县	Changjiang	1				1

14－7 各市县旅游饭店接待旅游人数
Number of Tourists Received by Tourism Hotel by City and County

单位:人次 (person)

市 县	City and County	接待旅游人数 Total Number of Tourists	境外游客 Total Number of International Tourists Arrival to China	外国人 Foreigners	港澳同胞 Compatriots from Hong Kong and Macao	台湾同胞 Compatriots from Taiwan	境内游客 Total Number of Domestic Tourists
全省合计	**Total**	**12585053**	**616932**	**465750**	**99468**	**51714**	**11968121**
海口市	Haikou	3621460	131105	80124	25457	25524	3490355
三亚市	Sanya	4549036	388818	311710	58470	18638	4160218
五指山市	Wuzhishan	155720	1119	583	13	523	154601
文昌市	Wenchang	203044	5484	3966	596	922	197560
琼海市	Qionghai	687429	14678	8802	3839	2037	672751
万宁市	Wanning	2123876	69461	57283	9198	2980	2054415
定安县	Dingan	184861	2705	1155	1117	433	182156
屯昌县	Tunchang	47988					47988
澄迈县	Chengmai	23131	227	225		2	22904
临高县	lingao	41684					41684
儋州市	Danzhou	386505					386505
东方市	Dongfang	74593	211	211			74382
乐东县	ledong	46732	36	27	9		46696
琼中县	qiongzhong	20066					20066
保亭县	Baoting	95125	763	303	453	7	94362
陵水县	Lingshui	257669	2325	1361	316	648	255344
白沙县	Baisha						
昌江县	Changjiang	66134					66134

主要统计指标解释

旅游者人数

⑴入境国际旅游者人数：指来中国参观、访问、旅行、探亲、访友、休养、考察、参加会议和从事经济、科技、文化、教育、宗教等活动的外国人、华侨、港澳同胞和台湾同胞的人数。不包括外国在我国的常驻机构，如使领馆、通讯社、企业办事处的工作人员；来我国常住的外国专家、留学生以及在岸逗留不过夜人员。

⑵出境居民人数：指大陆居民因公务活动或私人事务短期出境的人数。公务活动出境居民人数包括在国际交通工具上的中国服务员工，因私出境居民人数不包括在国际交通工具上的中国服务员工。

⑶国内旅游者人数：指我国大陆居民和在我国常住 1 年以上的外国人、华侨、港澳台同胞离开常住地在境内其他地方的旅游设施内至少停留一夜，最长不超过 6 个月的人数。

国际旅游(外汇)收入 指入境旅游的外国人、华侨、港澳同胞和台湾同胞在中国大陆旅游过程中发生的一切旅游支出，对于国家来说就是国际旅游(外汇)收入。

Explanatory Note on Main Statistical Indicators

Number of Tourists

(1) International tourists refer to foreigners, overseas Chinese, Chinese compatriots from Hong Kong, Macao and Taiwan coming to China for sight-seeing, visits, tours, family reunions, vacations, study tours, conferences and other activities of a business, scientific and technological, cultural, educational and religious nature. It does not include representatives and employees of resident institutions of foreign countries in China such as embassies, consulates, news agencies and offices of foreign companies and organizations, nor does it include long-term foreign experts or students residing in China, or persons in transition without spending a night in China.

(2) Chinese residents going abroad refer to Chinese residents going abroad for short terms for either public business or private purposes. Chinese employees working on international transport carriers are included in those going abroad for public business purpose, not in those for private purpose.

(3) Domestic tourists refer to residents of the mainland of China who stay for one night at least but no more than 6 months at tourist facilities in other places than their permanent residence within the territory of the mainland China, including foreigners, overseas Chinese and Chinese compatriots from Hong Kong, Macao and Taiwan who have resided in China for over one year.

Foreign Exchange Earnings from International Tourism refer to the total expenditures of foreigners, overseas Chinese, Chinese compatriots from Hong Kong, Macao and Taiwan during their stay in the mainland of China, which are earnings of foreign exchange from international tourism from the point of view from China.

资料整理: 李芙蓉

Arranged by Lifurong

15. 对外经济贸易

FOREIGN ECONOMY AND TRADE

进出口总额（亿美元）

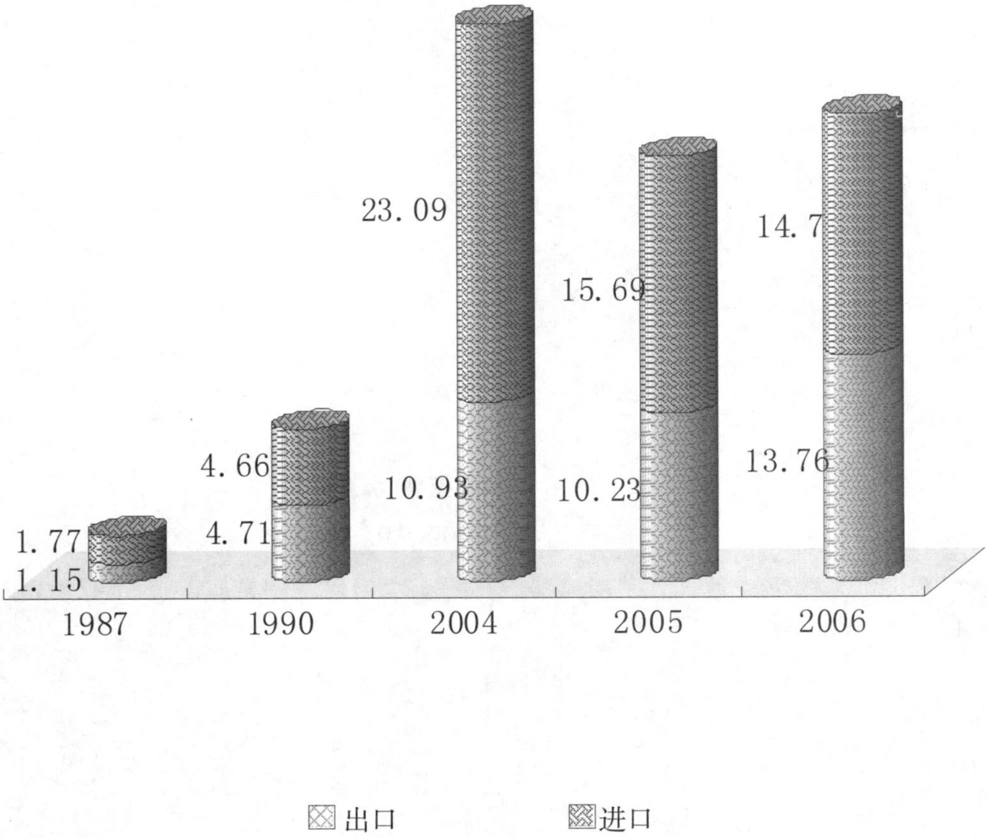

实际利用外资（亿美元）

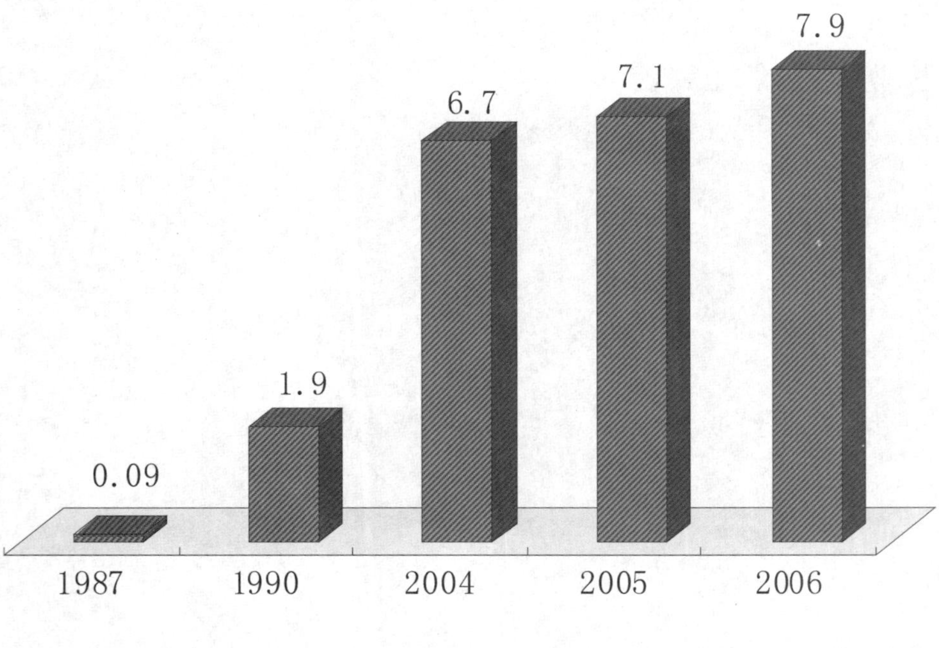

15－1 对外经济贸易基本情况
Foreign Trade and Economic Cooperation

指　标	Item	2004	2005	2006
进出口总额(万美元)	Total Imports and Exports(USD 100 million)	340168	259175	284607
出口总额	Total Exports	109252	102254	137562
进口总额	Total Imports	230916	156921	147045
进出口差额	Balance	-121664	-54667	-9483
对外签订利用外资合同项目	Number of Projects for Utilization of Foreign Capital in the Signed Agreements & Contracts	171	174	193
对外借款	Foreign Loans	2		2
外商直接投资	Foreign Direct Investments	169	174	191
对外签订利用外资合同金额(万美元)	Total Amount of Foreign Capital to Be Utilized in the Signed Agreements & Contracts (USD100 million)	74335	34211	108602
对外借款	Foreign Loans	4050		3490
外商直接投资	Foreign Direct Investments	70285	34211	105112
外商其他投资	Other Investments			
实际利用外资(万美元)	Total Amount of Foreign Capital Actually Used (USD 100 million)	66998	70711	79259
对外借款	Foreign Loans	2655	2310	4381
外商直接投资	Foreign Direct Investments	64343	68401	74878
外商其他投资	Other Investments			
对外经济合作(万美元)	Economic Cooperation with Foreign Countries & Territories (USD 100 million)			
合同金额	Contracted Value	238	890	307
完成营业额	Value of Business Fulfilled	68	715	246

15－2 对外贸易进出口总额
Total Value of Imports and Exports(Customs Statsics)

单位:万美元 (USD 10 000)

年 份 Year	进出口总额 Total Imports and Exports	出 口 Total Exports	进 口 Total Imports	差 额 Balance
1987	29241	11545	17696	-6151
1988	66462	29496	36966	-7470
1989	109620	36082	73538	-37456
1990	93697	47138	46559	579
1991	134876	66964	67912	-948
1992	169450	88120	81330	6790
1993	256866	90157	166709	-76552
1994	269719	98698	171021	-72323
1995	226744	83000	143744	-60744
1996	228667	84132	144535	-60403
1997	194901	88966	105935	-16969
1998	190913	88463	102450	-13987
1999	121867	74860	47007	27853
2000	128784	80289	48495	31794
2001	176238	80094	96144	-16050
2002	186686	81930	104756	-22826
2003	227871	86916	140939	-54023
2004	340168	109252	230916	-121664
2005	259175	102254	156921	-54667
2006	284607	137562	147045	-9483

15－3 向主要国家和地区出口商品金额
Value of Export Commodities with Main Countries and Territories

单位:万美元 (USD 10 000)

国家(地区)	Country (Territory)	2004	2005	2006
总计	**Total**	**109255**	**102254**	**137562**
#香港	Hong Kong, China	31649	32128	49088
台湾	Taiwan China	2576	1357	1824
日本	Japan	11992	11023	13399
韩国	South Korea	4591	4534	5057
新加坡	Singapore	1285	1096	2424
泰国	Thailand	2480	977	2539
马来西亚	Malaysia	2863	1637	2994
越南	Vietnam	1446	1053	2046
印度尼西亚	Indonesia	1481	955	1258
印度	India	1117	764	956
沙特阿拉伯	Saudi Arabia	249	425	738
阿联酋	United Arab Emirates	1241	1355	1459
俄罗斯	Russia	1176	1249	2082
波兰	Poland	510	321	419
匈牙利	Hungary	148	121	165
罗马尼亚	Romania	352	277	287
英国	United Kingdom	2291	2533	1836
法国	France	897	1239	1148
德国	Germany	1689	3073	2626
芬兰	Finland	129	127	229
意大利	Italy	1597	1573	1195
荷兰	Netherlands	1428	1759	2203
西班牙	Spain	985	1155	1625
比利时	Belgium	635	731	851
瑞典	Sweden	164	175	194
瑞士	Switzerland	420	361	197
南非	South Africa	787	1068	1101
美国	United State	13671	14385	20849
加拿大	Canada	758	641	873
澳大利亚	Australia	3687	921	1873

15－4 各市县对外贸易出口总额

Value of Export Commodities by City and County(Customs Statsics)

单位:万美元 (USD 10 000)

市县	City and County	2004	2005	2006
全省总计	**Total**	109255	102254	137562
海口市	Haikou	25100	21588	27897
三亚市	Sanya	2686	2200	3651
五指山市	Wuzhishan			
文昌市	Wenchang	1243	487	1670
琼海市	Qionghai	1005	1420	3308
万宁市	Wanning	288	279	205
定安县	Dingan	490	952	2038
屯昌县	Tunchang			4
澄迈县	Chengmai	738	282	576
临高县	lingao			
儋州市	Danzhou	1081	1152	1243
东方市	Dongfang	10441	3776	3856
乐东县	Ledong	13		
琼中县	Qiongzhong	8	8	37
保亭县	Baoting			2
陵水县	Lingshui	58	55	59
白沙县	Baisha			2
昌江县	Changjiang	55		391

注:全省总计包括省属专业公司及其他企业数字在内。
a)Data of Total include the Specializd Company Belong to Province and Other Enterprises.

15－5 对外贸易出口商品分类金额

Value of Exports by Category of Commodities (Customs Statistics)

单位:万美元 (USD 10 000)

商品类别	Categories of Commodities	2004	2005	2006
总　　额	**Total Value**	**109255**	**102254**	**137562**
动物产品	Animal Products	7403	9244	6564
植物产品	Vegetables; Fruits and Cereals	1910	1822	3443
动植物油脂及分解产品、精制食用油脂	Animal and Vegetable Oils; Refined Edible Oils and Fats	16	3	4
食品;饮料、酒及醋;烟草及代用品的制品	Food; Beverages; Liquor and Vinegar; Tobacco and Tobacco Substitutes	2555	3669	15697
矿产品	Minerals	19018	21871	22838
化学工业及其相关工业品	Chemicals and Related Products	15364	9400	10210
塑料及其制品;橡胶及其制品	Plastics and Related Products; Rubber and Relatted Products	2584	2365	2274
革、毛皮及制品;箱包	Leather; Furs and Related Products; Cases and Bags,Handgags	2806	1140	1170
木及制品;木炭;软木	Wood and Wooden Products; Charcoal;Cork	3808	2373	3206
木浆等;废纸;纸、纸板及其制品	Paper Pulp; Paper Waste; Paper; Paperboard and Related Products	548	783	438
纺织原料及纺织制品	Textile Materials and Products	19755	18716	18965
鞋帽伞等;羽毛品;人造花	Shoes; Hats and Umbrellas; Feather Products; Artificial Furs	1872	2294	2235
矿物材料制品;陶瓷品	Mineral Material Products;Cermics	1773	2967	2701
珠宝、贵金属及制品等	Lewelry; Precious Metals and Related Products	837	621	760
贱金属及其制品	Base Metals and Related Products	10251	7431	9871
机电、音像设备及其零件	Mechanical and Electrical Equipment Pecorders; Video Recorders and Accessories	6746	6639	9094
车辆、航空器、船舶及运输设备	Locomotives; Vehicles; Aircraft; Ship and Related Transportation Equipment	2444	1536	18479
光学、医疗等仪器;钟表、乐器	Optical; Medical Instruments; Clocks; Musicas Instruments	950	1898	1718
其他	Others	8616	7485	7894

15－6 对外贸易进口总额
Total Value of Imports(Customs Statsics)

单位:万美元 (USD 10 000)

项 目	Item	2004	2005	2006
进口总额	**Total Imports and Exports**	**230915**	**156921**	**147045**
按贸易方式分	**By Trade Pattern**			
一般贸易	Original Trade	159668	116093	111965
补偿贸易	Compensation Trade			
来料加工装配贸易	Processing and Assembly Trade	1408	1854	1119
进料加工贸易	Processing Trade for Imported Material	6463	7595	7999
外商投资企业进口设备	Imported Equipment and Materials as Investment of Foreign Funded Investment Enterprises for Processing and Sold Inside Country	912	357	682
免税外汇商品	Tax-free Foreign Exchange Commodities			
国际组织华侨及港澳同胞捐款	Donation of Compatriots from International Associations; Hong Kong; Macao	28	21	
其 他	Others	62436	31001	25280
按贸易国别(地区)分	By Country Territory			
香 港	Hong Kong	6920	3145	516
台 湾	Taiwan China	6730	5046	6664
日 本	Japan	48162	39380	34811
韩 国	South Korea	5145	1742	4616
新加坡	Singapore	2266	3244	2976
泰 国	Thailand	3328	2255	2758
马来西亚	Malaysia	3828	3053	6170
越 南	Vietnam	4944	7656	8713
印度尼西亚	In donesia	608	2016	4912
俄罗斯	Russia	1507	1519	1033
法 国	France	1762	5318	10704
德 国	Germany	22676	13897	17341
意大利	Italy	2207	2557	2347
美 国	USA	77523	41482	24560

15－7 对外贸易进出口主要商品数量和金额
Main Imports and Export Commodities in Volume and Value (Customs Statistics)

品　名	Item	数量 Voume	金额（万美元） Value(USD 10000)
进口主要商品	**Imports Commodities**		
机械及设备(价值)	Mechanical and Equipment (value)		28918
钢铁及制品(价值)	Steel (value)		10395
飞机（架）	Aircraft (unit)	9	33337
电器及电子产品(价值)	Appliances and Electrical Products		2856
动植物油(价值)	Animal and Vegetable Oils(value)		543
木及木制品(价值)	Wood and Wooden Products(value)		5752
药品(价值)	Medical and Pharmaceutical Products(value)		7871
有机化学品(价值)	Organic Chemistry Products(value)		1520
塑料及其制品(价值)	Plastic Products(value)		1296
出口主要商品	**Export Commodities**		
天然气(万吨)	Natural Gas(10 000 tons)	195	22033
衣服及衣着附件(价值)	Clothing and Accessories (value)		12719
家　具(价值)	Furniture(value)		5493
肥料(吨)	Chemical Fertilizers Ma nufactured(ton)	62440	1543
水海产品(价值)	Aquatic and Seawater Products(value)		21187
机电产品(价值)	Mechanical and Electrical Products (value)		33015
皮革及制品(价值)	Leather and RelatedProducts(value)		1160
蔬菜及水果(价值)	Vegetable and Fruits(value)		791
茶叶胡椒(吨)	Tea and Pepper(ton)	7006	1709

15－8 历年利用外资签约及投资

Number of Signed Agreements and Contracts and Foreign Investments

年份 Year	合计 Total	对外借款 Foreign Loans	外商直接投资 Foreign Direct Investment	合资企业 Joint Venture Enterprises	合作企业 Cooperative Operation Enterprises	独资企业 Foreign Enterprises	外商投资股份制企业 Shane issuing Enterprise of the foreing Investments	其他投资 Other Foreign Investment
新签协议(合同)(宗) Number of New Signed Agreements and Contracts on Foreign Capital to Be Utilized (unit)								
1980	35		4		4			31
1981	5		5		5			
1982	12		9	2	7			3
1983	27	1	22	6	16			4
1984	126	4	120	25	95			2
1985	96	5	85	35	47	3		6
1986	27	1	24	10	14			2
1987	55		25	11	13	1		30
1988	489	2	463	204	121	138		24
1989	383	5	378	151	62	165		
1990	261	9	252	98	30	124		
1991	476	6	470	205	35	230		
1992	1844	14	1830	530	79	1221		
1993	3106	15	3091	654	23	2414		
1994	810	8	802	232	18	552		
1995	410	21	389	133	15	241		
1996	268	29	239	87	9	143		
1997	241	14	227	66	6	155		
1998	187	13	174	52	7	115		
1999	170	12	158	52	5	101		
2000	187	3	184	132	50	2		
2001	182	1	181	58	7	116		
2002	238	5	233	44	6	183		
2003	171	7	164	40	5	118	1	
2004	171	2	169	51	6	112		
2005	174		174	66	3	105		
2006	193	2	191	75	6	109	1	

15-8 续 1 (continued 1)

年份 Year	合计 Total	对外借款 Foreign Loans	外商直接投资 Foreign Direct Investment					其他投资 Other Foreign Investment
				合资企业 Joint Venture Enterprises	合作企业 Cooperative Operation Enterprises	独资企业 Foreign Enterprises	外商投资股份制企业 Shane issuing Enterprise of the foreing Investments	
协议合同外商投资额(万美元)Total Amount of Foreign Capital to Be Utilized through the Signed Agreements and Contracts								
1980	186		50		50			136
1981	3087		3087		3087			
1982	378		310	149	161			68
1983	1433	200	930	211	719			303
1984	12300	313	11803	2862	8941			184
1985	6132	244	5560	2411	2413	736		328
1986	777		713	251	462			64
1987	1438		1361	335	1023	3		77
1988	39868	526	38189	7119	9911	21159		1153
1989	33213	5153	28060	8128	4072	15860		
1990	16204	3322	12882	3853	1188	7841		
1991	53339	13972	39367	17473	6829	15065		
1992	259337	33223	226114	72117	17168	136829		
1993	449519	30042	419477	69965	15627	333885		
1994	156530	34058	122472	34851	13621	74000		
1995	306968	28891	278077	32978	8284	236815		
1996	112558	85164	27394	14952	4532	7910		
1997	67421	39235	28186	17249	4108	6829		
1998	73343	59022	14321	7629	826	5866		
1999	142644	63468	79176	6697	5397	66708		
2000	15940	2235	13705	8242	4946	517		
2001	15373	180	15193	7905	1565	5723		
2002	25063	1990	23073	4064	3881	15128		
2003	34575	5390	29185	5070	7662	13711	2742	
2004	74335	4050	70285	10885	2357	57034		
2005	34211		34211	10483	788	22940		
2006	108602	3490	105112	24512	9747	70543	310	

15-8 续 2(continued2)

年份 Year	合计 Total	对外借款 Foreign Loans	外商直接投资 Foreign Direct Investment	合资企业 Joint Venture Enterprises	合作企业 Cooperative Operation Enterprises	独资企业 Foreign Enterprises	外商投资股份制企业 Shane issuing Enterprise of the foreing Investments	其他投资 Other Foreign Investment
实际利用外资额（万美元）Total Amount of Foreign Capital Actually Used								
1980	28		10		10			18
1981	109		109		109			
1982	83		83	83				
1983	438	200	192	25	167			46
1984	1784	313	1162	96	1066			309
1985	2643	244	2095	606	1489			304
1986	3259		3073	462	2611			186
1987	911		893	165	728			18
1988	12771	526	11421	2283	2314	6824		824
1989	16097	5153	10707	5436	784	4487		237
1990	18982	8911	10055	4816	1412	3827		16
1991	22232	4570	17606	4051	2538	11017		56
1992	53160	8000	45160	18908	5361	20891		
1993	128584	23800	104784	48194	2315	54275		
1994	126441	39000	87441	24482	2196	60763		
1995	145501	40000	105501	32090	6620	66791		
1996	118960	40000	78960	33853	7585	37522		
1997	112134	41000	71134	27642	2014	37023		
1998	109715	38000	71715	27136	1472	38379		
1999	84149	35700	48449	15753	411	29848		
2000	61280	18200	43080	22910	17287	2762	121	
2001	57291	10600	46691	17015	3118	26038	520	
2002	99878	48700	51178	14843	6339	29626	370	
2003	61782	3720	58062	10820	2206	44998	38	
2004	66998	2655	64343	11292	10878	35811	6362	
2005	70711	2310	68401	10239	2700	50192	5271	
2006	79259	4381	74878	28277	4109	42021	470	

15－9 对外借款情况
Utilization of Foreign Loans

		2004	2005	2006
对外借款合同数(宗)	Number of Contracts(Unit)	2		2
国外政府贷款	Government Loans	2		2
国际金融组织贷款	Loans from International Financial Organnizations			
出口信贷	Export Loans			
国际商业贷款	Commercial Loans			
对外借款合同金额(万美元)	Value of Contracts(USD 10 000)	4050		3490
国外政府贷款	Government Loans	4050		3490
国际金融组织贷款	Loans from International Financial Organnizations			
出口信贷	Export Loans			
国际商业贷款	Commercial Loans			
实际对外借款(万美元)	Used Value(USD 10 000)	2655	2310	4381
国外政府贷款	Government Loans	2330	1940	3988
国际金融组织贷款	Loans from International Financial Organnizations	325	370	393
出口信贷	Export Loans			
国际商业贷款	Commercial Loans			

15－10 对外承包工程与劳务合作
Contracted Projects and Labor Services with Foreign Countries & Territories

		2004	2005	2006
签订合同数(宗)	Number of Contracts(unit)	69	1	1
合同金额(万美元)	Contracted Value(USD 10 000)	238	890	307
营业额(万美元)	Value of Business Fulfilled (USD 10 000)	68	715	246
派出人数(人)	Persons be Sent Abroad(person)	122	59	76
期末在外人数(人)	Persons in Abroad(Year-end)(person)	385	333	386

主要统计指标解释

进出口总额指实际进出我国国境的货物总金额。包括对外贸易实际进出口货物，来料加工装配进出口货物，国家间、联合国及国际组织无偿援助物资和赠送品，华侨、港澳台同胞和外籍华人捐赠品，租赁期满归承租人所有的租赁货物，进料加工进出口货物，边境地方贸易及边境地区小额贸易进出口货物(边民互市贸易除外)，中外合资企业、中外合作经营企业、外商独资经营企业进出口货物和公用物品，到、离岸价格在规定限额以上的进出口货样和广告品(无商业价值、无使用价值和免费提供出口的除外)，从保税仓库提取在中国境内销售的进口货物，以及其他进出口货物。进出口总额用以观察一个国家在对外贸易方面的总规模。我国规定出口货物按离岸价格统计，进口货物按到岸价格统计。

利用外资 指我国各级政府、部门、企业和其他经济组织通过对外借款、吸收外商直接投资以及用其他方式筹措的境外现汇、设备、技术等。

对外借款 是我国利用外资的重要部分。指通过对外正式签订借款协议，从境外筹措的资金，包括外国政府贷款、国际金融组织贷款、外国银行商业贷款、出口信贷以及对外发行债券等。1996 年及以前还包括对外发行股票。

外商直接投资 指外国企业和经济组织或个人(包括华侨、港澳台胞以及我国在境外注册的企业)按我国有关政策、法规，用现汇、实物、技术等在我国境内开办外商独资企业、与我国境内的企业或经济组织共同举办中外合资经营企业、合作经营企业或合作开发资源的投资(包括外商投资收益的再投资)，以及经政府有关部门批准的项目投资总额内企业从境外借入的资金。

外商其他投资 指除对外借款和外商直接投资以外的各种利用外资的形式。包括企业在境内外股票市场公开发行的以外币计价的股票(目前主要是在香港证券市场发行的 H 股和在境内证券市场发行的 B 股)发行价总额，国际租赁进口设备的应付款，补偿贸易中外商提供的进口设备、技术、物料的价款，加工装配贸易中外商提供的进口设备、物料的价款。

对外承包工程 指各对外承包公司以招标议标承包方式承揽的下列业务：(1)承包国外工程建设项目，(2)承包我国对外经援项目，(3)承包我国驻外机构的工程建设项目，(4)承包我国境内利用外资进行建设的工程项目，(5)与外国承包公司合营或联合承包工程项目时我国公司分包部分，(6)对外承包兼营的房屋开发业务。对外承包工程的营业额是以货币表现的本期内完成的对外承包工程的工作量，包括以前年度签订的合同和本年度新签订的合同在报告期内完成的工作量。

对外劳务合作 指以收取工资的形式向业主或承包商提供技术和劳动服务的活动。我国对外承包公司在境外开办的合营企业，中国公司同时又提供劳务的，其劳务部分也纳入劳务合作统计。劳务合作营业额按报告期内向雇主提交的结算数(包括工资、加班费和奖金等)统计。

Explanatory Note on Main Statistical Indicators

Total Imports and Exports at Customs refer to the value of commodities imported into and exported from the boundary of China. They include the actual imports and exports through foreign trade, imported and exported goods under the processing and assembling trades and materials, supplies and gifts as aid given gratis between governments and by the United Nations and other international organizations, and contributions donated by overseas Chinese, compatriots in Hong Kong and Macao and Chinese with foreign citizenship, leasing commodities owned by tenant at the expiration of leasing period, the imported and exported commodities processed with imported materials, commodities trading in border areas (excluding mutual exchange goods), the imported and exported commodities and articles for public use of the Sino-foreign joint ventures, cooperative enterprises and ventures exclusively with foreign own investment. Also included are import or export of samples and advertising goods for whose CIF or FOB value are beyond the permitted ceiling (excluding goods of no trading or use value and free commodities for export), imported goods sold in China from bonded warehouses and other imported or exported goods. The indicator of the total imports and exports at customs can be used to observe the total size of external trade in a country. In accordance with the stipulation of the Chinese government, imports are calculated at CIF, while exports are calculated at FOB

Utilization of Foreign Capital refers to remittance,equipment and technology financed from abroad, by loans, foreign direct investment and other forms undertaken by the Chinese governments at all levels, by various departments, enterprises and other economic units.

Foreign Borrowings an important part of Chinas utilization of foreign capital, it refer to funds borrowed from abroad through formal signing of borrowing agreements with foreign institutions, including loans of foreign governments, loans of international financial institutions, commercial loans of foreign banks, export credit, and funds raised by Chinese bonds (and shares before 1996) issued abroad.

Direct Investment by Foreign Entrepreneurs refers to the investments inside China by foreign enterprises and economic organizations or individuals (including overseas Chinese, compatriots from Hong Kong and Macao, and Chinese enterprises registered abroad), following the relevant policies and laws of China, for the establishment of ventures exclusively with foreign own investment, Sino-foreign joint ventures and cooperative enterprises or for co-operative exploration of resources with enterprises or economic organizations in China. It includes the re investment of the foreign entrepreneurs with the profits gained from the investment and the funds that enterprises borrow from abroad in the total investment of projects which are approved by the relevant department of the government.

Other Investment by Foreign Entrepreneurs refers to all forms of utilization of foreign capitals other than foreign borrowings and foreign direct investment. It includes the total value of stock shares in foreign currencies issued by enterprises at domestic or foreign stock exchanges (now mainly consisting of H shares issued at Hong Kong Security Market and B shares issued at domestic security markets), rent payable for the imported equipment through international leasing arrangement, cost of imported equipment, technology and materials provided by foreign counterparts in compensation trade and processing and assembly trade.

Contracted Projects with Foreign Countries refer to projects undertaken by Chinese contractors (project contracting companies) through bidding process. They include: (1)overseas civil engineering construction projects financed by foreign investors; (2)overseas projects financed by the Chinese government through its foreign aid programs; (3)construction projects of Chinese diplomatic missions, trade offices and other institutions stationed abroad; (4)construction projects in China financed by foreign investment; (5)sub-contracted projects to be taken by Chinese contractors through a joint umbrella project with foreign contractor(s); (6)housing development projects. The business income from international contracted projects is the work volume of contracted projects completed during the reference period, expressed in monetary terms, including completed work on projects signed in previous years.

Service Cooperation with Foreign Countries refers to the activities of providing technology and labour services to employers or contractors in the forms of receiving salaries and wages. Labour services providing by contractual joint ventures of Chinese international contracting corporations should be included in the statistics of service co-operation with foreign countries. The business income of labour service co operation is the income in the form of wages and salaries, overtime pay, bonuses and other remuneration received from the employers during the reference period.

资料整理：罗　玲
Arranged by Luoling

16. 金融和保险
BANKING AND INSURANCE

全社会金融机构存款余额（亿元）

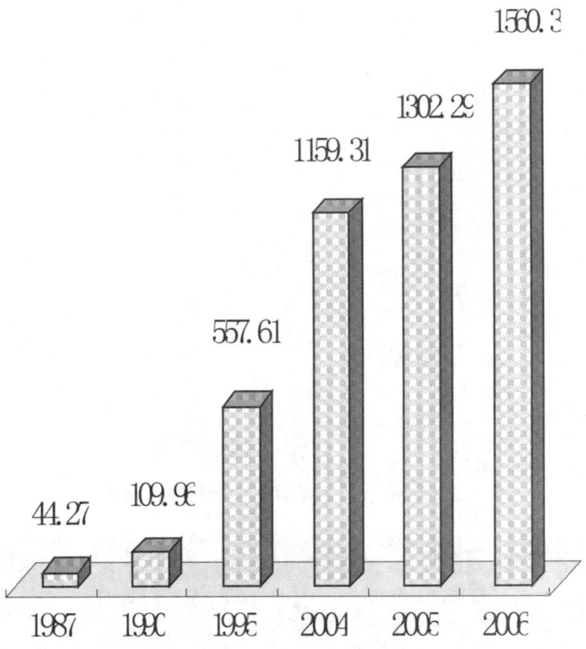

全社会金融机构贷款余额（亿元）

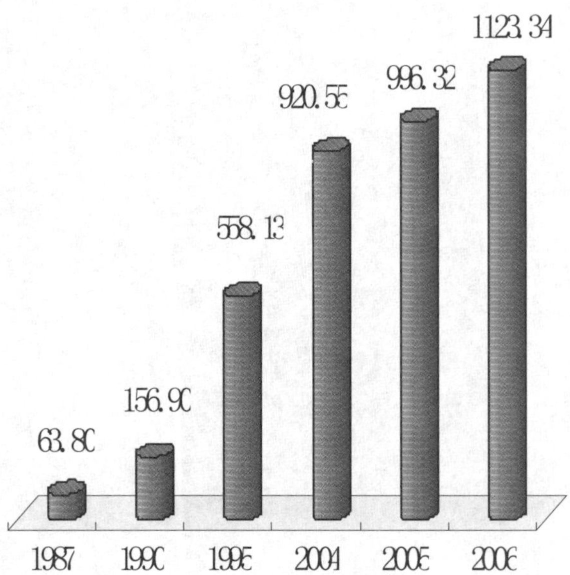

16－1 金融系统机构、人员数

Number of Institutions and Employed Persons in Finance Institutions

指标	Item	合计 Total	省级 Provincial Branches	地市级 Prefecture/ City Branches	县(市)级 County Branches	办事处 分理处 Business Offices	储蓄所 营业所 Saving Offices or Business Departments	其他 Others
机构数(个)	**Number of Institutions(Unit)**	1283	8	430	845	579	364	
中国人民银行	The People's Bank of China	19	1	1	17			
政策性银行	Policy Banks	19	2	3	14			
国家开发银行	National Development Bank	1	1					
农业发展银行	Agricultural Development Bank	18	1	3	14	14		
大型商业银行	Other Commercial Bank	505	5	254	246	437		
工商银行	Industrial and Commercial Bank	115	1	66	48	111		
农业银行	Agricultural Bank	215	1	87	127	211		
中国银行	Bank of China	92	1	49	42	89		
建设银行	Construction Bank	67	1	37	29	11		
交通银行	Bank of Communications	16	1	15		15		
股份制商业银行	Holding Commercial Banks	12		12		11		
光大银行	Everbright Bank	8		8		7		
深圳发展银行	Shenzhen Development Bank Co.,Ltd	4		4		4		
农村信用社	Rural Credit unions	388		78	310	131	25	
邮政储蓄	Postal Savings	339		81	258		339	
南洋商业银行	Nanyang Commercial Banks	1		1				
职工人数(人)	**Number of Employed Persons (person)**	18026	2790	6569	8667	8408	4418	
中国人民银行	The People's Bank of China	957	375	82	500			
政策性银行	Policy Banks	386	159	42	185	185		
国家开发银行	National Development Bank	77	77					
农业发展银行	Agricultural Development Bank	309	82	42	185	185		
大型商业银行	Other Commercial Bank	10733	2203	4529	4001	7984		
工商银行	Industrial and Commercial Bank	2483	439	1212	832	1716		
农业银行	Agricultural Bank	3881	348	1460	2073	3470		
中国银行	Bank of China	2081	632	821	628	1304		
建设银行	Construction Bank	1963	613	882	468	1350		
交通银行	Bank of Communications	325	171	154		144		
股份制商业银行	Holding Commercial Banks	318		318		239		
光大银行	Everbright Bank	178		178		99		
深圳发展银行	Shenzhen Development Bank Co.,Ltd	140		140		140		
农村信用社	Rural Credit unions	2834		682	2152		1635	
邮政储蓄	Postal Savings	2783	53	901	1829		2783	
南洋商业银行	Nanyang Commercial Banks	15		15				

16－2　保险系统机构、人员数
Number of Institutions and Employed Persons in Insurance System

指　标	Item	2005	2006
机构数(个)	Number of Institutions(Unit)	196	229
省级公司	Provincial Branches	9	12
地(市)级公司	Prefecture/City Branches	8	10
县级支公司(营业部)	County Branches,Business Offices	41	48
营销服务部	Selling Business Department	138	159
人员数(人)	Number of Employees (person)	5343	6150
省级公司	Provincial Branches	2019	2535
地(市)级公司	Prefecture/City Branches	701	696
县级支公司	County Branches,Business Offices	1686	1772
营销服务部(包括营销员)	Selling Business Department (includes marketing officer)	937	1147

1、2006 年末人员数中未包括中国大地财产保险股份有限公司海南分公司的人员。
2、本表中人员数包括保险营销员人数。
1. The number of personnel by the end of 2006 does not include the personnel of Hainan Branch of Continent Property Casualty Insurance Company of China.
2. The number of personnel in this form includes the number of insurance sales.

16－3 农村信用社机构、人员数
Number of Institutions and Employed Persons in Rural Credit Unions

指 标	Item	2004	2005	2006
机构数(个)	**Number of Institutions(Unit)**	**410**	**399**	**387**
独立核算机构	Independent Accounting Institutions	235	232	231
市县联社		19	19	19
乡镇信用社	Township Credit Unions	216	213	212
非独立核算机构	Non-Independent Accounting Institutions	175	167	156
信用分社	Credit Unions Branch	147	141	131
储蓄所(营业所)	Saving BANK (Business Departments)	28	26	25
职工人数(人)	**Number of Employees (person)**	**2900**	**2864**	**2834**
合同职工	Contract Employees	2805	2771	2748
信用社临时职工	Temporary Employee of Credit Unions	95	93	86

16－4 全社会金融机构存贷款余额
Total Deposit and Loan Balances of Financial Institutions

单位:万元 (10000 yuan)

指 标	Item	2004	2005	2006
全社会存款余额	**Total Deposit Balance**	**11593066**	**13022868**	**15603046**
国家银行	National Bank	9761981	10856985	12933712
其他金融机构	Other Financial Institutions	1831085	2165883	2672334
城市信用社	Urban Credit Unions	478	478	478
农村信用社	Rural Credit Unions	763830	834747	958716
信托投资公司	Trust & Investment Companies			
其 他	Others	1066777	1330658	1713140
全社会贷款余额	**Total Loan Balance**	**9205490**	**9963226**	**11233427**
国家银行	National Bank	8038339	8604769	9401638
其他金融机构	Other Financial Institutions	1167151	1358457	1831789
城市信用社	Urban Credit Unions	2916	2916	2916
农村信用社	Rural Credit Unions	462279	489255	530397
信托投资公司	Trust & Investment Companies			
其 他	Others	701956	866286	1298476

1、2006 年数字包括人民币和外币存贷款。2、"其他" 项包括交通银行、光大银行、深圳发展银行、南洋商业银行。
1. The number in including the deposit and loan of RMB and foreign correncey.
2.Others include Bank of Communications、Everbright Bank、Shenzhen Development Bank Co.,Ltd、Lease Company、Nanyang Commercial Bank.

16－5 金融机构存贷款项目构成
Composition of Deposits and Loans of Financial Institutions

单位:万元 (10000 yuan)

项 目	Item	2004	2005	2006
年末存款余额	**the Year-end Deposit Balance**	**11108268**	**12621622**	**15136894**
企业存款	Enterprise Deposits	3612069	3939222	5165070
其中:活期存款	Demand	3031612	3011778	4022302
定期存款	Time	580457	927444	1142768
财政存款	Treasury Deposits	202807	192614	364770
机关团体存款	Deposits of Government Agencies and Organizations	412507	551129	721071
储蓄存款	Urban and Rural Saving Deposits	6159162	6975744	7905740
其中:按储蓄时间分:	By saving Time			
活期储蓄	Demand	2923956	3269925	3862207
定期储蓄	Time	3235206	3705819	4043533
按储蓄对象分:	By Saving Target			
城镇居民储蓄	Urban and Rural Saving Deposits	5461655	6219155	6947024
农民存款	Peasant Deposits	697507	756589	958716
农业存款	Agricultural Deposits	186069	198054	86120
信托存款	Trusted Deposits	138	132	119
委托存款	Consignment Deposits	-22877	12011	13459
其他存款	Others	558390	752715	880545
年末贷款余额	**Year-end Loans Balance**	**8012059**	**8743246**	**9937819**
短期贷款	Short-term Loans	2634273	2537093	2386989
工业贷款	Industrial Loans	567789	421724	441931
商业贷款	Commercial Loans	444295	422821	515320
建筑业贷款	Construction Loans	48546	51074	36991
农业贷款	Agricultural Loans	573886	635946	435036
乡镇企业贷款	Loans to Township Enterprises	83233	45299	65225
三资企业贷款	Loans to Sino-Foreign Joint Venture and Cooperative Enterprises and Foreign-funded Enterprises	35548	11197	18285
私营企业及个体贷款	Loans to Private Enterprises and Individuals	14243	5074	5281
其他短期贷款	Other Short-term Loans	866733	943958	868921
中期流动资金贷款	Medium-term Working Capital Loans	362004		
中长期贷款	Medium-term & Long-term Loans	4710368	5838461	7178073
其中:基本建设贷款	Capital Construction Loans	2939110	3420732	4061839
技术改造贷款	Technical Innovation Loans	111557	104449	35777
其他中长期贷款	Other Medium-term & Long-term Loans	1659701	2316280	3080457
信托贷款	Credit Loans			
委托贷款	Trusted Loans			
其他贷款	Other Loans	305414	367692	372757

注:此表不包括南洋商业银行海口分行的数据。
Note: Data on the table do not include Deposits and Loans of NanYang Commercial Bank ,HaiKou Branch.

16－6 各市县金融机构存贷款余额
Deposit and Loan Balances of Financial Institutions by Region

单位:万元 (10000 yuan)

市县	Region	存款余额 Deposit Balance			贷款余额 Loan Balance		
		2004	2005	2006	2004	2005	2006
海口市	Haikou	6641923	7600163	9248686	5679459	6150427	8497958
三亚市	Sanya	1021400	1211105	1606233	498863	587047	756641
五指山市	Wuzhishan	83821	107668	129137	71870	94888	87529
文昌市	Wenchang	411296	456165	568974	172039	166745	167248
琼海市	Qionghai	457982	528980	685656	190000	180250	203448
万宁市	Wanning	267079	289985	372323	100801	100062	98232
定安县	Dingan	128725	146817	179241	57409	55346	50221
屯昌县	Tunchang	103590	118549	140751	65290	63520	50745
澄迈县	Chengmai	202032	230460	279011	120831	109474	90174
临高县	Lingao	129090	147116	174508	82275	77751	76455
儋州市	Danzhou	385216	437551	503967	193082	197978	169835
东方市	Dongfang	238742	282867	395148	68803	63929	71739
乐东县	Ledong	141450	167478	213184	79790	76064	71339
琼中县	Qiongzhong	105636	126574	148401	40463	41839	34532
保亭县	Baoting	68458	61872	75562	46365	9045	9324
陵水县	Lingshui	117191	150740	231342	75010	72167	70798
白沙县	Baisha	88531	106613	128382	41059	31308	25667
昌江县	Changjiang	165908	197454	233744	68453	57123	51122
洋浦	Yangpu	349454	253128	272526	360201	608279	650425

16－7 国家银行存贷款余额
Deposit and Loan Balances of National Bank

单位:万元 (10000 yuan)

指 标	Item	2004	2005	2006
年末存款余额	**Year-end Deposit Balance**	**9329677**	**10494249**	**12538776**
企业存款	Deposits of Enterprises	2862899	2996007	4003121
财政存款	Treasury Deposits	201033	190618	359292
机关团体存款	Deposits of Government Agencies and Organizations	398685	544517	688417
储蓄存款	Savings Deposits	5230695	5937829	6701590
农业存款	Agricultural Deposits	135978	135172	13990
其他存款	Others	500386	690105	772366
年末贷款余额	**Year-end Loan Balance**	**6859840**	**7407559**	**8126238**
短期贷款	Short-term Loans	1916026	1848855	1615222
#工业贷款	Industrial Loans	548429	379343	370681
商业贷款	Commercial Loans	422409	401247	480334
农业贷款	Agricultural Loans	313542	322372	163797
私营及个体贷款	Loans to Private Enterprises and Individuals	5125	258	362
其他短期贷款	Other Short-term Loans	550649	676343	584350
中期流动资金贷款	Medium-term Working Capital Loans	306432		
中长期贷款	Medium-term & Long-term Loans	4350749	5258128	6184318
#技术改造贷款	Technical Innovation	111557	101249	33847
基本建设贷款	Capital Construction	2904690	3317218	3880196
其他中长期贷款	Other Medium-term & Long-term Loans	1334502	1839661	2270275
信托及其他贷款	Credit and Other Loans	286633	300576	326698

16－8 各市县国家银行存贷款余额
Deposit and Loan Balances of National Bank by Region

单位:万元 (10000 yuan)

市 县	Region	2004	2005	2006
年末存款余额	**Year-end Deposit Balance**			
海口市	Haikou	5524147	6203827	6282606
三亚市	Sanya	888875	1042502	1264264
五指山市	Wuzhishan	69622	92959	89959
文昌市	Wenchang	314150	346714	357093
琼海市	Qionghai	367911	437364	507637
万宁市	Wanning	222155	243458	227981
定安县	Dingan	104412	121431	114613
屯昌县	Tunchang	86736	100463	86674
澄迈县	Chengmai	160218	187708	178695
临高县	Lingao	99073	113709	94285
儋州市	Danzhou	312635	361651	335732
东方市	Dongfang	223855	265204	330131
乐东县	Ledong	121227	146451	128861
琼中县	Qiongzhong	91168	109377	89807
保亭县	Baoting	58055	50548	36036
陵水县	Lingshui	105544	138816	176007
白沙县	Baisha	75384	92712	71601
昌江县	Changjiang	154965	186214	182520
洋浦	Yangpu	349454	253128	265122
年末贷款余额	**Year-end Loan Balance**			
海口市	Haikou	4935749	5337837	3638661
三亚市	Sanya	419063	412491	432333
五指山市	Wuzhishan	63581	86782	74702
文昌市	Wenchang	118268	110190	93834
琼海市	Qionghai	142505	128621	136584
万宁市	Wanning	68141	66329	49467
定安县	Dingan	38613	36229	24045
屯昌县	Tunchang	53679	51103	33090
澄迈县	Chengmai	94304	82128	45063
临高县	Lingao	58707	51483	33740
儋州市	Danzhou	154681	155536	89531
东方市	Dongfang	58577	52798	53113
乐东县	Ledong	64666	60687	45563
琼中县	Qiongzhong	37259	37983	26027
保亭县	Baoting	40337	2524	2320
陵水县	Lingshui	60231	57420	48214
白沙县	Baisha	32744	22607	16167
昌江县	Changjiang	58538	46529	33611
洋浦	Yangpu	360201	608279	650425

16－9 农村信用社存贷款余额
Deposit and Loan Balances of Rural Credit Unions

单位:万元 (10000 yuan)

市县	Region	年末存款余额 Year-end Deposit Balance	储蓄存款 Urban and Rural Savings Deposits	其他存款 Other Savings	年末贷款余额 Year-end Deposit Balance	农业贷款 Agricultural Deposits	其他贷款 Other Loans
全省总计	**Total**	**958716**	**870965**	**87751**	**530397**	**260976**	**269421**
海口市	Haikou	229343	190506	38837	108698	47416	61282
三亚市	Sanya	84469	76489	7980	48216	18303	29913
五指山市	Wuzhishan	16742	13555	3187	8681	2357	6324
文昌市	Wenchang	121825	115691	6134	59270	28453	30817
琼海市	Qionghai	100412	97179	3233	54416	23090	31326
万宁市	Wanning	60467	51582	8885	39330	25743	13587
定安县	Dingan	27537	26981	556	19862	13590	6272
屯昌县	Tunchang	20519	20270	249	12520	8961	3559
澄迈县	Chengmai	47564	45682	1882	27989	16585	11404
临高县	Lingao	38297	35403	2894	26859	14067	12792
儋州市	Danzhou	88246	84782	3464	46392	10169	36223
东方市	Dongfang	19524	17498	2026	12806	8774	4032
乐东县	Ledong	28720	27624	1096	16400	13011	3389
琼中县	Qiongzhong	19490	15972	3518	4525	1382	3143
保亭县	Baoting	12927	10973	1954	7004	3495	3509
陵水县	Lingshui	15445	14889	556	16096	12150	3946
白沙县	Baisha	14832	13950	882	9500	5810	3690
昌江县	Changjiang	12357	11939	418	11833	7620	4213

16－10 金融机构现金收支
Cash Income and Expenditure of National Bank

单位:万元 (10000 yuan)

指 标	Region	2004	2005	2006
现金收入合计	**Total Cash Income**	**27190761**	**27287136**	**28729390**
商品销售收入	Income from Commodity Sales	1939212	1730727	1641248
服务事业收入	Income from Services	1115336	1010245	1042432
税款收入	Income from Taxes	150282	154253	175147
城乡个体经营收入	Income from Individual Business	475746	455697	403279
储蓄存款收入	Income from Saving Deposits	21387742	21899489	23613933
其他金融机构收入	Income from Other Financial Institutions	71262	28313	82957
汇兑收入	Income from Remittances	143682	106602	92379
有价证券收入	Income from Securities	47709	31706	24564
其他收入	Other Income	1751837	1755856	1553635
现金支出合计	**Total Cash Expenditure**	**27069835**	**27196557**	**28633979**
工资性支出	Wages	1483838	1428663	1348020
# 国家工资及奖金支出	Expenditures for Wages and Bonus from Government	645352	589682	480087
国家对个人其他支出	Other Payments to Individuals from Government	294745	256798	234018
农副产品收购支出	Purchases of Agricultural and Sideline Products	585591	517273	611385
行政企业管理费支出	Government and Enterprise Overhead	1357789	1229340	1255268
城乡个体经营支出	Expenditure for Individual Business	653437	632320	506749
储蓄存款支出	Expenditure for Savings Deposits	20948634	21492977	23117423
其他金融机构支出	Expenditure for Other Financial Institutions	89996	45108	58489
汇兑支出	Expenditure for Remittances	89532	66237	69630
有价证券支出	Expenditure for Securities	24156	8805	11309
其他支出	Other Expenditure	1534498	1527020	1417568
货币净投放(+)或净回笼(-)		**-120926**	**-90579**	**-95411**

16－11 国家银行现金收支
Cash Income and Expenditure of National Bank

单位:万元 (10000 yuan)

指 标	Region	2004	2005	2006
现金收入合计	**Total Cash Income**	21710435	22365538	24106122
商品销售收入	Income from Commodity Sales	1664688	1566177	1544423
服务事业收入	Income from Services	1037692	957961	1009711
税款收入	Income from Taxes	115327	127377	151783
城乡个体经营收入	Income from Individual Business	310374	290279	280734
储蓄存款收入	Income from Saving Deposits	17116576	18075358	19823872
其他金融机构收入	Income from Other Financial Institutions	50486	23447	66322
居民归还贷款收入	Income from Household Loan Recovery	20063	21961	18554
汇兑收入	Income from Remittances	140589	102805	83048
有价证券收入	Income from Securities	46694	28075	22746
其他收入	Other Income	1207948	1172099	1104929
现金支出合计	**Total Cash Expenditure**	21559613	22292528	24160655
工资性支出	Wages	1379556	1374247	1311273
#国家工资及奖金支出	Expenditures for Wages and Bonus from Government	605639	578582	472396
国家对个人其他支出	Other Payments to Individuals from Government	268186	250119	230372
其他单位工资性支出	Expenditures for Wages of Other Units	376876	431821	499652
农副产品收购支出	Purchases of Agricultural and Sideline Products	569412	493021	584358
工矿产品采购支出	Purchases of Industrial & Mineral Products	177697	152773	155067
行政企业管理费支出	Government and Enterprise Overhead	1040314	977484	1028641
城乡个体经营支出	Expenditure for Individual Business	452448	392885	331757
储蓄存款支出	Expenditure for Savings Deposits	16657166	17685906	19534745
其他金融机构支出	Expenditure for Other Financial Institutions	51074	36480	44629
居民提取贷款支出	Expenditure for Household Loan Drawn	8539	4477	2727
汇兑支出	Expenditure for Remittances	88691	63215	58502
有价证券支出	Expenditure for Securities	23043	7781	10479
其他支出	Other Expenditure	1111673	1104260	1098478

16－12 各市县国家银行现金收支
Cash Income and Expenditure of National Bank by Region

单位:万元 (10000 yuan)

市县	Region	2004	2005	2006
现金收入	**Cash Income**			
海口市	Haikou	11525828	11373798	12238064
三亚市	Sanya	2165411	2424229	2798259
五指山市	Wuzhishan	147895	193065	214997
文昌市	Wenchang	1133827	1110656	1001275
琼海市	Qionghai	1343380	1329093	1440093
万宁市	Wanning	841589	852546	908158
定安县	Dingan	302353	302649	336065
屯昌县	Tunchang	284868	331823	357582
澄迈县	Chengmai	437539	514101	532344
临高县	Lingao	250875	244362	277796
儋州市	Danzhou	1005787	1165670	1296117
东方市	Dongfang	385851	399971	423576
乐东县	Ledong	330486	349520	414954
琼中县	Qiongzhong	130179	155347	181908
保亭县	Baoting	95893	50031	60156
陵水县	Lingshui	434798	434611	442631
白沙县	Baisha	100348	117625	140811
昌江县	Changjiang	336710	381562	378767
洋浦	Yangpu	448992	557432	648957
现金支出	**Cash Expenditure**			
海口市	Haikou	11220201	11142794	11921942
三亚市	Sanya	2073942	2332945	2666239
五指山市	Wuzhishan	156988	201380	231685
文昌市	Wenchang	1140885	1130134	1037769
琼海市	Qionghai	1332404	1311578	1462369
万宁市	Wanning	832734	852895	930937
定安县	Dingan	316881	317666	344662
屯昌县	Tunchang	296789	343896	366253
澄迈县	Chengmai	465737	543045	599339
临高县	Lingao	260887	257474	286546
儋州市	Danzhou	1017398	1171440	1304082
东方市	Dongfang	398476	418644	473352
乐东县	Ledong	341591	362058	472297
琼中县	Qiongzhong	151527	175138	199963
保亭县	Baoting	107342	54072	65688
陵水县	Lingshui	443942	432130	474135
白沙县	Baisha	130409	145773	169084
昌江县	Changjiang	364603	413505	413373
洋浦	Yangpu	499883	634920	730165

16－13 各市县城乡居民储蓄存款余额

Deposit Balances of the Urban and Rural Resident by Region

单位:万元 (10000 yuan)

市县	Region	2005 合计 Total	2005 城镇居民 Urban Resident	2005 农民 Peasant	2006 合计 Total	2006 城镇居民 Urban Resident	2006 农民 Peasant
全省总计	**Total**	**6975744**	**6219155**	**756589**	**7905634**	**7034669**	**870965**
海口市	Haikou	3560938	3394890	166048	3912312	3721806	190506
三亚市	Sanya	655656	595405	60251	791857	715368	76489
五指山市	Wuzhishan	77379	65019	12360	87217	73662	13555
文昌市	Wenchang	397059	293482	103577	458849	343158	115691
琼海市	Qionghai	387091	299455	87636	438899	341720	97179
万宁市	Wanning	245510	201258	44252	289094	237512	51582
定安县	Dingan	123373	98686	24687	140852	113871	26981
屯昌县	Tunchang	97455	79624	17831	114363	94093	20270
澄迈县	Chengmai	191953	151497	40456	223112	177430	45682
临高县	Lingao	118955	87757	31198	138640	103237	35403
儋州市	Danzhou	329750	256261	73489	377464	292682	84782
东方市	Dongfang	134675	119644	15031	154980	137482	17498
乐东县	Ledong	130416	110942	19474	158877	131253	27624
琼中县	Qiongzhong	92860	77867	14993	105912	89940	15972
保亭县	Baoting	44353	34795	9558	55286	44313	10973
陵水县	Lingshui	96037	84110	11927	121257	106368	14889
白沙县	Baisha	74010	60804	13206	84052	70102	13950
昌江县	Changjiang	128837	118489	10348	146252	134313	11939
洋浦	Yangpu	89110	89110		106360	106360	

16－14 金融机构外汇存贷款

Deposit and Loan of Foreign Exchanges of Financial Institutions

单位:万美元 (USD 10000)

项目	Item	2004	2005	2006
存款合计	**Total Deposits**	**58575**	**49719**	**59696**
境内机构存款	Deposit of Churchyard Institution	10740	9245	20994
外商投资企业存款	Deposit of Foreign-funded Enterprises	1744	1700	2461
储蓄存款	Savings Deposits	35723	30236	27674
信托存款	Trusted Deposits			
保证金存款	Security Deposits			
其他存款	Other Deposits	10368	8538	8567
贷款合计	**Total Loans**	**144195**	**151171**	**165919**
境内机构贷款	Loans of Churchyard Institution	123417	104455	124683
外商企业贷款	Loans of Foreign-funded Enterprises		26018	21845
信托贷款	Trusted Loans			
租赁融资	Lease Financing			
其他贷款	Other Loans	20778	20698	19391

16－15 全省保险业务总量
Total Province Insurance Business

单位:万元 (USD 10000)

指　标	Item	保费收入 Income of Premiums		赔款及给付 Claim and Payment	
		2005	2006	2005	2006
总　计	**Total**	149512.89	177184.93	38828.43	42567.26
财产保险公司	**Total Property Insurance**	56527.16	69895.76	29095.77	27237.51
企业财产保险	Enterprise Property Insurance	8486.43	8550.02	9371.27	7223.96
家庭财产保险	Family Property Insurance	62.49	118.14	24.73	12.62
机动车辆保险	Motor Vehicle Insurance	25537.38	35348.29	14026.21	16028.41
工程保险	Engineering Insurance	1688.76	1199.86	671.82	1003.04
责任保险	Projects Insurance	1036.01	1634.92	329.45	359.48
信用保险	Reposal Insurance		0.00		0.00
保证保险	Guarantee Insurance	1520.03	1297.23	467.71	195.94
船舶保险	Shipping Insurance	1797.84	1797.69	500.56	404.06
货运保险	Freight Transport Insurance	2393.9	2679.16	1191.25	594.83
特殊风险保险	Special Insurance	11135.13	13982.72	1590.28	57.21
农业保险	Agriculture Insurance	341.48	158.30	466.89	6.66
其他保险	Other Insurance	2527.71	3129.43	455.6	1351.30
人寿保险公司	**Total Life Insurance**	92985.73	107289.17	9732.66	15329.75
寿险	Life Insurance	81656.71	93989.16	7014.63	12790.76
健康保险	Health Insurance	7682.24	9081.56	1781.71	1794.68
人身意外伤害险	Unforeseen Injury Insurance	3646.78	4218.45	936.32	744.30

注：本表数据未包括中国大地财产保险股份有限公司海南分公司的数据。

Note:The number is not include the persennel of Hainan Branch of Continent Property Casualty insurance company of China.

主要统计指标解释

信贷资金 指金融机构以信用方式积聚和分配的货币资金。金融机构信贷资金的来源有各项存款、对国际金融机构负债、流通中货币、银行自有资金及当年结益等;信贷资金的运用有各项贷款、黄金占款、外汇占款、财政借款及在国际金融机构中的资产等。

存款 指企业、机关、团体或居民根据资金必须收回的原则,把货币资金存入银行或其他信用机构保管并取得一定利息的一种信用活动形式。根据存款对象的不同可划分为企业存款、财政存款、机关团体存款、基本建设存款、城镇储蓄存款、农村存款等科目。它是银行信贷资金的主要来源。

贷款 指银行或其他信用机构根据资金必须归还的原则,按一定利率,为企业、个人等提供资金的一种信用活动形式。我国银行贷款分为流动资金贷款、固定资产贷款、城乡个体工商户贷款以及农业贷款等科目。

保险公司 在中国境内的、经过保险监督部门批准设立,并依法登记注册的各类商业保险公司。

保险金额 指保险人承担赔偿或者给付保险金责任的最高限额。

保费 指投保人为取得保险人在约定范围内所承担赔偿责任而支付给保险人的费用。

赔款 指保险人根据保险合同的规定,向被保险人支付的赔偿保险责任损失的金额。

给付 包括死伤医疗给付和满期给付。死伤医疗给付是指保险人根据人寿保险及长期健康保险合同的规定,因被保险人在保险期内发生保险责任范围内的保险事故支付给被保险人(或受益人)的金额。满期给付是指被保险人生存期满,保险人按人寿保险合同规定支付给被保险人的满期保险金额。

Explanatory Note on Main Statistical Indicators

Credit Funds refer to the funds issued as loans by banking institutions. The sources of credit funds of the banking institutions included deposits, liabilities to international financial institutions, currency in circulation, self-owned funds and current retained profits, etc. The credit funds can be used in forms of loans, gold, foreign exchange, government debt and assets in the international financial insitutions.

Deposit is a form of credit by which enterprises, institutions, organizations or households can put money into banks and other credit institutions for safekeeping and interest earning under the principle of free withdrawal. According to different depositors, deposits are divided into enterprise deposits, treasury deposits, deposits of government agencies and organizations, capital construction deposits, urban savings deposits, rural deposits and other deposits. Deposits are major sources of the credit funds of banks.

Loan is a form of credit by which banks and other credit institutions provide funds at certain interest rate to enterprises and individuals in the light of the principle of unconditional repayment. Loans from Chinese banks include circulating capital loans, fixed assets loans, loans to urban and rural individuals engaged in industrial and commercial business and agricultural loans.

Insurance Companies refer to commercial insurance companies of various forms registered by law and established in China with the approval of insurance regulatory agencies.

Amount Insured refers to the maximum that the insurant will get for the claim of the case insured.

Premium is the fee paid by the insurant to the insurer to obtain the obligation of compensation from the insurance within the agreed terms.

Settled Claim is the compensation paid by the insurer to the insurant in accordance with the insurance contract.

Payment includes payment for death, injury or medical treatment and mature payment. Payment for death, injury or medical treatment refers to the money paid to the insurant (or the beneficiary) in accordance with the life or health insurance contract when the insurant encounters accidents within the insured period covered in the contract. Mature payment refers to the mature payment to the insurant in accordance with the life insurance contract at the end of the insured period.

资料整理: 陈绪曦　胡　薇

Arranged by –Chengxuxi Fuwei

17. 企业集团和景气

ENTERPRISES GROUP AND ENTERPRISES BUSINESS

企业家信心指数

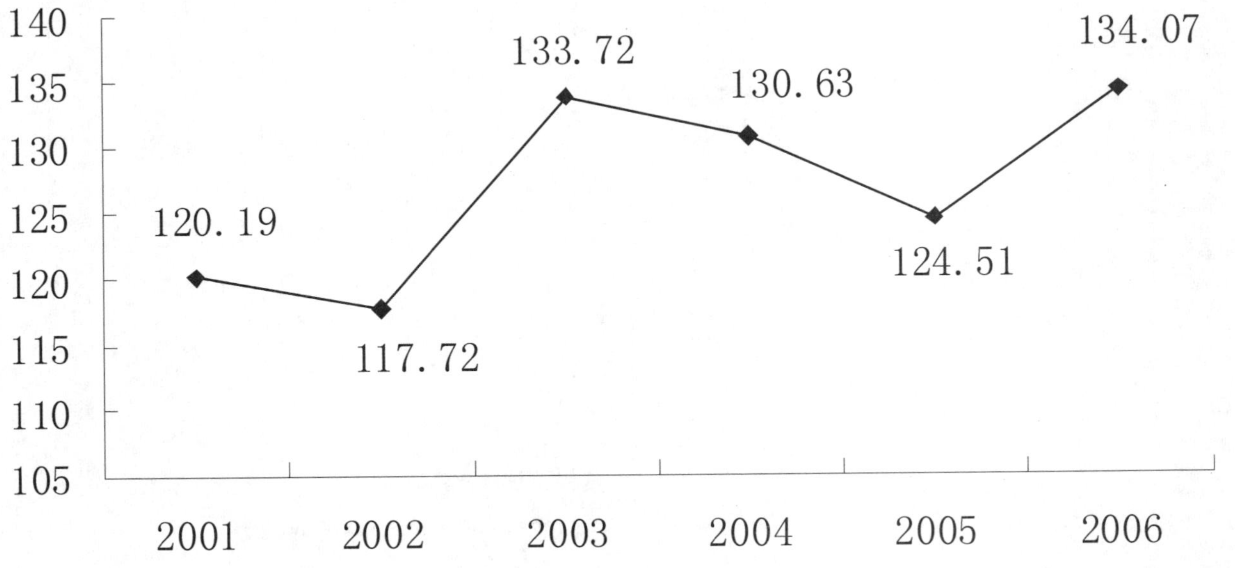

企业景气指数

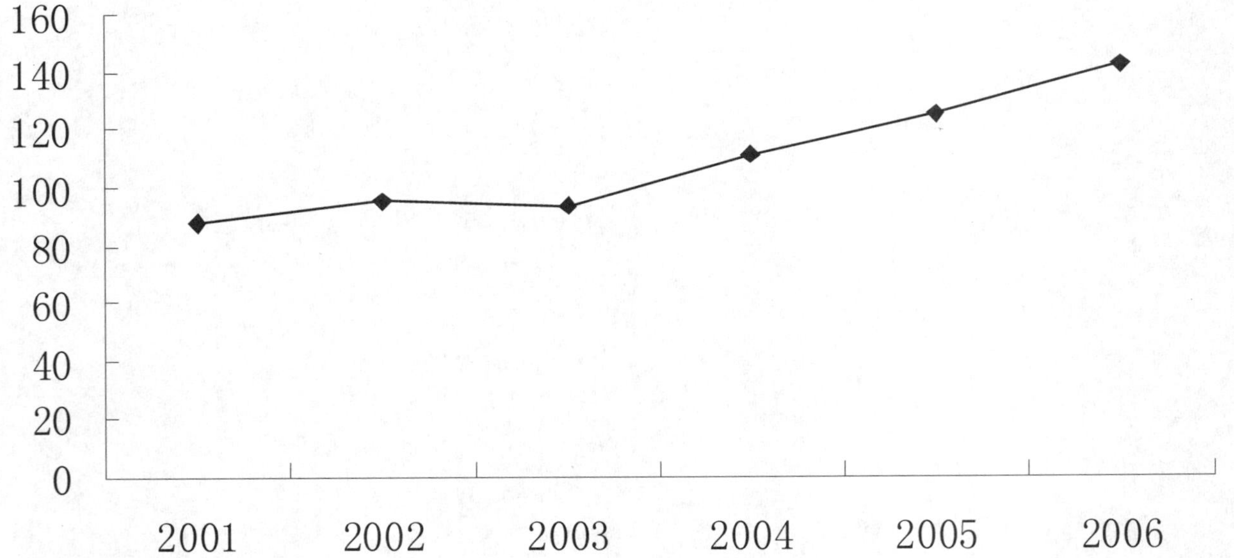

17－1 企业集团主要经济指标
Main Economic Indication of Enterprises(Group)

单位:万元 (10000 yuan)

指　标	Item	2005	2006
单位个数(个)	Number of Enterprises(unit)	8	9
年末资产总计	Total Assets(Year-end)	5973848	6452539
固定资产原价	Original Value of Fixed Assets	3788161	3855532
累计折旧	Total Depreciation Drawn Accumulated	809565	904269
#本年折旧	Drawn Accumulated This Year	136756	80702
累计对外投资	Total Outward Investment	194913	233041
#本年对外投资	External Investment This Year	12522	36766
存货	Inventory	161889	204296
流动资产年平均余额	Annual Average Balance of Circulating Funds	1556731	1916127
应收帐款	Account Receivable	126582	125513
年末负债合计	Total Liabilities(Year-end)	4183989	4596408
流动负债	Liquid Liabilities	2133041	2508209
#银行借款	Bank loan		965996
年末少数股东权益	Equity of a Few Shareholder(Year-end)	1047274	1073787
年末所有者权益合计	Total Equity of Shareholder(Year-end)	742585	782344
股本(实收资本)	Capital Stock(Capital Hold)	570546	587674
营业收入	Business Income	1715354	2381153
主营业务收入	Major Business Revenue	1688910	2331580
#主营业务成本	Major Business Costs	1326576	1870223
主营业务税金及附加	Major Business Tax and Extra Charges	44777	60665
其他业务收入	Other Business Income	26444	49573
新产品销售收入	Sales Revenue of New Products	2076	8445
#出口销售总额	Total Sales Exported	3998	5959
营业费用	Business cost		135427
管理费用	Manage ment cost		165176
#税金	Tax	603	2347
劳动、待业保险费	Labour and Unemployment Insurance	774	1289
职工教育费	Employee educational expenses		498
财务费用	Financiocl cost		124092
利息支出	Expenses of Interest	117424	124344
投资收益	Investment Income	41525	20367
利润总额	Total Profits	2614	51317
应交所得税	Income Tax Payable	8080	11501
应缴增值税	Value Added Tax Payable	6180	11532
固定资产投资完成额	Total Investment Completed in Fixed Assets	467039	240157
研究开发费用	Funds for Research and Development	106	38620

17－2 企业家信心指数
Enterpreneur Expectation Index

项 目	Item	一季度 1st. Quarter	二季度 2nd. Quarter	三季度 3rd. Quarter	四季度 4th. Quarter
总指数	**Total Index**	**131.9**	**125.36**	**121.99**	**134.07**
按行业分	**By Sector**				
工 业	Industry	126.41	125.6	117.97	124.09
建筑业	Construction	148.56	136.97	143.16	142.47
交通运输仓储及邮政业	Transport, Storage, Postal services	155.59	140.22	156.7	152.68
批发和零售业	Wholesale & Retail Trade	110.54	121.99	112.2	144.03
房地产业	Real Estate	113.64	105	110	115
社会服务业	Social Services	123.72	62.28	65.56	127.78
信息传输、计算机服务和软件业	Information Transmission, Computer Services and Software	153.33	157.14	146.15	138.28
住宿和餐饮业	Hotele and Catering Trade	140.37	93.48	93.99	129.32
按经济类型分	**By Ownership**				
国有企业	State-owned Enterprises	125.62	110.62	107.05	135.35
集体企业	Collective-owned Enterprises	112.5	125	137.5	137.5
有限责任公司	Limited-liability Companies	127.4	110.41	112.64	118.76
股份有限公司	Share Holding Ltd. Companies	153.1	161.99	159.89	165.58
私营企业	Private	166.67	120	125	150
外商及港、澳、台投资企业	Enterprises Funded by Foreigners, Businessmen from Hong Kong and Macao	128.69	125.02	113.96	118.92
按规模分	**By Size of Enterprises**				
大型	Large	157.61	157.98	152.03	156.44
中型	Medium	127.93	121.7	113.59	128.43
小型	Small	122.31	104.5	108.91	124.21
特殊分组	**Special Classification**				
上市公司	Share Listed Companies	162.65	169.01	164.08	180.98
国有控股公司	State-owned Holding Shares	131.69	120.88	118.14	135.83
高新技术企业	Enterprises of High-technology and New Technology	123.96	120.98	109.67	113.73

17－3 企业景气指数
Enterprises Business Climate Index

项 目	Item	一季度 1st. Quarter	二季度 2nd. Quarter	三季度 3rd. Quarter	四季度 4th. Quarter
总指数	**Total Index**	129.59	130.34	131.74	131.69
按行业分	**By Sector**				
工 业	Industry	120.17	128.62	132.07	129.56
建筑业	Construction	126.42	133.86	133.86	132.39
交通运输仓储及邮政业	Transport, Storage, Postal services	151.64	139.37	151.83	140.72
批发和零售业	Wholesale & Retail Trade	134.87	133.76	141.62	137.74
房地产业	Real Estate	113.64	125	115	95
社会服务业	Social Services	95.07	87.28	88.77	129.57
信息传输、计算机服务和软件业	Information Transmission, Computer Services and Software	158.85	163.06	152.52	138.28
住宿和餐饮业	Hotele and Catering Trade	131.07	92.47	84.4	126.76
按经济类型分	**By Ownership**				
国有企业	State-owned Enterprises	111.04	122.9	113.77	135.67
集体企业	Collective-owned Enterprises	100	100	112.5	87.5
有限责任公司	Limited-liability Companies	122.58	121.63	125.52	116.25
股份有限公司	Share Holding Ltd. Companies	152.05	155.69	155.18	164.39
私营企业	Private	183.33	140	200	175
外商及港、澳、台投资企业	Enterprises Funded by Foreigners, Businessmen from Hong Kong and Macao	138.71	130.45	126.37	125.53
按规模分	**By Size of Enterprises**				
大型	Large	156.67	155.28	162.23	168.91
中型	Medium	117.12	126.42	117.48	125.49
小型	Small	123.14	115.32	119.8	114.74
特殊分组	**Special Classification**				
上市公司	Share Listed Companies	163.45	174.71	159.3	175.23
国有控股公司	State-owned Holding Shares	121.69	129.69	126.23	140.9
高新技术企业	Enterprises of High-technology and New Technology	126.94	132.92	128.19	128.04

17-3 续 1(continued 1)

项　目	Item	一季度 1st. Quarter	二季度 2nd. Quarter	三季度 3rd. Quarter	四季度 4th. Quarter
工业	**Industry**				
企业家信心指数	Enterpreneur Expectation Index	126.41	125.6	117.97	124.09
企业景气指数	Enterprises Business Cilmate Index	120.17	128.62	132.07	129.56
生产成本	Production Cost	86.56	77.77	73.71	65.79
生产总量	Total Production Quantity	84.96	124.3	119	131.47
产品订货	Production Order	106	116.05	116.77	136.42
产品销售	Products Sales	84.27	115.92	129.46	131.64
产品销售价格	Selling Price of Products	97.29	111.38	79.8	104.07
产成品库存	Inventory of Products	129.68	133.84	118.16	129.53
盈利(亏损)变化	Changes in Profits (loses)	87.44	132.57	121.61	109.75
流动资金	Circulating Funds	82.87	92.85	93.43	99.42
企业融资	Enterprise's Financing	80.27	94.03	85.77	85.38
货款拖欠	Payment Delinquent	91.79	100.71	92.5	101.17
劳动力需求	Labour Demand	94.37	110.35	111.87	114.85
固定资产投资	Investment in Fixed Assets	97.8	106.65	107.61	106.72
科技创新	Input of Scientific and Technical	114.22	120.52	128.1	123.19
原材料及能源购进价格	Purchasing Price of Raw Materials and Energy	58.48	50.1	48.34	49.51
原材料及能源供应	Supply of Raw Materials and Energy	119.83	107.96	123.81	114.01
建筑业	**Construction**				
企业家信心指数	Enterpreneur Expectation Index	148.56	136.97	143.16	142.47
企业景气指数	Enterprises Business Cilmate Index	126.42	133.86	133.86	132.39
工程合同数	Assignment of Project Contracts	90.42	102.28	106.32	129.79
建筑工程量	Volume of Projects in Physical Unit	99.51	119.3	107.55	125.33
新开工工程量	Stated Projects This Year	85.28	114.37	102.82	142.68
技术设备能力	Technological equipment capability	166.74	155.98	166.75	166.75
工程进度	Project schedule	113.64	141.42	128.35	146.68
工程结算收入	Income from Project Settlement	78.54	111.75	116.6	127.37
建筑材料购进价格	Purchasing Price of Construction Materials	99.71	52.63	66.18	47.37
工程结算成本	Cost of Project Settlement	80.55	69.92	71.68	70.09
盈利（亏损）变化	Changes in Profits (loses)	87.42	114.04	117.83	141.12
流动资金	Circulating Funds	75.15	56.67	67.19	60.7
企业融资	Enterprise's Financing	50.38	37.5	47.51	35.29
货款拖欠	Payment Delinquent	74.45	51.4	65.88	97.21
劳动力需求	Labour Demand	76.78	108.29	112.81	147.26
固定资产投资	Investment in Fixed Assets	90.91	90.53	86.49	94.98
交通运输仓储及邮政业	**Transport, Storage, Postal Services**				
企业家信心指数	Enterpreneur Expectation Index	151.64	139.37	151.83	140.72
企业景气指数	Enterprises Business Cilmate Index	145.58	117.14	144.55	145.83
业务需求量	Business Volume	151.14	128.26	133.43	123.61
业务收费价格	Business Charges	133.75	146.09	139.18	128.92

17-3 续 2(continued 2)

项　目	Item	一季度 1st. Quarter	二季度 2nd. Quarter	三季度 3rd. Quarter	四季度 4th. Quarter
营业成本	Business Cost	81.37	58.77	69.89	51.87
盈利（亏损）变化	Changes in Profits (loses)	125.09	104.52	95.14	89.58
流动资金	Circulating Funds	137.88	116.38	122.13	134.35
企业融资	Enterprise's Financing	117.95	114.35	118.15	105.12
货款拖欠	Payment Delinquent	77.97	95.17	111.61	81.32
劳动力需求	Labour Demand	111.3	104.89	105.37	112.28
固定资产投资	Investment in Fixed Assets	94.18	112.6	115.18	121.06
批发和零售业	**Wholesale & Retail Trade**				
企业家信心指数	Enterpreneur Expectation Index	110.54	121.99	112.2	144.03
企业景气指数	Enterprises Business Cilmate Index	134.87	133.76	141.62	137.74
商品购进	Commodity Purchases	68.54	89.39	91.25	87.77
商品购进价格	Purchasing Price of Commodities	74.87	79.15	82.91	76.83
商品销售	Sales of Commodities	123.5	69.2	108.75	114.84
商品销售价格	Selling Price of Commodities	92.7	95.14	90.76	102.79
商品库存	Inventory of Commodities	95.29	112.96	120.72	127.54
经营费用	Business Expenditure	94.82	70.12	70.45	46.37
盈利(亏损)变化	Changes in Profits (loses)	117.78	85.96	98.5	127.36
流动资金	Circulating Funds	98.75	97.83	108.18	120.65
企业融资	Enterprise's Financing	81.48	107.79	105.52	102.87
货款拖欠	Payment Delinquent	108.91	115.14	103.75	97.73
劳动力需求	Labor Demand	97.3	93.99	109.78	93.82
固定资产投资	Investment in Fixed Assets	101.02	101.17	123.48	106.71
房地产业	**Real Estate**				
企业家信心指数	Enterpreneur Expectation Index	113.64	105	110	115
企业景气指数	Enterprises Business Cilmate Index	113.64	125	115	95
土地开发面积	Area of Land Development	81.82	75	75	90
完成投资	Completed Investment	100	115	85	120
新开工面积	New Construction in Current Year	90.91	80	85	100
房屋竣工面积	Floor Space Completed	81.82	75	70	85
商品房预售面积	Presale Space of Commercial Buildings	68.18	85	80	85
商品房销售面积	Sold Space of Commercial Buildings	77.27	85	85	90
商品房销售价格	Selling Price of Commercial Buildings	90.91	105	105	100
空置商品房面积	Vacant Space of Commercial Buildings	136.36	135	130	125
盈利（亏损）变化	Changes in Profits (loses)	81.82	60	80	70
流动资金	Circulating Funds	72.73	90	85	85
企业融资	Enterprise's Financing	85.71	70	85	90
货款拖欠	Payment Delinquent	113.64	130	130	130
劳动力需求	Labour Demand	104.55	100	90	105
固定资产投资	Investment in Fixed Assets	104.55	90	100	105
社会服务业	**Social Services**				
企业家信心指数	Enterpreneur Expectation Index	123.72	62.28	65.56	127.78

17-3 续 3(continued 3)

项 目	Item	一季度 1st. Quarter	二季度 2nd. Quarter	三季度 3rd. Quarter	四季度 4th. Quarter
企业景气指数	Enterprises Business Cilmate Index	95.07	87.28	88.77	129.57
服务预订	Service booking	102.57	45	47.37	119.69
旅游客源	Tourists	90.66	43.75	56.25	131.21
业务收费价格	Business (services) Charges	131.63	156.38	135.43	134.87
业务需求量	Business Volume	86.96	55	57.89	147.46
营业成本	Business Expenditure	54.16	62.28	52.63	44.44
盈利(亏损)变化	Changes in Profits (loses)	101.98	57.28	33.98	137.4
流动资金	Circulating Funds	67.78	91.61	103.11	111.11
企业融资	Enterprise's Financing	72.05	67.72	75.84	88.24
货款拖欠	Payment Delinquent	110.68	115	100	105.56
劳动力需求	Labour Demand	113.04	65	70.82	124.5
固定资产投资	Investment in Fixed Assets	102.36	90	102.86	97.46
信息传输、计算机服务和软件业	**Information Transmission,Computer Services and Software**				
企业家信心指数	Enterpreneur Expectation Index	153.33	157.14	146.15	138.28
企业景气指数	Enterprises Business Climate Index	158.85	163.06	152.52	138.28
产品销售	Products Sales	117.71	147.55	92.31	190
产品订货	Products Order	125.52	134.49	101.32	140
竞争能力	Competitive Power	153.33	157.14	138.46	180
销售价格	Price of Products Sales	106.67	92.86	100	71.72
营业收入	Business Revenue	117.71	140.4	115.38	143.44
营业成本	Business Cost	82.29	52.45	76.92	66.56
盈亏变化	Changes of Seek Profits and Loss	97.71	126.12	135.82	158.28
流动资金	Circulating Funds	92.19	84.49	114.06	128.28
企业融资	Enterprise's Financing	57.14	40	18.18	33.33
货款拖欠	Payment Delinquent	86.67	100	100	100
劳动力需求	Labour Demand	118.85	126.12	121.76	151.72
固定资产投资	Investment in Fixed Assets	106.67	104.69	128.13	148.28
住宿和餐饮业	**Hotels and Catering Trade**				
企业家信心指数	Enterpreneur Expectation Index	140.37	93.48	93.99	129.32
企业景气指数	Enterprises Business Climate Index	131.07	92.47	84.4	126.76
业务量	Business Volume	118.15	46.51	70.9	166.67
竞争能力	Competitive Power	136.65	112.09	120.49	122.05
客房出租	Rent of Guest Rooms	103.51	59.38	37.41	110.96
业务收费价格	Business (services)Charges	111.17	67.44	69.4	129.75
营业收入	Business Revenue	134.43	46.51	60.9	161.54
营业成本	Business Cost	91.54	115.26	94.1	66.76
盈亏变化	Changes of Seek Profits and Loss	122.8	56.2	45.9	151.8
流动资金	Circulating Funds	120.84	93.86	83.4	102.05
企业融资	Enterprise's Financing	88.81	81.03	73	92.66
货款拖欠	Payment Delinquent	105.76	100	108.1	94.34
劳动力需求	Labour Demand	82.32	84.18	75.9	136.42
固定资产投资	Investment in Fixed Assets	100.46	100.46	104.4	110.76

主要统计指标解释

景气指数 又称景气度，它是对企业景气调查中的定性指标通过定量方法加工汇总，综合反映某一特定调查群体或某一社会经济现象所处的状态或发展趋势的一种指标。其计算原理是：在调查的各类企业中，通过问卷的形式让企业经营决策者回答本企业本期经营状况相对于前期是上升、持平还是下降，然后经过加权、汇总，求出企业景气指数，即景气指数值 = 回答上升的企业所占比重 - 回答下降的企业所占比重。景气指数取值 0–200 之间，100 为景气指数的临界值，当景气指数大于 100 时，表明经济状况趋于上升或改善，处于景气状态；当景气指数小于 100 时，表明经济状况趋于下降或恶化，处于不景气状态。

企业景气指数 是根据企业家对本企业综合生产经营情况的判断与预期而编制的指数，用以综合反映企业的生产经营状况。

企业家信心指数 是根据企业家对企业外部市场经济环境与宏观政策的认识、看法、判断与预期而编制的指数，用以综合反映企业家对宏观经济环境的感受与信心。

Explanatory Note on Main Statistical Indicators

Boom Index refers to the qualitative index which is qualitatively processed and summarized in the investigation enterprises prosperity .It is an index reflecting a status or developmental trend of certain body or a certain social economic phenomenon under investigation. Its calculation principle: among the various enterprises investigated , the enterprise decision-maker is enquired in a written from to reply whether the present operation is better, equal to or poorer than before. The results are then weighted and summarized to obtain the boom index of the enterprise, i., e., Value of boom index=proportion of positive answer-proportion of negative answer. The value of boom index is between 0-200 and 100 is the critical value of boom index. When the boom index is greater then 100, the economic status tends to rise or improve, which proves in boom status; When the boom index is less than 100, the economic status tends to fall or deteriorate, which proves in slump status.

Enterprise's Boom Index (also called Enterprise's Macro-economic Boom Index) refers to the index compiled according to the enterprise's judgment and forecast to the enterprise's comprehensive production and operation. It is used to reflect the enterprise's comprehensive production and operation.

Enterprise's Confidence Index (also called Enterprise's comprehensive Operation economic Boom Index) refers to the index compiled according to the enterprise's realization, opinion, judgment and forecast to the external market economic environment and macro-policies. It is used to reflect the feeling and confidence in the enterprise's macro-economic environment.

资料整理: 邢　炜　俞祥初
Arranged by Xingwei Yuxiangchu

18. 教育、文化和科技

EDUCATION CULTURE SCIENCE AND TECHNOLOGY

在校学生数（万人）

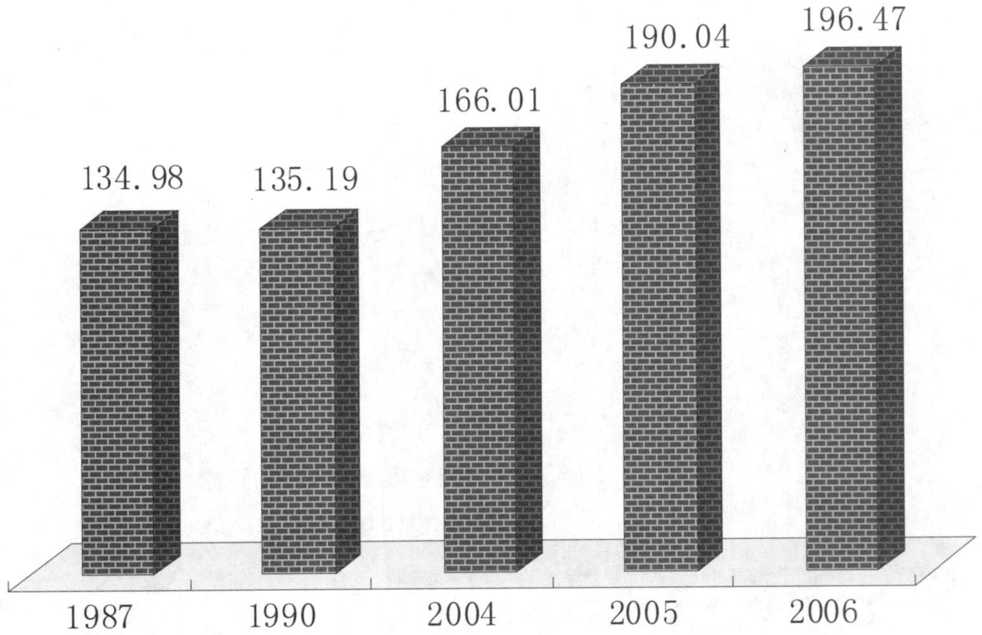

科技活动人员数（人）

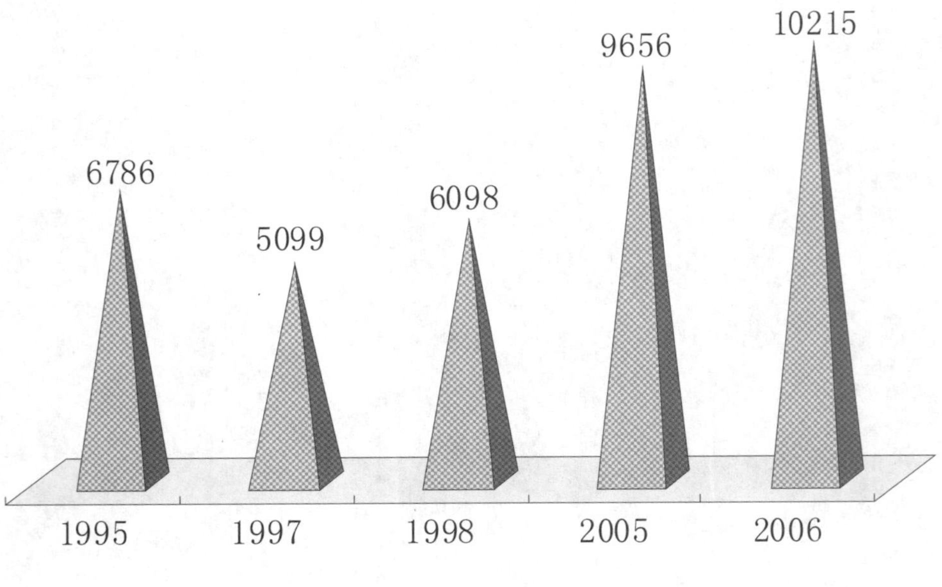

18－1 各级各类学校和教职工数
Number of Teachers and Staff by Level and Type of School

项 目	Item	2000	2001	2002	2003	2004	2005	2006
学校数(间)	**Number of Schools**							
普通高等学校	Regular Institutions of Higher Education	5	9	9	11	14	15	15
中等专业技术学校	Secondary Schools	47	46	46	42	41	37	38
普通中专学校	Regular Specialized Secondary Schools	34	35	34	30	27	23	24
技工学校	Technical Schools	13	11	12	12	14	14	14
普通中学	Regular Secondary Schools	503	527	535	542	554	563	574
职业中学	Vocational Secondary Schools	41	42	49	46	44	45	49
小 学	Primary Schools	4167	3399	3320	3287	3192	3106	3050
幼儿园	Kindergartens	706	642	619	662	708	721	865
教职工数(人)	**Number of Teachers and Staff (person)**							
普通高等学校	Regular Institutions of Higher Education	3848	3885	4356	5157	6311	7698	8638
中等专业技术学校	Technical Secondary Schools	3990	3777	3733	3423	3275	3071	3069
普通中专学校	Regular Specialized Secondary Schools	3284	3148	3071	2627	2349	2106	2093
技工学校	Technical Schools	706	629	662	796	926	965	976
普通中学	Regular Secondary Schools	29461	29987	30883	31537	32936	34331	36686
职业中学	Vocational Secondary Schools	1354	1395	1440	1268	1177	1200	1385
小 学	Primary Schools	56307	54827	55161	54869	55433	56516	57578
幼儿园	Kindergartens	6921	7236	7230	7685	8015	8672	10074
教师数(人)	**Number of Teachers (person)**							
普通高等学校	Regular Institutions of Higher Education	1571	1640	2125	2699	3636	4620	5294
中等专业技术学校	Technical Secondary Schools	2515	2382	2403	1850	1891	1827	1793
普通中专学校	Regular Specialized Secondary Schools	1809	1753	1741	1480	1271	1173	1145
技工学校	Technical Schools	706	629	662	370	620	654	648
普通中学	Regular Secondary Schools	22776	23163	24044	24903	26436	27652	29756
高 中	Senior Secondary Schools	3523	3805	4213	4768	5608	6590	7712
初 中	Junior Secondary Schools	19253	19358	19831	20135	20828	21062	22044
职业中学	Vocational Secondary Schools	1027	979	980	864	817	834	917
小 学	Primary Schools	50339	49347	49945	49367	50108	50598	51635
幼儿园	Kindergartens	6055	4058	6459	7685	4466	4845	5612

18－2 各级各类学校学生数
Number of Students Enrollment by Level and Type of School

项 目	Item	2002	2003	2004	2005	2006
在校学生数(人)	**Student Enrollment (person)**					
普通高等学校	Regular Institutions of Higher Education	34711	43498	57450	69984	90138
中等专业技术学校	Technical Secondary Schools	37570	44180	52200	60317	67628
普通中专学校	Regular Specialized Secondary Schools	31813	36427	42152	48643	52716
技工学校	Technical Schools	5757	7753	10048	11674	14912
普通中学	Regular Secondary Schools	476295	507886	541724	584351	613339
高 中	Senior Secondary Schools	78313	88946	102632	118165	137974
初 中	Junior Secondary Schools	397982	418940	439092	466186	475365
职业中学	Vocational Secondary Schools	8536	7105	7920	8888	10778
小 学	Primary Schools	1021696	1008860	1001835	1056730	1047236
幼儿园	Kindergartens	112359	113367	116820	120178	135578
招生数(人)	**New Student Enrollment (person)**					
普通高等学校	Regular Institutions of Higher Education	14648	17006	20142	24480	35264
中等专业技术学校	Technical Secondary Schools	13003	17400	20598	24285	26343
普通中专学校	Regular Specialized Secondary Schools	10559	13180	16432	19835	20528
技工学校	Technical Schools	2444	4220	4166	4450	5815
普通中学	Regular Secondary Schools	179468	189270	198242	214152	224025
高 中	Senior Secondary Schools	29970	32620	39634	46433	54135
初 中	Junior Secondary Schools	149498	156650	158608	167719	169890
职业中学	Vocational Secondary Schools	3931	3515	4179	4332	5581
小 学	Primary Schools	166168	164629	161941	182702	173749
毕业生数(人)	**Graduates(person)**					
普通高等学校	Regular Institutions of Higher Education	3939	5560	7673	11788	16436
中等专业技术学校	Technical Secondary Schools	7390	11423	11647	12188	14065
普通中专学校	Regular Specialized Secondary Schools	6191	9637	9761	10222	11362
技工学校	Technical Schools	1199	1786	1886	1966	2703
普通中学	Regular Secondary Schools	132085	141421	150468	161022	177716
高 中	Senior Secondary Schools	20076	22299	26749	30677	32472
初 中	Junior Secondary Schools	112009	119122	123719	130345	145244
职业中学	Vocational Secondary Schools	2834	2326	2095	1984	2389
小 学	Primary Schools	163422	173992	167544	171364	178501

18－3 普通高等学校学生和教职员工数
Number of Students, Teachers and Staff in Normal Higher Education

单位：人 (person)

年 份 Year	学校数（间） Schools	毕业生人数 Graduates	招生人数 New Student Enrollment	在校学生数 Student Enrollment	教职员工人数 Teachers and Staff	专任教师 Full-time Teachers
1950	2		46	219	92	42
1952	2	44	102	158	67	11
1958	5	301	780	702	114	57
1962	3	172	143	1332	411	181
1965	4		329	1008	472	190
1975	3		443	1322	553	340
1976	4	387	670	1581	1204	396
1977	6	579	763	1689	1161	609
1978	6	382	1168	3045	1426	610
1979	6	264	337	3174	1598	679
1980	6	810	857	2711	1658	698
1981	4	317	679	2531	1818	580
1982	4	484	713	2963	1883	699
1983	5	1105	1093	3054	2302	821
1984	3	1098	1621	3763	2327	938
1985	3	998	1525	4048	2959	994
1986	3	877	2371	5581	2968	1043
1987	4	1203	1886	6096	3043	1104
1988	4	2016	4630	9133	3403	1222
1989	5	2168	2406	9475	3445	1199
1990	5	3999	2460	7652	2294	1215
1991	5	2296	2525	7631	2947	1236
1995	5	3145	3739	12041	3460	1334
1998	5	3504	4324	13532	3456	1362
1999	5	3700	4903	14569	3607	1436
2000	5	3834	7940	18504	3848	1571
2001	9	3860	10851	26050	3885	1640
2002	9	3939	14648	34711	4356	2125
2003	11	5560	17006	43498	5157	2699
2004	14	7673	20142	57450	6311	3636
2005	15	11788	24480	69984	7698	4620
2006	15	16436	35264	90138	8638	5294

18－4 普通高等院校分科学生数

Student Enrollment in Institutions of Normal Higher Education by Field of Study

单位:人 (person)

科类	Item	毕业生人数 Graduates	本科 University	专科 College	招生人数 New Student enrollment	本科 University	专科 College	在校学生数 Student Enrollment	本科 University	专科 College
总计	Total	16436	6189	10247	35264	14525	20739	90138	41414	48724
其中:女	Female	6695	2207	4488	18087	7243	10844	44592	20048	24544
哲学	Phislosophy									
经济学	Economics	832	278	554	2040	784	1256	5137	2329	2808
法学	Law	449	313	136	1707	616	1091	4342	1686	2656
教育学	Education	1205	201	1004	3343	597	2746	7402	1771	5631
文学	Literature	2971	1048	1923	5992	3056	2936	15147	8193	6954
历史学	Fistory	53	53		120	120		253	253	
理学	Science	703	703		1581	1581		4330	4330	
工学	Engineering	3295	994	2301	8603	2434	6169	21135	7267	13868
农学	Agronomy	1331	765	566	1370	1043	327	4719	3533	1186
医学	Medicine	1078	533	385	2138	1115	1023	5944	3776	2168

18－5 普通中等专业、技工学校学生和教职员工数

Number of Students, Teachers and Staff in Regular Secondary Schools and Technical Schools,

单位：人　（含中等师范学校）(Uninclude Teacher Secondary Schools)　(person)

年 份 Year	学校数（间） Number of Schools	毕业生人数 Graduates	当年招生人数 New Student Enrollment	在校学生数 Student Enrollment	教职员工人数 Number of Teachers and Staff	专任教师 Full-time Teachers
1970	67		3524	4241	414	244
1971	65	6761	3700	4153	531	275
1972	61	3037	2856	2352	913	475
1973	44	1240	1792	2593	633	317
1974	41		1354	1400	494	266
1975	36		1852	3849	742	385
1976	28	1485	1530	3061	681	287
1977	29	1751	1820	3578	811	383
1978	29	1807	2435	3667	1126	529
1979	26	1600	2468	5387	1273	580
1980	23	2271	2505	5809	1477	632
1981	23	2756	2233	6117	1714	744
1982	24	2142	2683	6778	1810	787
1983	23	2241	2046	6044	1532	687
1984	25	2687	2662	6526	1661	701
1985	26	1870	3130	7884	1744	773
1986	28	1680	3674	9006	2033	873
1987	28	2893	3032	7313	2130	969
1988	28	2447	3278	8339	2219	1093
1989	27	3676	3773	9926	2115	1008
1990	36	4456	5239	12767	2677	1344
1991	43	4519	5990	13998	2908	1856
1992	31	2615	4949	11448	2170	982
1993	32	3622	6221	13826	2323	1038
1994	34	3962	6319	13818	2436	1198
1995	42	6431	10448	24461	3627	1716
1996	42	7434	9706	26530	3777	1958
1997	45	8146	10743	29014	3865	2070
1998	47	9565	11809	30056	4119	2096
1999	48	9759	11824	32824	4011	2180
2000	47	9767	12966	35668	3990	2118
2001	46	10736	12194	34967	3777	2172
2002	54	12778	16090	47163	4722	2700
2003	48	13200	18887	46734	3423	1850
2004	41	16933	18104	72233	5244	3196
2005	38	12188	24285	60317	3071	1827
2006	38	14065	26343	67628	3069	1793

18－6 普通中等专业学校分科类学生数

Number of Students by Field of Study in Regular Technical Secondary Schools

单位:人 (person)

科类	Item	毕业生人数 Graduates	当年招生人数 New Student Enrollment	招初中毕业生 Graduates of Junior Secondary Schools	在校学生数 Student Enrollment
总计	Total	11362	20528	20302	52716
#女性	Female	6411	10774	10669	27434
农林类	Agriculure and Forestry	546	648	353	1236
能源类	Energy	147	330	330	840
土木水利工程类	Civil Engineering and Water Conservancy	56	213	213	505
加工制造类	Processing and Manufacturing	630	1982	1974	4808
交通运输类	Transportation	919	1861	1855	5184
信息技术类	Informatiom Technology	1393	3138	3076	6921
医药卫生类	Medicine and Health	1736	3672	3672	9421
商贸与旅游类	Commerce and Tourism	1988	3341	3308	8625
财经类	Finance and Economics	711	1705	1701	4194
文化艺术与体育类	Culture Arts and Sports	342	555	555	1710
社会公共事业类	Social Pubic Affairs	141	341	341	725
师范类	Teacher Training	2280	2231	2231	7554
其他	Others	473	451	451	933

18 – 7 技工学校学生和教职员工数
Number of Students, Staff and Teachers in Technical Schools

单位:人 (person)

年 份 Year	学校数(间) Schools	毕业生人数 Graduates	招生数 New Student enrollment	在校学生数 Student Enrollment	教职工数 Teachers and Staff	专任教师 Full-time Teachers
1987		319	520	1075	301	118
1990	10	1143	1070	2770	518	243
1991	12	1143	1517	2821	610	274
1992	12	620	1933	4026	687	281
1993	12	1053	2269	4918	715	310
1994	12	2002	2425	5178	684	336
1995	12	1848	2509	5392	739	255
1996	12	1813	1765	5175	782	393
1997	13	1744	1588	5110	743	411
1998	14	1727	1411	4299	712	367
1999	13	1468	1570	4425	773	444
2000	13	1154	2015	4946	706	309
2001	11	1158	2024	4779	629	419
2002	12	1199	2444	5757	662	335
2003	12	1786	4220	7753	796	370
2004	14	1886	4166	10048	926	620
2005	14	1966	4450	11674	965	654
2006	14	2703	5815	14912	976	648

18－8 普通中学学生和教职员工数

Number of Students, Teachers and Staff in Regular Secondary School

单位：人 (person)

年 份 Year	学校数（间） Schools	毕业生人数 Graduates	招生数 New Student enrollment	在校学生数 Student Enrollment	教职工数 Teachers and Staff	专任教师 Full-time Teachers
1950	37	1358		12155	881	522
1951	32	2034		13633	876	529
1952	32	2165	9926	18070	1044	584
1965	139	11190	17105	50449	3630	2511
1966	137	14156	19021	53431	3512	2528
1967	100			42774	2935	2083
1968	177			88083	4168	3209
1969	218	33261	86314	135316	5717	4745
1970	308	79987	150015	234709	10898	9058
1971	442	127955	120947	248901	11955	9819
1972	301	106677	97238	213514	11967	8954
1973	297	89576	84617	184384	10888	8764
1974	306	82218	96567	190331	10957	8836
1975	429	87730	89659	257878	15348	11870
1976	458	97541	156303	303757	16972	13216
1977	487	113236	174090	345176	18823	14503
1978	487	108860	134468	338232	19845	14549
1979	510	108144	115745	305390	20231	14321
1980	501	85489	110755	301818	20740	14054
1981	503	91369	98437	264813	21562	14350
1982	489	80029	103462	257512	21293	13845
1983	485	65995	96811	255788	21417	13847
1984	480	68400	105401	280690	22078	14314
1985	480	73833	112320	304132	22324	14485
1986	483	82952	114244	336920	24113	16144
1987	479	90725	106772	325733	24956	16995
1988	480	98494	104042	303348	26127	17868
1989	480	89429	90086	264230	26276	17845
1990	481	77965	87404	252013	26329	18034
1991	474	73859	89594	247601	26054	17993
1995	478	84132	127641	317092	26613	18958
1999	501	112756	157303	412376	29546	22442
2000	503	118797	159425	435789	29461	22776
2001	527	120850	167275	446098	29987	23163
2002	535	132085	179468	476295	30883	24044
2003	542	141421	189270	507886	31537	24903
2004	554	150468	198242	541724	32936	26436
2005	563	161022	214152	584351	34331	27652
2006	574	177716	224025	613339	36686	29756

18－9 按城乡分普通中学学生和教职员工数
Number of Regular Secondary School Students,Teachers and Staff by Urban and Rural

项 目	Item	2000	2001	2002	2003	2004	2005	2006
普通中学(间)	Schools	503	527	535	542	554	563	574
城 市	City	47	54	65	76	87	90	90
县 镇	Town	69	273	256	241	246	255	263
农 村	Country	387	200	214	225	221	218	221
当年招生数(人)	New Student Enrollment	159425	167275	179168	189270	198242	214152	224025
城 市	City	16265	19178	22006	33694	36916	38466	41472
#高 中	Senior Secondary Schools	4455	4792	5774	10054	13211	14838	17016
县 镇	Town	42667	115179	115046	110780	117238	127709	138023
#高 中	Senior Secondary Schools	13942	19200	21984	20012	23643	27637	32577
农 村	Country	100493	32918	42416	44796	44088	47977	44530
#高 中	Senior Secondary Schools	4489	1728	2212	2554	2780	3958	4542
毕业生数(人)	Graduates	118797	120850	132088	26313	150468	161022	177716
城 市	City	11768	12783	14852	19320	27865	31472	33659
#高 中	Senior Secondary Schools	2923	3448	4048	6993	8564	10452	11004
县 镇	Town	33898	87673	93739	84264	89250	93394	107794
#高 中	Senior Secondary Schools	9035	11680	14793	14070	16509	17910	18935
农 村	Country	73131	20394	23494	30844	33353	36156	36263
#高 中	Senior Secondary Schools	2052	1006	1235	1236	1676	2315	2533
在校学生数(人)	Student Enrollment	435789	446098	476295	507886	541724	584351	613339
城 市	City	44488	50937	58267	91622	103129	110004	114605
#高 中	Senior Secondary Schools	11986	13276	15264	28153	34180	38841	44869
县 镇	Town	121585	312976	309984	299179	317590	346591	375031
#高 中	Senior Secondary Schools	37796	50776	57584	54827	61646	69906	82041
农 村	Country	269716	82185	108044	117085	121005	127756	123703
#高 中	Senior Secondary Schools	10075	4243	5465	5966	6806	9418	11064
教职员工数(人)	Teachers and Staff	29461	29987	30883	31537	32936	34331	36686
城 市	City	3642	4088	4735	6719	7385	7877	8581
#专职教师	Full-time Teachers	2846	3133	3534	5080	5616	6174	6672
县 镇	Town	8439	19321	18530	17459	18171	18671	20047
#专职教师	Full-time Teachers	6171	15311	14897	14091	14905	15292	16690
农 村	Country	17380	6578	7618	7359	7380	7783	8058
#专职教师	Full-time Teachers	13759	4719	5613	5732	5915	6186	6394
附:职业中学(间)	Attch:Vocational Secondary Schools	41	42	49	46	44	45	49
当年招生数(人)	New Student Enrollment	3563	3606	3931	3515	4179	4332	5581
在校学生数(人)	Student Enrollment	8459	8822	8536	7105	7920	8888	10778
教职员工数(人)	Teachers and Staff	1354	1395	1440	1480	2576	1200	1385

18－10 各市县普通中学学生和教职工数

Number of Students,Teachers and Staff in Regular Secondary School by City and Country

单位：人 (person)

		学校数(间) Schools	县镇 Town	农村 Country	毕业生 Graduates	县镇 Town	农村 Country	招生数 New Student Enrollment	县镇 Town	农村 Country
全省合计	Total	574	263	221	177716	107794	36263	224025	138023	44530
海口市	Haikou	108	23	10	37665	7915	1498	45636	9732	1643
三亚市	SanYa	44	6	23	12042	2758	3877	15500	3258	5031
五指山市	Wuzhishan	12	6	6	2994	1731	1263	3577	2246	1331
文昌市	Wenchang	33	19	14	10675	8877	1798	12312	10570	1742
琼海市	Qionghai	30	16	14	10934	8630	2304	10869	8796	2073
万宁市	Wanning	33	19	14	13899	9106	4793	14026	9366	4660
定安县	Dingan	24	17	7	6046	5510	536	7329	6579	750
屯昌县	Tunchang	19	10	9	5467	4519	948	6164	4950	1214
澄迈县	Chengmai	32	26	6	9806	8727	1079	11249	10040	1209
临高县	Lingao	23	15	8	8198	6433	1765	11528	9148	2380
儋州市	Dangzhou	50	31	19	18344	12585	5759	29884	21440	8444
东方市	Dongfang	25	17	8	8832	8530	302	12670	11766	904
乐东县	Ledong	30	15	15	10825	8747	2078	14617	12006	2611
琼中县	Qiongzhong	26	11	15	4016	2196	1820	4750	2864	1886
保亭县	Baoting	18	7	11	3286	2001	1285	4076	2477	1599
陵水县	Lingshui	23	14	9	6582	5053	1529	8824	6767	2057
白沙县	Baisha	23	6	17	3102	1609	1493	4184	2406	1778
昌江县	Changjiang	21	5	16	5003	2867	2136	6830	3612	3218

18-10 续(continued)

		在校学生数 Student Enrollment	县镇 Town	农村 Country	教职员工数 Teachers and Staff	县镇 Town	农村 Country	教师数 Teachers	县镇 Town	农村 Country
全省合计	Total	613339	375031	123703	36686	20047	8058	29756	16690	6394
海口市	Haikou	126133	27094	4689	8877	1462	305	7059	1287	244
三亚市	SanYa	43052	8966	13831	2737	409	857	2157	357	656
五指山市	Wuzhishan	9805	5982	3823	706	420	286	576	335	241
文昌市	Wenchang	35899	30518	5381	2362	1938	424	1953	1618	335
琼海市	Qionghai	32928	26330	6598	2056	1536	520	1770	1347	423
万宁市	Wanning	39326	26167	13159	2273	1456	817	1766	1115	651
定安县	Dingan	20389	18380	2009	1241	1027	214	934	794	140
屯昌县	Tunchang	16961	13711	3250	1016	761	255	857	664	193
澄迈县	Chengmai	31571	28243	3328	1897	1627	270	1452	1255	197
临高县	Lingao	32204	25468	6736	1530	1155	375	1270	977	293
儋州市	Dangzhou	76652	54320	22332	3847	2577	1270	3166	2153	1013
东方市	Dongfang	31736	29700	2036	1461	1306	155	1181	1057	124
乐东县	Ledong	39015	31834	7181	1917	1510	407	1656	1326	330
琼中县	Qiongzhong	13043	7626	5417	968	519	449	754	420	334
保亭县	Baoting	11204	6757	4447	814	505	309	684	426	258
陵水县	Lingshui	23489	17785	5704	1270	931	339	1107	815	292
白沙县	Baisha	11227	6206	5021	783	398	385	600	313	287
昌江县	Changjiang	18705	9944	8761	931	510	421	814	431	383

18－11 小学学生和教职员工数
Number of Students, Teachers and Staff in Primary Schools

单位:人 (person)

年 份 Year	学校数(间) Schools	毕业生人数 Graduates	当年招生人数 New Student enrollment	在校学生数 Student Enrollment	教职员工人数 Teachers and Staff	专任教师 Full-time eachers
1965	5027	85383	140499	511900	21067	17185
1966	5082	38541	94430	549807	20889	19716
1967	5289			519174	19600	17836
1968	5038			547108	19811	18028
1969	5120	83756	141298	527938	24259	21590
1970	5269	97032	153813	490502	21600	19298
1971	5275	76058	184118	548834	22545	18298
1972	4744	64233	163251	596107	24825	20258
1973	4559	57563	173116	666944	26785	21754
1974	4766	93721	136012	710591	27003	22231
1975	5570	96592	158805	829422	35589	29753
1976	5635	112967	180636	846721	34507	28610
1977	5604	128121	183134	856499	34693	29347
1978	5439	115723	194219	887920	38019	31504
1979	5569	104560	189757	882605	42463	34824
1980	5399	106122	175664	898676	44957	26610
1981	5302	99471	179595	904499	47212	38749
1982	5171	104881	167188	886926	45463	37039
1983	5122	109482	150903	847029	44370	35769
1984	5957	112051	169458	864560	43545	34637
1985	4905	117810	154640	872473	42082	34015
1986	4900	121518	162431	883942	43704	35412
1987	4830	119967	166567	890387	44363	36624
1988	4781	119967	169806	903500	45299	37296
1989	4759	94204	174566	918914	46065	37451
1990	4676	83352	175044	964724	46963	39002
1991	4659	90664	177649	1010528	47642	40656
1995	4430	139244	180493	1117457	49857	42583
1996	4330	149926	184641	1113621	51376	43606
1997	4330	151546	176491	1090799	57490	49470
1998	4249	152847	165948	1071910	56521	49868
1999	4199	153093	161165	1051079	56417	50130
2000	4167	154099	156735	1035810	56307	50339
2001	3399	153683	166419	1025278	54827	49347
2002	3320	163422	166168	1021696	55161	49945
2003	3287	173992	164629	1008860	54869	49367
2004	3192	167544	161941	1001835	55433	50108
2005	3106	171364	182702	1056730	56516	50598
2006	3050	178501	173749	1047236	57578	51635

18－12 按城乡分小学学生和教职员工数

Number of Students,Teachers and Staff in Primary School by Urban and Rural Areas

单位:人 (person)

项 目	Item	2000	2001	2002	2003	2004	2005	2006
学校数(间)	Schools	4167	3399	3320	3287	3192	3106	3050
城　市	City	128	128	135	160	163	149	117
县　镇	Town	137	136	317	304	302	308	284
农　村	Country	3902	2910	2868	2823	2727	2649	2649
当年招生数(人)	New Student Enrollment	156735	166419	166168	164629	161941	182702	173749
城　市	City	14806	18015	19398	22757	21615	22118	23038
县　镇	Town	17501	39862	36567	34975	35844	40609	40828
农　村	Country	124428	108542	110203	106897	104482	119975	109883
毕业生数(人)	Graduates	154099	153683	163422	173992	167544	171364	178501
城　市	City	12659	13656	16959	22392	22732	21660	21876
县　镇	Town	20369	43651	45753	44555	43095	47442	51219
农　村	Country	121071	96376	100710	107045	101717	102262	105406
在校学生数(人)	Student Enrollment	1035810	1025278	1021696	1008860	10018359	1056730	1047236
城　市	City	92484	107229	113029	136246	139490	142629	139257
县　镇	Town	119069	261443	241981	229977	242451	270242	278746
农　村	Country	824257	65606	666686	642637	619894	643859	629233
教职员工数(人)	Teachers and Staff	56307	54827	55161	54869	55433	56516	57578
城　市	City	4742	5593	6121	8070	7694	7894	7666
# 专职教师	Full-time Teachers	3952	4532	5009	6884	6310	6387	6125
县　镇	Town	6917	14387	13682	13363	13771	14655	14766
# 专职教师	Full-time Teachers	5965	12885	12225	11917	12294	12840	12956
农　村	Country	44648	34847	35358	33925	33968	33967	35146
# 专职教师	Full-time Teachers	40422	31930	32711	31251	31504	31371	32554

18－13 普通小学分年龄人口入学情况
Statistics for Primary Schools by Age

年 龄	Age	学龄儿童人口总数(人) School Age Children	女性 Female	学龄儿童在校数(人) Student Enrollment	女性 Female	入学率(%) Enrollment Rate	女性 Female
总 计	Total	985836	440440	983999	439717	99.81	99.84
6岁	Age6	36641	15944	36558	15911	99.77	99.79
7岁	Age7	162012	71850	161859	71804	99.91	99.94
8岁	Age8	161359	71055	161206	71007	99.91	99.93
9岁	Age9	164310	73445	164136	73388	99.89	99.92
10岁	Age10	170980	76476	170692	76369	99.83	99.86
11岁	Age11	172717	78380	172434	78259	99.84	99.85
12岁	Age12	117817	53290	117114	52979	99.40	99.42
城 市	City	131502	55543	131460	55528	99.97	99.97
6岁	Age6	20497	8726	20488	8723	99.96	99.97
7岁	Age7	20992	8891	20984	8887	99.97	99.97
8岁	Age8	21817	9283	21812	9281	99.98	99.98
9岁	Age9	22651	9562	22644	9560	99.97	99.98
10岁	Age10	23708	9855	23700	9853	99.97	99.98
11岁	Age11	21837	9226	21832	9224	99.98	99.98
12岁	Age12						
县 镇	Town	262209	110643	261575	110434	99.76	99.81
6岁	Age6	2958	1259	2944	1248	99.53	99.13
7岁	Age7	38604	16431	38568	16420	99.91	99.93
8岁	Age8	39520	16266	39481	16256	99.90	99.94
9岁	Age9	42461	17883	42416	17869	99.89	99.92
10岁	Age10	46267	19603	46161	19567	99.77	99.82
11岁	Age11	50156	21467	50069	21436	99.83	99.86
12岁	Age12	42243	17734	41936	17638	99.27	99.46
农 村	Country	592125	274254	590964	273755	99.80	99.82
6岁	Age6	13186	5959	13126	5940	99.54	99.68
7岁	Age7	102416	46528	102307	46497	99.89	99.93
8岁	Age8	100022	45506	99913	45470	99.89	99.92
9岁	Age9	99198	46000	99076	45959	99.88	99.91
10岁	Age10	101005	47018	100831	46949	99.83	99.85
11岁	Age11	100724	47687	100533	47599	99.81	99.82
12岁	Age12	75574	35556	75178	35341	99.48	99.40

18－14 各市县普通小学学生和教职工数

Number of Primary School Students,Teachers and Staff by City and County

单位:人 (person)

市 县	City and County	学校数 Schools	县 镇 Town	农 村 Country	毕业生 Graduates	县 镇 Town	农 村 Country	招生数 New Student enrollment	县 镇 Town	农 村 Country
全省合计	Total	3050	284	2649	178501	51219	105406	173749	40828	109883
海口市	Haikou	386	23	269	31723	4355	9848	34561	3619	12400
三亚市	SanYa	150	5	122	13123	746	8021	13305	606	8203
五指山市	Wuzhishan	51	3	48	1917	755	1162	1377	322	1055
文昌市	Wenchang	220	22	198	9309	3124	6185	8751	2744	6007
琼海市	Qionghai	206	21	185	7919	2893	5026	6776	2658	4118
万宁市	Wanning	217	20	197	12095	3532	8563	11511	3164	8347
定安县	Dingan	138	13	125	5998	2393	3605	5274	1669	3605
屯昌县	Tunchang	105	11	94	5360	1763	3597	4953	1441	3512
澄迈县	Chengmai	227	17	210	11299	3691	7608	12043	2968	9075
临高县	Lingao	157	21	136	9972	4278	5694	11089	3828	7261
儋州市	Dangzhou	346	44	302	24405	9198	15207	24547	7000	17547
东方市	Dongfang	175	17	158	9030	4032	4998	10527	3239	7288
乐东县	Ledong	205	15	190	11456	2882	8574	10866	2165	8701
琼中县	Qiongzhong	101	9	92	4258	1143	3115	2693	642	2051
保亭县	Baoting	75	8	67	3169	755	2414	2402	587	1815
陵水县	Lingshui	122	14	108	7921	2345	5576	5349	1835	3514
白沙县	Baisha	74	5	69	3876	827	3049	3305	528	2777
昌江县	Changjiang	95	16	79	5671	2507	3164	4420	1813	2607

18－14 续(continued)

市 县	City and County	在校学生数 Student Enrollment	县 镇 Town	农 村 Country	教职员工数 Teachers and Staff	县 镇 Town	农 村 Country	教师数 Teachers	县 镇 Town	农 村 Country
全省合计	Total	1047236	278746	629233	57578	14766	35146	51635	12956	32554
海口市	Haikou	196988	22751	61342	11377	1355	3626	9705	1285	3369
三亚市	SanYa	79103	4131	48610	3865	242	2353	3396	205	2117
五指山市	Wuzhishan	9822	3586	6236	801	217	584	749	195	554
文昌市	Wenchang	51374	17687	33687	2982	942	2040	2815	892	1923
琼海市	Qionghai	40563	15838	24725	2730	886	1844	2412	776	1636
万宁市	Wanning	62326	18587	43739	3955	1185	2770	3431	976	2455
定安县	Dingan	31640	11317	20323	2412	756	1656	2258	669	1589
屯昌县	Tunchang	29677	9358	20319	1849	535	1314	1779	515	1264
澄迈县	Chengmai	64799	18948	45851	3701	1069	2632	3233	864	2369
临高县	Lingao	59633	24146	35487	2886	1157	1729	2643	1010	1633
儋州市	Dangzhou	152719	51556	101163	6609	2205	4404	6008	1882	4126
东方市	Dongfang	63650	24452	39198	2908	1082	1826	2625	950	1675
乐东县	Ledong	71939	16377	55562	3369	827	2542	3097	718	2379
琼中县	Qiongzhong	19427	5350	14077	1483	392	1091	1384	347	1037
保亭县	Baoting	15766	3948	11818	1299	311	988	1132	265	867
陵水县	Lingshui	41142	12963	28179	2188	666	1522	2038	594	1444
白沙县	Baisha	22034	4725	17309	1383	321	1062	1255	262	993
昌江县	Changjiang	34634	13026	21608	1781	618	1163	1675	551	1124

18－15 平均每万人口在校学生数和大、中、小学生构成
Student Enrollment Per 10 Thousand Population and Its Composition

年份 Year	各级学校在校学生占总人口(%) Students as Percentage of Total Population	平均每万人口在校学生数(人) Number of Student Enrollment Per 10000 Population			大、中、小学校占学生总数(%) Students as Percentage of Total Student		
		大学 University Students	中学 Secondary School Students	小学 Primary School Students	大学 University Students	中学 Secondary School Students	小学 Primary School Students
1961	15.67	5.4	196	1366	0.4	12.5	87.1
1962	15.36	4.0	172	1361	0.3	11.2	88.5
1963	14.50	3.7	150	1296	0.3	10.3	89.4
1964	16.94	2.8	152	1539	0.1	9.0	90.9
1965	16.21	2.7	157	1390	0.2	3.5	86.3
1966	16.15		156	1456	0.1	9.7	90.2
1967	14.62		121	1340		8.3	91.7
1968	16.32		229	1403		14.0	86.0
1969	16.25		331	1293		20.4	79.6
1970	17.00		557	1143		32.8	67.2
1971	18.21		614	1207		33.7	66.3
1972	17.65		461	1274		26.6	73.4
1973	17.81	2.1	390	1391	0.1	21.8	78.1
1974	18.50	1.5	397	1457	0.1	21.2	78.7
1975	21.96	2.7	527	1669	0.1	24.9	76.0
1976	22.87	3.1	607	1676	0.1	26.6	73.3
1977	23.34	3.3	675	1659	0.1	28.9	71.0
1978	23.48	5.8	647	1680	0.3	27.7	72.0
1979	22.15	5.9	575	1634	0.3	26.0	73.7
1980	21.88	4.9	557	1626	0.2	25.5	74.3
1981	21.02	4.5	485	1613	0.2	23.1	76.7
1982	20.21	4.8	464	1552	0.2	23.0	76.8
1983	19.25	5.3	461	1452	0.3	23.9	75.8
1984	19.69	6.4	495	1467	0.3	25.2	74.5
1985	20.03	6.8	523	1460	0.3	26.8	72.9
1986	20.55	9.2	586	1459	0.5	28.5	71.0
1987	20.10	9.9	553	1448	0.5	27.5	72.0
1988	19.59	14.6	505	1439	0.7	25.8	73.5
1989	18.86	14.8	434	1439	0.8	23.0	76.2
1990	19.19	11.8	425	1481	0.6	22.2	77.2
1991	19.63	11.5	424	1528	0.6	21.6	77.8
1995	20.59	17.1	451	1591	0.8	21.9	77.3
1996	20.01	17.0	467	1517	0.8	23.3	75.8
1997	22.72	17.0	518	1506	0.9	25.4	73.7
1998	21.64	18.0	512	1424	0.8	23.6	75.6
1999	22.13	19.6	555	1414	0.9	25.1	74.0
2000	20.89	23.5	554	1316	1.3	29.2	69.5
2001	18.82	32.7	561	1289	1.7	29.8	68.5
2002	21.71	44.6	612	1295	2.1	28.3	69.6
2003	19.34	53.6	627	1245	2.7	32.6	64.7
2004	19.58	70.8	662	1225	3.6	33.8	62.6
2005	21.74	84.52	706	1276	4.1	34.1	61.8
2006	21.88	107.8	734	1253	5.1	35.0	59.8

18－16 各类成人教育学校学生和教职员工数

Number of Students,Teachers and Staff in Adult Schools by Level and Type

项 目	Item	2002	2003	2004	2005	2006
成人高等学校(间)	Adult Education College(unit)	1	1	1	1	1
毕业生人数(人)	Graduates(person)	917	6520	9501	7075	4510
当年招生数(人)	New Student Enrollment(person)	1022	10568	12943	9421	8672
在校学生数(人)	Student Enrollment(person)	2059	27507	20556	21581	22074
教职员工数(人)	Teachers and Staff(person)	95	105	108	107	106
# 专职教师	Full-time Teachers	59	66	66	67	67
成人中等专业学校(间)	Secondary Schools for Adults(unit)	19	14	10	9	8
毕业生人数(人)	Graduates(person)	268	702	511	392	336
当年招生数(人)	New Student Enrollment(person)	414	421	522	68	176
在校学生数(人)	Student Enrollment(person)	635	1117	1119	893	641
教职员工数(人)	Teachers and Staff(person)	620	416	284	188	281
# 专职教师	Full-time Teachers	285	229	162	93	170
成人中学校数(间)	Middle Schools for Adults(unit)	4	7	5	7	8
毕业生人数(人)	Graduates(person)	20	302	254	704	3127
在校学生数(人)	Student Enrollment(person)	206	206	98	745	2692
教职员工数(人)	Teachers and Staff(person)	15	39	15	51	61
# 专职教师	Full-time Teachers	8	8	8	17	32
成人初等学校数(间)	Primary Schools for Adults(unit)	187	589	390	603	570
毕业生人数(人)	Graduates(person)	3834	5188	532	5218	4342
在校学生数(人)	Student Enrollment(person)	4834	5719	630	6221	4246
教职员工数(人)	Teachers and Staff(person)	126	628	415	859	771
# 专职教师	Full-time Teachers	70	134	314	345	299
在成人初等教育中	Literacy Sourses of Primary Schools for Adults(unit)					
扫盲班(间)	Literacy Courses(unit)	172	1213	349	390	357
毕业生人数(人)	Graduates(person)	3297	196065	364	1363	568
在校学生数(人)	Student Enrollment(person)	4146	145517	500	2340	787
教职员工数(人)	Teachers and Staff(person)	110	1399	194	293	206
# 专职教师	Full-time Teachers	60	136	103	121	89

18－17 技工学校学生和教职员工数
Number of Students, Staff and Teachers in Technical Schools

单位：人 (person)

年 份 Year	学校数(间) Schools	毕业生数 Graduates	招生数 New Student enrollment	在校学生数 Student Enrollment	教职工数 Teachers and Staff	专任教师 Full-time eachers
1987		2301	7259	14126	1230	702
1990			4975	12232	1571	44
1991			5031	11843	1567	44
1992			4153	10202	1309	
1993			4234	9762	1359	
1994			4144	9303	1373	
1995			3777	8559	1350	933
1996	37	2607	3164	7609	1390	928
1997	35	2391	3221	7749	1400	979
1998	37	2439	3189	7446	1392	1053
1999	43	2925	4107	9411	1488	1086
2000	41	3134	3563	8459	1354	1027
2001	42	3076	3606	8822	1395	979
2002	49	2834	3931	8536	1440	980
2003	46	2326	3515	7105	1268	864
2004	44	2095	4179	7920	1177	817
2005	45	1984	4332	8888	1200	834
2006	49	2389	5581	10778	1385	917

18－18 幼儿园在园幼儿和教职员工数
Number of Students, Teachers and Staff in Kindergartens

单位：人 (person)

年份 Year	园数(所) Number of Kindergartens	在园幼儿数 Students Enrollment	教职员工人数 Teachers and Staff	教养员 Teachers
1961	174	8293	803	281
1962	177	8205	678	285
1963	141	8466	768	294
1964	198	10986	902	348
1965	268	11445	1036	434
1966	343	17591	1321	641
1967	89	9583	757	363
1968	84	7194	579	277
1969	39	4275	210	101
1970	107	6637	317	223
1971	211	7733	700	571
1972	100	7898	353	190
1973	155	8366	343	157
1974	163	8708	386	206
1975	682	20877	1387	886
1976	3524	108059	6223	4532
1977	2130	71570	3882	3162
1978	1894	69140	3557	2752
1979	1818	64817	3529	2135
1980	1670	63332	3949	2175
1981	1285	60614	4164	2543
1982	1349	61176	4328	2603
1983	1110	64741	4180	2410
1984	1200	77892	4476	2788
1985	783	72428	3481	2348
1986	1170	86039	4227	2806
1987	1409	106190	4788	3368
1988	623	97074	4170	2830
1989	385	93082	4235	2855
1990	384	102545	4466	3078
1991	306	109285	5158	3628
1995	477	130780	5678	4400
1996	512	133663	6160	5446
1997	499	138332	7009	6165
1998	516	119878	6426	5296
1999	652	124656	7077	6033
2000	706	128139	6921	6055
2001	642	115466	7236	6494
2002	619	112359	7230	6459
2003	662	113367	7685	4308
2004	708	116820	8015	4466
2005	721	120178	8672	4845
2006	865	135578	10074	5612

18－19 幼儿园基本情况表
Basic Statistics for Kindergartens

项 目		园数(所) Number of Kindergartens	班数(个) Number of Classes	入园人数(人) New Student Enrollment	学前班 Preschool Class	在园人数(人) New Students Enrollment	学前班 Preschool Class	教职工人数(人) Teachers and taff	教师 Teachers	保健员 Health Worker
总　计	**Total**	**865**	**5276**	**88068**	**45497**	**135578**	**57446**	**10074**	**5612**	**1268**
其中:女性	Female			36321	19000	55419	23561	9282	5513	1206
按经济类型分	Units by Type									
教育部门和集体办	Run by Educational Department	66	1565	33304	27218	41941	30302	1590	1068	84
社会力量办	Run by Social Organization and Citizens	695	3042	42212	11128	73807	17674	7117	3831	988
其他部门办	Run by Other Department	104	669	12552	7151	19830	9470	1367	713	196
按城乡分	Grouped by Urban and Rural Areas									
城　市	City	309	1613	19827	4959	38576	9428	4578	2484	532
县　镇	Town	356	1779	34316	14959	54006	19773	3883	2267	456
农　村	Country	200	1884	33925	25579	42996	28245	1613	861	280

18－20 文化、艺术、广播电视事业基本情况
Basic Statistics of Culture,Art,Broadcasting and Television

项 目	Item	2000	2001	2002	2003	2004	2005	2006
文化馆(间)	Cultural Centers	18	18	18	18	18	18	18
博物馆、纪念馆(间)	Museum and Memorial Hall	15	16	16	17	16	16	15
乡(镇)文化站(座)	Cultural Stations(set)	306	288	214	223	221	213	209
档案馆(座)	Chancery(set)	27	27	27	29	30	30	30
广播电台电视台(座)	Brpadcasting StationTelevision Stationss(set)	20	20	20	19	19	19	19
电视发射差转台(座)	Transmitters(set)	22	22	22	21	14	21	23
电视覆盖率(%)	Viewer Rating(%)	93.5	94.1	94.1	94.47	94.52	95	95

18－21 图书、报纸、杂志印刷出版

Number of Books,Newspaper,Magazines Published

项 目	Item	种类数(种) Number of Pubications(kind)	总刷数 (万册、万份) Printed Copies (10000 copies)	总张印数 (千印张) Printed Sheets (1000 sheets)
图　书	Books	1996	4918	381761
报　纸	Newspaper	20	23520	724720
综合报	Ceneral Newspaper	12	15181	572893
专业报	Specialized Newspaper	8	8339	151827
省级	Provincial Level	18	21248	660708
地(市)级	Municapal Level	2	2272	64012
杂　志	Magzines	41	1059	69396
综合类	Ceneral	15	535	34408
哲学、社会科学类	Philosophy and Social Science	7	90	4468
自然科学、技术类	Natural Science and Sechnoloty	10	67	3958
文化、教育类	Cultural and Education	6	334	24182
文学、艺术类	Lierature and Art	3	33	2379
画　刊	Picturial			

18－22 图书发行量

Composition of Books Published

单位:万册　(10 000copies)

项目	Item	总计 Total	哲学社会科学 Philosophy and Social Science	文化教育 Culture and Education	文学艺术 Literature and Arts	自然科学技术 Natural Science	少儿读物 Children Books	大中专教材 Teaching Material of University and Callege	课本 Textbook	图片 Photograph	其他出版物 Other Publisheds
销　售	Sell	9,277	350	430	72	143	350	101	7,831		3
库　存	Stock	3,380									

18－23 公共图书馆藏书

Collection Books of Pulic Libraries

级别	Item	机构数(个) Number of Institution	藏书合计(千册) Callection Books (1000copies)	图书 Books Published	古籍 Ancient Books	报刊 Newspaper and Magzines	缩微制品 Microfilm Products	其他 Others	在藏量中:开架书刊
总　计	Total	20	1927	1576	8	320		30	1020
地(市)级	Prefecture and City Level	2	487	434	6				196
县　级	County Level	17	1140	1142	2			30	824

18－24 企业、事业单位各类专业技术人员数
Number of Scientific and Technical Personnel in Enterprises and Institutions

单位：人 (person)

项目	Item	合计 Total	农林牧渔业 Agriculture, Forestry, Animal Iusbandry, Fishery	采矿业 Mining and Quarrying	制造业 Prodcts	电力、煤气及水的生产和供应业 Production and Supply of Electric Power Gas and Water	建筑业 Construction	交通运输仓储和邮政业 Transport, Storage, Postal Services	信息传输、计算机服务和软件业 Information Transmission, Computer Services and Software	批发和零售业 Wholesale & Retail Trade	住宿和餐饮业 Hotels and Catering Trade
总　计	**Total**	**138697**	**24545**	**1742**	**1683**	**819**	**864**	**2817**	**292**	**759**	**71**
工程技术人员	Engineering	9810	1336	606	752	664	680	1246	240	125	15
农业技术人员	Agriculture Research	3791	3435	7	7	1		6			3
科学研究人员	Scientific Research	524	16						8		
卫生技术人员	Health Care	23139	4106	210	165	2	4	98		58	1
教学人员	Teaching	85671	10072	391	140	3	2	132	1	3	2
其他	Others	15762	5580	528	619	149	178	1335	43	573	50

18－24 续(continued)

项目	Item	金融业 Banking and Insurance	房地产业 Real estate and Social Services	租赁和商务服务业 Rent and Business Affair Services	科学研究、技术服务和地质勘查业 Scientific Research, Polytechnic Services and Geological Prospecting	水利、环境和公共设施管理业 Water Conservancy, Environmental and Public Installations Management Services	居民服务和其他服务业 Resident Services and Other Social Services	教育 Education	卫生、社会保障和社会福利业 Culture, Sports and Recreational Services	文化、体育和娱乐业 Culture, Sports and Recreational Services	公共管理和社会组织 Public Management and Social Organizations
总　计	**Total**	**74**	**201**	**227**	**2202**	**1288**	**155**	**75993**	**19275**	**2825**	**2865**
工程技术人员	Engineering		68	11	1668	803	110	169	161	468	688
农业技术人员	Agriculture Research			1	90	57		32	58	1	93
科学研究人员	Scientific Research				196	9		248	11	5	31
卫生技术人员	Health Care		9	6	4	78	5	316	18022	23	32
教学人员	Teaching		17	6	4	59		74201	137	78	423
其他	Others	74	107	203	240	282	40	1027	886	2250	1598

18－25 科技活动人员数
Number of Personnel Engaged in Scientific and Technological Activities

指 标	Item	合计 Total	科研机构 Scientific Research and Development Institute	高等学校 Higher Education	大中型工业企业 Large-scale and Medium-scale Industrial Enterprises	其他 Others
单位数(个)	Number of Enterprises and Institutions	894	68	21	82	723
#有科技活动单位数	Number of Enterprises and Institutions Having S&T Activities	186	64	10	18	94
科技活动人员(人)	S&T Personnel (person)	10215	2848	871	1864	4632
#科学家与工程师	Scientists ang Engineers	5790	1206	768	1331	2485
#有研究与试验发展活动单位数	Number of Enterprises Andinstitutions Having R&D Activities	78	13	10	10	45
研究与试验发展人员(人)	R&D Personnel (person)	1745	433	328	244	740
#全时人员	Full-time Equivalent	1264	346	102	197	619
科学家与工程师	Scientists and Engineers	1518	330	322	209	657
基础研究	Basic Research	424	201	208		15
应用研究	Applied Reseatch	604	187	106		311
试验发展	Expermental Development	718	45	14	244	415

注:科研机构包括科技厅下属的科研机构、转制企业及综合技术服务机构。
a)The scientific research institutions including the scientific research institutions undering the scientic and technical hall the enterprise which changed the system and technical serving institutions.

18－26 科技活动经费情况

Basic Statistics on S&T Expenditure of Enterprises and institutions

单位:万元 (10 000yuan)

指 标	Item	合计 Total	科研机构 Scientific Research and Development Institute	高等学校 Higher Education	大中型工业企业 Large-scale and Medium-scale Industrial Enterprises	其他 Others
科技经费筹集额	Sources of Funds for S&T	123157	38927	6232	46042	31956
政府拨款	Government Funds	37032	31000	5328	70	634
企业资金	Enterprises Funds	78244	3173	162	45972	28937
事业单位资金	Institutions Funds	5301	3950	543		808
其他	Other	2580	804	199		1577
科技经费	Intramural Expenditure	117116	31823	5673	50393	29227
内部支出	Expenditures for S&T	108716	31486	5543	49596	22091
#劳务费	Labor Expenses	23018	9443	1733	4994	6848
固定资产购建	Expenses on Fixed Assets	44280	6108	1632	29786	6754
研究与试验发展经费支出	Expenditures for R&D	24494	8561	2497	4208	9228
#基础研究	Basic Research	4767	2984	1586		197
应用研究	Applied Reseatch	8430	2991	767		4672
试验发展	Expermental Development	9095	498	89	3998	4510

18－27 科技活动成果情况

Basic Statistics on Scientific and Technological Achievements of Enterprises and Institutions

项 目	Item	专利申请数(项) Number of Patent Applications Examined(unit)	发明 Inventions	拥有发明专利数(项) Number of Inventions Owned(unit)	发表科技论文(篇) S&T Papers	出版科技著作(种) S&T works
总 计	Total	131	53	60	3295	120
按机构类型分	Grouped by Institute					
科研机构	Scientific Research and Development Institute	18	9	8	776	33
高等院校	Higher Education	19	18	10	2031	85
大中型工业企业	Large and Medium Industrial Enterprises	37	2			
其他	Others	57	24	42	488	2
按地区分	By Region					
海口市	Haikou	14	12	11	488	2
三亚市	Sanya					
其他市县	Others	117	41	49	2807	118

18－28 科技活动机构情况
Statistic For Institutions In Science and Technology Activities

		机构数（个）Number of Institutions	机构从事科技活动人员(人) Personnel Engaged In Science and Technology	科学家和工程师 Scientist ang Engineer	机构科技经费内部支出(万元) Internal Expenditur S & T Activities	经费 R&D	机构年末固定资产原价(万元) Original Value of Fixed Assets at the Year-end	仪器设备 Inqupment
总　　计	Total	163	5874	1994	41433	10118	64891	60419
按数据来源分组	**Grouped by Source of Data**							
科研机构	Scientific Research and Development Institute	68	2848	959	31486	8561	46112	14074
高等院校	Higher Education	20	148	67	810	589	4086	3185
大中型工业企业	Large and Medium Industrial Enterprises	16	606	418	4293			37129
其他	Others	59	2272	550	4844	968	14693	6030
按学科分组	**Grouped by Course**							
自然科学	Natural Sciences	8	318	157	6095	3858	7316	4546
农业科学	Agriculture Science	52	2147	661	21700	5058	27163	7583
医药科学	Medical Science	24	236	171	3013	863	9798	4424
工程与技术科学	Engineering and Technical Science	73	2950	942	9610	310	18633	42874
人文与社会科学	Humanities and Social Sciences	6	223	63	1014	30	1980	992
按服务的国民经济行业分组	**Grouped by Sector**							
农业	Farming	25	1132	521	15743	4326	20201	7286
林业	Forestry	6	204	30	832		897	215
畜牧业	Animal Husbandry	3	23	7	260	113	559	127
渔业	Fishery	1	33	20	484		1973	
农、林、牧、渔服务业	Agricultural Services	17	1079	159	6246	1202	8926	2707
农副食品加工业	Agriculture and Non－Staple Food Processing	1	20	10	71	69	675	512
食品制造业	Food Manufacturing	8	106	91	172	26	300	28613
饮料制造业	Beverages Manufacturing	5	49	35	91		66	47
纺织业	Textiles	1	165	165	615			103
木材加工及、竹、藤、棕、草制品业	Timber Processing Bambov cane palm Fiber and straw	1	12	5	1			5000
家具制造业	Futnitnre Manufacturing	1	8		1			2
造纸及纸制品业	Papermaking and Paper Products	1	250	113	2933			2760
化学原料及化学制品制造业	Raw Chemical Materials and Chemical Products	7	26	17	106			27
医药制造业	Medical and Pharmaceutical Products	19	252	213	3998	718	6891	4563
塑料制品业	Plastic Products	2	30	23	145			103
黑色金属冶炼及压延加工业	Smelting and Pressing of Ferrous Metals	1	39	39	20			250

18-28 续(continued)

		机构数(个) Number of Institutions	机构从事科技活动人员(人) Personnel Engaged In Science and Technology	科学家和工程师 Scientist ang Engineer	机构科技经费内部支出(万元) Internal Expenditur S & T Activities	经费 R&D	机构年末固定资产原价(万元) Original Value of Fixed Assets at the Year-end	仪器设备 Inqupment
有色金属冶炼及压延加工业	Smelting and Pressing of Nonferrous Metals	1	4	4	15			10
专用设备制造业	Equipment for Special Purposes	5	51	29	73	10	107	15
交通运输设备制造业	Transport Equipment	2	45	35	152	142	5438	202
电气机械及器材制造业	Electric Equipment and Machinery	2	70	70	381	60	300	210
通信设备、计算机及其他电子设备制造业	Telecommunications Equipment Computer and Other Electronic Equipment	4	115	94	505		23	87
仪器仪表及文化、办公用机械制造业	Instruments Meters Cultural and Clerical Machinery	2	21	19	76		280	281
工艺品及其他制造业	Industrial Arts and other Manufacturing	1	3	3	10		4	4
废弃资源和废旧材料回收加工业	Recovery and Processing of Discarded Resoures and Weste Material							
房屋和土木工程建筑业	House and Civil Engine ering	11	1621					
计算机服务业	Computer Services							
研究与试验发展	R&D	6	198	157	5017	3295	4370	2615
专业技术服务业	Service Trade of the Professional Technique	2	131	75	2607		10941	2996
科技交流和推广服务业	Scientific and Technological Exchange and Popularizing the Senice Trade	4	26		77		73	24
环境管理业	Environmental Management Industry	1	22		549		29	20
公共设施管理业	Public in stallations Management Services							
教育	Education	3	8	5	5		5	4
卫生	Health	5	54	30	37	29	1793	792
广播、电视、电影和音像业		9	43	16	125	103	911	772
娱乐业	Recreational Services	6	34	9	84	27	129	55
按机构类型分组	**Grouped by Institute**							
与国内高等学校合办	Co-sponsored whit Domesti Colleges and Universities							
与国内独立科研机构合办	Co-sponsored whit Independent Domestic Scientific Agencies							
与境内注册外商独资企业合办	Co - sponsored whit Foreign Enterprises Registered in China	1	10	9	75	0	429	346
与境内注册其他企业合办	Co - sponsored whit Other Enterprises Registered in China							
单位自办	Self-sponsored	159	5856	1980	41353	10118	64457	60068
其他	Others	3	8	5	5		5	4
按隶属关系分组	**Grouped by Administraitive Relationship**							
中央	Central	15	1426	606	23487	8308	31122	12790
地方	Local	148	4448	1388	17944	1810	33768	47628
按地区分组	**Grouped by Region**							
海口市	Haikou	21	322	284	2994	967	14693	4300
三亚市	Sanya							
其他	Others	142	5552	1710	38439	9151	50198	56119

主要统计指标解释

普通高等学校 指按照国家规定的设置标准和审批程序批准举办，通过国家统一招生考试，招收高中毕业生为主要培养对象，实施高等教育的全日制大学、独立设置的学院和高等专科学校、短期职业大学。

成人高等学校 指按照国家有关规定审批，招收通过全国成人高教统一招生考试的具有高中毕业或同等学历的在职从业人员，利用脱产、半脱产、业余或函授等多种形式对其实施高等学历教育，培养高等教育专科或本科毕业水平的专门人才，修业年限、课程设置和总学时数均按高等学历教育要求付诸实施的学校。包括广播电视大学、职工高等学校、农民高等学校、管理干部学院、教育学院、独立设置的函授学院等。

小学学龄儿童入学率 指调查范围内已入小学学习的学龄儿童占校内外学龄儿童总数（包括弱智儿童，不包括盲聋哑儿童）的比重。计算公式为:

小学学龄儿童入学率 = 已入学的小学学龄儿童数 / 校内外小学学龄儿童总数 *100%

科技活动 指在自然科学、农业科学、医药科学、工程与技术科学、人文与社会科学领域（简称科学技术领域）中，与科技知识的产生、发展、传播和应用密切相关的有组织的活动。可分为研究与试验发展（R&D）、研究与试验发展成果应用及相关的科技服务三类活动。

科技活动人员 指直接从事科技活动、以及专门从事科技活动管理和为科技活动提供直接服务的人员。累计从事科技活动的实际工作时间占全年制度工作时间 10%及以上的人员。(1) 直接从事科技活动的人员包括: 在独立核算的科学研究与技术开发机构、高等学校、各类企业及其他事业单位内设的研究室、实验室、技术开发中心及中试车间（基地）等机构中从事科技活动的研究人员、工程技术人员、技术工人及其它人员；虽不在上述机构工作，但编入科技活动项目（课题）组的人员；科技信息与文献机构中的专业技术人员；从事论文设计的研究生等。(2) 专门从事科技活动管理和为科技活动提供直接服务的人员包括: 独立核算的科学研究与技术开发机构、科技信息与文献机构、高等学校、各类企业及其他事业单位主管科技工作的负责人，专门从事科技活动的计划、行政、人事、财务、物资供应、设备维护、图书资料管理等工作的各类人员，但不包括保卫、医疗保健人员、司机、食堂人员、茶炉工、水暖工、清洁工等为科技活动提供间接服务的人员。

科学家与工程师 指科技活动人员中具有高、中级技术职称（职务）的人员和不具有高、中级技术职称（职务）的大学本科及以上学历人员。

研究与试验发展（R&D）指在科学技术领域，为增加知识总量、以及运用这些知识去创造新的应用而进行的系统的创造性的活动，包括基础研究、应用研究、试验发展三类活动。

基础研究 指为了获得关于现象和可观察事实的基本原理的新知识（揭示客观事物的本质、运动规律，获得新发现、新学说）而进行的实验性或理论性研究，它不以任何专门或特定的应用或使用为目的。其成果以科学论文和科学著作为主要形式。

应用研究 指为获得新知识而进行的创造性研究，主要针对某一特定的目的或目标。应用研究是为了确定基础研究成果可能的用途，或是为达到预定的目标探索应采取的新方法（原理性）或新途径。其成果形式以科学论文、专著、原理性模型或发明专利为主。

试验发展 指利用从基础研究、应用研究和实际经验所获得的现有知识，为产生新的产品、材料和装置，建立新的工艺、系统和服务，以及对已产生和建立的上述各项作实质性的改进而进行的系统性工作。其成果形式主要是专利、专有技术、具有新产品基本特征的产品原型或具有新装置基本特征的原始样机等。在社会科学领域，试验发展是指把通过基础研究、应用研究获得的知识转变成可以实施的计划（包括为进行检验和评估实施示范项目）的过程。人文科学领域没有对应的试验发展活动。

研究与试验发展人员 指参与研究与试验发展项目研究、管理和辅助工作的人员，包括项目（课题）组人员，企业科技行政管理人员和直接为项目（课题）活动提供服务的辅助人员。

研究与试验发展人员全时当量 指全时人员数加非全时人员按工作量折算为全时人员数的总和。例如: 有两个全时人员和三个非全时人员（工作时间分别为 20%、30%和 70%），则全时当量为 2+0.2+0.3+0.7=3.2 人年。

专业技术人员 指从事专业技术工作和专业技术管理工作的人员，即企事业单位中已经聘任专业技术职务从事专业技术工作和专业技术管理工作的人员，以及未聘任专业技术职务，现在专业技术岗位上工作的人员。包括工程技术人员，农业技术人员，科学研究人员，卫生技术人员，教学人员，经济人员，会计人员，统计人员，翻译人员，图书资料、档案、文博人员，新闻出版人员，律师、公证人员，广播电视播音人员，工艺美术人员，体育人员，艺术人员及企业政治思想工作人员，共十七个专业技术职务类别。

科技活动经费筹集 指从各种渠道筹集到的计划用于科技活动的经费，包括政府资金、企业资金、事业单位资金、金融机构贷款、国外资金和其他资金等。

政府资金 指从各级政府部门获得的计划用于科技活动的经费，包括科学事业费、科技三项费、科研基建费、科学基金、教育等部门事业费中计划用于科技活动的经费以及政府部门预算外资金中计划用于科技活动的经费等。

企业资金 指从自有资金中提取或接受其他企业委托的、科研院所和高校等事业单位接受企业委托获得的，计划用于科研和技术开发的经费。不包括来自政府、金融机构及国外的计划用于科技活动的资金。

金融机构贷款 指从各类金融机构获得的用于科技活动的贷款。

科技活动经费内部支出 指报告年内用于科技活动的实际支出包括劳务费、科研业务费、科研管理费，非基建投资购建的固定资产、科研基建支出以及其他用于科技活动的支出。不包括生产性活动支出、归还贷款支出及转拨外单位支出。

劳务费 指以货币或实物形式直接或间接支付给从事科技活动人员的劳动报酬及各种费用。包括各种形式的工资、津贴、奖金、奖金、福利、离退休人员费用、人民助学金等。

固定资产购建费 指报告年内使用非基建投资购建的固定资产和用于科研基建投资的实际支出额，即固定资产实际支出和科研基建投资实际完成额之和。固定资产是指长期使用而不改变原有实物形态的主要物资设备、图书资料、实验材料和标本以及其他设备和家具、房屋、建筑物。

新产品 指采用新技术原理、新设计构思研制、生产的全新产品，或在结构、材质、工艺等某一方面比原有产品有明显改进，从而显著提高了产品性能或扩大了使用功能的产品。既包括政府有关部门认定并在有效期内的新产品，也包括企业自行研制开发，未经政府有关部门认定，从投产之日起一年之内的新产品。

专利 是专利权的简称，是对发明人的发明创造经审查合格后，由专利局依据专利法授予发明人和设计人对该项发明创造享有的专有权。包括发明、实用新型和外观设计。

发明 指对产品、方法或者其改进所提出的新的技术方案。

文化事业机构 指从事专业文化工作和为专业文化工作服务的独立建制的单位。不包括这些单位另外举办独立核算的其他机构和各部门的业余文化组织。

艺术表演团体 指从事戏曲、音乐、舞蹈、杂技等专业艺术表演，有独立帐户的单位，不包括半工半艺、半农半艺和民间职业剧团。

电影放映单位 指具有放映机器设备、固定或不固定的放映场所与专职或兼职的放映技术人员，经有关部门登记批准，经常为一定的观众对象放映电影的机构。包括经批准对外开放进行营业，并与电影发行放映管理机构分帐的专用放映单位和军委系统租片单位。

Explanatory Note on Main Statistical Indicators

Regular Institutions of Higher Learning refer to educational establishments set up according to the government evaluation and approval procedures, enrolling graduates from senior secondary schools and providing higher education courses and training for senior professionals. They include full-time universities, colleges, high professional schools and short-term professional universities.

Institutions of Higher Learning for Adults refer to educational establishments, set up in line with relevant rules approved by the government, enrolling staff and workers with senior secondary school or equivalent education ,and providing higher education courses in many forms of full time, part time, spare time, or correspondence for adults. Professionals thus trained receive a qualification equivalent to graduates studying regular courses at regular universities, colleges and professional colleges. Institutions of higher learning for adults include Radio and TV universities, schools of high education for staff and workers and peasants, colleges for management cadres, pedagogical colleges, independent correspondence colleges.

Enrollment Rate of Primary School Age Children refers to the proportion of school age children enrolled at schools to the total number of school age children both in and outside schools (including retarded children ,but excluding blind, deaf and mute children). The formula is:

Enrollment Rate of Primary School-age Children = (Total Primary School-age Children at Schools) (Total Primary School age Children Both at and Outside Schools) 100%

Scientific and Technological Activities (S&T Activities) refer to organized activities which are closely related with the creation, development, dissemination and application of the scientific and technical knowledge in the fields of natural sciences, agricultural science, medical science, engineering and technological science, humanities and social sciences (referred to as scientific and technological fields). S&T activities can be classified in to 3 categories: research and development (R&D) activities, application of R&D results, and related S&T services.

Personnel Engaged in S&T Activities refer to personnel directly engaged in S&T activities, in the management of S&T activities, and in providing direct service to S&T activities, who spend over 10% of the total working hours in a year in S&T activities. (1) Personnel directly engaged in S&T activities include researchers, engineers, technicians and other related personnel engaged in S&T activities in independent-accounting R&D institutions, institutions of higher learning, and in research institutes, laboratories, technology development centers and central experiment workshops under enterprises and institutions. Also included are people working in S&T research project teams, professional and technical personnel working in S&T information archiving institutes, and graduate students working on the design of their thesis. (2) Personnel engaged in the management of S&T activities and in providing direct service to S&T activities include senior management people responsible for S&T activities in independent-accounting R&D institutions, S&T information archiving institutes, institutions of higher learning, and in enterprises and institutions where S&T activities are undertaken. Also included are people responsible for the planning, administration, personnel management, financial management, logistics supply, equipment maintenance, information and library management that are related with S&T activities. People providing indirect services are excluded, such as security, medical service, drivers, plumbers, cleaners and those providing catering and related service.

Scientists and Engineers refer to persons engaged in S&T activities who have obtained titles of senior and middle level professional positions, and those without such position but have completed university or higher education.

Research and Development (R&D) refers to systematic and creative activities in the field of science and technology aiming at increasing the knowledge and using the knowledge for new application. R&D includes 3 categories of activities: basic research, applied research and experiments and development.

Basic Research refers to empirical or theoretical research aiming at obtaining new knowledge on the fundamental principles of phenomena of observable facts to reveal the nature and law of movement of objects and to acquire new discoveries or new theories. Basic research takes no specific or designated application as the aim of the research. Results of basic research are mainly released or disseminated in the form of scientific papers or monographs.

Applied research refers to creative research aiming at obtaining new knowledge on a specific objective or target. Purpose of the applied research is to identify the possible use of results from basic research, or to explore new (fundamental) methods or new approaches. Results of applied research are expressed in the form of scientific papers, monographs, fundamental models or invention patents.

Experiments and Development refer to systematic activities aiming at using the knowledge from basic and applied researches or from practical experience to develop new products, materials and equipment, to establish new production process, systems and services, or to make substantial improvement on the existing products, process or services. Results of experiment and development activities are embodied in patents, exclusive technology, monotype of new products or equipment. In social sciences, experiment and development activities refer to the process of converting the knowledge from basic or applied researches into feasible programmes (including conduct of demonstration projects for assessment and evaluation). There is no experiment and development activities in the science of humanities.

R&D Personnel refer to persons engaged in research, management and supporting activities of R&D, including persons in the project teams, persons engaged in the management of S&T activities of enterprises and supporting staff providing direct service to the research projects.

Full-time Equivalent of R&D Personnel refers to the sum of the full-time persons and the full-time equivalent of part-time persons converted by workload. For instance, if there are 2 full-time persons and 3 part-time workers (20%, 30% and 70% of working hours respectively on R&D activities), the full-time equivalent is 2+0.2+0.3+0.7=3.2 person-years.

Professional and Technical Personnel refer to person engaged in professional and technical work or in the management of professional and technical activities, i.e., people with professional or technical positions who are engaged in professional and technical work or in the management of professional and technical activities, and people without professional or technical positions but are working on professional or technical posts. They include professionals and technicians working in 17 categories of technical occupations including engineering, agriculture, scientific researches, medical service, teaching, economic research and application, accounting, statistics, translation, libraries, archives, cultural and museum service, journalism and publication, lawyers, notarization service, radio and television broadcasting, handicraft and fine arts, sports, performing art, and political workers in enterprises.

Funding for S&T Activities refers to funds obtained from various sources for S&T activities, including government funds, self-raised funds by enterprises, self-raised funds by institutions, loans from financial institutions, foreign funds and other funds.

Government Funds refer to funds obtained from government agencies at all levels to be used for S&T activities, including fund for scientific undertakings, 3 kinds of fund for S&T activities, fund for capital construction for scientific researches, science fund, funds from education expenditures by education departments for S&T activities, and extra-budget fund from government agencies for S&T activities.

Self-raised Funds by Enterprises refers to self-raised funds by enterprises from their own expenditure or from other enterprises and funds received by universities or research institutions from enterprises for scientific research or technical development projects. Excluded in this category are funds from government agencies, financial institutions or from foreign institutions.

Loans from Financial Institutions refer to loans from various financial institutions for S&T activities.

Internal Expenditures on S&T activities refer to the actual expenditures on S&T activities during the reference year, including service fees, expenditure on research activities, expenditure on research management, purchase or construction of fixed assets not included in the investment for capital construction, expenditure on capital construction for scientific researches, and other expenditures on S&T activities. Not included are expenditure on production activities, repayment of loans and transfer expenditure.

Service Fees refer to direct or indirect payment, in cash or in kind, made to personnel engaged in S&T activities as remuneration and other fees. They include, in various forms, salaries, subsidies, bonus, benefits, retirement pension, stipend, etc.

Purchase or Construction of Fixed Assets refers to the fixed assets purchased or constructed using funds other than the investment in capital construction, and the actual expenditure on capital construction for scientific researches. In other words, it is the sum of the actual expenditure on fixed assets and the accomplished investment in capital construction for scientific researches. Fixed assets refer to main materials and equipment, literatures and documents in libraries, materials for experiments, specimen, instruments, furniture, buildings and constructions that can be used for a long time without changing the form and shape of those articles or constructions.

New Products refer to new products produced with new technology and new design, or products that represent noticeable improvement in terms of structure, material, or production process so as to improve significantly the character or function of the older versions. They include new products certified by relevant government agencies within the period of certification, as well as new products designed and produced by enterprises within a year without certification by government agencies.

Patent is an abbreviation for the patent right and refers to the exclusive right of ownership by the inventors or designers for the creation or inventions, given from the patent offices after due process of assessment and approval in accordance with the Patent Law. Patents are granted for inventions, utility models and designs.

Inventions refer to the new technical proposals to the products or methods or their modifications.

Cultural Institutions refer to units which have their own organizational system and independent accounting system and specialize in or serve cultural development. They exclude other establishments run by these cultural institutions and amateur cultural groups established by various departments.

Art Troupe refers to the troupe which is engaged in drama, opera, music, dance, acrobatics or other art performance, opens independent accounts with banks and has self–supporting accounting system; excluding the troupes which are engaged partly in industrial or agricultural activities, partly in art performance and the professional troupes organized by the people.

Film Projection Units refer to units with film projection equipment, full or part time projectionists, permanent or non permanent places, approved by related administrative departments to show films regularly for certain groups of audience, including those film projection units which have been approved to give commercial shows and run business with independent accounting system as well as those film–renting units of the military system.

资料整理: 俞祥初

Arranged by Yuxiangchu

19. 卫生和体育
HEALTH AND SPORTS

专业卫生人员（人）

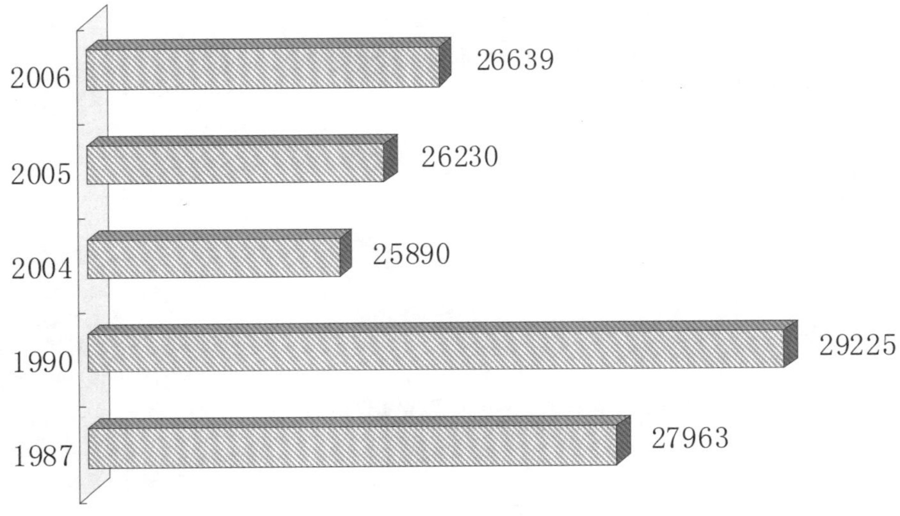

卫生机构病床位数（张）

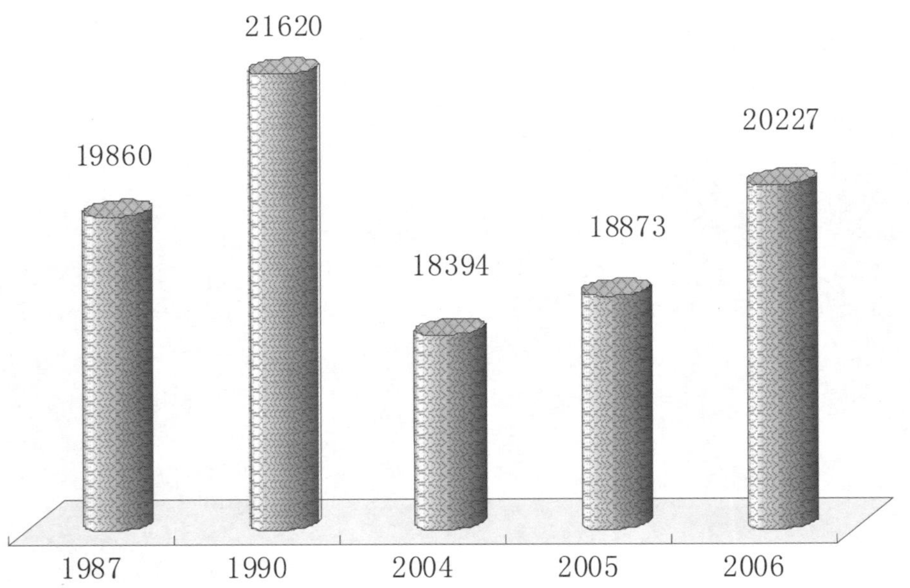

19－1 卫生机构、床位和人员数
Number of Health Institutions,Beds and Personnel

年 份 Year	卫生机构数（间）Number of Health Institutions(unit)	医院（含卫生院）Hospitals	床位数（张）Number of Beds(bed)	医院（含卫生院）Hospitals	卫生机构人员总数（人）Total Number of Persons in Health Institutions(person)
1961	1967	350	6737	5689	10973
1962	2171	228	7540	6227	11737
1963	1998	159	9236	6067	11645
1964	2229	185	9792	6647	12288
1965	2692	177	10026	6862	12533
1966	2744	174	9814	6865	12899
1972	3144	426	15720	15642	19286
1973	3224	430	16511	16288	20367
1974	3210	444	16624	16419	20362
1975	3082	447	17108	16935	20916
1976	3261	456	17657	17523	22243
1977	3175	462	18420	18266	23651
1978	3308	464	18687	18562	24730
1979	3493	468	18855	18649	25834
1980	3492	459	18885	18648	27666
1981	3703	458	18688	18404	22230
1982	3656	461	18589	18310	31181
1983	3978	459	18587	18309	31705
1984	3901	457	18582	18336	32750
1985	3877	417	18997	18672	33727
1986	3729	422	19313	18941	34121
1987	3702	427	19860	19542	34840
1988	3764	426	20643	20265	35208
1989	2911	428	20833	20479	35269
1990	3167	429	21620	21083	36290
1991	3154	427	21402	20857	36796
1992	2517	438	22397	21772	37681
1993	1646	446	22830	22053	38327
1994	1647	469	22658	21885	39167
1995	1653	473	22383	21684	39374
1996	2420	482	22283	21435	40047
1997	2595	485	21704	20777	40824
1998	2545	485	21480	20659	40394
1999	2460	488	20518	19889	39063
2000	2689	492	20550	15352	38539
2001	2712	488	19288	14784	38125
2002	2840	504	19120	17411	36310
2003	2655	503	18312	13018	32725
2004	2515	505	18394	17040	36835
2005	2464	502	18873	17475	37189
2006	2337	502	20227	18630	38199

19－2 各类卫生机构数
Number of Health Institutions by Type

单位：个 (unit)

年 份 Year	卫生机构总数 Number of Health Institutions	医院 (含卫生院) Hospitals	县及县以上医院 At and Above County Level	疗养院、所 Sanatorium	门诊部、所 Clinics	专科防治所、站 Specialiaed Stations
1950	15	14				
1977	3175	462	149		2612	20
1978	3308	464	152		2732	21
1979	3493	468	155	2	2908	23
1980	3492	459	149	2	2897	23
1981	3703	458	149	3	3117	25
1982	3656	461	151	3	3068	25
1983	3978	459	149	3	3391	25
1984	3901	457	148	3	3314	25
1985	3877	417	146	3	3335	22
1986	3729	422	149	2	3184	23
1987	3702	427	152	2	3148	23
1988	3764	426	153	2	3208	27
1989	2911	428	155	2	2349	27
1990	3167	429	156	2	2601	28
1991	3154	427	155	2	2585	32
1995	1653	473	164	2	1014	43
1996	2420	482	172	2	1760	44
1997	2595	485	175	2	1929	44
1998	2545	485	175	2	1877	44
1999	2460	488	177	2	1789	44
2000	2689	492	180	2	2017	42
2001	2712	488	177	2	2045	42
2002	2840	504		2	1905	43
2003	2655	503		2	1802	40
2004	2515	505		2	1860	37
2005	2464	502		2	1812	36
2006	2337	502		2	1451	33

19-2 续(continued)

年 份 Year	卫生防疫站 Sanitation and Antiepiedemic Agencies	妇幼保健所、站 Maternity and Child Care Centers	药品检验所、站 Medicines and Chemical Reagent Test Labs	医学科研机构 Scientific and Technical Institutions	其他卫生机构 Others Health Institutions
1950					1
1977	20	18	4	1	38
1978	20	18	9	5	39
1979	21	18	10	4	39
1980	21	19	12	4	55
1981	22	19	12	3	44
1982	22	19	11	4	43
1983	22	19	11	4	44
1984	22	19	11	4	46
1985	23	19	12	4	42
1986	25	20	12	4	37
1987	27	20	13	4	38
1988	25	20	14	4	34
1989	26	20	14	4	44
1990	26	20	14	4	43
1991	26	20	14	4	40
1995	32	19	14		36
1996	33	21	14	4	44
1997	33	21	14	4	47
1998	33	22	14	4	48
1999	31	22	14	4	50
2000	31	21	13	3	52
2001	31	21	12	3	52
2002	31	26		2	37
2003	29	25		2	35
2004	30	25		2	34
2005	29	26		2	34
2006	28	26		2	33

19－3 各类卫生机构床位数
Number of Beds in Health Institutions by Type

单位:张 (bed)

年份 Year	病床位总数 Total	医院(含卫生院) Hospitals	县及县以上医院 At and Above County Level	疗养院、所 Sanatorium	门诊部、所 Clinics	其他卫生机构 Others Health Institutions	每千人口医院床位数 Number of Beds per 1000 Population
1950	680	680					0.26
1952	1244	1134					0.44
1977	18420	18266	12935		154		3.54
1978	18687	18562	13216		125		3.51
1979	18855	18649	13383	100	106		3.45
1980	18885	18648	13339	140	97		3.38
1981	18691	18404	13473	180	104	3	3.28
1982	18589	18310	13479	180	99		3.20
1983	18587	18309	13867	160	118		3.15
1984	18582	18336	13991	137	103	6	3.11
1985	18997	18672	14436	180	145		3.13
1986	19313	18941	14605	160	212		3.13
1987	19860	19542	15164	160	141	17	3.23
1988	20643	20265	15895	170	179	29	3.29
1989	20822	20479	16217	170	135	49	3.26
1990	21620	21083	16802	300	195	42	3.32
1991	21402	20857	16577	250	221	35	3.15
1992	22397	21772	17457	250	197	125	3.24
1993	22830	22053	17472	250	130	329	3.23
1994	22658	21885	17336	250	119	295	3.28
1995	22383	24684	17096	200	119	292	3.19
1996	22283	21435	16885	250	119	492	3.06
1997	21704	20777	16276	250		493	2.87
1998	21480	20659	16047	250	18	361	2.85
1999	20518	19889	15418	250	5	179	2.69
2000	20550	19897	15352	250	5	268	2.70
2001	19924	19288	14784	250		247	2.50
2002	19120	13355		250	320	519	2.45
2003	18312	17411		250	150	453	2.32
2004	18394	17040		330	91	250	2.28
2005	18873	17253		330	145	250	2.17
2006	20227	18630		330	100	300	2.27

19－4 卫生机构、床位、人员数
Number of Health Institutions, Beds and Personnel

项目	Item	机构数(个) Number of Health Institutions (unit)	床位数(张) Beds (bed)	人员总数(人) Personnel (person)	执业医师 Doctors	执业助理医师 Assistant Doctors	注册护士 Registration Junior Nurses	药剂人员 Persons Engaged in Drug Work	检验人员 Laboratory Technical Personnel
总　计	**Total**	**2337**	**20227**	**38199**	**9373**	**2822**	**11508**	**2043**	**1533**
医　院	Number of Hospitals	190	13890	21199	5010	1234	7000	1166	799
综合医院	Comprehensive Hospitals	145	11380	18110	4325	1127	5977	904	669
中医院	Hospital of Traditional Chinese Medicine	18	1153	1894	436	71	576	210	86
中西结合医院	Combination Hospitals of Chinese and Western	3	50	64	11	1	24	5	3
专科医院	Specialized Hospital	24	1307	1131	238	35	423	47	41
卫生院	Number of Public Health Center	312	4740	7744	1211	818	1871	520	285
街道卫生院	Public Health Center in Neighbourhood	3		33	14	5	8		1
乡镇卫生院	Public Health Center in Township and Towns	309	4740	7711	1197	813	1863	520	284
门诊部	Out-patients Department	100	100	713	215	40	211	36	20
诊所	Clinics	1351		3090	1305	322	1078	136	17
卫生所、医务室	Clinics(Medical Stations)	182		536	210	51	198	25	6
社区卫生服务站	Community Health Service Stations	58		522	190	65	210	21	17
急救中心	Center for Emergency Treatment	3		26	5	4	4	3	1
采供血机构	Institute of Collecting and Supplying Blood	1		122	12	8	40	1	25
妇幼保健院	Maternity and Child Care Centers	26	823	1441	7	42	489	61	81
专科防治所	Specialized Prevention and Treatment Stations	33	24	632	138	68	111	39	53
疾病控制中心	Centers for Diseases Control and Prevention	28		1377	548	102	126	18	195
卫生监督所	Sanitation Supervision Stations	8		101	34	11	4	4	5
医学科研机构	Researh Institutes of Medical Sciences	2		40					1
健康教育所	Health Education Stations	5		19	2				
疗养院	Sanatorium	2	330	173	15		42	6	7
社区卫生服务中心	Centers for Community Health Service	3	20	27	3	3	4	3	1
其他卫生机构	Others Health Institutions	33	300	437	98	54	120	3	20

19－5 各市县卫生机构、床位、人员数(不含诊所等)

Number of Health Institutions,Beds and Personnel by City and County(excluding Clinics)

市 县	City and County	机构数(个) Number of Health Institutions (unit)	医院 Hospitals	卫生院 Public Health Center	床位数(张) Beds (bed)	人员总数(人) Personnel (person)	卫生技术人员 Medical Technical Personnel	执业医师 Doctors
总 计	**Total**	**746**	**190**	**312**	**20227**	**34051**	**26639**	**7668**
海口市	Haikou	161	40	36	6886	11772	9118	3035
三亚市	SanYa	37	15	15	1681	3014	2251	751
五指山市	Wuzhishan	23	5	9	721	723	525	110
文昌市	Wenchang	37	7	25	903	1551	1200	296
琼海市	Qionghai	51	9	21	940	1658	1431	395
万宁市	Wanning	34	8	18	922	1769	1339	340
定安县	Dingan	24	5	14	335	853	703	133
屯昌县	Tunchang	27	8	11	450	815	663	168
澄迈县	Chengmai	33	8	20	843	1211	925	197
临高县	Lingao	28	4	17	698	1253	996	234
儋州市	Danzhou	59	20	26	1915	2724	2091	558
东方市	Dongfang	34	9	17	752	1357	1071	296
乐东县	Ledong	31	11	15	830	1459	1169	287
琼中县	Qiongzhong	49	13	14	517	943	805	196
保亭县	Baoting	24	7	12	387	610	516	135
陵水县	Lingshui	28	5	17	469	760	582	206
白沙县	Baisha	30	10	14	445	755	592	151
昌江县	Changjiang	36	6	11	533	824	662	180

19-5 续(continued)

市 县	City and County	执业助理医师 Assistant Doctors	注册护士 Registration Junior Nurses	药剂人员 Persons Engaged in Drug Work	检验人员 Laboratory Technical Personnel	其他技术人员 Other Technical Personne;	管理人员 Manangerial Personnel	工勤人员 Logistics Workers
总 计	**Total**	**2384**	**10022**	**1860**	**1493**	**882**	**2894**	**3636**
海口市	Haikou	297	3723	623	566	534	921	1199
三亚市	SanYa	172	754	141	129	127	249	387
五指山市	Wuzhishan	29	238	24	34	12	83	103
文昌市	Wenchang	121	407	180	85	22	159	170
琼海市	Qionghai	130	530	134	84	1	131	95
万宁市	Wanning	187	513	108	63	37	138	255
定安县	Dingan	88	232	79	31	5	75	70
屯昌县	Tunchang	93	220	46	36	20	70	62
澄迈县	Chengmai	180	308	52	41	18	132	136
临高县	Lingao	75	400	63	36	11	102	144
儋州市	Danzhou	254	845	130	107	52	196	385
东方市	Dongfang	118	380	76	61	28	122	136
乐东县	Ledong	159	369	67	60	0	114	176
琼中县	Qiongzhong	162	261	32	34	0	87	51
保亭县	Baoting	103	178	23	25	0	57	37
陵水县	Lingshui	45	201	22	31	11	81	86
白沙县	Baisha	103	189	23	28	2	86	75
昌江县	Changjiang	68	274	37	42	2	91	69

19－6 分市县举办体育活动情况
Situation of Sports Activities Held by City and County

市 县 City and County	举办运动会或比赛 Sports Meets		举办全民健身活动 Sports Activities Attending All the People		
	综合运动会次数(次) Number of Synthetic Sports Meets(time)	单项比赛次数(次) Number of Individual Competition(time)	全民健身活动次数(次) Number of Sports Activities Attending All the People(time)	#1000人以上的活动(次) Sports Activities Attending above 1000 People(time)	参加活动人数(人) Number of Persons Attending Activities (person)
全省合计 Total	**28**	**237**	**215**	**69**	**621666**
省属小计		7	6	5	15000
地方小计	28	230	209	64	606666
海口市 Haikou	2	17	32	16	376800
三亚市 SanYa	6	14	0	0	0
五指山市 Wuzhishan	2	13	3	1	8200
文昌市 Wenchang	1	4	20	8	32000
琼海市 Qionghai	8	36	34	0	5460
万宁市 Wanning		6	3	0	2000
定安县 Dingan		60	4	0	5850
屯昌县 Tunchang	2	4	5	1	16000
澄迈县 Chengmai		10	2	1	1570
临高县 Lingao		19	9	3	5500
儋州市 Dangzhou	2	20	15	2	18956
东方市 Dongfang	3	8	7	5	5000
乐东县 Ledong		0	8	2	2050
琼中县 Qiongzhong		6	24	6	55000
保亭县 Baoting		1	1	1	1000
陵水县 Lingshui	2	6	2	2	3100
白沙县 Baisha		3	39	15	66950
昌江县 Changjiang		3	1	1	1230

主要统计指标解释

卫生机构 包括医疗机构、疾病预防控制中心(防疫站)、采供血机构、卫生监督及监测(检验)机构、医学科研和在职培训机构、健康教育所等。

医疗机构 包括医院、社区卫生服务中心(站)、疗养院、卫生院、门诊部、诊所(卫生所、医务室)、妇幼保健院(所、站)、专科疾病防治院(所、站)、急救中心(站)和临床检验中心。医疗机构分为非赢利性医疗机构和赢利性医疗机构。

医院 包括综合医院、中医医院、中西医结合医院、民族医院、各类专科医院和护理院。

卫生技术人员 指卫生事业机构支付工资的全部固定职工和合同制职工中现任职务为卫生技术工作的人员。包括中医师、西医师、中西医结合高级医师、护师、中药师、西药师、检验师、其他技师、中医士、西医士、护士、助产士、中药剂士、西药剂士、检验士、其他技士、其他 中医、护理员、中药剂员、西药剂员、检验员、其他初级卫生技术人员。

医生 指经卫生部门审查合格,从事医疗工作的专业人员。分为中医医生和西医生。包括卫生技术人员中的 中医师、西医师、中西医结合高级医师、中医士、西医士 和其他中医。

Explanatory Note on Main Statistical Indicators

Health agencies include medical agencies, disease prevention and control centers (epidemic stations), blood collection and supply agencies, health supervision and monitoring (inspection) agencies, medical research agencies, medical on-job training agencies, health education institutes, etc.

Medical agencies include hospitals, community health service centers (stations), convalescent hospitals, health centers, outpatient hospitals, clinics (health station and medical rooms), maternal and child health hospitals (institutions, stations), specialized disease prevention and treatment hospitals (institutions, stations), first-aid centers (stations) and clinic inspection centers. Medical agencies are classified as profitable medical agencies and non-profitable medical agencies.

Hospitals include comprehensive hospitals, Chinese medicine hospitals, western and Chinese medicine hospitals, ethnic hospitals, al sorts of specialized hospitals and nursing hospitals

Medical Technical Personnel refers to all medical staff and workers employed by medical institutions, including doctors of Chinese and Western medicine, senior doctors who integrate traditional Chinese therapeutics with Western therapeutics in practice, senior nurses, pharmacists of Chinese and Western medicine, laboratory specialists, other specialists, paramedics of Chinese and Western medicine, nurses, midwives, druggists in Chinese and Western medicine, laboratory technicians, other technicians, other practitioners of Chinese medicine, nursing attendants, pharmacological workers of Chinese and Western medicine, laboratory workers, and other primary medical personnel.

Doctors refer to qualified professional medical workers approved to practice by public health departments. They are classified into doctors of Chinese medicine, doctors of Western medicine, senior doctors who integrate traditional Chinese therapeutics with Western therapeutics in practice, paramedics of Chinese medicine and Western medicine, and other specialists of Chinese medicine.

资料整理: 俞祥初

Arranged by Yuxiangchu

20. 社会福利和保障

SOCLAL WELFARE ANDSOCIAL SECURITY

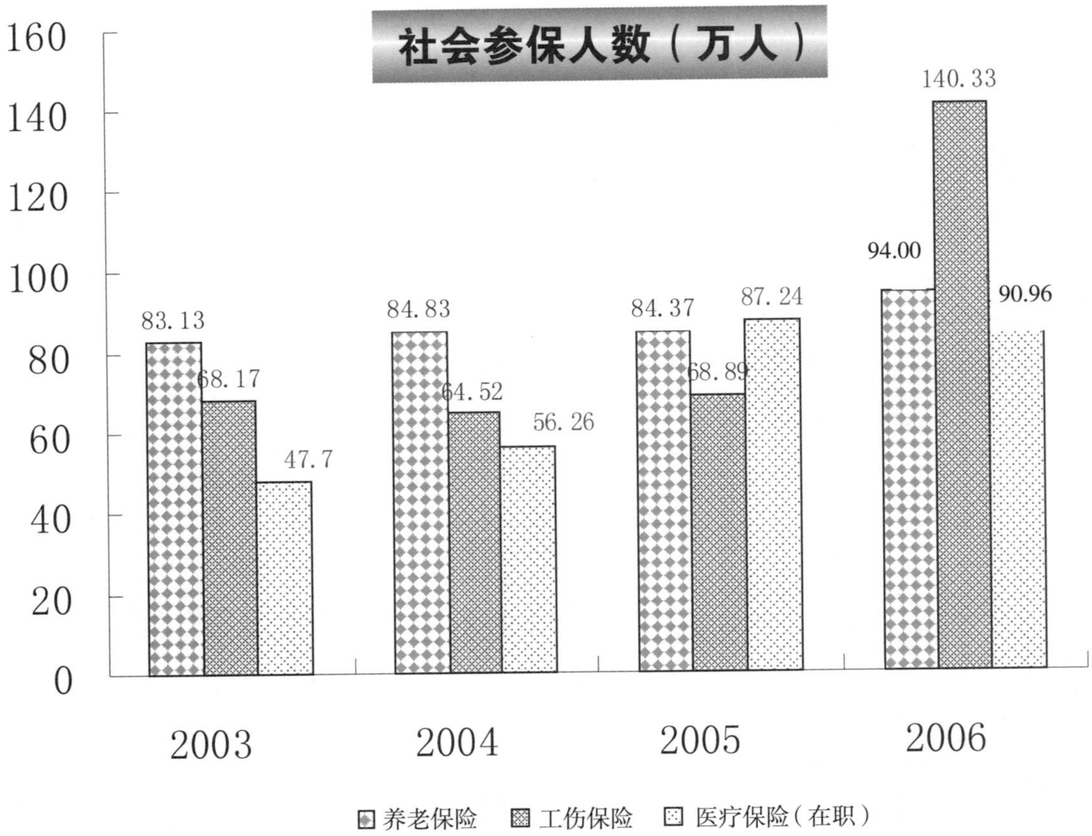

社会参保人数（万人）
160
140
120
100
80
60
40
20
0
83.13
68.17
47.7
84.83
64.52
56.26
84.37
68.89
87.24
94.00
140.33
90.96
2003
2004
2005
2006
养老保险
工伤保险
医疗保险（在职）

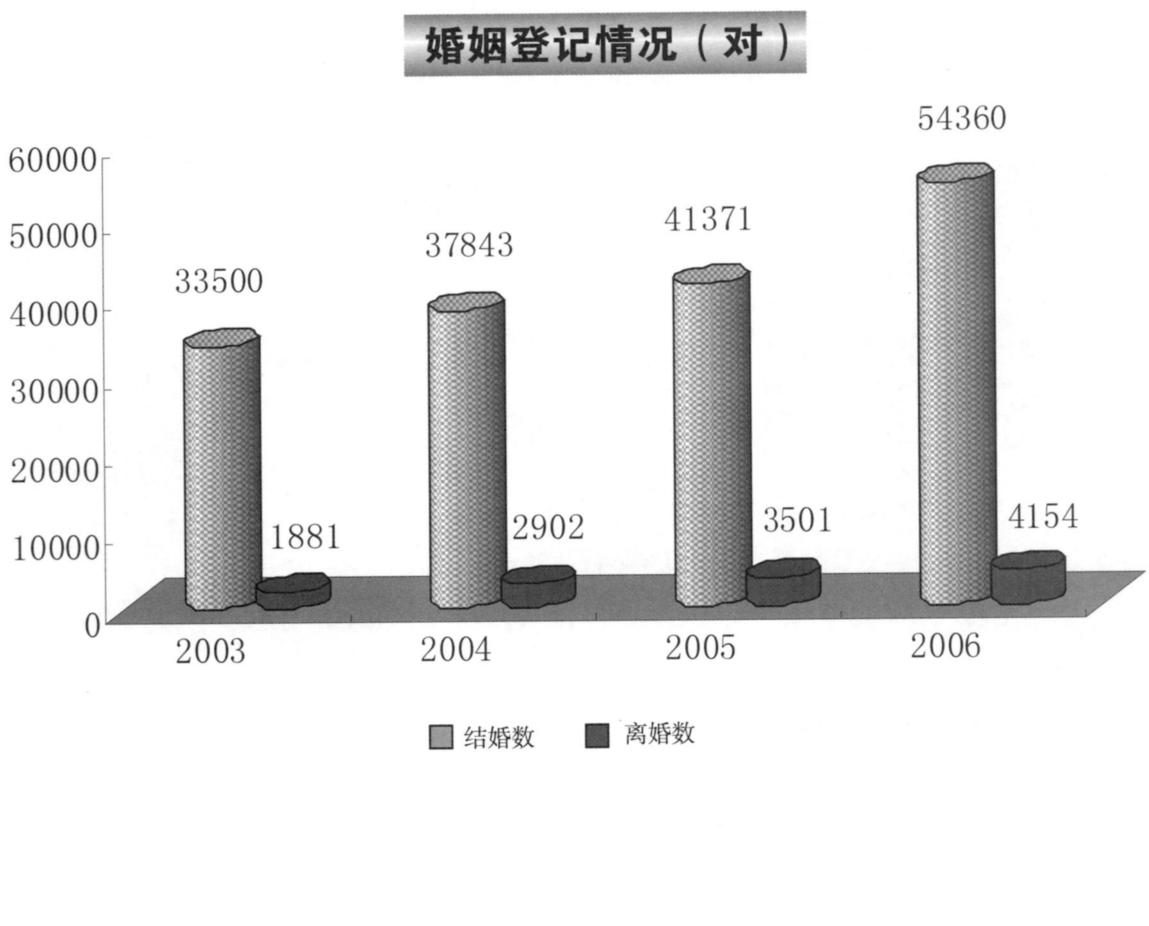

婚姻登记情况（对）
60000
50000
40000
30000
20000
10000
0
33500
1881
37843
2902
41371
3501
54360
4154
2003
2004
2005
2006
结婚数
离婚数

20-1 优抚对象人员情况
Situation of Family Members of Martyrs and Disable Veterans

市县	City and County	享受定期抚恤金人数 Enjoy Fixed Pension People	烈属 Members of a Revolutionary Martyr' Family	牺牲军人家属 Sacrticial Armyman Family	病故军人家属 Die of Illness Armyman Family	优待优抚对象户数 Family Number of Giving Special Treatment and Comfort
全省总计	Total	24600	4859	189	211	14875
海口市	Haikou	3181	711	5	14	3018
三亚市	SanYa	429	99	8	5	365
五指山市	Wuzhishan	450	29	1	6	424
文昌市	Wenchang	2839	1016	12	13	2991
琼海市	Qionghai	1960	491	8	33	851
万宁市	Wanning	2442	455	8	14	396
定安县	Dingan	878	104	11	15	420
屯昌县	Tunchang	1114	53	6	7	602
澄迈县	Chengmai	2191	396	14	10	435
临高县	Lingao	1869	373	43	19	428
儋州市	Danzhou	2122	355	25	15	336
东方市	Dongfang	818	319	9	8	1722
乐东县	Ledong	1507	161	23	11	261
琼中县	Qiongzhong	576	14		12	635
保亭县	Baoting	558	1	5	7	813
陵水县	Lingshui	586	157	8	14	490
白沙县	Baisha	658	8		7	160
昌江县	Changjiang	422	117	3	1	528

20-1 续(continued)

市县	City and County	优待军属户数 Special Treatment Armyman Family	享受定期补助人数 Enjoy Fixed Assistance People	在乡复员军人 Illness Demobilized army men which return to their hometown	带病回乡退伍军人 Illness Demobilized army men which return to their hometown	红军失散人员 Separated Staff of Red-Army
全省总计	Total	5552	16833	14298	1104	374
海口市	Haikou	1146	1875	1152	42	17
三亚市	SanYa	365	251	229	21	1
五指山市	Wuzhishan	153	380	373	7	
文昌市	Wenchang	161	1597	1505	54	38
琼海市	Qionghai	283	1283	1143	36	70
万宁市	Wanning	396	1630	1327	270	33
定安县	Dingan	270	646	535	61	16
屯昌县	Tunchang	172	976	929	35	12
澄迈县	Chengmai	435	1567	1421	51	95
临高县	Lingao	428	1271	810	331	65
儋州市	Danzhou	256	1527	1498	29	
东方市	Dongfang	330	385	370	15	
乐东县	Ledong	261	1225	1126	76	23
琼中县	Qiongzhong	135	500	485	15	
保亭县	Baoting	113	506	505	1	
陵水县	Lingshui	375	361	323	34	4
白沙县	Baisha	160	617	369	24	
昌江县	Changjiang	113	236	198	2	

20－2 革命伤残人员享受抚恤情况
Funds for Family Members of Martyrs and Disable Veterans

市 县	City and County	合计 Total	一级 One Grode	二级 Two Grode	三级 Three Grode	四级 Four Grode	五级 Five Grode	六级 Sit Grode	七级 Seven Grode	八级 Eight Grode	九级 Nine Grode	十级 Ten Grode
全省总计	**Total**	**2508**	**8**	**1**	**60**	**7**	**176**	**486**	**860**	**877**	**31**	**2**
海口市	Haikou	576	3		6	2	40	111	212	196	6	
三亚市	SanYa	66			2	1	5	10	23	25		
五指山市	Wuzhishan	34					2	7	12	13		
文昌市	Wenchang	201	1		9		15	38	60	75	2	1
琼海市	Qionghai	145	1		2		5	25	68	43	1	
万宁市	Wanning	335			9	2	31	105	109	79		
定安县	Dingan	102	2		2		20	24	35	19		
屯昌县	Tunchang	72			1		2	17	30	21	1	
澄迈县	Chengmai	204			2		12	36	71	82	1	
临高县	Lingao	163			3		7	30	44	79		
儋州市	Danzhou	200	1		10	1	17	16	70	84	1	
东方市	Dongfang	97			1		3	24	31	37		1
乐东县	Ledong	87			6	1	4	8	31	36	1	
琼中县	Qiongzhong	50			5		6	12	12		15	
保亭县	Baoting	39						8	1	30		
陵水县	Lingshui	46					2	3	16	22	3	
白沙县	Baisha	26					1	7	10	8		
昌江县	Changjiang	65		1	2		4	5	25	28		

20－3 国内婚姻登记情况
Marriage Registration of Domestic

市县	City and County	结婚数(对) Permitting Marriage Registration (couples)	登记结婚人数 Permitting Marriage	初婚人数(人) First Marriage (person)	再婚人数(人) Second Marriage (person)		再婚中恢复结婚(对) Resuming Marriage	登记离婚数(对) Permitting Divorce (couples)
						女 Man		
全省总计	**Total**	**54360**	**108720**	**99475**	**9245**	**3836**	**436**	**4154**
海南省本级	**Provincial**	**2049**	**4098**	**2792**	**1306**	**627**	**1**	
海口市	Haikou	13693	27386	24704	2682	1150	159	1827
三亚市	SanYa	3777	7554	7332	222	90	10	322
五指山市	Wuzhishan	976	1952	1932	20	10	5	61
文昌市	Wenchang	4220	8440	8140	300	135	6	397
琼海市	Qionghai	3228	6456	3886	2570	988	6	382
万宁市	Wanning	3095	6190	6110	80	31		132
定安县	Dingan	2007	4014	3703	311	178	3	130
屯昌县	Tunchang	1747	3494	3440	54	24	1	
澄迈县	Chengmai	2803	5606	5504	102	43	5	109
临高县	Lingao	1123	2246	2110	136	32	136	50
儋州市	Danzhou	4508	9016	8109	907	305	10	325
东方市	Dongfang	3114	6228	6192	36	10	16	112
乐东县	Ledong	1286	2572	2478	94	55	15	95
琼中县	Qiongzhong	1424	2848	2828	20	6		74
保亭县	Baoting	758	1516	1512	4	1		58
陵水县	Lingshui	2224	4448	4410	38	10	2	48
白沙县	Baisha	678	1356	1293	63	23	2	32
昌江县	Changjiang	1650	3300	3000	300	118	59	

20－4 涉外及华侨、港澳台同胞婚姻情况
Registered Marriages with Foreigner and the Citizen of Hong Kong,Macao, Taiwan

项 目	Item	2000	2001	2002	2003	2004	2005	2006
准予登记结婚对数(对)	Permitting Marriage Registration(couple)	1347	1524	1240	1067	1016	1354	2049
准予登记结婚人员分类(人)	Grouped by Permitting Divorce(person)							
国内公民	Domestic Resdents	1347	1524	1240	1067	1016	1354	2049
男	Man	70	116	133	87	136	201	348
女	Female	1277	1408	1107	980	880	1153	1701
港澳同胞	Citizen of Hong Kong,Macao	532	637	546	471	479	707	1341
台 胞	Citizen of Taiwan	666	660	503	393	325	451	524
华 侨	Overseas Chinese	22	22	44	13	22	26	26
外国人	Foreigner	127	296	147	190	190	170	158
申请离婚对数(对)	Divorce Examined(couple)	82	70	76	88	35	60	61
# 准予登记离婚(对)	Permitting Divorce(couple)	82	70	76	1881	35	60	61

20－5 离休、退休、退职人员人数及保险福利费用
Insurance and Welfare Funds of Retired and Resigned Staff and Workers

项 目	Item	离休退休退职人数（人）Number of Retired and Resigned Staff and Workers (Person)	女性 Female	离休人员 Retired Veterans	退休人员 Retired Persons
总 计	Total	354294	172051	4361	349933
城镇单位	Urban-owned Units	350413	169706	4352	346061
企 业	Enterprises	286247	147962	2411	283836
国有企业	State-owned	254974	132520	2091	252883
集体企业	Collective-owned	23369	11880	197	23172
事 业	Institution	47591	17802	600	46991
机 关	Agencies	16575	3942	1341	15234
其 他	Others	3881	2345	9	3872

20-5 续(continued)

项 目	Item	保险福利费总额（千元）Expenditures on Labour Insurance and Welfare	离休金 Pensions for Retired Veterans for Retired Veterans	退休金 Pensions for Retired Veterans	其他 Others
总 计	**Total**	**2959586**	**122195**	**2747336**	**90055**
城镇单位	Urban-owned Units	2926269	121955	2714515	89799
企 业	Enterprises	1816728	65959	1686686	64083
国有企业	State-owned	1595853	55679	14881107	59067
集体企业	Collective-owned	176557	5067	167244	4246
事业	Institution	794417	19533	758948	15936
机关	Agencies	315124	36463	268881	9780
其他	Others	33317	240	32821	256

20－6 各市县离休退休、退职人员人数及保险福利费用

Insurance and Welfare Funds of Retired and Resigned Staff and Workers by City and County

项 目	Item	离休退休退职人数(人) Number of Retired and Resigned Staff and Workers (Person)	离休人员 Retired Veterans	退休人员 Retired Persons	保险福利费总额(千元) Expenditures on Labour Insurance and Welfare	离休金 Pensions for Retired Veterans for Retired Veterans	退休金 Pensions for Retired Veterans	其他 Others
总 计	**Total**	**354294**	**4361**	**349933**	**2959586**	**122195**	**2747336**	**90055**
海 口 市	HaiKou	63845	1017	62828	751371	29456	707313	14602
三 亚 市	SanYa	10769	142	10627	123435	3390	117461	2584
五指山市	WuZhiShan	1024	72	952	12790	1090	11291	409
文 昌 市	WenChang	14052	357	13695	142453	8592	131962	1899
琼 海 市	QiongHai	8721	168	8553	108015	4056	100803	3156
万 宁 市	WanNing	5550	182	5368	78395	4010	72746	1639
定 安 县	DingAn	5989	188	5801	67829	3959	62487	1383
屯 昌 县	TunChang	4194	91	4103	47839	2171	44282	1386
澄 迈 县	ChengMai	2725	76	2649	43969	2065	41904	
临 高 县	LinGao	4907	108	4799	47438	1553	45885	
儋 州 市	DanZhou	13035	262	12773	120308	6499	113018	791
东 方 市	DongFang	6468	141	6327	70731	4254	58473	8004
乐 东 县	LeDong	9104	198	8906	84449	5041	78815	593
琼 中 县	QiongZhong	3312	116	3196	16140	2661	10689	2790
保 亭 县	BaoTing	1990	31	1959	30324	1846	28478	
陵 水 县	LingShui	5480	99	5381	54322	2660	51662	
白 沙 县	BaiSha	2862	58	2804	20269	5400	14869	
昌 江 县	ChangJiag	12349	238	12111	99103	5111	92100	1892
洋 浦	YangPu	168	1	167	3209	21	2561	627
农 垦	Nongken	177750	816	176934	1037197	28360	960537	48300

20－7 社会保障参保情况
Condition of Social Insurance and Insured

市 县	City and County	保障机构数(个) Number of Institution	参保项目人数(人)Contributors(person) 养老保险 Endowment Insurance	工伤保险 Injury Insurance	医疗保险(在职) Medical Insurance
全省总计	**Total**	22	940012	1403338	909605
海口市	Haikou	1	168765	209548	156582
三亚市	SanYa	1	48989	76121	58211
五指山市	Wuzhishan	1	7500	22143	7686
文昌市	Wenchang	1	20508	39626	31923
琼海市	Qionghai	1	22412	35649	19260
万宁市	Wanning	1	20103	44191	17950
定安县	Dingan	1	12058	14543	10946
屯昌县	Tunchang	1	9784	14236	9112
澄迈县	Chengmai	1	17830	29686	18588
临高县	Lingao	1	13298	27128	13262
儋州市	Danzhou	1	22886	41443	26083
东方市	Dongfang	1	15577	30989	18002
乐东县	Ledong	1	13230	18684	15177
琼中县	Qiongzhong	1	6668	13037	5310
保亭县	Baoting	1	7996	11754	7836
陵水县	Lingshui	1	12569	12656	9641
白沙县	Baisha	1	7993	13167	7923
昌江县	Changjiang	1	10828	17668	15050
省 直	Province	1	258558	323321	251142
洋浦开发区	YangPu	1	7901	10873	6126
农垦系统	Nongken	1	234559	380773	189765
海南钢铁公司	iron Compang	1		16102	14030

20－8 养老保险基本情况
Survey of Retirement Pension Insurance

市 县	City and County	参加人数(人) Active Contributors (person)	参加职工工资总额(万元) Total wage of Active Contributors (10000yuan)	参加统筹的离退休人数(人) Retirees(person)
全省总计	**Total**	**940012**	**891618**	**380456**
海口市	Haikou	168765	141995	42138
三亚市	SanYa	48989	47535	10735
五指山市	Wuzhishan	7500	5041	2045
文昌市	Wenchang	20508	20614	11240
琼海市	Qionghai	22412	20150	7749
万宁市	Wanning	20103	17195	6163
定安县	Dingan	12058	10661	5365
屯昌县	Tunchang	9784	8695	3763
澄迈县	Chengmai	17830	16290	7174
临高县	Lingao	13298	9881	4820
儋州市	Danzhou	22886	21044	7828
东方市	Dongfang	15577	12161	3990
乐东县	Ledong	13230	13277	4746
琼中县	Qiongzhong	6668	8926	2782
保亭县	Baoting	7996	5943	1671
陵水县	Lingshui	12569	9472	4090
白沙县	Baisha	7993	7253	1699
昌江县	Changjiang	10828	11865	3212
省直	Province	258558	343706	70540
洋浦开发区	YangPu	7901	9831	126
农垦系统	Nongken	234559	150083	178580
海南钢铁公司	iron Compang	0	0	0

主要统计指标解释

基本养老保险（参保）职工人数：指报告期末按照国家法律、法规和有关政策规定参加基本养老保险并在社保经办机构已建立缴费记录档案的职工人数，包括中断缴费但未终止养老保险关系的职工人数，不包括只登记未建立缴费记录档案的人数。

基本医疗保险参保人数：指报告期末按国家有关规定参加基本医疗保险的人数。包括参加保险的职工人数和退休人员人数。

失业保险参保人数：指报告期末按照国家法律、法规和有关政策规定参加了失业保险的城镇企业事业单位的职工及地方政府规定参加失业保险的其他人员的人数。

工伤保险参加保险人数：指报告期末依据国家有关规定参加工伤保险的职工人数。

离休、退休、退职人员保险福利费用：指离休、退休、退职人员实际得到的生活费用总额，包括从社会保险经办机构和单位得到的费用。

1.离休金：指按规定支付给离休人员的生活费用。

2.退休金：指按规定支付给退休人员的生活费用。

3.退职生活费：指按规定支付给退职人员的生活费用。

4.医疗卫生费：指单位直接支付给离休、退休、退职人员的医疗费、住院费以及住院伙食补助等费用。

5.其他：指离休金、退休金、退职生活费和医疗卫生费以外的其他保险福利费用，如丧葬抚恤救济费、生活补贴、物价补贴、冬季取暖补贴等。

Explanatory Note on Main Statistical Indicators

Number of staff covered by basic aged insurance refers to the number of staff who are covered by basic aged insurance and have established payment archive in social security agency at the end of reporting period according to state laws, regulations and related policies, including the number of staff who have terminated payment but have not terminated aged insurance relationship, not including the number of staff who have only got registered but failed to establish payment archive.

Number of staff covered by basic medical insurance refers to the number of personnel covered by basic medical insurance at the end of reporting period according to related state stipulations, including the number of staff and number of retired personnel covered by medical insurance.

Number of staff covered by unemployment insurance refers to the number of staff who work in urban enterprises and institutions covered by unemployment insurance and the number of other personnel covered by unemployment insurance according to related stipulations of local governments at the end of reporting period.

Number of staff covered by on-job injury insurance refers to the number of staff covered unemployment insurance at the end of reporting period according to related state stipulations.

Insurance and welfare expense for retired and resigned staff refers to total expense actually obtained by the honorary retired staff, retired staff and resigned staff, including the expenses obtained from social security agencies.

1. Honorary Retirement fund refers to the living expense paid to honorary retired staff.

2. Retirement fund refers to the living expense paid to retired staff

3. Living expense for resigned staff refers to the living expense paid to the retired staff.

4. Medical and healthcare expense refers to medical expense, hospitalization expense as well as food subsidy directly paid to retired and resigned staff.

5. Others refer to honorary retirement fund, retirement fund, living expense for resigned staff, other insurance and welfare other than medical and healthcare expense such as funeral subsidy, living subsidy, price subsidy, subsidy for winter warming, etc.

海口市文化体育局

海口市文化体育局是市政府主管文化、艺术、体育工作的职能部门。

2006年在市委、市政府领导下,文体事业成绩显著:

创作了一批能够代表海南、代表海口,具有地方、民族特色的文化精品。大型现代琼剧《百年苍翠》参加了国家地方戏曲展演并获奖。

公共文化事业持续发展,群众文化事业迈上新台阶。1、群众文化活动蓬勃开展。以"建设共同的家园"和"情系百姓"主题开展文化下乡活动。先后组织全市专业、业余文艺团体32个,举行文化下乡活动3711场次;把"广场文化"作为开展群众文化活动的重要内容来抓,先后举行大型群众广场文艺演出61场,观看广场文艺演出的观众达百万人次。2、抓群众文化活动精品,加快群众文化的发展。举办了海口市第五届少儿"蒲公英"声乐、器乐、舞蹈比赛;组队参加海南省东西南北中广场文艺汇演,节目获得一、二等奖;组队参加中央文明办、文化部联合举办的全国"四进社区"文艺展演,节目获得金奖、铜奖。《邻里情》代表海南省进京参加了展演。3、贯彻科学发展观,加强公共文化服务体系建设,充分发挥基层文化阵地作用。

节庆舞台色彩缤纷,丰富了"娱乐之都"的文化内涵。精心策划组织了2006年新春系列群众文化活动——万春会、第五届冼夫人文化节系列活动,"五一"黄金周期间的文体活动和欢乐节开幕式组织、演出工作,为海口市民献上了一场场可口的文化大餐。

加强文物保护工程建设,历史文化保护与利用更上一层楼。海口历史文化名城更名申报工作取得阶段性进展;文物保护单位保护管理工作取得成效,完成对4处国保单位的安防方案修改完善工作。

加强文化市场管理,促进市场健康发育。大力整顿和规范文化市场秩序,先后查处违规网吧122家,音像店189家次,书报刊32家次,游戏机房105家次,印刷厂9家次,收缴盗版音像制品112568张,淫秽色情音像5367件,非法电子出版物8491张,非法图书18356册。扶持高雅艺术和本土艺术的演出。

体育竞技以训练工作为中心,狠抓竞技能力的提高。大力培养高水平的体育人才,狠抓竞技能力的提高,组队参加全国各类赛事上获3银1铜、第四名1个、第六名2个。在海南省少年锦标赛上我市共获得95枚金牌、56枚银牌、40枚铜牌,8个团体总分第一。成功承办了"中国移动杯"2006年环海南岛国际公路自行车赛。该赛事是一项国际性高水平的赛事,通过这一平台提高海口的知名度。

群众体育健康发展。我市群众体育及全民健身活动继续坚持以"生活奔小康,身体要健康"为主题,开展了10次群众体育活动。全市目前有50多个全民健身点,近100多条健身路径,每天可供10万多人进行各类形式的锻炼活动。

成功举办具有"平民奥运"之称的《城市之间》中国区总决赛,提升了海口城市形象,对打造"阳光海口、娱乐之都",吸引更多的游客来海口休闲、度假起到积极作用。

海南省注册会计师协会

海南省注册会计师协会（以下简称“省注协”）于1991年1月29日成立，属海南省财政厅下属事业单位，业务上接受中国注册会计师协会的指导。省注协的主要职能是管理我省注册会计师行业，宗旨是“服务、监督、管理、协调”，组织机构有会员代表大会、常务理事会、理事会和各专业委员会，秘书处为常设办事机构。

省注协的主要职能有：

1、自律管理全省注册会计师行业；

2、对注册会计师执业质量和职业道德进行监督检查和内部惩戒；

3、负责注册会计师的审批；

4、组织贯彻注册会计师执业准则；

5、组织注册会计师任职资格和执业情况的年度检查；

6、组织实施全国注册会计师资格统一考试；

7、组织实施注册会计师后续教育培训；

8、组织行业内外交流；

9、及时向政府有关部门反映注册会计师的意见和建议，维护注册会计师的合法权益；

10、加强注册会计师执业标准建设，加强对事务所的业务指导，提高注册会计师执业水平；

11、办理授权或委托办理的其他事宜。

省注协自成立以来，认真履行职责，积极推进我省注册会计师事业健康、快速发展。截止2006年12月31日，全省共有会计师事务所43家，注册会计师402人，注册会计师非执业会员254人，2006年业务收入达6484万，同比去年增长了14%。

2006年，省注协在财政厅党组的领导和在中注协的指导下，在社会各界的大力支持以及广大会员的共同努力下，全面树立和落实科学发展观，认真履行法定职能，开展了一系列富有成效的工作：紧紧围绕行业诚信建设，开展治理商业贿赂工作；以“2006质量年”活动为契机，在行业内树立起了“以质量求生存、以质量求发展”的执业理念；推进事务所内部治理机制建设，推动事务所做强做大；贯彻落实人才战略，提升行业竞争力；加强行业宣传，树立注册会计师行业的良好形象；以巩固共产党员先进性教育成果为契机，加强行业党支部建设；加强秘书处自身建设，增强服务意识，提高服务水平，不断提高行业管理和服务水平。

海口市美兰区政法委员会

近年来，在市委、市政府的正确领导下，美兰区以实施“平安美兰”为载体，全力维护社会稳定，促进经济社会协调发展。

重点抓好五方面工作：

一、创新机制、强化措施，全力抓好维稳工作。建立健全维稳分析评估机制、目标量化考核机制、应急预警机制和矛盾纠纷排查机制，全面启动治安与维稳问责制，定期对各部门和基层单位进行检查督促、考核评估，确保各项工作措施的落实，有效地控制和化解了基层的各种矛盾，特别是妥善处置了美兰机场、白沙门、鲁能等一批省市挂牌督办的重大矛盾纠纷，维护了美兰社会的稳定，确保了重点建设项目的顺利实施。

二、专群结合、严厉打击，解决社会治安突出问题。全面开展严打专项斗争，努力将严打方针贯彻落实到侦查破案、批捕起诉、定罪量刑等各个环节，突出“打击战略、打击方式、打击重点”的四个转变，始终保持对刑事犯罪分子的高压态势。

三、打惩并举、帮教并重，深入开展禁毒人民战争。紧紧围绕创建“全省禁毒优秀市县”的目标，强化禁毒一把手责任制，积极开展“五大战役”，实施“四个一百”和启动“4321”工程，确保禁毒工作取得了显著成效。

四、抓住关键、创新思路，构建社区网格化防范体系。形成公安、联防队员和治安专管员联动防范的网格化防范机制，推进了联户联防和群防群治工作，提升了城区治安防控能力。同时，大力改革联防队伍管理体制，把联防队伍的管理权限下放到基层，有针对性地适时调整防范力量，强化社会面的防范控制，取得了良好的成效。

五、领导重视，把平安建设纳入经济社会发展规划。落实“平安美兰”领导责任制，实施“一把手”工程，区委高度重视，区主要领导亲自挂帅、亲自抓，区人大定期检查督办，区政府在人力、物力、财力等方面给予支持和倾斜，并拨款600万元作为平安建设的专项经费，确保“平安美兰”工程顺利实施。

海口市美兰区人民法院

2006年，我院在上级法院和区委的正确领导下，在区人大的监督下，在区政府的支持下，以邓小平理论和“三个代表”重要思想为指导，深入贯彻党的十六届五中全会精神和全国、全省法院院长会议精神，按照上级法院和区委的统一部署，认真开展社会主义荣辱观和社会主义法治理念教育活动，切实落实司法为民措施，全面开展审判工作和其它各项工作，不断加强法院队伍建设，取得了一定的成绩，为创建“和谐美兰、富裕美兰、文明美兰、平安美兰”提供了强有力的司法保障。

充分发挥职能作用，全面开展各项审判工作。2006年（截止到10月20日止），我院共受理各类审判案件2382件，比去年同期受理的2595件少出213件，综合结案1706件，比去年结案的1962件少出256件，结案率72%。受理执行案件1060件，比去年的1020件多出40件，执结521件，比去年执结的425件多出96件，结案率49%。刑事审判工作：全年共受理刑事案件324件，审结296件，结案率达91%。一是依法严厉打击严重刑事犯罪，二是依法严厉惩处严重经济犯罪，三是认真做好少年案件审理工作。民商事审判工作：全年共受理各类民商事案件1782件，审结1187件，结案率为67%。围绕做好新时期民商事审判工作，坚持调解与判决并重的原则，充分发挥民事调解的作用，一是依法审理各类债权案件，二是妥善处理人身权和婚姻家庭类案件，三是积极审理涉及公民基本生活权益的案件，四是积极审理房屋类纠纷案件，五是妥善处理金融纠纷案件，六是认真审理涉及农业和农村的经济案件，七是加大矛盾易激化纠纷的调处。行政审判工作：全年共受理行政案件96件，审结81件，结案率为84%。执行和申诉信访工作：我院始终把执行工作和申诉信访当做一把手工程来抓，统一思想，研究措施，狠抓落实，切实维护司法权威，确保司法公正。

强化法院队伍建设，提高审判服务。今年以来，我院“规范司法行为，促进司法公正”专项整改活动为载体，全面加强队伍思想建设和业务建设，进一步提高队伍素质。抓好党风廉政建设责任制的落实；认真落实“五条禁令”；开展司法为民工作；做好案件管理清理工作；加强法官队伍的培训和考核；推进法院改革，强化司法管理，确保司法公正；广泛接受监督，共促司法公正；积极参与社会治安综合治理，延伸审判服务。

海口市
美兰区安全生产监督管理局

2006年，我局在区委区政府的领导下，在省市安监部门的指导下，认真贯彻国务院和省政府《关于进一步加强安全生产工作的决定》，坚持“安全第一、预防为主、综合治理”的方针，突出“以人为本、安全第一”的主题，认真执行《安全生产法》，大力开展安全生产宣传教育活动，深入开展各项安全生产检查，加大专项整治和执法力度，完善监管体系，增强安全意识，排除安全隐患，努力把安全生产落到实处，有效遏制特重大安全事故的发生，确保人民群众生命财产安全。

2006年，全区没有发生重特大安全生产事故。

安全生产工作情况：

1、加强制度建设，促使安全生产工作逐步走向正轨；

2、落实工作目标责任制，进一步明确安全生产职责；

3、加强安全生产检查，做到防患于未然；

4、认真做好重大安全隐患整治工作，消除重大安全隐患；

5、深入开展安全生产专项整治，做好危险源的防控工作；

6、积极开展非公企业安全生产监管试点推行工作，为全面开展非公企业安全生产工作做好准备；

7、认真抓好节假日安全生产大检查活动，确保节假日的安全；8、积极开展安全生产月活动，进一步提高安全生产意识。

琼山区城市管理行政执法局
琼山区城市管理行政执法大队

琼山区城市管理行政执法局是主管全区城市管理行政执法工作的职能部门。琼山区城市管理行政执法大队是副科级全额拨款事业单位，隶属琼山区城市管理行政执法局，业务上接受海口市城市管理行政执法局及支队的指导，受区城市管理行政执法局委托，行使辖区内市容环境卫生管理、城市规划管理、城市绿化管理、市政设施管理、建筑市场管理、燃气管理方面法律、法规、规章规定的全部处罚权，行使环境保护管理、工商行政管理、公安交通管理方面法律、法规、规章规定的部分行政处罚权，按职责权限查处违法违章案件。2003 年 1 月，海口和琼山两市合并后，设立琼山区城市管理局，2006 年 9 月改称琼山区城市管理行政执法局，内设办公室、案件处理室，有工作人员 5 人。琼山区城市管理行政执法大队内设办公室、五个辖区中队、一个机动中队、一个特勤中队。有工作人员 160 人。

2003 年以来主要工作：

1、坚持教育与管理并重，大力加强队伍建设，不断提高城管执法队伍的整体素质，切实抓好业务培训和法律教育，不断深化制度创新和内部管理。

2、以整治占道经营为重点，切实提升工作水平，积极营造良好的出行居住环境。

3、围绕解决热点难点问题，不断加大执法力度，各类违章活动得到有效遏制。户外广告管理规范有序，车辆停放管理日趋规范，乱搭乱建得到有效清理，违法建筑得到依法拆除，“三车”营运整顿工作不断加强，各项保障工作有力到位。

4、全力打造坚强的领导核心，积极推进班子建设，充分发挥总支一班人的模范带头作用。切实抓好政治理论学习、规章制度的落实，勤政廉洁风气，自身形象的塑造。2005 年被评为城市管理工作先进单位；2006 年被区评为优秀党总支。

海口市琼山区府城镇

2006年，在区委、区政府的正确领导下，区有关部门的大力支持下，府城镇委、镇政府坚持以邓小平理论和“三个代表”重要思想为指导，认真贯彻落实党的十六届五中、六中全会精神，落实科学发展观，努力构建和谐新府城，带领全镇人民解放思想，发挥优势，真抓实干，较好地完成了全年的各项工作任务，推动了府城经济发展和社会各项事业的进步。

一、全镇经济稳步发展，主要经济指标持续增长。2006年全镇农林牧渔总产值完成4062万元，同比增长10.1%，人均农业总产值增长10.2%，乡镇工业总产值7538万元，同比增长6.1%，人均乡镇工业总产值增长6.6%，社会消费品零售总额10亿元，同比增长11%，城镇居民人均可支配收入8050元，增长8%，农民年人均纯收入3680元，同比增加323元，增长9.4%。养殖、加工和第三产业有新的发展，畜牧业产值达1689万元，年均增长10.3%，粮食播种面积9068亩，无公害瓜菜播种面积8387亩，产值1749万元。农村工副业、运输业和第三产业，年产值6360万元。招商引资带动经济发展，新引进的一汽集团公司投资1000万元兴建的解放商用汽车展销中心已建成开业，一批小型企业继续在我镇落户经营，家具、木制品、水泥制品加工企业发展到73家，年产值达7538万元。这些项目对增加我镇经济总量，促进经济发展将发挥积极作用。

二、以“三农”工作为重点，改变农村落后面貌。镇委、镇政府加大投入，不断改善农民生产生活条件，切实解决农村存在的突出问题，今年来，投入农村基础设施建设资金75万元，效果显著。一是加大农田水利建设投入，确保农业生产用水；二是切实解决饮水难问题；三是继续抓好农村土地纠纷调处，维护农村稳定；四是抓生态文明村建设。

三、加强社区建设管理，提高小街道环境卫生水平，改善居民生活条件。一是配合区建设部门抓好小街道的整治改造；二是落实新增硬板化小街巷清扫保洁人员共24人；三是抓好社区建设，逐步改善办公环境和完善社区服务功能；四是组织力量配合区政府组织的共三批100多宗违章建筑的拆除行动；五是治理城中坟。

四、开展第三批先进性教育活动，加强农村党的基层组织建设。一是抓好第三批先进性教育，二是抓好党建工作和党风廉政建设，三是做好政务公开，村务公开。

五、着力抓好各部门工作，促进社会各项事业协调发展。一是切实抓好人口与计划生育属地管理，较好地完成各项考核指标；二是发展文化教育事业；三是加强社会治安综合治理；四是民政工作落到实处；五是卫生工作有新成效。

海口市琼山区会计管理中心

海口市琼山区会计管理中心(以下简称"中心")于2001年6月成立,并于2002年1月正式运作。其机构性质为副科级事业单位,主要职能是负责对全区区直属行政事业单位、财政拨款或实行收支两条线单位和国兴街道办事处的会计委派工作的管理以及对各镇财务核算站的业务指导。

五年来,特别是两市合并后,在区委、区人大、区政府的正确领导和区财政局党组的直接领导下,在区纪委、监察、审计、人事等部门及各委派单位的大力支持和配合下,中心本着"三集中"(资金集中核算、账户集中管理、人员集中委派)和"两不变"(单位资金的所有权不变、使用权不变)的原则,采取集中委派的方式向全区97家直属行政事业单位和8个镇财务核算站委派会计,实行集中核算。

近年来,我们主要抓好如下几个方面的工作:

一、大力抓好中心的网络建设。通过网络系统将全区97家直属行政事业单位的会计监督和资金管理及各镇财务核算站的资金管理一并纳入统一的电脑网络进行集中管理,实现信息的直达和资源的共享,促进财务系统管理网络化。

二、加强制度建设,完善会计委派制。我们建立健全各项规章制度,规范了中心内部各项管理和业务流程,把各项工作纳入制度化、规范化的轨道,使整个中心操作有章可循。

三、设立镇财务核算站,推行镇财务零户统管制。2004年我们扩大会计委派范围,在各镇设立财务核算站,推行镇财务零户制。进一步规范了各镇财务管理工作,并加强对各镇财务核算站的业务指导。

四、加大沟通力度,提高服务质量。我们要求每一个会计把单位"满意不满意"作为工作的最高准则,为单位理好财,服好务。同时,明确服务内容,建立反馈渠道,把中心建成优质高效的服务单位。

中心通过五年来的运作,各项会计核算业务逐步走上轨道,财务监督进一步加强,会计基础工作进一步完善,基本实现了会计程序的规范化、科学化,促进了勤政廉政建设。一是加强财务监督,控制不合理开支:五年来,拒付内容不齐全的原始凭证254张,共49万元;拒付各种不合理的支出和超标准的差旅费、业务招待费527次,共65万元;二是严格预算执行,强化了预算结果:五年来,在执行预算的过程中,我们共拒付无预算的支出42次,金额295万元;拒付不按规定自行调剂使用的专项资金9次,金额115万元。三是促进了各镇会计管理工作进一步规范和完善。

海口市琼山区水务局

一年来，在区委、区政府的正确领导下，在省、市水务局的指导和支持下，努力拼搏，锐意进取，大力推进城乡水务一体化建设和社会各项事业全面协调发展，圆满完成了预定的各项工作目标，在三个文明建设项目和党的执政能力建设中，取得了显著成绩。

2006年全区农田水利基本建设及人畜饮水、防洪楼建设总投资3210万元，其中：省级以上资金1726万元，市财政投资970万元，区财政投资514万元，实施人畜饮水项目113宗，解决128个村庄2.346万多人的饮水难问题；加固病险水库四宗，防渗渠道两条共7.2公里，同时全面维修各种渠道32条，长265公里，整治田洋6个，增加灌溉面积0.5万亩，改造灌溉面积1.2万亩，恢复灌溉面积0.38万亩，改造低产田0.8万亩，大大增强了我区水利基础设施的实力，为确保我区国民经济的稳定增长，为农业增产，农民增收，社会增效做出了重大贡献。

一、筹措资金，加快我区农田水利建设，为建设社会主义新农村事业打下基础。一年来，在突出全面清理维修基础上，投入资金2376万元，重点抓好“六洋四库两渠道”工程建设。

二、争取上级资金，推进我区农业基础设施建设。2006年我区共争取上级资金1696万元，基本完成我区被洪水侵袭村庄的防洪项目建设，做到了抗击自然灾害以人为本，以防为主，深受广大人民群众的称赞。

三、一丝不苟，做好各项工程专项资金的稽查审计工作。2006年是中央国债资金项目进行督查和各项专项资金项目工程全面审计的一年，经过三个月的稽查审计，由于我们工作踏实，在稽查审计中分别受到各级部门的好评。同时完成了三年来的各项专项资金的审计工作。

四、加强值班，有备无患，做好防风防汛工作。抓好防汛物料的储备和补充，积极培训有关技术骨干，提高我区的防风防汛抗旱能力。在整个汛期做到不误时误事，不瞒报漏报，科学准确地向上级领导和主管部门提供信息。科学防汛，适量蓄水，确保水库安全渡汛和今冬明春的生产用水。

五、认真实践“三个代表”重要思想，开展“八荣八耻”教育活动。组织干部职工学习党的十六届五中、六中全会精神，学习胡锦涛总书记提出的“八荣八耻”内容，购买学习资料和江泽民文选，用“八荣八耻”的道德标准规范行为，指点工作。通过教育活动，干部职工思想觉悟得到进一步提高。

海口市秀英区财政局

海口市秀英区财政局成立于1991年，现任局长李坚，副局长吴群杰、李山泉。财政系统共有人员69人（其中：局机关11人，局下属单位会计核算中心有23人，6个镇财政所共有33人）。经过17年的风风雨雨，有艰辛、有喜悦、有坎坷、也有收获。秀英财政的成长凝聚着广大财政干部的辛勤汗水，包含了秀英财政人的不懈努力和孜孜追求。

2007年财政总体思路和工作重点是：在支持经济发展，积极培植财源，促进财力增长的同时，按照保工资、保运转和促发展的要求，关注民生，节用裕民，调整和优化支出结构，促进秀英和谐发展。

秀英财政担负着解决6,000多名财政供养人员和30余万人口的民生问题，承担着保证区镇两级政权正常运转等职责。

秀英财政随着海南经济的起伏发展，也经历了从起步到高潮，又从低谷进入回升，步入稳步发展的时期。区级财政收入一年上一个新台阶，从成立当年的财政收入完成787万元，发展至2006年财政收入完成44,898万元，实现又好又快发展。

秀英财政贯彻落实科学发展观，不断推进财政各项改革，实现全区行政事业单位人员由银行代发工资，政府采购、部门预算及国库集中支付等项改革，也开展的有声有色。

财政局办公地址位于丘海大道与秀华路交汇处，市内1路、2路、3路及17路公交车在此经过，交通十分便利。

财政局办公室电话：089868663091

传真电话：089868663091

邮政编码：570311

地址：海口市秀英区秀华路4号

海南省彩票管理中心

该中心1999年5月经省政府批准成立，隶属于省财政厅的正处级事业单位，承担对全省彩票市场进行监督管理，维护彩票市场秩序的主要职责，具体指导市县稽查打击非法彩票营销活动；协助省财政厅对彩票销售内容的合法性、程序上的合规性进行审查和监管；协助省财政厅督促彩票公益金、发行经费及时足额上缴；提出扩大彩票发行的意见和建议。中心下设办公室、监督科、稽查科、财审科。根据打击私彩的需要，省政府成立了全省打击私彩联合行动领导小组办公室，办公室设在彩票管理中心，负责日常具体事务。

2006年我中心在开展彩票监管工作中始终贯穿着"打击私彩，扶持公彩，严格监管，热情服务"的工作指导思想，加强对市县打击私彩工作的指导，充分依靠各级政府组织力量打击私彩。彭运洪主任亲自带领调研组进行多次明查暗访，走遍海口、三亚、东方、乐东等十八个市县，加强对打击私彩工作指导，我们感到各地都能贯彻执行省政府[2005]34号文件精神，打击私彩领导小组健全，设立举报电话，坚持巡逻制度，实施辖区责任制，基本上遏制了私彩的公开摆卖，但同时我们发现一些问题仍较为突出，各地打击私彩力度不平衡，缺乏长期性，有效性，存在私彩"死角"等，针对这些问题，我们及时向当地主管部门反馈，要求他们认真整改。我中心还注意抓好打击私彩的宣传工作，在海口市的主要街道和繁华市区悬挂横幅1000多条，同时制作流动宣传车在海口、澄迈、定安等市县进行巡回宣传，并拟出宣传标语口号，下发市、县要求配合专项治理行动，进行悬挂横幅宣传和张贴，让广大群众从宣传中知道私彩的危害性，从而达到自觉抵制私彩，扶持公彩的目的。

为确保我省彩票电脑系统发行销售彩票安全运营，我们依据财政部和省财政厅的有关政策规定，发挥职责作用，全面掌握体彩、福彩各种彩票的游戏规则变化及相应的安全管理规程，密切关注彩票的动态。

海南彩票市场较为复杂，我们深入市场调研时，注意收集彩民的意见，关注市场的变化，为政府有关部门决策提供参考依据。我们认为要根治海南的私彩，促进公彩发展，根本出路在于搞好彩票改革。

海口市琼山区府城医院

创建优质快捷的服务品牌

府城医院始创于1957年，是一所集医疗、保健、预防、康复治疗为一体的综合性医院，拥有卫生部评比的“爱婴医院”、“百姓放心医院”等光荣称号，是海南省和海口市医疗保险的定点医院，也是新型农村合作医疗定点服务机构。近年来府城医院对外加大合作力度，对内狠抓医疗质量，先后与全国著名的安贞医院、海口市急救中心120合作，使府城医院的医疗技术水平从合作中得到了快速提高，也使病患就医得到了质量的保障。现在的府城医院每年接待门诊患者达20万人次、住院患者4000人次，其设备优良，人才荟萃，环境优美。医院全体员工，始终以质量为根本、以服务为导向，不断努力打造优质快捷的服务品牌！

人性化的服务理念，人性化的门诊设施，亲切的医务人员使前来就医的患者感到放心、愉快。设各专科门诊有：

急诊科：同海口市120合作，能为您提供全天候的服务，由内、外、妇、儿、五官、中医、医技的优秀医护人员提供服务，病友的需求就是我们的义务。24小时呼叫热线65881001

内科：由诊疗经验丰富的副主任医师、主治医师合理的诊断与治疗，使广大内科门诊患者对我院的诊疗水平有很高的评价。

外科：已成功开展甲状腺、乳腺、肝胆、胃肠、泌尿、胸部等多部位手术，可进行多种肿瘤根治术。脊柱外科与微创手术的开展使得外科的技术水平登上了更高的阶梯。

妇产科：医院的品牌科室，设备齐全：无影灯、薄膜光、海扶刀超声妇科治疗仪、可视性人流机等先进设备。对治疗各类妇科疾患，经验丰富。

儿科：呵护关爱儿童的健康，擅长儿科常见病、多发病、新生儿疾病诊治。

中西医结合科：对常见病、多发病有很好的治疗效果，特别是对支气管哮喘和慢性支气管炎更是独特显著、名播一方。

眼科：对诊治各种眼科疾病有丰富的经验，开展各类手术如：白内障、青光眼、斜弱视矫治等。咨询电话：65801084

口腔科：建立早、技术好，是府城地区最具规模的口腔专科。采用先进的专业设备和高温高压的消毒设施，为广大患者提供镶牙、补牙、洁牙等可靠科学的口腔医疗服务。咨询电话：65895783

康复理疗科：开设按摩、针灸、电疗、体疗、药疗、特色疗法，主治骨质增生症、腰椎间盘突出症、肩周炎、颈椎病、风湿性关节炎以及多种内科、外科、妇科、儿科病症。咨询电话：65887500

皮肤科：主治各类常见病、多发病，对治疗皮肤瘙痒、皮肤过敏有较好的疗效。

影像科：是全院拥有先进设备最多的科室，能开展腹部、心脏、妇产科以及小器官的超声检查，同时还可开展介入性超声检查。常规胃镜和无痛胃镜的开展满足了患者对消化系统疾病检查的需要，超声碎石技术的应用更是解决了结石患者的痛苦。咨询电话：65800320

放射科：开展CT全身检查，X光拍片、透视。已开展各类造影检查如：消化道造影、尿路造影、子宫、输卵管造影、T管造影、瘘管造影等。同时开展：肿瘤介入治疗。咨询电话：65899291

检验科：开展常规、生化、免疫、肝功能、肾功能、心功能、妇科疾病的检验。咨询电话：65893047

防保科：提供免疫疫苗、妇幼保健系列服务，儿童发育早期教育中心，为孩子塑造最佳的人生开端。

医学美容科：配置先进的美容设备，安全高效，提供个性化的服务，将医学美容与生活美容完美结合。咨询电话：65800062

社区服务科：社区以健康咨询服务为中心，在与“中国疾病控制中心”“健康管理业务”合作后，系统建立个人档案，科学评估个人健康状况，提供与您的健康有关的信息，管理您的健康。咨询电话：65898314

海南省血液中心

海南省血液中心建于1989年,隶属海南省卫生厅,承担着海南全省临床用血采集、制备、贮存、供应和临床输血技术的科研和推广任务。中心设有六个科室、一个专业研究室和儋州、琼海、三亚三个分中心。

1996年,中心确立"靠质量求生存,向管理要效率,在改革中发展,在创新中提高"的发展思路,励精图治,开拓创新,在省财政没有投入的情况下,在只有一栋2280立方米的业务楼、固定资产不足300万元、员工30人、日采血量不足15人份、90%的临床用血靠从外省调剂的艰难困境上奋力拼搏、锐意改革,创建了具有海南特色的"中心辐射型采供血网络",做到全省统一规划采供血,统一管理血液;开展ISO9002质量体系认证活动并顺利通过认证,确保了全省医疗用血的需求和安全。

近几年来,中心获国债项目支持兴建的省血液中心和三个分中心相继投入使用,中心已发展成员工百人、占地30亩、近12000立方米的建筑面积、固定资产4500万元、现代花园式工作环境的省级血液中心,硬件设施及软件服务大大提高,为无偿献血提供更放心、舒适的献血环境,为医疗机构提供安全的血液产品和快捷、方便的送血服务,为海南采供血事业的可持续发展打下了坚实的基础。

2001年5月起,无偿献血满足全省临床用血需求,确保了安全血液的来源;2004年全省取消指导性献血指标,无偿献血实现真正的自愿、无偿。

海口市社会治安综合治理委员会办公室

省市领导视察滨濂村流动人口管理工作

海口市社会治安综合治理委员会办公室（简称海口市综治办），成立于1991年，是海口市社会治安综合治理委员会的常设办事机构，编制6人。其主要职责是：根据市委、市政府和市综治委的部署，研究、分析当前治安状况，提出解决问题的措施和建议；掌握各区、市直各部门治安综治工作进展情况，及时向综治委及上级综治部门反映；开展调查研究，推动综治各项措施在基层的落实；总结交流典型经验，鼓励先进，推动后进。

近年来，我市综治工作坚持以“三个代表”重要思想和科学发展观为指导，以建设“平安海口”为载体，采取有力措施，严厉打击各类刑事犯罪活动，积极预防处置矛盾纠纷和群体性事件，整治治安突出问题，加强社会治安管理，健全治安防控体系，治安综治各方面工作有了明显提升，群众安全感进一步增强，为全面建设小康社会和构建和谐海口营造了良好的治安环境。

2006年，我市综治工作主要取得了五个方面突出成效：一是全力推进“平安海口”建设，平安创建活动深入人心。市委、市政府高度重视平安建设工作，制定了实施方案和创建目标，为平安创建活动提供了有力的组织保障和经费保障。市综治办、平安办深入开展平安创建宣传活动，广泛发动基层开展平安创建活动，有26个街镇、231个村（社区）、学校、单位等达到平安创建标准。产生了平安创建工作先进集体60个，平安创建工作先进个人65名。2006年11月，中央综治委检查组到我市检查指导综治工作，对我市平安建设工作给予了高度评价。二是掌握化解矛盾纠纷主动权，解决了一大批信访突出问题，调处了一大批民间纠纷，妥善处置了一批群体性事件。三是坚持“严打”方针，有效打压控制可防性案件犯罪空间，刑事案件持续下降，治安形势持续好转。刑事案件发案率与去年相比下降5.3%，“两抢”犯罪案件从2004年的日均12起，下降到2006年底的日均6.8起。四是强化部门责任，社会管理能力进一步提高。坚持打防并举的方针，开展了一系列的专项整治活动。开展了扫黄打非的“百日反盗版”行动、禁毒的“清瘤”收戒行动，毒患严重地区挂牌整治、公共娱乐场所、停车场、城市小区、学校及周边治安整治等一系列专项整治活动，取得了明显成效。五是严密治安防控体系，科技防控能力得到强化。城市报警与监控体系建设一期工程完成，“社会面”科技监控网初步形成；五级联防、群防群治进一步完善，专群结合为我市社会稳定做出了积极贡献。

中央综治委检查组到我市检查近年综治暨平安建设工作情况

见义勇为表彰大会

海口市龙华区治安联防大队成立十五周年庆祝大会

海口市外事侨务办公室

海口市外事侨务办公室是海口市人民政府负责外事、侨务、引进国外智力和国际交流工作的职能部门。先后多次获得全国侨办系统先进集体、全国侨务信访工作先进单位、全省侨务系统先进单位等荣誉称号。改革开放以来，该办充分发挥职能作用，坚持外事侨务工作为中央总体外交服务，为海口的开放和发展服务，为侨服务，为树立海口良好的国际形象服务，致力于“办大外事，打好‘侨牌’，让世界了解海口，让海口走向世界”，外事侨务工作取得了骄人的成绩。至2006年，外事部门共受理公务出访团组2517个、7917人次，出访国有50多个国家和地区，大力推介了海口，提高了海口的国际知名度，促进了海口与世界各国的交流与合作。1989年起，该办精心打造国际友城平台，先后与国外8个城市结为友好城市，友城遍布五大洲。海口市是海南的第三大侨乡，侨力资源丰富，旅居海外的华侨华人、港澳同胞50多万人，归侨侨眷30多万人。该办致力于打好“侨牌”，主动与海外社团、侨领开展广泛联谊，积极开展以侨引资引智工作，吸引了众多的侨商在海口市投资兴业。建省以来，在海口市投资的侨港澳资企业5000多家，实际投资416000万美元，其中侨资企业和侨资均占外资企业和实际利用外资总数的80%，有力推动了海口市经济社会的发展。我们坚持“以人为本，为侨服务”的宗旨，热情接待华侨华人来访，尽力为他们排忧解难，维权护侨工作成绩显著，海外联谊日趋活跃，进一步促进了海口与海外世界海南社团的联系和友好合作，侨务工作呈现喜人的局面。海口市外事侨务办公室紧紧围绕促进经济建设，促进科技进步开展引智工作，二十多年来共为海口市各行各业申报引进外国人才项目300多个，引进国外、境外人才1500多人次，选派各类专业技术管理人才出国培训团组20多个、200多人次，为海口市的经济发展和重点项目建设做出了重要贡献。

2005年9月26日，市领导在波兰格丁尼亚市与该市什楚莱克市长签署“海口市和格丁尼亚市结为友好城市”意向书

市领导会见韩国21C韩中交流协会会长金汉圭、韩国东海市市长金振东

2005年7月，市政府与沃尔玛公司签署合作意向书

海口市外事侨务办公室领导会见英国专家约翰·格林

海口市双拥办

近年来，海口市双拥工作在市委、市政府的正确领导下，以“三个代表”重要思想和胡锦涛总书记关于做好双拥工作重要指示为指导，通过全市军民的共同努力，在创建“全国双拥模范城”活动中，已连续五次获此殊荣,有力地促进了我市经济社会发展和部队全面建设。

原省委常委、市委书记王为璐（左二）、原市长、现省委常委、市委书记陈辞（左三）慰问驻海南省军区某部

市人大常委会主任高锦全（右三）与省军区政治部副主任刘新（左三）在“援建军营图书室”活动中向驻市某通讯总站赠书

海口市美兰区首创“区片联创、军警互动”军民共建社会主义生态文明村模式，得到中央有关领导、部委的高度关注与评价。

市政协主席黄行光（左）在我市双拥表彰大会上向模范单位、先进个人颁奖

市委常委、警备区政委（右一）右与琼山区区委书记钟万荣（左一）在调研建设社会主义新农村现场

去年我省遭遇30年不遇的特大台风“达维”，驻市军警部队在抢险救灾

海口市法律援助中心

124法律援助送温暖活动

"维护军人军属合法权益、构建和谐海口"法律援助、法律宣传活动

法律援助是一项具有浓郁社会性和服务性的司法救济政策，海口市法律援助工作1997年才正式启动，起步相对较晚，但在市委、市政府的正确领导下，在各区的高度重视和公安局、检察院、法院及财政、人劳、建设等有关单位的协助支持下，全市各级司法行政机关和广大法律援助工作者，开拓进取，扎实工作，经过近十年的探索和实践，使法律援助从无到有，从小到大，取得了可喜的变化和显著的成绩。特别是自2005年起，市委、市政府坚持以人为本，着力解决困难群众打官司难问题，连续三年将法律援助列入"为民办实事工程"项目，并每年拨出专款150万元作经费保障，有力地促进了法律援助的快速发展，使之在维护人民群众合法权益，实现司法公正，维护社会稳定和促进海口和谐发展方面发挥了更加积极的作用。主要表现在以下几个方面：

一、降低门槛，扩大范围，让更多的困难群众享受到了党委政府的关怀。

二、加强网络建设，畅通服务渠道，为法律援助工程顺利实施奠定了良好的基础。

三、加强制度建设，规范工作程序，推动了法律援助工作健康有序的发展。

四、创新援助形式，加大便民力度，最大限度地满足了困难群众对法律援助的需求。

五、加强宣传，扩大影响，提高了法律援助的社会认知度。

六、化解社会矛盾，维护安定团结，有效促进了海口和谐发展。

两年来，法律援助这一"为民办实事工程"取得了显著的社会效益，先后共为2229人提供了诉讼法律援助，为2364人提供了非诉讼法律援助，解答法律咨询45000多人（次），为当事人挽回经济损失和争取经济补偿742万元，让符合条件申请法律援助的困难群众及农民工获得了及时有效的法律援助，被广大人民群众称为民心工程、阳光工程，法律援助也成为党和政府联系人民群众的"连心桥"。

送法进军营

受益群众的感谢

深入基层开展法律援助宣传活动，增强群众维权意识

降低门槛，让更多的困难群众享受到了党委政府的关怀

海南省海口市烟草专卖局

公司（局）定期召开党组理论中心组学习（扩大）会议

举办中层干部拓展训练

2006年，在海南省烟草专卖局（公司）党组和当地政府的正确领导下，海南省烟草公司海口公司（局）始终以“三个代表”重要思想为指导，在全体干部职工的扎实工作和努力拼搏下，各项工作进展情况良好，经济运行质量和效益稳步提高。全年销售完成省局（公司）下达全年计划的103.79%，同比增长4.83%。实现销售收入154,128万元，同比增长16.87%。实现税利1.028亿元，同比增长30.6%，其中：税金3443万元，同比增长27.3%；利润6840万元，同比增长32.3%。全片区共查处各类违法案件1224宗；为国家挽回经济损失700多万元；公检法依法刑事拘留犯罪嫌疑人44名，逮捕12名，判刑9名，网上追逃5名。

2006年，公司被市国资委评为“先进基层党组织”；被海口市人民政府办公厅评为“2006年度政务服务工作暨优质服务月活动三等奖”单位;被海口市统计局评为“2006年全市批发和零售业、住宿和餐饮业统计工作先进单位”。

海南海昌会计师事务所
海南海昌工程造价咨询有限公司

所长：郭渝丽

海南海昌会计师事务所（以下简称海昌所）是于1994年3月成立的一家专业审计和资产评估机构，1998年12月改制为合伙会计师事务所，几年来，海昌所已以其专业风范和周到服务，在客户中树立良好的职业形象，并在业界树立了广泛的影响。2003年5月设立海南海昌工程造价咨询有限公司，取得工程造价咨询乙级资质证书。2004年4月29日加入华德联营盟及CPAAI国际会计师组织。

业务范围：验证注册资本、审计财务报表、评估企业资产、资产重组破产清算、财务顾问咨询、经济案件鉴证、财会人员培训、建设工程估算、工程预决算编审、工程标底标书编制、工程可行性研究、工程造价咨询。

海南省残疾人劳动就业服务中心

海南省残疾人劳动就业服务中心是隶属海南省残疾人联合会，其主要职能是开展残疾人劳动力资源和社会用工调查、劳动能力评估、求职登记、就业咨询、职业培训、职业介绍、分散按比例安排残疾人就业，管理残疾人就业保障金，落实扶持措施以及帮助残疾人个体从业。

本中心坚持以提高残疾人劳动就业技能和实现就业为宗旨，采取中、短期培训相结合的方式，以自身培训基地和社会培训机构为依托，开展形式多样的实用型培训，为残疾人掌握一技之长，实现就业创造有利条件。“十五”期间，共培训残疾人1731人次，收缴残疾人就业保障金1654万元。2005年本中心被海南省残疾人工作委员会授予按比例安排残疾人就业工作先进单位，2006年中心主任钟川同志被省直机关工作委员会授予“精神文明建设先进工作者”的光荣称号。

尽管残疾人劳动就业服务工作依然任重而道远，但只要社会各界的大力支持，我们将不断克服前进道路上的各种困难，其前景无疑是灿烂而美好的，并必将为我国和谐社会的建设做出贡献。

省委常委、统战部部长（中）、省政府领导（右）、省政协领导（左）出席表彰大会

省领导（右三）、省就业局副局长王开初（右一）和钟川主任（右二）在残疾人职业技能竞赛现场亲切问候参赛选手

省残联副理事长黎世章（左三）、省残疾人劳动就业服务中心主任钟川（左四）出席开班仪式

海口市职业技术培训中心

海口市职业技术培训中心于1985年经市政府批准成立，隶属市人事劳动保障局，是一所培养初、中级职业技术人才的培训机构。其主要职责是：负责市属机关、企事业单位工人技术等级培训，劳动预备制人员上岗前培训，下岗失业人员再就业转岗培训，以及部队军地两用人才培训等。根据社会经济发展需要，中心先后开设的培训项目有：电子、家电、空调制冷、通信设备维修，电、焊工操作，厨师、面点师，机动车驾驶，电脑操作，服装裁剪，美容、美发、家政服务等。中心自成立来，先后举办各类中、短期培训班600多期，培训各类技能人才28000多人，为海南的经济发展，社会稳定做出了应有的贡献。

海口市土地储备整理中心

司马坡岛生态实景

林明勇主任在地产论坛上发表演讲

海口市土地储备整理中心是隶属海口市国土环境资源局的法人事业单位，其主要职能是受市政府委托，负责全市国有一级市场建设用地的经营管理和土地开发整理工作。中心下设综合财务部、储备部、规划运营部、开发整理部、征地部等五个部门。

中心在局党组领导下以文明单位创建为载体，以提高干部职工素质为重点，以完善制度规范服务为着力点，坚持科学发展观，紧紧围绕服务经济建设，推进城乡协调发展的目标，开拓进取，大胆创新，贯彻执行党的基本路线方针政策，认真完成市委市政府布置的各项工作任务目标，取得了较大的进展：一是创新土地经营模式，提升土地价值。2005年，成功策划、包装、推介，挂牌美丽沙土地以后，现继续推进司马坡岛、西海岸起步区、金沙湾、新港等片区项目的策划包装及推介招商工作；二是拓宽储备资金渠道，创新和完善土地储备制度体系和机制建设，极大地扩大了我市土地储备总量，为城市的可持续发展创造了良好的条件；三是积极推进征地工作改革。把服务城市建设和维护农民权益作为征地工作出发点和落脚点，确保被征地农民的征地补偿款及时到位的同时，积极推进被征地农民的社会保障制度建设，解决失地农民的长久生计，保证重点项目的建设；四是土地整理工作成效明显，大大地推动了城乡的协调发展。通过土地整理，新增耕地3000多亩，在保障城市发展的同时，推进了市新农村建设。

中心通过高效、规范化的运作，竭诚提供优质服务。2004年度被评为中国城市土地营商环境50佳；2005年被市政府授予集体三等功；连续3年被局评为市国土局先进单位、连续3年被局评为先进党支部。

中心年度工作总结会议

金沙湾实景

海口市工人文化宫

消防日在文化宫前举行宣传活动

流动电影队到工地慰问

2006年，海口市工人文化宫积极开展政治宣传教育的同时，富有成效地加强职业技能和文化艺术培训，大力组织文化艺术演出活动，注重经营管理，取得了较好的成绩，体现了工人文化宫的“职工学校和乐园”的作用。

尤其突出的是市文化宫被定为“海口市农村劳动力转移阳光工程培训基地”、“海南省总工会农民工业余学校”，贯彻执行《2003-2010年全国农民工培训规划》，落实市政府2006年为民办实事第十七项“解决农村富余劳动力培训就业”问题，积极组织农民工的培训，并推荐其就业。2006年共办农村富余劳动力培训班4期，参加培训的有851人，就业601人，就业率达85%，受到了市农业局、劳动就业局等部门的好评。这一年还培训下岗职工125人、城市待业人员60人、文化艺术方面的培训361人。职业技能培训人数和推荐就业人数之多，效益之好，是文化宫培训工作的新发展。

市工人文化宫组织文化艺术活动也更为广泛和深入。一方面，与有关单位联合在宫内举办文艺晚会6场，另一方面，于6月份，组建了“海口职工艺术团”，已先后在宫内和下乡、下社区演出13场。职工艺术团的成立是海口市史无前例的，艺术力量较强，演出效益较好，特别是在市委宣传部和市总工会主办的纪念红军长征胜利70周年文艺晚会上的演出，受到省、市领导的肯定和新闻媒体的报道。同时，文化宫的工人影剧院和文龙电影城共6个放映厅放映电影，还有两个流动电影放映队，下乡镇、社区、工地、学校，送电影上门，尤其是专场为农民工免费放映，开展“工会与农民工心连心”活动，支援三门坡镇西鲁村、新坡镇塘柳村建设文明生态村。

市工人文化宫在市委、市政府和市总工会的重视、支持和领导下正在引资合作，筹备改造，推进发展。

面点老师在示范蛋糕制作的操作

纪念红军胜利70周年文艺晚会

海口市琼山区财政局

局长：冯所勇

富有朝气，开拓进取的领导班子

琼山财政大厦

2006年，在区委、区政府的正确领导和市财政局的大力支持下，局党组紧紧围绕区委、区政府的中心工作，充分发挥财政职能作用，着力构建财政支持社会经济发展的长效机制，努力实现“收入持续增长，支出有效保障，效益不断提高”的综合管理目标，狠抓财政收入，规范财政管理，加强财政监督，有力促进了我区社会经济协调发展，为“十一五”规划开了一个好头。

2006年，全区财政收入完成52159万元，比上年增长23.7%，完成年度预算103.29%，一般预算支出完成42670万元（含省、市下达专款），比上年增长4.72%，完成年度预算114.1%；完成非税收入1489万元；完成对全区12个单位的财政专项资金检查，金额8700多万元；完成政府采购金额7298011元，节约资金70564元；完成种粮农民149348.83亩田，金额3497749.6元的综合直补发放任务；完成54家国有企业的调查摸底工作，掌握其所有“家底”；深入开展精神文明创建活动，进一步促进了人的思想素质的提升，进一步加强了机关作风建设，等等。

2006年的财政工作，确保了全区工资、离退休人员离退休费、专项资金、政府机构正常运转等经费支出，有力地支持和促进了全区经济发展和社会各项事业建设。

海口市琼山区规划建设局

琼山区规划建设局是琼山区城乡规划建设工作的主管部门，内设行政、市政、公用、报建、质安和人防等办公室，其主要职能是配合海口市有关部门做好辖区内重点项目建设的协调工作，对辖区的规划建设、市政公用设施的日常维护及建筑行业、建筑工地安全施工进行指导和管理。

2006年，我局坚持以邓小平理论和“三个代表”重要思想为指导，认真贯彻党的十六大和十六届历次重要会议精神，按照市、区党委和政府的工作部署，以科学发展观统领城乡建设工作，扎扎实实地开展了琼山城乡建设的各项业务工作：共完成了125条小街小巷道路和124条小巷路灯改造任务；开展了琼州大道、凤翔路街道立面改造工程；积极配合市政府及有关单位开展海端大桥、海府立交大桥、滨江西路、货运大道、中山南路、振兴路、绕城高速公路等重点项目建设和府城老城区污水管网改造；完成了红旗、龙塘、云龙、旧州、三门坡、大坡、甲子等7个小城镇建设总规、红旗镇控规和城郊示范村的规划编制工作；积极配合有关部门开展文明生态村等。从而加快了城区基础设施建设、小城镇建设和社会主义新农村建设的步伐，大大改善了城乡投资环境，促进了琼山区城乡建设事业的蓬勃向前发展。

法定代表人：龙舒华

单位地址：海口市琼山区府城镇新城路4号三楼

电话：65893676　　传真：65898983

城市建设突飞猛进

依法保护文物资源

海口市琼山区人民检察院

检察长：黄宏杰

黄宏杰检察长在全院干警大会上讲话

海口市琼山区人民检察院现任党组书记、检察长黄宏杰，人员74人，内设机构有：反贪污贿赂局、办公室、政工科、侦查监督科、公诉科、控告申诉科、反渎职侵权局、民事行政检察科、职务犯罪预防科、司法警察大队、业务监督管理中心，琼山区人民检察院是国家法律监督机关，依法履行法律监督职能，保证国家法律的统一实施，受海口市人民检察院领导，向琼山区人民代表大会及其常委会负责并报告工作。

一、反贪污贿赂局：反贪局现有人员13人，负责侦查辖区内的贪污贿赂、挪用公款、巨额财产来源不明、隐瞒境外存款、私分国有资产、私分罚没财物等案件。

二、公诉科：现有干警7名，负责刑事案件的审查起诉、出庭公诉、退回补充侦查和审查不起诉工作、依法对同级人民法院刑事审判活动实行监督，对确有错误的刑事判决、裁定依法提出抗诉或提请上级检察院提出抗诉。我院在办案过程中，认真履行法律职责，努力把好起诉关，做到有法必依、违法必究、执法必严、秉公执法、严格执法，坚持从严从快的方针，严厉打击各种刑事犯罪。

三、侦查监督科：现有人员6名，主要负责对刑事犯罪案件犯罪嫌疑人的批捕和立案监督、侦查活动监督工作。我院始终把维护社会稳定作为首要任务，加强与公安、法院密切配合，不断加大对各种刑事案件的打击力度。

办公地点：海口市琼州大道

办公电话：0898-65873424

琼山区人事劳动保障局
琼山区劳动和社会保障管理中心

2006年，在区委区政府的高度重视下，在市、区两级主管部门的具体指导下，我们认真学习贯彻党和国家及省、市有关就业再就业和企事业离退休人员社会化管理服务等文件精神，以促进经济发展，确保社会稳定为根本，以促进扩大就业再就业，全面落实扶持再就业各项优惠政策措施为前提，团结拼搏，克服各种困难，优质服务，坚持不懈抓好抓实就业再就业工作，切实做好离退休人员社会化管理和自主择业军转干部管理服务工作，取得了一定的成绩，并获得共青团中央、农业部、教育部、科技部、劳动和社会保障部、国务院扶贫办、民进中央七部委评为：全国农村青年转移就业“先进单位”。

劳动就业主要工作成效：

一、积极开发新增就业岗位，全力推荐实现就业再就业。一年来，共开发挖掘新增就业岗位5111个，组织2313人参加“海口市第四届人才劳动力现场招聘会”活动。

二、增强服务意识，全面落实就业再就业培训优惠政策的实施。一年来，开展多种形式的就业再就业培训和劳动技能培训。一是利用现有培训基地，开展电脑、厨师、商品营业员、政策法规法律、岗前培训及农村劳动力转移阳光工程引导性培训等项目；二是与市人劳保障局、市农业局及海口诚信职工培训学校、省技工学校联合办班，共举办各类培训班30期，免费培训富余劳动力、城镇待业人员和各类企业新增岗位人员及下岗事业人员等共计2908人次。

三、全面开展就业再就业援助活动。一年来，共为1402名国有、集体企业的下岗失业人员及享受最低生活保障并且失业一年以上的城镇其他失业人员办理《再就业优惠证》1302份；为6家招用持《再就业优惠证》的下岗失业、低保人员实现再就业的用人单位办理社会保险补贴10余宗；为自谋职业、自主创业、灵活就业的下岗失业人员办理小额担保贷款申请手续20人次。

区委区政府三套班子领导欢送琼山区农村劳动力赴外省就业会场

区委区政府三套班子领导欢送琼山区农村劳动力赴外省就业

海口市政府副市长蒙国海、市就业管理局局长麦珠丹等领导亲临我区指导“春风行动”政策咨询活动，区委副书记谭忠庭向上级领导做简要的情况介绍

农村劳动力转移阳光工程培训班

海口市琼山区民政局

琼山区民政局在区委区政府的正确领导下，认真贯彻落实党和国家有关民政工作的方针政策，以民为本，关注民生，为民解困工作落到实处，为构建和谐琼山做出积极贡献。2006年共发放低保金829万元，确保城乡困难群众105884户次210632人次的基本生活，实现应保尽保。下拨救灾救济款534万元，大病救助款37万元，帮助优抚对象、五保户、特困户、孤儿、灾民解决生活难14590户，治病难521户，住房难468户，安排好各大节日优抚对象、五保户和困难户的生活。拨冬令资金60多万元，购买棉被、衣服、毛毯、蚊帐、棉衣、大米、食油等物资，帮助三千多户困难群众安全过冬。

该局2006年被民政部《中国民政》评为民政宣传工作先进单位，被区委、区政府评为机关年度工作一等奖，区双拥办被评为省、市拥军优属先进单位，局长王业权同志被评为全省民政工作先进个人。

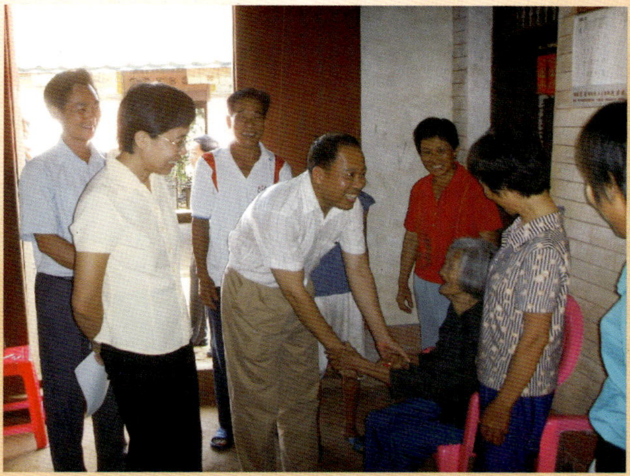

区、局领导走访慰问红军老战士

局领导及时将救灾物资运往灾区

关注民生　构建和谐

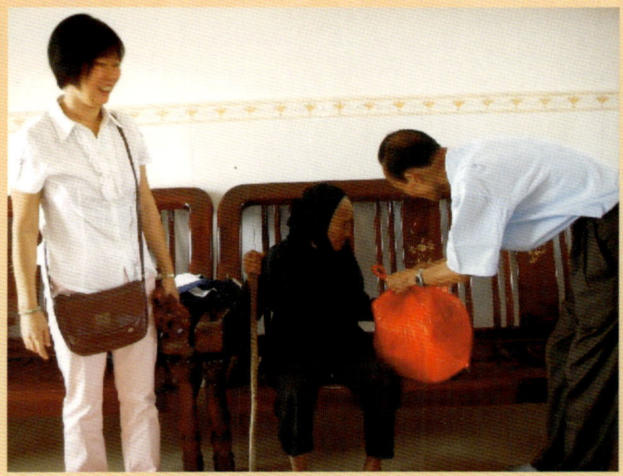

组织慰问百岁老人

开展维护老年人权益宣传活动

琼山区教科局

市领导到旧州中学指导危改工作

局长：朱材棱

市领导在旧州中学项目工地指导视察

市教育局领导下到琼山一小调研工作

今年来，我局在区委、区政府的正确领导下，在上级主管部门的关心指导下，认真贯彻全国、省、市农村教育工作会议精神，坚持以人为本的科学发展观总揽全局，在“创新”上求发展，在“突破”上做文章，在“改革”中动真格，在“落实”上求实效，进一步提高和巩固“两基”成果，高质量高标准发展琼山教育，使我局各项工作取得新的成效。我局被评为“海南省新闻宣传教育工作一等奖”、“海南省勤工俭学先进单位”、“海南省教育督导工作优秀奖”，同时我区也在被评为省科技先进区的基础上，并推荐评选全国科技先进区。中小学危改攻坚工程比市政府下达的时间提前一个月完成任务，得到市政府的肯定，海口市获得全省危改工作一等奖。全区教师参加省市教学评优和论文、案例、书画等项竞赛共有214人次，学生参加各种学艺竞赛获奖107人次；在今年海口市第二届小学生田径会上我区学校包揽前四名。

一、以迎接教育工作督导评估为动力，大力发展农村教育：成立领导小组，做好迎接督导评估的各项工作；加大布局调整的力度，优化教育资源配置；狠抓“控辍保学”，积极实施“扶孤助贫”阳光工程；高度重视学校安全工作，加强安全防患意识思想。

二、以危房改造为切入点，不断提高农村中小学办学水平。

三、以培育骨干教师为重点，极力提高教育教学水平：加强了学校德育工作；加强教师队伍建设，提高教育教学质量。

四、以提高为“三农”服务水平为基点，切实贯彻“科技兴区”和“科技兴农”的战略思想。

海口市琼山区农林局

省新农村建设试点工作现场会的省、市代表到琼山区红旗镇本立村参观指导

琼山区农林局在云龙镇、旧州镇等举办农民技术培训班

2006年，在区委、区政府的正确领导下，在上级主管部门的指导下，我局按照省、市、区农村工作会议要求，扎实抓好农业和新农村建设工作，较好地完成了区委、区政府和上级主管部门交给的各项任务。省、市春季农业生产，调整农业结构，香蕉下水田，“一村一品”，市早造水稻生产等7个现场会议在我区召开，参加全省农业工作现场会的各市县领导以及与会代表也到我区红旗镇本立村参观新农村建设试点现场。在农村沼气建设、造林绿化及防火、畜牧业发展、农村土地纠纷、罗非鱼等淡水养殖5项工作取得较好成绩，被评为市先进单位。

一、农业和农村经济持续增长。农业总收入12.81亿元，增长10.72%；乡镇企业营业总收入9.1亿元，增长5.7%；农民人均纯收入3558元，增长8.7%。

二、主要农产品产量完成情况良好，较上年均有增长。

三、农业农村工作成绩显著。农村经济结构调整78例增收示范村建设工作进展顺利；畜牧业与渔业生产持续升温，专业村、专业户有所增加；超额完成造林任务；畜禽春秋防措施到位，疫情零发生；植物检测检疫网络初步形成，农产品质量得到提高；农产品产销“两旺”；农村沼气建设进度快，生态循环农业发展势头好；村级债务债权真清实核，管理规范；农村经营管理规范，农村社会秩序持续稳定；农民科技培训量大，效果好。

海口市琼山区园林管理局

海口市琼山区园林管理局是海口市琼山区政府直属的正科级事业单位，主要职责有：

一、贯彻执行国家省、市、区有关城市园林绿化工作的方针、政策和法律、法规。

二、拟定全区园林绿化发展规划和管理方法，并组织实施。

三、负责区级公园、主干道绿化建设管理和古树古木的保护管理。

四、负责审查、指导、协调区内各项新建、扩建、改建工程和开发区、住宅区项目配套绿化工程的规划、建设和管理工作。

五、主管和参与区内重点工程及限额以上工程绿化竣工验收工作。

六、配合区政府有关部门部署和指导全区义务植树活动。

七、负责宣传贯彻执行有关园林绿化的法律、法规和检查监督执行。

八、承办区政府交办的其他事项。

地址：海口市琼山区府城镇高登街75号

电话：（0898）65876005　65877526

海口市琼山区总工会

2006年琼山区总工会深入贯彻党的十六大精神，巩固党的先进性教育成果，围绕工会的性质和职能，结合琼山区委和海口市总工会年度大局，推进工会年度计划工作的完成，工会工作取得了新的成绩。

一、结合工会实际贯彻“三会”精神。2006年琼山区总工会召开了十二届三次会议扩大会议，紧紧围绕区委区政府和市总工会全年的工作任务结合工作实际，我区各级工会组织和广大干部贯彻执行“组织起来，切实维权”的工作方针，认真履行工会各项职能，完善工会组织领导下的维权机制，推进企业工会建设，提高职工素质，团结动员广大职工为实现我区“十一五”规划，在构建社会主义和谐社会中发挥工人阶级主力军作用。

二、加强基层组织建设。全区新建立基层工会50个，新增加会员2125人。

三、高度重视职工维权工作。1、加强企业的民主管理工作，2006年全区46家私营个体企业签订劳动合同2354份；2、积极与劳动保障部门进行企业劳动用工检查和上诉案件的调处，及时解决了职工、农民工待遇问题；3、积极配合区安委会、区禁毒委开展6·11安全生产咨询活动并在海口市总工会的统一部署下，组织37个基层工会，在6·24开展声势较大的“职工拒绝毒品零计划行动宣传”，区委常委符勇同志参加了本次工会组织的咨询活动，区禁委林海涛同志也到场指导。

四、积极组织职工开展文化娱乐活动。

五、认真开展劳模推荐评选工作。

六、努力为职工办好事实事。1、2006年，区总工会“送温暖”工作有声有色，共投入慰问资金5.5万元。争取市总拨款3万元，解决全区200多名外来工、农民工春节生活问题。2、区总工会参与的“低保”核查工作无一差错，基本上做到应保尽保。3、区总女工部积极发动职工参加女职工“安康保险”。4、争取市总1.6万元和区总拿出经费1万元，对我区13名当年考上大学的企业困难职工子女进行资助，把“金秋助学”活动推向高潮。

海口市美兰区爱卫办

工作人员在进行灭“四害”工作

灭“四害”工作认真、规范

为贯彻落实中共海口市委十届六次全会提出的争创全国文明城市、国家卫生城市的目标，海口市美兰区扎扎实实地开展各方面的创建工作，总结如下：

一、加强领导，认真构建创建的组织网络。为了加强创建国家卫生城市工作的指导，海口市美兰区成立了以时任区委副书记、区长袁光平同志为组长的创建工作领导小组，并制定了实施方案，规定了各项创建的目标、任务和要求，督促各参与实施创建部门认真开展工作。我区在三级爱卫组织网络的基础上，构建了150个创建国家卫生城市工作领导小组，使创建工作通过严密构建各级爱卫组织网络，有条不紊地扎实开展。

二、标本兼治，不断完善巩固除四害达标成果。1、对城区除四害工作，从治标与治本两方面抓好除四害达标成果巩固。坚持科学的防治原则，加强四害孳生地治理、物理防治及化学防治工作。第一、加强四害孳生地环境治理，紧紧抓住清理卫生死角、垃圾及时清运、填埋陈年积水坑这一课题，从治本目标上铲除四害孳生。今年以来，我办协调各街道、驻区单位及区环卫局，清理各类大中型卫生死角和四害孳生地180处，共计580吨。有效减少四害孳生，降低了四害的密度。第二、加强完善防鼠、防蚊、防蝇设施的建设。第三、加强除四害药物化学防治，对居委会下水道灭蟑投放混配药液，对驻地区省委、省政府、美兰机场、市医院等多个驻区单位进行消杀，通过不间断化学防治，有效地控制城区内四害密度，巩固已取得除四害达标成果。2、对城乡结合部农村的除四害工作，主要从预防“登革热”、“流行性乙型脑炎”的发生流行两方面开展。

三、提高认识，不断改善城乡健康教育工作。注重从城区社区的健康教育和城乡结合部农村健康教育两个方面着手，侧重做好重点人群健康教育。

海口市美兰区人民检察院

倪家壮检察长

市院调研

下乡慰问困难群众

对未成年被告人宣布不诉

2006年，我院在区委和上级检察院的领导下，在区人大的监督和区政府的支持下，以“三个代表”重要思想为指导，全面落实科学发展观，紧紧围绕全区工作大局，大力加强法律监督能力建设，突出检察工作主题，落实检察工作总体要求，各项检察工作取得了显著成绩，为维护社会稳定、构建和谐美兰做出了积极贡献。

一、 围绕全区工作大局，全面履行法律监督职责。

（一）、依法严厉打击刑事犯罪活动，全力维护社会稳定。我院始终把维护稳定、服务经济建设作为首要任务，积极参与打黑除恶专项斗争，加强与公安、法院等部门的配合，充分发挥审查批捕和起诉职能作用，依法严厉打击各类严重刑事犯罪。共受理移送审查批捕案件426件605人，批准逮捕566人，共受理移送审查起诉的各类刑事案件440件641人。

（二）、加大查办职务犯罪工作力度，促进反腐败斗争深入开展。我院严格执行“三个一律”的要求，落实办案安全防范责任制，规范办案活动，进一步推动查办职务犯罪工作。共受理贪污贿赂犯罪案件线索24件，安排初查63件，查结55件，立案侦查贪污贿赂案件8件10人；共受理渎职犯罪案件线索12件，全部安排初查，查结14件，立案侦查玩忽职守案件1件2人。通过查办职务犯罪挽回国家集体直接经济损失233.75万元。

（三）、不断深化职务犯罪预防工作，努力实现从源头上治理腐败的目标。在注重打击的同时，我院坚持“打防结合，标本兼治”的方针，把预防职务犯罪工作作为服务大局的一项重要任务，不断深化职务犯罪预防工作。

（四）、强化诉讼监督，努力维护司法公正。我院认真履行诉讼监督职责，进一步强化立案监督、侦查监督和审判监督，着力纠正有罪不究、以罚代刑、超期羁押、重罪轻判、司法不公等违法现象，取得了较好的监督效果。

二、大力加强队伍建设，努力提高队伍整体素质和执法水平。一是加强思想政治建设；二是加强业务培训，提高队伍的业务素质；三是落实党风廉政建设责任制，加强队伍教育、监督和管理；四是加强组织建设。

三、检务保障进一步加强，检察宣传工作迈上新台阶。加强计财装备工作，严格财务管理，切实做到了精打细算，开支合理。严格遵守“收支两条线”的规定，对赃款、赃物”一物一卡、一案一帐”，管理规范。检察宣传工作迈上新台阶，今年被评为全国检察宣传先进单位。

海口市美兰区财政局

2006年，我区财税部门认真按照区委区政府的统一部署，积极组织财政收入，努力优化支出结构，强化财政监督管理，确保了财政收入平稳增长，基本保证了我区政权运转和社会各项事业发展的需要，财政预算执行情况良好。

2006年，全区财政收入149，866万元，完成预算的100.3%，同比增长13.4%。区本级财政支出22，834万元，完成预算的100.2%，同比增长8.2%。

一、2006年财政收入特点

企业效益普遍提高，所得税大幅增收成为增长的亮点；重点项目建设对税收发展的带动作用逐渐显现；固定资产投资成倍增加，相关行业税收增长强劲；旅游业迅速发展，带动第三产业稳步增长。

二、2006年财政支出特点

2006年，我区按照构建社会主义和谐社会的要求，坚持集中财力办大事，高度关注民生福祉，加大对各项社会事业发展的支持力度，财政支出体现了“四个提高”、“六个倾斜”。

体现“四个提高”，即提高公用经费标准，提高一线工作人员待遇，提高职工福利，提高总预备费

体现“六个倾斜”，即向“三农”倾斜，向“基层”倾斜，向“弱势群体”倾斜，向“民生工程”倾斜，向“维护社会稳定”倾斜，向“教育等社会事业”倾斜。

三、2006年财政主要工作

1、建立良好机制，稳固壮大辖区税源。完善镇街财政管理体制。新的镇街财政管理体制侧重于对新增税源的培植，且财力适当向基层倾斜，对镇、街优化环境、服务企业、发展经济产生了推动作用；建立走访企业制度，区领导和各职能部门定期走访企业，帮助企业解决实际困难，以及为企业做好税务登记、变更及纳税等方面的协调服务工作，努力做到“安商、稳商”；建立政府税收联席会议制度，及时帮助税务部门解决税收征管过程中存在的问题；健全税源监控服务制度，将年纳税5万元以上的企业都纳入重点监控服务范围，从企业的生产经营、纳税申报到入库都实行跟踪服务。

2、挖掘增收潜力，确保收入稳定增长。完善目标管理责任制，严格考核兑现；全面推广税收征管信息综合软件，充分应用科技加管理的有利条件，加强征管质量考核；组织开展各项税务稽查、清查、清欠活动，整顿和规范税收秩序；加强零散税收的勤征细管，确保应收尽收。

3、积极推进财政改革，强化财政监督管理。为了规范农村经济运行秩序，提高镇级财务透明度，对镇实行会计委派，对村级财务实施“村财镇监管”；有条不紊的推进国库集中支付改革，努力提高资金使用效益；主动配合审计部门工作，积极利用审计成果，并尽可能对财政资金使用情况进行事前、事中、事后评价。

海口市美兰区农林局

美兰区无公害瓜菜生产技术培训班

在美兰区委、区政府的正确领导下，海口市美兰区农林局全面贯彻落实科学发展观，紧紧围绕建设社会主义新农村这一主题，以调整农业产业结构为主线，以增加农民收入为目标，扎实抓好农业各项工作，促进农业快速健康发展。2006年全区农业总产值达14.2亿元，同比增长9.7%；农民人均纯收入4105元，同比增长6.3%。

（一）创新模式，产业结构调整步伐加快。一是抓好生产技术培训，提高农民生产和操作技能，共举办各种技术培训班33期，参加人数达6600多人次；二是大胆推行“五统一分”新经营模式调整产业结构，2006年新增花、果、菜面积6960亩。现有花卉种植面积1.57万亩，规模在50亩以上的花卉基地68个；三是实施经济结构调整增收100例，发挥辐射带头作用。

（二）注重防控，畜牧养殖产业健康发展。一是认真抓好重大动物疫病防控工作，畜禽免疫率达100%，确保无规定动物疫病示范区目标的实现；二是积极引导农民发展畜禽养殖业，2006年畜禽养殖量达365万只（头），实现产值5.9亿元，占农业总产值的41.5%。

（三）贴息支农，专业合作组织不断壮大。2006年区政府出台《美兰区支农贷款贴息管理办法》，全区已累计发放支农贷款贴息资金549万元，遍及88个村庄，239户。目前，全区有农民专业合作经济组织11个，参加的农户达353户，种植面积8879亩，累计投入开发资金1321.7万元，年总产值达2663.7万元。

（四）再接再厉，农村生态环境明显改善。2006年实现造林7022.5亩，完成市下达6000亩造林任务的117%，其中国债造林311亩，一般造林1993.5亩，四旁植树4718亩，浆纸林6029.5亩。依照“创办瓜果菜生产基地的优先、有示范带动作用的优先、有建设沼气原料的优先、有群众基础的优先”的工作原则，共建沼气池229个，完成市下达的建设任务。

美兰区的大中型沼气池正在建设

美兰区灵山镇大昌无公害瓜菜生产基地南瓜长势良好

全区生猪养殖年出栏量达12.5万头

中共海南省委党校
海南省行政学院
海南省社会主义学院

省领导来校视察

中共海南省委党校、海南省行政学院、海南省社会主义学院实行“三位一体”的管理模式。现任领导有罗保铭（省委副书记、省长兼党校校长）、吴国干（常务副校长）、廖逊（副校长、社会主义学院院长）、彭京宜（副校长、行政学院院长）、薛梅艳（校<院>教育长）。

校（院）有处级机构23个，在职人员204人，其中专业技术人员67人（教授7人，副教授21人，讲师及其他技术人员39人）。享受国务院特殊津贴专家2人、省优秀专家9人。

校园占地面积96亩。现有4栋学员宿舍（有220个不同规格的套间，可同时供450人住宿）；有大小餐厅2个（可同时容纳700人就餐）。

2006年，省委党校各项工作都上了一个新台阶：

一、教学工作有了新突破，校（院）共举办主体班次有18期，培训学员2028人。呈现了班次多、类型多、人数多、效果好的特点。

二、科研工作有了新提高。全年科研立项21项，完成课题28项，发表论文170篇，调研报告27篇，出版专著、编著（含教材）24本，撰写专题调查报告27篇。在海南省第五次社会科学优秀成果评奖中，我们是专著获奖最多，奖项最高的单位，共获得各种奖项6个，其中专著一等奖1个（全省2个），专著二等奖2个（全省6个），专著奖3个（全省8个）。

三、行政、后勤服务有了新改善。一是狠抓制度建设，共完善制度16项；二是积极改善办学条件：1、学校对2000多平方米的学员楼进行装修；2、完成了综合报告厅项目的立项工作；三是改善教职工生活和居住条件：1、新建了两幢教职工宿舍；2、加强管理服务，校园环境进一步美化，2006年被评为海口市卫生红旗单位和卫生先进单位。

海南省卫生学校

省卫生学校教育管理工作会议

教学大楼

海南省卫生学校建立于1977年，2004年进入国家级重点中专行列。2006年护理专业进入国家示范性专业。现任校长陈雪峰是全国教育系统劳动模范、国务院特殊津贴专家；校党总支书记邢福音同志。

本校是培养省内各类卫生人员的重要基地。现有在职人员175人。其中教学人员130人，本科学历占90%。技术职称结构：高级职称35人、中级职称54人、初级31人，在职攻读研究生学位的教师8人，师资力量较强。学科设置为：普通学科、医学基础学科、临床学科、专业学科。现设置专业有：护理、社区医学、药剂、妇幼医学、全科医学、医学影像技术、医学美容、医学检验、助产、中西医结合、针灸推拿、口腔医学、卫生监督、卫生保健、康复技术医学、眼视光技术等专业。2000年开始与海南医学院、江西医学院联办招收五年制高职班、成人大专班、本科班，为学生入学后建立进入“中专大专本科”的立交桥。学校教学设备完善，教学质量保证，在省内历年参加护士执业考试和省卫生厅直属卫生学校的科目统考中，成绩均名列前茅。2002年我校护士执业考试及格率为87%，进入全国合格水平的前列，是省内中专学校考生报考最热门的学校之一。

建校28年来，在党的教育方针和卫生工作方针的指引下，学校以“社会为本、育人为本、质量为本”的办学宗旨，坚持“加强管理，从严治校”为校风建设，以“明德、博学、自强、笃行”为校训，树立“求一等学识、立一等合格、成一等事业”的教育理念，实行“教书育人、管理育人、环境育人、活动育人”为教育模式，培养学生的自我教育，自我管理，自我服务的能力，取得明显成效。注重“电脑、英语、书法、写作”四项内容的训练，并成立180人的学生艺术团，提升学生的艺术素养，在省内获得较好声誉。建校以来培养卫生技术人员1万名，遍布全省各医疗单位。学生以专业基础知识牢固，临床技能熟练，而深受用人单位的好评，有些已成为医疗单位的骨干，许多学生成为基层卫生单位的中坚力量，为海南卫生事业作出了应有的贡献。目前，我校朝着全国卫生职业教育示范性学校的办学目标而努力奋斗。

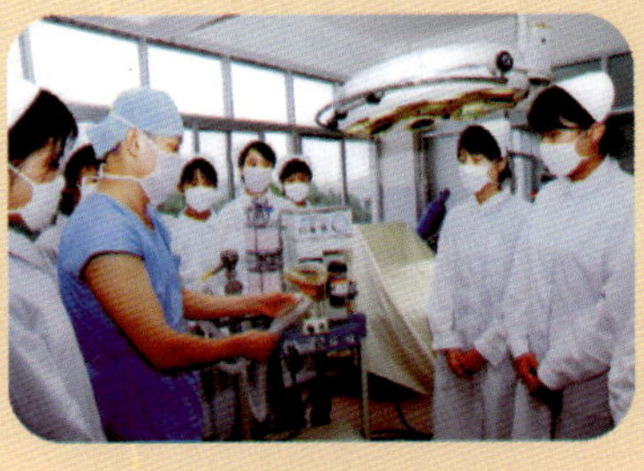

学生在外科实验室见习

奋进中的海南医学院

李书记和焦院长亲切交谈

环境优美的校园

历史广场

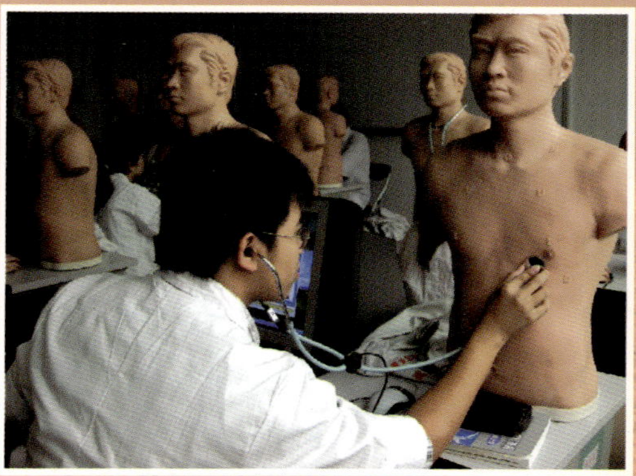

先进的仿真实验室

海南医学院座落于南国旅游名城海口市，是海南省唯一的一所高等医学院校。其前身为私立海南大学和私立海强医事技术学校。1993年经国家教委批准成立海南医学院。2004年起与北京大学联合招收硕士研究生，2005年被教育部高等教育评估中心评为本科教学水平“良好”。

学院占地面积830余亩，分龙华和城西两个校区，并将兴建占地1500余亩的西海岸校区。现有教职工（含附院）1400余人，专任教师632人，其中高级职称137人，中级职称141人；享受国务院特殊津贴专家10人，突出贡献奖1人，省级优秀专家16人；现有在校生8000余人，留学生150余人。学院下设临床学院、高等职业教育学院、国际教育学院、预防医学系等3院6系5部；现有省级重点学科2个，省级重点实验室2个，省级精品课程4门，省级重点课程3门； 6个基础实验室、5个专业实验室，设立附属医院3家，病床总数2320张；临床教学（实习）医院20家，开放病床数6433张，另有教学基地9个。

目前，海南医学院正抓住创新型国家建设、新一轮高等教育发展的历史性机遇，积极推进体制创新，在创新中加快发展。学院第二次党代会确立了“三步走”发展战略目标，即从2004年起，力争用十年左右时间，建成国内独树一帜的热带医学医疗教育中心，进而把学院建设成为具有鲜明热带特色的现代化的医药大学。

我们相信，不久的将来，一座学科齐全、环境优美、设施先进、办学水平高的现代化医药大学将屹立在南国宝岛！

党委书记：李永春　院 长：焦解歌

地址：海南省海口市龙华区学院路3号

邮编：571101　电话：0898-66893398

传真：0898-66893761

网址：www.hainmc.edu.cn

电邮：hainmcpublic@hainmc.edu.cn

投资近1亿的现代化图书馆

琼台师范高等专科学校

学校党委书记谢越华（左三）、校长詹道祥（左一）陪同省、厅领导视察我校

琼台师范高等专科学校是经海南省人民政府同意、国家教育部批准成立的全日制普通高等院校，是海南省小学、幼儿园教师的主要培养培训基地。学校前身是创办于1705年的琼台书院，1902年改制创办现代学校，三百年来为海南的教育文化事业做出了突出的贡献。2005年学校被评为全国“文明单位”，学校学生合唱团赴京参加全国第一届大学生艺术展演荣获声乐节目一等奖。学校现有在校生6000多人，专任教师281人，其中副高以上职称81人，省优专家2人，特级教师5人，6人被省教育厅聘为“基础教育课程改革”专家组成员，兼职教授、副教授13人。

学校新校区座落在海南省省会城市海口市美兰区高校园区，占地1151亩，交通便利，环境优雅，条件优越。学校建有高标准的教学大楼、电教中心、科艺馆、图书馆和宽敞舒适的学生公寓，配置了高规格的微格教学系统、电子图书阅览室、各学科实验和多媒体教室，建成了千兆校园网，实现了教学管理信息化。学校坚持人才培养和培训、教学与科研一体化，师范专业与非师范专业并存，省内生源与省外生源兼顾的原则，设置有八系一部一中心、即文史系、数理系、美术系、音乐系、体育系、学前教育系、现代教育技术系、英语系、公共教学部、省小学幼儿师资研究培训中心。2006年我校新增加了“新闻采编与制作”、“计算机网络技术”、“文化事业管理”、“学前（英语）教育”等专业。

学校制订了一系列助学措施，确保学生顺利完成学业，近年毕业生就业率达96%以上。

校 门

教学楼

琼台书院奎星楼

海南职业技术学院

林虎院长鼓励学生到基层创业

与法国合作办学

刚刚竣工投入使用的第二教学大楼

学生餐饮中心

海南职业技术学院正式成立于 2000 年 1 月，是海南省第一所独立设置的多科性普通高等职业技术学校，隶属于海南省人民政府。学院实行“产权股份化、运作企业化、后勤建设社会化”的办学模式和董事会领导下的院长负责制的管理体制。创办七年来，学院以发展快、效率高、体制新的办学模式，被国内教育理论界专家誉为我国高等教育八大模式之一，是中国高等教育多元化投资、股份制办学模式的代表。

经过 7 年的发展，学院总投资已达 2.3 亿元，学院占地 232 亩，桂林洋新校区 850 亩正在筹建中。现有教学楼、办公楼、电教楼、实训楼、教师宿舍楼、学生公寓楼、图书馆、餐饮中心等大楼，建筑总面积 18.3 万 m^2；教学仪器设备总值 2725.35 万元，设备利用率达到 90% 以上；馆藏图书 46.58 万册，图书资料利用率达到 97%；教学用计算机 1438 台，语音室 8 间 674 座，多媒体教室 14 间 2916 座，与 95 家企事业单位签订了校外实习实训基地（点）131 个。

学院现有教职工 787 人，专兼职教师总数达到 554 多人，其中高级职称教师占专任教师的 31.7%，研究生教师占专任教师的 6.7%。学院面向全国 30 个省（直辖市、自治区）招生，全日制在校生 9043 人，近三年的毕业生一次就业率达到了 65%，对毕业生的跟踪调查显示，用人单位对学院毕业生的满意率达到了 83%。

学院设有 8 个教学系（部），已开设 51 个专业，其中畜牧专业被确定为第一批国家级高职高专精品专业和第四批高职高专部级教学改革试点专业，汽车运用技术专业被确定为海南省首批高职高专教学改革试点专业。《动物遗传育种繁育学》等 3 门课程被评为省级精品课程，其中《网络营销实务》获评国家级精品课程，这是全省高职高专院校唯一获此殊荣的课程。

学院先后与加拿大爱德华王子岛荷兰学院、同济大学等国内外高校和企事业单位签订了联合办学协议，共同培养人才。目前已选送 28 名品学兼优的学生到法国深造，并接收 20 名法国留学生到海南实习，是海南省唯一选派学生到外国留学的高职院校。

在短短七年内，学院由仅有一幢闲置 8 年的“半拉子”楼的一片荒地发展成为蜚声省内外的国家重点建设的万人大学。2002 年，学院被推选为中国高等职业技术教育研究会常务理事单位；被国家教育部和财政部确定为“中央财政重点支持建设示范性职业院校”；2003 年，通过了教育部合格评估，成为全国首批通过高职高专人才培养工作水平合格评估院校之一。

学院的办学业绩，受到了国内教育专家的高度评价，林虎院长先后被授予“中国改革百名优秀人物”、“中国职业教育杰出校长”等荣誉称号。全国人大副委员长成思危等领导亲临学院视察并给予充分肯定，《中国教育报》等 30 多家新闻媒体先后报道了学院的办学成就。

校园远景

海南省高级技工学校

海南省高级技工学校座落在海口市琼山区，是省人事劳动保障厅下属的一所国家重点技校，是我省最早的一家高级技工学校和唯一一家同时荣获机电项目和电子信息项目的国家高级技能人才培训基地，担负着海南省中、高级技能人才的培养任务。我校创办以来，秉承教书育人、管理育人、服务育人的宗旨，根据我省就业再就业工作的需要，积极开展职业教育和培训，为我省劳动者素质的提高、为就业和再就业工作做出应有的贡献，为我省经济和社会发展培养了大批技能型人才。

学校占地面积80亩，目前全日制在校生总人数6000多人，建筑面积7万多平方米，固定资产总值8800多万元，教学、生活环境优越，师资力量雄厚，配备了先进水平的教学设备和设施完善的教学、实习实验场所，建有金工、钳工、电焊、汽修等实习车间45间，总工位数达2000多个，能满足学生的各种实验实习要求。

2004年荣获国家级最高奖项“国家技能人才培育突出贡献奖”，并在参加的“广州数控杯”全国技工学校技能竞赛中成为十所获得“优秀教学组织奖”的学校之一。2005年学校被有关部门确定为“国务院扶贫办贫困地区劳动力转移培训示范基地”、“机械工业职业技能鉴定海南省分中心”；2006年学校被授予全国劳动保障系统先进集体。

地址：海口市琼山区府城镇大园路77号　　邮编：571100

电话：0898-65903747　　传真：0898-65908374

2004年我校选手参加全国技工学校技能竞赛载誉归来

电工成套设备实验室

综合大楼

嘉积中学

刘晓朝校长陪同教育部周济部长视察我校

嘉积中学创办于1917年，原名“崇实学堂”，历经传承演变，1923年改称“广东省立第十三中学”，是当时海南岛唯一的省立中学，也是当时海南最高学府，1933年，“十三中”易名为“广东省立琼崖中学”，中华人民共和国成立后更名为“嘉积中学”，1993年嘉积中学成为中国名校，2005年相继被评为海南省一级甲等高级中学和中国百强中学，这是嘉积中学办学史上的重大里程碑。

嘉中校园环境优美，风景如画，行政综合大楼红楼，古朴典雅，巍峨壮观。近年来，嘉中人又进一步精心治理校园，图书馆、科学馆、学生公寓、李强学苑综合教学楼等建筑群拔地而起，气势雄伟，新老建筑交相辉映，相得益彰。嘉中校园更加多姿多彩。

嘉积中学名师荟萃，英才云集。学校现有专任教师210人，国家级骨干教师 5 人，省级骨干教师 9 人，市级骨干教师 28 人，现有教学班59个，在校生3541人。校长刘晓朝，系全国优秀教师，海南省十佳校长，国家级骨干校长，刘校长带领嘉中人创业十年来，硕果累累，各项办学指标均列海南省前茅，每年都有一大批嘉中学子走进清华、北大等名校校园。近年来，一大批中青年教师脱颖而出，在教育界崭露才华，担当起嘉中在新世纪新阶段再铸辉煌的历史重任。

“求知在嘉中，成长在嘉中”。九十年来，一代代嘉中学子胸怀祖国、探求真理、薪火相传。近年来学校大力推行素质教育，注重培养学生自主学习的能力和研究性探究能力，“爱国、守纪、严教、勤学”八字校风不断发扬光大。物华天宝，人杰地灵。嘉积中学这所如诗如画的中国名校，开启了多少催人奋进的青春之旅，奏响了气势恢宏的创业乐章。在2007年高考中，嘉积中学高三林婵娟、陈杨同学分获海南省高考文、理科第一名！

九十年的风雨，九十年的磨砺，九十年的辉煌。站在新世纪的起点上，嘉中人正充满信心，豪迈地走向美好未来！

日前，嘉中正朝着“省内一流、国内知名、海外有影响”的国家级示范性高级中学的目标奋勇迈进！

办公室电话：0898-62822451　31692345

传　　真：0898-62835208

学校网址：http://www. hnjjzx.net

电子信箱：jiazhongban@163.com

校　长：刘晓朝

书　记：程为群

李强学苑

嘉积中学的象征性建筑——红楼

海口市妇幼保健院
海口市妇女儿童医院

院长：饶世立

坐落在海南省海口市国兴大道文坛路的海口市妇幼保健院、海口市妇女儿童医院，是全省最具规模和现代化的妇女儿童专科医院。

医院设有病床300张，拥有温馨病房、电梯、自动扶梯、中央空调、中央供氧、中心吸引、自动传输系统、电子传呼系统、电子监控系统、电视播音系统等一流的设施，并开设了儿童乐园、购物走廊、咖啡吧、健康书屋、营养餐厅等辅助设施，生态环境良好。

医院拥有美国GE公司的螺旋CT、德国西门子数字式800mAX光机、500mAX光机、乳腺钼靶X光机、四维彩色超声诊断仪、全自动电泳扫描仪、日立7080全自动生化仪、乳腺超细光纤导管内视镜，胎儿及双胞胎监护系统、高危产妇监护系统、腹腔镜、宫腔镜、阴道镜、小儿胃（肠）镜、全自动生化分析仪等国内外一流的先进设备，形成了完整的医疗、保健、监护、急救体系。

目前，医院设有妇女保健科、儿童保健科、成人健康体检管理中心、儿童健康体检管理中心、生殖健康科、健康教育科、产科、妇科、新生儿科、小儿内科、小儿外科、乳腺病科、急诊室、手术室、麻醉科、检验科、病理科、影像科、功能检查科以及专家门诊、专科专病门诊等，可为广大妇女儿童的健康提供全方位的医疗保健服务。

医院在2004年2月通过了ISO9001国际质量认证，成为我省第一家取得国际质量认证的专科医院；同时，医院还引进了医院形象设计（CIS），极具人性化特色的医院文化获得了广大妇女儿童的赞誉。2005年6月，被中国医学基金杨崇瑞妇幼卫生奖励基金管委会评为先进单位；2004、2005年连续两年获得海南省医疗信用单位；2006年4月，医院又荣获了中国国际商务信用企业，信用级别为：AA，成为了全省医疗系统唯一获得此殊荣的医院。

医院的使命：一切为了健康！医院的承诺：关爱妇女、关爱儿童、关爱健康、关爱生命

海南省农业学校

校长、高级讲师：薛国献

校党总支书记：陆红专

海南省农业学校创办于1946年，原名为国立琼山高级农业职业学校，原址在海口得胜沙路，经七次搬迁，1987年搬到现址海口市城西路。

该校新校址校园面积105亩，实习农场面积513亩，校舍建筑面积40000多平方米，有各类专业实验室20余间，多媒体电脑室、电化教室10间，有宽带校园网等现代化的教学设备；学校有种植、养殖、信息工程、医药四大类共19个专业，在校生2073人；教职工130人，其中高级讲师35人，讲师30人，“双师型”教师26人。

该校不断深化教育教学改革，确立了“以就业为导向，开拓市场；以学生为中心，教书育人”的办学理念和“以职业岗位需要为目标，以综合职业能力为基础，办出特色、服务海南，培养德、智、体、美全面发展的应用型农业技术人才”的办学培养目标。六十年来，共为国家输送一万多名中等农业技术人才和管理人才，大多数毕业生已成为各行业特别是农业战线的骨干力量，其中许多毕业生成为专业技术带头人、企业家和农村致富带头人。设在该校的“国家第四十职业技能鉴定所”，是农业部科教司首批认定的全国44个农业职业技术教育培训示范基地之一。2003年学校被教育部授予“全国职业指导工作先进学校”，是国家级重点中等职业学校。

如今，学校正在积极推行“依据省情办职教、以校为本谋发展，因材施教重技能、以人为本抓管理，打造品牌创特色、以精为本求效益”的强校方略，努力把学校办成在国内有一定影响的现代化热带农业教育特色的重点中等职业学校。

教学区俯瞰

校　门

海口市中医药学校

海口市中医药学校为政府公办全日制普通中专，系海南省人民政府批准成立的目前全省唯一的一所中医药教育机构，建校于1959年，前身为海口市卫生学校。座落于风景秀丽的海口市海甸二西路，学校占地面积近万平方米，有造型新颖、风格独特、雄伟壮观的教学大楼（5000㎡）；师资队伍健全，现有专、兼任教师70名。现开设的专业有中西医结合医疗、中药、护理、针灸推拿。学校现拥有一流的教学设备与设施，供现代化教学多媒体设备教室4个，各学科实习与实验室的设备齐全，为强化学生在校时间的专业理论教学和提高操作技能提供了有力的保障。

教学工作成效显著：学校全面推进素质教育，改革教育教学方法，做到因材施教、因人施教，教学形式多样化，并能用现代化教学手段提高教学质量；2006年，教师撰写的教育教学论文有3篇在国家教育杂志上发表，有15篇在省级刊物上发表，有2篇选送到第八届全国说课年会；学校还十分注重学生实际操作能力的培养，在校外各市县建立若干个实习基地，为提高学生的动手能力创造了条件。

学校招生生源充足，2006年秋季招生319名；就业率较高，2006年召开供需见面会，有32个企业在校内设场招聘人才，有137名毕业生的初次就业率达92.7%。

校　长：张邦帅（法人代表）　　地　址：海口市海甸二西路18号

党委书记：张德川　　电　话：0898-66181798

海南省特殊教育学校

海南省特殊教育学校是一所省教育厅直属，省内唯一的、面向全省招生的十二年一贯制全日制公立特殊教育学校。

学校创办于1990年，座落在海口市琼山区府城镇，占地面积39960平方米。全校在岗教职工113名，学生416人，36个教学班。学校建有人性化的听障教学楼、视障教学楼、运动场。配备了标准化的听力测试、语言矫正、律动、电脑绘画、糕点制作、烹饪、缝纫校长操作、美容美发、电焊、多媒体等具有特殊教育特色的教室，开通了校园宽带网，实现了校园绿化，校道硬化，校舍楼房化。

校长：许书创

学校有语言康复、听障、视障、职教4个教学部，严格按照部颁标准设置课程，坚持以服务为宗旨，以就业为导向，开设了糕点制作、烹饪、绘画、电焊、电脑打字、美容美发、缝纫等职业技能课程。

目前，海南特殊教育学校是一所集残疾儿童康复、特殊教育教学、科研和师资培训为一体的综合性特殊教育机构，各项工作已挤身全国同类学校前列。今后，学校将加大改革与科研力度，力争办成全国示范特殊教育学校。

第22个教师节省政协付秘书长潘慧丽给何瑞金送来600元慰问金

我校毕业生在制药厂参加工作

海口市社会福利院

海口市社会福利院、海口市儿童康复院是由市政府兴建的全民所有制综合性福利事业单位。目前是一套机构、两块牌子，隶属于海口市民政局，始建于1951年，位于海甸福利路8号。主要任务是完成政府交给的收养社会上无依无靠、无家可归、无生活来源的孤、老、残、幼人员，对他们实行终身供养。同时，利用现有设施，面向社会开放，对家庭不便照料的病残患者实行自费抚养和临终关怀项目。对北方退休老人开展“北雁南飞”休闲度假项目。现有编制工作人员110人，下设办公室、儿童部、老人部、后勤保障部、医疗康复中心、社区服务中心（老年公寓）。

我院占地71928平方米，建筑面积26000平方米，院内建有一幢综合办公大楼，11幢庭院式老人公寓，一幢集生活、起居、康复、娱乐等功能为一体的儿童康复大楼。并建有医疗康复中心、食堂、洗衣房、健身房等。院内草坪、花园等绿地占可绿化面积的90%以上，有各种各样花草树木一百多个品种，一年四季绿树成荫、花木葱郁，衬以假山、凉亭，环境优雅、空气清新；收养人员居室内有空调、电扇、热水。安装了有线电视，设有棋牌室、娱乐厅、文化室等，内容丰富，条件舒适，是孤、老、残、幼人员休闲、养老、疗养的良好场所。

省领导“六一”节慰问儿童

我院以“真诚奉献、慈爱至上”全心全意为收养人员服务为宗旨，加强职业道德建设，发扬爱岗敬业、无私奉献的精神，全体职工齐心协力、勤奋工作、甘于奉献、为孤、老、残、幼人员倾注了无尽的爱心，使市社会福利院从一个初级福利院发展成为省一级福利院。

法人代表：邓桂添
联系电话：66268012
办公地址：海口市福利路8号

福利院儿童“六一”节表演节目

环境优雅、干净卫生的福利院

海南省疾病预防控制中心

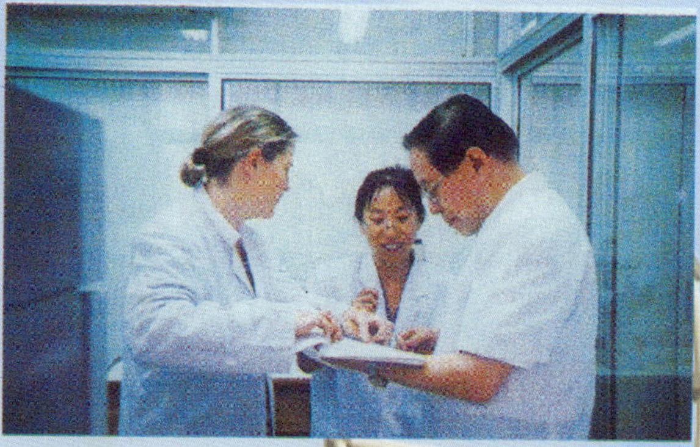

世界卫生组织官员和中国CDC脊灰实验室主任张礼璧教授（右一）来我中心考核脊灰实验室

省领导视察海南省疾病预防控制中心

海南省疾病预防控制中心是2003年1月在原海南省卫生防疫站、海南省热带病防治研究所、海南省结核病防治研究所、海南省健康教育研究所的基础上合并组建成立的，是我省疾病控制、应对突发公共卫生事件、监测检验指导中心和预防医学人才培训中心。

中心现已拥有一批具有国内先进水平的实验室，达到省级疾控机构的等级标准。海南省艾滋病监测中心HIV抗体确认实验室已通过国家卫生部评审，脊髓灰质炎实验室多次通过世界卫生组织的考核验收，卫生毒理实验室通过国家功能实验室的评审。2006年7月，中心还获得了中国实验室国家认可证书并通过了国家级计量认证。

年轻的省疾控中心在防病领域取得了显著成绩，全省传染病发病率连续下降，无重大疫情发生。特别是在全省防治非典型肺炎、禽流感等重大突发公共卫生事件应急处理工作中，经受住严峻的考验，为捍卫海南无疫区做出了突出贡献。全省计划免疫“四苗”接种率由建省前的10.8%提高到95%以上，提前实现了海南省消灭脊髓灰质炎的目标，从一个落后省份一跃进入全国先进省份行列，为全省人民的健康、经济发展、社会进步做出了突出的贡献。多年来，中心还担负来琼考察工作的中央首长和国内外政要的食品卫生安全保障工作，同时中心还出色完成博鳌亚洲论坛、世界小姐总决赛等国际大型活动的食品安全保障工作，屡获省政府表扬。

在省卫生厅的领导下，在中心领导班子的带领下，经过全体职工的共同努力，精神文明和物质文明取得了双丰收。近几年来中心获得中央文明委授予的“全国文明单位”、“全国创建文明行业工作先进单位”、卫生部授予“全国卫生系统先进集体”、“全国卫生系统抗击非典先进集体”“全国计划免疫工作先进集体”、“全国消灭脊髓灰质炎工作先进集体”、“全国预防与控制艾滋病性病先进集体”、“全国卫生系统行业作风建设先进集体”等国家级荣誉10项，省委省政府授予“文明单位”、“海南省防治非典型肺炎先进单位”等省级荣誉12项。

近年来还获得了26项卫生部及省、厅科技进步成果奖，其中省科技进步奖一等奖1项，二等奖1项，三等奖16项，四等奖3项，省卫生厅科技进步奖一等奖 1 项，卫生部科技进步奖（合作）二等奖3项，三等奖1项，部分成果已达到国内先进水平。

中心将以科技为依托，以疾病控制为重点，以人为根本，以改革为动力，以发展为核心，为建设一个功能齐全、装备精良、保障有力、反应迅速、技术过硬的疾病预防控制中心而努力奋斗。

法人代表：潘先海（中心主任、党委书记）

建设中的海南省疾病预防控制中心效果图

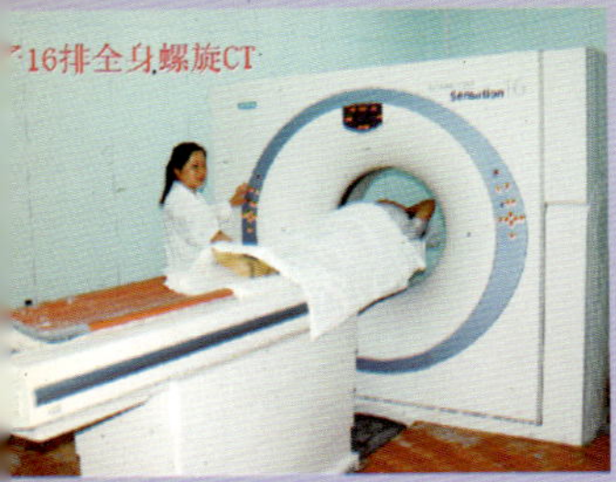

医疗设备(1)

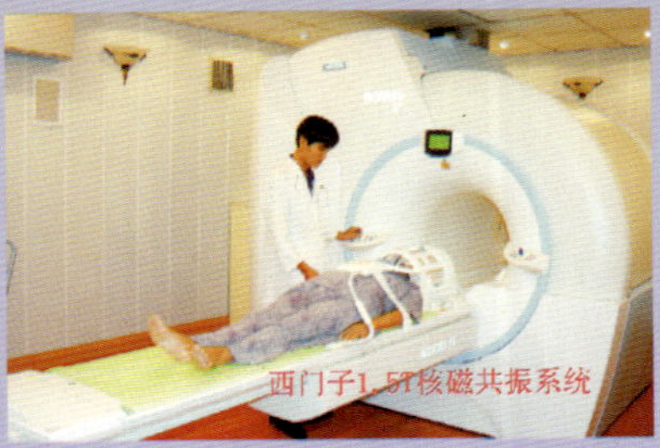

医疗设备(2)

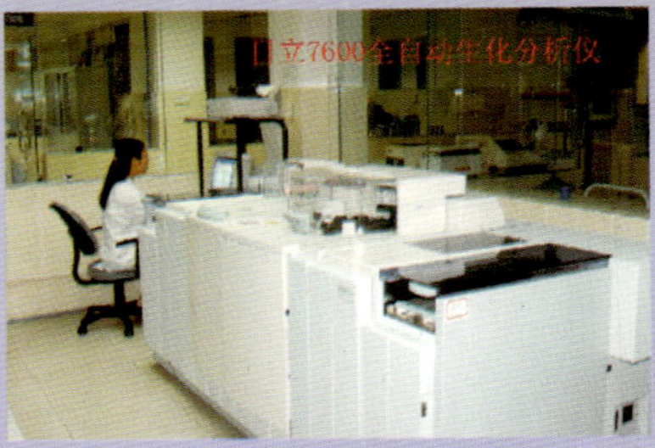

医疗设备(3)

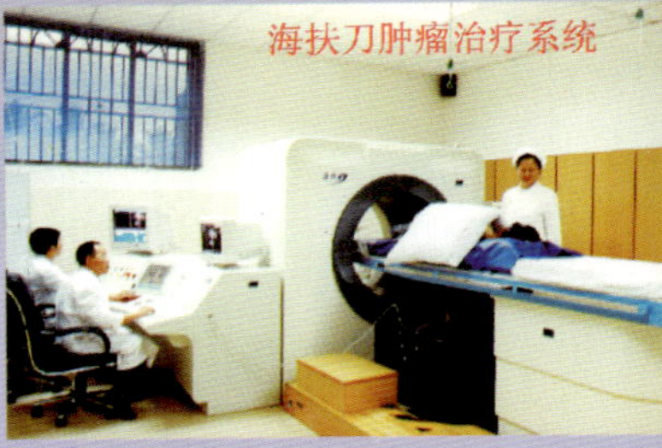

医疗设备(4)

海口市人民医院

中南大学湘雅医学院附属海口医院

医院简介

海口市人民医院是已有105年历史的综合性“三甲”医院，是中南大学湘雅医学院（原湖南医科大学）的附属医院，卫生部国际紧急救援中心网络医院。

海口市人民医院开放病床700张，设43个临床、医技专科和3个综合门诊部。1500多名员工中，有教授、主任医师54人，副教授、副主任医师111人，中级职称技术人员326人。有国家特殊津贴专家6人，省优专家8人。有硕士生导师17人，博士7人，硕士40人。年住院病人2.3万余人次，手术5000余例，门诊50万余人次，各项技术业务指标均处于海南省内前列。

专科特色

神经外科、急危重症专科和心血管介入诊疗科是经省卫生厅评审的重点优势专科。神经外科和血液科在省内唯一开展的颅脑“锁孔”手术和造血干细胞移植治疗白血病，技术达到国际先进水平。

神经外科、泌尿外科、肝胆外科、骨科、耳鼻咽喉科、心胸外科、妇产科等各外科率先在省内成功开展内窥镜微创先进新技术，通过花生米粒大小的小孔做大手术，具有创伤小，病人痛苦小，疤痕小，住院时间短，恢复快等优势。

肿瘤治疗形成了手术、化疗、X-刀治疗、海扶超声聚焦刀治疗、超声介入性治疗、放射介入性治疗、粒子刀治疗等最先进最完善的综合肿瘤治疗体系，为各种肿瘤病人提供全方位的治疗选择。

引进德国、美国等国际先进设备，总值2.08亿余元。总量3886台，10万元以上的130多台。如西门子16排全身螺旋CT、西门子1.5T核磁共振、VoLusin730实时四维彩超等，保证高质量的诊断和治疗，促进了临床、教学和科研等各项工作的顺利开展。

2003年8月8日，海口市人民政府、中南大学及海口市人民医院签约，共同创办“中南大学湘雅医学院附属海口医院”

综合大楼

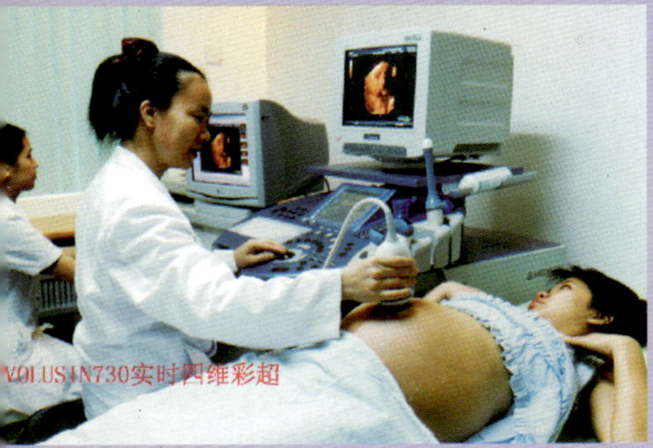

医疗设备(5)

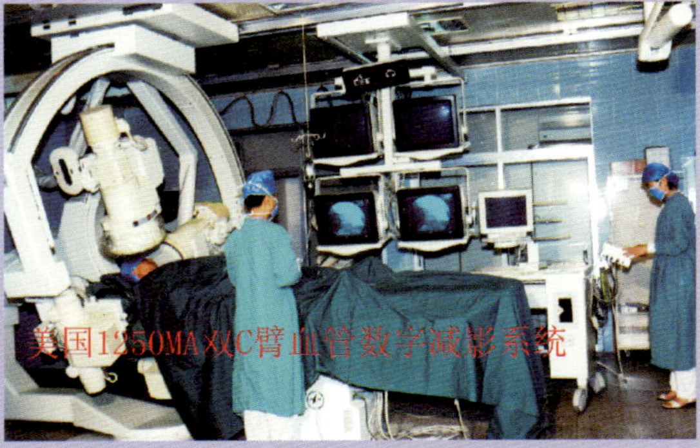

医疗设备(6)

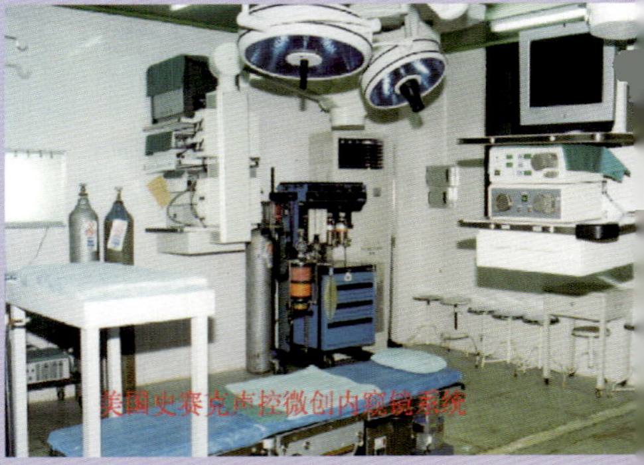

医疗设备(7)

海南省中医院

海南省中医院建院于1954年，是集医疗、教学、科研、预防、保健和康复为一体的综合性三级甲等中医医院，是广州中医药大学和海南省各医学院校的临床教学医院，国家药品临床研究基地，是海南省、海口市等医疗保险服务定点医院。近几年来，医院先后获得“全国卫生系统先进集体”、“爱婴医院”、“全省环境优美十佳医院”、“社会公认满意”、“全省最佳企业创新奖”等荣誉称号。

▶服务礼仪培训

医院拥有雄厚的中医、中药和中西医结合的医疗技术力量，现有国家特贴专家3人，省优秀专家5人，全国老中医药学术经验继承导师4人，副主任医师、副教授以上高级职称74人，主治医师、讲师等中级职称164人。医院开设病床360张，现代化仪器设备有700多台（件），总价值人民币2280万元，其中万元以上设备有螺旋CT、碎石机、彩色经颅多普勒血流分析仪、800、500毫安X光机和C臂X光机、全自动生化分析仪、中央监护系统等133台（件）。医院科室设置齐全，有中西医结合急救中心、重症病区、中医男科治疗研究中心、中西医结合骨伤治疗研究所、中风治疗康复科、肿瘤康复科、特诊科、内科、外科、肝胆科、肛肠科、妇产科、儿科、皮肤科、眼科、口腔科、耳鼻喉科、针灸科、推拿按摩科和预防保健科等临床一级科室18个，二级科室8个和门诊部3个。男性病治疗研究中心，在国内外享有盛誉，被中国中医药学会男科学会指定为性功能障碍委员会的唯一挂靠单位；骨伤科为我省优势专科和国家中医药管理局重点建设专科。

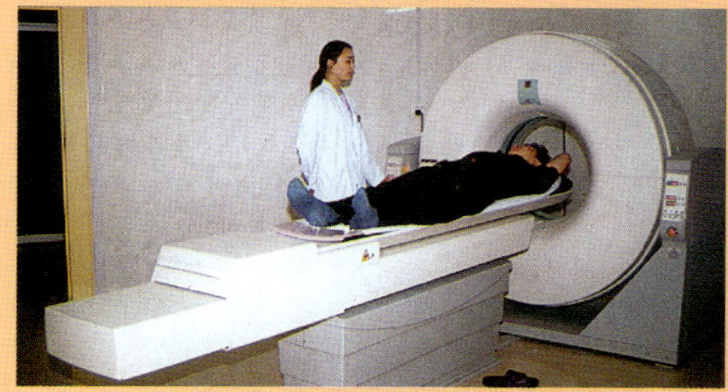

▶海南省中医院CT室

医院始终奉行“病人至上，质量第一”的办院宗旨，倡导“求真、奉献、拼搏、高效”的医院精神，加强精神文明建设，规范医疗服务行为，实行“病人选择医生”、“医疗收费一日清单”等多项便民服务措施，为患者提供优美的环境，高效的医疗，温馨的护理，一流的服务。

海南省安宁医院

省领导在卫生厅简梁盛厅长、陈少仕院长等陪同下视察安宁医院并看望病人

海南省安宁医院（海南省脑科医院）是一所创建于1960年的精神病专科医院，系海南省卫生厅直属机构，占地60余亩，总院地处海口市中心南海大道东10号，交通便利，环境优美,设施设备齐全，医疗环境整洁舒适。

总院拥有床位310张，设6个临床科室，其中4个精神科、1个戒毒科、1个心理康复科，3个门诊部（综合门诊、心理咨询治疗门诊、美沙酮戒毒维持治疗门诊）。属下机构：海南省精神疾病防治中心、海南省精神卫生研究所、海南省心理咨询治疗中心、海南省戒毒治疗指导中心、海南省毒品检测中心、海南省医学院教学医院。现有职工300余人，精神科专业技术人员221人，其中高级职称24人，中级职称89人。拥有视频脑电地形图、动态脑电图、彩超仪、数字X光机、酶标仪、血细胞分析仪、全自动生化分析仪、尿液分析仪，以及无抽搐电疗机、心理测验软件等先进专科设备。是省内集精神卫生教学、防治、科研、心理咨询、心理康复、戒毒技术指导为一体的规模最大、设备先进、技术领先、管理科学的三级精神病专科医院，是征兵、升学、招工工作进行毒品检测的权威机构。

该院长期以来一直本着“以病人为中心”的服务宗旨开展各项工作，狠抓医疗质量，使病人较好地回归社会。几年来在各级政府的支持下，在全院职工的共同努力下，医疗护理质量不断改善，医疗服务水平大幅度提高，医院发展势头良好，经济效益与社会效益同步协调发展，“十五”期间被评为全省、全国残疾人康复工作先进集体。

党组书记、院长：符永健

地址：海南省海口市南海大道东10号

电话：0898-66988629

邮编：571100

E-mail:lzh20@163.com

宽敞明亮的门诊楼大厅

中共海南老城经济开发区工作委员会书记、老城经济开发区管理委员会主任：曾能

海南老城经济开发区管委会领导班子

开发区管委会办公大楼鸟瞰图

风景如画的盈滨半岛旅游度假区

21世纪希望之城

海南老城

海南老城经济开发区的前身为澄迈县老城开发区，创建于 1988 年 5 月 23 日，属国务院批准的海口市城市总体规划三大组团之一的马村工业组团（国函 [1990]54 号），是《海南省城镇体系规划》确定的琼岛北部综合工业区的重要组成部分。为适应开发区发展形势的需要，2006 年 3 月份，经海南省人民政府批准（琼府函 [2006]22 号），澄迈县老城开发区正式更名为海南老城经济开发区，升格为省级开发区，并通过国家发改委的审核公告。

海南老城经济开发区区位优势明显。北依琼州海峡，西临北部湾；距海南省会城市海口市仅 20 公里，距海口美兰国际机场 35 公里；国家重点工程项目粤海铁路海口北站距海南老城经济开发区 2.8 公里，粤海铁路海口南站、铁路物流配送中心就在区内。开发区拥有 16.5 公里海岸线，6 个深水码头，年吞吐能力达 800 万吨。国家一类对外开放口岸马村口岸，已开通航线达日本、韩国、新加坡等十多个国家和地区。开发区公路四通八达、纵横交错，海南环岛西线高速公路、海口南海大道、海口西海岸景观大道西延线以及海口绕城高速公路均在区内交汇。

海南老城经济开发区基础设施完善，各项配套设施齐全。基础设施已经实现“六通一平”，10 万 m^3/d 供水工程即将建成供水。届时，开发区基础设施建设将实现“七通一平”，具备国际良好的开发条件。开发区内商贸、银行、通讯网点应有尽有，科教文卫配套设施齐全。

为减少办事环节，简化审批程序，提高服务意识和服务质量，开发区制订实施《服务承诺制》、《项目跟踪责任制》、《服务限时制》、《首问负责制》和《社会治安保障制》，成立投资服务中心和“马上办”，推行“一站式”服务，“保姆式”跟踪。2003 年 9 月，因一贯的诚信作风及良好的投资环境，海南老城经济开发区被评为“中国 50 家投资环

经济开发区

境诚信安全区”。获此殊荣的，海南省仅此一家。

截止 2006 年底，开发区共引进 309 家企业 481 个项目，累计投资 134.88 亿元。其中，2006 年开发区共引进 110 个项目，计划投资 206.06 亿元，实际投入资金 19.45 亿元，同比增长 27.16%。由于不断强化招商引资工作，开发区的经济也取得了跨越式发展。2006 年区内企业总产值达 78.13 亿元，同比增长 24.83%；生产总值 24.76 亿元，同比增长 28.08%；上缴国地税 3.65 亿元，占全县国地税收入的 69.61%，同比增长 9.88%。特别令人振奋的是，2006 年开发区出口贸易方面克服了出口交货值基数过小的瓶颈，突破了 3 亿元大关达 3.24 亿元，同比增长 161.72%；全区固定资产投资达 17.02 亿元，同比增长 26.84%，占全县固定资产投资的 85.74%。

现在，投资者到海南老城经济开发区投资置业不仅可以参照执行全省各地区颁布实施的各种优惠政策，还可以享受海南省高新技术产业示范区特殊招商优惠政策。

海南老城经济开发区是一方充满商机和希望的热土，这里每天都孕育着成功的机会，来开发区投资将是您最佳的选择，开发区热忱欢迎您！

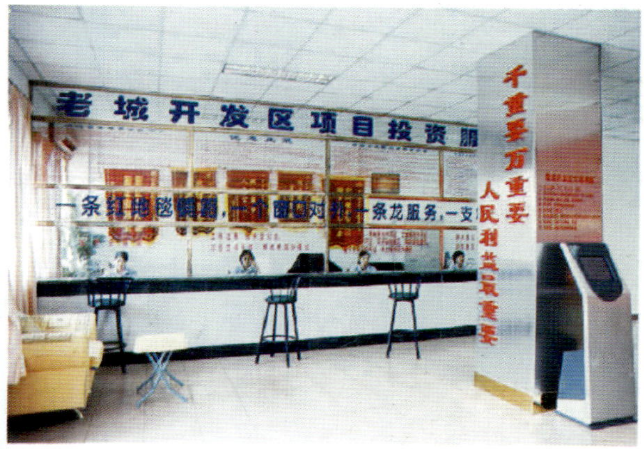

开发区管委会项目投资服务中心

中国石化股份有限公司海南油气分公司马村油库

中海石油管道输气有限公司老城接收站

武钢集团海南有限责任公司生产车间

海口市琼山人民医院

吴邦发正在为病人义诊

琼山人民医院始建于清光绪二十二年（1896年）间的爱生医院，至今已有106年的历史。是一所历史悠久，绿树成荫、环境优美的花园式医院。

琼山人民医院是国家卫生部授予“二级甲等医院”、“爱婴医院”的综合性医疗单位，先后荣获中华医院管理学会授予全国首批“百姓放心医院”、省政府授予全省环境优美“十佳医院”等50多项荣誉称号。

医院现有土地31亩，拥有建筑面积39241.6㎡，医院用房21924.14㎡，绿化面积13795㎡，全院高级职称30人，中级职称102人，现有3个门诊部、一个社区卫生服务站、29个临床医技科室。同时不断更新医疗设备，先后投资144，779，600元，增设日本全新东芝CT机，多功能彩超机、500毫安X光机、全自动生化分析仪、动态心电图仪、脑中风预测仪、血气分析仪、电解质分析仪等国内外先进医疗设备70余种。全院开放病床360张，可容纳700人次/日门诊量，年门诊量12多万次，住院病人逾5000多人次。

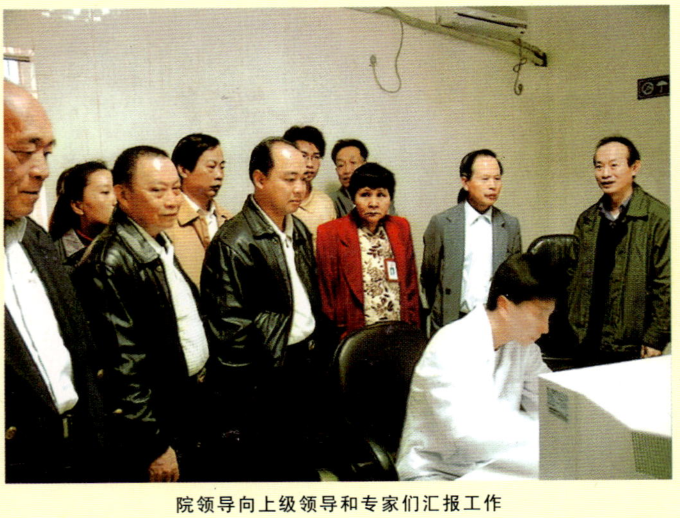

院领导向上级领导和专家们汇报工作

上街为群众义诊

海南省临高工商行政管理局

省工商局局长黄成模到该局西门工商所调研

临高工商局局长：陈德清

该局在3.15期间开展宣传咨询活动

执法人员开展农资市场专项整治

临高工商行政管理局是海南省工商行政管理局的直属机构，履行市场监督，行政执法的职能，现有国家公务员150名，内设5个股、室，下设12个基层工商所。

近几年来，全局紧紧围绕系统目标管理，以建立和维护市场经济秩序为目标，以打造“服务型工商”为方向，全面加强规范化建设，加大市场监管力度，积极促进地方经济发展。先后被国家工商总局和人事部评为先进集体；省委、省政府授予创建文明行业先进单位和文明单位；省工商局和省人劳厅给该局记集体二等功；被省工商局评为党风廉政建设先进单位；被国家工商总局评为2005年全国红盾护农先进单位。

前进中的琼海市邮政局

琼海市邮政局党组书记、局长：吴泽春

七年的风雨兼程，琼海市邮政局在改革发展中逐步壮大。在以吴泽春局长为首的领导班子的带领下，琼海市邮政局从无到有，从年业务收入500多成元，年亏损400多万元的国有老企业，发展到2006年完成邮政业务总量2300万元，邮政业务收入2185万元，上缴收支差475万元，全员劳动生产率达12.8万元/人，邮政服务用户满意度达86分的初具现代化的邮政企业。

琼海市邮政局在全市共设29个支局所，服务涵盖全市各个乡镇，20个邮政储蓄网点布局合理，全部实现全国联网；5条共478公里的自办汽车邮路覆盖全市城乡，46条共638公里的农村投递　邮路全部实现了摩托化。邮政业务逐步发展成邮政金融类、邮务类、信息代办类业务的“三业”并举局面。

邮政金融类业务：全市20个储蓄网点全部实现全国联网，5个ATM自动取款机全天候服务，邮储余额达7.04亿元；邮储中间业务提供代收电信资费、代发工资（养老金）、代理保险、代售国债等业务，并积极开拓“银联卡”类业务市场，汇兑业务在实现版本更新、电子联网基础上，致力开拓商务汇兑业务，先后开发了代收烟草款、代收中石化、中石油款项。

邮务类业务：报刊发行、信函、集邮、包裹、汇兑业务稳步发展，努力拓宽传统业务发展路子，促进“老树开新芽”，力争树立商业信函、特快专递、个性化邮品、西联汇兑等新品牌，打造服务优质，方便快捷的新型邮政。

信息代办类业务：建立健全11185客户服务中心平台，力争做大做强“登记易”业务、“代售火车票”、“鲜花礼仪”、商品配送等精品业务；努力开拓“邮政短信”服务，为邮政业务客户提供信息反馈服务；办理信息代理业和，为客户提供代办电信服务。

井然有序的报刊分发

琼海市房产管理局

符积良局长

琼海市房产管理局，系独立核算，自收自支的行政性事业单位。系琼海市房地产管理机构，贯彻执行党和国家及省有关房地产管理工作的方针政策、法律法规；依法拟定并组织实施本市房地产管理工作的政策、法规规章和规划、计划。

琼海市房产管理局，局长：符积良，主持全面工作。机构分别为：办公室、房地产交易中心、测绘所、房管股、产权股。

根据国家有关规定，开展的主要业务有：管理国家经租改造房屋、房屋权属初始登记，房地产转移登记，房地产抵押登记、房屋租赁登记、房地产变更登记、商品房预售登记、物业管理等。

服务大厅

大　楼

琼海市农村信用社联合社

一、今日信合

琼海市农村信用社是经中国银行业监督管理委员会批准设立，社员入股组成，实行民主管理，主要为社员提供金融服务的合作金融机构。历经50多年的发展，各项业务迅猛壮大，资金实力不断增强。截止2006年8月末，资产总额11亿元，存款总额9.9亿元，贷款总额5.2亿元。全辖共有34个营业网点，其中法人社19个，分社和储蓄所15个，网点遍布琼海城乡。在职职工214人，退休职工113人；在职职工中，大专以上学历171人，占比80%；高级职称1人，中级职称8人，初级职称82人，目前已发展成为支持琼海地方经济发展的重要金融力量。

二、贴心服务

琼海市农村信用社始终坚持“以农为本、为农服务”的办社宗旨，切实转换经营机制，定位“三农”，充分发挥农村信用社支农主力军和联系农民的纽带作用。近几年已累放各项贷款2亿多元，其中农业贷款占比80%以上，为农民脱贫致富作出了积极的贡献，有效地支持了农业产业结构调整和农村经济发展，满足了农业生产资金需求，推动了社会主义新农村的全面建设，实现了社会效益和经济效益的双丰收，琼海农民的生活水平和农村经济发展水平持续位居全省前列。

如今，当您走进琼海农村信用社，就会感受到宽敞、明亮的办公营业环境带给您的舒适，感受到真诚、热情的农信员工带给您的贴心服务，再加上工资自保、担保贷款、商业贷款、助学贷款等新品种的相继推出和以绿色贷款证为载体的信用工程的创建以及大小额支付系统的正式运行，必将为琼海广大客户朋友提供更加快捷、高效、优质、全面的金融服务。

三、展望未来

琼海农村信用社时时处处沐浴着琼海人民的悉心关怀与精心呵护，我们将站在农村金融的最前沿，及时把握时代脉搏，为服务“三农”尽职，为农民奔小康添力，面对您们的关注、信赖和期盼，我们深感责任重大。展望未来，我们将以更广阔的视角、更前沿的经营理念、更丰富的金融服务，建立一个管理科学、经营规范、效益显著、员工素质较高的现代金融企业，以优异的业绩回馈社会，服务琼海民众。“信用为本/合作成金”，也衷心希望社会各界一如既往地关心我们，支持我们。

单位地址：琼海市爱华路156号
联系电话：0898－36828555

琼海市妇幼保健院

琼海市妇幼保健院创建于1956年，其前身为“琼海县妇幼保健所”，1997年改所设院，经过40多年的励精图治，规模在不断扩大，现已发展成为以妇女儿童为主要服务对象的医疗保健专科医院，担负着保障全市妇女儿童身心健康的重任，是全市妇幼保健工作的业务指导和技术培训中心。

目前医院占地面积930m²，建筑面积3850m²，拥有36张病床；有职工62人，医疗技术人员占94%，其中中级以上职称10人；业务科室设有妇幼保健科、妇产科、儿科、门诊部、医技、功能检查科室；主要设备有救护车、普通B超、彩超、遥控200MA X线电视诊断系统、心电监护仪、麻醉机、红外线乳腺检查仪、电子阴道镜、妇科治疗仪、胎儿监护仪、婴儿培养箱、儿童智测仪、全自动血球计数仪、生化分析仪、酶标仪、尿十项分析仪等。主要开展孕产期保健、接生助产、妇产科疾病诊治、计划生育“四术”和儿童保健、儿科疾病诊治等妇女儿童医疗保健服务项目；能开展剖宫产、子宫全（次）切、妇科肿瘤剔除等手术，具备对疑难、急、危重病人的抢救治疗能力。

琼海市妇幼保健院遵循“团结、奉献、拼搏、创新”的宗旨，开拓进取，求实创新，先后荣获“琼海市卫生工作先进单位”、海南省“青年文明号”、“爱婴医院”、“海南省妇幼卫生工作先进单位”、海南省“文明单位”、“全国巾帼文明示范岗”等多项荣誉。

院长：陈晓

儋州第一人民医院

儋州市人民医院院长：李雪娟

儋州市人民医院主楼

医院前身是1926年美国基督教会福音医院，1952年属海南人民医院那大分院，1958年易名儋县第一人民医院，1993年更名儋州市第一人民医院。医院占地138亩，编制床位300张。现有职工354人，其中主任医师4人、副主任医师16人、中级90人。医院设1个门诊部，10个临床科室，16个医科技室。主要设备有：全身CT扫描机、彩色多普勒、电子胃肠镜、全自动生化分析仪等。

外科系统成功开展胃切除、心脏修补、食道和贲门癌根治、颅内肿瘤摘除、颅骨成形、断肢（指）离体再植、带肌皮瓣移植等重大手术；妇产科能开展巨大子宫肌瘤和宫颈癌根治、子宫脱垂曼氏改良、动脉插管化疗、内儿科系统在急性心肌梗塞、颅内出血及休克等急危重疾病的诊治方面，积累了丰富经验。

最近5年，医院先后投资3000余万元，兴建了外产科大楼（8500m²）、内科大楼（3500m²）、传染病区（1640m²）与工伤医疗康复中心，病房配备了电视、电话、空调、热水器、卫生间及阳台等现代化设施，病床及床上用品焕然一新，院内草坪如茵，绿树婆娑，病房整洁明亮、温馨舒适，是琼西地区医疗条件最好的综合性二级甲等医院。

曾先后荣获“全国五一劳动奖状”、“全国残疾人三项康复工作先进单位”、“海南省环境优美十佳医院”、“海南省文明单位”等称号。国务院特帖专家、妇产科主任医师李雪娟院长，先后荣获“全国五一劳动奖章”、“海南省十佳巾帼”等称号。

法人代表：李雪娟

地址：儋州市那大人民中路128号

总值（投诉）电话：0898－23322459　　急救电话：120

儋州市农税局

党组书记、局长：许勤强

儋州市农税局是负责全市农税征收管理工作的部门，行政级别为正科级行政单位，实行省地方税务局与儋州市政府双重管理，以儋州市政府管理为主的管理体制，并对各基层所（站）实行垂直管理，成立于2001年，现有干部职工102人。

几年来，该局根据国家法律、法规和国家税务总局提出的“完善稳定税制、强化税收征管”的税收工作指导思想，做好“依法治税、从严治队、科技加管理”三篇文章。以与时俱进、开拓创新的精神状态，坚持“向法律要税收、向管理要税收”的工作思路，积极推进并完善新的征管模式。创办全省第一家农税办税服务厅，积极推进信息化建设，打破传统的上门收税做法，实行集中申报、集中管理、集中征收、按章纳税、以征控税，征、管、查相推进的方法，提高征管质量和工作效率，降低了征收成本，减少征收阻力，自成立以来年年超额完成年度税收任务。2004、2005、2006年连续三年被儋州市委评为“先进基层党组织”，2004年被市委市政府评为“文明单位”。

2005年农税收入1329万元，同比增收947万元，增长248%。对当年全市税收增收额的贡献达到50%，所占税收比率也从年初预算的5%翻一番，提高到10%。

2006年农税收入2362万元，同比增收1033万元，增长78%。其中清理了历年欠税1000多万元，完成年初预算任务152%，增收812万元，取得更好成绩，所占税收比率从预算的10.8%翻一番，提高到20.3%。该局工作得到省地税局及市委、市政府的充分肯定。

地址：儋州市那大镇东风路152号

电话：0898-23336007

邮箱：nsj@danzhou.gov.cn

市领导亲临办税服务厅指导工作

领导班子

文昌市财政局

文昌市市委书记、人大主任谢明中同志带领部分市领导莅临财政局指导工作

文昌市财政局党组书记、局长：黄壮

2003年以前，文昌财政举步艰难，收支矛盾突出，为经济发展和政权运转提供财力保障倍感疲惫，已是不争的事实。2003年黄壮局长上任后，立足现状，紧紧围绕新一届市领导班子制定的“三抓”总要求和七大经济发展思路，适时提出“从规范财政管理入手，强化增收节支，坚决摆脱财政困境”。根据这一思路，三年来，新一届局领导班子带领全体同志群策群力，牢固树立科学的发展观，围绕“科学、发展、创新、服务、务实、高效、爱民、廉洁”十六字方针打造新型财政机关，在加强税费征管和努力争取上级财政支持的同时，认真贯彻“一保工资、二保工作、三保重点工程”方针，按照“量入为出，收支平衡”原则，科学把握预算指标，进一步理顺财政资金分配与国民经济、社会发展规划和政府施政目标紧密结合的关系，使财政资金在不同部门或公共领域之间得到合理配置。

三年来，财政收入实现跨越式增长。特别是2006年，全市财政总收入58691万元（按增长态势预测），比2002年的30557万元增收28134万元，增长92%。2003-2006年全市财政总收入年均增长17.1%。财政支出在保障工资、政府运转经费支出的同时，稳步增加对“三农”、教育、科技、公共卫生、社会保障等重点领域的投入，充分发挥了财政资金在提供保障、实施调控、促进平衡、统筹发展等方面的有效作用。2006年全市财政总支出58666万元（按支出进度预测），比2002年的31460万元增支27206万元，增长86%。2003-2006年全市财政总支出年均增支16.7%。

目前，文昌市经济社会稳定发展，城市面貌焕然一新，农村环境有效改善，农民收入稳步提高，干部职工工资水平与全省先进市县零差距，财政实现收支平衡，且略有节余，彻底结束了在支持经济建设和公共事业发展方面只能因财力有限而望洋兴叹的历史，扭转了被动的财政局面。

文昌市财税大厦

文昌市发展和改革局

文昌市发展和改革局是负责研究提出全市国民经济和社会发展战略、规划、总量平衡、结构调整的市政府组成部门。市国民经济动员办公室是市国防动员委员会的正局级办理机构，挂牌市发展和改革局。文昌市招商局是正局级职能机构，挂靠文昌市发展和改革局。共设10个股级职能机构：人事秘书股、规划和体制改革综合股、经济发展股、固定资产投资股、社会科技发展股、工交、能源股、社会投资招商综合股、招商服务中心、价格股、价格监督管理股。

二、主要职责

（一）贯彻执行党和国家有关国民经济、社会发展的方针政策、法律法规规章；拟订并组织实施全市国民经济和社会发展战略、中长期规划和年度计划；提出全市国民经济发展和优化重大经济结构的目标和政策；提出运用各种经济手段和政策的建议；受市政府委托向市人大作国民经济和社会发展计划的报告。

（二）研究分析全市经济形势和发展情况，进行宏观经济的预测、预警；研究涉及省及本市经济安全的重要问题，提出宏观调控政策建议，综合协调经济社会发展；负责全市日常经济运行的调节，组织解决经济运行中的有关重大问题，并向市政府提出意见和建议。

（三）负责汇总和分析财政、金融等方面的情况，拟订并组织实施全市产业政策和价格政策；综合分析财政、金融、产业、价格政策的执行效果，监督检查产业政策、价格政策的执行；制定和调整市政府管理的重要商品价格与收费标准；负责全市全口径外债的总量控制、结构优化和监测工作。

（四）研究全市经济体制改革和对外开放的重大问题，组织拟定全市综合性经济体制改革方案，协调有关专项经济体制改革方案；提出完善我市社会主义市场经济体制、以改革开放促进发展的建议，指导和推进全市总体经济体制改革。

（五）提出全市全社会固定资产投资总规模，规划重大项目和生产力布局；安排财政性建设资金儿建设项目，指导和监督国外贷款建设资金的使用，指导和监督政策性贷款的使用方向；引导民间资金用于固定资产投资的方向；研究提出利用外资和境外投资的规划和政策；参与管理省和市财政拨款建设项目、重大外资项目、境外投资项目；负责全市重大项目的稽察工作。

（六）推进全市产业结构战略性调整和升级；提出全市国民经济重要产业的发展战略和规划；研究并协调全市农业和农村经济社会发展的有关重大问题，衔接全市农村专项规划和政策；指导全市工业发展，推进工业化和信息化；制定全市能源发展规划；推动全市高技术产业发展，实施技术进步和产业现代化的宏观指导；指导全市引进的重大技术和重大成套装备的消化创新工作。

（七）研究分析全市区域经济和城镇化发展情况，提出区域经济协调发展，提出全市城镇经发展战略和重大政策措施；负责全市地区经济协作的统筹协调。

（八）研究分析市场的供求状况，负责全市重要商品的总量平衡和宏观调控；编制全市重要农产品、工业品和原材料进出口总量计划，监督计划执行情况，并根据经济运行情况对进出口总量计划进行调整；提出全市现代物流业发展的战略和规划。

（九）做好全市人口和计划生育、科学技术、教育、文化、卫生等社会事业以及国防建设与国民经济发展的衔接平衡；提出全市经济与社会协调发展、相互促进的政策，协调社会事业发展的重大问题。

（十）推进可持续发展战略，研究拟订全市资源节约综合利用规划，组织编制生态市建设规划，提出资源节约综合利用的政策，协调生态建设和资源节约综合利用的重大问题；组织协调全市环保产业工作。

（十一）研究全市多种所有制经济的状况，提出优化所有制结构和企业组织结构的建议，促进全市各种所有制企业的公平竞争和共同发展；研究提出促进全市中小企业和非国有经济发展的政策措施，协调发展中的重大问题。

（十二）参与研究促进全市就业、调整收入分配、完善社会保障与经济协调发展的政策。

（十三）拟订和制定全市国民经济和社会发展以及经济体制改革、对外开放的有关行政法规和规章，参与有关行政法规的起草和实施。

（十四）承办市政府和上级部门交办的其他事项。

局长：史君超　局长办公电话：63330465　行政秘书股电话：63330236

文昌市国家税务局在改革创新中前进

近年来，在省国税局和文昌市委、市政府的正确领导下，文昌市国家税务局坚持以邓小平理论和“三个代表”重要思想为指导，认真学习贯彻党的十六大和十六届四中、五中、六中全会精神，树立科学的税收发展观，切实推进依法治税，深化税收改革，强化科学管理，加强队伍建设，促进该局各项工作全面发展，税收收入任务连年超额完成，为文昌经济的发展和构建社会主义和谐社会做出了积极的贡献，树立了文昌国税良好的社会形象。3年多来，该局先后被国家税务总局授予“全国税务系统文明单位”、“全国税务系统税收信息化建设先进单位”、办税服务厅被授予“全国青年文明号”，局文建里宿舍区被评为“全国学习型家庭创建示范社区”；被省委省政府评为“全省创建文明行业先进单位”、“全省文明单位”、“海南省先进基层党组织”、“海南省学习型组织先进单位”、“海南省群众体育先进单位”；多次被省国税局评为“全省国税系统先进单位”、“全省国税系统三个文明建设先进单位”、“全省国税系统文明示范单位”、“党风廉政建设先进单位”、“税收宣传工作先进单位”、“全省国税系统先进领导班子”等100多项荣誉称号。

①书记、局长：林电

②国家税务总局领导在海南省国税局局长孙利军（左三）、文昌市政府副市长吕诗强（右二）和市国税局局长林电（右一）等领导的陪同下视察文昌国税基层建设情况，并予以肯定。

③全市国税工作会议

海南省文昌工商行政管理局

局长：黄泽恩

局长在换装仪式上讲话

2006年，我局在省工商局和市委市政府的正确领导下，以邓小平理论、“三个代表”重要思想和科学发展观为指导，以保持先进性教育和社会主义荣辱观教育活动为动力，紧紧围绕省工商局下达的管理目标和市委市政府提出的“三抓”总要求与七大发展思路，以及我局“一二九”工作思路，以六个“以”为抓手，坚持与时俱进，努力开拓进取，真抓实干，有力推进了队伍教育管理、规范化建设、服务与发展市场主体、整顿与规范市场经济秩序、执法办案、执收执罚等工商行政管理工作迈上新台阶，取得新成果，为构建和谐社会，促进文昌经济发展做出积极的贡献。

2006年主要工作情况：

（一） 以先进性教育活动为契机，进一步加强队伍建设。

（二） 以维护经济秩序为目标，全力抓好市场监管执法。

（三） 以促进经济发展为根本，大力发展市场主体。

（四） 以增加财政收入为着眼点，积极抓好执收执罚工作。

（五） 以制度建设为切入点，切实抓好规范化建设。

（六） 以明确的责任为要求，全力服务市委中心工作。

2006年7月1日换装仪式

2007年努力方向：我局将按照省工商局和市委、市政府的部署与要求，再接再厉，与时俱进，开拓创新，求真务实，进一步抓好政治理论学习，加强队伍建设、廉政建设、规范化建设和业务建设；继续为市场主体发展服务，促进市场主体的持续健康快速发展；强化市场监管执法，全面实施重点商品准入制度，不断完善“经济户口”监管机制，把食品市场安全专项整治、旅游市场整治、“红盾护农”、网吧专项整治、商业贿赂等市场专项整治行动不断引向深入，为我市经济发展、社会进步做出新的贡献。

局领导在研究工作

局长：许达超

文昌市文化广电出版体育局

文昌市文化广电出版体育局是主管全市文化、艺术、文物、广播电影电视、新闻出版、版权和体育工作的市政府组成部门。局现有19人，内设行政秘书股、文化管理股、广电管理股、出版管理股、体育管理股。局对市体育管理局、广播电视台、文化馆、图书馆、博物馆、孔庙管理处、电影公司、琼剧团、业余体校等下属单位负有领导责任，并指导和帮助其开展各项活动。

文昌市文化广电出版体育局的主要职责是：（1）制定我市文化、广电、出版、体育工作的发展规划、计划、管理规定，并组织实施；（2）组织和指导全市的文化、广电、出版、体育工作；（3）负责对下属单位贯彻执行上级方针、政策、法律、法规的检查监督，对其发展规划、计划进行指导、协调，在业务上检查指导各镇、办事处（场）文化站、广播电视站的工作；（4）依法对文化、广电、出版、体育工作的各种经营项目进行审批和管理。

近年来，我市的经费建设取得了丰硕成果，文化广电出版体育事业也蓬勃发展。1999年初被文化部授予“全国文化先进市”光荣称号，艺术、广播电视、体育事业也多次获得国家和省的表彰。尤其是广播电视事业，2004年7月建设了118米高的广播电视发射塔。该塔的建成，对于丰富广大人民群众的文化生活，巩固广播电视“村村通”工程建设成果具有重大的意义，是一项功在当代、利在千秋的公益事业。另外，2005年3月，国家沙滩排球训练基地在我市高隆湾落户，对我市的体育运动起到了很大的推动作用。

文昌市图书馆、文化馆综合楼

文昌市教育局

近年来，新一届市委、市政府高度重视发展教育事业，促进全市教育事业取得了令人瞩目的成绩：中小学办学条件不断改善，素质教育全面推进，教育质量不断提高，教育各项工作始终走在全省前列，文昌教育步入了历史上最辉煌的时期。

“普九”成果进一步巩固和提高、各级各类教育持续健康发展。全市现有小学234所，中学26所，中等职业学校2所，初中阶段入学率达97.1%，高中阶段毛入学率57.1%。成人教育、劳动者职业培训、继续教育成绩显著，我市基本建立起了比较完善的现代国民教育体系。

办学条件日臻完善。3年来，共筹措6.8亿元用于中小学的建设，办学条件得到大幅度的改善，文昌最美的地方便是校园了。

农村文明生态学校建设亮点多。中小学文明生态学校建设，共投入资金2202万元，文明生态学校建设体现出“量多、面广、质高”的特点，深受省和各市县领导的好评，教育局多次被评为“文明生态学校建设组织工作先进单位”。

信息化教育步伐加快。全市拥有计算机教室145个，总装机量为3600台，全市28所中学（含职中）、80所小学实现了计算机教学，有28所中小学添置了多媒体教室，56个教学点装置了教学光盘播放点、225所中小学校建没了卫星教学收视点，教育现代化教学水平得到提高。

教育人事制度改革不断深化，教师队伍建设不断加强。初步形成教师队伍的上岗竞争机制、有序流动机制和有效激励机制，全市涌现出了一大批省、市级优秀教师、业务骨干教师和师德标兵。

未成年人思想道德水平明显提高。被国家五部委命名为“全国青少年校外活动示范基地”，国家十部委组织评比的中国青少年社会教育“银杏奖”、“优秀团队奖”，市教育局党委、党组书记薛英炳被评为“突出贡献奖”。

全面推进素质教育，不断提高教育教学质量。引导教师积极推进教育教学改革，促使教育教学工作再上新台阶：高考录取人数2212人，本科第一批511人，其中清华大学2人，北京大学2人，高考录取率高达89.2%；中考综合评价位居全省前列。

回首过去的三年，文昌市的教育事业保持持续健康的发展势头，教育改革和发展取得了显著的成绩。展望未来，我们信心百倍！我们决心在市委、市政府的正确领导下，为打造侨乡教育的品牌、创建全省教育强市做出不懈的努力。

国务院“两纲”工作督导评估领导（右一）在省教育厅石秀慧（中）、市教育局党组、党委书记薛英炳的陪同下，到我市琼台师专附属幼儿园视察幼儿教育情况

省政协领导（前排左二），在市教育局局长潘正怀的陪同下，到我市职业学校了解职业教育情况

省教育厅厅长黄国泰（左五）、退休干部李光邦（左六），在市教育局党组、党委书记薛英炳（左四）和市教育局局长潘正怀的陪同下，在昌洒华侨小学与爱乡华侨符明潮先生等亲切合影

和谐发展的定安邮政

定安邮政发扬勇于拼搏、艰苦创业的精神，坚持以“发展、改革、服务、增效”为经营主线，以“客户的需求就是定安邮政的追求”为服务理念，以“迅速、准确、安全、方便”为质量方针，努力开拓经营、强化管理、改善服务，企业经营发展迈上新的台阶。

超额完成全年邮政业务总量、业务收入计划目标，邮政储蓄净增余额占全县新增余额的38%，储蓄专业收入比上年增14.56%。全面完成省局下达的各项通信质量和安全生产考核指标，用户满意度达86分。

邮政信息化建设不断取得新的进展，先后完成邮政储蓄国际金融系统、客户管理系统、报刊发行系统工程和集邮业务管理系统等上线运行工作，把信息技术作为业务发展和强化管理的重要保证和支撑，提升了我局信息化管理水平。加快网点标准化和邮政网络建设，进一步落实服务承诺，细化服务细节，优化服务流程，组建大中专生服务专柜，已建成电子化网点6个，邮政普遍服务能力得到不断增强。文明行业建设坚持与时俱进，积极参与社会公益事业活动，为扶贫点困难老党员、老支书、残疾人困难家庭等送上节日的温暖，邮政真诚回报社会的举动，得到社会各界群众的称赞，被省委、省政府评为“文明单位”。王浩局长被省委、省政府评为“精神文明建设积极分子”。

开展丰富多彩的文艺活动，丰富职工生活

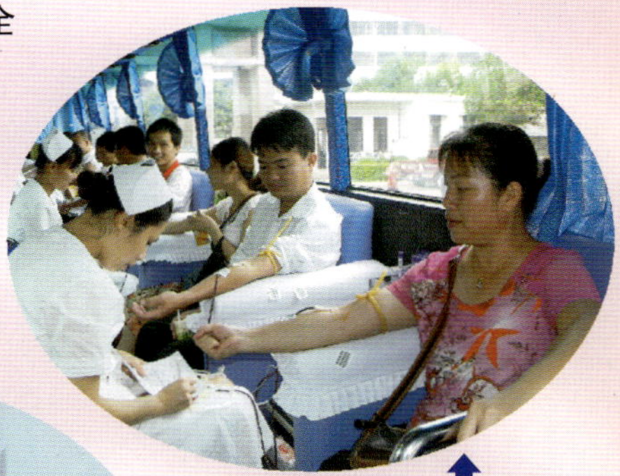

我局职工积极参与社会公益活动

宽敞明亮的标准化邮政网点

海口市殡葬管理所

海口市殡葬管理所作为海口市殡葬工作的具体管理与协调、服务与推行改革的行政管理事业性单位，现有在编人员50人。下设殡仪服务公司、颜春岭安乐园管理处、殡葬管理监察队。

海口殡仪馆始建于1964年，当时的生产、工作条件极为简陋：火化采用的是土窑式，防腐采用的是药物防腐，追悼厅也是一间不到60平方的小房子。1995年，海南省从省情出发，考虑海南是旅游大省，优越的热带旅游风光为全国所独有，宝贵的土地资源必须得到有效的保护，在省委、省政府的主持下，《海南省殡葬管理暂行办法》出台，海口、三亚划定为土葬改革区，大力倡导火化、改革土葬。同时，由政府投入2000多万重建海口市殡仪馆。重建后的殡仪馆占地近百亩，拥有四个追悼厅共1500多平方，其中追悼厅面积达500多平方，设施豪华，还有办公楼、骨灰寄存楼、职工宿舍等建筑。

海口市殡仪馆年火化量达到1200具，同时有能力承办各类大、中、小型追悼会。

殡仪馆重建后，历任馆领导均为争创国家一级馆而努力。2005年，市民政局对各基层领导进行“轮岗”，殡仪馆产生新领导班子。新领导班子上任后，把争创国家一级馆作为工作目标，大力改善馆内环境，同时推行优质服务，对前来办业务的家属采取“点对点”式服务，丧事办完后，我所的跟踪服务小组继续跟踪了解家属对我所服务质量的满意程度。这样在软、硬两方面同时提高我所的服务档次。

在海口市政府的大力推行下，于2005年8月10日正式在全市范围内实行土葬改革。凡本市行政区域内所有街道办事处管辖区域和府城镇所设立居委会的管辖区域定为火葬区，火葬区内死亡遗体除另有规定外，一律实行火葬，禁止土葬。土葬改革既是海口市殡葬事业的一座里程碑，又为海口这个优美的滨海城市的健康发展提供了有利保障。

为配合海口市土葬改革的进行，海口市殡葬管理监察队进一步加强全市

大追悼厅

行业统管，有效控制了不正当的行业竞争，依法监理殡葬用品市场制造销售的合法性，对地下行为与不公平行为逐步进行改正与平衡，使我市殡仪服务宗旨正确、明朗，使殡葬服务市场合理、有序。

我所将遵照省、市两级政府提出的建设旅游大省和"美化椰城"的战略部署，将我馆的服务档次和馆内环境再提高一个档次。同时，我馆也将从实际出发，参照国内一些优秀同行，在适当的时候申报国家一级殡仪馆。

绿树成荫的办公区域

办公区

业务办理处

服务车

HAIKOU SHI BINZANG GUANLI SUO